EXOTIC OVERLAYS

How to get BIG payoffs from the Pick Six, the Pick Three, exactas, triples, doubles and superfectas

Bill Heller

Bonus Books, Inc., Chicago

00   99   98   97   96   5   4   3   2   1

Library of Congress Cataloging-in-Publication Data
Heller, Bill.
    Exotic overlays : how to get big payoffs from the Pick Six, the
  Pick Three, exactas, trifectas, doubles, and superfectas / Bill
  Heller.
     p. cm.
  ISBN 1-56625-064-1 (alk. paper)
    1. Horse racing—Betting. I. Title.
  SF331.H44   1996
  798.401—dc20   96-19797

Bonus Books, Inc.
160 East Illinois Street
Chicago, Illinois 60611

1995 racing forms © 1995 by Daily Racing Form, Inc.; 1996 racing forms
© 1996 by Daily Racing Form, Inc. Reprinted with permission of copyright
owner.

Cover photo of Desert Stormer in 1995 sprint
courtesy of the Breeders' Cup, Ltd.

Composition by E. T. Lowe Publishing Co., Nashville, Tennessee.

Printed in the United States of America

To Bubba, the sunshine in my life

Contents

Acknowledgements

My deep appreciation goes to Steve Crist of the New York Racing Association, who graciously consented to sharing his Pick Six opinions and strategies. My close friend Bob Gersowitz, an excellent handicapper and bettor in his own right, was kind enough to read the manuscript and offer suggestions. Another friend and top handicapper, Dick Powell of the New York Racing Association, let me borrow several of his *Daily Racing Form*s (mine were too marked up to be legible). Mark Sanino of the *Daily Racing Form* was extremely helpful and quick to respond to my plea for permission to reproduce entries and charts. He also directed me to Debbie Hernandez of the *Form,* who sent me back issues I used as examples in *Exotic Overlays*. Todd Schrupp of Calder Raceway's Public Relations Department was extremely helpful. My wife, Anna, offered her suggestions. Our seven-year-old son, Bubba (a.k.a. Benjamin), was an immense help in sifting through piles of *Daily Racing Form*s for examples. He is the sharpest handicapping second grader in America.

Definitions

Bounce — When a horse runs a bad race after an extremely good one.

Bullet — The fastest work of the day of the horses who trained at the same distance on the same track.

Carryover — When no bettor connects on the Pick Six, a portion of the pool is distributed to those bettors with five winners (or, when nobody has five, four winners). The remaining money is carried over to the following day's Pick Six pool. If nobody connects on Day Two, the money is carried over to a third day. Note that on the final day of any meet, if the Pick Six is missed, the Pick Six pool is split among those bettors with the highest number of winners.

Criss-cross — Using a specific number of horses in the two halves of a double to cover every combination. Criss-crossing two horses in the first race with three in the second costs $12. Criss-crossing three in each race costs $18.

Daily Double — Picking the winner of the first and second races. Most tracks have a Late Double and/or other doubles. The principle is the same.

Exacta — Picking the first two horses in exact order.

Exacta Box — Betting two horses in an exacta to cover them finishing 1-2 or 2-1. A two-horse, $2 exacta box costs $4. Boxing three horses costs $12; four horses $24, and so on.

Exacta Wheel — This is an exacta bet keying one horse to

win and using every other horse in the race to finish second, or keying one horse to finish second and using every other horse to win. In a 10-horse field, a $2 exacta wheel costs $18. Using him for second is called a Back Wheel.

Overlay — A horse whose odds are higher than you think they should be.

Overlay, Overlay — A great handicapping book that makes a lovely holiday gift.

Pick Three — Picking the winners of three consecutive races.

Pick Six — Picking the winners of six straight races.

Quiniela — Picking the first two horses in either order with the payoff approximately half of an exacta. A very popular bet at greyhound tracks.

Superfecta — Picking the first four horses in exact order.

Triple (trifecta) — Picking the first three horses in exact order.

Triple Box — Covers every triple combination of a specified number of horses. A $2 triple box of three horses costs $12. Boxing four horses costs $48, et cetera.

Triple Key/Part Wheel — Use one horse to finish first, second or third, and cover a specified number of other horses to complete the triple. As an example, key the one horse to win and use four other horses in your triples, covering every combination. For $2 triples, the cost is $24. Using five other horses increases the cost to $40.

Introduction

You've likely heard of an overlay. You may have read *Overlay, Overlay* and *Harness Overlays*. Now it's time for *Exotic Overlays*.

As the late '90s spin toward the 21st century, horse racing has been forever changed by simulcasting and home betting.

Not that many years ago, if you wanted to make a bet on a horse race, you had to actually go to the track. When you did, you bet win, place or show. The only multiple bet offered was the Daily Double.

Now? Not only are there doubles, quinielas, exactas, triples (trifectas), Pick Threes, Pick Sixes and superfectas available non-stop, there is also full-card simulcasting from other tracks offering their own complex betting menus. Now, not only can you bet at an off-track betting parlor, you can bet from your home if you have a phone account and watch the races live in your living room.

You are literally flooded with wagering options. What's a bettor to do?

For openers, get with the times. Know, understand and evaluate all the different bets you encounter. Also, take the time to check out the available bets at each simulcasting track you are tracking.

In *Overlay, Overlay*, we tried to help you identify vulnerable favorites and legitimate overlays, horses whose odds are higher than you think they should be. *Exotic Overlays* takes you a giant step farther. If you bet straight, finding an overlay or two makes your day. If you bet exotics, you don't need an overlay a day. An exotic overlay can carry your week, your month or maybe even your year.

It's time to take a plunge and go after those juicy exotic payoffs which can reach three, four or even five figures.

To help you, we've enlisted Steve "Mr. Pick Six" Crist of the

New York Racing Association. He was kind enough to share his valuable Pick Six strategies, insights and opinions.

For openers, the first chapter offers easy and effective ways of improving your handicapping.

So what are you waiting for?

1

Improve Yourself

For the uninitiated, the racetrack is a confusing place; the *Daily Racing Form* resembles hieroglyphics, and handicapping is more difficult than calculus.

But the laws of horse racing are simple. Unlike the lottery, there are winners in every single race, and winners of every type of bet. Bettors are not betting against the track, rather against each other in pari-mutuel wagering.

It is not a simple game, but it is a rewarding one when you handicap correctly. To do so, you should take every single edge you can find. Knowledge is a powerful ally.

Here are ways you can improve your handicapping:

1. Always read past performance lines (PPs) from the bottom (least recent) to the top. Doing so means you won't miss important information. Yes, it takes more time, but we're not talking hours, rather minutes. It's time well spent if you discover that two or three horses raced against each other four or five starts back. Or that a layoff horse did run well fresh in a similar situation.

2. Use all the information the *Racing Form* provides. The *Form* has changed dramatically for the better in recent years. Especially important are the analysis boxes accompanying each horse. Many times, there is vital information there. The most obvious example is a maiden race with a bunch of first-time starters. The analysis presents statistics on both the sire and the dam. Additionally, the analysis may provide trainers' records with first-time starters. The *Form* now also presents important statistical information daily, such as trainers and jockeys' records with different types and different distances of races. This is a quantum leap from what the *Form* provided 10 years ago. Take advantage of it.

3. Take a few minutes out to do a simple exercise to improve your knowledge and your handicapping. If you are looking at a turf race, instead of simply looking at each horse's turf record, guess whether his record is good or bad by analyzing the breeding. Then see if you're correct. In doing this, you will increase your knowledge about turf breeding, which could be very valuable when you assess horses making their first start on turf. Do the same exercise with horses' records on wet tracks. Again, you'll learn more, and it may come in handy at a future date. At the worst, you'll have wasted a few minutes. Finally, take a minute and jot down the odds you expect all the horses in a certain race will go off. Then write down the actual post-time odds. Soon, you'll begin discovering which horses have odds that are higher than they should be: overlays — which are exactly what we are hoping to find.

4. Ignore tips. Usually, tips reveal themselves on the tote board. You can then judge the hot horse's odds for yourself. Over-bet tip horses create overlays on every other horse in a race.

5. Check the TV monitors for potential payoffs in doubles and Pick Threes. Before the first race, potential Daily Double payoffs will give you guidance for who is and who is not being bet in the second half of the double. The same holds true for the final leg of Pick Threes. In the Pick Three and the Pick Six, you

can see who is being bet in the first leg before you bet, which may help you make your decisions.

6. There is no substitute for watching races. Any time you can see the races live or on TV, do so. It gives you an edge over bettors who handicap solely from reading the *Racing Form*. A two- or three-word comment at the end of each horse's race in the *Form* can't do the horse's trip justice. See and judge for yourself whether a horse had a legitimate excuse, or how wide his trip was, or just how brave he was on the lead. If you're going to the track one afternoon and haven't seen the previous day's races, go a little early to watch yesterday's replays. In doing so, you'll learn if the track had a bias, favoring either speed or closers.

7. Beware of the following advice from well-meaning friends:

"They didn't ship this horse here without a reason." — Do all the other trainers who ship horses here do it because they think they will lose?

"He didn't beat anybody in his last start." — Maybe not. But would any other horse your friend likes have beaten those lesser horses by a substantially greater margin?

"The figs don't lie." — That means the Beyer speed figures don't lie, which implies that the horses with the best Beyers always win. They don't. Speed is an important aspect of handicapping, but so are class and form. Don't rule a contender out just because he doesn't have the best "figs." In fact, if you like a horse whose figs aren't the best, you may get an overlay, as the top Beyer figure horses are sometimes over-bet.

2

A Frame of Mind

Hitting exotic overlays frequently requires a mind set. In *Overlay, Overlay*, we stressed reality: the reality that nobody on the planet has the magic handicapping answers which uncover one winner after another. The favorite wins 25 to 35 percent of the time year after year at tracks around the country. Accept the fact that as a handicapper and a bettor, you are going to be wrong many times in the course of a day if you bet every single race. There are no sure things. The idea is to maximize the payoffs when you are correct by choosing your spots, identifying beatable favorites and locating overlays.

To cash exotic overlays, you must open your mind to consider horses which might not be the most logical choices. Some handicappers may find this objectionable, but their reasoning is unsound if they fool themselves into believing they always have the right horse. In dealing with reality, we understand that we do not have the correct answer in every race. Recognizing that fact is a strength, because we all know we occasionally encounter races where we don't have a clue who is going to win, or a race where we don't even know which horses will contend. Or we may like a single horse and dislike the chances of all of his

4

competitors. By identifying such races, we find situations where exotic overlays come to life time and time again. We recognize when it's a good time to wheel a horse in an exacta or a Daily Double. We define the races where we should use several or possibly all horses in one race of a Pick Three or Pick Six.

This doesn't guarantee you'll win all those bets, and, even when you do, it may produce results which will have your friends busting your chops because you invested $60 to hit a $40 Daily Double or spent $40 to hit a Pick Three which returned $25. Let them laugh, because it's going to happen sporadically while you're trying to catch an exotic overlay. But when you hit one, you will be laughing all the way to the bank. And they can be hit. Not time after time, but some of the time. And that is all you need.

3

The Bankroll Hit

Being a public handicapper is an interesting way to make a living. If you are at the top of your game, you are right between 25 to 35 percent of the time, because you are doing it a day before the races to get your selections into the daily newspaper. That's not an excuse; it's reality. Remember, the betting public is only right 25 to 35 percent of the time when it establishes the favorite with every last second detail included: scratches, track condition, jockey changes, and so forth.

Doing a bankroll in a newspaper is an invitation to a public flogging, because, it, too, must be done a day ahead of time. Just think how hard it is to win betting at the last minute. For a comparison, check out football handicappers in newspapers and see how well they prosper. And they only have two possibilities for every game they pick.

So I didn't do cartwheels when Butch Walker, my sports editor at the *Daily Gazette* in Schenectady, N.Y., told me in the summer of 1995 that he wanted me to do a mythical bankroll for arguably the country's most difficult meet on which to handicap and wager: Saratoga.

I had a brush with Saratoga bankrolls in my previous life

with the *Gazette*'s rival, the *Times Union* in Albany. It hadn't been pretty. While I held my own handicapping against other local and New York City papers year after year, the bankroll had pretty much been a disaster. The first year, I started with $500 and finished with $3. One year, I did manage to finish ahead. You want to talk about cheap? I told the managing editor of the *Times Union* that I needed more than $500 to start the bankroll for the 24-day meet, and he wouldn't give it to me. I think it was the first time a man was ever denied a mythical raise.

I hadn't done a bankroll in 10 years until last summer when the *Gazette* told me to do one. The *Gazette*, however, gave me $1,000 to start, a realistic amount for the Saratoga meet, which had been extended to 34 days.

Going into closing day, I was actually proud to have $819.30 left in the bankroll, because I was betting as much as $50 to $100 a day. I had hit a low of $733.50 one week earlier, but hadn't panicked, and, as a result, made some headway back to the break-even point, though I hardly expected to close the gap on the final afternoon of racing.

Then again, I never expected to hit an exotic overlay for more than $1,000 on a $2 bet.

Scratches reduced my $118 of action to $90. Forty dollars went out the window in Daily Doubles, leaving only bets on the sixth race and in the late Pick Three (races 6 through 8).

With only a field of six horses in both the sixth and seventh races — each containing a heavy favorite — and a field of eight in the eighth — with seemingly only three legit contenders — it was hard to imagine fireworks on the way.

But they were, because I realized that the heavy favorite in both the sixth and seventh races were vulnerable, at least vulnerable enough to make saver bets, both in the bankroll and real life.

The sixth race was a non-winners of three (two other than maiden and claimer) allowance for three-year-olds and up on the inner turf course at one mile. The field in post position order:

6 Saratoga

1 MILE. (Inner Turf). (1:34⁴) ALLOWANCE. Purse $36,000. 3-year-olds and upward which have not won two races other than maiden, claiming or starter. Weights: 3-year-olds, 117 lbs. Older, 122 lbs. Non-winners of $24,000 at one mile or over since May 3, allowed 3 lbs. Of $19,200 twice since February 2, 5 lbs. Of $15,000 twice in 1995, 8 lbs. (Races where entered for $50,000 or less not considered in allowances.)

Gilder

Own: Pitfield Ward C

LOVATO F JR (27 1 2 3 .04)

B. g. 4
Sire: Smile (Ln Reality)
Dam: Rythmical (Fappiano)
Br: Genter F A Stable Inc (Ky)
Tr: Hamtwald Philip M (10 2 1 0 .20)

114

	Lifetime Record:	4 2 1 0	$45,948	
1995	1 0 0 0		Turf	0 0 0 0
1994	2 1 1 0	$29,425	Wet	1 1 0 0	$23,205
Sar ①	0 0 0 0		Dist ①	0 0 0 0

WORKOUTS: Aug 21 Sar 4f fst :51¹ B 30/21   Aug 15 Sar tr.t 4f fst :51³ B 15/30   Jly 28 Sar tr.t 3f fst :36⁴ H 3/77   Jly 21 Sar tr.t 4f fst :51¹ B 13/21   Jly 9 CD 5f fst 1:03¹ B 3/13   Jly 4 CD 4f fst :48² B 16/28

Jets Over Miami

Own: Ackerman Kenny

DAY P (102 21 26 25 .17)

Dk. b or br c. 3 (Mar)
Sire: Far Out East (Raja Baba)
Dam: Jeanne's Lassie (Northern Fling)
Br: Kelly Thomas J (Ky)
Tr: Kelly Larry (7 1 1 0 .14)

112

	Lifetime Record:	17 4 1 1	$79,462	
1995	8 4 0 0	$67,610	Turf	6 2 0 0	$29,430
1994	9 0 1 1	$11,852	Wet	5 2 1 0	$45,177
Sar ①	1 0 0 0	$1,080	Dist ①	2 1 0 0	$11,910

Jostled, tight quarters start

WORKOUTS: ● Aug 21 Sar 3f fst :36 H 1/11   Jly 23 Sar 3f fst :37¹ B 16/20   Jly 10 AP 3f fst :37 B 3/12

Boulder Drive

Own: Willowett Stables

BAILEY J D (100 43 22 22 .23)

B. c. 3 (Jan)
Sire: Danzig (Northern Dancer)
Dam: Hidden Garden (Mr. Prospector)
Br: Farish William S (Ky)
Tr: Vestal Peter M (23 5 2 5 .22)

109

	Lifetime Record:	4 2 1 0	$35,608	
1995	4 2 1 0	$35,608	Turf	0 0 0 0
1994	0 M 0 0		Wet	1 1 0 0	$12,000
Sar ①	0 0 0 0		Dist ①	0 0 0 0

WORKOUTS: Aug 16 Sar 3f fst :38² B 15/17   Aug 5 Sar 4f fst :47² H 1/45   Jly 29 Sar 4f fst :48¹ H 3/42   Jly 23 Sar 4f fst :36⁴ H 7/28   Jly 17 CD 3f fst :38³ B 12/12

Kefalonians

Own: Amvroussias A & Vangelatos P

VELAZQUEZ J R (134 24 28 9 .18)

B. c. 3 (Mar)
Sire: Val de l'Orne (Fr) (Val de Loir)
Dam: Donnaa (Dewan)
Br: Rock Hill Farm (Ont-C)
Tr: Sciacca Gary (73 7 9 6 .10)

114

	Lifetime Record:	9 2 0 0	$39,600	
1995	9 2 0 0	$39,600	Turf	6 2 0 0	$39,600
1994	0 M 0 0		Wet	1 0 0 0
Sar ①	1 0 0 0		Dist ①	4 1 0 0	$19,200

Disqualified and placed 6th

WORKOUTS: Aug 28 Bel 4f fst :50 B 6/27   Jly 30 Bel 4f fst :49⁴ B 17/46   Apr 28 Bel 4f fst :48 H 2/57   Jan 11 Bel 4f fst :51³ B 5/59

Crimson Guard
Own: Dokwurthowski Henryk
SMITH M E (178 30 22 34 .17)

B. c. 3 (Apr)
Sire: Danzig (Northern Dancer)
Dam: Wedding Reception (Round Table)
Br: Kennelot Stables Ltd. (Ky)
Tr: Mott William I (54 17 6 6 .31)

112

Lifetime Record:	8	2	3	1	$106,279						
1995	5	2	2	1	$97,879	Turf	4	1	2	1	$82,159
1994	3	M	1	0	$8,400	Wet	0	0	0	0	
Sar ⓣ	0	0	0	0		Dist ⓣ	1	0	1	0	$16,800

Entered 27Aug95- 7 SAR

27May95- 9GS fm 1 1/16 ⓣ :24 :47² 1:11³ 1:43 JerseyDerby-G2 91 6 2 25 24½ 43½ 31¼ Smith M E 123 5.10 95-09 Da Hoss119½ Claudius119¹¼ Crimson Guard123no Mild rally 10
13May95- 8Bel fm 1 ⓣ :22⁴ :45² 1:09¹ 1:33³ Saranac-G3 81 1 2 21 21 25 212½ Perez R B 122 *1.70 82-12 Debonair Dan112¹² Crimson Guard122¹¼ Treasurer114⁸ Chased, no match 7
9Apr95- 8Kee fm 1 1/16 ⓣ :22³ :46² 1:11² 1:44 Transylvania60k 93 9 6 63½ 63½ 61½ 2nk Smith M E 118 13.20 86-12 DOps Smile113nk Crimson Guard118nk DHawk Attack113²½ 9
Altered course inside, finished fast Placed first through disqualification.
6Mar95- 6GP fst 1 1/16 :23² :47² 1:12¹ 1:46¹ Md Sp Wt 82 6 3 2½ 1hd 1½ 1¾ Smith M E 120 *1.80 77-24 Crimson Guard120¾ Palm Freezer120hd Play The Gold120¹¼ Driving, inside 11
4Feb95- 6GP fst 1 1/16 :23² :47¹ 1:13¹ 1:47 Md Sp Wt 77 10 4 31 2hd 23 25½ Smith M E 120 7.80 67-26 Da Bull120⁵½ Crimson Guard120³ Crimson120¹⁰ Rallied 11
20Nov94- 5Aqu fst 1 ⓦ :23⁴ :47² 1:12³ 1:37⁴ Md Sp Wt 62 5 4 32½ 33½ 48 411 Migliore R 118 3.40 68-25 Nostra113¹¼ Storm Hawk118⅞ Paragallo's Hope118⁵½ Lacked rally 10
8Nov94- 3Aqu fm 1 1/16 ⓣ :22² :46⁴ 1:11¹ 1:44⁴ Md Sp Wt 70 1 2 22 23½ 23 23 Smith M E 118 *1.45 82-13 Debonair Dan118³ Crimson Guard118⁵ Crowning Halo118¹⁰ Second best 8
16Oct94- 3Bel fst 7f :23¹ :47² 1:12³ 1:25² Md Sp Wt 48 6 10 108 97½ 811 614 Smith M E 118 4.20 62-18 Stauder113nk Devious Course118⁴½ Slice Of Reality113⁴½ Pinched break 11
WORKOUTS: Aug 21 Bel tr.t 7f fst 1:28 B 1/1 Aug 10 Bel tr.t 5f fst 1:02⁴ B 2/2 Aug 4 Bel tr.t 4f fst :49² B 6/29 Jun 24 Bel 6f fst 1:16 B 10/17

Thirty Good Ones
Own: Austin Stables Inc
SELLERS S J (56 11 13 10 .11)

B. c. 4
Sire: Clever Trick (Icecapade)
Dam: Cup of Honey (Raise a Cup)
Br: Hurstland Farm Inc (Ky)
Tr: Richards Robert J Jr (4 0 0 0 .00)

114

Lifetime Record:	22	2	5	4	$55,047						
1995	10	2	4	0	$35,385	Turf	17	2	5	4	$53,547
1994	6	M	0	3	$12,490	Wet	1	0	0	0	
Sar ⓣ	2	0	0	0	$2,700	Dist ⓣ	1	0	1	0	$5,940

Entered 27Aug95- 7 SAR

28Jly95- 4Sar fm 1 1/16 Ⓣ :23¹ :46 1:11² 1:42² 3+ Alw 36000N2X 81 8 3 21 21½ 31½ 54¾ Sellers S J 113 25.50 82-07 Debonair Dan108½ Check Ride113nk Comstock Lode113³ Chased, tired 10
Hand timed
6Jly95- 5Crc fm *1 1/16 ⓣ 1:43 3+ Alw 15500N1X 85 1 1 11½ 11½ 12 12¾ Castillo H Jr L 119 b *.70 89-16 Thirty Good Ones119²¾ Buck Call119¹½ T. T.'s Eskimo119nk Ridden out 6
1Jun95- 8Crc fm *1 1/16 ⓣ 1:43¹ 3+ Alw 17200N1X 83 4 2 2½ 2½ 11½ 2hd Castillo H Jr L 122 b 4.60 88-16 BirdieKing119hd ThirtyGoodOns122² Powrtron122²½ Gave way grudgingly 8
13May95-11Hia fm 1 1/16 ⓣ 1:43² 3+ Alw 15550N1X 72 4 2 2hd 2hd 1hd 43½ Castillo H Jr L 120 b *1.50 77-19 Troy's Turn Again117nk Birdie King117¹¾ Powertron123¹½ Weakened 11
1May95- 9Hia gd *1 3/16 ⓣ 1:51¹ Alw 16500N1X 52 1 2 22 1hd 21½ 813 Boulanger G L 122 b 2.60 63-27 Promising Pidgeon114½ Roto114³ Beau Ric114¹½ Faded 10
11Apr95- 4Hia fm *1 1/16 ⓣ 1:43 Md Sp Wt 86 1 1 13½ 12½ 15 110 Castillo H Jr L 122 b *.40 87-11 Thirty Good Ones122¹⁰ Double Redouble122⁵ Media Buy122¹¾ Ridden out 10
21Mar95-11Hia fm *1 1/16 ⓣ 1:41³ Md Sp Wt 76 9 3 34 21½ 2½ 2¾ Ramos W S L 122 b *1.30 93-09 LnchngPwdr122¾ ThrtyGdOns122nk Chstr'sGld122²½ Gave way grudgingly 11
14Mar95- 3GP gd 1 1/16 :24 :47⁴ 1:12⁴ 1:45² Md Sp Wt 73 2 1 1hd 1½ 1hd 45¾ Ramos W S L 120 b 6.80 75-24 Pleasant Interlude120⁴¾ Request A Star120nk Bluffy120¾ Weakened 6
10Feb95- 6GP fm *1 1/16 ⓣ :48 1:12¹ 1:36¹ 1:49⁴ + Md Sp Wt 79 1 3 23½ 22½ 2hd 2no McCauley W H L 120 b *1.10 96-03 Exclusive Casino120no Thirty Good Ones120²½ Seminole Slew120nk Rallied 10
20Jan95- 2GP fm *1 1/16 ⓣ :47⁴ 1:13¹ 1:38² 1:51⁴ + Md Sp Wt 77 10 4 32½ 21½ 12 22½ McCauley W H L 120 b 8.20 84-13 Gem Seeker120²½ Thirty Good Ones120¹¾ Dixieland King120nk Gamely 10
WORKOUTS: Aug 5 Sar 4f fst :51⁴ B 44/46 Jly 18 Crc 6f fst 1:17 B 1/1 Jly 3 Crc 6f fst 1:18 B 8/9 Jun 24 Crc 5f sly 1:02² B (d)2/23 Jun 12 Crc 4f fst :50³ B 21/29

1 — Gilder — This four-year-old gelding had obvious physical problems because he began his career, November 11, 1993, and had only made four starts, all on dirt. He won his debut wire to wire by six lengths; was second in an allowance, May 29, 1994; won an allowance on November 9, 1994, and, in his '95 debut at Saratoga, July 30, 1995, finished sixth by 11½ lengths in a six-furlong sprint. But this race was on grass, and as the accompanying analysis in the *Racing Form* told readers, Gilder was the first foal out of a grass stakes-winning mare, Rythmical. Gilder's sire was Smile, whose offspring have had success on grass, but not especially in their first starts on grass.

2 — Jets Over Miami — He won his last start on dirt, a $75,000 claimer for three-year-olds, by four lengths, and had two wins in six grass starts. In his last grass race, a similar non-winners of three, he was fifth by seven lengths at 17-1.

3 — Boulder Drive — This three-year-old had two wins and a second in four dirt starts, but was making his grass debut. He had a strong grass pedigree on the top, being sired by Danzig, a son of

Northern Dancer, but his broodmare sire was Mr. Prospector, more renowned for his outstanding success as a sire of dirt horses.

4 — Kefalonians — Though he'd won two of six grass starts, he was a badly beaten sixth and eighth in his last two starts, both on grass.

5 — Crimson Guard — The obvious favorite, trained by Bill Mott, the leading trainer at Saratoga and as good a trainer as anyone anywhere. Crimson Guard had four grass starts, all very sharp performances: second by three lengths to future stakes winner Debonair Dan; second by a neck, but placed first on a disqualification in the Transylvania Stakes; a distant second in the Saranac to Debonair Dan, and, in his last start, May 27, 1995, a close third in the Jersey Derby behind Da Hoss and Claudius. But he had no races in three months since.

Crimson Guard obviously had a class advantage here, and Mott is certainly adept at bringing horses back off a layoff successfully. But common sense said Mott hadn't been pointing to this allowance race while planning the rest of Crimson Guard's three-year-old season, rather he was using it as a tightener for future stakes endeavors. In his only previous start off a layoff, when he made his three-year-old debut at Gulfstream Park, February 4, 1995, off a similar layoff as today, Crimson Guard was second by 5½ lengths on the dirt.

6 — Thirty Good Ones — He'd run fifth by 4¾ lengths to Debonair Dan in his last start, a slightly longer grass allowance at Saratoga, July 28, 1995. He had a record of 2-5-4 in 17 grass starts, and he also had early speed. In the nine turf past performance lines (PPs) in the *Form*, Thirty Good Ones had been on the lead twice, second at the first call five times, and third twice. Of the four horses in the field who had raced on turf, he was the only one that had made the lead.

Conclusions? Crimson Guard was the horse to beat if ready, but if he wasn't, Gilder and Thirty Good Ones figured to have a chance. In my selections, I picked Crimson Guard first despite the layoff. In the bankroll, I bet $10 exactas using Crimson Guard on top of both Gilder and Thirty Good Ones, and $2 saver exactas using Gilder and Thirty Good Ones on top of Crimson Guard. I also bet $5 Pick Threes (races 6 through 8) using Crimson Guard in the sixth and $2 Pick Threes using Gilder and Thirty Good Ones in the sixth.

SIXTH RACE	1 MILE. (Inner Turf)(1.34⁴) ALLOWANCE. Purse $36,000. 3-year-olds and upward which have not won two races other than maiden, claiming or starter. Weights: 3-year-olds, 117 lbs. Older, 122 lbs.
Saratoga AUGUST 28, 1995	Non-winners of $24,000 at one mile or over since May 3, allowed 3 lbs. Of $19,200 twice since February 2, 5 lbs. Of $15,000 twice in 1995, 8 lbs. (Races where entered for $50,000 or less not considered in allowances.)

Value of Race: $36,000 Winner $21,600; second $7,200; third $3,960; fourth $2,160; fifth $1,080. Mutuel Pool $337,147.00 Exacta Pool $548,678.00

Last Raced	Horse	M/Eqt. A.Wt	PP	St	¼	½	¾	Str	Fin	Jockey	Odds $1
30Jly95 4Sar6	Gilder	4 114	1	1	$1^{1\frac{1}{2}}$	$1^{\frac{1}{2}}$	$1^{\frac{1}{2}}$	$1^{\frac{1}{2}}$	$1^{1\frac{1}{2}}$	Lovato F Jr	18.20
27May95 9GS3	Crimson Guard	3 113	5	5	3^1	$3^{\frac{1}{2}}$	$3^{1\frac{1}{2}}$	$3^{\frac{1}{2}}$	2^{nk}	Smith M E	0.75
28Jly95 4Sar5	Thirty Good Ones	b 4 114	6	6	2^2	2^1	$2^{\frac{1}{2}}$	$2^{1\frac{1}{2}}$	3no	Sellers S J	6.90
5Aug95 4Sar1	Jets Over Miami	b 3 112	2	4	6	6	6	5^3	$4^{\frac{1}{2}}$	Day P	4.30
17Aug95 7Sar1	Boulder Drive	3 112	3	2	4^1	4^1	$4^{\frac{1}{2}}$	$4^{1\frac{1}{2}}$	$5^{5\frac{1}{2}}$	Bailey J D	4.20
6Aug95 4Sar8	Kefalonians	3 114	4	3	5^2	5^3	5^{hd}	6	6	Velazquez J R	18.60

OFF AT 3:40 Start Good. Won driving. Time, :23⁴, :48¹, 1:11⁴, 1:35³ Course firm.

$2 Mutuel Prices:

1–GILDER	38.40	9.10	5.40
5–CRIMSON GUARD		2.70	2.20
6–THIRTY GOOD ONES			3.30

$2 EXACTA 1–5 PAID $92.50

B. g, by Smile–Rythmical, by Fappiano. Trainer Hauswald Philip M. Bred by Genter F A Stable Inc (Ky).

GILDER sprinted clear in the early stages, set the pace under pressure for six furlongs, drifted out a bit while maintaining a narrow lead into upper stretch, dug in when challenged inside the furlong marker then edged clear under brisk urging. CRIMSON GUARD settled just off the pace from outside to the top of the stretch, then closed late to nip THIRTY GOOD ONES for the place. THIRTY GOOD ONES forced the pace from outside for six furlongs, drew on nearly even terms with the winner in midstretch, then weakened in the final sixteenth. JETS OVER MIAMI trailed to the turn then rallied belatedly. BOULDER DRIVE raced in close contention along the inside to the top of the stretch and lacked a strong closing bid. KEFALONIANS raced within striking distance to the turn and lacked a further response.

Owners— 1, Pitfield Ward C; 2, Dekwiatkowski Henryk; 3, Anstu Stable & Subotnick Stuart; 4, Ackerman Kenny; 5, Willmott Stables; 6, Amvrosiatos A & Vangelatos P

Trainers— 1, Hauswald Philip M; 2, Mott William I; 3, Richards Robert J Jr; 4, Kelly Larry; 5, Vestal Peter M; 6, Sciacca Gary

Overweight: Crimson Guard (1), Boulder Drive (3).

Gilder went wire to wire, paying $38.40. Crimson Guard, sent off at 3-5, came on again to edge Thirty Good Ones for second by a neck, with Jets Over Miami just another nose behind. The two-dollar exacta paid $92.50. The $2 Pick Threes were alive with Duda and La Turka, the horses I picked 1-2 in the seventh in my selections, and Golden Attraction and Western Dreamer, the horses I picked 1-2 in the eighth, the Spinaway Stakes for two-year-old fillies.

The scratches of Market Booster and Oh Nonsense reduced the field in the seventh, the Waya Stakes for fillies and mares at 1⅜ miles on the inner turf course, to six.

7 Saratoga

1⅜ MILES. (Inner Turf). (2:13¹) 4th Running of THE WAYA. Purse $50,000 Added. Fillies and mares, 3-year-olds and upward. By subscription of $50 each, which should accompany the nomination, $250 to pass the entry box, $250 to start, with $50,000 added. The added money and all fees to be divided 60% to the winner, 20% to second, 11% to third, 6% to fourth and 3% to fifth. Weights: 3-year-olds, 115 lbs. Older, 123 lbs. Non-winners of $50,000 twice over a mile and a quarter on the turf since October 31, allowed 3 lbs. $30,000 twice over a mile and a furlong on the turf in 1995, 5 lbs. $30,000 over a mile and a quarter since September 1, 9 lbs. Starters to be named at the closing time of entries. Trophies will be presented to the winning owner, trainer and jockey. The New York Racing Association reserves the right to transfer this race to the main track. Closed Saturday, August 12 with 35 nominations.

Coupled – Oh Nonsense and Softina

Irving's Girl

Owner: Annin Stable

B. m. 5
Sire: Badger Land (Codex)
Dam: Card Table (Bold Bidder)
Br: Spring Farm & Assoc (Bel-C)
Tr: Schulhofer Flint S ($2 7 9 12 .13)

114

Lifetime Record: 32 7 6 5 $254,111

SAMYN J L ($1 7 2 8 .14)

Oh Nonsense

Owner: Sheppard Jonathan E

Dk. b or br. f. 4
Sire: Oh Say (Hoist the Flag)
Dam: Ba Binh (King's Bishop)
Br: Sheppard Jonathan E (Pa)
Tr: Sheppard Jonathan E ($8 6 6 1 .21)

114

Lifetime Record: 9 4 1 2 $50,828

RICE D S (1 0 1 0 .00)

Sofitina

Owner: Augustin Stable

B. f. 4
Sire: Alydar (Raise a Native)
Dam: Waya (Faraway Son)
Br: Brant Peter M & Strawbridge George Jr. (Pa)
Tr: Sheppard Jonathan E ($8 6 6 1 .21)

114

Lifetime Record: 14 3 3 1 $62,378

KRONE J A (141 14 24 21 .18)

Duda

Owner: Paulson Madeleine A

Dk. b or br. f. 6
Sire: Theatrical (Ire) (Nureyev)
Dam: Noble Times (Drums of Time)
Br: Paulson Allen E (Ky)
Tr: Mott William I ($4 17 6 6 .21)

117

Lifetime Record: 13 5 2 2 $176,578

BAILEY J D (100 43 22 22 .23)

Kudos For Sweets

Own: Taylor Anthony
CHAVEZ J F (175 23 22 18 .13)

B. f. 4
Sire: Buck Dance (Water Prince)
Dam: Custard Creme (Restivo)
Br: Houbeck Elmer Jr & Harriet C (Fla)
Tr: Hulbert Howard A (2 1 1 0 .50)

114

Lifetime Record: 34 5 8 4 $131,890										
1995	9	2	3	2	$73,620	Turf	2	0	0	0	$840
1994	15	1	3	2	$37,540	Wet	8	1	1	1	$30,995
Sar Ⓣ	0	0	0	0		Dist Ⓣ	0	0	0	0	

16Aug95-8Sar fst 7f	:224 :454 1:10 1:23 3+ ⒻAlw 40000N$Y	93 7 1 11½ 2½ 2½ 2½	Chavez J F	121	19.50	90-14	Twist Afleet121½ Kudos ForSweets1214 Aly's Conquest121no	Game effort	7
6Aug95-6Sar wf 6f	:223 :461 :584 1:12 3+ ⒻAlw 42000N$Y	79 1 5 2hd 3nk 2hd 1hd	Chavez J F	113	3.30	81-17	KdosForSwts113hd Wllspynow122nk MssProspctr116¾	Broke slowly, game	5
21May95-6Hia sly 5½f ⊗	:214 :45 :583 1:04 3+ ⒻAlw 24200N$Y	84 1 4 43½ 45 41½ 31¾	Verenzuela J L	115	4.10	100-13	Gipsy Countess115nk Nezzie Baby1191½ Kudos For Sweets115nk	Late rally	7
16May95-10Hia fst 6f	:224 :451 :574 1:102 ⒻAlw 22000N$Y	89 2 2 13½ 1hd 11 2¾	Madrid S O	115	*2.30	88-21	SlyMid115¾ KudosForSwets115nk FuturAnswr1151½	Gave way grudgingly	7
9Apr95-10Hia fst 6f	:214 :441 1:092 3+ ⒻChris EvertH50k	71 8 1 64¾ 65½ 55 511	Vasquez J	115	22.70	83-16	Sigrun1152½ Goldarama1161½ Gipsy Countess113nk	Tired	9
28Mar95-4OTC fst 1 1/16	:24 :484 1:142 1:463 3+ ⒻFlaTBOA DstF35k	87 9 6 52½ 4½ 2hd 2nk	Vasquez J	116	-	97-04	Shouldnt Say Never122nk Kudos For Sweets116no Cavada1222		12
Wide 1st turn, led into stretch									
11Mar95-1GP fst 6f	:223 :452 :573 1:101 ⒻAlw 35000N3X	91 7 1 21 2hd 1½ 12¾	Bailey J D	116	2.70	89-11	KudosForSwets1162¾ VrySntimntl1183¾ LightExrcis1161½	Driving, six wide	7
23Feb95-9GP fst 7f	:224 :461 1:11 1:233 ⒻAlw 29000N3X	86 6 3 1hd 1hd 1hd 31½	Bailey J D	116	16.90	83-20	LottDncing116¾ VrySntimntl118¾ KudosForSwts1164½	Weakened, inside	8
19Jan95-9GP fst 7f	:221 :444 1:101 1:233 ⒻAlw 41500N$Y	77 4 2 5¾ 43½ 54½ 64½	Bailey J D	114	34.70	78-21	Goldarama1143 Tenacious Tiffany1181½ Mary Morning114hd	Faded	8
27Dec94-1Crc fst 6f	:22 :453 :58 1:111 ⒻAlw 22500NC	81 4 3 43½ 35½ 37 37¾	Velasquez J	114	16.10	83-21	Miss Gibson County1146 Beau Blush1141¾ Kudos For Sweets1142	4-wide	5

WORKOUTS: Jly 25 Rkm 5f my 1:03 B (d) 1/1 Jly 22 Rkm 4f fst :51 B 11/15 Jly 14 Rkm 4f fst :482 B 7/18 ●Jun 29 Rkm 4f fst :472 H 1/6

La Turka

Own: De Hechavarria Luis
SANTOS J A (161 19 21 24 .12)

Dk. b or br m. 5
Sire: Turkoman (Alydar)
Dam: Ansha (Believe It)
Br: Jayeff B Stables (Ky)
Tr: Tagg Barclay (16 4 0 1 .25)

114

Lifetime Record: 32 9 4 8 $212,237										
1995	7	3	1	1	$83,101	Turf	27	7	3	7	$178,472
1994	14	3	1	5	$73,186	Wet	0	0	0	0	
Sar Ⓣ	2	2	0	0	$44,400	Dist Ⓣ	1	0	0	1	$5,200

6Aug95-7Sar gd 1 3/16 Ⓣ	:474 1:122 1:383 1:574 3+ ⒻAlw 44000N$mY	97 1 2 31 1hd 11½ 11½	Bailey J D	114 b	3.85	76-21	La Turka1141½ Symphony Lady1141 Chelsey Flower1221½	Edged clear	6
9Jly95-3Lrl fst 1 1/16 ⊗	:243 :49 1:133 1:444 3+ ⒻAlw 30400NC	82 4 2 21 21 2½ 1no	Reynolds L C	L 119 b	1.90	86-23	La Turka119no Mz. Zill Bear1172½ Nellie Custis11911	Driving	4
11Jun95-9Pim fm 1½ Ⓣ	:49 1:134 2:024 2:292 3+ ⒻApril Run34k	75 10 6 56½ 57 54½ 48	Johnston M T	L 119 b	*1.70	85-11	Nellie Custis1173 Joy Of Ireland1192 Open Toe1173	No menace	11
2Apr95-11Hia fm 1 1/16 Ⓣ	1:39 3+ ⒻHia Bud BCH107k	79 2 6 77¾ 78 88½ 88¾	Ramos W S	L 114 b	30.60	94 —	Cox Orange120nk Apolda1121½ P J Floral114nk	Faded	11
24Feb95-4GP fm *1 1/16 Ⓣ	:234 :484 1:124 1:423 + ⒻAlw 40000N$mY	94 9 7 41½ 3½ 3½ 1no	Smith M E	L 114 b	7.90	95 —	La Turka114no Shir Dar116hd Icy Warning114nk		9
Seven wide top str, driving									
29Jan95-3GP fm 1⅜ Ⓣ	:494 1:142 1:382 2:144 ⒻHandicap40k	87 4 1 1½ 1hd 21½ 33	Smith M E	L 114 b	2.80	89-06	Northern Emerald1151½ Petiteness1131½ La Turka1141½	Weakened	7
13Jan95-4GP fm *1½ Ⓣ	:504 1:172 2:084 2:331 ⒻHandicap40k	93 1 1 12 2½ 2½ 23	Smith M E	L 113 b	7.40	72-16	Abigailthewife1183 La Turka1131½ Petiteness1121	Gamely	9
27Dec94-10Crc fm 1 1/16 Ⓣ	:24 :491 1:133 1:442 3+ ⒻAlw 21000NC	87 2 5 73½ 74 41½ 32¾	Smith M E	L 115 b	*1.40	76-21	Urus1151½ Track Gossip115¾ La Turka115nk	Bid, hung	9
29Oct94-9Lrl fm 1 1/16 Ⓣ	:233 :473 1:132 1:444 3+ ⒻAlw 23000N4X	89 9 3 34 3nk 11½ 3¾	Prado E S	L 117 b	2.30	77-27	Night Fax115¾ Promiseville114no La Turka1172½	Hung	9
7Oct94-7Med fm 1 70 Ⓣ	:222 :461 1:11 1:403 3+ ⒻAlw 35000N$mY	88 5 11 106 62½ 2½ 2hd	Krone J A	L 115 b	*1.20	88-13	My Marchesa115hd La Turka1153½ Kira's Dancer119¾	Caught, final strides	12

WORKOUTS: Aug 25 Sar tr.t Ⓣ 5f fm 1:021 B (d) 2/4 Aug 18 Sar tr.t Ⓣ 4f fm :502 B (d) 30/35 ●Aug 1 Lrl Ⓣ 4f fm :484 H (d) 1/10 Jly 25 Lrl Ⓣ 4f fm :503 B (d) 3/3 ●Jly 3 Lrl 5f fst :59 H 1/10 ●Jun 28 Lrl 5f gd 1:01 H 1/

Market Booster

Own: Moyglare Stud Farm
DAY P (182 31 26 25 .17)

B. m. 6
Sire: Green Dancer (Nijinsky II)
Dam: Final Figure (Super Concorde)
Br: Moyglare Stud Farm Ltd (Ky)
Tr: Lukas D Wayne (35 7 5 2 .20)

123

Lifetime Record: 36 9 6 5 $783,366										
1995	7	1	2	1	$134,393	Turf	32	9	6	4	$774,366
1994	12	3	0	3	$213,858	Wet	2	0	0	0	
Sar Ⓣ	2	0	0	1	$5,624	Dist Ⓣ	4	1	0	1	$83,154

29Jly95-8Sar fm 1½ Ⓣ	:471 1:13 2:004 2:252 3+ SwordDancerH-G1	96 11 4 31 21 43 67¾	Day P	112 b	7.90	95-08	Kiri's Clown114hd Awad1211½ King's Theatre1132	Bid, tired	13
9Jly95-9Bel fm 1¼ Ⓣ	:48 1:114 1:354 1:594 3+ ⒻNew York H-G2	103 1 4 54 52½ 51½ 31	Day P	119 b	2.55	88-14	Irish Linnet119hd Danish1161 Market Booster119hd	Boxed in, checked late	6
25Jun95-9CD fm 1⅛ Ⓣ	:481 1:121 1:353 1:472 3+ ⒻLocustGroveH110k	98 1 2 2½ 31½ 21 21½	Barton D M	L 120 b	*1.00	92-06	Memories1141½ Market Booster1201½ Thread1152¾	Lacked solid bid	7
4Jun95-9Bel fm 1⅜ Ⓣ	:482 1:132 1:381 2:133 3+ ⒻShepshdBayH-G2	97 3 3 31½ 41½ 31½ 54¼	Smith M E	121 b	*1.10	86-08	Duda1121½ Danish116¾ Chelsey Flower112nk	Boxed in, took up 1/8	7
Placed 4th through disqualification.									
27Apr95-8Kee fm 1½ Ⓣ	:481 1:134 2:04 2:291 ⒻBewitch-G3	101 4 2 21 2hd 1hd 1½	Day P	L 119 b	*1.20	99-08	Market Booster119½ Memories1131½ Abigailthewife1144	Hand urging	7
12Mar95-10GP sf 1½ Ⓣ	:502 1:15 2:051 2:29 3+ ⒻOrchid H-G2	101 4 3 43½ 53½ 33 2½	Day P	L 116 b	7.30	74-25	Exchange120½ Market Booster116hd Northern Emerald115½	Rallied	10
19Feb95-9GP fm 1⅜ Ⓣ	:483 1:14 1:381 2:142 3+ ⒻVery One H50k	96 6 2 1½ 1hd 1hd 42½	Bailey J D	L 117 b	2.20	92-03	P J Floral1131½ Trampoli118¾ Memories113hd	Faded	6
17Dec94-10Crc gd 1½ Ⓣ	:484 1:132 2:034 2:284 3+ ⒻLaPrevoyanteH-G2	93 2 5 35 42 33½ 35	Day P	L 118 b	*.90	81-14	Abigailthewife1144¾ Trampoli118nk MrketBooster1182	Bid between, hung	14
12Nov94-8Aqu gd 1½ Ⓣ	:51 1:153 2:071 2:314 3+ ⒻLongIslandH-G2	103 2 6 31 12 17 15¾	Luzzi M J	115 b	7.70	97-03	Market Booster1155¾ Tiffany's Taylor114no Lady Affirmed113¾	Mild drive	12
28Oct94-8Kee fm 1½ Ⓣ	:48 1:123 2:05 2:311 3+ ⒻDowager46k	89 4 3 2hd 2hd 1hd 11½	Day P	L 123 b	2.90	89-14	MarketBooster1231½ MyMandy114¾ FairyGrden115nk	Well ridden, driving	10

WORKOUTS: Aug 22 Sar Ⓣ 5f fm 1:00 H (d) 1/3 Aug 15 Sar tr.t 4f fst :54 B 25/30 ●Jly 23 Sar Ⓣ 5f fm 1:02 B (d) 1/4 Jun 20 Bel 4f fst :484 B 14/31 Jun 14 Bel tr.t 4f gd :504 B 13/30 May 31 Bel 4f fst :502 B 58/73

Petiteness

Own: Harbor View Farm
SMITH M E (178 30 22 34 .17)

B. f. 4
Sire: Chief's Crown (Danzig)
Dam: Affirmatively (Affirmed)
Br: Wolfson Mr & Mrs L & Jacobs Mrs E D (Ky)
Tr: Jerkens H Allen (44 8 4 6 .18)

114

Lifetime Record: 26 3 5 7 $142,521										
1995	5	0	1	1	$16,540	Turf	23	3	5	5	$134,453
1994	16	3	3	4	$110,923	Wet	2	0	0	1	$6,468
Sar Ⓣ	3	1	1	0	$27,240	Dist Ⓣ	3	0	2	1	$17,800

17Aug95-5Sar fm 1 1/16 Ⓣ	:233 :464 1:113 1:413 3+ ⒻAlw 44000N$Y	78 4 4 48 51¾ 51¾ 45½	Samyn J L	119 f	6.30	85-12	Lady Reiko1192 Falconese119½ Uncharted Waters1143	No late bid	7
12Mar95-10GP sf 1½ Ⓣ	:502 1:15 2:051 2:29 3+ ⒻOrchid H-G2	89 8 7 97¾ 95¾ 99½ 97	Samyn J L	111	43.60	68-25	Exchange120½ Market Booster116hd Northern Emerald115½	Gave way	10
22Feb95-8GP fm *1⅛ Ⓣ	:471 1:12 1:364 1:483 + ⒻAlw 30000N3X	87 4 4 58 64 51½ 42½	Samyn J L	116 f	*1.90	99 —	Joy Of Ireland1181 Park Valley116no Duda1191½	Lacked response	10
29Jan95-3GP fm 1⅜ Ⓣ	:494 1:142 1:382 2:144 ⒻHandicap40k	89 1 4 47 45½ 34 21½	Samyn J L	113 f	4.60	90-06	Northern Emerald1151½ Petiteness1131½ La Turka1141½		7
Seven wide top str, rallied									
13Jan95-4GP fm *1½ Ⓣ	:504 1:172 2:084 2:331 ⒻHandicap40k	90 4 5 33 3½ 34 34½	Samyn J L	112	8.00	71-16	Abigailthewife1183 La Turka1131½ Petiteness1121	Lacked response	9
17Dec94-10Crc gd 1½ Ⓣ	:484 1:132 2:034 2:284 3+ ⒻLaPrevoyntH-G2	89 13 11 1311 107½ 86½ 47	Rodriguez P A	110	25.40f	79-14	Abigailthewife1144¾ Trampoli118nk Market Booster1182		14
Lacked room backstretch									
3Dec94-9Crc gd 1⅛ Ⓣ	:49 1:131 1:38 1:503 3+ ⒻMy Charmer H100k	78 12 12 1214 1212 1214 1210½	Boulanger G	111	*2.40e	— —	Caress114no Putthepowdertoit1142 Cox Orange116nk	Slow start	12
12Nov94-8Aqu gd 1½ Ⓣ	:51 1:153 2:071 2:314 3+ ⒻLongIslandH-G2	~86 8 7 84½ 43 58½ 49½	Samyn J L	108	*1.45e	88-03	Market Booster1155¾ Tiffany's Taylor114no LadyAffirmed113¾	No late bid	12
26Oct94-7Aqu gd 1⅛ Ⓣ	:482 1:132 1:381 1:504 3+ ⒻAlw 36000N3X	87 1 8 85½ 62½ 54 32	Samyn J L	116	*1.05e	84-15	Caress119nk Manila Lila1171¾ Petiteness116nk	Late gain	10
22Sep94-8Bel fm 1 1/16 Ⓣ	:24 :464 1:11 1:44 3+ ⒻAlw 34000N2X	89 5 8 810 56 35 11	Samyn J L	115	3.10e	76-18	Petiteness1151 Great Lady Mary1152 Bold Rosa Lined1175	Driving	8

WORKOUTS: Aug 9 Sar tr.t 5f fst 1:053 B 8/10

The seventh was almost a carbon copy of the sixth: a six-horse grass race with Billy Mott sending out the heavy favorite off a layoff. This time it was the 3 horse, Duda, a top-class filly who sported a turf record of 4-2-2 in 11 starts and earnings of $158,748. She'd won her lone start at this distance in stakes company, taking the Grade II Sheepshead Bay Handicap by a length and a quarter at Belmont Park. But she had not raced since finishing a close fourth as the favorite in the New York Handicap, July 9, 1995, at Belmont.

In her PPs, she showed four starts off layoffs and had won three of them.

Of the others:

1 — Irving's Girl — The hard-hitting mare had been in the money 15 of 28 grass starts, but was only three for 18 the past two years. She was a threat on best.

2 — Softina — The Delaware shipper had one win in 10 grass starts and appeared to be way over her head.

4 — Kudos For Sweets — A sprinter stretching way out who had not lit the board in two previous grass tries. No way.

5 — La Turka — This improving mare had a turf record of 7-3-7 in 27 starts, and had won her last grass appearance in the third start off a layoff, an allowance race at Saratoga, racing without Lasix for the first time in her 10 PPs. (Lasix became legal in New York State four days later when racing shifted from Saratoga to Belmont.) She had also won her previous race on dirt. A quick look at her PPs showed that she'd been eighth and a distant fourth in two stakes races, losing the first to the ultra-talented Cox Orange. But if you took the time to read the *Form* analysis next to her PPs, you discovered that the horse she just beat at Saratoga, Symphony Lady, came back to beat Cox Orange in a stakes at Monmouth.

Every single year at Saratoga there are repeat overlay winners, horses who come back and win a second straight start at Saratoga at generous odds. Every year.

6 — Petiteness — A dull fourth in her return, an allowance race at Saratoga, and three for 23 lifetime on grass. Starting at the bottom of her and La Turka's PPs, we pick up that they raced against each other twice at Gulfstream in January of '95, splitting two decisions. But Petiteness was in top shape then, and now

was making a second start off a layoff after a dull fourth in an easier spot. She certainly had a chance to win, but if anybody was going to upset Duda, it figured to be La Turka.

She did.

SEVENTH RACE
Saratoga
AUGUST 28, 1995

1¾ MILES. (Inner Turf)(2.13¹) 4th Running of THE WAYA. Purse $50,000 Added. Fillies and mares, 3-year-olds and upward. By subscription of $50 each, which should accompany the nomination, $250 to pass the entry box, $250 to start, with $50,000 added. The added money and all fees to be divided 60% to the winner, 20% to second, 11% to third, 6% to fourth and 3% to fifth. Weights: 3-year-olds, 115 lbs. Older, 123 lbs. Non-winners of $50,000 twice over a mile and a quarter on the turf since October 31, allowed 3 lbs. $30,000 twice over a mile and a furlong on the turf in 1995, 5 lbs. $30,000 over a mile and a quarter since September 1, 9 lbs. Starters to be named at the closing time of entries. Trophies will be presented to the winning owner, trainer and jockey. The New York Racing Association reserves the right to transfer this race to the main track. Closed Saturday, August 12 with 35 nominations.

Value of Race: $55,290 Winner $33,190; second $11,050; third $6,077; fourth $3,315; fifth $1,656. Mutuel Pool $403,407.00 Exacta Pool $671,941.00

Last Raced	Horse	M/Eqt. A.Wt	PP	¼	½	¾	1	Str	Fin	Jockey	Odds $1
6Aug95 ⁷Sar¹	La Turka	b 5 114	5	2½	2¹	1¹	1¹	1hd	1hd	Santos J A	4.90
9Jly95 ⁹Bel⁴	Duda	4 117	3	5¹	4hd	4¹	3hd	2²	2¹½	Bailey J D	0.70
16Jly95 ¹⁰Del⁷	Sofitina	4 114	2	6	6	2hd	4²	3⁴	3⁵	Krone J A	10.40
6Aug95 ⁸Rkm³	Irving's Girl	5 114	1	3¹	3hd	5½	5³	4¹	4⁶	Samyn J L	6.80
17Aug95 ⁵Sar⁴	Petiteness	f 4 114	6	4½	5¹	3½	2½	5¹⁰	5⁹	Smith M E	7.00
16Aug95 ⁸Sar²	Kudos For Sweets	4 114	4	1¹½	1½	6	6	6	6	Chavez J F	10.90

OFF AT 4:11 Start Good. Won driving. Time, :24⁴, :50⁴, 1:16⁴, 1:40³, 2:04¹; 2:16¹ Course firm.

$2 Mutuel Prices:

5-LA TURKA	11.80	3.80	3.00
3-DUDA		2.50	2.20
1A-SOFITINA			3.00

$2 EXACTA 5-3 PAID $23.40

Dk. b. or br. m, by Turkoman–Aneka, by Believe It. Trainer Tagg Barclay. Bred by Jayeff B Stables (Ky).

LA TURKA forced the early pace from outside, opened a clear advantage along the backstretch, continued on the front into the stretch, dug in when challenged in midstretch then turned back DUDA under brisk urging. DUDA settled just off the pace while between horses for a mile, rallied inside the winner to challenge in midstretch, but couldn't overtake that one in the final eighth. SOFITINA trailed for five furlongs, moved up steadily while three wide to contest the pace along the backstretch, remained a factor into upper stretch then lacked a strong closing response. IRVING'S GIRL raced in close contention while saving ground to the far turn and gradually tired thereafter. PETITENESS reserved early, moved into contention along the backstretch, made a run to threaten midway on the turn, flattened out. KUDOS FOR SWEETS set the early pace along the inside, gave way after going six furlongs.

Owners— 1, De Hechavarria Luis; 2, Paulson Madeleine A; 3, Augustin Stable; 4, Anstu Stable; 5, Harbor View Farm; 6, Taylor Anthony
Trainers—1, Tagg Barclay; 2, Mott William I; 3, Sheppard Jonathan E; 4, Schulhofer Flint S; 5, Jerkens H Allen; 6, Hulbert Howard A
Scratched— Oh Nonsense (13Aug95 ⁹PEN³), Market Booster (29Jly95 ⁸SAR⁶).

Duda was hammered down to 3-5 and La Turka dispatched as the second choice at 9-2. La Turka took the lead midway through the race, then tenaciously held Duda off in the lane to win by a head, paying $11.80 to win and presenting potential Pick Three payoffs that were all four figures for our $2 tickets.

Eight two-year-old fillies went to post in the seven-furlong Spinaway Stakes. The Pick Three payoffs for our two live tickets were $1,033 and $1,574 for Golden Attraction and Western Dreamer, respectively.

8 Saratoga

7 Furlongs (1:20²) 104th Running of THE SPINAWAY. Purse $200,000. Grade I. Fillies, 2-year-olds. By subscription of $200 each which should accompany the nomination, $1,000 to pass the entry box, $1,000 to start. The purse to be divided 60% to the winner, 20% to second, 11% to third, 6% to fourth and 3% to fifth. Weight, 121 lbs. Starters to be named at the closing time of entries. Trophies will be presented to the winner owner, trainer and jockey. Closed Saturday, August 12 with 26 nominations.

7 FURLONGS

Zee Lady

Own: Eiserman M & Fishbein K & Silver E
Dk. b or br f. 2 (Mar)
Sire: Unreal Zeal (Mr. Prospector)
Dam: Try to Be a Lady (Sham)
Br: Eric A. DelValle (Fla)
Tr: Rice Linda (6 0 1 0 .00)
SANTOS J A (161 19 21 24 .12) 121

Lifetime Record: 4 2 0 0 $49,320
1995 4 2 0 0 $49,320 Turf 0 0 0 0
1994 0 M 0 0 Wet 0 0 0 0
Sar 1 0 0 0 Dist 0 0 0 0

21Jly95-8Sar fst 6f :21³ :44³ :57¹ 1:10⁴ ⒻSchuylrvill-G2 43 1 3 3² 4² 45½ 718½ Santos J A 118 5.00 68-10 GoldnAttrcton1212½ DylghtCm112nk WstrnDrmr1213½ Saved ground, tired 8
21Jun95-8Bel fst 5½f :22¹ :46 :58⁴ 1:05⁴ ⒻAstoria BC64k 78 4 3 1¹ 1¹ 1⁵ 17½ Santos J A 114 2.15 86-18 Zee Lady1147½ Not Brite Brilliant1124½ Dynasty1142½ Lugged in, driving 5
6May95-3CD fst 5f :22² :45² :57³ WHAS92k 50 11 14 1111 1119 914 618½ Davis R G 114 *2.50e 94 — Western Dreamer1142 Rosie O'greta1141½ Great Southern1133 14
Reared start, improved position, always wide
19Apr95-2Aqu fst 4½f Ⓢ :22² :46² :53 ⒻMd Sp Wt — 4 3 1½ 1⁷ 1¹⁰ Santos J A 115 *.65 102-13 Zee Lady11510 Little Notice115hd Bring Me Flowers115no Ridden out 10
WORKOUTS: ●Aug 23 Sar 5f fst :59¹ H 1/21 Aug 17 Sar 6f fst 1:14² H 1/2 Aug 11 Sar 5f fst 1:01 H 7/35 Aug 5 Sar 4f fst :48³ B 8/46 Jly 17 Bel 3f fst :39⁴ B 15/15 Jun 16 Bel 4f fst :51³ B 78/80

Summer Squeeze

Own: Dogwood Stable
Ch. f. 2 (Mar)
Sire: Summer Squall (Storm Bird)
Dam: Sugar Hill Chick (Fit to Fight)
Br: Farish W S & Webber W Temple Jr (Ky)
Tr: Vestal Peter M (23 5 2 5 .22)
DAY P (182 31 26 25 .17) 121

Lifetime Record: 4 2 0 1 $32,955
1995 4 2 0 1 $32,955 Turf 0 0 0 0
1994 0 M 0 0 Wet 0 0 0 0
Sar 1 1 0 0 $19,200 Dist 1 1 0 0 $19,200

14Aug95-6Sar fst 7f :23 :45⁴ 1:11² 1:24¹ ⒻAlw 32000N2L 92 3 8 4³ 3³ 2½ 1⁵ Day P 115 3.90 85-19 Summer Squeeze1155 Wild 'n' Nasty1123 My Flag1182 Drew off 9
26Jly95-8EIP fst 6f :22³ :46¹ :59¹ 1:11⁴ ⒻMd Sp Wt 76 6 3 31½ 3¹ 1hd 1⁴ Martinez W 117 *1.00 87-19 Summer Squeeze1174 Trillium Trick1171 Mariuka11711 Inside, driving 12
9Jly95-5EIP fst 5f :22³ :46 :58⁴ ⒻMd Sp Wt 71 11 6 42½ 3³ 32½ 3nk Martinez W 117 8.10 94-10 Natural Genius117nk Currency Quest117no Summer Squeeze1174 11
Altered course inside, deep stretch, hung
25Jun95-4CD fst 5½f :22¹ :46 :57⁴ 1:04² ⒻMd Sp Wt 45 2 7 12¹⁵ 12¹³ 10¹⁶ 714½ Martinez W 120 20.80 86-03 Grab The Cash120½ Oxford Scholar120hd Mariuka120½ 12
Checked, opening 1/16, never close
WORKOUTS: Aug 24 Sar 4f fst :48² H 5/25 Aug 9 Sar 5f fst 1:01² H 12/40 Jly 21 CD 5f fst 1:02² B 7/17 Jly 6 CD 4f gd :51 B 15/18 ●Jun 21 CD 4f fst :48 B 1/45 Jun 14 CD 5f fst 1:02⁴ Bg 19/37

Golden Attraction

Own: Young William T
B. f. 2 (Jan)
Sire: Mr. Prospector (Raise a Native)
Dam: Seaside Attraction (Seattle Slew)
Br: Overbrook Farm (Ky)
Tr: Lukas D Wayne (35 7 5 2 .20)
STEVENS G L (4 2 0 0 .50) 121

Lifetime Record: 4 3 1 0 $195,587
1995 4 3 1 0 $195,587 Turf 0 0 0 0
1994 0 M 0 0 Wet 1 0 1 0 $40,000
Sar 1 1 0 0 $65,940 Dist 0 0 0 0

6Aug95-8Mth sly 6f :21² :45 :57³ 1:10⁴ ⒻSorority-G3 80 6 1 3⁴ 1hd 2¹ 2¾ Barton D M 119 *.70 84-14 CrftyButSweet119¾ GoldenAttrction1194½ CrelessHirss1192 Outfinished 6
21Jly95-8Sar fst 6f :21³ :44³ :57¹ 1:10⁴ ⒻSchuylrvill-G2 90 6 2 2hd 2hd 1hd 12½ Barton D M 121 3.15 87-10 GoldenAttrction1212½ DylightCome112hd WesternDrmr1213½ Dueled, game 8
2Jly95-10CD fst 5½f :22 :45³ :57³ 1:04 ⒻDebutante H105k 82 2 5 1½ 1½ 12½ 1½ Barton D M 115 *1.20e 103-04 GoldenAttraction115½ WesternDremer1213½ TipiclyIrish1152 Ridden out 9
4Jun95-2Hol fst 5f :22 :46 :58² ⒻMd Sp Wt 72 7 4 21½ 21½ 1¹ 14½ Stevens G L B 118 *.40 92-10 Golden Attraction1184½ Fillycap118hd Woodyoubelieveit1183½ Ridden out 7
WORKOUTS: ●Aug 22 Mth 5f fst 1:00⁴ B 1/14 Aug 16 Mth 5f fst :59⁴ H 2/21 Jly 31 Mth 4f fst :48³ B 4/39 Jly 15 Bel 5f fst 1:00⁴ H 4/30 ●Jun 25 CD 5f fst :59 H 1/36 Jun 17 CD 5f fst 1:01² B 7/30

Crafty But Sweet

Own: Moira & My Jo Lee Stable & Resee
Ch. f. 2 (Mar)
Sire: Crafty Prospector (Mr. Prospector)
Dam: Keys Special (Chieftain)
Br: Mischief Inc. (Ky)
Tr: Barbara Robert (30 6 3 4 .20)
SANTAGATA N (—) 121

Lifetime Record: 2 2 0 0 $138,000
1995 2 2 0 0 $138,000 Turf 0 0 0 0
1994 0 M 0 0 Wet 1 1 0 0 $120,000
Sar 1 1 0 0 $18,000 Dist 0 0 0 0

6Aug95-8Mth sly 6f :21² :45 :57³ 1:10⁴ ⒻSorority-G3 82 3 5 22½ 2hd 1¹ 1¾ Santagata N 119 11.50 85-14 CraftyButSweet119¾ GoldenAttraction1194½ CrelessHeiress1192 Driving 6
21Jly95-6Sar fst 5½f :21⁴ :45² :58 1:05 ⒻMd Sp Wt 81 7 6 2¹ 2hd 1hd 1nk Migliore R 119 13.70 96-10 Crafty But Sweet119nk Fast Busy1196 Afirmada119hd Fully extended 9
WORKOUTS: Aug 19 Sar 5f fst 1:01² H 9/25 Aug 1 Sar 4f fst :48 B 2/30 Jly 15 Bel 5f fst 1:01¹ H 11/30 Jly 6 Bel 5f fst 1:01³ H 3/16 Jun 30 Bel 4f fst :49¹ Hg21/53 Jun 24 Bel tr.t 4f fst :49⁴ B 26/37

Strawberry Clover

Own: Sabine Stable
Gr/ro f. 2 (Apr)
Sire: Darn That Alarm (Jig Time)
Dam: Strawberry Burrah (Princely Pleasure)
Br: Sabine Stables (Fla)
Tr: Barbara Robert (30 6 3 4 .20)
DAVIS R G (171 28 25 27 .12) 121

Lifetime Record: 2 1 0 0 $21,288
1995 2 1 0 0 $21,288 Turf 0 0 0 0
1994 0 M 0 0 Wet 1 1 0 0 $18,000
Sar 1 0 0 0 $3,288 Dist 0 0 0 0

9Aug95-9Sar fst 6½f :22¹ :45³ 1:10² 1:16³ ⒻAdirondack-G2 65 1 7 77¾ 7⁸ 69½ 511¾ Davis R G 112 b 29.50 80-11 FltFleetFeet113nk StedyCt112nk WesternDremr1201½ Broke slowly, drifted 7
26May95-2Bel sly 5f :22 :45³ :59 ⒻMd Sp Wt 67 6 5 31½ 1½ 1¹ 11½ Davis R G 115 *1.40 91-10 StrwbrryClvr1151½ Onthrghtwckt1152½ Thsky'sthlmt115no Drifted, gamely 8
WORKOUTS: ●Aug 24 Sar 3f fst :35⁴ H 1/9 Aug 19 Sar 5f fst 1:01 H 4/25 Aug 5 Sar tr.t 5f fst 1:04³ B 18/16 Jly 29 Sar 5f fst 1:01¹ H 8/37 Jly 23 Sar 4f fst :48³ B 14/54 Jly 17 Bel 3f fst :37² B 5/15

Western Dreamer

Own: Miller J Fred III
Ch. f. 2 (Apr)
Sire: Gone West (Mr. Prospector)
Dam: Dream Launch (Relaunch)
Br: Jayeff B Stables (Ky)
Tr: Beagle Barbara (2 0 0 2 .00)
PERRET C (42 4 3 9 .10) 121

Lifetime Record: 5 2 1 2 $125,733
1995 5 2 1 2 $125,733 Turf 0 0 0 0
1994 0 M 0 0 Wet 1 1 0 0 $19,406
Sar 2 0 0 2 $24,145 Dist 0 0 0 0

9Aug95-9Sar fst 6½f :22¹ :45³ 1:10² 1:16³ ⒻAdirondack-G2 92 2 6 64¾ 41½ 3nk 3½ Perret C 120 f 4.80 91-11 Flat Fleet Feet113nk Steady Cat112nk Western Dreamer1201½ Sharp try 7
21Jly95-8Sar fst 6f :21³ :44³ :57¹ 1:10⁴ ⒻSchuylrvill-G2 83 2 4 42½ 31½ 32½ 32½ Perret C 121 f *2.10 84-10 GoldnAttrction1212½ DylghtCm112hd WstrnDrmr1213½ Well placed, no rally 8
2Jly95-10CD fst 5½f :22 :45³ :57³ 1:04 ⒻDebutante H105k 81 3 4 84¾ 7⁴ 32½ 2½ Perret C L 121 f 1.60 102-04 GoldenAttrction115½ WesternDremer1213½ TipicHyIrish1152 Closed well 9
6May95-3CD fst 5f :22² :45² :57³ WHAS92k 82 9 8 8⁸ 62¾ 2² 1¾ Perret C L 114 f 6.80 104 — Western Dreamer1142 Rosie O'greta1141½ Great Southern1133 14
Bobbled start, 4-wide, driving
21Apr95-3Kee my 4½f :22⁴ :46 :52² ⒻMd Sp Wt 75 7 10 7⁵ 3⁴ 1hd Hughes L L5 L 110 f 6.30 99-07 WesternDremer110hd HevenlyVlly1173 MidnightTrin117no Fully extended 11
WORKOUTS: ●Aug 26 Sar 4f fst :46⁴ H 1/36 Aug 7 Sar 3f fst :36 B 3/27 Aug 2 Sar 5f fst 1:01³ H 3/34 Jly 19 Sar 3f fst :36 H 3/7 ●Jun 29 CD 3f fst :35¹ H 1/18 Jun 21 CD 6f fst 1:16 B 2/4

Birr

Own: Prestonwood Farm
Dk. b or br f. 2 (May)
Sire: Farma Way (Marfa)
Dam: Here's Your Tower (Irish Tower)
Br: Duncan Lloyd (Ky)
Tr: Walden W Elliott (12 1 2 3 .08)
BAILEY J D (188 43 22 22 .23) 121

Lifetime Record: 1 1 0 0 $10,800
1995 1 1 0 0 $10,800 Turf 0 0 0 0
1994 0 M 0 0 Wet 0 0 0 0
Sar 1 1 0 0 $10,800 Dist 0 0 0 0

2Aug95-4Sar fst 6f :22¹ :45⁴ :58¹ 1:11¹ ⒻMd 50000 92 6 6 2hd 1² 1³ 1⁹ Smith M E 117 b 4.20 85-19 Birr1179 Celestial Glance1174 Bright Plank1174½ Drifted, ridden out 9
WORKOUTS: ●Aug 23 Sar 4f fst :47 H 1/22 Aug 15 Sar 3f fst :36² B 3/15 Jly 31 Sar 4f fst :48² Hg11/55 Jly 25 Sar 5f fst 1:01³ B 4/28 Jly 19 Bel 4f fst :49 Hg30/66 Jly 14 Bel 5f fst 1:00² H 6/32

Flat Fleet Feet

Own: Kimmel Caesar P & Solondz Philip
Ch. f. 2 (Apr)
Sire: Afleet (Mr. Prospector)
Dam: Czar Dancer (Czaravich)
Br: Ollie A. Cohen (Ky)
Tr: Kimmel John C (33 5 7 9 .15)
SMITH M E (178 30 22 34 .17) 121

Lifetime Record: 3 2 1 0 $89,760
1995 3 2 1 0 $89,760 Turf 0 0 0 0
1994 0 M 0 0 Wet 0 0 0 0
Sar 2 2 0 0 $83,760 Dist 0 0 0 0

9Aug95-9Sar fst 6½f :22¹ :45³ 1:10² 1:16³ ⒻAdirondack-G2 93 3 4 3² 3¹ 1hd 1nk Smith M E 113 *.80 92-11 Flat FleetFeet113nk SteadyCat112nk WesternDreamer1201½ Fully extended 7
21Jly95-2Sar fst 5½f :21⁴ :45¹ :57² 1:03⁴ ⒻMd Sp Wt 99 2 2 2½ 2hd 1² 1⁹ Smith M E 119 *1.30 102-10 Flat Fleet Feet1199 Gold Sunrise119hd Oxford Scholar1193½ Mild drive 6
3Jly95-6Bel fst 5f :22 :46 :58³ ⒻMd Sp Wt 88 3 4 4⁶ 3³ 2½ 2nk Smith M E 115 4.30 93-14 Desiderosa115nk Flat Fleet Feet1156 Ontheright wicket1154½ Sharp try 6
Aug 22 Sar 5f fst 1:01 B 3/9 Aug 7 Sar 4f fst :50³ B 44/64 Aug 3 Sar 5f fst 1:03⁴ B 21/27 Jly 16 Bel 4f fst :49³ B 20/36 Jun 28 Bel 4f fst :48 Hg2/50 Jun 16 Bel tr.t 4f fst :48¹ H 5/44

I thought Golden Attraction, trained by D. Wayne Lukas, would be odds-on. She'd won her first three starts, including the Schuylerville Stakes at Saratoga, before finishing second by three-quarters of a length on a sloppy track at Monmouth in the Sorority Stakes to Crafty But Sweet, who was also in today's Spinaway.

Many times, top horses reveal more in defeat than they do in victories. When a good horse is beaten, does he or she fight it out for second or third, or completely pack it in? A classic example was the unbelievable performance of Seattle Slew when he finished second by a nose to Exceller in the Jockey Club Gold Cup. Many believe it was Slew's greatest race, and some argue it was one of the best races of all time, when Slew battled Affirmed into defeat in blazing fractions on a sloppy track in a mile and a half race. Exceller went by Slew easily at the top of the stretch, but Slew found something extra, coming back at Exceller and actually getting past him a few strides past the wire.

Golden Attraction is not Seattle Slew, but in her loss at Monmouth, which was simulcast at Saratoga, she held the lead, lost it to Crafty But Sweet, but came back at her again, holding second place safe by 4½ lengths. Her tenacity in defeat impressed me, and I fully expected her to be 4-5 in the Spinaway. Instead, she went off at 2-1.

Western Dreamer, our other live filly, was a closer who had two wins, a second and two thirds in five starts. Stretching out from 6½ furlongs, when she was third in her last start by half a length to Flat Fleet Feet in the Adirondack Stakes at Saratoga, to seven furlongs in the Spinaway figured to help her. She went off the 3-1 second choice.

The horse I left out in the Pick Threes and my third pick in my selections, Flat Fleet Feet, figured to be right there. After losing her first race by a neck, she won a maiden at Saratoga by nine lengths, then gamely held off Steady Cat and Western Dreamer, by a neck and half a length, respectively, in the Adirondack. She went off the 3-1 third choice.

Of the others, Zee Lady had been trounced by Golden Attraction in the Schuylerville, and Strawberry Clover was a distant fifth in the Adirondack. Summer Squeeze and Birr were stepping up from allowance and maiden claiming wins, respectively. I dismissed Crafty But Sweet. Her lone start on a fast track was a maiden win by a neck, and her Sorority win came on a sloppy track. As a daughter of speedy Crafty Prospector, she figured to have trouble stretching out from six furlongs to seven.

Golden Attraction and Crafty But Sweet went head to head early. When Golden Attraction put her away after a half mile, up came Flat Fleet Feet on the rail. They battled head to head, when, at the top of the stretch, Feet took the lead by half a length as Western Dreamer began to rally behind them. But Golden Attraction wasn't done, coming on again to beat Feet by three-quarters of a length, with Western Dreamer another length behind in third.

The Pick Three paid $1,033. The bankroll finished at $1,854.80, a profit of $854.80 for 34 days of top racing at Saratoga. Think about the Pick Three. It contained a 2-1 favorite (who could have been much lower), a second choice at 9-2 (who should have been much lower) and a longshot at 18-1, the fifth favorite in a field of six (Kefalonians went off at a higher 18-1). The key to the Pick Three was beating two vulnerable heavy favorites: Crimson Guard and Duda. The key to all exotic overlays is finding similar, beatable chalks. You don't beat all of them. You don't even beat most of them. But when you do, the exotic overlay can be huge.

EIGHTH RACE

Saratoga

AUGUST 28, 1995

7 FURLONGS. (1.20²) 104th Running of THE SPINAWAY. Purse $200,000. Grade I. Fillies, 2-year-olds. By subscription of $200 each which should accompany the nomination, $1,000 to pass the entry box, $1,000 to start. The purse to be divided 60% to the winner, 20% to second, 11% to third, 6% to fourth and 3% to fifth. Weight, 121 lbs. Starters to be named at the closing time of entries. Trophies will be presented to the winner owner, trainer and jockey. Closed Saturday, August 12 with 26 nominations.

Value of Race: $200,000 Winner $120,000; second $40,000; third $22,000; fourth $12,000; fifth $6,000. Mutuel Pool $409,460.00 Exacta Pool $491,790.00 Triple Pool $433,265.00

Last Raced	Horse	M/Eqt. A.Wt	PP	St	¼	½	Str	Fin	Jockey	Odds $1
6Aug95 ⁸Mth²	Golden Attraction	2 121	3	3	1½	1¹½	2²	1½	Stevens G L	2.30
9Aug95 ⁹Sar¹	Flat Fleet Feet	2 121	8	1	4ʰᵈ	4¹½	1½	2¹	Smith M E	3.45
9Aug95 ⁹Sar³	Western Dreamer	f 2 121	6	5	7ʰᵈ	6½	3ʰᵈ	3³½	Perret C	3.35
21Jly95 ⁸Sar⁷	Zee Lady	2 121	1	6	3²	3ʰᵈ	4¹	4¹½	Santos J A	8.30
14Aug95 ⁶Sar¹	Summer Squeeze	2 121	2	7	6½	7¹⁰	5²½	5¹	Day P	5.90
2Aug95 ⁴Sar¹	Birr	b 2 121	7	4	5¹½	5³	6¹	6⁶½	Bailey J D	11.10
6Aug95 ⁸Mth¹	Crafty But Sweet	2 121	4	2	2²½	2½	7	7	Santagata N	13.40
9Aug95 ⁹Sar⁵	Strawberry Clover	b 2 121	5	8	8	8	—	—	Davis R G	48.50

Strawberry Clover:Eased

OFF AT 4:45 Start Good. Won driving. Time, :22, :45¹, 1:10¹, 1:23⁴ Track fast.

$2 Mutuel Prices:

3—GOLDEN ATTRACTION	6.60	3.30	2.70
8—FLAT FLEET FEET		3.80	2.90
6—WESTERN DREAMER			2.90

$2 EXACTA 3–8 PAID $21.80 $2 TRIPLE 3–8–6 PAID $55.50

B. f, (Jan), by Mr. Prospector–Seaside Attraction, by Seattle Slew. Trainer Lukas D Wayne. Bred by Overbrook Farm (Ky).

GOLDEN ATTRACTION dueled inside CRAFTY BUT SWEET along the backstretch, opened a clear advantage on the far turn, relinquished the lead to FLAT FLEET FEET in upper stretch, then battled back from outside to prevail in a long drive. FLAT FLEET FEET settled in good position while saving ground, took up chase after the winner on the turn, moved through along the rail to gain the lead nearing the furlong marker, maintained a slim lead into deep stretch, then weakened in the final sixteenth. WESTERN DREAMER devoid of early speed, was unhurried for a half, steadily gained to reach contention in upper stretch, but could't overtake the top two. ZEE LADY stalked the early pace while three wide, remained a factor to the top of the stretch, then weakened in the drive. SUMMER SQUEEZE outrun for a half, closed the gap while saving ground into the stretch, but couldn't sustain her rally. BIRR raced within striking distance while four wide to the turn and lacked a further response. CRAFTY BUT SWEET forced the pace outside the winner to the turn, drifted out while giving way at the top of the stretch. STRAWBERRY CLOVER checked in tight at the start, trailed for a half, drifted wide on the turn, and was eased in the lane.

Owners— 1, Young William T; 2, Kimmel Caesar P & Solondz Philip; 3, Miller J Fred III; 4, Eiserman M & Fishbein K & Silver E; 5, Dogwood Stable; 6, Prestonwood Farm; 7, Moira & My Jo Lee Stable & Rosee; 8, Sabine Stable

Trainers— 1, Lukas D Wayne; 2, Kimmel John C; 3, Beagle Barbara; 4, Rice Linda; 5, Vestal Peter M; 6, Walden W Elliott; 7, Barbara Robert; 8, Barbara Robert

---

$2 Pick–3 (1–5–3) Paid $1,033.00; Pick–3 Pool $234,148. $2 Pick–6 (7–9–7–1–5–3) 5 Correct 46 Tickets Paid $3,130.00; 4 Correct 1,188 Tickets Paid $40.40; Pick–6 Pool $256,021.

4

The Game Plan

O ne great aspect of handicapping is that you can always improve at it as long as you don't delude yourself into the notion that you already know everything there is to know, or that there is a magic formula to handicapping that reveals the winner of each and every race. There is no single factor to handicapping which does that: not speed, class, form, trips, trainer patterns, track bias. Rather there are tenets which every handicapper uses as a framework. Here are five which can lead to hitting an exotic overlay:

1. Young horses improve. Some handicappers and bettors hate maiden races. I love them because, invariably, young horses will show whether or not they want to beat other horses. They may do this by showing speed, then weakening, sometimes badly. They may do this by rallying from far back to beat a few horses without threatening to win the race.

At first glance, one could dismiss a horse's first race if he led and tired to a badly beaten sixth, or if he was eighth the whole way and passed three horses to get fifth. Don't dismiss these horses, especially if they have a second race and show even modest improvement. If a horse gets the lead, holds it for two furlongs and spits out the bit in his first race, then shows speed in his second start and keeps the lead for four furlongs before tiring, he is telling you that he is getting better. Expect him to continue that improvement in his third start, especially if he has a good workout after his second race.

The same logic applies for horses who come from behind or make a middle move in their first start, then improve even a little in their second. The improvement may be subtle. As an example, a horse breaks slowly from the gate in his first start, then rallies from 10th to finish fifth. In his second start, he gets away from the gate okay and rallies from seventh to get third. Conclude that he has overcome his fear of the starting gate, wants to beat other horses and is likely sitting on a big effort.

2. Turf and dirt racing are two different ballgames. As the incomparable Cigar proved in 1995, horses can be completely different performers on dirt and grass. He was mediocre at best on turf and a killer on dirt. Conversely, horses who show no ability on dirt, but are bred well for turf, may come out running in their first grass start, quite possibly at juicy odds, as Gilder did at Saratoga in 1995. However, if a horse is well-bred for turf and has run on it more than one or two times without showing any ability, his breeding becomes worthless as a handicapping tool, unless he caught an unfavorable soft or yielding course in his races, or if he is getting a blinker change or adding Lasix for the first time on grass.

Also, in turf racing, jockeys take on greater significance. Some riders are simply better on turf. They are more successful avoiding the common problem of being boxed in on the inside and more adept at getting decent position from an outside post to save at least some ground on the turns. Other jockeys are less adept on grass. The *Form* now shows each jockey's separate grass record. Use that information. The same information is provided in the *Form* for trainers and is also useful. Some trainers rarely win a grass race, while others are proficient year after year.

3. Horses race in cycles. Cigar was an aberration, finishing 1995 a perfect 10 for 10. Ninety to 95 percent of horses don't maintain their good form for more than a few weeks. That's why it's so crucial to start evaluating a horse's PPs from the bottom up. Seeing how a horse is coming into today's race is vital information which gives you an edge over bettors who read each horse's PPs by skimming the top two or three races.

4. Clue-less races may be an asset in hitting exotic overlays. Again, don't be so smug as to think you can handicap every single race. Now and then, all of us handicap a race and reach the conclusion that we have no idea who is going to win. Recognizing these races for what they are can lead you to wheeling horses in exotic bets.

5. Horses are not machines; they don't always fire. This point would seem obvious, but it cannot be overstated. Anybody can excuse a horse's poor race when the *Form* tells you he was taken up, bothered, carried wide, raced on a wet track, had an outside turf post position, got a poor ride, or needed the race after a layoff. But what do you do when a horse shows good form for three or four races, then throws in a single, poor one? Can you excuse it? This tough handicapping question must be answered in degrees: there is a whale of a difference between finishing a dull fifth by five or six lengths and finishing dead last and losing by double-digit lengths with no apparent excuse. Throw out the latter horse, but don't necessarily dismiss the former, especially if he threw in a good workout after the dull effort. Once more, starting from a horse's bottom PPs can provide valuable information. Did this horse throw in a poor race and bounce back with a good one in his previous 10 PPs? If so, he might do it again. But you would never know that by looking only at his most recent two or three PPs. Spend the time by starting from the bottom. It's worth it.

5

When Favorites Lose

Annually, at every thoroughbred racing track in America, favorites win between 25 to 35 percent of the time. When do they lose? There are patterns which repeat themselves. Tapping into them to discover vulnerable favorites is a major edge. They won't reveal every single losing favorite, because doing so is leaving the framework of reality we talked about earlier. You will never identify all the losing favorites. Realistically, you shouldn't expect such success. But discovering one or two a day, or even a week, can connect you to an exotic overlay. Look for the following situations, when the favorite is:

- A chronic loser who gets over-bet

- Breaking from a poor post position on grass or dirt

- Facing a different type of off track for the first time

- Off a significant layoff

- Going against a track bias

- Coming off an exceptionally poor comeback race or races

- Getting a bad jockey switch

- Trying something for the first time

- A two-year-old in a maiden race

Chronic Losers Who Are Over-Bet

They're easy to spot and smart to bet against, especially when they're the favorites or taking any serious money. Any maiden who's had more than nine starts without a win — unless part of the horse's bad record was on a different surface or on wet tracks — is prone to lose again. The same for allowance horses or claimers sporting lifetime winning percentages less than 10. The lower the percentage, the better they are to bet against.

Crafty Lady took a one-for-19 win record into an allowance race at Aqueduct, December 10, 1995, and was bet down to 2-1 favoritism. She was second by six lengths. In her following start, December 27, she was hammered down to 1-2. How can you possibly bet an odds-on favorite with her record? She ran second again by 1¾ lengths.

Classi Envoy, who was zero for 20 the past two years, was sent off at even money in a claiming race at Aqueduct Park, December 14, 1995. She was third.

Lorene's Prospect ended her 1995 season in New York with a lifetime record of zero for 22. Yet in her last 10 '95 starts, she went off the favorite three times at 2-1, 7-5 and 9-5, and also at 5-2, 5-1, 9-2 and 6-1 in four other starts.

A few other examples:

Iain's Storm — He took a two-for-25 mark into a claiming race at Philadelphia Park, November 12; was bet down to 2-1 favoritism and finished fourth by nine lengths. He finished '95 two for 29 lifetime.

Psychic Spirit — Went off at even money with a zero-for-nine record at Saratoga, August 13, 1995, and was third by 16 lengths.

Robber Baron — He took a one-for-19 record into a claiming race at Aqueduct, February 5, 1995, and was bet down to 6-5, ostensibly because he was second by a length in his last start after finally breaking his maiden the race before. He finished sixth by 17½ lengths.

Wild Reflection — Distant fifth at 5-2 at The Meadowlands, November 17, 1995, despite his zero-for-17 record.

Carr De La Carr — Second at 3-5 at the Finger Lakes, November 5, 1995, despite a one-for-18 record.

You get the idea. Sure, some of those horses do win eventually — usually when there's a whole field of them in the same race — but you're getting absolutely no value in playing them. And, by getting rid of chronic losers who are over-bet, we find contenders with enhanced odds.

At the opposite end of the horse spectrum are horses like Gene's Gary Girl. She always gives it her best shot, which is why she started 1996 with 18 wins and 14 seconds in 54 lifetime starts.

If you are going to bet a favorite in exotics, bet ones who win at least some of the time. Bet against the ones who don't.

Bad Post Positions on Turf

Outside post positions on turf courses can be a huge disadvantage, which is really common sense, since a track's turf course is inside its dirt track. This means the turns are sharper, and thereby conducive to penalizing horses for racing wide. Take a minute out and check the winning turf post positions record in the *Form* for whatever tracks the *Form* carries. You'll almost always see horses from outside post positions winning less frequently, or occasionally, not at all. A sample:

At The Meadowlands' 1995 fall meet, through the end of November, horses from post positions nine through 12 went one for 44; four for 35; one for 16, and one for seven, respectively, in turf route races.

At Calder from November 4 through December 30, posts 10, 11 and 12 went one for 36, zero for 11, and zero for nine, respectively, in turf routes.

At Aqueduct's 1995 fall meet, posts eight through 12 were a combined one for 21 in turf races.

If the favorite has the 10, 11 or 12 post in a 12-horse turf field, he might be very vulnerable.

Bad Post Positions on Dirt

Outside post positions are a negative on dirt when the distance of the race sends horses into a turn quickly. This happens most frequently in New York in five-furlong maiden races. Racing wide is never a plus, but it can be even harder on inexperienced two-year-olds. If a two-year-old's lone race or races were from outside post positions in races with a short run into a turn, give the horse the benefit of the doubt if he shows speed or any ability at all. Moving inside to a better post position could help such a horse a lot, maybe at a price. When a two-year-old shows up hot on the tote board, especially if it's his first race, and he has the outside post position, he may not overcome it.

There can also be a disadvantage from having the rail. At some tracks, when horses race from a chute, the inside post position can get a horse squeezed if he doesn't have good early speed. Some handicappers don't like a first-time starter breaking from the rail.

Different Wet Track Conditions

The *Form* now provides a horse's lifetime record on wet tracks, but there are major differences from racing on a sloppy, muddy, good, or wet-fast surface. Again, starting at the bottom of a horse's PPs will ensure you don't miss an important PP, which may exactly match today's wet track condition. With shippers, wet tracks may vary, meaning that a sloppy track at Belmont Park is not identical to a sloppy track at Saratoga, though a horse may excel, or not perform at all, on both.

On the turf course, soft and yielding conditions must be noted, because frequently horses who do well on firm courses can't hack going on wet or drying-out grass.

If a horse hasn't encountered the type of off track on dirt or turf which he is competing on today, be wary.

Layoffs

Most horses need a race or two to get back in shape off a significant layoff — Crimson Guard provided a perfect example against Gilder at Saratoga in 1995. Any time a horse is off more than two months, proceed with caution. Layoff horses do win, and there are trainers who routinely accomplish that feat — which is usually noted in the *Racing Form*'s horse by horse analysis. However, because these trainers are successful with layoff horses, they frequently are over-bet, creating underlays, which in turn makes other contenders in the race overlays.

This is yet another reason to start from each horse's bottom PPs in the *Form*. The horse may have previously raced off a similar layoff. That's a powerful bit of knowledge when debating the chances of a layoff horse, especially if he gets heavily played.

Going Against a Track Bias

First be sure there is a bias at the track you're betting. Don't watch a front-runner win the first race and conclude there is a speed-favoring bias. But if four of the first five winners go wire to wire, then you may be onto something. Especially if the other winner raced from near the lead. In that situation, if the favorite in the next race is a come-from-way-behind closer, mark him as vulnerable and proceed accordingly. If he runs well but loses, remember that he raced against a track bias when he makes his next start.

Try to avoid stereotypes and generalizations. Everyone in the world knows Aqueduct's inner dirt track used in the winter is speed-favoring. But for several weeks in the winter of '95-96, closers were winning consistently, which at the very least indicated the track was playing fairer than normal.

Has an Exceptionally Poor Comeback Race or Races

Montreal Red was one of 1994's top two-year-olds, winning four of six starts including the Sanford Stakes, Saratoga Special and Belmont Futurity. He was second as the 7-10 favorite in the Hopeful Stakes, and in his final two-year-old start, was fourth by 7¼ lengths, chasing Timber Country in the 11-horse Grade I Champagne Stakes.

When he came back in 1995, it wasn't until mid-July, when he was bet down to 2-1 in a high-tier allowance race at Belmont Park. He finished seventh by 15½ lengths. In his next start, he moved up in company in the Grade II Kings Bishop at Saratoga, took some action at 9-2, and finished last in the field of 10 by 18¼ lengths. He was freshened for two months, returned in an allowance race at Belmont and was last in a field of eight by 16¾ lengths at 12-1. In his next start in a slightly easier allowance spot at Aqueduct 13 days later, he was sent off at 3-1 despite showing that he was in terrible form — for whatever reason. He was sixth by 17¾ lengths. It didn't take a veterinarian or a clairvoyant to know that something was wrong with him. Don't settle for 3-1 on horses sending out messages that he is not the same horse he was before.

It's worth noting that trainer Scotty Schulhofer then tried Montreal Red on the grass, and he woke up to finish second by a neck in an allowance race at Calder to Clint Essential. That gave Clint Essential three straight wins, his last loss coming when he was third by 5½ lengths to our old pal Gilder in a mid-September allowance race in Kentucky.

Getting a Bad Jockey Switch

Einstein was right, though he probably didn't have jockeys in mind when he produced the theory of relativity. Jockey changes are most important when there is a significant difference, bad or good, between two riders. It doesn't make a heck of a lot of difference if a horse who had been ridden by Jerry Bailey and Gary Stevens switches to Mike Smith. They're all good. But if the switch is from one of those three to a jockey with an inordinately low winning percentage — remember the *Form* gives you all the riders' records to check — then take note. And if this same horse is a favorite despite the rider switch, it's frequently wise to consider that horse vulnerable. Bet against him.

Trying Something for the First Time

Harvey Pack, the thoroughly enjoyable host of NYRA's daily recap TV show on SportsChannel, has hammered this point home for years — and he is correct: be wary of a favorite who is trying to do something for the first time, be it a sprinter stretching out, a route horse cutting back to a sprint, or a horse making his turf or wet-track debut. This isn't saying they don't win. They do — sometimes. Other times, they are vulnerable.

A Two-year-old in a Maiden Race

When a two-year-old shows up hot on the toteboard in a maiden race, especially if he's a first-time starter, check the analysis in the *Form* to see if it gives the trainer's and the horse's sire's record with two-year-olds and first-time starters. If the horse's trainer and/or sire's winning percentages are weak, take a stand against him.

6

Wheeling and Dealing with Clue-less Races

W heeling horses in exactas or doubles can be a humbling experience, occasionally even when you're correct. However, the embarrassment of spending $20 to catch a $14 Daily Double is quickly forgotten when the same strategy catches an exotic overlay in triple figures.

The best time to wheel a horse is:

1. In the first or second half of a double when one of the races is wide-open or clue-less.

2. On the top of an exacta when you think there is no stand-out second choice.

For the moment, we'll differentiate between wheeling a horse and using all horses in one race in a Pick Three or Pick Six. Those exotic bets have their own chapters later in the book.

Here are a couple of exotic overlays from winning handicap selections I had in the *Gazette* in the 1995 Saratoga meet.

Austrian Empress seemed to be the best horse in the first race, July 23, a six-furlong claiming sprint for fillies and mares, despite a tough post (12).

1

Saratoga

6 Furlongs (1:08) CLAIMING. Purse $24,000. Fillies, 3–year–olds. Weight: 121 lbs. Non–winners of three races, allowed 3 lbs. Two races, 6 lbs. Maidens, 9 lbs. Claiming price $35,000.

Coupled – Arctic Patience and Showsnap

A Wild Favor
Own: Dorsey Charles

Dk. b or br f. 3 (Apr)
Sire: Wild Again (Icecapade)
Dam: Curried Favor (Raja Baba)
Br: Mary A. Sullivan (Ky)
Tr: Cordero Angel Jr (—)

VELASQUEZ J (1 0 0 0 .00) $35,000   115

Lifetime Record:	13 1 3 2	$32,110
1995	3 0 1 0	$5,390	Turf	2 0 0 0	
1994	10 1 2 2	$26,720	Wet	3 0 0 0	$2,850
Sar	1 0 0 0	$300	Dist	2 0 0 1	$1,920

Arctic Patience
Own: Sommer Viola

Dk. b or br f. 3 (Mar)
Sire: Northern Jove (Northern Dancer)
Dam: Viola Sommer (Ky)
Tr: Martin Frank (—)

NELSON D (1 0 0 0 .00) $35,000   115

Lifetime Record:	14 1 3 4	$33,130
1995	10 1 2 3	$27,090	Turf	0 0 0 0	
1994	4 M 1 1	$6,040	Wet	2 0 1 0	$3,780
Sar	0 0 0 0		Dist	2 0 1 2	$22,650

Wilmick
Own: Due Process Stable

Ch. f. 3 (Apr)
Sire: Spend a Buck (Buckaroo)
Dam: August Poetry (Vaguely Noble)
Br: Due Process Stables Inc. (Ky)
Tr: Nobles Reynaldo H (—)

BAILEY J D (7 1 1 1 .14) $35,000   112

Lifetime Record:	7 1 1 2	$18,430
1995	3 1 0 1	$11,670	Turf	1 0 0 0	$1,800
1994	4 M 1 1	$6,760	Wet	0 0 0 0	
Sar	0 0 0 0		Dist	2 0 0 1	$2,070

Carols World
Own: Roberts Richard H

B. f. 3 (Feb)
Sire: Shanekite (Hoist Bar)
Dam: My Sister Joyce (Gummo)
Br: Hale Farms (Cal)
Tr: Levine Bruce N (1 0 0 0 .00)

BELMONTE L A (—)   114⁷

Lifetime Record:	14 3 2 4	$56,700
1995	7 2 0 2	$34,575	Turf	1 0 0 1	$3,450
1994	7 1 2 2	$22,125	Wet	2 0 0 0	$11,575
Sar	0 0 0 0		Dist	9 3 0 2	$46,175

Devilette

Own: Wachtel Edwin H

MIGLIORE R (2 1 0 0 .50) $35,000   115

Dk. b or br f. 3 (Mar)
Sire: Claramount (Policeman)
Dam: Dukette (Unpredictable)
Br: Edwin Wachtel (NY)
Tr: Destefano John M Jr (—)

Lifetime Record :	14 1 4 1	$48,885
1995	7 0 3 0	$15,495 Turf	1 0 0 0
1994	7 1 1 1	$33,390 Wet	2 0 2 0	$8,200
Sar	0 0 0 0	Dist	4 0 0 1	$5,585

Whispering Leaves

Own: Yemec George

LUZZI M J (2 0 0 0 .00) $35,000   118

B. f. 3 (Apr)
Sire: Evzone (Peace Corps)
Dam: Aspenetta (Baldski)
Br: George Yemec (Ont-C)
Tr: Johnstone Bruce (1 0 0 0 .00)

Lifetime Record :	13 2 3 2	$45,087
1995	9 1 3 1	$35,220 Turf	0 0 0 0
1994	4 1 0 1	$9,867 Wet	2 0 0 0	$1,590
Sar	0 0 0 0	Dist	2 0 0 1	$24,847

Carson Kitty

Own: Farmergan Stable

SMITH M E (6 1 1 0 .17) $35,000   121

Dk. b or br f. 3 (Apr)
Sire: Carson City (Mr. Prospector)
Dam: Nalley's Comeback (Key to the Kingdom)
Br: Crescent Hill Farm & Reed W A (Ky)
Tr: Friedman Mitchell (—)

Lifetime Record :	14 3 0 5	$42,752
1995	10 3 0 4	$39,455 Turf	0 0 0 0
1994	4 M 0 1	$3,297 Wet	3 0 0 1	$4,267
Sar	0 0 0 0	Dist	10 2 0 5	$33,495

Claimed from Spath Allen H, Biusiewicz Leon J Trainer

Enhearten

Own: Pomerantz Lawrence J

PEREZ R B (2 0 0 0 .00) $35,000   121

Dk. b or br f. 3 (May)
Sire: Smarten (Cyane)
Dam: Biava (Kennedy Road)
Br: Blue Seas Music Inc (WV)
Tr: Barbara Robert (1 1 0 0 1.00)

Lifetime Record :	9 4 0 1	$66,524
1995	8 3 0 1	$61,904 Turf	1 0 0 0
1994	1 1 0 0	$4,620 Wet	1 0 0 0	$3,264
Sar	0 0 0 0	Dist	7 4 0 0	$61,464

Capote's Cookie

Own: Terrill William V

CHAVEZ J F (5 0 2 1 .00) $35,000   112

Dk. b or br f. 3 (Apr)
Sire: Capote (Seattle Slew)
Dam: Miss Prestigious (Secretariat)
Br: Woodrow D. Marriott (Ky)
Tr: Terrill William V (1 0 0 0 .00)

Lifetime Record :	2 M 1 0	$2,800
1995	1 M 1 0	$2,800 Turf	0 0 0 0
1994	1 M 0 0	Wet	1 0 1 0	$2,800
Sar	0 0 0 0	Dist	0 0 0 0

Prospective Green
Own: Gorey John J
VELAZQUEZ J R (4 1 0 1 .25) $35,000
Ch. f. 3 (Feb)
Sire: Aloha Prospector (Native Prospector)
Dam: Quick Trick (Clever Trick)
Br: John J. Gorey (Md)
Tr: Hough Stanley M (—)
115
Lifetime Record: 7 1 1 0 $15,100
1995 3 0 1 0 $4,060 Turf 1 0 0 0
1994 4 1 0 0 $11,040 Wet 0 0 0 0
Sar 0 0 0 0 Dist 2 1 1 0 $10,600

13Jly95-2Bel fst 6f :22 :454 :583 1:112 ⓕClm 20000 64 10 9 67 53½ 31 2¾ Velazquez J R 115 b 21.90 83-17 Chrmless115¾ ProspectiveGren115nk ShrwdPnny1152 Four wide, led late 10
3Jly95-3Bel fst 7f :224 :464 1:122 1:252 ⓕClm 30000 50 3 7 75 74½ 58½ 513½ Smith M E 115 b 13.00 60-14 Ride The Wind1152¾ A Wild Favor115½ Amaysing Diane1144¾ No threat 8
16Jun95-5Bel fm 1¹⁄₁₆ [T] :241 :473 1:114 1:424 ⓕClm 45000 35 5 6 62¾ 63½ 98½ 1020¾ Smith M E 114 b 7.80 61-12 Aljinda1165½ My Song114¾ Aidan's Breath116½ Faded 10
23Dec94-5Aqu fst 170 [•] :23 :471 1:14 1:462 ⓕAlw 32000N1X 44 2 6 616 611 514 418½ Davis R G 116 13.00 48-28 Foxy Scarlet11615 A Wild Favor1111½ Ring By Spring1161¾ No factor 6
9Dec94-9Aqu fst 170 [•] :24 :48 1:132 1:452 ⓕAlw 32000N1X 55 7 8 815 77¾ 46½ 47½ Davis R G 116 26.50 64-25 F Sharp1184 Pleasantry1161½ Limit1112 Broke slowly 8
12Nov94-9Aqu fst 6f :224 :464 :592 1:124 ⓕMd 30000 62 5 6 57½ 58½ 45 1½ Davis R G 113 22.00 78-19 Prospective Green113½ Nay Nay Renay115½ Crafty Josie1151½ Driving 9
30Oct94-3Aqu fst 7f :224 :463 1:12 1:26 ⓕMd 45000 36 3 10 1013 914 812 717 Davis R G 113 13.40 57-18 Sadie's Glory1139 A Wild Favor1122 Aerosilver1133 Broke slowly 10

WORKOUTS: Jun 30 Bel 4f fst :484 B 8/52 Jun 24 Bel 4f fst :513 B 84/90 Jun 9 Bel 5f fst 1:014 Hg 11/29 Jun 2 Bel 5f fst 1:012 H 12/24 May 25 Bel [T] 4f fm :48 B (d) 4/18 May 21 Bel 4f fst :484 B 34/113

Rich Seam
Own: Humphrey G Watts Jr
LOVATO F JR (—) $35,000
B. f. 3 (Feb)
Sire: Mining (Mr. Prospector)
Dam: Straight South (Hail the Pirates)
Br: Gunther John (Ky)
Tr: Arnold George R II (1 1 0 0 1.00)
112
Lifetime Record: 3 M 1 0 $7,850
1995 3 M 1 0 $7,850 Turf 0 0 0 0
1994 0 M 0 0 Wet 1 0 1 0 $6,300
Sar 0 0 0 0 Dist 2 0 0 0 $1,550

Entered 22Jly95- 3 SAR
21Jun95-4CD fst 6f :213 :453 :58 1:112 3+ ⓕMd Sp Wt 56 12 2 74½ 61¾ 56 59¼ Barton D M L 112 7.80 79-12 Tup Take Too1126 Your Moon112½ Exotic Beauty1123 No late threat 12
18Mar95-6CD sly 6½f :23 :464 1:122 1:191 3+ ⓕMd Sp Wt 68 2 4 1hd 1½ 2hd 22 Walls M K L 114 6.10 81-14 Good N Gorgeous1142 Rich Seam1141 MidnightOil1112 Dueled, 2nd best 11
19Apr95-5Kee fst 6f :22 :454 :581 1:11 ⓕMd Sp Wt 67 10 7 85½ 97 56½ 47½ Walls M K L 121 5.40 75-13 Queen Tutta1216 Pausing1211 Tulira121½ 12
Wide stretch, improved position

WORKOUTS: Jly 20 Sar tr.t 3f fst :37 B 2/16 Jly 5 Bel 3f fst :381 B 11/21 ●Jun 18 CD 3f fst :35 H 1/30 Jun 13 CD 5f fst 1:053 B 35/37 Jun 3 CD 5f my 1:03 B 18/25 May 11 CD 5f fst 1:012 B 7/40

Amaysing Diane
Own: Oakridge Stable
BECKNER D V (5 0 0 0 .00) $35,000
Ch. f. 3 (Mar)
Sire: Known Fact (In Reality)
Dam: Miss Czara (Czaravich)
Br: W. L. Reynolds (Ky)
Tr: Samuel Philip (—)
121
Lifetime Record: 19 6 1 4 $83,745
1995 14 5 1 4 $76,090 Turf 1 0 0 0 $155
1994 5 1 0 0 $7,655 Wet 3 1 0 0 $11,500
Sar 0 0 0 0 Dist 9 2 1 3 $33,030

3Jly95-3Bel fst 7f :224 :464 1:122 1:252 ⓕClm c-25000 71 6 3 43½ 2½ 21½ 33¾ Alvarado F T 114 fb 3.20 71-14 Ride The Wind1152¾ AWildFavor115½ AmaysingDiane1144¾ Bid, weakened 8
Claimed from Boto Stable, Galluscio Dominic G Trainer
15Jun95-9Bel wf 6f :224 :464 :593 1:131 ⓕClm c-18000 71 3 8 65½ 64 33 11¾ Alvarado F T 115 fb *2.05 75-20 Amaysing Diane1151¾ Henbane's Girl115no Charmless115hd Rallied inside 10
Claimed from Davis Barbara J, Moschera Gasper S Trainer
1Jun95-3Bel fst 6f :223 :463 :591 1:124 ⓕClm 35000 73 7 7 53¾ 53½ 33½ 22 Alvarado F T 116 fb 2.75 75-17 Ray'sCrftyLdy1162 AmysingDine116nk CrsonKitty1111 Rallied four wide 7
11May95-6Bel my 1¹⁄₁₆ ⊗ :231 :46 1:111 1:453 ⓕClm 50000 37 2 3 22 33 34½ 49½ Perez R B5 113 fb *1.55 61-22 Northern Five1129 Halloween Mask112nk Heliopause109nk Lacked rally 7
6May95-3Bel fst 1¹⁄₁₆ :232 :464 1:114 1:422 3+ ⓕAlw 36000N2X 51 3 3 32 45½ 516 527¼ Alvarado F T 113 b 8.30 59-15 Golden Bri11311 Our Springwater1143½ Mega1126 Done after 5/8's 5
17Apr95-6Aqu fst 1 :232 :462 1:113 1:383 ⓕAlw 32000N1X 68 3 1 11 1hd 11 1nk Perez R B5 110 b *1.65 76-24 Amaysing Diane110nk Holley's Heart116½ Whispering Leaves1136¾ All out 7
10Apr95-6Aqu fst 6f :221 :451 :572 1:101 ⓕClm 55000 81 2 6 43½ 43½ 32½ 32 Perez R B5 111 b 4.20 89-12 Nappelon118no Pleasantry1162 Amaysing Diane1112 Broke slowly 6
31Mar95-5Aqu fst 6f :232 :474 :593 1:113 3+ ⓕAlw 30000N1X 63 5 8 64½ 75 34½ 38 Samyn J L 111 b 1.60 76-19 Crafty Jam1101 Miss Shoplifter1197 Amaysing Diane1111½ Wide, no rally 9
23Mar95-4Aqu fst 6½f :23 :473 1:123 1:191 ⓕClm c-35000 78 2 6 55½ 2½ 13 14 Samyn J L 118 b 1.85 84-17 Amaysing Diane1184 Showsnap1162 Risen Tower1073 Ridden out 6
Claimed from Team Ten Stable & Werbowsky Irwin R, Galluscio Dominic G Trainer
17Feb95-5GP fst 7f :22 :451 1:111 1:26 ⓕClm 32000 55 7 3 51¾ 43½ 34 54 Samyn J L L 118 b *1.20 69-21 Emma's First114½ Rock N Bowl116nk Talcountess114¾ 11
Six wide top str, lacked response

Austrian Empress
Own: Hardwick Stable
KRONE J A (5 0 2 0 .00) $35,000
Dk. b or br f. 3 (Jan)
Sire: Exclusive Gem (Exclusive Native)
Dam: Decorated Empress (Well Decorated)
Br: Elisabeth Jerkens (Fla)
Tr: Jerkens H Allen (1 0 0 0 .00)
118
Lifetime Record: 11 2 3 3 $47,990
1995 7 1 2 3 $33,250 Turf 1 0 0 0 $400
1994 4 1 1 0 $14,740 Wet 3 0 1 2 $11,980
Sar 0 0 0 0 Dist 10 2 3 3 $47,590

12Jly95-2Bel fst 6f :22 :451 :573 1:102 ⓕClm 40000 73 4 1 41½ 41½ 21 22 Krone J A 112 3.60 87-14 So Cheerful1162 Austrian Empress1122 Ride The Wind116nk Willingly 8
1Jly95-4Bel sly 6f :22 :454 :581 1:114 3+ ⓕClm 35000 66 3 2 31 23 23 35½ Krone J A 106 *2.60 77-14 RunwyFling1195 You'renotlistening116nk AustrinEmprss1064 Weakened 6
26May95-7Bel my 6f :223 :453 :572 1:10 3+ ⓕAlw 32000N1X 77 5 2 43 32½ 23½ 34¾ Dunkelberger T L5 105 11.90 84-10 Dybydybydy1124 FntsticWomen1102½ AustrinEmprss105nk Bid, weakened 7
12May95-6Bel my 6f :221 :453 :573 1:101 ⓕClm 50000 73 4 5 35½ 35 24 28 Dunkelberger T L5 110 2.50 82-15 Daybydaybyday1138 Austrian Empress110nk Carson Kitty1197 Held place 6
20Apr95-7Aqu fst 6f :23 :471 :592 1:12 ⓕAlw 32000N2X 79 5 1 1½ 11 1½ 31½ Dunkelberger T L5 108 13.80 81-16 KhlifOfKushog114¾ CrftyJm118½ AustrinEmprss1086 Speed, weakened 5
17Feb95-9GP fm *1 ⓣ :241 :47 1:102 1:352 ⓕAlw 40000NC 29 10 3 45½ 59 918 1030¼ Samyn J L 114 22.90 72 — MissUnionAvenue1143 ShockingPlesure1144 LdyShIsToo1144¾ Stopped 10
21Jan95-4GP fst 6f :224 :461 :59 1:123 ⓕClm 35000 72 1 4 21 2hd 12 1nk Samyn J L 116 7.80 77-17 AustrianEmpress116nk Three'sACrowd1161½ Metlbne1161½ Fully extended 9
21Dec94-6Aqu fst 6f [•] :224 :463 :593 1:131 ⓕClm 47500 57 4 4 31 63¾ 46 46 Samyn J L 116 5.80 71-20 Lawana Go Fast1122 Showsnap1102 Wonaria1092 No solid bid 9
1Dec94-1Aqu fst 6f :231 :473 1:002 1:14 ⓕMd 45000 65 5 3 11 13 15 14 Samyn J L 113 3.70 72-24 Austrian Empress1134 Mega1091½ Risen Tower1176 Mild drive 8
20Nov94-9Aqu fst 6f :23 :473 :594 1:122 ⓕMd 35000 61 3 1 11 11 2½ 23½ Samyn J L 113 f *1.90 76-16 Mcfanny1173½ Austrian Empress1131 Arctic Patience1175¾ Held place 10

WORKOUTS: Jly 10 Bel tr.t 4f fst :48 H 2/10 Jun 15 Bel tr.t 6f fst 1:18 B 3/3 Jun 9 Bel tr.t 5f fst 1:03 B 3/8

Shrewd Penny
Own: Haley Terrence W & Wickman Joseph F
DAVIS R G (4 1 0 0 .25) $35,000
B. f. 3 (May)
Sire: Buckaroo (Buckpasser)
Dam: Penny's Chelly (Rizdal)
Br: Harriet C. Heubeck & Elmer Heubeck Jr. (Fla)
Tr: Lake Robert P (—)
115
Lifetime Record: 11 1 0 3 $16,910
1995 8 0 0 2 $7,310 Turf 0 0 0 0
1994 3 1 0 1 $9,600 Wet 2 0 0 0 $840
Sar 0 0 0 0 Dist 7 1 0 2 $14,110

13Jly95-2Bel fst 6f :22 :454 :583 1:112 ⓕClm 20000 63 7 8 43½ 32 1½ 31 Davis R G 115 b 12.70 83-17 Charmless115¾ Prospective Green115nk Shrewd Penny1153 Gamely 10
23Jun95-1Bel wf 1 :223 :46 1:12 1:384 ⓕClm 25000 37 6 5 63½ 62¾ 66½ 612½ Smith M E 116 b 4.50 56-23 Pageant Princess1165½ Shady Baby1122 Gin And Ice1113½ No threat, wide 7
5Apr95-6Aqu fst 1 :234 :47 1:131 1:403 ⓕClm 26000 59 4 3 42 51½ 31½ 31½ Santos J A 115 b 11.90 65-27 HalloweenMsk1121 Soquickly115nk ShrewdPenny1156 Block 1/4, alt crse 7
24Mar95-2Aqu fst 1⅛ :49 1:151 1:42 1:561 ⓕClm 27500 57 7 6 31 31½ 54½ 64¾ Dunkelberger T L5 110 b 18.20 54-38 RunwySmok118¾ Gntlmn'sCopy1161½ Adn'sBrth1161 Five wide trip, tired 7
10Mar95-9Aqu fst 1¹⁄₁₆ [•] :23 :474 1:141 1:491 ⓕClm 30000 45 6 4 54½ 53½ 37 511½ Perez R B5 111 b 6.20 47-33 Domina1164 Halloween Mask1123½ Sammi De1093½ Wide, flattened out 8
19Feb95-2Aqu fst 6f [•] :231 :473 1:01 1:143 ⓕClm c-22500N2L 48 7 6 74¾ 64½ 32½ 44½ Lovato F Jr 114 b 7.40 66-22 Risen Tower109¾ Tara's Flame1113 Soquickly114½ Flattened out 10
Claimed from Heubeck Harriet C, Kelly Michael J Trainer
29Jan95-2Aqu fst 6f [•] :232 :481 1:011 1:143 ⓕClm 32500N2L 53 3 8 57 54½ 44½ 44¾ Lovato F Jr 114 8.30 66-26 NyNyReny1173 BrodwyAndPine1091½ Tr'sFlme107no Broke slowly, rallied 8
7Jan95-1Aqu my 6f [•] :23 :473 1:004 1:141 ⓕClm 25000N2L 36 2 2 32½ 35½ 37¾ 411¾ Lovato F Jr 118 f *2.20 60-28 Nappelon11610 Call My Agent114nk Sadie's Glory1161 No rally 5
14Dec94-1Aqu fst 6f [•] :24 :483 1:011 1:141 ⓕMd 32500 51 1 8 2hd 31 21½ 11 Lovato F Jr 115 9.70 72-21 Shrewd Penny1151 Northern Five1031½ Nay Nay Renay1177 Driving 8
8Dec94-3Med fst 6f :224 :463 :59 1:113 ⓕMd 30000 45 3 5 41½ 42¾ 45 47½ Martin C W 114 10.00 76-16 Laugh Out119hd Hanging Fire1135½ Eloquent Crusader1151½ Even trip 6

WORKOUTS: Jly 5 Bel tr.t 4f fst :473 H 2/27 Jun 30 Bel 5f fst 1:004 H 3/35 Jun 18 Bel 4f fst :49 H 11/32 Jun 10 Bel 4f fst :49 H 7/33 Jun 6 Bel 6f fst 1:162 B 2/3 Jun 2 Bel 6f fst 1:18 B 7/8

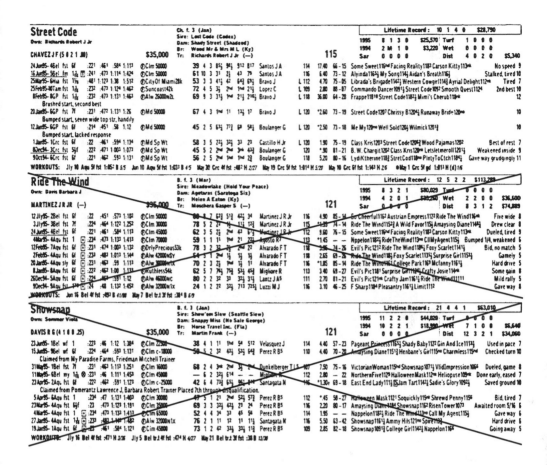

Austrian Empress was sent off at just under 3-1 with Julie Krone and won by a neck to return $7.90. A $2 Daily Double wheel of her with all the horses in the second — a maiden race for two-year-old New York-Bred fillies, cost $22 and returned a chintzy $63.50 when 7-1 Lizzie Worthington ($16) nosed out Little Notice at 41-1. The winning parlay would have paid nearly $64, and a good double should always pay more than a parlay. However, a $2 exacta wheel of Austrian Empress would have cost the same $22 and made you very happy when 30-1 Rich Seam got up for second. The exacta paid $453.

FIRST RACE
Saratoga
JULY 23, 1995

6 FURLONGS. (1.08) CLAIMING. Purse $24,000. Fillies, 3-year-olds. Weight: 121 lbs. Non-winners of three races, allowed 3 lbs. Two races, 6 lbs. Maidens, 9 lbs. Claiming price $35,000. (Day 3 of a 34 Day Meet. Cloudy. 85.)

Value of Race: $24,000 Winner $14,400; second $4,800; third $2,640; fourth $1,440; fifth $720. Mutuel Pool $291,863.00 Exacta Pool $454,620.00

Last Raced	Horse	M/Eqt.	A.	Wt	PP	St	¼	½	Str	Fin	Jockey	Cl'g Pr	Odds $1
12Jly95 2Bel2	Austrian Empress		3	118	12	5	2hd	21½	21½	1nk	Krone J A	35000	2.95
21Jun95 4CD5	Rich Seam		3	114	10	3	1½	1hd	1hd	2½	Lovato F Jr	35000	30.75
15Mar95 8GP6	Wilmick	f	3	115	8	12	4hd	3½	4½	3½	Bailey J D	35000	3.15
3Jly95 3Bel2	A Wild Favor	b	3	115	1	10	8½	8hd	61½	4½	Velasquez J	35000	7.10
13Jly95 2Bel3	Shrewd Penny	b	3	115	13	2	6½	5½	51½	5no	Davis R G	35000	f-19.80
12Jly95 2Bel4	Carson Kitty	b	3	121	6	6	71½	41½	3hd	62	Smith M E	35000	5.40
13Jly95 2Bel2	Prospective Green	b	3	115	9	7	9hd	9½	9½	7½	Velazquez J R	35000	f-19.80
12Jly95 2Bel5	Enhearten		3	121	7	14	111½	101½	7hd	8¾	Perez R B	35000	6.30
24May95 4Bel4	Whispering Leaves		3	118	5	8	14	121½	102	9hd	Luzzi M J	35000	22.60
1Jly95 4Bel5	Arctic Patience		3	115	2	4	5½	6½	8½	102	Nelson D	35000	36.75
3Jly95 3Bel3	Amaysing Diane	bf	3	121	11	9	103	11½	111	111	Beckner D V	35000	20.20
21Jun95 6GG8	Carols World	b	3	114	4	13	13hd	132	121	122½	Belmonte L A7	35000	16.60
24Jun95 4Bel8	Street Code		3	115	14	1	31	72	134	135	Chavez J F	35000	f-19.80
14Jun95 1Bel2	Capote's Cookie		3	114	8	11	122	14	14	14	Decarlo C P	35000	45.75

f-Mutuel Field: Shrewd Penny and Prospective Green and Street Code.

OFF AT 1:01 Start Good. Won driving. Time, :22, :454, :581, 1:113 Track fast.

$2 Mutuel Prices:

11-AUSTRIAN EMPRESS	7.90	4.20	3.30
9-RICH SEAM		32.40	13.80
3-WILMICK			4.20

$2 EXACTA 11-9 PAID $453.00

Dk. b. or br. f, (Jan), by Exclusive Gem–Decorated Empress, by Well Decorated. Trainer Jerkens H Allen. Bred by Elisabeth Jerkens (Fla).

AUSTRIAN EMPRESS dueled for the lead from outside into midstretch, then wore down RICH SEAM in the final twenty yards. RICH SEAM took the lead soon after the start, battled heads apart inside the winner into deep stretch and yielded grudgingly. WILMICK checked while breaking outward at the start, rushed up along the inside, angled out to threaten at the top of the stretch, but couldn't overtake the top two. A WILD FAVOR reserved for a half, rallied belatedly. SHREWD PENNY raced within striking distance while five wide to the top of the stretch, and lacked a strong closing bid. CARSON KITTY checked between horses nearing the half mile pole, made a steady run to threaten in upper stretch, then flattened out. ENHEARTEN broke awkwardly, raced well back to the turn then failed to threaten while improving her position. WHISPERING LEAVES never reached contention. ARCTIC PATIENCE up close while saving ground, gave way on the turn. AMAYSING DIANE was never a factor. CAROLS WORLD was never close after breaking slowly. CAPOTE'S COOKIE returned bleeding.

Owners— 1, Hardwick Stable; 2, Humphrey G Watts Jr; 3, Due Process Stable; 4, Dorsey Charles; 5, Haley Terrence W & Wickman Joseph F; 6, Farmorgan Stable; 7, Gorey John J; 8, Pomerantz Lawrence J; 9, Yemec George; 10, Sommer Viola; 11, Oakridge Stable; 12, Roberts Richard H; 13, Richards Robert J Jr; 14, Terrill William V

Trainers—1, Jerkens H Allen; 2, Arnold George R II; 3, Nobles Reynaldo H; 4, Cordero Angel Jr; 5, Lake Robert P; 6, Friedman Mitchell; 7, Hough Stanley M; 8, Barbara Robert; 9, Johnstone Bruce; 10, Martin Frank; 11, Samuel Philip; 12, Levine Bruce N; 13, Richards Robert J Jr; 14, Terrill William V

Corrected weight: Wilmick (115) **Overweight:** Rich Seam (2), Capote's Cookie (2).

Scratched— Devilette (29Jun95 8BEL6), Ride The Wind (12Jly95 2BEL3), Showsnap (23Jun95 1BEL5)

Did I have it? No way. I didn't have the double either. But, I did catch the following double in the bankroll and in real life, too. Procryptic looked extremely imposing in the first race at Saratoga, August 21, a maiden race for two-year-old New York-Breds.

1 Saratoga

7 Furlongs (1:202) **MAIDEN SPECIAL WEIGHT. Purse $30,000. 2-year-olds foaled in New York State and approved by the New York State-Bred Registry. Weight, 118 lbs. (Preference to horses that have not started for a claiming price.)**

Columbia County
Own: Zaretsky Martin
ALVARADO F T (51 4 6 4 .08)
Dk. b or br c. 2 (Feb)
Sire: Go and Go (Be My Guest)
Dam: Stuttsman County (Damascus)
Br: Jerry Bilinski (NY)
Tr: Bond Harold James (15 6 2 1 .40)
118
Lifetime Record: 1 M 0 0 $0
1995 1 M 0 0 | Turf 0 0 0 0
1994 0 M 0 0 | Wet 1 0 0 0
Sar 1 0 0 0 | Dist 1 0 0 0
12Aug95- 2Sar sly 7f ⊗ :222 :463 1:12 1:251 Md Sp Wt 35 4 6 31½ 32 35 6 13½ Alvarado F T 118 13.40 64-15 Spicy Fact1184½ Jetting Robert1184 Tuning Up118no Chased, tired 8
WORKOUTS: Aug 9 Sar 5f fst 1:033 B 39/48 Aug 3 Sar 6f fst 1:16 Bg3/6 Jly 24 Sar 5f gd 1:022 Hg5/11 Jly 17 Sar 4f fst :511 B 40/41 Jly 7 Bel 5f fst 1:02 Hg11/30 Jun 29 Bel 4f fst :50 Bg28/49

Dance the Wind
Own: Ryan Daniel M
PEREZ R B (68 8 5 7 .12)
B. g. 2 (Feb)
Sire: Noble Nashua (Nashua)
Dam: Daisy Dancer (Dancing Count)
Br: Romando Emil Jr (NY)
Tr: Donk David (17 3 3 2 .18)
118
Lifetime Record: 2 M 0 1 $3,300
1995 2 M 0 1 $3,300 | Turf 0 0 0 0
1994 0 M 0 0 | Wet 1 0 0 0
Sar 2 0 0 1 $3,300 | Dist 0 0 0 0
7Aug95- 2Sar fst 6f :232 :48 1:003 1:132 [S]Md Sp Wt 31 8 4 3½ 32 36 311 Perez R B 118 11.80 63-19 I'llNotCmply1182 Iwllbkng1189 DncThWnd1184 Forced pace, weakened 9
24Jly95- 2Sar wf 5½f :222 :461 :584 1:051 [S]Md Sp Wt 48 5 4 67½ 78½ 77¼ 67¼ Perez R B 118 67.50 87-08 Severe Clear118nk Procryptic118nk Tropicool1183 Evenly 12
WORKOUTS: Aug 6 Sar 3f fst :371 B 4/9 Aug 2 Sar 4f fst :523 B 36/38 Jly 13 Bel 5f fst 1:012 H 13/30 Jly 8 Bel 5f fst 1:02 Hg15/27 Jly 4 Bel 4f fst :50 Bg47/71 Jun 28 Bel 3f fst :382 Bg18/26

Mr. M. O.
Own: Beecher Aaron
RYDOWSKI S R (22 1 2 2 .05)
Dk. b or br g. 2 (Jun)
Sire: Claramount (Policeman)
Dam: Miss M. O. (Prove Out)
Br: Edwin Wachtel (NY)
Tr: Gullo Gary P (11 2 1 0 .18)
118
Lifetime Record: 0 M 0 0 $0
1995 0 M 0 0 | Turf 0 0 0 0
1994 0 M 0 0 | Wet 0 0 0 0
Sar 0 0 0 0 | Dist 0 0 0 0
WORKOUTS: Aug 17 Sar 5f fst 1:023 H 11/17 Aug 11 Sar tr.t 5f fst 1:07 B 8/10 Jly 29 Sar 3f fst :37 Bg7/16

Out to Win
Own: Brennan Bernard F
KRONE J A (114 11 19 16 .10)
B. g. 2 (Mar)
Sire: Carr de Naskra (Star de Naskra)
Dam: Etoile Joyeux (L'Heureux)
Br: J. Watson Lynch & Dr. Bernard F. Brennan (NY)
Tr: Brennan Brian (1 0 0 1 .00)
118
Lifetime Record: 1 M 0 1 $3,300
1995 1 M 0 1 $3,300 | Turf 0 0 0 0
1994 0 M 0 0 | Wet 0 0 0 0
Sar 1 0 0 1 $3,300 | Dist 0 0 0 0
7Aug95- 4Sar fst 6f :23 :47 :594 1:132 [S]Md Sp Wt 55 5 3 32 2hd 21 31¼ Krone J A 118 4.20 73-19 Goodthngstocom118nk LoustrousTurn1181 OutToWn118¾ Bid, weakened 7
WORKOUTS: Aug 16 Mth 4f fst :51 B 21/26 Aug 2 Mth 5f fst 1:04 B 10/14 Jly 26 Mth 5f fst 1:012 Hg4/16 Jly 20 Mth 4f fst :49 B 7/22 Jly 15 Mth 5f fst 1:031 B 11/19 ●Jly 9 Mth 3f fst :36 B 1/8

Curtain Up
Own: Chevalier Stable
SAMYN J L (32 6 1 5 .19)
Gr. c. 2 (Apr)
Sire: Forever Silver (Silver Buck)
Dam: Private Theatrics (Private Account)
Br: Chevalier Stable (NY)
Tr: Shapoff Stanley R (23 0 2 4 .00)
118
Lifetime Record: 3 M 0 0 $0
1995 3 M 0 0 | Turf 0 0 0 0
1994 0 M 0 0 | Wet 1 0 0 0
Sar 1 0 0 0 | Dist 0 0 0 0
7Aug95- 2Sar fst 6f :232 :48 1:003 1:132 [S]Md Sp Wt 2 3 8 916 99¼ 912 923 Graell A 118 f 28.00 51-19 I'll Not Comply1182 Iwillbking1189 Dance The Wind1184 Checked break 9
2Jly95- 6Bel my 6f ⊗ :23 :47 :59 1:111 Md Sp Wt 23 3 3 75 55 611 620¾ Beckner D V 116 30.00 64-13 Ok By Me11611 Erskine1161 [D]Tuning Up116¾ No threat 8
6May95- 2Bel fst 5f :222 :454 :581 Md Sp Wt 35 2 5 612 67 69 612 Graell A 116 17.00 83-06 Unclear Gamble116½ Justinthemiddle1165½ Lonsdale1161 Checked break 6
WORKOUTS: Aug 17 Sar tr.t [T] 4f fm :51 B (d)6/9 Aug 3 Sar 4f fst :49 H 9/40 Jly 29 Sar tr.t 3f fst :392 B 12/15 Jun 30 Bel tr.t 4f fst :48 H 3/12 Jun 25 Bel tr.t 5f sly 1:034 B 2/3 Jun 21 Bel 4f fst :491 H 31/71

Iwillbking
Own: Chuckolow Stable
MIGLIORE R (60 4 6 14 .07)
Dk. b or br g. 2 (Apr)
Sire: Secret Prince (Cornish Prince)
Dam: Iamhavinfun (Don Rickles)
Br: Philip Chuck (NY)
Tr: Anderson William D (1 0 1 0 .00)
118
Lifetime Record: 2 M 2 0 $12,000
1995 2 M 2 0 $12,000 | Turf 0 0 0 0
1994 0 M 0 0 | Wet 0 0 0 0
Sar 1 0 1 0 $6,000 | Dist 0 0 0 0
7Aug95- 2Sar fst 6f :232 :48 1:003 1:132 [S]Md Sp Wt 53 6 3 1½ 1hd 2hd 22 Migliore R 118 b *2.45 72-19 I'll Not Comply1182 Iwillbking1189 Dance The Wind1184 Dueled inside 9
7Jly95- 2Bel fst 5½f :224 :464 :584 1:051 [S]Md Sp Wt 60 6 4 32½ 31 23½ 26 Migliore R 116 b 14.40 83-10 Meadowtime1166 Iwillbking116nk Squeaky Clean1161¾ Held place 9
WORKOUTS: Aug 17 Mth 5f fst 1:021 B 4/9 Aug 3 Mth 4f fst :513 B 13/15 Jly 25 Mth 5f my 1:013 Bg2/14 Jly 19 Mth 5f fst 1:042 B 18/25 Jun 30 Mth 5f fst 1:024 Bg10/20 Jun 23 Mth 5f fst 1:022 Bg11/35

Tri Line
Own: Morrell Sam F
CHAVEZ J F (144 20 18 11 .14)

B. c. 2 (Apr)
Sire: Crafty Prospector (Mr. Prospector)
Dam: Great Birdie (Proud Birdie)
Br: Calverley Farm Inc (NY)
Tr: Sciacca Gary (56 6 7 2 .11)

118

Lifetime Record :	1 M 0 1	$3,300			
1995	1 M 0 1	$3,300	Turf	0 0 0 0	
1994	0 M 0 0		Wet	0 0 0 0	
Sar	1 0 0 1	$3,300	Dist	0 0 0 0	

31Jly95- 2Sar fst 6f :224 :463 :591 1:12 [S]Md Sp Wt 49 1 4 1½ 1½ 32 39¾ Chavez J F 118 4.20 71-16 CarrbineSpecil1185½ TlcAboutJune1184 TriLine118nk Bumped early, rank 11

WORKOUTS: Aug 19 Sar 3f fst :353 H 3/21 Jly 26 Sar 4f fst :49 Bg 17/52 Jly 19 Sar tr.t 4f fst :502 B 9/20 Jly 3 FL 4f fst :503 Hg 14/32 Jun 23 FL 3f fst :36 Hg 3/17 ●Jun 16 FL 3f fst :371 Hg 1/21

Procryptic
Own: Paraneck Stable
DAVIS R G (139 14 22 24 .10)

B. c. 2 (Feb)
Sire: Distinctive Pro (Mr. Prospector)
Dam: Crypto Game (Secreto)
Br: Delehanty Stock Farm (NY)
Tr: Aquilino Joseph (21 2 4 1 .10)

118

Lifetime Record :	2 M 2 0	$12,000			
1995	2 M 2 0	$12,000	Turf	0 0 0 0	
1994	0 M 0 0		Wet	1 0 1 0	$6,000
Sar	2 0 2 0	$12,000	Dist	0 0 0 0	

3Aug95- 6Sar fst 5½f :223 :463 :583 1:05 Md Sp Wt 77 3 1 11 1½ 2hd 22¼ Davis R G 118 3.05 94-12 Roar1182¼ Procryptic11812 Tom N' Kath1184¾ Speed, game 6

24Jly95- 2Sar wf 5½f :222 :461 :584 1:051 [S]Md Sp Wt 68 12 6 32 2½ 1hd 2nk Davis R G 118 23.80 95-08 Severe Clear118nk Procryptic118nk Tropicool1183 Drifted late, game 12

WORKOUTS: Aug 14 Sar tr.t 5f fst 1:044 B 17/35 Jly 16 Aqu 5f fst 1:03 B 2/4 Jly 12 Aqu 5f fst 1:003 H 2/4 Jly 7 Aqu 3f fst :36 H 2/13 Jly 3 Aqu 3f fst :363 Hg 1/3 Jun 29 Aqu 4f fst :473 H 2/25

Hooray for Evan
Own: Schwartz Herbert
LUZZI M J (93 11 5 7 .12)

B. g. 2 (Apr)
Sire: Cormorant (His Majesty)
Dam: Raise Some Thunder (Thunder Puddles)
Br: Schwartz Herbert (NY)
Tr: Schwartz Scott M (8 1 2 0 .13)

118

Lifetime Record :	1 M 0 0	$0		
1995	1 M 0 0		Turf	0 0 0 0
1994	0 M 0 0		Wet	0 0 0 0
Sar	1 0 0 0		Dist	0 0 0 0

31Jly95- 2Sar fst 6f :224 :463 :591 1:12 [S]Md Sp Wt 9 2 6 64 66 911 925¼ Luzzi M J 118 b 33.50 55-16 Carrbine Special1185½ Talc About June1184 Tri Line118nk Bumped early 11

WORKOUTS: Aug 17 Sar 5f fst 1:011 H 4/17 Aug 8 Sar 4f fst :482 H 7/33 Jly 23 Sar 5f fst 1:012 H 13/30 Jly 13 Aqu 4f fst :482 Hg 3/13 Jly 9 Aqu 4f fst :523 B 10/11 Jly 4 Aqu 4f fst :521 Bg 11/11

Mac in N. Y.
Own: Festa Charles E Jr
LEON F (40 2 4 4 .05)

Dk. b or br c. 2 (Mar)
Sire: Love That Mac (Great Above)
Dam: In a N. Y. Minute (Amber Pass)
Br: Charles E. Festa Jr. (NY)
Tr: Reynolds Patrick L (8 0 1 0 .00)

118

Lifetime Record :	1 M 0 0	$0		
1995	1 M 0 0		Turf	0 0 0 0
1994	0 M 0 0		Wet	1 0 0 0
Sar	1 0 0 0		Dist	0 0 0 0

24Jly95- 2Sar wf 5½f :222 :461 :584 1:051 [S]Md Sp Wt 21 2 12 1219 1113 1115 1117¼ Velasquez J 118 48.75 77-08 Severe Clear118nk Procryptic118nk Tropicool1183 Broke slowly 12

WORKOUTS: Aug 14 Sar tr.t 3f fst :373 B 9/20 Aug 9 Sar tr.t 4f fst :511 B 6/13 Jly 9 Aqu 4f fst :522 Bg 8/11 Jly 5 Aqu 3f fst :364 H 3/6 Jun 30 Aqu 4f fst :511 Bg 7/10 Jun 24 Aqu 3f fst :36 H 2/12

Superb Fleet
Own: Kupferberg Max & Saul J
DAY P (142 23 18 23 .16)

B. c. 2 (Apr)
Sire: Afleet (Mr. Prospector)
Dam: Sherry Mary (Superbity)
Br: Martin Michael T Racing Stables (NY)
Tr: Margotta Anthony Jr (18 1 5 3 .06)

118

Lifetime Record :	0 M 0 0	$0		
1995	0 M 0 0		Turf	0 0 0 0
1994	0 M 0 0		Wet	0 0 0 0
Sar	0 0 0 0		Dist	0 0 0 0

WORKOUTS: Aug 14 Sar 3f fst :372 Hg 7/21 Aug 7 Sar 4f fst :511 B 50/64 Jly 27 Sar 4f fst :501 Bg 16/24

Golden Axe
Own: Behrendt John T
BAILEY J D (153 36 19 18 .24)

B. c. 2 (Apr)
Sire: Gold Seam (Mr. Prospector)
Dam: Axkernish (Drone)
Br: James Hettinger (NY)
Tr: Donk David (17 3 3 2 .18)

118

Lifetime Record :	0 M 0 0	$0		
1995	0 M 0 0		Turf	0 0 0 0
1994	0 M 0 0		Wet	0 0 0 0
Sar	0 0 0 0		Dist	0 0 0 0

WORKOUTS: Aug 16 Sar 5f fst 1:013 Hg 4/27 Aug 9 Sar 5f fst 1:03 H 34/48 Aug 5 Sar 5f fst 1:032 Hg 17/31 Jly 31 Sar 4f fst :494 Hg 33/55 Jly 26 Sar 5f fst 1:023 H 21/47 Jly 13 Bel 5f fst 1:013 B 17/30 Jly 8 Bel 5f fst 1:023 H 19/27 Jly 4 Bel tr.t 4f fst :494 B 12/17 Jun 27 Bel tr.t 4f gd :494 B 9/18 Jun 21 Bel 4f fst :491 B 31/71

In both of his previous starts, Procryptic was a hard-fought second. Better yet, the times of those two races were superior to all of his opposition who had run before, which was duly reflected by his vastly superior Beyer speed figures. It hardly made me a genius to figure this out. Procryptic won by six lengths at 3-5, paying $3.20. A $2 exacta wheel would have cost $20. I passed, and Out To Win finished second at 7-1, producing a $16.20 exacta.

FIRST RACE

Saratoga

AUGUST 21, 1995

7 FURLONGS. (1.28²) MAIDEN SPECIAL WEIGHT. Purse $30,000. 2-year-olds foaled in New York State and approved by the New York State–Bred Registry. Weight, 118 lbs. (Preference to horses that have not started for a claiming price.)(Day 28 of a 34 Day Meet. Clear. 86.)

Value of Race: $30,000 Winner $18,000; second $6,000; third $3,300; fourth $1,800; fifth $900. Mutuel Pool $221,450.00 Exacta Pool $370,460.00

Last Raced	Horse	M/Eqt. A.Wt	PP	St	¼	½	Str	Fin	Jockey	Odds $1
3Aug95 6Sar²	Procryptic	2 118	7	5	2hd	1hd	11½	16	Davis R G	0.60
7Aug95 4Sar³	Out to Win	2 118	3	8	51½	5hd	21½	26	Krone J A	7.90
31Jly95 2Sar³	Tri Line	b 2 118	6	6	33	2½	33	33	Chavez J F	4.40
31Jly95 2Sar³	Hooray for Evan	b 2 118	8	4	1hd	3½	41½	43½	Luzzi M J	65.50
7Aug95 2Sar³	Dance the Wind	2 118	1	9	7hd	74	77	53	Perez R B	28.50
7Aug95 2Sar²	Iwillbking	b 2 118	5	7	4hd	610	6½	6nk	Migliore R	10.10
	Golden Axe	2 118	11	2	64	4½	53	78	Bailey J D	20.60
7Aug95 2Sar⁹	Curtain Up	f 2 118	4	10	11	11	8½	8nk	Samyn J L	68.75
	Superb Fleet	2 118	10	1	83	81½	91	9¾	Day P	20.30
24Jly95 2Sar¹¹	Mac in N. Y.	2 118	9	3	9hd	10¼	101½	105½	Leon F	77.75
	Mr. M. O.	2 118	2	11	10⁴	9½	11	11	Rydowski S R	86.50

OFF AT 1:02 Start Good. Won driving. Time, :22¹, :45³, 1:11⁴, 1:25² Track fast.

$2 Mutuel Prices:

8–PROCRYPTIC	3.20	2.60	2.20
4–OUT TO WIN		4.50	2.90
7–TRI LINE			2.70

$2 EXACTA 8–4 PAID $16.20

B. c, (Feb), by Distinctive Pro–Crypto Game, by Secreto. Trainer Aquilino Joseph. Bred by Delehanty Stock Farm (NY).

PROCRYPTIC dueled between horses to the turn then drew off under intermittent urging. OUT TO WIN settled in good position while saving ground for a half, made a run to threaten in upper stretch but was no match for the winner while clearly second best. TRI LINE dueled inside the winner to the turn and gradually tired thereafer. HOORAY FOR EVAN stalked the pace while three wide into upper stretch and lacked a further response. DANCE THE WIND failed to threaten while saving ground. IWILLBKING raced just off the pace while three wide to the turn and lacked the needed response when called upon. GOLDEN AXE moved up steadily while four wide to reach contention approaching the stretch and flattened out. CURTAIN UP never reached contention after breaking slowly. SUPERB FLEET was never a factor. MAC IN N. Y. was outrun, as was MR. M. O.

Owners— 1, Paraneck Stable; 2, Brennan Bernard F; 3, Morrell Sam F; 4, Schwartz Herbert; 5, Ryan Daniel M; 6, Chuckolow Stable; 7, Behrendt John T; 8, Chevalier Stable; 9, Kupferberg Max & Saul J; 10, Festa Charles E Jr; 11, Beecher Aaron

Trainers—1, Aquilino Joseph; 2, Brennan Brian; 3, Sciacca Gary; 4, Schwartz Scott M; 5, Donk David; 6, Anderson William D; 7, Donk David; 8, Shapoff Stanley R; 9, Margotta Anthony Jr; 10, Reynolds Patrick L; 11, Gullo Gary P

Scratched— Columbia County (12Aug95 2SAR6), Compellance

Instead, I went for the $2 Daily Double wheel in the bankroll, because I thought the second race, a 1¹⁄₁₆-mile maiden turf race for two-year-olds, might produce an upset with four of the nine two-year-olds making their grass debuts.

2 Saratoga

1 1/16 MILES. (Inner Turf). (1:39^4) MAIDEN SPECIAL WEIGHT. Purse $32,000. 2-year-olds. Weight, 118 lbs.
(Preference to horses that have not started for a claiming price.)

INNER TURF COURSE
1 1/16 MILES
START FINISH

Touch of Honey

Own: Gentile Aurelio P
CRUGUET J (15 0 2 0 .00)

B. c. 2 (Mar)
Sire: Obligato (Northern Dancer)
Dam: Champetre (Policeman)
Br: Aurelio Gentile (NY)
Tr: O'Brien Colum (9 0 1 0 .00)

118

Lifetime Record:	2 M 0 0		$0
1995	2 M 0 0	Turf	0 0 0 0
1994	0 M 0 0	Wet	1 0 0 0
Sar Ⓣ	0 0 0 0	Dist Ⓣ	0 0 0 0

14Aug95-2Sar wf 5½f :22^1 :46^2 1.13 1:19^4 [S]Md Sp Wt 33 11 2 8^{7¾} 10^{8¾} 11^{9¾} 10^{14} Cruguet J 118 55.25 62-19 Shoppers Gold118^{nk} Talc About June118^{1½} Tropicool118^{4¾} No factor 12
31Jly95-2Sar fst 6f :22^4 :46^3 :59^1 1:12 [S]Md Sp Wt 14 10 1 8^6 8^{6½} 8^{10} 8^{23¼} Cruguet J 118 62.50 57-16 Carrbine Special118^{5½} Talc About June118^4 Tri Line118^{nk} No threat, wide 11
WORKOUTS: Aug 9 Sar 4f fst :49 H 6/26 Jly 28 Sar tr.t 5f fst 1:04^3 B 7/14 Jly 15 Bel 5f fst 1:01^2 H 13/30 Jly 7 Bel 4f fst :49 Hg 21/47 Jun 17 Bel 4f fst :52 Bg 57/63

Star of Theatrical

Own: Spence James C
SANTOS J A (128 16 19 17 .13)

Ch. c. 2 (Mar)
Sire: Theatrical (Ire) (Nureyev)
Dam: Dynawite (Vigors)
Br: Cole Mrs Harold (Ky)
Tr: Lukas D Wayne (29 6 5 2 .21)

118

Lifetime Record:	1 M 0 0		$0
1995	1 M 0 0	Turf	1 0 0 0
1994	0 M 0 0	Wet	0 0 0 0
Sar Ⓣ	0 0 0 0	Dist Ⓣ	0 0 0 0

13Jly95-6Bel fm 6f Ⓣ :22 :46^1 :58^3 1:11 Md Sp Wt 46 10 4 3^1 1^{hd} 4^{1½} 7^6 Santos J A 116 3.30 75-19 Harpsichord116^{¾} Old Chapel116^{hd} Erskine116^1 Dueled, greenly 12
WORKOUTS: Aug 15 Sar tr.t 5f fst 1:07 B 12/13 Aug 7 Sar tr.t 5f fst 1:06^4 B 16/16 Jly 31 Sar tr.t 5f fst 1:05 B 9/12 Jly 8 Bel 6f fst 1:16^2 Bg 1/1 Jly 1 Bel 5f fst 1:03^3 B 27/33 Jun 23 Bel 4f gd :49^4 Hg 19/38

Togher

Own: Condren William & Cornacchia Joseph
DAY P (142 23 18 23 .16)

Ch. c. 2 (Jun)
Sire: Irish River (Riverman)
Dam: Bally Knockan (Exclusive Native)
Br: Phil Owens, Evelyn Owens, et al. (Ky)
Tr: Zito Nicholas P (43 8 5 10 .19)

118

Lifetime Record:	1 M 0 0			$900
1995	1 M 0 0 $900	Turf	1 0 0 0	$900
1994	0 M 0 0	Wet	0 0 0 0	
Sar Ⓣ	0 0 0 0	Dist Ⓣ	0 0 0 0	

16Jly95-6Bel fm 6f Ⓣ :22^2 :46^2 :58^1 1:10^1 Md Sp Wt 57 2 12 9^{12} 7^5 5^{4¾} 5^7 Krone J A 116 9.30 78-15 Game's On116^{2¾} Vibrations116^1 Cornwall116^{nk} Poor break, wide 12
WORKOUTS: Aug 17 Sar tr.t 5f fst 1:04^3 B 5/7 Aug 1 Sar tr.t 5f fst 1:03^3 B 4/12 Jly 14 Bel 3f fst :37^2 B 5/17 Jly 7 Bel 5f fst 1:01^4 H 8/30 Jun 30 Bel 3f fst :36 H 3/44 Jun 23 Bel 4f gd :48^1 Hg 4/38

Wish You Goboy

Own: Mongru Madhan P
MAPLE E (64 9 8 8 .14)

Ch. g. 2 (Jan)
Sire: Lyphard's Wish (FR) (Lyphard)
Dam: Warm and Soft (Caracolero)
Br: Arnold Farms (Ky)
Tr: Barbara Robert (26 5 3 4 .19)

118

Lifetime Record:	1 M 0 0		$0
1995	1 M 0 0	Turf	1 0 0 0
1994	0 M 0 0	Wet	0 0 0 0
Sar Ⓣ	0 0 0 0	Dist Ⓣ	0 0 0 0

16Jly95-6Bel fm 6f Ⓣ :22^2 :46^2 :58^1 1:10^1 Md Sp Wt 41 11 4 8^{10} 9^{7½} 8^{9¼} 8^{13½} Maple E 116 38.50 72-15 Game's On116^{2¾} Vibrations116^1 Cornwall116^{nk} No threat 12
WORKOUTS: Aug 15 Sar 4f fst :49^1 B 10/29 Aug 3 Sar 4f fst :50 H 26/40 Jly 9 Bel 4f fst :52 B 47/48 Jun 24 Bel 3f fst :37^2 Bg 19/38 Jun 9 Bel 3f fst :37^3 B 12/25 Jun 3 Bel tr.t 3f fst :37^4 B 8/17

Officious

Own: Amherst Stable
BECKNER D V (58 1 5 3 .02)

Ch. c. 2 (Apr)
Sire: Magesterial (Northern Dancer)
Dam: Madam Guilletine (Blakeney)
Br: Amherst Stable (Ky)
Tr: Johnson Philip G (17 2 0 1 .12)

118

Lifetime Record:	1 M 0 0		$0
1995	1 M 0 0	Turf	0 0 0 0
1994	0 M 0 0	Wet	0 0 0 0
Sar Ⓣ	0 0 0 0	Dist Ⓣ	0 0 0 0

14Jly95-6Bel fst 5f :22 :45^2 :57^1 Md Sp Wt –0 6 6 8^{9½} 8^{10} 8^{18} 8^{32½} Beckner D V 116 28.25 68-07 Bright Launch116^{¾} Hashid116^{10} Gun Approval116^5 Bumped break 8
WORKOUTS: Aug 15 Sar 5f fst 1:01^4 B 25/47 Jly 30 Sar 4f fst :48^3 H 8/24 Jly 25 Sar 3f fst :38^1 B 23/26 Jly 12 Bel tr.t 3f fst :36^2 B 3/9 Jly 5 Bel tr.t 4f fst :47^3 H 2/27 Jun 30 Bel tr.t 5f fst 1:03^1 B 5/5

Grey Relic

Own: Paraneck Stable
CHAVEZ J F (144 20 18 11 .14)

Ch. c. 2 (Feb)
Sire: Black Tie Affair (Miswaki)
Dam: Lana's Relic (Olden Times)
Br: Sexton Hargus & Sandra (Ky)
Tr: Aquilino Joseph (21 2 4 1 .10)

118

Lifetime Record:	1 M 0 0		$0
1995	1 M 0 0	Turf	0 0 0 0
1994	0 M 0 0	Wet	0 0 0 0
Sar Ⓣ	0 0 0 0	Dist Ⓣ	0 0 0 0

29Jly95-2Sar fst 6f :22^1 :45^1 :57^2 1:10^1 Md Sp Wt –0 2 7 5^4 9^{11} 9^{18} 9^{36½} Chavez J F 119 14.80 53-13 Louis Quatorze119^{5½} Beefchopper119^{7½} Hey You Weasel119^{3½} Brief speed 9
WORKOUTS: Aug 18 Sar tr.t 5f fst 1:04^1 B 6/10 Jly 26 Sar tr.t 3f fst :38 B 8/15 Jly 22 Sar tr.t 5f fst 1:03 B 4/9 ● Jly 16 Aqu 5f fst 1:02^4 B 1/4 ● Jly 12 Aqu 3f fst :35^4 Hg 1/5 Jly 7 Aqu 3f fst :37^2 Hg 6/13

Green Manor

Own: Thompson Roland E
SMITH M E (143 25 18 23 .17)

Dk. b or br c. 2 (Mar)
Sire: Green Dancer (Nijinsky II)
Dam: Riasly (Raise a Native)
Br: Roland E. Thompson (Ky)
Tr: Skiffington Thomas J (13 3 1 2 .23)

118

Lifetime Record:	0 M 0 0		$0
1995	0 M 0 0	Turf	0 0 0 0
1994	0 M 0 0	Wet	0 0 0 0
Sar Ⓣ	0 0 0 0	Dist Ⓣ	0 0 0 0

WORKOUTS: Aug 14 Sar tr.t 3f fst :38 B 12/20 Aug 8 Sar tr.t 4f fst :52 B 19/24 Aug 2 Sar 3f fst :37^4 Bg 10/13 Jly 27 Sar tr.t 4f fst :52^2 B 13/16 Jly 15 Bel [T] 4f fm :51 B (d) 2/3 Jun 24 Bel 3f fst :38^2 B 24/38
Jun 20 Bel 4f fst :52^2 B 30/31

Dangerous Ground
Own: Sullivan Robert J

BELMONTE L A (59 3 9 4 .05)

Gr/ro g. 2 (Jan)
Sire: Lear Fan (Roberto)
Dam: Oigaway (Mr. Prospector)
Br: Marion G. Montanari (Fla)
Tr: Blengs Vincent L (11 1 2 4 .09)

113⁵

	Lifetime Record :	1 M 0 0	$140
1995	1 M 0 0	$140	Turf	0 0 0 0
1994	0 M 0 0		Wet	0 0 0 0
Sar ⊕	0 0 0 0		Dist ⊕	0 0 0 0

30Mar95- 3Hia fst 3f   .22²   .33⁴   Md Sp Wt   — 6 6   10¹⁰10¹¹¼ Duys D C   11⁶ 8.50 81–16 Cahill Bay113ⁿᵏ Laplander114¾ Cashier Coyote116¹¼   No factor 11
WORKOUTS: Aug 16 Sar tr.t① 7f fm 1:33 B t/t Aug 9 Sar tr.t 5f fst 1:06⁴ B 10/10 ●Jly 31 Lrl 3f fst :36 H 1/6 Jly 11 Lrl 4f fst :51 Bg 34/36 May 21 Lrl 3f fst :37³ B 2/4

River Quest
Own: Kelly Edward J Jr

SAMYN J L (32 6 1 5 .19)

Dk. b or br c. 2 (Mar)
Sire: Riverman (Never Bend)
Dam: Personable Lady (No Robbery)
Br: Mohan Mr & Mrs John C (Ky)
Tr: Schulhofer Flint S (30 5 9 9 .15)

118

	Lifetime Record :	1 M 0 0	$0
1995	1 M 0 0		Turf	0 0 0 0
1994	0 M 0 0		Wet	1 0 0 0
Sar ⊕	0 0 0 0		Dist ⊕	0 0 0 0

5Aug95- 2Sar wf 6½f   .22² .45⁴ 1:11¹ 1:17⁴ Md Sp Wt   45 4 5 1ʰᵈ 3¹½ 3⁷¼ 6.15½ Santos J A   11⁸ 7.50 70–13 Sir Cat118¾ J P Hamer118¾ Jack Teagarden118²   Dueled, tired 7
WORKOUTS: Aug 19 Sar 4f fst :47³ H 2/27 Aug 14 Sar 4f fst :49¹ B 30/63 Jly 31 Sar 5f fst 1:02⁴ B 10/34 Jly 25 Sar 4f fst :47³ Hg 2/52 Jly 21 Sar 4f fst :49¹ H 14/50 Jly 15 Bel 3f fst :36¹ Hg Xt/30

Our Theme
Own: Malmstrom Ivar W

DAVIS R G (139 14 22 24 .10)

B. c. 2 (Apr)
Sire: Our Native (Exclusive Native)
Dam: Durham's Theme (Lord Durham)
Br: Thomas Dooley & Mary Alice Dooley (Mich)
Tr: Destasio Richard A (13 1 0 1 .08)

118

	Lifetime Record :	2 M 0 0	$0
1995	2 M 0 0		Turf	1 0 0 0
1994	0 M 0 0		Wet	0 0 0 0
Sar ⊕	0 0 0 0		Dist ⊕	0 0 0 0

13Jly95- 6Bel fm 6f ① .22 .46¹ .58³ 1:11   Md Sp Wt   36 1 2 1½ 2ʰᵈ 2¹ 9¹⁰ Davis R G   11⁶ 34.50 71–19 Harpsichord116¾ Old Chapel116ʰᵈ Erskine116¹   Dueled inside 12
24Jun95- 2Bel fst 5f   .22 .46²   .59⁴ Md Sp Wt   10 2 3 4³ 5⁴ 7¹² 7¹⁴ Davis R G   11⁵ 47.00 71–15 Cobb's Creek116¹ Tax Break116¾ Game's On116¾   Brief speed 7
WORKOUTS: Aug 15 Sar tr.t 4f fst :51³ B 15/30 Aug 8 Sar tr.t 4f fst :51² B 15/24 Aug 2 Sar tr.t 4f fst :53¹ B 12/12 Jly 27 Sar tr.t 4f fst :51² B 8/16 Jly 4 Bel tr.t 4f fst :50³ B 14/17 Jun 16 Bel tr.t 4f fst :48⁴ B 11/44

One of them, Officious, trained by P.G. Johnson and ridden by Dale Beckner, beat the 6-5 favorite Togher by a neck at 29-1, paying $60.50 to win, good for a double payoff of $146 on an $18 investment (using a $2 wheel). Of course, if Togher had won, the double was paying something like $11. And yes, I would have felt sheepish hitting the double and losing $7. But one good one like this produced a profit of $128 by wheeling a 3-5 shot.

SECOND RACE   1₁₆ MILES. (Inner Turf)(1.39⁴) MAIDEN SPECIAL WEIGHT. Purse $32,000. 2-year-olds. Weight, 118 lbs. (Preference to horses that have not started for a claiming price.)

Saratoga
AUGUST 21, 1995

Value of Race: $32,000 Winner $19,200; second $6,400; third $3,520; fourth $1,920; fifth $960. Mutuel Pool $218,583.00 Exacta Pool $321,406.00 Quinella Pool $77,645.00

Last Raced	Horse	M/Eqt. A.Wt	PP	St	¼	½	¾	Str	Fin	Jockey	Odds $1
14Jly95 6Bel8	Officious	2 118	5	3	4³	42½	4½	1hd	1nk	Beckner D V	29.25
16Jly95 6Bel5	Togher	2 118	3	9	8½	6½	5½	5½	2¹	Day P	1.35
	Green Manor	f 2 118	7	5	3½	3½	3¹	3¹	3nk	Smith M E	6.10
13Jly95 6Bel7	Star of Theatrical	2 118	2	6	9	9	9	7hd	42½	Santos J A	2.65
29Jly95 2Sar9	Grey Relic	2 118	6	4	2³	22½	2½	2¹	5nk	Chavez J F	31.25
13Jly95 6Bel9	Our Theme	2 118	9	7	5²	5½	6½	6½	6nk	Davis R G	20.30
30Mar95 3Hia10	Dangerous Ground	b 2 113	8	8	7hd	8hd	8hd	8²	7hd	Belmonte L A5	6.20
16Jly95 6Bel8	Wish You Goboy	2 118	4	1	6½	7²	7½	4½	8⁶	Maple E	14.20
14Aug95 2Sar10	Touch of Honey	2 118	1	2	1hd	1½	1hd	9	9	Cruguet J	30.50

OFF AT 1:32 Start Good. Won driving. Time, :23³, :48⁴, 1:14², 1:39³, 1:45⁴ Course firm.

$2 Mutuel Prices:

5–OFFICIOUS	60.50	15.60	9.20
3–TOGHER		3.10	2.50
7–GREEN MANOR			3.70

$2 EXACTA 5–3 PAID $182.00 $2 QUINELLA 3–5 PAID $74.00

Ch. c, (Apr), by Magesterial–Madam Guillotine, by Blakeney. Trainer Johnson Philip G. Bred by Amherst Stable (Ky).

OFFICIOUS settled in good position while between horses for six furlongs, split horses in upper stretch, surged to the front in midstretch then was all out to hold off TOGHER in the final strides. TOGHER outrun early, moved up gradually while four wide along the backstretch, continued wide advancing into the stretch, then finished fastest in the middle of the track but could not get up. GREEN MANOR stalked the pace while three wide into upper stretch, made a run to threaten in midstretch, but was no match for the top two. STAR OF THEATRICAL trailed for six furlongs, circled five wide into the stretch, lugged in while gaining in upper stretch, rallied belatedly. GREY RELIC dueled between horses to the turn, gained a slim lead in upper stretch then weakened under pressure in the final eighth. OUR THEME reserved for five furlongs, raced in traffic while between horses on the turn and failed to threaten thereafter. DANGEROUS GROUND outrun for six furlongs, while saving ground, raced in traffic along the inside in upper stretch, then lacked a further response. WISH YOU GOBOY rated in the middle of the pack for six furlongs, made a run along the rail to reach contention in upper stretch, steadied along the rail in midstretch, and was never close thereafter. TOUCH OF HONEY dueled along the rail to the top of the stretch and gave way.

Owners— 1, Amherst Stable & Spruce Pond Stable; 2, Condren William & Cornacchia Joseph; 3, Thompson Roland E; 4, Spence James C; 5, Paraneck Stable; 6, Malmstrom Ivar W; 7, Sullivan Robert J; 8, Mongru Madhan P; 9, Gentile Aurelio P

Trainers— 1, Johnson Philip G; 2, Zito Nicholas P; 3, Skiffington Thomas J; 4, Lukas D Wayne; 5, Aquilino Joseph; 6, Destasio Richard A; 7, Blengs Vincent L; 8, Barbara Robert; 9, O'Brien Colum

Scratched— River Quest (5Aug95 2SAR6), Northern Shaker (31Jly95 2SAR5), Pro Doc (12Aug95 2SAR8), Peace Process, R.s.v.p. Requested, Bombardier (5Aug95 2SAR5), Semper K (7Jly95 2BEL9), Lonsdale (12Aug95 6SAR4)

$2 Daily Double (8–5) Paid $146.00; Daily Double Pool $397,590.

The final day of 1995 racing at Aqueduct, December 31, produced a spectacular exotic overlay in the fifth, a six-furlong maiden race for fillies and mares, three-year-olds and up.

I begin handicapping a race by eliminating horses I don't think can win.

Scratches left a field of 12:

5 Aqueduct

6 Furlongs (Inner Dirt). (1:08³) **MAIDEN SPECIAL WEIGHT.** Purse $29,000 (plus up to $11,383 NYSBFOA).
Fillies and mares, 3–year–olds and upward. Weights: 3–year–olds, 120 lbs. Older, 122 lbs.

Coupled – Princess Harriet and Reputable

Northville
Own: Coffey Marialice
Ch. f. 3 (Apr)
Sire: Nostrum (Dr. Fager)
Dam: Distant Lullaby (Duns Scotus)
Br: Coffey Marialice (NY)
Tr: Coffey Marialice (2 0 0 .00)
LEON F (44 2 1 3 .05)   120

Lifetime Record:	8 M 0 2	$3,224
1995	4 M 0 2	$3,224	Turf	0 0 0 0
1994	4 M 0 0		Wet	2 0 0 0
Aqu	1 0 0 0		Dist	3 0 0 2	$2,354

Bestofbothaccounts
Own: Minassian Harry
Dk. b or br f. 3 (Feb)
Sire: Private Account (Damascus)
Dam: Bestofbothworlds (Globe)
Br: Titly Foster Farms (NY)
Tr: Serpe Philip M (15 2 3 .13)
CHAVEZ J F (236 42 42 25 .18)   L 120

Lifetime Record:	10 M 1 1	$8,410
1995	10 M 1 1	$8,410	Turf	1 0 0 0
1994	0 M 0 0		Wet	2 0 0 1	$3,280
Aqu	0 0 0 0	$330	Dist	5 0 1 1	$5,680

Going Too Farr
Own: Oliver James H & Walbert Susan J
Dk. b or br f. 3 (Apr)
Sire: Carr de Naskra (Star de Naskra)
Dam: Going To (Flit–to)
Br: Walbert Sue (NY)
Tr: O'Connell Richard (22 2 4 1 .08)
VELAZQUEZ J R (147 27 19 22 .18)   L 120

Lifetime Record:	3 M 0 0	$300
1995	3 M 0 0	$300	Turf	0 0 0 0
1994	0 M 0 0		Wet	0 0 0 0
Aqu	1 0 0 0		Dist	2 0 0 0	$300

Sunsational Girl
Own: Schwartz Herbert
Ch. f. 3 (Feb)
Sire: Sunny's Halo (Halo)
Dam: Jimmy's Girl (Proudest Roman)
Br: Schwartz Ariane (NY)
Tr: Schwartz Scott M (12 1 1 1 .08)
LUZZI M J (146 18 12 14 .12)   L 120

Lifetime Record:	9 M 1 1	$10,670
1995	9 M 1 1	$10,670	Turf	0 0 0 0
1994	0 M 0 0		Wet	2 0 1 0	$7,480
Aqu	2 0 1 0	$5,800	Dist	4 0 1 0	$5,800

Paul's On Call
Own: Lostritto Joseph A
B. f. 3 (Mar)
Sire: Dr. Blum (Dr. Fager)
Dam: Amour Moi (Smoggy)
Br: Lostritto Joseph (NY)
Tr: Lostritto Joseph A (20 4 2 0 .20)
CORDOVA D W (135 14 10 14 .10)   L 120

Lifetime Record:	8 M 0 0	$5,340
1995	8 M 0 0	$5,340	Turf	0 0 0 0
1994	0 M 0 0		Wet	5 0 0 0	$2,760
Aqu	0 0 0 0		Dist	3 0 0 0	$1,680

Lorene's Prospect
Own: Paraneck Stable
B. f. 3 (Mar)
Sire: Northern Prospect (Mr. Prospector)
Dam: Fateful Prospect (Dactylographer)
Br: Quirk Equine Inc (Ky)
Tr: Aquilino Joseph (60 4 8 5 .07)
MADRID A JR (146 15 3 3 0 .05)   L 120

Lifetime Record:	21 M 5 4	$30,135
1995	14 M 4 4	$24,195	Turf	10 0 4 1	$17,010
1994	7 M 1 0	$5,940	Wet	3 0 1 2	$10,300
Aqu	2 0 1 1	$7,120	Dist	5 0 1 2	$3,255

Wild Plum
Own: Murphy Betty Jean
BRAVO J (48 5 6 2 .13)
B. f. 3 (Mar)
Sire: Once Wild (Baldski)
Dam: Plum Island Girl (Rexson)
Br: Richard Curtin (Fla)
Tr: Reid Robert E Jr (23 2 0 5 .09)
120

Lifetime Record:	1 M 0 1	$1,980			
1995	1 M 0 1	$1,980	Turf	0 0 0 0	
1994	0 M 0 0		Wet	1 0 0 1	$1,980
Aqu ⊡	0 0 0 0		Dist	1 0 0 1	$1,980

22Jun95-2Bel sly 6f :22 :451 :574 1:103 3+ ⒻMd 50000 56 4 5 57½ 56 57½ 310 Smith M E 113 *1.30 78-16 Houston Elegance1106 WishIMay1134 WildPlum1132 Improved position 7
WORKOUTS: Dec 23 Bel tr.t 5f fst :59 Hg2/36 Dec 13 Bel tr.t 4f fst :483 H 22/70 Dec 8 Bel tr.t 5f fst 1:02 H 7/28 Dec 2 Bel tr.t 5f fst 1:013 B 4/36 Nov 25 Bel tr.t 4f fst :483 H 10/52 Nov 18 Bel 4f fst :492 B 20/37

Glowing
Own: Hidden Lane Farms Inc
MIGLIORE R (191 21 25 27 .11)
Ch. f. 4
Sire: Sunny's Halo (Halo)
Dam: Go Gina Go (Horatius)
Br: Jack Mendel (Ky)
Tr: Preciado Guadalupe (6 1 0 1 .17)
L 122

Lifetime Record:	4 M 1 3	$9,255			
1995	3 M 1 2	$7,770	Turf	0 0 0 0	
1994	1 M 0 1	$1,485	Wet	0 0 0 0	
Aqu ⊡	1 0 0 1	$3,080	Dist	2 0 0 2	$4,565

20Dec95-5Pha fst 7f :231 :48 1:142 1:274 3+ ⒻMd Sp Wt 45 6 4 43 5½ 31½ 31 McCarthy M J L 122 fb 1.90 66-23 UltrPower120hd ColonilCurrncy1201 Glowing1222½ Lacked room, good try 9
29Jan95-1Lrl fst 1 1/16 :243 :49 1:154 1:483 ⒻMd Sp Wt 54 1 1 1½ 1hd 2½ 2no Wilson R L 122 fb *.70 67-26 Val De Vol122no Glowing1223 Miss Star Verse1222½ Willingly 7
5Jan95-9Aqu fst 6f ⊡ :224 :462 :592 1:13 ⒻMd Sp Wt 52 6 5 54½ 46½ 38 35½ Velazquez J R 122 fb 5.30 73-20 Limited Edition1222½ Compound Girl1222¾ Glowing1228 Finished evenly 8
18Dec94-6Pha fst 6f :223 :463 :59 1:12 3+ ⒻMd Sp Wt 38 7 5 42½ 53½ 56½ 39 Black A S 120 b 3.60 72-21 Bail Requested1204½ Rex Hannah122½ Glowing120½ 12
Came in, impeded rival
WORKOUTS: Dec 24 Pha 5f fst 1:022 B 5/22 Nov 24 Pha 6f fst 1:161 Bg1/1 Nov 7 Pha 5f fst 1:034 B 15/28 Oct 31 Pha 4f fst :491 B 11/32

Amaryllis
Own: Woodside Stud
PEREZ R B (125 12 13 10 .10)
B. f. 3 (May)
Sire: Cormorant (His Majesty)
Dam: Cupid's Play (Silent Screen)
Br: Eaglestone Farm Inc (Ky)
Tr: Alpers Sue P (6 2 1 0 .33)
120

Lifetime Record:	4 M 1 0	$6,500			
1995	4 M 1 0	$6,500	Turf	0 0 0 0	
1994	0 M 0 0		Wet	1 0 0 0	
Aqu ⊡	0 0 0 0		Dist	2 0 0 0	$900

1Dec95-5Aqu my 6f :22 :452 :582 1:111 3+ ⒻMd Sp Wt 46 8 9 99½ 108½ 79½ 711¾ Perez R B 119 f 3.70 74-18 Covija1193½ Sea Tempest1192½ Dare To Be Me1191 Five wide, no threat 11
16Nov95-5Aqu fst 6½f :224 :464 1:122 1:19 3+ ⒻMd Sp Wt 72 2 7 77 74 43½ 2½ Krone J A 119 f 12.20 84-15 Callas' Aria119½ Amaryllis1192½ Covija119hd Finished well 8
19Oct95-4Bel fst 1 1/16 :232 :464 1:12 1:433 3+ ⒻMd Sp Wt 51 4 6 76 75½ 78 717¾ Davis R G 117 12.10 63-24 Blonde Actress1174 Deo Devil1179½ Callas' Aria117½ No factor 9
2Oct95-1Bel fst 6f :231 :461 1:002 1:133 3+ ⒻMd Sp Wt 58 2 11 89½ 108½ 84½ 53½ Krone J A 119 f 13.00 69-22 Playful Katie1191 Devil's Mine119½ Bali Magic1192 Bumped break 11
WORKOUTS: Dec 24 Bel tr.t 5f fst 1:03 B 26/44 Dec 19 Bel tr.t 4f gd :501 B 14/29 Dec 13 Bel tr.t 4f fst :471 H 3/70 Nov 26 Bel tr.t 4f fst :52 B 61/65 Nov 11 Bel 4f fst :482 H 13/65 ●Nov 6 Bel 3f fst :36 H 1/18

Lady Sundquist
Own: Valentino John
NELSON D (73 3 4 7 .04)
B. f. 4
Sire: He's Bad (Rambunctious)
Dam: Suntanning (Jig Time)
Br: Valentino John (NY)
Tr: Ortiz Juan (10 1 0 1 .10)
122

Lifetime Record:	0 M 0 0	$0		
1995	0 M 0 0		Turf	0 0 0 0
1994	0 M 0 0		Wet	0 0 0 0
Aqu ⊡	0 0 0 0		Dist	0 0 0 0

WORKOUTS: Dec 18 Bel tr.t 4f fst :51 B 41/74 Dec 10 Aqu ⊡ 6f fst 1:18 B 1/2 Dec 3 Aqu 6f fst 1:182 Bg5/5 Nov 25 Aqu 5f fst 1:031 B 4/5 Nov 17 Aqu 5f fst 1:031 B 5/12 Sep 21 Aqu 3f fst :373 B 1/3

Ol' Pink
Own: Tri Richard Stable
SWEENEY K H (7 0 0 0 .00)
Ch. f. 3 (Apr)
Sire: Raise a Man (Raise a Native)
Dam: Jamara (J. O. Tobin)
Br: Friedman Lewis & Milfer Farm (NY)
Tr: Sedlacek Michael C (16 0 0 0 .00)
120

Lifetime Record:	2 M 0 0	$0		
1995	2 M 0 0		Turf	0 0 0 0
1994	0 M 0 0		Wet	0 0 0 0
Aqu ⊡	1 0 0 0		Dist	2 0 0 0

22Dec95-1Aqu fst 6f ⊡ :224 :464 :593 1:122 3+ ⒻMd 25000 31 6 10 109 107¾ 612 68¼ Sweeney K H 119 b 65.75 73-13 Shawklit Souffle1193 Is It WorthIt1192 MeetMeInHeaven114¾ Steadied 11
17Nov95-4Aqu fst 6f :223 :463 :594 1:133 3+ ⒻⓈMd Sp Wt 21 11 9 97¾ 1012 1020 1016¾ Rydowski S R 119 b 43.00 57-21 Easy Virtue119nk Missy Mims1122¾ Toyaholic119nk No threat 13
WORKOUTS: Dec 12 Aqu ⊡ 4f fst :524 B 1/1 Dec 8 Aqu ⊡ 4f fst :51 B 5/7 Nov 26 Aqu 5f fst 1:03 B 9/12 Nov 11 Aqu 4f fst :492 Hg4/24 Nov 5 Aqu 6f fst 1:183 B 3/4 Oct 30 Aqu 3f fst :373 B 3/5

Princess Harriet
Own: Krakower Lawrence J
CASTILLO H JR (135 12 11 14 .09)
Ch. f. 3 (May)
Sire: Mt. Livermore (Blushing Groom)
Dam: Nearly a Princess (Prince John)
Br: Waggoner George Stables Inc (Ky)
Tr: Pierce Joseph H Jr (23 2 3 2 .09)
120

Lifetime Record:	2 M 0 0	$900		
1995	2 M 0 0	$900	Turf	0 0 0 0
1994	0 M 0 0		Wet	1 0 0 0
Aqu ⊡	1 0 0 0		Dist	1 0 0 0

17Dec95-2Aqu my 6f ⊡ :232 :471 1:00 1:132 3+ ⒻMd Sp Wt 52 5 4 89¾ 912 79¼ 64 Cordova D W 120 22.80 72-15 J'approve120½ Lorene's Prospect1202½ Dare To Be Me120no No factor 9
10Aug95-5Sar fst 6½f :221 :452 1:101 1:164 3+ ⒻMd Sp Wt 39 6 6 88½ 711 815 522¾ Chavez J F 117 8.10 68-13 Wish I May11716 Mason Dixie117nk In Conference1173 Five wide trip 11
WORKOUTS: Dec 1 Med 5f fst 1:02 Bg10/27 Nov 25 Med 5f fst 1:004 H 7/27 Nov 18 Med 4f fst :48 B 4/70 Nov 11 Med 3f fst :364 B 12/34

1 — Northville — Seventh by 20 lengths at 40-1 in a New York-Bred maiden race and now trying open company. No.

2 — Bestofbothaccounts — Not closer than 4¾ lengths in 10 tries, losing her last two by seven and 16¼ lengths, at odds of 13-1 and 26-1, respectively. Uh-uh.

3 — Going Too Farr — Another New York-Bred moving up to open company after finishing 10th by 27 lengths at 2-1 in her return. No thanks.

4 — Sunsational Girl — This New York-Bred was a distant third and second in her last two tries, but was zero for nine and moving up. No.

5 — Paul's On Call — She moved up from New York-Breds to open company in her last start and was 11th by 30¾ lengths at 18-1. No.

6 — Lorene's Prospect — Closed 10½ lengths to finish second by half a length in a great try in last. That made her zero for 21 lifetime with five seconds and four thirds. A chronic loser we've already documented. No way.

7 — Wild Plum — Went off at 6-5 in her only start, and finished third by 10 lengths on a sloppy track in a $50,000 maiden claimer, June 22. She had two strong works for her return, but she was off six months and moving up. Contender.

8 — Glowing — In the money all four starts, including her last, a seven-furlong try at Philadelphia, when she was third by a length at 9-5 in her first start in better than 10 months. What was not to like?

9 — Amaryllis — Two starts back, she was second by half a length at 12-1. But in her last start, which was on a muddy track, she was seventh by 11¾ lengths, beaten 4¾ lengths by Bestofbothaccounts. Was the mud a valid excuse? Hard to tell. Contender.

10 — Lady Sundquist — The only first-timer in the field had questionable breeding and slow works, a bad combination. No.

11 — Ol' Pink — Moving up from a $25,000 maiden claimer when she was sixth by 8¼ lengths at 65-1. Pass.

12 — Princess Harriet — Off a distant fifth in her debut at Saratoga, August 10, she returned to the races December 17 at Aqueduct, closing eight lengths to finish sixth by four lengths in an improved performance. Contender.

Conclusion? Easy. Glowing looked clearly the best and was my pick in the *Gazette*. She went off a very generous 5-1, perhaps because of a late rider switch from Richard Migliore to Mike Mc-Carthy, who'd ridden her in in her last start in Philly. Benefitting from a good ride by McCarthy, she won by a neck, paying $13.80. Wild Plum, the layoff horse, was bet down to 8-5 favoritism and finished a decent sixth.

Wheeling Glowing in the exacta would have gotten you set for the new year. Northville, at 98-1, held off 9-2 Amaryllis by a head for second. The exacta paid $774.

FIFTH RACE

Aqueduct

DECEMBER 31, 1995

6 FURLONGS. (Inner Dirt)(1.08³) MAIDEN SPECIAL WEIGHT. Purse $29,000 (plus up to $11,383 NYSBFOA). Fillies and mares, 3-year-olds and upward. Weights: 3-year-olds, 120 lbs. Older, 122 lbs.

Value of Race: $38,450 Winner $17,400; second $7,250; third $3,190; fourth $1,740; fifth $870. Mutuel Pool $226,772.00 Exacta Pool $318,948.00 Trifecta Pool $276,821.00

Last Raced	Horse	M/Eqt. A.Wt	PP	St	¼	½	Str	Fin	Jockey	Odds $1
2Dec95 5Pha³	Glowing	Lbf 4 122	8	6	5¹	5½	22½	1nk	McCarthy M J	5.90
15Dec95 4Aqu⁷	Northville	3 120	1	4	1¹	1¹	1½	2hd	Leon F	98.50
1Dec95 5Aqu⁷	Amaryllis	f 3 120	9	10	10¹½	10¹	3½	31½	Perez R B	4.50
10Dec95 1Aqu⁵	Bestofbothaccounts	Lb 3 120	2	8	7½	7hd	41½	4½	Chavez J F	8.20
17Dec95 2Aqu²	Lorene's Prospect	Lb 3 120	6	11	9½	9hd	7¹	5¹	Madrid A Jr	6.90
22Jun95 2Bel³	Wild Plum	3 120	7	7	6hd	8hd	5hd	6½	Bravo J	1.85
17Dec95 2Aqu⁶	Princess Harriet	3 120	12	1	11hd	11⁷	8½	72½	Castillo H Jr	19.70
15Dec95 4Aqu²	Sunsational Girl	L 3 120	4	3	2½	2½	6hd	8²	Luzzi M J	19.70
	Lady Sundquist	4 122	10	12	8½	4hd	9³	94½	Nelson D	19.90
15Dec95 4Aqu¹⁰	Going Too Farr	Lb 3 120	3	5	4¹½	6¹½	10²	10hd	Velazquez J R	27.00
22Dec95 1Aqu⁶	Ol' Pink	b 3 120	11	9	12	12	12	113½	Sweeney K H	89.75
1Dec95 5Aqu¹¹	Paul's On Call	Lb 3 120	5	2	31½	3²	11²	12	Cordova D W	16.40

OFF AT 2:21 Start Good. Won driving. Time, :23¹, :47², 1:00³, 1:14¹ Track fast.

$2 Mutuel Prices:

9-GLOWING	13.80	6.40	4.00
2-NORTHVILLE		56.50	21.60
10-AMARYLLIS			4.30

$2 EXACTA 9-2 PAID $774.00 $2 TRIFECTA 9-2-10 PAID $4,111.00

Ch. m, by Sunny's Halo-Go Gina Go, by Horatius. Trainer Preciado Guadalupe. Bred by Jack Mondel (Ky).

GLOWING put a head in front of NORTHVILLE a sixteeth out, then was kept to pressure to hold sway. NORTHVILLE made the pace, then battled gamely when challenged to drop a close decision. AMARYLLIS raced four wide and finished well to hold for a share. BESTOFBOTHACCOUNTS finished evenly along the rail. LORENE'S PROSPECT failed to menace. WILD PLUM failed to reach serious contention. LORENE'S PROSPECT raced with mud caulks.

Owners— 1, Hidden Lane Farms Inc; 2, Coffey Marialice; 3, Woodside Stud; 4, Minassian Harry; 5, Paraneck Stable; 6, Murphy Betty Jean; 7, Krakower Lawrence J; 8, Schwartz Herbert; 9, Valentino John; 10, Oliver James H & Walbert Susan J; 11, Tri Richard Stable; 12, Lostritto Joseph A

Trainers— 1, Preciado Guadalupe; 2, Coffey Marialice; 3, Alpers Sue P; 4, Serpe Philip M; 5, Aquilino Joseph; 6, Reid Robert E Jr; 7, Pierce Joseph H Jr; 8, Schwartz Scott M; 9, Ortiz Juan; 10, O'Connell Richard; 11, Sedlacek Michael C; 12, Lostritto Joseph A

Scratched— Cathedral Choir (1Dec95 5AQU⁹), Cupid's Touch (3Nov95 1AQU¹⁰), Reputable (15Dec95 4AQU⁴)

7

The Double

You don't have to uncover a 20-1 shot to reap the benefits of an exotic overlay. In fact, you can occasionally use favorites, if you use them creatively. Golden Attraction was the favorite in the 1995 Spinaway at Saratoga, yet was part of a $1,000-plus Pick Three. It was the second consecutive day a D. Wayne Lukas-trained star was part of an exotic overlay, which is amazing. Lukas' live horses usually get over-bet fiercely in New York, especially at Saratoga. Yet his Hennessy, the dominant two-year-old in the country at the time, was indeed part of an exotic overlay — thanks to the late double.

The purpose of betting a double is to get a payoff better than a win parlay, hopefully a lot better. But using a win parlay as a comparison to a double payoff is only valid when you bet one single double combination, not if you use multiple selections in one or both halves. As Hennessy demonstrated, it is possible to bet a single double combination and connect on an exotic overlay.

Only six other two-year-olds chose to challenge Hennessy in the seven-furlong Hopeful Stakes. One was Maria's Mon, who was two for two at the time. Maria's Mon would lose the Hopeful this day, win the Champagne Stakes at Belmont Park, and go on to be named two-year-old champion.

But Hennessy was my Hopeful pick, and it did not take a lot of thinking. After losing his maiden race by a head as the 3-2 favorite, he'd won a maiden race by 6½ lengths at 2-5, the Hollywood Juvenile Championship by 5½ lengths at 1-2, and, in his first appearance in the East, the Sapling at Monmouth by 9¾ lengths at 2-5. The *Form*'s Hopeful analysis was absolutely justified when it said Hennessy "enters the race as the country's most accomplished juvenile colt."

Of the others in the Hopeful, Built For Pleasure was a distant second in the Sapling. Maria's Mon was picking up seven pounds off his impressive 2¼-length win in the Sanford at Saratoga. Seeker's Reward had been second in the Sanford. Lukas-trained Bright Launch, running as an uncoupled entrymate of Hennessy, had been life and death to win the Saratoga Special in a mediocre time and was picking up 10 pounds. Nick Zito's Louis Quatorze had won a maiden race at Saratoga impressively in his second start, but had lost to Maria's Mon by 10½ lengths in his first. Feather Box was fourth in the Saratoga Special.

---

8 **Saratoga**

7 Furlongs (1:20²) 91st Running of THE HOPEFUL. Purse $200,000. Grade I. 2-year-olds. By subscription of $200 each which should accompany the nomination, $1,000 to pass the entry box, $1,000 to start. The purse to be divided 60% to the winner, 20% to second, 11% to third, 6% to fourth and 3% to fifth. Weight, 122 lbs. Starters to be named at the closing time of entries. Trophies will be presented to the winning owner, trainer and jockey. Closed Saturday, August 12 with 28 nominations.

Built for Pleasure		Lifetime Record : 4 2 2 0 $65,670	

Seeker's Reward
Own: Lewis Debbie & Lee
PERRET C (39 4 3 8 .10)

B. c. 2 (Jan)
Sire: Gone West (Mr. Prospector)
Dam: Willamar (Northjet)
Br: Gord Capuccitti (Ont-C)
Tr: Hennig Mark (42 7 9 6 .17)

122

Lifetime Record: 3 1 1 1 $48,815
1995 3 1 1 1 $48,815 Turf 0 0 0 0
1994 0 M 0 0 Wet 0 0 0 0
Sar 1 0 1 0 $22,780 Dist 0 0 0 0

21Jly95-7Sar fst 6f :213 :45 :573 1:104 Sanford-G3 84 5 7 75¼ 43½ 22 22¼ Perret C 115 3.80 85-10 Maria's Mon1152¼ Seeker's Reward1156 Frozen Ice112hd Finished well 11
1Jly95-9CD fst 6f :211 :452 :58 1:112 BshfrdManor-G3 84 3 8 86½ 64¾ 33 31¼ Perret C 115 10.10 88-11 A. V. Eight1151 Aggie Southpaw115nk Seeker's Reward115no 8
Stumbled start, in tight, bumped 3/8ths
20May95-1CD fst 5f :222 :453 :581 Md Sp Wt 72 5 4 73¼ 43¼ 32 1hd Sellers S J 121 6.80 101-07 Seeker's Reward121hd Moro Oro1214¼ Trust My Funds121hd 12
Angled out late, fully extended
WORKOUTS: Aug 22 Sar 5f fst 1:03 B 8/9 ●Aug 16 Sar 5f fst 1:00 H 1/27 Jly 31 Sar 4f fst :482 H 11/55 ●Jly 16 Sar 4f fst :483 H 1/8 Jun 24 CD 5f my 1:013 B 6/20 Jun 13 CD 5f fst 1:03 B 13/37

Bright Launch
Own: Spence James C
SANTOS J A (156 19 21 24 .12)

B. c. 2 (Feb)
Sire: Relaunch (In Reality)
Dam: Burnished Bright (Well Decorated)
Br: Carrion Jamie S (Ky)
Tr: Lukas D Wayne (33 7 5 2 .21)

122

Lifetime Record: 4 2 2 0 $97,140
1995 4 2 2 0 $97,140 Turf 0 0 0 0
1994 0 M 0 0 Wet 0 0 0 0
Sar 1 1 0 0 $66,540 Dist 0 0 0 0

10Aug95-9Sar fst 6½f :22 :452 1:111 1:174 Sar Special-G2 77 1 6 11 1hd 12 1nk Santos J A 112 2.05 86-13 Bright Launch112nk Devil's Honor1141½ Severe Clear1134 Drifted, all out 8
14Jly95-6Bel fst 5f :22 :452 :571 Md Sp Wt 85 2 1 1hd 1hd 2hd 1¾ Santos J A 116 *.90 100-07 Bright Launch116¾ Hashid11610 Gun Approval1165 Dueled, game 8
10Jun95-1CD fst 5½f :22 :451 :571 1:034 Md Sp Wt 72 4 1 1hd 2½ 23 25 Barton D M 119 2.60 99-07 A. V.Eight1195 BrightLaunch1192 Don'tTakeForever1193¼ Pace, 2nd best 12
27May95-3CD fst 5f :224 :462 :58 Md Sp Wt 65 2 8 95¼ 76 33 23¼ Gryder A T 118 10.20 98-04 Blow Out1183¼ Bright Launch1181¼ Rush Did It118¾ Inside, 2nd best 11
WORKOUTS: Aug 22 Sar tr.t 4f fst :513 B 8/19 Aug 5 Sar tr.t 4f fst :504 B 5/18 Jly 30 Sar tr.t 5f fst 1:034 B 3/10 Jly 24 Sar tr.t 4f fst :484 H 2/30 Jly 8 Bel 5f fst 1:021 B 17/27 Jun 28 CD 4f fst :492 B 11/32

Louis Quatorze
Own: Condren & Cornacchia & Hofmann
SMITH M E (172 29 21 33 .17)

B. c. 2 (Mar)
Sire: Sovereign Dancer (Northern Dancer)
Dam: On to Royalty (On to Glory)
Br: Hofmann Georgia E (Ky)
Tr: Zito Nicholas P (51 10 6 11 .20)

122

Lifetime Record: 2 1 0 0 $18,000
1995 2 1 0 0 $18,000 Turf 0 0 0 0
1994 0 M 0 0 Wet 0 0 0 0
Sar 1 1 0 0 $18,000 Dist 0 0 0 0

29Jly95-2Sar fst 6f :221 :451 :572 1:101 Md Sp Wt 92 7 3 21 2hd 11 15¼ Smith M E 119 *.75 90-13 LouisQutorze1195¼ Beefchopper1197¼ HyYouWsl1193¼ Intermitent urging 9
4Jly95-2Bel fst 5½f :23 :464 :583 1:043 Md Sp Wt 63 1 7 66½ 53½ 38 210¼ Smith M E 116 2.15 81-17 Mr'sMon11610 [D]LousQutorz1163¼ ShwkltPowr1163¼ Chckd, swerved in 1/4 7
Disqualified and placed 6th
WORKOUTS: ●Aug 21 Sar tr.t 5f fst 1:023 B 1/17 Aug 14 Sar tr.t 5f fst 1:021 B 4/36 ●Aug 7 Sar tr.t 4f fst :491 B 1/40 Jly 22 Sar tr.t 4f fst :523 B 7/8 Jly 14 Bel 5f fst 1:01 H 10/32 Jun 30 Bel 4f fst :49 B 15/53

Hennessy
Own: Lewis Beverly J & Robert B
STEVENS G L (4 2 0 0 .50)

Ch. c. 2 (Mar)
Sire: Storm Cat (Storm Bird)
Dam: Island Kitty (Hawaii)
Br: Overbrook Farm (Ky)
Tr: Lukas D Wayne (33 7 5 2 .21)

122

Lifetime Record: 4 3 1 0 $202,900
1995 4 3 1 0 $202,900 Turf 0 0 0 0
1994 0 M 0 0 Wet 0 0 0 0
Sar 0 0 0 0 Dist 0 0 0 0

12Aug95-10Mth fst 6f :214 :454 :581 1:104 Sapling-G2 77 5 6 21½ 11½ 14½ 19¾ Barton D M 122 *.40e 85-14 Hennessy1229¾ Built ForPleasure1221½ CashierCoyote1221½ Mild hand ride 7
24Jly95-8Hol fst 6f :212 :442 :563 1:094 HolJuvnlChm-G2 91 7 2 51½ 1½ 12 15¾ Stevens G L B 117 *.50 91-09 Hennessy1175¾ Reef Reef117nk Desert Native1174 4 wide, ridden out 7
2Jly95-4Hol fst 5f :22 :45 :57 Md Sp Wt 91 7 1 2½ 1hd 11½ 16¼ Stevens G L B 118 *.40 99-05 Hennessy1186¼ Dubious Connection1183¼ Brazoria118nk Ridden out 8
3Jun95-3Hol fst 5f :214 :444 :57 Md Sp Wt 88 5 2 2hd 1hd 2hd 2hd Stevens G L B 118 *1.50 99-08 Andthelivinisesy118hd Hennessy1185¼ RegntAct1184¼ Rail, brushed, gamely 6
WORKOUTS: Aug 22 Mth 4f fst :493 B 14/34 Aug 5 Mth 4f gd :49 B 9/41 Jly 19 SA 4f fst :494 B 20/26 Jly 12 SA 4f fst :471 H 7/46 Jun 27 SA 5f fst 1:00 H 2/30 Jun 20 SA 5f fst 1:012 H 14/31

Feather Box
Own: Buckland Farm
MIGLIORE R (71 6 7 14 .08)

B. c. 2 (Feb)
Sire: Cherokee Colony (Pleasant Colony)
Dam: Center Box (Run the Gantlet)
Br: Evans T M (Ky)
Tr: Cordero Angel Jr (14 0 0 3 .00)

122

Lifetime Record: 3 1 1 0 $23,496
1995 3 1 1 0 $23,496 Turf 0 0 0 0
1994 0 M 0 0 Wet 0 0 0 0
Sar 1 0 0 0 $6,654 Dist 0 0 0 0

10Aug95-9Sar fst 6½f :22 :452 1:111 1:174 Sar Special-G2 64 4 4 53¼ 43 53¼ 45¾ Migliore R 114 21.60 80-13 Bright Launch112nk Devil's Honor1141½ Severe Clear1134 No late bid 8
11Jly95-5Lri fst 5½f :223 :463 :59 1:05 Alw 17500N2L 62 6 1 3½ 31 1hd 21 Douglas F G 120 *1.40 93-15 Bug River1201 Feather Box120hd Alisa Smartie1174¾ Unruly prerace 6
22Jun95-7Lri fst 5f :232 :471 :593 Md Sp Wt 60 4 2 2hd 2hd 1½ 15¼ Douglas F G 120 16.80 89-17 Feather Box1205¼ Chili Society120no Another Miracle1204¾ Driving 9
WORKOUTS: Aug 20 Sar tr.t 6f fst 1:17 B 1/3 Aug 7 Sar tr.t 3f fst :374 B 3/10 Jly 31 Sar tr.t 5f fst 1:03 B 3/12 Jly 23 Sar tr.t 5f fst 1:06 B 8/8 Jly 7 Mid 4f fst :502 B 1/1 Jun 3 Mid 5f fst 1:04 B 1/1

Expecting Hennessy to go off at 1-5 or 2-5, I hardly expected to find any value in betting him, until I checked the late double payoffs. I had planned to bet my *Gazette* pick, Little Moe S., in the ninth, a maiden turf race (love those maiden races, especially on grass).

Ten horses went postward in the ninth. In post position order:

9 Saratoga

1 1/16 MILES. (Inner Turf). (1:39⁴) MAIDEN SPECIAL WEIGHT. Purse $32,000. 3-year-olds and upward. Weights: 3-year-olds, 115 lbs. Older, 121 lbs. (Preference to horses that have not started for a claiming price.)

Hasty Data
Own: Paxson Mrs Henry D
KRONE J A (136 13 23 20 .10)

B. c. 4
Sire: Fit to Fight (Chieftain)
Dam: Olden Charade (Hagley)
Br: Paxson Mrs Henry D (Ky)
Tr: Dickinson Michael W (6 0 2 0 .00)
121

Lifetime Record: 3 M 1 1 $6,860
1995 1 M 0 0 $960 Turf 0 0 0 0
1993 2 M 1 1 $5,900 Wet 1 0 1 0 $2,900
Sar ⓣ 0 0 0 0 Dist ⓣ 0 0 0 0

2Aug95-5Sar fst 1⅛ :474 1:131 1:392 1:523 3+ Md Sp Wt 81 4 1 1hd 1hd 42 56¾ Krone J A 122 10.30 66-30 Crimson1151¾ Ransom Me Daddy1152 Little Moe S.115¾ Pressured, tired 12
23Dec93-9Aqu fst 6f ⊡ :224 :47 :593 1:124 Md Sp Wt 66 4 4 42 53 34½ 33¾ Davis R G 118 f 4.40 75-20 More To Tell1183½ Watrals Gone West118½ Hasty Data1189 Finished well 8
4Dec93-4Pha my 6f :22 :452 :582 1:114 Md Sp Wt 62 4 3 11½ 13½ 11½ 22 Salvaggio M V 122 b 3.20 80-19 Running Rock1152 Hasty Data1222½ Bonnerdale1227 8
Came in start, bumped rivals

WORKOUTS: Aug 14 Fai 5f (W) fst 1:01 B 1/2 Jly 24 Fai 5f (W) fst 1:052 B 2/2 Jly 2 Del 7f my 1:263 H 1/1 Jun 19 Fai 5f (W) fst 1:032 B 2/2 Jun 6 Fai ⓣ 6f fm 1:16 B (d)2/3

Cryptologist
Own: Low Lawana L & Robert E
VELAZQUEZ J R (132 24 20 9 .18)

B. g. 3 (May)
Sire: Cryptoclearance (Fappiano)
Dam: Routine (Northern Dancer)
Br: Flamingo Partnership & Vinery (Ky)
Tr: Peitz Daniel C (12 2 2 0 .17)
115

Lifetime Record: 4 M 0 0 $900
1995 2 M 0 0 $900 Turf 0 0 0 0
1994 2 M 0 0 Wet 1 0 0 0 $900
Sar ⓣ 0 0 0 0 Dist ⓣ 0 0 0 0

11May95-5Bel my 7f :223 :46 1:102 1:223 Md Sp Wt 50 10 2 22 22 46½ 516 Davis R G 120 b 38.00 72-11 Cat Be Nimble12010 Second Childhood1204 Goldsider1201½ Chased, tired 10
21Apr95-10OP fst 6f :22 :453 :581 1:103 3+ Md Sp Wt 51 4 10 86¾ 810 613 613½ Lester R N 114 b 15.20 74-13 Finally Legal114nk Dr. Kat's Cure1165 Sand Saint1146 Shuffled back 11
31Dec94-3Aqu fst 6f ⊡ :224 :46 :583 1:114 Md Sp Wt 50 7 9 99½ 911 916 919 Lovato F Jr 118 68.75 65-22 Angle Of Pursuit1188¾ Caro's Echo118¾ Hanging Road1131 Outrun 11
8Dec94-3Aqu fst 6f ⊡ :223 :463 :59 1:114 Md Sp Wt 57 5 4 55 67 79 711 Mojica R Jr 118 47.50 73-18 Bid Baby1185½ Screen Oscar118½ Guadalcanal1182½ No factor 8

WORKOUTS: Aug 21 Sar tr.t 5f fst 1:054 B 11/17 Aug 14 Sar tr.t 5f fst 1:024 B 6/36 Aug 1 Sar tr.t 4f fst :52 B 10/15

Shinhopple
Own: Boto Stable
RODRIGUEZ R R (2 0 0 0 .00)

Ch. g. 3 (May)
Sire: Smart Style (Foolish Pleasure)
Dam: Northern Diamond (Northern Hawk)
Br: BOTO Thoroughbreds Inc (NY)
Tr: Pichette Ray A (1 0 0 0 .00)
115

Lifetime Record: 1 M 0 0 $0
1995 1 M 0 0 Turf 0 0 0 0
1994 0 M 0 0 Wet 0 0 0 0
Sar ⓣ 0 0 0 0 Dist ⓣ 0 0 0 0

20Aug95-4Sar fst 6f :223 :462 :584 1:114 3+ Md Sp Wt 23 10 8 1019 1020 1038 1021¼ Rodriguez R R 116 114.25 61-18 Call Home116¾ As Time Flys By1161 Court Jester1162¼ Trailed, green 10

WORKOUTS: Aug 15 Sar 6f fst 1:192 B 3/5 Aug 10 Sar 5f fst 1:05 B 23/25 Jly 22 Sar 5f fst 1:05 B 11/12 Jly 16 Sar TR3 5f fst 1:04 Hg5/7

Royal Groomsman
Own: Knoebel Suzanne B
DAVIS R G (169 20 24 27 .12)

Dk. b or br c. 3 (Jan)
Sire: Runaway Groom (Blushing Groom)
Dam: Her Elegancy (His Majesty)
Br: Suzanne B. Knoebel (Fla)
Tr: Ward John T Jr (7 0 3 1 .00)
115

Lifetime Record: 6 M 1 2 $9,865
1995 1 M 1 0 $6,400 Turf 3 0 1 2 $9,445
1994 5 M 0 2 $3,465 Wet 1 0 0 0 $140
Sar ⓣ 1 0 1 0 $6,400 Dist ⓣ 2 0 1 1 $7,850

17Aug95-2Sar fm 1 1/16 ⓣ :232 :464 1:11 1:422 3+ Md Sp Wt 67 8 3 3½ 31½ 33 36¼ Davis R G 116 b 6.40 81-12 Hard Charger116nk DMr Market1166 Royal Groomsman1167 10
Bumped soundly, forced out 3/16 pl Placed second through disqualification.
28Dec94-2Crc fm *1⅛ ⓣ 1:534 Md Sp Wt 55 9 5 12 1½ 2½ 37 Velasquez J 119 b *1.60 43-49 Shellybird1195½ No Lollygagging1191½ Royal Groomsman1192 Gave way 10
27Nov94-6Crc fm 1 1/16 ⓣ :234 :482 1:131 1:453 Md Sp Wt 72 7 9 107 97½ 43½ 34 Velez J A Jr 118 b 9.70 68-29 Cuzzin Jeb1183¾ Our Opening118hd Royal Groomsman1187½ 6 wide, rallied 12
12Nov94-6Crc sly 7f :23 :462 1:124 1:264 Md Sp Wt 56 7 3 83¾ 86½ 75¼ 75¾ Velasquez J 119 10.40 72-20 Casperoo119¾ MollysPotShot1191½ NoLollygging119½ Failed to menace 11
29Oct94-6Crc fst 6f :222 :464 :594 1:134 Md Sp Wt 50 3 6 76½ 65½ 55½ 53½ Velasquez J 118 15.70 75-18 Perfect Spiral1181 Fortunate Tune118nk Clever Effort118hd Belated bid 9
8Oct94-6Crc fst 6f :22 :453 :584 1:121 Md Sp Wt 44 5 11 1212 1115 912 911¼ Castaneda M 118 65.80 74-16 Pleasant Too1181½ Escorted Flight1184 To Be Missed118½ Showed little 12

WORKOUTS: Aug 9 Sar 6f fst 1:144 H 4/11 Aug 3 Sar 6f fst 1:15 Hg2/6 Jly 29 Sar 4f fst :491 H 21/42 Jun 16 Crc 1 fst 1:483 B 3/4 Jun 11 Crc 6f fst 1:18 B 3/3 Jun 6 Crc 5f sly 1:053 B (d)12/14

Exemplar
Own: Dogwood Stable
SELLERS S J (94 11 13 10 .12)

B. c. 3 (Feb)
Sire: Nijinsky II (Northern Dancer)
Dam: Past Example (Buckpasser)
Br: Bruce Hutson & Marie D. Jones (Ky)
Tr: Alexander Frank A (32 2 1 5 .06)
115

Lifetime Record: 5 M 0 1 $6,790
1995 2 M 0 1 $3,080 Turf 0 0 0 0
1994 3 M 0 0 $3,710 Wet 1 0 0 0 $1,500
Sar ⓣ 0 0 0 0 Dist ⓣ 0 0 0 0

15Apr95-1Aqu fst 7f :23 :461 1:114 1:234 Md Sp Wt 52 4 8 75 76½ 79¾ 617¼ Velazquez J R 121 10.50 68-17 FlyingChevron1215 LstEffort121¾ SecondChildhood121¾ Steadied early 10
1Apr95-5Aqu fst 6½f :222 :452 1:111 1:18 Md Sp Wt 62 5 8 66½ 57 33½ 35½ Velazquez J R 120 7.20 84-13 Davenport1204 Dazz1201½ Exemplar1201 Broke awkwardly 8
19Aug94-5Sar sly 7f :23 :462 1:104 1:231 Md Sp Wt 47 2 8 41½ 43½ 45 415¾ Perret C 118 23.60 73-09 Top Account1181¾ Mr. Greeley11811 Jackson1182½ Saved ground 8
4Aug94-3Sar fst 7f :223 :46 1:12 1:251 Md Sp Wt 46 7 6 85½ 53½ 53 47½ Luzzi M J 118 10.60e 71-15 Bick1181½ Arezzano1182½ Confessor1184 Checked break 9
8Jly94-8EIP fst 5½f :223 :473 :593 1:061 Md Sp Wt 42 8 9 85½ 84½ 77½ 48 Martinez J R Jr 118 *1.40e 81-16 Bare Knuckle Bob1185 Bungee Jumper1182 Northern Stone1181 9
Bumped 1/8 pole, no threat

WORKOUTS: Aug 21 Sar 5f fst 1:03 B 13/29 Aug 14 Sar 5f fst 1:03 B 28/46 Aug 6 Sar 5f fst 1:022 B 8/21 ●Jly 29 Bel 5f sly 1:023 B 1/4 Jly 14 Bel 4f fst :492 H 13/40 Jun 26 Aik 3f fst :40 B 1/2

Mi Maestro
Own: Little Timothy M & Morgan Anne C
PERRET C (39 4 3 8 .10)

Ro. g. 3 (Mar)
Sire: Marfa (Foolish Pleasure)
Dam: To the Moon (Northjet)
Br: G. Watts Humphrey & Pamela H. Firman (Ky)
Tr: Morgan Anne C (3 0 1 0 .00)
115

Lifetime Record: 4 M 1 0 $8,320
1995 3 M 1 0 $8,320 Turf 1 0 1 0 $6,400
1994 1 M 0 0 Wet 2 0 0 0 $1,920
Sar ⓣ 1 0 1 0 $6,400 Dist ⓣ 1 0 1 0 $6,400

14Aug95-3Sar wf 1⅛ ⊗ :49 1:142 1:394 1:523 3+ Md Sp Wt 31 4 8 814 811 716 733¼ Perret C 115 22.60 40-25 Ransom Me Daddy115nk Kadrmas1154 Little Moe S.1152 No speed 8
4Aug95-6Sar my 1⅛ ⊗ :482 1:133 1:394 1:531 3+ Md Sp Wt 38 2 6 611 68½ 414 427 Perret C 115 f 5.90 43-26 Kazan12116 Crowned Crane1157 Devon's Tune11514 No threat 6
23Jly95-3Sar fm 1 1/16 ⓣ :232 :481 1:124 1:441 3+ Md Sp Wt 54 8 10 96½ 73¾ 66¾ 29 Leon F 115 56.25 69-15 Classic Arbitrage1229 Mi Maestro115no Excelleet115hd In traffic 1/4 pl 10
29Aug94-5Sar fst 6f :221 :453 :581 1:112 Md Sp Wt –0 9 8 918 1015 1015 1033 Carr D 118 64.40 51-13 Reality Road1188 Admiralty1185½ Cherokee Saga118nk Outrun 10

WORKOUTS: Aug 23 Sar 3f fst :371 H 6/23 ●Jly 16 Sar TR3 5f fst 1:023 Hg1/7 Jly 13 Sar 4f fst :50 B 7/9 Jly 8 Sar tr.t 5f fst 1:06 B 4/4 Jun 28 Sar ⓣ 4f fm :502 B (d)3/5 Jun 19 Sar tr.t 3f fst :393 B 3/3

Newport
Own: Donnelly & Ray & Shapiro
SMITH M E (172 29 21 33 .17)
Ch. g. 3 (Mar)
Sire: Silver Hawk (Roberto)
Dam: Here's Your Hat (Search for Gold)
Br: Jones Brereton C (Ky)
Tr: Walden W Elliott (11 0 2 3 .00)
115
Lifetime Record: 5 M 0 3 $11,180
1995 4 M 0 3 $10,470 Turf 4 0 0 2 $7,660
1994 1 M 0 0 $710 Wet 1 0 0 1 $3,520
Sar (T) 2 0 0 1 $3,520 Dist (T) 3 0 0 2 $6,950

17Aug95-10Sar fm 1 1/16 (T) :222 :461 1:113 1:424 3+ Md Sp Wt 74 9 5 57 52½ 3½ 31½ Day P 116 b 4.10 84-12 Paulo116nk Excelleet1161 Newport1162 Wide bid, weakened 9
4Aug95-1Sar my 1⅛ (X) :481 1:132 1:393 1:531 3+ Md Sp Wt 71 1 1 1½ 2½ 36 36½ Day P 115 5.00 63-26 Know It All1156 Golden Note115½ Newport11516 Dueled, weakened 8
26Jly95-6Sar fm 1 1/16 (T) :23 :471 1:12 1:423 3+ Md Sp Wt 58 6 7 75½ 105¾ 910 89½ Day P 115 3.75 76-11 Sublime Season115¾ Runaway Crusader1152 Golden Note110¾ 12
Checked early, steadied 3/8 pl
24Jun95-1CD fm 1 1/16 (T) :233 :48 1:123 1:44 3+ Md Sp Wt 70 2 2 1hd 21 42 35 Perret C 112 5.30 79-11 Vast War1135 Big Bruiser121no Newport112nk Dueled, weakened 10
6Jly94-7EIP fm 5½f (T) :221 :451 :58 1:043 Md Sp Wt 38 5 6 66¾ 55¾ 57 45¾ Martinez J R Jr 118 4.20 — — Tough1185 NapoleonDynamite118no CertinAsTheSun115hd No late threat 8
WORKOUTS: Jly 20 Sar 5f fst 1:01 H 3/24 Jly 13 CD 4f fst :491 B 4/21 Jun 20 CD (T) 4f fm :51 B (d) 1/3 Jun 13 CD (T) 6f gd 1:182 B (d) 2/3 ●Jun 6 CD (T) 6f fm 1:16 B (d) 1/4 May 27 CD 5f fst 1:023 B 18/41

Mr Market
Own: Klaravich Stables
CHAVEZ J F (169 23 21 17 .14)
B. g. 3 (Apr)
Sire: Carnivalay (Northern Dancer)
Dam: Puzzlement (Tentam)
Br: Rathbun Mr & Mrs Henry T (Md)
Tr: Sciacca Gary (71 7 9 5 .10)
115
Lifetime Record: 13 M 1 4 $20,060
1995 9 M 1 3 $16,460 Turf 10 0 1 4 $19,820
1994 4 M 0 1 $3,600 Wet 0 0 0 0
Sar (T) 1 0 0 1 $3,520 Dist (T) 7 0 0 4 $16,200

17Aug95-2Sar fm 1 1/16 (T) :232 :464 1:11 1:422 3+ Md Sp Wt 80 6 2 2hd 1½ 1hd 2nk Chavez J F 116 fb 3.20 87-12 HrdChrger116nk (D)MrMrkt1166 RoylGroomsmn1167 Swerved out 3/16 pl 10
Disqualified and placed third
15Jly95-3Bel fm 1 1/16 (T) :231 :46 1:103 1:411 3+ Md Sp Wt 69 4 2 11 11½ 21½ 37 Alvarado F T 114 fb 10.00 85-08 The Author114hd The Greek One1137 Mr Market1141½ Dueled, weakened 10
3Jly95-10Bel yl 1 1/16 [T] :241 :473 1:114 1:431 3+ Md Sp Wt 73 6 1 13 11½ 21½ 37½ Alvarado F T 114 fb 18.90 72-26 Validate1146½ Palm Freezer1141 Mr Market1143 Hustled, weakened 10
8Jun95-4Bel fm 1¼ [T] :472 1:12 1:363 2:004 3+ Md Sp Wt 56 6 3 3½ 2½ 47 516¾ Velazquez J R 112 fb 12.40 68-17 Menzies112¾ Kazan1178½ Banquet1143 Bid, tired 12
14May95-5Bel fm 1 1/16 (T) :222 :453 1:10 1:414 Clm 45000 74 7 3 21 2½ 32 43¾ Ramos W S 114 fb 3.65 85-12 GlitteringWolf113nk FerlessAndFre1121½ Bldski'sGmbl1162 Rushed, tired 10
19Apr95-6Hia fm *1⅛ (T) 1:493 Md Sp Wt 72 4 1 1½ 11 13 2hd Chavez S N 121 fb 8.50 84-15 TaterNorth121hd MrMarket1213½ Backwardtion121½ Gave way grudgingly 10
20Mar95-4Hia fm *1⅛ (T) 1:481 Md Sp Wt 64 2 1 11½ 12 23½ 510 Fires E 121 b 21.90 81-11 Senor Doria1213½ Backwardation1214½ Tater North121nk Faded 11
16Feb95-6GP fm *1 1/16 (T) :231 :48 1:123 1:434+ Md Sp Wt 38 4 2 21 2hd 68 820 Bracho J A 120 b 6.50 69-13 Social Approval1203½ OhSoFabulous120no RansomMeDaddy1201¾ Faltered 9
6Feb95-10GP fst 1 1/16 :231 :471 1:122 1:471 Md Sp Wt 60 10 1 1hd 2½ 22½ 911½ Bracho J A 120 54.70 60-28 Deceptive Stroke1205½ Make Your Choice120nk Paulo1203 Gave way 12
20Nov94-5Aqu fst 1 (X) :234 :472 1:123 1:374 Md Sp Wt 40 7 9 911 88 1016 1023 Chavez J F 118 5.80e 56-25 Nostra1131¾ Storm Hawk118¾ Paragallo's Hope1188½ Outrun 10
WORKOUTS: Aug 14 Sar tr.t 4f fst :502 B 10/38 Aug 7 Sar tr.t 4f fst :501 B 5/40 Jly 27 Bel 4f fst :48 H 3/21 Jun 24 Bel 4f fst :484 B 21/91 May 28 Bel 4f fst :483 B 17/93

Little Moe S.
Own: Safier Gary
SANTOS J A (156 19 21 24 .12)
Gr. c. 3 (Feb)
Sire: Skip Trial (Bailjumper)
Dam: She's Our Funny (Funny Fellow)
Br: DeVries Edward R (Fla)
Tr: Schulhofer Flint S (50 7 9 12 .14)
115
Lifetime Record: 7 M 2 3 $14,945
1995 7 M 2 3 $14,945 Turf 2 0 0 1 $1,800
1994 0 M 0 0 Wet 2 0 0 1 $4,080
Sar (T) 0 0 0 0 Dist (T) 1 0 0 1 $1,600

14Aug95-3Sar wf 1⅛ (X) :49 1:142 1:394 1:523 3+ Md Sp Wt 77 2 3 32 31 42 34½ Samyn J L 115 b 3.15 69-25 Ransom Me Daddy115nk Kadrmas1154 Little Moe S.1152 No late bid 8
2Aug95-5Sar fst 1⅛ :474 1:131 1:392 1:523 3+ Md Sp Wt 85 5 3 31½ 31 53½ 33¾ Bailey J D 115 b 3.90 69-30 Crimson1151¾ Ransom Me Daddy1152 Little Moe S.115¾ Held well 12
23Jly95-4Mth fm 1 (T) :231 :464 1:11 1:371 3+ Md Sp Wt 72 5 10 911 89¼ 67½ 53¾ McCauley W H 114 b *2.80 80-16 Greenbo114nk S.h. Builder1141½ Recanted114nk 10
Jostled, squeezed back start
15Jun95-6Crc fst 1 1/16 :242 :483 1:133 1:471 3+ Md Sp Wt 73 5 3 3½ 2hd 2hd 21½ Castillo H Jr 115 b 3.30 82-22 Navy Knight1151½ Little Moe S.1154½ Francis Albert11517 Best of rest 7
3Jun95-5Crc wf 7f :223 :454 1:121 1:252 3+ Md Sp Wt 62 11 2 99 910 77¾ 46½ Pincay L Jr 117 *3.70 78-11 Ultimatim1152 Disapproved115nk Navy Knight1154 Belated bid 12
20May95-5Hia yl 1 1/16 (T) 1:441 Md Sp Wt 59 3 5 48½ 55½ 45 35½ Douglas R R 121 *2.40 72-19 Techster121nk Ricky's Shadow1215 Little Moe S.1213 Late rally 12
8May95-4Hia fst 7f :241 :47 1:11 1:241 Md Sp Wt 67 6 9 95 75½ 45½ 22½ Boulanger G 121 8.30 85-11 Senor Roo1212½ Little Moe S.1212 Runaway Racer121¾ Rallied 9
WORKOUTS: Aug 22 Sar 4f fst :491 B 6/22 Aug 10 Sar 4f fst :483 H 5/26 Jly 19 Sar 5f fst 1:03 B 8/12 Jly 14 Sar 5f fst 1:023 B 3/5 Jly 9 Sar tr.t 5f fst 1:04 B 1/3 Jly 4 Sar tr.t 5f fst 1:041 B 2/3

Meet Approval
Own: Live Oak Plantation
PEREZ R B (75 10 6 8 .13)
Ch. c. 3 (Mar)
Sire: With Approval (Caro)
Dam: Damask Sky (Damascus)
Br: Live Oak Stud (Fla)
Tr: Kelly Patrick J (29 3 4 2 .10)
115
Lifetime Record: 6 M 0 0 $4,560
1995 4 M 0 0 $2,880 Turf 3 0 0 0 $2,880
1994 2 M 0 0 $1,680 Wet 1 0 0 0
Sar (T) 2 0 0 0 $2,880 Dist (T) 2 0 0 0 $2,880

17Aug95-10Sar fm 1 1/16 (T) :222 :461 1:113 1:424 3+ Md Sp Wt 70 7 4 34½ 2½ 2½ 43½ Perez R B 116 b 18.60 82-12 Paulo116nk Excelleet1161 Newport1162 Led, weakened 9
2Aug95-5Sar fst 1⅛ :474 1:131 1:392 1:523 3+ Md Sp Wt 32 12 4 42½ 53 1220 1237 Maple E 115 25.25 36-30 Crimson1151¾ Ransom Me Daddy1152 Little Moe S.115¾ Wide, tired 12
23Jly95-3Sar fm 1 1/16 [T] :232 :481 1:124 1:441 3+ Md Sp Wt 49 9 8 73¾ 63¼ 46½ 511½ Maple E 115 10.50 67-15 Classic Arbitrage1229 Mi Maestro115no Excelleet115hd Steadied first turn 10
13Jly95-9Bel fm 1 (T) :223 :46 1:103 1:351 3+ Md Sp Wt 55 3 2 2½ 3½ 77½ 812 Maple E 113 8.40 75-13 Mr. Bluebird1222½ Visible King113nk H. J. Baker113hd Forced pace 10
10Dec94-7Aqu wf 170 [•] :242 :483 1:143 1:442 Alw 32000N1X 47 5 6 57¾ 63½ 67½ 716¾ Maple E 117 16.10e 60-23 Devil'sBrew117nk Krabbie1176½ TheGenerlsAngel1174 Bump brk, std turn 7
1Dec94-5Aqu fst 6½f :231 :464 1:114 1:182 Md Sp Wt 61 5 5 615 615 511 411½ Maple E 118 49.00 77-24 Judge Me Not1131½ Hoolie1188 Private Rite1182 Broke slowly 6
WORKOUTS: Aug 18 Sar 3f fst :36 H 2/18 Jly 8 Bel 3f fst :374 B 15/27 Jun 25 Bel 3f sly :382 B (d) 6/6

1 — Hasty Data — We could excuse him losing to Little Moe S. on dirt, but his turf breeding was nothing special for his grass debut.

2 — Cryptologist — Layoff horse who showed nothing on dirt.

3 — Shinhopple — Lone start had been a disaster.

4 — Royal Groomsman — Been third in all three grass races, including his troubled '95 debut in last, when he was placed second thanks to a disqualification. Certainly a contender.

5 — Exemplar — Off since April 15. Had never been farther

that seven furlongs in five dirt races. Apt to need a race back even if he liked grass, which was not certain from his breeding.

6 — Mi Maestro — Second by nine lengths in his lone turf start. Contender.

7 — Newport — Strong third on grass in last with blinkers added, losing by a length to Excelleet, whom Mi Maestro had beaten by a nose July 23. Contender.

8 — Mr Market — In the money five of 10 grass starts without a win, and was zero for 13 overall. A chronic loser who was second by a neck in last and disqualified to third for fouling Royal Groomsman, though he beat him by six lengths.

9 — Little Moe S. — He was in the money four of five dirt starts, including a pair of thirds in his last two races. In his grass debut, he was bet down to 2-1 favortism and rallied for third on a yielding course at Hialeah. As the 5-2 favorite in his second grass start at Monmouth, he was "jostled, squeezed back at the start," according to the *Form*, and rallied from 10th to fifth. Clearly he had shown good intentions on turf: he wanted to beat other horses. The horse to beat.

10 — Meet Approval — A fourth in his third turf start in last was an improvement, as he finished two lengths behind Newport. Maybe.

The *Form* analysis labeled Little Moe S. as "the top contender," in the ninth, and I was thinking he could be anywhere from 3-1 to 6-1. So I was shocked to see the late double of Hennessy and Little Moe S. paying well over $30 a few minutes before post time for the Hopeful. I quickly bet a $20 late double of Hennessy-Little Moe S.

Hennessy went off at 4-5 and won by 3¼ lengths to pay $3.60. Little Moe S. went off at 5-1; was carried out extremely wide on the first turn, and won by four lengths anyway to pay $13.60. The late double paid $34.80. The return was $348.

A $20 win bet on Little Moe S. would have returned $136. A $20 win parlay of Hennessy and Little Moe S. would have returned $244.80.

EIGHTH RACE

Saratoga
AUGUST 27, 1995

7 FURLONGS. (1.20²) 91st Running of THE HOPEFUL. Purse $200,000. Grade I. 2-year-olds. By subscription of $200 each which should accompany the nomination, $1,000 to pass the entry box, $1,000 to start. The purse to be divided 60% to the winner, 20% to second, 11% to third, 6% to fourth and 3% to fifth. Weight, 122 lbs. Starters to be named at the closing time of entries. Trophies will be presented to the winning owner, trainer and jockey. Closed Saturday, August 12 with 28 nominations.

Value of Race: $200,000 Winner $120,000; second $40,000; third $22,000; fourth $12,000; fifth $6,000. Mutuel Pool $741,963.00 Exacta Pool $540,999.00 Triple Pool $378,172.00 Minus Show Pool $24,393.00

Last Raced	Horse	M/Eqt. A.Wt	PP	St	¼	½	Str	Fin	Jockey	Odds $1
12Aug95 ¹⁰Mth¹	Hennessy	2 122	6	3	5²	4²½	1¹	1³½	Stevens G L	0.80
29Jly95 ²Sar¹	Louis Quatorze	2 122	5	4	3²	2hd	2¹	2³½	Smith M E	3.35
21Jly95 ⁷Sar¹	Maria's Mon	2 122	2	7	1½	1hd	3⁷	3⁹	Davis R G	3.10
10Aug95 ⁹Sar⁴	Feather Box	b 2 122	7	1	6½	6½	4¹½	4⁶	Migliore R	65.00
21Jly95 ⁷Sar²	Seeker's Reward	2 122	3	5	7	7	7	5¹	Perret C	11.70
10Aug95 ⁹Sar¹	Bright Launch	2 122	4	2	2hd	3½	5¹½	6¹¾	Santos J A	21.30
12Aug95 ¹⁰Mth²	Built for Pleasure	2 122	1	6	4½	5hd	6½	7	Sellers S J	43.75

OFF AT 5:17 Start Good. Won driving. Time, :22², :45³, 1:10², 1:23² Track fast.

$2 Mutuel Prices:

6–HENNESSY	3.60	2.60	2.10
5–LOUIS QUATORZE		3.50	2.10
2–MARIA'S MON			2.10

$2 EXACTA 6–5 PAID $13.80 $2 TRIPLE 6–5–2 PAID $24.20

Ch. c, (Mar), by Storm Cat–Island Kitty, by Hawaii. Trainer Lukas D Wayne. Bred by Overbrook Farm (Ky).

HENNESSY settled in good position just behind the early speed duel, launched a rally four wide leaving the far turn, drew alongside LOUIS QUATORZE to challenge at the quarter pole, opened a clear advantage in midstretch, then drew away under steady left hand encouragement. LOUIS QUATORZE forced the early pace while three wide, surged to the front gaining a brief lead on the turn, battled gamely inside the winner into midstretch, but couldn't stay with that one in the final furlong. MARIA'S MON rushed up along the inside after breaking a bit slowly, set the pace under pressure to the turn then weakened from his early efforts. FEATHER BOX unhurried for a half, circled four wide on the turn, lacked a strong closing response. SEEKER'S REWARD devoid of early speed, never reached contention. BRIGHT LAUNCH dueled between horses for a half then gave way leaving the far turn. BUILT FOR PLEASURE up close early, was finished after going a half. LOUIS QUATORZE wore mud caulks.

Owners— 1, Lewis Beverly J & Robert B.; 2, Condren & Cornacchia & Hofmann; 3, Rosenthal Mrs Morton; 4, Buckland Farm; 5, Lewis Debbie & Lee; 6, Spence James C; 7, Heard Thomas H Jr

Trainers—1, Lukas D Wayne; 2, Zito Nicholas P; 3, Schosberg Richard; 4, Cordero Angel Jr; 5, Hennig Mark; 6, Lukas D Wayne; 7, Heard Thomas H Jr

$2 Pick–3 (12–9–6) Paid $106.00; Pick–3 Pool $244,229. $2 Pick–6 (4–4–4–12–9–6) 6 Correct 5 Tickets Paid $17,376.00; 5 Correct 164 Tickets Paid $176.50; Pick–6 Pool $154,229.

NINTH RACE   1¹⁄₁₆ MILES. (Inner Turf)(1.39⁴) MAIDEN SPECIAL WEIGHT. Purse $32,000. 3-year-olds and upward. Weights: 3-year-olds, 115 lbs. Older, 121 lbs. (Preference to horses that have not started for a claiming price.)

Saratoga
AUGUST 27, 1995

Value of Race: $32,000. Winner $19,200; second $6,400; third $3,520; fourth $1,920; fifth $960. Mutuel Pool $410,436.00 Exacta Pool $445,070.00 Triple Pool $589,084.00

Last Raced	Horse	M/Eqt. A.Wt	PP	St	¼	½	¾	Str	Fin	Jockey	Odds $1
14Aug95 3Sar3	Little Moe S.	b 3 115	9	10	8¹½	8⁴	4½	3¹½	1⁴	Santos J A	5.80
14Aug95 3Sar7	Mi Maestro	f 3 115	6	9	9³	9¹⁰	7½	5hd	2¹	Perret C	14.90
17Aug95 10Sar4	Meet Approval	b 3 115	10	8	7³	5³	3hd	2¹½	3³	Perez R B	22.30
2Aug95 5Sar5	Hasty Data	4 121	1	1	1½	1½	1hd	1½	4⁴½	Krone J A	3.85
11May95 5Bel5	Ⓓ Cryptologist	bf 3 115	2	2	5¹	7hd	8¹	4¹	5²½	Velazquez J R	36.75
17Aug95 10Sar3	Newport	b 3 115	7	6	2²	2¹	2²½	6⁵	6⁸	Smith M E	5.10
15Apr95 1Aqu6	Exemplar	3 115	5	5	6hd	6½	9³⁰	7²	7⁴	Sellers S J	10.50
17Aug95 2Sar3	Royal Groomsman	b 3 115	4	4	3hd	3hd	5hd	9⁴⁰	8¹½	Davis R G	3.70
17Aug95 2Sar2	Mr Market	bf 3 115	8	7	4³	4³	6²	8½	9	Chavez J F	3.50
20Aug95 4Sar10	Shinhopple	3 115	3	3	10	10	10	10	—	Rodriguez R R	113.00

Shinhopple:Distanced
Ⓓ—Cryptologist disqualified and placed 10th.

OFF AT 5:45 Start Good. Won driving. Time, :22³, :46³, 1:11², 1:36⁴, 1:43¹ Course good.

$2 Mutuel Prices:

9-LITTLE MOE S.	13.60	6.50	4.60
6-MI MAESTRO		15.80	11.60
10-MEET APPROVAL			13.40

$2 EXACTA 9-6 PAID $209.50 $2 TRIPLE 9-6-10 PAID $3,424.00

Gr. c, (Feb), by Skip Trial–She's Our Funny, by Funny Fellow. Trainer Schulhofer Flint S. Bred by DeVries Edward R (Fla).

LITTLE MOE S. swerved out sharply going extremely wide to avoid the trouble on the first turn, raced well back for a half, circled four wide while closing the gap on the turn, then finished well in the middle of the track to win going away. MI MAESTRO outrun for five furlongs, circled five wide on the turn, closed late to edge MEET APPROVAL for the place. MEET APPROVAL steadied while being carried out on the first turn, moved up steadily along the backstretch, saved ground on the turn, angled out entering the stretch, made a run to challenge inside the furlong marker but couldn't sustain his bid. HASTY DATA set the pace along the rail into midstretch and weakened. CRYPTOLOGIST drifted out, causing considerable crowding on the first turn, raced in the middle of the pack for a half, dropped back on the far turn, and failed to threaten thereafter. NEWPORT forced the pace from outside to the turn and tired. EXEMPLAR steadied sharply between horses while being bothered on the first turn, failed to seriously threaten thereafter. ROYAL GROOMSMAN checked in tight approaching the first turn, raced up close for five furlongs and tired. MR MARKET faded after going six furlongs. SHINHOPPLE veered out sharply when bothered by CRYPTOLOGIST on the first turn, was never close thereafter. Following a stewards inquiry into the incident on the first turn, CRYPTOLOGIST was disqualified from fifth and placed last for interference on the first turn.

Owners— 1, Safier Gary; 2, Little Timothy M & Morgan Anne C; 3, Live Oak Plantation; 4, Paxson Mrs Henry D; 5, Low Lawana L & Robert E; 6, Donnelly & Ray & Shapiro; 7, Dogwood Stable; 8, Knoebel Suzanne B; 9, Klaravich Stables; 10, Boto Stable

Trainers— 1, Schulhofer Flint S; 2, Morgan Anne C; 3, Kelly Patrick J; 4, Dickinson Michael W; 5, Peitz Daniel C; 6, Walden W Elliott; 7, Alexander Frank A; 8, Ward John T Jr; 9, Sciacca Gary; 10, Pichette Ray A

Scratched— Seattle's Revenge (17Aug95 2SAR5), Ruffed Grouse (31Jly95 5SAR2)

$2 Daily Double (6-9) Paid $34.80; Daily Double Pool $373,579.

Though hardly a bonanza, that double was certainly an exotic overlay. But let's look at a couple other doubles which featured triple figure returns.

Winter racing at Aqueduct is about as far removed from Saratoga as you can go in New York racing. The Daily Double on November 24, 1995, featured a maiden claiming race ($40,000-

$50,000) for two-year-olds in the first, followed by a $12,000-$14,000 claimer for fillies and mares. The races were at 6½ furlongs and six, respectively.

The first race had a flock of non-contenders in a field of 12. Four were first-time starters. In post position order:

1 Aqueduct

6½ Furlongs (1:15) MAIDEN CLAIMING. Purse $16,000 (plus up to $6,280 NYSBFOA). 2-year-olds. Weight, 118 lbs. Claiming price $50,000, for each $5,000 to $40,000, allowed 2 lbs.

Hardshell Crab
Own: Kushner Herbert W
KRONE J A (69 13 9 11 .19) $45,000
Dk. b or br g. 2 (Jun)
Sire: Aaron's Concorde (Super Concorde)
Dam: Princess Pipit (Cornish Prince)
Br: Kushner Arlene E (Md)
Tr: Dutrow Richard E (5 1 2 0 .20)
116
Lifetime Record: 0 M 0 0 $0
1995 0 M 0 0 | Turf 0 0 0 0
1994 0 M 0 0 | Wet 0 0 0 0
Aqu 0 0 0 0 | Dist 0 0 0 0
Entered 23Nov95- 1 AQU
WORKOUTS: Nov 18 Aqu 5f fst 1:032 B 11/19 Nov 11 Aqu 5f fst 1:04 B 7/10 Nov 5 Aqu 5f fst 1:014 H 4/7 Oct 25 Aqu 5f fst 1:011 H 4/14 Oct 18 Aqu 5f fst 1:01 B 2/6 Oct 11 Aqu 5f fst 1:01 H 2/5 Oct 2 Aqu 4f fst :49 Bg 1/3 Sep 25 Aqu 3f fst :362 B 2/5 Sep 16 Aqu 4f fst :521 Bg 20/21 Sep 2 Aqu 4f fst :483 Bg 2/11

Trail City
Own: Mott William I & Verchota Robert
BAILEY J D (72 9 10 6 .13) $50,000
Dk. b or br c. 2 (Apr)
Sire: Red Ransom (Roberto)
Dam: Willow Runner (Alydar)
Br: Prestonwood Farm (Ky)
Tr: Mott William I (16 2 2 3 .13)
118
Lifetime Record: 3 M 0 0 $0
1995 3 M 0 0 | Turf 1 0 0 0
1994 0 M 0 0 | Wet 1 0 0 0
Aqu 1 0 0 0 | Dist 1 0 0 0
2Nov95- 1Aqu sly 1 :222 :452 1:112 1:382 Md 40000 38 6 1 12½ 2½ 47 716½ Bailey J D 118 b *2.15 60-28 Newsbreaker1143 Glowing Tru1165 Glade1183½ Used in pace 11
28Aug95- 2Sar fm 1 1/16 ① :232 :481 1:13 1:432 Md Sp Wt 45 6 3 32½ 31½ 67½ 813 Perez R B 118 15.20 69-08 Jetting Robert118¾ Togher1183 Vibrations118nk Stalked, tired 12
10Aug95- 6Sar fst 6½f :222 :454 1:101 1:163 Md Sp Wt 43 5 9 31½ 32 611 722 Bailey J D 118 5.80 70-13 Diligence11811 Gold Fever1182½ Surround Sound1181 Used up 10
WORKOUTS: Nov 20 Bel tr.t 5f fst 1:013 B 9/29 Nov 14 Bel 4f fst :481 H 2/27 Oct 31 Bel 4f fst :491 B 18/56 Oct 23 Sar tr.t 5f my 1:031 B 1/3 Oct 17 Sar tr.t 6f fst 1:17 B 1/2 Sep 30 Sar tr.t 1 fst 1:443 B 2/2

In the Rain
Own: Hobeau Farm
CORDOVA D W (43 2 4 3 .05) $45,000
B. g. 2 (Apr)
Sire: Fortunate Prospect (Northern Prospect)
Dam: Raininsky (Nijinsky II)
Br: Hobeau Farm (Fla)
Tr: Jerkens H Allen (16 4 1 4 .25)
116
Lifetime Record: 4 M 0 1 $5,880
1995 4 M 0 1 $5,880 | Turf 0 0 0 0
1994 0 M 0 0 | Wet 1 0 0 0 $1,680
Aqu 2 0 0 0 $1,680 | Dist 0 0 0 0
10Nov95- 1Aqu fst 7f :223 :454 1:121 1:261 Md 45000 46 4 3 11 11½ 2½ 65 Samyn J L 116 b *1.30 68-17 Magna Carta1191 Stalingrad1191 Night School1131 Gave way 9
4Nov95- 2Aqu wf 6f :222 :461 :583 1:112 Md Sp Wt 55 1 9 56 55 46 48¼ Samyn J L 119 8.10 77-14 Sea Horse119no Joe Jones1191¼ Ultimate Sanction1196¾ Ducked in break 9
25Oct95- 6Bel fst 6f :224 :462 :582 1:103 Md Sp Wt 52 1 5 51¼ 62¾ 54¼ 512 Samyn J L 118 17.90 76-13 KnownAccomplc118¾ SwngAndMss1183 Alln'sRnbow1183¾ Bobbled turn 10
30Sep95- 2Bel fst 6f :222 :463 :582 1:124 Md Sp Wt 65 5 4 32¾ 31 32¼ 33¼ Samyn J L 118 6.10 73-22 Citified1181 Turning Fifty1182¾ In The Rain1181 Svd grnd, even finish 9
WORKOUTS: Nov 22 Bel tr.t 3f fst :372 B 9/24 Oct 23 Bel tr.t 4f fst :491 B 14/28 Oct 18 Bel tr.t 6f fst 1:184 B 1/1 · Oct 10 Bel tr.t 4f fst :504 B 18/22 Sep 28 Bel 5f fst 1:01 H 8/29 Sep 25 Bel 6f fst 1:144 H 4/8

Ernie the King
Own: Federico Gino
MIGLIORE R (58 3 10 14 .04) $40,000
Dk. b or br g. 2 (May)
Sire: Silver Buck (Buckpasser)
Dam: My Dear Cathy (Honest Moment)
Br: Federico Gino (Fla)
Tr: Badgett William Jr (14 2 3 0 .14)
114
Lifetime Record: 0 M 0 0 $0
1995 0 M 0 0 | Turf 0 0 0 0
1994 0 M 0 0 | Wet 0 0 0 0
Aqu 0 0 0 0 | Dist 0 0 0 0
Entered 23Nov95- 1 AQU
WORKOUTS: Nov 21 Bel tr.t 4f fst :483 H 4/47 Nov 14 Bel tr.t 5f fst 1:041 B 18/25 Nov 7 Bel 4f fst :481 Bg 11/47 Oct 30 Bel 5f fst 1:013 H 12/36 Oct 24 Bel 5f fst 1:012 B 22/47 Oct 16 Bel 4f fst :51 Bg 41/50

Early Echoes
Own: Fox Hill Farm
SANTOS J A (30 6 4 5 .20) $50,000
Ch. c. 2 (Mar)
Sire: Eastern Echo (Damascus)
Dam: Candlestick (El Baba)
Br: Carter John B & Farish W S (Ky)
Tr: Servis John C (11 5 1 2 .45)
118
Lifetime Record: 0 M 0 0 $0
1995 0 M 0 0 | Turf 0 0 0 0
1994 0 M 0 0 | Wet 0 0 0 0
Aqu 0 0 0 0 | Dist 0 0 0 0
WORKOUTS: ●Nov 16 Aqu 4f fst :48 Hg 1/7 Nov 9 Aqu 6f fst 1:16 B 1/3 Nov 1 Aqu 4f fst :502 Bg 2/3 Oct 25 Aqu 6f fst 1:164 B 2/3 Oct 18 Aqu 4f fst :494 B 3/11 Oct 12 Aqu 5f fst 1:04 B 8/10 Sep 28 Aqu 4f fst :50 Bg 5/5 Sep 18 Aqu 4f sly :493 B 1/2 Sep 8 Mth 3f fst :373 B 6/9

Rosa in Bloom
Own: Rosenthal Mrs Morton
LUZZI M J (42 6 4 3 .14) $50,000
Gr/ro g. 2 (Feb)
Sire: Lee Castelli (Sovereign Dancer)
Dam: Is Rosalind (Mr. Leader)
Br: Rosenthal Mrs Morton (Ky)
Tr: Destefano John M Jr (11 3 1 1 .27)
118
Lifetime Record: 1 M 0 0 $0
1995 1 M 0 0 | Turf 0 0 0 0
1994 0 M 0 0 | Wet 0 0 0 0
Aqu 0 0 0 0 | Dist 0 0 0 0
27Jly95- 2Sar fst 6f :22 :453 :574 1:104 Md Sp Wt 37 11 3 53¾ 66¾ 911 919½ Velazquez J R 118 14.00e 67-12 Honour And Glory11810 Blushing Jim1183½ Jetting Robert118nk Tired 12
WORKOUTS: ●Nov 13 Bel tr.t 5f fst 1:00 H 1/18 Nov 5 Bel tr.t 5f fst 1:013 H 8/29 Oct 27 Bel tr.t 5f fst 1:04 B 17/20 Oct 16 Bel tr.t 4f fst :51 B 5/8 Oct 10 Bel tr.t 3f fst :372 B 3/9 Oct 3 Bel tr.t 3f fst :38 B 5/13

Hurry West
Own: Hough Stanley M
ALVARADO F T (71 3 11 9 .04) $45,000
Dk. b or br c. 2 (Feb)
Sire: Gone West (Mr. Prospector)
Dam: Line of Duty (Buffalo Lark)
Br: Foxfield (Ky)
Tr: Hough Stanley M (18 4 3 4 .22)
116

Lifetime Record:	0 M 0 0	$0			
1995	0 M 0 0		Turf	0 0 0 0	
1994	0 M 0 0		Wet	0 0 0 0	
Aqu	0 0 0 0		Dist	0 0 0 0	

WORKOUTS: Nov 17 Bel 5f fst 1:021 Bg 13/34 Nov 11 Bel 3f fst :36 Hg 4/20 Nov 6 Bel 5f fst 1:042 B 49/52 Oct 31 Bel 5f fst 1:044 B 37/39 Oct 25 Bel 4f fst :494 B 28/49 Oct 19 Bel 4f fst :503 B 23/35 Oct 13 Bel 3f fst :371 H 7/14

Thegiantkiller
Own: Black Marlin Stable
NELSON D (28 0 0 4 .00) $45,000
B. g. 2 (Feb)
Sire: Danzig Connection (Danzig)
Dam: Determined 'n Bold (Exclusive Native)
Br: Haras Pemale (Ky)
Tr: Jerkens Steven T (1 0 0 0 .00)
116

Lifetime Record:	2 M 0 0	$1,800			
1995	2 M 0 0	$1,800	Turf	0 0 0 0	
1994	0 M 0 0		Wet	0 0 0 0	
Aqu	0 0 0 0		Dist	1 0 0 0	

25Oct95-2Bel fst 6½f :224 :46 1:111 1:18 Md 45000 34 1 1 1hd 32 68¾ 815½ Nelson D 116 f 16.20 69-13 Ima Good Gamble1187¾ Grey Relic118½ Magna Carta1182¾ Dueled, tired 11
11Jun95-2Bel fst 5f :222 :463 :59 Md Sp Wt 47 5 5 21 21½ 45½ 414 Nelson D- 116 14.10 77-25 Grindstone1165 Sierra Grande1168 Fig Fest1161 Stalked, tired 5
WORKOUTS: Nov 20 Bel tr.t 5f fst 1:03 B 16/29 Nov 5 Bel tr.t 5f fst 1:05 B 29/29 ●Oct 28 Bel tr.t 5f fst 1:01 H 1/10 Oct 17 Bel tr.t 5f fst 1:022 B 4/6 Oct 14 Bel tr.t 6f fst 1:19 B 3/3 ●Oct 8 Bel tr.t 4f fst :474 H 1/24

Rev Owen G
Own: Flynn Pierce J
PEREZ R B (35 3 5 1 .06) $40,000
B. g. 2 (Jan)
Sire: Tiffany Ice (Icecapade)
Dam: Palms in the Sky (Great Above)
Br: Flynn Pierce J (Ky)
Tr: Destasio Richard A (11 0 0 1 .00)
L 114

Lifetime Record:	4 M 0 0	$1,200			
1995	4 M 0 0	$1,200	Turf	0 0 0 0	
1994	0 M 0 0		Wet	2 0 0 0	$660
Aqu	0 0 0 0		Dist	2 0 0 0	$660

25Oct95-2Bel fst 6½f :224 :46 1:111 1:18 Md 45000 35 2 3 3nk 22 44 615 Alvarado F T 116 19.70 70-13 Ima Good Gamble1187¾ Grey Relic118½ Magna Carta1182¾ Chased, tired 11
27Sep95-2Bel my 6½f :221 :454 1:114 1:181 Md 50000 53 4 10 33 43 42½ 56½ Alvarado F T 114 14.40 77-19 Fenton Lane1161 Grey Relic1185 Tellerico's Fire118nk Broke awkwardly 10
1Sep95-1Bel fst 6f :221 :454 :572 1:113 Md 50000 48 8 11 78½ 76½ 56 54½ Chavez J F 118 26.50 79-08 Ideal State1182¾ Gamble Junior1181½ Night School118hd Broke slowly 12
12Aug95-6Sar sly 5½f :214 :453 :583 1:052 Md Sp Wt 31 6 9 89½ 1010 1013 914¾ Chavez J F 118 20.80 79-15 StatePrize118nk VlidVictor1184½ NorthernPursuit1181 Broke slowly, tired 10
WORKOUTS: Nov 20 Bel tr.t 4f fst :501 B 26/35 Nov 14 Bel tr.t 4f fst :501 B 25/40 Nov 6 Bel tr.t 4f fst :50 B 23/53 Oct 20 Bel tr.t 5f fst 1:022 B 4/10 Sep 22 Bel tr.t 4f fst :492 H 10/20 Sep 16 Bel tr.t 5f fst 1:021 B 2/7

Justinthemiddle
Own: Cohen Robert B
SANTAGATA N (41 3 3 3 .07) $40,000
Gr/ro c. 2 (Feb)
Sire: Darn That Alarm (Jig Time)
Dam: Rive Gauche (Star Envoy)
Br: Kingwell R A (Fla)
Tr: Shapoff Stanley R (10 0 1 1 .00)
114

Lifetime Record:	7 M 2 2	$16,840			
1995	7 M 2 2	$16,840	Turf	0 0 0 0	
1994	0 M 0 0		Wet	2 0 0 0	
Aqu	1 0 0 0		Dist	1 0 0 0	

Entered 23Nov95- 1 AQU
2Nov95-1Aqu sly 1 :222 :452 1:112 1:382 Md 35000 42 1 8 34½ 54 69½ 614¾ Santagata N 116 f 6.90 62-28 Newsbreaker1143 Glowing Tru1165 Glade1183½ Saved ground, tired 11
13Sep95-2Bel fst 7f :23 :463 1:122 1:253 Md 35000 54 5 4 1½ 3nk 2½ 32½ Maple E 118 f 4.00 71-20 Tea Attack1181½ Lonsdale118¾ Justinthemiddle1185 Dueled inside 13
2Sep95-2Bel fst 1 :23 :454 1:103 1:37 Md Sp Wt 40 1 2 31 53½ 59 615¾ Maple E 118 8.70 62-16 Pirate Performer118¾ Fortitude1182 Hey You Weasel11810 Dueled, tired 8
5Aug95-2Sar wf 6½f :222 :454 1:111 1:174 Md Sp Wt 40 7 1 64½ 75½ 710 718 Maple E 118 6.30 68-13 Sir Cat118¾ J P Hamer1189½ Jack Teagarden1182 No threat, wide 7
22Jly95-2Sar fst 5½f :222 :462 :584 1:051 Md Sp Wt 53 4 5 43 42½ 44 36½ Maple E 120 4.30 89-07 Sunny Side1206 NorthernPursuit120nk Justinthemiddle1202 Sved ground 12
17May95-2Bel fst 5f :22 :46 :59 Md Sp Wt 63 1 2 3½ 32½ 33 24½ Santagata N 116 3.40 86-13 VictorySpech1164½ Justinthmiddl116¾ MdiumTurn1167 Green, up for 2nd 6
6May95-2Bel fst 5f :222 :454 :581 Md Sp Wt 70 5 3 21½ 2½ 1½ 2½ Santagata N 116 2.15 94-06 Unclear Gamble116½ Justinthemiddle1165½ Lonsdale1161 Couldn't last 6
WORKOUTS: Nov 21 Bel tr.t 3f fst :353 H 2/17 Nov 11 Bel tr.t 5f fst 1:023 B 5/26 ●Oct 29 Bel tr.t 4f fst :49 H 1/4 Oct 23 Bel tr.t 5f fst 1:03 B 14/20 Oct 19 Bel tr.t 4f fst :501 B 10/14 Oct 12 Bel tr.t 4f fst :494 B 3/9

Going for the Gold
Own: Kimmel Caesar P & Nicholson Ronald
SAMYN J L (34 3 1 5 .09) $50,000
Ch. g. 2 (May)
Sire: Afleet (Mr. Prospector)
Dam: Forlassy (Forli)
Br: Nydrie Stud (Va)
Tr: Toner James J (10 1 0 0 .10)
L 118

Lifetime Record:	5 M 1 0	$6,400			
1995	5 M 1 0	$6,400	Turf	1 0 1 0	$6,400
1994	0 M 0 0		Wet	0 0 0 0	
Aqu	1 0 0 0		Dist	0 0 0 0	

15Nov95-4Aqu gd 1⅛ :481 1:134 1:404 1:55 Md Sp Wt 24 5 3 2½ 41½ 610 623½ Samyn J L L 118 b 12.00 42-28 Dustin's Dream118½ Adorjinsky1183¾ Criminal Suit11813 Used up 8
18Oct95-2Bel fst 1 1/16 :233 :464 1:113 1:444 Md Sp Wt 45 6 2 2hd 43 610 713¾ Samyn J L L 118 b 12.50 61-21 Shining Promise1182 Dothebucket1182¾ Quite A Story118¾ Dueled, tired 11
13Sep95-6Bel fm 1 1/16 [T] :23 :461 1:104 1:431 Md Sp Wt 67 5 1 2½ 43½ 38½ 27½ Samyn J L L 118 b 38.25 72-20 Togher1187½ GoingForTheGold118nk Bombardier1184 Dueled, came again 8
4Sep95-2Bel fst 5½f :223 :461 :58 1:041 Md Sp Wt 36 9 8 64 85¾ 811 818 Chavez J F L 118 b 13.00 76-08 Sole City1186 Criminal Suit118nk Hashid1185½ Carried wide 9
4Jly95-6Bel fst 5½f :224 :463 :592 1:061 Md Sp Wt 40 1 1 2½ 32 77½ 710 Bailey J D 116 5.20 74-17 Choice Shift1161 Game's On1163 Head Minister116no Forced pace, tired 8
WORKOUTS: Nov 11 Bel 5f fst 1:014 H 17/56 Nov 5 Bel tr.t 5f fst 1:014 B 9/29 Oct 27 Bel tr.t 4f fst :483 H 6/47 Oct 13 Bel tr.t 5f fst 1:031 B 7/9 Oct 7 Bel tr.t 4f fst :503 B 15/22 Oct 1 Bel 5f fst 1:01 H 18/38

Mack's Oscar
Own: Robinson J Mack
DAVIS R G (94 21 14 10 .22) $50,000
Ch. c. 2 (Mar)
Sire: Academy Award (Secretariat)
Dam: Roberto Belle (Roberto)
Br: Robinson J Mack (Fla)
Tr: Alexander Frank A (14 0 0 4 .00)
118

Lifetime Record:	3 M 0 0	$300			
1995	3 M 0 0	$300	Turf	0 0 0 0	
1994	0 M 0 0		Wet	0 0 0 0	
Aqu	1 0 0 0	$300	Dist	0 0 0 0	

11Nov95-2Aqu fst 1 :234 :47 1:121 1:374 Md Sp Wt 54 6 9 64 74½ 69½ 514¾ Davis R G 118 f 30.50 65-19 Prince Of Thieves1186¾ Circle Of Light1185½ Chenlo118¾ No factor 9
27Oct95-1Bel fst 7f :223 :454 1:104 1:234 Md Sp Wt 59 7 8 129½ 119½ 79 711½ Stevens G L 118 f 61.75 70-11 Robb1187¾ Traffic Circle1181½ Footloose118½ No threat 12
22Jly95-2Sar fst 5½f :222 :462 :584 1:051 Md Sp Wt 27 8 11 1121 1117 1012 915¾ Smith M E 120 f 36.75 79-07 SunnySide1206 NorthernPursuit120nk Justinthemiddle1202 Broke slowly 12
WORKOUTS: Nov 20 Bel tr.t 3f fst :36 H 4/13 Nov 6 Bel 5f fst 1:004 H 6/52 Oct 19 Bel 4f fst :49 Hg 10/35 Oct 12 Bel 5f fst 1:014 B 8/19 ●Oct 5 Bel 3f gd :362 B (d) 1/10 Sep 29 Bel 4f fst :501 B 35/61

1 — Hardshell Crab — A firster with uninspiring breeding and unspectacular works from a very talented trainer, Dick Dutrow, with Julie Krone up. Pass.

2 — Trail City — A well-bred two-year-old from top trainer

Billy Mott and top jockey Jerry Bailey who had done nothing but disappoint people in his first three starts, the first two in maiden special weights. He debuted at Saratoga at 5-1 against Diligence — Nick Zito's promising winner that day — and was third early before tiring badly at 6½ furlongs, finishing seventh by 22 lengths. His second start was a maiden turf route and he again was third early before packing it in and finishing eighth. Mott responded by by giving him 10 weeks off. In his return race, Mott dropped him into a $40,000 maiden claimer at one mile on a sloppy track with the addition of blinkers. Trail City made a clear lead this time by posting fractions of :22^2/$_5$ and :45^2/$_5$, before tiring to a badly beaten seventh. Though it looked like just another bad race from a bad horse, he had nonetheless showed a sign of life by making the lead in a race — his first start in 10 weeks — that he probably needed. Cutting back from one mile to 6½ furlongs today would help, too. Hardly a star, but I couldn't eliminate him considering the competition. The *Form* analysis erred this time in saying "he's valueless mutuelly."

3 — In The Rain — He was a strong third in his debut then fifth and fourth, all three starts in maiden special weights. In his fourth start, Allen Jerkens added blinkers and dropped him into a maiden claimer. He led, showed good speed (:22^3/$_5$ and :45^4/$_5$) and tired late. An obvious contender.

4 — Ernie The King — An okay-bred firster with a couple good drills. Pass.

5 — Early Echoes — Bullet-work (but only of seven horses) for this firster. Pass.

6 — Rosa In Bloom — Bullet work for return from a maiden special debut disaster when ninth by 19½ lengths as part of a 14-1 entry. Liked the drop and the bullet, but that lone race was real bad. Maybe.

7 — Hurry West — Well-bred firster from a top two-year-old trainer, Stanley Hough, but the works were dull. Pass.

8 — Thegiantkiller — Named for Allen Jerkens and trained by his son, Steven. Showed speed in his second start, but faded real badly to finish eighth by 15½ lengths. No.

9 — Rev Owen G — Exited the same race, beating The Giant Killer by half a length at 19-1. No.

10 — Justinthemiddle — Caught a sloppy track in his re-

turn and was a badly beaten sixth. But he needed the race, and had a good work since. Had two seconds and two thirds in six starts previously, five of them in maiden special weights. Cutting back to a sprint and catching a fast track could make him the one to beat.

11 — Going For The Gold — One good performance in five starts was on the turf. Drops into a maiden claimer for the first time. Had some early speed. Pass.

12 — Mack's Oscar — Drops into a maiden claimer for the first time and adds blinkers off three terrible races. No.

My picks in the *Gazette* were Just In The Middle — because he had by far the best dirt sprints of any horse in here — and Trail City for second because he had at least shown improvement in his return.

The scratch of Our Dear Dana reduced the field in the second race to nine:

2 Aqueduct

6 Furlongs (1:08) CLAIMING. Purse $13,000. Fillies and mares, 3-year-olds and upward. Weights: 3-year-olds, 120 lbs. Older, 122 lbs. Non-winners of three races since September 27, allowed 2 lbs. A race since October 19, 4 lbs. A race since October 8, 6 lbs. Claiming price $14,000, if for $12,000, allowed 2 lbs. (Races where entered for $10,000 or less not considered.)

6 FURLONGS

Victorian Woman
Own: Gullo Gary P & Gedash Barbara
MIGLIORE R (68 3 10 14 .04) $14,000
B. f. 3 (Apr)
Sire: Jeblar (Alydar)
Dam: Pull Up (Well Decorated)
Br: Farnsworth Farms & M & M Bloodstock (Fla)
Tr: Gullo Gary P (10 1 0 1 .10)
L 114

Lifetime Record: 34 7 2 7 $60,875

1995	20	3	2	1	$37,950	Turf	1	0	0	0	$155
1994	14	4	0	6	$22,925	Wet	8	1	0	3	$9,900
Aqu	6	1	2	0	$16,430	Dist	14	2	0	4	$17,320

15Nov95-2Aqu gd 6f	:22 :46 :584 1:124	ⒻClm 15000	51 7 1 84¾ 86¾ 55¾ 53¾	Chavez J F	L 114 b	6.00	74-18	Tara's Flame114nk Charmless114¾ Henbane's Girl1141¾	No threat	11
4Nov95-1Aqu wf 6f	:222 :461 :584 1:113 3↑	ⒻClm 18000	61 7 1 42 44 54¾ 67¾	Persaud R10	L 102 b	32.25	76-14	Indian Paradise1161½ Now I Hope1201½ Promised Relic109nk	Tired	7
20Oct95-2Bel fst 6f	:22 :444 :573 1:112 3↑	ⒻClm 14000	51 4 3 22 33¾ 35¾ 56¾	Samyn J L	L 111 b	16.00	78-15	PromisedRelic1073½ FastNicole1011 OurDerDn1141¾	Bumped break, tired	8
11Oct95-5Bel fst 6½f	:224 :461 1:114 1:182	ⒻClm 18000	55 2 5 96 96¼ 84¾ 96¾	Samyn J L	L 112 b	15.70	77-16	Quaker Street1152 Kathey's Attitude1072 Nay Nay Renay115nk	No factor	11
27Sep95-9Bel my 6f	:221 :452 :583 1:114	ⒻClm 25000	60 10 12 1213 1012 79 59	Samyn J L	L 115 b	78.75	73-19	Attack Me Not1124 Showsnap1151½ Joe's Workingirl1152	Pinched break	12
15Sep95-5Bel fst 7f	:224 :46 1:112 1:25	ⒻClm 30000	45 8 3 117 1212 129¾ 1211½	Chavez C R5	L 108 b	78.50	65-14	Birthday115¾ Fine Wine113hd Emergency1172	No speed	12
1Sep95-9Bel fst 1	:222 :452 1:103 1:361	ⒻClm 25000	61 8 5 44 53 55¾ 58¾	Belmonte L A5	L 110 b	24.25	73-21	Blackburn1152½ A Wild Favor115nk Charmless1153¼	Evenly	10
21Jly95-1Sar fst 7f	:22 :451 1:104 1:241 3↑	ⒻAlw 32000n1x	50 2 8 64¾ 87¾ 87¾ 816	Leon F	107 b	31.50	69-10	Blind Trust107¾ Cana119¾ Crafty Jenny1147	No threat	9
29Jun95-9Bel fst 6f	:222 :47 1:00 1:133	ⒻClm c-18000	52 7 6 810 75¾ 45¾ 37¾	Belmonte L A7	111 b	5.90	65-22	Henbane'sGirl116¾ RisenTower1167 VictorianWomn1111	Steadied 3/8 pl	11
Claimed from Beecher Aaron, Gullo Gary P Trainer										
23Jun95-1Bel wf 1	:223 :46 1:12 1:384	ⒻClm 22500	40 1 4 21 3½ 33¼ 411	Chavez J F	114 b	3.35	58-23	Pageant Princess1165¾ Shady Baby1122 Gin And Ice1113¼	Bobbled break	7

Tara's Tempest
Own: Connaughton Bernard
MAYSONETT F (1 0 0 0 .00) $14,000
Dk. b or br f. 4
Sire: Talc (Rock Talk)
Dam: Lotus Delight (Mongo)
Br: Lane Glenn E (NY)
Tr: O'Brien Colum (11 0 1 2 .00)
L 1097

Lifetime Record: 22 4 3 3 $95,540

1995	7	2	1	1	$48,740	Turf	2	0	0	0	$1,900
1994	11	1	1	1	$24,710	Wet	6	0	0	2	$8,020
Aqu	4	2	0	0	$29,130	Dist	5	2	0	0	$32,100

24May95-1Bel fst 6½f	:224 :463 1:12 1:183	ⒻClm 16000	64 9 8 96 75 67¾ 510¾	Martin G J5	117 b	5.50	71-19	Yazma1063 EuphoricInterlude1161 PalmBechDewey114no	Steadied 1/4 pl	9
4May95-7Bel fst 6½f	:23 :463 1:113 1:182 3↑	ⒻⓈAlw 34000n2x	68 5 4 43¾ 42¾ 1hd 1nk	Martin G J5	116 b	5.30	83-13	Tr'sTempest116nk ADyToRemember1141 Frisky'sFinle112nk	Wide, all out	8
28Apr95-9Aqu fst 6f	:223 :47 1:00 1:131 3↑	ⒻⓈAlw 30000n1x	65 3 7 67 63¾ 1hd 12¾	Martin G J7	112 b	10.30	76-16	Tara's Tempest1122¾ Where Is It1071 Jazzpacked1191	Pinched break	7
10Mar95-7Aqu fst 170 ⊡	:24 :482 1:141 1:46	ⒻⓈAlw 32000n1x	43 6 6 57 56¾ 69¾ 615¾	Martin G J7	109 b	2.25	52-33	Frisky's Finale1071¼ Parmelina1073 Woodland Gal1145¾	Dull effort	6
26Feb95-3Aqu fst 1⅛ ⊡	:502 1:161 1:422 1:553	ⒻⓈAlw 32000n1x	66 4 6 67 54 42¾ 32	Martin G J7	110 b	2.95	56-38	Longleaf117nk Frisky's Finale1101¾ Tara's Tempest110nk	Late gain	7
10Feb95-7Aqu fst 1 1/16 ⊡	:242 :493 1:144 1:484	ⒻⓈAlw 34000n2x	50 5 10 1111 109¾ 1010 1012	Chavez J F	113 b	5.20	49-38	Hillis Lee119no Carr Star1062 New York Flag1081¼	Checked early	11
5Feb95-3Aqu fst 1 1/16 ⊡	:242 :493 1:152 1:504	ⒻⓈAlw 32000n1x	71 6 3 32 2hd 2hd 2¾	Chavez J F	117 b	2.25	50-47	Hillis Lee117¾ Tara'sTempest1177 PureVintage1171¼	Wide bid, weakened	6
24Dec94-6Aqu my 1⅛ ⊡	:474 1:142 1:414 1:551 3↑	ⒻⓈAlw 32000n1x	55 2 5 51¾ 31¾ 36¾ 39¾	Martin G J7	108 b	*2.05	50-32	Critical Crew115¾ Call Today1159 Tara's Tempest1083	No rally	7
16Dec94-7Aqu fst 1 1/16 ⊡	:24 :493 1:151 1:482 3↑	ⒻⓈAlw 32000n1x	62 5 9 82¾ 52¾ 32¾ 23¾	Martin G J7	108 b	6.30	60-30	Lihue1173¼ Tara's Tempest1084 Hillis Lee117¾	Up for place	10
27Nov94-2Aqu fst 1⅛	:501 1:16 1:421 1:554 3↑	ⒻClm 35000n2L	61 1 7 62¾ 31¾ 1½ 11	Martin G J7	108 b	16.80	57-33	Tara's Tempest1081 Lone Star Gale1103 Monster Order1085¼	Driving	7

WORKOUTS: Nov 18 Bel 6f fst 1:164 B 3/3 Nov 11 Bel tr.t 4f fst :491 H 13/45 Nov 5 Bel tr.t 5f fst 1:03 B 15/29 Oct 30 Bel tr.t 4f fst :53 B 27/28

Green Reader

Own: Benincasa Joseph & Gulle Giacomo
CHAVEZ J F (87 14 14 6 .16) $12,000

Ch. m. 5
Sire: Buckaroo (Buckpasser)
Dam: Green Magazine (Green Forest)
Br: Evans T M (Ky)
Tr: Odintz Jeff (6 1 0 0 .17)

L 118

Lifetime Record:	53 9 5 9	$116,605			
1995	17 4 2 2	$45,585	Turf	2 0 0 0	
1994	20 3 2 4	$37,200	Wet	9 3 2 2	$33,870
Aqu	12 1 1 5	$19,445	Dist	6 2 0 1	$17,310

9Nov95- 9Aqu fst 1 :232 :472 1:14 1:404 3↑ ⒻClm 14000 40 10 2 11 1hd 75½ 810 Agosto R7 L 113 f 6.90 55-26 Frisky's Finale1141¼ Forever Proud111nk Fast Nicole103hd Speed, tired 10
23Oct95- 9Bel fst 1 1/16 :231 :463 1:12 1:462 3↑ ⒻClm 14000 61 8 4 31½ 22½ 11 1hd Agosto R7 L 108 fb 10.60 67-23 Green Reader108hd Ogy's Threat1154 Monster Order115½ All out 8
9Oct95- 9Bel fst 7f :23 :464 1:121 1:26 3↑ ⒻClm 14000 28 1 8 74½ 107¾ 1015 1019¾ Chavez C R7 L 108 fb 24.75 51-18 Gene's Gray Girl1163½ Fast Nicole1031¾ Indian Paradise116½ Outrun 10
28Sep95- 2Bel fst 6f :221 :453 :573 1:102 3↑ ⒻClm 14000 54 3 3 58½ 59½ 712 714½ Perez R B L 115 4.50 74-16 Accipiter's Star11511 Personaltestimony1082 Fast Nicole1011 Gave way 8
17Sep95- 1Bel sly 7f :222 :451 1:103 1:242 3↑ ⒻClm 14000 56 3 1 3½ 47½ 25 23 Perez R B L 114 fb 3.30 76-11 Needles Last1143 Green Reader1145½ Saratoga April116¾ Clear second 7
4Sep95- 1Bel fst 1 :23 :463 1:114 1:382 3↑ ⒻClm 16000 31 2 1 21 76½ 810 819¾ Perez R B 116 b 5.80 51-16 Muko1161 Rabs Lil Brit Brit1163¾ Alkris116¾ Dueled, tired 9
13Jly95- 3Bel fst 7f :221 :451 1:111 1:244 ⒻClm 18000 53 4 6 710 711 68¾ 611½ Davis R G 112 b 7.80 66-17 Madrona112¾ IndianPrdise1133 EuphoricInterlude1162½ Stumbled break 7
2Jly95- 2Bel my 1 1/16 :231 :471 1:124 1:452 ⒻClm c-14000 56 6 4 31 2½ 35 39¾ Perez R B5 115 fb *.60 62-27 Doc's Josephine1163¾ Muko1166 Green Reader1152¾ Flattened out 6
Claimed from Hauman Eugene E & Schwartz Barry K, Hushion Michael E Trainer
21Jun95- 2Bel fst 1 1/16 :234 :472 1:123 1:462 3↑ ⒻClm 30000 66 6 3 53½ 41½ 43½ 45½ Valdivia J7 112 fb *1.85 61-31 BoundingBeliever1123½ GeorgiaAnna1191½ SartogApril117½ Wide, no rally 7
8Jun95- 3Bel fst 1 :224 :463 1:114 1:373 ⒻClm 17000 83 5 4 41½ 11 15 16 Valdivia J7 107 fb *1.95 75-31 Green Reader1076 Doc's Josephine1162 Dancing Lacey1164 Rail trip 7

WORKOUTS: Oct 19 Aqu 3f fst :39 B 7/7 Aug 30 Aqu 3f fst :36 H 2/3 Aug 25 Aqu 3f fst :383 B 3/4

Keeping Fit

Own: Friendship Stable & Mogru Madhan
PEREZ R B (35 3 5 1 .09) $14,000

B. m. 5
Sire: Fit to Fight (Chieftain)
Dam: Keep Believing (Believe It)
Br: Nuckols Charles Jr & Sons (Ky)
Tr: Barbara Robert (28 5 5 1 .18)

L 116

Lifetime Record:	22 3 3 2	$48,280			
1995	9 1 1 1	$20,610	Turf	0 0 0 0	
1994	10 1 2 0	$18,790	Wet	3 0 0 0	$2,310
Aqu	5 2 0 0	$15,000	Dist	12 3 1 2	$39,180

26Oct95- 4Bel fst 6f :221 :453 :574 1:102 3↑ ⒻClm 35000 59 4 6 67 67½ 59 511¾ Santos J A L 116 b 13.10 77-17 Accipiter'sStr116¾ MidwyGl1189 EuphoricInterlude116no Pinched break 6
11Oct95- 9Bel fst 6f :223 :454 :58 1:11 3↑ ⒻClm 25000 30 4 8 85 911 1016 1020½ Smith M E L 116 b 5.60 66-16 Showsnap1135 Fortune Wand1161 Waqueen1142 No factor 11
11May95- 2Bel my 6½f :222 :452 1:10 1:162 ⒻClm 20000 51 1 4 44½ 53½ 55½ 513 Ramos W S 116 b 5.20 80-11 Indian Paradise1116 Jake'sSister1112 WildsBestTurn1181 Saved ground 7
28Apr95- 2Aqu fst 6f :22 :462 :584 1:114 ⒻClm 30000 57 1 7 67½ 76¾ 75½ 64½ Perez R B5 109 b 5.30 74-18 ReachForClever112no FortuneWand1165 RunawyFling1162½ Broke slowly 7
16Mar95- 6Aqu fst 6½f :224 :464 1:124 1:193 ⒻAlw 30000N1X 50 4 7 65 65 74 85¾ Perez R B5 110 b *.70 76-15 Alytude114nk Sun Attack1141½ Limited Edition110¾ Wide, dull 8
1Mar95- 3Aqu gd 6f ⊡ :223 :462 :584 1:11 ⒻClm 30000 84 2 5 57 31½ 2½ 13 Perez R B5 110 b 7.60 88-15 Keeping Fit1103 Whenourshipcomesin117nk Jake's Sister1151 Good trip 6
20Feb95- 2Aqu fst 6f ⊡ :232 :47 :593 1:123 ⒻClm 25000 75 2 5 34½ 32½ 34½ 23 Perez R B5 111 b 2.75 77-25 Biddy Mulligan1083 Keeping Fit111½ King's Sweetest1164 Up for place 5
8Feb95- 4Aqu fst 6f ⊡ :234 :481 1:01 1:133 ⒻClm 25000 74 6 3 2½ 2½ 21 32 Perez R B5 112 b 5.20 73-27 Be Myself1172 Wilds Best Turn117no Keeping Fit1123½ Forced pace 6
2Jan95- 7Aqu my 6f ⊡ :23 :472 1:002 1:134 ⒻAlw 30000N1X 54 1 7 77½ 76 59½ 48 Velazquez J R 117 b 9.00 66-27 CleverlyIntended1173¾ MiteyJenny117nk Jessica'sTwoStep1174 No factor 7
26Dec94- 6Aqu fst 6f ⊡ :23 :464 :591 1:121 3↑ ⒻAlw 30000N1X 56 2 4 43½ 53½ 58½ 410 Velazquez J R 117 b 9.50 72-21 For Sport1151 Mitey Jenny1154 Jackie Ramos1155 Outrun 5

WORKOUTS: Sep 23 Bel tr.t 5f gd 1:013 H 1/2 Sep 16 Bel tr.t 4f fst :492 B 13/25 Sep 6 Bel tr.t 3f fst :372 B 5/8

Our Dear Dana

Own: Ferriola Ingrid A & Saks Martin
LEON F (21 1 1 1 .05) $12,000

Dk. b or br m. 6
Sire: Robellino (Roberto)
Dam: Hazel Marsh (Assert)
Br: Derry Meeting Farm (Pa)
Tr: Ferriola Peter (15 3 6 1 .20)

114

Lifetime Record:	47 7 5 16	$116,410			
1995	9 0 0 5	$8,810	Turf	3 0 0 0	
1994	12 4 2 4	$56,840	Wet	1 0 0 0	
Aqu	14 4 0 5	$41,250	Dist	31 6 4 9	$90,430

20Oct95- 2Bel fst 6f :22 :444 :573 1:112 3↑ ⒻClm 14000 56 2 8 67 68 57 34½ Nelson D 114 fb 20.70 79-15 PromisedRelic1073½ FastNicole1011 OurDerDn1141¾ Checked break, wide 8
9Oct95- 9Bel fst 7f :23 :464 1:121 1:26 3↑ ⒻClm 14000 42 5 10 63¾ 75½ 711 712¾ Nelson D 114 f 24.50 58-18 Gene'sGrayGirl1163½ FstNicole1031¾ IndinPrdise116½ Brk slowly, six wide 10
16Jly95- 3Bel fst 6f :224 :463 :59 1:121 ⒻClm 12000 51 7 9 85¾ 86½ 87½ 87½ Beckner D V 112 fb 4.00 73-16 PlmBechDewey120nk ShellCrist1163 Personltstimony116¾ Pinched break 9
21Jun95- 1Bel fst 1 1/16 :233 :471 1:123 1:454 ⒻClm 12000 72 4 1 14 1hd 21½ 35 Beckner D V 112 fb 4.70 65-31 DancingLcey1162 Doc'sJosephine1163 OurDerDn1123½ Speed, weakened 7
16Jun95- 3Bel fst 6f :224 :47 1:00 1:131 ⒻClm 12000 63 8 7 42½ 3½ 31 31½ Beckner D V 112 fb 8.60 74-21 PlmBechDewy1161 WinConnoissur116nk OurDrDn1123½ Stalked four wide 8
24Mar95- 1Bel fst 6½f :224 :463 1:12 1:183 ⒻClm 14000 65 3 6 31½ 85½ 57 410 Beckner D V 112 fb 5.20 72-19 Yzm1063 EuphoricInterlude1161 PlmBechDwy114no Saved ground, tired 9
7Apr95- 4Aqu fst 1 :232 :464 1:124 1:391 ⒻClm 15500 56 5 3 42 44½ 48 411¾ Graell A 112 fb 5.20 61-28 Tainted Angel1126½ Turner's Bid1162½ Vallation1122¾ Wide, tired 6
11Mar95- 1Aqu fst 6f ⊡ :232 :47 :594 1:123 ⒻClm c-11000 70 7 2 41 41 52½ 31½ Graell A 112 fb 4.50 78-16 Bow Creek109nk Personaltestimony1121½ Our Dear Dana1121¾ Mild rally 8
Claimed from Corrado Fred L, Debonis Robert Trainer
6Jan95- 5Aqu fst 1 1/16 ⊡ :243 :49 1:134 1:48 ⒻClm 14000 48 5 2 2hd 23½ 37½ 310 Martin G J7 110 fb *1.50 55-21 Country Red Neck1174½ Nasty Shot1135½ Our Dear Dana110½ No late bid 8
4Dec94- 2Aqu fst 1 :232 :474 1:13 1:392 ⒻClm c-14000 58 5 5 54½ 55 47½ 38½ Migliore R 119 fb *1.05 63-34 Nikki's Rose112nk Ski At Dawn1178 Our Dear Dana119no No factor 6
Claimed from Hauman Eugene E, Hushion Michael E Trainer

WORKOUTS: Nov 18 Aqu 5f fst 1:031 B 10/19 Sep 13 Aqu 5f fst 1:031 B 8/10 Aug 30 Aqu 5f fst 1:021 B 2/7

Satans Archangel

Own: Bissett Joan B
NELSON D (20 0 0 4 .00) $12,000

Ch. f. 4
Sire: Here's Honor (Northern Dancer)
Dam: Cabala Rouge (Crimson Satan)
Br: Bissett Joan B (NY)
Tr: Lenzini John J Jr (6 0 0 1 .00)

L 114

Lifetime Record:	8 2 2 0	$36,440			
1995	5 2 1 0	$28,600	Turf	0 0 0 0	
1994	3 M 1 0	$7,840	Wet	3 0 1 0	$3,880
Aqu	3 1 0 0	$19,200	Dist	5 1 2 0	$15,560

3May95- 6Bel wf 1 1/16 :232 :462 1:11 1:421 3↑ ⒻⓈAlw 36000N2X 54 4 3 31½ 44½ 510 621½ Nelson D 122 b 4.90 66-16 Varsity Gold11015 Bitta's Charm1206 Shiani120no Checked break, tired 6
13Apr95- 3Aqu fst 1 1/8 :48 1:123 1:393 1:532 3↑ ⒻⓈAlw 32000N1X 71 1 1 11½ 15 18 110 Nelson D 119 b 2.20 73-24 Satans Archangel11910 Shady Baby1103½ Funky Diva119½ Kept to task 6
17Mar95- 6Aqu fst 6f :223 :462 :592 1:124 ⒻⓈAlw 30000N1X 41 7 8 32½ 32 74 78½ Nelson D 114 b 3.35 70-17 Lone Star Gale1144½ No Frost1141 MillwardLane114hd Checked 3/16, tired 10
9Feb95- 1Aqu fst 6f ⊡ :231 :474 1:011 1:151 ⒻMd 35000 59 10 1 11 11½ 13 16 Nelson D 122 b *.70 67-29 Satans Archangel1226 Weekend Leave118nk Dar's Delight120½ Drew off 12
20Jan95- 9Aqu sly 6f ⊡ :222 :452 :574 1:112 ⒻMd 25000 57 3 2 21½ 24 24 21 Nelson D 122 b *1.35 85-14 Time To Tender1171 Satans Archangel1229 Merci'ocain1152 Steady gain 7
8Nov94- 9Aqu fst 6f :221 :462 :592 1:122 3↑ ⒻⓈMd Sp Wt -0 8 2 22 35 816 1227 Nelson D 120 b *1.65 53-19 I'mabaroness1154 Compound Girl12011 Personal Nurse115hd Gave way 12
27Sep94- 9Bel sly 6½f :22 :46 1:124 1:20 3↑ ⒻⓈMd Sp Wt 33 6 8 1½ 1hd 32½ 46½ Nelson D 118 b *1.80 66-18 Klassy Charade113½ Iron Fence1183 Alytune1183 Broke slowly, tired 10
14Sep94- 9Bel fst 6f :224 :462 :584 1:121 3↑ ⒻⓈMd Sp Wt 56 9 12 1hd 1hd 2½ 2nk Nelson D 118 9.50 80-13 Cirastaire118nk Satans Archangel1182 Compound Girl1181½ Gamely 14

WORKOUTS: Nov 7 Aqu 5f fst 1:022 Bg2/3 Oct 31 Aqu 5f fst 1:031 B 7/10 Oct 24 Aqu 5f fst 1:022 B 5/11 Oct 17 Aqu 5f fst 1:024 B 5/7 Sep 30 Aqu 4f fst :48 H 2/5 Sep 14 Aqu 3f fst :371 B 1/3

Waqueen

Own: Jakubovitz Jerome R
DAVIS R G (94 21 14 10 .22) $14,000

Ro. f. 4
Sire: Waquoit (Relaunch)
Dam: Gunny's Turn (Caucasus)
Br: Ford Eugene F (Md)
Tr: Myer Pat (5 1 0 0 .20)

L 116

Lifetime Record:	27 4 3 5	$100,866			
1995	10 1 0 2	$16,752	Turf	2 0 0 0	$2,934
1994	9 1 2 2	$36,460	Wet	3 0 0 0	$1,675
Aqu	1 0 0 0	$495	Dist	7 1 0 3	$16,495

4Nov95- 1Aqu wf 6f :222 :461 :584 1:113 3↑ ⒻClm 20000 62 1 7 74 77 66 57 Davis R G L 116 b 10.00 77-14 IndinPrdis1161½ NowIHop1201½ PromisdRlic109nk Brk slow, saved ground 7
11Oct95- 9Bel fst 6f :223 :454 :58 1:11 3↑ ⒻClm 20000 66 8 2 21 3½ 34 36 Davis R G L 114 b 11.50 80-16 Showsnap1135 Fortune Wand1161 Waqueen1142 Forced pace 11
17Sep95- 1Bel sly 7f :222 :451 1:103 1:242 3↑ ⒻClm c-16000 42 4 2 42½ 37 37½ 49¼ Luzzi M J L 118 b *.95 70-11 Needles Last1143 Green Reader1145½ Saratoga April116¾ Wide, tired 7
Claimed from Ford Eugene F, Motion H Graham Trainer
6Sep95- 3Bel fst 6½f :23 :462 1:112 1:173 3↑ ⒻClm 20000 69 4 2 2½ 2hd 1hd 53¼ Smith M E L 116 b 7.40 84-14 Dixie Brat1161½ Madrona116nk Roses For Regina114¾ Dueled, weakened 8
6Aug95- 4Pim sly 1 1/16 ⊗ :241 :48 1:124 1:463 3↑ ⒻAlw 14500s 70 2 1 2hd 2hd 21½ 67 Reynolds L C L 117 b *1.60 68-27 Ivorgot Again1172 Ernucbobray1173 Kippen117½ Gave way 7
18Jly95- 3Lrl fst 1 1/16 :24 :481 1:13 1:443 3↑ ⒻClm 25000 76 7 2 21½ 2hd 2½ 32¾ Reynolds L C L 117 b 6.00 84-13 Proud Angela1171 You Slewz You Lose1171¾ Waqueen1171¾ Weakened 7
8Jly95- 5Lrl fst 7½f :222 :454 1:111 1:31 3↑ ⒻClm 14500 76 9 2 57 46 11 1¾ Delgado A L 117 b 5.50 92-13 Wqueen117¾ Goldgorin'sAlden113no SongAndASmil1195½ Wide, lugged in 10
18Jun95- 8Lrl fst 6f :221 :452 :572 1:094 3↑ ⒻAlw 21000N3X 37 2 3 32½ 47 512 721¾ Reynolds L C L 117 b 5.40 69-17 Oh Summer1137¾ I Am Me R. G.117hd Lost Leaf11711 Faded 7
29May95- 8Del fst 1 :242 :474 1:121 1:373 3↑ ⒻAlw 12000N4L 56 5 2 2hd 52¾ 58 413¾ Umana J L L 116 b 1.80 81-08 EasilyMajestic1114 CmpbellSlewp1165½ Devil'sBlld1194½ Pinched far turn 6
4May95- 6Pim fst 6f :233 :464 :591 1:114 3↑ ⒻAlw 19600N3X 59 3 4 21½ 43 44½ 57 Reynolds L C L 117 b *.80 82-12 Stonewall Sue117no Made For Satin1174½ Devil's Glen1172 Faded 5

WORKOUTS: Nov 21 Bel tr.t 3f fst :383 B 15/17 Oct 27 Bel 4f fst :493 B 31/65 Oct 7 Bel tr.t 4f fst :494 B 13/22 Sep 2 Lrl 4f fst :49 B 7/33

Straight Jacket (Chi)
Own: Delehanty Farm
CASTILLO H JR (35 3 2 4 .09) $14,000
B. f. 4
Sire: Noisy When Hot (Cannonade)
Dam: Quacks Darlin' (Quack)
Br: Haras Paulina (Chi)
Tr: Penna Angel Jr (5 0 0 0 .00)
L 116
Lifetime Record: 10 3 2 0 $13,716
1995 5 0 0 0 $870 | Turf 5 1 1 0 $4,784
1994 5 3 2 0 $12,846 | Wet 1 0 0 0 $170
Aqu 1 0 0 0 $540 | Dist 2 0 0 0 $710

16Nov95-3Aqu fst 6f :222 :462 :59 1:121 3+ [F]Clm 25000 53 8 4 64½ 54 56½ 54½ Castillo H Jr L 116 11.50 72-15 EuphoricInterlude1162½ PromisedRelic1093¾ FortuneWand1162½ No threat 8
30Jly95-1Mth fm 1 [T] :233 :472 1:131 1:394 3+ [F]Clm 20000 62 11 8 64¾ 31 43 68¾ Velez J A Jr L 115 16.50 62-24 Speedy Colleen1174 Aswillow115nk Dame Wollaston113½ Bid, tired 12
11Jly95-6Mth my 6f :214 :444 :571 1:101 3+ [F]Clm 25000 52 1 7 3½ 67½ 69 512½ Santagata N L 116 12.10 75-16 Lucky Cassie1162 Tilloola116nk Z Rated1163¾ Gave way 7
18Jun95-6Bel fm 1 1/16 [T] :234 :464 1:102 1:413 3+ [F]Alw 38000N3X 41 4 6 710 89½ 818 824½ Samyn J L 119 27.75 64-10 Firm Friend119hd Shocking Pleasure1123¾ Upper Noosh1123½ No threat 8
2Jan95 ♦ Club Hippico(Chi) gd *1 [T]RH 3+ Clasico Eugenia (Listed) 8 124 - Further Information unavailable
24Dec94 ♦ Hipodromo(Chi) gd *7f LH Allowance Race 1 114 - Further Information unavailable
26Nov94 ♦ Hipodromo(Chi) gd *7f LH Allowance Race 2 117 - Further Information unavailable
5Nov94 ♦ Hipodromo(Chi) gd 6½f LH Allowance Race 1 117 - Further Information unavailable
13Oct94 ♦ Club Hippico(Chi) gd 5½f [T]RH Maiden Race 1 119 - Further Information unavailable
26Sep94 ♦ Club Hippico(Chi) gd 6f [T]RH Maiden Race 2 119 - Further Information unavailable
WORKOUTS: ●Nov 13 Bel 3f fst :352 H 1/7 Nov 6 Bel 6f fst 1:154 B 2/8 Oct 31 Bel 5f fst 1:022 B 24/39 Oct 25 Bel 4f fst :522 B 47/49 Oct 18 Bel 4f fst :50 B 29/46 Oct 9 Bel 4f fst :49 B 22/60

Sadie's Glory
Own: Ostman & Toscano & Twilite Tee Stb
TREJO J (34 2 1 4 .06) $14,000
Ch. f. 3 (Feb)
Sire: Claim (Mr. Prospector)
Dam: Fragile Dream (Turn and Count)
Br: Stoops W R (Ky)
Tr: Toscano John T Jr (3 0 0 0 .00)
1077
Lifetime Record: 10 1 2 2 $21,030
1995 6 0 2 1 $9,990 | Turf 0 0 0 0
1994 4 1 0 1 $11,040 | Wet 2 0 0 1 $1,540
Aqu 6 1 1 1 $15,090 | Dist 8 0 2 2 $11,430

4Nov95-1Aqu wf 6f :222 :461 :584 1:113 3+ [F]Clm 20000 58 2 6 64 65½ 76½ 78¾ Trejo J7 107 20.90 75-14 Indian Paradise1161½ Now I Hope1201½ PromisedRelic109nk Bobbled break 7
1Jun95-3Bel fst 6f :223 :463 :591 1:124 [F]Clm 35000 61 3 4 42¾ 43 54 77 Valdivia J7 109 7.50 70-17 Ry'sCrftyLdy1162 AmysingDin116nk CrsonKitty1111 Saved ground, tired 7
4May95-1Bel fst 6f :22 :454 :581 1:11 [F]Clm 30000 77 6 8 55 51½ 2½ 21 Valdivia J7 108 7.60 85-13 So Cheerful1151 Sadie's Glory108¾ Jam Tart1154 Four wide bid 8
23Apr95-2Aqu fst 6f :222 :462 :591 1:123 [F]Clm 25000 60 4 8 84¾ 55 43 32¾ Valdivia J7 109 16.00 76-18 East End Lady111½ [D]Jam Tart1142½ Sadie's Glory1092¾ Rallied wide 10
Placed second through disqualification.
13Apr95-9Aqu fst 6f :221 :46 :582 1:111 [F]Clm 18000 51 8 9 76½ 64¾ 64½ 57¾ Valdivia J7 109 5.90 78-10 Time For Allaire1163½ EastEndLady1181½ NayNayRenay1161¾ Broke slowly 9
7Jan95-1Aqu my 6f [•] :23 :473 1:004 1:141 [F]Clm 25000N2L 39 3 4 2½ 23 25 310¾ Nelson D 116 2.70 61-28 Nappelon11610 Call My Agent114nk Sadie's Glory1161 Even trip 5
21Dec94-6Aqu fst 6f [•] :224 :463 :593 1:131 [F]Clm 47500 15 7 7 51¾ 42½ 913 923 Nelson D 114 12.60 54-20 Lawana Go Fast1122 Showsnap1102 Wonaria1092 Outrun 9
11Nov94-6Aqu fst 7f :234 :473 1:13 1:254 [F]Alw 30000N1X 52 6 4 51½ 2hd 42½ 68¾ Frost G C 114 15.60 66-20 MoroccnMgic1144 [D]WlnutPoint1192½ CollgPrk114½ Wide, flattened out 6
30Oct94-3Aqu fst 7f :224 :463 1:12 1:26 [F]Md 45000 72 2 6 11 11 16 19 Frost G C 113 3.75 74-18 Sadie's Glory1139 A Wild Favor1122 Aerosilver1133 Ridden out 10
20Oct94-3Aqu fst 6f :222 :462 :584 1:12 [F]Md 35000 57 5 5 31½ 23 26 37¾ Frost G C 117 4.10 74-18 Pleasantry1175 Nay Nay Renay1132¾ Sadie's Glory1171¾ Lacked rally 8
WORKOUTS: Oct 27 Aqu 5f fst 1:013 H 2/5 Oct 12 Aqu 4f fst :484 H 3/7 Sep 16 Aqu 3f fst :361 H 3/6

Nicky's Amber
Own: Towne James T Jr
ALVARADO F T (71 3 11 9 .04) $12,000
Gr. f. 4
Sire: Amber Pass (Pass Catcher)
Dam: Givitgas (North Sea)
Br: Bruno Joseph L (NY)
Tr: Galluscio Dominic G (8 2 0 0 .25)
L 114
Lifetime Record: 11 3 2 2 $49,390
1995 5 1 1 1 $4,530 | Turf 0 0 0 0
1994 6 2 1 1 $44,860 | Wet 1 0 0 0
Aqu 2 2 0 0 $34,800 | Dist 8 3 2 1 $46,030

4Nov95-8FL fst 6f :22 :462 1:00 1:133 3+ [F]Clm 11000N4L 50 7 2 43½ 41¾ 21 24½ Hiraldo J L L 119f 2.45 71-28 Stars All Around1164½ Nicky's Amber1191½ Makin Melody1162 No match 7
14Oct95-6FL fst 6f :222 :46 :583 1:121 3+ [F]Clm 11000N3L 55 7 2 32½ 31½ 1hd 1½ Hiraldo J L L 116f 1.45 83-17 Nicky's Amber116½ Many Colored Roses1162 TopkapiJewel1161½ Driving 7
24Sep95-10FL fst 6f :23 :474 1:01 1:142 3+ [F]Clm 11000N4L 57 3 3 45 33 21½ 31½ Hiraldo J L L 116f 3.75 70-29 Lady In Love116½ Brace's Dolly1161 Nicky's Amber1161½ Hung 7
4Sep95-1Bel fst 1 :23 :463 1:114 1:382 3+ [F]Clm 16000 31 8 6 66 53½ 78½ 915¾ Migliore R L 114f 13.30 51-16 Muko1161 Rabs Lil Brit Brit1163¾ Alkris116¾ Gave way 9
17Aug95-3Sar fst 6f :221 :46 :583 1:113 3+ [F]Clm 25000 44 8 1 58 87¼ 87 815½ Beckner D V 114f 21.80 68-17 Midway Gal1172¾ Gene's Gray Girl1221 Madrona1171 Done early 8
17Dec94-2Aqu fst 6f [•] :233 :473 1:00 1:123 [F]Clm 25000 50 3 5 63 42½ 68¾ 511½ Chavez J F 116 7.40 68-17 Jake's Sister118¾ Mitey Jenny1113½ Indian Paradise1166¾ Tired 6
15Nov94-7Aqu fst 6f :231 :473 1:00 1:124 3+ [F][S]Alw 30000N1X 62 1 6 42½ 41 31 1¾ Smith M E 117 2.35 78-17 Nicky's Amber117¾ Miss Halo Country115no Frisky's Finale1101 Driving 7
29Oct94-5Aqu fst 6f :224 :47 1:002 1:14 3+ [F][S]Md Sp Wt 53 4 3 810 77½ 22 1nk Smith M E 119 *1.10 72-19 Nicky's Amber119nk I'mabaroness1142½ Rumba Lession1192 Driving 12
20Sep94-1Bel fst 7f :231 :47 1:114 1:244 3+ [F][S]Md Sp Wt 56 1 3 34½ 33½ 34 37½ Beckner D V5 113 *1.30 72-19 Shell Crist1184½ Now I Hope1183 Nicky's Amber1135 No late bid 6
9Sep94-9Bel fst 6f :23 :471 :593 1:12 3+ [F][S]Md Sp Wt 64 12 7 62½ 3nk 1½ 22 Beckner D V5 113 4.60 79-18 Nanny Brow1182 Nicky's Amber1137½ High Tor118no Rallied wide 14
WORKOUTS: Oct 25 FL 4f fst :511 B 5/13 Sep 17 FL 3f fst :371 B 4/12 Aug 29 Bel 5f fst 1:014 B 9/16

1 — Victorian Woman — Hadn't raced well since the claim nine starts back, but her fifth by 3½ lengths in last wasn't that bad. Maybe.

2 — Tara's Tempest — Off since May 24. No.

3 — Green Reader — Wildly inconsistent mare had enough ability to win this, though her last start at six furlongs four races back was awful. Contender.

4 — Keeping Fit — Taking a sharp drop off two poor races. Demand to see a sign of life before trying these. No.

5 — Satans Archangel — Speedster had run well fresh previously, but hadn't been out since May 3. She was dropping, but I passed.

6 — Waqueen — Another drop-down who was one for seven lifetime at six furlongs. Had some speed. Pass.

7 — Straight Jacket — Fifth in return and drops, but had shown nothing since shipping in from Chile. Pass.

8 — Sadie's Glory — Beaten by Waqueen in last, but it was her first race off a layoff and she bobbled at the start. Zero for eight record at six furlongs. Maybe.

9 — Nicky's Amber — Finger Lakes shipper had been in the money seven of her last 10 starts. If you read her PPs from the top, you saw three poor races in New York, one at Belmont, Saratoga and Aqueduct, and maybe tossed her. But two of those three were in $25,000 claimers, and the other was at $16,000, at one mile. If you started at the bottom of her PPs, you discover she had two wins and a second in three previous six-furlong tries in New York against New York-Breds. Her record at six furlongs was 2-3-1 in eight starts, and she was a perfect two for two on Aqueduct's main track. She was dropping five pounds off a second at 2-1 at Finger Lakes, and was picking up the services of Frank Alvarado, one of Aqueduct's best jockeys. In a field lacking quality, she seemed the best to me, and I picked her first in the *Gazette*.

Well, Trail City, my second choice in the first race, won and paid $14.80. Nicky's Amber won the second race by a length and paid $25.40. The Daily Double paid $407.

Connecting on that double could have been accomplished by simply criss-crossing my top two picks, a cost of $8, or by criss-crossing three picks in each race for $18. If you catch one juicy exotic overlay double, you'll more than cover a daily investment of $8 or $18. Big bettors can simply multiply the $2 double bets by anything they're comfortable with spending. It's the idea which is valid, not the amount of the investment.

FIRST RACE

Aqueduct

NOVEMBER 24, 1995

6½ FURLONGS. (1.15) MAIDEN CLAIMING. Purse $16,000 (plus up to $6,280 NYSBFOA). 2-year-olds. Weight, 118 lbs. Claiming price $50,000, for each $5,000 to $40,000, allowed 2 lbs. (Day 18 of a 44 Day Meet. Clear. 38.)

Value of Race: $16,000 Winner $9,600; second $3,200; third $1,760; fourth $960; fifth $480. Mutuel Pool $169,511.00 Exacta Pool $274,359.00

Last Raced	Horse	M/Eqt. A.Wt	PP	St	¼	½	Str	Fin	Jockey	Cl'g Pr	Odds $1
2Nov95 1Aqu7	Trail City	b 2 118	2	11	6hd	41½	11½	11	Bailey J D	50000	6.40
25Oct95 2Bel6	Rev Owen G	L 2 114	9	9	5½	31½	21½	23½	Perez R B	40000	16.80
11Nov95 2Aqu5	Mack's Oscar	bf 2 118	12	3	8½	61½	44	34½	Davis R G	50000	8.00
25Oct95 2Bel8	Thegiantkiller	f 2 116	8	1	1hd	2½	3½	4nk	Nelson D	45000	38.50
15Nov95 4Aqu6	Going for the Gold	Lb 2 118	11	4	10½	9½	71	52	Samyn J L	50000	16.70
10Nov95 1Aqu6	In the Rain	2 116	3	7	7½	7hd	61	62	Cordova D W	45000	4.40
2Nov95 1Aqu6	Justinthemiddle	f 2 114	10	2	12	11½	8hd	72½	Santagata N	40000	15.00
	Ernie the King	b 2 114	4	12	113	8½	92½	81½	Migliore R	40000	23.40
	Hardshell Crab	2 116	1	5	2½	1½	5hd	91	Krone J A	45000	12.90
	Hurry West	bf 2 116	7	10	9½	10½	112	10½	Alvarado F T	45000	11.80
	Early Echoes	2 118	5	6	3½	5hd	10½	111	Santos J A	50000	4.10
27Jly95 2Sar9	Rosa in Bloom	2 118	6	8	4hd	12	12	12	Luzzi M J	50000	5.00

OFF AT 12:30 Start Good. Won driving. Time, :223, :462, 1:112, 1:18 Track good.

$2 Mutuel Prices:				
	2-TRAIL CITY	14.80	12.40	6.50
	9-REV OWEN G		13.60	9.30
	12-MACK'S OSCAR			6.50

$2 EXACTA 2-9 PAID $341.50

Dk. b. or br. c, (Apr), by Red Ransom—Willow Runner, by Alydar. Trainer Mott William I. Bred by Prestonwood Farm (Ky).

TRAIL CITY raced in good position while saving ground to the turn, accelerated to the front in upper stretch then turned back REV OWEN G under brisk urging. REV OWEN G steadily gained while four wide in upper stretch but couldn't stay with the winner in the lane. MACK'S OSCAR steadily worked his way forward while four wide on the turn and finished willingly for a share. THEGIANTKILLER dueled for the lead from outside for a half and weakened. GOING FOR THE GOLD outrun for a half, failed to threaten while improving his position. IN THE RAIN was never a serious threat. JUSTINTHEMIDDLE never reached contention while racing wide. ERNIE THE KING checked in tight at the start, was never close thereafter. HARDSHELL CRAB dueled along the rail to the turn and gave way. HURRY WEST was never close after being shuffled back in the early stages. EARLY ECHOES was used up chasing the early leaders. ROSA IN BLOOM showed only brief speed. REV OWEN G, IN THE RAIN, JUSTINTHEMIDDLE and HURRY WEST wore mud caulks.

Owners— 1, Mott William I & Verchota Robert; 2, Flynn Pierce J; 3, Robinson J Mack; 4, Black Marlin Stable; 5, Kimmel Caesar P & Nicholson Ronald; 6, Hobeau Farm; 7, Cohen Robert B; 8, Federico Gino; 9, Kushner Herbert W; 10, Hough Stanley M; 11, Fox Hill Farm; 12, Rosenthal Mrs Morton.

Trainers— 1, Mott William I; 2, Destasio Richard A; 3, Alexander Frank A; 4, Jerkens Steven T; 5, Toner James J; 6, Jerkens H Allen; 7, Shapoff Stanley R; 8, Badgett William Jr; 9, Dutrow Richard E; 10, Hough Stanley M; 11, Servis John C; 12, Destefano John M Jr

SECOND RACE

Aqueduct

NOVEMBER 24, 1995

6 FURLONGS. (1.08) CLAIMING. Purse $13,000. Fillies and mares, 3-year-olds and upward. Weights: 3-year-olds, 120 lbs. Older, 122 lbs. Non-winners of three races since September 27, allowed 2 lbs. A race since October 19, 4 lbs. A race since October 8, 6 lbs. Claiming price $14,000, if for $12,000, allowed 2 lbs. (Races where entered for $10,000 or less not considered.)

Value of Race: $13,000 Winner $7,800; second $2,600; third $1,430; fourth $780; fifth $390. Mutuel Pool $216,054.00 Exacta Pool $312,839.00 Quinella Pool $68,435.00

Last Raced	Horse	M/Eql. A. Wt	PP St	¼	½	Str	Fin	Jockey	Cl'g Pr	Odds $1
4Nov95 8FL2	Nicky's Amber	Lf 4 116	9 2	7½	5½	2½	1¹	Alvarado F T	12000	11.70
4Nov95 1Aqu5	Waqueen	Lb 4 116	6 1	1hd	1½	11½	2¹½	Davis R G	14000	1.70
26Oct95 4Bel5	Keeping Fit	Lb 5 116	4 7	6hd	8²	6⁴	3nk	Perez R B	14000	5.90
16Nov95 3Aqu5	Straight Jacket-CH	L 4 116	7 3	4¹	4½	4¹	4¹½	Castillo H Jr	14000	20.40
4Nov95 1Aqu7	Sadie's Glory	3 107	8 6	5²	2²	3¹	5¹½	Trejo J7	14000	10.70
24May95 1Bel5	Tara's Tempest	Lb 4 109	2 9	8½	6¹	5½	6½	Maysonett F7	14000	13.90
9Nov95 9Aqu8	Green Reader	Lbf 5 118	3 5	9	9	7²½	7¹⁰	Chavez J F	12000	5.00
15Nov95 2Aqu5	Victorian Woman	Lb 3 114	1 4	2½	3½	8½	8nk	Migliore R	14000	15.40
3May95 6Bel6	Satans Archangel	Lb 4 114	5 8	3½	7½	9	9	Nelson D	12000	5.30

OFF AT 12:55 Start Good. Won driving. Time, :22³, :46⁴, :59², 1:12¹ Track good.

$2 Mutuel Prices:	9–NICKY'S AMBER	25.40	7.80	4.20
	6–WAQUEEN		3.70	2.80
	4–KEEPING FIT			3.40

$2 EXACTA 9–6 PAID $85.00 $2 QUINELLA 6–9 PAID $36.20

Gr. f, by Amber Pass–Givitgas, by North Sea. Trainer Galluscio Dominic G. Bred by Bruno Joseph L (NY).

NICKY'S AMBER reserved early, circled five wide on the turn then wore down WAQUEEN in the final sixteenth. WAQUEEN dueled slightly off the rail for a half, opened a clear advantage in upper stretch but couldn't withstand the winner's late charge. KEEPING FIT reserved early, steadily between horses, dropped back while lacking room on the turn, rallied belatedly in the middle of the track. STRAIGHT JACKET went evenly. SADIE'S GLORY reserved early, made a run from outside to threaten at the quarter pole and flattened out. TARA'S TEMPEST away slowly, lodged a mild rally while angling four wide on the turn but couldn't sustain her bid. GREEN READER never reached contention after breaking in tight at the start. VICTORIAN WOMAN dueled along the inside to the turn and tired. SATANS ARCHANGEL up close early, gave way on the turn.

Owners— 1, Towne James T Jr; 2, Jakubovitz Jerome R; 3, Friendship Stable & Mogru Madhan; 4, Delehanty Farm; 5, Ostman & Toscano & Twilite Tee Stb; 6, Connaughton Bernard; 7, Benincasa Joseph & Gullo Giacomo; 8, Gullo Gary P & Godash Barbara; 9, Bissett Joan B

Trainers—1, Galluscio Dominic G; 2, Myer Pat; 3, Barbara Robert; 4, Penna Angel Jr; 5, Toscano John T Jr; 6, O'Brien Colum; 7, Odintz Jeff; 8, Gullo Gary P; 9, Lenzini John J Jr

Corrected weight: Nicky's Amber (116).

Waqueen was claimed by Frankel Richard M; trainer, Galluscio Dominic G.

Scratched— Our Dear Dana (20Oct95 2BEL3)

$2 Daily Double (2–9) Paid $407.00; Daily Double Pool $294,854.

The blizzard of 1996 played havoc with January racing at Aqueduct. On Saturday, January 14, the jockeys voted to cancel the card after the second race. By then, a criss-cross of my *Gazette* picks would have produced an outrageous exotic overlay.

The first two races were claimers for three-year-olds at a mile and 70 yards, the first for fillies ($35,000 to $40,000), and the second open to colts and geldings ($30,000 to $35,000).

Handicapping the first race, it quickly became evident that several of the 10 fillies entered had no desire to be in a route race. The field:

1

Aqueduct

1 MILE 70 YARDS (Inner Dirt). (1:39³) CLAIMING. Purse $25,000 (plus up to $4850 NYSBFOA). Fillies, 3-year-olds. Weight, 120 lbs. Non-winners of two races at a mile or over, allowed 2 lbs. Such a race since December 12, 4 lbs. Such a race since November 26, 6 lbs. Claiming price $40,000, if for $35,000, allowed 2 lbs. (Races where entered for $30,000 or less not considered.)

Thirty Six Gold

Own: West Point Thoroughbreds

MARQUEZ C H JR (38 2 11 .07) $35,000

B. f. 3 (May)
Sire: Thirty Six Red (Slew o' Gold)
Dam: Banner Hit (Oh Say)
Br: Losey, Ezzell, McGinty & Brophy (Ky)
Tr: Dowd John F (9 2 0 0 .22)

L 112

Lifetime Record: 11 1 2 2 $16,705

1995	11 1 2 2	$16,705	Turf	0 0 0 0	
1994	0 M 0 0		Wet	2 0 1 0	$3,330
Aqu⊡	3 1 0 0	$8,130	Dist	0 0 0 0	

Tri Irish

Own: Woodfield Stables

ALVARADO F T (114 15 19 14 .13) $40,000

Entered 12Jan96– 3 AQU

Dk. b or br f. 3 (Apr)
Sire: Irish Sur (Surreal)
Dam: Tri Maw (Tri Jet)
Br: Right Angle Stable (Fla)
Tr: Sciacca Gary (43 1 4 3 .02)

L 114

Lifetime Record: 6 1 1 0 $10,150

1995	6 1 1 0	$10,150	Turf	0 0 0 0	
1994	0 M 0 0		Wet	1 1 0 0	$5,600
Aqu⊡	0 0 0 0		Dist	1 0 0 0	$165

WORKOUTS: Dec 2 Crc 4f fst :51 B 40/57   Nov 11 Crc 4f fst 1:05 B 36/43   Nov 6 Crc 4f fst :50 B 6/24   Nov 1 Crc 3f fst :36³ B 2/18   Oct 18 Crc 3f sly :37³ B (d) 3/17

Cheerful

Own: Blake Pavel

TREJO J (64 7 6 8 .11)   107⁷

Gr/ro f. 3 (Apr)
Sire: Proud Truth (Graustark)
Dam: Cheerful Reward (Double Edge Sword)
Br: Amoss Hamilton & MacDermott Mr & Mrs Kieran (Md)
Tr: Carroll Del W II (11 2 2 1 .18)

Lifetime Record: 3 1 0 0 $7,590

1995	3 1 0 0	$7,590	Turf	0 0 0 0	
1994	0 M 0 0		Wet	1 0 0 0	
Aqu⊡	0 0 0 0	$7,200	Dist	1 0 0 0	$7,200

WORKOUTS: Jan 10 Bel tr.t 5f fst 1:03 B 3/5   Dec 24 Bel tr.t 4f fst :50 B 85/147   Dec 18 Bel tr.t 5f fst 1:04³ B 18/23   Dec 8 Bel tr.t 4f fst :53 B 41/41   Nov 21 Bel tr.t 4f fst :50¹ B 12/24   Nov 14 Bel tr.t 3f fst :38¹ B 6/14

She's all Class

Own: Paraneck Stable

CORDOVA D W (90 10 11 15 .10) $40,000

B. f. 3 (Mar)
Sire: Rahy (Blushing Groom)
Dam: Fast Nellie (Ack Ack)
Br: Makk Mr & Mrs Laszlo (Ky)
Tr: Ryerson James T (9 2 1 2 .22)

L 114

Lifetime Record: 9 1 1 0 $17,990

1995	9 1 1 0	$17,990	Turf	2 0 0 0	
1994	0 M 0 0		Wet	1 0 0 0	$10,260
Aqu⊡	1 0 1 0	$4,600	Dist	1 0 1 0	$4,600

WORKOUTS: Dec 24 Bel tr.t 4f fst :49² B 56/147   ●Dec 19 Bel tr.t 3f gd :37¹ B 1/18   Nov 18 Bel 4f fst :50² B 29/37   ●Oct 23 Bel tr.t 4f fst :49 H 1/20

Lake Jacqueline

Own: Edition Farm

NELSON D (52 2 7 4 .04) $40,000

Entered 12Jan96– 3 AQU

Gr/ro f. 3 (Apr)
Sire: Jacques Who (Grey Dawn II)
Dam: Cambridge Cutie (Harvard Man)
Br: Edition Farm (NY)
Tr: Daggett Michael H (9 1 0 2 .11)

L 114

Lifetime Record: 10 2 0 2 $28,790

1995	10 2 0 2	$28,790	Turf	0 0 0 0	
1994	0 M 0 0		Wet	1 0 0 0	$900
Aqu⊡	3 1 0 0		Dist	1 0 0 0	

WORKOUTS: ●Dec 31 Bel tr.t 4f fst :47¹ H 1/65   Dec 24 Bel tr.t 5f fst 1:02³ B 19/47   Dec 19 Bel tr.t 4f gd :51² B 23/29   Dec 7 Bel tr.t 4f fst :49² B 8/22   Nov 28 Bel tr.t 6f fst 1:15⁴ B 1/2   Nov 21 Bel tr.t 4f fst :49¹ B 11/40

Pocket the Cash
Own: Chevalier Stable
RYDOWSKI S R (10 0 0 3 .00) $40,000
Ch. f. 3 (Feb)
Sire: Tunerup (The Pruner)
Dam: Fleet Pocket (Full Pocket)
Br: Casse Justin & Norman (Fla)
Tr: Shapoff Stanley R (12 0 1 1 .00)
114

Lifetime Record:	9 1 0 2	$21,760			
1995	9 1 0 2	$21,760	Turf	0 0 0 0	
1994	0 M 0 0		Wet	2 0 0 0	$2,760
Aqu ⊡	1 0 0 1	$3,080	Dist	0 0 0 0	

8Dec95- 3Aqu fst 6f ⊡ :232 :463 :59 1:121 ⒻClm 45000 50 3 3 67½ 67½ 416 312 Nelson D 113 8.80 70-19 CelstilGlnc1168 Don'tLtnyonknow1144 PocktThCsh1133 No threat, wide 6
22Nov95- 4Aqu fst 6f :232 :47 :594 1:124 ⒻClm 35000 58 1 7 56¼ 65 45 33½ Nelson D 116 21.90 75-19 Jumberca1182 Little Miss Fast1161½ Pocket The Cash116¾ Rallied inside 9
14Sep95- 3Bel wf 6f :222 :46 :582 1:111 ⒻAlw 32880N1X 56 4 6 616 66 54½ 57¾ Krone J A 112 27.25 77-16 Gold Sunrise1161 Top Secret116¾ Logical Manner1161 Broke slowly 6
14Aug95- 6Sar fst 7f :23 :454 1:112 1:241 ⒻAlw 32000N2L 19 2 9 913 922 918 935¼ Chavez J F 112 33.50 50-19 Summer Squeeze1155 Wild 'n' Nasty1123 My Flag1182 Broke slowly 9
29Jun95- 2Bel fst 5f :231 :473 1:003 ⒻMd 40000 59 7 3 3½ 1hd 11 1nk Maple E 115 3.75e 83-22 PocketTheCsh115nk BrkThrough1156 Fortuitousmiss115hd Drifted, game 8
18Jun95- 2Bel fst 5½f :224 :47 :592 1:053 ⒻMd Sp Wt 54 5 5 53 42½ 53½ 511½ Maple E 115 20.00 75-20 Steady Cat1156¾ Lemon Dove1151½ Irma1152¾ Flattened out 9
7Jun95- 2Bel gd 5f :22 :452 :574 ⒻMd Sp Wt 64 8 8 78¼ 55½ 56 47½ Maple E 115 10.90 89-09 Dynasty1155¾ Not Brite Brillant115nk Lizzy's Pleasure1151½ Mild gain 8
26May95- 2Bel sly 5f :22 :453 :59 ⒻMd Sp Wt 55 2 7 78 78½ 55 44 Maple E 115 4.10 87-10 StrwbrryClovr1151½ Onthrghtwckt1152¾ Thsky'sthlmt115no Checked break 8
4May95- 2Bel fst 5f :221 :461 :59 ⒻMd Sp Wt 52 8 4 32 43 52½ 45 Maple E 115 3.70 86-13 Five Corners1152 Jumberca1151¾ Lizzy's Pleasure1151½ Wide, evenly 8
WORKOUTS: Jan 12 Bel tr.t 3f fst :382 B 30/42 Dec 18 Bel tr.t 5f fst 1:05 B 19/33 Dec 1 Bel tr.t 4f fst :503 B 28/43 Nov 28 Bel tr.t 3f fst :384 B 13/13 Nov 13 Bel tr.t 5f fst 1:021 B 7/10 Nov 6 Bel tr.t 5f fst 1:023 B 18/29

Don'tletanyoneknow
Own: Casse Norman E
VELAZQUEZ J R (111 20 8 18 .18) $40,000
B. f. 3 (Apr)
Sire: Danzatore (Northern Dancer)
Dam: Coaxing (L'Enjoleur)
Br: Scott Dr C G (Ont-C)
Tr: Levine Bruce N (32 2 6 1 .06)
L 114

Lifetime Record:	7 1 1 1	$33,756			
1995	7 1 1 1	$33,756	Turf	0 0 0 0	
1994	0 M 0 0		Wet	0 0 0 0	
Aqu ⊡	1 0 1 0	$5,600	Dist	0 0 0 0	

Entered 12Jan96- 3 AQU
8Dec95- 3Aqu fst 6f ⊡ :232 :463 :59 1:121 ⒻClm 45000 60 2 2 32 23 28 28 Velazquez J R L 114 3.10 74-19 ClstlGlnc1168 Don'tLtnyonknw1144 PcktThCsh1133 No match, 2nd best 6
12Nov95- 3Aqu gd 1 :23 :462 1:122 1:391 ⒻAlw 32000N1X 48 4 2 31 42½ 68 617¾ Chavez J F 112 8.70 56-29 Ontherightwicket113¾ BreakThrough1136 MeritWings1163¼ Forced pace 7
28Oct95-11WO fst 6f :214 :443 :573 1:11 ⒻⓇFanfrluche-G3C 66 1 1 42½ 33½ 24 48¾ Husbands P 113 15.40 80-13 Highland Vixen1145 Heavenly Valley121¾ Northern Hilite1193 Inside try 7
7Oct95- 9WO fst 7f ⊗ :224 :461 1:114 1:254 ⒻMd Sp Wt 61 3 5 21 23 12 12½ Husbands P 114 7.30 80-16 Don'tLtnyonknow1142½ WnnngSprs1141½ QnsNVgbonds1191 Driving clear 8
6Sep95- 4WO fst 5f :222 :461 :59 ⒻMd 40000 47 9 5 75½ 76¾ 68¾ 35¾ Husbands P 114 2.80 81-11 AimIsTrue115nk NotSoWild1155½ Don'tletnyonknow1141½ Closed between 10
24Jun95- 9WO fst 5½f :223 :461 1:053 ⒻⓇShady Well-G3C 51 1 4 41½ 53¾ 44½ 46½ Kabel T K 114 16.25 81-12 Heavenly Valley1142 Autumn Slew114½ Mooncoin1144 Saved ground 5
10Jun95- 9WO fst 5f :221 :454 :583 ⒻMy Dear-G3C 49 7 8 89 58 712 510¾ Husbands P 114 29.40 79-15 Rosie O'greta1162 Miners Mirage1162¾ Timely Search1164 8
Squeezed break, mild wide rally
WORKOUTS: Dec 23 Aqu ⊡ 5f fst 1:04 B 3/9 Oct 22 WO tr.t 4f my :51 H 6/8

Artistic Fire
Own: Schmidt Hilmer C
CHAVEZ J F (145 27 21 17 .19) $40,000
Dk. b or br f. 3 (May)
Sire: Badger Land (Codex)
Dam: All My Marys (Page Page)
Br: Tackett Paul (Ky)
Tr: Kimmel John C (17 3 4 1 .18)
114

Lifetime Record:	2 1 0 0	$10,080			
1995	2 1 0 0	$10,080	Turf	0 0 0 0	
1994	0 M 0 0		Wet	1 1 0 0	$9,600
Aqu ⊡	0 0 0 0		Dist	0 0 0 0	

30Nov95- 3Aqu sly 7f :23 :47 1:122 1:253 ⒻMd 50000 57 4 5 1hd 12½ 15 16 Alvarado F T 118 4.20 76-14 Artistic Fire1186 Revelation Bay1183 ColorfulCharacter118½ Drew away 8
17Nov95- 3Aqu fst 6f :23 :471 :594 1:131 ⒻMd 50000 42 2 8 86¾ 75½ 59½ 510 Vives L5 112 5.60 66-21 Three Decades1062 Celestial Glance1176½ No Hastle1171½ No threat 9
WORKOUTS: Jan 11 Bel tr.t 5f fst 1:05 B 18/25 Jan 5 Bel tr.t 4f fst :52 B 18/30 Dec 30 Bel tr.t 5f fst 1:033 B 19/23 Dec 24 Bel tr.t 4f fst :53 B 142/147 Nov 7 Med 5f fst 1:01 Bg7/30 Oct 26 Med 5f fst 1:011 Bg6/17

Fresh Look
Own: Dichiaro Michael & My Jo Lee Stable
LUZZI M J (108 14 7 15 .13) $35,000
Ch. f. 3 (Apr)
Sire: Mister Frisky (Marsayas)
Dam: Sun Creme (Koluctoo Bay)
Br: Hagan Leslie Ann (Fla)
Tr: Miceli Michael (12 1 0 2 .08)
L 112

Lifetime Record:	10 2 0 1	$19,790			
1995	10 2 0 1	$19,790	Turf	0 0 0 0	
1994	0 M 0 0		Wet	2 0 0 1	$1,650
Aqu ⊡	3 1 0 0	$11,400	Dist	0 0 0 0	

21Dec95- 4Aqu fst 6f ⊡ :222 :462 :591 1:12 ⒻClm 20000 62 4 1 2hd 2hd 1hd 11 Luzzi M J L 114 b 26.75 83-13 Fresh Look1141 Theransomspaid111nk Heavenly Glance114no Driving 7
6Dec95- 6Med fst 6f :223 :463 :584 1:112 ⒻClm 16000 40 3 4 3nk 1hd 54¾ 59½ Pezua J M L 115 b 6.40 72-19 God's Pic115½ Lil Magic Twig1155½ Halos Wonder1153 Tired 6
22Nov95- 4Aqu fst 6f :232 :47 :594 1:124 ⒻClm 30000 46 2 6 77½ 76½ 67½ 68¾ Pezua J M L 112 b 41.25 70-19 Jumberca1182 Little Miss Fast1161½ Pocket The Cash116¾ No threat 9
16Nov95- 4Med fst 6f :223 :462 :59 1:121 ⒻMd 20000 51 1 7 41½ 1hd 13 14¼ Pezua J M L 117 b 9.50 78-19 Fresh Look1174¼ Holy Bolla117½ Thirty Six Gold1174½ Rail trip, driving 8
9Nov95- 2Aqu fst 7f :232 :482 1:152 1:282 ⒻMd 35000 37 3 10 1½ 1½ 31 510½ Luzzi M J L 115 b 51.25 51-23 BornTwice1183 ColorMeGold108½ Copewiththefutur118½ Dueled inside 12
12Oct95- 1Bel fst 7f :231 :472 1:122 1:251 ⒻMd 30000 37 2 8 63½ 74 512 415 Luzzi M J L 114 b 11.70 60-16 Court Dispute1144 Born Twice117no Clamorosa11711 Broke slowly 8
6Oct95- 1Bel my 1 :232 :48 1:153 1:432 ⒻMd 30000 38 4 2 2hd 1hd 33½ 36 Santos J A L 114 b 13.40 40-35 NoblestDrem1144 Thebstfromtxs1142 FrshLook1144 Dueled, weakened 9
27Sep95- 1Bel my 6f :223 :471 :594 1:121 ⒻMd 35000 29 2 8 97 96¾ 79¾ 613 Luzzi M J L 117 b 38.25e 67-19 She's All Class1174 Kim's World1142 DarnThatKrissy1171¾ Five wide trip 13
19Apr95- 2Aqu fst 4½f ⊡ :222 :462 :53 ⒻMd Sp Wt — 3 4 44½ 712 720 Brocklebank G V 115 b 14.50 82-13 Zee Lady11510 Little Notice115hd Bring Me Flowers115no Done early 10
5Apr95- 2Aqu fst 4½f ⊡ :234 :473 :534 ⒻMd Sp Wt — 5 6 53½ 616 729½ Brocklebank G V 115 4.20 68-21 Rosie O'greta11511 Jumberca1152 Court Dispute11512 Wide, tired 9
WORKOUTS: Nov 6 Aqu 3f fst :39 B 7/8 Nov 1 Aqu 4f fst :491 B 1/3 Oct 24 Aqu 5f fst 1:02 B 4/11 Oct 19 Aqu 5f fst 1:022 Bg5/8

Lady Tymatt
Own: Seaman Casey
BRAVO J (63 6 13 5 .09) $35,000
Dk. b or br f. 3 (Apr)
Sire: His Majesty (Ribot)
Dam: Lady Lister (Lord Lister)
Br: Hancock Arthur B III (Ky)
Tr: Velazquez Alfredo (1 0 1 0 .00)
L 112

Lifetime Record:	12 4 1 1	$36,650			
1995	12 4 1 1	$36,650	Turf	0 0 0 0	
1994	0 M 0 0		Wet	1 1 0 0	$4,200
Aqu ⊡	0 0 0 0		Dist	3 1 0 0	$11,030

22Dec95- 6Lrl fst 1 1/16 :24 :49 1:15 1:484 ⒻClm 25000 62 8 4 31 1hd 1hd 1no Klinger C O L 114 9.50 66-33 Lady Tymatt114no Marrakech Dawn1163 Name In Print1161½ Driving 8
28Nov95- 8Pha fst 1 :25 :501 1:161 1:431 ⒻAlw 16350N1X 67 1 1 2hd 2hd 1hd 13½ Glasser T P7 L 106 10.70 62-39 Lady Tymatt1063½ Bow Guard1131¾ Seattle Suzzy121nk Inside, drew clear 7
16Nov95- 9Med fst 170 :223 :47 1:132 1:443 ⒻAlw 20000N1X 27 5 8 97 96¾ 910 814 Unsihuay A L 113 20.30 55-24 Miss Kim Liberty1131 Roadie1131¾ Marrakech Dawn117¾ Outrun 9
4Nov95- 8Pha fst 6f :224 :472 1:004 1:142 ⒻClm 20000 26 7 6 64½ 77½ 68 69¼ Glasser T P7 L 111 *1.40 60-23 Princess Audrey1165 It Was Inevitable116hd P. X. Dancer1171½ Wide 7
27Oct95- 7Pha fst 6f :214 :451 :583 1:123 ⒻAlw 17092N1X 36 6 6 77¾ 79½ 68½ 45¼ Glasser T P7 L 108 *1.80 73-18 SmartLady1151½ EyefulPower1171½ Mtt'sMinistress1102½ Showed nothing 7
12Oct95- 3Bel fst 6½f :222 :461 1:114 1:183 ⒻClm 50000 47 4 5 510 511 410 39½ Glasser T P7 L 105 18.60 72-16 HelloBrian1169 ExtremeChange116½ LadyTymtt1057 Improved position 5
3Oct95- 6Pha fst 6f :221 :463 1:001 1:132 ⒻClm 20000 47 5 7 711 65¼ 1hd 11½ Glasser T P7 L 110 10.70 74-20 Lady Tymatt1101½ Bold Impression115¾ TheLastShananie1154 Very wide 7
18Sep95- 2Pha wf 7f :222 :453 1:131 1:271 ⒻMd 15000 31 4 6 64½ 611 33 1½ Black A S L 120 *1.80 70-14 Lady Tymatt120½ Proud By You1208½ Ultra Lily1202½ Wide, just up 8
20Aug95-11RD fst 170 :23 :464 1:121 1:451 B C Rascal45k -0 2 10 1118 1126 1144 1142½ Fiorentino C T LB 115 67.80 42-17 Grant Road1174 City By Night1145½ Johnsaidnoproblem114½ Never close 11
5Aug95- 8Pha fst 6f :223 :463 1:00 1:134 ⒻMd 15000 35 8 5 43½ 44½ 32 2no Hughes L L5 L 114 14.20 72-18 Smarten's Ida119no Lady Tymatt1145 Elite One119½ Wide, missed 9

1 — Thirty Six Gold — One for 11 overall, her 10 PPs in the *Form* were all sprints. She was dropping from allowance company, but had graduated three races back in a maiden $30,000 claimer. She had speed, but there was no reason to think she'd make a mile and 70 yards. No.

2 — Tri Irish — While she showed a decent fourth in a
$35,000 claiming sprint in her last start, the Calder shipper had
been in one route race, finishing ninth by 27 lengths at 18-1 in a
non-winners of two. No.

3 — Cheerful — She won a $1\frac{1}{16}$-mile maiden $25,000 claimer
in last, but was stepping up. No.

4 — She's All Class — This speedster was a solid front-
running second in a $1\frac{1}{16}$-mile $35,000 claimer in her last, losing by
$2\frac{3}{4}$ lengths while beating the third horse by $6\frac{3}{4}$. Top contender.

5 — Lake Jacqueline — The New York-Bred filly showed all
her 10 starts. She'd won a New York-Bred maiden race and an
open allowance race at Finger Lakes, but both were $5\frac{1}{2}$-furlong
sprints. She's run an okay fourth in the six-furlong New York
Stallion Stakes two starts back, but in her lone try at a route in
her last race, the East View Stakes for New York-Bred fillies, she
was eighth by $39\frac{3}{4}$ lengths at 31-1. Now she was dropping in
company and losing blinkers (her first three starts were without
blinkers) off a bullet work. If this was a sprint, I would have
given her a big shot. But at a route? No.

6 — Pocket The Cash — Only one of her nine starts was
longer than six furlongs. In a seven furlong non-winners of two
at Saratoga, she was ninth by $35\frac{1}{4}$ lengths at 33-1. She'd been
third in two claiming sprints in her last two races. Maybe.

7 — Don'tletanyoneknow — She was second by eight
lengths in a six-furlong claiming sprint — beating Pocket The
Cash by four lengths — in her last start with Lasix added. In her
lone route try the race before, a non-winners of two at one mile,
she was sixth by $17\frac{1}{4}$ lengths at 8-1. On the plus side, she had
won a maiden race at seven furlongs and showed a pair of
fourths and a fifth in three ambitiously-placed stakes appear-
ances at Woodbine in Canada before shipping to New York. Contender.

8 — Artistic Fire — After a dull fifth by 10 lengths in her six-
furlong maiden claiming debut, she won a seven-furlong maiden
claimer on a sloppy track by six lengths wire to wire. But that
was November 30. She didn't show a workout until December
24, and that workout and three others for this race were very
slow. No.

9 — Fresh Look — She was stepping up and stretching out

off a front end, six-furlong, $20,000 claiming win by a length at 26-1. Previously, she had raced twice at seven furlongs and once at a mile, tiring in each one. No.

10 — Lady Tymatt — An intriguing shipper. After finishing second by a nose in a $15,000 maiden claimer at Philadelphia in her third career start (she had 12 lifetime races and her bottom PP was therefore her third start), her connections placed her in a mile and 70 yards stakes race against colts at River Downs. She was a distant last. Then she won a maiden $15,000 claimer at seven furlongs and a $20,000 claimer at six at Philadelphia. Off those two wins, she shipped to Belmont in a 6½-furlong, $50,000 claimer and was a rallying third by 9½ lengths in a field of just five, with a *Form* comment of "Improved position." She then was fourth and sixth at Philadelphia in sprints. Next came a non-winners of two try at a mile and 70 yards at The Meadowlands, when she was eighth by 14 lengths at 20-1. On Nov. 28, she won a one mile, non-winners of two at Philadelphia Park by 3½ lengths at 10-1, and, in her last start, shipped to Laurel and won a 1¹⁄₁₆-mile, $25,000 claimer by a nose at 9-1. She was moving up a bit today to $35,000 and dropping two pounds. Pitted against fillies who couldn't get out of a non-winners of two, and/or showed great difficulty racing at a distance, she made eminent sense, and the *Form* analysis cast her as a "big player." I made her my pick in the *Gazette* and was stunned, not that she won, but that she paid $14.80 in winning her third straight race.

RACES 3-9 WERE CANCELLED

FIRST RACE
Aqueduct
JANUARY 14, 1996

1 MILE 70 YARDS. (Inner Dirt)(1.39^3) CLAIMING. Purse $25,000 (plus $4850 NYSBFOA). Fillies, 3-year-olds. Weight, 120 lbs. Non-winners of two races at a mile or over, allowed 2 lbs. Such a race since December 12, 4 lbs. Such a race since November 26, 6 lbs. Claiming price $40,000, if for $35,000, allowed 2 lbs. (Races where entered for $30,000 or less not considered.)(Day 10 of a 65 Day Meet. Clear. 41.)

Value of Race: $25,000 Winner $15,000; second $5,000; third $2,750; fourth $1,500; fifth $750. Mutuel Pool $130,924.00 Exacta Pool $228,852.00

Last Raced	Horse	M/Eqt.	A.	Wt	PP	St	¼	½	¾	Str	Fin	Jockey	Cl'g Pr	Odds $1
22Dec95 ^{6}Lrl^{1}	Lady Tymatt	L	3	114	10	9	$8^{2\frac{1}{2}}$	5^{1}	4^{2}	$2^{2\frac{1}{2}}$	$1^{1\frac{1}{4}}$	Bravo J	35000	6.40
8Dec95 ^{3}Aqu^{2}	Don'tletanyoneknow	L	3	114	7	7	$4^{1\frac{1}{2}}$	2^{1}	2^{3}	$1^{1\frac{1}{2}}$	$2^{3\frac{1}{4}}$	Velazquez J R	40000	4.80
21Dec95 ^{4}Aqu^{1}	Fresh Look	Lb	3	114	9	10	$9^{\frac{1}{2}}$	$8^{1\frac{1}{2}}$	$5^{\frac{1}{2}}$	$4^{2\frac{1}{2}}$	$3^{2\frac{3}{4}}$	Luzzi M J	35000	30.25
29Dec95 ^{1}Aqu^{1}	Cheerful	b	3	107	3	4	$7^{\frac{1}{2}}$	$7^{\frac{1}{2}}$	$7^{1\frac{1}{2}}$	$5^{1\frac{1}{2}}$	$4^{1\frac{1}{2}}$	Trejo J^{7}	40000	23.90
21Dec95 ^{10}Crc^{4}	Tri Irish	Lf	3	114	2	3	$5^{2\frac{1}{2}}$	$6^{1\frac{1}{2}}$	$8^{1\frac{1}{2}}$	$6^{\frac{1}{2}}$	5^{nk}	Chavez J F	40000	4.10
8Dec95 ^{3}Aqu^{3}	Pocket the Cash		3	114	6	6	6^{hd}	$9^{\frac{1}{2}}$	10	$8^{1\frac{1}{2}}$	6^{5}	Rydowski S R	40000	18.50
31Dec95 ^{4}Aqu^{6}	Thirty Six Gold	Lbf	3	113	1	1	$1^{3\frac{1}{2}}$	1^{2}	1^{hd}	3^{hd}	7^{hd}	Marquez C H Jr	35000	8.20
30Nov95 ^{3}Aqu^{1}	Artistic Fire	f	3	114	8	8	10	10	$9^{1\frac{1}{2}}$	$7^{\frac{1}{2}}$	$8^{\frac{3}{4}}$	Alvarado F T	40000	3.05
10Dec95 ^{8}Aqu^{8}	Lake Jacqueline	L	3	114	5	5	$3^{\frac{1}{2}}$	4^{3}	$6^{\frac{1}{2}}$	$9^{\frac{1}{2}}$	$9^{5\frac{3}{4}}$	Nelson D	40000	23.10
31Dec95 ^{2}Aqu^{2}	She's all Class	Lf	3	114	4	2	2^{2}	$3^{1\frac{1}{2}}$	$3^{1\frac{1}{2}}$	10	10	Cordova D W	40000	5.30

OFF AT 12:30 Start Good. Won driving. Time, :23^{3}, :48^{1}, 1:14, 1:42, 1:46^{2} Track sloppy.

$2 Mutuel Prices:

10-LADY TYMATT	14.80	7.80	5.40
7-DON'TLETANYONEKNOW		6.40	4.90
9-FRESH LOOK			19.40

$2 EXACTA 10-7 PAID $105.00

Dk. b. or br. f, (Apr), by His Majesty–Lady Lister, by Lord Lister. Trainer Velazquez Alfredo. Bred by Hancock Arthur B III (Ky).

LADY TYMATT unhurried early while five wide, closed the gap on the far turn, made a run in the middle of the track to challenge inside the furlong marker, then edged away in the final seventy yards. DON'TLETANYONEKNOW settled in good position while three wide, overtook the pacesetter to gain the lead on the turn, opened a clear advantage in upper stretch, continued on the front into deep stretch but couldn't hold the winner safe. FRESH LOOK outrun for five furlongs after breaking slowly, closed steadily while saving ground on the turn, angled out a bit entering the stretch, rallied mildly to gain a share. CHEERFUL unhurried for six furlongs while four wide, failed to threaten while improving her position. TRI IRISH was never a factor. POCKET THE CASH never reached contention. THIRTY SIX GOLD sprinted clear in the early stages, maintained a clear lead for five furlongs, then gave way on the turn. ARTISTIC FIRE had no speed. LAKE JACQUELINE faded after going a half. SHE'S ALL CLASS up close early while saving ground, gave way after going six furlongs. DON'TLETANYONEKNOW, CHEERFUL, TRI IRISH and ARTISTIC FIRE wore mud caulks.

Owners— 1. Seaman Casey; 2. Casse Norman E; 3. Dichiaro Michael & My Jo Lee Stable; 4. Blaho Pavel; 5. Woodfield Stables; 6. Chevalier Stable; 7. West Point Thoroughbreds; 8. Schmidt Hilmer C; 9. Edition Farm; 10. Paraneck Stable

Trainers— 1. Velazquez Alfredo; 2. Levine Bruce N; 3. Miceli Michael; 4. Carroll Del W II; 5. Sciacca Gary; 6. Shapoff Stanley R; 7. Dowd John F; 8. Kimmel John C; 9. Daggett Michael H; 10. Ryerson James T

Corrected weight: Lady Tymatt (114) **Overweight:** Fresh Look (2), Thirty Six Gold (1).

Artistic Fire was claimed by R Kay Stable; trainer, Araya Rene A.

The scratches of Dance The Wind, Thirty Six Madison and Lucky Meridian reduced the field in the second race to nine:

2 Aqueduct

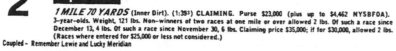

1 MILE 70 YARDS **(Inner Dirt). (1:393) CLAIMING. Purse $23,000 (plus up to $4,462 NYSBFOA). 3-year-olds. Weight, 121 lbs. Non-winners of two races at one mile or over allowed 2 lbs. Of such a race since December 13, 4 lbs. Of such a race since November 30, 6 lbs. Claiming price $35,000; if for $30,000, allowed 2 lbs. (Races where entered for $25,000 or less not considered.)**

Coupled - Remember Lewie and Lucky Meridian

Remember Lewie
Own: Rudina Stable
CHAVEZ J F (145 27 21 17 .19) $35,000
Dk. b or br g. 3 (Apr)
Sire: Golden Choice (Val de l'Orne)
Dam: Pococurante (Nain Bleu)
Br: Lucille Wakefield (Ont-C)
Tr: Meyer Jerome C (14 2 3 0 .14)
L 115

Lifetime Record: 7 2 0 1 $22,479
1995 7 2 0 1 $22,479 | Turf 0 0 0 0
1994 0 M 0 0 | Wet 0 0 0 0
Aqu 0 0 0 0 | Dist 4 2 0 0 $20,730

2Dec95- 7WO fr 1 1/16 :23 :463 1:104 1:42 ⓇKingarvie82k 35 8 10 96½ 1012 1024 1030½ Platts R L 115 b 41.90 73-05 Kristy Krunch1195½ Bartholomew Bandy1153¾ Barley Talk115no No mishap 10
24Nov95- 9WO fst 1 1/16 :24 :49 1:142 1:464 Clm 20000 65 4 1 11 12 14 19½ Landry R C L 113 b 4.55 79-21 Remember Lewie1139½ All Approved113hd Forrest G.1174¾ Much the best 8
25Oct95- 6WO fst 1 1/16 :231 :473 1:141 1:482 Clm 20000 46 2 7 48 72½ 64½ 56¾ Landry R C L 114 b 2.75 64-19 Silver Classic1195 Forrest G.1151 Affirmed Fling117nk Steadied far turn 8
18Oct95- 1WO fst 1 1/16 :232 :48 1:132 1:484 Md 11500 52 2 4 1hd 12 15 19½ Landry R C L 113 b *2.15 69-24 Remember Lewie1139½ Mr. Confidence1161½ DanceForBuck1116½ Drew off 6
22Sep95- 5WO fst 6f :221 :451 :582 1:13 Md 20000 24 6 8 911 1013 812 812 Montpellier C 115 b 10.90 67-19 Fun To Run1152½ Horseplay1151½ Chocolate Thundra1151 No factor 10
8Sep95- 5WO fst 7f :231 :464 1:123 1:251 Md 37500 25 8 8 86½ 77¾ 713 718½ Montpellier C 113 b 10.55 65-14 Intended Passage1162½ Reel Easy1162½ Prince Of Olympic115hd No factor 8
1Sep95- 3WO fst 6f :23 :474 1:011 1:151 Md 20000 34 5 8 65 43½ 34 33 Montpellier C 115 b 13.35 65-26 Rare Runner1202 Copy Cat1171 Remember Lewie1152 Late bid 8
WORKOUTS: Dec 31 Aqu 6f fst 1:173 B 1/2 Dec 28 Aqu 6f fst 1:18 Bg1/1 Dec 22 Aqu 7f fst 1:302 B 1/2 Dec 18 Aqu 6f fst 1:17 H 3/4 Nov 14 WO 5f my 1:021 H 8/21 Nov 4 WO 4f fst :493 B 10/18

Dance the Wind
Own: Ryan Daniel M
PEREZ R B (83 9 9 7 .11) $30,000
B. g. 3 (Feb)
Sire: Noble Nashua (Nashua)
Dam: Daisy Dancer (Dancing Count)
Br: Romando Emil Jr (NY)
Tr: Donk David (12 0 1 2 .00)
L 113

Lifetime Record: 7 1 0 1 $23,400
1995 7 1 0 1 $23,400 | Turf 0 0 0 0
1994 0 M 0 0 | Wet 3 0 0 0
Aqu 1 0 0 0 | Dist 0 0 0 0

15Dec95- 3Aqu my 6f :233 :471 :592 1:122 Clm 25000 37 3 5 64¾ 65½ 68 610¾ Perez R B L 114 b 17.10 70-17 Lucky Meridian1141 American Irish1162 Panama Jay1167¾ Outrun 6
3Nov95- 6Aqu sly 1 :224 :453 1:112 1:371 ⓈAlw 32000N1X 47 7 6 58 710 711 880 Perez R B 116 b 40.00 63-21 CurrncyArbitrg1168 Goodthingstocom114½ NorthrnShkr11411 No threat 8
4Oct95- 4Bel fst 1 :234 :481 1:144 1:412 ⓈMd Sp Wt 49 8 5 4¾ 1½ 1½ 12½ Perez R B 118 b 25.50 56-35 Dance The Wind1182½ How Goes118hd Killer Koupe1187½ Five wide, clear 9
28Sep95- 1Bel fst 1 :23 :47 1:124 1:39 Md 35000 35 9 7 83½ 75¾ 811 715½ Luzzi M J 117 b 16.20 52-29 Silent Intruder1141½ Harrowman1175 Panama Jay1171 Steadied 7/16 pl 11
21Aug95- 1Sar fst 7f :221 :453 1:114 1:252 ⓈMd Sp Wt 38 1 9 78¾ 712 711 518½ Perez R B 118 28.50 60-15 Procryptic1186 Out To Win1186 Tri Line1183 Saved ground 11
7Aug95- 2Sar fst 6f :232 :48 1:003 1:132 ⓈMd Sp Wt 32 8 4 3½ 32 36 311 Perez R B 118 11.80 63-19 I'llNotCmply1188 Iwllbkng1189 DncThWnd1184 Forced pace, weakened 9
24Jly95- 2Sar wf 5½f :222 :461 :584 1:054 ⓈMd Sp Wt 48 5 4 67½ 78½ 77¾ 67½ Perez R B 118 67.50 87-08 Severe Clear118nk Procryptic118nk Tropicool1183 Evenly 12
WORKOUTS: Dec 4 Bel tr.t 3f fst :364 B 7/14 Nov 28 Bel tr.t 3f fst :363 B 2/28 Nov 23 Bel tr.t 5f fst 1:024 B 2/8 Nov 18 Bel tr.t 5f fst 1:032 B 13/22 Nov 13 Bel tr.t 4f fst :484 B 8/22 Oct 30 Bel tr.t 4f fst :494 B 12/29

Glendi
Own: Kouray Athena C
TREJO J (64 7 6 8 .11) $35,000
Gr/ro g. 3 (Apr)
Sire: Fire Dancer (Northern Dancer)
Dam: Swift Delight (Restless Native)
Br: Reinhart Jacquelyn A (Fla)
Tr: Carroll Del W II (11 2 2 1 .18)
L 1087

Lifetime Record: 10 1 2 0 $14,980
1996 1 1 0 0 $6,600 | Turf 1 0 0 0
1995 9 M 2 0 $8,380 | Wet 2 0 1 0 $2,400
Aqu 2 1 1 0 $9,000 | Dist 1 0 0 0 $960

3Jan96- 3Aqu fst 6f :234 :48 1:01 1:142 Md 25000 53 5 8 811 87 52½ 1¾ Trejo J7 L 112 3.30 71-25 Glendi112¾ Justinthemiddle114nk Ernie The King1192½ Driving 8
6Dec95- 4Aqu wf 6f :232 :473 1:00 1:123 Md 30000 47 1 10 66 75½ 69½ 27½ Trejo J7 L 108 12.40 72-19 Rosa In Bloom1187½ Glendi108½ AppealingBandit1082½ Brk slow, in traffic 10
15Nov95- 3Aqu gd 1⅛ :464 1:124 1:401 1:542 Md 35000 5 9 5 49½ 54½ 826 839 Lovato F Jr L 116 b 14.20 29-28 Tom N' Kath11810 Erskine1147 Glowing Tru1182½ Gave way 9
4Nov95- 5Aqu wf 1 :23 :463 1:13 1:392 Md Sp Wt 38 8 4 53½ 63¾ 710 715 Lovato F Jr L 118 25.00 57-19 Mariner1183 Dothebucket1187 Beino Village1183 Wide trip 9
25Oct95- 2Bel fst 6½f :224 :46 1:111 1:18 Md 40000 46 6 8 109¾ 89½ 58½ 410½ Lovato F Jr L 116 29.75 74-13 Ima Good Gamble1187½ Grey Relic118½ Magna Carta1182½ Mild gain 11
16Oct95- 2Bel fst 1 :232 :471 1:123 1:391 Md 40000 52 7 6 55½ 44 44 46 Lovato F Jr L 115 9.50 61-30 Hrrowmn1183 JustCountOnM1141 Stlingrd1182 Checked, bumped break 9
9Oct95- 2Bel fst 7f :23 :464 1:131 1:264 Md 35000 55 7 9 64½ 64½ 23½ 22½ Lovato F Jr L 118 16.80 65-18 Magic Of Stars1152½ Glendi118hd Designer Prospect1184½ Finished well 11
20Sep95- 6Bel fst 1 1/16 :224 :461 1:113 1:433 Md Sp Wt 35 1 8 56 55 520 528¾ Luzzi M J 118 40.50 52-21 Blushing Jim11813 Lonsdale11810 Captain Charlie118¾ No threat 9
25Aug95- 6Sar fm 1 1/16 Ⓣ :23 :47 1:114 1:433 Md Sp Wt 53 2 9 85 64½ 64½ 97 Luzzi M J 118 44.75 74-07 Defacto118nk Bombardier1184 Dontanswerthefour118nk Checked early 11
17Aug95- 6Sar fst 6½f :23 :47 1:13 1:193 Md 45000 16 4 5 53½ 41¾ 77½ 721 Luzzi M J 118 9.10 56-17 Viktor1201 Nello B1153 Holmes1208 Bumped break 7
WORKOUTS: Dec 31 Bel tr.t 3f fst :372 B 18/30 Dec 24 Bel tr.t 4f fst :492 B 56/147 Dec 18 Bel tr.t 3f fst :392 B 32/38 Dec 3 Bel tr.t 3f fst :374 B 11/19 Nov 11 Bel tr.t 3f fst :372 B 8/23

Panama Jay
Own: Capecci B & Kupferberg S
PEZUA J M (104 17 17 18 .16) $30,000
Ch. g. 3 (Jan)
Sire: Badger Land (Codex)
Dam: Goodness Sakes (The Real McCoy)
Br: Forbush Richard J (Ky)
Tr: Margotta Anthony Jr (15 3 2 2 .20)
L 115

Lifetime Record: 7 1 0 2 $13,340
1995 7 1 0 2 $13,340 | Turf 1 0 0 0 $180
1994 0 M 0 0 | Wet 2 1 0 1 $9,890
Aqu 1 0 0 1 $2,090 | Dist 0 0 0 0

15Dec95- 3Aqu my 6f :233 :471 :592 1:122 Clm 25000 57 2 6 53½ 32 33½ 33 Velazquez J R L 116 b 3.00 78-17 Lucky Meridian1141 American Irish1162 Panama Jay1167¾ Even finish 6
1Dec95- 1Aqu my 1 :222 :442 1:093 1:374 Md 30000 56 6 5 56½ 45 31½ 11¾ Chavez J F L 115 b 11.00 80-12 Panama Jay1151¾ Crypto Duck115½ Ohsaykid1181½ Rallied wide 12
15Nov95- 3Aqu gd 1⅛ :464 1:124 1:401 1:542 Md 35000 35 1 3 59½ 43 414 420 Chavez J F L 116 b 4.60 48-28 Tom N' Kath11810 Erskine1147 Glowing Tru1182½ No rally 9
26Oct95- 7Med gd 170 Ⓣ :223 :474 1:133 1:441 Md Sp Wt 48 7 3 33 45 613 610 Marquez C H Jr L 118 7.60 60-31 Darn That Erica1184½ Belfour118½ Tanzia108½ Tired 11
9Oct95- 2Bel fst 7f :23 :464 1:131 1:264 Md 35000 46 10 4 53 31½ 33½ 47 Beckner D V L 118 *2.05 60-18 Magic Of Stars1152½ Glendi118hd Designer Prospect1184½ Four wide, tired 11
28Sep95- 1Bel fst 1 :23 :47 1:124 1:39 Md 35000 51 10 5 41½ 3½ 33½ 36¾ Beckner D V 117 4.40 61-29 Silent Intruder1141¾ Harrowman1175 Panama Jay1171 Stalked, no rally 11
26Aug95- 2Sar fst 6f :222 :46 :582 1:111 Md Sp Wt 20 10 1 68 910 916 824½ Beckner D V 119 117.00 56-16 Unbridled's Song1198½ Strangelove119½ Rage1195½ No response 10

Trading Genius
Own: Woodfield Stables
VELAZQUEZ J R (111 20 8 18 .18) $35,000
Ch. c. 3 (May)
Sire: Beau Genius (Bold Ruckus)
Dam: Just a Drizzle (Mickey McGuire)
Br: Penn Oscar & Vinery (Ky)
Tr: Sciacca Gary (43 1 4 3 .02)
115

Lifetime Record: 7 1 0 1 $13,280
1995 7 1 0 1 $13,280 | Turf 1 0 0 0
1994 0 M 0 0 | Wet 3 1 0 1 $12,200
Aqu 1 0 0 1 $3,080 | Dist 0 0 0 0

6Dec95- 3Aqu wf 6f :231 :463 :583 1:112 Clm 45000 42 4 7 713 610 514 316 Velazquez J R 112 b 22.30 70-19 NonstopOlivia1194 VonGroovey11912 TradingGenius1121 Steadied break 7
3Nov95- 3Aqu my 6f :224 :464 :591 1:121 Md 35000 69 8 6 55½ 42½ 33 1¾ Velazquez J R 116 b 4.90 81-20 Trading Genius116¾ Darn That Krissy1161½ Barlow1198¾ Rallied wide 9
25Oct95- 2Bel fst 6½f :224 :46 1:111 1:18 Md 40000 34 10 11 1115 1113 914 715¼ Smith M E 114 b 29.25 69-13 Ima Good Gamble1187½ Grey Relic116½ Magna Carta1182½ Checked brea 11
16Oct95- 2Bel fst 1 :232 :471 1:123 1:391 Md 50000 48 8 4 44 55 56 68½ Velazquez J R 118 b 5.40 59-30 Harrowman1183 Just Count On Me1141 Stalingrad1182 Gave way 9
27Sep95- 2Bel my 6½f :221 :454 1:114 1:181 Md 60000 54 10 1 87½ 78½ 67 46½ Chavez J F 118 b 15.50 78-19 Fenton Lane1161 Grey Relic1185 Tellerico's Fire118nk No threat 10
25Aug95- 6Sar fm 1 1/16 Ⓣ :23 :47 1:114 1:433 Md Sp Wt 54 5 10 107½ 96¾ 74½ 76½ Velazquez J R 118 b 10.50 74-07 Defacto118nk Bombardier1184 Dontanswerthefour118nk Saved ground 11
17Aug95- 6Sar fst 6½f :23 :47 1:13 1:193 Md 50000 36 5 6 78½ 78¾ 67 412 Velazquez J R 120 b 3.95e 65-17 Viktor1201 Nello B1153 Holmes1208 Checked, broke inward 7
WORKOUTS: Jan 12 Bel tr.t 3f fst :38 B 22/42 ●Jan 7 Bel tr.t 3f fst :373 B 1/22 Dec 30 Bel tr.t 4f fst :483 H 4/48 Dec 24 Bel tr.t 3f fst :372 B 25/50 Dec 18 Bel tr.t 3f fst :39 B 24/38 Nov 28 Bel tr.t 3f fst :38 B 17/28

Thirty Six Madison
Own: Lussier Frank P
MIGLIORE R (108 19 17 18 .18) $35,000
B. c. 3 (Mar)
Sire: Thirty Six Red (Slew o' Gold)
Dam: Northern Meeting (Lee Castelli)
Br: Brophy B Giles & Peregrine B[illegible] (Fla)
Tr: Domino Carl J (45 5 2 0 .33)
115

Lifetime Record:	0 M 0 0		$0					
1996	0 M 0 0		Turf	0	0	0	0	
1995	0 M 0 0		Wet	0	0	0	0	
Aqu ⊡	0 0 0 0		Dist	0	0	0	0	

WORKOUTS: Jan 11 Bel tr.t 3f fst :384 Bg 21/22 Dec 23 Bel tr.t 4f fst :50 Bg 27/37 Dec 7 Bel tr.t 5f fst 1:044 B 14/16 Dec 1 Bel tr.t 4f fst :524 B 41/43

Zordon
Own: Two Sisters Stable
CASTILLO H JR (95 9 12 11 .09) $35,000
Ch. c. 3 (Feb)
Sire: Master Derby (Dust Commander)
Dam: Millian (Temperence Hill)
Br: Hager David E II (Ky)
Tr: Pierce Joseph H Jr (21 1 2 1 .05)
115

Lifetime Record:	4 1 1 0	$9,860						
1995	4 1 1 0	$9,860	Turf	0	0	0	0	
1994	0 M 0 0		Wet	1	0	0	0	
Aqu ⊡	3 1 0 0	$7,860	Dist	1	1	0	0	$7,200

28Dec95- 1Aqu fst 1 1/16 ⊡ :23 :481 1:153 1:492	Md 25000	59 2 7 72¾ 41½ 21 1hd	Castillo H Jr	118	*3.10e	58-37	Zordon118hd Firestix1187½ Doctor Cool118no	Driving	11
22Dec95- 2Aqu fst 6f ⊡ :224 :464 :591 1:114	Md 25000	40 8 3 63½ 64½ 68¼ 48¼	Cordova D W	118	5.70	75-13	Glowing Tru1184¼ Mr. M. O.1183½ The Craigster118¾	Improved position	11
6Dec95- 4Aqu wf 6f ⊡ :232 :473 1:00 1:123	Md 35000	28 8 8 87 97¼ 913 815½	Chavez J F	118	*1.95	65-19	Rosa In Bloom1187½ Glendi108¾ Appealing Bandit1082¾	No threat	10
22Nov95- 7Med fst 6f :224 :462 :591 1:123	Md 25000	53 5 4 41¾ 43¾ 44½ 21¾	Ortiz F L	118	10.60	74-28	Northern Hawthorne1181¾ Zordon118¾ Woodbine Perk114no	Up for place	6

WORKOUTS: ●Dec 3 Med 3f fst :37 B 1/7 Nov 18 Med 4f fst :49 Bg 26/70 Nov 11 Med 5f fst 1:021 Bg 23/40 Nov 4 Med 5f gd 1:031 Bg 26/37 Oct 21 Med 4f gd :504 B 19/26

Jerobuck
Own: Biancolli Pam & Gullo Gina
CHAVEZ C R (83 6 13 8 .07) $30,000
Gr/ro c. 3 (Apr)
Sire: Jeblar (Alydar)
Dam: Erobuck (Silver Buck)
Br: Farnsworth Farms & Robins Gerald (Fla)
Tr: Gullo Gary P (14 0 3 1 .00)
L 108[5]

Lifetime Record:	11 2 2 2	$17,808						
1995	11 2 2 2	$17,808	Turf	0	0	0	0	
1994	0 M 0 0		Wet	3	0	2	0	$4,335
Aqu ⊡	1 0 0 0		Dist	1	0	0	0	

30Dec95- 6Aqu fst 1 1/16 ⊡ :234 :482 1:142 1:48	Alw 33000N1X	— 5 3 52½ 99¼ 936 —	Castillo H Jr	L 114 b	29.25	— 24	Criminal Suit1191 Magna Carta11313 Crypto Duck1131¾	Eased	9
14Dec95- 1Crc fst 1 :24 :481 1:14 1:423	Clm 25000	53 2 1 1hd 2hd 27 39	Boulanger G	115	6.50	65-23	All Alone1174¾ Mr. Chan1154¾ Jerobuck115nk	Used on pace	6
25Nov95- 1Crc fst 1 :243 :493 1:153 1:441	Clm 18000	56 3 1 1hd 1½ 1hd 1½	Boulanger G	113	5.60	66-30	Jerobuck113½ A MasterRun1152¼ Youmissedthepoint115no	3 wide, driving	6
4Nov95- 6Crc fst 1 :25 :504 1:161 1:422	Clm 16000	53 6 2 2½ 31½ 35 310	Madrid S O	115	*1.40	65-22	Lycurgus Kiah1155¾ Pallets1094¾ Jerobuck115nk	Weakened	7
17Oct95- 4Crc sly 1 :242 :49 1:142 1:42	Clm 25000	56 2 2 2hd 2hd 23 23	Madrid S O	115	3.70	74-23	All Alone1153 Jerobuck115no He's Wistlin Dixie115¾	Gamely	5
9Oct95- 3Crc fst 7f :231 :47 1:132 1:27	Md 20000	57 5 2 2hd 2hd 11½ 13½	Madrid S O	118	2.10	76-16	Jerobuck1183½ D. Gemini Jo1182½ Three B One1181	Ridden out	6
21Sep95- 3Crc fst 6f :221 :46 :584 1:124	Md 50000	12 5 3 31 46 721 726	Henry W T	117	16.40	57-18	Damien's Fantasy115nk Predicted Wildcat1177 Primasea1175¾		7

Drifted out top str, six wide, stopped

9Sep95- 6Crc wf 6f :22 :461 :592 1:131	Md Sp Wt	45 4 4 53 44½ 36 410¼	Henry W T	117	7.10	70-15	Valid Romeo1174¾ Primasea1171½ Recycled Code1175¾	Weakened	7
26Aug95- 3Crc sly 6f :222 :462 1:00 1:141	Md 40000	58 5 2 1hd 1hd 2hd 2nk	Henry W T	116	17.80	76-20	Noble Zipper111nk Jerobuck1166¾ FirstBuckToGo116nk	Yielded grudgingly	7
13Aug95-12Crc fst 7f :232 :47 1:131 1:264	Md Sp Wt	-0 4 10 1015 1025 1226 1232¼	Boulanger G	116	20.10	45-16	Termidator1165¾ Laughing Dan116nk Predicted Wildcat1161½	No factor	12

WORKOUTS: Dec 11 Crc 4f fst :50 B 10/22 Dec 5 Crc 5f sly 1:051 B 25/28 Nov 28 Crc 5f fst 1:031 B 15/28 Nov 12 Crc 4f gd :49 B 2/25 Nov 3 Crc 3f fst :39 B 25/26 Oct 25 Crc 4f fst :513 B 24/33

Torch Carrier
Own: Muckamal Steven
LUZZI M J (188 14 7 15 .13) $35,000
B. g. 3 (Apr)
Sire: Moment of Hope (Timeless Moment)
Dam: Content in Camelot (Key to Content)
Br: Holt Dana (Ky)
Tr: Labeccetta Frank (9 1 2 2 .11)
L 115

Lifetime Record:	5 1 0 0	$12,200						
1995	5 1 0 0	$12,200	Turf	0	0	0	0	
1994	0 M 0 0		Wet	2	0	0	0	$2,820
Aqu ⊡	3 0 0 0	$4,800	Dist	1	0	0	0	$1,980

30Dec95- 6Aqu fst 1 1/16 ⊡ :234 :482 1:142 1:48	Alw 33000N1X	55 8 4 3½ 41½ 310 415¾	Luzzi M J	L 114 b	13.60	49-24	Criminal Suit1191 Magna Carta11313 Crypto Duck1131¾	No factor	9
15Dec95- 3Aqu my 6f ⊡ :233 :471 :592 1:122	Clm c-25000	38 6 3 31 42¾ 46½ 410¾	Chavez J F	L 114 fb	*1.40	70-17	Lucky Meridian1141 American Irish1162 Panama Jay1167½	Even trip	6

Claimed from Hough Stanley M & Team Canonie Stb, Hough Stanley M Trainer

6Dec95- 3Aqu wf 6f ⊡ :231 :463 :583 1:112	Clm 45000	39 2 5 2½ 32 310 417	Santos J A	L 112 b	4.10	69-19	NonstopOlivi1194 VonGroovy11912 TrdingGnus1121	Bumped break, tired	7
23Nov95- 2Aqu fst 6½f :221 :453 1:111 1:182	Clm 50000	62 5 7 56 44 35 46¼	Pezua J M	L 110	3.40	82-13	NonstopOlivia1184 HighTerrce1152 Newsbreker114nk	Four wide, no rally	7
25Sep95- 2Bel fst 6f :223 :452 :584 1:12	Md 35000	66 1 10 62½ 31 1½ 1hd	Bailey J D	117 f	*.90	81-12	DH TrchCrrr117 DH H'yThrTSx1148¾ MAndMx114nk	Brk slow, checked 3/8	11

WORKOUTS: Dec 3 Bel tr.t 4f fst :482 H 3/66 Nov 11 Bel 5f fst 1:02 H 19/56 ●Oct 26 Bel 5f fst :594 H 1/17 Oct 20 Bel 4f fst :483 H 11/57

Crypto Duck
Own: Paraneck Stable
CORDOVA D W (98 10 11 15 .10) $35,000
B. c. 3 (Feb)
Sire: Cryptoclearance (Fappiano)
Dam: Pretendyouraduck (Quack)
Br: Robinson Lance K (Ky)
Tr: Aquilino Joseph (36 3 5 7 .08)
L 119

Lifetime Record:	11 1 1 1	$19,070						
1995	11 1 1 1	$19,070	Turf	1	0	0	0	
1994	0 M 0 0		Wet	2	0	1	0	$4,400
Aqu ⊡	2 1 0 1	$12,030	Dist	2	1	0	1	$12,030

30Dec95- 6Aqu fst 1 1/16 ⊡ :234 :482 1:142 1:48	Alw 33000N1X	58 3 7 75½ 65 410 314	Cordova D W	L 113 b	23.80	51-24	Criminal Suit1191 Magna Carta11313 Crypto Duck1131¾	Mild bid	9
14Dec95- 1Aqu fst 1 1/16 ⊡ :231 :472 1:14 1:482	Md 35000	65 1 5 59 47 2hd 1¾	Cordova D W	L 116 b	*1.10	63-28	Crypto Duck116¾ Salty 'n Sterling1132¼ Appealing Bandit1098	Driving	10
1Dec95- 1Aqu my 1 :222 :442 1:093 1:374	Md 30000	53 12 3 2½ 21½ 2½ 21¾	Cordova D W	L 115 b	23.20	78-12	Panama Jay1151¾ Crypto Duck115¾ Ohsaykid1181½	Sharp try	12
15Nov95- 3Aqu gd 1⅛ :464 1:124 1:401 1:542	Md 35000	18 2 6 613 77½ 723 630½	Chavez C R7	L 109 b	15.20	37-28	Tom N' Kath11810 Erskine1147 Glowing Tru1182½	No factor	9
2Nov95- 3Aqu sly 1⅛ :484 1:132 1:391 1:522	Md Sp Wt	53 3 3 3½ 21 411 413	Chavez C R7	L 111 b	25.75	65-28	Hail To The Lion1188 Lonsdale1184 Quite A Story1181	Chased, tired	7
9Oct95- 2Bel fst 7f :23 :464 1:131 1:264	Md 35000	42 11 8 1013 1011 89¾ 59	Chavez C R7	L 111 b	4.40e	58-18	MagicOfStars1152¼ Glendi118hd DesignerProspect1184¾	Improved position	11
28Sep95- 1Bel fst 1 :23 :47 1:124 1:39	Md 35000	49 11 8 73 41 45 47¾	Chavez C R7	L 110 b	14.60	60-29	SilentIntruder1141¾ Harrowman1175 PanamJy1171	Four wide, flattened	11
13Sep95- 2Bel fst 7f :23 :463 1:122 1:253	Md 35000	41 2 6 116¾ 109¾ 77½ 54¾	Chavez C R7	L 111 b	20.70	64-20	Tea Attack1181½ Lonsdale118¾ Justinthemiddle1185	Saved ground	13
28Aug95- 2Sar fm 1 1/16 Ⓣ :232 :481 1:13 1:432	Md Sp Wt	34 5 12 1110 1011 1013 1018	Martinez J R Jr	118	92.75	64-08	Jetting Robert118¾ Togher1183 Vibrations118nk	Pinched break, wide	12
19Aug95- 6Sar fst 7f :23 :464 1:122 1:254	Md Sp Wt	25 6 5 98 915 811 820¼	Rydowski S R	118	41.00	57-15	Head Minister1182 Chenlo118¾ Change Partners118nk	No speed	9

WORKOUTS: Nov 27 Aqu 3f fst :353 H 2/3 Oct 25 Aqu 5f fst 1:014 B 5/14

Silent Intruder
Own: Biamonte Ralph J
MADRID A JR (60 4 5 3 .07) $30,000
B. g. 3 (Mar)
Sire: Cryptoclearance (Fappiano)
Dam: Speak Lovingly (Speak John)
Br: Stolich Ronald & Tannenbaum Edward (Ky)
Tr: Rice Linda (11 0 1 0 .00)
113

Lifetime Record:	7 1 0 0	$11,550						
1995	7 1 0 0	$11,550	Turf	1	0	0	0	
1994	0 M 0 0		Wet	1	0	0	0	
Aqu ⊡	2 0 0 0	$990	Dist	2	0	0	0	$990

30Dec95- 6Aqu fst 1 1/16 ⊡ :234 :482 1:142 1:48	Alw 33000N1X	54 9 8 97¾ 87¾ 714 516	Madrid A Jr	114 b	41.00	49-24	Criminal Suit1191 Magna Carta11313 Crypto Duck1131¾	No factor	9
6Dec95- 3Aqu wf 6f ⊡ :231 :463 :583 1:112	Clm 50000	28 3 6 58½ 713 616 721½	Alvarado F T	114 b	19.60	65-19	Nonstop Olivia1194 VonGroovey11912 TradingGenius1121	Checked break	7
7Nov95- 3Aqu fst 7f :222 :451 1:104 1:241	Clm 40000	62 6 2 64½ 64½ 410 410¾	Alvarado F T	114	4.30	73-16	Barely Nothing1157 Nonstop Olivia1153 Tea Attack112nk	No speed	6
29Oct95- 4Bel sf 1 1/16 Ⓣ :251 :51 1:18 1:521	Alw 34000N1X	15 5 8 88¾ 710 626 632¾	Alvarado F T	113	52.50	— 58	Marlin11511 Courtney'smercedes112½ Termidator11211	Pinched break	8
12Oct95- 4Bel fst 1 1/16 :234 :472 1:12 1:444	Alw 34000N1X	51 1 3 53 67 69½ 615½	Luzzi M J	114	35.25	60-26	Gator Dancer1162½ Crafty Friend1144 Hey You Weasel116nk	Brief speed	6
28Sep95- 1Bel fst 1 :23 :47 1:124 1:39	Md 30000	63 5 6 62½ 52½ 1½ 11¾	Santos J A	114	5.40	68-29	SilentIntruder1141¾ Harrowman1175 PanamJy1171	Split rivals, drew off	11
13Sep95- 2Bel fst 7f :23 :463 1:122 1:253	Md 35000	39 1 13 63½ 74¾ 67 69½	Santos J A	118	5.60	63-20	TeaAttack1181½ Lonsdale118¾ Justinthemiddle1185	Broke slowly, rushed	13

WORKOUTS: Jan 11 Bel tr.t 4f fst :521 B 37/45 Dec 28 Bel tr.t 4f fst :51 B 15/21 Dec 19 Bel tr.t 4f gd :50 B 12/29 Dec 14 Bel tr.t 4f fst :49 B 26/52 Dec 4 Bel tr.t 3f fst :363 B 2/14 Nov 28 Bel tr.t 4f fst :494 B 9/42

Lucky Meridian
Own: Rudina Stable
BRAVO J (63 6 13 5 .08) $30,000

Dk. b or br c. 3 (Jan)
Sire: Gold Meridian (Seattle Slew)
Dam: Lucky a Go Go (Classic Go Go)
Br: DelValle Eric A (Fla)
Tr: Meyer Jerome C (14 2 3 0 .14)

L 113

Lifetime Record:	9	1	0	1	$15,923					
1995	9	1	0	1	$15,923	Turf	1	0	0	0
1994	0	M	0	0		Wet	2	1	0	0 $11,400
Aqu ⊡	1	1	0	0	$11,400	Dist	2	0	0	0 $1,320

15Dec95-3Aqu	my	6f	⊡ $:23^3$ $:47^1$ $:59^2$ $1{:}12^2$	Clm 25000	84 1 4 1^1 1^2 $1^{1\frac{1}{2}}$ 1^1	Santagata N	L 114 fb	31.50	81-17	Lucky Meridian114^1 American Irish116^2 Panama Jay$116^{7\frac{1}{2}}$	Driving 6
7Dec95-10Med	fst	6f	$:23$ $:47^2$ $1{:}00^2$ $1{:}14^2$	Md 22500	37 8 2 $3^{2\frac{1}{2}}$ 3^2 $2^{4\frac{1}{2}}$ 4^5	Velez J A Jr	L 116 fb	21.40	62-31	Zesty Zeal$118^{3\frac{1}{2}}$ Ultra Hi$118^{\frac{3}{4}}$ Cheeca Blue118^1	Even finish 8
26Nov95-1WO	gd	5f	$:22^4$ $:47^1$ $:59^3$	Md 20000	36 4 2 3^{nk} 3^1 2^4 $3^{11\frac{3}{4}}$	Callaghan S	L 120 fb	6.40	73-18	Taiwan115^{10} Executive Move$117^{1\frac{3}{4}}$ Lucky Meridian120^4	Early speed 6
16Nov95-2WO	sly	6f	$:22^3$ $:47^1$ $1{:}01$ $1{:}15^2$	Md 20000	33 7 4 $6^{5\frac{1}{2}}$ 5^5 $6^{7\frac{1}{2}}$ $7^{8\frac{1}{4}}$	Ramsammy E	L 120 fb	8.50	58-33	GrntMeAWin$114^{2\frac{1}{2}}$ SweetwterCounty$106^{1\frac{1}{2}}$ DoctorCool111^{no}	Mild bid turn 9
19Oct95-1WO	fst	7f	$:23^2$ $:47^1$ $1{:}14^2$ $1{:}28^2$	Md 20000	34 6 1 1^{hd} 1^1 2^{hd} $4^{2\frac{1}{2}}$	Willey K M	L 120 fb	5.65	64-23	Majestic Pass120^1 J. J.'s Ferdie115^{nk} Albera$115^{1\frac{1}{2}}$	Weakened late 6
11Oct95-2WO	fst	$1\frac{1}{16}$	$:24^1$ $:49^1$ $1{:}15^1$ $1{:}48^3$	Md 35000	28 6 4 3^1 $4^{\frac{3}{4}}$ 3^7 4^{17}	Callaghan S	L 116 fb	21.60	53-28	Slam Try120^2 Tuttodoro120^{15} Tackle That118^{hd}	Wide throughout 6
20Sep95-5WO	fst	$1\frac{1}{16}$	$:23^2$ $:48^3$ $1{:}15^2$ $1{:}49^3$	Md 30000	2 8 2 2^{hd} $5^{1\frac{1}{2}}$ 9^{15} $9^{25\frac{3}{4}}$	Ramsammy E	120 b	27.95	39-24	Justlikepunch$113^{5\frac{1}{2}}$ Tackle That$120^{\frac{1}{2}}$ Trinity Park117^5	Dueled, faded 9
9Sep95-5WO	fm	7f	ⓣ $:22^2$ $:45^3$ $1{:}10^3$ $1{:}23^3$	Md Sp Wt	28 1 5 $5^{2\frac{1}{2}}$ $8^{6\frac{1}{4}}$ 10^{10} $10^{20\frac{3}{4}}$	Bahen S R	120 b	61.90	76-04	Morangie115^{no} Red Shadow$120^{1\frac{1}{4}}$ Firm Dancer$115^{1\frac{1}{2}}$	Done early 10
4Sep95-7WO	fst	5f	$:22^3$ $:46^4$ $:59^4$	Md Sp Wt	11 9 9 9^{11} $9^{9\frac{3}{4}}$ 9^{16} $9^{14\frac{3}{4}}$	Luciani D	120 b	60.35	68-17	Polish Prediction$120^{\frac{1}{2}}$ Nicholia115^3 Regal Slipper$115^{2\frac{1}{2}}$	Trailed 9

WORKOUTS: Jan 10 Aqu ⊡ 6f fst $1{:}19^3$ B 2/4 Dec 31 Aqu ⊡ 6f fst $1{:}17^3$ B 1/2 Dec 5 WO 3f fst $:37^4$ B 2/2

1 — Remember Lewie — Woodbine shipper had been clobbered in a stakes in his last start, but won two of his three previous races by identical 9½-length margins: an $11,500 maiden claimer and a $20,000 claimer. Both victories were on the front end. He was nowhere near the lead in his five other starts. Major player.

2 — Glendi — He was one for nine on dirt, including a good second in a field of 11 at seven furlongs. He'd finished fifth in a maiden special weight, then fourth, seventh and eighth in maiden claimers in his four route tries. The last was three starts back at 1⅛ miles when blinkers were added. The blinkers were promptly removed, and Glendi responded with his best two races. In two six-furlong maiden claiming sprints at $30,000 and $25,000, he was second by 7½ lengths at 12-1, and, first by half a length, making up 11 lengths closing from eighth, at 3-1. He was stepping up and stretching out today, while dropping four pounds. Major player off the improved two races.

3 — Panama Jay — In the money three of six dirt starts, including a $30,000 maiden claiming win at a mile, and a good third in a $25,000 claiming sprint in his last two tries. Starting from his bottom PPs, we note that in his third start, a seven-furlong maiden claimer, he was fourth by seven lengths, beaten 4¾ lengths by Glendi. Subsequently, at 1⅛ miles, he beat Glendi by 19 lengths despite finishing fourth by 20 lengths. Major player.

4 — Trading Genius — Had a poor start when third by 16 lengths in a $45,000 claiming sprint in last. In his lone route try, a $50,000 maiden claimer at one mile, he was sixth by 8¼ lengths. No.

5 — Zordon — Won his route debut, a maiden $25,000 claimer, by a head. Stepping up today. Maybe.

6 — Jerobuck — Eased in an allowance try at 29-1 in last after success with cheaper claimers than these at Calder. Not off that last one, despite the drop.

7 — Torch Carrier — Exited the same race as Jerobuck when he was fourth by 15¾ lengths at 13-1. Beaten 7½ lengths by Panama Jay in a sprint the race before. No.

8 — Crypto Duck — Third by 14 lengths, beating Torch Carrier in last, after winning a $35,000 maiden claiming route. In the race before, he was second by 1¾ lengths to Panama Jay. Contender.

9 — Silent Intruder — Fifth by 16 lengths at 41-1 behind Crypto Duck and Torch Carrier in last. No thanks.

Conclusion? Panama Jay was the horse to beat, and Glendi was a horse who had beaten him, a point I noted to myself when I briefly thought of reversing my top two *Gazette* picks. I didn't, leaving Panama Jay as my top pick and Glendi second. I made Remember Lewie my third choice.

Why Glendi was not played at all, to win or in the double, amazed me. Remember Lewie, who had graduated by winning an $11,500 maiden claimer in Canada, was bet down to 3-2, and ran second. Panama Jay went off the second choice at 7-2 and was a soundly-beaten sixth. Glendi, who had graduated by winning a $25,000 maiden, and who had split two decisions with Panama Jay, won by six lengths at 28-1, paying $59 to win and producing a Daily Double worth $448.50.

SECOND RACE

Aqueduct

JANUARY 14, 1996

1 MILE 70 YARDS. (Inner Dirt)(1.39³) CLAIMING. Purse $23,000 (plus up to $4,462 NYSBFOA). 3-year-olds. Weight, 121 lbs. Non-winners of two races at one mile or over allowed 2 lbs. Of such a race since December 13, 4 lbs. Of such a race since November 30, 6 lbs. Claiming price $35,000; if for $30,000, allowed 2 lbs. (Races where entered for $25,000 or less not considered.)

Value of Race: $23,000 Winner $13,800; second $4,600; third $2,530; fourth $1,380; fifth $690. Mutuel Pool $160,212.00 Exacta Pool $264,951.00 Quinella Pool $57,410.00

Last Raced	Horse	M/Eqt. A.Wt	PP	St	¼	½	¾	Str	Fin	Jockey	Clg Pr	Odds $1
3Jan96 ³Aqu¹	Glendi	L 3 108	2	1	7³½	5²	4¹	1⁴	1⁶	Trejo J⁷	35000	28.50
2Dec95 ⁷WO¹⁰	Remember Lewie	Lb 3 115	1	3	1ʰᵈ	11½	1²	2²	2²	Chavez J F	35000	1.50
30Dec95 ⁶Aqu³	Crypto Duck	Lb 3 119	8	7	4¹½	4⁴	5⁸	3³	3²½	Cordova D W	35000	5.10
28Dec95 ¹Aqu¹	Zordon	3 115	5	5	8¼	7²	7²½	7¹²	4¼	Castillo H Jr	35000	24.50
6Dec95 ³Aqu³	Trading Genius	b 3 115	4	8	6½	6⁵	6³	6½	5⁵	Velazquez J R	35000	5.60
15Dec95 ³Aqu³	Panama Jay	Lb 3 115	3	2	2½	3⁴	3½	4¹½	6¹	Pezua J M	30000	3.80
30Dec95 ⁶Aqu⁴	Torch Carrier	Lb 3 115	7	6	3⁵	2½	2ʰᵈ	5½	7	Luzzi M J	35000	9.40
30Dec95 ⁶Aqu⁵	Silent Intruder	b 3 114	9	9	9	8³	8³⁰	8	—	Madrid A Jr	30000	24.50
30Dec95 ⁶Aqu⁹	Jerobuck	L 3 108	6	4	5²	9	9	—	—	Chavez C R⁵	30000	17.10

Silent Intruder:Eased; Jerobuck:Eased

OFF AT 12:56 Start Good. Won driving. Time, :24², :47⁴, 1:13³, 1:40², 1:45 Track sloppy.

$2 Mutuel Prices:	2-GLENDI	59.00	15.00	7.70
	1-REMEMBER LEWIE		4.00	2.80
	8-CRYPTO DUCK			3.30

$2 EXACTA 2-1 PAID $209.00 $2 QUINELLA 1-2 PAID $73.50

Gr/ro g, (Apr), by Fire Dancer-Swift Delight, by Restless Native. Trainer Carroll Del W II. Bred by Reinhart Jacquelyn A (Fla).

GLENDI unhurried for a half, rapidly gained while five wide on the turn, took charge in upper stretch, then drew off while being kept to the task. REMEMBER LEWIE set the pace along the inside into upper stretch and held well for the place. CRYPTO DUCK raced just off the pace while four wide to the turn and lacked a strong closing bid. ZORDON unhurried for six furlongs, failed to threaten while improving his position. TRADING GENIUS was pinched back at the start, raced just inside the winner for five furlongs, then lacked the needed response when called upon. PANAMA JAY dueled early between horses, faded after going six furlongs. TORCH CARRIER stalked three wide to the turn, then steadily tired thereafter. SILENT INTRUDER never reached contention and was eased late. JEROBUCK was finished early and eased in the stretch.

Owners— 1, Kouray Athena C; 2, Rudina Stable; 3, Paraneck Stable; 4, Two Sisters Stable; 5, Woodfield Stables; 6, Capecci B & Kupferberg S; 7, Muckamal Steven; 8, Biamonte Ralph J; 9, Bianculli Pam & Gulio Gina

Trainers— 1, Carroll Del W II; 2, Meyer Jerome C; 3, Aquilino Joseph; 4, Pierce Joseph H Jr; 5, Sciacca Gary; 6, Margotta Anthony Jr; 7, Laboccetta Frank; 8, Rice Linda; 9, Gullo Gary P

Overweight: Silent Intruder (1).

Crypto Duck was claimed by Garren Murray M; trainer, Martin Carlos F.

Scratched— Dance the Wind (15Dec95 ³AQU⁶), Thirty Six Madison, Lucky Meridian (15Dec95 ³AQU¹)

$2 Daily Double (10-2) Paid $448.50; Daily Double Pool $244,907.
Consolation Pick-3 (2/2-4-5-6-7-8-9-10/1-2-3-5-6-8-10) Paid $61.50; Pick-3 Pool $70,506.

8

Exactas

To box — or not to box?

Box. Box. And keep boxing.

Bettors who bet cold exactas without reversing the combination are just asking to get crushed, economically and emotionally.

Say you love the 2 horse, who is the favorite at 2-1. And you bet two cold $20 exactas with a couple of longshots, say the 3 horse at 4-1 and the 4 horse at 8-1. So if it comes in 2-3 or 2-4, you make a good hit.

But what happens, if — and this seems to happen a lot — it comes in 3-2 or 4-2, or even 3-4 or 4-3? You get nothing. Zilch. Despite the fact that you handicapped the race correctly.

Betting cold exactas is almost an act of arrogance. You're sure the 2 will win and the 3 or 4 will be second, but you won't even consider the possibility that you may be close to being right without betting it right?

There's no written law that says because you bet a $20 2-3 that you have to bet a $20 3-2 to cover yourself. Or that you have to split the bets and bet a $10 2-3 and $10 3-2. If you are intent on betting just $20 on that one exacta, take at least $2 of it and bet a

3-2 to cover yourself. If it comes in 2-3, you'll still have an $18 winning ticket. And if it comes in 3-2, you cash. That way, you don't feel like a moron if 3-2 comes in, and you also might get enough of a payoff to still produce a profit.

It's the same idea if you plan to bet $20 cold exactas of 2-3 and 2-4, an investment of $40. Bet a $2 3-2, a $2 4-2 and even a $2 3-4 and a $2 4-3 to complete the box. That still leaves you $16 cold exactas of 2-3 and 2-4, which will make you enough money if you're correct. Or slash the saver exactas in half and bet $1 exactas of 3-2, 4-2, 3-4 and 4-3 to cover yourself. That'll leave $18 cold exactas of 2-3 and 2-4, and not significantly cut into your immediate profit. In the long run, you will make money by catching some exotic overlays, even if they're modest ones.

Another point: if you are planning to play a $20 cold exacta without reversing it, using the 2 on top, and the 2 is the favorite, then fine. But if the 2 isn't the favorite, at least bet a small amount to win on the horse. Even $2 to win on an 8-1 shot eases the pain if your exacta bet loses. Don't completely waste being right on an 8-1 shot. They're too hard to find.

One last suggestion: if you're in a hole, don't chase a profit by betting cold exactas. You're better off betting a wheel and hoping for a longshot to finish second.

But you don't have to wheel horses to get exotic overlays in exactas, and the exotic overlays you do hit in exactas don't have to be mind-boggling to reinforce the idea that you did indeed make a smart bet with unexpectedly good value.

Three examples from Saratoga's 1995 meet follow.

The fourth race, July 30, was a non-winners of three (two other than maiden, claiming or starter) at six furlongs. A field of eight entered:

4 Saratoga

6 Furlongs (1:08) **ALLOWANCE. Purse $34,000. 3-year-olds and upward which have not won two races other than maiden, claiming or starter. Weights: 3-year-olds, 117 lbs. Older, 122 lbs. Non-winners of $21,000 twice in 1995, allowed 3 lbs. $18,000 twice since October 28, 6 lbs. $12,000 twice since April 7, 9 lbs. (Races where entered for $40,000 or less not considered in allowances.)**

6 FURLONGS

Taddarruj (GB)

Own: Shadwell Stable
CHAVEZ J F (48 7 9 1 .18)

B. c. 4
Sire: Gulch (Mr. Prospector)
Dam: Casual (Care*Ir)
Br: Crescent Ltd (GB)
Tr: Skiffington Thomas J (1 0 0 1 .00)

113

Lifetime Record: 12 2 0 1 $33,690

1995	1	0	0	0	$270	Turf	2	0	0	0
1994	9	2	0	1	$31,800	Wet	1	0	0	0
Sar	0	0	0	0		Dist	1	0	0	0

9Jan95-7GP fst 7f :221 :45 1:10 1:224 Alw 27000N2X 34 4 8 910 912 922 929 Krone J A L 119 14.30 60-09 Waldoboro119¾ Convince1221½ Cool Bandit1191½ 10

Broke inward start, no factor

23Nov94-6Aqu fst 6f :221 :461 :582 1:104 3+ Alw 32000N2X 64 7 5 74 73¾ 711 716¾ Smith M E 115 5.20 71-21 Thru 'n Thru115½ Catchin Air1157 Bull Inthe Heather1171 Outrun 7

28Oct94-6Aqu fst 1 :222 :443 1:094 1:353 3+ Alw 34000N2X 61 5 6 65½ 55½ 613 623 Krone J A 114 3.15 67-23 Cigar1178 Golden Plover1193½ Gulliviegold1092 Outrun 6

2Oct94-4Bel gd 7f :223 :453 1:102 1:231 3+ Alw 30000N1X 90 2 5 24 26 1½ 17¾ Krone J A 114 3.90 87-14 Taddarruj1147¾ Matthew Red Dog114nk Lulu's Little Boy114¾ Ridden out 6

8Sep94-6Bel fst 7f :223 :454 1:103 1:232 3+ Alw 30000N1X 84 6 11 106¼ 72 33 53¾ Krone J A 113 28.50 83-15 FiveStrGenerl1171 GoldstrRod114¾ Lightnin'Ct108¾ Wide, flattened out 11

6Aug94-8Sar yl 1 1/16 Ⓣ :234 :483 1:132 1:444 3+ Alw 30000N1X 57 8 10 128½ 126½ 118½ 1013½ Perret C 112 12.70e 57-24 Darby Stubbles112nk Henry S.114no Cadence Count117¾ Wide turn 12

19Jly94-7Bel fm 1 1/16 Ⓣ :234 :463 1:111 1:42 3+ Alw 30000N1X 60 7 6 56 42 77¾ 712¾ Perret C 112 20.70 76-11 DutchessFirst116¾ GrouchoGaucho117nk GallntGuest1116 Flattened out 10

21May94-9Bel fst 1 1/16 :224 :453 1:093 1:404 3+ Alw 30000N1X 50 2 1 21½ 32¾ 716 733 Maple E 112 11.10 65-12 Unaccounted For11514 Jo RanExpress1105 LordWollaston112nk Gave way 7

22Apr94-3Kee fst 1⅛ :474 1:14 1:42 1:562 Md Sp Wt 77 2 3 33 31 12 1½ Perret C 116 3.10 52-44 Taddarruj116½ Stylish Prospector1161 Texas Falls1162 Steady drive 11

22Mar94-4Hia fst 7f :23 :461 1:113 1:244 Md Sp Wt 65 6 11 74½ 63¾ 33½ 3¾ Maple E 122 5.80 84-13 Seattle Pioneer122nk Head Trip122½ Taddarruj1221½ 11

Seven wide top str, late rally

WORKOUTS: Jly 28 Sar tr.t 3f fst :362 H 2/17 Jly 23 Sar tr.t 4f fst :51 B 12/27 Jly 17 Bel 5f fst 1:033 B 20/22 Jly 12 Bel 3f fst :372 B 27/30 Jly 5 Bel 7f fst 1:294 B 1/1 Jun 28 Bel 5f fst 1:00 Hg 7/42

Placid Fund

Own: Rosenthal Mrs Morton
DAVIS R G (38 5 4 7 .13)

Ch. c. 3 (Mar)
Sire: Dixieland Band (Northern Dancer)
Dam: Sunset Strait (Naskra)
Br: Morton Rosenthal (Ky)
Tr: Schosberg Richard (7 3 0 1 .43)

111

Lifetime Record: 10 2 2 2 $53,860

1995	9	2	2	2	$53,860	Turf	2	0	0	1	$4,760
1994	1	M	0	0		Wet	2	0	1	1	$6,940
Sar	1	0	0	0		Dist	1	1	0	0	$19,200

9Jly95-7Bel fst 6f :222 :452 :574 1:094 3+ Alw 32000N1X 103 6 4 45½ 44½ 2½ 15 Davis R G 112 b 5.20 92-18 Placid Fund1125 Law Of The Sea1111¾ Judge Me Not111no Going away 7

31May95-6Bel fm 1 1/16 Ⓣ :223 :454 1:103 1:43 3+ Alw 34000N2L 82 8 3 33½ 31 32 53½ Davis R G 112 8.60 79-21 Kefalonians114no Navillus1132 Jelly Roll Jive112no No rally 10

20May95-9Bel gd 1 Ⓣ :222 :453 1:102 1:363 3+ Alw 34000N1X 84 1 4 51¾ 31½ 22 41 Luzzi M J 112 b 6.80 79-18 MarqueeStar110½ DKefalonians112nk GoneDancingAgin120nk Weakened 11

Placed third through disqualification.

11May95-8Bel my 7f :221 :443 1:093 1:214 3+ Alw 32000N1X 77 8 5 89½ 74½ 46 38 Smith M E 112 b 4.80 84-11 Flying Chevron1124 Viva Sabona1104 Placid Fund112¾ Four wide 8

27Apr95-4Aqu fst 1 :224 :453 1:104 1:361 Md Sp Wt 97 3 1 2hd 11 14 112¾ Davis R G 120 b 3.65 88-12 Placid Fund12012 Diplomacy120¾ Cozy Drive1203 Kept to task 8

8Apr95-3Aqu fst 1⅛ :47 1:12 1:393 1:54 Md Sp Wt 52 8 4 45 47 66½ 611 Madrid A Jr 120 b 2.90 59-22 Bob'sProspect120¾ PersonalMatter1201¾ CozyDrive1205 Four wide, tired 8

25Mar95-5Aqu fst 1 :234 :473 1:134 1:392 Md Sp Wt 83 10 1 2hd 1hd 2½ 2¾ Madrid A Jr 120 b 18.60 71-25 Treasure Cay120¾ Placid Fund1204¾ Classy Moment1204½ Dueled, gamely 11

26Feb95-3GP wf 7f :222 :454 1:112 1:244 Md 57500 69 9 2 5¾ 4½ 1hd 2¾ Davis R G 118 10.60 78-18 Quick Study120¾ Placid Fund1183 Brave Warrior1203¾ 10

Brushed leaving bkstr, second best

12Feb95-3GP fst 7f :224 :462 1:113 1:252 Md 50000 56 9 11 106½ 99¾ 77½ 57¾ Davis R G 120 12.80 68-20 Dancing Lad1203 Traveling Jeff1201 Tonya's Dancer1201½ Mild bid 11

11Aug94-3Sar fst 5f :224 :462 :59 Md Sp Wt 38 1 1 79½ 86½ 76½ 611¼ Luzzi M J 118 23.40 77-14 Magical Call118no Mountain Of Laws1184 Hopkins Forest1182¾ No threat 8

WORKOUTS: Jly 25 Sar 4f fst :491 B 17/43 Jun 28 Bel tr.t 4f fst :491 B 12/37 Jun 21 Bel tr.t 4f fst :511 B 10/18 May 7 Bel tr.t 4f fst :49 B 3/13

Ghostly Moves

Own: Evans Edward P
SANTOS J A (35 1 7 4 .03)

Gr. c. 3 (May)
Sire: Silver Ghost (Mr. Prospector)
Dam: Dance Teacher (Smarten)
Br: Evans Edward P (Va)
Tr: Hennig Mark (11 1 2 3 .09)

111

Lifetime Record: 7 2 2 2 $43,705

1995	5	1	2	1	$33,165	Turf	0	0	0	0	
1994	2	1	0	1	$10,540	Wet	0	0	0	0	
Sar	0	0	0	0		Dist	2	0	1	0	$6,420

23Jun95-5CD fst 1 1/16 :231 :46 1:103 1:421 3+ Alw 40380N2X 96 5 3 45½ 21 1hd 21½ Barton D M L 106 3.70 101-12 TenntsHrbor1141½ GhostlyMoves1062 Convinc1135 Bid, led, second best 8

29May95-8CD fst 6½f :221 :451 1:101 1:163 3+ Alw 38820N2X 92 4 4 43 21 2½ 32½ Hebert T J 109 *.90 93-08 Gold Groovy115no Red Mcfly1152½ Ghostly Moves1092½ Came up empty 8

6May95-1CD fst 6½f :23 :454 1:094 1:16 Alw 30600N2L 95 1 2 31 41½ 11½ 11½ Stevens G L 115 *2.00 99 — Ghostly Moves1151½ Kelly Time1211 Count The Blues121nk Hand urging 12

14Apr95-4Kee fst 6f :211 :442 :561 1:081 Alw 33950N2L 84 9 6 43½ 31 33 53½ Bailey J D 115 1.40 88-10 Muhtafal1215 Butter You Up1211½ Hobgoblin1181½ Bid, tired 9

16Mar95-8GP fst 6f :214 :434 :563 1:102 Alw 31000N2L 91 10 2 31 2hd 2hd 2nk Bailey J D 122 8.40 88-14 Jealous Crusader122nk Ghostly Moves122½ Dodge City1223½ 12

Seven wide top str, just missed

24Jly94-5Lrl fst 5½f :223 :461 :582 1:05 Md Sp Wt 80 1 2 11 11½ 13 15¾ Pino M G 120 *2.20 96-11 Ghostly Moves1205¾ Premier Punch1202¾ Western Echo1201¾ Driving 11

28Jun94-7Lrl fst 5f :224 :464 :592 Md Sp Wt 52 8 10 1013 1014 69 33½ Skinner K 120 20.10 88-14 Skehanagh120nk Lucky Trend1203½ Ghostly Moves1201¾ Stumbled start 11

WORKOUTS: Jly 24 Sar 4f gd :502 B 17/23 Jly 16 Sar 5f fst 1:03 B 3/8 Jly 8 CD 3f fst :372 B 4/9 Jun 14 CD 4f fst :484 B 3/37 May 21 CD 5f fst 1:023 B 23/47 ●Apr 30 CD 4f fst :482 H 1/35

Gilder

Own: Pitfield Ward C
LOVATO F JR (3 0 2 0 .00)

B. g. 4
Sire: Smile (In Reality)
Dam: Rythmical (Fappiano)
Br: Genter F A Stable Inc (Ky)
Tr: Hauswald Philip M (—)

113

Lifetime Record: 3 2 1 0 $45,948

1994	2	1	1	0	$29,425	Turf	0	0	0	0	
1993	1	1	0	0	$16,523	Wet	1	1	0	0	$23,205
Sar	0	0	0	0		Dist	1	1	0	0	$23,205

9Nov94-6CD sly 6f :213 :453 :571 1:111 3+ Alw 33300N1X 103 9 5 6½ 21 2½ 11½ Day P L 112 2.60 90-17 Gilder1121½ Wheelin Dealin1144½ Shelby Mist113½ Inside, driving 11

29May94-7CD fst 6½f :221 :454 1:103 1:17 Alw 30400N2L 85 7 8 75 52½ 44½ 23½ Johnson P A 121 3.80 90-11 Goldseeker Bud1213½ Gilder121nk Mutuality1184 Fully extended 10

11Nov93-6CD fst 7f :224 :463 1:123 1:253 Md Sp Wt 79 3 5 1½ 11 12 16 Stacy A T 121 6.20 82-13 Gilder1216 Eccentric1212½ Babylouka121no Ridden out 12

WORKOUTS: Jly 28 Sar tr.t 3f fst :364 H 3/17 Jly 21 Sar tr.t 4f fst :511 B 13/21 Jly 9 CD 5f fst 1:031 B 9/13 Jly 4 CD 4f fst :493 B 16/20 Jun 25 CD 5f fst 1:043 B 32/36 Jun 17 CD 4f fst :49 B 11/47

Stock Power

Own: Farish W S & Webber Temple Jr
SMITH M E (51 3 7 10 .06)

B. c. 3 (Feb)
Sire: Seeking the Gold (Mr. Prospector)
Dam: Under Oath (Deputed Testamony)
Br: Farish W S (Ky)
Tr: Howard Neil J (4 1 0 0 .25)

108

Lifetime Record: 3 2 0 0 $23,705

1995	1	1	0	0	$12,000	Turf	0	0	0	0	
1994	2	1	0	0	$11,705	Wet	0	0	0	0	
Sar	0	0	0	0		Dist	2	1	0	0	$13,505

3Jly95-6AP fst 6f :222 :454 :582 1:113 Alw 20000N1X 93 6 7 43½ 21½ 21½ 13½ Day P 116 2.30 86-19 Stock Power1163½ Daring David1161¾ Proper Texan1161½ Ridden out, wide 9

17Dec94-6Crc fst 7f :222 :462 1:123 1:253 Md Sp Wt 82 9 2 32 1hd 12 13¾ Ramos W S 120 *1.20 84-17 Stock Power1203¾ Native Tribe120¾ Outta My Way Man120no Ridden out 11

18Nov94-5CD fst 6f :213 :454 :581 1:112 Md Sp Wt 73 5 7 33 42 45½ 45½ Woods C R Jr 121 6.60 83-14 G H's Pleasure121½ Prory1213 Ziploose1212 No late response 12

WORKOUTS: Jly 25 Sar 5f fst 1:023 B 17/28 Jly 19 Sar 3f fst :361 H 4/7 Jly 13 CD 4f fst :484 B 3/21 Jun 30 AP 4f fst :472 Hg 2/65 ●Jun 25 AP 6f fst 1:13 H 1/7 Jun 19 AP 5f fst 1:01 H 4/26

Fort Edward

Own: Brida Dennis J
MIGLIORE R (16 3 1 2 .19)

B. g. 4
Sire: Marl's Book (Northern Dancer)
Dam: Reine Doree (Medaille d'Or)
Br: Coleman Lise Anne (NY)
Tr: Brida Dennis J (4 0 1 1 .00)

113

Lifetime Record: 5 2 0 2 $43,260

1995	5	2	0	2	$43,260	Turf	1	0	0	0	
1994	0	M	0	0		Wet	1	1	0	0	$19,200
Sar	1	0	0	1	$3,960	Dist	2	2	0	0	$36,000

22Jly95-7Sar fst 7f :223 :452 1:094 1:223 3+ Alw 36000N$Y 91 6 3 62¾ 32½ 21½ 31¾ Migliore R 119 b 31.50 91-07 Top Account117¾ Yeckley1151 Fort Edward1193 Wide, flattened out 7

16Jun95-7Bel fm 1 Ⓣ :223 :451 1:102 1:344 3+ ⓈAlw 36000N2X 63 2 8 67½ 63½ 79½ 711¾ Migliore R 120 b 5.00 77-12 Silver Safari1203 FearlessAndFree1121 RightForward120½ Broke slowly 9

27May95-5Bel wf 6f :223 :454 :58 1:104 3+ ⓈAlw 32000N1X 78 4 9 32 2½ 11 1nk Santos J A 119 b 2.30 87-09 Fort Edward119nk Wee Laddie1192½ Sea Raven1121½ Broke slowly, all out 9

15Apr95-4Aqu fst 7f :23 :462 1:114 1:251 Alw 30000N1X 70 3 8 910 87 53½ 31½ Samyn J L 119 10.80 76-17 Framed In Gold1151½ Lulu's LittleBoy114nk FortEdward1191½ Belated rally 10

26Mar95-5Aqu fst 6f :23 :471 :594 1:13 Md Sp Wt 64 8 8 41¾ 2hd 1hd 1¾ Samyn J L 122 4.80 77-17 Fort Edward122¾ Frisco Gold1223¾ Lovubaby12213 Checked break, wide 8

WORKOUTS: Jly 19 Sar 3f fst :374 B 6/7 Jly 14 Bel 4f fst :50 B 22/39 Jly 7 Bel 4f fst :50 B 33/47 Jun 15 Bel tr.t 3f fst :373 B 4/15 ●May 21 Bel tr.t 4f fst :472 H 1/39 May 13 Bel tr.t 3f fst :372 B 11/18

Bid Baby
Own: Sahn Robert I
BAILEY J D (42 11 1 8 .26)

B. g. 3 (Feb)
Sire: Loustrous Bid (Illustrious)
Dam: Barking Baby (Avatar)
Br: Paxson Mrs Henry D (NY)
Tr: Levine Bruce N (7 0 0 0 .00)

111

Lifetime Record:	4 2 2 0	$48,160			
1995	1 1 0 0	$19,200	Turf	0 0 0 0	
1994	3 1 2 0	$28,960	Wet	0 0 0 0	
Sar	0 0 0 0		Dist	4 2 2 0	$48,160

9Jly95-4Bel fst 6f :22^3 :46 :58 1:10^2 3+ Alw 32000N1X 94 5 5 1½ 1hd 1^{1½} 1^1 Luzzi M J 112 *1.00 89-18 Bid Baby112^1 Mountain Of Laws113^{2¼} Hearts Of Home113^8 Dueled, clear 8
29Dec94-7Aqu fst 6f ⊡ :23^1 :48 1:01 1:13^4 Alw 30000N1X 82 3 4 1^{1½} 1^{2½} 1^1 2½ Luzzi M J 122 *.80 73-29 Churka112½ Bid Baby122^5 Gin On Land117^{3½} Second best 5
8Dec94-3Aqu fst 6f ⊡ :22^3 :46^3 :59 1:11^4 Md Sp Wt 85 8 1 1½ 1½ 1^3 1^{5½} Luzzi M J 118 *.25 84-18 Bid Baby118^{5½} Screen Oscar118½ Guadalcanal118^{2¾} Mild drive 8
17Nov94-5Aqu fst 6f :22^3 :46^2 :58^1 1:10 Md Sp Wt 91 6 2 1^2 2hd 2^1 2^{3½} Bailey J D 118 6.30 88-16 Cryptic Bid118^{3½} Bid Baby118^3 Trailblazer118^2 Second best 7
WORKOUTS: ● Jly 21 Sar 4f fst :46^3 H 1/50 Jly 4 Aqu 6f fst 1:13^2 H 1/2 Jun 28 Aqu 5f gd 1:00^1 H 3/7 Jun 20 Aqu 5f fst 1:00^1 H 1/2 ● Jun 15 Aqu 4f fst :47^3 H 1/13 Jun 10 Aqu 4f fst :48^3 H 3/11

Goodbye Doeny
Own: Valande Elizabeth J
KRONE J A (35 1 10 2 .03)

B. c. 4
Sire: Storm Cat (Storm Bird)
Dam: Evangelic (Halo)
Br: Hancock A B III & Overbrook Farm (Ky)
Tr: Schulhofer Flint S (11 1 1 2 .09)

113

Lifetime Record:	12 2 4 0	$87,030			
1994	5 0 1 0	$8,340	Turf	1 0 0 0	
1993	7 2 3 0	$78,690	Wet	0 0 0 0	
Sar	3 1 0 0	$14,100	Dist	2 0 1 0	$6,160

11Aug94-6Sar fst 7f :22^3 :45^2 1:10 1:23^1 3+ Alw 30000N2X 59 2 5 5^{2½} 7^{6¾} 8^{7¾} 8^{20} Krone J A 112 7.70 69-14 Prenup117^{1¾} Golden Larch112^{2½} Malmo112^4 Outrun 8
29Jun94-7Bel fst 7f :23 :45^4 1:10^1 1:23 3+ Alw 30000N2X 92 6 3 3^1 2^1 2hd 2^{2½} Krone J A 111 11.60 85-16 Famous Fan122^{2½} Goodbye Doeny111^{1¾} Not For Love119^4 Bid, weakened 6
9Jun94-6Bel fm 1$\frac{1}{16}$ ⓣ :23 :46 1:09 1:39^4 3+ Alw 32000N2X 41 8 8 8^5 10^{8½} 10^{14} 10^{28} Krone J A 111 17.90 71-07 Lahint113^5 Pennine Ridge112no Warm Wayne112^{2½} Outrun 10
22Apr94-8Aqu fst 7f :22^4 :46^1 1:11^2 1:24^2 Alw 29000N2X 58 3 6 3^{1½} 3^3 5^5 5^{12½} Santos J A 117 2.30 69-17 Mccullough110^{3½} Southern Claim117nk N Dever117^4 Gave way 6
1Apr94-7Aqu fst 6½f :22^1 :45^1 1:09^4 1:16^2 Alw 29000N2X 68 2 3 2^{2½} 2^2 3^{7½} 4^{14} Santos J A 117 2.40 85-16 Jericho Blaise117^7 Gold Tower117½ Memories Of Linda117^{6½} Tired 5
27Nov93-8CD fst 1$\frac{1}{16}$:23^4 :48 1:13^2 1:46^3 BW Ky JC-G3 74 10 5 3^{1½} 4^4 6^{5¾} 8^{9½} Martinez W 113 4.20 72-22 War Deputy112^{2½} Tarzans Blade122nk Rustic Light119^{1½} Tired 11
24Oct93-8Kee fst 1$\frac{1}{16}$:23^2 :47^2 1:11^1 1:42^1 Brdrs Fty-G2 87 5 2 2^1 2^1 2^{1½} 2^5 Bailey J D 121 5.00 93-17 Polar Expedition121^5 Goodbye Doeny121^2 Solly's Honor121^1 8
Came in, bumped start, 2nd best
10Oct93-4Kee fst *7f :22^4 :45^3 1:11^3 1:25^1 Alw 22320N2L 76 4 5 3½ 3^1 1hd 1^{1½} Bailey J D 118 3.80 98-05 Goodbye Doeny118^{1½} Ocean Crest121½ Turkomatic118^5 Steady drive 10
25Sep93-7Bel fst 6f :22^3 :46^1 :58^2 1:11^1 Alw 28000N1X 77 3 3 2½ 2hd 2½ 2^5 Santos J A 117 1.90 79-19 Crary117^5 Goodbye Doeny117^6 Mobile117nk No match 5
2Sep93-7Bel fst 6½f :22 :44^1 1:09^4 1:17 Alw 28000N2X 75 1 6 3^{1½} 3^3 3^3 2^7 Santos J A 117 5.60 81-15 Holy Bull119^7 Goodbye Doeny117^3 End Sweep119½ Up for place 6
WORKOUTS: Jly 25 Sar 4f fst :48 B 2/43 Jly 20 Sar 3f fst :38^2 B 10/11 Jly 12 Bel 4f fst :47^2 H 3/60 Jly 6 Bel 4f fst :48^2 H 8/30

1 — Taddarruj — Off since January 9, when he was ninth by 29 lengths at 14-1 at Gulfstream. Next.

2 — Placid Fund — His entire 10-race career was contained in his PPs today. Though he lost his lone start as a two-year-old at Saratoga, he'd progressed nicely as a three-year-old. Discarding two fair turf tries, he had two wins, two seconds and a third out of his last six dirt races, the only bad one at 1⅛ miles. In his last start at Belmont, he'd won a non-winners of two by five lengths in a fast 1:09⅘. He was moving up today, but was an obvious contender.

3 — Ghostly Moves — In the money six of seven lifetime, he was cutting back to a sprint off a good second at Churchill Downs with Lasix added. Without Lasix the race before there, he was third by 2½ lengths at 9-10 in a 6½-furlong sprint. Contender.

4 — Gilder — Our turf horse to be was making his first start since November and was apt to need a race back. Pass.

5 — Stock Power — He won his '95 six-furlong debut at Arlington Park, a non-winners of two, by 3¼ lengths at 2-1, and was dropping eight pounds. Contender.

6 — Fort Edward — Toss out his turf try and he had two wins and two thirds in four starts, including a strong third in his last at Saratoga in a fast seven-furlong sprint. Contender.

7 — Bid Baby — This speedster smacked of quality. He was

second in his two-year-old debut to the very good Cryptic Bid; won his maiden by 5½ lengths at 1-5, and ran second by half a length at 4-5 in three starts as a two-year-old, all at six furlongs. In his '95 debut at Belmont Park, July 9, he won a six furlong non-winners of two by a length at even money in a solid 1:10²/₅. He followed that by working a bullet four furlongs in :46³/₅, the best of 50 workouts that day at this distance. The obvious one to beat in a race lacking early speed. In fact, out of the other horses' combined 47 PPs, there were only two where a horse led after the first call.

8 — Goodbye Doeny — Idle nearly a year since finishing eighth by 20 lengths in a seven-furlong allowance race at Saratoga. No way off the layoff.

Conclusion? Bid Baby was an easy pick in the *Gazette*. He went off a slight favorite over Ghost Moves, both at 5-2. They finished 1-2. The exacta with the two favorites in order in a field of eight? $31.60.

FOURTH RACE

Saratoga
JULY 30, 1995

6 FURLONGS. (1.08) ALLOWANCE. Purse $34,000. 3-year-olds and upward which have not won two races other than maiden, claiming or starter. Weights: 3-year-olds, 117 lbs. Older, 122 lbs. Non-winners of $21,000 twice in 1995, allowed 3 lbs. $18,000 twice since October 28, 6 lbs. $12,000 twice since April 7, 9 lbs. (Races where entered for $40,000 or less not considered in allowances.)

Value of Race: $34,000 Winner $20,400; second $6,800; third $3,740; fourth $2,040; fifth $1,020. Mutuel Pool $476,107.00 Exacta Pool $601,287.00 Quinella Pool $124,463.00

Last Raced	Horse	M/Eqt. A.Wt	PP	St	¼	½	Str	Fin	Jockey	Odds $1
9Jly95 4Bel1	Bid Baby	3 112	7	1	2²	1¹	1²	1¹	Bailey J D	2.65
23Jun95 5CD2	Ghostly Moves	3 112	3	8	6hd	4hd	3¹	2¹	Santos J A	2.95
22Jly95 7Sar3	Fort Edward	b 4 114	6	6	4¹	2½	2½	3²	Migliore R	6.80
3Jly95 6AP1	Stock Power	3 113	5	7	8	3½	4²	4²½	Smith M E	5.30
9Jly95 7Bel1	Placid Fund	b 3 112	2	5	5¹	8	5½	5⁵	Davis R G	3.80
9Nov94 6CD1	Gilder	4 114	4	3	3hd	6hd	6¹	6¼	Lovato F Jr	8.00
11Aug94 6Sar8	Goodbye Doeny	4 113	8	4	7²	5¹	7⁴	7¹⁰	Krone J A	35.00
9Jan95 7GP9	Taddarruj-GB	4 113	1	2	1hd	7¹½	8	8	Chavez J F	40.00

OFF AT 2:35 Start Good. Won driving. Time, :22, :45², :57², 1:10 Track fast.

$2 Mutuel Prices:

7–BID BABY	7.30	4.00	3.10
3–GHOSTLY MOVES		4.00	3.00
6–FORT EDWARD			3.60

$2 EXACTA 7-3 PAID $31.60 $2 QUINELLA 3-7 PAID $15.20

B. c, (Feb), by Loustrous Bid–Barking Baby, by Avatar. Trainer Levine Bruce N. Bred by Paxson Mrs Henry D (NY).

BID BABY dueled for the early leader from outside, shook off TADDARRUJ to get clear on the turn, extended his lead in upper stretch, then turned back GHOSTLY MOVES under brisk urging. GHOSTLY MOVES reserved early, steadily gained between horses on the turn, then finished with good energy for the place. FORT EDWARD never far back, made a run outside the winner to threaten at the top of the stretch, but couldn't sustain his bid. STOCK POWER checked at the start, trailed along the backstretch, circled five wide leaving the turn, made a run to reach contention in upper stretch then finished evenly. PLACID FUND raced just off the early pace, steadied along the inside while lacking room through the turn and failed to threaten thereafter. GILDER settled just behind the dueling leaders while slightly off the rail, dropped back on the turn, then lacked the needed response when called upon. GOODBYE DOENY lodged a mild rally between horses while four wide on the turn and flattened out. TADDARRUJ was used up battling for the early lead.

Owners— 1, Sahn Robert I; 2, Evans Edward P; 3, Brida Dennis J; 4, Farish W S & Webber Temple Jr; 5, Rosenthal Mrs Morton; 6, Pitfield Ward C; 7, Valando Elizabeth; 8, Shadwell Stable

Trainers—1, Levine Bruce N; 2, Hennig Mark; 3, Brida Dennis J; 4, Howard Neil J; 5, Schosberg Richard; 6, Hauswald Philip M; 7, Schulhofer Flint S; 8, Skiffington Thomas J

Overweight: Bid Baby (1), Ghostly Moves (1), Fort Edward (1), Stock Power (5), Placid Fund (1), Gilder (1).

The fifth race at Saratoga, August 3, was a $25,000 claimer for three-year-olds and up at seven furlongs. A field of 12, minus the scratch of Glenfiddich Lad, went to post:

5 Saratoga

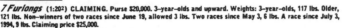

7 Furlongs (1:20²) CLAIMING. Purse $20,000. 3-year-olds and upward. Weights: 3-year-olds, 117 lbs. Older, 121 lbs. Non-winners of two races since June 19, allowed 3 lbs. Two races since May 3, 6 lbs. A race since July 3, 1994, 9 lbs. Claiming price $25,000.

Maastricht Accord
Own: Goose Creek Farm
ALVARADO F T (17 2 11 .12) $25,000
Dk. b or br h. 5
Sire: D'Accord (Secretariat)
Dam: Sky Contessa (Cutlass)
Br: Melhado E Noel Harwerth (NY)
Tr: Kimmel John C (12 1 3 3 .00)
112

Lifetime Record: 18 3 2 4 $72,560
1995 4 1 0 1 $25,780 Turf 1 0 0 0
1994 9 0 2 2 $14,200 Wet 3 1 1 0 $29,080
Sar 3 0 0 0 Dist 5 0 0 1 $1,740

I'm No Quacker
Own: Terranova John P II
BECKNER D V (24 0 3 1 .00) $25,000
Dk. b or br g. 7
Sire: Irish Tower (Irish Castle)
Dam: Quick Quack (Quack)
Br: Sabarese Theodore M (Fla)
Tr: Terranova John P II (1 0 0 0 .00)
112

Lifetime Record: 34 5 2 6 $108,805
1995 3 1 0 0 $9,600 Turf 1 0 0 0
1994 13 2 0 2 $36,000 Wet 5 0 0 0 $3,330
Sar 4 0 1 0 $8,090 Dist 6 0 1 3 $18,280

Come On Talc
Own: Zablewitz Karen S
LUZZI M J (38 3 0 2 .08) $25,000
Dk. b or br c. 4
Sire: Talc (Rock Talk)
Dam: Come On Miss Jay (Noble Jay)
Br: Middle Creek Farm (NY)
Tr: Parisella John (6 0 0 1 .00)
112

Lifetime Record: 10 3 0 1 $63,960
1995 7 1 0 1 $27,960 Turf 0 0 0 0
1994 3 2 0 0 $36,000 Wet 1 0 0 0 $1,800
Sar 0 0 0 0 Dist 3 0 0 0

Lightning Surge
Own: Beecher Aaron
RYDOWSKI S R (10 1 1 1 .10) $25,000
Dk. b or br c. 4
Sire: Fortunate Prospect (Northern Prospect)
Dam: Try to Be a Lady (Sham)
Br: Lematta Andrea (Fla)
Tr: Gullo Gary P (4 1 0 0 .25)
112

Lifetime Record: 23 3 4 4 $37,230
1995 10 1 1 1 $8,380 Turf 0 0 0 0
1994 11 2 3 3 $27,790 Wet 2 0 0 0
Sar 1 0 0 0 Dist 3 0 0 0 $320

Maraud
Own: G Lack Farms
MIGLIORE R (24 3 2 4 .13) $25,000
Ch. h. 6
Sire: Sunny's Halo (Halo)
Dam: Alpha Flight (Oxford Flight)
Br: Wolff A Don (WV)
Tr: Klesaris Robert P (4 0 1 0 .00)
118

Lifetime Record: 49 12 3 14 $176,601											
1995	5	3	0	0	$21,630	Turf	1	0	0	0	$350
1994	15	4	2	5	$65,320	Wet	6	1	0	1	$17,311
Sar	4	0	2	2	$13,370	Dist	8	1	1	3	$23,706

15Jly95-1Bel fst 6f :22 :45 :573 1:10 Clm 12000 96 6 3 3½ 2½ 12 13 Migliore R 114 f *2.15 91-11 Maraud1143 Prioritizer1162½ Nowhere Man116nk Well placed 9
4Jly95-4Bel fst 1$\frac{1}{16}$:232 :461 1:11 1:433 Clm 22500 76 4 3 35½ 45 47 512½ Santos J A 114 f 10.10 69-18 Advanced Placement1164 Zeezaroo1121¾ A Call To Rise1165½ Lacked rally 11
18Jun95-1Bel fst 6f :223 :462 :59 1:121 Clm 14000 85 3 7 83 51¾ 1hd 11½ Migliore R 116 4.90 80-20 Maraud1161½ Prioritizer116hd Cross Ice Pass1151 Rallied five wide 12
14May95-3Bel fst 6½f :221 :46 1:114 1:183 Clm c-14000 60 1 11 66½ 74 75 99½ Davis R G 116 f 3.60 72-17 Zeezaroo1162 Nowhere Man1181½ Proper Bounder1164 Saved ground 13
Claimed from Hackel Kenneth S, Galluscio Dominic G Trainer
14Apr95-2Aqu fst 6f :223 :463 :584 1:112 Clm 10000 69 5 7 51¾ 41 31½ 1nk Beckner D V 114 f *1.55 85-10 Maraud114nk Poets Pistol107no Numbered Accord1041½ Fully extended 9
12Oct94-6Bel fst 7f :223 :454 1:104 1:241 3↑ Clm c-32500 83 7 3 36 33½ 52½ 44¾ Migliore R 115 f *.90 77-21 Imaging110nk Giant Leap1151½ Change Of Fortune1153 Wide, evenly 8
Claimed from Hauman Eugene E, Hushion Michael E Trainer
22Sep94-2Bel fst 6f :224 :454 :573 1:093 3↑ Clm 45000 96 2 5 53 41½ 3nk 2hd Migliore R 113 f 3.50 93-15 Dibbs N' Dubbs113hd Maraud1131½ Boss Soss1172 Sharp try 5
7Sep94-6Bel fst 6½f :224 :46 1:10 1:16 3↑ Clm 32500 98 6 7 74½ 72½ 1hd 12¾ Migliore R 115 f 6.80 93-14 Maraud1152¾ Ocean Splash1172 Carrnac119¾ Blocked, driving 9
17Aug94-4Sar fst 1$\frac{3}{16}$:473 1:114 1:373 1:573 3↑ Clm 32500 88 6 1 1½ 11 3nk 36 Migliore R 115 f *3.00 85-15 Ambush Alley117hd Decoder1175¾ Maraud1151½ Weakened 7
6Aug94-10Sar fst 1⅛ :47 1:114 1:374 1:511 Clm 32500 88 8 2 21 12 11½ 2¾ Migliore R 115 6.00 79-17 A Call To Rise117¾ Maraud1152 Carney's Kid1173 Couldn't last 9
WORKOUTS: ●Jun 5 Bel tr.t 4f fst :491 B 1/4

Island Dash
Own: Paraneck Stable
BELMONTE L A (25 2 2 1 .08) $25,000
Ch. c. 4
Sire: Island Whirl (Pago Pago)
Dam: Southern Dash (Exuberant)
Br: Elliott Fuentes & Alice Hayman (Fla)
Tr: Aquilino Joseph (8 0 2 0 .00)
1075

Lifetime Record: 14 3 1 3 $63,800											
1995	10	2	1	2	$41,360	Turf	1	0	0	0	
1994	3	1	0	1	$22,270	Wet	3	0	0	0	$1,250
Sar	1	0	0	0		Dist	2	0	0	1	$3,000

24Jly95-5Sar wf 6f :22 :453 :574 1:10 3↑ Clm 25000 55 12 2 31½ 21 106 1214½ Migliore R 114 7.60 76-08 Love Jazz113nk Chispaviva1141½ Sun Valley Sundae1132 Used in pace 13
12Jly95-4Bel fst 7f :222 :444 1:092 1:223 Clm 45000 60 5 1 1½ 11 67½ 617 Rodriguez R R 114 19.70 71-14 Frmonthefrewy1161 Tnochtitln1205 ConcordsProspct120hd Used in pace 8
21Jun95-10Mth fst 6f :213 :444 :573 1:103 3↑ Alw 22000N3X 53 1 6 32 32½ 54½ 512¾ Bravo J L 116 1.90 73-17 Love That Siew1163 Gallant Warfare116nk For All The Bills116no 6
Steadied slightly near lane, gave way
29May95-7Mth fst 6f :212 :443 :574 1:114 3↑ Alw 22000N3X 79 3 3 3½ 22½ 23 34 Wilson R L 116 4.10 76-27 Lighting Force1162¾ Gallant Warfare1161½ Island Dash116hd Weakened 7
12May95-7Bel my 6½f :221 :452 1:092 1:154 3↑ Alw 36000N3X 43 3 1 11 3½ 516 525½ Rydowski S R 119 2.20 70-15 Kings Fiction1106½ Mccullough1193 Memories OfLinda1193 Used in pace 5
14Apr95-7Kee fm 5½f Ⓣ :212 :45 :571 1:033 Alw 36450N3X 64 5 8 53½ 63½ 99½ 911½ Bravo J L 115 7.10 86-03 Long Suit1122 Pharmeadow1122 Toli Paid112nk Finished early 9
30Mar95-8TP fst 6f :221 :454 :582 1:12 Alw 26320N2X 88 7 2 1hd 12½ 13 13½ Rydowski S R L 113 *1.00 85-21 Island Dash1133½ Fit 'n Pepi1131 Exhilarator115no Dueled, driving 8
24Feb95-9GP fst 6f :212 :44 :564 1:101 Alw 27000N2X 93 2 3 21 1hd 1hd 3½ Bravo J L 122 *1.00 88-17 [D]Pro Brite119no Over Doer119½ Island Dash1221 Weakened 9
Placed second through disqualification.
28Jan95-4GP fst 6f :213 :44 :57 1:104 Alw 25000N1X 94 9 4 2hd 12½ 13 12½ Bravo J L 119 *1.50 86-16 Island Dash1192½ Turn West1223¾ Count Joseph1191½ 11
Bumped start, rushed, driving
18Jan95-8GP fst 7f :223 :452 1:101 1:23 Alw 25000N1X 81 1 8 11½ 11½ 2hd 35¾ Bravo J L 119 3.20 82-18 April Christmas1192¾ Turkomatic1193 Island Dash1191½ Weakened 9
WORKOUTS: ●Jly 1 Aqu 4f fst :46 H 1/11 ●May 9 GS 5f fst 1:00 H 1/14

Stolen Zeal
Own: Cohn Seymour
CHAVEZ J F (64 10 12 3 .16) $25,000
Ch. g. 5
Sire: Unreal Zeal (Mr. Prospector)
Dam: One Alone (One for All)
Br: Hartigan John H Estate (Fla)
Tr: Terrill William V (11 0 0 0 .00)
118

Lifetime Record: 39 8 3 2 $143,017											
1995	13	4	0	0	$28,275	Turf	0	0	0	0	
1994	1	0	0	0		Wet	4	3	0	0	$52,200
Sar	3	0	0	0		Dist	4	3	0	0	$30,600

15Jly95-1Bel fst 6f :22 :45 :573 1:10 Clm 14000 82 2 1 21 31½ 32 45½ Bailey J D 118 4.20 85-11 Maraud1143 Prioritizer1162½ Nowhere Man116nk Forced pace 9
1Jly95-2Bel sly 7f :22 :452 1:10 1:231 Clm 12000 88 7 1 11½ 11 12½ 17½ Chavez J F 112 *1.85 85-14 Stolen Zeal1127½ Proper Bounder1167½ Publicized1141 Wide, ridden out 9
18Jun95-1Bel fst 6f :223 :462 :59 1:121 Clm 13000 68 10 8 73 94¾ 95¾ 96¾ Belmonte L A7 108 4.90 73-20 Maraud1161½ Prioritizer116hd Cross Ice Pass1151 Wide, no threat 12
29May95-10Bel gd 1 :23 :46 1:112 1:373 Clm 25000 51 4 3 32½ 31½ 98¾ 919¾ Bailey J D 116 7.00 55-17 Le Risky1122 Zeezaroo1161¾ Runaway Chris114no Gave way 10
17May95-3Bel fst 1 :233 :464 1:122 1:38 3↑ Alw 36000N2X 70 5 1 1hd 1hd 44 614½ Ramos W S 120 7.20 58-32 Final Clearance1206½ Slice Of Reality112½ Heavenwood1155 Dueled, tired 6
4May95-9Bel fst 6f :223 :46 :58 1:102 Clm 15000 88 7 2 12 11 13 15½ Bailey J D 114 5.60 89-13 Stolen Zeal1145½ Proper Bounder116hd Prioritizer116nk Ridden out 10
29Apr95-1Aqu fst 7f :224 :46 1:113 1:244 Clm 10000 77 5 4 21 33 12½ 15 Chavez J F 119 *1.75 80-18 Stolen Zeal1195 Mr Vincent1072¾ Slews Gold114½ Ridden out 10
21Apr95-2Aqu fst 6f :223 :46 :583 1:113 Clm 12000 69 7 2 74½ 74½ 73¾ 64 Dunkelberger T L5 107 9.40 80-15 Gallant Step118nk Callisto1162 Mr Sledge1091½ No threat 9
12Apr95-3Aqu fst 7f :222 :451 1:101 1:23 Clm 20000 65 3 4 66 79 97 712½ Davis R G 112 21.90 77-14 Regal Mike116hd Fabian1182 Baypark1201 No threat 9
30Mar95-5Aqu fst 6f :222 :453 :58 1:102 Clm 18000 80 1 1 31½ 42½ 53½ 55 Dunkelberger T L5 107 27.00 85-17 Pension Fraud1133 Baypark1201¾ Groovy Attire118no Checked 1/2 pl 7
WORKOUTS: Jly 26 Sar tr.t 4f fst :53 B 25/27 Jun 16 Bel 3f fst :374 B 16/38 Jun 9 Bel tr.t 4f fst :504 B 9/17

Giant Leap
Own: Jakubovitz Jerome R
DAVIS R G (57 6 6 11 .11) $25,000
Dk. b or br g. 7
Sire: Conquistador Cielo (Mr. Prospector)
Dam: Leap of the Heart (Nijinsky II)
Br: Mellon Paul (Va)
Tr: Myer Pat (—)
112

Lifetime Record: 54 8 11 11 $173,045											
1995	9	1	3	1	$31,460	Turf	1	0	0	0	
1994	16	2	4	2	$45,570	Wet	11	2	4	3	$43,890
Sar	4	2	0	0	$25,740	Dist	21	5	5	4	$85,065

18Jly95-8Mth fst 1$\frac{1}{16}$:224 :461 1:11 1:45 3↑ Clm 30000 73 1 3 34 24 34 34½ Santagata N L 115 fb 3.70 75-21 Dynamic Brush1151¾ Halo Of Merit1152¾ Giant Leap1151¾ Saved ground 6
28Jun95-6Bel fst 7f :224 :461 1:112 1:242 Clm 30000 88 3 1 22½ 21½ 2½ 22 Davis R G 112 fb *1.90 77-22 Baypark1122 Giant Leap1126½ Wissie's Wish114nk Bid, clear 2nd 7
11Jun95-1Bel fst 7f :222 :453 1:112 1:244 Clm 25000 88 10 1 53½ 44 22 22 Davis R G 116 fb 12.20 75-25 Heavenwood1162 Giant Leap1163 Inside Connection1163 Bid, no match 10
18May95-9Bel gd 7f :224 :46 1:11 1:241 Clm c-20000 65 6 2 31 43 85 88½ Chavez J F 116 fb *2.05 71-16 Baypark116nk Le Risky1121½ Fire Devil116½ Used up 9
Claimed from Hagedorn Charles C & Rottkamp John, Odintz Jeff Trainer
10Apr95-7Aqu fst 6½f :222 :45 1:09 1:151 Alw 32000N2X 85 1 4 43½ 43 55 58¾ Chavez J F 114 fb 6.20 95-12 West Quest1192 Scherbo1191½ Lake Ali1143 Stumbled break 5
26Mar95-4Aqu fst 7f :233 :464 1:114 1:241 Alw 32000N2X 89 4 2 31 42 2½ 2no Chavez J F 114 b 3.15 83-17 Here's Noah119no Giant Leap1141 Heavenwood110¾ Four wide, gamely 5
16Mar95-9Aqu fst 1 :224 :454 1:111 1:373 Clm 30000 85 7 4 43 4¾ 1½ 1nk Chavez J F 116 fb 3.70 81-24 Giant Leap116nk A Call To Rise116½ Hot Siew1162 Wide, all out 8
26Feb95-5Aqu fst 6f ⊡ :232 :47 :593 1:12 Clm 25000 80 7 8 67½ 64½ 52¾ 42½ Chavez J F 117 b 8.40 80-19 Dernier's Lass117¾ Nymphist1191¾ Panico117hd Belated rally 9
16Feb95-7Aqu fst 6f ⊡ :231 :463 :59 1:112 Alw 32000N2X 63 4 2 63½ 65 65½ 611½ Mojica R Jr 117 fb 6.20 74-21 Expressed117½ Bay Dancer1154 Fog Storm1144¾ No speed 6
10Dec94-6Aqu wf 6f ⊡ :23 :461 :582 1:104 3↑ Clm 35000 85 8 2 55½ 76½ 54 43 Mojica R Jr 117 b 7.10 86-20 Current Impact1191½ Nowhere Man117½ Boss Soss1091½ Rallied wide 8
WORKOUTS: Jun 4 Bel 4f fst :54 B 22/22 May 8 Aqu 4f fst :511 B 3/4

Jido
Own: Downturn Stable
VELASQUEZ J (27 1 0 3 .04) $25,000
B. c. 4
Sire: Slew City Slew (Seattle Slew)
Dam: Platinum Poster (Poster Prince)
Br: Mara Thomas D (Ky)
Tr: Martin Jose (10 1 1 2 .10)
112

Lifetime Record: 18 6 0 1 $92,040											
1995	1	0	0	0	$2,100	Turf	9	4	0	0	$61,200
1994	12	4	0	0	$63,060	Wet	1	0	0	1	$1,680
Sar	0	0	0	0		Dist	1	0	0	0	

12Jly95-6Bel fst 1$\frac{1}{16}$ ⊗ :23 :453 1:094 1:422 Clm 55000 75 1 1 1½ 43½ 47½ 412½ Velasquez J 112 f 11.20 74-23 Dibbs N' Dubbs1169½ Sole Bird1163 Arz114no Used up 5
5Nov94-1Aqu yl 1$\frac{1}{16}$ Ⓣ :241 :482 1:134 1:464 3↑ Alw 36000N3X 63 7 3 31 2½ 88 914½ Beckner D V5 110 f 2.50 60-25 GoneForRel1171½ Threehrvrdvenue114¾ GrndContinntl1174¾ Forced pace 10
8Oct94-5Bel fm 1 Ⓣ :23 :453 1:094 1:34 3↑ Kelso H-G3 66 5 1 13½ 3½ 710 719¾ Beckner D V 106 f 16.40 72-15 Nijinsky's Gold114no Lure1282¾ A In Sociology117nk Gave way 7
16Sep94-7Bel fm 1 Ⓣ :23 :452 1:083 1:33 3↑ Alw 34000N2X 94 7 1 13 13½ 15 12½ Beckner D V5 108 f 3.40 97-13 Jido1082½ Bermuda Cedar1142 Limited War1132 Driving 11
4Sep94-1Bel fm 1$\frac{1}{16}$ [T] :241 :47 1:103 1:412 Clm 50000 91 10 1 11½ 11 14 13¾ Beckner D V5 112 3.70 89-10 Jido1123¾ Grand Continental117nk Baling Wire1131¾ Driving 10
24Aug94-4Sar gd 1$\frac{1}{16}$ Ⓣ :234 :472 1:12 1:424 Clm 35000 97 7 1 11½ 12 18 18 Beckner D V5 112 f *2.10 80-22 Jido1128 Dizzy Devil1172½ Magic's Cause117no Kept to drive 8
15Aug94-4Sar yl 1$\frac{1}{16}$ Ⓣ :232 :464 1:111 1:424 Clm 70000 43 10 6 76½ 87½ 711 623 Chavez J F 113 f 5.10 57-21 Head Trip1172 Best Of Music1137 Natural Fact1171½ Wide, tired 10
7Aug94-7Sar gd 1⅛ [T] :474 1:114 1:371 1:492 3↑ Alw 32000N2X 80 8 1 11 11 2½ 84 Velazquez J R 112 f 12.50 84-18 Palace Piper119½ Whitney Tower1121 Jesse F113no Used in pace 8
3Jun94-6Bel fm 1 Ⓣ :22 :451 1:094 1:35 Clm 35000 83 2 6 66½ 43½ 1hd 11½ Chavez J F 117 f *1.20 87-16 Jido1171½ Johnny North1172 Sean's World1171½ Checked 3/8 pl, drvg 10
12May94-1Bel fm 1 Ⓣ :23 :464 1:113 1:353 Clm 70000 75 5 2 2½ 2½ 41½ 54½ Chavez J F 113 f 7.60 79-21 Mr.Imptienc1131¾ OutFromUndr1131 BstOfMusic113no Forced pace, tired 8
WORKOUTS: Jly 26 Sar 4f fst :491 H 19/52 ●Jly 8 Bel tr.t 5f fst 1:004 H 1/5 Jly 1 Bel 6f fst 1:164 H 5/8 Jun 24 Bel 6f fst 1:151 H 7/17 Jun 16 Bel 6f fst 1:17 Hg6/8 Jun 11 Bel tr.t 4f fst :50 B 12/21

Change of Fortune

Own: Fink Morton

KRONE J A (49 4 10 2 .08) $25,000

Dk. b or br g. 6
Sire: Time for a Change (Damascus)
Dam: Tasty Kiss (Sauce Boat)
Br: Granite David S (Ont-C)
Tr: Levine Bruce N (9 1 0 0 .11)

112

Lifetime Record: 46 6 11 8 $195,211											
1995	3	0	0	0	$1,020	Turf	2	0	0	0	
1994	14	2	1	4	$43,020	Wet	3	0	0	0	$1,020
Sar	0	0	0	0		Dist	16	1	5	2	$59,108

8Jly95-1Bel	fst	6f	:224 :454 :573 1:10	Clm 30000	80	2	4	85¾	75½	84¼	64	Alvarado F T	116 fb	12.20	87-16	Fini Cassette116½ Ocean Splash1141 Country Sky1161	No threat	8
24Jun95-10Bel	wf	6½f	:221 :453 1:112 1:181	Clm 18000	80	7	7	109¾	97¼	64	42½	Alvarado F T	114 fb	16.50	81-15	Ocean Splash1162 Francis Marion116½ Nowhere Man112no	Finished well	11
11Jan95-3Aqu	fst	6f ⊡	:231 :463 :59 1:121	Clm 25000	69	3	9	1011	1011	99¾	96½	Alvarado F T	117 fb	7.50	76-22	Raja'sCharter110nk MagicRuckus117no Baypark1172½	Checked break, wide	10
16Dec94-1Aqu	fst	170 ⊡	:233 :48 1:131 1:43	3↑ Clm 30000	74	4	6	52½	44	57	412¼	Chavez J F	113 fb	6.50	71-30	Country Sky1082 Advanced Placement1172¼ Alpstein1178	No rally	7
29Nov94-2Aqu	wf	7f	:232 :47 1:114 1:242	3↑ Clm 30000	71	3	4	67½	68	67½	69	Davis R G	113 b	3.40e	73-21	Yeckley1174 Current Impact122hd Birdie's Fly1173	No factor	7
18Nov94-4Aqu	fst	6f	:223 :461 :582 1:11	3↑ Clm 32500	87	6	5	710	59	46	33	Davis R G	115 fb	5.70	84-14	Imaging117hd Nowhere Man1103 Change Of Fortune1151	Mild gain	7
22Oct94-6Aqu	fst	1	:234 :471 1:12 1:371	3↑ Clm 32500	89	2	7	75½	63½	43½	32	Davis R G	115 fb	3.10	80-23	CurrentImpct115¾ Gllpit'sMoment1171¼ ChngOfFortun115hd	Rallied wide	7
12Oct94-6Bel	fst	7f	:223 :454 1:104 1:241	3↑ Clm 32500	89	3	4	59	57	42	31¾	Davis R G	115 fb	6.10	80-21	Imaging110nk Giant Leap1151½ Change Of Fortune1153	Mild gain	8
5Sep94-2Bel	fst	7f	:231 :461 1:102 1:231	3↑ Clm 25000	89	1	8	810	84½	53	2nk	Alvarado F T	117 fb	7.00	87-14	PeerlessPerformer117nk ChngOfFortun117hd HotSlw117½	Checked 3/16 pl	9
13Jly94-4Bel	fst	7f	:221 :45 1:101 1:231	Clm 45000	76	5	8	812	812	77	79¼	Alvarado F T	114 fb	7.20	77-15	Boss Soss117¾ Senor Cielo1173 Le Risky1152¼	Outrun	8

WORKOUTS: May 28 Aqu 5f fst 1:02 B 7/11

Glenfiddich Lad

Own: Calabrese Frank C

PEREZ R B (27 0 1 3 .00) $25,000

Gr. g. 6
Sire: Procida (Mr. Prospector)
Dam: Chepstow Vale (Key to the Mint)
Br: McBean Peter (Ky)
Tr: Dutrow Richard E (3 0 0 0 .00)

112

Lifetime Record: 41 11 10 4 $279,195											
1995	6	1	0	0	$22,595	Turf	35	5	8	2	$167,150
1994	12	3	4	1	$116,110	Wet	5	1	1	1	$26,665
Sar	0	0	0	0		Dist	0	0	0	0	

22Jly95-4AP	yl	1 ⓣ	:233 :47 1:123 1:382	3↑ Clm 40000	77	5	10	1013	1010	87½	85¾	Lasala J	L 117 b	3.00	76-20	Star Turner117no Broken Code1171½ War Machine117no	Late wide bid	10
8May95-8Spt	sly	1	:243 :491 1:142 1:38	Alw 26000N$Y	75	5	4	44	44	58½	512¾	Lasala J	L 119 fb	2.00	77-16	Dancing Jon1141½ Michislew1147½ Inca Trail1222½	No rally rail	5
22Apr95-7Kee	fm	1⅛ ⓣ	:473 1:121 1:371 1:494	Alw 40800C	86	6	6	64½	74¼	65¼	66	Torres F C	L 113 b	4.50	82-15	Wolf Prince1122½ Smart Enough1151½ Final Waltz114no		8
Swerved in start, saved ground, no rally																		
18Mar95-11Spt	fst	1	:232 :47 1:123 1:382	Alw 32000NC	93	2	4	49½	48	21½	1nk	Lasala J	L 117 b	*1.50	88-15	Glenfiddich Lad117nk Brookshire122nk Inca Trail117no	Driving 3 wide	7
12Feb95-8GP	fm	*1 1/16 ⓣ	:231 :46 1:10 1:401	+ Alw 40000N$mY	95	5	9	910	65½	55	42¼	Ramos W S	L 117 b	10.40	105 —	WeekendMadness113nk Solenzno1151½ DominntProspect115¾	Belated bid	10
13Jan95-8GP	fm	*1⅛ ⓣ	:481 1:13 1:37 1:502	+ Alw 40000N$mY	96	3	5	511	510	63½	53¾	Smith M E	L 119 b	4.50	89-16	Awad115hd Brazany1151¾ Country Coy115hd		9
Six wide top str, failed to menace																		
29Dec94-10Crc	fm	7½f ⓣ	:232 :472 1:11 1:30	3↑ Alw 20000NC	97	5	7	811	710	65	1½	Smith M E	L 117 b	*2.20	93-07	GlenfiddichLad117½ ClintEssentil1161½ CourtLrk119nk	5-wide, fast finish	8
5Nov94-4Haw	sly	170 ⊗	:233 :472 1:122 1:404	3↑ RFCareyMemH100k	91	4	7	77½	68½	37	310	Martin E M Jr	L 114 b	4.40	87-16	Recoup The Cash1198 Road Of War1152 Glenfiddich Lad1145½	3 wide bid	7
23Oct94-9Kee	fm	1⅛ ⓣ	:462 1:121 1:383 1:511	3↑ Alw 32900N$mY	102	3	8	712	57	22	1nk	Martin E M Jr	L 114 b	*2.40	81-19	GlenfiddichLd114nk LittleBroLntis1232 DivinWrning114nk	Fully extended	8
25Sep94-3Due	gd	*1½ ⓣ	2:312	3↑ SamHouston H300k	84	12	11	1111	31½	710	711½	Bourque C C	L 116 b	16.50	59-29	Lindon Lime1134 Sir MarkSykes118½ DrummerBoy1151	Inside bid, hung	12

WORKOUTS: Jly 2 AP 5f fst 1:031 B 15/31 Jun 17 AP 4f fst :49 B 6/13 Jun 1 Spt 4f fst :533 B 21/29 May 3 Haw 5f fst 1:03 B 6/8

Nowhere Man

Own: Ahearn Joseph M

BAILEY J D (62 16 4 9 .26) $25,000

Ch. g. 6
Sire: Fountain of Gold (Mr. Prospector)
Dam: Sister Aggie (Great Above)
Br: Matthews Karen & P (Fla)
Tr: Terracciano Neal (2 0 0 0 .00)

112

Lifetime Record: 52 10 8 9 $180,188											
1995	12	1	1	3	$20,880	Turf	1	0	0	0	
1994	14	3	5	0	$63,380	Wet	10	3	3	3	$52,708
Sar	0	0	0	0		Dist	3	0	0	0	$260

15Jly95-1Bel	fst	6f	:22 :45 :573 1:10	Clm 14000	82	4	9	44½	53¾	53¼	35¼	Davis R G	116 fb	3.10	86-11	Maraud1143 Prioritizer1162½ Nowhere Man116nk	Checked break	9
24Jun95-10Bel	wf	6½f	:221 :453 1:112 1:181	Clm 18000	80	1	1	11	11½	1½	32½	Sweeney K H	112 fb	10.40	81-15	OceanSplash1162 FrancisMrion116½ NowhereMn112no	Dueled, weakened	11
18Jun95-1Bel	fst	6f	:223 :462 :59 1:121	Clm 13000	79	11	3	1hd	1hd	3½	42½	Martinez J R Jr	114 fb	8.20	78-20	Maraud1161¼ Prioritizer116hd Cross Ice Pass1151	Dueled, weakened	12
11Jun95-1Bel	fst	7f	:222 :453 1:112 1:244	Clm 22500	60	4	3	2hd	31½	46½	815¼	Martinez J R Jr	114 fb	12.90	62-25	Heavenwood1162 GintLep1163 InsideConnection1163	Forced pace, tired	10
14May95-3Bel	fst	6½f	:221 :46 1:114 1:183	Clm c-14000	77	11	3	11½	11	2½	22	Alvarado F T	118 b	4.70	80-17	Zeezaroo1162 Nowhere Man1181¼ Proper Bounder1164	Held well	13
Claimed from Davis Barbara J, Moschera Gasper S Trainer																		
22Apr95-1Aqu	fst	6f	:22 :454 :583 1:114	Clm 20000	73	4	3	2hd	4½	52½	64½	Martinez J R Jr	116 b	9.60	79-17	Groovy Attire118½ Publicized1162 Pension Fraud115hd	Dueled, tired	7
8Apr95-5Aqu	fst	6f	:22 :45 :574 1:11	Clm 16000	83	5	3	31	32½	2hd	1hd	Martinez J R Jr	116 b	4.10	87-10	Nowhere Man116hd Unreal Mot116½ Appealing Tracy1131½	Fully extended	7
18Mar95-7Aqu	fst	6½f	:223 :461 1:102 1:163	Alw 42000N$Y	28	1	7	21	44	711	730	Luzzi M J	114 b	13.80	67-15	Mr. Tyler1172¼ Able Buck1141¾ Golden Cloud1106½	Broke slowly, rushed	7
19Feb95-7Aqu	fst	6f ⊡	:23 :464 :591 1:12	Alw 42000N$Y	92	2	2	11	1hd	3nk	4¾	Alvarado F T	114 b	4.50	82-22	Rocking Josh114½ Imaging114no Golden Cloud112hd	Gamely	5
22Jan95-4Aqu	gd	6f ⊡	:221 :451 :572 1:10	Alw 42000N$Y	53	5	5	2½	21½	68	616¾	Alvarado F T	117 b	2.85e	76-11	Frmonthefreewy1172 Yeckly1172¼ CurrntImpct117¾	Brk slow, used early	6

WORKOUTS: Jun 4 Aqu 4f fst :473 H 1/3 May 24 Aqu 4f fst :48 H 1/2 May 8 Bel tr.t 4f fst :483 B 4/10

Mr. Stalwart

Own: Raymond Terry

DAY P (57 10 7 7 .18) $25,000

Ch. g. 7
Sire: Stalwart (Hoist the Flag)
Dam: Blue Bidder (Bold Bidder)
Br: Conway James D (Ky)
Tr: Romans Dale (4 0 0 1 .00)

112

Lifetime Record: 62 10 14 10 $235,266											
1995	12	2	4	2	$61,180	Turf	2	0	0	0	
1994	11	2	1	2	$30,603	Wet	12	2	3	3	$44,841
Sar	0	0	0	0		Dist	5	1	3	1	$29,311

2Jly95-11CD	fst	1 1/16	:242 :48 1:123 1:44	Clm 40000	71	1	1	11½	1hd	33	58½	Bourque K	L 116 b	6.00	85-04	Lord Gordon1162 CrownLease1122½ SafeAndLegal116no	Out in strip, tired	7
18Jun95-4CD	fm	1⅛ ⓣ	:464 1:111 1:364 1:491	3↑ Alw 42800N4X	75	2	2	2½	2hd	44½	59½	Bourque K	L 116 b	8.40	76-13	Shades Of Silver118no Flops1185 Lordly Prospect116hd	Pressed, tired	7
28May95-10CD	sly	1 1/16	:241 :48 1:131 1:471	Clm 25000	87	4	4	42	42½	3½	1½	Bourque K	L 117 b	*3.10	78-26	Mr. Stalwart117½ The Jettster1191 Prognosticator1171½		11
Ducked in start, checked in tight 1st turn, hard drive																		
5May95-10CD	fst	1 1/16	:24 :472 1:124 1:442	Clm 25000	87	9	5	54	41	2½	21¼	McCauley W H	L 117 b	8.30	91-07	Lord Gordon1171¼ Mr. Stalwart1171 GoldenCan117nk	Bid, led, second best	9
23Apr95-1Kee	fst	1 1/16	:232 :47 1:122 1:46	Clm 25000	85	8	3	21½	1½	2hd	31¾	Davis R G	L 119 b	*2.30	77-23	Colonial Winter1171¼ Eaton Row117¾ Mr. Stalwart1191½	Weakened late	11
29Mar95-7TP	fst	1	:234 :474 1:14 1:401	Clm 25000	85	2	2	1½	11	11½	21	Fox T L	L 115 b	*1.80	68-32	S U Twenty Nine1141 Mr. Stalwart115no Mr. Memphis114¾	Held on well	7
15Mar95-9TP	fst	1 1/16	:232 :472 1:12 1:444	Alw 37500N3X	95	3	2	2hd	2hd	1hd	1nk	Fox T L	L 112 b	5.50	84-26	Mr. Stalwart112nk Prince Scoundral1137 Lord Gordon113½		6
Exchanged brushes 3/16, driving																		
5Mar95-8TP	sly	1	:232 :472 1:132 1:41	Clm 20000	91	6	5	33	31	21	2no	Fox T L	L 113 b	5.90	65-35	Macheath114no Mr. Stalwart1134½ Estill1131		6
Brushed 3-16, missed																		
24Feb95-5TP	gd	1 1/16	:244 :502 1:163 1:52	Clm 16000	82	1	1	12	11	11	2¾	Fox T L	L 115 b	*2.30	47-62	Leggo My Mako112¾ Mr. Stalwart1158 Bold Return113¾	Could not last	9
10Feb95-7TP	fr	1	:223 :463 1:113 1:37	Clm 20000	77	1	4	32½	31½	44½	49¾	Fox T L	L 110 b	6.40	75-19	Colony Sound1121 Payment Era109¾ Artic Harry1188	Flattened out	6

WORKOUTS: Jly 24 Sar tr.t 4f fst :511 B 16/29 ● Jun 9 CDT 4f fst :48 B 1/12

1 — Maastricht Accord — Failed badly in a $30,000 claimer in last. No.

2 — I'm No Quacker — Had beaten cheaper in his '95 debut three starts back. Was a distant fifth in a shorter sprint in last, and stretching out to a distance at which he was zero for six. Pass.

3 — Come On Talc — Overmatched in allowance company in his lone start at seven furlongs. Was a decent fifth as the favorite in his return in last at six furlongs as the favorite, but was wearing front bandages, never an encouraging sign. Pass.

4 — Lightning Surge — Did okay against weaker at the bottom of his PPs, but his last six starts were abysmal. No.

5 — Maraud — This hard-hitter usually gave it his best shot — his career record was 12-3-14 in 49 starts. At seven furlongs, he was 1-1-3 in eight starts. He won his last by three lengths at Belmont, but was moving up from a $12,500 to $25,000, and was stretching out from six furlongs to seven. With his back class, he could pull it off. Contender.

6 — Island Dash — Had speed, but was stopping badly and was stretching out from six furlongs to seven. No thanks.

7 — Stolen Zeal — Moving way up in company despite getting beaten soundly by Maraud in both a $13,000 claimer and a $14,000 claimer in two of his last three starts. In his other start, he won a seven-furlong, $12,500 claimer on a sloppy track by 7½ lengths as the 8-5 favorite. He was three for four on a wet track and three for four at seven furlongs. But the track today would be fast. Pass.

8 — Giant Leap — Didn't like the fact that he had raced on Lasix out of town in last, when he was third in a a route try for $30,000 claimers, but he had raced in New York without Lasix in all his previous starts and had done well. He was a specialist at seven furlongs with a record of 5-5-4 in 21 starts, including a pair of seconds at Belmont two and three races back. Major player.

9 — Jido — Front-runner who was taking a sharp drop off a poor fourth in his '95 debut. He'd been more successful on turf than dirt and better at route races, but had won two of nine on dirt. Unlikely with Nowhere Man apt to press him early.

10 — Change Of Fortune — Dropping a notch off a so-so sixth at six furlongs. At seven, he'd been in the money eight of 16 starts with one win. Prime material for an exacta. Julie Krone

was replacing Frank Alvarado, which was no big deal, as Alvarado has become an extremely capable rider in New York, and Julie always gets over-bet at Saratoga.

11 — Nowhere Man — Speedster who didn't fire in his last race at six furlongs; was moving up from $14,000 to $25,000, and hadn't been in the money in three tries at seven furlongs. A certain pace factor, but that's all.

12 — Mr. Stalwart — This intriguing also-eligible drew in. He was dropping from $40,000 to $25,000; had won at this level; could race on the lead or off the pace, and had been in the money four of five starts at seven furlongs, though only one was a win. Major player.

Conclusion? Giant Leap looked solid and was my pick in the *Gazette*. Of the others, Maraud, Change Of Fortune and Mr. Stalwart seemed best. As the 5-2 favorite in a field of 12, Giant Leap was not an overlay, though he won by a length and paid $7.60. The real value was in the exacta. Change Of Fortune, who was the fifth choice in the field at 9-1, got second, beating 16-1 Nowhere Man by half a length. The exacta paid $67.50.

FIFTH RACE	7 FURLONGS. (1.20²) CLAIMING. Purse $20,000. 3-year-olds and upward. Weights: 3-year-olds, 117 lbs. Older, 121 lbs. Non-winners of two races since June 15, allowed 3 lbs. Two races since May 3, 6 lbs. A race since July 3, 1994, 9 lbs. Claiming price $25,000.

Saratoga
AUGUST 3, 1995

Value of Race: $20,000 Winner $12,000; second $4,000; third $2,200; fourth $1,200; fifth $600. Mutuel Pool $301,759.00 Exacta Pool $483,296.00 Triple Pool $428,082.00

Last Raced	Horse	M/Eqt. A.Wt	PP	St	¼	½	Str	Fin	Jockey	Cl'g Pr	Odds $
18Jly95 8Mth³	Giant Leap	bf 7 112	8	7	6²	5³	2¹½	1¹	Davis R G	25000	2.80
8Jly95 1Bel⁶	Change of Fortune	bf 6 112	10	3	11³	9¹	3¹	2½	Krone J A	25000	9.70
15Jly95 1Bel³	Nowhere Man	bf 6 112	11	1	2¹	1¹	1½	3¹	Bailey J D	25000	16.70
8Jly95 1Bel⁵	Come On Talc	bf 4 112	3	11	10½	10½	6²	4²	Luzzi M J	25000	4.10
2Jly95 11CD⁵	Mr. Stalwart	b 7 112	12	2	9²	8ʰᵈ	5¹	5ⁿᵏ	Day P	25000	6.30
24Jly95 5Sar⁵	I'm No Quacker	bf 7 112	2	9	7¹	7½	4½	6ⁿᵏ	Beckner D V	25000	23.60
22Jun95 7Bel⁶	Maastricht Accord	5 114	1	12	12	12	7ʰᵈ	7ⁿᵏ	Alvarado F T	25000	22.90
12Jly95 6Bel⁴	Jido	4 113	9	8	8½	11²	8²	8⁹	Velasquez J	25000	10.90
15Jly95 1Bel¹	Maraud	f 6 118	5	10	5ʰᵈ	3ʰᵈ	9²	9ʰᵈ	Migliore R	25000	4.70
24Jly95 5Sar⁸	Lightning Surge	b 4 112	4	6	3¹	4½	10ʰᵈ	10¹½	Rydowski S R	25000	83.00
15Jly95 1Bel⁴	Stolen Zeal	5 118	7	4	4²	6½	11²¹	11¹⁸	Chavez J F	25000	17.90
24Jly95 5Sar¹²	Island Dash	b 4 108	6	5	1¹½	2¹½	12	12	Belmonte L A⁵	25000	43.20

OFF AT 3:05 Start Good. Won driving. Time, :21³, :44³, 1:16³, 1:24⁴ Track fast.

$2 Mutuel Prices:

8-GIANT LEAP	7.60	4.30	3.00
10-CHANGE OF FORTUNE		8.20	5.40
11-NOWHERE MAN			8.30

$2 EXACTA 8-10 PAID $67.50 $2 TRIPLE 8-10-11 PAID $863.00

Dk. b. or br. g, by Conquistador Cielo-Leap of the Heart, by Nijinsky II. Trainer Myer Pat. Bred by Mellon Paul (Va).

GIANT LEAP reserved early, launched a rally four wide on the turn, made a run to challenge in midstretch then turned back CHANGE OF FORTUNE under brisk urging. CHANGE OF FORTUNE far back for a half, circled five wide rallying into the stretch then finished with good energy for the place. NOWHERE MAN forced the early pace from outside, took the lead on the far turn continued on the front into midstretch then weakened in the final eighth. COME ON TALC far back early, checked in traffic on the turn, angled out in upper stretch then rallied belatedly. MR. STALWART unhurried for a half, gained a bit between horses in upper stretch, lacked a strong closing bid. MAASTRICHT ACCORD trailed to the turn, angled seven wide entering the stretch then lacked a strong closing bid. I'M NO QUACKER raced in the middle of the track for a half, lodged a mild rally to reach contention in upper stretch and flattened out. JIDO never reached contention. MARAUD lodged a mild rally between horses on the turn, then faded in the drive. LIGHTNING SURGE saved ground and tired. STOLEN ZEAL raced six wide then gave way ISLAND DASH was used up setting the early pace.

Owners— 1, Jakubovitz Jerome R; 2, Fink Morton; 3, Ahearn Joseph M; 4, Zablowitz Karen S; 5, Raymond Terry; 6, Terranova John P II; 7, Goose Creek Farm; 8, Downturn Stable; 9, G Lack Farms; 10, Beecher Aaron; 11, Cohn Seymour; 12, Paraneck Stable.

Trainers—1, Myer Pat; 2, Levine Bruce N; 3, Terracciano Neal; 4, Parisella John; 5, Romans Dale; 6, Terranova John P II; 7, Kimmel John C; 8, Martin Jose; 9, Klesaris Robert P; 10, Gullo Gary P; 11, Terrill William V; 12, Aquilino Joseph.

Overweight: Maastricht Accord (2), Jido (1), Island Dash (1).

Giant Leap was claimed by Joques Farm; trainer, Moschera Gasper S.,
Mr. Stalwart was claimed by Lewis Mark J; trainer, Galluscio Dominic G.

Scratched— Glenfiddich Lad (22Jly95 4AP⁸).

You'd think that a field of five would preclude finding an exacta with value. But you'd be wrong. See, it never hurts to check those monitors to see what the exotics are paying. The scratches of Defrere and Rank And File left these five going 1⅛ miles on the main track in a non-winners of three, the eighth race at Saratoga, August 17:

8 Saratoga

1⅛ MILES. (1:47) ALLOWANCE. Purse $36,000. 3-year-olds and upward which have not won two races other than maiden, claiming or starter. Weights; 3-year-olds, 117 lbs. Older, 123 lbs. Non-winners of $22,800 since May 3, allowed 3 lbs. Of $18,000 twice in 1995, 5 lbs. Of $15,000 twice in 1995, 8 lbs. (Races where entered for $50,000 or less not considered in allowances.)

Wayfarer
B. g. 4
Sire: Fappiano (Mr. Prospector)
Dam: Roxy Spectre (Nijinsky II)
Br: Burning Daylight Farms Inc (Va)
Tr: Nafzger Carl A (10 2 1 3 .20)

Own: Burning Day Farm

KRONE J A (99 9 18 13 .09)

115

	Lifetime Record:	12 2 1 5	$55,065
1995	5 0 1 2	$12,950 Turf	4 0 0 2	$5,750
1994	7 2 0 3	$42,115 Wet	3 2 1 0	$41,600
Sar	3 2 1 0	$41,400 Dist	3 2 1 0	$41,400

Da Bull
Gr. c. 3 (Apr)
Sire: Country Pine (His Majesty)
Dam: Brekke (Al Hattab)
Br: Pelican Stable (Fla)
Tr: Walden W Elliott (9 0 1 2 .00)

Own: Lamastar Bill

SELLERS S J (70 7 7 8 .10)

112

	Lifetime Record:	8 2 2 2	$67,475
1995	6 2 1 2	$55,555 Turf	0 0 0 0	
1994	2 M 1 0	$11,920 Wet	1 0 0 1	$15,000
Sar	0 0 0 0	Dist	0 0 0 0	

Crary
Own: Condren & Cornacchia & Paulsen
DAY P (122 20 14 19 .16)

Ch. c. 4
Sire: Mt. Livermore (Blushing Groom)
Dam: Royal Alydar (Alydar)
Br: Paulson Allen E (Ky)
Tr: Zito Nicholas P (36 5 4 8 .14)

115

Lifetime Record: 16 2 4 1 $173,555
1995 7 0 2 0 $19,235 Turf 1 0 0 0
1994 6 0 1 1 $13,420 Wet 4 0 1 1 $10,320
Sar 0 0 0 0 Dist 2 0 0 0

28Jly95-4Sar fm 1⅛ T :231 :46 1:112 1:422 3+ Alw 36000N2X 79 2 4 42 33 54 65¼ Day P 113 7.80 82-07 DebonirDn109½ CheckRide113nk ComstockLode1133 Saved ground, tired 10
Hand timed
1Jly95-5Bel sly 1⅛ ⊗ :224 :452 1:10 1:414 3+ Alw 36000N3L 83 6 5 47 35 39¼ 216½ Belmonte L A7 113 6.40 73-18 Kerfoot Corner12016 Crary1133½ Spanish Charge11114 Up for place 7
10Jun95-3Bel fst 1⅛ :233 :463 1:111 1:441 3+ Alw 36000N2X 91 6 4 53½ 54 33¼ 72¼ Belmonte L A7 113 8.10e 75-25 Amathos1202½ Crary1132 Reality Road1123 Rallied wide 9
28May95-7Bel fst 1⅛ :233 :463 1:104 1:423 3+ Alw 36000N2X 76 4 2 42½ 64¼ 68 615 Day P 120 4.40 71-22 West Buoyant115nk Silver Fox12011 Pops Is Tops115no Brief speed 7
6May95-9CD fst 6½f :221 :45 1:092 1:154 3+ Alw 42900N$Y 82 5 10 99¼ 610 610 46¼ Antley C W L 115 3.40e 94 — Ojai1154¼ Top Account1121¼ Keepscratching114nk Rallied 12
15Apr95-5Kee fst 7f :223 :453 1:102 1:23 Alw 43240N$Y 92 8 10 94¾ 74¼ 65 42¼ Krone J A L 112 12.90 84-16 Can't Be Denied112no Air Craft1211¼ Stacey's Bird1131 11
Seven wide stretch, mild gain
10Mar95-10GP fst 7f :222 :451 1:09 1:214 Alw 33000N2X 70 5 2 35¼ 67¾ 512 519 Sellers S J 119 2.70e 75-15 Our Emblem1191¾ Imtoocool1191¾ Turkomatic1229 Faded 7
30Apr94-10CD sly 1 :231 :453 1:10 1:371 Derby Trial-G3 82 4 6 612 610 613 619¼ Sellers S J L 114 9.30 80-20 Numerous1152 Dynamic Asset114nk Exclusive Praline1192¾ 6
Drifted out backstretch, wide trip, dull
16Apr94-9Aqu my 1⅛ :472 1:112 1:362 1:49 Wood Mem-G1 75 1 7 94¾ 77 713 520¾ Luzzi M J 123 *.90e 70-19 Irgun1231¼ Go For Gin1238¾ Shiprock1236¼ No threat 9
12Mar94-10GP fst 1⅛ :46 1:10 1:344 1:472 Fla Derby-G1 82 3 9 97¾ 811 815 819¾ Bravo J 122 *2.40e 80-06 Holy Bull1225¾ Ride The Rails122no Halo's Image1221 No threat 14
WORKOUTS: Aug 8 Sar tr.t 5f fst 1:06 B 7/7 Jly 23 Sar tr.t 4f fst :532 B 24/27 Jly 15 Bel 4f fst :51 B 28/31 Jly 9 Bel 4f fst :504 B 36/48 Jun 20 Bel 5f fst 1:04 B 14/17 Jun 6 Bel 4f fst :50 B 42/58

~~**Defrere**~~
Own: Due Process Stable
BAILEY J D (136 28 17 17 .21)

Dk. b or br c. 3 (Apr)
Sire: Deputy Minister (Vice Regent)
Dam: Sister Dot (Secretariat)
Br: Due Process Stable Inc (Ky)
Tr: Nobles Reynaldo H (12 4 2 2 .33)

112

Lifetime Record: 4 2 1 1 $48,500
1995 4 2 1 1 $48,500 Turf 0 0 0 0
1994 0 M 0 0 Wet 0 0 0 0
Sar 1 1 0 0 $19,200 Dist 0 0 0 0

22Jly95-5Sar fst 7f :221 :44 1:083 1:22 3+ Alw 32000N1X 102 5 5 2½ 2hd 1hd 12¾ Bailey J D 114 f *1.45 96-07 Defrere1142¾ Prospect Bay1142 Investor1082 Hard drive 10
31May95-7Bel fst 6½f :224 :461 1:101 1:162 3+ Alw 32000N2L 93 3 3 42 21½ 23 25¾ Bailey J D 112 f *.65 87-16 Hoolie1125¾ Defrere1127 Smart Little Boy110½ Four wide, no match 6
16Apr95-9Hia fst 7f :232 :454 1:093 1:222 Bahamas50k 93 1 4 42 21½ 33 31¾ Bailey J D 112 f *.30 95-14 Koennecker1171 Hail Orphan112¾ Defrere11212 5
Angled outside upper str, rallied
11Mar95-2GP fst 6f :222 :452 :574 1:094 Md Sp Wt 97 7 8 2hd 1hd 1½ 11¾ Bailey J D 120 f *.90 91-11 Defrere1201¾ Cayeli1207 Phidias Frieze1204½ 12
Bobbled start, driving
WORKOUTS: ●Aug 5 Mdl 5f fst 1:003 B 1/6 Jly 31 Mdl 4f fst :48 B 2/7 ●Jly 15 Mdl 5f fst :593 B 1/12 ●Jly 10 Mdl 6f fst 1:13 B 1/5 ●Jly 3 Mdl 5f fst :59 B 1/8 ●Jun 28 Mdl 4f my :48 B 1/6

~~**Rank And File**~~
Own: Am W D Stable
CHAVEZ J F (126 20 17 6 .16)

Ch. c. 3 (Feb)
Sire: Forty Niner (Mr. Prospector)
Dam: Princess Accord (D'Accord)
Br: Cheveley Park Stud (Ky)
Tr: Schettino Dominick A (14 1 1 0 .07)

109

Lifetime Record: 8 2 0 0 $33,240
1995 6 2 0 0 $33,240 Turf 3 0 0 0
1994 2 M 0 0 Wet 3 1 0 0 $20,400
Sar 3 1 0 0 $22,440 Dist 2 1 0 0 $22,440

5Aug95-6Sar wf 1⅛ :483 1:132 1:383 1:52 Alw 34000N1X 85 2 1 11 1½ 12 1hd Bailey J D 112 6.90 76-23 Rank And File112hd Slip1121¼ Knackattack1171 All out 6
24Jly95-7Sar fst 1⅛ :471 1:114 1:373 1:501 3+ Alw 34000N1X 81 2 2 21 2hd 1½ 44 Bailey J D 112 17.10 81-13 Jo Ran Express1121 Law Of The Sea106hd Cresson Springs1113 Bid, tired 7
4Jly95-3Bel fst 7f :223 :453 1:114 1:253 3+ Md 45000 72 3 8 42 31½ 1hd 13¾ Bailey J D 112 11.50 73-17 Rank And File1123¾ Point Man1151¼ Kadrmas1151 Altered course 1/4 pl 8
8Jun95-4Bel fm 1¼ T :472 1:12 1:363 2:004 3+ Md Sp Wt 50 7 2 2½ 31½ 810 819 Samyn J L 112 61.25 65-17 Menzies112¾ Kazan1178½ Banquet1143 Dueled, tired 12
21May95-10Bel fm 1⅛ T :234 :473 1:121 1:432 3+ Md Sp Wt 64 4 3 31½ 21 31½ 64¾ Santos J A 114 12.90 74-15 Hypo Runner1142 Come Talk To Me113½ Mactou1131¼ Bid, flattened 10
6May95-4Bel gd 1 T :244 :48 1:134 1:372 3+ Md Sp Wt 49 7 9 106¾ 54½ 78 714¾ Samyn J L 113 16.60 61-22 Fidgetyfeet1131 Forest Thunder114½ Paulo1131 Four wide, flattened 12
24Sep94-3Bel my 7f :223 :461 1:103 1:234 Md Sp Wt 44 4 3 33½ 42 411 516 Krone J A 118 5.50 71-13 Composer1182½ Nostra1138 Leap To Flame1189 No factor 5
21Aug94-3Sar sly 7f ⊗ :221 :452 1:112 1:253 Md Sp Wt 26 3 5 2hd 23½ 59¼ 720 Bailey J D 118 8.40 57-20 Manila Thriller1181¼ Noble 'n Heart1185 Banquet1185¼ Brief speed 8
WORKOUTS: Jly 17 Bel 4f fst :464 H 2/62 Jly 1 Bel 4f fst :481 H 4/52 Jun 26 Bel 4f gd :512 B 17/19 Jun 5 Bel 4f fst :49 B 19/36 May 30 Bel 3f sly :382 B (d)2/7 May 20 Bel 3f my :373 B 3/7

Jo Ran Express
Own: Stasi Randy
MAPLE E (52 7 7 7 .13)

B. g. 4
Sire: Gate Dancer (Sovereign Dancer)
Dam: Kennedy Express (Exuberant)
Br: Opstein Kenneth (Fla)
Tr: Ortiz Paulino O (3 1 1 0 .33)

115

Lifetime Record: 13 2 3 4 $71,160
1995 5 1 1 1 $34,800 Turf 0 0 0 0
1994 6 1 2 1 $31,200 Wet 2 0 0 1 $1,920
Sar 1 1 0 0 $20,400 Dist 3 1 2 0 $33,800

24Jly95-7Sar fst 1⅛ :471 1:114 1:373 1:501 3+ Alw 34000N1X 88 1 7 712 67½ 42½ 11 Maple E 112 3.05 85-13 JoRanExpress1121 LawOfTheSe106hd CressonSprings1113 Strong finish 7
8Jly95-4Bel fst 1⅛ :452 1:111 1:363 1:50 3+ Alw 34000N1X 86 7 4 48½ 31 21 22 Maple E 120 3.00 80-21 SaveTheWhale1132 JoRnExpress1202½ CressonSprings113nk Bid, 2nd best 7
24Jun95-3Bel fst 1⅛ :23 :461 1:11 1:44 3+ Alw 34000N1X 83 4 7 76 63 41½ 41½ Maple E 120 4.30 77-24 Tymtodyn1131 Save The Whale113nk Slip111nk Wide, hung 7
10Jun95-1Bel fst 1 :23 :452 1:102 1:372 3+ Alw 34000N1X 85 1 8 810 87½ 55 43½ Martin G J5 115 9.00 72-25 Jackson110no Northern Ensign1133 Tymtodyn114½ Belated rally 8
21May95-7Bel fst 6f :222 :461 :583 1:114 3+ Alw 32000N1X 80 5 3 108½ 96 53½ 32½ Martin G J5 114 29.50 79-22 Jump The Shadow1121¼ Frisco Gold1211½ Jo Ran Express114¾ 12
Bumped early, took up 7/16 pl
18Jly94-6Bel sly 1 :232 :462 1:103 1:363 3+ Alw 30000N1X 64 5 6 618 612 614 613 Alvarado F T 113 3.30 67-22 Fleethoof117¾ CommodoreAdmiral111nk InsideTheBeltwy112nk No factor 7
6Jly94-5Bel fst 1⅛ :234 :472 1:122 1:433 3+ Alw 30000N2L 80 2 1 1hd 2hd 51¾ 56¾ Velazquez J R 111 3.60 77-23 Final Clearance113½ Chrys1164 Track Topper117nk Dueled inside 6
25Jun94-5Bel fst 1⅛ :46 1:103 1:364 1:501 3+ Alw 30000N1X 80 4 2 21 1hd 1½ 2nk Velazquez J R 111 *1.70 80-25 Wajir119nk Jo Ran Express1111¼ Sangre De Toro1123¾ Gamely 6
21May94-9Bel fst 1⅛ :224 :453 1:093 1:404 3+ Alw 30000N1X 84 4 6 64 44 27 214 Velazquez J R 110 4.70 84-12 UnccontdFor11514 JoRnExprss1105 LordWllstn112nk Circled turn, rallied 7
10May94-7Bel fst 1⅛ :23 :462 1:111 1:424 3+ Alw 30000N2L 81 4 5 85½ 84 43½ 33½ Velazquez J R 110 6.70 85-10 Sky Hero110½ Final Clearance1132¾ Jo Ran Express110nk Rallied wide 8
WORKOUTS: Aug 11 Bel tr.t 4f fst :491 B 5/20 Jly 21 Bel 4f fst :502 B 11/17 Jun 20 Bel tr.t 4f fst :51 B 9/11 Jun 5 Bel 5f fst 1:041 B 15/16

Royal Haven
Own: Davis Barbara J
LUZZI M J (79 7 5 6 .09)

Dk. b or br g. 3 (Apr)
Sire: Hail Emperor (Graustark)
Dam: Cruising Haven (Shelter Half)
Br: Robert T. Manfuso (Md)
Tr: Moschera Gasper S (37 6 6 4 .16)

109

Lifetime Record: 4 3 1 0 $44,340
1995 4 3 1 0 $44,340 Turf 0 0 0 0
1994 0 M 0 0 Wet 2 2 0 0 $26,700
Sar 1 1 0 0 $21,000 Dist 0 0 0 0

6Aug95-3Sar wf 7f :222 :453 1:11 1:242 Clm c-75000 87 4 5 34½ 42¾ 31 12 Luzzi M J 118 3.30 84-17 Royal Haven1182 Dakota's Trick1201¼ Winwithwalker1183½ Going away 6
Claimed from Manfuso Robert T, Voss Katharine M Trainer
30Jun95-7Lrl fst 7f :23 :46 1:103 1:23 3+ Alw 24500N1X 82 7 5 31 53½ 2hd 11¾ Hamilton S D L 114 12.40 94-14 Royal Haven1141¾ Pleasant Dancer1173¾ Sovereign Mac117hd Driving 12
6Jun95-6Pim fst 6f :231 :462 :582 1:111 Alw 17500N2L 73 3 7 68 67½ 35 24¾ Hamilton S D L 115 18.30 87-13 Cat Be Nimble1174¾ Royal Haven115¾ Scrub Brush1175 Rallied 7
18May95-5Pim sly 6f :231 :464 :594 1:13 3+ Md 18500 57 8 3 31½ 23 2½ 12½ Hamilton S D 114 32.30 83-14 Royal Haven1142½ Real Hip1143¾ Preamplifier114no Driving 9
WORKOUTS: Aug 2 Sar 6f fst 1:182 B 6/8 Jly 25 Bow 5f fst 1:03 B 3/11 Jun 26 Bow 6f gd 1:143 B 1/1 Jun 2 Bow 5f fst 1:011 B 2/6

1 — Wayfarer — Four of his last five starts had been on turf, but in the dirt start, a 1⅛-mile allowance on a wet fast track at Saratoga, he was a good second by three lengths. In fact, he had two wins and a second in three starts at this distance. Given that,

I still didn't like him. He'd lost eight straight races, and I didn't like his last start. Even though it was on grass, he was 10th by 20 lengths after finishing third in his previous two grass starts.

2 — Da Bull — He'd chased some good three-year-olds, including Wild Syn and Composer, and was an okay third in the Fairmont Derby in his last start on a sloppy track. He'd been in the money six of eight starts. He raced on the lead in five of his eight starts and was stretching out to 1⅛ miles for the first time.

3 — Crary — This once promising two-year-old was now a four-year-old who hadn't won in 13 starts stretching out over two years. His last race was on turf, so you could toss it. He was second on dirt in his previous two starts at 1¹/₁₆ miles. As a son of Mt. Livermore, whose progeny favor speed, it was hard to imagine him as a force at nine furlongs. But his lone two poor tries at 1⅛ miles — which were his bottom two PPs in the *Form* — were in the Florida Derby against Holy Bull and in the Wood Memorial against Irgun and Go For Gin. Still, how do you fall in love with a horse who hasn't won in two years?

4 — Jo Ran Express — Stepping up off a 1⅛-mile allowance win at Saratoga. An obvious contender.

5 — Royal Haven — Gaspar Moschera claimed this Maryland shipper for $75,000 in his last start, a seven-furlong win at Saratoga by two lengths. That gave him three wins and a second in four lifetime starts. He was stretching out past seven furlongs for the first time, but he raced from off the pace and was a grandson of distance loving Graustark. Another definite plus was that he got in at 109 pounds, receiving three to six pounds from the other four horses.

I loved Royal Haven this day, picked him in the *Gazette* and bet him at 5-2. But I also cased out the exacta payoffs and played exactas with him and Da Bull and Jo Ran Express.

Royal Haven went off at 5-2. Da Bull was the 2-1 favorite, with Wayfarer a slightly shorter 5-2, Jo Ran Express at 4-1 and Crary at 7-1. Using the speed built in from his sprints, Royal Haven went wire to wire under a heady ride by Mike Luzzi to score by two lengths. Da Bull sat second the entire way and finished second, three lengths in front of Crary.

The exacta — in this field of five — with a 5-2 shot over a 2-1 favorite, paid $23.40.

EIGHTH RACE
Saratoga
AUGUST 17, 1995

1½ MILES. (1.47) ALLOWANCE. Purse $36,000. 3-year-olds and upward which have not won two races other than maiden, claiming or starter. Weights; 3-year-olds, 117 lbs. Older, 123 lbs. Non-winners of $22,800 since May 3, allowed 3 lbs. Of $18,000 twice in 1995, 5 lbs. Of $15,000 twice in 1995, 8 lbs. (Races where entered for $50,000 or less not considered in allowances.)

Value of Race: $36,000 Winner $21,600; second $7,200; third $3,960; fourth $2,160; fifth $1,080. Mutuel Pool $420,985.00 Exacta Pool $559,363.00

Last Raced	Horse	M/Eqt. A.Wt	PP	St	¼	½	¾	Str	Fin	Jockey	Odds $1
6Aug95 3Sar1	Royal Haven	3 109	5	4	1¹	1½	1hd	11½	1²	Luzzi M J	2.75
6Aug95 8FP3	Da Bull	bf 3 112	2	3	2⁴	2⁴	2²	2³	2³	Sellers S J	2.05
28Jly95 4Sar6	Crary	b 4 115	3	5	3hd	4⁵	3hd	3hd	3nk	Day P	7.20
6Aug95 4Sar10	Wayfarer	4 115	1	1	4¹	3hd	43½	4²	41½	Krone J A	2.70
24Jly95 7Sar1	Jo Ran Express	4 115	4	2	5	5	5	5	5	Maple E	4.00

OFF AT 4:38 Start Good. Won driving. Time, :24¹, :48², 1:13², 1:38, 1:50⁴ Track fast.

$2 Mutuel Prices:

6-ROYAL HAVEN	7.50	4.30	3.00
2-DA BULL		3.70	2.90
3-CRARY			3.80

$2 EXACTA 6-2 PAID $23.40

Dk. b. or br. g, (Apr), by Hail Emperor-Cruising Haven, by Shelter Half. Trainer Moschera Gasper S. Bred by Robert T. Manfuso (Md).

ROYAL HAVEN rushed up to gain the early advantage, set the pace under pressure to the top of the stretch, shook off DA BULL to get clear in midstretch then drew away under pressure. DA BULL angled to the outside on the first turn, forced the pace outside the winner into upper stretch, but couldn't stay with that one through the lane. CRARY reserved early, closed the gap a bit midway on the turn, but couldn't sustain his rally. WAYFARER raced just inside CRARY the entire way and lacked a strong closing bid. JO RAN EXPRESS trailed throughout.

Owners— 1, Davis Barbara J; 2, Lamaster Bill; 3, Condren & Cornacchia & Paulson; 4, Burning Day Farm; 5, Stasi Randy
Trainers—1, Moschera Gasper S; 2, Walden W Elliott; 3, Zito Nicholas P; 4, Nafzger Carl A; 5, Ortiz Paulino O
Scratched— Defrere (22Jly95 5SAR1), Rank And File (5Aug95 6SAR1)

9

Triples

There are many roads to travel to locate an exotic overlay. One is by identifying an overlay and using him to wheel other horses in an exacta because you think the second finisher could be anybody else in the field. Another way is by taking an overlay horse and eliminating those other horses in the race that you think have no chance at all to finish second or third.

This triple (trifecta) was highlighted by a winner I picked in the *Gazette* at Saratoga in 1995 and bet, unfortunately for me, straight only.

A field of 11 New York-Bred maiden three-year-olds and up went to bat in the fifth race, August 18, at 1⅛ miles on the inner turf course:

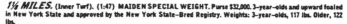

5 Saratoga

1⅛ MILES. (Inner Turf). (1:47) MAIDEN SPECIAL WEIGHT. Purse $32,000. 3-year-olds and upward foaled in New York State and approved by the New York State-Bred Registry. Weights: 3-year-olds, 117 lbs. Older, 122 lbs.

Irish Patriot
Own: Delaney Austin
DAY P (125 21 15 19 .17)
Dk. b or br g. 3 (Apr)
Sire: Fortunate Prospect (Northern Prospect)
Dam: Nara (Green Forest)
Br: Delaney Austin (NY)
Tr: O'Brien Leo (41 5 6 4 .12)
117
Lifetime Record: 12 M 4 2 $32,180
1995 7 M 4 1 $28,500 | Turf 5 0 1 1 $3,700
1994 5 M 0 1 $3,600 | Wet 0 0 0 0
Sar ⓣ 1 0 0 0 | Dist ⓣ 2 0 0 1 $3,300

31Jly95-5Sar fm 1⅛ ⓣ :461 1:111 1:371 1:493 3+ ⓢMd Sp Wt 55 2 9 109½ 108¾ 73½ 95½ Day P 117 *.85e 81-08 Striver117¾ Ruffed Grouse122no Make No Mistake122no 11
Steadied early, blocked stretch
12Jly95-5Bel fst 1 :23 :463 1:114 1:383 3+ ⓢMd Sp Wt 61 7 3 41 2½ 2½ 22 Velazquez J R 113 b *.55 68-23 Raising Peas1152 Irish Patriot1133 Worldly Slew108hd Bid, hung 9
3Jly95-5Bel yl 1¼ ⓣ :481 1:133 1:39 2:051 3+ ⓢMd Sp Wt 64 9 3 22½ 2½ 2hd 62½ Velazquez J R 113 *.55 59-26 Il Grappa113½ Segrenti1141½ Billy King122nk Bid, tired 12
7Jun95-5Bel gd 1 1/16 ⓣ :231 :462 1:112 1:431 3+ ⓢMd Sp Wt 93 3 4 43 31 1hd 2nk Velazquez J R 113 *.85 82-22 Identity113nk Irish Patriot11320 Uncle Twist111nk Bid, game 10
25May95-3Bel fst 1 1/16 :234 :472 1:123 1:452 3+ ⓢMd Sp Wt 71 1 1 11½ 2hd 1½ 2no Smith M E 113 *.85 72-29 Duchess's Secret114no Irish Patriot1138 Il Grappa113¾ Dueled, game 7
29Apr95-9Aqu fm 1⅛ ⓣ :47 1:113 1:37 1:493 3+ ⓢMd Sp Wt 76 10 6 77½ 74½ 35 34 Martin G J5 108 *1.90 88-05 Sounds Like Scott1133¾ New York Lights113hd IrishPatriot1082 Late gain 10
17Apr95-1Aqu fst 1⅛ :49 1:15 1:414 1:544 3+ ⓢMd Sp Wt 48 1 5 53½ 62½ 34½ 210½ Martin G J7 106 10.70 55-24 Winfield D. H.11310 Irish Patriot1062½ Identity1131½ Check early, svd grnd 11
9Nov94-9Aqu fst 1 :24 :482 1:142 1:412 ⓢMd Sp Wt 48 6 3 42 3nk 2½ 33¾ Chavez J F 118 6.90 57-33 Dig Zig118½ Identity1183¾ Irish Patriot118¾ No late bid 10
3Nov94-2Aqu fst 6f :221 :46 :582 1:11 ⓢMd Sp Wt 42 6 8 107¾ 78 611 515 Moran M T 118 19.80e 72-15 Raimondo118hd Mine'spro11810 Fearless And Free1083 Steadied 3/8 pl 10
5Oct94-3Bel fst 7f :23 :464 1:121 1:254 ⓢMd Sp Wt 48 3 11 85¾ 98¾ 46½ 59 Moran M T 118 3.90e 65-27 Count J. R.1181½ Slew's Miner118½ Maltbie1187 Broke slowly 11
WORKOUTS: May 21 Bel 5f fst 1:014 H 26/54

A. J. Warbucks
Own: Schaeffer Carol
LOVATO F JR (14 1 2 1 .07)
B. g. 6
Sire: Rallying Cry (Hoist the Flag)
Dam: Elsada (Iron Warrior)
Br: Yageda Stanley (NY)
Tr: Schaeffer Stephen W Jr (—)
122
Lifetime Record: 28 M 4 3 $39,470
1995 1 M 0 0 $1,920 | Turf 20 0 4 2 $36,230
1994 9 M 1 0 $9,120 | Wet -1 0 0 1 $3,240
Sar ⓣ 3 0 1 0 $5,610 | Dist ⓣ 3 0 0 0

14Jly95-9Bel fm 1 ⓣ :223 :454 1:101 1:35 3+ ⓢMd Sp Wt 58 4 8 85½ 64½ 35½ 48 Lovato F Jr 122 b 26.25 80-12 Top Tapper1223 Lunatic Luke1135 Church St. Dancer115hd Flattened out 10
26Nov94-2Aqu sf 1⅛ ⓣ :494 1:152 1:413 1:544 3+ Md Sp Wt 33 5 8 55½ 75½ 914 919¾ Rodriquez E M 122 b 27.25 46-29 Sir Bert1202 Poulet Chasseur1204½ Right Forward1201½ Faded 10
28Oct94-2Aqu fm 1⅛ ⓣ :473 1:132 1:392 1:522 3+ ⓢMd Sp Wt 42 6 12 714 65 610 513½ Pezua J M 122 b 9.00 64-18 Crosskate1196 TripleFst1141¾ TkesomeBelieving1145½ Improved position 12
14Sep94-3Bel fm 1 1/16 ⓣ :233 :472 1:12 1:423 3+ Md Sp Wt 42 7 9 912 97½ 911 818¾ Chavez J F 122 b 22.50 64-14 Yokohama1182 Super Twenty Five1181¾ Hawkeye Bay1183 Outrun 10
2Sep94-1Bel fm 1 1/16 ⓣ :241 :474 1:121 1:434 3+ ⓢMd Sp Wt 64 2 7 52¾ 51¾ 51½ 63½ Bailey J D 122 b 4.10 74-17 Crooked Heels1181½ Lord Basil118nk Al's Rose118hd Lacked rally 10
Placed 5th through disqualification.
12Aug94-5Sar fm 1 1/16 ⓣ :24 :483 1:131 1:434 3+ Md Sp Wt 45 5 10 84¾ 42½ 96½ 912½ Lovato F Jr 122 b 20.00 68-10 RiskYourWlth117hd Yokohm1173½ GonDncngAgn1173½ Wide, flattened out 10
26Jun94-9Bel fm 1 1/16 ⓣ :224 :453 1:102 1:424 3+ ⓢMd Sp Wt 52 8 10 97 84½ 85½ 89½ Chavez J F 122 b 3.60 75-16 Jacsonzac1222½ North Forty Four1171½ Ace The Test122no Broke slowly 10
4Jun94-3Bel fm 1 1/16 ⓣ :223 :454 1:101 1:412 3+ ⓢMd Sp Wt 70 4 10 88 74½ 33 27 Chavez J F 122 b 4.90 84-10 RainAlert1227 A.J.Warbucks1222½ NrrowRiver1144 Checked break, wide 10
14May94-5Bel fm 1¼ ⓣ :501 1:141 1:39 2:033 3+ ⓢMd Sp Wt 71 3 8 63 11½ 3½ 43¾ Chavez J F 124 b *2.60 68-20 Mr Hydro124no The Bank Man1082 Watrals Sea Trip1151¾ 12
Steadied, took up, middle move
27Apr94-5Aqu gd 1 1/16 ⓣ :234 :483 1:124 1:45 3+ Md Sp Wt 59 4 9 711 59 516 414½ Chavez J F 124 b 7.40 69-14 Electric Image11512 Juan In A Million1151½ Price Rise115½ Four wide 10
WORKOUTS: Aug 8 Bel tr.t 4f fst :502 B 21/29 Jly 13 Bel tr.t 3f fst :38 B 11/16 Jun 1 Bel tr.t 5f fst 1:033 B 4/4

Plattkin
Own: Martino Phyllis
DECARLO C P (19 0 4 2 .00)
B. g. 4
Sire: Late Act (Stage Door Johnny)
Dam: Glut's Kin (Water Prince)
Br: Galloping Acres Farm (NY)
Tr: Martino Phyllis (1 0 0 0 .00)
122
Lifetime Record: 10 M 0 0 $720
1995 10 M 0 0 $720 | Turf 0 0 0 0
1994 0 M 0 0 | Wet 0 0 0 0
Sar ⓣ 0 0 0 0 | Dist ⓣ 0 0 0 0

10Aug95-2Sar fst 6½f :222 :462 1:121 1:192 3+ ⓢMd Sp Wt 33 2 8 109½ 1011 89½ 810½ Lovato F Jr 121 b 73.25 68-13 Biggie Munn1212½ Decimal Place117no DapperDutchman117¾ No response 11
13Apr95-4Aqu fst 1 :232 :462 1:114 1:371 Md Sp Wt — 4 6 62¾ 65½ 617 — Santagata N 121 b 65.50 — 24 ErumpentO'rolli1144½ Bluffy1162¾ DiggersWell1211¾ Checked break, eased 6
26Mar95-5Aqu fst 6f :23 :471 :594 1:13 Md Sp Wt 21 3 7 78½ 58 512 617½ Rodriquez E M 122 b 55.75 59-17 Fort Edward122¾ Frisco Gold1223¾ Lovubaby12213 Broke slowly 8
22Mar95-1Aqu fst 6½f :23 :474 1:141 1:21 Md 25000 15 4 8 42 53 55½ 715 Cruguet J 120 20.70 60-20 LonlyGmblr120½ ChocltWzrd120no SpWthThDvl1203 Saved ground, tired 9
15Mar95-5Aqu fst 6½f :234 :461 1:124 1:193 Md Sp Wt 40 1 7 54 67½ 76½ 77½ Rodriquez E M 120 74.00 75-14 Abtwil1201½ Whose On First120hd Erumpent O'rolli113no Saved ground 8
5Mar95-6Aqu fst 170 ⊡ :233 :474 1:142 1:462 Md Sp Wt — 1 4 58 59½ 716 — Rodriquez E M 122 39.75 — 33 It'sJohn'sTim122nk PrsonlAffir1155 PoltclProspct122hd Done early, eased 7
20Feb95-5Aqu fst 1⅛ ⊡ :493 1:151 1:414 1:551 Md Sp Wt 25 1 9 915 822 827 832¾ Madrid A Jr 122 18.40 27-29 ClerSense1222½ PoliticlProspct1224¾ It'sJohn'sTim1225½ Lacked response 9
16Feb95-1Aqu fst 6f ⊡ :233 :473 1:003 1:134 Md Sp Wt 41 4 6 716 718 78¾ 67½ Rodriquez E M 122 30.00 67-21 DnzigsPride122½ LevThFlg1223½ ChocoltWizrd122nk Stead, pinched break 7
1Feb95-2Aqu fst 6f ⊡ :224 :464 :594 1:134 Md 35000 38 2 8 713 613 513 410½ Rodriquez E M 122 56.00 64-21 John Karavas1186½ Instant Grudge1223¾ The Boz'n115no Broke slowly 9
28Jan95-5Aqu fst 6f ⊡ :24 :482 1:011 1:143 Md 35000 11 10 8 1011 914 917 921¾ Rodriquez E M 122 95.50 48-29 Szczepnkowski1222¾ AccordingToCole1222½ ChngingRhy1183½ Never close 11
WORKOUTS: Jly 28 Sar 4f fst :50 B 17/23 Jly 5 Sar tr.t 3f fst :392 B 4/5 May 31 Sar ⓣ 4f fm :52 B (d)3/7

I Know The Family
Own: Kelly Michael J
DAVIS R G (124 12 18 24 .10)
B. g. 3 (Mar)
Sire: Personal Flag (Private Account)
Dam: It's My Family (Dr. Carter)
Br: Dragone Allan R (NY)
Tr: Kelly Michael J (6 0 1 2 .00)
117
Lifetime Record: 2 M 0 0 $0
1995 2 M 0 0 | Turf 1 0 0 0
1994 0 M 0 0 | Wet 0 0 0 0
Sar ⓣ 0 0 0 0 | Dist ⓣ 0 0 0 0

14Jly95-9Bel fm 1 ⓣ :223 :454 1:101 1:35 3+ ⓢMd Sp Wt 42 2 9 99½ 87½ 710 715½ Davis R G 113 b 5.90 72-12 Top Tapper1223 Lunatic Luke1135 Church St. Dancer115hd Broke slowly 10
17Jun95-1Bel fst 6f :223 :462 :584 1:113 3+ ⓢMd Sp Wt 42 2 7 55½ 54 79¼ 715½ Leon F 113 b 21.40 68-19 Tintinnabular1222¾ All For You1121 Matthew W.1136½ Hustled, tired 12
WORKOUTS: Aug 10 Sar 1 fst 1:43 B 1/1 Jly 29 Sar 7f fst 1:303 B 1/1 ●Jly 8 Bel 5f fst :594 H 1/27 Jly 4 Bel 4f fst :484 B 15/71 Jun 7 Bel 6f fst 1:154 Hg3/4 Jun 2 Bel 5f fst 1:011 H 8/24

Speediation
Own: Fiore John & Joseph & Nicholas J
BECKNER D V (58 1 5 2 .02)
Gr. g. 4
Sire: Cojak (Cohoes)
Dam: Fair Jeanine (Pontoise)
Br: J. N. J. Stables & Alt-Ran Stable (NY)
Tr: Fiore Nicholas J (—)
122
Lifetime Record: 6 M 0 0 $0
1995 6 M 0 0 | Turf 0 0 0 0
1994 0 M 0 0 | Wet 0 0 0 0
Sar ⓣ 0 0 0 0 | Dist ⓣ 0 0 0 0

15Jly95-2Bel fst 6f :224 :462 :584 1:113 3+ ⓢMd Sp Wt 27 3 8 129½ 108½ 912 1018½ Graell A 122 b 103.75 65-11 Matthew W.1143 Scanner Pro1132½ Programable1143 No speed 12
29Jun95-5Bel fst 7f :23 :471 1:13 1:26 3+ ⓢMd Sp Wt 18 6 9 85½ 85½ 910 1026¾ Graell A 123 b 76.00 44-22 Sunny Ghost1145½ Programable1149 Freeze The Raise116½ No factor 11
17Jun95-1Bel fst 6f :223 :462 :584 1:113 3+ ⓢMd Sp Wt 44 1 11 1113 107½ 89½ 615 Graell A 122 b 59.75 68-19 Tintinnabular1222¾ All For You1121 Matthew W.1136½ Checked break 12
21Apr95-3Aqu fst 6f :223 :461 :584 1:12 3+ ⓢMd Sp Wt 32 4 6 65 66½ 711 716¾ Rydowski S R 123 31.00 65-15 Lovubaby1236 Selected Sauce1142½ Fouldre116nk Done early 8
14Apr95-3Aqu fst 1 :232 :461 1:113 1:374 Clm 30000N2L 13 1 5 43 77½ 720 731½ Dunkelberger T L5 113 26.75 49-13 GallntGuest1114 FinlRelity108¾ GrduteSchool1184½ Broke slowly, outrun 7
30Mar95-9Aqu fst 6½f :222 :454 1:114 1:183 ⓢAlw 30000N1X 48 2 9 810 97¾ 87 79¾ Lovato F Jr 114 40.25 77-17 Gate Six114nk Best Aquarian1141½ Accordion1142½ Broke slowly, green 9
WORKOUTS: Aug 1 Bel tr.t 3f fst :363 B 2/7 Jly 10 Aqu 3f fst :371 B 2/4 Jun 27 Aqu 3f sly :364 H (d)1/2 Jun 13 Aqu 4f my :49 H 2/3 ●Jun 3 Aqu 5f fst 1:013 Hg1/5 May 29 Aqu 3f gd :381 B 3/4

My Song

Own: Engel Karen K & Richard L

BAILEY J D (138 30 17 17 .22)

Dk. b or br f. 3 (Mar)
Sire: Personal Flag (Private Account)
Dam: Accipiter's Song (Accipiter)
Br: Dr. J. K. Griggs (NY)
Tr: O'Connell Richard (26 2 4 0 .08)

112

Lifetime Record:	9 M 2 0	$16,520			
1995	9 M 2 0	$16,520	Turf	5 0 2 0	$16,520
1994	0 M 0 0		Wet	1 0 0 0	
Sar Ⓣ	1 0 1 0	$6,800	Dist Ⓣ	2 0 1 0	$8,600

30Jly95-9Sar	fm	1⅛ [T]	:461 1:102 1:361 1:484	3+ Ⓕ[S]Alw 34000N1X	66	11	4	52¼	1hd	2½	28	Bailey J D	112 f	13.00	83-09	Sweetzie1138 My Song112¾ Through The Tulips1163	Held place	12
7Jly95-5Bel	fm	1 1/16 [T]	:241 :472 1:11 1:441	3+ Ⓕ[S]Md Sp Wt	67	4	1	1½	22½	23½	44	Velazquez J R	113	*.90	71-22	FollowJoanne1222 CallToPrayer113nk Mpleline1131¾	Bumped break, tired	10
16Jun95-5Bel	fm	1 1/16 [T]	:241 :473 1:114 1:424	ⒻClm 45000	69	3	1	11	1½	2½	25½	Velazquez J R	114	11.20e	76-12	Alyinda1165½ My Song114½ Aidan's Breath116½	Dueled, held 2nd	10
25May95-6Bel	fm	1 1/16 Ⓣ	:23 :46 1:102 1:42	ⒻClm 60000	60	2	2	1hd	1hd	41¾	612¼	Santos J A	114 b	15.80	76-18	Pitchunia1164¾ Mega112nk Darlin Danika1165	Dueled, tired	7
29Apr95-9Aqu	fm	1⅛ Ⓣ	:47 1:113 1:37 1:493	3+ [S]Md Sp Wt	72	3	7	53	32	45	46	Velazquez J R	110 b	30.50	86-05	SoundsLikeScott1133¾ NwYorkLights113hd IrishPtriot1082	Flattened out	10
23Mar95-1Aqu	fst	1	:233 :473 1:144 1:424	ⒻMd 25000	18	3	5	62¾	64½	710	817½	Nelson D	120 b	47.00	38-34	Northern Five1206½ Heliopause115nk [DH]Stellina113	Tired	9
9Mar95-9Aqu	wf	170 [•]	:24 :49 1:144 1:452	Ⓕ[S]Md Sp Wt	19	7	5	63	89½	916	922¾	Madrid A Jr	120 b	42.00	48-24	Bo Bo's Sister1201½ Cool Babe120nk Razzita Margrita1202	Wide, tired	9
24Feb95-5Aqu	fst	1 1/16 [•]	:234 :493 1:16 1:491	Ⓕ[S]Md Sp Wt	26	7	3	21½	2½	610	717½	Madrid A Jr	121 b	14.40	41-29	Positive Tally116nk [D]Baby's In A Fog1211 Leah Ray114no	Used in pace	9
11Feb95-1Aqu	fst	6f [•]	:234 :49 1:03 1:17	Ⓕ[S]Md Sp Wt	22	9	8	911	89½	89½	810¾	Madrid A Jr	120 b	*1.55e	47-33	Doroteo Arango1202½ Baby's In A Fog120nk Bo Bo's Sister1202¾	No threat	10

WORKOUTS: Aug 16 Sar 4f fst :524 B 28/28 Aug 10 Sar 4f fst :503 H 21/25 Jly 25 Sar 4f fst :492 B 21/44 Jly 19 Bel 4f fst :50 B 47/66 Jly 6 Bel 3f fst :38 B 12/19 Jun 29 Bel 4f fst :494 B 24/49

Make No Mistake

Own: Foss Monty & Schwartz Gary

CHAVEZ J F (130 20 17 8 .15)

Ch. g. 6
Sire: Thunder Puddles (Speak John)
Dam: Restless Gerry (Peace Corps)
Br: Garofalo Juliana (NY)
Tr: Contessa Gary C (16 1 2 2 .06)

122

Lifetime Record:	13 M 3 2	$22,840			
1995	2 M 0 1	$3,520	Turf	8 0 2 1	$14,740
1994	1 M 0 0		Wet	0 0 0 0	
Sar Ⓣ	4 0 1 1	$9,130	Dist Ⓣ	3 0 1 1	$9,130

31Jly95-5Sar	fm	1⅛ [T]	:461 1:111 1:371 1:493	3+ [S]Md Sp Wt	62	6	2	2hd	2hd	3½	32½	Rydowski S R	122	10.70	84-08	Striver1172½ Ruffed Grouse122no Make No Mistake122no	Dueled outside	11
23Jly95-3Sar	fm	1 1/16 [T]	:232 :481 1:124 1:441	3+ Md Sp Wt	36	3	5	52	53	810	817½	Rydowski S R	122	8.40	61-15	Classic Arbitrage1229 Mi Maestro115no Excelleet115hd	Tired	10
26Jun94-9Bel	fm	1 1/16 Ⓣ	:224 :453 1:102 1:424	3+ [S]Md Sp Wt	56	2	1	1½	1hd	5¾	77	Alvarado F T	122 f	5.50	77-16	Jacsonzac1222½ North Forty Four1171½ Ace The Test122no	Gave way	10
21Aug93-3Sar	yl	1⅛ Ⓣ	:49 1:14 1:391 1:511	3+ Md Sp Wt	—	7	2	21½	—	—	—	McCarron C J	122	3.40	— 22	Majesty's Darby117½ Rain Alert1173 Wild West1171½	Pulled up lame	11
13Aug93-5Sar	fm	1⅛ Ⓣ	:473 1:114 1:363 1:491	3+ [S]Md Sp Wt	75	10	1	11	11½	2½	22½	Migliore R	122	3.70	80-15	Bye And Comply1172½ Make No Mistake1223 Over Point1171¾	Gamely	12
8Jly93-2Bel	fm	1 1/16 Ⓣ	:23 :461 1:094 1:40	3+ Md Sp Wt	67	4	1	11½	1½	32	59	Migliore R	122 f	3.20	87-09	Nobiz Like Showbiz1161½ Wills1225½ Luciano P.116hd	Speed, tired	10
2Jun93-9Bel	gd	1⅜ Ⓣ	:473 1:123 1:38 2:153	3+ [S]Md Sp Wt	79	2	1	13½	11	1½	2nk	Alvarado F T	122	10.00	89-16	Musical Storm122nk Make No Mistake1229 Warner Wolf1225	Gamely	11
23May93-3Bel	fst	7f	:231 :47 1:121 1:251	3+ [S]Md Sp Wt	62	5	4	61¾	63½	63¾	55½	Leon F7	117	13.00	71-23	Sky Carr1152 Small Pack115no World Flag1153	Evenly	11
6May93-9Bel	gd	1 1/16 Ⓣ	:233 :473 1:123 1:44	3+ [S]Md Sp Wt	60	11	4	31½	1½	3½	56¾	Rodriguez R R5	119	6.20	69-19	Noble Romancer1245 Jacsonzac115no Stopped Silence1151	Bid, tired	12
25Apr93-5Aqu	fst	6f	:223 :462 :592 1:13	3+ [S]Md Sp Wt	53	4	2	42¾	32	33½	54	Santagata N	124	8.80	73-18	Dr. Messina115¾ Cannon Row124¾ Small Pack1152	Tired	8

WORKOUTS: Jly 17 Bel 7f fst 1:272 B 1/1 Jly 9 Bel 7f fst 1:272 H 1/1 Jun 29 Bel 5f fst 1:044 B 25/28 Jun 17 Bel 4f fst :51 B 49/63 May 23 Bel 4f fst :50 B 25/42

Demanding Terms

Own: Boto Stable

MAPLE E (54 7 8 7 .13)

Ro. c. 3 (Feb)
Sire: Private Terms (Private Account)
Dam: Demand Attention (Al Hattab)
Br: Boto Thoroughbreds Inc (NY)
Tr: Kelly Timothy D (11 0 1 1 .00)

117

Lifetime Record:	3 M 0 0	$2,760			
1995	3 M 0 0	$2,760	Turf	1 0 0 0	
1994	0 M 0 0		Wet	1 0 0 0	$960
Sar Ⓣ	0 0 0 0		Dist Ⓣ	0 0 0 0	

10Aug95-2Sar	fst	6½f	:222 :462 1:121 1:192	3+ [S]Md Sp Wt	49	7	11	65½	43	56	43½	Alvarado F T	117	3.65	75-13	BiggieMunn1212½ DecimlPlce117no DpprDutchmn117¾	Reared break, wide	11
3Jly95-5Bel	yl	1¼ [T]	:481 1:133 1:39 2:051	3+ [S]Md Sp Wt	48	10	10	98½	53½	66	89¾	Alvarado F T	114 b	17.20e	52-26	Il Grappa113½ Segrenti1141¼ Billy King122nk	Flattened out	12
25Jun95-3Bel	my	1 1/16	:232 :47 1:121 1:44	3+ Md Sp Wt	52	2	4	31	56¼	511	518¾	Alvarado F T	114 b	21.00	60-31	ClernceCod1135¾ ThnSom1132 ScondChildhood1141	Saved ground, tired	7

WORKOUTS: Aug 2 Sar 5f fst 1:013 H 3/34 Jly 30 Sar 3f fst :372 H 9/19 Jly 23 Sar 4f fst :491 B 31/54 ●Jly 15 Bel 3f fst :35 H 1/30 Jun 15 Bel 5f gd 1:021 Bg6/14 Jun 10 Bel 4f fst :51 Bg26/33

Watrals Finesse

Own: Watral Michael

MIGLIORE R (57 4 6 13 .07)

Dk. b or br f. 3 (May)
Sire: Overskate (Nodouble)
Dam: Shawanna (Graustarkian)
Br: Michael Watral (NY)
Tr: Brida Dennis J (19 2 2 4 .11)

112

Lifetime Record:	6 M 1 2	$16,100			
1995	6 M 1 2	$16,100	Turf	5 0 1 2	$16,100
1994	0 M 0 0		Wet	0 0 0 0	
Sar Ⓣ	1 0 0 0	$960	Dist Ⓣ	1 0 0 1	$3,300

7Aug95-3Sar	gd	1⅜ [T]	:484 1:143 1:40 2:183	3+ ⒻMd Sp Wt	60	9	9	86½	45	67½	56½	Migliore R	115	7.20	66-18	Winner's Edge1151½ Sean's Woodman1152½ Shallah115no	Flattened out	9
17Jly95-4Bel	fm	1¼ [T]	:461 1:114 1:364 2:024	3+ Ⓕ[S]Md Sp Wt	64	9	5	412	41¾	45½	35¾	Migliore R	114	3.05	68-18	ABlinkAndANod122nk JustFlirting1135½ WatrlsFinesse1141	Flattened out	12
14Jun95-6Bel	gd	1 1/16 Ⓣ	:233 :473 1:121 1:451	3+ Ⓕ[S]Md Sp Wt	69	4	7	73¾	42	31	2nk	Migliore R	114	8.80e	72-25	Lamplight114nk Watrals Finesse1142 Dennie Mae109hd	Split horses, game	11
31May95-5Bel	fm	1¼ [T]	:48 1:132 1:383 2:031	3+ ⒻMd Sp Wt	57	4	9	95½	63¾	59½	413	Nelson D	113	25.50	59-21	Klfo1127½ ARoseForShnnon1125½ SocilSovereign112hd	Steadied first turn	12
20May95-1Bel	gd	1 1/16	:24 :48 1:16 1:491	3+ Ⓕ[S]Md Sp Wt	16	5	4	53	75½	99	915¾	Martinez J R Jr	112	2.35	37-24	Overtake107nk Stellina1122 Hold You1121½	Wide, gave way	9
30Apr95-1Aqu	fm	1⅛ Ⓣ	:471 1:122 1:38 1:502	3+ Ⓕ[S]Md Sp Wt	61	8	11	1014	76½	39	310	Martinez J R Jr	112	24.75e	78-09	Sweetzie1076 Great Beginnings1124 Watrals Finesse1123	Bumped break	11

WORKOUTS: Aug 2 Sar 4f fst :50 B 18/38 Jly 1 Bel 4f fst :522 B 50/52

Micky Maccar

Own: Barrow Paul & Macarelli Gerald C

RYDOWSKI S R (18 1 1 2 .06)

Ch. g. 3 (Jun)
Sire: Ends Well (Lyphard)
Dam: Hawaiian Cutlass (Hawaii)
Br: Gus Schoenborn Jr & Stanley Greene (NY)
Tr: Barrow Paul (—)

117

Lifetime Record:	6 M 1 1	$4,048			
1995	5 M 1 0	$2,872	Turf	0 0 0 0	
1994	1 M 0 1	$1,176	Wet	1 0 0 0	$60
Sar Ⓣ	0 0 0 0		Dist Ⓣ	0 0 0 0	

28Jly95-8FL	fst	6f	:223 :464 :594 1:132	3+ [S]Md Sp Wt	44	2	4	64½	63	42	2no	Messina R	115 b	5.00	77-17	Lotta Brass122no Micky Maccar115nk Laughing Roman115nk	Gamely	7
6Jly95-8FL	my	1	:234 :472 1:131 1:40	3+ Md Sp Wt	31	2	4	39	611	613	624	Whitley K	115 b	8.30	57-20	Evening At Home12212 Chief Harry1151 Esprit Du Lac1155	Done early	8
24Jun95-10FL	fst	5½f	:23 :471 1:001 1:07	3+ Md Sp Wt	41	6	7	46	45½	57	56	Whitley K	114 b	4.60	73-21	Annscrest114¾ Evening At Home1222 Calculating1141	Bumped start	10
13Jun95-12FL	fst	6f	:223 :47 1:001 1:141	3+ [S]Md Sp Wt	49	11	2	75¾	56¾	46½	56½	Whitley K	114	4.60	66-26	El Noor Jihad1223¾ Cash Me Out114no Tip For Jasper1142½	No solid bid	12
3Jun95-10FL	fst	5½f	:224 :481 1:013 1:083	3+ Md Sp Wt	49	2	6	75¾	66	63¼	42	Whitley K	114	4.30	69-25	Splendid Doc1221½ Emosewa122hd Lucky Bleu114½	5 wide turn	11
2Dec94-6FL	fst	6f	:224 :461 :591 1:114	[S]Md Sp Wt	38	2	8	53	34½	35	39¼	Messina R	121	*2.05	78-15	BrzilinMichel1215¾ Imgonnbityounow1213½ MickyMccr1213¾	Finished well	9

WORKOUTS: ●May 28 FL 5f fst 1:03 B 1/9 May 22 FL 5f fst 1:033 Hg2/12

Seventhofdecember

Own: Marbet Stable

MARTINEZ J R JR (30 1 4 0 .03)

Ch. g. 4
Sire: Settlement Day (Buckpasser)
Dam: Northern Haily (Northern Baby)
Br: Dileo Philip (NY)
Tr: Varvaro Vincent (1 0 0 0 .00)

122

Lifetime Record:	9 M 0 1	$3,800			
1995	4 M 0 0	$560	Turf	1 0 0 0	
1994	5 M 0 1	$3,240	Wet	0 0 0 0	
Sar Ⓣ	1 0 0 0		Dist Ⓣ	0 0 0 0	

6Aug95-9Sar	gd	1⅜ [T]	:481 1:152 1:411 2:193	3+ Md Sp Wt	35	4	1	11	75½	915	825	Martinez J R Jr	121 b	53.00	43-21	Hawkeye Bay1213 Fast Ace1151 Paulo1152	Used in pace	9
30Jun95-1Bel	fst	1 1/16	:231 :463 1:122 1:462	3+ Md 35000	36	8	4	33½	24	612	723½	Martinez J R Jr	122 b	23.00	43-33	King Of The City1146½ Chosen Country114½ Brave Warrior1126	Tired	10
14Jun95-6Rkm	fst	6f	:22 :452 :582 1:114	3+ Md Sp Wt	43	2	6	66	613	515	47¾	Molinari E	B 122 fb	4.20	81-09	SlickDefense1154½ GallantSinger1161½ SlantSix1152	Angled out wide turn	8
3Jun95-10FL	fst	5½f	:224 :481 1:013 1:083	3+ Md Sp Wt	42	9	2	2hd	33	53	84¾	Faine C	122 f	*3.20	66-25	Splendid Doc1221½ Emosewa122hd Lucky Bleu114½	Lugged in stretch	11
29Aug94-9Sar	fst	7f	:22 :451 1:11 1:241	3+ Md Sp Wt	39	3	5	2½	53½	75	920½	Mojica R Jr	117	33.30	63-13	Silver Fox117nk Andover Road11711 Iron Mountain1175	Used up	11
13Aug94-10Sar	fst	1⅛	:484 1:141 1:412 1:552	3+ [S]Md Sp Wt	46	3	4	31½	56	74½	78¾	Cruguet J	117	12.20	50-23	Uncle Pockets1173 Sir Noble1171¾ Top Tapper112nk	Lacked rally	11
1Aug94-5Sar	fst	1⅛	:482 1:14 1:403 1:543	3+ [S]Md Sp Wt	46	3	2	1½	2hd	32	39¾	Cruguet J	117	26.00	53-26	Rogersdividends1172¾ SirNobl1177 Svnthofdcmbr117no	Dueled, weakened	9
1Jly94-9Bel	fst	1 1/16	:224 :462 1:12 1:461	3+ Md 35000	54	9	4	117¾	107¾	89½	812½	Frost G C	116	69.80	59-32	Buck Mulligan1182¾ Charmed Prospect116¾ Blue Eyed Bob1121	Outrun	12
14Jun94-5Bel	fst	7f	:223 :452 1:103 1:234	3+ [S]Md Sp Wt	41	6	9	107½	1021	1012	717¾	Frost G C	114	51.60	66-15	Alanne1154 Elocat's Banner1092 Carrdomain1143	No factor	10

WORKOUTS: Jly 28 Sar 5f fst 1:043 B 27/28 Jly 19 Sar tr.t 4f fst :522 B 19/20 ●May 23 Sar tr.t 3f fst :37 H 1/7

1 — Irish Patriot — A beaten favorite six straight times (the last as part of an entry), four of them on grass and the last five of them at odds-on. As part of a 4-5 entry in a similar spot in his last, a 1⅛-mile turf race at Saratoga, he got into trouble early and late, struggling home ninth by 5¾ lengths in the field of 11. Lifetime, he was zero for 12, but in the money six times. On turf, he had a second and a third in five starts. A must in exactas and triples, but certainly vulnerable if he was bet down to favortism again.

2 — A.J. Warbucks — Zero for 28 lifetime, 20 of them on dirt. Not in a zillion years.

3 — Plattkin — Had turf breeding on his sire side (a grandson of Stage Door Johnny), but 10 PPs which were just plain ugly. He was also trying 1⅛ miles in a turf debut off a single, awful sprint, his first start in nearly eight months. No.

4 — I Know The Family — Equally bad in one start on turf and one on dirt. No thanks.

5 — Speediation — Incredibly bad on dirt with no indication of grass breeding which would turn him around. Pass.

6 — My Song — Had a couple things going against her: She was a three-year-old filly taking on colts, some of them older, and was zero for nine. Unlike horses 2 through 5, though, she also had some positives. In five turf starts, she had been: fourth against colts; sixth versus winning $60,000 claimers; second versus winning $45,000 claimers; fourth at 4-5 versus New York-Bred maiden fillies, and, in her last start at Saratoga, second by eight lengths, sporting front bandages for the first time in a 1⅛-mile allowance race against a runaway, legit winner, Sweetzie. Dropping back to a maiden race, she figured as a major player despite facing colts.

7 — Make No Mistake — Front-runner was a good third in his second start off a 13-month layoff, beating Irish Patriot in the process. The race had to help. However, he was still a maiden at the age of 6, with a turf record of 0-2-1 in eight starts and a lifetime mark of 0-3-2 in 13 starts. Had to use him in exotics, though hardly a value play given his career numbers.

8 — Demanding Terms — Unlike some of the others, he'd only had three starts, a distant fifth on dirt, an eighth on a yielding grass course at 1¼ miles, and, in his last start at Saratoga, a

much improved fourth by 3¼ lengths in a 6½-furlong sprint with blinkers removed. He had a good turf broodmare sire (Al Hattab), so whether or not you played him depended on your evaluation of that single turf race. Was it bad because it was: a) a yielding course; b) a mile and a quarter in only his second lifetime start; c) because of a bad post (10); d) because he raced with blinkers, or e) because he had no ability on turf. With "a" through "d" all possibilities, and also because of the lack of competition in here, I threw out "e" and decided to give him another try on grass. Am I a nice guy or what?

9 — Watrals Finesse — In the money three of five grass starts. She was fifth in open company in her last start, and her return to New York-Breds stamped her as a top contender versus colts.

10 — Micky Maccar — The shipper from Finger Lakes was nosed in his last start, and he was bred both sides for turf, with Ends Well by Lyphard on the sire line and Hawaii as the broodmare sire. A possibility, though his poor post position on the inside of two turf courses was a big negative. Not today.

11 — Seventhofdecember — His lone turf race was in a 1⅜-mile marathon in open company in his last start. He showed speed and finished eighth by 25 lengths at 53-1. Cutting back in distance and switching to New York-Breds would help, but probably not enough to overcome the 11 post. Pass.

Conclusions? Demanding Terms was an overlay because Irish Patriot was again made the favorite at 2-1, My Song, a filly facing colts, went off at 3-1, and zero-for-13 Make My Mistake was made 5-1, a shorter 5-1 than Demanding Terms.

Using Demanding Terms on top, and boxing the only four horses we thought had a legitimate shot to finish second underneath him (Irish Patriot, My Song, Make No Mistake and Watrals Finesse at 7-1), would have cost $24 for $2 triples. Demanding Terms won by four lengths and paid $13.80. He was followed by the two favorites in inverse order, My Song and Irish Patriot, and the triple returned a generous $241. The exacta was also an overlay at $78 for a 5-1 shot over the 3-1 second choice.

FIFTH RACE
Saratoga
AUGUST 18, 1995

1⅛ MILES. (Inner Turf)(1.47) MAIDEN SPECIAL WEIGHT. Purse $32,000. 3-year-olds and upward foaled in New York State and approved by the New York State-Bred Registry. Weights: 3-year-olds, 117 lbs. Older, 122 lbs.

Value of Race: $32,000 Winner $19,200; second $6,400; third $3,520; fourth $1,920; fifth $960. Mutuel Pool $462,416.00 Exacta Pool $540,317.00 Triple Pool $519,954.00

Last Raced	Horse	M/Eqt.	A.	Wt	PP	St	¼	½	¾	Str	Fin	Jockey	Odds $1
10Aug95 2Sar4	Demanding Terms		3	117	8	8	2hd	2^1	2^1	1^1½	1^4	Maple E	5.90
30Jly95 9Sar2	My Song	f	3	112	6	4	4^1	4^2½	4^2	4^2	2^2½	Bailey J D	3.05
31Jly95 5Sar9	Irish Patriot		3	117	1	1	7^1	8^1	7hd	3hd	3½	Velazquez J R	2.05
14Jly95 9Bel4	A. J. Warbucks	b	6	122	2	3	11	10^4	9^1	6½	4½	Lovato F Jr	26.25
6Aug95 9Sar8	Seventhofdecember	b	4	122	11	9	3½	3hd	3½	5^2	5^3½	Martinez J R Jr	64.25
31Jly95 5Sar3	Make No Mistake	f	6	122	7	7	1½	1½	1½	2hd	6nk	Chavez J F	5.10
7Aug95 3Sar6	Watrals Finesse	b	3	114	9	10	9^4	7½	8^2	7^2	7^2½	Migliore R	7.10
14Jly95 9Bel7	I Know The Family	b	3	117	4	6	8½	9^2	10^6	8^1	8^3	Davis R G	25.00
28Jly95 8FL2	Micky Maccar	b	3	117	10	11	6hd	6^1	5hd	10½	9nk	Rydowski S R	14.60
10Aug95 2Sar8	Plattkin		4	122	3	2	10^1	11	11	11	10^2	Decarlo C P	95.25
15Jly95 2Bel10	Speediation		4	122	5	5	5½	5hd	6hd	9^2½	11	Beckner D V	89.25

OFF AT 3:07 Start Good. Won driving. Time, :23^2, :47^4, 1:12^3, 1:37^2, 1:49^2 Course firm.

$2 Mutuel Prices:			
8-DEMANDING TERMS	13.80	7.00	4.40
6-MY SONG		4.40	2.90
1-IRISH PATRIOT			2.80

$2 EXACTA 8-6 PAID $78.00 $2 TRIPLE 8-6-1 PAID $241.00

Ro. c, (Feb), by Private Terms–Demand Attention, by Al Hattab. Trainer Kelly Timothy D. Bred by Boto Thoroughbreds Inc (NY).

DEMANDING TERMS stalked the pace from outside to the turn, accelerated to the front in upper stretch, then drew away under good handling. MY SONG raced just off the pace while saving ground to the turn and finished willingly to outfinish IRISH PATRIOT for the place. IRISH PATRIOT steadied along the inside on the first turn, raced well back for six furlongs, closed the gap while saving ground on the turn, made a run along the inside to threaten in midstretch then flattened out. A. J. WARBUCKS pinched back at the start, raced far back to the turn, angled five wide to launch his bid at the top of the stretch, rallied belatedly. SEVENTHOFDECEMBER stalked the pace three wide to the turn and weakened in the drive. MAKE NO MISTAKE set the pace along the inside into upper stretch and tired from his early efforts. WATRALS FINESSE failed to threaten while between horses. I KNOW THE FAMILY never reached contention. MICKY MACCAR raced within striking distnace while four wide to the turn and tired.

Owners— 1, Boto Stable; 2, Engel Karen K & Richard L; 3, Delaney Austin; 4, Schaeffer Carol; 5, Marbet Stable; 6, Foss Monty & Schwartz Gary; 7, Watral Michael; 8, Kelly Michael J; 9, Barrow Paul & Macarelli Gerald C; 10, Martino Phyllis; 11, Fiore John & Joseph & Nicholas J

Trainers—1, Kelly Timothy D; 2, O'Connell Richard; 3, O'Brien Leo; 4, Schaeffer Stephen W Jr; 5, Varvaro Vincent; 6, Contessa Gary C; 7, Brida Dennis J; 8, Kelly Michael J; 9, Barrow Paul; 10, Martino Phyllis; 11, Fiore Nicholas J

Overweight: Watrals Finesse (2).

Can you play favorites and catch an exotic overlay triple? Yes. Here's a good example: the fourth race at Keeneland, October 18, 1995. Two scratches left a field of 10 maidens going seven furlongs.

4 **Keeneland**

About 7 Furlongs (1:24^3) **MAIDEN SPECIAL WEIGHT. Purse $31,000 (includes $6,200 KTDF). 3-year-olds and upward. Weights: 3-year-olds, 119 lbs. Older, 121 lbs. (Preference to Horses that have not started for less than $25,000).**

Perry James
Own: Gottlieb Roy & Rosenthal Myron
MARTINEZ W (44 5 9 3 .11)

B. c. 4
Sire: Deputy Minister (Vice Regent)
Dam: Dame Amour (Iron Ruler)
Br: ReaLaw Farm & Myron Rosenthal (Ky)
Tr: Lopresti Charles (1 1 0 0 1.00)

121

Lifetime Record:	3 M 0 0	$2,430		
1995	3 M 0 0	$2,430	Turf	0 0 0 0
1994	0 M 0 0		Wet	1 0 0 0
Kee	0 0 0 0		Dist	0 0 0 0

28Sep95-6TP	fst	1	:22^4	:46^3	1:12	1:39	3↑ Md Sp Wt	57	2	2	1hd	2^3	2^7	4^12½	Martinez W	122 b	23.60	62-28	ProspectForLove118^12 LightHert118½ Chris'Plsur122hd	Dueled, weakened 11
20Sep95-3TP	sly	6½f	:22^4	:45^1	1:11^4	1:18^1	3↑ Md Sp Wt	49	2	8	8^5½	7^2½	8^12	7^14½	Bruin J E	122	8.60	71-14	Kaily119^1½ Canadian Gold119^2 Pro Irish122^2½	No factor 11
1Sep95-7EIP	fst	6½f	:22^2	:45^3	1:10^4	1:17^1	3↑ Md Sp Wt	55	7	5	6^4½	4^8	4^12	4^13½	Bruin J E	122	7.30	75-16	Cream Station122^3 Undeniable119^10 Gleam119½	No rally 7

WORKOUTS: Oct 16 CmF 3f fst :37 B 1/1 Oct 11 CmF 5f fst 1:02 B 2/2 Sep 11 CmF 4f fst :49^2 B 2/3 Aug 28 CmF 4f fst :49 B 1/7 Aug 19 CmF 6f fst 1:19 Bg 1/1 Aug 7 CmF 4f fst :51 Bg 1/2

Crack Willow
B. f. 3 (May)
Sire: Wolf Power (SA) (Flirting Around)
Dam: Hankow Willow (No Robbery)
Br: Hunter Barbara (Ky)
Tr: Rieser Steven M (2 1 0 0 .50)
Own: Hunter Barbara
VASQUEZ J (18 2 1 1 .11) 116

Lifetime Record: 1 M 0 0 $0
1995 1 M 0 0 | Turf 0 0 0 0
1994 0 M 0 0 | Wet 1 0 0 0
Kee 0 0 0 0 | Dist 0 0 0 0

18May95-3CD sly 6½f :223 :461 1:114 1:182 3+ (F)Md Sp Wt 34 5 10 116¾ 810 1019 1021½ Vasquez J 114 35.20 65-14 Graceful Minister114¾ Cordovesa1115 Apalachee Lassie114nk 11
Sluggish start, outrun
WORKOUTS: Oct 13 CD 6f fst 1:153 B 6/7 ●Oct 7 CD 6f fst 1:153 B 1/6 Sep 30 CD 5f fst 1:03 B 6/14

Preservation Blues
Ch. c. 3 (Mar)
Sire: Dixieland Band (Northern Dancer)
Dam: Windmill Gal (Gallant Romeo)
Br: Lazy Lane Stables Inc (Ky)
Tr: Brothers Frank L (7 1 1 1 .14)
Own: Lazy Lane Farms Inc
GRYDER A T (40 4 6 3 .10) 119

Lifetime Record: 4 M 1 0 $7,680
1995 4 M 1 0 $7,680 | Turf 0 0 0 0
1994 0 M 0 0 | Wet 0 0 0 0
Kee 0 0 0 0 | Dist 0 0 0 0

28Sep95-6TP fst 1 :224 :463 1:12 1:39 3+ Md Sp Wt 56 10 5 63¾ 46½ 612 613½ Gryder A T 118 *2.80 62-28 Prospect For Love11812 Light Heart118½ Cheris' Pleasure122hd Tired 11
24Aug95-3EIP fst 6f :224 :454 :581 1:113 3+ Md Sp Wt 64 7 5 75¾ 810 610 44¼ Bruin J E 118 *1.20 80-15 InspectorMcmhon118¾ ClevelndWy122¼ Dmibrt118nk Mild gain, six wide 9
30Jun95-7CD fst 6f :212 :453 :582 1:112 3+ Md Sp Wt 74 3 3 52¾ 62¾ 41½ 2nk Barton D M 111 9.50 89-08 Black Balled111nk Preservation Blues1111½ Mandamus1134 Rallied 12
8Jun95-3CD fst 6f :214 :453 :58 1:103 3+ Md Sp Wt 62 11 3 51¾ 72 66¾ 77¼ Sellers S J 113 8.00 86-05 Aziano1121½ Tough Guy112¾ Majestic Ransom112½ Tired after 1/2 12
WORKOUTS: ●Oct 10 Kee 5f fst 1:01 Bg 1/21 Sep 23 CD 6f fst 1:162 B 2/3 Sep 18 CD 5f fst 1:044 B 35/36 Sep 12 CD 4f fst :504 B 22/37 Aug 23 CD 3f fst :38 B 14/17 Aug 16 CD 5f fst 1:023 B 6/17

Sgt. Imboden
Dk. b or br c. 3 (Apr)
Sire: Staff Writer (Northern Dancer)
Dam: Fete Champetre (Cox's Ridge)
Br: Thomas C Mueller (Ky)
Tr: Wiggins Hal R (1 0 0 0 .00)
Own: Mueller Thomas C
DAY P (32 6 3 4 .19) 119

Lifetime Record: 0 M 0 0 $0
1995 0 M 0 0 | Turf 0 0 0 0
1994 0 M 0 0 | Wet 0 0 0 0
Kee 0 0 0 0 | Dist 0 0 0 0

WORKOUTS: Oct 13 CD 5f fst 1:022 Bg 13/24 Oct 7 CD 6f fst 1:164 B 3/6 Sep 28 CD 5f fst 1:033 Bg 18/28 ●Aug 30 BRD 4f fst :481 Bg 1/5 Aug 27 BRD 4f fst :481 Bg 4/10 Aug 20 BRD 4f fst :484 B 8/14

Timeless Ways
Dk. b or br c. 3 (May)
Sire: Wop Wop (Bold Dun-Cee)
Dam: Best in Turn (Best Turn)
Br: Donna C. Ward (Ky)
Tr: Ward John T Jr (6 1 1 1 .17)
Own: Ward Donna C
MAPLE S (2 0 0 1 .00) 119

Lifetime Record: 2 M 0 0 $140
1995 2 M 0 0 $140 | Turf 0 0 0 0
1994 0 M 0 0 | Wet 0 0 0 0
Kee 0 0 0 0 | Dist 1 0 0 0 $140

30Jun95-7CD fst 6f :212 :453 :582 1:112 3+ Md Sp Wt 58 4 12 1215 119¾ 97¾ 66¾ Maple S 114 103.30 82-08 Black Balled111nk Preservation Blues1111½ Mandamus1134 Broke slow 12
28Mar95-4Hia fst 7f :24 :47 1:12 1:253 Md Sp Wt 29 3 9 914 916 812 713½ McCauley W H 121 9.30 67-15 Mr. Affirmed1211¾ Cool Star1211 Proud Destiny1217½ Showed little 9
WORKOUTS: Oct 11 Kee 5f fst 1:02 B 3/9 Sep 28 Kee 5f fst 1:032 B 4/5 Aug 28 Sar 5f fst 1:033 B 9/9 Aug 19 Sar 5f fst 1:012 Hg 9/25 Aug 3 Sar 5f fst 1:024 B 12/27 Jly 25 Sar 5f fst 1:034 B 24/28

Elusive Groom
Gr. g. 3 (Apr)
Sire: Runaway Groom (Blushing Groom)
Dam: Alydarla (Alydar)
Br: English James E (Ky)
Tr: Ebert Dennis W (6 0 0 1 .00)
Own: Drey Alan
COOKSEY P J (11 0 0 1 .00) L 119

Lifetime Record: 11 M 3 2 $17,095
1995 11 M 3 2 $17,095 | Turf 2 0 0 1 $2,550
1994 0 M 0 0 | Wet 0 0 0 0
Kee 2 0 0 0 $1,550 | Dist 2 0 0 1 $3,860

8Oct95-2Kee fst 1⅛ :473 1:131 1:394 1:523 3+ Md Sp Wt 52 7 1 12 1½ 64¾ 614 Cooksey P J L 118 b 8.60 57-16 Shining Treasures1183½ Big Bruiser121hd Le Duke1211 11
Dueled, tired, checked 1/4 pole
2Sep95-11AP fm 1 (T) :24 :473 1:12 1:364 3+ Md Sp Wt 73 1 1 1½ 11½ 1hd 32¼ Albarado R J L 117 b 7.80 88-11 Bonnie Rob1171¾ Rio Vista117½ Elusive Groom1172¼ Faded rail 12
12Aug95-6AP fst 6f :221 :45 :572 1:103 3+ Md Sp Wt 60 7 4 65¾ 78 79¾ 610¼ Baird E T L 117 fb 5.30 80-12 Mississippi Chat1172¼ Thereitis Hoop1171 Nicaros1171¼ Evenly wide 9
31Jly95-4AP fst 7f :223 :454 1:113 1:253 3+ Md Sp Wt 61 3 4 2hd 43 35½ 35¼ Fires E L 115 fb 2.40 73-21 Ad Valorem1151¾ Eastern Danger1153¼ Elusive Groom1152¼ Faded 8
15Jly95-7AP fst 6f :221 :453 :582 1:112 3+ Md Sp Wt 74 3 3 31½ 42½ 33 23¼ Baird E T L 115 fb 4.80 83-12 Sir Cognac1223¼ Elusive Groom1151½ Eastern Danger115¾ Altered course 9
10Jun95-2Spt fst 6f :222 :46 :58 1:103 3+ Md Sp Wt 61 1 3 11½ 12 21½ 26 Baird E T L 114 b 1.90 85-10 Do It Again1136 Elusive Groom1141½ Vin Sec1131 Faded rail 6
22May95-7Spt fst 6f :223 :464 :593 1:133 3+ Md Sp Wt 56 1 7 31 31½ 21½ 21½4 Meier R L 113 b *1.30 74-21 GenrlGridlock1141½ DH ElusivGroom113 DH AdVlorm1141½ Three wide bid 9
22Apr95-5Kee fst 7f :221 :45 1:104 1:241 Md Sp Wt 71 5 10 86 75¾ 46½ 45½ Fires E L 119 b 41.30 74-14 Seven N Seven1191¾ Nuclear Treaty1193 Nine Innings119¾ 11
Bore in, bumped start, no late threat
28Mar95-6Hia fm *1⅛ (T) 1:47 Alw 16500N1X 56 8 1 13 11½ 4¾ 612½ Turner T G L 113 b 66.20 85-04 Trucking Baron1131½ Noble 'n Heart1161¾ Default1132 Weakened 10
6Mar95-6GP fst 1 1/16 :232 :472 1:121 1:461 Md Sp Wt 45 9 1 1½ 32½ 714 722 Turner T G L 120 b 49.20 55-24 Crimson Guard1202¼ Palm Freezer120nk Play The Gold1201½ Faded 11
WORKOUTS: Sep 30 Kee 5f fst 1:021 B 5/17

Serial
Dk. b or br c. 3 (Feb)
Sire: Slew O' Gold (Seattle Slew)
Dam: Series (Mr. Prospector)
Br: Claiborne Farm (Ky)
Tr: Walden W Elliott (14 3 1 1 .21)
Own: Fehsenfeld Mac
SELLERS S J (43 7 9 5 .16) L 119

Lifetime Record: 1 M 0 0 $0
1995 1 M 0 0 | Turf 0 0 0 0
1994 0 M 0 0 | Wet 1 0 0 0
Kee 0 0 0 0 | Dist 0 0 0 0

21May95-6CD my 1 :231 :46 1:111 1:364 3+ Md Sp Wt 58 7 6 83½ 109 918 1017½ Crump D L 114 19.80 76-08 Cape Doctor1102 Nine Innings1103 Vast War1144 Done early 17
WORKOUTS: Oct 3 Kee 5f fst 1:02 H 6/17 Sep 27 CDT 5f fst 1:03 Bg 4/7 Sep 19 CDT 5f fst 1:014 B 5/9 Sep 9 CD 5f fst 1:02 B 4/17 Aug 31 CD 4f fst :502 B 14/21 Aug 25 CD 3f fst :373 B 12/20

Sparkster
B. g. 3 (Apr)
Sire: Sparkly (Halo)
Dam: Lasting Queen (Selari)
Br: Wornall Perry W (Ky)
Tr: Mitchell Sherman S (1 0 0 0 .00)
Own: Looker D & Warner P & Wiley L
SARVIS D A (3 0 0 1 .00) 119

Lifetime Record: 6 M 1 0 $5,620
1995 3 M 0 0 $1,000 | Turf 0 0 0 0
1994 3 M 1 0 $4,620 | Wet 2 0 1 0 $3,420
Kee 1 0 0 0 | Dist 0 0 0 0

28Sep95-6TP fst 1 :224 :463 1:12 1:39 3+ Md Sp Wt 54 3 6 74 64½ 713 714½ Romero R P 118 f 18.90 61-28 Prospect For Love11812 Light Heart118½ Cheris' Pleasure122hd No threat 11
9Sep95-11TP wf 1 :232 :473 1:134 1:411 3+ Md Sp Wt 58 12 11 107¾ 76¾ 68 57¾ Romero R P 118 f 13.50 56-25 OplMoon1223 SummerKnight1182½ NewEdinburg118nk Improved position 12
9Aug95-8EIP fst 1 :233 :463 1:122 1:393 3+ Md Sp Wt 56 6 8 86¾ 85 43½ 43¾ Sarvis D A 116 f 20.20 72-27 Early Conquest116no New Edinburg1162¾ Gnarl1161 No late response 11
30Nov94-1TP fst 1 1/16 :224 :462 1:121 1:45 Md Sp Wt 54 12 10 1018 87½ 56½ 414 Troilo W D 121 f 12.40 68-21 RememberThRor121hd MinInspctor12112 J.P.Gold1212 Improved position 12
16Nov94-5CD sly 1 :23 :47 1:142 1:414 Md 30000 65 3 12 1210 97¾ 46½ 23 Troilo W D 119 f 25.70 65-27 Garland1193 Sparkster1193 Tin Soldier1101½ Mild rail gain 12
29Oct94-2Kee fst 6½f :222 :462 1:114 1:18 Md Sp Wt 31 11 10 1110 109½ 77 814 Barton D M 118 f 49.50 72-15 DixiesAngel118hd QuietDeception1186 PrsonlMttr118½ Passed tired ones 12
WORKOUTS: Jly 25 KHC 3f fst :384 B 4/4

Coth Cho
B. g. 3 (Apr)
Sire: Halo (Hail to Reason)
Dam: Bambina Linda (Liloy (FR))
Br: Hancock A B III & Way Oak Cliff Stable (Ky)
Tr: Nowacki Carl C (—)
Own: Nowacki Carl C
DAY P (32 6 3 4 .19) L 119

Lifetime Record: 6 M 1 1 $11,400
1995 6 M 1 1 $11,400 | Turf 2 0 0 0
1994 0 M 0 0 | Wet 1 0 1 0 $6,400
Kee 0 0 0 0 | Dist 0 0 0 0

6Oct95-3TP fst 1 1/16 :232 :472 1:13 1:464 3+ Md Sp Wt 62 2 3 32½ 31½ 31½ 3¾ Johnston J A L 119 b 6.80 73-22 Bridge Play119½ Sunrise Again122nk Coth Cho1193 9
Lacked room 3/16, no late response
20Aug95-2AP fst 1 :232 :462 1:12 1:392 3+ Md 25000 61 3 3 31½ 24 38 410 Guidry M 115 b 2.10 62-28 FlyingPadre1113 MysticalCnyon1154¾ OldMn'sRun115hd Brief wide speed 6
6Aug95-9Sar gd 1⅜ [T] :481 1:152 1:411 2:193 3+ Md Sp Wt 36 7 2 21 32 815 925 Perez R B 115 b 12.70 43-21 Hawkeye Bay1213 Fast Ace1151 Paulo1152 Gave way 9
15Jly95-3Bel fm 1 1/16 (T) :231 :46 1:103 1:411 3+ Md Sp Wt 46 2 5 42 52½ 78 618 Perez R B 113 b 7.30 74-08 The Author114hd The Greek One1137 Mr Market1141½ Checked 1/4 pl 10
1Jly95-11Bel sly 1 (X) :222 :454 1:12 1:382 3+ Md Sp Wt 63 7 2 21 31½ 23 210½ Chavez J F 114 b 6.70 60-18 Other Intentions11410 Coth Cho1146 Legally Bryan1145 Late gain 8
27Apr95-4Aqu fst 1 :224 :453 1:104 1:361 Md Sp Wt 66 7 7 74½ 77½ 69½ 416½ Perez R B5 115 b 12.60 71-12 Placid Fund12012 Diplomacy120¾ Cozy Drive1203 No threat 8
WORKOUTS: ●Oct 1 Beu 5f fst :592 B 1/4 Sep 26 Beu 5f fst 1:033 H 1/1 Aug 30 AP 4f fst :493 B 14/33 Aug 3 Bel tr.t 4f fst :49 B 3/16

Will Run
Own: Prestonwood Farm Inc
TROSCLAIR A J (13 1 1 1 .08)
Dk. b or br c. 3 (Apr)
Sire: Proper Reality (In Reality)
Dam: Willow Runner (Alydar)
Br: Prestonwood Farm (Ky)
Tr: Holthus Robert E (6 0 1 0 .00)
L 119

Lifetime Record:	0 M 0 0		$0
1995	0 M 0 0	Turf	0 0 0 0
1994	0 M 0 0	Wet	0 0 0 0
Kee	0 0 0 0	Dist	0 0 0 0

WORKOUTS: Oct 16 CD 5f fst 1:02^3 B 13/38 Oct 9 CD 4f fst :48^4 B 2/38 Oct 3 CD 3f my :37^2 B 6/15 Aug 24 CD 6f fst 1:16^2 Bg 1/2 ●Aug 17 CD 5f fst 1:01^4 Bg 1/9 Aug 8 CD 5f gd 1:02^2 B 8/17 Aug 2 CD 5f fst 1:02 B 3/21 Jly 26 CD 4f fst :48^4 B 4/29 Jly 20 CD 4f fst :51^3 B 19/20 Jly 14 CD 4f fst :50^2 B 18/27 Jly 8 CD 3f fst :37 B 3/9 Jun 29 CD 3f fst :37^2 B 12/18

Prince Capote
Own: Taylor Anthony
LESTER R N (9 1 1 2 .11)
B. g. 3 (Apr)
Sire: Capote (Seattle Slew)
Dam: Precisely Paris (Verbatim)
Br: Peter Haisall Invstmnts Inc & Phoenix Corp (Fla)
Tr: Taylor Anthony (1 1 0 0 1.00)
119

Lifetime Record:	2 M 0 0		$51		
1995	1 M 0 0		Turf	0 0 0 0	
1994	1 M 0 0	$51	Wet	0 0 0 0	
Kee	0 0 0 0		Dist	0 0 0 0	

4Sep95-13Rkm fst 6f	:22^2 :46 :58^4 1:12^1 3+ Md Sp Wt	-0	9	3	4^1	10^{16}	10^{26}	10^{24}	Rivera L Jr	B 118	82.60	63-11	Keys And Socks118½ Made In U. S. A.118½ JustAFlopper118^{nk}	Brief speed 10
29Apr94-5Tam fst 3f	:24^3 :36^2 Md Sp Wt	—	4	5			6^8	6^{9}½	Stannard G S	117	19.50	— —	Jazzy Jeb117^3 Miss Double Jet114^3 Fearless And Free122^{1}½	Weakened 8

WORKOUTS: Oct 12 Kee 5f fst 1:02^3 B 8/14

Lonely Capote
Own: Roberts Royce G
JOHNSTON J A (2 0 0 0 .00)
Dk. b or br c. 3 (Apr)
Sire: Capote (Seattle Slew)
Dam: Just Say Whoa (Secretariat)
Br: Brylynn Farms (Fla)
Tr: Wingfield Robert E (—)
L 119

Lifetime Record:	5 M 0 2	$11,725			
1995	4 M 0 2	$10,950	Turf	0 0 0 0	
1994	1 M 0 0	$775	Wet	0 0 0 0	
Kee	0 0 0 0		Dist	1 0 0 0	$3,000

27Sep95-1TP fst 6f	:22^2 :46^2 :58^4 1:11^3 3+ Md Sp Wt	51	4	5	6^{4}¾	6^{4}½	5^{8}½	3^{12}½	Johnston J A	L 119	2.60	74-15	MadBomber119^{3}½ LivelySauce119^9 LonelyCapote119^{1}½	Improved position 7
16Mar95-2OP gd 1$\frac{1}{16}$	:23^2 :48^2 1:15^1 1:49 Md Sp Wt	56	5	5	3^{2}½	3½	5^6	5^{10}½	Gryder A T	L 120	1.90	51-35	Brushy120^{2}½ Sir Spellbinder120^1 Change The Key120^2	Bid, tired 9
26Feb95-8RP fst 7f	:22 :45 1:10^3 1:23^3 Budweiser50k	79	8	11	11^{6}½	8^{5}½	9^{7}½	4^7	Vasquez J	LB 113	12.00	81-18	Our Gatsby120^1 Only Cash113^2 Dazzling Falls120^4	Five wide turn 11
28Jan95-6SA fst 6f	:21^4 :45^1 :57^3 1:10 Md Sp Wt	76	3	10	6^{4}¾	6^{2}¾	3^{3}½	3^{3}½	Stevens G L	LB 118	7.70	84-11	HighStkesPlyer118½ PrinceOtto118^{2}¾ LonelyCpot118¾	Wide move, hung 10
24Dec94-7Hol fst 6½f	:21^3 :44^2 1:09 1:15^2 Md Sp Wt	79	3	12	12^{16}	10^{12}	5^{6}½	5^{8}½	Stevens G L	LB 119	15.50	84-11	ProspectiveBeau119^{1}½ RegalFighter119½ GraceOfDrby119^1	Bore in start 12

WORKOUTS: Aug 30 TP 4f fst :50^3 B 6/13

There were two obvious favorites: Coth Cho and Lonely Capote. Both had finished third in separate returns, and would go off at 9-5 and 5-2, respectively. If you thought these two stood out — and the betting reflected it as the next favorite, Elusive Groom, was 6-1 — you could have keyed them in triples by playing Coth Cho-Lonely Capote-all and Lonely Capote-Coth Cho-all. For $2 triples, it would have cost $32. Coth Cho won, Lonely Capote was second, and when Sparkster ran third at 37-1, the triple came back $314.40.

FOURTH RACE
Keeneland
OCTOBER 18, 1995

ABOUT 7 FURLONGS. (1.24^3) MAIDEN SPECIAL WEIGHT. Purse $31,000 (includes $6,200 KTDF). 3-year-olds and upward. Weights: 3-year-olds, 119 lbs. Older, 121 lbs. (Preference to Horses that have not started for less than $25,000).

Value of Race: $29,760 Winner $19,406; second $4,960; third $3,100; fourth $1,550; fifth $744. Mutuel Pool $159,675.00 Exacta Pool $110,470.00 Trifecta Pool $105,013.00

Last Raced	Horse	M/Eqt.	A.	Wt	PP	St	¼	½	Str	Fin	Jockey	Odds $1
6Oct95 3TP3	Coth Cho	Lb	3	119	8	2	3^{1}½	2^{1}½	1^1	1^5	Day P	1.90
27Sep95 1TP3	Lonely Capote	Lb	3	119	10	4	1^1	1^2	2^2	2^{hd}	Perret C	2.50
28Sep95 6TP7	Sparkster	bf	3	119	7	8	8^2	8^3	6^{1}½	3¾	Sarvis D A	37.70
8Oct95 2Kee6	Elusive Groom	Lb	3	119	5	1	4^{hd}	5^{hd}	3^{1}½	4^{nk}	Cooksey P J	6.00
28Sep95 6TP4	Perry James	b	4	121	1	7	6^4	6^3	5^{hd}	5½	Martinez W	7.20
18May95 3CD10	Crack Willow	b	3	116	2	6	5^{1}½	3^1	4^1	6^{hd}	Vasquez J	27.00
	Sgt. Imboden		3	119	3	9	9^3	10	8^3	7¾	Borel C H	20.60
21May95 6CD10	Serial	Lf	3	119	6	5	7½	7^{hd}	7^{hd}	8^{hd}	Sellers S J	6.20
30Jun95 7CD6	Timeless Ways		3	119	4	10	10	9½	9^6	9^9	Maple S	16.40
4Sep95 13Rkm10	Prince Capote		3	119	9	3	2½	4^1	10	10	Lester R N	105.90

OFF AT 2:35 Start Good. Won driving. Time, :22^3, :45^3, 1:11^3, 1:28^1 Track fast.

$2 Mutuel Prices:				
	9-COTH CHO	5.80	3.20	2.80
	12-LONELY CAPOTE		4.00	3.20
	8-SPARKSTER			7.60

$2 EXACTA 9-12 PAID $21.80 $2 TRIFECTA 9-12-8 PAID $314.40

B. g, (Apr), by Halo–Bambina Linda, by Liloy (FR). Trainer Nowacki Carl C. Bred by Hancock A B III & Way Oak Cliff Stable (Ky).

COTH CHO stalked the leaders while four abreast early, moved from that position to take over in the upper stretch and widened under intermittent left-handed urging. LONELY CAPOTE gained the lead soon after the start, edged inside, moved clear but was no match for the winner in the drive. SPARKSTER, outsprinted for a half, made a mild late gain. ELUSIVE GROOM saved ground in a striking position but had no late response. PERRY JAMES swerved in sharply at the start, then raced evenly. CRACK WILLOW, well placed despite swerving badly at the start, came up empty in the drive. SGT. IMBODEN was outrun. SERIAL was no factor. TIMELESS WAYS was wide in the stretch run and never prominent. PRINCE CAPOTE stopped.

Owners— 1, Nowacki Carl C; 2, Roberts Royce G; 3, Looker D & Warner P & Wiley L; 4, Drey Alan; 5, Gottlieb Roy & Rosenthal Myron; 6, Hunter Barbara; 7, Mueller Thomas C; 8, Fehsenfeld Mac; 9, Ward Donna C; 10, Taylor Anthony

Trainers— 1, Nowacki Carl C; 2, Wingfield Robert E; 3, Mitchell Sherman S; 4, Ebert Dennis W; 5, Lopresti Charles; 6, Rieser Steven M; 7, Wiggins Hal R; 8, Walden W Elliott; 9, Ward John T Jr; 10, Taylor Anthony

Scratched— Preservation Blues (28Sep95 6TP6), Will Run

How about a triple race where there are three obvious favorites? Here's a good example. The late vet scratch of Annapolis Gold left a field of 11 maiden claimers ($30,000 to $32,000) going 1 1/16 miles in the 10th race at Gulfstream Park, February 9, 1996. We'll discuss each horse, but let you make your own conclusions.

In post position order:

10   Gulfstream Park

1 1/16 MILES. (1:40¹) MAIDEN CLAIMING. Purse $12,000. 3-year-olds. Weight, 120 lbs. Claiming price $32,000, if for $30,000, allowed 2 lbs.

Noble Houston

Own: Sugar Hill Farm & Training Center
BAIN G W (49 3 4 5 .06) $30,000
B. c. 3 (Feb)
Sire: Houston (Seattle Slew)
Dam: Vague Game (Vaguely Noble)
Br: Guntovitch Carlos (Ky)
Tr: Bennett Gerald S (11 1 0 1 .09)
118
Lifetime Record: 4 M 0 0 $977
1996 1 M 0 0 $800 | Turf 0 0 0 0
1995 3 M 0 0 $177 | Wet 0 0 0 0
GP 1 0 0 0 $800 | Dist 1 0 0 0 $800

22Jan96-1GP fst 1 1/16 :231 :472 1:132 1:474 Md 45000 42 2 4 43¾ 35½ 38½ 414¾ Bain G W 118 b 85.10 54-23 MckenzieStr1209 NobleMission1204 AllegedPrinc120½ Inside, weakened 7
8Dec95-6Crc fst 6f :223 :464 1:00 1:14 Md 30000 39 8 5 87 811 811 810 Nunez E O 118 b 31.70 67-22 Gamble The Throne1204½ MightyProspect118nk ToroNegro1181½ Very wide 8
18Jly95-1EIP fst 5½f :223 :47 1:002 1:071 Md 12500 17 3 6 68 810 913 913½ Thorwarth J O L 117 b 10.20 70-18 J. J. Ray1172 Chilly Leader1172 Raja's Best Swing1172 Done early 11
29Jun95-2EIP fst 5f :23 :47 :592 Md 17500 21 3 7 912 814 811 812½ Miller S E L 117 3.30 79-13 Triple Play1174½ Impulsive Bid1171½ [D]Mr. Roger1173 Never close 12
WORKOUTS: ●Feb 6 Tam 3f fst :36 H 1/10 Jan 31 Tam 4f fst :52 B 10/11 Jan 19 Tam 3f fst :381 B 8/14 Jan 12 Tam 6f gd 1:16 H 1/2 Jan 6 Tam 4f fst :49 H 5/37 Dec 30 Tam 5f fst 1:034 B 14/23

Matthew's Jeb

Own: Giacopelli Rich
TURNER T G (32 3 1 3 .09) $32,000
Ch. g. 3 (Apr)
Sire: Jeblar (Alydar)
Dam: Laughing Place (Iron Ruler)
Br: Farnsworth Farms (Fla)
Tr: Sciametta Anthony Jr (7 1 2 1 .14)
L 120
Lifetime Record: 4 M 0 0 $2,280
1996 1 M 0 0 $600 | Turf 0 0 0 0
1995 3 M 0 0 $1,680 | Wet 0 0 0 0
GP 1 0 0 0 $600 | Dist 1 0 0 0 $600

24Jan96-3GP fst 1 1/16 :234 :481 1:131 1:473 Md 32000 44 6 1 12½ 1hd 31 411¾ Santos J A L 120 b 2.80 58-24 ForkliftHelmr1182½ Glde1204½ SirMichel'sSon1185 Wknd, drifted out late 8
22Nov95-7Med fst 6f :224 :462 :591 1:123 Md 25000 51 2 2 2hd 1hd 21½ 42¾ Marquez C H Jr 118 b *1.40 74-28 Northern Hawthorne1181½ Zordon118¾ Woodbine Perk114no Weakened 6
10Nov95-4Med fst 6f :22 :451 :572 1:101 Md Sp Wt 52 8 2 31½ 32 48 411½ Lopez C C 118 b 27.00 76-11 Devil's Touch1181½ Roy Boy Roy1189 Syrian Knight1181½ Even trip 8
27Oct95-1Med fst 6f :221 :45 :572 1:103 Md Sp Wt 44 2 3 11 2½ 47½ 514 Rocco J 118 18.60 72-15 Deserves Another118hd Devil's Touch1189¾ ImminentFirst1185 Used early 9
WORKOUTS: ●Feb 5 Hia 3f fst :37 B 1/11 ●Jan 11 Hia 5f fst 1:011 H 1/4 Jan 2 Hia 6f fst 1:152 B 1/3 Dec 23 Hia 4f gd :484 B 7/12 Dec 18 Hia 3f fst :364 B 4/5

Annapolis Gold

Own: Brazil Stables
RIVERA J A II (82 3 4 7 .04) $30,000
Gr/ro c. 3 (Apr)
Sire: Blue Ensign (Hoist the Flag)
Dam: Planet of Gold (John's Gold)
Br: Brazil Stable (NY)
Tr: Wayar Manuel J (7 2 0 0 .29)
L 118
Lifetime Record: 1 M 0 0 $90
1996 1 M 0 0 $90 | Turf 0 0 0 0
1995 0 M 0 0 | Wet 0 0 0 0
GP 0 0 0 0 | Dist 0 0 0 0

2Jan96-12Crc fst 7f :23 :471 1:141 1:284 Md 25000 [illegible] 8 8 54½ 43½ 711 610 Gryder A T 120 11.10 56-23 Toby's Pride1202 Perpetual Shine1201 Superior Rex120½
In close start, tired badly inside
WORKOUTS: Feb 7 Crc 3f fst :37 B 4/8 Feb 1 Crc 5f fst 1:021 Bg 4/16 Jan 24 Crc 4f fst :51 B 8/15 Jan 12 Crc 5f fst 1:03 B 6/18 Dec 27 Crc 5f fst 1:033 B 15/24 Dec 19 Crc 4f fst :50 B 10/28

Alysham

Own: Kligman Herbert
KRONE J A (145 21 18 22 .14) $32,000
Ch. c. 3 (May)
Sire: Alysheba (Alydar)
Dam: Baby Duck (Quack)
Br: Cardiff Stud & Sahadi Fred (Ky)
Tr: Plesa Edward Jr (41 9 6 6 .22)
L 120
Lifetime Record: 8 M 2 1 $6,980
1996 1 M 0 0 $600 | Turf 1 0 0 0 $145
1995 7 M 2 1 $6,380 | Wet 2 0 0 0 $750
GP 1 0 0 0 $600 | Dist 5 0 2 0 $5,370

5Jan96-3GP fst 1 1/16 :234 :483 1:143 1:48 Md 32000 60 6 5 43 43½ 52 44 Gryder A T L 120 b 5.70 64-26 Royal Robe120¾ Glade1201½ Arnies Alarm1181¾ 9
4-wide, shied stretch, bumped
24Dec95-3Crc fst 1 1/16 :233 :481 1:141 1:494 Md 32000 60 2 7 67½ 69 56½ 24½ Gryder A T L 119 b 3.70 66-22 Thundering Storm1194½ Alysham119hd Forge1192 5-wide, late gain 7
15Dec95-6Crc fst 1 1/16 :234 :484 1:15 1:492 Md Sp Wt 50 1 7 76½ 65 411 410¾ McCauley W H L 119 b 3.10 61-28 He's Exciting1192¾ Rough Opening1193¾ Mckenzie Star1194½ 4-wide 11
30Nov95-3Crc fst 1 :243 :494 1:161 1:44 Md 32000 47 2 3 32 43½ 35½ 32 Gryder A T L 118 b *.80 65-24 Little Villain1161¾ Arnies Alarm118nk Alysham1181 Late gain inside 7
9Nov95-10Crc fm *1 1/16 ① 1:444 Md Sp Wt 54 10 8 64¾ 76½ 86¾ 56 Boulanger G 118 4.50 74-18 Jazz Time Star1182 J. W. Blue1182½ Red Medieval118¾ Mild bid 10
17Oct95-3Crc sly 1 1/16 ⊗ :24 :49 1:142 1:483 Md Sp Wt 39 2 5 69½ 410 414 414½ Boulanger G 117 2.70 61-23 RecycledCode117¾ AnotherIntention1177½ SilvrLprchun1176½ Belated bid 6
2Oct95-10Crc fst 1 1/16 :242 :50 1:15 1:501 Md 25000 49 8 11 1112 912 58½ 24½ Boulanger G 117 8.00 63-22 Keybascan1174½ Alysham1171½ Freebie Two1173½ 11
Seven wide top str, rallied
23Jun95-10Crc sly 4½f :223 :481 :55 Md 35000 22 4 5 79½ 68 66 Castillo H Jr 115 6.80 81-16 Meddbumps117½ Termidator117nk Flame Dodger1174½ No threat 8
WORKOUTS: Feb 1 Crc 1 fst 1:46 B 1/2 Jan 16 Crc 1 fst 1:47 B 3/3 Dec 9 Crc 1 fst 1:49 B 2/3 Nov 20 Crc 5f fst 1:043 Bg 19/20

Goodbye Mickey

Own: Dichiaro Michael & My Jo Lee Stable
GRYDER A T (110 6 16 21 .05) $32,000
B. g. 3 (Feb)
Sire: Caveat (Cannonade)
Dam: Always Pretty (Naskra)
Br: New Farm Breeding Inc (NJ)
Tr: Sciametta Anthony Jr (7 1 2 1 .14)
L 120
Lifetime Record: 7 M 1 1 $5,985
1996 1 M 1 0 $2,160 Turf 0 0 0 0
1995 6 M 0 1 $3,825 Wet 1 0 0 0
GP 1 0 1 0 $2,160 Dist 1 0 1 0 $2,160

18Jan96-7GP fst 1 1/16 :241 :483 1:14 1:483 Md 30000 56 1 4 32 42 23½ 21½ Gryder A T L 118 fb 17.90 64-24 Krystie's Boy1201½ Goodbye Mickey1181½ Arnies Alarm1201½ 11
Bumped final turn, six wide, rallied
9Dec95-7Med fst 6f :224 :462 :583 1:11 [S]Md Sp Wt 43 2 6 51½ 72½ 78½ 712¾ Ferrer J C L 118 fb 35.30 71-17 Red Light Rambler1182¾ Back Off Bob1183½ Batoni1181 No factor 9
5Dec95-6Med fst 6f :222 :453 :583 1:12 [S]Md 22500 40 2 5 52¾ 64 66 56½ Marquez C H Jr L 116 fb 4.90 73-15 Jinsky's Star1181½ Jimmy Tomato1141 Jersey Justis1142¾ No rally 6
24Nov95-2Med fst 6f :23 :462 :584 1:114 [S]Md Sp Wt 39 1 5 56 75½ 57 57½ Turner T G L 118 fb 4.00 72-16 Talk Over1181¾ Messer1181½ Brielle Landing118hd No factor 8
2Nov95-3Aqu sly 1⅛ :484 1:132 1:391 1:522 Md Sp Wt 7 1 1 1hd 33 633 642 Santagata N 118 b 14.00 36-28 Hail To The Lion1188 Lonsdale1184 Quite A Story1181 Dueled inside 7
28Sep95-4Med fst 6f :22 :45 :58 1:114 [S]Md Sp Wt 32 9 4 44½ 26 48½ 710 Bravo J 118 b 4.60 70-17 Paddy Time1183 Jinsky's Star1184½ Gak Attack118hd Tired 11
14Sep95-1Med fst 6f :23 :471 1:00 1:13 [S]Md Sp Wt 36 1 3 1hd 1hd 3nk 34½ Bravo J 118 b *.80 69-16 Sir Dun Cee1183 Talk Over1111½ Goodbye Mickey118no Weakened 6
WORKOUTS: Feb 5 Hia 4f fst :51 B 14/21 Jan 11 Hia 5f fst 1:013 H 2/4 Jan 2 Hia 6f fst 1:16 B 3/3 Dec 23 Hia 5f gd 1:03 B 2/5 Nov 18 Med 3f fst :374 B 19/33

Majestic Review

Own: Pecoraro Matteo
VALLES E S (23 3 0 0 .13) $30,000
Ch. g. 3 (May)
Sire: Buckaroo (Buckpasser)
Dam: Majestic North (Vent du Nord)
Br: Barbazon Joseph & Smith Paul (Fla)
Tr: Pecoraro Anthony (16 3 3 0 .19)
L 118
Lifetime Record: 2 M 0 0 $100
1996 1 M 0 0 $40 Turf 0 0 0 0
1995 1 M 0 0 $60 Wet 0 0 0 0
GP 0 0 0 0 Dist 0 0 0 0

14Jan96-5Tam fst 7f :231 :463 1:114 1:253 Md 11500 -0 8 4 3½ 45 730 731½ Valles E S L 115 3.00 56-15 Son Of Lomond1181½ Sailing Sain1189½ Tramonti1187 Blocked into turn 9
28Dec95-3Crc fst 6f :224 :473 1:01 1:15 Md 12500 21 5 8 65 59 59½ 58½ Valles E S L 120 10.60 64-24 Call Me Later1201 Unreal Intensity1201 T's Cee Jim120hd 9
Rough trip early, wide
WORKOUTS: Jan 29 Hia 5f fst 1:024 B 9/12 Jan 22 Hia 5f fst 1:022 B 6/7 Dec 26 Hia 4f fst :49 Bg 10/16 Dec 19 Hia 5f fst 1:02 B 6/9 Dec 4 Crc 5f sly 1:042 B (d) 11/15 Nov 26 Crc 4f fst :522 Bg 22/24

Chenlo

Own: Paulson Allen E
DAY P (158 23 28 23 .15) $32,000

Ch. c. 3 (Feb)
Sire: Mt. Livermore (Blushing Groom)
Dam: Mehtar (Green Dancer)
Br: Paulson Allen E (Ky)
Tr: Zito Nicholas P (45 12 6 4 .27)

L 120

Lifetime Record:	10 M 2 2	$20,800			
1996	2 M 1 0	$3,650	Turf	0 0 0 0	
1995	8 M 1 2	$17,150	Wet	4 0 1 0	$3,780
GP	2 0 1 0	$3,650	Dist	2 0 0 1	$3,200

14Jan96-2GP	fst	6f	:231 :461 :583 1:112	Md 57500	31 7 1 31 44 410 418¼	Day P	L 118 b	3.50	65-18	Ultimate Sanction1184 Jaded Gold1206 Prime Avenue1208¼		8
Six path, weakened												
3Jan96-3GP	sly	6f	:221 :452 :582 1:113	Md 50000	64 4 5 32 31½ 35½ 28¼	Day P	L 120 b	3.30	74-18	Tarquin Joe1208¼ Chenlo1202 Neartheridge120½	4-wide, no match	8
29Nov95-4Aqu	sly	1⅛	:474 1:13 1:38 1:511	Md Sp Wt	54 2 4 34 33 412 519½	Perez R B	L 118	3.10e	64-20	CriminlSuit1188 MdowGypsy1185 CirclOfLight1186	Saved ground, tired	8
11Nov95-2Aqu	fst	1	:234 :47 1:121 1:374	Md Sp Wt	59 7 2 2½ 3nk 36 312¼	Smith M E	L 118	10.80	68-19	Prince Of Thieves1186¼ Circle Of Light1185½ Chenlo118½	Forced pace	9
21Oct95-3Kee	fst	1 1/16	:23 :472 1:132 1:46	Md Sp Wt	69 9 6 67 53¾ 23 36	Sellers S J	L 116	10.50	73-23	Rebecca's Storm1164½ Summer Squeal1161½ Chenlo116¾	Came up empty	12
5Oct95-2Bel	sly	1 1/16	:224 :453 1:111 1:462	Md Sp Wt	— 4 1 21½ 38 829 —	Krone J A	L 118	7.00	— 26	Change Partners1189 Lonsdale1181½ Country Cuzzin1181½	Dueled, eased	9
23Sep95-6Bel	my	7f	:23 :46 1:101 1:221	Md Sp Wt	27 6 2 21 21 514 829	Bailey J D	118	2.10	61-08	Crafty Friend11815 Country Cuzzin1183¼ Mariner118¾	Forced pace, tired	9
2Sep95-2Bel	fst	1	:23 :454 1:103 1:37	Md Sp Wt	44 3 1 1hd 2½ 47 413¼	Day P	118	*.95	65-16	Pirate Performer118¾ Fortitude1182 Hey You Weasel11810	Dueled wide	8
19Aug95-6Sar	fst	7f	:23 :464 1:122 1:254	Md Sp Wt	63 8 1 1½ 1½ 21 22	Day P	118	13.20	75-15	Head Minister1182 Chenlo118¾ Change Partners118nk	Held well	9
3Aug95-6Sar	fst	5½f	:223 :463 :583 1:05	Md Sp Wt	32 6 4 31½ 32½ 410 418¾	Day P	118	9.90	77-12	Roar1182¼ Procryptic11812 Tom N' Kath1184½	Gave way	6

WORKOUTS: Feb 5 GP 5f fst 1:004 H 2/41 Jan 28 GP 4f fst :493 B 18/40 Jan 22 GP 5f fst 1:042 B 30/33 Dec 21 GP 5f fst 1:02 B 4/22 Dec 11 GP 5f fst 1:03 B 6/18 Nov 25 Bel tr.t 4f fst :492 H 23/52

Glade

Own: Dogwood Stable
DAVIS R G (166 18 21 17 .11) $32,000

Ch. g. 3 (Mar)
Sire: Gulch (Mr. Prospector)
Dam: Vaguely Foelish (Vaguely Noble)
Br: Firman Pamela H (Ky)
Tr: Alexander Frank A (16 1 4 0 .06)

L 120

Lifetime Record:	11 M 3 2	$9,750			
1996	2 M 2 0	$4,440	Turf	1 0 0 0	
1995	9 M 1 2	$5,310	Wet	3 0 1 1	$3,330
GP	2 0 2 0	$4,440	Dist	2 0 2 0	$4,440

24Jan96-3GP	fst	1 1/16	:234 :481 1:131 1:473	Md 32000	60 2 7 58 44 42 22¼	Davis R G	L 120 b	*1.10	68-24	Forklift Helmar1182¼ Glade1204½ Sir Michael's Son1185		8
Five wide top str, rallied												
5Jan96-3GP	fst	1 1/16	:234 :483 1:143 1:48	Md 32000	66 4 8 64½ 54 2½ 2¾	Davis R G	L 120 b	5.70	67-26	Royal Robe120¾ Glade1201½ Arnies Alarm1181¾	Shied 1/8 pole	9
23Dec95-3Crc	sly	6f	:223 :471 :594 1:13	Md 32000	52 7 2 74¾ 66 47½ 27¾	Sellers S J	L 120 b	3.30	74-18	For Larry1207¾ Glade120¾ Fortunate Leader118½	5-wide, no threat	8
1Dec95-1Aqu	my	1	:222 :442 1:093 1:374	Md 35000	24 9 7 710 610 68½ 917¼	Santos J A	L 118 b	3.50	63-12	Panama Jay1151¾ Crypto Duck115½ Ohsaykid1181¼	Saved ground	12
2Nov95-1Aqu	sly	1	:222 :452 1:112 1:382	Md 40000	55 8 9 76½ 32 35 38	Davis R G	118 b	10.70	69-28	Newsbreaker1143 Glowing Tru1165 Glade1183½	Four wide, flattened	11
25Oct95-2Bel	fst	6½f	:224 :46 1:111 1:18	Md 50000	27 5 4 65¾ 67½ 812 918½	Stevens G L	118 b	4.10	66-13	Ima Good Gamble1187½ Grey Relic118½ Magna Carta1182¼	Faded	11
11Oct95-1Bel	fst	6f	:221 :454 :59 1:12	Md 50000	61 11 12 96¼ 86½ 52½ 32½	Davis R G	117 b	13.30	78-16	FlyStraight1172 UltimateSanction113½ Glade117hd	Checked brk, six wide	12
28Aug95-2Sar	fm	1 1/16 Ⓣ	:232 :481 1:13 1:432	Md Sp Wt	39 7 9 107½ 99¾ 911 916	Davis R G	118 b	67.25	66-08	Jetting Robert118¾ Togher1183 Vibrations118nk	No menace	12
29Jly95-2Sar	fst	6f	:221 :451 :572 1:101	Md Sp Wt	16 8 2 85 711 716 729½	Santos J A	119 b	18.50	60-13	Louis Quatorze1195½ Beefchopper1197½ Hey You Weasel1193½	No threat	9
4Jly95-6Bel	fst	5½f	:224 :463 :592 1:061	Md Sp Wt	44 4 2 44 53 56½ 68½	Davis R G	116	21.80	75-17	Choice Shift1161 Game's On1163 Head Minister116no	No rally	8

WORKOUTS: Jan 18 GP 5f fst 1:032 B 9/12 Jan 1 GP 3f gd :39 B (d)6/6 Dec 15 GP 4f fst :49 B 3/30 Nov 27 Bel tr.t 4f fst :491 B 20/48 Nov 20 Bel tr.t 4f fst :491 B 16/35 Nov 13 Bel 5f fst 1:014 H 8/22

Chrispatricks Halo

Own: Whalen Florence
DUYS D C (33 2 1 1 .06) $30,000

Dk. b or br c. 3 (May)
Sire: Prospector's Halo (Gold Stage)
Dam: Song of Amad (Minshaanshu Amad)
Br: Dennis K. Whalen (Fla)
Tr: Whalen Dennis K (3 0 0 0 .00)

L 118

Lifetime Record:	8 M 1 1	$4,015			
1996	3 M 0 0	$460	Turf	0 0 0 0	
1995	5 M 1 1	$3,555	Wet	0 0 0 0	
GP	2 0 0 0	$370	Dist	3 0 1 1	$3,275

4Feb96-6GP	fst	1⅛ ⊗	:484 1:15 1:413 1:541	Alw 26000N2L	35 11 9 108½ 1113 1124 1133	Duys D C	L 117 b	122.60	33-30	Harrowman1173½ Latin Reign1203 Woodman's Image120nk	No factor	11
15Jan96-2GP	fst	7f	:232 :471 1:14 1:27	Md 32000	29 8 11 119½ 117 55¾ 610¾	Smith M E	L 120 b	2.80	58-17	Tax Code1204¾ Fearless Gator1201¾ Pro Doc1182½		11
Failed to menace, wide												
2Jan96-12Crc	fst	7f	:23 :471 1:141 1:284	Md 25000	41 1 10 106¼ 87 611 53¾	Duys D C	L 120 b	3.10	62-23	Toby's Pride1202 Perpetual Shine1201 Superior Rex120½		11
Bumped hard start, 5-wide rally												
21Dec95-2Crc	fst	1 1/16	:241 :484 1:153 1:512	Md 20000	52 5 2 2½ 2½ 21½ 2nk	Duys D C	L 119 b	*1.60	62-34	J. J.'s Ferdie119nk Chrispatricks Halo119¾ Superior Rex119nk	Sharp try	8
11Dec95-1Crc	fst	1 1/16	:25 :502 1:16 1:503	Md 22500	56 6 3 43 22½ 22½ 32½	McCauley W H	L 117	*.70	63-33	Sir Dusty1191¾ Superior Rex117¾ Chrispatricks Halo11716	Lacked rally	6
25Nov95-5Crc	fst	1 1/16	:231 :484 1:15 1:503	Md 20000	52 3 8 87½ 76¼ 43 45	Boulanger G	L 118	23.80	61-30	Silver General1182½ Irish Bacon118¾ Thundering Storm1181¾		10
5 wide, lost whip stretch												
11Apr95-6Hia	fst	3f	:22 :332	Md Sp Wt	— 5 11 119¾ 119½	Chapman K L	118	41.60	85-20	Grayson Bay1181¾ Cashier Coyote118no Hooie1181	Outrun	11
30Mar95-3Hia	fst	3f	:222 :334	Md Sp Wt	— 4 8 1112 1114¼	Valdivia J7	109	20.30	79-16	Cahill Bay113nk Laplander114½ Cashier Coyote1161½	Outrun	11

WORKOUTS: ●Jan 26 Hia 4f my :482 H 1/9 Jan 12 Hia 5f fst 1:022 B 12/21 Dec 18 Crc 3f fst :371 Bg4/12 Nov 21 Crc 3f fst :37 Bg4/15 Nov 16 Crc 6f fst 1:182 B 3/3 Nov 10 Crc 6f fst 1:18 Bg2/2

1 — My Brother Nick — Showed a couple of improved efforts in his fourth and fifth starts with the addition of Lasix, but in his sixth start at Gulfstream, January 18 — a near identical spot to today's — he was eighth by 16 lengths at 14-1, losing to other horses in today's race.

2 — Justaold Frank — He lost to My Brother Nick by a neck at Calder two starts back, then beat him by 12 lengths in his last at Gulfstream.

3 — Chee Kee Bee — Fourth by nine lengths in his sprint return. Stretching out off a good work.

4 — Noble Houston — Dropping off a distant fourth off a bullet work at Tampa.

5 — Matthew's Jeb — Added Lasix for his return race, his first route try, and led, then weakened to a distant fourth, 9½ lengths behind Glade, the 10 horse today. Also worked a bullet since.

6 — Alysham — Even fourth, beaten 3¼ lengths by Glade, with traffic problems noted by the *Form*: "4 wide, shied stretch, bumped."

7 — Goodbye Mickey — He, too, had an eventful trip in his last: "Bumped final turn, six wide, rallied," and ran a much improved second at 17-1 in his seventh career start.

8 — Majestic Review — Moving up off two horrid lines at Calder and Tampa.

9 — Chenlo — Taking a sizable drop from a $57,500 maiden claiming sprint, when he was a distant fourth at 7-2. He had been in the money four of nine previous starts, three in maiden special weights, and two of those at one mile and 1¹⁄₁₆ miles.

10 — Glade — Zero for 11, but after a poor ninth on a muddy track in his first start with Lasix, had reeled off three consecutive seconds, the last two at this distance. In his last, the *Form* noted he had been five wide.

11 — Chrispatricks Halo — Back to reality after being foolishly placed in an allowance race. Previously, had a couple decent tries in slightly cheaper maiden claimers at Calder.

Your conclusions?

The bettors at Gulfstream identified three favorites, and sent off Chenlo a slight choice over Glade, both at 2-1. Alysham was 3-1. Goodbye Mickey was the fourth choice at 8-1 and everyone else was double digits.

Two of the favorites, Chenlo and Glade, made sense. You could have tossed Alysham, because he had lost to Glade by 3¼ lengths.

Then what? A minimum of five of the others seemed to have a reasonable chance to run well. But don't stop there. If you had made the correct decision to identify Alysham as vulnerable, take it the whole way. Bet Chenlo-Glade-all and Glade-Chenlo-all. This time the cost was $36. And, if Alysham had run third, you would have gotten a lot of grief from your friends for hitting a triple which could have paid all of $50. But that didn't happen. Glade won by five lengths. Chenlo finished second, seven lengths ahead of Chrispatricks Halo at 63-1, with Matthew's Jeb another 3½ lengths back in fourth at 10-1. Alysham dropped back to 10th and was pulled up in distress by jockey Julie Krone. The triple using a pair of 2-1 shots for first and second returned $531.60.

TENTH RACE **1$\frac{1}{16}$ MILES. (1.40^{1}) MAIDEN CLAIMING. Purse $12,000. 3-year-olds. Weight, 120 lbs. Claiming price $32,000, if for $30,000, allowed 2 lbs.**

Gulfstream

FEBRUARY 9, 1996

Value of Race: $12,000 Winner $7,200; second $2,160; third $1,200; fourth $600; fifth $120; sixth $120; seventh $120; eighth $120; ninth $120; tenth $120; eleventh $120. Mutuel Pool $270,658.00 Exacta Pool $247,720.00 Trifecta Pool $230,512.00 Superfecta Pool $77,150.00

Last Raced	Horse	M/Eqt.	A.	Wt	PP	St	¼	½	¾	Str	Fin	Jockey	Cl'g Pr	Odds $1
24Jan96 ^{3}GP^{2}	Glade	Lb	3	120	10	10	$6^{2\frac{1}{2}}$	$5^{1\frac{1}{2}}$	3^{5}	$1^{\frac{1}{2}}$	1^{5}	Davis R G	32000	2.40
14Jan96 ^{2}GP^{4}	Chenlo	L	3	120	9	9	3^{hd}	3^{5}	2^{4}	$2^{3\frac{1}{2}}$	2^{7}	Day P	32000	2.20
4Feb96 ^{6}GP^{11}	Chrispatricks Halo	Lb	3	118	11	11	9^{hd}	$8^{1\frac{1}{2}}$	7^{2}	$4^{2\frac{1}{2}}$	$3^{3\frac{1}{2}}$	Duys D C	30000	63.30
24Jan96 ^{3}GP^{4}	Matthew's Jeb	Lb	3	120	5	2	$2^{\frac{1}{2}}$	1^{hd}	1^{hd}	3^{5}	4^{nk}	Turner T G	32000	10.70
18Jan96 ^{7}GP^{2}	Goodbye Mickey	Lbf	3	120	7	8	$8^{3\frac{1}{2}}$	7^{3}	$5^{\frac{1}{2}}$	$5^{1\frac{1}{2}}$	$5^{6\frac{1}{2}}$	Gryder A T	32000	8.00
18Jan96 ^{7}GP^{4}	Justaold Frank	b	3	118	2	3	11	11	$9^{1\frac{1}{2}}$	$7^{2\frac{1}{2}}$	6^{1}	Velasquez J	30000	16.80
15Jan96 ^{2}GP^{4}	Chee Kee Bee	b	3	120	3	5	$1^{\frac{1}{2}}$	2^{hd}	$4^{2\frac{1}{2}}$	$6^{1\frac{1}{2}}$	$7^{\frac{3}{4}}$	Wilson R	32000	17.10
18Jan96 ^{7}GP[illegible]	My Brother Nick	Lb	3	118	1	1	7^{hd}	$9^{1\frac{1}{2}}$	10	9^{2}	$8^{1\frac{1}{4}}$	Beitia A O	30000	51.10
22Jan96 ^{1}GP^{4}	Noble Houston	b	3	118	4	4	5^{hd}	$6^{\frac{1}{2}}$	$8^{1\frac{1}{2}}$	$8^{1\frac{1}{2}}$	$9^{3\frac{1}{4}}$	Bain G W	30000	64.80
14Jan96 ^{5}Tam^{7}	Majestic Review	L	3	118	8	7	4^{5}	$4^{1\frac{1}{2}}$	$6^{\frac{1}{2}}$	10	10	Valles E S	30000	270.80
5Jan96 ^{3}GP^{4}	Alysham	Lb	3	120	6	6	$10^{3\frac{1}{2}}$	10^{5}	—	—	—	Krone J A	32000	3.00

Alysham:Pulled up

OFF AT 5:09 Start Good. Won driving. Time, :23^{3}, :47^{1}, 1:12^{2}, 1:40^{2}, 1:47^{3} Track fast.

$2 Mutuel Prices:				
	11–GLADE	6.80	3.40	2.80
	10–CHENLO		3.60	3.20
	12–CHRISPATRICKS HALO			10.60

$2 EXACTA 11 & 10 PAID $24.80 $2 TRIFECTA 11–10–12 PAID $531.60
$2 SUPERFECTA 11–10–12–5 PAID $3,908.80

Ch. g, (Mar), by Gulch–Vaguely Foolish, by Vaguely Noble. Trainer Alexander Frank A. Bred by Firman Pamela H (Ky).

GLADE reserved early, made a run leaving the backstretch, came into the stretch seven wide, then, under left handed urging, outfinished CHENLO. The latter wide on the first turn while vying for the early lead, gained command leaving the final turn in between calls, but was no match for the winner in the drive while being best of the rest. CHRISPATRICKS HALO unhurried early, came into the stretch ten wide, then while drifting inward, rallied to take down the show. MATTHEW'S JEB vied for the early lead outside of CHEE KEE BEE, moved to the fore down the backstretch, lost the lead leaving the final turn, then weakened. GOODBYE MICKEY reserved early, then closed with a belated bid. JUSTAOLD FRANK trailed the field early, came into the stretch wide, then made a mild late bid.CHEE KEE BEE sprinted to a slim lead inside, then faded. MY BROTHER NICK reserved early, then tired. NOBLE HOUSTON reserved inside, then gave way. MAJESTIC REVIEW, within striking distance early, came into the stretch extremely wide, then stopped. ALYSHAM void of early foot, then pulled up on the final turn in distress. ANNAPOLIS GOLD WAS ORDERED SCRATCHED BY THE STEWARDS' ON THE ADVICE OF THE VETERINARIAN. ALL MONIES WAGERED ON ANAPOLIS GOLD WERE REFUNDED AND A CONSOLATION DOUBLE WAS PAID.

Owners— 1, Dogwood Stable; 2, Paulson Allen E; 3, Whalen Florence; 4, Giacopelli Rich; 5, Dichiaro Michael & My Jo Lee Stable; 6, Ambrosio Anne M & Astling J; 7, Paraneck Stable; 8, Gemini Stables Inc; 9, Sugar Hill Farm & Training Center; 10, Pecoraro Matteo; 11, Kligman Herbert

Trainers—1, Alexander Frank A; 2, Zito Nicholas P; 3, Whalen Dennis K; 4, Sciametta Anthony Jr; 5, Sciametta Anthony Jr; 6, Francy Kate A; 7, Ryerson James T; 8, Carlisi Frank C; 9, Bennett Gerald S; 10, Pecoraro Anthony; 11, Plesa Edward Jr

Scratched— Annapolis Gold (2Jan96 ^{12}CRC^{6})

Let's do one more triple at Gulfstream. A field of nine three-year-old fillies went to post in a six-furlong allowance for non-winners of three races in the 10th race, February 4, 1996:

10 Gulfstream Park

6 Furlongs **(1:07⁴) ALLOWANCE. Purse $26,000. Fillies, 3-year-olds which have not won two races other than maiden, claiming or starter. Weight, 120 lbs. Non-winners of such a race since December 1, allowed 3 lbs.**

1 Supah Avalanche
Own: Bee Bee Stables Inc
PENNA D (72 6 12 5 .08)
Gr/ro f. 3 (Apr)
Sire: Darn That Alarm (Jig Time)
Dam: Bucks Silver Belle (Silver Buck)
Br: Bush John (Fla)
Tr: Tortora Emanuel (37 2 8 5 .05)
L 120

Lifetime Record: 7 2 2 0 $29,945											
1996	1	0	0	0		Turf	0	0	0	0	
1995	6	2	2	0	$29,945	Wet	2	0	1	0	$2,365
GP	1	0	0	0		Dist	1	0	0	0	

6Jan96-9GP fst 6f :21³ :44² :57³ 1:10³ ⒻOld Hat50k 69 4 3 66½ 79½ 710 79½ Gryder A T L 113 24.60 78-14 J J'sdream1161½ Mindy Gayle1122½ Nic's Halo1131½ No factor 8
24Dec95-7Crc fst 7f :23 :47² 1:13² 1:26² ⒻAlw 18200N1X 75 4 1 21½ 1hd 13½ 14½ Chapman K L L 120 *1.40e 79-18 Supah Avalanche1204½ Supah Halo117nk Fleur De Nuit1202½ Hand ride 7
9Dec95-10Crc fst 1 1/16 :24² :50² 1:15³ 1:48 ⒻBoca Raton100k 69 8 2 2hd 61½ 64½ 710 Chapman K L L 115 3.80e 69-19 Plum Country1153½ Supah Jen117¾ Frosty's Girl112³ Tired badly 8
25Nov95-8Crc fst 7f :22³ :45⁴ 1:12 1:25⁴ ⒻAlw 18875N1X 78 6 3 31 2hd 2hd 2¾ Chapman K L L 120 5.90e 81-22 RareBlend117¾ SupahAvalanche120³ OurDerHelen1171½ Held well, inside 11
2Nov95-3Crc fst 5f :22 :47 1:00¹ ⒻMd Sp Wt 68 2 3 31½ 33½ 2hd 11½ Chapman K L L 119 *.70 88-18 SupahAvalanche1191½ GretLookingMiss1193½ Longlenndlnky119½ Driving 8
14Oct95-6Crc sly 5f :22³ :47⁴ 1:01² ⒻMd Sp Wt 55 5 3 34 24 23 2nk Chapman K L L 118 9.90 82-18 Cuttolast118nk Supah Avalanche1182½ Sweet Secret1181½ Rallied 9
28Sep95-10Crc sly 5½f :22¹ :46³ :59³ 1:06² ⒻMd Sp Wt 48 6 5 64 57½ 612 69 Chapman K L 117 *2.00e 82-15 Upity Lady1176 Sweet Secret117¾ Supah Gold1171 No threat 8
WORKOUTS: Jan 31 Crc 4f fst :49¹ B 6/24 Jan 24 Crc 4f fst :48² H 2/15 Jan 19 Crc 4f fst :50¹ B 9/25 Dec 18 Crc 3f fst :36² B 2/12 Dec 4 Crc 4f sly :49² B (d) 5/24 Nov 20 Crc 4f fst :50³ B 14/31

2 Silk Appeal
Own: Robsham E Paul
BOULANGER G (123 18 16 18 .08)
B. f. 3 (Mar)
Sire: Valid Appeal (In Reality)
Dam: Silk Stocks (Medieval Man)
Br: Robsham E Paul (Fla)
Tr: White William P (44 2 4 8 .05)
120

Lifetime Record: 3 2 1 0 $26,640											
1996	1	1	0	0	$12,300	Turf	0	0	0	0	
1995	2	1	1	0	$14,340	Wet	0	0	0	0	
GP	0	0	0	0		Dist	2	1	1	0	$15,340

2Jan96-9Crc fst 6f :22 :46² :59² 1:13¹ ⒻAlw 18700N2L 75 7 1 12 14 15 13½ Boulanger G 120 *.50 81-23 Silk Appeal1203½ Splittin' Eights1107 Dancing Mercedes120nk 7
Ducked out start, strong handling
10Dec95-10Crc fst 6f :22¹ :46¹ :59¹ 1:13² ⒻAlw 16000N1X 72 1 8 1½ 11 2hd 2¾ Boulanger G 117 *.90 79-20 GoldMemory117¾ SilkAppeal117¾ AwesomeB1172 Bobbled start, rushed 8
26Jun95-6Crc fst 4½f :22 :46¹ :52² ⒻMd Sp Wt 88 5 3 12½ 13½ 17 Boulanger G 117 *.60 100-13 Silk Appeal1177 Emily's Star117nk Supah Jen1171 Handily 8
WORKOUTS: ●Jan 29 Crc 5f fst 1:00² H 1/21 Jan 18 Crc 5f fst 1:02¹ B 4/22 Dec 31 Crc 3f fst :37² B 4/10 Dec 24 Crc 5f gd 1:04 B 11/23 Dec 9 Crc 3f fst :37³ B 11/22 Dec 3 Crc 5f fst 1:03¹ B 12/22

3 Great Looking Miss
Own: Sunshine Bloodstock Inc
LOPEZ R D (15 0 1 0 .00)
B. f. 3 (Apr)
Sire: Great Above (Minnesota Mac)
Dam: Native Look (Native Royalty)
Br: Mangurian Harry T Jr (Fla)
Tr: Herrera Humberto (4 0 0 0 .00)
L 117

Lifetime Record: 6 1 3 0 $19,165											
1995	6	1	3	0	$19,165	Turf	1	0	0	0	$120
1994	0	M	0	0		Wet	1	0	0	0	$130
GP	0	0	0	0		Dist	2	1	1	0	$13,310

17Dec95-6Crc fst 6f :22 :46² 1:00 1:14² ⒻMd Sp Wt 52 1 9 1½ 12 12 11¾ Lopez R D 120 *1.90 75-20 GrtLookingMiss1201¾ Copwiththfutur1201½ PrncssRobyn120hd Drifted out 10
30Nov95-6Crc fst 5f :22³ :47² 1:00¹ ⒻMd Sp Wt 60 2 2 11½ 11 11½ 23½ Bain G W 119 *.60 84-20 Sports Authority1193½ Great LookingMiss1191½ Reallywaki1191¾ No match 7
12Nov95-6Crc fst 6f :22³ :47 1:00 1:13² ⒻMd Sp Wt 68 7 3 11 1½ 1hd 2¾ Bain G W 119 2.20 79-16 Kipper Kim119¾ Great Looking Miss1197¼ Haute119nk Yielded grudgingly 10
2Nov95-3Crc fst 5f :22 :47 1:00¹ ⒻMd Sp Wt 64 3 7 53¾ 44½ 42½ 21½ Bain G W 119 9.80 86-18 SupahAvalanche1191½ GretLookingMiss1193½ Longlenndinky119½ Rallied 8
16Oct95-6Crc sly 1 1/16 ⊗ :23² :47⁴ 1:13³ 1:47⁴ ⒻMd Sp Wt 44 4 1 2hd 23 513 521½ Bain G W 117 32.00 59-19 All Milady1177½ Allstar Baby117½ Silver Coin1173½ Faded 7
14Sep95-10Crc gd *1 1/16 Ⓣ 1:46³ ⒻMd Sp Wt — 2 2 — — — — Perez R A 116 26.80 — 29 Linesplasher1164½ Womanwithanattitud1163½ Swing To The Beat1167½ 10
Lost footing, fell going into first turn
WORKOUTS: Jan 24 Hia 4f fst :50³ B 23/33

4 Bright Time
Own: New Farm
WILSON R (57 8 10 7 .14)
B. f. 3 (Apr)
Sire: High Brite (Best Turn)
Dam: Last in Time (Time to Explode)
Br: Lynda K. Conway (Ky)
Tr: Perkins Benjamin W (14 5 3 1 .36)
120

Lifetime Record: 2 2 0 0 $25,800										
1996	1	1	0	0	$15,000	Turf	0	0	0	0
1995	1	1	0	0	$10,800	Wet	1	1	0	0
GP	1	1	0	0	$15,000	Dist	1	1	0	0

7Jan96-9GP sly 7f :22⁴ :46⁴ 1:13² 1:26⁴ ⒻAlw 25000N1X 77 9 1 2½ 21 14 11½ Wilson R 120 *1.00 70-20 Bright Time1201½ Torch1204 Exquisite Affair1172½
1Dec95-4Med fst 6f :22 :45² :58 1:11¹ ⒻMd Sp Wt 74 5 3 2hd 11 14 17½ Wilson R 117 1.80 83-19 Bright Time1177½ Personal Call117hd Juba Jane117¾
WORKOUTS: Jan 31 GP 4f fst :48³ B 3/37 Jan 24 GP 4f fst :48³ H 5/59 Jan 17 GP 5f fst 1:00³ H 4/27 Dec 29 GP 5f fst 1:01³ Hg 7/35 ●Dec 23 GP 3f sly :36 H (d) 1/8 Dec 16 GP 4f fst :48⁴ B 3/29

5 Oxford Scholar

Ch. f. 3 (Mar)
Sire: Seeking the Gold (Mr. Prospector)
Dam: Fulbright Scholar (Cox's Ridge)
Br: MJAKA I Stable (Ky)
Tr: Hennig Mark (32 8 6 4 .25)
Own: Evans Edward P
BAILEY J D (150 39 23 23 .26)
117

Lifetime Record: 6 2 3 1 $74,610
1995 6 2 3 1 $74,610 Turf 0 0 0 0
1994 0 M 0 0 Wet 0 0 0 0
GP 0 0 0 0 Dist 3 2 1 0 $58,430

10Oct95-8Bel fst 6f :221 :454 :582 1:12 ⒻValleyStream54k 85 1 2 21½ 21½ 2½ 12 Bailey J D 112 4.40 81-19 OxfordScholar1122 ZeeLady1204¾ StormyKrissy1127 Saved ground, clear 5
16Sep95-8Med fst 6f :213 :444 :574 1:112 ⒻJerseyJumper40k 73 3 4 41½ 21½ 1hd 2nk Santos J A 117 2.30 82-13 Mystic Rhythms117nk Oxford Scholar1171¾ Stormy Krissy117hd Game try 7
25Aug95-2Sar fst 6f :224 :463 :583 1:114 ⒻMd Sp Wt 84 1 2 11 1½ 11 11½ Perret C 118 *.70 82-22 OxfordScholr1181½ WnnngActrss1188½ NwhllRod1183 Repulsed challenge 8
21Jly95-2Sar fst 5½f :214 :451 :572 1:034 ⒻMd Sp Wt 73 4 1 1½ 1hd 22 39 Perret C 119 1.85 93-10 FltFleetFeet1199 GoldSunrise119hd OxfordScholr1193½ Dueled, weakened 6
25Jun95-4CD fst 5½f :221 :46 :574 1:042 ⒻMd Sp Wt 85 6 1 12 11 1½ 2½ Perret C 120 *.70 100-03 Grab The Cash120½ Oxford Scholar1208 Mariuka120½ Could not last 12
4Jun95-1CD fst 5½f :224 :461 :582 1:051 ⒻMd Sp Wt 73 7 10 1½ 1hd 1hd 2hd Perret C 119 *.90 97-09 TipicallyIrish119hd OxfordScholr1193 TrustTheDrem119no Pace, good try 10
WORKOUTS: Jan 28 GP 5f fst 1:014 B 9/23 Jan 20 GP 5f fst 1:013 B 7/34 Jan 12 GP 5f fst 1:013 H 2/26 Jan 6 GP 5f fst 1:02 B 11/47 Dec 31 GP 4f fst :481 H 3/53 Dec 24 GP 4f fst :503 B 39/76

6 Nic's Halo

Dk. b or br f. 3 (Mar)
Sire: Prospector's Halo (Gold Stage)
Dam: Pat Mags (Highland Blade)
Br: Diamond L Farm (Fla)
Tr: Hale Robert A (15 0 6 1 .00)
Own: Hale Kay & Robert A & Rousseau S O
SELLERS S J (160 39 19 13 .24)
117

Lifetime Record: 8 2 4 1 $38,325
1996 1 0 0 1 $5,500 Turf 2 0 2 0 $7,220
1995 7 2 4 0 $32,825 Wet 1 0 1 0 $1,425
GP 1 0 0 1 $5,500 Dist 4 2 0 1 $28,350

6Jan96-9GP fst 6f :213 :442 :573 1:103 ⒻOld Hat50k 81 8 1 12½ 12½ 12 33¾ Bain G W 113 b 23.50 83-14 J J'sdream1161½ Mindy Gayle1122½ Nic's Halo1131½ Tired inside 8
22Dec95-8Crc fm *5f Ⓣ :581 ⒻAlw 23100NC 75 3 3 1hd 2hd 1½ 2nk Bain G W 115 b 2.00 93-07 Courtlin113nk Nic's Halo1152 Ms. Phoenix1132¾ Stubbornly 7
21Nov95-9Crc fm *5f Ⓣ :583 ⒻAlw 18500N2X 74 5 3 2hd 1½ 11 2no Bain G W 120 b 3.70 91-09 Gleason117no Nic's Halo1203¾ Cuttolast117hd Yielded grudgingly 8
12Nov95-8Crc fst 6f :214 :46 :591 1:131 ⒻAlw 18575N1X 72 4 3 12½ 1½ 12 11¾ Bain G W 117 b 1.80e 81-16 Nic's Halo1171¾ No Winking1201 Fight Over Jeani117nk Driving 7
27Oct95-6Crc fst 6f :221 :46 :584 1:121 ⒻMd 45000 72 6 2 1hd 11½ 13½ 1nk Bain G W 116 b 7.70 86-18 Nic's Halo116nk Stroozer1185 Splittin' Eights1161½ Driving 7
7Oct95-3Crc sly 5½f :221 :462 :594 1:063 ⒻMd 32000 62 7 2 12½ 13 12 21¾ Rivera J A II 118 b 2.40 88-13 Tri Irish1161¾ Nic's Halo1189½ [D]Ellen's Wing1163 Best of others 7
25Sep95-6Crc fst 5f :222 :464 1:001 ⒻMd 25000 62 4 6 2½ 21 23½ 21¼ Rivera J A II 117 b 2.80 87-17 My Lucky Baby1151¼ Nic's Halo1174 Flo's Z Fury1173½ 7
Steadied leaving bkstr, tight quarters inside, rallied
15Sep95-10Crc fst 6f :221 :463 1:00 1:134 ⒻMd 30000 39 7 3 3½ 2hd 3½ 54¾ Beitia A O 115 6.10 71-22 EllsChanaDonn117nk SweetHotPepper1172½ UnrulyDowdy1151½ Weakened 10
WORKOUTS: Jan 31 Crc 4f fst :49 B 4/24 Jan 27 Crc 3f fst :381 B 19/23 Nov 11 Crc 3f fst :38 B 29/41

7 Ms. Phoenix

Ch. f. 3 (Mar)
Sire: Habitonia (Habitony)
Dam: Miss Yippie (Mad Lane)
Br: Wm. Nienstedt (Mich)
Tr: Ashor Jacob (3 0 0 0 .00)
Own: Ashor Jacob & Mizrahi Ralph H
NUNEZ E O (81 5 7 9 .06)
117

Lifetime Record: 10 2 1 2 $20,035
1996 2 0 0 0 $270 Turf 1 0 0 1 $2,730
1995 8 2 1 2 $19,765 Wet 4 1 0 0 $10,331
GP 1 0 0 0 $140 Dist 3 1 0 0 $3,860

11Jan96-5GP fst 6f :23 :461 :59 1:114 ⒻClm 22500 29 12 1 106½ 97½ 1115 1118 Davis R G 115 10.10 63-21 Ucntstopthmusc1171¾ YoSoAndSo117hd Longlnndlnky1194 Showed little 12
1Jan96-7Crc my 7f :23 :464 1:132 1:262 ⒻClm 32000 37 7 1 21 21 35½ 616½ Nunez E O 117 10.70 61-19 [D]Hurricane Viv1194½ WildSociety1171½ Alda'sWill1154 Dueled, weakened 8
Placed 5th through disqualification.
22Dec95-8Crc fm *5f Ⓣ :581 ⒻAlw 23100NC 69 4 6 43½ 43½ 42 32¾ Nunez E O 113 27.90 91-07 Courtlin113nk Nic's Halo1152 Ms. Phoenix1132¾ 4-wide bid 7
11Nov95-9Det sly 170 :231 :482 1:153 1:473 Ⓕ[S]MiJuvFillies69k 59 13 12 76½ 41¾ 1hd 47¾ Gonzalez L A 122 53.30 54-42 Agiftfrom Bertie1226 Leading Memories122¾ Bet Twice Princess1221 14
Very wide to 2nd turn, then 5 wide
21Oct95-7Det my 6f :214 :452 :582 1:122 Ⓕ[R]MichiganSire86k 51 3 8 2½ 2hd 45 69 Martinez L 119 15.20 70-24 Srh'sLil'Lucie119nk AgiftfromBertie1193 MissHbitoni1193½ No excuse rail 13
11Oct95-4Det fst 6f :223 :462 :591 1:133 ⒻAlw 6200N2L 48 4 2 13 13 14 1½ Moore B G 115 5.70 73-24 Ms. Phoenix115½ [D]Sunny Black1132 Royal Mum1201½ Lasted inside 6
22Sep95-5Det sly 5½f :224 :473 1:012 1:083 Ⓕ[S]Md 40000 40 1 6 11 12 13 12 Allen R D Jr 117 *.70 72-28 Ms. Phoenix1172 Lac La Tina1166 Ashfords Doll1171½ Hustled off rail 8
2Sep95-10Det fst 5½f :222 :461 :581 1:053 Ⓕ[S]Temptress45k 20 10 2 42½ 56 816 918½ Allen R D Jr 119 44.00 69-23 BtTwicPrincss1192½ Srh'sLil'Luci119½ MissHbiton1193 Outrun 3 furlongs 10
23Aug95-2Det fst 5½f :23 :473 1:02 1:092 Ⓕ[S]Md 40000 22 6 7 21 2hd 2hd 31 Gonzalez L A 116 *.60 67-29 Miss Charlie Mac113¾ Steffie J.118nk Ms. Phoenix116no 8
Stumbled early, hustled
13Aug95-6Det fst 5½f :231 :474 1:013 1:083 Ⓕ[S]Md Sp Wt 29 4 8 67½ 43½ 32½ 2hd Gonzalez L A 118 3.00 72-23 Pessian Ann118hd Ms. Phoenix1182½ Steffie J.118¾ 6 wide, 2nd best 10
WORKOUTS: Jan 27 Hia 4f fst :50 B 20/35 Dec 16 Hia 3f fst :382 B 10/14 Nov 7 Det 5f fst 1:042 B 5/8

8 Proper Dance

Dk. b or br f. 3 (Apr)
Sire: Nureyev (Northern Dancer)
Dam: Sophisticated Girl (Stop the Music)
Br: Mabee Mr & Mrs John C (Ky)
Tr: Lukas D Wayne (33 5 6 6 .15)
Own: Overbrook Farm
DAY P (133 19 23 21 .14)
L 117

Lifetime Record: 8 2 1 1 $59,955
1996 1 0 0 1 $3,380 Turf 1 0 0 0 $2,130
1995 7 2 1 0 $56,575 Wet 0 0 0 0
GP 1 0 0 1 $3,380 Dist 2 2 0 0 $38,485

12Jan96-3GP fst 7f :23 :464 1:123 1:253 ⒻAlw 26000N2X 71 6 2 31½ 31½ 3½ 3nk Day P 117 *.60 76-23 Relic Rhythm117no Hurricane Viv120nk Proper Dance1172¾ 6
Broke outward start, seven wide top str, rallied, just missing
25Nov95-8CD fst 1 1/16 :241 :481 1:13 1:452 ⒻGolden Rod-G3 71 1 1 11 1hd 42½ 96½ Barton D M 113 7.70e 81-08 Gold Sunrise113½ Birr119no Solana113hd Pace, tired 11
8Nov95-5CD gd 1 Ⓣ :233 :474 1:13 1:383 ⒻAlw 42600NC 63 5 5 46½ 46½ 36½ 46½ Barton D M 109 2.70 73-22 Colcon1152 Supreme Silver1151½ Wistfully1123 10
Bumped start, no rally
19Oct95-8Kee fst 7f :221 :453 1:11 1:241 ⒻIndianSummer54k 83 2 4 31½ 31½ 21½ 21½ Barton D M 118 2.40 78-17 J. D. And Water1211½ Proper Dance1182 Prissy One1152½ Inside, 2nd best 6
23Sep95-6TP fst 1 :23 :462 1:112 1:374 ⒻKyCupJuvFlly100k 83 2 2 31½ 32 45 45 Barton D M 114 2.10 76-15 Tipically Irish1151½ Birr1141 Summer Squeeze1142½ 6
Bobbled start, weakened inside
7Sep95-6TP fst 6f :222 :471 1:00 1:131 ⒻAlw 27350N2L 88 7 2 1hd 11½ 17 114 Barton D M 121 1.30 79-28 Proper Dance12114 Gone For Gusto1217 Quiet Lucky1142½ Ridden out 9
27Aug95-8Dmr fst 7f :214 :441 1:09 1:222 ⒻDmrDbutante-G2 66 12 2 41½ 31½ 57½ 710 Barton D M B 115 15.00 79-10 Batroyale1194 Proud Dixie1172 General Idea1161 4 wide to turn 12
19Aug95-4Dmr fst 6f :221 :451 :572 1:094 ⒻMd Sp Wt 82 5 3 1½ 11 13 12¾ Flores D R B 118 19.90 92-06 Proper Dance1182¾ Jade Hawk1185 Stepandrepeat118½ Clearly best 12
WORKOUTS: Jan 31 GP 4f fst :502 B 21/37 Jan 24 GP 4f fst :493 B 28/59 Jan 6 GP 5f fst 1:01 B 2/47 Dec 31 GP 4f fst :502 B 28/63 Nov 19 CD 5f fst 1:013 B 3/29

9 Marfa's Finale

Dk. b or br f. 3 (May)
Sire: Marfa (Foolish Pleasure)
Dam: Final Bow (Stop the Music)
Br: Stoneworth Farm (Md)
Tr: Donovan Patrick (7 1 1 0 .14)
Own: Our Old Gang Stable
TURNER T G (27 3 1 2 .11)
L 117

Lifetime Record: 6 2 2 1 $52,264
1996 2 0 1 0 $18,000 Turf 0 0 0 0
1995 4 2 1 1 $34,264 Wet 1 0 1 0 $7,495
GP 2 0 1 0 $18,000 Dist 4 1 1 1 $24,097

24Jan96-9GP fst 7f :23 :461 1:104 1:242 ⒻForward Gal-G2 85 7 2 2hd 2½ 23½ 23½ McCauley W H L 113 b 12.90 78-21 Mindy Gayle1123½ Marfa's Finale1132 Supah Jen114½ 7
Drifted out top str, eight wide, second best
6Jan96-9GP fst 6f :213 :442 :573 1:103 ⒻOld Hat50k 78 1 6 32½ 33 32 45 McCauley W H L 113 7.50 82-14 J J'sdream1161½ Mindy Gayle1122½ Nic's Halo1131½ Tired inside 8
7Nov95-7Lrl sly 6f :22 :451 :574 1:104 ⒻFair Star37k 80 5 5 35 48 25 25 Bracho J A L 114 4.40e 81-20 Secret Prospect1155 Marfa's Finale1142¾ No Comment Baby120hd Rallied 9
29Oct95-6Lrl fst 6f :22 :452 :581 1:112 ⒻAlw 17500N1X 78 8 1 21½ 24 21½ 1nk Bracho J A L 117 *1.00 83-17 Marfa's Finale117nk Wide River1202½ Quick Sassy Sue1153½ Driving 8
7Sep95-8Pim fst 6f :224 :452 :574 1:104 ⒻDebby's Turn32k 56 9 1 21½ 24 24 38¾ Bracho J A 114 5.70 85-11 Season's Flair1134½ Chapter Seven1144½ Marfa's Finale1141½ Weakened 11
20Aug95-3Pim fst 5½f :222 :463 :592 1:061 ⒻMd Sp Wt 61 9 3 1hd 11 15 14½ Bracho J A 119 5.50 90-14 Marfa's Finale1194½ Buckaroo Zoo1191½ Know The Code1196 Driving 10
WORKOUTS: Jan 16 GP 6f fst 1:163 B 2/5 Dec 28 GP 4f fst :492 B 3/30 Dec 24 GP 3f fst :393 B 39/40 Dec 2 GP 6f fst 1:173 B 3/3

1 — Supah Avalanche — Had two wins and two seconds in six starts with Lasix added. Her two poor lines were in stakes company. In her last, the Old Hat, she was seventh, beaten 4¾ lengths by Nic's Halo, the 6 horse today. Pass.

2 — Silk Appeal — Speedster was stepping up off two wins and a second in three starts, all at odds-on. Add in a bullet work for this. Prefer others.

3 — Great Looking Miss — Jumping up two classes off a layoff from a maiden win. Had made the lead in her last three starts. Certainly capable of pressing the pace, but that was all.

4 — Bright Time — Two for two, the last at even money at seven furlongs on a sloppy track. She sat a close second at the first call in both her starts.

5 — Oxford Scholar — In the money all six starts, including a close second and a two-length win in stakes company, but idle a little more than four months. Her works were steady. Obviously, the horse to beat if she was ready. But would she be?

6 — Nic's Halo — In the money seven straight starts, including a front-running third in the Old Hat at 23-1. Certainly a contender.

7 — Ms. Phoenix — Moving up from two awful races in claimers. Next.

8 — Proper Dance — Hadn't shown quite as much ability as Oxford Scholar as a two-year-old — note that she was fourth by five lengths to Tipically Irish in the Kentucky Cup Juvenile Filly, and that Oxford Scholar was second by a head to Tipically Irish in her debut — but she had something that Oxford Scholar did not: a race back. And it was a good one, overcoming a poor break and a seven-wide trip to finish third by a neck at 3-5 in a seven-furlong allowance. Today, she was adding Lasix. A top contender.

9 — Marfa's Finale — In the money five of six starts. Fourth by five lengths in the Old Hat in her '96 debut, then a solid second in the seven-furlong Forward Gal stakes. Contender.

Conclusions? Ms. Phoenix and Great Looking Miss clearly didn't belong. Overlays are useless if the horses have no chance, and these two did not, going off at prices of 208-1 and 68-1, respectively.

Of the remaining seven, Super Avalanche had been beaten pretty soundly by Nic's Halo. That left six.

Silk Appeal and Bright Time were stepping up. Bright Time looked to be the better of the two.

That left five. Here were there odds:

Oxford Scholar and Proper Dance went off at 2-1, with the former a slight favorite. Marfa's Finale and Nic's Halo went off at 5-1 and Bright Time at 6-1.

The key was Oxford Scholar. It was reasonable to expect her to need a race back after a four month layoff and moderate workouts. At 2-1, she was a vulnerable favorite.

Boxing the four others would have cost $48.

Nic's Halo won by three-quarters of a length over Proper Dance to return $13.00. Bright Time was another neck behind in third, 1½ lengths in front of Maria's Finale. Oxford Scholar broke inward at the start; bumped with Bright Time hard, rushed up to challenge for the lead and stopped badly, finishing last by 26 lengths.

The triple with horses at odds of 5-1, 2-1 and 6-1 paid $346.40, not a candidate for the Guiness Book of Records, but a good example of a different approach to land an exotic overlay.

TENTH RACE

Gulfstream

FEBRUARY 4, 1996

6 FURLONGS. (1.074) ALLOWANCE. Purse $26,000. Fillies, 3–year–olds which have not won two races other than maiden, claiming or starter. Weight, 120 lbs. Non–winners of such a race since December 1, allowed 3 lbs.

Value of Race: $26,000 Winner $15,600; second $4,680; third $3,120; fourth $1,300; fifth $260; sixth $260; seventh $260; eighth $260; ninth $260. Mutuel Pool $310,646.00 Exacta Pool $286,316.00 Trifecta Pool $278,962.00

Last Raced	Horse	M/Eqt. A.Wt	PP	St	1/4	1/2	Str	Fin	Jockey	Odds $1
6Jan96 9GP3	Nic's Halo	b 3 117	6	3	1$\frac{1}{2}$	2$\frac{1}{2}$	1hd	1$\frac{3}{4}$	Sellers S J	5.50
12Jan96 3GP3	Proper Dance	L 3 117	8	1	6$\frac{1}{2}$	4$\frac{1}{2}$	4$\frac{1}{2}$	2nk	Day P	2.20
7Jan96 9GP1	Bright Time	3 120	4	9	7^4	6$\frac{1}{2}$	6^8	3$\frac{1}{2}$	Wilson R	6.20
24Jan96 9GP2	Marfa's Finale	Lb 3 117	9	2	3hd	3hd	3hd	4$\frac{1}{2}$	Turner T G	5.10
6Jan96 9GP7	Supah Avalanche	L 3 120	1	8	5hd	7^9	5$\frac{1}{2}$	5$\frac{2}{2}$	Penna D	36.70
2Jan96 9Crc1	Silk Appeal	3 120	2	6	2$\frac{1}{2}$	1hd	2$\frac{2}{2}$	6^9	Boulanger G	10.80
17Dec95 6Crc1	Great Looking Miss	L 3 117	3	4	8$\frac{1}{2}$	8$\frac{1}{2}$	8^5	7^{10}	Lopez R D	68.40
11Jan96 5GP11	Ms. Phoenix	3 117	7	7	9	9	9	8$\frac{1}{2}$	Nunez E O	208.40
10Oct95 8Bel1	Oxford Scholar	3 117	5	5	4^1	5$\frac{1}{2}$	7^3	9	Bailey J D	2.10

OFF AT 5:11 Start Good. Won driving. Time, :22^4, :46^2, 1:00, 1:13^1 Track fast.

$2 Mutuel Prices:	6–NIC'S HALO	13.00	5.40	3.60
	8–PROPER DANCE		3.60	3.00
	4–BRIGHT TIME			4.80

$2 EXACTA 6 & 8 PAID $52.80 $2 TRIFECTA 6–8–4 PAID $346.40

Dk. b. or br. f, (Mar), by Prospector's Halo–Pat Mags, by Highland Blade. Trainer Hale Robert A. Bred by Diamond L Farm (Fla).

NIC'S HALO alternated for the early lead, came into the stretch six wide, gained command midstretch, then, under right handed urging, held PROPER DANCE safe. The latter reserved early, made a run leaving the backstretch to be within striking distance, came into the stretch eight wide, rallied in the drive just missing. BRIGHT TIME bumped hard at the start, steadied on the turn when lacking racing room, came into the stretch wide, then closed with a good late rally. MARFA'S FINALE vied for the lead from the beginning, came into the stretch seven wide, then lacked the needed late response. SUPAH AVALANCHE, within striking distance early, then lacked the needed late response in the drive. SILK APPEAL dueled for the early lead, then faded. GREAT LOOKING MISS was no threat. MS. PHOENIX showed little. OXFORD SCHOLAR broke inward start, bumped BRIGHT TIME hard, rushed to vie for the early lead, then stopped.

Owners— 1, Hale Kay & Robert A & Rousseau S O; 2, Overbrook Farm; 3, New Farm; 4, Our Old Gang Stable; 5, Bee Bee Stables Inc; 6, Robsham E Paul; 7, Sunshine Bloodstock Inc; 8, Ashor Jacob & Mizrahi Ralph H; 9, Evans Edward P

Trainers— 1, Hale Robert A; 2, Lukas D Wayne; 3, Perkins Benjamin W; 4, Donovan Patrick; 5, Tortora Emanuel; 6, White William P; 7, Herrera Humberto; 8, Ashor Jacob; 9, Hennig Mark

10

Superfectas

When you connect on a superfecta — correctly tabbing the first four finishers in a race — the payoff should be exotic. It's not a high percentage investment, because it's an extremely difficult bet.

An old friend proved that to me many years ago at Monticello Raceway, a harness track 90 miles northwest of New York City. Mark became enamored with the superfecta, offered nightly on the last race. He invested $72 every single night he went to the track, two to four times a week, for an entire summer. And he finally hit one in late August. It paid something like $210.

If you play the superfecta, wait for an overlay horse you like strongly enough to key on top to play against a vulnerable favorite. Then box all the contenders, including the favorite, underneath him. Remember, the beatable favorite can still finish second, third or fourth and be part of the superfecta.

Boxing four horses underneath your key horse costs $48 for every two dollars you invest. Five horses cost $120, and so on. Betting an extra $1 or $2 exacta wheel with your horse on top as a saver will ensure that if your key horse wins and you miss the superfecta, you don't completely waste the overlay winner.

If you key a favorite on top in the superfecta, you're risking getting a chintzy return, which you can't afford to do, because you're not going to be right a high percentage of time on such a difficult wager. So maximize the ones you do hit by focusing on an overlay, not the favorite, as a key on top of your superfecta boxes.

The second race at Calder, December 7, 1995, presented such an opportunity. The scratch of Kapellmeister left a field of nine three-year-old claimers ($9,000 to $10,000) in a seven-fur-long sprint.

2 **Calder Race Course**

7 Furlongs (1:22) CLAIMING. Purse $6,000. 3-year-olds and upward which have never won two races. Weights: 3-year-olds, 121 lbs. Older, 122 lbs. Claiming price $10,000, if for $9,000, allowed 2 lbs.

Uncle Haley	B. g. 3 (Apr) Sire: Garbomi (Believe It) Dam: Prodigal Princess (Majestic Prince)		Lifetime Record: 23 1 1 2 $11,337
Own: Establo Mandarria	Br: Billy C. Ballard (Ky) Tr: Casado Luis (8 0 0 0 .00)	L 119	1995 12 1 1 2 $10,442 Turf 0 0 0 0
NUNEZ E O (149 15 31 13 .13) $9,000			1994 11 M 0 0 $1,495 Wet 4 0 0 1 $345
			Crc 16 0 0 1 $2,880 Dist 5 0 1 1 $2,238

Space Card	Ch. g. 3 (May) Sire: Spare Card (Paris Dust) Dam: Hal Snowden Jr. (Ill)		Lifetime Record: 13 1 4 2 $11,988
Own: Demora Julian	Br: Hal Snowden Jr. (Ill) Tr: Cosimano Anthony (12 1 3 1 .08)	L 121	1995 13 1 4 2 $11,988 Turf 1 0 0 0 $120
BETTIA A O (38 4 5 2 .11) $10,000			1994 0 M 0 0 Wet 2 0 1 0 $1,380
			Crc 12 1 4 2 $11,868 Dist 1 0 1 0 $1,083

Lucky Liaison	Ch. c. 3 (Apr) Sire: Foreign Holding (Damascus) Dam: My Lucky Wish (Lyphard's Wish (FR))		Lifetime Record: 12 1 4 1 $9,390
Own: Tsanadis James G	Br: Fedra Tsanadis (Fla) Tr: Gianos George (20 3 3 1 .15)	L 119	1995 12 1 4 1 $9,390 Turf 1 0 0 0 $160
CHAPMAN K L (68 6 9 12 .08) $9,000			1994 0 M 0 0 Wet 1 0 0 0 $70
			Crc 11 1 4 1 $9,230 Dist 1 0 0 0 $780

Cutler Ridge
Own: Arango Frank
DIAZ S (47 6 5 7 .13) $9,000

B. c. 3 (Apr)
Sire: Cutlass (Damascus)
Dam: Wajiliat (Wajima)
Br: Joseph Iantosca (Fla)
Tr: Estevez Manuel A (15 0 4 1 .00)

L 112⁷

Lifetime Record:	8 1 2 1	$8,168			
1995	7 1 2 1	$8,113	Turf	2 0 0 0	$583
1994	1 M 0 0	$55	Wet	1 0 1 0	$1,980
Crc	2 0 1 0	$1,255	Dist	3 1 1 1	$6,240

28Nov95-4Crc fst 5f :23 :474 1:011 3+ Clm 9000n2L	52 4 6 65 64½ 42½ 21 Diaz S7	L 112 fb 2.30 82-21	BoldSilverBuck1191 CutlerRidge112hd SkipABrth120nk	Swung out stretch	6
15May95-9Hia fm *1⅛ Ⓣ 1:413 Clm 30000	54 3 7 89 811 59½ 510¼ Duarte J C	114 b 6.60 83-09	Tune M Up1192½ Royal Rumor1124 Kilmer116hd	Failed to menace	10
10Apr95-8Hia fm *1⅛ Ⓣ 1:48 Clm 30000	57 8 8 89½ 911 57½ 48½ Velez J A Jr	114 b 8.30 83-12	Bufalo Erik1161½ Prince Ensign1165 Royal Rumor1121½	Belated bid	9
2Apr95-5Hia fst 7f :233 :471 1:123 1:26 Md 14000	61 3 8 52½ 51½ 11½ 17½ Velez J A Jr	117 b *.90 79-22	Cutler Ridge1177½ ⒹStar Fiance121½ Racing Tokyo121no	Ridden out	10
20Mar95-2Hia fst 7f :234 :464 1:112 1:25 Md 14000	58 8 10 73½ 53 31 3¾ Rivera J A II	117 b 7.70 83-12	Party Fame121½ Quite Soxy117no Cutler Ridge1172½		10
Six wide top str, lacked response					
13Mar95-4GP sly 7f :222 :463 1:14 1:281 Clm 10000	38 4 10 84½ 85 33½ 21½ Ramos W S	117 b 15.70 60-23	Christina Prince1171½ Cutler Ridge117¾ Demi's Pal117nk		11
Six wide top str, drifted out drive, rallied					
9Feb95-5GP fst 6f :222 :463 :59 1:124 Clm 10000	44 6 11 910 813 89½ 511 Rivera J A II	117 28.10 65-22	Red On Top1198½ Starwans Reality1191½ Leap Fire117hd	Mild bid	12
27Dec94-11Crc fst 6f :224 :472 1:004 1:144 Md c-12500	21 1 12 1215 1220 1116 1012¾ Jurado E M	120 8.40 60-21	Charging Charger120½ G'night Nic1282½ Racing Tokyo1201½	Poor start	12
Claimed from Iantosca Joseph, Wolfson Martin D Trainer					

WORKOUTS: Nov 11 Crc 5f fst 1:042 B 27/43

Kapellmeister
Own: Marablue Farm
GONZALEZ M A (89 10 7 14 .11) $10,000

B. g. 5
Sire: Country Pine (His Majesty)
Dam: Allouette (Proud Birdie)
Br: Marablue Farms (Fla)
Tr: Richards Robert J Jr (28 0 3 5 .00)

L 122

Lifetime Record:	20 1 3 3	$29,090			
1995	8 0 1 1	$2,726	Turf	2 0 0 0	
1993	8 1 2 0	$22,863	Wet	3 1 0 1	$13,898
Crc	10 0 1 2	$4,546	Dist	3 0 0 1	$1,290

27Nov95-7Crc fst 1⅛ :234 :483 1:151 1:583 3+ Clm 10000n2L	51 7 2 1hd 1½ 4¾ 54½ Gonzalez M A	L 122 fb 12.70 61-26	Duke Dikkish1201½ Purple Toe120no Air Rill111nk	Tired	7
12Nov95-5Crc fst 1⅛ :24 :484 1:144 1:494 3+ Clm 10000n2L	50 11 4 42½ 44½ 68½ 94½ Ramos W S	L 122 fb 11.70 65-33	Marroquin120nk Duke Dikkish120½ Wayzata120¾	Gave way	11
22Oct95-4Crc fst 1 :243 :484 1:142 1:41 3+ Clm 10000n2L	67 2 3 31 51¾ 44½ 26 Bain G W	L 122 fb 5.60 76-20	Sea Voyage1206 Kapellmeister1222 Racing Tokyo1194½	Rallied	7
15Oct95-12Crc sly 7f :231 :464 1:122 1:252 3+ Clm 10000n2L	59 2 4 43 49½ 410 46¾ Bain G W	L 122 fb *2.30 72-20	HankTheHmmer1132 RcingTokyo1201½ UncleHley1183	Lacked response	9
23Sep95-7Crc fst 7f :23 :462 1:124 1:252 3+ Clm 10000n2L	61 4 7 52 54½ 65½ 44½ Bain G W	L 122 fb 4.00 74-20	Flummox1192½ Bold Silver Buck112½ Racing Tokyo1191½		9
Eight wide top str, lacked response					
11Sep95-2Crc wf 7f :231 :473 1:132 1:262 3+ Clm 10000n2L	60 4 3 3hd 3½ 46 34 Bain G W	L 122 fb 12.10 75-18	Forever Smiles1122 Per Pop1222 Kapellmeister1223	Lacked response	7
20Aug95-2Crc fst 1⅛ :234 :484 1:134 1:404 3+ Clm 10000n2L	40 9 3 22½ 68½ 814 816½ Boulanger G	122 fb 8.00 58-25	P Val117hd Crimson Claim1174 Fran's Book128¾	Gave way	9
6Aug95-8Crc fst 1⅛ :232 :48 1:144 1:483 3+ Clm 10000n2L	53 12 4 59¾ 55½ 811 816½ Boulanger G	122 b 6.90 66-20	Super120nk Pooks Count117¾ P Val1171½	Gave way	12
31Oct93-2CD my 1⅛ :243 :484 1:161 1:493 3+ Md Sp Wt	74 1 2 11½ 1½ 13 16½ Martinez W	118 fb 6.50 66-30	Kapellmeister1186½ Cherokee Fox118no Play Groom1184½	Driving, clear	12
9Oct93-2Kee fst 1⅛ :481 1:124 1:38 1:502 3+ Md Sp Wt	65 4 10 94 51½ 63½ 65½ Martinez W	117 b 3.80 70-16	Swinging Speeder117½ Arthurian1171½ Play Groom1172½	No factor	11

WORKOUTS: ●Dec 6 Crc 3f sly :353 B 1/17 Oct 6 Crc 5f sly 1:03 B (d)3/14 Sep 8 Crc 5f sly 1:023 B (d)3/17

Upper Action
Own: Dwoskin Steven
VALLES E S (38 1 4 2 .03) $10,000

Ch. g. 3 (Apr)
Sire: Upper Nile (Nijinsky II)
Dam: Dish Baby (Noble Grow)
Br: Rupert B. Brown (Fla)
Tr: Dwoskin Steven (19 3 3 0 .16)

L 121

Lifetime Record:	4 1 0 0	$3,622			
1995	4 1 0 0	$3,622	Turf	1 0 0 0	$130
1994	0 M 0 0		Wet	1 0 0 0	$135
Crc	3 1 0 0	$3,492	Dist	0 0 0 0	

27Oct95-8Crc fst 6f :221 :454 :59 1:123 3+ Clm 10000n2L	44 11 11 94 810 1012 79½ Griffis D M	L 120 15.40 75-18	Commemort'sCopy1181½ Deliverble120¾ SuddnSm120nk	Failed to menace	12
15Oct95-9Crc sly 6f :223 :463 :591 1:12 Alw 14500n1x	47 6 5 68 63½ 610 614½ Griffis D M5	L 114 9.50 70-20	Worth Noting1193½ El Torreon1193½ Silver Cyclone1191½	No factor	6
30Sep95-3Crc yl *1⅛ Ⓣ 1:444 Alw 14000n2L	49 5 5 79½ 714 612 617½ Griffis D M5	112 23.20 63-14	Copy Editor1289½ Cool Star1282½ Naked Inspiration1289½	Showed little	7
15Sep95-2Crc fst 6f :221 :463 1:00 1:14 3+ Md 12500	53 5 8 56 2½ 12½ 12½ Griffis D M5	114 6.80 77-22	Upper Action1142½ Bea Slick119½ Distribution1191½	Driving	8

WORKOUTS: Nov 25 Crc 3f fst :372 B 14/32 Oct 26 Crc 3f fst :382 B 16/22 Oct 11 Crc 4f fst :492 B 7/43 Sep 25 Crc 4f fst :513 B 34/39 Sep 14 Crc 3f fst :382 B 15/20

Catch This
Own: Ullmann J
BAIN G W (78 9 12 5 .13) $10,000

Ro. h. 5
Sire: Wolf Power (SA) (Flirting Around)
Dam: Catcha Shiningstar (Accipiter)
Br: Aldila Farm (Ky)
Tr: Trivigno Michael (14 3 1 0 .21)

122

Lifetime Record:	7 1 2 0	$12,050			
1995	3 0 2 0	$2,150	Turf	1 0 0 0	$1,620
1994	1 0 0 0	$1,680	Wet	2 1 0 0	$6,600
Crc	3 0 2 0	$2,150	Dist	0 0 0 0	

23Nov95-9Crc fst 6f :221 :461 :593 1:132 3+ Clm 10000n2L	43 4 11 118½ 1111 87½ 77½ Bain G W	122 f 4.90 72-20	I. C. Pine119½ Space Card121¾ Deliverable1211	Mild bid	12
1Jly95-2Crc fst 6f :223 :471 :594 1:123 3+ Clm 10000n2L	62 1 5 42 65 52¾ 36½ Bain G W	122 f *1.10 77-17	Charging Charger1174½ ⒹIron In The Fire1171½ Catch This1221		8
Ckd hvg bkstr inside, angled out turn, eight wide top str, late rally Placed second through disqualification.					
17Jun95-5Crc fst 6f :222 :453 :582 1:113 3+ Clm 10000n2L	66 6 3 21 22½ 22½ 25½ Bain G W	122 f 2.90 84-12	Virginian Snow1225½ Catch This122nk Iron In The Fire1154		7
Seven wide top str, drifted out str, gamely					
1Jun94-7Bel fst 6f :222 :451 :571 1:101 3+ Alw 28000n1x	77 4 6 611 63½ 57 57½ Luzzi M J	119 29.90 83-20	CommncheTril1123½ MdiclPro106hd FmousFn1191½	Broke slowly, bobbled	6
Awarded fourth purse money					
27Oct93-3Aqu wf 6f :232 :481 1:003 1:131 3+ Md 35000	73 8 7 63 4¾ 1½ 13¾ Davis R G	119 *1.50 76-20	Catch This1133¾ Color Me Speed1153 Varricchio11910	Wide, driving	8
8Oct93-7Bel fm 1⅛ Ⓣ :223 :462 1:111 1:424 3+ Md Sp Wt	70 10 8 97½ 93½ 63¾ 45½ Alvarado F T	119 5.10 77-18	Delray1194 Rain Alert119¾ A. J. Warbucks122½	Broke slowly, wide	10
27Sep93-9Bel sly 6f :22 :461 :584 1:121 3+ Md Sp Wt	67 1 6 720 715 77 53 Alvarado F T	118 20.40 76-22	Franz118no Rise To Rule122no Eyesight118½	Strong finish	8

WORKOUTS: Nov 19 Crc 5f fst 1:044 B 21/25 Nov 4 Crc 4f fst :492 B 4/49 Oct 28 Crc 5f fst 1:051 B 29/31

Birdies Crescent
Own: Condry L & Karpf L
HENRY W T (83 13 8 11 .16) $10,000

Dk. b or br g. 3 (Mar)
Sire: Proud Birdie (Proud Clarion)
Dam: Star Wish (Cutlass)
Br: Joseph Rothenberger (Fla)
Tr: Catanese Joseph C III (11 2 3 1 .18)

L 121

Lifetime Record:	18 1 1 5	$9,292			
1995	18 1 1 5	$9,292	Turf	1 0 0 0	$140
1994	0 M 0 0		Wet	3 0 1 1	$1,952
Crc	13 1 1 5	$8,745	Dist	5 1 0 1	$4,435

23Nov95-9Crc fst 6f :221 :461 :593 1:132 3+ Clm 10000n2L	51 11 4 109½ 1010 76½ 64½ Henry W T	L 121 b 9.10 75-20	I. C. Pine119½ Space Card121¾ Deliverable1211	Belated bid	12
5Nov95-2Crc fst 7f :23 :463 1:121 1:254 3+ Clm 10000n2L	63 7 1 51¾ 42½ 33½ 32½ Henry W T	L 121 b *1.70 80-17	BasketBallCrd1212 BoldSilverBuck112nk BirdiesCrescent1212½	Late rally	7
26Oct95-2Crc fst 7f :224 :461 1:122 1:262 3+ Md 12500	65 9 2 31 32 21½ 13½ Henry W T	L 120 b 2.60 79-16	Birdies Crescent1203½ Lake Emerald1201½ Aly Abby1201½	Driving	9
15Oct95-2Crc sly 1⅛ :24 :484 1:144 1:49 3+ Md 12500	63 3 2 32½ 21½ 2hd 21 Henry W T	L 119 b 14.50 73-14	Air Rill1191 Birdies Crescent1193½ One Above1191	Second best, inside	7
28Sep95-1Crc sly 1⅛ :234 :48 1:142 1:491 3+ Md 12500	53 1 4 47 35½ 35 35½ Griffis D M5	L 113 b 6.20 67-26	Mosbemyluckydy1181½ OneAbov1183½ BirdisCrscnt1138	Lacked response	6
18Sep95-6Crc gd 1⅛ ⊗ :23 :48 1:144 1:493 3+ Md 22500	23 1 4 77½ 812 716 625 Cedeno L M7	L 109 b 26.70 46-23	Fashionable Lies1225½ Bjorn11610 Stout Ole Fellow1115	Tired	8
7Sep95-2Crc fst 1⅛ :24 :48 1:144 1:49 3+ Md 12500	54 6 2 32 35 37 38½ Griffis D M5	L 113 b 13.60e 66-28	GallantSelection1181½ LuckyLiison1186½ BirdiesCrescent1131	Weakened	9
20Aug95-1Crc fst 1⅛ :234 :482 1:144 1:492 3+ Md 12500	43 3 3 31 34½ 39 314½ Griffis D M5	L 112 b 35.00 57-26	Flummox1126½ Lucky Liaison1178½ BirdiesCrescent1122½	Lacked response	8
3Aug95-6Crc sly 1⅛ :241 :484 1:142 1:493 3+ Md 12500	41 2 5 616 623 614 614½ Bain G W	117 b 33.60 57-28	Exclusive Bon Bon117¾ Air Rill1175 Flummox1122½		8
Bumped start, failed to menace					
28Jly95-3Crc fst 6f :23 :472 1:00 1:13 3+ Md 12500	22 4 4 31 68½ 715 720½ Gonzalez M A	117 b 32.40 62-15	Skybird1172½ Sneak Out Frosty1172½ Orchid King1171½	Tired	9

WORKOUTS: Nov 16 Crc 4f fst :494 B 3/25 Nov 3 Crc 4f fst :522 B 31/34 Oct 24 Crc 3f fst :381 B 11/14 Sep 17 Crc 3f fst :393 B 19/19

Don'tsellgeorge
Own: Muncy Charles D & Winklet James C
MADRID S O (111 16 18 18 .14) $10,000

B. g. 3 (Jan)
Sire: No Sale George (Raise a Native)
Dam: Impressively Regal (Regal and Royal)
Br: Paul Phipps & Marianne Rublee (Fla)
Tr: Vivian David A (25 7 4 5 .28)

121

Lifetime Record:	4 1 1 0	$6,756			
1995	4 1 1 0	$6,756	Turf	0 0 0 0	
1994	0 M 0 0		Wet	0 0 0 0	
Crc	2 1 0 0	$5,525	Dist	0 0 0 0	

27Nov95-4Crc fst 6f :22¹ :46² :59² 1:12³ Clm 16000 68 1 3 4² 53½ 5³ 45½ Madrid S O 119 4.30 79-22 WorthNoting1174½ ChrgingChrgr115nk NightTmRun117¾ Early foot inside 6
16Nov95-6Crc fst 6f :22¹ :46¹ :59² 1:12⁴ 3+ Md 25000 68 5 3 22½ 21½ 1½ 1⁴ Madrid S O 121 2.60 83-16 Don'tsellgeorge1214 Hey Hombre1213½ Sharp Pleasure1121¾ Driving 8
16Apr95-3Hia fst 6f :22⁴ :45³ :58 1:10³ Md 40000 48 2 4 52½ 54½ 4⁷ 416 Rivera J A II 118 5.20 72-14 Traveling Jeff11814 Sez It All1181½ L. C. Pine111hd Belated bid 8
18Mar95-6Tam fst 6f :22² :46¹ :59 1:12 Md Sp Wt 64 4 7 56½ 36½ 2⁵ 23½ Garcia J J 118 12.30 88-14 Palecari1183½ Don'tsellgeorge1184½ Tales Of War1181 Best of rest 12
WORKOUTS: Nov 11 Crc 5f fst 1:02² B 4/43 Nov 4 Crc 5f fst 1:03 Bg 13/42 Oct 28 Crc 4f fst :49⁴ B 11/45 Oct 20 Crc 4f fst :49³ B 8/47 Oct 13 Crc 3f fst :37 B 2/27

Tara's Sword
Own: L E S Stables Inc
GRYDER A T (27 6 2 2 .22) $10,000

Ch. c. 3 (Mar)
Sire: Sword Dance (Nijinsky II)
Dam: Tara Too (Laomedonte)
Br: Richard J. Forbush (Ky)
Tr: McMullen James (10 2 2 1 .20)

L 121

Lifetime Record:	13 1 0 2	$7,650			
1995	12 1 0 2	$7,560	Turf	1 0 0 0	$240
1994	1 M 0 0	$90	Wet	1 0 0 0	$90
Crc	4 0 0 0	$535	Dist	2 0 0 0	$210

23Nov95-9Crc fst 6f :22¹ :46¹ :59³ 1:13² 3+ Clm 10000N2L 52 12 1 1hd 2½ 3¹ 5⁴ Madrid S O L 121 b 35.40 76-20 I. C. Pine119½ Space Card121¾ Deliverable1211 Weakened 12
10Nov95-2Crc fst 5f :22² :46³ :59⁴ 3+ Clm 10000N2L 50 7 5 4³ 45½ 59½ 48¾ Madrid S O L 121 b 10.90 81-19 Dig This Buck1214½ True Coyotie1123½ Private Tech118¾ 7
Eight wide top str, lacked response
16Oct95-9Haw fst 6½f :22¹ :44⁴ 1:10 1:16³ 3+ Clm 12500N2L 33 8 2 2½ 2³ 89½ 819¾ Sibille R L 118 fb 32.90 75-09 Kaseykan1154½ Foolish Bob1131½ Cayman Slough1135½ Brief speed 9
1Oct95-6Haw fst 6½f :22² :45 1:11⁴ 1:19 3+ Md 10000 62 4 2 1hd 2¹ 1hd 13½ Sibille R L 116 fb 4.50 83-19 Tara's Sword1163½ Grecian Pride1163½ Isle Of Torque1164½ Drew out drv 12
10Sep95-6Haw fst 6f :22³ :46² :59¹ 1:12² 3+ Md 10000 52 1 6 2² 43½ 3³ 3⁵ Enriquez I D L 115 fb 3.40 76-17 Sir Lil Bit110½ Java Man1204½ Tara's Sword1152½ Lacked rally 10
2Sep95-3AP fm 1 ⓣ :23⁴ :47 1:11⁴ 1:36³ 3+ Md Sp Wt 49 1 2 2¹ 3³ 410 614½ Enriquez I D L 117 b 40.50 76-11 Daddy Watch1172¾ Bad Desire122½ Black Stairs1176½ Broke wide 10
17Aug95-1AP fst 7f :22³ :45² 1:11⁴ 1:26 3+ Md 16000 14 3 5 2² 6⁷ 716 723 Enriquez I D L 113 fb 5.30 53-24 Kaldi117nk Stolen Phone117¾ Kaseykan117hd Faltered 7
4Aug95-3AP sly 6f :22² :46¹ :58⁴ 1:12 3+ Md 20000 31 11 2 4² 3² 48½ 615¾ Toribio A R L 117 fb 8.80 68-19 Dantrick1172½ Flying Padre117³ Stolen Phone1173¾ Wide, tired 11
21Jly95-3AP fst 6f :22³ :46² :59¹ 1:12² 3+ Md 20000 67 3 4 2¹ 2¹ 41¾ 34½ Toribio A R L 111 b 11.10 78-19 Sympatacular1221¾ Dantrick1152½ Tara's Sword111no Loomed boldly 10
26Jan95-6GP fst 7f :22³ :47³ 1:12⁴ 1:26⁴ Md 32000 39 4 5 1hd 3nk 65½ 810½ Fires E 120 b 5.30 59-27 Forchuck118hd Pyrite Blue1204½ Pure And Simple1112½ Gave way 11
WORKOUTS: Sep 25 Haw 4f fst :49² B 11/51

The 7-5 favorite was Don'tsellgeorge, who was dropping from a fourth place finish by 5¼ lengths in a $16,000 claimer. Dropping to $10,000 certainly justified him getting attention, but at 7-5? He had just four starts, all at six furlongs. In stretching out to seven, he was attempting a distance for the first time. Did it mean he couldn't make it? No. Did it make him a vulnerable favorite? Yes.

Space Card seemed to be a more logical favorite. In his last start, a $10,000 claimer at six furlongs, he closed strongly from eighth to finish second by half a length to I.C. Pine, beating four other horses in here. Notice from his PPs, that in his four starts with Lasix, he'd yet to run a bad race. The only time he was out of the money in those four starts was when he was fourth in a field of eight in a maiden special weight. Every horse in this race (except the scratched one) who had a maiden win in his PPs, including Space Card, had gotten his initial victory in a maiden claimer.

So give Space Card credit for improvement with the addition of Lasix. Since he closed strongly at six furlongs, he would certainly benefit from stretching out to seven. But, perhaps because he went off at 10-1 the start before, he was dispatched at a generous 5-1.

The key, of course, was deciding who to use with him.

There were four others in here who had been in the I.C. Pine race. Uncle Haley had rallied from seventh to fourth, losing by 2¼ lengths at 23-1, beating Tara's Sword, Birdies Crescent and Catch This, who rallied from 11th to seventh in his first start in nearly five months. The two to use of these four were Uncle Haley, who got completely ignored and went off at 23-1, and Catch This, who figured to step forward in his second start. Remember, we expect horses to need a race back off a layoff.

Of the other three horses, Lucky Liaison was cutting back to a sprint off a good fourth. He'd been in the money six of 12 lifetime starts and had to be used. Cutler Ridge closed strongly for second in a shorter return race with the addition of Lasix and had to be used. Upper Action had shown little in his last two starts despite the addition of Lasix and could be tossed.

If you used Space Card on top and boxed four horses underneath him, you would have had to throw out one of these five: favored Don'tsellgeorge at 7-5, Cutler Ridge at 3-1, Lucky Liaison at 7-1, Catch This at 9-1 and Uncle Haley at 23-1 again. Since we are pursuing exotic overlays, the horse we definitely would not have tossed was Uncle Haley, who was ignored at the windows. Perhaps it was because of his big odds in his previous start, or because he was picking up seven pounds, which would have been a greater concern in a route race rather than a sprint.

If you tossed Catch This or Don'tsellgeorge, you lost, because they ran third and fourth, respectively.

If you tossed Cutler Ridge or Lucky Liaison, you won.

Or, if you went to a five horse box instead of four — turning your $48 investment into $120 for $2 tickets — you won.

And you won big because Uncle Haley finished second, losing by just a neck. Space Card paid $12 to win; the exacta $134.60; the triple $1,215.80 and the $2 superfecta $5,978.60.

If you bet $48 or $120 to win on Space Card, you would have gotten back $288 or $720, respectively. But the superfecta is an extremely difficult bet; one many tracks don't offer, and one I never could really get enthused about. Maybe Mark's experience soured me for life. Regardless, the Pick Three and Pick Six are much better investments.

SECOND RACE

Calder

DECEMBER 7, 1995

7 FURLONGS. (1.22) CLAIMING. Purse $6,000. 3-year-olds and upward which have never won two races. Weights: 3-year-olds, 121 lbs. Older, 122 lbs. Claiming price $10,000, if for $9,000, 2 lbs.

Value of Race: $6,000 Winner $3,600; second $1,000; third $220; fourth $300; fifth $60; sixth $60; seventh $60; eighth $60; ninth $60. Mutuel Pool $74,468.00 Exacta Pool $86,436.00 Trifecta Pool $79,123.00 Superfecta Pool $19,657.00

Last Raced	Horse	M/Eqt.	A.	Wt	PP	St	¼	½	Str	Fin	Jockey	Cl'g Pr	Odds $1
23Nov95 9Crc2	Space Card	Lb	3	121	2	7	7½	5hd	1hd	1nk	Toribio A R	10000	5.00
23Nov95 9Crc4	Uncle Haley	Lb	3	119	1	8	6²	6²	5²½	2²½	Nunez E O	9000	23.90
23Nov95 9Crc7	Catch This	f	5	122	6	3	2hd	3hd	2hd	3no	Bain G W	10000	9.10
27Nov95 4Crc4	Don'tsellgeorge		3	121	8	4	3¹½	2hd	3hd	4½	Madrid S O	10000	1.40
23Nov95 9Crc5	Tara's Sword	Lb	3	121	9	2	1¹½	1³	4¹½	5¹½	Gryder A T	10000	14.50
28Nov95 4Crc2	Cutler Ridge	Lbf	3	112	4	9	9	7½	7²	6½	Diaz S7	9000	3.40
27Nov95 7Crc4	Lucky Liaison	Lb	3	119	3	5	4½	4¹½	6hd	7¹½	Chapman K L	9000	7.20
23Nov95 9Crc6	Birdies Crescent	Lb	3	121	7	1	5hd	8²	8²	8nk	Henry W T	10000	12.60
27Oct95 8Crc7	Upper Action	L	3	121	5	6	8¹	9	9	9	Valles E S	10000	52.70

OFF AT 12:56 Start Good. Won driving. Time, :22⁴, :46⁴, 1:13⁴, 1:27² Track fast.

$2 Mutuel Prices:

2—SPACE CARD	12.00 6.60	4.20
1—UNCLE HALEY	17.80	7.80
6—CATCH THIS		6.00

$2 EXACTA 2–1 PAID $134.60 $2 TRIFECTA 2–1–6 PAID $1,215.80 $2
SUPERFECTA 2–1–6–8 PAID $5,978.60

Ch. g, (May), by Spare Card–Golden Gal, by Golden Ruler. Trainer Cosimano Anthony. Bred by Hal Snowden Jr. (Ill).

SPACE CARD raced four wide into the stretch, reached the front a furlong out and lasted over UNCLE HALEY. The latter, behind a wall of horses after entering the stretch, swung out five wide for room near the final furlong and finished gamely. CATCH THIS made a run between horses leaving the turn but weakened under pressure. DON'TSELLGEORGE, a factor to the stretch while racing four wide, lacked a late response. TARA'S SWORD showed speed into the stretch while saving ground and weakened. CUTLER RIDGE, away slowly, failed to seriously menace. LUCKY LIAISON tired between horses. BIRDIES CRESCENT was finished early. UPPER ACTION raced wide.

Owners— 1, Demora Julian; 2, Establo Mandarria; 3, Uliano J; 4, Muncy Charles D & Winkler James C; 5, L E S Stables Inc; 6, Arango Franz; 7, Tsanadis James G; 8, Condry L & Karpf L; 9, Dwoskin Steven

Trainers—1, Cosimano Anthony; 2, Casado Luis; 3, Trivigno Michael; 4, Vivian David A; 5, McMullen James; 6, Estevez Manuel A; 7, Gianos George; 8, Catanese Joseph C III; 9, Dwoskin Steven

Don'tsellgeorge was claimed by M A H Stables Inc; trainer, Olivares Jon.

Scratched— Kapellmeister (27Nov95 7CRC5)

11

The Pick Three

Let's face it: hitting a $1,000-plus payoff on a $2 bet at Saratoga in 1995 certainly increased my appreciation of the Pick Three. But the truth is I've always thought it to be one of the best wagers at the track. In *Harness Overlays*, I detailed a Pick Four — a cousin of the Pick Three — I caught at Saratoga Harness for a four-figure payoff of $1,970 on a $1 bet. The principle is the same. Beat one vulnerable favorite and you can cash a generous exotic overlay. Beat favorites in two races and you may be filling out tax statements when you cash your ticket.

Be sure of this: they do happen.

This one would have qualified. I say "would have" because I only picked one of the three winners in the *Gazette* that day, and I can only wish I had been the least bit creative betting Pick Threes that day, because it was a lu-lu.

The three legs of the late Pick Three at Saratoga, August 18, 1995, featured:

A field of six high-priced claimers in the sixth.

A field of six allowance fillies on the turf in the seventh.

A field of nine fillies and mares in the $125,000 Diana Handicap on the turf in the featured eighth.

Billy Mott, Saratoga's leading trainer in '95, figured prominently in the sixth and seventh, sending out Golden Larch and Kalfo, respectively. Both would go off heavy favorites.

What was interesting was that Mott named Bailey to ride Kalfo, but gave young jockey Ramon Perez a break by naming him on Golden Larch. As it was, Golden Larch went off at 6-5. If Bailey, Saratoga's leading rider was up, the horse could have been 2-5.

Accordingly, Kalfo was bet down to 3-2 in the seventh. If Perez was aboard, the horse would have been the 5-2 or 3-1 he deserved — or higher. Because, unlike Golden Larch in the sixth, he did not stand out. And he certainly did not deserve to be 3-2.

With perfect hindsight, it would turn out that there was value in betting Golden Larch and betting against Kalfo in the Pick Three. I didn't do it, but it doesn't mean I can't learn from the experience. You can, too.

Let's take a look at the two races:

The scratch of Golden Tent left six high-priced claimers ($75,000 to $100,000) going seven furlongs in the sixth. In post position order:

6   **Saratoga**

7 Furlongs (1:20²) CLAIMING. Purse $38,000. 3-year-olds and upward. Weights: 3-year-olds, 119 lbs. Older, 123 lbs. Non-winners of $24,000 since May 1, allowed 2 lbs. Of two races since February 14, 4 lbs. Of a race since then, 6 lbs. Claiming price $100,000; for each $5,000 to $75,000, allowed 1 lb. (Races where entered for $70,000 or less not considered.)

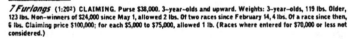

Golden Tent — racing past performance lines (struck through with an X indicating scratch).

Say Dance

Own: Winbound Farms
CHAVEZ J F (130 20 17 8 .15) $75,000
Dk. b or br g. 7
Sire: Fire Dancer (Northern Dancer)
Dam: Bestsayes (Marsayas)
Br: Bowling & Devers (Fla)
Tr: Sciacca Gary (47 6 6 1 .13)
112

Lifetime Record: 63 11 14 7 $343,462
1995 3 0 0 0 $1,440 | Turf 24 3 5 2 $105,614
1994 14 1 1 3 $51,170 | Wet 12 4 2 2 $109,160
Sar 4 0 1 2 $22,948 | Dist 2 0 1 0 $2,340

8Jly95-8Bel fm 7f Ⓣ :214 :434 1:074 1:201 Alw 44000N$Y 81 8 2 2½ 2¾ 7⁶ 7⁸¾ Santos J A 115 b 30.00 90-01 Grand Continental115nk Compadre1151¾ Worldwide1183 Used up 8
23Jun95-7Bel wf 1 1/16 ⊗ :224 :452 1:102 1:42 Alw 48000C 80 2 1 1½ 1½ 3⁴½ 5¹³¾ Chavez J F 112 b 7.20 75-23 Party Manners1185 Electrojet1118½ Artema112nk Used in pace 6
29May95-11Crc fm 1⅛ Ⓣ :471 1:101 1:344 1:47 3+ MemorialDayH50k 81 2 1 1hd 1hd 5² 10⁵ Madrid S O L 114 b 30.50 100-06 Mr. Light Tres113hd Fabulous Frolic112½ Flying American116hd Gave way 11
16Oct94-2Bel fm 1 1/16 [T] :234 :462 1:101 1:401 3+ Clm 75000 70 4 1 1½ 2½ 6⁶ 6¹⁰¾ Lantz J A5 112 b 12.60 84-12 Scott The Great1121½ Chief Master110¾ Royal Ninja1173 Used up 8
29Sep94-8Bel fst 1 :232 :463 1:112 1:361 3+ Handicap50k 44 6 1 1hd 4³ 6¹⁵ 6³³ Santos J A 115 b 12.60 49-22 Key Contender1182 Contract Court1142 Crafty Coventry1114½ Gave way 6
9Sep94-5Bel fm 1 Ⓣ :222 :444 1:092 1:341 3+ Clm 75000 82 1 1 1²½ 1¹ 2¹½ 4⁶½ Chavez J F 117 b 3.10 85-11 Bonus Award1172 Scannapieco117nk Scott The Great1174 Used in pace 7
19Aug94-4Sar sly 1⅛ ⊗ :462 1:111 1:372 1:502 3+ Clm 85000 87 1 1 1¹ 1½ 2hd 3¾ Chavez J F 116 b *.90 84-18 Shower Of Silver112hd Final Sunrise122nk Say Dance11612 Gamely 5
1Aug94-4Sar gd 1 1/16 Ⓣ :242 :482 1:124 1:431 Clm 90000 90 5 1 1³½ 1½ 4²½ 4³½ Migliore R 118 b 6.10 74-18 Pride Of Summer1181 Scannapieco116no Personal Draw118²½ Tired 7
24Jly94-7Sar gd 1 [T] :241 :473 1:12 1:353 3+ Alw 44000C 82 4 1 1² 3¹ 5⁵ 5¹³ Krone J A 117 b 6.50 86-01 Fourstardave1175 Dignitas1222 Final Sunrise117no Tired 7
9Jly94-7Bel fm 1 1/16 Ⓣ :23 :452 1:091 1:394 3+ Alw 44000N$mY 102 4 1 1²½ 1½ 2½ 3³½ Chavez J F 122 b 14.50 95-19 Royal Mountain Inn1173 River Majesty117½ Say Dance1221 Weakened 7

WORKOUTS: Aug 14 Sar tr.t 3f fst :37 B 5/20 Aug 2 Sar tr.t 4f fst :51 B 4/12 Jly 26 Sar tr.t 4f fst :494 B 3/27 Jly 20 Sar tr.t 4f fst :492 H 3/28 Jly 5 Bel tr.t 3f fst :362 B 2/17 Jun 16 Bel 4f fst :481 H 7/80

Gallapiat's Moment

Own: Ferriola Ingrid A
KRONE J A (101 10 18 13 .10) $85,000
B. g. 5
Sire: Gallapiat (Buckpasser)
Dam: Timeless Reason (Timeless Moment)
Br: Harrison Dale (Fla)
Tr: Ferriola Peter (12 2 3 0 .17)
120

Lifetime Record: 52 11 16 7 $276,394
1995 12 3 4 2 $103,930 | Turf 0 0 0 0
1994 17 3 5 2 $71,640 | Wet 10 1 3 2 $35,162
Sar 3 0 1 0 $4,180 | Dist 5 2 0 0 $25,218

8Jly95-7Bel fst 1 :234 :464 1:113 1:363 Alw 48000N$Y 100 7 2 2½ 2hd 1hd 1¹½ Krone J A 119 fb *1.00 80-21 Gallpit'sMoment1191½ BermudCedr119¾ Torowep112²½ Dueled, drew clear 7
24Jun95-6Bel wf 1 :233 :461 1:104 1:364 Clm 70000 97 7 3 3³ 3½ 1hd 2½ Krone J A 112 fb 2.85 78-24 Private Plan109½ Gallapiat's Moment1123 Rocking Josh1161 Bid, game 7
1Jun95-7Bel fst 6½f :221 :452 1:111 1:18 Clm 45000 96 5 2 3² 2² 1¹ 2no Krone J A 116 fb 3.00 85-17 Jericho Blaise111no Gallapiat's Moment1161¾ Expressed116hd Couldn't last 7
21May95-6Bel fst 6f :221 :453 :581 1:111 Clm 50000 94 3 2 4⁴ 4³ 1½ 1nk Krone J A 114 fb *2.10 85-22 Gallapit'sMoment114nk Expressed1161½ Miron'sGentlemn1121½ Hard drive 7
3May95-3Bel my 6f :222 :451 :57 1:084 Clm 55000 98 5 5 3³ 3² 3¹ 3¹ Krone J A 112 fb 5.10 96-02 LakeAli116no ToughHeart1161 Gllpit'sMoment1121½ Four wide, flattened 5
6Apr95-6Aqu fst 6½f :222 :452 1:10 1:162 Clm 35000 94 1 4 4³ 3²½ 2½ 2¹½ Krone J A 112 fb 17.10 96-08 Fabersham1111½ Gallapiat's Moment1123 Medical Pro1164 Gamely 6
23Mar95-6Aqu fst 7f :23 :463 1:111 1:234 Clm 35000 72 3 4 2½ 2hd 4⁵ 5¹⁰½ Agosto R7 111 fb 5.00 75-17 Fini Cassette118no Love Jazz118²½ Rocking Josh1227 Dueled, tired 6
15Mar95-6Aqu fst 1⅛ :473 1:122 1:372 1:503 Clm 42500 74 2 1 1¹ 2hd 6⁵½ 7¹¹½ Leon F 117 fb 6.10 76-20 Five Star General116³½ Flying Groom1161¾ Private Plan114½ Used in pace 7
4Mar95-7Aqu fst 170 [•] :241 :483 1:131 1:43 Alw 46000N$mY 71 3 4 4³ 4³ 4⁷½ 4¹² Leon F 118 fb 4.40 71-21 Won Song1133 Local Problem1101 [D]Prank Call1138 Lacked response 6
Placed third through disqualification.
20Feb95-6Aqu fst 1 1/16 [•] :242 :493 1:144 1:46 Alw 36000N3X 97 6 1 1hd 1hd 1² 1nk Leon F 117 fb *1.25 75-29 Gallapit'sMoment117nk OcenSplsh112½ PrivtePln1173 Pressured, gamely 7

WORKOUTS: Aug 9 Sar 5f fst 1:014 H 17/48 Jly 26 Sar 4f fst :482 H 9/52 Jun 21 Aqu 5f fst 1:012 H 3/4

Rum'n Cope

Own: Sommer Viola
LUZZI M J (82 7 5 6 .09) $75,000
B. c. 4
Sire: Copelan (Tri Jet)
Dam: Lively Maid (Lord Rebeau)
Br: Hooper Fred W (Fla)
Tr: Martin Frank (18 3 3 5 .17)
114

Lifetime Record: 46 10 8 4 $136,230
1995 13 2 1 1 $43,795 | Turf 4 0 0 0 $1,130
1994 21 7 3 1 $80,470 | Wet 9 4 1 0 $51,595
Sar 0 0 0 0 | Dist 5 2 0 0 $10,100

16Jly95-8Bel fst 1 1/16 :232 :462 1:104 1:43 3+ Alw 38000N3X 80 1 6 5³½ 6⁵½ 7⁷¾ 6⁹ Perez R B 120 b 20.10 75-22 Yourmissinthepoint120nk WildEscapade1114 FifthSet120²¾ Saved ground 8
2Jly95-7Bel my 6½f :224 :451 1:10 1:164 3+ Alw 34000N2X 94 1 3 3⁵ 3⁶½ 2⁴ 1nk Luzzi M J 119 b 8.60 91-13 Rum'n Cope119nk Scherbo1197½ Get Behind Me11423 Checked 3/16, up late 5
24Jun95-6Bel wf 1 :233 :461 1:104 1:364 Clm 70000 86 6 4 4⁴½ 5²½ 5³¾ 5⁶½ Luzzi M J 112 b 4.30 72-24 PrivtePln109½ Gllpit'sMomnt1123 RockingJosh1161 Four wide, no rally 7
27May95-10Bel fst 1 1/16 ⊗ :234 :463 1:111 1:44 Clm 50000 86 7 2 2¹½ 2¹ 2¹½ 2hd Luzzi M J 116 b 8.10 79-18 Crooked Heels108hd Rum'n Cope116²¾ Klondike Clem1181½ Stalked, game 7
14May95-6Bel fst 1 1/16 :224 :46 1:103 1:434 Clm 50000 89 3 8 8¹¹ 8⁸½ 5⁵ 5⁶½ Samyn J L 116 b 27.75 74-29 PrivatePlan1143 FiveStarGenerl1182 StormyJv116½ No threat, five wide 9
3May95-4Bel gd 1 1/16 :234 :464 1:112 1:421 3+ Alw 36000N2X 71 5 1 2½ 2hd 6⁴½ 6¹² Pezua J M 120 b 11.50 76-16 Bull Inthe Heather120¾ Hunting Hard1131 Silver Fox1206 Dueled, tired 7
13Apr95-8Aqu fst 7f :222 :45 1:093 1:22 Alw 34000N3X 83 1 6 3³½ 4⁴ 6³½ 6⁶½ Pezua J M 114 b 37.75 87-10 Vallata Lane114½ Peace Baby1144½ Here's Noah115no Tired 10
2Apr95-7Aqu fst 1⅜ :483 1:124 1:38 1:564 Alw 46000N$Y 84 3 4 4⁶ 3³½ 6⁷½ 6¹⁴ Davis R G 112 b 10.50 80-23 Iron Gavel1155 Kristen's Baby1121 Call Me Anytime1152 Bobbled break 7
2Mar95-5GP fst 1 1/16 :23 :463 1:112 1:443 Clm c-32000 85 8 9 8¹³ 8⁹ 5⁶½ 5⁷½ Boulanger G L 119 b 16.00 77-21 Tri To Watch1176 Danc'n Jake115nk Benchwarrant1171 Mild bid 9
Claimed from White Cross Stable, Poulos Luke E Trainer
18Feb95-11GP fst 1 1/16 :231 :47 1:114 1:45 Clm c-25000 81 3 8 7⁶½ 5⁵ 3²½ 3³½ Suckie M C L 119 b 4.20 79-16 Tri To Watch1171½ Fire Devil1172½ Rum'n Cope119¾ Lacked response 10
Claimed from Farrington Stables Inc, Hurtak Daniel C Trainer

WORKOUTS: Aug 15 Sar 4f fst :473 H 4/29 Aug 7 Sar 4f fst :483 H 10/64 Jly 30 Sar 3f fst :363 H 6/19 Jly 12 Bel tr.t 4f fst :473 H 2/31 Jun 16 Bel tr.t 4f fst :473 H 2/44 ●Jun 8 Bel tr.t 4f fst :473 H 1/14

Golden Larch

Own: Al Maktoum Mohammed
PEREZ R B (60 6 4 7 .10) $100,000
Ch. g. 4
Sire: Slew O' Gold (Seattle Slew)
Dam: Golden Petal (Mr. Prospector)
Br: Firestone Mr & Mrs Bertram R (Va)
Tr: Mott William I (36 12 4 4 .33)
117

Lifetime Record: 17 5 4 3 $148,967
1995 6 1 1 2 $52,209 | Turf 2 0 0 1 $4,400
1994 10 3 3 1 $84,200 | Wet 4 2 1 0 $58,320
Sar 2 0 1 1 $10,200 | Dist 6 2 2 0 $47,638

10Aug95-8Sar fm 1 1/16 Ⓣ :234 :471 1:103 1:403 3+ Alw 40000C 94 5 3 3²½ 4³½ 4² 3² Perez R B 122 8.40 94-06 Lost Soldier1162 Beware The Quest116hd Golden Larch1221¾ Willingly 8
1Jly95-8Bel sly 1 1/16 :23 :454 1:101 1:413 Alw 48000N$Y 97 2 4 4¹½ 2³ 2⁶ 2⁹½ Perez R B5 112 4.70 81-18 Unaccounted For120⁹½ Golden Larch1124 Private Plan1142 Rallied inside 6
10Jun95-5Bel fm 1 1/16 [T] :251 :483 1:12 1:411 Alw 48000C 88 6 4 4² 5³ 8⁴¾ 8⁵½ Perez R B5 116 8.30 84-06 Siberian Summer118½ Lower Egypt114¾ Solenzano113½ Tired 10
4May95-8Bel fst 1 1/16 :223 :452 1:10 1:42 Alw 48000N$mY 89 1 4 4⁶ 5³½ 5⁴¾ 5⁸½ Perez R B5 111 7.30 81-18 Slick Horn113nk As Indicated113nk Key Contender1181½ Faded 5
16Jan95-8Aqu gd 1 1/16 [•] :231 :46 1:093 1:41 3+ Aqueduct H-G3 96 3 3 3⁷½ 3⁹ 3⁷ 3⁹ Perez R B 112 *1.20 91-20 Dnzig'sDnce1115 KeyContendr1154 GoldnLrch1124 Bump 3/8 pl, no rally 8
7Jan95-7Aqu my 1 1/16 [•] :231 :471 1:123 1:453 Alw 46000N$mY 109 1 4 4²½ 3²½ 1hd 1⁶¾ Perez R B5 117 *.85 77-35 Golden Larch1176¾ Yeckley115no Won Song11515 Driving 5
23Dec94-7Aqu fst 1 1/16 [•] :222 :461 1:114 1:442 3+ Alw 38000N4X 110 1 3 3⁵ 3³ 1hd 2nk Perez R B5 112 *1.05 83-28 More To Tell115nk Golden Larch1127¾ Yeckley1177 Bid, missed 7
25Nov94-6Aqu fst 1 :232 :461 1:104 1:361 3+ Alw 36000N3X 102 1 4 2hd 1hd 1½ 1¹ Perez R B5 110 *.80 87-13 Golden Larch1101 Gallapiat's Moment1177½ Iron Gavel1194½ Driving 6
9Nov94-5Aqu fst 7f :224 :46 1:111 1:233 3+ Alw 34000N3X 102 1 5 4³ 4² 2½ 1¹ Perez R B5 110 *1.65 86-14 [D]Golden Larch1101 Advanced Placement1172½ Fighting Daddy1171¾ 7
Caused crowding 1/4 pl, driving Disqualified and placed 7th
18Oct94-7Aqu fst 7f :231 :46 1:102 1:224 3+ Alw 34000N3X 95 2 4 2½ 1hd 2¹½ 2² Perez R B5 111 4.10 88-15 Mr. Tyler1142 Golden Larch111nk More To Tell1166 Held place 9

WORKOUTS: Aug 5 Sar 4f fst :49 B 13/46 Jly 20 Bel 4f fst :482 H 4/13 Jly 13 Bel 4f fst :482 B 5/66 Jun 30 Bel 3f fst :36 H 3/44 Jun 24 Bel 4f fst :513 B 85/91 Jun 7 Bel 4f fst :49 B 11/46

Absent Minded
Own: Cohen Robert B
SMITH M E (126 24 17 20 .19) $75,000
B. g. 4
Sire: Polish Navy (Danzig)
Dam: Wimbledon Star (Hoist the Flag)
Br: Brushwood Stable (Pa)
Tr: Shapoff Stanley R (21 0 2 4 .00)
116

Lifetime Record: 17 4 7 2 $126,811											
1995	6	3	1	0	$62,840	Turf	2	0	0	0	
1994	11	1	6	2	$63,971	Wet	1	1	0	0	$16,200
Sar	1	1	0	0	$16,200	Dist	2	0	1	0	$5,211

28Jly95-6Sar fm 1 1/16 (T) :23 :461 1:102 1:403 3+ Alw 38000C 4 4 3 63 77½ 722 742½ Luzzi M J 115 b 14.50 53-07 Older But Smarter112nk Head Trip115nk Lost Soldier113¾ Done early 7
17Mar95-7Aqu fst 1 1/8 :474 1:121 1:373 1:503 Alw 36000N3X 94 4 2 2½ 1hd 1hd 19 Santagata N 122 b *1.35 87-13 DH AbsentMinded122 DH CllMAnytim1169 SkyCrr113½ Hard drive, game 5
24Feb95-7Aqu fst 1 [•] :232 :462 1:103 1:364 Alw 34000N2X 95 2 3 2½ 1hd 11 13 Santagata N 119 b *1.80 — — AbsentMinded1193 LevelLnd1141 Geret'sJewel1134 Stalked, drew clear 5
12Feb95-5Aqu fst 1 1/8 [•] :494 1:143 1:41 1:542 Alw 32000N1X 95 5 1 1½ 12 16 13 Santagata N 117 b *1.65 64-39 Absent Minded1173 King Protea1077½ Swift Tern117¾ Drew off 8
16Jan95-9Aqu gd 1 1/16 [•] :231 :462 1:111 1:434 Alw 34000N2X 88 4 3 2hd 2hd 1hd 42¼ Chavez J F 117 b 2.70 84-20 D OceanSplash1121 CallMeAnytime1171¼ MeanPncho119no Dueled inside 6
4Jan95-8Aqu fst 170 [•] :231 :47 1:124 1:441 Alw 34000N2X 91 2 2 22½ 2½ 2½ 22 Santagata N 117 b 6.00 75-35 FiveStarGeneral1172 AbsentMinded117¾ OcenSplsh117hd Bid, weakened 8
15Dec94-4Aqu fst 1 1/16 [•] :233 :474 1:124 1:461 3+ Alw 32000N1X 84 6 3 32 33½ 34½ 33 Santagata N 115 b *2.15 71-29 Goldstar Road1152 Timeless Dream1081 Absent Minded1152¾ Even trip 11
20Nov94-7Aqu fst 1 :232 :464 1:12 1:372 3+ Alw 32000N1X 80 7 3 33½ 31½ 33½ 23 Davis R G 115 b *1.35 78-25 Churkin1153 Absent Minded1151 Bailadoro110¾ Up for place 8
9Nov94-2Aqu fst 1 1/8 :481 1:131 1:391 1:524 3+ Alw 32000N1X 82 6 1 11 1½ 21 21½ Maple E 115 b *.45 70-33 Sophie's Friend1151½ Absent Minded1151¼ Churkin1153½ Held place 6
6Oct94-6Bel fst 1 1/16 :24 :473 1:113 1:424 3+ Alw 32000N1X 85 5 4 53½ 2½ 21½ 22¾ Maple E 114 b *.40 85-20 Golden Plover1142¾ Absent Minded1143 Timeless Dream1099 No match 5
WORKOUTS: Aug 11 Sar 4f fst :484 H 8/24 ● Aug 6 Sar 6f fst 1:143 H 1/5 Jly 25 Sar tr.t 4f fst :50 B 4/28 Jly 20 Sar 6f fst 1:13 H 1/2 Jly 11 Bel 7f sly 1:284 B (d) 2/2 Jly 5 Bel tr.t 6f fst 1:184 B 5/9

Passing Attack
Own: R Kay Stable
SANTOS J A (114 15 15 15 .13) $100,000
Dk. b or br g. 5
Sire: Red Attack (Alydar)
Dam: Lt A J (Lt. Stevens)
Br: Freib & Phister & Smith & Youngblood (Ky)
Tr: Araya Rene A (13 1 0 1 .08)
123

Lifetime Record: 24 4 6 4 $133,592											
1995	9	2	2	0	$57,845	Turf	3	1	0	0	$30,485
1994	12	2	4	4	$74,087	Wet	2	0	0	1	$2,400
Sar	1	0	0	0		Dist	0	0	0	0	

14Aug95-9Sar wf 1 1/8 :482 1:12 1:371 1:504 3+ Alw 44000N2m 94 4 4 33½ 33 43½ 83¾ Santos J A 115 19.20 78-25 Swindle115½ Brilliant Patriot110½ Hopkins Forest115nk Bobbled break 10
26Jly95-10Sar fm 1 1/8 (T) :472 1:11 1:351 *:471 3+ Clm c-75000 81 9 7 76 76½ 87¾ 67 Day P 122 4.00 84-11 My Mogul1131 Scannapieco1142 Hollywood Handsome113no No threat 11
Claimed from Denson Joe B, Jacobs Jeff Trainer
24Jun95-8CD fm 1 1/8 (T) :471 1:103 1:352 1:474 3+ Alw 46900N$Y 105 5 7 55 44½ 12½ 17 Borel C H L 120 8.50 92-11 Passing Attack1207 Devlin1204½ Hyper Shu116nk 10
Lunged out start, driving, rail
7Jun95-6CD fm 1 1/16 (T) :233 :464 1:11 1:422 3+ Alw 43020N$Y 87 8 8 86¾ 63½ 52¼ 52¾ Perret C L 120 10.30 89-03 Deputy Slew116½ Dividend Option116½ Flops118½ No factor 9
19May95-4CD fst 1 1/16 :232 :472 1:121 1:434 Clm c-50000 86 2 5 55 42½ 23 21¼ Sellers S J 116 2.60 94-12 Golf BallHill1161¼ PassingAttack1162 CozzyGrey112nk Inside, second best 6
Claimed from Smith Thomas V & Youngblood John, Smith Thomas V Trainer
6Apr95-9OP fst 1 :232 :464 1:111 1:362 Alw 39000N$Y 89 1 5 45 34 34½ 46 Trosclair A J 119 22.10 91-18 Class O Lad122¾ Bucks Nephew1162 Rowdy Rowdy Rowdy119½ Inside 5
25Mar95-7OP fst 1 1/16 :232 :472 1:124 1:444 Alw 28000N$Y 75 5 5 52¾ 63¼ 87½ 810 Trosclair A J 119 6.20 73-19 Tyus116nk Bat Que1161 Simple Grace1196 4-wide 2nd turn 9
23Feb95-10OP fst 1 1/16 :223 :461 1:12 1:44 Alw 24000N2X 89 4 8 810 63 2½ 1hd Borel C H 116 2.80 87-17 Passing Attack116hd Nilwon1162½ Mattingly1162½ Driving 8
8Feb95-8OP fst 1 1/16 :231 :471 1:122 1:45 Alw 24000N2X 89 6 5 56 52½ 31½ 21½ Compton P 115 12.70 80-19 Simple Grace1181½ Passing Attack1151 Nilwon115nk Up for place 10
2Dec94-8TP fst 1 :23 :461 1:104 1:372 3+ Alw 26160N2X 84 5 6 69 59 55½ 63½ Gomez G K 122 3.50 81-21 Judge Vonsteubon1141½ Quito Bonito116nk Best Of Music114½ No factor 11
WORKOUTS: Aug 6 Sar tr.t 4f fst :493 B 5/24 Jly 20 Sar 5f fst 1:013 H 7/24 Jly 9 CD 4f fst :50 B 15/22 Jun 19 CD 5f fst 1:022 B 14/32 Jun 4 CD 4f fst :512 B 60/69

1 — Say Dance — This speedster was one for 17 the last two years. Now seven, he'd had only three starts in '95, stopping in all of them, though two were on turf. A majority of his dirt races were in routes, and the *Form* showed he'd made just two career starts at seven furlongs, finishing second once. A pace factor certainly, but that was it.

2 — Gallapiat's Moment — Here's a horse as honest as there is. He had a lifetime record of 11-16-7 in 52 starts, but only five were at seven furlongs. He won two of them with no seconds or thirds. He'd been in the money six straight times, and won his last start at Belmont in allowance company easily at even money. He raced close to the lead and could be compromised by Say Dance.

3 — Rum'n Cope — Back to claimers off a poor allowance race. He won the start before, an easier allowance try, but the race before that was beaten six lengths by Gallapiat's Moment. In his lone seven-furlong race showing in his PPs, he was a non-threatening sixth, though he was two for five at the distance with no seconds or thirds.

4 — Golden Larch — Dropping into a claimer for the first

time in his PPs. He'd been beaten 8¼ lengths by Slick Horn on May 4 at 1¹⁄₁₆ miles, but that was his first start since January 16. He was then eighth on turf, then second by 9½ lengths to Unaccounted For, who was tons better than these, while beating a solid horse, Private Plan, by four lengths on a sloppy track at 1¹⁄₁₆ miles. In his last start, he was a good third on turf. He was dropping five pounds today and cutting back to a distance where he had two wins and two seconds in six starts. There seemed to be an arrow pointing out that in his return to dirt today, his third dirt start and fifth overall start off a layoff, he was sitting on a big race.

5 — Absent Minded — His awful return on turf, which was his first start since March 17, was only a tightener for this. He'd won his previous three starts on dirt, all on or near the front end, against much easier horses. He also preferred routes, and had one second to show for two starts at seven furlongs. Probably needed another race back.

6 — Passing Attack — He was picking up eight pounds off a troubled but close eighth in an allowance try. His game was going longer, too, as he showed no starts lifetime at seven furlongs. His best race of his last 10 PPs was a seven-length turf win with Lasix, which he didn't have today. Seemed out of his element.

Conclusion? Golden Larch looked much the best, especially since Gallapiat's Moment and Say Dance could dispute the pace, which would set him up nicely. If you were playing Pick Threes, he was a key, the only horse to use in the first leg.

Now, here's the seventh at 1⅜ miles on turf.

The scratches of Polish Profit and Rara Avis left these six:

7 Saratoga

1⅜ MILES. **(Inner Turf). (2:131) ALLOWANCE. Purse $34,000. Fillies and mares, 3-year-olds and upward which have not won a race other than maiden, claiming, optional or hunt meet. Weights: 3-year-olds, 116 lbs. Older, 123 lbs. Non-winners of $19,200 over nine furlongs in 1995, allowed 3 lbs. $16,400 over a mile since November 25, 5 lbs. $12,000 on the turf since October 31, 8 lbs. (Races where entered for $40,000 or less not considered in allowances.)**

Kyle's Pet

Own: Whiteley David A

VELASQUEZ J (49 1 4 6 .02)

B. m. 5
Sire: Stately Don (Nureyev)
Dam: La Petite Flo (French Colonial)
Br: Whiteley David A (Ky)
Tr: Whiteley David A (2 0 0 1 .00)

115

Lifetime Record:	11	1	2	0	$26,150						
1995	2	0	1	0	$6,800	Turf	9	1	2	0	$25,930
1994	5	1	1	0	$19,210	Wet	0	0	0	0	
Sar (T)	1	0	0	0		Dist (T)	1	0	0	0	

3Aug95-10Sar fm 1⅛ (T) :472 1:12 1:373 1:493 3+ (F)Alw 34000N2L 32 7 5 55½ 1010 1015 1023½ Velasquez J 119 8.30 55-14 Last Approach1103½ Royal Fandango1162 Star Of Light113½ Gave way 10

13Jly95-7Bel fm 1 1/16 (T) :232 :461 1:101 1:421 3+ (F)Alw 34000N1X 81 8 6 75½ 85½ 74½ 2¾ Velasquez J 120 22.50 84-13 Ski At Dawn115¾ Kyle's Pet120hd Sisterella1131 Belated rally 8

21Jun94-8Bel fm 1⅜ (T) :493 1:151 1:393 2:162 3+ (F)Alw 30000N1X 58 8 7 74¾ 52½ 67 613½ Bailey J D 122 *1.60 58-23 Knocknock111no Miss Carmella1193¾ Petiteness111nk Flattened out 8

3Jun94-5Bel fm 1¼ (T) :481 1:132 1:38 2:014 3+ (F)Md Sp Wt 80 9 9 96¾ 31½ 11½ 15½ Bailey J D- 122 3.00 81-16 Kyle's Pet1225½ Sudana114½ Viva La Dance114no Mild drive 11

12Apr94-11Hia fm *1 1/16 (T) 1:44 (F)Md Sp Wt 74 3 7 612 53 21½ 21½ Castillo H Jr 122 8.00 80-18 Silly's Philly1221½ Kyle's Pet1227 Al's Memory1222¾ Best of others 10

15Mar94-2GP fm 1⅛ (T) :471 1:104 1:353 1:474+ (F)Md Sp Wt 55 12 11 1113 1013 810 69 Turner T G 121 31.50 84-05 Super Chef1211½ Alinam121¾ Silly's Philly1213¾ Mild bid 12

20Jan94-4GP fst 1 1/16 :233 :48 1:131 1:461 (F)Md Sp Wt 48 3 10 109½ 109¾ 99¾ 94¾ Vasquez J 120 22.90 70-11 Royalty On Ice120¾ Bland120hd Mrs. Marcos1201½ No threat 12

23Dec93-5Crc fm *1 1/16 (T) 1:501 3+ (F)Md Sp Wt 61 9 8 77 53 52¾ 54 Vasquez J 120 18.80 64-24 Dabir120hd Kris's Kiss1201¾ Alinam1201½ 9
Bothered start, tired

4Nov93-9Aqu fst 1 :232 :464 1:123 1:394 3+ (F)Md Sp Wt 35 2 6 76 85¾ 1016 1018¾ Santos J A 120 11.70 46-32 Key To The Peace113nk Manila Lila120nk Turk's Flirt1205¾ No factor 12

18Oct93-5Bel sf 1 1/16 (T) :241 :481 1:133 1:463 3+ (F)Md Sp Wt 53 5 10 94½ 94 67 612 Santos J A 119 4.70 51-35 Julia Reins119¾ Crandall1196 Pigeon Pea1193¾ Checked break 12

WORKOUTS: Jly 31 Sar 3f fst :392 B *9/10* Jly 10 Bel 4f fst :501 B *30/37* Jly 4 Bel 3f fst :382 B *20/24* Jun 28 Bel 3f fst :392 B *25/26* Jun 1 Bel 4f fst :494 B *20/40* May 25 Bel 4f fst :50 B *24/36*

Winner's Edge

Own: December Hill Farm

SMITH M E (125 24 17 20 .19)

Dk. b or br f. 3 (May)
Sire: Seeking the Gold (Mr. Prospector)
Dam: Lucky Us (Nijinsky II)
Br: Bender Virginia Knott (Ky)
Tr: Kimmel John C (24 4 6 5 .17)

116

Lifetime Record:	7	1	2	0	$35,720						
1995	5	1	2	0	$34,040	Turf	1	1	0	0	$19,200
1994	2	M	0	0	$1,680	Wet	3	0	1	0	$8,080
Sar (T)	1	1	0	0	$19,200	Dist (T)	1	1	0	0	$19,200

7Aug95-3Sar gd 1⅜ (T) :484 1:143 1:40 2:183 3+ (F)Md Sp Wt 72 8 7 43½ 2hd 15 11½ Smith M E 115 4.00 73-18 Winner's Edge1151½ Sean's Woodman1152½ Shallah115no Mild drive 9

14Jly95-3Bel fst 1 1/16 :232 :464 1:122 1:454 3+ (F)Md Sp Wt 62 1 1 2hd 2hd 2hd 2½ Krone J A 113 *.50 69-27 Sarabi114½ Winner's Edge1131½ Shallows11312 Dueled throughout 6

2Jly95-3Bel my 1 1/16 :224 :46 1:11 1:432 3+ (F)Md Sp Wt 72 1 3 32½ 32½ 21 21½ Chavez J F 113 2.70 80-27 Zakiyya1131½ Winner's Edge1134 Bank Approval1116 Rallied inside 6

18Jun95-4Bel fst 7f :23 :463 1:124 1:264 3+ (F)Md Sp Wt 59 7 5 64½ 44 44 44½ Smith M E 113 13.90 63-20 SilentAllnt1132 JustForFun1132 PsychicSpirit122nk Wide, checked 1/8 pl 9

8Jan95-3GP fst 1 1/16 :234 :48 1:131 1:47 (F)Md Sp Wt 51 7 6 57 55 56½ 58 Krone J A 120 5.70 67-22 SmplyPlsnt120¾ BoyntnCnyn1202½ MjstcRhpsdy1203½ No threat, wide str 7

29Nov94-5Aqu wf 1 :233 :471 1:131 1:393 (F)Md Sp Wt 46 4 2 22 32 57 511 Velazquez J R 117 5.10 59-24 Surprise Girl117¾ Just For Fun117¾ Jah1171 Forced pace 8

6Nov94-3Aqu wf 6f :224 :47 :592 1:121 (F)Md Sp Wt 53 6 7 51½ 3nk 42½ 47 Krone J A 117 9.00 74-17 Crafty Jam1172½ Lizzie Toon1172 Country Blue1172½ Flattened out 8

WORKOUTS: ●Aug 3 Sar tr.t 4f fst :49 H *1/16* Jly 27 Sar 4f fst :504 B *20/24* Jun 11 Bel tr.t 4f fst :484 H *2/21* Jun 5 Bel tr.t 5f fst 1:022 B *2/2* May 30 Bel tr.t 5f gd 1:04 B *1/2* May 22 Bel tr.t 4f fst :493 B *10/22*

In Time

Own: Shields Joseph V Jr

SELLERS S J (72 7 7 8 .10)

B. f. 4
Sire: Cozzene (Caro)
Dam: En Tiempo (Bold Hour)
Br: Hamilton Mrs Emory A (Ky)
Tr: Connors Robert F (3 0 1 0 .00)

115

Lifetime Record:	24	1	4	2	$30,398						
1995	6	0	1	0	$4,520	Turf	21	1	4	2	$29,564
1994	12	1	2	2	$18,888	Wet	0	0	0	0	
Sar (T)	3	0	0	0		Dist (T)	0	0	0	0	

3Aug95-10Sar fm 1⅛ (T) :472 1:12 1:373 1:493 3+ (F)Alw 34000N2L 60 10 10 109 88 77 711 Sellers S J 116 b 55.00 68-14 Last Approach1103½ Royal Fandango1162 Star Of Light113½ No threat 10

22Jly95-4Mth gd 1⅛ (T) :483 1:122 1:373 1:494 3+ (F)Clm 25000 75 7 5 65 53 72½ 43 Lopez C C L 115 b 27.00 79-15 Tarot Card1153 Winning Trip115no Make No Law108no Fin. well 10

12Jly95-9Del fm *1 1/16 (T) :232 :48 1:121 1:424 3+ (F)Alw 12600N1X 64 7 4 43½ 54 46½ 24½ Lynch H D L 116 b 11.20 92-08 Silver Nibblets1164½ In Time1162¼ Shiviat119hd Closed 10

20Jun95-10Del fm 1 1/16 (T) :232 :473 1:112 1:423 3+ (F)Alw 12000N1X 52 11 9 75 87 911 810¾ Lynch H D L 116 b 4.50 82-07 Selari's Gold Star1162¾ Golden Lucy1162 Love Spanish1162¼ Outrun 12

30May95-10Del fm 1 (T) :23 :46 1:114 1:384 3+ (F)Alw 11500N2X 67 2 7 613 76 52½ 42 Jones E L L 116 b 5.50 81-18 Lear's Lady116nk Talented Empress1011½ Alan's Turn116hd Willingly inside 11

13May95-8Del fst 1 :244 :49 1:142 1:411 3+ (F)Alw 9500N2L 40 3 4 51½ 52¾ 53½ 44¾ McCarthy M J L 116 b 8.70 72-18 Rockpoint Miss111no Marie C1081¾ Bestsofar1163 Needed rally 7

11Oct94-10Del fst 1 :25 :494 1:154 1:43 3+ (F)Alw 8800N2L 46 3 2 42 68 67½ 58¾ Price A L L 113 b 4.70 60-33 Frank's Persuasion1164¾ Wise Corrine114¾ Katie Ledyard112¾ Tired 7

16Sep94-9Pim fm 1⅛ (T) :474 1:123 1:382 1:513 3+ (F)Alw 18500N1X 65 11 8 813 810 610 56½ Umana J L L 112 b 5.70 70-21 Eurostar1141½ Game Hit1132½ Cappalade117¾ Checked 1/4 11

31Aug94-10Del fm *1 1/16 (T) :24 :481 1:134 1:483 3+ (F)Alw 8800N2L 67 1 2 33 33½ 22 21½ Taylor K T L 109 b 1.90 66-34 Never Ever1161½ In Time1094 Snow Cove1162½ Second-best 10

9Aug94-10Del fm 1 (T) :234 :472 1:114 1:374 3+ (F)Alw 8400N1X 70 9 8 86¾ 99 46 31½ Taylor K T L 109 b 6.30 92-05 Secondary Offering1151 Don't Blush Doctor116nk In Time109nk Too late 10

WORKOUTS: Jly 31 Sar tr.t 3f fst :372 B *2/7*

Star Of Light

Own: Hechavarria Luis De

MAPLE E (54 7 8 7 .13)

Ch. f. 3 (May)
Sire: Risen Star (Secretariat)
Dam: Grand Luxe (Sir Ivor)
Br: McCombs & Jones & Robert S. Folsom (Ky)
Tr: Tagg Barclay (12 3 0 1 .25)

108

Lifetime Record:	3	1	1	1	$20,515						
1995	3	1	1	1	$20,515	Turf	3	1	1	1	$20,515
1994	0	M	0	0		Wet	0	0	0	0	
Sar (T)	1	0	0	1	$3,740	Dist (T)	0	0	0	0	

3Aug95-10Sar fm 1⅛ (T) :472 1:12 1:373 1:493 3+ (F)Alw 34000N2L 72 2 4 34½ 33½ 32 35½ Santos J A 113 4.40 73-14 Last Approach1103½ Royal Fandango1162 Star Of Light113½ No late bid 10

16Jly95-5Bel fm 1 1/16 (T) :233 :471 1:112 1:421 (F)Alw 34000N2L 76 6 8 96¾ 94½ 77½ 26¾ Day P 117 3.50 80-13 Hawaiian Brave1176¾ Star Of Light1171 Lamplight117nk Took up break 10

10Jun95-3Pim fm 1 1/16 (T) :223 :472 1:122 1:442 3+ (F)Md Sp Wt 79 9 11 1111 97½ 41½ 13 Reynolds L C 113 4.30 82-15 Star Of Light1133 Big Bad Bunny1142 Landholder1155 Driving 12

WORKOUTS: Jly 4 Lrl (T) 4f yl :523 B (d) *4/4* Jun 30 Lrl 5f fst 1:04 B *6/7* Jun 25 Lrl 4f gd :494 B *11/12* Jun 20 Lrl 4f fst :49 B *11/29* Jun 3 Lrl 4f fst :48 Hg *?/15* May 28 Lrl 4f sly :50 B *7/12*

Gweibo
Own: Merven Stud Farm
DAY P (125 21 15 19 .17)

Ch. f. 3 (Mar)
Sire: Woodman (Mr. Prospector)
Dam: Vanities (Nureyev)
Br: Merven Stud, Ltd. (Ky)
Tr: Schulhofer Flint S (34 6 8 7 .18)

116

Lifetime Record:	4 1 0 0	$24,060			
1995	4 1 0 0	$24,060	Turf	3 1 0 0	$22,140
1994	0 M 0 0		Wet	1 0 0 0	$1,920
Sar ⓣ	0 0 0 0		Dist ⓣ	0 0 0 0	

17Jly95-7Bel fm 1¼ Ⓣ :482 1:131 1:373 2:011 3+ⒻAlw 34000N2L 78 5 5 54 61½ 64½ 54¾ Smith M E 114 b 6.10 77-18 Look Daggers1122¾ Royal Fandango1191 Retained Earning1141½ Evenly 12
15Jun95-3Bel gd 1¼ Ⓣ :47 1:122 1:38 2:024 3+ⒻMd Sp Wt 82 6 5 57 2½ 12 110 Bailey J D 112 b 2.85 74-20 Gweibo11210 Hippy Hippy Heart1113 Winter Fling112nk Ridden out 10
24May95-3Bel fm 1 ⓣ :22 :45 1:093 1:344 3+ⒻMd Sp Wt 67 2 5 63½ 42 31½ 44¾ Santos J A 114 9.60 85-07 Space Warning1123 Bank Approval1071½ Bemmalou112no Flattened out 10
3May95-9Bel wf 1 ⊗ :224 :46 1:111 1:36 3+ⒻMd Sp Wt 30 5 7 73¾ 54 514 427 Santos J A 114 14.10 56-16 Ravishing Raven11415 Bank Approval1105 Kalfo1127 Four wide 8
WORKOUTS: Aug 16 Sar 3f fst :362 H 4/17 Aug 11 Sar 4f fst :474 H 2/24 Aug 6 Sar 4f fst :493 B 17/38 Jly 30 Bel 4f fst :494 B 32/45 Jly 25 Bel 4f fst :492 B 6/15 Jly 13 Bel 4f fst :514 B 64/66

Kalfo
Own: Paulson Allen E
BAILEY J D (138 38 17 17 .22)

B. f. 3 (Mar)
Sire: Dahar (Lyphard)
Dam: Cruella (Tyrant)
Br: Paulson Allen E (Ky)
Tr: Mott William I (36 12 4 4 .33)

116

Lifetime Record:	7 1 1 2	$36,460			
1995	3 1 0 1	$24,760	Turf	3 1 1 0	$27,840
1994	4 M 1 1	$11,700	Wet	1 0 0 1	$3,520
Sar ⓣ	1 0 0 0	$2,040	Dist ⓣ	0 0 0 0	

9Aug95-10Sar fm 1⅛ ⓣ :463 1:11 1:353 1:474 3+ⒻAlw 34000N1X 76 9 4 43½ 42 42¾ 45 Bailey J D 114 *2.95 83-09 JustWonderful1141½ Francia1143 Mrth'sVineyrd109½ Four wide, no rally 11
31May95-5Bel fm 1¼ Ⓣ :48 1:132 1:383 2:031 3+ⒻMd Sp Wt 86 10 4 32 1½ 15 17½ Bailey J D 112 *1.35 72-21 Kalfo1127½ A Rose For Shannon1125½ Social Sovereign112hd Mild drive 12
3May95-9Bel wf 1 ⊗ :224 :46 1:111 1:36 3+ⒻMd Sp Wt 43 7 6 43½ 43½ 311 320 Bailey J D 112 4.10 63-16 Ravishing Raven11415 Bank Approval1105 Kalfo1127 No late bid 8
3Dec94-4Hol fm 1 1/16 ⓣ :231 :474 1:121 1:431 ⒻMd Sp Wt 75 1 5 52½ 32 21½ 21 Antley C W L 119 5.00 79-16 Ladies Ballet1191 Kalfo1191¾ The Jody Grind1193½ No match late 10
19Nov94-6Hol fst 1 1/16 :224 :464 1:12 1:442 ⒻMd Sp Wt 40 9 3 31½ 54 99¾ 817¾ Antley C W LB 118 *.90e 62-12 Kindred Soul1182½ Sarajen118no Castleberry1184½ 4-wide into lane 11
23Oct94-9SA fst 6½f :22 :451 1:10 1:163 ⒻMd Sp Wt 74 9 5 62½ 41½ 32½ 32 Antley C W LB 117 5.90 87-08 Real Operator117hd Silverbulletlover1172 Kalfo11710 Wide trip 9
10Sep94-6Dmr fst 6½f :212 :432 1:093 1:161 ⒻMd Sp Wt 61 3 9 79 717 814 610 Antley C W LB 118 *.80e 80-08 Comstock Queen1184 Juddy1184½ Inthefastlane118hd Off bit slow, wide 9
WORKOUTS: Aug 2 Bel tr.t 7f fst 1:31 B 1/1 Jly 26 Bel 5f fst 1:031 B 4/7 May 21 Bel 6f fst 1:17 B 22/22

Polish Profit
Own: Sioumis Nicholas
LEON F (31 2 4 3 .06)

B. m. 5
Sire: Polish Navy (Danzig)
Dam: Nuotare (Sir Ivor)
Br: Cox E A Jr (Ky)
Tr: Ortiz Paulino O (3 1 1 0 .33)

115

Lifetime Record:	24 1 2 2	$32,340			
1995	12 0 1 0	$12,100	Turf	8 0 0 0	$1,020
1994	8 1 0 2	$12,600	Wet	5 0 0 1	$3,450
Sar ⓣ	1 0 0 0	$1,020	Dist ⓣ	0 0 0 0	

3Aug95-10Sar fm 1⅛ ⓣ :472 1:12 1:373 1:493 3+ⒻAlw 34000N2L 67 9 8 87½ 66 53½ 57½ Leon F 116 44.75 71-14 LastApproach1103½ RoyalFandango1162 StarOfLight113½ Checked break 10
17Jly95-7Bel fm 1¼ Ⓣ :482 1:131 1:373 2:011 3+ⒻAlw 34000N2L 65 8 6 65 85½ 98 1010½ Belmonte L A7 112 b 41.50 71-18 Look Daggers1122¾ Royal Fandango1191 Retained Earning1141½ Faded 12
8Jly95-3Bel fst 6½f :22 :452 1:111 1:181 3+ⒻAlw 32000N1X 46 1 6 57 67 56½ 513 Maple E 119 b 16.40 71-16 Lil's Lass113½ Crafty Casa1136 Faith In Dreams119½ No threat 6
7Jun95-7Bel gd 1¼ Ⓣ :48 1:13 1:381 2:03 3+ⒻAlw 34000N2L 62 6 7 54 66 79½ 79½ Martin G J5 115 25.00 65-22 Cavalanche114nk BellaDawn113nk RoyalFandango1201 Four wide, no rally 10
1Jun95-8Bel fm 1 ⓣ :221 :444 1:093 1:36 3+ⒻAlw 34000N2L 62 9 9 910 910 77 69½ Martin G J5 114 15.10 73-20 Heirloom Wish119½ Mystic Mel109¾ Just Wonderful1192½ No threat 10
27May95-4Bel wf 1 1/16 :234 :464 1:111 1:43 3+ⒻAlw 34000N1X 68 1 8 76¾ 77½ 68 610 Leon F 119 12.30 74-18 Ravishing Raven1122¾ Rabs Lil Brit Brit1191 Spire1105½ Broke slowly 9
7May95-7Bel fm 1 ⓣ :222 :452 1:10 1:354 3+ⒻAlw 36000N3L 66 10 6 711 810 88 612 Maple E 119 18.40 72-18 Lady She Is Too1093 Swamp Cat1192½ Wadaz119nk No threat 12
30Apr95-7Aqu fst 1 :234 :473 1:134 1:394 3+ⒻAlw 32000N1X 68 7 2 21½ 2½ 11½ 2nk Leon F 120 9.20 70-26 Judicial Girl113nk Polish Profit1204½ Holley's Heart114hd Sharp try 7
6Apr95-8Aqu fst 1 :223 :45 1:111 1:39 ⒻAlw 32000N1X 57 5 10 1013 95½ 54½ 44¾ Leon F 113 6.60 70-26 Bow Creek1061 Judicial Girl113nk Fire Attack1133 Broke slowly 10
16Mar95-6Aqu fst 6½f :224 :464 1:124 1:193 ⒻAlw 30000N1X 57 6 3 77½ 77 63 42¾ Leon F 114 19.50 79-15 Alytude114nk Sun Attack1141½ Limited Edition110¾ In tight break 8
WORKOUTS: Jly 31 Bel 5f fst 1:05 B 18/20 Jly 3 Bel 4f fst :494 B 13/23

1 — Kyle's Pet — The five-year-old mare could handle the distance. She'd won at 1¼ miles on grass at Belmont by 5½ lengths back in '94. She then was a distant sixth at this distance as the 8-5 favorite. Something obviously went wrong, since she didn't race again for almost 13 months. In her return, July 13, 1995, at Belmont, she was second by three-quarters of a length at 22-1 at 1 1/16 miles. She followed that with a terrible 10th at 1⅛ miles in her most recent start. You want to say she's a throw-away, but the fact that she won easily at 1¼ miles prevents you from doing that. Was the last race a bounce or a sign of decline? Tough read.

2 — Winner's Edge — Tough not to respect since she won her turf debut at Saratoga at this distance by a length and a quarter against older fillies and mares. An obvious contender.

3 — In Time — One for 24 lifetime, and one for 21 on turf. Racing without Lasix for the first time in her PPs, she was sev-

enth by 11 lengths at 55-1 in her last start. In doing so, however, she'd beaten Kyle's Pet by 12½ lengths. Still a throw-out.

4 — Star Of Light — After a win and a second in her lone two starts, she was a good third to Last Approach at Saratoga at 1⅛ miles, clobbering In Time and Kyle's Pet in the process. Today, she dropped five pounds while switching jockeys from Jose Santos to Eddie Maple, a slightly bad switch on grass. Obvious contender.

5 — Gweibo — Throw out her first start on dirt. In her turf debut, she finished fourth at one mile. With blinkers added, she won her maiden in her next start at 1¼ miles by 10 lengths. Surprisingly, off that monster maiden win, she was sent off at 6-1 in her next race, in allowance company at the same distance. She ran an even but dull fifth by 4¾ lengths. She had two strong workouts since. Obvious contender, but certainly no lock.

6 — Kalfo — She was freshened by Mott after winning a 1¼-mile grass maiden race by 7½ lengths at 6-5 at Belmont, May 31. In her return, August 9 at Saratoga at 1⅛ miles, she, too, was dull, finishing fourth by five lengths as the 5-2 favorite. Obviously, she needed the race. Top contender, but again no lock.

Conclusion? In a field of six, at least four fillies had a chance. The fifth, Kyle's Pet, was a maybe, and the only throw-out, In Time, had beaten Kyle's Pet.

In the eighth, the scratches of Grand Charmer and Graffin left a field of nine fillies and mares in the 1⅛-mile Diana Handicap on turf. The race seemed wide open.

8 Saratoga

1⅛ MILES. **(Turf). (1:45²) 57th Running of THE DIANA HANDICAP. Purse 125,000 Added. Grade II. Fillies and mares, 3-year-olds and upward. By subscription of $125 each which should accompany the nomination, $625 to pass the entry box, $625 to start with $125,000 added. The added money and all fees to be divided 60% to the winner, 20% to second, 11% to third, 6% to fourth and 3% to fifth. Weights Sunday, August 13. Starters to be named at the closing time of entries. Trophies will be presented to the winning owner, trainer and jockey. The New York Racing Association reserves the right to transfer this race to the main track. Closed Saturday, August 5, with 35 nominations.**

Northern Emerald

Own: Polk Hiram & Richardson David
PEREZ R B (60 6 4 7 .10)
B. m. 5
Sire: Green Dancer (Nijinsky II)
Dam: Tromphe de Naskra (Naskra)
Br: Oakbrook Farm (Ky)
Tr: Mott William I (36 12 4 4 .33)
115
Lifetime Record: 22 7 2 6 $256,587
1995 8 3 0 3 $126,806 Turf 22 7 2 6 $256,587
1994 5 1 0 1 $43,061 Wet 0 0 0 0
Sar [T] 1 1 0 0 $17,100 Dist [T] 6 3 1 1 $79,538

22Jly95-7Atl fm 1⅛ [T] :473 1:11 1:352 1:54 3+ [F]Matchmaker-G2 100 5 7 66½ 66½ 53¼ 3nk Perez R B L 113 5.90 91-16 Avie's Fancy113no Plenty Of Sugar118hd Northern Emerald1131¾ 8
Broke in air, 5 wide upper stretch
25Jun95-8Bel sf 1¼ [T] :504 1:16 1:403 2:06 [F]Alw 48000N$mY 102 3 3 31½ 2hd 11½ 12 Perez R B5 115 2.10 58-42 NorthernEmerld1152 Abigilthwif1221 ChlsyFlowr1132 Well placed, clear 7
4Jun95-9Bel fm 1⅜ [T] :482 1:132 1:381 2:133 3+ [F]ShepshdBayH-G2 101 4 1 2½ 2½ 2½ 42 Perez R B 116 6.40 88-08 Duda1121¼ Danish116½ Chelsey Flower112nk Drifted in 1/8 pl 7
Disqualified and placed 5th
19May95-8GS yl 1⅛ [T] :471 1:12 1:374 1:482 3+ [F]Vineland H-G3 100 4 6 76 62¾ 31 12¾ Perez R B L 115 *2.20 107-03 Northern Emerald1152¾ Kris's Kiss1092¼ Kira's Dancer113hd Mild drive 8
27Apr95-8Kee fm 1½ [T] :491 1:134 2:04 2:291 [F]Bewitch-G3 91 5 4 43 43½ 45½ 45¾ Perret C L 114 5.40 93-08 Market Booster119½ Memories1131¼ Abigailthewife1144 No rally 7
12Mar95-10GP sf 1½ [T] :502 1:15 2:051 2:29 3+ [F]Orchid H-G2 101 10 2 32 1hd 21½ 3½ Perret C L 115 27.50 74-25 Exchnge120½ MrketBoostr116hd NorthrnEmrld115½ Gave way grudgingly 10
29Jan95-3GP fm 1⅜ [T] :494 1:142 1:382 2:144 [F]Handicap40k 92 2 3 34 31½ 11½ 11½ Perret C L 115 *1.30 92-06 Northern Emerald1151½ Petiteness1131½ La Turka1141½ 7
Six wide top str, driving
20Jan95-9GP fm *1⅛ [T] :223 :464 1:121 1:444+ [F]Alw 33000N4X 87 3 6 57 31 1½ 32½ Perret C L 117 3.80 82-13 Afaladja1171½ Ma Guerre1191 Northern Emerald1173½ Weakened 10
26Nov94-7CD gd 1⅛ [T] :224 :474 1:132 1:464 3+ [F]Alw 40260C 69 7 9 912 910 75½ 68 Perret C 116 *2.20 64-27 Nice Mistake1162½ Fleeting Ways116½ Nasdoria1162 No factor 10
5Jun94-8AP fm 1⅛ [T] :483 1:122 1:373 1:56 3+ [F]Modesty H-G3 89 4 5 75½ 96¾ 84¾ 84¾ Guidry M 114 4.40 82-13 [D]Aube Indienne114¾ Assert Oneself1151½ One Dreamer1171¾ 6 wide bid 9
WORKOUTS: Aug 15 Sar 4f fst :491 B 10/29 Aug 9 Sar 5f fst 1:013 H 15/48 Aug 3 Bel tr.t 4f fst :51 B 9/16 Jly 19 Bel 4f fst :492 B 37/66 Jly 13 Bel 4f fst :501 B 44/66 Jly 6 Bel [T] 5f fm 1:053 B (d) 15/15

Perfect Arc

Own: Brazil Stables
VELAZQUEZ J R (97 14 14 8 .14)
B. f. 3 (Mar)
Sire: Brown Arc (Alleged)
Dam: Podeica (Petronisi)
Br: Delehanty Stock Farm (NY)
Tr: Penna Angel Jr (5 2 2 0 .40)
113
Lifetime Record: 6 5 0 1 $126,315
1995 4 4 0 0 $108,315 Turf 4 4 0 0 $108,315
1994 2 1 0 1 $18,000 Wet 0 0 0 0
Sar [T] 0 0 0 0 Dist [T] 1 1 0 0 $17,400

23Jun95-8Bel yl 1 1/16 [T] :252 :483 1:121 1:43 [F]SandsPoint H82k 106 4 1 11 1½ 12½ 15 Velazquez J R 117 1.60 81-19 PerfectArc1175 MissUnionAvenue1233 TransientTrend11012 Drifted late 5
24May95-7Bel fm 1 1/16 [T] :231 :462 1:10 1:391 3+ [F]Alw 38000N3X 103 1 1 11 11 13 15 Velazquez J R 109 *2.05 102-07 Perfect Arc1095 Joy Of Life1191½ Aucilla1192 Ridden out 10
1Apr95-6Hia fm *1 1/16 [T] 1:404 [F]Bal Harbour31k 85 1 2 11 1½ 11½ 12½ Ramos W S 114 2.00 98-02 Perfect Arc1142½ Another Legend1142 Remda1134 Driving 12
2Mar95-7GP fm *1⅛ [T] :484 1:134 1:374 1:492+ [F]Alw 29000N1X 83 3 6 31 31 3½ 1nk Ramos W S 118 8.50 98-02 Perfect Arc118nk Another Legend1185½ Two Elk121nk Fully extended 10
31Jly94-3Sar fst 6f :222 :464 :594 1:131 [F][S]Md Sp Wt 57 9 9 62¾ 3nk 11 12½ Davis R G 117 4.00 75-16 Perfect Arc1172½ Courtney Kelsey M.1172 Dominated Way1171½ Driving 12
12Jly94-5Bel fst 5½f :232 :472 :593 1:06 [F][S]Md Sp Wt 36 6 7 54½ 53½ 35 310½ Davis R G 115 7.30 74-16 Miss Wild1159 Cascade Canyon1151½ Perfect Arc1154 Wide, weakened 9
WORKOUTS: ●Aug 14 Sar 6f fst 1:134 H 1/13 Aug 7 Sar 4f fst :483 H 10/64 Jly 28 Sar 5f fst 1:003 H 3/28 Jly 15 Bel 5f fst 1:00 H 2/30 Jly 1 Bel 3f fst :391 B 16/21 Jun 20 Bel 4f fst :474 H 4/31

Grand Charmer

Own: Farish W S & Webber Temple Jr
DAY P (125 21 15 19 .17)
B. f. 3 (Feb)
Sire: Lord Avie (Lord Gaylord)
Dam: Regal Feeling (Clever Trick)
Br: Farish W S & Webber W T Jr (Tex)
Tr: Howard Neil J (13 3 0 1 .23)
111
Lifetime Record: 17 6 4 5 $210,087
1995 9 3 2 3 $156,567 Turf 5 2 1 2 $120,567
1994 8 3 2 2 $53,520 Wet 4 2 0 1 $41,070
Sar [T] 1 0 0 1 $12,486 Dist [T] 3 2 1 0 $99,819

2Aug95-9Sar fm 1 1/16 [T] :231 :472 1:12 1:414 [F]Nijana-G3 87 8 6 53 31 41½ 33¾ Day P 120 5.10 86-08 BailOutBecky115¾ FashionStar1123 GrandChrmer120nk Wide, weakened 9
Run in divisions
1Jly95-9AP fm 1⅛ [T] :481 1:123 1:372 1:492 [F]Pucker Up-G3 89 4 7 31½ 52 54 1½ Day P L 116 2.50 90-11 GrndChrmer116½ UpperNoosh116nk StMStright1141½ Late four wide rush 8
8Jun95-9CD fm 1⅛ [T] :481 1:12 1:354 1:474 3+ [F]Alw 46560N$mY 96 1 3 42 52¾ 4¾ 1½ Hebert T J L 108 6.10 92-06 Grand Charmer108½ Olden Lek1182 Lismore Lass1232 6
Carried out wire, bumped, hard drive
13May95-9CD yl 1 1/16 [T] :244 :484 1:131 1:45 [F]Regret83k 92 1 5 58 48 46 3¾ Perret C L 117 4.00 78-23 Christmas Gift122nk BailOutBecky122½ GrandCharmer1172 Finished well 7
20Apr95-8Kee gd 1⅛ [T] :47 1:112 1:364 1:494 [F]Palisades65k 92 1 4 45½ 47 33 22½ Smith M E L 114 4.30 85-14 MissUnionAvenue1212½ GrndChrmer1141½ UpperNoosh1194½ Bid, 2nd best 7
1Apr95-10TP fst 1 :23 :464 1:121 1:384 [F]Bourbonette100k 87 5 8 89½ 76½ 36½ 31 Nakatani C S L 115 5.70 75-20 Sherzarcat115¾ Minister Wife118nk Grand Charmer1156 9
Went to knees at start, finished fast
13Mar95-10GP sly 1 1/16 [⊗] :231 :471 1:122 1:454 [F]Alw 34000N2X 82 7 5 47½ 32 1hd 13½ Smith M E L 118 *1.20 79-18 Grand Charmer1183½ Ayrial Delight1183½ Lady She Is Too1184½ 9
Nine wide top str, drifted in final sixteenth, driving
20Feb95-1GP fst 1 1/16 :241 :474 1:123 1:451 [F]Alw 28000N2X 86 3 2 32 41½ 31½ 2nk Smith M E L 118 3.20 82-18 With A Princess118nk Grand Charmer1183 Hip Hip Hur Rahy11812 5
Seven wide bkstr, nine wide top str, rallied
15Jan95-9FG gd 6f :221 :462 :592 1:114 [F]Thelma H43k 63 9 8 88½ 815 78 710½ Woods C R Jr 119 7.40 77-16 Broad Smile1195½ Irish And Foxy114hd Glare Ice112no No factor 10
3Dec94-7Hou fst 6f :224 :461 :584 1:12 [F][S]SusnnaDckrsn25k 73 11 2 44 32 24 1¾ Woods C R Jr 116 *.60e — — Grand Charmer116¾ Pure Imagination116½ Abner Lenore1163½ Up late 12
WORKOUTS: Aug 16 Sar 5f fst 1:024 B 15/27 Aug 11 Sar 5f fst 1:024 B 28/35 Jly 30 Sar 5f fst 1:03 B 14/20 Jly 20 Sar 5f fst 1:01 H 3/24 Jly 11 CD 4f fst :484 B 4/32 Jun 28 CD 4f fst :484 B 4/32

Coronation Cup

Own: Rokeby Stables
BAILEY J D (138 30 17 17 .22)
B. f. 4
Sire: Chief's Crown (Danzig)
Dam: Glowing Tribute (Graustark)
Br: Mellon Paul (Va)
Tr: Miller MacKenzie (15 1 3 3 .07)
110
Lifetime Record: 12 3 2 1 $158,904
1995 4 0 2 0 $38,250 Turf 12 3 2 1 $158,904
1994 8 3 0 1 $120,654 Wet 0 0 0 0
Sar [T] 3 1 0 1 $91,692 Dist [T] 2 0 0 1 $16,602

28Jly95-8Sar fm 1 1/16 [T] :232 :47 1:11 1:401 3+ [F]Sar Bud BCH-G3 95 6 6 63½ 73½ 52½ 44 Bailey J D 112 7.90 94-07 WeekendMadness1171¾ IrishLinnet1202 AllezLesTrois115hd Saved ground 7
15Jly95-7Bel fm 1 [T] :232 :462 1:094 1:334 3+ [F]Alw 48000N$Y 83 2 4 42½ 63½ 56 47 Bailey J D 124 *1.05 87-08 Great Lady Mary1153¾ Statuette118nk Jiving Around1153 No rally 7
11Jun95-9Bel fm 1 [T] :221 :444 1:082 1:322 3+ [F]JustAGame II82k 97 2 4 46 43 34¾ 25 Bailey J D 119 2.35 96-08 Caress1195 Coronation Cup1191 Grafin1173 Up for place 5
28May95-8Bel fm 1 1/16 [T] :23 :461 1:10 1:404 [F]Alw 48000N$mY 92 3 6 66½ 74½ 65½ 24 Bailey J D 118 2.45 90-14 Grafin1184 Coronation Cup118¾ Statuette121no Blocked 1/4 pl 8
29Oct94-8Kee fm 1⅛ [T] :471 1:113 1:362 1:484 [F]QnElizbthII-G1 99 4 9 83½ 74½ 76 63¾ Bailey J D L 121 3.50 89-15 Danish1212½ Eternal Reve121nk Avie's Fancy121¾ 10
Bumped start, no factor
8Oct94-7Kee fm 1 1/16 [T] :221 :453 1:103 1:422 [F]ValleyViewBC81k 96 3 8 814 712 67½ 42½ Sellers S J L 121 2.80 91-10 Pharma121no Mariah's Storm1212½ Thread121no 9
Bobbled, broke awkwardly, mild gain, wide stretch
10Sep94-8Bel fm 1 1/16 [T] :233 :462 1:102 1:392 3+ [F]NobleDamslH-G3 86 8 8 910 104½ 88½ 610 Bailey J D 108 4.70 89-11 Irish Linnet1176½ Statuette1131 Cox Orange117¾ No factor 10
14Aug94-9Sar sf 1⅛ [T] :501 1:143 1:392 1:52 3+ [F]Diana H-G2 98 5 5 75½ 74½ 34 33 Day P 108 3.80 72-25 Via Borghese1152 Blazing Kadie1101 Coronation Cup1085 Saved ground 7
3Aug94-7Sar yl 1 1/16 [T] :233 :474 1:122 1:434 [F]Nijana-G3 102 5 6 64½ 32 21½ 15 Bailey J D 114 *2.00 75-25 Coronation Cup1145 Stretch Drive1144 Golden Tajniak1181 Driving 7
Run in divisions
17Jly94-6Bel fm 1 1/16 [T] :232 :471 1:102 1:404 3+ [F]Alw 32000N2X 78 3 4 55 75 87½ 75 Bailey J D 112 *.60 87-09 Jiving Around117½ Arctic Aaria117¾ Chelsey Flower111nk Dull try 8
WORKOUTS: ●Aug 16 Sar 3f fst :35 H 1/17 Aug 11 Sar 5f fst 1:004 H 4/35 Aug 4 Sar tr.t 4f sly :511 B 2/2 Jly 26 Sar 3f fst :353 H 2/19 Jly 11 Bel 7f sly 1:274 B (d) 1/2 ●Jly 4 Bel 6f fst 1:144 B 1/6

Icy Warning

Own: Team Valor Stables
WOODS C R JR (—)

Ro. m. 5
Sire: Caveat (Cannonade)
Dam: Northern Sting (Northern Jove)
Br: Ryehill Farm (Md)
Tr: Hennig Mark (29 2 5 6 .07)

110

Lifetime Record: 41 8 8 9 $417,352
1995 7 2 1 1 $149,324 Turf 29 7 6 6 $389,008
1994 12 1 4 2 $106,714 Wet 0 0 0 0
Sar T 1 0 1 0 $20,526 Dist T 5 0 2 1 $53,250

16Jly95-13RD fm 1 1/16 T :233 :464 1:103 1:41 3+ F RD Bud BC157k 99 2 4 35 2hd 12 12 Woods C R Jr LB 119 b 4.30 98-02 IcyWarning1192 ShadowMiss1101½ MarinaPrk1141 Bumped backstretch 8
1Jly95-8CD fm 1 T :233 :473 1:121 1:351 3+ F Alw 41300N$mY 96 8 5 31½ 2½ 1hd 12½ Woods C R Jr L 116 b *.70 96-04 Icy Warning1162½ Mari's Key1233½ Shadow Miss116nk Driving 7
3Jun95-3Cby fm 1 T :23 :462 1:094 1:332 3+ F LadyCantrbyH100k 93 1 9 99½ 49 47 46½ Alvarado F T LB 117 b 4.20 111 — Go Go Jack1121 Words Of War1192½ Romy1213 Outside bid 2nd turn 9
6May95-4CD fm 1 T :232 :471 1:111 1:343 3+ F ProvidnMile86k 94 2 9 106¾ 97½ 54 23 Delahoussaye E L 116 b 15.90 96-02 Bold Ruritana1233 Icy Warning1161¼ Rapunzel Runz114no 10
4-wide 1/4, closed well
13Apr95-8Kee fm 1 1/16 T :233 :473 1:114 1:431 F Jenny Wiley-G3 95 6 9 96¾ 96½ 54¾ 52½ Samyn J L L 113 b 15.30e 88-18 Romy118hd Weekend Madness121nk Bold Ruritana121½ 9
Sluggish start, 6-wide stretch, no late gain
11Mar95-7GP fm 1 1/16 T :233 :484 1:132 1:432+ 3+ F BuckramOakH-G3 93 2 3 41¾ 31 52½ 62½ Santos J A L 114 b 14.50 77-18 Cox Orange1181¼ Weekend Madness118nk Ma Guerre113hd Tired 11
24Feb95-4GP fm *1 1/16 T :234 :484 1:124 1:423+ F Alw 40000N$mY 94 6 3 3½ 41½ 2hd 3nk Santos J A L 114 b 4.70 95 — La Turka114no Shir Dar116hd Icy Warning114nk 9
Gave way grudgingly, inside
23Nov94-8CD fm 1 T :241 :48 1:122 1:37 3+ F Alw 40180C 85 3 7 79½ 76¾ 78¼ 75½ Gomez G K L 121 b 5.50 83-17 Elizabeth Bay1213½ Smile N Betsy111no Mystical Path116hd No factor 10
5Nov94-3CD fm 1⅛ T :48 1:12 1:362 1:481 3+ F Cardinal H117k 81 4 4 42½ 21 75¼ 88 Santos J A L 114 b 10.80 82 — Bold Ruritana116¾ Eternal Reve1172 Monaassabaat113½ Bid, tired 11
10Oct94-10Lrl yl 1⅛ T :484 1:134 1:394 1:53 3+ F R MdMllnLadies118k 91 1 4 54 45½ 32 22½ Santos J A 121 2.20 62-34 Mz. Zill Bear1232½ Icy Warning121½ Verbal Volley1236½ Rallied 6
WORKOUTS: Aug 14 Sar 4f fst :504 B 55/69 Aug 5 Sar 5f fst 1:023 B 3/31 Jly 11 CD 4f fst :494 B 16/32 Jun 27 CD 4f fst :481 B 2/33 Jun 20 CD T 5f fm 1:03 B (d)2/5 Jun 14 CD 4f fst :493 B 7/37

Grafin

Own: Godolphin Racing Inc
LUZZI M J (82 7 5 6 .09)

Ch. f. 4
Sire: Miswaki (Mr. Prospector)
Dam: Reigning Countess (Far North)
Br: Robertson Corbin J (Ky)
Tr: McLaughlin Kiaran P (12 2 1 5 .17)

108

Lifetime Record: 12 4 1 3 $128,119
1995 6 1 0 2 $43,172 Turf 9 4 1 2 $125,669
1994 6 3 1 1 $84,947 Wet 0 0 0 0
Sar T 0 0 0 0 Dist T 0 0 0 0

25Jun95-8Bel sf 1¼ T :504 1:16 1:403 2:06 F Alw 48000N$mY 91 2 1 11 1hd 21½ 45 Velazquez J R 120 *1.75 53-42 NorthernEmerld1152 Abigilthewife1221 ChelseyFlowr1132 Used in pace 7
11Jun95-9Bel fm 1 T :221 :444 1:082 1:322 3+ F JustAGameH182k 95 3 2 22 2½ 23½ 36 Velazquez J R 117 2.65 95-08 Caress1195 Coronation Cup1191 Grafin1173 Bid, weakened 5
28May95-8Bel fm 1 1/16 T :23 :461 1:10 1:404 F Alw 48000N$mY 101 2 1 11½ 11 13 14 Velazquez J R 118 17.20 94-14 Grafin1184 Coronation Cup118½ Statuette121no Drew off 8
7May95-8Bel fst 1 :231 :461 1:111 1:37 F Alw 40000N4X 76 2 6 66½ 75 66 611½ Antley C W 115 12.00 66-23 Future Pretense1133½ Regal Solution113½ Chatta Code114¾ Broke slowly 8
5Mar95 ♦ NadAlSheba(UAE) fst *1¼ LH 2:061 3+ Handicap (Class 2) 731 Hind G 129 - Rehlat Farah1295 Royal Fandango127no Ijlal1161 8
Tr: Hilal Ibrahim Hcp 13600
At rear,pushed along 4f out,faded,not persevered with.No betting
8Jan95 ♦ NadAlSheba(UAE) fst *1¼ LH 2:043 3+ Allowance Race 33 Carroll J 127 - Luhuk1271 Rainbow Heights1232 Grafin1278 4
Alw 16300
Tracked leader,led 2-1/2f to 1f out,one-paced to line.No betting
1Oct94-8Bel sf 1 1/16 T :243 :49 1:141 1:463 F RarePerfumH-G2 72 1 5 63 83½ 79½ 713½ Perret C 122 *2.00 50-37 Jade Flush1116½ Lady Affirmed117¾ Saxuality117no Lacked response 8
28Aug94 ♦ Deauville(Fr) yl *1¼ T RH 2:144 F Prix de la Nonette-G3 1½ Head F 128 6.20 Grafin128½ Maidment128½ Danish1281½ 7
Tr: Francois Boutin Stk 62900
Tracked in 4th,bid 1f out,hard ridden to lead final 16th,held
4Aug94 ♦ Deauville(Fr) gd *1 T RH 1:412 F Prix de la Calonne (Listed) 11 Asmussen C 123 *.70e Grafin1231 Moivouloirtoi1231½ Sarmatie1234 9
Stk 38600
Well placed in 3rd, led 70y out, driving
3Jly94 ♦ Saint-Cloud(Fr) gd *7f T LH :241 F Prix Amandine (Listed) 32½ Asmussen C 128 *1.50e Shamaniya1281 Blue Burgee1281½ Grafin128hd 9
Stk 38700
Unruly pre-start,3rd on rail,evenly late
WORKOUTS: Aug 15 Sar 5f fst 1:002 H 5/47 Aug 7 Sar 5f fst 1:013 H 11/40 Aug 1 Sar 4f fst :51 B 20/30 Jly 26 Sar 5f fst 1:014 H 8/47 Jly 19 Bel 4f fst :483 H 24/66 Jly 13 Bel 4f fst :50 B 36/66

Statuette

Own: Blum Peter E
SANTOS J A (114 15 15 15 .13)

B. m. 5
Sire: Pancho Villa (Secretariat)
Dam: Mine Only (Mr. Prospector)
Br: Blum Peter E (Ky)
Tr: Clement Christophe (16 2 2 3 .13)

112

Lifetime Record: 24 6 7 7 $335,820
1995 6 1 2 3 $68,469 Turf 21 5 6 6 $302,556
1994 8 1 2 2 $75,417 Wet 0 0 0 0
Sar T 1 1 0 0 $55,980 Dist T 2 0 0 0 $2,000

15Jly95-7Bel fm 1 T :232 :462 1:094 1:334 3+ F Alw 48000N$Y 90 6 5 73¾ 21½ 31½ 23¾ Stevens G L 118 2.80 90-08 GretLdyMry1153¾ Sttuett118nk JivingAround1153 Brk slow, saved ground 7
8Jun95-8Bel fm 1 1/16 T :242 :481 1:12 1:412 F Alw 48000C 89 5 6 53 41½ 32 24 Smith M E 119 *1.90 85-17 Tiffany's Taylor1134 Statuette119hd Irving's Girl1191¾ Up for place 8
28May95-8Bel fm 1 1/16 T :23 :461 1:10 1:404 F Alw 48000N$mY 91 1 8 88 84¾ 44 34½ Smith M E 121 *1.00 89-14 Grafin1184 Coronation Cup118½ Statuette121no Bumped 1/4 pl 8
30Apr95-8Aqu fm 1 1/16 T :222 :454 1:103 1:42 3+ F Beaugay H-G3 93 5 8 717 87 54½ 33½ Smith M E 116 *1.35 95-09 Caress1132¾ Shir Dar113¾ Statuette1161½ Wide, belated rally 8
17Apr95-7Aqu fm 1 T :233 :481 1:124 1:372 3+ F Handicap50k 98 7 6 65½ 53 3½ 12 Smith M E 118 *.90 93-10 Statuette1182 Teasing Charm117no Tee Kay1152½ Wide, going away 7
5Mar95-10GP fm *1 1/16 T :233 :47 1:104 1:404+ F Alw 44000N$mY 97 5 7 65 55 2hd 3nk Smith M E 114 2.90 104 — Irving's Girl114no Romy114nk Statuette1142¾ 10
Lacked response, inside
18Oct94-8Aqu fm 1⅛ T :481 1:121 1:364 1:483 3+ F Athenia H-G3 87 3 9 96½ 104 73 55 Smith M E 112 *1.90e 92-03 Lady Affirmed1111¾ Irving's Girl1101½ Cox Orange116no 11
Blocked 1/4 pl, steadied late
7Oct94-9Med fm 1 1/16 T :234 :481 1:114 1:423 3+ F Violet H-G3 92 1 10 85½ 75½ 44½ 42 Smith M E 114 *2.40 86-13 It's Personal1111½ Carezza115½ Artful Pleasure109no Finished well 11
10Sep94-8Bel fm 1 1/16 T :233 :462 1:102 1:392 3+ F NobleDamsIH-G3 94 5 10 1010 83½ 45½ 26½ Smith M E 113 *1.20e 92-11 Irish Linnet1176½ Statuette1131 Cox Orange117¾ Rallied inside 10
7Aug94-10Rkm fm *1⅛ T 1:473 3+ F SpicyLivngH-G3 84 7 8 75½ 78 47 67½ McCauley W H B 115 3.70 88-18 SuspectTerrain1113 IcyWrning1152½ BelleNuit112½ Inside, flattened out 11
WORKOUTS: Aug 14 Bel tr.t 3f fst :38 B 4/12 ●Aug 8 Bel tr.t 4f fst :473 H 1/29 Aug 2 Bel tr.t 4f fst :48 H 6/23 Jly 25 Bel 4f fst :50 B 12/15 Jly 12 Bel 4f fst :49 B 32/60 Jly 5 Bel 4f fst :52 B 51/57

Memories (Ire)

Own: Haynes Alvin & New Phoenix Stables
SELLERS S J (72 7 7 8 .10)

B. f. 4
Sire: Don't Forget Me (Ahonoora)
Dam: Ardmelody (Law Society)
Br: Grangemore Stud (Ire)
Tr: Kessinger Burk Jr (12 1 1 1 .08)

116

Lifetime Record: 17 6 3 2 $302,345
1995 8 4 1 2 $271,526 Turf 17 6 3 2 $302,345
1994 7 1 2 0 $25,328 Wet 0 0 0 0
Sar T 0 0 0 0 Dist T 4 4 0 0 $229,933

23Jly95-9WO yl 1⅛ T :462 1:101 1:343 1:471 3+ F WO Bud BCH-G1C 101 7 6 65½ 63¾ 41½ 1hd Sellers S J 116 1.85 101 — Memories116hd Bold Ruritana122½ Ballerina Queen113½ 7
Blocked stretch, bid between, just in time
25Jun95-9CD fm 1⅛ T :481 1:121 1:353 1:472 3+ F LocustGroveH110k 101 5 1 12½ 11½ 11 11½ Sellers S J 114 2.40 94-06 Memories1141½ Market Booster1201½ Thread1152½ Driving 7
3Jun95-8CD gd 1 1/16 T :234 :481 1:124 1:443 3+ F Alw 42420N$mY 96 6 3 33½ 31½ 1hd 14 Sellers S J 118 *1.30 81-25 Memories1184 Shadow Miss116½ Seventies1202 Driving, clear 9
20May95-9CD fm 1 1/16 T :241 :483 1:122 1:423 F MintJulep H84k 98 5 3 21½ 21½ 21½ 31¾ Sellers S J 113 *1.90 89-08 Romy1181½ Olden Lek114nk Memories113nk No late response 6
27Apr95-8Kee fm 1½ T :491 1:134 2:04 2:291 F Bewitch-G3 100 3 1 11 1hd 2hd 2½ Sellers S J 113 4.30 98-08 Market Booster119½ Memories1131½ Abigailthewife1144 Pace, good try 7
9Apr95-9Kee fm 1⅛ T :471 1:122 1:374 1:501 F Alw 33150N2X 98 3 3 33 1hd 14 14½ Sellers S J 113 2.10 86-12 Memories1134½ Dance Of Sunshine1172 Polar Princess113¾ Ridden out 9
12Mar95-10GP sf 1½ T :502 1:15 2:051 2:29 3+ F Orchid H-G2 92 1 10 108 84¼ 88¼ 65¾ Boulanger G 112 8.40 69-25 Exchange120½ Market Booster116hd Northern Emerald115½ Mild bid 10
19Feb95-9GP fm 1⅜ T :493 1:14 1:381 2:142 3+ F Very One H50k 96 5 5 2½ 2hd 2hd 32¼ Perret C 113 12.10 92-03 P J Floral1131¼ Trampoli118¾ Memories113hd Weakened 6
25Sep94 ♦ Curragh(Ire) hy 1⅛ T RH 2:044 3+ Solonaway Stakes (Listed) 1no Carson W 119 9.00 Memories119no Wandering Thoughts132no Karikata123nk 9
Tr: J G Burns Stk 23400
Unhurried in 6th,4th 2f out,rallied to lead final strides
11Sep94 ♦ Curragh(Ire) sf 1 T Str 1:413 3+ F Matron Stakes-G3 54½ Dettori L 121 12.00 Eternal Reve1211 Andromaque1261 Girl From Ipanema1212 9
Stk 38600
Rated in 6th,4th 2f out,one-paced to line
WORKOUTS: Aug 16 Sar tr.t T 3f fm :372 B 4/6 Aug 14 Sar T 4f gd :513 B (d)1/1 Aug 9 Sar T 4f fm :491 B (d)2/2 Jly 19 WO tr.t T 5f fm 1:024 B 8/11 ●Jly 13 CD 3f fst :363 B 1/6 ●Jun 22 CD 3f fst :36 H 1/12

```
Danish (Ire)                                   B. f. 4                                                   Lifetime Record :  15 4 3 3   $249,594
Own: McCalmont Harry                           Sire: Danehill (Danzig)                                   1995   4 0 2 0   $47,520  Turf    14 4 3 3  $248,214
                                               Dam: Tea House (Sassafras)                                1994   6 3 0 3  $187,839  Wet      0 0 0 0
                                               Br:  McCalmont Major V (Ire)                      118     Sar Ⓣ  0 0 0 0            Dist Ⓣ   1 1 0 0  $124,000
KRONE J A (101 10 18 13 .10)                   Tr:  Clement Christophe (16 2 2 3 .13)
9Jly95-9Bel fm 1¼ [T] :48 1:114 1:354 1:594 3+ ⒻNew York H-G2   105 3 3 32 31½ 31 2hd Krone J A  116 3.10 89-14 Irish Linnet118hd Danish1161 Market Booster119hd  Steady gain 6
4Jun95-9Bel fm 1⅜ [T] :482 1:132 1:381 2:133 3+ ⒻShepshdBayH-G2 103 7 6 63½ 63 52½ 21½ Krone J A 116 3.20 89-08 Duda1121½ Danish116½ Chelsey Flower112nk  Belated rally 7
18May95-8Bel fm 1 Ⓣ :232 :463 1:104 1:352 ⒻAlw 40000N4X  86 4 8 76¾ 62¾ 52¼ 43¾ Krone J A  113 *.65 82-14 Great Lady Mary1131¾ Vice On Ice1131¾ Great Triumph114nk  8
  Blocked 1/4 pl, lacked room stretch
14Apr95-7Aqu fst 1⅛ :463 1:103 1:361 1:492 ⒻAlw 46000N$mY  79 3 2 25 33½ 46½ 511½ Krone J A  119 3.80 81-13 Little Buckles1172½ Sovereign Kitty1195½ Forcing Bid114hd  Gave way 7
29Oct94-8Kee fm 1⅛ Ⓣ :471 1:113 1:362 1:484 ⒻQnElizbthII-G1 107 5 7 63 62½ 21½ 12½ Krone J A  121 11.80 93-15 Danish1212½ Eternal Reve121nk Avie's Fancy121¾  10
  Leaned in bumped start, driving, clear
24Sep94-9Bel sf 1¼ [T] :49 1:141 1:401 2:052 3+ ⒻFlowerBowlH-G1 84 2 2 2½ 23 28 313¼ Krone J A  113 29.50 50-37 Dahlia's Dreamer11213 Alywow114nk Danish113nk  Weakened 12
28Aug94 ♦ Deauville(Fr)  yl *1¼ ⓉRH 2:144  ⒻPrix de la Nonette-G3   31 Dubroeucq G  128 25.00  Grafin128½ Maidment128½ Danish1281½  7
  Tr: John Hammond                               Stk 62900                                             Led to 150y out, no answer to first two
27Jly94 ♦ La Teste(Fr)  fm *1 ⓉRH  ⒻPrix La Sorellina (Listed)   1hd Dubroeucq G  119 3.50  Danish119hd Fire and Sword1191½ Amy Ride119½  9
                                                 Stk 31500                                             Led after 1f, held gamely. Time not taken
21Jun94 ♦ Saint-Cloud(Fr)  gd *1 ⓉLH 1:414  Prix Bosalino   11½ Marcus B  120 4.80  Danish1201½ White Girl120½ Most Beautiful117nk  9
                                                 Alw 25900                                             Wire to wire, driving
23May94 ♦ Wissembourg(Fr) gd *7½f ⓉLH  Prix Martine Lutz   34½ Gruhn D  123  Sigismond1384 Son Brondo136½ Danish123½  11
                                                 Alw 7100                                              Time not taken
WORKOUTS: Aug 14 Sar tr.t 4f fst :513 B 23/30  Aug 7 Bel tr.t 4f fst :494 B 10/17  Jly 21 Bel 4f fst :502 B 11/17  Jly 7 Bel 3f fst :362 B 5/30  Jun 30 Bel [T] 5f gd 1:003 H (d)2/7  Jun 23 Bel 4f gd :484 B 9/38

Avie's Fancy                                   Dk. b or br f. 4                                          Lifetime Record :  20 10 4 3   $402,909
Own: Smith Stanton J Jr                        Sire: Lord Avie (Lord Gaylord)                            1995   4 3 1 0  $162,200  Turf    12 6 4 1  $323,000
                                               Dam: Fancy Pan (Paavo)                                    1994   9 4 2 1  $175,070  Wet      2 2 0 0   $47,160
                                               Br:  Gunsmith Stables (NJ)                        118     Sar Ⓣ  0 0 0 0            Dist Ⓣ   3 1 0 1   $80,000
MCCAULEY W H (2 0 0 0 .00)                     Tr:  Perlsweig Mark (—)
6Aug95-9Rkm yl *1⅛ Ⓣ 1:501 3+ ⒻSpicyLivingH100k  101 1 4 35½ 33½ 11½ 14 McCauley W H  B 117 *1.20 82-18 Avie'sFncy1174 PlntyOfSugr118nk Irving'sGirl113½  Rated 2 path, driving 7
22Jly95-7Atl fm 1⁵⁄₁₆ Ⓣ :473 1:11 1:352 1:54 3+ ⒻMatchmaker-G2  100 6 3 43 4½ 3½ 1no McCauley W H  113 6.30 91-16 Avie'sFancy113no PlentyOfSugr118hd NorthernEmerld1131¾  4 wide 5/16ths 8
2Jly95-9Rkm fm 1¹⁄₁₆ Ⓣ :231 :472 1:121 1:441 3+ ⒻRkm Bud BCH104k  93 10 1 14 12 11½ 21½ Ferrer J C  B 116 *1.30 93-11 PlentyOfSugr1131½ Avie'sFncy1161½ GryMood1142  Rated rail,outfinished 10
18Jun95-9Mth fm 1¹⁄₁₆ Ⓣ :233 :463 1:094 1:402+ 3+ ⒻRumson35k  93 4 1 12 11½ 12½ 11½ Ferrer J C  113 *1.00 96-05 Avie's Fancy1131½ Plenty Of Sugar113nk Nezzie Berlin1142½  Driving 8
19Nov94-8CD fm 1¹⁄₁₆ Ⓣ :241 :482 1:13 1:434 ⒻMrs. Revere116k  92 8 6 65½ 85 52½ 22 Day P  119 *1.30 85-18 Mariah's Storm1222 Avie's Fancy1193 Bear Truth119no  10
  Six wide stretch, second best
29Oct94-8Kee fm 1⅛ Ⓣ :471 1:113 1:362 1:484 ⒻQnElizbthII-G1  101 10 1 1½ 1½ 11½ 32¾ Ferrer J C  121 20.80 90-15 Danish1212½ Eternal Reve121nk Avie's Fancy121¾  Pace, weakened 10
8Oct94-9Lrl yl 1¹⁄₁₆ Ⓣ :232 :48 1:13 1:451 ⒻMWashington-G3  94 2 3 32½ 21½ 21½ 21¼ Ferrer J C  119 *.60 75-24 Tee Kay1151¼ Avie's Fancy1193½ Lady Ellen115¾  Hung 8
5Sep94-9Med fm 1¹⁄₁₆ Ⓣ :23 :471 1:111 1:412 ⒻBoilnSprngH-G3  98 5 1 11 11 13 13 Ferrer J C  119 2.60 94-12 Avie's Fancy1193 Teasing Charm1131¼ Knocknook1151¾  Mild drive 7
21Aug94-6Mth gd 1¹⁄₁₆ Ⓣ :232 :471 1:12 1:441+ ⒻThomsJMalley40k  96 8 4 35½ 1hd 13 16 Ferrer J C  121 6.30 77-27 Avie's Fancy1216 Cavada121¾ Accountinquestion116nk  Driving 9
30Jly94-11Mth sly 1¹⁄₁₆ ⊗ :234 :474 1:123 1:451 ⒻLittleSilver35k  85 2 1 12 1½ 11 13¾ Ferrer J C  116 f *1.00 79-14 Avie's Fancy1163¾ Tj's Tuff As Nails1125¾ Sea Ditty1126  Driving 7
WORKOUTS: Jly 21 Mth 3f fst :363 B 4/16  Jly 15 Mth 6f fst 1:16 B 2/3  Jly 1 Mth 3f fst :38 B 32/44  Jun 17 Mth 3f fst :354 H 7/52  ● Jun 10 Mth 6f fst 1:15 B 1/7  Jun 5 Mth 5f fst 1:023 B 3/12

Tiffany's Taylor                               B. m. 6                                                   Lifetime Record :  45 11 10 4   $382,967
Own: Maher Theresa                             Sire: Titanic (Alydar)                                    1995   3 2 0 1   $66,450  Turf    24 7 7 1  $276,353
                                               Dam: Tiffany Dream (Blue Ensign)                          1994  12 2 4 1  $132,477  Wet     12 1 3 2   $54,519
                                               Br:  Giardina Jay A (NY)                          112     Sar Ⓣ  5 2 3 0   $62,714  Dist Ⓣ   5 1 1 0   $36,960
SMITH M E (126 24 17 20 .19)                   Tr:  O'Brien Leo (41 5 6 4 .12)
12Jly95-8Bel fm 1¹⁄₁₆ [T] :234 :464 1:10 1:402 3+ Ⓕ[S]Mt Vernon H53k  102 2 4 42 2½ 13½ 16 Velazquez J R  118 fb 2.80 94-06 Tiffny'sTylor1186 Kris'sKiss1151 ADyToRemmbr1103  Well placed, clear 6
22Jun95-8Bel sly 1 ⊗ :221 :444 1:101 1:372 ⒻAlw 46560C  42 2 3 33 37½ 310 315¾ Velazquez J R  115 fb 2.75 60-22 UnlawfulBehavior1121¾ UnrealCupcake11114 Tiffny'sTylor11524  Gave way 4
8Jun95-8Bel fm 1¹⁄₁₆ [T] :242 :481 1:12 1:412 ⒻAlw 48000C  98 6 3 31½ 2hd 1½ 14 Velazquez J R  113 fb 5.00 89-17 Tiffany's Taylor1134 Statuette119hd Irving's Girl1191¾  Drew away 8
4Dec94-8Aqu fst 1⅛ :493 1:143 1:392 1:52 3+ Ⓕ[S]Montauk H54k  81 3 7 66½ 53 46 48 Migliore R  119 b 1.80e 68-34 Beloved Bea1136 Hey Baba Lulu116¾ Lottsa Talc1191½  No threat 7
12Nov94-8Aqu gd 1½ Ⓣ :51 1:153 2:071 2:314 3+ ⒻLongIslandH-G2  88 7 9 94¾ 53¼ 27 28½ Migliore R  114 b 14.90 88-03 MarketBooster1158½ Tiffany'sTaylor114no LdyAffirmed113¾  Up for place 12
18Oct94-8Aqu fm 1⅛ Ⓣ :481 1:121 1:364 1:483 3+ ⒻAthenia H-G3  84 8 10 106¾ 94 104¾ 66½ Cruguet J  113 b 12.30 90-03 Lady Affirmed1111¾ Irving's Girl1101½ Cox Orange116no  No threat 11
15Oct94-7Bel fm 1¹⁄₁₆ [T] :25 :483 1:112 1:403 3+ Ⓕ[S]TiconderogaH75k  78 11 9 87½ 88 77 59½ Migliore R  118 b *.60e 83-05 Putthepowdertoit1155 Great Triumph1121½ Irish Linnet1261  Late gain 11
27Sep94-8Bel sly 1 ⊗ :222 :444 1:093 1:363 3+ [S]AshlyTCole H56k  81 1 5 55¾ 44¼ 43½ 46½ Velazquez J R  114 b 3.30 74-23 Terrorist1084 Corma Ray1152 My Mogul112nk  Saved ground 7
29Aug94-7Sar fm 1⅜ [T] :501 1:153 1:403 2:164 3+ ⒻWaya55k  95 6 2 45 43 2hd 2nk Velazquez J R  113 b 2.30e 82-18 SaratogaSource113nk Tiffny'sTylor113½ MrketBooster122½  Rallied inside 7
21Aug94-7Sar sly 1⅛ ⊗ :472 1:124 1:394 1:534 3+ ⒻClm 100000  78 2 2 2½ 2hd 1½ 2no Velazquez J R  122 b 2.80 67-25 SchwayBabySwy114no Tiffny'sTylor1222 EenieMeenieMiney1147½  Gamely 5
WORKOUTS: ● Jly 30 Sar tr.t 3f fst :361 H 1/8  Jun 1 Bel [T] 7f fm 1:31 B (d)2/2  May 21 Bel 6f fst 1:14 H 3/22
```

1 — Northern Emerald — Beaten three-quarters of a length by Danish, though disqualified, three starts back in the Sheepshead Bay at Belmont. Won an allowance race easily, and then was third by a neck in the Matchmaker Stakes at Atlantic City. Contender.

2 — Perfect Arc — A perfect four for four on grass. Though the only three-year-old filly in here, she had beaten older horses in an allowance race. Her layoff didn't seem important, because she was two for two off layoffs and worked a bullet for this. She won her last three turf races wire to wire, but had come from third to win her first grass race. The scratch of the front-running Graffin certainly helped her chances. Top contender.

3 — Coronation Cup — This talented filly had lost eight straight, including two allowance tries, after winning three of her first four grass races. She clearly was not at the top of her game.

4 — Icy Warning — Had won her last two starts out of town and was taking a sizable step up in company. Pass.

5 — Statuette — Hard-hitting mare had been in the money six straight starts and 17 times in 21 career grass races. Contender.

6 — Memories — Shipped down from Canada off a three-race win streak, two in stakes. Top contender.

7 — Danish — Second in the Sheepshead Bay and the New York Handicap to two fine grass mares, Duda and Irish Linnet, in her last two starts. Top contender.

8 — Avie's Fancy — Had six wins, four seconds and a third in 12 grass starts, including wins in the Matchmaker and Spicy Living her last two tries. Beaten 2¾ lengths last year by Danish in the Queen Elizabeth. Top contender.

9 — Tiffany's Taylor — Stepping up off a runaway New York-Bred grass stakes win, but three starts back beat Statuette easily in a four length allowance win. Contender.

What to do? Memories would go off a slight favorite over Perfect Arc, both at 3-1. Danish was 5-1, Northern Emerald 6-1. Avie's Fancy 7-1 and Tiffany's Taylor 8-1.

If you liked Perfect Arc, you might not have thought 3-1 was a great price. Unless you liked her enough to key her in the third leg of the Pick Three with Golden Larch in the sixth and all six horses in the seventh at a cost of $12. Or if you used her and one other Diana contender in the third leg with the same strategy at a cost of $24. Either way, you were rich.

Golden Larch won the sixth at 6-5 and paid $4.40. Perfect Arc remained undefeated on turf by winning the Diana by 2½ lengths under a heady ride by John Velazquez to pay $8.30 in the eighth.

In the interim, 28-1 In Time beat 3-2 Kalfo by a neck in the seventh to pay $58.50. The Pick Three with horses at 6-5 and 3-1 and one longshot in a field of six paid a whopping $1,446.

SIXTH RACE
Saratoga
AUGUST 18, 1995

7 FURLONGS. (1.28^{2}) CLAIMING. Purse $30,000. 3-year-olds and upward. Weights: 3-year-olds, 119 lbs. Older, 123 lbs. Non-winners of $24,000 since May 1, allowed 2 lbs. Of two races since February 14, 4 lbs. Of a race since then, 6 lbs. Claiming price $100,000; for each $5,000 to $75,000, allowed 1 lb. (Races where entered for $70,000 or less not considered.)

Value of Race: $30,000 Winner $22,000; second $7,600; third $4,100; fourth $2,200; fifth $1,140. Mutuel Pool $430,704.00 Exacta Pool $635,255.00

Last Raced	Horse	M/Eqt.	A.	Wt	PP	St	¼	½	Str	Fin	Jockey	Cl'g Pr	Odds $1
10Aug95 ^{8}Sar^{3}	Golden Larch		4	117	4	3	3^{hd}	$4^{2\frac{1}{2}}$	3^{hd}	$1^{2\frac{1}{2}}$	Perez R B	100000	1.20
14Aug95 ^{9}Sar^{6}	Passing Attack		5	123	6	2	5^{1}	3^{hd}	$1^{\frac{1}{2}}$	2^{1}	Santos J A	100000	13.30
8Jly95 ^{7}Bel^{1}	Gallapiat's Moment	bf	5	120	2	4	$2^{2\frac{1}{2}}$	$2^{1\frac{1}{2}}$	$2^{\frac{1}{2}}$	3^{3}	Krone J A	85000	2.55
8Jly95 ^{8}Bel^{7}	Say Dance	b	7	112	1	1	$1^{1\frac{1}{2}}$	$1^{\frac{1}{2}}$	4^{3}	$4^{\frac{1}{2}}$	Chavez J F	75000	8.60
16Jly95 ^{8}Bel^{6}	Rum'n Cope	b.	4	114	3	5	4^{1}	$5^{\frac{1}{2}}$	5^{4}	5^{3}	Luzzi M J	75000	15.80
28Jly95 ^{6}Sar^{7}	Absent Minded	bf	4	116	5	6	6	6	6	6	Smith M E	75000	3.55

OFF AT 3:39 Start Good. Won driving. Time, :23^{1}, :46^{2}, 1:11^{1}, 1:23^{3} Track fast.

$2 Mutuel Prices:			
5–GOLDEN LARCH	4.40	3.30	2.30
7–PASSING ATTACK		8.00	3.10
3–GALLAPIAT'S MOMENT			2.30

$2 EXACTA 5–7 PAID $34.20

Ch. g, by Slew O' Gold–Golden Petal, by Mr. Prospector. Trainer Mott William I. Bred by Firestone Mr & Mrs Bertram R (Va).

GOLDEN LARCH reserved early, steadied while boxed in along the rail on the turn, checked while lacking room, altered course to the outside in upper stretch, then unleashed a strong late run to win going away. PASSING ATTACK raced just outside GOLDEN LARCH while three wide on the turn, surged to the front in upper stretch but couldn't withstand the winner's late charge. GALLAPIAT'S MOMENT forced the pace from outside for a half, battled heads apart between horses into upper stretch then weakened in the lane. SAY DANCE sprinted clear in the early stages, set the pace into upper stretch then gave way. RUM'N COPE faded after going a half. ABSENT MINDED trailed throughout.

Owners— 1, Al Maktoum Mohammed; 2, R Kay Stable; 3, Ferriola Ingrid A; 4, Winbound Farms; 5, Sommer Viola; 6, Cohen Robert B

Trainers—1, Mott William I; 2, Araya Rene A; 3, Ferriola Peter; 4, Sciacca Gary; 5, Martin Frank; 6, Shapoff Stanley R

Golden Larch was claimed by Schwartz Barry K; trainer, Hushion Michael E.

Scratched— Golden Tent (23Jly95 ^{4}SAR1)

SEVENTH RACE
Saratoga
AUGUST 18, 1995

1⅜ MILES. (Inner Turf)(2.13^{1}) ALLOWANCE. Purse $34,000. Fillies and mares, 3-year-olds and upward which have not won a race other than maiden, claiming, optional or hunt meet. Weights: 3-year-olds, 116 lbs. Older, 123 lbs. Non-winners of $19,200 over nine furlongs in1995, allowed 3 lbs. $16,400 over a mile since November 25, 5 lbs. $12,000 on the turf since October 31, 8 lbs. (Races where entered for $40,000 or less not considered in allowances.)

Value of Race: $34,000 Winner $20,400; second $6,800; third $3,740; fourth $2,040; fifth $1,020. Mutuel Pool $478,883.00 Exacta Pool $704,458.00

Last Raced	Horse	M/Eqt.	A.	Wt	PP	¼	½	¾	1	Str	Fin	Jockey	Odds $1
3Aug95 ^{10}Sar^{7}	In Time	b	4	115	3	$5^{\frac{1}{2}}$	4^{2}	4^{5}	$4^{2\frac{1}{2}}$	$2^{\frac{1}{2}}$	1^{nk}	Sellers S J	28.25
9Aug95 ^{10}Sar^{4}	Kalfo		3	116	6	2^{1}	$2^{1\frac{1}{2}}$	$2^{1\frac{1}{2}}$	2^{2}	$1^{1\frac{1}{2}}$	2^{3}	Bailey J D	1.55
17Jly95 ^{7}Bel^{5}	Gweibo	b	3	116	5	3^{3}	3^{2}	$3^{\frac{1}{2}}$	$3^{\frac{1}{2}}$	$3^{\frac{1}{2}}$	$3^{\frac{1}{2}}$	Day P	2.05
3Aug95 ^{10}Sar^{3}	Star Of Light		3	112	4	6	$5^{\frac{1}{2}}$	5^{3}	5^{3}	$4^{\frac{1}{2}}$	4^{7}	Maple E	4.30
7Aug95 ^{3}Sar^{1}	Winner's Edge		3	116	2	$1^{1\frac{1}{2}}$	1^{1}	1^{1}	$1^{\frac{1}{2}}$	5^{10}	5^{4}	Smith M E	4.70
3Aug95 ^{10}Sar^{10}	Kyle's Pet		5	115	1	4^{1}	6	6	6	6	6	Velasquez J	13.70

OFF AT 4:11 Start Good. Won driving. Time, :23^{4}, :47^{2}, 1:12^{1}, 1:37^{1}, 2:02^{2}, 2:14^{4} Course firm.

$2 Mutuel Prices:			
3–IN TIME	58.50	13.20	4.30
6–KALFO		3.70	2.50
5–GWEIBO			2.80

$2 EXACTA 3–6 PAID $196.00

B. f, by Cozzene–En Tiempo, by Bold Hour. Trainer Connors Robert F. Bred by Hamilton Mrs Emory A (Ky).

IN TIME reserved early while between horses, moved up three wide to reach contention on the turn, then closed steadily from outside to wear down KALFO in the final strides. KALFO stalked the pace from outside for a mile, opened a clear advantage in upper stretch, continued on the lead into deep stretch, and yielded grudgingly. GWEIBO was rated just behind the leaders to the turn, raced in traffic while making a run to threaten in upper stretch then lacked a strong closing bid. STAR OF LIGHT unhurried for a mile, rallied along the rail to reach contention in upper stretch, raced in traffic in midstretch, then flattened out. WINNER'S EDGE set the pace under pressure to the turn and tired. KYLE'S PET never reached contention.

Owners— 1, Shields Joseph V Jr; 2, Paulson Allen E; 3, Morven Stud Farm; 4, Hechavarria Luis De; 5, December Hill Farm & Dragone Chris; 6, Whiteley David A

Trainers—1, Connors Robert F; 2, Mott William I; 3, Schulhofer Flint S; 4, Tagg Barclay; 5, Kimmel John C; 6, Whiteley David A

Overweight: Star Of Light (4).

Scratched— Polish Profit (3Aug95 ^{10}SAR5), Rara Avis (4Aug95 ^{7}SAR2)

EIGHTH RACE
Saratoga
AUGUST 18, 1995

1⅛ MILES. (Turf)(1.46²) 57th Running of THE DIANA HANDICAP. Purse 125,000 Added. Grade II. Fillies and mares, 3-year-olds and upward. By subscription of $125 each which should accompany the nomination, $625 to pass the entry box, $625 to start with $125,000 added. The added money and all fees to be divided 60% to the winner, 20% to second, 11% to third, 6% to fourth and 3% to fifth. Weights Sunday, August 13. Starters to be named at the closing time of entries. Trophies will be presented to the winning owner, trainer and jockey. The New York Racing Association reserves the right to transfer this race to the main track. Closed Saturday, August 5, with 35 nominations.

Value of Race: $141,875 Winner $85,125; second $20,375; third $15,606; fourth $8,513; fifth $4,256. Mutuel Pool $586,827.00 Exacta Pool $582,582.00 Triple Pool $500,219.00

Last Raced	Horse	M/Eqt.	A.	Wt	PP	St	¼	½	¾	Str	Fin	Jockey	Odds $1
23Jun95 8Bel1	Perfect Arc		3	113	2	1	3½	4½	41½	21½	12½	Velazquez J R	3.15
9Jly95 9Bel2	Danish-IR		4	118	7	5	1½	1½	1½	1½	22	Krone J A	5.20
12Jly95 8Bel1	Tiffany's Taylor	bf	6	113	9	9	7½	71	7hd	32	3no	Smith M E	8.30
22Jly95 7Atl3	Northern Emerald		5	115	1	2	61	61	81	5½	41	Perez R B	6.50
28Jly95 8Sar4	Coronation Cup		4	111	3	3	81	81	6hd	6½	53½	Bailey J D	10.30
15Jly95 7Bel2	Statuette		5	114	5	7	9	9	9	4hd	6nk	Santos J A	27.25
6Aug95 9Rkm1	Avle's Fancy		4	118	8	8	2½	31½	3hd	810	7nk	McCauley W H	7.80
23Jly95 9WO1	Memories-IR		4	116	6	6	5½	51	5½	71½	818	Sellers S J	3.00
16Jly95 13RD1	Icy Warning	b	5	110	4	4	41	2hd	2hd	9	9	Woods C R Jr	18.30

OFF AT 4:45 Start Good. Won driving. Time, :23¹, :46⁴, 1:11, 1:35¹, 1:46⁴ Course firm.

$2 Mutuel Prices:

2-PERFECT ARC	8.30	5.00	4.00
9-DANISH-IR		5.90	4.10
11-TIFFANY'S TAYLOR			5.10

$2 EXACTA 2-9 PAID $59.00 $2 TRIPLE 2-9-11 PAID $359.50

B. f, (Mar), by Brown Arc–Podelca, by Petronisi. Trainer Penna Angel Jr. Bred by Delehanty Stock Farm (NY).

PERFECT ARC settled in good position while saving ground for six furlongs, steadied along the rail while lacking room on the turn, slipped through along the fence to launch her bid leaving the quarter pole, closed steadily to take the lead inside the furlong marker then pulled away under mild encouragement. DANISH hustled up to gain the early advantage, dug in when challenged along the backstretch, extended her lead on the far turn, maintained a clear advantage into midstretch but couldn't withstand the winner's late charge. TIFFANY'S TAYLOR was unhurried for six furlongs, launched a rally four wide leaving the far turn, closed the gap to reach contention in upper stretch and finished willingly for a share. NORTHERN EMERALD was rated in the middle of the pack between horses, dropped back slightly on the far turn, raced in traffic while gaining at the top of the stretch, then failed to threaten with a mild late rally. CORONATION CUP outrun for five furlongs while saving ground, gained a bit along the inside on the far turn, steadied behind the winner through the turn then failed to threaten thereafter. STATUETTE trailed for six furlongs, closed the gap while rallying five wide into the stretch then flattened out. AVIE'S FANCY settled just behind DANISH on the first turn, moved up to contest the pace between horses along the backstretch, remained a factor for six furlongs, then gave way leaving the far turn. ICY WARNING steadied between horses on the first turn, moved up three wide to contest the pace along the backstretch, raced up close to the turn, steadied between horses while giving way at the quarter pole. MEMORIES raced in the middle of the pack between horses for seven furlongs and lacked a further response.

Owners— 1, Brazil Stables; 2, McCalmont Harry; 3, Maher Theresa; 4, Polk Hiram & Richardson David; 5, Rokeby Stables; 6, Blum Peter E; 7, Smith Stanton J Jr; 8, Haynes Alvin & New Phoenix Stables; 9, Team Valor Stables

Trainers—1, Penna Angel Jr; 2, Clement Christophe; 3, O'Brien Leo; 4, Mott William I; 5, Miller MacKenzie; 6, Clement Christophe; 7, Perlsweig Mark; 8, Kessinger Burk Jr; 9, Hennig Mark

Overweight: Tiffany's Taylor (1), Coronation Cup (1), Statuette (2).

Scratched— Grand Charmer (2Aug95 9SAR3), Grafin (25Jun95 8BEL4)

$2 Pick-3 (5-3-2) Paid $1,446.00; Pick-3 Pool $227,627. $2 Pick-6 (3-2-8-5-3-2) 5 Correct 21 Tickets Paid $1,366.00; Pick-6 Pool $153,008; Carryover Pool $86,067.

Now, let's head west for an interesting day of racing at Santa Anita, October 20, 1995.

Santa Anita and Hollywood Park feature several consecutive Pick Threes every day, and the cost of playing them is $3 a pop, not the $2 it is in New York. So, for purposes of comparison, keep in mind that these Pick Three payoffs are automatically inflated by 50 percent just because of the cost of the bet. But there was still money to be made this day by using favorites in two races and "all" the other horses in the third.

In the space of just four races, 5 through 8, you could have caught two exotic overlays in two different Pick Threes, each one using two heavy favorites.

The key to cashing these Pick Threes was determining which of three heavy favorites in races 5 through 8 were vulnerable, and betting Pick Threes accordingly.

The scratch of Push'm High in the fifth race left 11 three-year-old claimers ($10,500 to $12,500) going 6½ furlongs. The even money favorite would be Keen Rate.

5 **Santa Anita Park**

6½ FURLONGS

6½ Furlongs **(1:14) CLAIMING. Purse $12,000. 3-year-olds. Weight, 120 lbs. Non-winners of two races since August 15, allowed 3 lbs. Of a race since September 15, 5 lbs. Claiming price $12,500, if for $10,500, allowed 2 lbs. (Maiden or races when entered for $10,000 or less not considered.)**

Seal Your Fate
Own: Fairmeade Farm
BLACK C A (57 10 8 7 .18) $12,500
Dk. b or br c. 3 (Feb)
Sire: Flying Paster (Gummo)
Dam: Bold Array (Bold Tactics)
Br: Fairmeade Farm (BC-C)
Tr: Molina Mark S (3 0 0 0 .00)
L 115
Lifetime Record: 9 1 0 1 $28,050
1995 9 1 0 1 $28,050 Turf 0 0 0 0
1994 0 M 0 0 Wet 0 0 0 0
SA 6 1 0 1 $23,575 Dist 2 0 0 0 $2,925

8Oct95-2SA fst 6f :214 :444 :573 1:102 Clm 20000 48 1 8 31 73¾ 87½ 813½ Black C A LB 116 26.40 71-16 Rubicon1151½ Tsarskoie Selo115nk Another Great One1101½ Brief speed 8
16Sep95-10Fpx fst 6f :221 :461 :583 1:11 Clm 32000 58 2 6 65½ 74½ 77¾ 510 Sorenson D LB 116 9.70 84-10 Fly Home1162 Purdue Cadet1092½ Wali Esquire1163½ 7
Crowded early, 4 wide into lane
31May95-7Hol fst 1 1/16 :231 :46 1:102 1:431 Clm 40000 17 1 5 54 611 720 738¾ Pedroza M A LB 116 13.60 46-12 SlewCitySims116hd LastTimeAtBt117no Pplote11616 Rail,steadied 1st turn 7
10May95-7Hol fst 6½f :212 :44 1:091 1:16 Clm 50000 73 1 7 712 68½ 66½ 47¼ Nakatani C S LB 115 12.30 82-11 Desert Pirate1154 Prince Of Darkness1131½ Sunnybrook1151¾ Off bit slow 7
19Apr95-7SA gd 6f :213 :451 :573 1:101 Clm 62500 54 4 6 66½ 53¾ 46 416 Nakatani C S LB 115 8.40 70-17 Ruby Beads1165½ Dutch1175 Busy Count1155½ Weakened 7
26Mar95-2SA fst 1 1/16 :234 :472 1:11 1:424 Alw 46000N1X 61 1 6 67 65¾ 69½ 715½ Solis A LB 117 b 11.90 65-15 Capote's Promise120nk Chocolate Threads1172 Gastown1177 Outrun 7
16Mar95-3SA fst 6f :221 :444 :563 1:09 Alw 42000N1X 79 3 4 42½ 44½ 34 38 Solis A LB 117 11.40 84-12 Houston Sunrise1203 Venus Genus1205 Seal Your Fate117¾ Inside bid 5
22Feb95-6SA fst 6f :213 :444 :573 1:103 Md 50000 82 7 9 1111 77 43 1½ Solis A LB 118 7.00 84-14 Seal Your Fate118½ Lucky Difference1182 Devils Duffle1132½ Just up 12
4Feb95-6SA fst 6½f :213 :442 1:10 1:17 Md Sp Wt 51 3 8 79½ 56 710 710½ Black C A B 118 18.00 77-08 Huge Gator118hd Freon1182 Tru's Heritage1184 Off slow 8
WORKOUTS: ●Oct 15 SA 3f fst :35 H 1/19 Oct 2 SA 4f fst :484 H 17/27 Sep 25 SA 5f fst 1:001 H 9/32 ●Sep 9 Dmr 6f fst 1:13 Hg 1/10 Aug 24 Dmr 5f fst 1:02 Hg 38/58 Aug 18 Dmr 5f fst 1:011 H 35/61

Push'm High
Own: Earnhardt Hal J III
BLANC B (55 4 3 4 .07) $12,500
Gr. g. 3 (Apr)
Sire: Swing Till Dawn (Grey Dawn II)
Dam: Marilyn H. (Raise A Native)
Br: Walter Mr & Mrs Robert H (Cal)
Tr: Baffert Bob (14 1 1 2 .07)
L 110[5]
Lifetime Record: 4 1 2 0 $18,550
1995 2 1 1 0 $15,350 Turf 0 0 0 0
1994 2 M 1 0 $3,200 Wet 1 0 1 0 $3,200
SA 1 0 0 0 Dist 0 0 0 0

9Sep95-10Dmr fst 5½f :223 :451 :582 1:044 3↑ Ⓢ Md 32000 67 5 3 2hd 1hd 13 12 York R LB 120 - 89-14 Push'm High1202 Moscow Mensch120hd Navy Bean1201 Clearly best 8
Rocking Chair Derby - Exhibition race for retired riders
23Aug95-9Dmr fst 6f :22 :451 :572 1:102 3↑ Ⓢ Md 32000 72 3 4 1½ 11½ 11 2no Pedroza M A LB 118 3.40 89-11 Purdue Cadet111no Push'm High1181½ HonorIsPower115½ Caught on wire 12
10Nov94-9Hol my 6f :22 :452 :574 1:103 Ⓢ Md 32000 58 5 4 1hd 1hd 2½ 25½ Pedroza M A B 119 4.00 81-12 Runaway Bay1195½ Push'm High119hd Seagull Bay1174½ Just held 2nd 9
15Oct94-6SA fst 6f :214 :45 :572 1:093 Ⓢ Md Sp Wt 2 9 1 31 88½ 1118 1232 Flores D R B 117 31.40 57-08 Testimony117½ Hunt For Missouri1174½ Short Order Chef1173½ Gave way 12
WORKOUTS: Oct 14 SA 5f fst 1:013 H 14/32 Oct 8 SA 6f fst 1:152 H 10/16 Oct 2 SA 6f fst 1:122 H 8/23 Sep 26 SA 5f fst 1:002 H 11/40 Sep 19 SA 4f fst :484 H 13/35 Sep 4 Dmr 5f fst :594 B 5/58

Keen Rate
Own: Mevorach Samuel
DESORMEAUX K J (59 13 8 7 .22) $12,500
Dk. b or br g. 3 (Mar)
Sire: Basic Rate (Valdez)
Dam: Keen Traveler (Peggy's Dancer)
Br: Rosenquist Jack (Ariz)
Tr: Lewis Craig A (12 3 0 1 .25)
L 115
Lifetime Record: 15 5 4 0 $44,480
1995 12 2 4 0 $33,170 Turf 0 0 0 0
1994 3 3 0 0 $11,310 Wet 0 0 0 0
SA 2 0 0 0 $1,050 Dist 3 1 1 0 $12,800

6Sep95-7Dmr fst 6f :212 :442 :57 1:094 Clm 20000 73 1 4 21 21½ 21 23 Desormeaux K J LB 116 fb 6.50 89-08 Second Emerald1153 Keen Rate1161¾ Rubicon1162 Inside trip 10
23Aug95-7Dmr fst 6½f :214 :442 1:093 1:162 Clm 25000 63 7 8 52 42 57½ 79½ Desormeaux K J LB 116 fb 5.30 79-11 Brick By Brick115nk Feathered Friend1163½ Plumeria Star1152½ Wide trip 11
9Aug95-6Dmr fst 6f :213 :443 :571 1:093 Clm 32000 68 1 5 2hd 1hd 3½ 67 Desormeaux K J LB 116 fb 4.60 86-07 Telefonzo1163½ ShingenWrrior115hd FetherdFrind1152 Dueled, weakened 8
31Jly95-5Dmr fst 1 :222 :451 1:10 1:361 Clm 32000 79 7 2 1hd 1½ 2hd 23½ Desormeaux K J LB 116 fb 2.90 85-09 HarbourDawn1173½ KeenRte1161 Stephntothemusic1161¾ Lugged out 7/8 10
4Jly95-7Hol fst 6½f :214 :441 1:083 1:151 Clm 16000 93 2 4 1hd 14 15 110 Desormeaux K J LB 116 fb *1.60 93-10 KeenRate11610 PromisingRuhler1163½ SpagettiFestivl118nk Much the best 10
18Jun95-5Hol fst 6f :212 :442 :57 1:104 Clm 16000 79 8 2 44 35 26 21½ Desormeaux K J LB 115 fb *1.50 85-14 Skol1161½ Keen Rate1154½ Deep Space1163½ Steady gain 11
4Jun95-1Hol fst 6f :214 :451 :573 1:102 Clm 25000 56 1 5 2hd 1hd 32 610½ Desormeaux K J LB 116 fb *1.80 78-10 Rivermeritsdream1151¾ First Rate Gift1183 Mike L1163½ Inside duel 8
21May95-7Hol fst 6½f :213 :44 1:09 1:152 Clm 20000 74 1 2 12½ 13½ 11½ 22 Desormeaux K J LB 116 fb 3.00 90-08 Rubicon1162 Keen Rate1161¾ Summertam1141¾ Speed, caught 7
19Apr95-7SA gd 6f :213 :451 :573 1:101 Clm 62500 48 3 3 21 32 56 618¾ Desormeaux K J LB 117 fb *2.30 68-17 Ruby Beads1165½ Dutch1175 Busy Count1155½ Gave way 7
8Mar95-7SA fst 6f :212 :442 :564 1:101 Clm c-50000 71 7 2 53½ 44 56½ 54½ Rollins C J LB 115 7.80 82-13 Drummin Around1151½ Tac Squad1151½ Alybobbob1151¾ Wide to turn 7
Claimed from Rosenquist John, Wright Robert F Trainer
WORKOUTS: Oct 15 SA 4f fst :474 H 8/63 Oct 7 SA 4f fst :464 H 2/37 Sep 19 Fpx 3f fst :37 H 6/12

Dasha

Own: Garvin Patricia

ATKINSON P (19 1 2 1 .05) **$12,500**

B. g. 3 (Feb)
Sire: Fatih (Icecapade)
Dam: Duchess Greg (Gregorian)
Br: Patricia Garvin (Cal)
Tr: Stute Melvin F (16 1 3 1 .06)

115

Lifetime Record:	3 1 0 0	$9,350		
1995	3 1 0 0	$9,350	Turf	0 0 0 0
1994	0 M 0 0		Wet	0 0 0 0
SA	1 0 0 0		Dist	1 0 0 0

11Oct95-5SA	fst	6½f	$:21^4$ $:44^3$ $1:09^4$ $1:16^1$	Clm 32000	35	2	7	2^{hd}	2^{hd}	12^{11}	$12^{19½}$	Atkinson P	B 115 b	122.40	72-11	SrvvlExprt117¾ NwAsprtons115^2 DncngIslndr115½	Dueled between foes	12
21Sep95-6Fpx	fst	6f	$:22$ $:46$ $:59$ $1:12^3$ 3↑	[S]Md 32000	59	5	5	4^4	3^3	$3^{2½}$	1^1	Valdivia J5	B 109 b	2.10	86-10	Dasha109^1 Power Of Prince114½ Glorious Country114¾	Steady handling	8
23Aug95-9Dmr	fst	6f	$:22$ $:45^1$ $:57^2$ $1:10^2$ 3↑	[S]Md 32000	56	9	9	$6^{2¾}$	$5^{3½}$	$7^{5¾}$	$8^{6½}$	Valdivia J5	B 113	22.90	83-11	Purdue Cadet111^{no} Push'm High$118^{1½}$ Honor Is Power115½	5 wide trip	12

WORKOUTS: ●Oct 17 SA 4f fst $:45^3$ H 1/46 Oct 5 SA 5f fst $:59^4$ H 2/30 Sep 30 SA 5f fst $:58^1$ H 2/57 Sep 13 Fpx 4f fst :48 H 3/21 Sep 5 Dmr 4f fst $:47^2$ H 6/44 Aug 30 Dmr 4f fst $:48^3$ Hg 24/65

Tate Express

Own: Tate Brad

PEDROZA M A (32 4 5 5 .13) **$12,500**

Ro. g. 3 (Mar)
Sire: Naevus (Mr. Prospector)
Dam: Dondamar (Champagne Charlie)
Br: Brad Tate (Tex)
Tr: Baffert Bob (14 1 1 2 .07)

L 115

Lifetime Record:	6 1 0 0	$15,100		
1995	6 1 0 0	$15,100	Turf	0 0 0 0
1994	0 M 0 0		Wet	0 0 0 0
SA	1 0 0 0	$450	Dist	0 0 0 0

8Oct95-2SA	fst	6f	$:21^4$ $:44^4$ $:57^3$ $1:10^2$	Clm 20000	73	4	6	$5^{1½}$	$4^{1½}$	$4^{¾}$	$5^{3¾}$	Desormeaux K J	LB 117	3.40	81-16	Rubicon$115^{1½}$ Tsarskoie Selo115^{nk} Another Great One$110^{1½}$	Bid, weakened	8
10Sep95-5Dmr	fst	6f	$:21^4$ $:44^4$ $:57^1$ $1:10$	Clm 32000	59	7	5	3^{nk}	$3^{1½}$	7^6	8^{10}	Pedroza M A	LB 115	13.90	81-11	GlitteringEvent116^{hd} TheWhdlr117^{nk} BrickByBrick115^{no}	Dueled, gave way	10
28Aug95-7Dmr	fst	7f	$:22$ $:44^3$ $1:09^3$ $1:23$	Clm 40000	57	7	3	$4^{½}$	3^1	5^4	$6^{10½}$	Pedroza M A	LB 115	*1.80	76-11	Rivermeritsdream117¾ Glittering Event116^{nk} Stalegacy$116^{3½}$	Wide trip	10
4Aug95-2Dmr	fst	6f	$:22$ $:45$ $:57$ $1:09^3$ 3↑	Md 40000	87	5	2	$2^{½}$	$1^{½}$	1^4	$1^{4½}$	Pedroza M A	LB 118	*.70	93-08	Tate Express$118^{4½}$ Florida Fury$118^{4½}$ MetroExpress118^1	Strong hand ride	7
25Jun95-10Hol	fst	6f	$:22$ $:44^4$ $:56^4$ $1:09$ 3↑	Md Sp Wt	64	8	4	$7^{3½}$	$4^{3½}$	4^5	$4^{10¾}$	Pedroza M A	LB 116	7.50	84-06	Suggest$116^{1½}$ Summer At Saratoga116^9 Cheval Sauvage116½		10
6 wide backstretch, bumped 4 1/2																		
20May95-4Hol	fst	6f	$:21^2$ $:44^2$ $:56^4$ $1:09^1$ 3↑	Md Sp Wt	74	8	3	1^1	$1^{½}$	$4^{¾}$	$7^{6¾}$	Pedroza M A	LB 115 b	*1.40	87-04	Private Interview115^{no} Contender$115^{4½}$ CutlassPro$115^{1½}$	Speed, weakened	8

WORKOUTS: Oct 5 SA 4f fst :49 H 10/25 Sep 30 SA 6f fst $1:11^4$ H 4/44 Sep 20 SA 4f fst :47 H 3/47 Sep 5 Dmr 5f fst $:58^3$ H 4/36 Aug 24 Dmr 5f fst $1:00^2$ H 17/58 Aug 19 Dmr 4f fst $:48^4$ H 31/56

Java Lee

Own: Stenger Richard

FLORES D R (—) **$12,500**

Dk. b or br g. 3 (Apr)
Sire: Java Gold (Key to the Mint)
Dam: Nana Lee (New Policy)
Br: Cally Stenger & Richard Stenger (Ky)
Tr: Gregson Edwin (6 0 1 2 .00)

L 115

Lifetime Record:	9 1 0 1	$12,915			
1995	7 1 0 1	$12,915	Turf	0 0 0 0	
1994	2 M 0 0		Wet	1 0 0 0	
SA	3 0 0 1	$3,150	Dist	3 0 0 0	$1,465

27Sep95-11Fpx	fst	6½f	$:21^4$ $:45^4$ $1:11^3$ $1:18$	Clm 12500	57	6	8	$8^{8¾}$	$7^{6¾}$	$6^{4¾}$	$6^{7½}$	Stevens S A	LB 116	8.20	82-10	Ron Warnock116^2 Luxury Box111^{nk} Yugo Fast$119^{3½}$	Off slowly	8
30Aug95-9Dmr	fst	6½f	$:21^3$ $:44^2$ $1:10^1$ $1:16^3$	Clm 12500	69	2	12	11^{16}	10^{18}	$9^{5¾}$	$4^{2¾}$	Solis A	LB 115	8.10	85-13	Yugo Fast115^1 Bettor League$115^{1¾}$ Luxury Box116½	Wide into lane	12
28Jly95-5Dmr	fst	1	$:21^3$ $:45^2$ $1:10^3$ $1:36$	Clm 20000	66	3	9	$9^{7½}$	6^5	5^8	$5^{13½}$	Pincay L Jr	LB 117	13.00	76-10	ChhuhuCty$115^{5½}$ RookrMontn116^5 Dstngshdnt115^{hd}	Squeezed back start	10
11May95-9Hol	fst	7½f	$:22^2$ $:45^4$ $1:11^2$ $1:30^1$ 3↑	Md 25000	75	9	8	$8^{4½}$	$6^{2¼}$	2^{hd}	1^1	Pincay L Jr	LB 117	3.50	83-11	Java Lee117^1 Mcsorley$122^{5½}$ Slate Dancer$122^{3½}$	Wide to turn	12
5Mar95-4SA	sly	1	$:23^1$ $:48^1$ $1:14^2$ $1:40^2$	Md 32000	16	3	6	2^2	$5^{6½}$	5^{22}	7^{36}	Pincay L Jr	LB 117 b	4.10	31-42	Matsu Moe$117^{8½}$ Northern Era115^8 Letthebigcajundoit$117^{7½}$	In tight 7/8	8
4Feb95-4SA	fst	1	$:23$ $:46^4$ $1:11^4$ $1:37^2$	Md 32000	68	6	7	7^{12}	7^6	5^7	$3^{5¾}$	Nakatani C S	LB 117	3.10	76-15	Mr Jim117^{nk} Trophy Time$117^{5½}$ Java Lee117¾	Circled field	7
22Jan95-2SA	fst	1	$:23^1$ $:47$ $1:12$ $1:38^1$	Md 32000	66	7	9	7^{10}	$7^{7½}$	$6^{4¾}$	$7^{3¾}$	Solis A	B 117	10.90	75-15	Western Flagship117^1 Seekside117^1 Hudson Drive117^{hd}	Bumped start	9
24Dec94-4Hol	fst	1 1/16	$:22^4$ $:46^2$ $1:11^1$ $1:43^1$	Md Sp Wt	60	7	8	$8^{8¾}$	$9^{7½}$	$7^{8½}$	$7^{16½}$	Solis A	B 118	47.50	69-24	Royal Surge$118^{7½}$ Flick$118^{3½}$ Kenai Lake118^2	No rally	9
27Nov94-10Hol	fst	6½f	$:22^1$ $:45^1$ $1:10^2$ $1:16^3$	Md Sp Wt	53	2	9	10^{10}	$10^{9¾}$	10^{12}	$10^{11½}$	Pincay L Jr	B 119	46.20	74-11	Score Quick119^2 Feather River One$119^{1½}$ Freon119^3	Bumped hard start	10

WORKOUTS: Oct 14 SA 5f fst $1:00^3$ H 9/32 Oct 8 SA 4f fst $:48^4$ B 20/42 Sep 23 SA 4f fst $:49^2$ H 28/52 Sep 17 SA 5f fst $1:00^1$ H 9/44 Aug 18 Dmr 3f fst $:37^3$ H 20/26 Jly 22 Dmr 6f fst $1:12^4$ H 2/3

Tomorrow's Flight

Own: Burke Gary W & Timothy R

SOLIS A (77 9 11 14 .12) **$12,500**

Ch. g. 3 (Mar)
Sire: Half a Year (Riverman)
Dam: Laura's Jet (Wajima)
Br: Mabee Mr & Mrs John C (Cal)
Tr: Mitchell Mike (9 4 2 1 .44)

L 115

Lifetime Record:	6 1 1 2	$22,825			
1995	3 1 1 0	$13,650	Turf	0 0 0 0	
1994	3 M 0 2	$9,175	Wet	0 0 0 0	
SA	2 0 0 1	$3,750	Dist	2 0 0 1	$4,525

8Oct95-2SA	fst	6f	$:21^4$ $:44^4$ $:57^3$ $1:10^2$	Clm 20000	71	5	3	1^{hd}	1^{hd}	2^{hd}	$7^{4½}$	Solis A	LB 115	3.90	80-16	Rubicon$115^{1½}$ Tsarskoie Selo115^{nk} Another Great One$110^{1½}$	Weakened late	8
13Sep95-6Dmr	fst	7f	$:22$ $:44^2$ $1:09^2$ $1:23$ 3↑	Md 32000	79	12	2	1^1	1^1	2^{hd}	$1^{½}$	Solis A	LB 118	*2.20	86-11	Tomorrow'sFlight118½ VidoVision$118^{3½}$ GtoRdg$115^{2½}$	Headed, came back	12
25Aug95-2Dmr	fst	5½f	$:21^3$ $:44^4$ $:57^1$ $1:03^4$ 3↑	Md 25000	75	6	2	2^2	2^2	$2^{1½}$	$2^{½}$	Flores D R	LB 118	2.50	93-07	FncyTckt118½ Tomorrow'sFlght118^5 MomntosDcsn$113^{4½}$	Slow late gain	10
28Dec94-2SA	fst	6½f	$:21^3$ $:44^2$ $1:09^4$ $1:16^4$	Md c-50000	65	6	3	4^3	$4^{3½}$	2^4	3^5	Solis A	B 118	9.90	83-10	Ruby Beads118^4 Valued One118^1 Tomorrow's Flight118^2	Drifted out 1/8	7
Claimed from Golden Eagle Farm, Cenicola Lewis A Trainer																		
26Nov94-6Hol	fst	6½f	$:22$ $:45^3$ $1:11^3$ $1:17^3$	[S]Md Sp Wt	45	4	6	5^4	$6^{5½}$	6^{10}	$5^{16½}$	Desormeaux K J	B 119	2.90	64-15	SnowKidd'n119^1 Onetimesoneisone119^7 SmokeyMy119^2	Crowded early	8
12Nov94-9Hol	fst	6f	$:21^4$ $:44^3$ $:56^4$ $1:09^3$	[S]Md Sp Wt	59	5	8	9^{10}	9^{13}	5^8	$3^{8½}$	Solis A	B 119	6.10	83-09	MasterfulSlew$119^{6½}$ MoCrystal119^2 Tomorrow'sFlight$119^{1½}$	Along for 3rd	10

WORKOUTS: Oct 16 Hol 4f fst $:48^4$ H 5/21 Oct 5 Hol 3f fst $:38^2$ H 9/10 Sep 30 Hol 3f fst :37 H 4/13 Sep 10 Dmr 3f fst $:36^1$ H 7/20 Aug 19 Dmr 5f fst :59 H 5/50 Aug 14 Dmr 3f fst $:36^4$ Hg 10/18

Kay's Darling

Own: Pinner John E

TOSCANO P R (29 2 1 1 .07) **$12,500**

B. g. 3 (Feb)
Sire: Cure The Blues (Stop the Music)
Dam: Green Eyed Kay (Northern Jove)
Br: Silky Green Inc. (Ky)
Tr: Velasquez Danny (4 0 0 0 .00)

L 115

Lifetime Record:	14 1 3 4	$28,980			
1995	14 1 3 4	$28,980	Turf	0 0 0 0	
1994	0 M 0 0		Wet	1 0 0 0	$500
SA	6 0 1 1	$7,900	Dist	5 1 1 1	$14,880

13Oct95-2SA	fst	1	$:22^2$ $:46$ $1:11^3$ $1:37^4$	Clm 16000	57	1	8	$7^{5¾}$	$7^{3¾}$	6^5	$5^{7¾}$	Toscano P R	LB 115	13.60	72-18	False Move115¾ Where's Lester$115^{2½}$ Glendower117¾	Rail to lane	8
28Sep95-6Fpx	fst	6½f	$:21^3$ $:45$ $1:10^3$ $1:17$	Clm 16000	76	6	1	6^6	$6^{7½}$	4^4	3^3	Toscano P R	LB 115	9.70	91-09	Rubicon$117^{2½}$ See The Wood114½ Kay's Darling115^{no}	Rail rally lane	6
20Sep95-4Fpx	fst	6½f	$:21^4$ $:45^3$ $1:12^2$ $1:18^4$ 3↑	Md 16000	69	9	6	$8^{5½}$	$6^{4¾}$	$5^{3½}$	$1^{1½}$	Toscano P R	LB 115	2.80	85-12	Kay's Darling$115^{1½}$ Osceola Lad109½ Catchy Prospect114^{no}	Closed gamely	10
28Aug95-4Dmr	fst	6½f	$:21^4$ $:45^1$ $1:10$ $1:16^2$ 3↑	Md 25000	65	2	10	10^{13}	$9^{8½}$	5^6	$5^{6¾}$	Blanc B5	LB 113	8.30	82-11	SheerLuxury$120^{5½}$ ClssicAngel113^{nk} MiswkiDlight118½	Improved position	11
3Aug95-6Dmr	fst	7f	$:22^1$ $:44^4$ $1:10^1$ $1:23^3$ 3↑	Md 28000	69	3	11	11^{15}	11^{13}	$6^{7½}$	$4^{2¾}$	Valenzuela F H	LB 116	11.80	80-12	SuprmSurvivor118½ LuckyDiffrnc118^{nk} GtoRdg115^2	Squeezed back start	12
14Jly95-2Hol	fst	6f	$:22$ $:45$ $:57^4$ $1:10^1$ 3↑	Md 25000	69	3	8	$10^{9¾}$	$8^{7¾}$	6^5	2^4	Blanc B5	LB 111	5.80	85-10	Medicine Man Jake109^4 Kay's Darling111^{nk} Ruhl The Mann116½		11
Off step slow, wide rally																		
23Jun95-2Hol	fst	6f	$:21^3$ $:45^1$ $:58$ $1:11$ 3↑	Md 25000	70	7	7	7^{13}	6^8	$5^{5½}$	$2^{¾}$	Blanc B5	LB 111	8.50	84-11	Dreamntechnicolors116¾ Kay's Darling$111^{6½}$ Certitude$116^{3½}$	Finished well	10
25May95-9Hol	fst	7f	$:22$ $:45^1$ $1:11$ $1:24^2$ 3↑	Md 25000	46	9	4	$5^{1½}$	$4^{1¾}$	3^3	$3^{12¼}$	Pedroza M A	LB 115 b	4.40	68-13	Cold War$122^{6½}$ Wonderful Man$116^{5½}$ [DH]Explode Time122	Cut to rail 4 1/2	11
4May95-9Hol	fst	6f	$:22^1$ $:45^2$ $:58$ $1:11^2$ 3↑	Md 25000	59	8	8	4^2	$4^{2½}$	$4^{1¾}$	$3^{¾}$	Pedroza M A	LB 115 b	2.70	82-10	Here's Jack115^{nk} Dixie Prospect122½ Kay's Darling115^1	Good effort	10
13Apr95-9SA	fst	6f	$:22$ $:45^1$ $:57^4$ $1:10^4$	Md 32000	51	6	7	8^5	$6^{4½}$	$6^{5½}$	8^{10}	Valenzuela P A	B 118	7.30	73-15	First Rate Gift$118^{1½}$ Papalote118^2 Stalegacy118½	Rail, no rally	11

WORKOUTS: Oct 7 SA 4f fst $:50^3$ H 30/37 Sep 14 SA 3f fst $:36^3$ H 5/13 Sep 7 Dmr 4f fst $:48^1$ H 12/46 Aug 25 Dmr 3f fst $:35^3$ H 3/16 Aug 20 Dmr 5f fst $1:01^4$ H 51/64 Aug 15 Dmr 5f fst $1:00^1$ H 21/62

Bye Bye Saga

Own: Flory & Lindsey

ALMEIDA G F (46 8 2 5 .17) **$10,500**

Ch. g. 3 (Feb)
Sire: In the Swing (Blushing Groom–Fr)
Dam: Fabulous Saga (Beau Buck)
Br: James J. Lindsey (Cal)
Tr: Stepp William T (2 1 0 0 .50)

L 113

Lifetime Record:	14 1 2 1	$15,265			
1995	14 1 2 1	$15,265	Turf	0 0 0 0	
1994	0 M 0 0		Wet	1 0 0 0	
SA	5 0 0 1	$4,000	Dist	3 0 0 1	$3,280

28Sep95-11Fpx	fst	6f	$:21^4$ $:45^2$ $:58^3$ $1:10^4$	Clm 10000	58	4	8	$8^{7¾}$	$7^{8½}$	$6^{4¾}$	$4^{8½}$	Blanc B5	LB 111	7.00	86-09	BettorLeaguer$111^{4½}$ CopaseticOrphn115^{hd} SuperFlyer116^4	Saved ground	9
21Sep95-5Fpx	fst	6½f	$:22^1$ $:46^2$ $1:11^2$ $1:17^4$	Clm 9000	56	3	7	$6^{3¾}$	$5^{2½}$	$6^{6¼}$	$6^{8½}$	Almeida G F	LB 112	*3.20	82-10	Ron Warnock116^{nk} Eminent Prospect112^6 BettorLeaguer115^2	Off slowly	7
14Sep95-4Fpx	fst	6f	$:21^4$ $:45^4$ $:58^4$ $1:12$	[S]Clm 9000	66	9	10	$7^{4½}$	$5^{2½}$	3^3	$2^{¾}$	Almeida G F	LB 112	28.20	88-09	Payoff116¾ Bye Bye Saga$112^{2½}$ Save One For Me117^{nk}	Good effort	10
25Aug95-3Dmr	fst	6f	$:22$ $:45^1$ $:57^3$ $1:10^2$	[S]Clm 14000	55	7	3	$7^{3¾}$	$6^{4½}$	$5^{5½}$	$5^{6½}$	Almeida G F	LB 113	27.50	82-07	Oat Couture$115^{3½}$ One For Papa115½ Save One For Me120^{nk}	No rally	7
2Aug95-5Dmr	fst	6f	$:22$ $:45$ $:57^1$ $1:10^1$	Clm 14000	60	7	12	$11^{7½}$	$8^{6½}$	$9^{9½}$	8^9	Blanc B5	LB 108	38.60	81-12	Brick By Brick$115^{4½}$ Tower Full115^{hd} Hud$117^{1¾}$	Broke in, bumped	12
24Jun95-3GG	fst	6f	$:22^1$ $:46$ $:58^1$ $1:11^1$	Clm 25000N2X	65	2	5	$6^{7½}$	6^7	5^4	5^6	Lopez A D	LB 119	16.70	77-14	Retsina Reel119½ Lotta Courage119^3 Power Within119^{no}	No rally	6
12Jun95-6GG	fst	5½f	$:21^2$ $:45^3$ $:58^3$ $1:05^1$	Clm 12500N2L	65	7	3	6^5	$6^{3½}$	2^1	$2^{¾}$	Meza R Q	LB 119	9.60	83-15	Navy Recruit119¾ Bye Bye Saga$119^{1½}$ Classy Friend119½	Good effort	8
27May95-1GG	fst	6f	$:21^3$ $:45^1$ $:58^3$ $1:12$	Md 13500	57	2	5	$4^{5½}$	3^2	1^{hd}	1^2	Meza R Q	LB 118	5.90	79-15	ByeByeSaga118^2 MrTylorRomulus$118^{1½}$ Hjji'sBbilee118^2	Closed gamely	9
11May95-9Hol	fst	7½f	$:22^2$ $:45^4$ $1:11^2$ $1:30^1$ 3↑	Md 22500	54	6	9	$10^{6½}$	$10^{4½}$	4^5	$5^{10½}$	Castanon A L	LB 115	44.40	72-11	Java Lee117^1 Mcsorley$122^{5½}$ Slate Dancer$122^{3½}$	Stumbled start	12
20Apr95-9SA	fst	6f	$:21^4$ $:45^2$ $:57^3$ $1:10^2$	[S]Md 28000	47	7	11	$9^{8¾}$	$7^{5¾}$	$5^{7½}$	$5^{12¼}$	Castanon A L	LB 116	102.90	73-15	King'sMarshll$118^{4½}$ SilentNick118^{nk} Benevolence118^4	Broke out, bumped	12

WORKOUTS: Oct 18 SA 3f fst $:34^4$ H 3/10 Sep 12 SA tr.t 3f fst $:35^3$ H 1/7 Sep 6 Dmr 4f fst :48 H 9/49 Aug 19 Dmr 6f fst 1:15 H 30/34 ●Jly 27 SA 3f fst $:34^4$ H 1/8

Toll Road
Own: Maras Libertad
NAKATANI C S (66 10 16 12 .15) $12,500
Dk. b or br g. 3 (Mar)
Sire: Toll Key (Nodouble)
Dam: Meneval's Star (Meneval)
Br: Walsh Adele (Cal)
Tr: Polanco Marcelo (4 1 0 0 .25)
L 115
Lifetime Record: 6 1 0 1 $14,875
1995 6 1 0 1 $14,875 Turf 0 0 0 0
1994 0 M 0 0 Wet 0 0 0 0
SA 1 0 0 0 $300 Dist 0 0 0 0

6Oct95-1SA fst 6f :212 :441 :561 1:091 Clm 12500 57 3 7 43 45½ 69 510 Douglas R R LB 115 f 11.80 81-07 Luxury Box1104 Bettor Leaguer117½ Yugo Fast1153 Bit awkward start 8
11Sep95-2Dmr fst 1 :223 :464 1:113 1:364 Clm 16000 54 6 2 21½ 41¾ 85¾ 814¾ Stevens G L LB 115 f 2.80 71-15 Conejo1151½ System1152 Ificouldaiwoulda115¾ Gave way 8
16Aug95-6Dmr fst 7f :221 :444 1:10 1:224 3↑ Ⓢ Md 32000 80 2 6 1hd 11 12 11 Stevens G L LB 118 f 5.20 87-10 Toll Road1181 Prince Saul1183 Moscow Mensch1181 Cleared, held 11
26Jly95-4Dmr fst 6f :221 :452 :574 1:103 3↑ Ⓢ Md 32000 68 8 2 73½ 63 42¾ 42¾ Stevens G L LB 118 f 4.60 85-06 Cheersitup118no Nor'easter118hd Lucky Spiff1202½ Broke in air 12
23Jun95-9Hol fst 6f :22 :452 :571 1:094 3↑ Ⓢ Md 32000 80 9 1 32 31½ 34½ 33½ Stevens G L LB 116 f 2.60 87-11 Fly Home1163 Glendower117½ Toll Road1167½ Best of rest 9
24May95-6Hol fst 6f :214 :451 :573 1:104 3↑ Ⓢ Md 32000 68 5 12 109½ 86 74½ 63¾ Stevens G L LB 115 8.90 82-11 Yo'rGoodToGo1161 Ptrotr116½ MscwMnsch115nk Hopped, pinched start 12
WORKOUTS: Oct 14 SA 3f fst :373 H 9/18 Sep 26 SA 4f fst :492 H 18/24 Sep 20 SA 3f fst :39 H 17/20 Sep 6 Dmr 5f fst 1:033 H 57/61 Aug 31 Dmr 4f fst :493 H 35/48 Aug 10 Dmr 4f fst :501 H 39/47

Bettor Leaguer
Own: Hanson Stock Farm
VALDIVIA J JR (44 4 3 4 .09) $12,500
B. g. 3 (Apr)
Sire: Big Leaguer (Bold Bidder)
Dam: Bettor Deb (Debonair Roger)
Br: Hanson Stock Farm (Cal)
Tr: Sise Clifford Jr (7 0 1 0 .00)
L 110⁵
Lifetime Record: 20 2 3 4 $38,065
1995 15 1 3 3 $22,265 Turf 0 0 0 0
1994 5 1 0 1 $15,800 Wet 1 0 0 0
SA 4 0 1 0 $3,075 Dist 6 0 2 1 $6,240

6Oct95-1SA fst 6f :212 :441 :561 1:091 Clm 12500 73 2 4 33 33½ 33½ 24 Desormeaux K J LB 117 b *2.10 87-07 Luxury Box1104 Bettor Leaguer117½ Yugo Fast1153 Rail to lane 8
28Sep95-11Fpx fst 6f :214 :452 :583 1:104 Clm 10000 80 6 2 32 32 1hd 14½ Valdivia J5 LB 111 b 2.10 95-09 Bettor Leaguer1114½ Copasetic Orphan115hd Super Flyer1164 Clearly best 9
21Sep95-5Fpx fst 6½f :221 :462 1:112 1:174 Clm 10000 62 7 3 4¾ 62½ 56 36½ Toscano P R LB 115 b 3.40 84-10 Ron Warnock116nk Eminent Prospect1126 Bettor Leaguer1152 Wide trip 7
8Sep95-1Dmr fst 5½f :214 :442 :562 1:03 Ⓢ Clm 14000 64 1 3 54 56 58 510½ McCarron C J LB 114 b 8.40 87-10 Holiday Dream1165 Fancy Ticket115¾ Busy Count115¾ Rail to lane 7
30Aug95-9Dmr fst 6½f :213 :442 1:101 1:163 Clm 12500 73 12 2 43½ 43 31½ 21 Flores D R LB 115 b 17.10 87-13 Yugo Fast1151 Bettor Leaguer1151½ Luxury Box116½ 4 wide into lane 12
16Aug95-9Dmr fst 6f :22 :444 :571 1:093 Clm 14000 61 10 1 41½ 43 66 68 Flores D R LB 114 b 12.40 87-10 Rubicon1161 Capichi's Jack117¾ Another Great One115¾ Wide trip 12
27Jly95-1Dmr fst 6f :221 :451 :572 1:101 Ⓢ Clm 20000 73 9 1 4¾ 62¾ 53½ 53 Flores D R LB 115 b 31.30 87-10 Tsarskoie Selo1151 Dancing Islander1151 Kalempress116no Wide trip 10
14Jly95-1Hol fst 6f :214 :451 :571 1:102 Clm 22500 63 5 1 4½ 3nk 21½ 35 Flores D R LB 115 b 31.40 83-10 Dreamntechnicolors1183 Another Great One1182 Bettor Leaguer115½ 7
Bit awkward start, dueled between foes
3Jun95-5Hol fst 6½f :22 :45 1:093 1:162 Clm 16000 47 10 1 1hd 2½ 56½ 813 Flores D R LB 115 b 29.60 74-08 Tsarskoie Selo1184 Deep Space1153 Valued One1151 Dueled, gave way 10
19May95-13TuP fst 6½f :223 :451 1:102 1:17 Alw 6500N2L 48 2 3 2½ 1hd 3½ 55½ Garrido O L L 117 b 3.00 79-16 Shannie River117¾ Big Sky Chester1203½ Gold Bon Bon1191 Tired 7
WORKOUTS: Aug 8 Dmr 4f fst :503 H 27/33

Shingen Warrior
Own: Takeda Kyohei
DOUGLAS R R (45 4 11 5 .09) $12,500
Gr. g. 3 (Apr)
Sire: Two Punch (Mr. Prospector)
Dam: Fast n Blonde (Fast Passer)
Br: Diane Richards & R. L. Roeper (Md)
Tr: Cross David C Jr (8 1 0 2 .13)
L 115
Lifetime Record: 13 1 4 1 $33,035
1995 13 1 4 1 $33,035 Turf 0 0 0 0
1994 0 M 0 0 Wet 1 0 1 0 $4,000
SA 6 0 1 1 $8,500 Dist 4 0 1 0 $5,835

8Oct95-2SA fst 6f :214 :444 :573 1:102 Clm 20000 72 7 2 2hd 2hd 1hd 64½ Stevens G L LB 115 6.70 81-16 Rubicon1151½ Tsarskoie Selo115nk Another Great One1101½ Bobbled start 8
23Sep95-7Fpx fst 6½f :22 :454 1:112 1:18 Alw 40000s 61 8 1 54½ 42½ 76 77½ Pedroza M A LB 117 4.90 82-08 Hard Workin' Guy117¾ Stalegacy117hd Sudden Fear1201½ Weakened 8
10Sep95-5Dmr fst 6f :214 :444 :571 1:10 Clm 32000 64 5 7 43½ 51¾ 64½ 78 Stevens G L LB 115 7.00 83-11 GlttrngEvnt116hd ThWhdlr117nk BrckBBrck115no Between foes, weakened 10
9Aug95-6Dmr fst 6f :213 :443 :571 1:093 Clm 32000 77 8 6 84½ 52½ 41 23½ Stevens G L LB 115 5.30 89-07 Telefonazo1163½ Shingen Warrior115hd Feathered Friend1152 4 wide turn 8
1Jly95-10Hol fst 6f :22 :451 :572 1:094 3↑ Md 32000 87 9 2 2½ 11 1hd 1hd Stevens G L LB 116 *.60 91-09 Shingen Warrior116hd What A Bandit1168½ Bold Banquet1171½ Gamely 10
15Jun95-9Hol fst 6f :213 :443 :563 1:092 3↑ Md 25000 88 1 3 31 2hd 1hd 21 Stevens G L LB 116 2.00 92-11 Hud1171 Shingen Warrior11610 Dixie Prospect1202½ Inside duel 12
21May95-1Hol fst 6½f :213 :441 1:093 1:16 3↑ Md 35000 71 6 1 31½ 2hd 2hd 45½ Pedroza M A LB 113 10.90 84-08 Major Funding117nk Key Sider1154 Gallant Soldier1221 Weakened 7
10May95-9Hol fst 6f :22 :452 :574 1:103 3↑ Md 32000 73 8 2 41½ 41½ 43 22½ Black C A LB 116 20.30 84-11 Factorage1222½ Shingen Warrior116½ Earth Rockett1163 Wide early 10
24Apr95-10SA fst 6f :214 :451 :574 1:11 Md 32000 55 8 5 86¾ 84½ 59 37 Garcia M S LB 118 13.10 75-15 Papalote1185 Another Great One1182 Shingen Warrior118nk Just got 3rd 12
1Apr95-10SA fst 1 :224 :47 1:121 1:383 Md 32000 -0 3 8 109¾ 1016 1025 1042 Antley C W LB 117 4.90 34-23 Hot Hooves1172¾ Chillin Out115½ Beauregard1171½ Done early 10
WORKOUTS: Sep 8 Dmr 3f fst :364 B 10/18 Aug 29 Dmr 6f fst 1:141 H 10/13 Aug 20 Dmr 6f fst 1:14 H 14/27 Aug 6 Dmr 5f fst 1:014 H 26/54 Aug 1 Dmr 5f fst 1:003 H 8/43 Jly 26 Dmr 5f fst 1:011 H 29/66

Keen Rate was dropping from a solid second in a $20,000 claimer to $12,500. While he certainly had every right to win this, he showed a grand total of one win in his last 10 starts, which was at this distance, wire to wire. He had high speed, chasing in second in his last start in fractions of :21⅖ and :44⅖. In his wire-to-wire win, he went an even faster first half on the lead: :44⅕, and in an earlier race had the lead through fractions of :21⅗ and :44.

But there was lots of early speed to push Keen Rate early. One, Push'm High, was scratched. The others weren't.

Dasha was a head off fractions of :21⅘ and :44⅗ before tiring badly in his last race, a $32,000 claimer. He was dropping further than Keen Rate.

Tomorrow's Flight had been on the lead in both of his last starts through fractions of :22 and :44⅖, and :21⅘ and :44⅘, respectively.

In one of his six races, Toll Road was on the lead through fractions of :22$^{1}/_{5}$ and :44$^{4}/_{5}$.

Bettor Leaguer showed one race on the lead through a first quarter of :22.

Shingen Warrior was a head off the lead through fractions of :21$^{4}/_{5}$ and :44$^{4}/_{5}$ in his last race.

When Keen Rate was pounded down to even money in a race loaded with other speed horses, he was certainly vulnerable. And in betting Pick Threes beginning with the fifth race, it would have been wise to use all the horses in the fifth, especially if you liked the two favorites in the sixth and seventh well enough to key them in the Pick Three. The cost would have been $33.

In the sixth, La Nativa would be bet down to 7-10 despite a two-month layoff because she was dropping into a maiden claimer for the first time, and had worked a bullet :59$^{2}/_{5}$ for this.

6 Santa Anita Park

6½ Furlongs (1:14) MAIDEN CLAIMING. Purse $17,000. Fillies and mares, 3-year-old and upward, bred in California. Weights: 3-year-olds, 120 lbs. Older, 122 lbs. Claiming price $32,000, if for $28,000, allowed 2 lbs.

[Past performance data for the following horses: Pyromoon, Qui's A Lady, It's Me Swingin]

Smoggy
Own: McCutcheon James R
ATKINSON P (19 1 2 1 .05) $28,000
Dk. b or br f. 3 (Apr)
Sire: Badger Land (Codex)
Dam: Ozone Gal (El Terresto)
Br: Lukas D Wayne (Cal)
Tr: McCutcheon James R (3 1 0 0 .33)
L 118

Lifetime Record:	5 M 0 0	$500		
1995	5 M 0 0	$500	Turf	0 0 0 0
1994	0 M 0 0		Wet	0 0 0 0
SA	0 0 0 0		Dist	0 0 0 0

29Sep95-6Fpx fst 6f :22 :454 :583 1:112 3↑[F][S]Md 32000 33 10 8 812 715 712 615¼ Fernandez A L LB 115 fb 95.30 76-10 Double Vanilla113½ Minislew109¾ First Tank1144 Off slowly 10
22Sep95-12Fpx fst 6f :222 :46 :584 1:113 3↑[F]Md 32000 22 4 10 89 1012 915 819 Garrido O L LB 116 b 25.30 72-13 Donya Chayo1111¼ Charbell1161¼ Slew In The Wind1163 Off bit slow 10
6Sep95-6Dmr fst 5½f :213 :454 :584 1:052 3↑[F][S]Md 28000 30 7 12 1221 1218 1111 87¾ Valenzuela F H LB 116 b 53.10 78-08 Nifty Edie1161¾ Shellac118nk [D]Movin Molly1162¼ Took up sharply start 12
Placed 7th through disqualification.
14Aug95-2Dmr fst 6f :214 :444 :57 1:094 3↑[F][S]Md 32000 23 3 8 44½ 510 714 820¼ Pedroza M A LB 118 12.50 72-07 LuckyMrge1138 Slew'sShrpie1162¾ SlewInTheWind1182¼ Inside, gave way 9
31Jly95-6Dmr fst 6f :214 :453 :581 1:102 3↑[F]Md 28000 45 11 3 915 97 89 712 Pedroza M A LB 116 27.50 77-10 Felice1161 Woodacres Lass1182 Liteup My Life118¾ Wide early 11
WORKOUTS: Oct 15 SA 4f fst :494 H 35/53 Oct 10 SA 3f fst :361 B 5/19 Sep 12 Fpx 3f fst :364 H 2/11 Sep 2 Dmr 3f fst :362 H 9/24 Aug 23 Dmr 3f fst :35 Hg4/28 Aug 7 Dmr 4f fst :483 H 21/65

Our Irish Miss
Own: Meehan & Meehan & Van Patten
VALENZUELA F H (34 1 3 2 .03) $32,000
Dk. b or br f. 3 (May)
Sire: Our Michael (Bolero)
Dam: Feudalism (Irish Ruler)
Br: Rancho Jonata (Cal)
Tr: Acerno John (1 0 1 0 .00)
L 120

Lifetime Record:	0 M 0 0	$0		
1995	0 M 0 0		Turf	0 0 0 0
1994	0 M 0 0		Wet	0 0 0 0
SA	0 0 0 0		Dist	0 0 0 0

WORKOUTS: Oct 15 SA 6f fst 1:123 H 2/26 Sep 23 SA 4f fst :514 H 52/52 Sep 16 SA 6f fst 1:13 Hg2/10 ●Aug 26 SA 5f fst 1:00 H 1/18 Aug 18 SA 5f fst 1:003 H 2/13 Aug 12 SA 4f fst :483 H 5/31
Aug 6 SA 4f fst :473 H 8/25 Jly 29 SA 4f fst :493 H 10/22 Jly 22 SA 3f fst :374 H 7/11

Slew In The Wind
Own: Hawthorne Nancy
ALMEIDA G F (46 8 2 5 .17) $32,000
Gr. f. 3 (Apr)
Sire: Slew the Bride (Seattle Slew)
Dam: Windy Doll (Windy Sands)
Br: Russell Tourville (Cal)
Tr: Hawthorne James W (—)
L 120

Lifetime Record:	6 M 0 4	$9,960			
1995	6 M 0 4	$9,960	Turf	0 0 0 0	
1994	0 M 0 0		Wet	0 0 0 0	
SA	0 0 0 0		Dist	2 0 0 1	$2,490

20Oct95-13Fpx fst 6½f :214 :461 1:12 1:183 3↑[F]Md 32000 60 6 6 53 45½ 32¼ 32¼ Castro J M LB 115 3.90 84-09 Charbell1141¼ Dawn Of Promise109¾ Slew In The Wind1153
Steadied, forced out 1/2
22Sep95-12Fpx fst 6f :222 :46 :584 1:113 3↑[F]Md 32000 62 10 8 21 21½ 32 33 Garcia M S LB 116 8.60 88-13 DonyaChayo1111¼ Chrbell1161¼ SlewInTheWind1163 Drifted out into lane 10
14Aug95-2Dmr fst 6f :214 :444 :57 1:094 3↑[F][S]Md 32000 47 7 5 35½ 35 37¾ 310¾ Almeida G F LB 118 14.60 81-07 LuckyMarge1138 Slew'sShrpie1162¾ SlewInTheWind1182¼ Best of others 9
28Jly95-4Dmr fst 6f :22 :45 :572 1:102 3↑[F][S]Md 32000 53 3 9 52½ 46 57¼ 610¾ Almeida G F B 118 20.50 78-12 Wonderful Copy118nk Ole' Sis1187 Fleet Princess111nk Gave way 10
14Jly95-9Hol fst 6½f :221 :45 1:10 1:163 3↑[F][S]Md 32000 52 7 4 3½ 43 46 510¼ Garcia M S B 116 21.90 75-10 SportingScene1161 Angelina'sCourt1177 LuckMeALady1162 Weakened 11
18Jun95-6Hol fst 6f :214 :452 :58 1:11 3↑[F][S]Md 32000 59 2 7 64½ 54½ 43 39 Garcia M S B 116 37.60 77-14 MySymphony1147¼ Angelina'sCourt116½ SlewInTheWind1162 Inside trip 11
WORKOUTS: Oct 12 Fpx 4f fst :483 H 2/5 ●Sep 9 Fpx 3f fst :344 H 1/16 ●Sep 2 Fpx 6f fst 1:143 H 1/4 ●Aug 9 Fpx 3f fst :35 H 1/6 Jly 25 Fpx 4f fst :501 H 2/2

Lori's Sunshine
Own: Sam Crivello Estate
DOUGLAS R R (45 4 11 5 .09) $28,000
Ch. f. 3 (Feb)
Sire: Simi Dancer (Riverman)
Dam: Green Eyed Lori (Blue Eyed Davy)
Br: Sam Crivello (Cal)
Tr: Bean Robert A (5 0 0 0 .00)
118

Lifetime Record:	3 M 0 0	$1,665			
1995	3 M 0 0	$1,665	Turf	0 0 0 0	
1994	0 M 0 0		Wet	0 0 0 0	
SA	1 0 0 0		Dist	1 0 0 0	$1,190

6Oct95-9SA fst 6f :212 :441 :562 1:091 3↑[F][S]Md 32000 49 11 8 1116 1010 710 713 Douglas R R B 120 b 24.30 78-07 Ole' Sis1206¼ Minislew120nk Pyromoon120¾ 12
Bumped into rail past 3/16
19Sep95-5Fpx fst 6½f :214 :454 1:123 1:193 3↑[F][S]Md 32000 50 9 5 57 510 47 43¾ Mawing L A5 B 109 b 7.40 77-11 Meria Breeze114nk Ole' Sis1143 Big Foot Mary114½ Saved ground 9
6Sep95-6Dmr fst 5½f :213 :454 :584 1:052 3↑[F][S]Md 32000 33 6 10 1017 1011 76¾ 66½ Mawing L A5 113 b 20.80 79-08 Nifty Edie1161¾ Shellac118nk [D]Movin Molly1162¼ Took up start 12
Placed 5th through disqualification.
WORKOUTS: Oct 14 Hol 5f fst 1:02 H 16/23 Sep 30 Hol 4f fst :484 H 4/21 ●Sep 15 SA 3f fst :344 H 1/12 ●Aug 31 SA 3f fst :354 H 1/13 Aug 24 SA 4f fst :472 Hg5/12 Aug 11 SA 6f fst 1:161 H 1/2

La Nativa
Own: Strader John & Scott
NAKATANI C S (66 10 16 12 .15) $32,000
B. f. 3 (Jun)
Sire: Native Prospector (Mr. Prospector)
Dam: Lakeland Beauty (Mummy's Pet)
Br: Lakeland Beauty Syndicate (Cal)
Tr: Perdomo A Pico (4 0 2 1 .00)
L 120

Lifetime Record:	5 M 0 0	$8,625			
1995	5 M 0 0	$8,625	Turf	1 0 0 0	$2,925
1994	0 M 0 0		Wet	0 0 0 0	
SA	1 0 0 0		Dist	1 0 0 0	

18Aug95-5Dmr fst 6f :214 :444 :57 1:10 3↑[F][S]Md Sp Wt 65 9 1 62¾ 53½ 52¾ 45½ Nakatani C S LB 118 b 12.80 86-10 FlyingWinner118¾ PowerfulLaunch1224 ValiantVaness118½ 5 wide early 9
6Jly95-4Hol fst 6f :22 :45 :573 1:10 3↑[F][S]Md Sp Wt 67 9 6 86½ 56 55 45½ Nakatani C S LB 116 b 5.60 85-11 RuhlingContessa1161¼ Letthelilsisroll116½ ValiantVness1163½ 4 wide turn 10
10Jun95-1Hol fst 1$\frac{1}{16}$:231 :463 1:111 1:432 3↑[F]Md Sp Wt 60 4 4 53½ 53½ 89¾ 816¼ Almeida G F LB 115 b 13.60 67-16 Response1161 Some Kinda Lady1153½ Pearl Garden116½ Gave way 8
13Apr95-1SA fm 1 [T] :231 :474 1:121 1:37 3↑[F]Md Sp Wt 72 6 3 31½ 3½ 2½ 43¼ Valenzuela P A LB 117 10.80 77-15 Jet Gray1232¼ Iolani123nk Supermaid116¾ Lugged in early & 1/16 7
26Mar95-1SA fst 6½f :214 :443 1:093 1:161 [F][S]Md Sp Wt 57 3 7 78½ 76¾ 77¼ 710¼ McCarron C J 117 11.50 80-09 Our SummerBid1176 PrincessAfleet1171½ Minislew117½ Off slow, rail trip 7
WORKOUTS: ●Oct 15 Hol 5f fst :592 H 1/23 Oct 9 Hol 5f fst 1:024 H 30/30 Oct 3 Hol 5f fst 1:032 H 13/25 Sep 27 Hol 4f fst :49 H 4/28 Aug 27 SA tr.t 4f fst :493 H 1/3 Aug 13 SA 5f fst 1:003 H 5/29

Especial Miss
Own: Buchmuller & Lyle & Stepp
PEDROZA M A (32 4 5 5 .13) $28,000
B. f. 3 (May)
Sire: Coach's Call (Alydar)
Dam: Epergne (Round Table)
Br: James J. Lindsey (Cal)
Tr: Stepp William T (2 1 0 0 .50)
118

Lifetime Record:	0 M 0 0	$0		
1995	0 M 0 0		Turf	0 0 0 0
1994	0 M 0 0		Wet	0 0 0 0
SA	0 0 0 0		Dist	0 0 0 0

WORKOUTS: Oct 18 SA 3f fst :344 H 3/10 Oct 12 SA 5f fst 1:013 Hg22/43 Oct 3 SA 5f fst 1:00 H 11/29 Sep 25 SA 6f fst 1:163 H 23/23 Sep 19 SA 4f fst :482 H 10/35 Sep 13 Dmr 6f fst 1:152 H 13/15
Sep 6 Dmr 5f fst 1:003 H 25/61 Sep 1 Dmr 5f fst 1:012 H 27/52 Aug 22 Dmr 5f fst 1:021 H 41/56 Aug 15 SA 4f fst :522 H 21/21 Aug 3 SA 4f fst :502 H 12/13 Jly 28 SA 4f fst :503 H 12/14

Lil' Lita Starr
Own: Kenis & 3 Plus U Stable
BLANC B (55 4 3 4 .07) $32,000
Dk. b or br f. 3 (Apr)
Sire: Prospective Star (Mr. Prospector)
Dam: Womanoftheeighties (Foreign Power)
Br: Jack Van Berg (Cal)
Tr: Van Berg Jack C (17 2 3 0 .12)
L 115⁵

Lifetime Record:	4 M 0 0	$425		
1995	4 M 0 0	$425	Turf	0 0 0 0
1994	0 M 0 0		Wet	0 0 0 0
SA	1 0 0 0	$425	Dist	1 0 0 0

6Oct95-9SA fst 6f :212 :441 :562 1:091 3↑[F][S]Md 32000 63 4 7 1011 78¾ 58 57¾ Pedroza M A LB 120 fb 76.20 83-07 Ole' Sis1206¼ Minislew120nk Pyromoon120¾ Improved position 12
7Sep95-6Dmr fst 6f :221 :46 :582 1:102 3↑[F]Md 25000 21 11 2 1hd 1hd 99¾ 1222 Pedroza M A LB 118 fb 30.80 67-13 FavoriteGift1188 Vee'sVice118¾ SeptiemeChnson118¾ Dueled, gave way 12
12Aug95-10Dmr fst 6½f :221 :452 1:101 1:162 3↑[F][S]Md 32000 14 6 1 87¾ 1116 1116 926¾ Gonzalez S Jr B 118 f 25.60 62-06 Ruthie Jane1187¼ Celtic Affair1182¾ Gypsy Grey1201¼ Lugged out 3 1/2 12
20Jly95-9Hol fst 6f :214 :451 :573 1:094 3↑[F][S]Md 32000 40 5 7 75¼ 86¾ 813 716¼ Almeida G F B 116 f 46.40 74-10 Hemet Eagle1228 Ruthie Jane1162¼ Ruff Tex1162¼ Drifted wide into lane 11
WORKOUTS: Oct 15 Hol 6f fst 1:154 Hg10/12 Oct 3 Hol 5f fst 1:052 H 24/25 Sep 26 Hol 5f fst 1:032 H 29/30 Sep 20 Hol 5f fst 1:032 H 22/26 Aug 28 Dmr 4f fst :484 H 27/43 Aug 21 Dmr 3f fst :371 H 17/22

Shellac
Own: Amazing Stable & Petrovsky
DOROCHENKO G (—) $32,000

B. f. 3 (Apr)
Sire: Native Prospector (Mr. Prospector)
Dam: Unpainted (Painted Wagon)
Br: Annabelle Stute (Cal)
Tr: Ward Cynthia (—)

L 120

Lifetime Record:	7 M 1 0	$6,210			
1995	5 M 1 0	$4,860	Turf	0 0 0 0	
1994	2 M 0 0	$1,350	Wet	0 0 0 0	
SA	1 0 0 0	$1,350	Dist	3 0 0 0	$160

24Sep95-3Fpx	fst	$1\frac{1}{16}$	:23	$:46^2$	$1:12^1$	$1:44^3$	Clm 12500	60	3	4	4^{14}	4^{12}	6^{13}	$5^{15\frac{1}{4}}$	Dorochenko G	LB 115	14.80	71-15	$FlyingRazz114^8$ $StrPotentil114^{1\frac{1}{2}}$ $Crig'sHoochie116^{2\frac{3}{4}}$	Off bit slow, outrun	6
15Sep95-6Fpx	fst	6½f	:22	$:46^2$	1:11	$1:17^2$	3↑ ⒻMd 32000	49	8	5	$10^{8\frac{3}{4}}$	$10^{9\frac{3}{4}}$	7^{11}	$7^{14\frac{1}{4}}$	Dorochenko G	LB 116	17.90	77-10	$Martha's Girl116^{3\frac{1}{4}}$ $First Tank116^6$ $Woodacres Lass116^{no}$	Wide into lane	10
6Sep95-6Dmr	fst	5½f	$:21^3$	$:45^4$	$:58^4$	$1:05^2$	3↑ ⒻⓈMd 32000	46	4	9	9^{16}	9^{11}	$6^{5\frac{3}{4}}$	$2^{1\frac{3}{4}}$	Dorochenko G	LB 118	97.70	84-08	$Nifty Edie116^{1\frac{3}{4}}$ $Shellac118^{nk}$ $ⒹMovin Molly116^{2\frac{1}{4}}$	Steadied start	12
27Jly95-2Dmr	fst	6½f	$:22^1$	$:45^2$	$1:10^3$	1:17	3↑ ⒻMd 25000	27	2	9	$11^{8\frac{1}{4}}$	12^{17}	12^{18}	11^{21}	Dorochenko G	LB 118	72.40	65-10	$Amazin Aim118^5$ $Southern Psychic117^2$ $Nobra118^{\frac{3}{4}}$	Outrun	12
16Jly95-2Hol	fst	6f	$:22^2$	$:45^4$	:58	$1:10^1$	3↑ Md 40000	53	4	4	8^9	$8^{6\frac{3}{4}}$	9^{10}	$7^{11\frac{1}{2}}$	Dorochenko G	LB 115	92.50	77-09	$KeySider116^{2\frac{1}{4}}$ $Glndowr117^{hd}$ $Htoldmsomthing116^3$	Bumped start, outrun	9
9Nov94-6Hol	fst	6½f	$:22^1$	$:45^3$	$1:10^4$	$1:17^2$	ⒻⓈMd 32000	16	3	5	8^8	10^{10}	8^{13}	$6^{22\frac{1}{4}}$	Nakatani C S	B 119	9.20	59-11	$Nicolletta119^{\frac{3}{4}}$ $No Bounty Paid119^{2\frac{3}{4}}$ $Malachia119^{5\frac{1}{4}}$	Checked 3 1/2	10
20Oct94-3SA	fst	6f	:22	$:45^2$	$:58^1$	$1:11^4$	ⒻⓈMd 32000	36	4	3	7^7	$7^{7\frac{3}{4}}$	$6^{5\frac{3}{4}}$	$4^{7\frac{1}{4}}$	Nakatani C S	B 118	5.70	70-15	$LdyCirBounty118^{3\frac{1}{4}}$ $FeminineVlue118^{1\frac{1}{4}}$ $PrfrrdRod118^{2\frac{3}{4}}$	Improved position	7

WORKOUTS: Oct 17 Hol 4f fst $:48^1$ H 4/30 ●Oct 1 Hol 3f fst $:35^4$ H 1/15 ●Sep 1 SA 4f fst $:46^4$ H 1/13 Aug 22 SA 4f fst $:49^1$ H 8/16

First Tank
Own: Garcia Eddie
SCOTT J M (14 0 1 0 .00) $32,000

Dk. b or br f. 3 (Apr)
Sire: Tank's Prospect (Mr. Prospector)
Dam: Bella Prima (Bold Hitter)
Br: Hi Card Ranch (Cal)
Tr: Spiker Charles L (—)

L 120

Lifetime Record:	7 M 1 2	$10,235			
1995	6 M 1 2	$10,235	Turf	0 0 0 0	
1994	1 M 0 0		Wet	0 0 0 0	
SA	1 0 0 0		Dist	3 0 1 1	$5,420

29Sep95-6Fpx	fst	6f	:22	$:45^4$	$:58^3$	$1:11^2$	3↑ ⒻⓈMd 32000	62	5	1	2^2	$2^{4\frac{1}{2}}$	$3^{3\frac{1}{2}}$	3^4	Scott J M	LB 114	3.60	88-10	$Double Vanilla113^{\frac{1}{2}}$ $Minislew109^{3\frac{1}{2}}$ $First Tank114^4$	Best of rest	10
15Sep95-6Fpx	fst	6½f	:22	$:46^2$	1:11	$1:17^2$	3↑ ⒻMd 32000	75	5	3	$4^{2\frac{1}{4}}$	3^1	2^2	$2^{3\frac{1}{2}}$	Scott J M	LB 116	13.20	88-10	$Martha's Girl116^{3\frac{1}{2}}$ $First Tank116^6$ $Woodacres Lass116^{no}$	Second best	10
14Aug95-6Dmr	fst	6½f	$:22^1$	$:45^1$	$1:10^4$	1:17	3↑ ⒻMd 32000	43	9	2	$3^{\frac{1}{2}}$	$4^{1\frac{3}{4}}$	8^5	8^9	Almeida G F	B 118	33.70	77-07	$Mist At Dawning113^{no}$ $Farr Bettor Miss118^{\frac{3}{4}}$ $Martha's Girl118^{nk}$	4 wide trip	11
28Jly95-4Dmr	fst	6f	:22	:45	$:57^2$	$1:10^2$	3↑ ⒻⓈMd 32000	61	6	8	$7^{4\frac{1}{4}}$	$6^{8\frac{3}{4}}$	4^7	$4^{7\frac{1}{2}}$	Garcia M S	B 118	3.30	81-12	$Wonderful Copy118^{nk}$ $Ole' Sis118^7$ $Fleet Princess111^{nk}$	Improved position	10
12Jly95-2Hol	fst	6½f	$:22^2$	$:45^3$	1:11	$1:17^2$	3↑ ⒻMd 32000	63	6	2	4^2	$4^{1\frac{1}{2}}$	$2^{1\frac{1}{2}}$	$3^{2\frac{1}{2}}$	Fuentes J A	B 116	60.50	80-11	$Chide116^{2\frac{1}{4}}$ $Mist At Dawning111^{hd}$ $First Tank116^{3\frac{1}{4}}$	4 wide turn	7
18Jun95-6Hol	fst	6f	$:21^4$	$:45^2$	:58	1:11	3↑ ⒻⓈMd 32000	54	11	6	$7^{4\frac{1}{2}}$	$6^{5\frac{3}{4}}$	5^6	4^{10}	Fuentes J A	B 116	73.80	75-14	$My Symphony114^{7\frac{1}{2}}$ $Angelina's Court116^{\frac{1}{2}}$ $SlewInTheWind116^2$	Wide trip	11
13Oct94-9SA	fst	6f	$:21^4$	$:45^2$	$:57^4$	$1:10^2$	ⒻⓈMd 32000	44	3	11	11^7	11^{11}	10^{11}	$7^{11\frac{1}{2}}$	Scott J M	B 117	130.20	73-13	$Piratesleadinglady117^2$ $Nicolletta117^{1\frac{3}{4}}$ $NoBountyPid117^{1\frac{1}{4}}$	Wide into lane	11

WORKOUTS: Sep 6 Fpx 5f fst $1:03^1$ H 2/5 Aug 26 Fpx 5f fst $1:03^3$ H 4/7

La Nativa won by 11 lengths.

SIXTH RACE
Santa Anita
OCTOBER 20, 1995

6½ FURLONGS. (1.14) MAIDEN CLAIMING. Purse $17,000. Fillies and mares, 3-year-old and upward, bred in California. Weights: 3-year-olds, 120 lbs. Older, 122 lbs. Claiming price $32,000, if for $28,000, allowed 2 lbs.

Value of Race: $17,000 Winner $9,350; second $3,400; third $2,550; fourth $1,275; fifth $425. Mutuel Pool $251,376.70 Exacta Pool $193,473.00 Trifecta Pool $250,960.00 Quinella Pool $35,980.00

Last Raced	Horse	M/Eq	L A.Wt	PP	St	¼	½	Str	Fin	Jockey	Cl'g Pr	Odds $1
18Aug95 ^{5}Dmr^4	La Nativa	LBb	3 120	7	1	$1^{1\frac{1}{2}}$	1^4	1^7	1^{11}	Nakatani C S	32000	0.70
	Our Irish Miss	L	3 120	4	10	$8^{\frac{1}{2}}$	$6^{1\frac{1}{2}}$	3^{hd}	2^{nk}	Valenzuela F H	32000	5.50
20Oct95 ^{13}Fpx^3	Slew In The Wind	LB	3 120	5	11	$5^{1\frac{1}{2}}$	3^{hd}	$2^{2\frac{1}{2}}$	3^2	Almeida G F	32000	6.60
29Sep95 ^{6}Fpx^3	First Tank	LB	3 120	11	7	10^8	$9^{\frac{1}{2}}$	5^{hd}	$4^{1\frac{1}{2}}$	Scott J M	32000	7.60
6Oct95 ^{9}SA^7	Lori's Sunshine	Bb	3 118	6	8	9^{hd}	7^{hd}	$4^{1\frac{1}{2}}$	$5^{2\frac{1}{4}}$	Douglas R R	28000	29.40
6Oct95 ^{9}SA^5	Lil' Lita Starr	LBbf	3 115	9	6	7^1	8^1	$8^{1\frac{1}{2}}$	6^2	Blanc B^5	32000	28.20
24Sep95 ^{3}Fpx^5	Shellac	LB	3 120	10	9	11	11	$10^{2\frac{1}{2}}$	7^1	Dorochenko G	32000	84.60
6Oct95 ^{9}SA^9	Qui's A Lady	LB	4 120	1	2	6^{hd}	$10^{4\frac{1}{2}}$	9^1	8no	Berrio O A	28000	73.30
29Sep95 ^{6}Fpx^6	Smoggy	LBbf	3 118	3	5	4^2	4^{hd}	$6^{\frac{1}{2}}$	$9^{3\frac{1}{2}}$	Flores D R	28000	139.50
	Especial Miss	Bb	3 118	8	3	$3^{\frac{1}{2}}$	2^1	7^{hd}	$10^{3\frac{1}{2}}$	Pedroza M A	28000	18.80
12Jun95 ^{9}Hol^6	It's Me Swingin	LB	3 120	2	4	2^{hd}	5^1	11	11	Toscano P R	32000	18.60

OFF AT 3:30 Start Good For All But SLEW IN THE WIND. Won handily. Time, $:22^2$, $:45^2$, 1:10, $1:16^3$ Track fast.

$2 Mutuel Prices:			
7–LA NATIVA	3.40	2.60	2.40
4–OUR IRISH MISS		4.40	3.60
5–SLEW IN THE WIND			3.00

$2 EXACTA 7–4 PAID $15.80 $2 TRIFECTA 7–4–5 PAID $53.80 $2 QUINELLA 4–7 PAID $11.40

B. f, (Jun), by Native Prospector–Lakeland Beauty, by Mummy's Pet. Trainer Perdomo A Pico. Bred by Lakeland Beauty Syndicate (Cal).

LA NATIVA quickly sprinted to a clear lead, opened up on the turn and proved much the best under a mild hand ride. OUR IRISH MISS steadied at the start, was sent between rivals leaving the backstretch, moved up wide into the lane and just got the place. SLEW IN THE WIND stumbled at the start, raced off the rail on the backstretch, continued four wide on the turn, got closest to the winner in upper stretch and just lost the place. FIRST TANK raced wide and improved position in the stretch but was not a threat. LORI'S SUNSHINE was sent between rivals early on the turn, raced out from the inside thereafter and lacked the needed late response. LIL' LITA STARR raced wide throughout. SHELLAC bobbled at the start and also raced wide. QUI'S A LADY saved ground until the end of the turn, swung out and weakened. SMOGGY went between rivals on the backstretch, raced outside IT'S ME SWINGIN on the turn, then gave way. ESPECIAL MISS tracked the early pace outside IT'S ME SWINGIN, remained closest to the winner on the turn, then gave way. IT'S ME SWINGIN raced close up inside ESPECIAL MISS but off the rail early, continued inside on the turn, then gave way.

Owners— 1, Strader John & Scott; 2, Meehan & Meehan & Van Patten; 3, Hawthorne Nancy; 4, Garcia Eddie; 5, Sam Crivello Estate; 6, Kenis & 3 Plus U Stable; 7, Amazing Stable & Petrovsky; 8, Cohen Milton S; 9, McCutcheon James R; 10, Buchmuller & Lyle & Stepp; 11, Hilaski Carl S & Evelyn J

Trainers—1, Perdomo A Pico; 2, Acerno John; 3, Hawthorne James W; 4, Spiker Charles L; 5, Bean Robert A; 6, Van Berg Jack C; 7, Ward Cynthia; 8, Perez Mag; 9, McCutcheon James R; 10, Stepp William T; 11, Van Berg Jack C

Scratched— Pyromoon (6Oct95 ^{9}SA^3)

$3 Pick Three (3–9–7) Paid $782.10; Pick Three Pool $60,441.

In the seventh, Chemolo would go off the 3-2 favorite after being nosed in his last start, his eighth straight finish in the money.

7 Santa Anita Park

6 Furlongs (1:07¹) CLAIMING. Purse $22,000. Fillies and mares, 3-year-olds and upward. Weights: 3-year-olds, 120 lbs. Older, 122 lbs. Non-winners of two races since August 15, allowed 3 lbs. Of a race since September 15, 5 lbs. Claiming price $25,000, if for $22,500, allowed 2 lbs. (Maiden or races when entered for $20,000 or less not considered.)

Winning Start

Own: Burke Gary W & Timothy R

VALDIVIA J JR (44 4 3 4 .09) $25,000

Dk. b or br m. 5
Sire: Sauce Boat (Key to the Mint)
Dam: One and Only (Victor's Pride)
Br: Copeland Draabon (Ky)
Tr: Mitchell Mike (9 4 2 1 .44)

L 117⁵

	Lifetime Record:	19 5 1 8	$107,101
1995	6 3 1 2	$65,650	Turf	0 0 0 0
1994	4 0 0 2	$9,701	Wet	0 0 0 0
SA	8 3 0 2	$49,300	Dist	13 2 1 6	$50,401

WORKOUTS: Sep 29 Hol 6f fst 1:15⁴ H 8/10 Sep 22 Hol 3f fst :38⁴ H 6/7 Aug 31 Dmr 4f fst :49³ H 15/40 Aug 14 Dmr 6f fst 1:14¹ H 18/23 Jly 27 Dmr 3f fst :36¹ H 4/17

Ferdie Le Grande

Own: Holmes J Stephen

BLANC B (55 4 3 4 .07) $25,000

B. f. 4
Sire: Ferdinand (Nijinsky II)
Dam: Scarp (Damascus)
Br: Bell Stanley (Ky)
Tr: MacDonald Brad (9 1 0 2 .11)

L 112⁵

	Lifetime Record:	8 1 0 1	$23,175
1995	7 1 0 1	$21,600	Turf	2 0 0 0	$4,075
1994	1 M 0 0	$1,575	Wet	0 0 0 0
SA	1 0 0 1	$3,900	Dist	2 0 0 0	$3,450

Bumped, shuffled back start

WORKOUTS: Oct 2 SA 3f fst :38³ H 13/13 Sep 25 SA 5f fst 1:00 H 6/32 Sep 19 SA 5f fst 1:00 H 5/37 Sep 13 SA 4f fst :48⁴ H 2/5 Aug 28 SA 4f fst :46² H 2/13 Aug 11 SA 4f fst :49² H 10/18

Chemolo

Own: McCaslin Robert F

PEDROZA M A (32 4 5 5 .13) $25,000

Ch. f. 4
Sire: Be a Native (Exclusive Native)
Dam: Eager Dusty (Eager Eagle)
Br: Burton Blackwell, Auby Blackwell ,et al. (Cal)
Tr: Keen Dallas E (8 1 1 1 .13)

L 117

	Lifetime Record:	19 7 5 3	$99,515
1995	13 4 5 2	$76,380	Turf	1 0 0 0
1994	4 1 0 1	$18,875	Wet	2 1 0 1	$19,950
SA	0 0 0 0		Dist	15 5 5 2	$80,755

WORKOUTS: ● Sep 25 Hol 3f fst :33³ H 1/9 Aug 24 Dmr 5f fst 1:02² H 44/58 ● Aug 18 Dmr 5f fst 1:00² H 27/61 Aug 12 Dmr 5f fst 1:01¹ H 36/55 Jly 26 Dmr 5f fst 1:03² H 50/65

Sovereign Allez
Own: Haras Libertad
DOUGLAS R R (45 4 11 5 .09) $25,000
B. f. 4
Sire: Sovereign Dancer (Northern Dancer)
Dam: Allez Texas (Shergar)
Br: Oak Cliff Breeders Inc (Ala)
Tr: Polanco Marcelo (4 1 0 0 .25)
L 117

Lifetime Record: 14 2 1 0 $32,265										
1995	6	1	0	0	$16,890	Turf	2	0 0	0	$875
1994	7	1	1	0	$15,375	Wet	2	0 1	0	$3,200
SA	4	0	0	0	$450	Dist	3	1 0	0	$9,350

15Sep95-11Fpx fst 1 1/16 :224 :47 1:124 1:444 3↑ ⒻAlw 37000N2X 63 6 3 31 41¼ 48½ 416 Almeida G F LB 117 14.50 70-16 Sea Of Serenity12012 Slick Silk1202½ China Sky1151½ Fractious gate 8
7Aug95-7Dmr fst 6f :221 :443 :563 1:083 3↑ ⒻAlw 42000N1X 64 4 2 41¾ 55 67 612¾ Black C A LB 117 87.30 85-07 RaduCool1151¼ Stephnie'sRod1175 BlushingHeiress1151 5 wide into lane 8
4Jun95-4Hol fst 6½f :22 :451 1:10 1:162 3↑ ⒻAlw 40000s 71 3 5 32½ 32½ 33½ 26½ Stevens G L LB 117 6.50 80-10 ⒹSllwoodFrn1176½ SvrgnAllz1173 Hllywd'sAct116½ Rail,steadied near 1/8 6
Placed first through disqualification.
16Apr95-4SA wf 6½f ⊗ :222 :454 1:10 1:161 ⒻClm 62500 64 6 4 3½ 41½ 65½ 611¾ Valenzuela F H LB 117 30.30 80-12 Blue Tess1172¾ Sham Pain1151¾ Desert Orchid116nk 4 wide, gave way 6
19Mar95-3SA fst 6f :212 :441 :562 1:091 ⒻAlw 42000N1X 67 5 5 56½ 68 68½ 611 Flores D R LB 118 44.80 80-06 Mock Orange121hd Madder Than Mad121½ Cathy'sDynasty1214½ No threat 6
5Feb95-7SA fm 1 Ⓣ :23 :464 1:111 1:363 ⒻAlw 46000N1X 71 9 2 2hd 2½ 43 64½ Flores D R LB 117 f 18.50 78-17 Political Process120¾ Leasears117hd Shirley Valentine121nk Used up 10
22Dec94-5Hol fm 5½f Ⓣ :221 :452 :58 1:05 3↑ ⒻAlw 35000N2L 75 1 8 75½ 77½ 55 52¼ Flores D R LB 117 9.70 78-20 SydneyExplorer1201 Cathy'sDynasty120½ Cozzenes'Lady119½ Inside bid 9
2Dec94-3Hol fst 6f :221 :453 :58 1:11 3↑ ⒻMd 32000 73 9 1 11½ 11½ 12 12½ Flores D R LB 120 *2.10 85-17 Sovereign Allez1202½ More Amour122nk Run For My Life120½ Driving 9
10Nov94-6Hol my 6½f :223 :461 1:104 1:17 3↑ ⒻMd 32000 69 3 2 11 11½ 2½ 2¾ Valenzuela F H LB 120 1.80 83-12 Tori's Pet118¾ Sovereign Allez1205½ Rullababy1201½ Game inside 8
6Oct94-2SA fst 1 1/16 :233 :482 1:13 1:451 3↑ ⒻMd 32000 58 1 1 1½ 2hd 32 55½ Valenzuela F H LB 118 4.30 64-19 ⒹErinova118hd Functionindisaster1181½ Fast A Foot1181¾ Rail trip 7
WORKOUTS: Oct 12 SA 5f fst 1:01 H 12/43 Oct 6 SA 5f fst 1:003 H 29/60 Sep 30 SA tr.t 4f fst :511 H 2/2 ●Sep 24 SA 3f fst :361 H 1/13 Sep 9 Dmr 4f fst :483 Hg24/46 Sep 3 Dmr 5f fst 1:024 H 54/62

Sidepocketsue
Own: Sardo Tony
PINCAY L JR (60 11 6 9 .18) $25,000
Dk. b or br m. 5
Sire: Mike Fogarty*Ir (Royal and Regal)
Dam: Carols Dewan (Dewan)
Br: Sardo Tony (Cal)
Tr: Dolan John K (—)
L 117

Lifetime Record: 34 5 8 4 $154,032										
1995	7	0	0	1	$15,375	Turf	3	0 0	1	$5,700
1994	13	2	4	2	$68,482	Wet	4	1 1	1	$28,450
SA	10	2	1	2	$58,300	Dist	14	3 5	3	$86,182

18Sep95-11Fpx fst 6½f :222 :454 1:10 1:162 3↑ ⒻⓇPio Pico49k 69 7 7 711 712 79¾ 712 Berrio O A LB 114 b 16.80 85-10 Salta's Pride1222½ Dezibelle's Star1152 Persistant Sal122hd Outrun 7
8Sep95-5Dmr fst 7f :223 :453 1:102 1:231 3↑ ⒻClm 40000 58 5 7 75½ 73¼ 64½ 69 Flores D R LB 117 b 11.50 76-10 Gambling Mistress117hd IslandOrchid117½ Cee'sMaryanne1173 No threat 7
3Aug95-7Dmr fst 6f :213 :443 :571 1:102 3↑ ⒻClm 40000 72 1 9 99¾ 95½ 77 52¾ Flores D R LB 117 b 16.30 86-12 Strong Colors1171 Carol117no Truce In Balance1171½ Improved position 9
16Apr95-5SA wf 6f :212 :45 :572 1:101 ⒻClm 40000 67 8 8 819 810 810 610½ Flores D R LB 116 b 18.10 75-12 Queen Gen1163 Gambling Mistress1161 Fast Reward1164¾ No threat 8
25Feb95-7SA fst 7f :222 :45 1:092 1:22 ⒻⓈWntrSolstice71k 78 6 8 813 812 86½ 48½ Flores D R LB 114 b 46.20 83-13 Pirte'sRevenge115hd SiyhNr1144 PrivtePersusion1154½ Improved position 8
19Jan95-1SA fst 7f :224 :46 1:101 1:23 ⒻClm 50000 66 7 7 57 55½ 46 48½ Nakatani C S LB 116 b 6.80 78-15 Livermore Lady1155 Wee Miss Bee1163½ Valid Betty115no Off step slow 7
5Jan95-7SA my 6f :221 :453 :581 1:111 ⒻClm 40000 70 1 5 511 511 57½ 38½ Flores D R LB 116 b 2.90 72-25 PrideAndPower1165 FstRewrd1173½ Sidepocketsue1167½ Off bit slow, rail 5
19Nov94-2Hol fst 6½f :214 :443 1:091 1:153 3↑ ⒻⓈAlw 36000N2X 66 1 8 815 811 68 59¾ Nakatani C S LB 116 b 7.90 81-10 ⒹFast Reward117nk Miss Lady Bug1151 Scoring Road1173 By tired ones 8
4Nov94-7SA fm *6½f Ⓣ :22 :45 1:09 1:153 3↑ ⒻAlw 42000N2X 69 4 8 1011 1010 1013 1011 Castanon A L LB 116 b 37.10 69-20 Miss Intergreen1104½ Simply Groovy118hd Amy Ride114½ Outrun 10
12Oct94-5SA fm *6½f Ⓣ :212 :434 1:074 1:14 3↑ ⒻAlw 38000N2X 68 1 9 914 914 98½ 38¾ Flores D R LB 116 b 25.00 79-12 Rabiadell116¾ DmeD'onzeHeures1168 Sidepocketsue1161¼ Drifted in late 9
WORKOUTS: Oct 12 SA 5f fst 1:013 H 22/43 Oct 6 SA 3f fst :362 H 9/26 Sep 2 SA 4f fst :501 H 25/28 Aug 19 SA 4f fst :472 H 6/25 Aug 12 SA 4f fst :484 H 9/31 Jly 28 SA 4f fst :484 Hg7/14

Wild Express
Own: Stolich Fran & Ron
DESORMEAUX K J (59 13 8 7 .22) $25,000
B. m. 5
Sire: Wild Again (Icecapade)
Dam: Jean Royale (Real Value)
Br: Baumohl & Calum & Inman & Koester (Ky)
Tr: Sise Clifford Jr (7 0 1 0 .00)
L 117

Lifetime Record: 29 4 4 6 $117,268										
1995	9	0	2	2	$21,565	Turf	3	0 0	1	$7,175
1994	12	2	1	3	$54,508	Wet	2	0 1	1	$9,050
SA	7	1	1	1	$28,400	Dist	14	1 1	3	$39,173

10Oct95-5Fpx fst 6f :221 :46 :581 1:101 3↑ ⒻClm 32000 77 6 2 42 31½ 43¾ 45¾ Pedroza M A LB 116 b 3.40 93-07 Silent Lord116no Chemolo1165 Brumbeau122nk Balked gate 6
16Sep95-5Fpx fst 6f :22 :454 :583 1:113 3↑ ⒻClm 32000 73 5 3 66 42½ 34 2nk Pedroza M A LB 116 b 5.40 91-10 Brumbeau116nk Wild Express116no Sharp Staker1154 Closed gamely 7
30Aug95-5Dmr fst 1 1/16 :222 :46 1:104 1:433 3↑ ⒻClm c-20000 71 10 3 44 1½ 1½ 34½ Desormeaux K J LB 117 b 14.90 79-18 PrettyNetGl1174 GoodLordBrbie117½ WildExpress1172½ Led, outfinished 11
Claimed from Stronach Frank H, Hollendorfer Jerry Trainer
16Aug95-5Dmr fst 1 :214 :45 1:101 1:363 3↑ ⒻClm 25000 61 8 4 33½ 42 72 68½ Pincay L Jr L 117 b 14.20 79-13 April's Benefit117nk Elias Beach1172 A Trifle To Spare1173½ 4 wide 7/8 8
30Jly95-5Dmr fst 6f :213 :444 :571 1:094 3↑ ⒻClm 25000 56 8 3 62½ 75½ 89½ 811¾ Baze R A LB 117 b 9.00 80-07 Icy Luck1181¾ Chemolo117hd Winning Start1171½ Gave way 10
9Jun95-6GG fst 5½f :211 :441 :564 1:033 ⒻClm 35000 57 4 2 41¾ 43 45 59½ Lopez A D LB 116 b *1.70e 82-16 Masterful Dawn1186 Kat Krazy1171 Balla Balla1161½ Through early 6
18Mar95-6GG wf 1 :23 :47 1:111 1:371 ⒻClm c-25000 74 4 2 22 22 22 21½ Espinoza V LB 116 b 2.00 82-18 MadmeBovry1181½ WildExpress116hd GospelMusic1162½ Wide stretch run 5
Claimed from Totman James W, Webb Bryan Trainer
8Mar95-7GG sly 6f :213 :442 :564 1:094 ⒻClm 35000 79 5 1 63¾ 42 31 31 Espinoza V LB 116 b 3.40 89-16 Chemolo1181 Hollyfrankie116hd Wild Express1161 Raced wide 6
3Feb95-3SA fst 6f :213 :443 :563 1:092 ⒻClm c-32000 66 5 1 4¾ 53½ 57½ 59 Almeida G F LB 117 b 7.20 81-12 Fast Reward117no Silent Lord117¾ You'renotlistening118no 4 wide 5
Claimed from Dunn Charles W, Lewis Gary Trainer
16Oct94-1SA fst 6½f :214 :442 1:093 1:161 3↑ ⒻClm 32000 86 6 4 41½ 33½ 31½ 11 Almeida G F LB 116 b 10.40 91-11 Wild Express1161 Sarita Sarita109½ Fast Reward1171 4 wide to turn 7
WORKOUTS: Oct 12 SA 4f fst :503 H 26/29 Aug 27 Dmr 4f fst :492 H 24/37 Aug 21 Dmr 4f fst :503 H 42/50 ●Aug 9 Dmr 4f fst :47 H 1/35 Jly 24 GG 6f fst 1:16 H 5/5

Sharper Bye One
Own: Harrington & Vander Houwen
DELAHOUSSAYE E (51 3 8 9 .06) $25,000
Dk. b or br f. 4
Sire: Sharper One (Drum Fire)
Dam: Nites 'n Bye (Night Time)
Br: Harrington & Vander Houwen (Wash)
Tr: Harrington Mike (4 0 0 0 .00)
L 117

Lifetime Record: 28 4 2 2 $83,345										
1995	7	0	1	1	$14,370	Turf	2	0 0	0	
1994	15	3	1	1	$52,350	Wet	0	0 0	0	
SA	8	2	0	1	$28,950	Dist	10	2 0	1	$34,825

25Sep95-8Fpx fst 6½f :22 :454 1:102 1:164 3↑ ⒻAlw 35640N2X 72 1 4 42½ 4¾ 34 66¼ Castro J M LB 117 14.00 89-09 Valid Symmetry1153½ Ruhling Contessa1151 RegalGentry1121 4 wide 5/16 7
8Sep95-5Dmr fst 7f :223 :453 1:102 1:231 3↑ ⒻClm 40000 57 1 6 54 63 75¼ 79½ Solis A LB 117 17.40 75-10 GmblingMistress117hd IslndOrchid117½ Cee'sMrynne1173 Inside, no rally 7
19Aug95-5Dmr fst 6½f :213 :44 1:083 1:153 3↑ ⒻClm 32000 77 6 8 88½ 76¼ 57½ 25 Solis A LB 117 8.50 88-06 WinningStrt1125 ShrperByeOn117hd GmblingMistrss117nk Awkward start 9
7Aug95-7Dmr fst 6f :221 :443 :563 1:083 3↑ ⒻAlw 42000N1X 78 6 1 64½ 65 54½ 47¼ Solis A LB 117 44.60 91-07 Radu Cool1151¼ Stephanie's Road1175 Blushing Heiress1151 No late bid 8
22Jun95-9Hol fst 6½f :212 :434 1:093 1:161 ⒻClm 25000 74 2 8 710 710 55 32½ Delahoussaye E LB 116 9.90 85-10 SpectculrFort1162 RodBuddy118½ ShrperByeOne116hd Off slow, rail trip 8
3Jun95-1Hol fst 6½f :22 :444 1:093 1:154 ⒻClm 20000 68 5 5 44½ 44½ 43½ 57½ Black C A LB 116 15.60 82-08 Smooth Wine1185½ Musical Pal116hd Toast The Table1161½ No late bid 8
22Jan95-9SA fst 6½f :22 :444 1:09 1:151 ⒻClm 20000 57 8 8 64¾ 76¾ 713 817¾ Pedroza M A LB 115 b 10.80 78-09 You'renotlistening11711 Icy Luck115½ Popcorn Magic1153½ Weakened 12
29Dec94-3SA fst 1 :223 :463 1:113 1:382 ⒻClm 35000 61 1 4 32 42½ 53½ 55½ Pedroza M A LB 113 b 8.30 71-18 Burning Desire117nk Our Passion1151¾ Lady Kariba115hd Weakened 7
21Dec94-1Hol fst 6½f :213 :45 1:103 1:171 ⒻClm 25000 69 6 1 35½ 53¼ 53 42¾ Valenzuela F H LB 116 b 5.00 80-13 Tiger Popcorn114nk Damsela1162 Icy Luck117½ Wide into lane 6
24Nov94-2Hol fst 6½f :22 :444 1:093 1:162 ⒻClm 40000 70 6 6 63¼ 64½ 77½ 66¼ Valenzuela F H LB 115 b 11.70 81-10 MissoulaLula115½ SiyahRelief1152½ GmblingMistress117¾ Wide, no rally 7
WORKOUTS: Oct 10 Hol 5f fst 1:003 H 3/10 Sep 3 Dmr 5f fst 1:002 H 17/62 Aug 3 Dmr 3f fst :353 H 2/22 Jly 28 Dmr 5f fst 1:002 H 7/51

Bandral
Own: Gann Edmund A
NAKATANI C S (66 10 16 12 .15) $25,000
B. f. 4
Sire: Dixieland Band (Northern Dancer)
Dam: General Charge (General Assembly)
Br: Gann Edmund (Ky)
Tr: Frankel Robert (10 1 3 2 .10)
L 117

Lifetime Record: 6 1 2 1 $27,850										
1995	6	1	2	1	$27,850	Turf	0	0 0	0	
1994	0	M	0	0		Wet	1	0 0	1	$3,000
SA	3	0	2	1	$15,000	Dist	4	0 1	1	$11,700

3Jly95-4Hol fst 5½f :214 :451 :574 1:043 3↑ ⒻMd 35000 68 6 3 2hd 1hd 12½ 11¼ Antley C W LB 120 3.30 88-10 Bandral1201¼ Martha's Girl116½ Five O'clock1175 Cleared, held 8
24Jun95-10Hol fst 6f :213 :451 :574 1:112 3↑ ⒻMd 32000 38 6 2 2hd 1hd 2hd 510 Flores D R LB 122 *1.20 73-13 Street Dancing1161½ Mist At Dawning111¾ Picaroon1142 Inside due [illegible]
27May95-10Hol fst 6f :214 :45 :572 1:101 3↑ ⒻMd Sp Wt 68 8 3 1hd 1hd 2hd 510¼ Nakatani C S LB 122 4.20 79-11 Rockroller1154½ RellyTlented122½ DreToBeMe1164 Dueled between foes 10
10Apr95-6SA fst 6f :22 :453 :573 1:093 ⒻMd Sp Wt 83 3 3 1hd 1hd 11 2½ Nakatani C S LB 120 *1.70 88-12 PhrosDiscovery115½ Bndrl1202 BrillintSunlight1201¾ Rail, caught on wire [illegible]
17Mar95-4SA fst 6½f :214 :444 1:102 1:17 ⒻMd 40000 72 6 5 21 1hd 12 21 Romero R P LB 120 3.50 86-09 Plum Flo1201 Bandral1201 Wild And Wonderful1184 Overtaken late 9
3Mar95-2SA wf 6f :214 :454 :582 1:114 ⒻMd 32000 64 5 6 44½ 2½ 21½ 32½ Romero R P B 120 4.30 75-16 House Of Dreams1202 Our Happy Day120½ Bandral1202¾ Off bit slow [illegible]
WORKOUTS: Oct 17 Hol 4f fst :474 H 2/30 ●Oct 11 Hol 5f fst 1:004 H 1/10 Oct 5 Hol 6f fst 1:144 H 5/13 Sep 29 Hol 6f fst 1:151 H 5/10 ●Sep 23 Hol 5f fst 1:002 H 1/24 Sep 17 Hol 5f fst 1:024 H 14/25

Chemolo won by 3½ lengths.

SEVENTH RACE
Santa Anita
OCTOBER 20, 1995

6 FURLONGS. (1.07¹) CLAIMING. Purse $22,000. Fillies and mares, 3-year-olds and upward. Weights: 3-year-olds, 120 lbs. Older, 122 lbs. Non-winners of two races since August 15, allowed 3 lbs. Of a race since September 15, 5 lbs. Claiming price $25,000, if for $22,500, allowed 2 lbs. (Maiden or races when entered for $20,000 or less not considered.)

Value of Race: $22,000 Winner $12,100; second $4,400; third $3,300; fourth $1,650; fifth $550. Mutuel Pool $273,543.00 Exacta Pool $288,325.00 Quinella Pool $55,869.00

Last Raced	Horse	M/Eqt. A.Wt	PP St	¼	½	Str	Fin	Jockey	Cl'g Pr	Odds $1
10ct95 ⁵Fpx²	Chemolo	LB 4 117	2 4	4 1½	3 hd	3½	1 3½	Pedroza M A	25000	1.50
18Sep95 ¹¹Fpx⁷	Sidepocketsue	LBb 5 117	4 7	7	5 1	4½	2²	Pincay L Jr	25000	16.30
25Sep95 ⁸Fpx⁶	Sharper Bye One	LB 4 117	6 6	6 1	7	6 hd	3 hd	Black C A	25000	10.30
15Sep95 ¹¹Fpx⁴	Sovereign Allez	LB 4 117	3 5	5 2½	6 1½	5 hd	4 1½	Douglas R R	25000	30.50
3Jly95 ⁴Hol¹	Bandral	LB 4 117	7 2	2³	2 2½	2 hd	5½	Nakatani C S	25000	6.80
5Oct95 ¹SA¹	Winning Start	LB 5 117	1 3	1 hd	11	1½	6 3½	Valdivia J Jr⁵	25000	1.90
10ct95 ⁵Fpx⁴	Wild Express	LBb 5 117	5 1	3 hd	4 1	7	7	Desormeaux K J	25000	5.90

OFF AT 3:59 Start Good. Won driving. Time, :21⁴, :44⁴, :57², 1:10 Track fast.

$2 Mutuel Prices:

2–CHEMOLO	5.00	3.20	2.40
4–SIDEPOCKETSUE		9.40	4.20
6–SHARPER BYE ONE			4.20

$2 EXACTA 2–4 PAID $54.60 $2 QUINELLA 2–4 PAID $46.60

Ch. f, by Be a Native–Eager Dusty, by Eager Eagle. Trainer Keen Dallas E. Bred by Burton Blackwell, Auby Blackwell, et al. (Cal.)

CHEMOLO settled inside WILD EXPRESS for a half mile, angled out into the stretch, swept to the front in midstretch and pulled clear under a strong hand ride. SIDEPOCKETSUE unhurried off the rail early, angled in for the turn and rallied along the inside for second. SHARPER BYE ONE raced well off the rail early, came wide into the stretch and got the show. SOVEREIGN ALLEZ also raced out from the inside, was no threat to the top pair but just missed the show. BANDRAL a bit reluctant to load, dueled outside WINNING START on the backstretch and turn, but between rivals in midstretch, then weakened. WINNING START held a slim lead inside to midstretch and weakened. WILD EXPRESS outside the winner for a half mile, came a bit wide into the stretch and gave way.

Owners— 1, McCaslin Robert F; 2, Sardo Tony; 3, Harrington & Vander Houwen; 4, Haras Libertad; 5, Gann Edmund A; 6, Burke Gary W & Timothy R; 7, Stolich Fran & Ron

Trainers—1, Keen Dallas E; 2, Dolan John K; 3, Harrington Mike; 4, Polanco Marcelo; 5, Frankel Robert; 6, Mitchell Mike; 7, Sise Clifford Jr

Chemolo was claimed by Auerbach James & Madeleine; trainer, Abrams Barry.
Bandral was claimed by Daley Ronald; trainer, Machowsky Michael.
Winning Start was claimed by Lewis & McCaslin; trainer, Keen Dallas E.
Scratched— Ferdie Le Grande (5Oct95 ¹SA³)

$3 Pick Three (9–7–2) Paid $558.00; Pick Three Pool $68,535.

The stunner was in the fifth, and the huge payoffs weren't confined to Pick Threes. Toll Road won at 27-1, paying $56.60. Seal Your Fate ran second at 48-1 and Kay's Darling third at 21-1. The $2 quiniela paid $812.80, the $2 exacta $1,490.40 and the $2 triple $32,140.80. If Santa Anita had superfecta wagering, it could have been a record one, as 101-1 Bye Bye Saga ran fourth. Keen Rate finished eighth by 10½ lengths after dueling with Toll Road, opening a clear lead and stopping.

FIFTH RACE
Santa Anita
OCTOBER 20, 1995

6½ FURLONGS. (1.14) CLAIMING. Purse $12,000. 3-year-olds. Weight, 120 lbs. Non-winners of two races since August 15, allowed 3 lbs. Of a race since September 15, 5 lbs. Claiming price $12,500, if for $10,500, allowed 2 lbs. (Maiden or races when entered for $10,000 or less not considered.)

Value of Race: $12,000 Winner $6,600; second $2,400; third $1,800; fourth $900; fifth $300. Mutuel Pool $287,306.00 Exacta Pool $215,672.00 Trifecta Pool $261,734.00 Quinella Pool $38,887.00

Last Raced	Horse	M/Eqt.	A	Wt	PP	St	¼	½	Str	Fin	Jockey	Cl'g Pr	Odds $1
6Oct95 ^{1}SA^{5}	Toll Road	LBf	3	115	9	2	$2^{1\frac{1}{2}}$	$2^{\frac{1}{2}}$	$1^{\frac{1}{2}}$	1no	Nakatani C S	12500	27.30
8Oct95 ^{2}SA^{8}	Seal Your Fate	L	3	117	1	11	$9^{1\frac{1}{2}}$	8^{hd}	$4^{1\frac{1}{2}}$	$2^{1\frac{1}{2}}$	Black C A	12500	48.60
13Oct95 ^{2}SA^{5}	Kay's Darling	LB	3	115	7	9	11	$10^{1\frac{1}{2}}$	6^{hd}	$3^{3\frac{1}{2}}$	Toscano P R	12500	21.70
28Sep95 ^{11}Fpx^{4}	Bye Bye Saga	LB	3	113	8	6	$8^{2\frac{1}{2}}$	6^{1}	$7^{\frac{1}{2}}$	$4^{\frac{1}{2}}$	Almeida G F	10500	101.20
8Oct95 ^{2}SA^{5}	Tate Express	LBb	3	115	4	7	4^{hd}	3^{1}	3^{hd}	$5^{\frac{1}{2}}$	Pedroza M A	12500	7.50
6Oct95 ^{1}SA^{2}	Bettor Leaguer	LBb	3	110	10	3	6^{1}	$7^{1\frac{1}{2}}$	8^{1}	$6^{\frac{1}{2}}$	Valdivia J Jr^{5}	12500	5.40
27Sep95 ^{11}Fpx^{6}	Java Lee	LB	3	115	5	10	$10^{1\frac{1}{2}}$	11	10^{1}	7^{4}	Flores D R	12500	23.00
6Sep95 ^{7}Dmr^{2}	Keen Rate	LBbf	3	117	2	4	1^{hd}	$1^{1\frac{1}{2}}$	2^{1}	8^{nk}	Desormeaux K J	12500	1.00
8Oct95 ^{2}SA^{7}	Tomorrow's Flight	LB	3	115	6	1	3^{hd}	4^{hd}	5^{hd}	$9^{1\frac{1}{2}}$	Solis A	12500	5.70
11Oct95 ^{5}SA^{12}	Dasha	B	3	115	3	8	7^{1}	$9^{1\frac{1}{2}}$	11	$10^{\frac{1}{2}}$	Atkinson P	12500	35.50
8Oct95 ^{2}SA^{6}	Shingen Warrior	LB	3	115	11	5	5^{1}	$5^{1\frac{1}{2}}$	$9^{1\frac{1}{2}}$	11	Douglas R R	12500	10.40

OFF AT 3:00 Start Good. Won driving. Time, :21^{3}, :44^{3}, 1:10^{2}, 1:17 Track fast.

$2 Mutuel Prices:				
	9–TOLL ROAD	56.60	20.80	12.60
	1–SEAL YOUR FATE		37.60	16.00
	7–KAY'S DARLING			9.20

$2 EXACTA 9–1 PAID $1,490.40 $2 TRIFECTA 9–1–7 PAID $32,140.80
$2 QUINELLA 1–9 PAID $812.80

Dk. b. or br. g. (Mar), by Toll Key–Meneval's Star, by Meneval. Trainer Polanco Marcelo. Bred by Walsh Adele (Cal).

TOLL ROAD dueled outside KEEN RATE on the backstretch, let that one slip away a bit on the turn, took the lead outside that rival in midstretch, inched clear, then just held off SEAL YOUR FATE under urging. SEAL YOUR FATE off a bit slowly, came off the rail on the turn, four wide into the stretch, lugged inward slightly in midstretch but finished well. KAY'S DARLING unhurried off the rail early, swung wide into the stretch and closed gamely. BYE BYE SAGA off the rail early, raced outside BETTOR LEAGUER on the turn, split rivals into the stretch and lacked the needed rally. TATE EXPRESS went up outside TOMORROW'S FLIGHT leaving the backstretch, raced between foes on the turn, bid inside the winner into the stretch, then weakened. BETTOR LEAGUER wide early, angled in to go between rivals early on the turn, was crowded a bit in midstretch and lacked the needed late kick. JAVA LEE drifted out on the backstretch and raced wide. KEEN RATE sped to the early lead inside, inched clear on the turn, had little left for the stretch, did not return to be unsaddled but was walked off. TOMORROW'S FLIGHT between foes early, found the rail on the backstretch, reamined inside and weakened. DASHA saved ground to no avail. SHINGEN WARRIOR raced wide on the backstretch, outside rivals on the turn, was crowded behind SEAL YOUR FATE in midstretch, and gave way.

Owners— 1, Haras Libertad; 2, Fairmeade Farm; 3, Pinner John E; 4, Flory & Lindsey; 5, Tate Brad, 6, Hanson Stock Farm; 7, Stenger Richard; 8, Mevorach Samuel; 9, Burke Gary W & Timothy R; 10, Garvin Patricia; 11, Takeda Kyohei

Trainers—1, Polanco Marcelo; 2, Molina Mark S; 3, Velasquez Danny; 4, Stepp William T; 5, Baffert Bob; 6, Sise Clifford Jr; 7, Gregson Edwin; 8, Lewis Craig A; 9, Mitchell Mike; 10, Stute Melvin F; 11, Cross David C Jr

Overweight: Seal Your Fate (2), Keen Rate (2).

Java Lee was claimed by Bent Tree Stable; trainer, Searing Jerry L.

Keen Rate was claimed by Alexander Alan; trainer, Villardi Anthony R.

Scratched— Push'm High (9Sep95 ^{10}DMR^{1})

$3 Pick Three (2–3–9) Paid $2,259.30; Pick Three Pool $69,824.

The $3 Pick Three in races 5 through 7 using Toll Road, La Nativa and Chemolo paid $558.00, not bad considering La Nativa paid $3.40 and Chemolo $5.

But wait. If you'd really liked La Nativa and Chemolo, you might have also used them in the Pick Three beginning with the sixth race.

The favorite in the eighth, Ivory Mint, had beaten three of her five rivals in her last start. But that was September 2. She'd worked sharply since, but a horse coming off a seven week layoff might not fire in her first start back.

8 Santa Anita Park

6 FURLONGS

6 Furlongs (1:071) ALLOWANCE. Purse $37,000. Fillies and mares, 3-year-olds and upward bred in California which are non-winners of $3,000 other than maiden or claiming or have never won two races. Weights: 3-year-olds, 120 lbs. Older, 122 lbs. Non-winners of a race other than maiden or claiming, allowed 3 lbs. Of a race other than claiming, 5 lbs.

Ivory Mint

Own: Keith Diane & Harold
MCCARRON C J (34 8 7 5 .24)
Ch. f. 3 (May)
Sire: Key to the Mint (Graustark)
Dam: Iverina (Sir Ivor)
Br: Eclipse Investments (Cal)
Tr: Dupuis Jean-Pierre (—)
L 117

Lifetime Record: 3 1 1 0 $28,750
1995 3 1 1 0 $28,750 | Turf 0 0 0 0
1994 0 M 0 0 | Wet 0 0 0 0
SA 0 0 0 0 | Dist 3 1 1 0 $28,750

2Sep95- 9Dmr fst 6f :22 :45 :57 1:091 3+ Ⓕ[S]Alw 42000N1X 86 9 3 3nk 1hd 11½ 23¼ Stevens G L LB 116 b *1.80 91-07 Swoon River1163¼ Ivory Mint116nk Sassyriver1182¼ Wide trip 10
22Jly95- 2Hol fst 6f :212 :444 :57 1:10 3+ Ⓕ[S]Md Sp Wt 88 5 3 3½ 2hd 11½ 110 Desormeaux K J LB 116 b *1.20 90-17 Ivory Mint11610 Letthelitsisroll1162¼ Powerful Launch1222 Ridden out 6
18Jun95- 2Hol fst 6f :214 :451 :574 1:104 3+ Ⓕ[S]Md Sp Wt 59 3 8 41½ 21 32½ 63 Desormeaux K J LB 116 b 2.20 77-14 Contentment1173¾ VlintVnss1162 BrillintSunlight1223 Came in start, rail 9
WORKOUTS: ●Oct 14 Hol 5f fst 1:001 H 1/23 Oct 7 Hol 5f fst :594 H 2/27 Sep 30 Hol 3f fst :384 H 10/13 Aug 26 Dmr 5f fst :584 H 4/70 Aug 19 Dmr 5f fst 1:021 H 41/50 Aug 12 Dmr 4f fst :482 H 22/53

Time For Saratoga

Own: Buss & Idelson & Rio Vsta Thrbs Inc
DOUGLAS R R (45 4 11 5 .09)
B. f. 4
Sire: Saratoga Six (Alydar)
Dam: Timely Touch (Dr. Fager)
Br: Rio Vista Rancho (Cal)
Tr: Buss Jim (8 0 2 0 .00)
L 117

Lifetime Record: 19 1 3 2 $47,755
1995 16 0 3 2 $43,005 | Turf 3 0 1 0 $8,400
1994 3 1 0 0 $4,750 | Wet 1 0 0 0 $900
SA 7 0 2 0 $18,625 | Dist 5 0 2 0 $12,300

6Oct95- 5SA fst 6½f :213 :44 1:09 1:154 3+ Ⓕ[S]Alw 37000N1X 67 6 4 66 69½ 66½ 55¼ Pedroza M A LB 117 50.40 88-07 Flying Winner1172¾ Rapidlaunch117hd Luz Daniela1192 No rally 7
24Sep95- 9Fpx fst 1 1/16 :231 :472 1:123 1:451 3+ ⒻAlw 12500s 63 7 4 42 54 69½ 610¾ Castro J M LB 115 f 14.50 73-15 That'debeme1163 Don Juan's Gal1151 April's Benefit1183 Weakened 7
2Sep95- 9Dmr fst 6f :22 :45 :57 1:091 3+ Ⓕ[S]Alw 42000N1X 75 8 6 95½ 105½ 95½ 67¼ Valenzuela F H LB 118 f 32.00e 87-07 Swoon River1163¼ Ivory Mint116nk Sassyriver1182¼ By tired ones 10
12Aug95- 5Dmr fm 1 1/16 Ⓣ :233 :48 1:122 1:432 3+ Ⓕ[S]Alw 46000N1X 68 9 7 77½ 85½ 79 712¼ Nakatani C S LB 117 14.00 74-15 Princess Afleet1136 We Got The Dinero117¾ Patriot Star1121 No rally 10
4Aug95- 5Dmr fst 6½f :221 :451 1:094 1:16 3+ Ⓕ[S]Alw 42000N1X 61 5 7 65½ 74¾ 97½ 611¼ Pedroza M A LB 119 7.20 80-08 Hemet Eagle1194 Mary Beverly118½ Rapidlaunch1192 Weakened 10
4Jly95- 8Hol fst 7f :214 :444 1:094 1:222 3+ Ⓕ[S]Alw 40000N1X 72 7 4 53 65½ 45 34¾ Nakatani C S LB 119 2.40 85-10 Contentment117¾ BonjourMdm1164 TimForSrtog1193¾ Late bid outside 7
18Jun95-13Hol fst 6½f :22 :451 1:104 1:173 3+ Ⓕ[S]Alw 40000N1X 67 1 5 53½ 51¾ 51½ 43¾ Pedroza M A LB 118 9.70 78-14 Juliandra114nk Bonjour Madame116¾ We Got The Dinero1202¼ 6
Lacked room lane; blocked, steadied past 1/16
8Jun95- 7Hol fm 5½f Ⓣ :21 :433 :561 1:023 ⒻClm 62500 73 6 3 89¾ 912 910 66 Almeida G F LB 117 6.10 88-06 Ballasecret1141¼ Janet Garrison1171 Lady Evening Belle1171 No rally 10
18May95- 8Hol fst 5½f ⊗ :213 :443 :564 1:031 ⒻClm 62500 71 1 4 49 49 48½ 35¾ Valenzuela P A LB 117 7.70 89-08 SalsaDancer116hd StrongColors1165½ TimeForSaratoga1172¾ Along for 3rd 5
24Apr95- 1SA fm *6½f Ⓣ :222 :45 1:082 1:143 ⒻAlw 42000N1X 85 7 3 42 1½ 11½ 21¼ Nakatani C S LB 117 8.00 84-13 Snowy's Mark1201¼ Time ForSaratoga1176 TashaShanny120hd 4 wide duel 8
WORKOUTS: Sep 19 SA 5f fst 1:024 H 34/37 Jly 30 Dmr 4f fst :49 H 22/54 Jly 23 Dmr 3f fst :372 B 5/11

Aly Sweet

Own: Rochelle Ben
PEDROZA M A (32 4 5 5 .13)
Ch. f. 4
Sire: Alydar (Raise a Native)
Dam: Very Subtle (Hoist the Silver)
Br: Rochelle Ben (Cal)
Tr: Lynch Brian A (1 0 0 1 .00)
L 119

Lifetime Record: 22 1 2 4 $71,125
1995 10 0 2 1 $33,325 | Turf 1 0 0 0
1994 12 1 0 3 $37,800 | Wet 1 0 1 0 $8,400
SA 7 0 1 2 $22,425 | Dist 6 0 0 3 $19,025

2Sep95- 9Dmr fst 6f :22 :45 :57 1:091 3+ Ⓕ[S]Alw 42000N1X 70 2 8 85½ 73¾ 85½ 79¼ Douglas R R LB 120 b 21.70 85-07 Swoon River1163¼ Ivory Mint116nk Sassyriver1182¼ No rally 10
19Aug95- 1Dmr fst 7f :222 :451 1:10 1:224 3+ Ⓕ[S]Alw 42000N1X 74 5 8 85¼ 84¼ 21 21¾ Douglas R R LB 119 b 8.00 85-06 BllOfAck1171¾ AlySwt1193 LondonConnction113hd 4 wide into lane, hung 8
4Aug95- 5Dmr fst 6½f :221 :451 1:094 1:16 3+ Ⓕ[S]Alw 42000N1X 73 4 6 53½ 51¾ 53 46½ Douglas R R LB 122 b 19.90 84-08 HemetEagle1194 MryBeverly118½ Rpidlunch1192 Lacked room into lane 10
14Jly95- 5Hol fm 1 1/16 Ⓣ :23 :464 1:104 1:422 3+ Ⓕ[S]Alw 43000N1X 45 3 2 2½ 2½ 99¾ 1117¼ Almeida G F LB 119 10.40 66-16 BigJune1141¼ WeGotTheDinero119½ AfleetFtle114no Btwn foes, gave way 11
22Jun95- 5Hol fst 1 1/16 :224 :46 1:102 1:443 3+ Ⓕ[S]Alw 43000N1X 75 7 6 66¾ 56½ 57½ 42¾ Almeida G F LB 120 9.30 75-22 Lite 'n Comfy1152 Elias Beach118½ New Bounty118nk 6 wide 7 1/2 8
2Jun95- 3Hol fst 6f :213 :444 :57 1:092 3+ Ⓕ[S]Alw 40000N1X 54 5 6 63½ 54 45½ 316 Almeida G F LB 122 5.10 77-12 Emerald Express12211 Fortunes Destiny1165 AlySweet1221¾ Along for 3rd 7
19May95- 3Hol fst 7f :221 :444 1:091 1:22 3+ Ⓕ[S]Alw 40000N1X 68 6 5 52¾ 32 32 46 Almeida G F LB 122 b 5.40 86-08 Guided Dancer1201¾ Miss Kyama1161¼ It Can B Done1203 Wide to turn 6
17Feb95- 7SA fst 7f :223 :452 1:101 1:224 Ⓕ[S]Alw 42000N1X 40 8 6 63¾ 53½ 64¾ 819¼ Solis A LB 120 b 6.00 68-15 Carol1172¾ Mystical Sky1181 Distant Call1172¼ Broke out, wide 8
29Jan95- 2SA fst 1 :223 :462 1:112 1:362 Ⓕ[S]Alw 46000N1X 76 7 7 79½ 53¾ 45½ 59 Pedroza M A LB 117 b 6.90 78-12 Melrose Wine1172½ Spanish Vixen1172 Carol1171¾ Saved ground 9
7Jan95- 2SA sly 7f :22 :452 1:103 1:243 Ⓕ[S]Alw 42000N1X 78 3 6 510 59 39 27 Pedroza M A LB 120 b 3.00 72-20 Damsela1207 Aly Sweet1202¾ Gold Shivers1206¼ Bumped 6 1/2 6
WORKOUTS: Oct 16 Hol 5f fst 1:00 H 5/29 Oct 10 Hol 6f fst 1:143 H 3/5 Oct 4 Hol 4f fst :503 H 25/34 Aug 26 SA 4f fst :50 B 15/20 Aug 13 SA 5f fst 1:032 H 25/29 Aug 2 SA 3f fst :371 H 3/10

Tabled With Saros

Own: Hughes David R
DESORMEAUX K J (58 13 8 7 .22)
Dk. b or br f. 3 (Mar)
Sire: Never Tabled (Never Bend)
Dam: Sweet Saros (Saros)
Br: Dave R. Hughes (Cal)
Tr: Hess R B (9 0 3 0 .00)
L 115

Lifetime Record: 6 3 0 0 $59,075
1995 3 1 0 0 $30,850 | Turf 0 0 0 0
1994 3 2 0 0 $28,225 | Wet 1 0 0 0 $2,500
SA 2 0 0 0 $3,775 | Dist 3 2 0 0 $35,925

22Sep95-11Fpx fst 1 1/16 :23 :47 1:114 1:434 Ⓕ[S]CTBA Marian48k 67 3 4 42½ 41½ 59½ 513 Douglas R R LB 114 *1.20 78-15 MdToPrfction1165 ShuBzAnn1143 BndThRuhls1144 Reserved, gave way 5
6Sep95- 3Dmr fst 6f :214 :443 :564 1:091 ⒻClm 62500 90 6 2 53½ 41½ 31½ 11¼ Solis A LB 115 4.40 95-08 TabledWithSros1151¼ VlidSymmetry116¾ Bueno115¾ Awaited room turn 6
7Jan95- 8SA sly 7f :221 :441 1:103 1:242 Ⓕ[S]Cal Br Champ109k 58 2 6 79½ 713 510 517¼ Nakatani C S LB 114 12.70 62-20 Cat's Cradle12114 Sound Wisdom1142 Grant Maker117½ Bumped start 7
15Dec94- 1Hol fst 7f :231 :47 1:114 1:243 Ⓕ[R]Alw 40000s 76 5 3 32 31½ 2½ 1nk Solis A LB 119 6.10 81-19 Tabled With Saros119nk Secluded Pugilist1163 Nicolletta116½ Gamely 6
23Nov94- 6Hol fst 6f :222 :46 :581 1:11 Ⓕ[S]Md 32000 63 8 1 2½ 31 2hd 1hd Solis A LB 119 *.90 85-13 TbledWithSros119hd OurSummerBid1193 TwntyTwoJwls119½ Long drive 12
13Oct94- 9SA fst 6f :214 :452 :574 1:102 Ⓕ[S]Md 32000 60 10 5 42 3½ 31 45 Nakatani C S B 117 *3.10 80-13 Piratesleadinglady1172 Nicolletta1171¾ No BountyPaid1171¼ Wide to turn 11
WORKOUTS: Oct 15 SA 4f fst :484 H 21/53 Oct 9 Hol 4f fst :473 H 3/26 Oct 4 Hol 4f fst :493 H 12/34 Sep 18 Hol 4f fst :474 H 3/25 Aug 30 Dmr 6f fst 1:133 H 8/12 ●Aug 24 Dmr 5f fst :584 H 1/58

Linda Lou B.

Own: Altman & Belmonte & Gowing
NAKATANI C S (66 10 16 12 .15)
Dk. b or br f. 4
Sire: Native Prospector (Mr. Prospector)
Dam: Robin's Sailor (Sailing Along)
Br: Belmonte Phillip B & Gowing A F (Cal)
Tr: Mitchell Mike (9 4 2 1 .44)
L 117

Lifetime Record: 16 2 5 1 $74,812
1995 4 0 1 0 $6,675 | Turf 1 0 0 0
1994 9 2 2 1 $54,112 | Wet 1 1 0 0 $12,100
SA 6 1 2 1 $28,375 | Dist 9 2 2 1 $51,807

29Sep95- 8BM fst 5½f :213 :451 :572 1:034 3+ ⒻAlw 25000N1X 75 9 1 2½ 2hd 1hd 22¼ Espinoza V LB 119 6.40 86-16 Rosey's Remark1192¼ Linda Lou B.1192¼ Southern Psychic1191½ Wide trip 10
14Sep95- 6BM fst 6f :224 :461 :581 1:103 3+ ⒻAlw 25000N1X 51 7 3 42½ 51¾ 56½ 510½ Baze R A LB 119 *1.20 77-14 ChisosFlyer1193 Rosey'sRemrk119½ OcnInMotion1193 Rank early, wide 8
2Sep95- 9Dmr fst 6f :22 :45 :57 1:091 3+ Ⓕ[S]Alw 42000N1X 76 5 1 1hd 3nk 42 57¼ Nakatani C S LB 118 10.10 88-07 Swoon River1163¼ Ivory Mint116nk Sassyriver1182¼ Dueled, weakened 10
19Aug95- 1Dmr fst 7f :222 :451 1:10 1:224 3+ Ⓕ[S]Alw 42000N1X 60 4 1 74¾ 73¾ 76½ 64¾ Nakatani C S LB 117 *1.70 79-06 Belle Of Ack1171¾ Aly Sweet1193 London Connection113hd No rally 8
9Dec94- 5Hol fm 5½f Ⓣ :223 :452 :564 1:032 ⒻClm 50000 55 4 10 108¾ 1011 811 812 Stevens G L LB 116 5.30 76-12 Brendas Wildindian1161¾ Antifreeze1161¾ StrongColors1172¼ Off step slow 10
5Nov94- 5SA fst 6½f :22 :45 1:093 1:161 3+ Ⓕ[S]Alw 39000N1X 76 7 1 4¾ 42 33½ 53¾ Antley C W LB 115 *1.20 87-13 Scoring Road1152 Mystical Sky1181 Afleet Floozie115½ 4-wide trip 9
6Oct94- 7SA fst 6½f :213 :441 1:084 1:152 ⒻClm 50000 87 3 1 21½ 24 35 23¼ Nakatani C S LB 118 5.60 91-12 BrendasWildindian1183¼ LindLouB.118½ MissLdyBug116¾ Mild late gain 8
14Sep94- 3Dmr fst 6f :22 :45 :572 1:101 ⒻClm 50000 84 6 1 56½ 75¾ 63½ 1no Nakatani C S LB 115 5.10 90-10 Linda Lou B.115no You'renotlistening115½ Falmora1171 Just up 7
22Aug94- 7Dmr fst 6½f :22 :444 1:092 1:154 ⒻClm 40000 85 5 2 2hd 1hd 2hd 2no Valenzuela P A LB 115 3.30 92-11 Fresh Parsley115no Linda Lou B.115hd Natural Game1151 8
Drifted out, bumped late
4Aug94- 7Dmr fst 6½f :214 :443 1:093 1:162 3+ Ⓕ[S]Alw 41276N1X 67 1 2 1hd 2hd 44½ 48¼ Valenzuela P A LB 115 22.90 81-10 You'renotlistening1171¼ Falmora1152¾ Fresh Parsley1154 Weakened 8
WORKOUTS: ●Oct 15 BM 5f fst :59 H 1/52 Oct 9 BM 4f fst :49 H 12/21 ●Sep 23 BM 3f fst :352 H 1/22 Sep 11 Dmr 4f fst :482 H 11/38 Aug 28 Dmr 5f fst 1:013 H 37/62 Aug 16 Dmr 4f fst :48 H 17/63

Golden Half

Own: Golden Eagle Farm
SOLIS A (77 9 11 14 .12)
Ch. f. 3 (Mar)
Sire: Half a Year (Riverman)
Dam: Golden Darling (Slew o' Gold)
Br: Mabee Mr & Mrs John C (Cal)
Tr: Cenicola Lewis A (10 1 1 3 .10)
L 115

Lifetime Record: 2 1 0 0 $13,225
1995 2 1 0 0 $13,225 | Turf 0 0 0 0
1994 0 M 0 0 | Wet 0 0 0 0
SA 1 0 0 0 $2,775 | Dist 1 1 0 0 $10,450

6Oct95- 5SA fst 6½f :213 :44 1:09 1:154 3+ Ⓕ[S]Alw 37000N1X 68 2 3 1hd 1hd 3½ 45 Solis A B 115 1.90 88-07 Flying Winner1172¾ Rapidlaunch117hd Luz Daniela1192 Inside duel 7
28Aug95- 6Dmr fst 6f :214 :443 :564 1:093 3+ ⒻMd 32000 88 4 2 11 14 16 18¼ Solis A B 118 4.90 93-11 Golden Half1188¼ Milda122¾ Fanfan118nk Handily 12
WORKOUTS: Oct 16 SA 4f fst :473 H 4/35 Sep 28 SA 6f fst 1:122 H 6/25 Sep 22 SA 5f fst :592 H 2/31 Sep 15 SA 4f fst :492 H 17/24 Sep 9 Dmr 4f fst :474 H 11/46 Aug 27 Dmr 3f fst :352 H 4/27

If you thought Ivory Mint was vulnerable, and you were particularly brilliant, you might have bet Pick Threes using La Nativa solely in the sixth, Chemolo alone in the seventh and all six horses in the eighth at a cost of $18. When Aly Sweet won the eighth at 45-1, the $3 Pick Three returned $1,033.50.

EIGHTH RACE
Santa Anita
OCTOBER 20, 1995

6 FURLONGS. (1.07¹) ALLOWANCE. Purse $37,000. Fillies and mares, 3-year-olds and upward t California which are non-winners of $3,000 other than maiden or claiming or have never won two Weights: 3-year-olds, 120 lbs. Older, 122 lbs. Non-winners of a race other than maiden or cl allowed 3 lbs. Of a race other than claiming, 5 lbs.

Value of Race: $37,000 Winner $20,350; second $7,400; third $5,550; fourth $2,775; fifth $925. Mutuel Pool $294,553.20 Exacta $239,602.00 Quinella Pool $44,341.00

Last Raced	Horse	M/Eqt.	A.	Wt	PP	St	¼	½	Str	Fin	Jockey
2Sep95 9Dmr7	Aly Sweet	LB	4	119	3	4	6	6	5 1½	1nk	Pedroza M A
2Sep95 9Dmr2	Ivory Mint	LBbf	3	117	1	6	2 2½	1hd	1 2½	2 2	McCarron C J
22Sep95 11Fpx5	Tabled With Saros	LB	3	117	4	2	4 3½	3 1	2hd	3 5½	Desormeaux K J
29Sep95 8BM2	Linda Lou B.	LB	4	117	5	1	3 2	4 3½	4½	4hd	Nakatani C S
6Oct95 5SA5	Time For Saratoga	LB	4	117	2	5	5 1	5hd	6	5 2	Douglas R R
6Oct95 5SA4	Golden Half	LB	3	115	6	3	1hd	2 1½	3½	6	Solis A

OFF AT 4:28 Start Good. Won driving. Time, $:21^2$, $:44^3$, :57, $1:09^3$ Track fast.

$2 Mutuel Prices:			
3-ALY SWEET	92.00	14.00	3.40
1-IVORY MINT		3.60	2.20
4-TABLED WITH SAROS			2.40

$2 EXACTA 3-1 PAID $200.60 $2 QUINELLA 1-3 PAID $58.20

Ch. f, by Alydar-Very Subtle, by Hoist the Silver. Trainer Lynch Brian A. Bred by Rochelle Ben (Cal).

ALY SWEET outside TIME FOR SARATOGA to the stretch, rallied strongly along the inside through the final furlong t IVORY MINT near the wire. IVORY MINT off a trifle slowly, quickly sprinted up inside GOLDEN HALF, dueled inside that o the stretch, got clear and just failed to hold off the winner. TABLED WITH SAROS drifted out early and again o backstretch, angled in to race inside LINDA LOU B. on the turn and gained the show. LINDA LOU B. floated out a bit early, r off the rail to the turn, outside TABLED WITH SAROS on the bend and lacked a rally. TIME FOR SARATOGA saved gr throughout. GOLDEN HALF floated out a bit early, dueled outside IVORY MINT to the stretch and weakened.

Owners— 1, Rochelle Ben; 2, Keith Diane & Harold; 3, Hughes David R; 4, Altman & Belmonte & Gowing; 5, Buss & Idelson & Rio Vsta Thrbs Inc; 6, Golden Eagle Farm

Trainers—1, Lynch Brian A; 2, Dupuis Jean-Pierre; 3, Hess R B; 4, Mitchell Mike; 5, Buss Jim; 6, Cenicola Lewis A

Overweight: Tabled With Saros (2).

$3 Pick Three (7-2-3) Paid $1,033.50; Pick Three Pool $72,521.

Once again, using all the horses in a field of just six wound up producing a gigantic exotic overlay in the Pick Three, just as it had in our Saratoga example earlier in this chapter, and in the $1,033 Pick Three Saratoga example in chapter three.

Let's look at one more Pick Three. In this one, February 8, 1996, at Aqueduct (races 2 through 4), I picked the winners of the second and third races in the *Gazette*. Both were overlays, and both won easily. I blew the fourth race, but it was a wide open one, a perfect candidate to use all nine horses in betting the Pick Three.

And betting the Pick Three made a lot of sense once a vulnerable favorite, Jido, was way over-bet in the second race.

2 Aqueduct

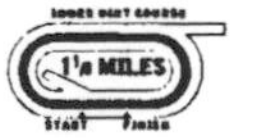

1⅛ MILES. **(Inner Dirt). (1:47¹) CLAIMING. Purse $12,000. 4-year-olds and upward. Weight, 122 lbs. Non-winners of two races at a mile or over since December 31, allowed 3 lbs. Such a race since then, 5 lbs. Such a race since December 9, 7 lbs. Claiming price $12,500, if for $10,500, allowed 2 lbs.**

Coupled – Jido and Royalty Affirmed

Jido
Own: Joques Farm
PEZUA J M (176 28 32 23 .16) $12,500
B. h. 5
Sire: Slew City Slew (Seattle Slew)
Dam: Platinum Pewter (Pewter Prince)
Br: Mara Thomas D (Ky)
Tr: Moschera Gasper S (110 22 24 17 .20)
L 117

Lifetime Record: 24 8 2 2 $119,890

1996	1	0	1	0	$3,100	Turf	9	4	0	0	$61,200
1995	6	2	1	1	$26,850	Wet	3	1	1	1	$14,000
Aqu ⊡	5	3	1	0	$37,600	Dist	1	0	0	0	$1,860

27Jan96- 1Aqu sly 1⅛ ⊡ :243 :484 1:13 1:471 Clm 14000 80 2 2 21½ 21½ 22 21¾ Pezua J M L 115 f *.30 67-26 Northern T.1151¾ Jido1153½ Gin On Land1177¾ Bid, no match 7
17Dec95- 1Aqu my 170 ⊡ :242 :49 1:131 1:414 3↑ Clm 14000 95 3 1 12½ 18 113 113½ Pezua J M L 114 f *.80 89-16 Jido11413 Connecticut Yankee1205 My Only Hope1143½ Ridden out 6
11Oct95- 3Bel fst 1⅛ :232 :463 1:112 1:441 3↑ Clm c-14000 78 6 2 2½ 1hd 2½ 31 Velasquez J L 116 f *1.45 77-24 Dependableness114¾ Royce Joseph116nk Jido1165 Bid, weakened 7
Claimed from Team Martin Stable, Martin Jose Trainer
30Sep95- 1Bel fst 1⅛ :233 :471 1:124 1:453 3↑ Clm 16000 78 3 1 2½ 1½ 21 24 Velasquez J L 120 f *2.60 67-30 Northern T.1164 Jido1201 Royce Joseph1141 Dueled, held well 13
8Sep95- 1Bel fst 1⅛ :232 :462 1:11 1:43 3↑ Clm 18000 90 1 1 14 12 12 11 Velasquez J L 114 4.20 84-17 Jido1141 Pride Prevails1162¾ Ambush Alley1161 Fully extended 10
3Aug95- 5Sar fst 7f :213 :443 1:103 1:244 3↑ Clm 25000 75 9 8 89¼ 118¾ 86¼ 85¼ Velasquez J 113 10.00 77-12 Giant Leap1121 Change Of Fortune112½ Nowhere Man1121 No threat 12
12Jly95- 6Bel fst 1⅛ ⊗ :23 :453 1:094 1:422 Clm 55000 75 1 1 1½ 43½ 47½ 412½ Velasquez J 112 f 11.20 74-23 Dibbs N' Dubbs1163½ Sole Bird1163 Arz114no Used up 5
5Nov94- 1Aqu yl 1⅛ ⓣ :241 :482 1:134 1:464 3↑ Alw 36000N3X 63 7 3 31 2½ 89 914½ Beckner D V5 118 f 2.50 60-25 GoneForRef1171½ Threehrvrdvenue114¾ GrndContinntl1174¾ Forced pace 10
8Oct94- 5Bel fm 1 ⓣ :23 :453 1:094 1:34 3↑ Kelso H-G3 66 5 1 13½ 3½ 710 718¾ Beckner D V 106 f 16.40 72-15 Nijinsky's Gold114no Lure1282¾ A In Sociology117nk Gave way 7
16Sep94- 7Bel fm 1 ⓣ :23 :452 1:083 1:33 3↑ Alw 34000N2X 94 7 1 13 13½ 15 12½ Beckner D V5 108 f 3.40 97-13 Jido1082½ Bermuda Cedar1142 Limited War1132 Driving 11
WORKOUTS: Jan 12 Bel tr.t 4f fst :492 B 9/77 Nov 22 Bel tr.t 4f fst :494 H 11/34

Teston (Arg)
Own: Gonzalez Nectalier A
MADRID A JR (117 12 7 8 .10) $12,500
Dk. b or br h. 5
Sire: Egg Toss (Buckpasser)
Dam: Textura (Major Gundry)
Br: Bello Nelson Moreira (Arg)
Tr: Alvarez Luis C (4 0 0 0 .00)
L 115

Lifetime Record: 24 3 3 4 $27,760

1996	1	0	0	0		Turf	3	0	1	0	$2,404
1995	12	1	0	2	$9,242	Wet	2	0	0	0	$616
Aqu ⊡	1	0	0	0		Dist	2	0	0	1	$1,245

27Jan96- 1Aqu sly 1⅛ ⊡ :243 :484 1:13 1:471 Clm 16000 37 5 7 714 718 728 727½ Madrid A Jr L 117 35.25 42-26 Northern T.1151¾ Jido1153½ Gin On Land1177¾ Trailed 7
2Dec95- 2Aqu gd 1⅛ :464 1:121 1:374 1:492 3↑ Clm 35000 46 7 5 59 68 719 732½ Perez R B 116 41.00 61-07 Private Plan1165½ Imperial Action1141 Gulpha Gorge1162½ No factor 7
19Oct95- 9Bel yl 1¼ ⓣ :49 1:14 1:382 2:034 3↑ Clm 45000 49 9 10 95 1113 1120 1021½ Velasquez J L 114 44.75 47-37 Zester1124 Same Old Wish1161 Summer Senate1127 No factor 11
9Oct95- 3Bel fst 1⅛ :231 :463 1:113 1:442 3↑ Clm 35000 81 5 9 910 95½ 86½ 75½ Velasquez J L 116 29.50 71-23 Le Risky116¾ Baypark116¾ Faviano114no No factor 9
6Jly95 ♦ La Plata(Arg) fst *7f LH 1:271 3↑ Premio Hyfton Pap 33 Rivero A 126 64.50 Vam Top1112½ Teston126½ Petit Breton119 11
Tr: Jorge Marsiglia Alw 7000 *Mid-pack,mild late gain*
27Jun95 ♦ La Plata(Arg) fst *1 LH 1:374 3↑ Especial I Correas 52 Rivero A 121 6.00 Tham Esperado121 At Sea121 Rockstone121 11
Alw 7500 *Mid-pack,finished well without threatening*
6Jun95 ♦ La Plata(Arg) gd *7f LH 1:292 Premio Pretexto 13 Ojeda J 123 3.75 Teston1233 Vam Top123 Rico Type123 12
Alw 7700 *Tracked in 3rd,led 1f out,drew clear*
30Apr95 ♦ La Plata(Arg) my *1¼ LH 2:082 Especial Juan Galvez 46½ Ojeda J 118 4.90 Mat's American118 El Estrellero118 Ecu Estrecho118 13
Alw 12300 *Chased in 6th,evenly late*
13Apr95 ♦ Hipodromo(Arg) fst *1 LH 1:35 Premio Tempero 410½ Valdivieso J 123 31.00 Berliner117 Mixer123 Punt E Mes114 8
Alw 12400 *Towards rear,passed tired ones*
9Apr95 ♦ Hipodromo(Arg) gd *1⅛ LH 1:504 Premio Ventanal 31¾ Falero P 123 25.60 Hondero1231 Bigbone123¾ Teston123 7
Alw 12400 *Tracked in 5th,bid 1-1/2f out,not good enough*
WORKOUTS: Feb 2 Bel tr.t 3f fst :363 H 3/14 Jan 22 Bel tr.t 6f fst 1:19 B 4/5 Jan 6 Bel tr.t 4f fst :521 B 16/22 Nov 11 Bel 4f fst :481 H 12/85

Lord Beer
Own: Perdue Edward C
LUZZI M J (101 23 15 22 .13) $12,500
Dk. b or br g. 6
Sire: Cormorant (His Majesty)
Dam: Bright Tribute (Barrera)
Br: Nielsen Gerald A (NY)
Tr: Perdue Edward C (9 2 0 2 .22)
115

Lifetime Record: 32 8 0 5 $179,183

1996	1	0	0	0		Turf	0	0	0	0	
1995	8	2	0	1	$21,545	Wet	2	0	0	0	$2,760
Aqu ⊡	17	6	0	3	$143,982	Dist	4	1	0	1	$16,200

28Jan96- 10Aqu my 6f ⊡ :223 :454 :574 1:10 Clm 16000 6C 10 1 45 510 713 713½ Chavez J F 117 f 15.70 83-13 Winwithwalker1176½ Opening Prayer1172½ On The Phone114no Gave way 10
8Nov95- 10FL fst 6f :223 :464 1:00 1:132 3↑ Ⓢ Alw 10100N3 58 4 5 61¾ 52½ 64½ 68¼ Davila J R Jr 116 2.95 69-29 Dealer Stands1192¾ MilitaryFriday1192¾ Talc'sRisingSon116½ No response 7
20May95- 9FL fst 170 :234 :481 1:133 1:46 3↑ Ⓢ Alw 10500N3 58 5 2 21½ 33½ 513 514¾ Davila J R Jr 119 *1.40 60-29 Nastifir116no Royal Spruce1167½ Go Buy The Mint1161 Tired 6
1May95- 9FL fst 1 :234 :474 1:151 1:43 3↑ Ⓢ Alw 10000N2 79 4 1 11½ 13 15 17¾ Hulet L 116 f *.70 66-39 Lord Beer1167¾ I'm Tired1162½ Allsing116nk Handily 6
14Apr95- 6FL fst 5f :224 :473 1:01 3↑ Ⓢ Alw 10000N2 60 1 4 33 44½ 55½ 43½ Hulet L 116 f *.75 79-21 Zig Off1161¾ Not So Nice1161½ Allsing116hd No response 6
30Mar95- 6Aqu fst 1 :231 :454 1:102 1:361 Clm 20000 83 6 2 31½ 1½ 2½ 36 Madrid A Jr 114 f 3.85 82-26 AdvncdPlcmnt1223 StudlyDoRight1123 LordBr1143½ Wide bid, weakened 6
15Mar95- 6Aqu fst 1⅛ :473 1:122 1:372 1:503 Clm 40000 78 1 2 21 3½ 75½ 68½ Madrid A Jr 113 f 4.80 78-20 FiveStarGenerl1163½ FlyingGroom1161¾ PrivtePln114½ Forced pace, tired 7
3Mar95- 9Aqu fst 1⅛ ⊡ :481 1:122 1:382 1:512 Clm 25000 93 1 1 11 1½ 13 12½ Madrid A Jr 117 f 5.70 79-26 Lord Beer1172½ Kristen's Baby117½ Mean Pancho1171½ Drew clear 7
16Feb95- 4Aqu fst 1⅛ ⊡ :224 :47 1:124 1:462 Clm 25000 73 3 5 58 22 46½ 48½ Madrid A Jr 117 f 9.10 65-30 Dixieland Music1101½ Kristen's Baby1173 Rohwer1034 Flattened out 7
16Dec94- 1Aqu fst 170 ⊡ :233 :48 1:131 1:43 3↑ Clm 35000 51 7 3 31½ 64½ 713 725 Madrid A Jr 117 fb *3.20 58-30 Country Sky1082 Advanced Placement1172½ Alpstein1178 Tired 7
WORKOUTS: Jan 19 Aqu ⊡ 5f my 1:032 B 1/1 Jan 4 Aqu ⊡ 4f gd :513 B 4/7 Dec 29 Aqu ⊡ 4f fst :512 B 5/5

Home Prospect
Own: Gorsky Bernard
TREJO J (134 17 17 13 .13) $12,500
Ch. g. 4
Sire: Allen's Prospect (Mr. Prospector)
Dam: Honora (Going Straight)
Br: Redmond C. S. Finney (Md)
Tr: Sorey Juan (55 11 12 7 .20)
L 1087

Lifetime Record: 28 3 4 4 $29,540
1996 1 0 0 0 $600 | Turf 0 0 0 0
1995 17 3 3 4 $26,855 | Wet 3 0 0 0 $1,145
Aqu ⊡ 1 0 0 0 $600 | Dist 1 0 0 0 $600

26Jan96- 9Aqu wf 1⅛ ⊡ :481 1:122 1:382 1:52 Clm 10000 75 5 1 11 13 12 42¾ Beckner D V L 113 fb 7.30 73-21 Lightning Runner1132 My Only Hope113no Since You Ask113¾ Weakened 10
28Nov95- 2Med fst 1 :233 :472 1:122 1:384 Clm 7500 72 2 1 13 14 17 19¾ Rocco J L 116 fb 4.70 84-17 Home Prospect1169¾ Military Trail1141 Pokhetailhego1131 Ridden out 8
7Nov95- 4Med sly 170 :223 :463 1:124 1:44 Clm 7500 49 6 1 1½ ½ 59 712¾ Turner T G L 115 fb 3.60 60-30 M J's Sultan115nk Furigno1081 Second City Slew1122¾ Tired 8
14Oct95- 3Med sly 170 :23 :462 1:122 1:452 Clm 10500 43 3 1 11½ 2½ 47½ 410¾ Bravo J L 111 fb 8.30 55-30 Peace Time1175 Raised By Natives1131½ Divine Courage1154 Tired 7
21Sep95- 6Med fst 1 1/16 :232 :464 1:114 1:443 Clm 12500 63 7 3 2½ 31½ 35½ 69 Bravo J L 115 fb 5.50 73-23 Peace Time1157½ Military Trail113hd Pay Buddy107nk Tired 7
12Sep95- 4Med fst 6f :222 :451 :573 1:102 Clm 16000 55 8 2 53½ 53½ 98¾ 98¼ Butler D P L 112 fb 28.10 78-18 Five Alarm116no Catch The Prospect1161¾ So Dazzling1161½ Tired 10
30Aug95- 6Mth fst 6f :223 :46 :584 1:12 Clm 14000 69 4 4 41½ 22 23½ 23¾ Butler D P L 112 fb 10.10 76-22 I Request More1143¾ Home Prospect1122¾ Standing Pat1167 Second best 7
5Aug95- 3Mth gd 6f :221 :451 :584 1:112 Clm 16000 48 2 5 ½ 12 32 39¾ Butler D P L 116 fb 3.80 73-14 Believe In Stanley1162¾ Standing Pat1165¾ Home Prospect1162½ 5
Drifted out some entering lane, tired
16Jly95- 3Mth fst 6f :221 :452 :58 1:111 Clm c-16000 46 4 5 34½ 45½ 47 410 Pezua J M L 116 b 2.40 73-15 IRqustMor1142¾ BlivInStnly111½ ExclusivBlnd1117¾ Broke bit awkwardly 6
Claimed from Gian Richard, Kopaj Paul Trainer
4Jly95- 3Mth fst 6f :222 :454 :583 1:114 Clm c-12500 71 6 2 32 3nk 2hd 2hd Marquez C H Jr L 116 fb *1.40 80-20 Ruxton Rider112hd Home Prospect1165¾ Sea Lure1111 6
Lugged in slightly 1/8, threw head briefly Claimed from Happy Tenth Stable, Tammaro John J III Trainer
WORKOUTS: Jan 6 GS 3f fst :382 B 32/54

Runaway Chris
Own: Acri Sam & Bertuzzi Michael
COLANERI M A (—) $10,500
Gr. g. 9
Sire: Runaway Groom (Blushing Groom–Fr)
Dam: Bear the Load (Vent du Nord)
Br: Stavola M J (NJ)
Tr: Imperio Joseph (27 0 3 5 .00)
L 1085

Lifetime Record: 108 15 14 15 $229,668
1996 2 0 0 0 $360 | Turf 5 0 0 0 $95
1995 19 3 4 4 $43,070 | Wet 17 4 3 2 $54,552
Aqu ⊡ 4 0 0 1 $1,900 | Dist 9 1 3 0 $22,099

26Jan96- 9Aqu wf 1⅛ ⊡ :481 1:122 1:382 1:52 Clm 10000 38 9 7 811 1012 1021 1025½ Migliore R L 114 4.20 51-21 Lightning Runner1132 My Only Hope113no Since You Ask113¾ No factor 10
1Jan96- 9Aqu fst 170 ⊡ :244 :502 1:154 1:453 Clm 12500 65 9 6 62½ 73½ 56½ 56¾ Mojica R Jr L 116 4.00 63-28 Sea Baba1153 Possibilities1131½ My Only Hope113¾ No threat 9
10Dec95- 9Aqu fst 1 1/16 ⊡ :234 :483 1:14 1:47 3↑ Clm 12000 66 7 8 82 63 4¾ 34 Santagata N L 114 5.70 66-29 ConnecticutYankee1162 RoylJudge1142 RunwyChris1141½ Flattened out 11
3Nov95- 9Aqu sly 1⅛ :473 1:13 1:392 1:523 3↑ Clm 14000 74 6 4 42 4½ 56 56½ Santagata N L 116 b *2.20 70-21 Eire Power116nk Hot Slew116½ Judge Time1085 Flattened out 8
22Oct95- 9Bel gd 1 1/16 :234 :472 1:13 1:453 3↑ Clm 16000 80 6 4 3nk 51½ 32 31½ Santagata N L 114 b 13.20 70-22 NorthernT.118½ MyOnlyHope116¾ RunawyChris114¾ Pinch brk, willingly 8
30Sep95- 1Bel fst 1 1/16 :233 :471 1:124 1:453 3↑ Clm 14000 72 8 6 94½ 126½ 77½ 77½ Chavez C R7 L 107 b 12.30 64-30 Northern T.1164 Jido1201 Royce Joseph1141 No threat, wide 13
18Sep95- 9Bel gd 1 :233 :463 1:111 1:362 3↑ Clm 16000 54 9 8 74½ 87 913 915 Beckner D V L 114 11.90 66-15 Le Risky1163 Northern T.1141 Eire Power116nk Pinched break, wide 12
8Sep95- 1Bel fst 1 1/16 :232 :462 1:11 1:43 3↑ Clm 18000 79 3 2 34 22 44 56½ Santagata N L 114 23.00 78-17 Jido1141 Pride Prevails1162¾ Ambush Alley1161 Chased, tired 10
22Jly95- 2Mth fst 1 :234 :463 1:12 1:391 3↑ Clm 12500 67 8 8 910 89 66½ 56¾ Santagata N L 115 5.00 75-20 Eyes Ofa Bandit1151¾ Nice 'n Proud119nk Is ItBlinking1104 Wide, mild bid 9
17Jun95-10Bel fst 1 1/16 :231 :464 1:131 1:454 Clm 14000 61 6 7 75½ 71½ 610 514½ Beckner D V 116 5.00 55-22 EirePower1163½ Dependableness108nk CountrySky11611 Five wide, no rally 12
WORKOUTS: ●Jan 16 Aqu ⊡ 4f fst :494 B 1/6 ●Dec 3 Aqu 3f fst :36 H 1/5

Basque's Ad
Own: Thompson J Willard
CASTILLO H JR (151 17 19 22 .11) $10,500
B. g. 7
Sire: Bounding Basque (Grey Dawn II)
Dam: Ellen's Ad (Our Michael)
Br: O'Mealia Joanne (Ky)
Tr: Thompson J Willard (25 0 3 2 .00)
L 113

Lifetime Record: 57 3 9 10 $96,625
1996 1 0 0 1 $1,100 | Turf 36 3 7 4 $71,960
1995 16 0 2 0 $12,005 | Wet 6 0 1 2 $8,630
Aqu ⊡ 2 0 0 1 $1,100 | Dist 2 0 1 1 $4,300

25Jan96- 2Aqu wf 1⅛ ⊡ :481 1:121 1:382 1:512 Clm 10000 69 1 6 66½ 34 33½ 39¾ Castillo H Jr L 114 b 8.10 70-21 Turkmenistan1083½ Royalty Affirmed1166 Basque's Ad1141¾ No late bid 9
30Dec95- 9Aqu fst 1 1/16 ⊡ :233 :474 1:132 1:474 3↑ Clm 16000 71 8 8 89½ 89½ 86½ 87½ Rocco J L 116 b 36.25 59-24 Glenbeigh114½ Limited War118nk Royce Joseph1143 No factor 10
9Dec95- 3Med fst 170 :231 :47 1:12 1:414 3↑ Clm 16000 82 3 2 21 31 42¾ 41½ Colton R E L 115 b 17.60 82-17 Bo Hagley115nk Will To Reign115¾ Wide Line104nk Even finish 6
18Nov95- 6Med fst 1 1/16 :24 :471 1:113 1:442 3↑ Clm 18000 71 3 5 53½ 56 58 59 Turner T G L 113 b 27.90 74-22 Barbada1153¾ Will To Reign1153½ Charlestown Bill1141½ No factor 7
31Oct95- 6Med fst 170 :231 :47 1:112 1:413 3↑ Clm 20000 75 1 3 31 66 55 56¾ Turner T G L 115 b 15.90 77-16 Doctor Fish1142¾ Will To Reign1142 Charlestown Bill114nk Tired 7
18Oct95- 4Med gd 1 1/16 Ⓣ :23 :473 1:122 1:443 3↑ Clm 25000 81 5 5 54½ 64 55 43½ Turner T G L 115 b 17.90 75-23 Juan In A Million1172½ Polesti115no Royal Ninja1151½ No factor 8
27Sep95- 6Med fst 1 1/16 ⊗ :241 :472 1:111 1:433 3↑ Clm 20000 73 1 4 52½ 44 45½ 46½ Colton R E L 114 b 5.40 81-17 Pitch In111nk Big Al's Country115no Barbada1156 No factor 5
4Sep95- 4Med fm 1 1/16 Ⓣ :241 :481 1:122 1:442 3↑ Clm 25000 82 7 4 57 53½ 52½ 41 McCauley W H L 115 b 4.30 79-17 Blazon Song114no Juan In A Million113no Add The Gold115¾ Needed more 8
23Aug95- 8Mth fm 1⅛ Ⓣ :504 1:144 1:383 1:504 3↑ Clm 20000 85 1 6 53 42½ 53¾ 53¾ Keim-Bruno P M5 L 106 b 19.00 73-21 Ozama117¾ Royal Ninja1151 Amy's Harold115¾ 7
Checked first turn, wide into lane
16Aug95- 4Mth fm *1⅛ Ⓣ :472 1:114 1:372 1:503 3↑ Clm 20000 86 6 7 63 43½ 22 2½ Wilson R L 115 b 3.50 87-15 Big Al's Country108½ Basque's Ad115¾ Comme Pink115no Gamely 8
WORKOUTS: ●Jan 28 Bel tr.t 5f fst 1:03 H 1/8 Dec 2 Med 4f fst :491 B 15/52

Lusty Dancer
Own: Evans Robert S
OTERO W P (25 1 5 4 .04) $10,500
Dk. b or br g. 4
Sire: Gate Dancer (Sovereign Dancer)
Dam: Lusty Lady (Star de Naskra)
Br: Evans Robert S (Fla)
Tr: Cordero Angel Jr (24 2 2 0 .08)
1085

Lifetime Record: 18 3 0 1 $34,656
1996 2 0 0 0 $720 | Turf 1 0 0 0
1995 16 3 0 1 $33,936 | Wet 5 0 0 0 $630
Aqu ⊡ 2 0 0 0 $720 | Dist 4 0 0 1 $2,970

25Jan96- 2Aqu wf 1⅛ ⊡ :481 1:121 1:382 1:512 Clm 10000 42 9 7 79½ 811 818 826¼ Mojica R Jr 114 b 14.40 53-21 Turkmenistan1083½ Royalty Affirmed1166 Basque's Ad1141¾ No factor 9
3Jan96- 4Aqu fst 1 1/16 ⊡ :24 :49 1:15 1:474 Clm 12500 64 3 6 74½ 42½ 44½ 47 Mojica R Jr 116 b 15.80 59-37 Royalty Affirmed1161 Eire Power1164 Uncle Julius1152 No factor 9
18Nov95- 1Aqu fst 1⅛ :491 1:141 1:392 1:522 3↑ Clm 18000 68 7 7 77½ 85¾ 79 810¾ Velazquez J R 113 b 16.70 68-12 Hot Slew1161½ Judge Time1081 Ocean Wave116¾ No factor 9
7Nov95- 9Aqu my 1 :23 :453 1:102 1:363 3↑ Clm 20000 53 4 10 1016 812 916 920¾ Alvarado F T 114 fb 23.00 65-14 Gulpha Gorge1111 Classi Envoy1141½ Gallant Guest1161 No response 11
25Oct95- 1Bel fst 1 1/16 :242 :481 1:124 1:44 Clm 30000 74 1 7 75½ 86¾ 55½ 54¾ Mojica R Jr 114 b 13.80 74-22 Dancing Gator114nk Babylonian115no Can't Believeit1152¾ No threat 8
12Oct95- 5Bel fst 1 :23 :461 1:113 1:38 Clm 22500 62 10 4 53½ 53 46 58¾ Velasquez J 116 b 4.90 66-26 Elk Basin1143 Foxy Jerry116¾ Judge Time1081 Four wide, tired 11
30Sep95- 3Bel fst 1 1/16 :233 :464 1:12 1:461 Clm 30000 73 3 8 813 67 45 43¾ Velasquez J 115 b 6.60 64-30 DancingGator115¾ Cn'tBelieveit112¾ VlidVirgo1082¾ Brk slowly, late gain 8
7Sep95- 5Bel fst 1 1/16 :231 :462 1:111 1:433 Clm 25000 69 9 4 75½ 65½ 312 410¾ Velasquez J 118 b *2.35 71-20 Cn'tBlivit1124½ Dot'sSilvrB.1163½ BoldlyArrognt1162½ Five wide, weakened 10
2Aug95-10Sar fst 1⅛ :473 1:134 1:402 1:534 Clm 35000 68 7 6 67 41½ 43 38 Velasquez J 113 b 6.90 59-30 Babylonian1143 Dancing Gator1165 Lusty Dancer1132 Mild wide rally 8
17Jly95- 5Bel fst 1 :23 :461 1:113 1:374 Clm 20000 76 12 9 86½ 43½ 2½ 13¾ Velasquez J 116 b 4.80 74-19 LustyDncer1163¾ CshThtTicket1131 Dot'sSilverB.1123 Wide, going away 12
WORKOUTS: Dec 24 Bel tr.t 5f fst 1:044 B 42/47

Burt's Bunch
Own: Jujugen Stable
ALVARADO F T (182 27 30 21 .15) $12,500
Dk. b or br g. 4
Sire: Valiant Lark (Buffalo Lark)
Dam: Nature's Witness (Strike Gold)
Br: Carroll Henry L (SC)
Tr: Moore N Calvin (15 1 3 1 .07)
119
Lifetime Record: 6 1 0 1 $10,500
1996 2 1 0 0 $8,520 | Turf 0 0 0 0
1995 4 M 0 1 $1,980 | Wet 2 1 0 0 $7,800
Aqu ⊡ 3 1 0 0 $9,180 | Dist 0 0 0 0

18Jan96- 1Aqu my 1 1/16 ⊡ :224 :463 1:131 1:40 Md 30000 60 6 10 922 58½ 2½ 12 Alvarado F T 116 b 25.25 65-33 Burt's Bunch1162 Uninvited1163 Canonbury115¾ Drew clear 11
3Jan96- 1Aqu fst 1 1/16 ⊡ :233 :481 1:142 1:483 Md 25000 57 3 2 21 2½ 35½ 47 Luzzi M J 120 b 11.30 55-37 Cherokee Assembly1201 Have Faith1205 Kaysfreq't Flyer1201 Tired 9
13Dec95- 1Aqu fst 6f ⊡ :231 :472 1:00 1:122 3↑ Md 25000 52 1 6 65 53½ 46½ 418½ Luzzi M J 119 b 3.65 71-18 Cryptologist1196 Toner's Value119¾ Watrals Gone West121½ No factor 8
30Nov95- 1Aqu sly 1 :224 :453 1:102 1:37 3↑ Md 30000 37 10 2 24 510 715 821½ Santos J A 115 b 4.00 62-17 MeetApproval112¾ LicenseRevoked1168 PrivateMtch119½ Chased, tired 10
15Nov95- 1Aqu gd 7f :221 :444 1:111 1:25 3↑ Md 35000 45 8 3 1hd 31 58½ 613 Luzzi M J 120 b 8.10 66-18 Pleasant Court1205½ Uninvited1174 Jumpin And Jivin117½ Dueled, tired 11
1Nov95- 1Aqu fst 6f :232 :472 :594 1:123 3↑ Md 30000 60 11 4 21 2½ 31 31 Santos J A 117 b 34.75 78-16 Believe It Seventy119½ Dazz117½ Burt's Bunch1171 Forced pace 11
WORKOUTS: Dec 28 Aqu ⊡ 4f fst :50 B 2/6 Nov 27 Aqu 3f fst :352 H 1/3

Firstontherun
Own: Fox Hill Farm
MARQUEZ C H JR (48 3 2 3 .06) $10,500
Ro. c. 4
Sire: Runaway Groom (Blushing Groom)
Dam: Sprawl (First Landing)
Br: Miller Fred J III (Fla)
Tr: Servis John C (19 2 4 2 .11)
L 113
Lifetime Record: 16 2 1 4 $33,270
1996 2 0 0 0 | Turf 2 0 0 0 $470
1995 10 1 1 3 $21,120 | Wet 2 1 0 0 $9,600
Aqu ⊡ 2 0 0 0 | Dist 1 0 0 0

26Jan96- 9Aqu wf 1⅛ ⊡ :481 1:122 1:382 1:52 Clm 10000 67 8 9 1012 912 711 77¼ Marquez C H Jr L 113 fb 11.90 69-21 Lightning Runner1132 My Only Hope113no Since You Ask113½ No speed 10
3Jan96- 4Aqu fst 1 1/16 ⊡ :24 :49 1:15 1:474 Clm 12500 58 9 4 53 53½ 76½ 716½ Marquez C H Jr L 116 fb 4.30 55-37 Royalty Affirmed1161 Eire Power1164 Uncle Julius1152 No rally 9
4Aug95- 6Mth fst 1 70 :224 :47 1:124 1:44 Clm 12500 73 1 5 59¾ 58½ 34½ 32½ Vives L5 L 110 b *1.40 80-23 Peace Time115hd Just Stunning1152½ Firstontherun1105¾ Fin. well 5
3Jly95- 1Mth fst 1 70 :224 :471 1:131 1:443 Clm 16000 63 8 4 31½ 1hd 3½ 32 Wilson R L 115 fb 5.90 77-24 Call Me J. R.1152 Just Stunning115no Firstontherun115½ Willingly 8
16Jun95- 6Bel fst 1 1/16 :233 :464 1:113 1:441 Clm 30000 41 5 5 68 611 714 726 Valdivia J7 106 b 6.40 52-25 Back Ring Al1163½ Myfriendwatts1148 Just Wild114hd No rally 7
21May95- 5Pim fst 1 1/16 :241 :473 1:12 1:452 Clm 25000 66 4 7 64½ 32 32½ 32 Wilson R L 112 *2.30 79-16 Gentleman JimT117no TimsAnchor1172 Firstontherun1121¼ Flattened out 7
22Apr95-12Hia fm 1 1/16 ⓣ 1:424 Alw 16500n1x 46 3 11 97¾ 713 916 918¾ Bisono J L 113 b 40.30 65-11 Tonidar1135 Charcoal Star1131½ Otto's Brother1141½ No threat 12
12Apr95- 9Hia fst 1 1/16 :234 :473 1:121 1:443 Alw 16500n1x 64 2 5 57½ 86½ 59 512 Boulanger G L 113 b 2.30 76-19 PhidisFrieze113¾ HRunsForDddy1214½ WinlotDncr1145½ Failed to menace 9
10Mar95- 8GP gd *1 1/16 ⓣ :234 :474 1:124 1:431+ Alw 32000n1x 64 2 7 810 1011 916 913 Bailey J D 119 b 5.30 79-14 Claramount Hill1191½ Indomable1192½ Count De Monnaie119nk Faltered 10
22Feb95- 5GP fst 1 1/16 :233 :474 1:123 1:46 Clm c-45000 77 7 4 42½ 41¾ 23½ 1½ Bailey J D 115 b 3.80 78-29 Firstontherun115½ No Lollygagging1191½ Dontstopthejukebox1157½ 7
Six wide top str, driving Claimed from Vittese Dominick, Vivian David A Trainer
WORKOUTS: Dec 16 Aqu ⊡ 6f my 1:19 B 1/1 Nov 28 Aqu 4f fst :51 B 6/7 Nov 20 Aqu 4f fst :472 H 2/7 Nov 13 Aqu 4f fst :483 B 2/6

Eire Power
Own: Pollard Damon
BRAVO J (133 12 18 16 .09) $12,500
B. h. 7
Sire: Irish Tower (Irish Castle)
Dam: Exploding Wind (Explodent)
Br: Miron Jodie (Ky)
Tr: Pollard Damon (13 1 1 3 .08)
L 115
Lifetime Record: 77 11 11 18 $207,190
1996 2 0 1 0 $3,240 | Turf 18 2 2 3 $45,010
1995 20 2 3 7 $41,880 | Wet 18 5 1 5 $66,225
Aqu ⊡ 17 4 5 3 $76,330 | Dist 24 4 5 4 $59,780

15Jan96-10Aqu my 1⅛ ⊡ :471 1:13 1:392 1:523 Clm 14000 80 9 10 1112 87 67 45½ Bravo J L 116 fb 9.60 67-26 Hugatag116hd Will To Reign1133½ Copper Mount1192 Belated rally 12
3Jan96- 4Aqu fst 1 1/16 ⊡ :24 :49 1:15 1:474 Clm 12500 74 2 9 99½ 85¾ 33 21 Bravo J L 116 fb *1.95 65-37 Royalty Affirmed1161 Eire Power1164 Uncle Julius1152 Up for place 9
1Dec95- 9Aqu my 1 :223 :451 1:102 1:36 3↑ Clm 18000 66 12 8 119 1010 98 713 Cordova D W L 114 fb 19.70 76-12 Copper Mount1146 Goldstar Road114no Hot Slew120nk No threat 13
18Nov95- 1Aqu fst 1⅛ :491 1:141 1:392 1:522 3↑ Clm 18000 78 6 8 89½ 75 64 43½ Alvarado F T L 116 b 10.10 74-12 Hot Slew1161¾ Judge Time1081 Ocean Wave116¾ Late gain 9
3Nov95- 9Aqu sly 1⅛ :473 1:13 1:392 1:523 3↑ Clm c-14000 84 7 6 710 63 2hd 1nk Davis R G L 116 fb 2.65 77-21 Eire Power116nk Hot Slew116½ Judge Time1085 Inside, driving 8
Claimed from Gullo Gary P & Godash Barbara, Gullo Gary P Trainer
23Oct95- 3Bel fst 1¼ :473 1:123 1:38 2:021 3↑ Clm 30000 64 3 5 52¾ 34 310 317½ Davis R G L 114 b 3.00 65-23 Malmo11614 Best Aquarian1223 Eire Power1144½ No late bid 5
30Sep95- 1Bel fst 1 1/16 :233 :471 1:124 1:453 3↑ Clm c-16000 74 5 10 116½ 104½ 66½ 66½ Luzzi M J L 116 b 3.85 65-30 Northern T.1164 Jido1201 Royce Joseph1141 No rally 13
Claimed from Pollard Damon, Pollard Damon Trainer
18Sep95- 9Bel gd 1 :233 :463 1:111 1:362 3↑ Clm 18000 75 8 11 109½ 78 54½ 34 Stevens G L L 116 b 4.40 77-15 Le Risky1163 Northern T.1141 Eire Power116nk Belated rally 12
8Sep95- 1Bel fst 1 1/16 :232 :462 1:11 1:43 3↑ Clm 20000 82 10 10 1019 98¾ 65 44¾ Smith M E L 116 b 11.00 79-17 Jido1141 Pride Prevails1162¾ Ambush Alley1161 Late gain 10
19Aug95- 1Sar fst 1⅛ :481 1:131 1:393 1:532 3↑ Clm 25000 80 3 5 53½ 56½ 43½ 53 Smith M E 115 b 4.70 66-22 Come On Talc115¾ Ambush Alley115nk My Only Hope115nk Saved ground 8
WORKOUTS: Dec 24 Bel tr.t 4f fst :54 B 146/147

Hot Slew
Own: Lewis Mark J
CHAVEZ J F (238 43 34 34 .18) $12,500
Ch. h. 6
Sire: Slew O' Gold (Seattle Slew)
Dam: Hot Topic (The Minstrel)
Br: Keswick Stables (Va)
Tr: Galluscio Dominic G (29 3 4 6 .10)
L 115
Lifetime Record: 36 5 6 5 $109,760
1996 1 0 0 0 | Turf 3 0 0 0 $1,200
1995 14 2 3 4 $56,340 | Wet 6 0 1 2 $8,910
Aqu ⊡ 13 2 4 2 $64,030 | Dist 11 2 2 1 $29,300

20Jan96-10Aqu gd 1⅛ ⊡ :492 1:14 1:392 1:52 Clm 22500 56 4 5 42 43 812 919½ Alvarado F T L 115 b 3.00 57-29 Geret's Jewel1174½ Electrojet117hd Crafty Coventry1131 Tired 9
27Dec95- 9Aqu fst 1⅛ ⊡ :471 1:123 1:391 1:52 3↑ Clm 25000 85 5 6 54 2½ 1hd 36½ Alvarado F T L 116 5.50 69-30 Copper Mount116hd Ambush Alley1166½ Hot Slew116nk Bid, weakened 9
15Dec95- 9Aqu my 1 1/16 ⊡ :23 :472 1:123 1:433 3↑ Clm 25000 79 9 6 57 43½ 37 39½ Alvarado F T L 114 f 13.00 77-12 Trevelyan1184½ Imperial Action1165 Hot Slew1146 Even finish 12
1Dec95- 9Aqu my 1 :223 :451 1:102 1:36 3↑ Clm c-20000 79 5 6 43 1½ 2hd 36 Pezua J M L 120 6.50 83-12 Copper Mount1146 Goldstar Road114no Hot Slew120nk Bid, weakened 13
Claimed from Davis Barbara J, Moschera Gasper S Trainer
18Nov95- 1Aqu fst 1⅛ :491 1:141 1:392 1:522 3↑ Clm 18000 84 3 2 22 21 11½ 11¾ Pezua J M L 116 *1.80 78-12 Hot Slew1161¾ Judge Time1081 Ocean Wave116¾ Stalked, clear 9
3Nov95- 9Aqu sly 1⅛ :473 1:13 1:392 1:523 3↑ Clm 14000 84 4 3 32 1hd 1hd 2nk Pezua J M L 116 6.20 77-21 Eire Power116nk Hot Slew116½ Judge Time1085 Gamely 8
3May95- 1Bel my 1 1/16 :23 :46 1:11 1:43 Clm 18000 34 6 2 33½ 33 88½ 828½ Pezua J M 112 3.15e 55-16 Churkin116nk Runaway Chris1132½ Mean Pancho1161½ Chased, gave way 9
23Apr95- 3Aqu fst 1 :24 :473 1:131 1:39 Clm 16000 74 5 1 2hd 1½ 2hd 44½ Perez R B5 111 2.45e 69-19 Churkin1161½ Cross Ice Pass1162½ Runaway Chris116¾ Dueled, weakened 9
10Apr95- 9Aqu fst 1 :223 :45 1:094 1:36 Clm 18000 76 1 4 32 42¾ 24 56½ Perez R B5 111 *1.95 83-18 Rogersdividends1164¾ Le Risky1121 Litigation Rex109nk Saved ground 9
22Mar95- 9Aqu fst 1⅛ :473 1:122 1:374 1:583 Alw 34000n2x 82 5 3 21 32½ 55½ 610½ Alvarado F T 114 5.10 76-21 Yourmissinthepoint119no Level Land1116 Krisanova1124 Wide, gave way 6

Royalty Affirmed
Own: Davis Barbara J
PEZUA J M (176 28 32 23 .16) $12,500
Ch. g. 6
Sire: Affirmed (Exclusive Native)
Dam: Eastman Star (Pia Star)
Br: Vreeland James (Cal)
Tr: Moschera Gasper S (110 22 24 17 .20)
L 119
Lifetime Record: 33 3 3 2 $47,335
1996 3 1 1 0 $9,200 | Turf 7 0 0 1 $6,520
1995 16 1 1 1 $24,160 | Wet 3 0 1 0 $3,500
Aqu ⊡ 8 3 2 0 $24,440 | Dist 3 0 1 0 $2,000

26Jan96- 2Aqu wf 1⅛ ⊡ :481 1:121 1:382 1:512 Clm 10000 79 2 2 21½ 11 2hd 23½ Pezua J M L 116 b *2.85 76-21 Turkmenistan1083½ Royalty Affirmed1166 Basque's Ad1141½ Couldn't last 9
11Jan96- 9Aqu fst 1⅛ ⊡ :482 1:13 1:391 1:523 Clm 18000 68 2 5 64½ 86 79 813 Pezua J M L 115 b 13.30 60-33 Limited War117nk GulphaGorge1125 GinOnLand115nk Saved ground, tired 10
3Jan96- 4Aqu fst 1 1/16 ⊡ :24 :49 1:15 1:474 Clm 12500 76 4 3 31½ 1hd 12 11 Pezua J M L 116 b 3.45 66-37 Royalty Affirmed1161 Eire Power1164 Uncle Julius1152 Driving 9
29Dec95- 9Aqu fst 1 3/16 ⊡ :482 1:14 1:401 1:591 3↑ Alw 33000n1x 62 4 2 32½ 32½ 814 921½ Pezua J M L 116 b 46.25 56-36 Then Some1175¾ Opal Moon1164 Point Man1132 Tired 10
14Dec95- 8Aqu wf 1 1/16 ⊡ :224 :472 1:12 1:441 3↑ Alw 33000n1x 62 7 7 51½ 74½ 813 718½ Pezua J M L 115 b 39.95 65-28 Stanley Silver1121½ Treasure Cay1126 Vega's Secret1141 Tired 8
5Nov95- 5Aqu fst 1⅛ :474 1:121 1:38 1:504 3↑ Alw 32000n1x 70 1 1 1½ 2hd 66½ 612½ Alvarado F T L 115 b 47.25 73-16 Poulo1123½ General Gus112no Paragram1126¾ Used in pace 10
29Oct95-10Bel fst 7f :222 :453 1:101 1:222 3↑ Alw 32000n1x 72 7 1 31 74¾ 66¾ 611½ Alvarado F T L 115 b 64.50 77-17 Sunny Rican114nk Big Blue1122 Treasure Cay1135 Brief speed 10
4Jly95-10Bel gd 1 1/16 ⓣ :233 :464 1:11 1:424 Clm 30000 64 2 10 108½ 104 99¾ 912 Santos J A 112 b 26.75 72-17 ⒹBonusAward1161½ KnownRanger112½ Threeharvrdvenue1123¾ No speed 10
23Jun95- 9Bel wf 1¼ ⊗ :491 1:14 1:393 2:05 Clm 30000 76 5 5 43½ 31 42 44 Valdivia J7 105 b 23.80 65-23 Geret's Jewel1163 Brett's Jet116hd Jessup North1221 Four wide, no rally 10
14Jun95- 5Bel gd 1¼ ⓣ :483 1:132 1:381 2:024 3↑ Alw 34000n1x 57 6 4 42½ 53 910 915¾ Valdivia J5 115 b 84.00 58-25 Bluffy1152½ Crafty Virginian110¾ Navillus1125¼ Four wide, gave way 12
WORKOUTS: Jan 22 Bel tr.t 4f fst :54 B 32/32 Nov 16 Bel tr.t 4f fst :494 B 11/28

Blaze Of The Sun

Dk. b or br g. 5
Sire: Halo (Hail to Reason)
Dam: Sol de Terre (Mr. Prospector)
Br: Overbrook Farm (Ky)
Tr: Araya Rene A (32 4 2 2 .13)

Own: R Kay Stable
VELAZQUEZ J R (192 32 19 30 .17) $12,500   115

Lifetime Record: 10 2 1 1 $37,610							
1995	5 0 0 1	$6,460	Turf	0 0 0 0			
1994	5 2 1 0	$31,150	Wet	2 1 0 0	$3,000		
Aqu	5 1 0 1	$23,110	Dist	1 1 0 0	$16,800		

WORKOUTS: Feb 5 Bel tr.4 fst .51³ B 3/6   Dec 24 Bel tr.4 5f fst 1:02 B 13/47   Nov 25 Bel tr.4 3f fst .37² B 6/15   Nov 11 Bel tr.4 3f fst .38¹ B 14/23

Since You Ask

B. g. 4
Sire: Cormorant (His Majesty)
Dam: Grand Marais (Mr. Justice)
Br: Kinsman Stud Farm (NY)
Tr: Shapoff Stanley R (23 1 1 5 .04)

Own: Gallo Michael
RYDOWSKI S R (32 2 0 7 .06) $12,500   L 115

Lifetime Record: 18 4 2 3 $28,830							
1996	2 0 0 1	$1,460	Turf	0 0 0 0			
1995	13 4 2 2	$26,470	Wet	4 1 0 1	$5,840		
Aqu	3 0 0 1	$2,360	Dist	1 0 0 1	$1,100		

WORKOUTS: Feb 6 Bel tr.4 4f fst .51³ B 19/29   Jan 21 Bel tr.4 5f fst 1:06 B 26/71   Dec 26 Bel tr.4 6f fst 1:18³ H 4/7   Dec 18 Bel tr.4 4f fst .52 B 57/78   Dec 8 Bel tr.4 4f fst .36⁴ H 6/16   Dec 5 Bel tr.4 3f fst .38 B 13/29

Personnel Director

Gr. g. 5
Sire: Personal Flag (Private Account)
Dam: Joanie's Hero (King's Bishop)
Br: Curpier Joy E (NY)
Tr: Battles Jake (3 0 0 1 .00)

Own: Canon Helen G & Lazzara Ed
HOLE T M (4 0 0 2 .00) $12,500   L 115

Lifetime Record: 39 7 1 4 $64,710							
1996	3 0 0 1	$2,300	Turf	2 0 0 0			
1995	14 2 0 2	$18,965	Wet	10 2 0 2	$15,319		
Aqu	17 3 0 1	$15,331	Dist	5 0 1 0	$6,380		

WORKOUTS: Dec 29 Pha Al fst .53 B 12/13

Gin On Land

Dk. b or br c. 4
Sire: Copelan (Tri Jet)
Dam: My Mom Ginny (Marvlaw)
Br: Parent Art (Fla)
Tr: Carlesimo Charles Jr (22 3 2 3 .14)

Own: Parent Arthur F
BRAVO J (133 12 18 16 .09) $12,500   L 115

Lifetime Record: 19 2 1 9 $51,080							
1996	2 0 0 2	$3,520	Turf	1 0 0 0			
1995	12 1 0 5	$26,840	Wet	3 0 0 3	$6,285		
Aqu	8 1 0 3	$17,790	Dist	1 0 0 1	$1,815		

WORKOUTS: Dec 31 Aqu ⊡ 5f fst 1:03 B 5/9   Dec 18 Aqu ⊡ 5f fst 1:02¹ H 2/19

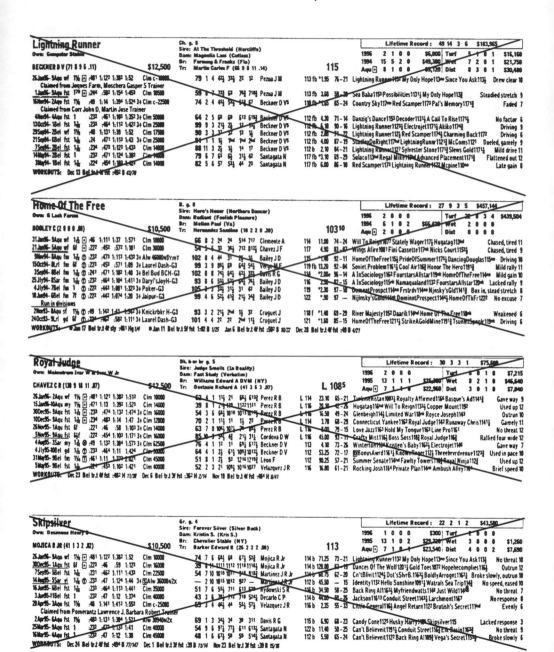

Let me go on the record as saying I've always liked Jido. He's a winning-type horse as shown by his eight for 24 lifetime record. But he had to be on the lead! And it showed in his PPs. His three wins, including one by 13½ lengths two starts back, were wire to wire.

Four starts back, he was second by half a length at the first call and finished second as the 5-2 favorite.

Three starts back, he was again second by half a length at the first call and finished third as the 7-5 favorite.

In his last start, he was sent off at 3-10 and didn't make the early lead, sitting second. And he finished second by a non-threatening 1¾ lengths.

Jido's chances today, and every day, were governed by the absence or presence of other speed horses.

But there was another negative for Jido. This race was at 1⅛ miles, a distance he'd tried just once on dirt and finished out of the money.

Of the 11 other claimers ($10,500 to $12,500) Jido was facing today, he had to deal with Home Prospect, who had raced on the lead in his last four starts. Jido was a classier horse than Home Prospect, but that wasn't the most relevant point here. What was important was that Home Prospect's presence compromised Jido's chances, and enhanced the prospects for all the closers in here. In the *Gazette*, I went with Eire Power, who was dropping a bit and had an excellent record at the distance. I made Hot Slew, another drop down who had beaten Eire Power in two of three recent meetings, my second choice and Jido my third pick.

Jido was bet down to even money. Hot Slew and Eire Power went off at 4-1 and 5-1, respectively.

Conclusion for the Pick Three? Use Eire Power alone or with Hot Slew.

Home Prospect outsprinted Jido to the early lead and held on well for second. Jido was third. Eire Power came from way back as he always did, and won going away by four lengths to return $12.60. Hot Slew fell back to last in the field of 12 and was eased.

SECOND RACE
Aqueduct
FEBRUARY 8, 1996

1⅛ MILES. (Inner Dirt)(1.47^{1}) CLAIMING. Purse $12,000. 4-year-olds and upward. Weight, 122 lbs. Non-winners of two races at a mile or over since December 31, allowed 3 lbs. Such a race since then, 5 lbs. Such a race since December 9, 7 lbs. Claiming price $12,500, if for $10,500, allowed 2 lbs.

Value of Race: $12,000 Winner $7,200; second $2,400; third $1,320; fourth $720; fifth $360. Mutuel Pool $170,405.00 Exacta Pool $258,999.00 Quinella Pool $53,287.00

Last Raced	Horse	M/Eqt.	A.	Wt	PP	St	¼	½	¾	Str	Fin	Jockey	Cl'g Pr	Odds $1
15Jan96 ^{10}Aqu^{4}	Eire Power	Lbf	7	115	10	11	11^{1}	9^{1}	7^{1}	2^{3}	1^{4}	Bravo J	12500	5.30
26Jan96 ^{9}Aqu^{4}	Home Prospect	Lbf	4	110	4	4	1^{5}	1^{6}	1^{7}	1^{3}	$2^{2\frac{1}{2}}$	Trejo J†^{5}	12500	9.20
27Jan96 ^{1}Aqu^{2}	Jido	Lf	5	117	1	1	$2^{1\frac{1}{2}}$	3^{1}	$2^{1\frac{1}{2}}$	3^{5}	3^{3}	Pezua J M	12500	1.05
26Jan96 ^{2}Aqu^{8}	Lusty Dancer	b	4	108	7	5	$9^{1\frac{1}{2}}$	$10^{\frac{1}{2}}$	$11^{\frac{1}{2}}$	$5^{\frac{1}{2}}$	$4^{1\frac{1}{4}}$	Otero W P^{5}	10500	42.00
26Jan96 ^{9}Aqu^{10}	Runaway Chris	L	9	108	5	6	7^{2}	8^{4}	$6^{\frac{1}{2}}$	4^{1}	5^{1}	Colaneri M A^{5}	10500	36.25
26Jan96 ^{9}Aqu^{7}	Firstontherun	Lb	4	113	9	9	6^{3}	6^{3}	$5^{\frac{1}{2}}$	8^{hd}	$6^{1\frac{1}{4}}$	Marquez C H Jr	10500	49.25
18Jan96 ^{1}Aqu^{1}	Burt's Bunch	b	4	119	8	10	$8^{\frac{1}{2}}$	7^{hd}	$8^{\frac{1}{2}}$	7^{1}	7no	Alvarado F T	12500	32.25
28Jan96 ^{10}Aqu^{7}	Lord Beer	f	6	115	3	2	4^{hd}	$4^{\frac{1}{2}}$	$3^{\frac{1}{2}}$	$6^{\frac{1}{2}}$	8^{hd}	Luzzi M J	12500	12.10
26Jan96 ^{9}Aqu^{3}	Since You Ask	Lbf	4	115	12	12	12	12	10^{2}	9^{hd}	$9^{1\frac{1}{2}}$	Rydowski S R	12500	29.00
26Jan96 ^{2}Aqu^{3}	Basque's Ad	Lb	7	114	6	7	10^{1}	$11^{\frac{1}{2}}$	12	10^{8}	10^{13}	Castillo H Jr	10500	36.00
27Jan96 ^{1}Aqu^{7}	Teston-AR	Lb	5	115	2	3	3^{hd}	2^{hd}	$4^{1\frac{1}{2}}$	11^{14}	11	Madrid A Jr	12500	56.50
20Jan96 ^{10}Aqu^{8}	Hot Slew	Lb	6	115	11	8	$5^{3\frac{1}{2}}$	5^{4}	9^{1}	12	—	Chavez J F	12500	4.10

Hot Slew: Eased

OFF AT 12:56 Start Good. Won driving. Time, :22^{1}, :46^{1}, 1:11^{3}, 1:38^{4}, 1:52^{4} Track fast.

$2 Mutuel Prices:				
	10-EIRE POWER	12.60	7.00	3.20
	4-HOME PROSPECT		10.20	4.70
	1-JIDO			2.40

$2 EXACTA 10-4 PAID $116.00 $2 QUINELLA 4-10 PAID $53.00

B. h, by Irish Tower–Exploding Wind, by Explodent. Trainer Pollard Damon. Bred by Miron Julie (Ky).

EIRE POWER unhurried for five furlongs, closed the gap while splitting horses on the turn then sustaining his run, wore down HOME PROSPECT to win going away. HOME PROSPECT sprinted clear in the early stages, opened a wide gap along the backstretch, set a rapid pace into the stretch then weakened in the final furlong. JIDO raced must behidn the pacesetter to the top of the stretch and lacked a strong closing bid. LUSTY DANCER far back for six furlongs, failed to threaten while improving his position. RUNAWAY CHRIS lodged a mild rally five wide on the turn and flattened out. FIRSTONTHERUN went evenly. BURT'S BUNCH checked at the start, and failed to threaten thereafter. LORD BEER raced just off the pace to the turn and tired. SINCE YOU ASK was never close after breaking slowly. BASQUE'S AD was never a factor. TESTON saved ground to the turn and gave way. HOT SLEW raced wide and tired. EIRE POWER and FIRSTONTHERUN wore mud caulks. BURT'S BUNCH bled.

Owners— 1, Pollard Damon; 2, Gorsky Bernard; 3, Joques Farm; 4, Evans Robert S; 5, Acri Sam & Bertuzzi Michael; 6, Fox Hill Farm; 7, Jujugen Stable; 8, Perdue Edward C; 9, Gallo Michael; 10, Thompson J Willard; 11, Gonzalez Nectalier A; 12, Lewis Mark J & Rossi Dawn Marie

Trainers— 1, Pollard Damon; 2, Serey Juan; 3, Moschera Gasper S; 4, Cordero Angel Jr; 5, Imperio Joseph; 6, Servis John C; 7, Moore N Calvin; 8, Perdue Edward C; 9, Shapoff Stanley R; 10, Thompson J Willard; 11, Alvarez Luis C; 12, Galluscio Dominic G

†Apprentice Allowance Waived: Home Prospect (2) **Overweight:** Basque's Ad (1).

Basque's Ad was claimed by Lamarca Stable; trainer, Kiesaris Robert P.

Scratched— Royalty Affirmed (26Jan96 ^{2}AQU^{2}), Blaze Of The Sun (30Dec95 ^{9}AQU^{6}), Personnel Director (31Jan96 ^{9}AQU^{6}), Gin On Land (27Jan96 ^{1}AQU^{3}), Lightning Runner (26Jan96 ^{9}AQU^{1}), Home Of The Free (31Jan96 ^{9}AQU^{7}), Royal Judge (26Jan96 ^{2}AQU^{6}), Skipsilver (26Jan96 ^{9}AQU^{5})

$2 Daily Double (3-10) Paid $50.00; Daily Double Pool $259,274.

The third race, 1¹⁄₁₆ miles for maidens, offered a classic example of the rewards of handicapping a horse's PPs from the bottom to the top.

3 Aqueduct

1 1/16 MILES. (Inner Dirt). (1:41) MAIDEN SPECIAL WEIGHT. Purse $31,000 (plus up to $6,014 NYSBFOA).
4-year-olds and upward. Weight, 121 lbs.

Canonbury
Own: Valentino John
TREJO J (134 17 17 13 .13)
B. h. 5
Sire: He's Bad (Rambunctious)
Dam: Vintage Champagne (Iron Warrior)
Br: Valentino John (NY)
Tr: Ortiz Juan (12 1 0 1 .08)
L 1147
Lifetime Record: 4 M 0 2 $4,620
1996 1 M 0 1 $1,430 | Turf 0 0 0 0
1995 2 M 0 1 $3,190 | Wet 1 0 0 1 $1,430
Aqu ⊡ 2 0 0 1 $1,430 | Dist 1 0 0 1 $1,430

18Jan96-1Aqu my 1 1/16 ⊡ :224 :463 1:131 1:48 Md 35000 52 11 1 14 12 1½ 35 Trejo J7 L 115 b 8.40 60-33 Burt's Bunch1162 Uninvited1163 Canonbury1153¼ Weakened 11
30Dec95-5Aqu fst 6f ⊡ :23 :471 1:001 1:132 3+ Md Sp Wt 37 5 1 41 52¼ 87¾ 913 Nelson D 122 23.50 63-19 Spirited Approval1203¼ Victory Sign120nk Classy Moment1203¾ Tired 9
20Dec95-3Aqu gd 6f :223 :462 :584 1:112 3+ Md Sp Wt 53 4 3 43 44 46 39¼ Nelson D 122 43.00 76-12 Real Silk1203¼ Court Jester1205¾ Canonbury1223 No threat 6
19Jly94-5Bel fst 7f :224 :454 1:112 1:243 3+ Md Sp Wt 48 9 4 42¼ 64¼ 89¼ 715¼ Mojica R Jr 116 22.00 65-19 Crafty Mist1161¼ Level Land1165¼ Fleet Stalker1163¼ Brief speed 9
WORKOUTS: Dec 23 Aqu ⊡ 5f fst 1:052 B 9/10 Nov 17 Aqu 6f fst 1:162 B 2/3

Evil Ways
Own: Hohensee Karl M
VELAZQUEZ J R (192 32 19 30 .17)
B. g. 4
Sire: Once Wild (Baldski)
Dam: Hammerlock (Tom Rolfe)
Br: Karl Hohensee (Fla)
Tr: Hohensee Elisabeth (1 0 0 0 .00)
121
Lifetime Record: 14 M 0 5 $12,970
1995 12 M 0 5 $12,690 | Turf 2 0 0 0 $930
1994 2 M 0 0 $280 | Wet 0 0 0 0
Aqu ⊡ 3 0 0 2 $6,380 | Dist 1 0 0 1 $3,300

14Dec95-11Crc fm *1⅛ ⓣ 1:514 3+ Md Sp Wt 60 10 2 1hd 31 67 86¼ Ramos W S 120 8.50 54-27 Bon Homme120½ Exaltado120½ Great Goltfrid120nk Used on pace 10
18Nov95-11Crc fm *1⅛ ⓣ 1:493 3+ Md Sp Wt 60 4 3 36 32¼ 38 511¼ Rivera J A II 120 13.90 60-20 Lucky Baldski1209 Warn J1201¼ Lawless Lad122nk 10
Bumped repeatedly bkstr, lacked response Placed 4th through disqualification.
31Oct95-2Crc fst 6f :223 :47 1:00 1:133 3+ Md 20000 49 1 4 3½ 32¼ 34 35¼ Ramos W S 120 2.30 74-18 Cut Linen1201¾ Jolie's Fountain1223¼ Evil Ways1204¼ Lacked response 6
20Oct95-10Crc fst 7f :224 :463 1:13 1:263 3+ Md 25000 48 1 4 2hd 1hd 32 38¼ Coa E M 120 *1.70 70-19 The Issue Is Power1206 Yaku1222¼ Evil Ways1202 Weakened 6
17Jun95-9Crc fst 6f :222 :46 :591 1:121 3+ Md Sp Wt 65 2 6 52¼ 64¼ 54¼ 32¼ Boulanger G 115 17.00 83-12 Silver Cyclone1151¾ Cossack Fighter115¾ Evil Ways1151 Late rally 8
17May95-4Bel fst 6f :223 :464 :59 1:112 Md Sp Wt 44 6 4 31 42 66¼ 616 Martinez J R Jr 120 fb 20.10 68-13 Big Blue1206¼ Dazz120¾ Kadrmas1202¼ Wide, tired 7
22Apr95-3Aqu fst 1⅛ :473 1:131 1:404 1:543 3+ Md Sp Wt 43 4 1 12¼ 2½ 48¼ 516 Santagata N 113 fb 16.80 51-21 Crafty Virginian113¼ Bluffy1184¼ Babylonian11310 Used in pace 5
5Apr95-3Aqu fst 6f :224 :471 1:001 1:14 Md 35000 50 8 6 74¾ 65¼ 54¼ 42¼ Santagata N 120 f 7.10e 69-21 Brutish's Secret111¼ Outen Delight120no NakedPrediction1162 Late gain 12
25Mar95-5Aqu fst 1 :234 :473 1:134 1:392 Md Sp Wt 46 5 10 97¼ 109¼ 1112 1020¾ Santagata N 120 27.50 51-25 Treasure Cay120¾ Placid Fund1204¾ Classy Moment1204¼ No response 11
11Mar95-5Aqu fst 1 1/16 ⊡ :24 :483 1:14 1:481 Md Sp Wt 67 4 5 54¼ 42 3nk 3½ Santagata N 120 18.50 63-25 Scooby Dooby Do120½ Gunslinger120no Evil Ways1203 Rallied, hung 7
WORKOUTS: Jan 20 BIS 5f gd 1:012 B 1/1

Uninvited
Own: Evans Robert S
MOJICA R JR (41 1 3 2 .02)
Ch. g. 4
Sire: Gate Dancer (Sovereign Dancer)
Dam: Casual Distinction (Secretariat)
Br: Evans Robert S (Fla)
Tr: Cordero Angel Jr (24 2 2 0 .08)
121
Lifetime Record: 7 M 2 0 $7,220
1996 2 M 1 0 $2,600 | Turf 1 0 0 0 $120
1995 5 M 1 0 $4,620 | Wet 2 0 1 0 $3,020
Aqu ⊡ 2 0 1 0 $2,600 | Dist 2 0 1 0 $2,600

18Jan96-1Aqu my 1 1/16 ⊡ :224 :463 1:131 1:48 Md 30000 57 5 3 310 34¼ 31¼ 22 Mojica R Jr 116 b 20.00 63-33 Burt's Bunch1162 Uninvited1163 Canonbury1153¼ Willingly 11
3Jan96-1Aqu fst 1 1/16 ⊡ :233 :481 1:142 1:483 Md 25000 42 6 8 67 46 510 616¼ Mojica R Jr L 120 b *.80e 46-37 Cherokee Assembly1201 Have Faith1205 Kaysfreq't Flyer1201 No factor 9
30Nov95-1Aqu sly 1 :224 :453 1:102 1:37 3+ Md 35000 52 3 6 68 49 410 513¼ Mojica R Jr 116 b *1.05e 70-17 Meet Approval1123¼ License Revoked1165 PrivateMatch119¾ No late bid 10
15Nov95-1Aqu gd 7f :221 :444 1:111 1:25 3+ Md 30000 61 2 8 73¼ 64 24 29¼ Mojica R Jr 117 b *.85 73-18 PlsntCourt1205¼ Uninvitd1174 JumpinAndJivn117¾ Saved grnd, clear 2nd 11
24Oct95-5Med gd 1 ⓣ :24 :482 1:151 1:414 3+ Md 35000 51 7 5 73¾ 66 619 611 Ferrer J C 117 13.20 53-36 Spare Me Not1153¼ Clear Memories1172 Imarebelrowser113¼ No factor 12
4Oct95-3Bel fst 7f :222 :453 1:101 1:223 3+ Md 35000 48 3 3 53 58¼ 413 422¼ Martinez J R Jr 118 10.90 65-14 Big Tall Dancer1189 Point Man1184 Sunny Lead1158¼ No rally 12
13Sep95-1Bel fst 7f :223 :453 1:103 1:24 3+ Md 35000 60 1 9 51¾ 910 67¼ 48¼ Martinez J R Jr 117 29.75 73-20 HangingRoad1176 DpperDutchmn117nk CrrPool1172 Broke slowly, green 10
WORKOUTS: Dec 24 Bel tr.t 4f fst :53 B 142/147 Nov 10 Bel tr.t 4f fst :501 B 15/26

Double Carr
Own: Snowberry Farm
MADRID A JR (117 12 7 8 .10)
Dk. b or br c. 4
Sire: Carr de Naskra (Star de Naskra)
Dam: Cardenessa (Olden Times)
Br: Snowberry Farm (NY)
Tr: Smith David S (3 0 0 0 .00)
L 121
Lifetime Record: 3 M 0 0 $1,740
1995 3 M 0 0 $1,740 | Turf 0 0 0 0
1994 0 M 0 0 | Wet 1 0 0 0
Aqu ⊡ 2 0 0 0 $1,740 | Dist 0 0 0 0

30Dec95-5Aqu fst 6f ⊡ :23 :471 1:001 1:132 3+ Md Sp Wt 37 6 8 910 99¾ 910 813 Madrid A Jr L 120 fb 67.25 63-19 Spirited Approval1203¼ Victory Sign120nk Classy Moment1203¾ Outrun 9
10Dec95-10Aqu fst 6f ⊡ :23 :472 1:002 1:134 3+ ⓈMd Sp Wt 40 3 6 44¼ 45¼ 48 48¾ Battaglini V L 140 fb 49.50 65-19 Balaka1406 Son Of A Bissett140½ Round Bid1402¾ Stumbled break 11
Amateur rider
30Nov95-4Aqu sly 6½f :223 :463 1:114 1:181 3+ ⓈMd Sp Wt -0 1 11 1115 1122 1137 1142 Migliore R L 120 fb 22.90 47-14 Campocologno120¾ Carr Power1201¾ Port O Gold120hd Broke slowly 11
WORKOUTS: Feb 2 Aqu ⊡ 3f fst :38 B 2/4 Jan 24 Aqu ⊡ 3f fst :403 B 8/8 Nov 23 Aqu 4f fst :504 B 3/4 Nov 14 Aqu 4f fst :404 B 4/5

Sun City
Own: Pultz Martha
CEBALLOS O F (1 0 0 0 .00)
Ch. c. 4
Sire: Tapping Wood (Roberto)
Dam: How's the Dancer (Fiddle Isle)
Br: Dr. Lawrence O. Pultz (Fla)
Tr: Schlesinger Renee A (1 0 0 0 .00)
L 121
Lifetime Record: 10 M 0 1 $6,581
1996 1 M 0 0 $1,860 | Turf 5 0 0 1 $3,793
1995 9 M 0 1 $4,721 | Wet 2 0 0 0 $1,860
Aqu ⊡ 1 0 0 0 $1,860 | Dist 3 0 0 0 $580

27Jan96-3Aqu sly 1⅛ ⊡ :491 1:14 1:40 1:533 Md Sp Wt 57 1 3 33¼ 32¼ 310 419 Ceballos O F L 120 fb 39.50 49-26 PrivteMtch12013 RobbersGold1205 Yoinde'sPet120½ Saved ground, tired 7
5Dec95-5Pha fst 170 :232 :473 1:141 1:473 3+ Md Sp Wt 48 8 5 65¼ 54¼ 54¼ 56¾ Espindola M A L 118 fb 47.40 55-42 Carr Pool1185 Palm Beach Playboy118¾ Showstopper Shorty118¾ Wide 8
4Nov95-4Pha wf 170 :231 :471 1:133 1:451 3+ Md Sp Wt 38 1 3 33¼ 45¼ 58¼ 616¼ Espindola M A L 118 fb 25.10 57-27 ClearMemories117¾ SolitaryShot117no HaveplnwillIrvel1173¼ Came in 1/4 10
14Sep95-5Med fm 1 1/16 ⓣ :222 :463 1:103 1:42 3+ Md Sp Wt 60 6 6 44¼ 47¼ 59 59¼ Ceballos O F L 116 fb 9.50 83-11 Devil's Fire1161¼ Parklo1164¾ Palm Beach Playboy1161¼ Even trip 10
1Sep95-10Mth fm 1 1/16 ⓣ :233 :472 1:123 1:441 + 3+ Md Sp Wt 68 4 1 2¾ 2hd 3nk 33¼ Prado A J L 116 fb 24.60 74-21 J J Hansel116hd Seminole Slew1223¼ Sun City1161¾ Weakened 9
10Aug95-6Del fst 1 :234 :474 1:13 1:403 3+ Md Sp Wt 24 2 4 57¼ 47¼ 513 519¼ Ceballos O F 115 fb 19.30 61-21 Mendel The Duke1157 Bid Yes1224¼ He's Almost Famous1152 Outrun 9
19Jly95-5Del fm *1⅛ ⓣ :481 1:133 1:40 1:524 3+ Md Sp Wt 45 9 2 13 3½ 43¼ 58¼ Ceballos O F 114 fb 10.70 68-16 Tsunaminator1142¾ Dark And Deadly122no Neige D'hiver1153¼ Used up 9
21Jun95-5Del fm 1 ⓣ :231 :463 1:11 1:37 3+ Md Sp Wt 43 4 6 59¼ 610 512 48¼ Jones E L 113 fb 8.40 83-09 Lear Classy1138 Rawlings Comet122no Pleasant Wizard113¼ In close 11
7Jun95-5Del fm 1 1/16 ⓣ :232 :471 1:113 1:431 3+ Md Sp Wt 46 1 9 86¾ 69¼ 610 612¼ Jones E L 113 f 44.20 78-14 Tiny Puddies113¾ Hero In Me113¾ Agapae1226¼ No menace 12
22May95-3Hia fst 1 1/16 ⊗ :233 :473 1:121 1:453 3+ Md Sp Wt 4 3 8 85¾ 1020 1026 1036¼ Nunez E O 113 f 32.30 46-21 Vany's Crusader1135 Midnite Danzig123nk Garnett Road1134¼ No factor 11
WORKOUTS: Jan 26 GS 3f fst :36 B 4/38 Jan 23 GS 4f fst :49 B 8/47 Jan 18 GS 1 gd 1:50 B 1/1 Jan 5 GS 5f fst 1:034 B 13/14 Jan 2 GS 4f my :503 B 2/5

Back Country Boy
Own: Silverbell Farm
CORDOVA D W (167 22 15 26 .13)
Ch. g. 6
Sire: Overskate (Nodouble)
Dam: Lady Temperence (Temperence Hill)
Br: Catella de Delley Jean de & Silver R S (NY)
Tr: Levine Bruce N (48 3 8 2 .06)
L 121
Lifetime Record: 11 M 3 0 $19,870
1996 2 M 1 0 $8,370 | Turf 2 0 0 0
1995 4 M 1 0 $6,000 | Wet 3 0 0 0 $930
Aqu ⊡ 2 0 1 0 $8,370 | Dist 1 0 1 0 $7,440

27Jan96-3Aqu sly 1⅛ ⊡ :491 1:14 1:40 1:533 Md Sp Wt 51 3 2 2½ 21 412 523 Cordova D W L 120 4.20 45-26 Private Match12013 Robbers Gold1205 Yolande's Pet120½ Forced pace 7
6Jan96-4Aqu fst 170 ⊡ :234 :484 1:153 1:461 Md Sp Wt 80 5 4 74 53 2½ 22¼ Cordova D W L 121 32.00 65-33 Voodoo Spell1212¼ Back Country Boy1215¼ Robbers Gold12110 Best of rest 9
30Nov95-4Aqu sly 6½f :223 :463 1:114 1:181 3+ ⓈMd Sp Wt 34 6 4 54¼ 43¼ 76¼ 714 Velazquez J R 122 14.50 75-14 Campocologno120¾ CrrPower1201¾ PortOGold120hd Four wide, flattened 11
5Nov95-1Aqu fst 6½f :23 :471 1:121 1:183 3+ ⓈMd Sp Wt 47 2 4 31½ 72¾ 87¼ 912¾ Bailey J D 122 4.10 74-11 Club Bud120nk All For You1225 Toni's Stargallant1221¾ Brief speed 12
8Oct95-1Bel fst 6f :224 :464 :59 1:12 3+ ⓈMd Sp Wt 40 1 3 32 42 56¼ 68¾ Bailey J D 122 *1.60 72-17 Winloc'sZachary119no Sacket'sSix1194 SonOfABissett119nk Chased, tired 9
9Sep95-3Bel fst 6f :23 :471 :593 1:121 3+ ⓈMd Sp Wt 57 7 3 3nk 2hd 2½ 21¼ Bailey J D 121 *2.55 79-19 ChrubBuck1141¼ BckCountryBoy121¼ TsunmSmmy117¾ Dueled, held 2nd 12
7Oct93-5Bel fst 6f :224 :47 :594 1:124 3+ ⓈMd Sp Wt 62 4 9 73¼ 52¼ 32 22¼ Sweeney K H 119 b 54.40 73-22 Twelve Cylinders1192¼ Back Country Boy119hd Mr. Decker1222¾ Willingly 13
22Sep93-7Bel my 7f :224 :462 1:122 1:261 3+ ⓈMd Sp Wt 42 5 10 63¼ 63¼ 56 718¾ Sweeney K H 118 b 40.50 61-26 Lake118nk Sweet Ralph1184 Gifted Traven1182 No threat 13
7Aug93-7Sar gd 1⅜ ⓣ :511 1:423 2:083 2:464 3+ Md Sp Wt — 9 2 1011 — — — Carr D 117 b 61.20 — 27 Stayed Too Long1221¼ Toasty A.1225 Lyons Hall1176¼ Pulled up 10
26May93-7Bel fm 1¼ Ⓣ :493 1:151 1:39 2:022 3+ Md Sp Wt 14 1 1 12 74 716 730 Santos J A 115 b 26.50 48-19 Shades Of Silver115nk Noble Sheba1155 Musical Storm1241¼ Used in pace 9
WORKOUTS: Jan 22 Aqu ⊡ 4f fst :483 H 1/3 Dec 31 Aqu ⊡ 3f fst :373 B 2/5 Nov 23 Aqu 5f fst 1:021 B 3/4

Robbers Gold
Own: Ritzenberg Milton
LUZZI M J (181 23 15 22 .13)
B. g. 4
Sire: Strike Gold (Mr. Prospector)
Dam: Fun Til Dawn (Grey Dawn II (Fr))
Br: Ritzenberg Milton (Va)
Tr: Johnstone Bruce (15 2 3 2 .13)
L 121
Lifetime Record: 8 M 1 2 $15,490
1996 2 M 1 1 $9,610 Turf 0 0 0 0
1995 6 M 0 1 $5,880 Wet 1 0 1 0 $6,200
Aqu ⊡ 6 0 1 2 $14,590 Dist 2 0 0 1 $3,410

27Jan96-3Aqu sly 1⅛ ⊡ :491 1:14 1:40 1:533 Md Sp Wt 66 5 5 45 43 210 213¾ Luzzi M J L 120 b 4.30 54-26 PrivteMtch12013 RobbersGold1205 Yolnde'sPet120¾ No match, clear 2nd 7
6Jan96-4Aqu fst 1 70 ⊡ :234 :484 1:153 1:461 Md Sp Wt 71 7 5 42½ 2½ 33½ 37¾ Luzzi M J L 121 b 3.40 59-33 VoodooSpell1212¾ BckCountryBoy1215½ RobbersGold12110 Bid, weakened 9
17Nov95-6Aqu fst 1 :232 :464 1:122 1:383 3+ Md Sp Wt 67 7 3 31½ 41½ 43½ 54¼ Davis R G L 118 b 11.50 68-27 Recorded1183 Prodigal Son1183¼ Musical Connection118¾ Stalked, tired 7
8Apr95-3Aqu fst 1⅛ :47 1:12 1:393 1:54 Md Sp Wt 43 7 6 67 812 89¼ 816½ Davis R G 120 b 12.90 53-22 Bob's Prospect120¾ Personal Matter1201¾ Cozy Drive1205 No threat 8
11Mar95-5Aqu fst 1 1/16 ⊡ :24 :483 1:14 1:481 Md Sp Wt 42 3 4 43½ 52¼ 710 715½ Luzzi M J 120 5.30 48-25 Scooby Dooby Do120½ Gunslinger120no Evil Ways1203 Dropped back 7
25Feb95-2Aqu fst 1⅛ ⊡ :484 1:141 1:412 1:552 Md Sp Wt 60 7 2 2½ 21 22 31½ Luzzi M J 122 3.25 58-32 LismoreBoy1221¼ Bbylonin122nd RobbrsGold1222½ Forced pace, weakened 8
3Feb95-5Aqu fst 6f ⊡ :231 :473 1:01 1:142 Md Sp Wt 52 2 10 813 85¾ 74½ 54¼ Luzzi M J 122 16.00 67-25 MountainOfLaws1223½ PrivateMtch117no LismoreBoy122½ Pinched break 10
22Jan95-2Aqu gd 6f ⊡ :223 :46 :582 1:112 Md Sp Wt 41 6 6 610 68 511 513¾ Luzzi M J 122 4.40 72-11 CountrySquir122¾ SrtogFonz1158 MrHwkins1222½ Broke slowly, greenly 6
WORKOUTS: Jan 21 Bel tr.t 5f fst 1:033 B 15/31 Dec 31 Bel tr.t 5f fst 1:01 H 2/32 Dec 14 Bel tr.t 6f fst 1:15 H 1/3 Dec 4 Bel tr.t 6f fst 1:144 B 2/4 Nov 28 Bel tr.t 4f fst :482 B 4/42

Invaluable
Own: Green Leonard C
LEON F (57 6 2 7 .11)
B. g. 4
Sire: Meadowlake (Hold Your Peace)
Dam: Valid Lady (Valid Appeal)
Br: Stark Fran & Ray (Ky)
Tr: Orseno Joseph (28 6 2 3 .21)
L 121
Lifetime Record: 1 M 0 0 $0
1996 1 M 0 0 Turf 0 0 0 0
1995 0 M 0 0 Wet 1 0 0 0
Aqu ⊡ 1 0 0 0 Dist 0 0 0 0

21Jan96-4Aqu wf 6f ⊡ :224 :462 :59 1:112 Md Sp Wt –0 10 3 65 915 1018 1027½ Chavez J F L 121 b 6.70 62-07 Amazonia Dancer1215½ Aga Aga1211¼ Ed's Bull Child1161½ Done early 10
WORKOUTS: Feb 2 Bel tr.t 4f fst :51 B 30/39 ●Jan 26 Bel tr.t 5f fst 1:01 Hg 1/13 Jan 12 Bel tr.t 3f fst :40 B 42/43 Jan 5 Bel tr.t 4f fst :513 B 15/30 Dec 23 Bel tr.t 5f fst 1:00 Hg 4/37 ●Dec 8 Med 5f fst 1:013 Bg 1/9

Victory Sign
Own: Trombly Wayne
MIGLIORE R (160 28 26 18 .18)
Dk. b or br g. 4
Sire: With Approval (Caro)
Dam: Fissure (Tentam)
Br: Live Oak Stud (Fla)
Tr: Kiesaris Robert P (27 5 4 3 .19)
L 121
Lifetime Record: 2 M 1 0 $5,800
1996 1 M 0 0 Turf 0 0 0 0
1995 1 M 1 0 $5,800 Wet 1 0 0 0
Aqu ⊡ 2 0 1 0 $5,800 Dist 0 0 0 0

21Jan96-4Aqu wf 6f ⊡ :224 :462 :59 1:112 Md Sp Wt 10 2 6 55 53½ 814 823½ Migliore R L 121 b *1.80 67-07 Amazonia Dancer1215½ Aga Aga1211¼ Ed's Bull Child1161½ Tired 10
30Dec95-5Aqu fst 6f ⊡ :23 :471 1:001 1:132 3+ Md Sp Wt 60 9 3 51¼ 41¼ 22½ 23½ Migliore R L 120 b 13.00 72-19 Spirited Approval1203½ Victory Sign120nk Classy Moment1203½ Held place 9
WORKOUTS: Jan 11 Bel tr.t 4f fst :523 B 38/45 Dec 23 Bel tr.t 5f fst 1:021 B 13/37 Dec 13 Bel tr.t 5f fst 1:004 H 6/33 Dec 4 Bel tr.t 4f fst :50 B 21/38 Nov 28 Bel tr.t 4f fst :494 B 20/42 Nov 22 Bel tr.t 3f fst :361 B 4/24

Yolande's Pet
Own: Scheftel Herbert
CHAVEZ J F (238 43 34 34 .18)
Ch. c. 4
Sire: Woodman (Mr. Prospector)
Dam: Courtney's Day (Roberto)
Br: Little Marvin Jr (Ky)
Tr: Veitch John M (6 0 0 2 .00)
L 121
Lifetime Record: 12 M 0 3 $13,980
1996 1 M 0 1 $3,410 Turf 3 0 0 0 $1,920
1995 9 M 0 2 $10,570 Wet 3 0 0 2 $7,860
Aqu ⊡ 4 0 0 1 $5,240 Dist 3 0 0 1 $4,420

27Jan96-3Aqu sly 1⅛ ⊡ :491 1:14 1:40 1:533 Md Sp Wt 58 4 4 610 611 515 318¾ Chavez J F L 120 6.20 49-26 Private Match12013 Robbers Gold1205 Yolande's Pet120¾ No threat 7
15Dec95-6Aqu my 1¼ ⊡ :494 1:15 1:404 2:054 3+ Md Sp Wt 49 5 6 69 58 514 521¾ Maple E L 119 b 4.10 77-12 Then Some1194 Private Match1198 Devon's Tune1191 No factor 7
5Nov95-4Aqu fst 1⅛ :484 1:134 1:393 1:521 3+ Md Sp Wt 66 11 11 1110 86 46½ 37 Maple E L 119 b 9.80 72-16 Excelleet1195¾ Then Some1191¾ Yolande's Pet1192 Mild wide rally 11
2Oct95-4Bel gd 1 1/16 T :242 :481 1:131 1:451 3+ Md Sp Wt 70 5 9 99½ 99¾ 77½ 45 Maple E L 118 b 10.80 65-26 AbsolutePlesure118nk Devon'sTune118nk Cellulrconnction1184½ Mild gain 10
18Sep95-4Bel my 1 1/16 ⊗ :23 :461 1:104 1:431 3+ Md Sp Wt 73 3 8 78 57½ 44½ 32¾ Maple E L 117 b 50.80 81-23 WildNightOut1171½ ProdiglSon117¾ Yolnd'sPt117hd Checked break, wide 8
21Jun95-5Bel fm 1¼ T :48 1:133 1:39 2:031 3+ Md Sp Wt 51 4 12 1219 86 810 813½ Smith M E 113 b 30.75 59-18 African Dancer1121 Banquet114hd Devon's Tune1121¾ Broke awkwardly 12
3Jun95-5Bel fm 1 T :231 :461 1:11 1:353 3+ Md Sp Wt 52 8 10 109¾ 106¾ 811 811¾ Davis R G 113 b 42.80 73-17 ForestThunder1141½ NorthernKing106nk TheGreekOn1135 Checked break 10
15Apr95-3Aqu fst 7f :221 :452 1:112 1:242 Md Sp Wt 32 2 8 76½ 810 813 823½ McCauley W H 121 b 38.75 59-17 Twosie Stamp1211¼ Fidgetyfeet1213 Cat Be Nimble121hd No threat 10
1Feb95-5Aqu fst 1 1/16 ⊡ :243 :494 1:154 1:492 Md Sp Wt 32 2 5 43½ 45 514 619 Madrid A Jr 122 b 19.40 39-28 Thayer1221¾ Glenbeigh117nk Wakeupthedevil11518 Broke slowly, wide 7
16Jan95-6Aqu gd 1 1/16 ⊡ :24 :484 1:143 1:462 Md Sp Wt 45 5 9 75½ 74½ 57½ 513 Madrid A Jr 122 b 60.25 60-20 ScreenOscar1223 HiddenVideo1225 Wakeupthedevil1155 Pinched break 10
WORKOUTS: Feb 2 Bel tr.t 3f fst :383 B 13/14 Jan 22 Bel tr.t 5f fst 1:05 B 15/19 Dec 31 Bel tr.t 4f fst :51 B 47/60 Dec 13 Bel tr.t 4f fst :492 B 43/70 Nov 26 Bel tr.t 4f fst :50 B 41/65 Nov 16 Bel 3f fst :38 B 9/16

Tiberian Gold
Own: Goldstein Morton
OTERO W P (25 1 5 4 .04)
Dk. b or br g. 7
Sire: Bold Agent (Bold Bidder)
Dam: Our Loveline (Rambunctious)
Br: Morton Goldstein (NY)
Tr: Goldstein Morton (9 0 1 1 .00)
116^5
Lifetime Record: 21 M 3 2 $20,640
1996 1 M 0 0 Turf 1 0 0 0
1993 12 M 2 2 $18,000 Wet 5 0 1 0 $5,610
Aqu ⊡ 7 0 0 1 $2,460 Dist 5 0 0 2 $5,700

21Jan96-4Aqu wf 6f ⊡ :224 :462 :59 1:112 Md Sp Wt 7 3 8 1016 1019 916 924½ Madrid A Jr 121 39.50 65-07 Amazonia Dancer1215½ Aga Aga1211¼ Ed's Bull Child1161½ No speed 10
13Oct93-1Bel gd 1¼ ⊗ :484 1:144 1:413 2:09 3+ Md Sp Wt 67 5 5 56 32 2½ 2hd Bisono C V 122 2.40 46-30 Luciano P.119hd Tiberian Gold12212 Count Badger1224½ Hung 5
1Oct93-1Bel fst 1 1/16 :232 :462 1:113 1:451 3+ Ⓢ Md Sp Wt 67 7 11 97½ 74¾ 35 32½ Leon F5 117 20.30 73-25 Normal Star119½ Sweet Ralph1192 Tiberian Gold1175 Wide turn 13
22Sep93-7Bel my 7f :224 :462 1:122 1:261 3+ Ⓢ Md Sp Wt 42 8 6 129½ 119½ 1010 811 Leon F5 117 f 15.20 61-26 Lake118nk Sweet Ralph1184 Gifted Traven1182 No factor 13
6Sep93-6Bel fst 7f :23 :462 1:122 1:254 3+ Ⓢ Md Sp Wt 46 5 10 1215 1112 86½ 63½ Lovato F Jr 122 45.90 64-19 Sorabosia1181 Sweet Ralph1183 Ti Dye1182½ Late gain 13
6May93-9Bel gd 1 1/16 T :233 :473 1:123 1:44 3+ Ⓢ Md Sp Wt 34 5 11 117¼ 105¾ 86½ 718½ Bravo J 124 7.40 57-19 Noble Romancer1245 Jacsonzac115no Stopped Silence1151 Broke slowly 12
22Apr93-9Aqu my 1⅛ ⊗ :493 1:152 1:414 1:554 3+ Md Sp Wt 60 1 2 22 2½ 29 27 Bravo J 124 f 5.00 50-40 GroomedToWin1157 TiberianGold1245 NobleRomncer1243½ Second best 7
9Apr93-3Aqu fst 1 :233 :472 1:124 1:39 3+ Md 35000 65 2 8 83½ 73½ 41½ 41½ Bravo J 124 12.50 67-29 BigCrouser111no RetirementAccount115nk Crter'sGold1151½ 5-Wide, hung 8
26Mar93-3Aqu fst 1 1/16 ⊡ :242 :492 1:141 1:463 Md 35000 54 4 6 41½ 32½ 33½ 37 Bravo J 122 9.70 65-23 SaratogaStorm1184¾ NobleRomncer1182½ TiberinGold1221½ Bid weakened 9
12Mar93-5Aqu fst 1 1/16 ⊡ :24 :482 1:142 1:472 Md 45000 59 5 7 73½ 56 45 49½ Santiago A 118 39.20 58-32 All Canadian1183½ Personal Draw1282½ Saratoga Storm1184 Saved ground 9
WORKOUTS: Jan 12 Bel tr.t 3f fst :392 B 36/43 Jan 6 Bel tr.t 5f fst 1:04 Bg 6/6 Dec 30 Bel tr.t 4f fst :52 B 43/48 Dec 24 Bel tr.t 3f fst :372 B 25/51 Dec 18 Bel tr.t 3f fst :39 B 24/30

If you look at Back Country Boy's most recent PP, fifth by 23 lengths on a sloppy track, and glanced at his zero-for-11 record, and noted that he was a New York-Bred taking on open company at the advanced age of six, you might have tossed him out quickly. But you'd have missed the boat.

Start with his bottom two PPs and toss them because they were on the turf back in 1993. But note that on September 22, 1993, he was a distant seventh on a muddy track. In his last '93 start on a fast track, he was second at 54-1 in a field of 13 New York-Breds.

He obviously had physical ailments, since he didn't return to race until September 9, 1995, when he was bet down to 5-2 despite the huge layoff and was second. He lost his next three starts against New York-Breds, the final one on a sloppy track.

But on January 6, 1996, he was moved up to open company, stretched out to a mile and 70 yards and given Lasix. At 32-1, he was a strong second, beating third-place finisher Robbers Gold by 5½ lengths. Bet down to 4-1 in his last start, he ran that distant fifth, losing to Robbers Gold by 10 lengths. But it was on a sloppy track! As the *Form* showed and his PPs verified, he'd raced three times on a wet track and never been in the money. So he couldn't handle an off track. Then, don't forget to subtract the two losses on turf. On a fast track, he had made six starts and finished second three times. He had shown in his race two starts back that, with Lasix, he was indeed competitive in open company.

Robbers Gold had been beaten soundly by Back Country Boy on a fast track, then bounced back to beat him on a sloppy track when he was second by 13½ lengths.

Back on a fast track today, bettors made Robbers Gold the 2-1 favorite in a field of 10.

Back Country Boy, my pick in the *Gazette*, won by seven lengths at a good 9-2, returning $11.80. Evil Ways held on for second at 10-1, and Robbers Gold, my second pick in the *Gazette*, was third.

THIRD RACE   1¼ MILES. (Inner Dirt)(1.41) MAIDEN SPECIAL WEIGHT. Purse $31,000 (plus up to $6,014 NYSBFOA). 4-year-olds and upward. Weight, 121 lbs.

Aqueduct
FEBRUARY 8, 1996

Value of Race: $34,720 Winner $22,320; second $6,200; third $3,410; fourth $1,860; fifth $930. Mutuel Pool $186,259.00 Exacta Pool $317,428.00

Last Raced	Horse	M/Eqt. A.Wt	PP	St	¼	½	¾	Str	Fin	Jockey	Odds $1
27Jan96 3Aqu5	Back Country Boy	L	6 121	6	4	7⁷	7¹½	3½	1³	1⁷½	Cordova D W	4.90
14Dec95 11Crc8	Evil Ways		4 121	2	1	1¹½	1¹	1¹½	2⁶	2⁶	Velazquez J R	10.00
27Jan96 3Aqu2	Robbers Gold	Lb	4 121	7	6	5½	3¹	4¹½	3¹½	3ʰᵈ	Luzzi M J	2.40
27Jan96 3Aqu3	Yolande's Pet	Lb	4 121	10	11	10¹½	9²½	8³½	7¹½	4ⁿᵏ	Chavez J F	8.30
30Dec95 5Aqu8	Double Carr	Lbf	4 121	4	10	11	11	9³½	8⁹	5⁴	Madrid A Jr·	96.75
27Jan96 3Aqu4	Sun City	Lbf	4 121	5	8	8³	8⁹	6³	5½	6²	Ceballos O F	62.00
18Jan96 1Aqu3	Canonbury	Lb	5 116	1	2	2ʰᵈ	2¹½	2²½	4¹	7³½	Trejo Jt⁵	3.05
18Jan96 1Aqu2	Uninvited	b	4 121	3	3	4¹	4ʰᵈ	5½	6½	8⁷	Mojica R Jr	8.90
21Jan96 4Aqu8	Victory Sign	Lb	4 121	9	7	6¹	6½	7²½	9²	9	Bravo J	8.80
21Jan96 4Aqu10	Invaluable	Lb	4 121	8	5	3¹½	5½	11	11	—	Leon F	51.25
21Jan96 4Aqu9	Tiberian Gold		7 116	11	9	9³½	10¹	10²	10⁸	—	Otero W P⁵	41.00

Invaluable:Eased; Tiberian Gold:Eased

OFF AT 1:23 Start Good. Won driving. Time, :23, :47⁴, 1:13¹, 1:39², 1:45⁴ Track fast.

$2 Mutuel Prices:

6-BACK COUNTRY BOY	11.80	6.60	3.90
2-EVIL WAYS		10.80	6.10
7-ROBBERS GOLD			2.90

$2 EXACTA 6-2 PAID $121.00

Ch. g, by Overskate–Lady Temperence, by Temperence Hill. Trainer Levine Bruce N. Bred by Catella de Delley Jean de & Silver R S (NY).

BACK COUNTRY BOY unhurried early while saving ground, launched a rally between horses leaving the far turn, took charge in upper stretch and drew away while being kept to the task. EVIL WAYS sprinted clear on the first turn, set the pace along the rail into upper stretch and held well for the place. ROBBERS GOLD raced just off the pace while three wide to the turn, and lacked a strong closing bid. YOLANDE'S PET outrun for six furlongs, failed to threaten while improving his position. DOUBLE CARR checked at the start and was never close thereafter. SUN CITY raced just behind the winner while between horses to the turn and lacked a further response. CANONBURY angled outside the pacesetter entering the backstretch, chased to the turn and gave way. UNINVITED up close early while saving ground, gave way on the turn. VICTORY SIGN raced in good position along the backstretch, gave way on the turn. INVALUABLE was finished early and eased in the stretch. TIBERIAN GOLD was outrun and eased late. BACK COUNTRY BOY, ROBBERS GOLD, YOLANDE'S PET, DOUBLE CARR and CANONBURY wore mud caulks.

Owners— 1, Silverbell Farm; 2, Hohensee Karl M; 3, Ritzenberg Milton; 4, Scheftel Herbert; 5, Snowberry Farm; 6, Pultz Martha; 7, Valentino John; 8, Evans Robert S; 9, Trombly Wayne; 10, Green Leonard C; 11, Goldstein Morton

Trainers— 1, Levine Bruce N; 2, Hohensee Elisabeth; 3, Johnstone Bruce; 4, Veitch John M; 5, Smith David S; 6, Schlesinger Renee A; 7, Ortiz Juan; 8, Cordero Angel Jr; 9, Klesaris Robert P; 10, Orseno Joseph; 11, Goldstein Morton

†Apprentice Allowance Waived: Canonbury (2).

I wasn't right about the fourth race, picking Ask Shananie,
a shipper from Suffolk.

4 Aqueduct

1 MILE 70 YARDS (Inner Dirt). (1:39³) CLAIMING. Purse $30,000 (plus up to $5,820 NYSBFOA). Fillies and mares, 4-year-olds and upward. Weight, 123 lbs. Non-winners of two races at a mile or over since January 4, allowed 2 lbs. Such a race since then, 4 lbs. A race since December 16, 6 lbs. Claiming price $50,000, for each $5,000 to $40,000, allowed 2 lbs. (Races where entered for $35,000 or less not considered.)

Ask Shananie

Own: Campbell Gilbert G

Dk. b or br m. 5
Sire: Shananie (In Reality)
Dam: Ask Directions (Darby Creek Road)
Br: Campbell Gilbert C (Fla)
Tr: Allard Edward T (9 0 3 1 .00)

KING E L JR (M 0 3 1 .00) $50,000 L 117

Lifetime Record:	36 11 5 4	$209,654
1996	1 0 0 1	$2,500	Turf	3 0 0 0	$750
1995	15 5 2 3	$66,240	Wet	7 3 0 2	$51,640
Aqu⊡	5 2 1 0	$69,302	Dist	18 7 2 2	$138,544

Dancer's Gate

Own: D M Glory Stable

B. m. 6
Sire: Gate Dancer (Sovereign Dancer)
Dam: Lilya's for Real (In Reality)
Br: Fuller Peter B (Fla)
Tr: Mettinis Louis N (ZZ 1 1 1 .05)

LEON F (57 6 2 7 .11) $50,000 L 117

Lifetime Record:	49 9 4 7	$234,123
1996	2 0 0 1	$3,300	Turf	4 0 0 0	
1995	20 1 2 3	$79,588	Wet	10 3 1 5	$98,235
Aqu⊡	15 3 2 2	$78,283	Dist	15 3 3 3	$76,540

Ruth's Revenge

Own: Gumpster Stable

Gr. m. 5
Sire: Far Out East (Raja Baba)
Dam: Vibes (Tudor Way)
Br: Jones Roger II & Penn Frank Jr (Ky)
Tr: Lopez Daniel J (—)

CASTILLO R E (—) $50,000 L 117

Lifetime Record:	24 5 5 5	$82,601
1995	8 1 2 1	$28,540	Turf	12 2 3 2	$43,361
1994	16 4 3 4	$54,061	Wet	1 1 0 0	$12,600
Aqu⊡	5 3 2 2	$52,098	Dist	3 1 0 1	$15,740

Minetonightsfirst

Own: Jim Tim Stables

B. m. 5
Sire: D'Accord (Secretariat)
Dam: Mine Tonight (Upper Nile)
Br: O'Brien James P (NY)
Tr: O'Brien Leo (54 1 5 4 .02)

BRAVO J (133 12 18 16 .08) $50,000 L 117

Lifetime Record:	14 3 2 0	$30,570
1995	6 0 1 0	$11,380	Turf	2 0 0 0	$1,750
1994	6 2 1 0	$15,190	Wet	1 0 0 0	$2,220
Aqu⊡	6 0 1 0	$15,380	Dist	3 0 0 0	$6,540

Miracle Zone

Own: Rich Jill P

BECKNER D V (71 8 9 6 .11) $40,000

Dk. b or br m. 6
Sire: Zoning (Hoist the Flag)
Dam: Baymira (Buffalo Lark)
Br: Rich Jill P & John C (NY)
Tr: Kott Donna M (—)

L 113

	Lifetime Record:	27 3 4 5	$33,345
1996	2 0 2 0	Turf	12 1 1 4	$10,480
1995	11 2 1 1	Wet	4 1 0 0	$6,500
Aqu	1 0 4 0	Dist	7 1 1 1	$10,400

31Jan96–5Suf fst 1   :251 :49 1:17 1:443   ④Alw 13720nx3x   63 2 6 6¾ 64 54   Bermudez J E   LB 116 b 6.20   64–30   BelieveInDoris116¾ MircleZone116½ NiffyDme116¾   4w 2nd, crr'd out str 6
21Jan96–5Suf fst 170   :241 :481 1:144 1:461   ④Alw 13720nx3x   68 5 5 51¾ 24 2½   Bermudez J E   LB 116 b 31.10   75–29   RefinedCollen11⁶¹ MircleZone116¹½ BlvnIaDoris116¹²   Slow start, outside 7
13Dec95–5Suf fst 1   :252 :504 1:172 1:45   ④Alw 12740nx3L   58 3 5 42 31¾ 3¾   Bermudez J E   LB 116 b 14.40   59–37   MiracleZone116¾ FullOfSkil16¾ RussinEnsign116ᵉᵈ   Carried wide into str 8
10ec95–5Suf fst 1   :233 :471 1:453 1:463 3+ ④Alw 12740nx3L   46 1 2 2¹ 3⁵ 6¹⁰ 4¹³   Bermudez J E   LB 119 b 21.10   38–49   True Style116ʰᵈ Russian Ensign116³ Vinnieanome116⁴   Dueled inside 9
12Nov95–6Aqu wf 1¼ ⊕ :482 1:15 1:404 1:53² 3+ⒼSAlw 34000n2x   46 8 10 10⁹ 9¹⁴ 5⁴⁶   Chavez J F   L 173   32.25   45–29   A Day ToRemember119½ Katie'sFlag113⁸ Elocat'sBurglar112⁹   No factor 10
16Oct95–9Rkm fm 1   ⊕ :23 :481 1:41 1:462 3+ ④Alw 11760nx3L   61 1 6 6¹² 64½ 66½ 54½   Thompson W A   LB 116 b 5.50   73–22   Loshellez116½ Maria Rosa116¹ Diplodelightful11⁴½   Tired inside 10
40ct95–10Rkm sly 1   ⊕ :23 :481 1:162 1:493 3+ ④Alw 10780nx2L   66 5 5 34½ 1½ 1⁵ 1⁵½   Thompson W A   LB 117 fb 3.80   75–15   Miracle Zone117⁵ DanceAllNight116⁴ Vinnieanome116¾   Rail, ridden out 7
18Sep95–8Rkm my 1¼ ⊕ :24 :481 1:132 1:46⁴ 3+ ④Alw 10780nx2L   — 6 1 3½ 6¹⁰ — —   Thompson W A   LB 116 b 3.00   — 24   Lady On Trial116⁴ Party Bowl116⁶ Vinnieanome117²½   Eased 7
6Sep95–8Rkm fst 1   ⊕ :233 :481 1:132 1:464 3+ ④Alw 10780nx2L   65 7 3 31¾ 31 34   Thompson W A   LB 116 b 5.30   77–16   Diplodelightful117² Lady On Trial116¹½ Miracle Zone116½   3 wide, hung 12
21Aug95–8Rkm fst 1¼ ⊕ :23 :472 1:124 1:451 3+ ④Alw 11760nx3L   75 5 4 4⁵ 31¼ 3⁵ 2³   Ma H C   LB 116 b 32.50   81–11   Niner116³ Miracle Zone116½ Loshellez113⁴   2 wide, mild gain 6

Zul

Own: Rahosa Farm Inc

MIGLIORE R (169 28 25 13 .18) $40,000

Ch. m. 5
Sire: North Prospect (Mr. Prospector)
Dam: Strichly'Az (Dancing Moss)
Br: Rahosa Farm Inc (Ky)
Tr: Romero Jorge E (2 1 0 0 .50)

113

	Lifetime Record:	17 1 7 0	$26,870
1996	2 1 0 0	Turf	3 0 0 0	$390
1995	7 M 3 0	Wet	3 1 1 0	$3,955
Aqu	2 1 0 0	Dist	4 1 1 0	$10,540

31Jan96–2Aqu wf 1¼ ⊗ :233 1:15³ 1:484   ④Md 25000   54 7 8 6½ 1¹ 1⁴ 1⁴¾   Leon F   120 fb *2.05   61–24   Zul120⁴ Who Sings120½ Be Reinvested120½   Bumped break, wide 8
20Jan96–4Aqu fst 1¼ ⊗ :472 1:13² 1:413 1:55¹   ④Md Sp Wt   31 7 3 3⁴ 7¹⁰ 71½   Leon F   120 fb 8.00   45–29   Molt120⁴½ Chinn House120² Princess Harriet120¹   Chased, tired 8
27Dec95–1Crc fst 6f   :221 :47 1:00 1:132 3+ ④Md Sp Wt   48 1 5 5ᵉᵈ 6½ 46¼   Lopez E C⁷   115 fb 7.50   79–21   Fancyful Francine121⁴ Shee Cat121² Livermore's Lass121¾   No excuse 8
10Dec95–2Crc fst 6f   :23 :471 :59³ 1:12³ 3+ ④Md Sp Wt   55 1 3 3ʰᵈ 32½ 31⅞ 45½   Velez J X   122 fb 14.00   74–20   Tempo121⁴ Shee Cat121⁴ Hippy Hippy Heart121¼   Tired badly 7
7Apr95–9Hia fst 1¼   :243 :49² 1:14 1:45³   ④Md Sp Wt   30 1 2 3½ 7¹² 7¹⁰ 7¹⁷¾   Velez J X   122 fb 2.80   62–15   Major Momma122³ Victorious Vice122⁷ Footsie Here122⁴   Faltered 8
20Mar95–7Hia fm 1½ ⊕ :23   1:49   ④Md Sp Wt   61 4 2 2¹ 11½ 21½ 41¾   Chavez S N   120 fb 5.40   79–11   Flower Delivery122¹ MajorMomma122²¼ ShesOurFastest122⁴   Weakened 11
15Mar95–3GP fst 1¼   :243 :50 1:15 1:48   ④Md Sp Wt   — 8 — — — —   Bravo J   120 fb 4.20   73   Sofitina120¹¾ Love Of Pam120¹¾ Love Dancing120¼   10
     Reared, hit head top gate, off extremely slow, pulled up in distress
23Feb95–3GP fst 7f   :223 :46 1:11³ 1:243   ④Md 30000   65 10 2 7⁴ 5³¾ 2³ 2³¼   Bravo J   120 fb *1.40   74–20   On Alert LL120½ Zul120⁴ Laura's Gold120¹   Best of others 11
18Jan95–9GP fst 1¼   :231 :482 1:13² 1:402 1:541   ④Md Sp Wt   63 7 9 7⁴½ 44 3⁵ 2⁴½   Bravo J   120 fb 4.40   61–25   Carefree Kate120⁵ Zul120¾ Shes Our Fastest120²   12
     Six wide top str, rallied
28Dec94–6Crc fm 1¼ ⊕   1:52³ 3+ ④Md Sp Wt   51 8 5 6½ 5¹² 51¾ 4½   Boulanger G   120 fb 15.10   42–49   Chrysocolla122⁵ Dragon Miss120³ Shes Our Fastest120¹¾   Wide, tired 9

WORKOUTS: Jan 17 Bel tr.4 4f sly :504 B 1/4   Dec 16 Hia 3f fst :36³ H 2/14   Dec 5 PBD 3f gd :39 Bg 1/7   Nov 28 PBD 3f gd :38 B 1/7

Sinful Hush

Own: Kennedy Rick W & Smither Bruce R

MADRID A JR (117 12 7 8 .10) $50,000

Ch. m. 5
Sire: No Louder (Nodouble)
Dam: Sinister Gold (Sinister Purpose)
Br: Frederiksen Erland R (Ont–C)
Tr: Aitfield Roger L (15 3 0 1 .20)

L 117

	Lifetime Record:	30 5 6 6	$123,688
1996	2 0 0 1	Turf	1 0 0 0	
1995	12 1 3 3	Wet	3 1 0 0	$8,580
Aqu	4 1 0 1	Dist	16 2 4 5	$79,477

21Jan96–7Aqu wf 1¼ ⊗ :231 1:141 1:41 1:434   ④Alw 37444nx3x   58 4 4 32 52½ 7¹⁵ 7¹⁷¾   Madrid A Jr   L 114 f 4.10e   62–17   Shoop113⁴ Enticing Miss113¾ Foxy Miss113⁵   Gave way 7
3Jan96–7Aqu fst 1¼ ⊗ :234 :491 1:153 1:493   ④Alw 37444nx3x   78 10 6 3¹ 34 3¹¾   Madrid A Jr   L 114 f 10.10   53–30   Safe At Home113¼ Enticing Miss113³ Sinful Hush114³   Even finish 10
23Dec95–7Aqu fst 170 ⊗ :234 :471 1:113 1:402 3+ ④Alw 62400nc   84 1 4 41¾ 31½ 3½ 2¹   Castillo H Jr   L 114 f 32.75   89–16   Restored Hope114ʰᵈ Sinful Hush114¹ Nappelon119³   Second best 8
4Dec95–10IWO fst 1¼   :224 :472 1:12 1:434 3+ ④OCIm 50000N   83 1 5 41¾ 3¹ 1ʰᵈ 2ⁿᵒ   McAleney J S   L 117 f 7.30   89–22   Quest For Lisa114ⁿᵒ Sinful Hush117¾ Mips115¹¾   Gamely 11
19Nov95–8IWO fst 7f   :222 :451 1:101 1:233 3+ ④OCIm 80000N   80 2 6 51¾ 41½ 2¹½ 2ⁿᵒ   McAleney J S   L 115 f 12.70   92–09   Elderberry Drive115¹ SinfulHush115¾ AviesCovergirl110³   Good rail rally 6
22Oct95–8IWO fst 7f   :224 :473 1:124 1:454 3+ ④OCIm 80000N   60 5 4 5⁶ 4⁸ 51⁵ 51⁹   McAleney J S   L 113 f 8.20   67–19   Quest For Lisa109½ Wings Of Erin117⁴½ Elegante Chica114²   No factor 6
8Oct95–7IWO fst 1¼   :224 :473 1:124 1:454 3+ ④Bessarabian H48k   76 5 3 3¹ 31½ 3½ 3¹½   McAleney J S   L 113 f 10.75   72–23   Steliarina119ʰᵈ Wings Of Erin114¹¼ Sinful Hush113ⁿᵒ   Dueled three wide 6
21Sep95–8IWO fst 1¼   :234 :473 1:124 1:454 3+ ④OCIm 80000N   80 4 3 4¹ 44 51¾ 37½   McAleney J S   L 114 f 7.75   79–18   Casual Rendezvous113³ Steliarina116½ Sinful Hush115⁴   Evenly 5
10Sep95–5IWO fst 1½   :23 :462 1:113 1:454 3+ ④OCIm 50000N   80 4 5 57½ 1¹ 1½ 1³¾   McAleney J S   L 117 f 6.85   87–13   Sinful Hush117¾ Alice's Hope117¾ Lady Merjo115¾   Driving wide 7
24Aug95–8IWO fst 1¼   :24 :491 1:131 1:461 3+ ④Alw 27400N2x   76 2 2 2¹ 4⁴ 5⁴¾ 54½   McAleney J S   L 116 f 9.00   78–21   Alice's Hope116½ Regal Galaxy116ᵒ Athena's Crown114¹½   7
     Away slowly, dueled, tired

Safe At Home

Own: Minnesian Harry

VELAZQUEZ J R (192 32 19 30 .17) $50,000

Dk. b or br m. 5
Sire: Homebuilder (Mr. Prospector)
Dam: Dazzled (Majestic Light)
Br: Pin Oak Stud Inc & Stilz Bros (Ky)
Tr: Serpe Philip M (11 2 1 3 .18)

L 121

	Lifetime Record:	35 7 9 9	$290,620
1996	2 1 0 0	Turf	2 0 0 1	$3,600
1995	12 2 1 2	Wet	3 0 0 0	$4,230
Aqu	5 2 1 1	Dist	5 2 1 1	$40,790

25Jan96–7Aqu my 1   ⊗ :232 :464 1:112 1:363   ④Alw 39000n4x   49 4 5 54½ 5¹ 51⁴ 52⁴   Chavez J F   L 119   7.00   71–16   Punkin Pie107ʰᵈ Shoop115¹ Madame Adolphe113²⁰   Gave way 5
5Jan96–8Aqu fst 1¼ ⊗ :234 :471 1:12¹ 1:453   ④Alw 37444nx3x   84 8 5 52½ 52½ 2¹½ 1½   Chavez J F   L 113   *2.90   57–30   Safe At Home113½ Enticing Miss113³ Sinful Hush114³   Up, final strides 10
21Dec95–7Aqu fst 1¼ ⊗ :464 1:113 1:374 1:50 3+ ④Alw 37000nx3x   84 6 5 7³ 73¾ 31¼ 3¹   Chavez J F   L 114   6.70   84–03   MadameAdolphe115¼ RavishingRven114²¼ SfeAtHome113¹   Finished well 8
25Nov95–5Aqu fst 7f   :233 :47 1:12¹ 1:234 3+ ④Alw 35000nx3x   80 3 8 74 6⁵ 6⁶ 6⁶   Bailey J D   L 114   11.80   79–12   Miss Golden Circle114² Crafty Jam113¹ Blind Trust112ⁿᵒ   No threat 9
5Nov95–3Aqu fst 1   :231 :47 1:12¹ 1:37 3+ ④Clm 35000N3x   86 3 4 42 41½ 2ʰᵈ 2²   Bailey J D   L 114   2.65   84–16   ADayToRemember114ⁿᵒ AngiAtMy116ʰ Dancer'sGte116¹½   Up for place 8
23Oct95–5Bel fst 1   :223 :452 1:10¹ 1:363 3+ ④Clm 40000   88 6 6 64¼ 7² 2½ 1½   Bailey J D   L 116   3.10   80–23   Safe At Home116½ Pastel Parade120¾ Sun Attack114ᵃᵏ   Long drive 7
13Oct95–5Bel fst 1   :223 :452 :573 1:101 3+ ④Alw 40120n3x   73 4 6 7⁶ 7⁴½ 7⁵½ 75½   Davis R G   L 115   9.30   84–18   Feasibility Study113ⁿ Beauty'sSake115¹½ KhalifOfKushog112¹½   No threat 7
29Sep95–8Bel fst 6½f   :22 :452 1:10 1:163 3+ ④Alw 40320n3x   89 3 5 51⁰ 5⁵½ 2¹½ 34   Bailey J D   L 116   15.40   85–20   LucyEllen116ʰᵉ ReturnOfMom116ᵒ SfAtHom116¹⁰   Bumped brk, willingly 7
26Aug95–2Sar fst 7f   :223 :452 1:103 1:243 3+ ④Clm 25000   87 7 3 7⁴½ 5⁶ 7¹ 1½½   Bailey J D   L 113   2.55e   83–16   SafeAtHome113¾ MidwayGal112¹½ Gene'sGryGirl121ⁿ Split horses, clear 8
9Aug95–9Sar fst 7f   :223 :453 1:101 1:232 3+ ④Clm 50000   73 9 2 7⁴½ 9⁶ 7¹ 67½   Luzzi M J   L 112   11.30   81–18   Skip One112¼ Runaway Fling117³ You'renotlistening112³   No threat 9

Angel At My Door

Own: Novak Katalin

CHAVEZ J F (236 43 34 34 .18) $45,000

B. m. 7
Sire: At the Threshold (Norcliffe)
Dam: Queen's Angel (Sette Bello)
Br: Weaver Frank & Irene (Fla)
Tr: Shapoff Stanley R (23 1 1 5 .04)

L 115

	Lifetime Record:	42 8 8 4	$126,955
1995	17 2 5 3	Turf	6 0 0 0	$2,243
1994	3 0 0 0	Wet	7 1 0 0	$11,110
Aqu	3 0 0 0	Dist	18 3 5 3	$59,040

8Dec95–4Crc fst 1¼   :234 :48 1:133 1:463 3+ ④Alw 23600NC   87 1 4 4⁶½ 31¾ 1¹½ 1½   Chapman K L   L 115 fb 14.70   80–28   Easter Doll117⁵½ Angel At My Door115⁴½ Sly Maid115³   No match 6
24Nov95–1Crc fst 1¼   :244 :491 1:462 3+ ④Alw 23100NC   85 5 2 3¹ 3¹½ 31½ 2½   Chapman K L   L 115 fb 9.80   81–20   Easter Doll115⁴½ Angel At My Door115²½ High Mio Royal115ᵉ   Second best 5
10ct95–9Crc fst 1¼   :231 :481 1:134 1:394 3+ ④Alw 19900n$mY   87 3 4 41½ 45 3½ 3½   Chapman K L   L 115 fb 6.20   80–14   Goldarama115²¾ Berga117⁴ Angel At My Door115ʰᵈ   5
     Six wide top str, late rally
21Sep95–7Crc fst 1¼   :241 :482 1:133 1:453 3+ ④Clm 25000   75 6 5 41¾ 44½ 31½ 3²½   Chapman K L   L 119 fb *1.60   76–21   DzzIMDrIng117½ DorothyBrown117ʰ AngIAtMyDr117½   Late rally, inside 7
27Aug95–4Crc sly 1¼   :242 1:133 1:481 3+ ④Clm 25000   74 5 3 31½ 3² 31½ 11½   Chapman K L   L 122 fb 2.30   74–17   ⒹCambridge Scholar112ᵏ Alluring Secretary117ⁿ Trouble Rips I1117⁴   6
4Aug95–1Crc gd 1¼   :242 :491 1:153 1:48 3+ ④Clm 25000   80 6 2 2ʰᵈ 1½ 1½ 1¾   Chapman K L   L 119 fb 2.10   82–20   Angel AtMyDoor119½ AlluringSecretary117¾ DorothyBrown117²   Driving 6
10July95–5Crc gd 1¼   :232 :48 1:143 1:481 3+ ④Clm 30000   74 2 2 21½ 2¹ 2¹ 1½   Chapman K L   L 115 fb *1.70   78–10   Angel At My Door115½ Mystic Tower117²¼ Cupid's Dream115²¾   6
     Angled inside top str, driving
9Jun95–8Crc fst 1¼   :24 :49 1:143 1:473 3+ ④Clm 25000   72 7 3 2½ 1ʰᵈ 1ʰᵈ 2ⁿ   Chapman K L   L 116 fb 3.40   81–17   Alluring Secretary116ⁿ Angel At My Door116¹ My Angel Maryon116¹   8
     Six wide top str, drifted out deep str, gave way grudgingly
26May95–7Crc fst 1¼   :241 :491 1:153 1:482 3+ ④Clm 25000   81 8 5 31½ 34 24 2ⁿ   Chapman K L   L 114 fb 12.60   80–14   Licorice Tfifet117½ AngelAtMyDoor114¾ AlluringScrtry116½   Second best 8
6May95–5Hia fst 1¼   :242 :491 1:153 1:484 3+ ④Clm 25000   66 5 5 4⁵ 54½ 5⁴ 4⁸   Chapman K L   L 116 fb 2.90   64–08   Huckster Rose117¹ Bronze Willow114¹½ Derby Morning116¾   Belated bid 6

WORKOUTS: ❍Jan 31 Bel tr.t 5f fst 1:02 H 1/11   Jan 26 Bel tr.t 4f fst :50 B 25/41   Dec 22 Bel tr.t 5f fst 1:024 B 12/14   Nov 18 Crc 4f fst :52³ B 53/57

Stop Right Here
Own: Riccio James A

Dk. b or br m. 5
Sire: Cherokee Colony (Pleasant Colony)
Dam: Stop Quick (Stop the Music)
Br: Evans T M (Va)
Tr: Serey Juan (55 11 12 7 .20)

TREJO J (134 17 17 13 .13) $40,000 L 1067

Lifetime Record:	30	7	5	7	$104,295						
1996	3	0	1	0	$6,260	Turf	1	0	0	0	$350
1995	9	4	0	1	$48,700	Wet	6	1	1	2	$16,565
Aqu ⊡	7	0	3	0	$16,820	Dist	15	5	2	3	$56,480

27Jan96-6Aqu sly	170 ⊡	:244 :483 1:131 1:431	ⒻClm 35000	82	1	1	12	1½	21½	23	Trejo J7	L 108 fb	2.65	79-26	Proud Angela1133 Stop Right Here1083½ MissPocketCourt1174	Held well	5
17Jan96-3Aqu my	1 1/16 ⊡	:234 :474 1:124 1:462	ⒻClm 30000	75	8	1	13	11½	41½	44½	Trejo J7	L 109 fb	6.20	68-28	MissPocketCourt116no ProudAngel1181½ CleverRsoning1132½	Speed, tired	8
5Jan96-6Aqu fst	1¼ ⊡	:501 1:16 1:43 2:093	ⒻClm 55000	36	2	2	2½	58	720	738	Rocco J	L 114 fb	3.55e	— 38	Shoop1163½ Punkin Pie1122 Miss Gold Peace1166	Tired	7
8Dec95-9Med fst	1 1/16	:24 :481 1:134 1:461 3↑	ⒻPrncssRooney35k	61	5	1	1hd	1½	69½	618½	Santagata N	L 113 fb	17.50	55-24	Flirty Frosty1171½ Why Be Normal11411 Footing1221	Tired	9
25Nov95-7Med fst	6f	:22 :443 :57 1:093 3↑	ⒻAlw 30000N$Y	69	6	4	65½	68	610	611½	Ortiz F L	L 115 fb	23.10	79-17	My RealStar1194 ThroughTheDoor1151 PleasantDilemma1191½	No factor	7
8Jly95-7Mth fm	1 1/16 Ⓣ	:23 :461 1:094 1:41 + 3↑	ⒻMth Beach35k	59	6	2	24	66	812	815	Butler D P	L 117 fb	21.10	78-06	Irving's Girl113½ Circus Music113hd Kira's Dancer1171½	Gave way	8
4Jly95-9Mth fst	1 1/16	:234 :464 1:101 1:434 3↑	ⒻMolPitcherH-G2	61	2	3	56½	513	521	528	Butler D P	L 110 fb	23.10	60-21	Inside Information1246½ Jade Flush1151½ Halo America1184½	Brief factor	5
3Jun95-6Mth fst	1	:234 :471 1:122 1:387 3↑	ⒻAlw 28000N1m	98	7	1	1hd	13	17	110½	Vives L5	L 111 fb	9.60	86-20	Stop Right Here11110 Why Be Normal1111½ Alphabulous1161½	Drew out	7
29May95-3Mth fst	170	:233 :481 1:14 1:453 3↑	ⒻClm c-40000	66	6	5	42	43	35½	37½	McCauley W H	L 117 b	2.80	66-23	AskShnnie1145½ NoHoldingDvid1172½ StopRightHere117½	No stretch bid	6
Claimed from Jones Anderson Farm, Lopez Daniel J Trainer																	
25Mar95-6Pha fst	170	:224 :47 1:123 1:43	ⒻClm c-32000	87	1	1	2hd	1½	12	13½	Taylor K T	L 116 b	4.30	85-21	StopRightHere1163½ DremLdyDrm1161½ MyLdyLynn114nk	Inside, drew off	6
Claimed from Buckland Farm, Weymouth Eugene E Trainer																	

WORKOUTS: Dec 2 Med 3f fst :364 Hg6/19 Nov 18 Med 6f fst 1:153 B 5/9

I thought this was the toughest race of the day to handicap, and I thought Ask Shananie would go off anywhere from 5-2 to 5 or 6-1 in the field of nine. Wrong. She got pounded down to 9-5.

Angel At My Door went off the 4-1 second choice, and Safe At Home, whom I thought had a big chance as my second *Gazette* pick, was next at 9-2. Sinful Hush was fourth choice at 7-1 and Dancer's Gate, Ruth's Revenge and Stop Right Here all went off at 8-1. Only Minetonightsfirst (22-1) and Miracle Zone (63-1) went off at double-digit odds.

The correct way to go in Pick Three bets was to treat this race as wide open and use all the horses in the fourth with Back Country Boy in the third and Eire Power with or without Hot Slew in the second. It would've cost either $18 or $36.

Ask Shananie and Stop Right Here dueled early, with Ask Shananie taking the lead. But Stop Right Here proved to be the stronger of the two, winning by 1¼ lengths over Ruth's Revenge. Dancer's Gate was third another two lengths back, half a length in front of Ask Shananie. Safe At Home was last.

FOURTH RACE
Aqueduct
FEBRUARY 8, 1996

1 MILE 70 YARDS. (Inner Dirt)(1.39^{3}) CLAIMING. Purse $30,000 (plus up to $5,820 NYSBFOA). Fillies and mares, 4-year-olds and upward. Weight, 123 lbs. Non-winners of two races at a mile or over since January 4, allowed 2 lbs. Such a race since then, 4 lbs. A race since December 16, 6 lbs. Claiming price $50,000, for each $5,000 to $40,000, allowed 2 lbs. (Races where entered for $35,000 or less not considered.)

Value of Race: $30,000 Winner $18,000; second $6,000; third $3,300; fourth $1,800; fifth $900. Mutuel Pool $220,750.00 Exacta Pool $317,209.00 Quinella Pool $65,366.00

Last Raced	Horse	M/Eqt.	A.	Wt	PP	St	¼	½	¾	Str	Fin	Jockey	Cl'g Pr	Odds $1
27Jan96 ^{6}Aqu^{2}	Stop Right Here	Lbf	5	108	9	6	2^{1}	2^{2}	1^{2}	1^{3}	$1^{1\frac{1}{4}}$	Trejo J†^{5}	40000	8.70
17Nov95 ^{9}Aqu^{2}	Ruth's Revenge	L	5	117	3	2	$4^{1\frac{1}{2}}$	$4^{1\frac{1}{2}}$	$3^{\frac{1}{2}}$	$3^{1\frac{1}{2}}$	2^{2}	Castillo R E	50000	8.50
26Jan96 ^{7}Aqu^{3}	Dancer's Gate	Lb	6	117	2	4	$8^{\frac{1}{2}}$	$8^{\frac{1}{2}}$	8^{1}	5^{2}	$3^{\frac{1}{2}}$	Leon F	50000	8.70
20Jan96 ^{8}Suf^{3}	Ask Shananie	L	5	117	1	1	$1^{1\frac{1}{2}}$	1^{hd}	$2^{1\frac{1}{2}}$	$2^{\frac{1}{2}}$	$4^{1\frac{1}{2}}$	King E L Jr	50000	1.95
8Dec95 ^{8}Crc^{2}	Angel At My Door	Lbf	7	115	8	9	9	9	9	$6^{\frac{1}{2}}$	$5^{\frac{3}{4}}$	Chavez J F	45000	4.40
31Jan96 ^{8}Suf^{2}	Miracle Zone	Lb	6	113	5	8	5^{hd}	$5^{\frac{1}{2}}$	$7^{1\frac{1}{2}}$	$4^{\frac{1}{2}}$	6^{4}	Beckner D V	40000	63.00
23Dec95 ^{4}Aqu^{7}	Minetonightsfirst	Lb	5	117	4	3	3^{hd}	3^{hd}	4^{hd}	7^{hd}	$7^{\frac{3}{4}}$	Bravo J	50000	22.80
21Jan96 ^{7}Aqu^{7}	Sinful Hush	Lf	5	117	6	5	6^{1}	$6^{1\frac{1}{2}}$	$5^{\frac{1}{2}}$	9	8^{1}	Madrid A Jr	50000	7.50
25Jan96 ^{7}Aqu^{5}	Safe At Home	L	5	121	7	7	7^{4}	7^{3}	6^{hd}	8^{hd}	9	Velazquez J R	50000	4.70

OFF AT 1:50 Start Good. Won driving. Time, :24, :48^{2}, 1:13^{2}, 1:39^{3}, 1:43^{4} Track fast.

$2 Mutuel Prices:

9-STOP RIGHT HERE	19.40	9.00	7.50
3-RUTH'S REVENGE		9.20	6.40
2-DANCER'S GATE			5.70

$2 EXACTA 9-3 PAID $147.00 $2 QUINELLA 3-9 PAID $80.00

Dk. b. or br. m, by Cherokee Colony–Stop Quick, by Stop the Music. Trainer Serey Juan. Bred by Evans T M (Va).

STOP RIGHT HERE forced the early pace from outside, opened a clear advantage on the turn, maintained a clear lead into midstretch then was fully extended to hold off RUTH'S REVENGE in the late stages. RUTH'S REVENGE raced in good position for five furlongs, launched a rally slightly off the rail leaving the turn then closed steadily but could not get up. DANCER'S GATE checked a bit at the start, raced well back for six furlongs, then rallied belatedly to gain a share. ASK SHANANIE sprinted clear in the early stages, set the pace for a half, relinquished the lead nearing the far turn, raced just behind the winner into midstretch then weakened. ANGEL AT MY DOOR away slowly, trailed to the turn then failed to threaten with a late run along the inside. MIRACLE ZONE raced in the middle of the pack for five furlongs, checked in traffic on the far turn and failed to threaten thereafter. MINETONIGHTSFIRST raced up close between horses to the top of the stretch and steadily tired thereafter. SINFUL HUSH raced just off the pace while four wide to the turn and gave way. SAFE AT HOME outrun for a half, rallied five wide on the turn and flattened out. DANCER'S GATE wore mud caulks.

Owners— 1, Riccio James A; 2, Gumpster Stable; 3, D M Glory Stable; 4, Campbell Gilbert G; 5, Novak Katalin; 6, Rich Jill P; 7, Jim Tim Stables; 8, Kennedy Rick W & Smither Bruce R; 9, Minassian Harry

Trainers— 1, Serey Juan; 2, Lopez Daniel J; 3, Meittinis Louis N; 4, Allard Edward T; 5, Shapoff Stanley R; 6, Kutt Donna M; 7, O'Brien Leo; 8, Attfield Roger L; 9, Serpe Philip M

†Apprentice Allowance Waived: Stop Right Here (2).

Ask Shananie was claimed by Hagedorn Charles G; trainer, Friedman Mitchell.

Scratched— Zul (31Jan96 ^{2}AQU^{1})

$2 Pick-3 (10-6-9) Paid $1,350.00; Pick-3 Pool $73,826.

The Pick Three with winners at 5-1, 9-2 and 8-1 returned $1,350.

They are out there; and they can be hit.

12

The Pick Six

There is probably no better authority on the Pick Six on the entire planet than the man who rightfully earned the nickname of "Mister Pick Six," Steve Crist, now a vice president with the New York Racing Association, which operates Belmont Park, Saratoga and Aqueduct.

Since joining NYRA in 1995, Steve has refrained from wagering on the Pick Six to avoid even the appearance of a conflict of interest. "I honestly don't even miss it," he said recently. "Obviously, when I see a four-day carryover, it presses some old buttons, but I'm busy what I'm doing. I'm not paying attention like I used to. It was a hell of a lot of work."

It was work handsomely rewarded, and Steve was duly acknowledged as the reigning king of racing's most difficult wager. "It was good for the old ego," he said. But there was a down side. "People didn't understand gambling etiquette," he said. "Strangers would come up to me and ask me if they could have five percent of my ticket. Friends would ask me, and I'd say, 'Only if you took the previous losses for the three days when it carried over.' "

Steve, the son of noted *TV Guide* critic Judith Crist, emerged as one of the nation's outstanding turf writers in a long career with the *New York Times*. He then took the bold step of tackling the *Daily Racing Form*, beginning the *Racing Times,* which gave the *Form* quite a tussle before folding a few years back (The author did a couple free-lance stories for the *Racing Times,* and, no, that is not why it folded!). The *Form*, to its credit, wound up taking several innovations of the *Racing Times* to improve its own publication. Steve was honored by being the only member of the media named to the New York State Legislature Advisory Committee on Racing, and served there before joining NYRA in the new regime of President Kenny Noe.

Steve graciously consented to share his Pick Six opinions, insights and actual strategies in *Exotic Overlays*.

He first became acquainted with the Pick Six in Florida in the early 1980s. "That's when I really was introduced to it," he said. "There was no Pick Six in New York at the time. I joined a little partnership with Andy Beyer, Paul Cornman and Mark Hopkins."

Beyer, of course, is an excellent writer, the author of several handicapping books, and the source of the Beyer speed figures now used by the *Racing Form*. Hopkins, one of his associates, is a columnist in the *Form*. Cornman, who owned the outstanding New York-Bred grass horse Win, trained by the late Sally Bailie, was a handicapper and commentator for NYRA's live Race Day TV analysis shown in house and on cable TV.

Steve continued:

> At the time, the Pick Six wasn't a big deal in Florida. You had to wait five of six days to make it worth it. We hit a few down there, nothing life-changing.
>
> What I saw early on was the logic of waiting and playing carryover. It's the only positive expectation bet in racing. There's more amount of money given out than in. You've beaten the takeout.

Steve, of course, is dead center accurate. The takeout on the Pick Six is taken out the first day. On days the Pick Six isn't hit, there is a Pick Five consolation, and the rest of the money is carried over to the next day. If you didn't bet that first day, but do bet the Pick Six the next, all that money is being placed into the Pick Six pool with none of your money included and the takeout already taken out. Ditto if the Pick Six carries into a third or fourth day.

This doesn't mean you should never play the first day of a Pick Six, but it certainly does mean you are getting relatively greater value if you wait and play only carryover days.

But Steve's brilliance was borne of his approach, one that fits perfectly into the theme of *Exotic Overlays*: open your mind to the idea that you can beat vulnerable favorites and that you can also be uncertain about a race and still make money by betting it.

"What I saw down there (in Florida) was that very few people had given a lot of thought to how to strategically play the bet," Steve said. He continued:

> Andy was the only one playing more than one ticket, but he was only doing two or three. I came up with the idea of really making out multiple tickets, like 15 of them. I began to think you could structure a ticket, if you were willing to sit down and fill out that many slips, that, if you were right in four of six races, could give you the opportunity to be less than a genius in the other races and hit it.
>
> It seems to me that people have misinterpreted the bet. In the Double, you're trying to pick the winners of two races. In the Pick Six, you're not trying to pick the winners, in so much as you're trying to get through the sequence. It's very egotistical to think, "I'm going to be right six straight times." Playing a Pick Six using two by two horses a race (only your top two selections in each of the six races) is a great way to waste $128. In any sequence of six races, there's going to be a race where you have to go more than two deep. That's the mistake I think most people make in the Pick Six. They figure out the costs to go two by two by two, or two by three by two, rather than recognizing that in a sequence of six races, you're going to have different situations. Where you might key one, or lock it up with only two horses, there are other races where you have to put in six horses.

Andy would always come in and say, "What's your strategy?" I'd say, "I don't have one. I just want to get through it." I have never felt good or bad about a Pick Six going in. I think anyone who does is committing a crime of hubris. Get through the thing and hope it breaks right for you.

I've heard guys say, "I'm playing the Pick Six because I love a 12-1 shot in the sixth race." I say, "If you do, then go bet it to win."

Other people come in and say, "It looks easy today," but something goofy always happens. If it does and it pays $10,000, I don't throw it back.

Steve suggests that a carryover Pick Six is not exclusive for major players and syndicates, but he does suggest a minimum investment to go after it: "I think it's a good bet for a small bettor, somebody who's going to put in $50 or $200, because it pays two or three times more than the parlay. I think putting in less than $50 is stupid."

Steve was never guilty of spending less than $50. He said his own comfort zone of investment chasing a Pick Six carryover was in the range of $600 to a one-time high of $4,000. His biggest payoff was for $162,000, which, amazingly, included two odds-on favorites and another favorite.

This was his betting strategy that day and every day:

He would construct tickets by classifying contending horses A, B or C. "The thing that is different in a Pick Six than playing exactas or triples is differentiating between horses who can and can't win," he said. "The biggest ones that I hit were not six As. My As aren't that different from any other persons. The difference is that I put in multiple tickets."

Here's how he did it:

His first ticket would consist of six As.

Then five As and one B.

Then five As and one C.

Then four As and two Bs.

"If that all came out to an odd number, I'd spend a little more with four As, one B and one C, a little insanity insurance," he said.

The key race of his $162,000 Pick Six hit was a maiden race at Belmont in July. There were eight horses, including four first-time starters. "The four who had run had terrible figures," Steve said. "What I did was put the four first-time starters on the main ticket (all As) and the four who had not run as Bs. One of the firsters did win, and he paid $30. The Pick Six paid $162,000. The last three winners were all favorites; the last two were odds-on."

Steve summarized:

> I see no point in playing non-carryover Pick Sixes with one exception: major stakes days, such as the Belmont Stakes or Travers. The pool is going to be big and there will be a lot of amateurs.
>
> The other trap that all too many people fall into is thinking that you have to beat all the favorites, or beat an odds-on favorite, for it to pay anything. If there's a 3-5, don't be a wise guy. Use him as a single.
>
> It is hit-able for the small bettor. On a big carryover day, because there's so much more money in the pool, there will be an overlay. It's worth the small guy getting involved. It's so good for the ego, to say, "I hit the Pick Six at Saratoga."

What's important to emphasize here is that you don't have to copy Steve's system. But copying his suggestions and his strategies fit exactly into our thinking: those juicy Pick Six pay-offs do come in. You're a fool to think you can hit all of them, but you don't have to be piggish about it. One or two will carry you a long, long way.

This one certainly could have. There was a carryover of $166,600 heading into Aqueduct's Friday card, February 2, 1996. When nobody picked six, the carryover reached a staggering $381,007.

You'd think there must have been several crazy longshots winning races 3 through 8, February 2, if nobody hit it. Well, there was only one.

Sea Tempest won the third and paid $7.10 as the second favorite. Favored Maraud won the fourth and paid $5.20. Nikki Jean was the second choice in the sixth and paid $9.80. Boom

Towner was the second choice in the seventh and paid $7.20. Accipiter's Star was the second choice in the eighth and paid $8.60.

Now, for a moment, forget about picking six. When nobody hit the Pick Six, your reward for picking five of six was a staggering $492.50! That is nearly $500 for coming up with one favorite and four second choices as the winners of five races.

If you had used those five logical contenders in their five races, and used all the horses in the fifth race, you would have had the Pick Six pool to yourself.

Of course, a huge longshot won the fifth, Seasons Comerant ($164.50) at 81-1. Was he impossible to come up with if you hadn't used all the horses in the race? You decide.

Two scratches reduced the field to 12 (including an entry) in the 1⅛-mile, non-winners of two, allowance race for New York-Bred fillies and mares.

5 Aqueduct

1⅛ MILES. **(Inner Dirt). (1:471) ALLOWANCE. Purse $33,000. Fillies and mares, 4-year-olds and upward foaled in New York State and approved by the New York State-Bred Registry which have not won a race other than maiden, claiming or starter. Weight, 122 lbs.**

Coupled - Deputy Snoop and Mon Drapeau

Miss S O S
Own: Ferrari Louis P
MIGLIORE R (148 27 25 17 .18)

B. f. 4
Sire: Titanic (Alydar)
Dam: Naive Misiya (Miswaki)
Br: Ferrari Louis P (NY)
Tr: Ferraro James W (22 4 0 2 .18)

L 119

Lifetime Record:	16	1	0	3	$25,140						
1996	1	1	0	0	$9,360	Turf	3	0	0	0	$1,990
1995	15	M	0	3	$15,780	Wet	6	1	0	1	$13,620
Aqu ⊡	3	1	0	1	$12,770	Dist	2	0	0	2	$6,710

19Jan96-2Aqu	my	1 1/16 ⊡	:253	:504	1:161	1:514	ⒻMd 35000	64	4	3	11½	13	12	11½	Migliore R	L 121 b	*2.15	46-49	Miss S O S121½ Leitrim Light11511 Diviso N'belle1213½	Steady urging	9
28Dec95-2Aqu	fst	1⅛ ⊡	:49	1:16	1:423	1:561 3↑	ⒻⓈMd Sp Wt	51	2	6	44	45½	26	36½	Migliore R	L 118 b	9.00	48-37	Reelherin1146½ Call To Prayer118hd Miss S O S11812	Even finish	12
10Dec95-1Aqu	fst	1 1/16 ⊡	:24	:484	1:154	1:493 3↑	ⒻMd Sp Wt	24	3	5	44	117	1014	1025	Rocco J	L 119 b	28.50	32-29	Merry Me Mary1191¾ Psychic Spirit12210 Flakes Of Gold1193	Gave way	11
23Nov95-3Aqu	fst	1	:224	:46	1:114	1:394 3↑	ⒻⓈMd Sp Wt	51	3	4	64½	43½	44½	34¾	Chavez C R7	L 111 b	22.40	65-20	Hardy Heart1183 Call To Prayer1131¾ Miss S O S111hd	Mild rally	11
2Nov95-2Aqu	sly	1⅛ ⊗	:474	1:132	1:411	1:551 3↑	ⒻⓈMd Sp Wt	41	3	3	34½	23½	22½	36	Chavez C R7	L 111 b	44.50	58-28	LightBrightHrt1215 Union'sComplinc1181 MissSOS111½	Led, weakened	12
22Oct95-4Bel	my	1	:224	:472	1:132	1:404 3↑	ⒻⓈMd Sp Wt	22	5	4	52½	66	811	711¾	Rydowski S R	L 118 b	40.25	47-29	Alytune117hd Easy Virtue1181¾ Flag Of Gold111no	Speed, tired	12
22Sep95-1Bel	my	1¼ ⊗	:481	1:141	1:422	2:111 3↑	ⒻⓈMd Sp Wt	23	8	7	812	710	610	513¼	Rydowski S R	L 116 b	41.00	25-30	Never Alone116nk Call To Prayer116¾ Light Bright Heart12211	No factor	9
24Aug95-2Sar	fst	7f	:223	:462	1:133	1:273 3↑	ⒻⓈMd Sp Wt	30	1	7	77½	615	59	510¾	Belmonte L A5	112 b	9.90	57-18	Miz Off The Cuff1174 Tahila1172 Missy Mims117¾	No threat	8
5Aug95-4Atl	gd	140 Ⓣ	:23	:47	1:131	1:44 3↑	ⒻMd Sp Wt	40	2	2	31	32	55½	67½	Mojica R Jr	115 b	8.40	67-23	ShezaSharpDnz1151¾ RoseRhpsody1152¾ M.S.Kimpinsky1172½	Had enough	11
17Jly95-4Bel	fm	1¼ Ⓣ	:461	1:114	1:364	2:024 3↑	ⒻⓈMd Sp Wt	44	10	3	613	610	612	615	Rydowski S R	113 b	68.25	59-18	A Blink And A Nod122nk Just Flirting1135½ Watrals Finesse1141	Evenly	12

WORKOUTS: Dec 24 Aqu ⊡ 5f fst 1:03 B *5/16* Nov 18 Aqu 6f fst 1:19 B *2/3*

Deputy Snoop
Own: Rosbsham E Paul
ALVARADO F T (162 24 26 20 .15)

B. m. 5
Sire: Deputy Minister (Vice Regent)
Dam: Star Snoop (Stage Door Johnny)
Br: Stone Ridge Farm (NY)
Tr: Terrill William V (28 0 4 1 .00)

L 113

Lifetime Record:	23	1	5	3	$53,956						
1995	7	0	2	0	$13,026	Turf	9	0	0	1	$5,490
1994	10	0	1	2	$10,620	Wet	6	0	2	2	$15,135
Aqu ⊡	0	0	0	0		Dist	1	0	1	0	$5,586

26Dec95-7Lrl	fst	7f	:23	:464	1:12	1:251 3↑	ⒻAlw 17500N1X	8	7	10	1014	1019	1024	1033½	Johnston M T	L 117 b	8.60	49-18	Star Pic1156½ Duchess Diva115½ Roughthekicker1153½	Outrun	10
7Dec95-6Lrl	fst	1 1/16	:242	:493	1:16	1:483 3↑	ⒻClm 20000N2L	39	5	7	76	75½	77¾	511¼	Reynolds L C	L 122 b	*1.20	56-34	Semele119½ Georgia K.1191 Joyful Paces1191¾	Awaited room 3 1/2	7
19Oct95-7Lrl	yl	1 1/16 Ⓣ	:234	:50	1:163	1:49 3↑	ⒻAlw 19000N1X	69	9	10	88	54½	55½	43½	Reynolds L C	L 117 b	*.40e	57-49	Glorious Bearfoot1173 Soft Spot122hd Please Dance113nk	No menace	12
26Sep95-4Pim	sly	1 1/16 ⊗	:231	:471	1:13	1:472 3↑	ⒻAlw 19000N2L	63	7	7	66½	43	32½	27¾	Reynolds L C	L 117	3.90	64-24	Beaded Moccasins11471¾ Deputy Snoop1173 Wolf Rosie O'shay11413	Wide	7
23Jly95-4Lrl	fm	1 1/16 Ⓣ	:23	:464	1:112	1:43 3↑	ⒻAlw 19000N1X	67	7	9	710	810	610	44½	Reynolds L C	L 117	6.90	86-11	One Accord1081¾ Hawk's Fortune1132 Ernucbobray117½	Wide	10
8Jly95-7Lrl	fst	1⅛ ⊗	:463	1:12	1:39	1:523 3↑	ⒻAlw 26600N1X	64	7	8	715	68¾	34	24½	Reynolds L C	L 117	8.10	70-16	Talcountess1144½ Deputy Snoop1171½ Glorious Bearfoot1173	Rallied	9
27Jun95-7Lrl	my	6f	:23	:473	1:00	1:121 3↑	ⒻAlw 24500N1X	53	4	9	99¼	85½	75¾	58	Reynolds L C	L 117	7.00	71-16	Honor Society1084½ Dazzling1142¾ Frigid Heiress117¾	Passed faders	9
12Oct94-9Med	fm	1 1/16 Ⓣ	:231	:48	1:121	1:432 3↑	ⒻAlw 20000N1X	55	10	9	94¾	106	96½	89	Santagata N	L 113	20.90	75-14	Peppy Broad111nk Crandall1162¾ Jessica's Two Step116nk	Outrun	10
22Sep94-9Med	sly	170	:23	:472	1:13	1:44 3↑	ⒻAlw 19000N1X	62	3	5	55¼	42	32	2½	Santagata N	L 113	2.90	75-18	Holyterial113½ Deputy Snoop1131½ More Margin1131¾	Up for place	6
31Aug94-8Mth	fm	1 1/16 Ⓣ	:233	:473	1:114	1:444 3↑	ⒻAlw 17000N1X	55	7	4	410	56	66	69	Santagata N	L 112	6.50	71-18	Goodonya Amy1122½ Senorita Cielo113hd Sly Maid113¾	No rally	10

WORKOUTS: Jan 26 Bel tr.t 4f fst :494 B *20/41* Jan 22 Bel tr.t 4f fst :502 B *15/32* Dec 5 Lrl 3f fst :37 B *5/10* Nov 30 Lrl 4f fst :492 B *8/12* Nov 24 Lrl 4f fst :49 B *3/11* Nov 19 Lrl 4f fst :491 B *6/10*

Cool Babe
Own: Piety Hill Stable
VELAZQUEZ J R (172 30 14 25 .17)

Ch. f. 4
Sire: Ends Well (Lyphard)
Dam: Icy Care (Caro (Ire))
Br: Bailie Sally (NY)
Tr: O'Connell Richard (18 0 2 1 .00)

L 113

Lifetime Record:	13 1 1 1	$31,800			
1995	10 1 1 1	$31,800	Turf	0 0 0 0	
1994	3 M 0 0		Wet	6 0 1 0	$6,900
Aqu ⊡	6 0 1 1	$12,000	Dist	2 1 0 0	$18,000

15Dec95-7Aqu my 1 1/16 ⊡ :233 :48 1:131 1:453 3↑ Ⓕ[S]Alw 33000N1X 36 3 7 67¾ 78¾ 718 824 Velazquez J R 113 f 37.00 53-12 Blind Truth1169 A Blink And A Nod1167¼ Igobacktotheking113nk Outrun 12
1Dec95-6Aqu my 1⅛ :483 1:121 1:381 1:514 3↑ Ⓕ[S]Alw 33000N1X 28 5 6 64 66 911 923¾ Velazquez J R 112 15.10 57-12 Hardy Heart1163 Hold You112½ A Blink And A Nod1152½ Wide, tired 9
15Nov95-8Aqu gd 6f :214 :453 :591 1:123 3↑ Ⓕ[S]Alw 30000N1X 30 4 10 1013 1012 1011 1013¼ Luzzi M J 114 46.00 65-18 PecockPlume1122 ILoveLydi1121 Irllynddthis1122 Broke slowly, outrun 10
13Apr95-2Aqu fst 1⅛ :49 1:143 1:413 1:552 Ⓕ[S]Md Sp Wt 53 5 6 64½ 31½ 1½ 1no Doran K 120 3.75 63-24 Cool Babe120no Flag Of Gold1131½ Pitchunia120nk All out 6
26Mar95-1Aqu fst 1 :233 :474 1:141 1:401 ⒻMd Sp Wt 29 1 7 77 76 610 417¼ Doran K 120 15.50 50-30 Seeking Account1202 Enchancement12016 CraftyLady1205 Broke slowly 7
9Mar95-5Aqu wf 170 ⊡ :24 :49 1:144 1:452 Ⓕ[S]Md Sp Wt 55 9 9 84½ 53¾ 43 21½ Doran K 120 9.30 69-24 BoBo'sSister1201½ CoolBabe120nk RazzitaMrgrit1202 Brk slow, in trffc 3/4 9
24Feb95-5Aqu fst 1 1/16 ⊡ :234 :493 1:16 1:491 Ⓕ[S]Md Sp Wt 53 5 9 53 52½ 41½ 41½ Doran K 121 10.90 58-29 Positive Tally116nk [D]Baby's In A Fog1211 Leah Ray114no 9
Checked break, boxed in turn, bumped, trapped 1/8 pl Placed third through disqualification.
16Feb95-2Aqu fst 170 ⊡ :234 :481 1:14 1:452 ⒻMd Sp Wt 51 2 6 69 55½ 49 413 Doran K 119 7.80 58-30 Your Approval1194 Chinn House1143 Mystic Mel1196 Poor break 6
21Jan95-4Aqu my 1 1/16 ⊡ :242 :49 1:143 1:491 ⒻClm 20000N2L 49 2 5 53½ 41½ 31½ 42¼ Doran K 112 23.90 56-26 CllMyAgent114nk Impediment1112 HlloweenMsk112nk Broke slowly, wide 5
4Jan95-5Aqu fst 6f ⊡ :23 :473 1:004 1:134 Ⓕ[S]Md Sp Wt 27 8 12 1114 107½ 911 716¾ Doran K 121 124.00 57-22 Patti's Purse1213¼ Star Personality1219 Baroness B.1211¾ No factor 12
WORKOUTS: Jan 20 Bel tr.t 4f fst :493 B 11/20 Jan 11 Bel tr.t 5f fst 1:023 B 3/25 Jan 5 Bel tr.t 4f fst :514 B 16/30 Dec 31 Bel tr.t 4f fst :484 B 9/67 Dec 24 Bel tr.t 4f fst :503 B 111/147 Nov 27 Bel tr.t 5f fst 1:02 B 5/24

Devilette
Own: Wachtel Edwin H
CHAVEZ C R (116 9 17 10 .08)

Dk. b or br f. 4
Sire: Claramount (Policeman)
Dam: Dukette (Unpredictable)
Br: Wachtel Edwin H (NY)
Tr: Destefano John M Jr (24 4 6 3 .17)

L 108⁵

Lifetime Record:	18 1 5 2	$59,965			
1996	1 0 1 0	$6,600	Turf	1 0 0 0	
1995	10 0 3 1	$19,975	Wet	2 0 2 0	$8,200
Aqu ⊡	2 0 1 0	$6,600	Dist	1 0 1 0	$6,600

3Jan96-7Aqu fst 1⅛ ⊡ :51 1:171 1:433 1:57 Ⓕ[S]Alw 33000N1X 50 3 2 2½ 2½ 21½ 24 Chavez C R5 L 108 b 10.20 47-37 Light Bright Heart1164 Devilette1081 ABlinkAndANod1143½ Second best 10
23Dec95-1Aqu fst 6f ⊡ :223 :463 :583 1:104 ⒻClm 18000 54 6 11 107½ 115½ 87¾ 611¼ Castillo H Jr L 115 b 24.50 78-10 Henbane's Girl1144½ Domina1151 Charmless1082 No factor 11
24Aug95-10Sar fst 7f :224 :463 1:121 1:251 3↑ Ⓕ[S]Alw 32000N1X 50 6 7 105½ 74½ 66½ 514 Krone J A 112 b 16.50 66-18 Katie's Flag1114½ Elocat's Burglar1125½ Angel Kate1172 Wide trip 11
28Jly95-1Sar fst 6½f :22 :452 1:112 1:18 3↑ Ⓕ[S]Alw 32000N2L 55 1 11 1116 1112 57½ 310½ Krone J A 114 b 10.80 74-15 Personal Coup111½ Kacie's Favor11710 Devilette114¾ Broke slowly 11
29Jun95-8Bel fst 7f :221 :461 1:122 1:26 3↑ Ⓕ[S]Alw 32000N1X 47 9 9 78½ 58 610 616 Krone J A 110 b 3.20 55-22 Green Strawberry1132 Katie's Flag1125½ BellaRansom1126 Saved ground 11
7Jun95-3Bel gd 1 1/16 :232 :464 1:13 1:471 3↑ Ⓕ[S]Alw 34000N1X 58 7 4 44½ 22½ 1½ 21½ Krone J A 109 b *1.30 62-29 Jazzpacked1191½ Devilette1092 Pink Syncopation1122½ Bid, couldn't last 7
26May95-3Bel sly 1 1/16 :232 :47 1:124 1:461 ⒻClm 25000 58 5 5 54½ 41½ 1hd 21½ Krone J A 116 b *1.05 67-20 Gentleman's Copy1161½ Devilette11613 Pick A Day1141½ Bid, weakened 6
18May95-1Bel my 6½f :221 :46 1:114 1:182 ⒻClm 20000 72 8 7 911 88 21½ 2no Krone J A 112 b *1.00e 83-18 Gin And Ice114no Devilette1123¼ Fast Nicole1161½ Lost bob 9
19Apr95-6Aqu gd 1 1/16 Ⓣ :231 :48 1:124 1:452 ⒻClm 45000 43 4 9 85½ 85¾ 812 816 Beckner D V 112 b 24.25 66-18 TwilightEncounter1121 ErinsRelity109hd Domin1141 Pinch brk, stead 3/8 9
12Apr95-4Aqu fst 1 :233 :464 1:122 1:39 Ⓕ[S]Alw 32000N1X 31 5 5 52¾ 74 710 616½ Velazquez J R 112 3.40 57-19 Darlin Danika1126½ Sammycat1121½ Untold Secret107hd Done after half 7
WORKOUTS: Jan 26 Bel tr.t 4f fst :50 B 26/41 Dec 19 Bel tr.t 4f gd :522 B 31/39 Dec 14 Bel tr.t 5f fst 1:03 B 14/18 Dec 7 Bel tr.t 4f fst :49 B 6/32 Dec 1 Bel tr.t 4f fst :491 H 5/43 Nov 23 Bel tr.t 3f fst :364 B 3/16

Pink Syncopation
Own: Davidson Herbert S & Wendel Arthur
NELSON D (82 3 12 7 .04)

Dk. b or br m. 5
Sire: Palace Panther (Crystal Palace)
Dam: Adforsyn (Advocator)
Br: Windylea Farm (NY)
Tr: Wendel Arthur (13 0 1 1 .00)

113

Lifetime Record:	25 1 0 1	$21,410			
1996	2 0 0 0	$990	Turf	3 0 0 0	
1995	19 1 0 1	$20,420	Wet	5 1 0 0	$10,830
Aqu ⊡	9 1 0 0	$10,650	Dist	4 0 0 0	$2,040

15Jan96-5Aqu my 1 1/16 ⊡ :231 :474 1:142 1:481 Ⓕ[S]Alw 33000N1X 47 2 7 913 812 611 511½ Decarlo C P 114 59.50 53-26 Patti's Purse113½ Positive Tally1132 A Blink And A Nod1143 No threat 10
3Jan96-7Aqu fst 1⅛ ⊡ :51 1:171 1:433 1:57 Ⓕ[S]Alw 33000N1X 38 9 3 63½ 108 710 711¾ Ward J5 108 88.75 39-37 Light Bright Heart1164 Devilette1081 A Blink And A Nod1143½ Tired 10
11Nov95-1Aqu fst 1 :233 :464 1:122 1:391 3↑ Ⓕ[S]Alw 32000N1X 47 11 9 104½ 109½ 1110 1011½ Belmonte L A5 111 79.50 62-19 SrtogCpers1141½ FollowTheFlg1142 WorkOfTheDvil1152½ No factor, wide 11
26Oct95-5Bel fst 1 1/16 :233 :473 1:132 1:461 3↑ Ⓕ[S]Alw 34000N1X 40 4 7 73¾ 82½ 65 512½ Chavez C R7 109 44.75 55-22 ClypsoVuh1142 WorkOfTheDvil1162 HoldYou1138 Saved grnd, no threat 9
18Oct95-9Bel fst 1 1/16 :231 :464 1:124 1:454 3↑ Ⓕ[S]Alw 34000N1X 37 2 9 99½ 96 710 615¾ Chavez C R7 109 51.00 54-21 SeasonalSplendor1133 WorkOfTheDevil1164 OnlyForever1144 No threat 10
6Oct95-7Bel gd 6f :23 :47 :591 1:121 3↑ Ⓕ[S]Alw 32000N1X 41 3 6 613 67 510 511¾ Chavez C R7 108 26.75 68-18 K. O. Lady1084½ Flannel Sheets116no Go With Flo113¾ No speed 6
14Jly95-5Bel fst 1 1/16 :234 :474 1:13 1:444 3↑ Ⓕ[S]Alw 34000N1X 32 3 6 75 77 715 727 Belmonte L A7 112 16.60 48-27 Bella Ransom11317 Crama1194 Peacock Plume110½ No factor 8
9Jly95-5Bel fm 1 Ⓣ :222 :46 1:11 1:361 3↑ Ⓕ[S]Alw 34000N1X 51 5 10 108¾ 107½ 89½ 812½ Belmonte L A7 112 45.50 70-14 Curled Waters1191½ Sweetzie1141 Bid O'powdre1113 No threat 10
22Jun95-9Bel sly 1 1/16 ⊗ :22 :45 1:103 1:451 3↑ Ⓕ[S]Alw 34000N1X 54 6 8 811 77½ 77½ 46 Belmonte L A7 112 13.50 67-22 Lady Trilogy119hd Igobacktotheking1092½ Lovelines Gold1193½ Late gain 9
7Jun95-3Bel gd 1 1/16 :232 :464 1:13 1:471 3↑ Ⓕ[S]Alw 34000N1X 55 5 7 711 65 31½ 33½ Belmonte L A7 112 29.00 60-29 Jazzpacked1191½ Devilette1092 Pink Syncopation1122½ Flattened out 7
WORKOUTS: Dec 24 Bel tr.t 4f fst :484 B 25/147 Dec 19 Bel tr.t 3f gd :392 B 17/18 Nov 27 Bel tr.t 3f fst :363 B 7/24

Seasons Comerant
Own: Micheletti John R
SHERMAN J M (5 0 0 0 .00)

B. m. 5
Sire: Cormorant (His Majesty)
Dam: Cosmic (Halo)
Br: Kinderhill Select Bloodstock Inc (NY)
Tr: Held Dieter K (5 0 0 0 .00)

103¹⁰

Lifetime Record:	6 1 0 0	$20,880			
1995	6 1 0 0	$20,880	Turf	0 0 0 0	
1994	0 M 0 0		Wet	0 0 0 0	
Aqu ⊡	4 1 0 0	$20,880	Dist	2 1 0 0	$18,000

13Apr95-3Aqu fst 1⅛ :48 1:123 1:393 1:532 3↑ Ⓕ[S]Alw 32000N1X — 3 2 32 511 620 — Cruguet J 119 b 6.60 — 24 Satans Archangel11910 Shady Baby1103½ Funky Diva119½ Gave way, eased 6
6Apr95-8Aqu fst 1 :223 :45 1:111 1:39 ⒻAlw 32000N1X 44 2 9 912 85 86 711½ Cruguet J 119 b 34.75 62-26 Bow Creek1061 Judicial Girl113nk Fire Attack1133 Broke slowly 10
10Mar95-7Aqu fst 170 ⊡ :24 :482 1:141 1:46 Ⓕ[S]Alw 32000N1X 54 4 2 24 36 48 49½ Cruguet J 119 8.00 58-33 Frisky's Finale1071½ Parmelina1073 Woodland Gal1145½ Used up 6
23Feb95-5Aqu fst 1⅛ ⊡ :494 1:15 1:42 1:554 ⒻMd Sp Wt 56 2 1 1½ 1½ 12 11½ Cruguet J 122 4.30 57-29 SeasonsComernt1221½ BlindTruth122no MissStrVerse1173 Fully extended 10
19Feb95-3Aqu fst 6f ⊡ :23 :464 1:00 1:134 ⒻMd Sp Wt 37 6 7 79 910 911 813 Chavez J F 120 10.90 61-22 Facul1201½ CompoundGirl1205 WendysTerms1201½ Outrun, checked 1/4 pl 10
19Jan95-5Aqu fst 6f ⊡ :233 :474 1:004 1:142 ⒻMd 50000 16 8 3 56 58½ 611 411 Lumpkins J 122 2.55 60-18 Fresser1223 Linda Lee Lou1184 Landing The Gold1084 Three wide 8
WORKOUTS: Jan 22 Aqu ⊡ 4f fst :511 B 3/3

Positive Tally
Own: Minnella Martin J
LUZZI M J (165 20 14 19 .12)

B. f. 4
Sire: D'Accord (Secretariat)
Dam: Royal Tali (Talc)
Br: McNulty Mr & Mrs David P & Akindale Farm (NY)
Tr: Kiesaris Steve (15 6 3 1 .40)

L 113

Lifetime Record:	8 1 2 0	$35,730			
1996	1 0 1 0	$6,600	Turf	0 0 0 0	
1995	5 1 1 0	$28,290	Wet	1 0 1 0	$6,600
Aqu ⊡	8 1 2 0	$35,730	Dist	0 0 0 0	

15Jan96-5Aqu my 1 1/16 ⊡ :231 :474 1:142 1:481 Ⓕ[S]Alw 33000N1X 65 3 3 35½ 32½ 22½ 2½ Luzzi M J L 113 b *2.05 63-26 Patti's Purse113½ Positive Tally1132 A Blink And ANod1143 Steady gain 10
29Dec95-6Aqu fst 6f ⊡ :231 :474 1:004 1:134 3↑ Ⓕ[S]Alw 31000N1X 55 9 10 107½ 84¾ 75¾ 53½ Luzzi M J 113 b 19.10 71-19 Alytune115nk Quality Control113hd Easy Virtue1121 Bumped, start 12
24Feb95-5Aqu fst 1 1/16 ⊡ :234 :493 1:16 1:491 Ⓕ[S]Md Sp Wt 55 4 5 32½ 32 2hd 1nk Perez R B5 116 *1.05 59-29 PositiveTally116nk [D]Bby'sInAFog1211 LehRy114no Well placed, prevailed 9
17Feb95-4Aqu fst 6f ⊡ :231 :464 :593 1:132 Ⓕ[S]Md Sp Wt 56 3 6 69½ 59½ 47 43 Perez R B5 116 5.30 73-21 Where Is It1141½ Quaker Street121hd Lamplight1211½ Rallied inside 10
11Jan95-5Aqu fst 1 1/16 ⊡ :234 :491 1:161 1:502 Ⓕ[S]Md Sp Wt 54 1 5 53 41¾ 34½ 2no Perez R B5 116 3.85 53-38 SammiDe121no PositiveTally1164 OurBlueDimond1215½ Lacked room turn 8
4Jan95-5Aqu fst 6f ⊡ :23 :473 1:004 1:134 Ⓕ[S]Md Sp Wt 33 5 8 95¾ 86¾ 69 414¼ Lumpkins J 121 26.25 60-22 Patti's Purse1213¼ Star Personality1219 Baroness B.1211¾ Some gain 12
26Dec94-9Aqu fst 6f ⊡ :224 :47 1:00 1:133 Ⓕ[S]Md Sp Wt 34 11 11 98 87½ 812 511¼ Lumpkins J 117 10.00 64-21 GreenStrwberry1173 StrPrsonlity117¾ RussinEnsign1172½ Passed faders 12
7Dec94-3Aqu fst 6f ⊡ :221 :453 :582 1:113 Ⓕ[S]Md Sp Wt 42 4 10 1017 1012 109½ 710 Davis R G 117 30.00 75-12 Quality Control1175 Where Is It1081½ Winloc's Peggy117hd Pinched brk 11
WORKOUTS: Dec 23 Bel tr.t 5f fst 1:03 B 28/37 Dec 14 Bel tr.t 5f fst 1:03 B 14/18 Nov 13 Suf 4f fst :51 B 13/24

Ultra Power

Own: Gelb Richard L

B. f. 4
Sire: Personal Flag (Private Account)
Dam: Fess Up (Sharpen Up (GB))
Br: Rusty Mac Stables (NY)
Tr: Fisher John R S (1 0 0 0 .00)

L 113

Lifetime Record :	5 1 0 0	$12,720	
1995	5 1 0 0	$12,720	Turf	0 0 0 0
1994	0 M 0 0		Wet	1 0 0 0
Aqu⊡	1 0 0 0		Dist	1 0 0 0	$1,800

CORDOVA D W (155 16 14 24 .10)

15Dec95-7Aqu my 1⅛ ⊡ :231 :48 1:131 1:453 3↑ ⑤Alw 33000N1x   9 10 6 7¾ 9⅛ 12⅝ 12⅞ Luzzi M J   113   27.25 37−12   Blind Truth116⅓ A Blink And A Nod116⁴½ Igobacktotheking113ᵐᵏ   Outrun 11
2Dec95-5Pha fst 1⅛   :231 :48 1:142 1:274 3↑ ⑤Md Sp Wt   47 2 6 1ʰᵈ 1½ 2ʰᵈ 1ⁿᵒ   120   3.60 67−23   Ultra Power120ⁿᵒ Colonial Currency120¹ Glowing122²⅛   Gamely 9
13Apr95-2Aqu fst 6f   :49 1:143 1:413 1:552   ⑤Md Sp Wt   50 2 2 1ʰᵈ 4⅝ 5¾ Luzzi M J   120   *.85 61−24   Cool Babe120ⁿᵒ Flag Of Gold113¼ Pitchunia120ᵐᵏ   Dueled inside 4
19Mar95-5Aqu fst 6f   :223 :463 :592 1:131   ⑤Md Sp Wt   48 4 5 63⅛ 44 44⅛ Chavez J F   120   4.30 71−19   Foxing Relity120¹½ StrPersonality120²½ HomhJSimon120½   Wide, no late bid 11
17Feb95-4Aqu fst 6f   :223 :461 :593 1:132   ⑤Md Sp Wt   34 5 5 79½ 58½ 51⁰ 512 Chavez J F   121   6.10 64−21   Where Is It114¾ Quaker Street121ᵐᵏ Lamplight121¹½   10
Steadied repeatedly, grass

WORKOUTS: ● Jan 23 Fai 4f fst :48³ B (d) 2/9   Dec 31 Fai 4f gd :50 B (d)3/4

Only Forever

Own: Roberts James K & Terian Peter G

Dk. b or br f. 4
Sire: Distinctive Pro (Mr. Prospector)
Dam: Forbidden Sight (Bagdad)
Br: Tierra Hill Farm (NY)
Tr: Martin Carlos F (62 9 7 11 .15)

L 113

Lifetime Record :	7 1 2 2	$37,920	
1996	1 0 0 0		Turf	0 0 0 0
1995	6 1 2 2	$37,920	Wet	1 1 0 0	$18,000
Aqu⊡	3 0 1 1	$9,280	Dist	0 0 0 0

CHAVEZ J F (218 41 32 30 .19)

11Jan96-6Aqu fst 6f   ⊡ :231 :47 :593 1:13   ⑤Alw 31000N1x   48 6 4 42½ 44 77½ 87½ Chavez J F   114 b   *1.40 74−18   Work Of The Devil114⁴ All Button114¹ Patti's Purse114²   Broke outward 11
13Dec95-5Aqu fst 6f   ⊡ :23 :464 :581 1:121 3↑ ⑤Alw 31000N1x   60 4 7 41½ 51⅓ 31 2ⁿᵒ Chavez J F   114 b   3.45 82−18   Crama114ⁿᵒ Only Forever114ⁿᵈ Easy Virtue112⅓   Just missed 11
15Nov95-3Aqu gd 6f   :214 :453 :581 1:123 3↑ ⑤Alw 30000N1x   48 2 5 60 78 56½ 34ʰᵈ Chavez J F   117   *1.65 72−18   Peacock Plume112² I Love Lydia112½ Ireallyneededthis112¾   No threat 10
1Nov95-3Aqu fst 6½f   ⊡ :23 :463 1:111 1:174 3↑ ⑤Alw 30000N1x   58 10 2 63⅛ 23½ 26 2⁹ Chavez J F   116   *1.65 82−14   SktersLustre114⁹ OnlyForevr116⁶½ WtrlsRidg114⅛   No match, clear second 11
18Oct95-8Bel fst 1½   ⊡ :231 :463 1:112 1:47 3↑ ⑤Alw 30000N1x   50 5 3 2⅛ 21 33 37 Chavez J F   114   2.40 63−21   SesonlSplendor113⅛ WorkOfTheDevil114⁴ OnlyForever114⁴   Chased, tired 11
5Oct95-1Bel sly 7f   :222 :463 1:131 1:27 3↑ ⑤Md Sp Wt   63 8 4 37 21 1½ 1ʰᵈ Chavez J F   118   *2.25 66−18   Only Forever118ʰᵈ Easy Virtue118¼ Lucy Brown121⁴   Ridden out 10
27Jun95-1Bel sly 6f   ⊡ :231 :481 1:014 1:154   ⑤Md Sp Wt   30 6 3 52 55½ 34½ Alvarado F T   121   *1.50 60−25   Darlin Danika121⁷ Escarrgot121¹½ Only Forever121ᵐᵏ   7
Shuffled back 1/4 pl, green

WORKOUTS: Jan 27 Bel tr.t 5f gd 1:04² B 1/7   Jan 5 Bel tr.t 3f fst :37² B 2/13   Dec 28 Bel tr.t 3f fst :37¹ B 5/11   Dec 8 Bel tr.t 4f fst :48¹ H 6/40

Go With Flo

Own: Boyd & Hangan & Walsh

Ch. f. 4
Sire: Nostrum (Dr. Fager)
Dam: All for Ollie (Shredder)
Br: Walsh Georgia (NY)
Tr: Walsh Thomas M (4 0 0 0 .00)

113

Lifetime Record :	12 1 0 1	$24,700	
1996	1 0 0 0	$1,980	Turf	1 0 0 0
1995	7 1 0 1	$22,720	Wet	3 1 0 0	$21,180
Aqu⊡	2 0 0 0	$1,980	Dist	0 0 0 0

ROCCO J (72 5 6 10 .07)

15Jan96-5Aqu my 1⅛ ⊡ :231 :474 1:142 1:481   ⑤Alw 33000N1x   57 7 2 2² 2¹ 44⅝ 45½ Ward J⁵   108   26.75 58−26   Patti's Purse113¾ Positive Tally113² A Blink AndA Nod114³   Forced pace 10
29Dec95-6Aqu fst 6f   :23 :464 1:00⁰ 1:134 3↑ ⑤Alw 31000N1x   47 2 8 64⅝ 52½ 53 48⅓ Persaud R   113   44.50 64−23   Alytune116ⁿᵒ Quality Control111ⁿᵈ Easy Virtue112¹   No factor 12
15Nov95-2Aqu gd 6f   :22 :46 :584 1:124   ⑤Clm 15000   35 11 9 94¾ 94½ 811 810½ Persaud R¹⁰   104   21.70 67−18   Tara's Flame114¾ Charmless114² Henbane's Girl114¹⅛   Wide trip 11
18Oct95-8Bel fst 1½   ⊡ :231 :464 1:124 1:454 3↑ ⑤Alw 34000N1x   31 5 4 3² 106½ 10123 1013½ Rydowski S R   113   8.20 51−21   SeasonalSplendor113³ WorkOfTheDevil114⁴ OnlyForever114⁴   Gave way 11
6Oct95-7Bel gd 6f   :23 :47 :591 1:123 3↑ ⑤Alw 34000N1x   59 4 5 5¹² 34 34½ Maple E   113   10.10 75−18   K. O. Lady108⅛ Flannel Sheets116ⁿᵒ Go WithFlo113⁵   Four wide, mild gain 6
16Aug95-5Sar fst 1½   :483 1:14 1:394 1:533 3↑ ⑤Alw 34000N1x   57 3 8 2⅛ 910 1016 1034 Maple E   112   37.50 34−32   Pro Finessa112⅛ Calypso Vuh113³⅛ Loveliines Gold112⁷   Checked break 11
14Jly95-5Bel fst 1½   :234 1:13 1:391 3↑ ⑤Alw 34000N1x   35 1 1 1½ 2¹ 513 519 Persaud R¹⁰   112   17.40 50−27   Bella Ransom113¹⁷ Crama119⁴ Peacock Plume118½   Dueled inside 8
15Oct94-5Bel sly 7f   :224 :463 1:121 1:48 3↑ ⑤Md Sp Wt   38 5 1 1½ 1¹ 1¹ 1⅛ Persaud R¹⁰   102   29.75 59−22   Go With Flo112¹½ Stellina112² Seasonal Splendor112½   Drifted, late 7
15Oct94-5Bel fst 1   :224 :454 1:101 1:354   ⑤Md Sp Wt   20 10 10 843 12 12171426 Maple E   117   49.30 56−18   Distinctive Ruby114² Quality Control117² Russian Ensign110½   Tired 14
20Sep94-5Bel gd 1 ⊕ :224 :454 1:101 1:354   ⑤Md Sp Wt   4 10 9 91⁷ 10¹⁵ 1219 12343 Sweeney K H   117   82.90 48−20   Erins Reality117⁶¾ High Sevens117ⁿᵏ Bank Approval117²½   Outrun 12

WORKOUTS: Jan 26 Bel tr.t 3f fst :37³ B 7/16   Jan 7 Bel tr.t 4f fst :51 B 15/45   Dec 24 Bel tr.t 4f fst :50¹ B 99/147   Dec 18 Bel tr.t 4f fst :50¹ B 25/70   Dec 8 Bel tr.t 5f fst 1:06 B 27/28   Nov 11 Aqu 4f fst :52 B 18/24

Mon Drapeau

Own: Cohn Seymour

B. f. 4
Sire: Personal Flag (Private Account)
Dam: Ardenay (Bon Mot)
Br: Hettinger John (NY)
Tr: Terrill William V (28 0 4 1 .00)

L 113

Lifetime Record :	14 1 1 3	$40,940	
1996	2 0 0 0	$1,980	Turf	6 0 0 2	$8,140
1995	5 1 0 1	$25,840	Wet	3 1 0 0	$21,300
Aqu⊡	2 0 0 0	$1,980	Dist	1 0 0 0	$1,980

BRAVO J (120 11 16 14 .09)

15Jan96-5Aqu my 1⅛ ⊡ :231 :474 1:142 1:481   ⑤Alw 33000N1x   39 8 8 8¹³ 91⁴ 8¹⁵ 716 Cordova D W   L 113 b   8.20 48−26   Patti's Purse113¾ Positive Tally113² A Blink And A Nod114³   No factor 10
3Jan96-7Aqu fst 1½ ⊡ :482 :51 1:171 1:433 1:57   ⑤Alw 33000N1x   43 2 4 42½ 5⁴⅓ 54½ 48⅛ Beckner D V   L 113 b   3.45 42−37   Light Bright Heart116⁴ Deviiette108¹ A Blink And A Nod114³⅛   Even trip 10
3Nov95-5Aqu sly 1 ⊕ :23 :454 1:11 1:38   ⑤Clm 50000   59 8 10 10⁹½ 9⅝ 43 43⅜ Migliore R   115   18.70 63−21   Crafty Jenny111½ New York Rainbow113⁴ Bid O'powdre113½   Wide trip 10
26Oct95-5Bel fst 1   :233 :473 1:132 1:461 3↑ ⑤Alw 34000N1x   — 8 9 9⁷⅝ 91⁷ 12¹ Smith M E   113   3.30 −22   Calypso Vuh114² Work Of The Devil116⁴ Hold You113⁸   No speed, eased 10
21Sep95-7Bel fm 1½ ⊕ :483 1:123 2:044 3↑ ⑤Alw 34000N2L   71 6 6 3¹ 31 53½ 55½ Bailey J D   115   5.80 58−26   Grand Chorus117⁴¾ Bella Dawn112ⁿᵒ Select Account117½   Stalked, tired 9
27Aug95-2Sar gd 1½ ⊕ :484 1:141 1:402 2:17¹ 3↑ ⑤Alw 32000N1x   67 6 3 1ʰᵈ 2ʰᵈ 2ʰᵈ 31⅛ Smith M E   117   10.60 77−20   Rara Avis112⅛ Space Warning109²⅛ Mon Drapeau117²⅝   Dueled, weakened 7
5Aug95-9DSar wf 1½ ⊕ :50¹ 1:154 1:404 2:012 3↑ ⑤Alw 34000N1x   64 11 6 4³ 5² 3¹ 11½ Day P   115   *1.30ᵉ 72−25   Mon Drapeau115¹½ Follow The Flag115²¾ Call To Prayer115³   Going away 11
24Nov94-3Aqu fst 7f   :23² :472 1:12¹ 1:48⁴   ⑤Md Sp Wt   52 8 1 6¹⁰ 6⁸ 4¹³ 31³⅓ Beckner D V⁵   115   12.30 55−24   Foxy Scarlet117¹² Symmetrical117ᵐᵏ Mon Drapeau117²³   No threat 9
18Nov94-3Aqu yl 1½ ⊕ :233 :50 1:16³ 1:484   ⑤Md Sp Wt   52 1 10 101¹ 9⁹⅝ 83 34½ Davis R G   117   *2.45 59−25   Silver Decor117⁷ Moni Woman117⅛ Spire112¹⅛   Outrun 10
9Oct94-3Bel fm 1½ ⊕ :231 :482 1:11 1:441   ⑤Md Sp Wt   66 6 11 9¹³ 81⁰ 53 31½ Davis R G   117   16.20 75−21   Rara Avis117⅛ Ivory Hunter117¹ Mon Drapeau117¾   Belated rally 12

WORKOUTS: Jan 26 Bel tr.t 4f fst :51 B 25/41   Dec 31 Bel tr.t 5f fst 1:02³ B 13/22   Dec 24 Bel tr.t 4f fst :52 B 134/147   Dec 18 Bel tr.t 4f fst :54 B 73/78   Dec 4 Bel tr.t 5f fst 1:06 B 9/11   Nov 25 Bel tr.t 4f fst :51¹ B 41/52

A Blink And A Nod

Own: Wallace Dana

Dk. b or br m. 5
Sire: Salutely (Hoist the Flag)
Dam: Wave of the Hand (Handsome Kid)
Br: Wallace Dana (NY)
Tr: Rea Michael (3 0 1 2 .00)

L 113

Lifetime Record :	22 2 1 5	$55,819	
1996	2 0 0 2	$7,260	Turf	8 1 0 0	$22,500
1995	20 2 1 3	$48,559	Wet	4 0 1 3	$17,380
Aqu⊡	5 0 1 2	$15,860	Dist	5 0 0 2	$9,540

CASTILLO N JR (140 15 18 20 .11)

15Jan96-5Aqu my 1⅛ ⊡ :474 1:142 1:481   ⑤Alw 33000N1x   62 5 9 71⁰ 54½ 3³ 32½ Castillo H Jr   L 114   3.20 61−26   Patti's Purse113¾ PositiveTally113² ABlinkAndANod114³   Bid, weakened 10
3Jan96-7Aqu fst 1½ ⊡ :51 1:171 1:433 1:57   ⑤Alw 33000N1x   48 4 9 7⁴ 63½ 31⅔ 3⁵ Castillo H Jr   L 114   7.30 46−37   Light Bright Heart116⁴ Deviiette108¹ A Blink And A Nod114³⅛   Mild bid 10
15Dec95-7Aqu my 1⅛ ⊡ :48 1:131 1:453 3↑ ⑤Alw 33000N1x   62 7 10 10¹¹ 64½ 3³ 3⁵ Castillo H Jr   L 116   7.00 68−12   BlindTruth116⅓ ABlinkAndANod116⁴½ Igobacktotheking113ᵐᵏ   Best of rest 12
1Dec95-4Aqu my 1¼   :483 1:121 1:381 1:514 3↑ ⑤Alw 33000N1x   60 7 8 7⁷ 7ᵐ 44 33½ Castillo H Jr   L 115   26.75 71−13   Hardy Heart115³ Hold You112¾ A Blink And A Nod115²½   Late gain 9
11Nov95-6Pha fst 1½   :23 :493 1:15 1:494 3↑ ⑤Clm 15000N2L   42 8 9 99½ 76½ 31½ 1ⁿᵒ Hollick W J   L 110   *2.10 63−29   A Blink And A Nod110ⁿᵒ Never Vein113²⅛ Kane's Cancer105⁴⅝   Just up 10
29Oct95-9Bel sf 1½ ⊕ :23 1:162 2:103 2:37 3↑ ⑤LongIslandH-G2   — 5 4 5² 71¹ 9¹³ — Hollick W J   L 108   125.00 − 58   Yenda114¹½ Windsharp1117 Market Booster118ᵐᵏ   Gave way, eased 10
12Oct95-8Bel gd 1¼ ⊕ :483 1:13¹ 1:384 2:03² 3↑ ⑤Alw 34000N2L   67 3 8 7⁷½ 66½ 79 59½ Hollick W J   L 109   63.00 62−17   Francia113⁴ Star Of Light111⁴ Bella Dawn113ᵐᵏ   Checked early 12
28Sep95-8Bel fst 1½   :50³ 1:154 1:42 2:08³ 3↑ ⑤Alw 34204N1x   45 3 1 2ᵐ 42 43⅔ 44½ Hollick W J   L 110   18.00 32−29   SelectAccount110⁴ RabsLilBritBric117¹¾ SpaceWrning110ⁿᵒ   Dueled, tired 5
21Sep95-7Bel fm 1½ ⊕ :493 1:141 1:393 2:044 3↑ ⑤Alw 34000N1x   70 4 5 5¹ 53 64½ 64½ Hollick W J   L 112   19.80 58−26   Grand Chorus117⁴¾ Bella Dawn112ⁿᵒ Select Account117½   No rally 7
19Aug95-5Sar fm 1½ ⊕ :241 :474 1:12 1:363 3↑ ⑤Alw 34000N1x   60 3 10 84⅛ 5⁸ 78½ Perez R B   123   6.70 86−05   Lamplight118² Bid O'powdre113¹⅓ Reel Talc118²   Wide, flattened 10

WORKOUTS:

Reelherin
Own: Valentine John
TREJO J (110 13 15 10 .12)

B. m. 7
Sire: He's Bad (Rambunctious)
Dam: Alfa's Sunrise (Hoist the Silver)
Br: Valentine John (NY)
Tr: Ortiz Juan (11 1 0 1 .09)

L 112^7

Lifetime Record:	21 1 5 3	$66,794			
1995	10 1 2 1	$43,980	Turf	0 0 0 0	
1994	7 M 3 2	$22,640	Wet	3 0 0 1	$5,040
Aqu ⊡	6 1 2 1	$33,760	Dist	3 1 1 0	$25,900

28Dec95-2Aqu fst	$1\frac{1}{8}$ ⊡	:49	1:16	1:42^3	1:56^1	3↑ⒻⓈMd Sp Wt	61	9	9	7^7	1^5	1^6	$1^{6\frac{1}{2}}$	Trejo J^7	L 114 b	2.70	55-37	Reelherin114$^{6\frac{1}{2}}$ Call To Prayer118^{hd} Miss S O S118^{12}	Driving 12
2Dec95-1Aqu gd	7f	:23	:46^2	1:12^4	1:26	3↑ⒻⓈMd Sp Wt	43	8	5	9^9	7^{10}	$4^{9\frac{1}{2}}$	4^7	Agosto R^5	L 116 b	3.90	67-12	LightTheLights119^2 MissyMims112$^{4\frac{3}{4}}$ SunsationlGirl119^{hd}	Mild gain, wide 11
20Oct95-3Bel fst	6f	:21^3	:44^2	:58	1:12	3↑ⒻⓈMd Sp Wt	45	7	7	8^{12}	8^{12}	$6^{8\frac{1}{2}}$	$5^{5\frac{1}{2}}$	Leon F	L 121	14.10	75-15	Accuracy118$^{3\frac{1}{2}}$ Missy Mims111^{nk} Star Personality118$^{\frac{3}{4}}$	Saved ground 12
18Sep95-3Bel my	1	:23^3	:47^3	1:13	1:39	3↑ⒻⓈMd Sp Wt	42	7	7	$8^{5\frac{1}{2}}$	$5^{5\frac{1}{2}}$	$6^{6\frac{1}{2}}$	$4^{10\frac{1}{2}}$	Chavez C R^7	L 114 b	7.70	57-23	FollowTheFlg116^7 FlgOfGold116$^{\frac{1}{2}}$ DivisoN'belle116^3	Four wide, no rally 12
9Jly95-3Bel fst	7f	:23	:47^2	1:13^1	1:26^4	3↑ⒻⓈMd Sp Wt	32	7	4	6^3	$6^{2\frac{3}{4}}$	3^6	$4^{9\frac{1}{2}}$	Krone J A	122 b	*1.15	57-18	TwentySixKrts108$^{6\frac{1}{2}}$ DomintedWy114$^{2\frac{1}{2}}$ FollowTheFlg114$^{\frac{1}{2}}$	Flattened out 10
2Jun95-3Bel fst	6f	:22^4	:47	1:00	1:13^2	3↑ⒻⓈMd Sp Wt	60	12	9	10^{14}	9^9	4^6	$3^{4\frac{1}{4}}$	Agosto R^7	115 b	6.00	70-25	Subversive Dancer113$^{3\frac{1}{2}}$ Honey Watral113$^{\frac{3}{4}}$ Reelherin115$^{1\frac{1}{2}}$	Belated rally 12
14May95-2Bel fst	$1\frac{1}{16}$	:23	:46^1	1:13^1	1:47^3	3↑ⒻⓈMd Sp Wt	52	7	10	$11^{8\frac{3}{4}}$	5^2	3^2	4^7	Perez R B^5	117 b	3.70	54-29	Forever Proud112$^{6\frac{1}{2}}$ Hold You112^{no} Stellina112$^{\frac{1}{2}}$	Five wide, flattened 14
8Apr95-1Aqu fst	1	:23^4	:47^3	1:13^2	1:39^4	ⒻMd Sp Wt	54	2	4	3^3	2^{hd}	$2^{\frac{1}{2}}$	$2^{\frac{3}{4}}$	Martin G J^7	114 b	4.10	69-22	PocketBeuty121$^{\frac{3}{4}}$ Reelherin114$^{5\frac{3}{4}}$ LerningTheRopes121^1	Brief lead, game 8
18Mar95-9Aqu fst	1	:23^4	:48^2	1:15^3	1:43	ⒻMd Sp Wt	47	4	4	$5^{2\frac{1}{2}}$	$4^{2\frac{1}{4}}$	3^1	2^2	Martin G J^7	114 b	3.60	52-31	Blind Truth121^2 Reelherin114^2 Be Reinvested121$^{\frac{3}{4}}$	Willingly 11
23Feb95-5Aqu fst	$1\frac{1}{8}$ ⊡	:49^4	1:15	1:42	1:55^4	ⒻMd Sp Wt	49	6	3	$2^{\frac{1}{2}}$	$2^{\frac{1}{2}}$	$3^{2\frac{1}{2}}$	$4^{4\frac{1}{4}}$	Martin G J^7	115 b	*2.00	53-29	SesonsComernt122$^{1\frac{1}{4}}$ BlindTruth122^{no} MissStrVrs117^3	Forced pace, tired 10

WORKOUTS: Jan 23 Aqu ⊡ 5f fst 1:02^1 B 5/8 Nov 10 Aqu 5f fst 1:03^3 B 2/5

~~**Hold You**~~
Own: Joques Farm
TREJO J (110 13 15 10 .12)

Dk. b or br f. 4
Sire: Stay the Course (Majestic Light)
Dam: Extended Charge (Full Extent)
Br: Galvin Michael (NY)
Tr: Moschera Gasper S (103 22 21 16 .21)

L 106^7

Lifetime Record:	26 1 5 4	$73,540			
1996	2 0 0 0		Turf	3 0 1 0	$6,400
1995	17 1 5 2	$52,880	Wet	8 1 2 1	$37,240
Aqu ⊡	6 0 0 0	$840	Dist	4 0 2 0	$14,920

15Jan96-5Aqu my	$1\frac{1}{16}$ ⊡	:23^1	:47^4	1:14^2	1:48^1	ⒻⓈAlw 33000N1X	20	8	4	4^5	4^4	7^{14}	$8^{22\frac{3}{4}}$	Pezua J M	L 113	9.80	41-26	Patti's Purse113$^{\frac{1}{2}}$ Positive Tally113^2 A Blink And A Nod114^3	Gave way 10
3Jan96-7Aqu fst	$1\frac{1}{8}$ ⊡	:51	1:17^1	1:43^3	1:57	ⒻⓈAlw 33000N1X	28	1	1	$1^{\frac{1}{2}}$	$1^{\frac{1}{2}}$	$4^{4\frac{1}{2}}$	$8^{18\frac{3}{4}}$	Chavez J F	L 113	*1.80	33-37	Light Bright Heart116^4 Devilette108^1 A Blink And A Nod114$^{3\frac{1}{2}}$	Tired 10
15Dec95-7Aqu my	$1\frac{1}{16}$ ⊡	:23^3	:48	1:13^1	1:45^3	3↑ⒻⓈAlw 33000N1X	38	6	1	3^3	2^6	3^{14}	6^{23}	Chavez J F	L 113	*1.60	54-12	Blind Truth116^9 A Blink And A Nod116$^{7\frac{1}{2}}$ Igobacktotheking113^{nk}	Tired 12
1Dec95-6Aqu my	$1\frac{1}{8}$	:48^3	1:12^1	1:38^1	1:51^4	3↑ⒻⓈAlw 33000N1X	61	4	2	$1^{\frac{1}{2}}$	$1^{\frac{1}{2}}$	$2^{\frac{1}{2}}$	2^3	Chavez J F	L 112	5.80	78-12	Hardy Heart116^3 Hold You112$^{\frac{1}{2}}$ A Blink And A Nod115$^{2\frac{1}{2}}$	Dueled, held 2nd 9
16Nov95-7Aqu fst	$1\frac{1}{8}$	:52^1	1:17^4	1:44	1:57^1	3↑ⒻⓈAlw 32000N1X	58	2	1	1^1	$1^{1\frac{1}{2}}$	$1^{\frac{1}{2}}$	2^{nk}	Chavez J F	L 112	*1.90	54-35	ThroughThTulps115^{nk} HoldYo112^{nk} TwntySxKrts108^1	Yielded grudgingly 8
11Nov95-1Aqu fst	1	:23^3	:46^4	1:12^2	1:39^1	3↑ⒻⓈAlw 32000N1X	61	4	4	2^1	5^3	$6^{6\frac{1}{2}}$	$7^{9\frac{1}{2}}$	Alvarado F T	L 114	8.00	63-19	SartogCoers114$^{1\frac{1}{2}}$ FollowTheFlg114^2 WorkOfTheDevil115$^{2\frac{1}{2}}$	Chased, tired 11
26Oct95-5Bel fst	$1\frac{1}{16}$	:23^3	:47^3	1:13^2	1:46^1	3↑ⒻⓈAlw 34000N1X	54	3	1	2^{hd}	1^{hd}	3^1	3^4	Alvarado F T	L 113	36.75	64-22	Calypso Vuh114^{hd} Work OfTheDevil116^2 HoldYou113^8	Dueled, weakened 9
18Oct95-9Bel fst	$1\frac{1}{16}$	:23^1	:46^4	1:12^4	1:45^4	3↑ⒻⓈAlw 34000N1X	45	8	5	$4^{2\frac{1}{2}}$	$3^{1\frac{1}{2}}$	4^7	4^{11}	Alvarado F T	L 114	28.25	59-21	SesonlSplendor113^3 WorkOfTheDevil116^4 OnlyForvr114^4	Flattened out 10
5Oct95-5Bel sly	1	:22^3	:45^3	1:11^1	1:39	3↑ⒻⓈAlw 34000N1X	18	4	4	5^4	10^{10}	11^{17}	11^{24}	Martinez J R Jr	L 112	13.60	44-26	DoroteoArngo112^{nk} WorkOfTheDevil116^{hd} SesonlSplendor113$^{1\frac{1}{2}}$	Gave way 11
29Jly95-9Sar fm	$1\frac{1}{8}$ Ⓣ	:46	1:11^3	1:36^2	1:49	3↑ⒻⓈAlw 34000N1X	6	6	3	4^3	$9^{9\frac{1}{2}}$	11^{28}	11^{33}	Martinez J R Jr	113	38.00	49-08	Simply Pleasant113^{no} Katie's Flag111^3 Aidan's Breath113$^{\frac{3}{4}}$	Gave way 12

WORKOUTS: Nov 7 Bel tr.t 5f fst 1:01^1 H 3/14

Of the 12, only three had won at $1\frac{1}{8}$ miles: Cool Babe, Seasons Comerant and Reelherin.

Among the others were Miss S O S at one for 16 lifetime, Deputy Snoop at one for 23, Devilette at one for 18, Pink Syncopation at one for 25, Go With Flo at one for 12, Mon Drapeau at one for 14 and A Blink And A Nod at two for 22. Cool Babe was one for 13 and Reelherin one for 21.

In fields of chronic losers, crazy things sometimes happen.

The perfectly legitimate 8-5 favorite was Positive Tally, who was second in her last start. She had a win and another second in seven previous starts.

The perfectly legitimate 2-1 second choice was Only Forever, who had a record of 1-2-2 in seven starts.

What of the winner?

Seasons Comerant deserved to be a longshot. She was a five-year-old mare making her first start since April 13, 1995, off only one slow published workout (four furlongs in :$51\frac{1}{5}$). But let's take a close look at her record of one win in six starts, starting, of course, at the bottom of her PPs.

Her first start was in a six-furlong, open maiden $50,000 claimer at Aqueduct, January 19, 1995. She was bet down to 5-2 in her debut and finished fourth by 11 lengths in the field of eight while three wide.

She moved up to an open maiden special weight for her second start, also at six furlongs, and ran eighth by 13 lengths at 10-1, but the *Form* noted she was checked at the quarter pole.

She remained in open maiden special weights in her third start while stretching out to 1⅛ miles. Sent off at 4-1 in the field of 10, she went wire to wire, winning by 1¼ lengths. Of all the other horses in today's race showing their maiden wins in their PPs, only one did not break her maiden against New York-Breds, and that was Miss S O S, who won an open maiden $35,000 claimer.

In her fourth start, Seasons Comerant moved up to a mile and 70 yards, New York-Bred, non-winners of two and was fourth by 9½ lengths in a field of six at 8-1.

She then went into an open filly non-winners of two with blinkers on. Sent off at 34-1, she was seventh by 11½ lengths in the one mile race after breaking slowly.

Her last race was 1⅛ miles, New York-Bred non-winners of two. Sent off at 6-1, she tired badly and was eased.

Today, she was racing without blinkers, and by using Jackie Sherman, a 10-pound apprentice rider, was carrying 103 pounds, getting from five to 16 pounds from every other horse in the race.

Was she a logical contender? No way.

Did I like her? No way.

But did she deserve to be 80-1, considering she not only won at the distance, but she did so in open company? No way. Despite the layoff, she had gone off at 6-1 in her previous start, was getting a blinker change and dropping 16 pounds.

This isn't about being a genius handicapper and coming up with an 80-1 longshot. It is about opening up your thinking, handicapping and wagering to occasionally allow such exotic overlays to grace your wallet.

And even sometimes when they don't, there is consolation. This Pick Five paying nearly $500 was an exotic overlay of its own.

$2 Pick–3 (1–5–2) Paid $40.00; Pick–3 Pool $86,309.

FIFTH RACE
Aqueduct
FEBRUARY 2, 1996

1⅛ MILES. (Inner Dirt)(1.47^{1}) ALLOWANCE. Purse $33,000. Fillies and mares, 4–year–olds and upward foaled in New York State and approved by the New York State–Bred Registry which have not won a race other than maiden, claiming or starter. Weight, 122 lbs.

Value of Race: $33,000 Winner $19,800; second $6,600; third $3,630; fourth $1,980; fifth $990. Mutuel Pool $193,075.00 Exacta Pool $275,572.00 Trifecta Pool $252,535.00

Last Raced	Horse	M/Eqt.	A.	Wt	PP	St	¼	½	¾	Str	Fin	Jockey	Odds $1
13Apr95 ^{3}Aqu^{6}	Seasons Comerant		5	105	6	2	1^{2}	1^{1}	$1^{\frac{1}{2}}$	$1^{1\frac{1}{2}}$	$1^{\frac{1}{2}}$	Sherman J M^{10}	81.25
15Jan96 ^{5}Aqu^{2}	Positive Tally	Lb	4	114	7	5	$5^{1\frac{1}{2}}$	5^{hd}	5^{1}	3^{1}	$2^{\frac{3}{4}}$	Luzzi M J	1.75
15Jan96 ^{5}Aqu^{3}	A Blink And A Nod	L	5	114	11	11	12	$11^{1\frac{1}{2}}$	$10^{1\frac{1}{2}}$	$4^{1\frac{1}{2}}$	$3^{\frac{1}{2}}$	Castillo H Jr	7.30
15Jan96 ^{5}Aqu^{4}	Go With Flo		4	113	9	8	4^{2}	3^{2}	3^{2}	$2^{\frac{1}{2}}$	4^{3}	Rocco J	27.25
28Dec95 ^{2}Aqu^{1}	Reelherin	Lb	7	112	12	12	$10^{1\frac{1}{2}}$	8^{1}	7^{1}	$5^{1\frac{1}{2}}$	$5^{2\frac{1}{4}}$	Trejo J^{7}	15.80
15Dec95 ^{7}Aqu^{8}	Cool Babe	Lb	4	113	3	3	$9^{\frac{1}{2}}$	9^{hd}	9^{2}	7^{3}	6^{nk}	Velazquez J R	17.50
11Jan96 ^{6}Aqu^{8}	Only Forever	Lb	4	113	8	7	2^{1}	$2^{\frac{1}{2}}$	$2^{\frac{1}{2}}$	$6^{\frac{1}{2}}$	7^{4}	Chavez J F	2.40
19Jan96 ^{2}Aqu^{1}	Miss S O S	Lb	4	114	1	1	$3^{\frac{1}{2}}$	$4^{1\frac{1}{2}}$	4^{1}	$9^{1\frac{1}{2}}$	8no	Migliore R	26.75
3Jan96 ^{7}Aqu^{2}	Devilette	Lb	4	108	4	6	6^{2}	6^{3}	$6^{\frac{1}{2}}$	$8^{\frac{1}{2}}$	9^{2}	Chavez C R^{5}	7.60
26Dec95 ^{7}Lrl^{10}	Deputy Snoop	L	5	114	2	9	11^{1}	12	12	12	10no	Alvarado F T	a-14.60
15Jan96 ^{5}Aqu^{5}	Pink Syncopation		5	113	5	4	8^{3}	10^{2}	11^{2}	$10^{\frac{1}{2}}$	11^{nk}	Nelson D	40.00
15Jan96 ^{5}Aqu^{7}	Mon Drapeau	L	4	113	10	10	7^{1}	7^{1}	$8^{\frac{1}{2}}$	$11^{1\frac{1}{2}}$	12	Bravo J	a-14.60

a–Coupled: Deputy Snoop and Mon Drapeau.

OFF AT 2:06 Start Good. Won driving. Time, :23^{1}, :48^{2}, 1:14, 1:41^{2}, 1:55 Track fast.

$2 Mutuel Prices:				
	6–SEASONS COMERANT	164.50	35.20	10.00
	7–POSITIVE TALLY		3.30	2.60
	10–A BLINK AND A NOD			3.40

$2 EXACTA 6–7 PAID $499.50 $2 TRIFECTA 6–7–10 PAID $2,959.00

B. m, by Cormorant–Cosmic, by Halo. Trainer Held Dieter K. Bred by Kinderhill Select Bloodstock Inc (NY).

SEASONS COMERANT sprinted clear in the early stages, shook off a challenge from ONLY FOREVER on the turn, regained a clear lead in upper stretch then lured back POSITIVE TALLY in the final sixteenth. POSITIVE TALLY settled in good position while saving ground to the turn, made a run to threaten leaving the furlong marker but couldn't overtake the winner. A BLINK AND A NOD far back seven furlongs, rallied belatedly along the rail. GO WITH FLO stalked the pace three wide for six furlongs, made a run to threaten in upper stretch but couldn't sustain her bid. REELHERIN gradually worked her way forward on the turn, then lacked a strong closing bid. COOL BABE never reached contention. ONLY FOREVER forced the pace from outside to the top of the stretch and gave way. MISS S O S raced up close to the turn and steadily tired thereafter. DEVILETTE went evenly for six furlongs then lacked the needed response when called upon. POSITIVE TALLY, REELHERIN and ONLY FOREVER wore mud caulks.

Owners— 1, Michelotti John R; 2, Minnella Martin J; 3, Wallace Dana; 4, Boyd & Hangan & Walsh; 5, Valentino John; 6, Piety Hill Stable; 7, Roberts James K & Terian Peter G; 8, Ferrari Louis P; 9, Wachtel Edwin H; 10, Rosbsham E Paul; 11, Davidson Herbert S & Wendel Arthur; 12, Cohn Seymour

Trainers— 1, Held Dieter K; 2, Klesaris Steve; 3, Rea Michael; 4, Walsh Thomas M; 5, Ortiz Juan; 6, O'Connell Richard; 7, Martin Carlos F; 8, Ferraro James W; 9, Destefano John M Jr; 10, Terrill William V; 11, Wendel Arthur; 12, Terrill William V

Corrected weight: Miss S O S (114) **Overweight:** Seasons Comerant (2), Positive Tally (1), A Blink And A Nod (1), Miss S O S (1), Deputy Snoop (1)

Scratched— Ultra Power (15Dec95 ^{7}AQU^{12}) Hold You (15Jan96 ^{5}AQU^{8})

But let's move from Pick Sixes nobody hit to ones that people did connect on.

The Pick Six at Belmont Park, October 19, 1995, had a carryover of $37,750. In the spirit of Steve Crist, let's see how hard it was to "get through it."

For openers, we could consider this Pick Six as a Pick Five because of the presence of Mesabi Maiden in the sixth. The scratch of Flume left a field of eight.

6 Belmont Park

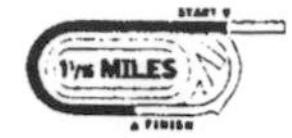

1 1/16 MILES. (1:39^4) **MAIDEN SPECIAL WEIGHT. Purse $32,000 (plus up to $12,560 NYSBFOA). Fillies, 2-year-olds. Weight, 117 lbs.**

Turn to the Queen
Own: Jayaraman K K & B J
STEVENS G L (82 17 10 14 .21)

B. f. 2 (Feb)
Sire: Lyphard's Ridge (Lyphard's Wish)
Dam: Riva's Queen (Riva Ridge)
Br: Jayaraman Dr K K & Dr Vilasini D (Ark)
Tr: Jolley Leroy (25 3 2 2 .12)

117

Lifetime Record:	3 M 0 0	$1,593			
1995	3 M 0 0	$1,593	Turf	1 0 0 0	
1994	0 M 0 0		Wet	0 0 0 0	
Bel	1 0 0 0	$900	Dist	0 0 0 0	

24Sep95-4Bel fst 7f :22^2 :45^2 1:10^2 1:23^3 ⒻMd Sp Wt 45 10 8 10^{8}¼ 8^{10} 6^{14} 5^{19} Sellers S J 117 90.25 64-15 StrtAtOnce117^3 MesbiMiden1171½ ScrletRinbow117^7 Improved position 10
7Sep95-9Bel fm 1 Ⓣ :23 :46 1:10^4 1:37 ⒻMd Sp Wt 36 10 12 11^{18} 11^{9}¾ 10^{13} 8^{15}¼ Velasquez J 117 51.25 62-21 SinfullyDelicious1171½ Illume117^{nk} Lizzy'sPlesur1174¼ Took up break, wide 12
20Aug95-3Pim fst 5½f :22^2 :46^3 :59^2 1:06^1 ⒻMd Sp Wt 28 8 6 7^{9}¼ 7^{6}¼ 4^{8}¼ 5^{12}¼ Hamilton S D 119 14.70 78-14 Marfa's Finale1194¼ Buckaroo Zoo1191½ Know The Code119^6 Wide 10

WORKOUTS: Oct 9 Bel tr.t 4f fst :48^3 H 5/25 Sep 21 Bel 4f fst :47^4 H 5/47 Sep 3 Bel 4f fst :47^4 H 4/46 Aug 15 Pim 4f fst :48^4 Hg2/8

Girton Gate
Own: Live Oak Plantation
SAMYN J L (86 9 10 13 .10)

B. f. 2 (Mar)
Sire: Gate Dancer (Sovereign Dancer)
Dam: Smart 'Nuff (Smarten)
Br: Live Oak Stud (Ont-C)
Tr: Kelly Patrick J (31 4 3 2 .13)

117

Lifetime Record:	2 M 0 0	$1,920			
1995	2 M 0 0	$1,920	Turf	1 0 0 0	
1994	0 M 0 0		Wet	1 0 0 0	$1,920
Bel	1 0 0 0	$1,920	Dist	1 0 0 0	$1,920

6Oct95-5Bel my 1 1/16 :23^4 :48^1 1:14 1:47 ⒻMd Sp Wt 50 4 4 6^{2}¾ 6^{4}½ 5^9 4^{9}¾ Samyn J L 117 33.75 54-35 Weekend In Seattle1171½ Honorably117^9 Reliable Lady117^{nk} Tired 9
7Sep95-9Bel fm 1 Ⓣ :23 :46 1:10^4 1:37 ⒻMd Sp Wt 35 4 11 12^{19} 12^{9}¾ 11^{15} 10^{16} Samyn J L 117 25.75 62-21 Sinfully Delicious1171½ Illume117^{nk} Lizzy's Pleasure1174¼ Broke slowly 12

WORKOUTS: Oct 16 Bel 3f fst :36^4 H 4/26 Sep 30 Bel 3f fst :36^3 B 3/17 Sep 25 Bel 4f fst :49 B 26/77 Sep 21 Bel tr.t 4f fst :49^4 B 8/17 Sep 15 Bel 4f fst :48^3 H 8/38 Sep 1 Bel 3f fst :37^1 Hg 13/21

Mesabi Maiden
Own: Janney Stuart S III
VELAZQUEZ J R (287 32 23 26 .15)

B. f. 2 (Apr)
Sire: Cox's Ridge (Best Turn)
Dam: Steel Maiden (Damascus)
Br: Stuart S. Janney III & Ogden Phipps (Ky)
Tr: McGaughey Claude III (31 3 9 5 .10)

117

Lifetime Record:	1 M 1 0	$6,000			
1995	1 M 1 0	$6,000	Turf	0 0 0 0	
1994	0 M 0 0		Wet	0 0 0 0	
Bel	1 0 1 0	$6,000	Dist	0 0 0 0	

24Sep95-4Bel fst 7f :22^2 :45^2 1:10^2 1:23^3 ⒻMd Sp Wt 80 9 6 5^{5}¼ 5^{7}¼ 3^7 2^3 Velazquez J R 117 11.00 80-15 Start AtOnce117^3 MesabiMaiden1171½ ScarletRainbow117^7 Finished well 10

WORKOUTS: Oct 17 Bel 4f fst :49 B 16/34 Oct 10 Bel 4f fst :49^1 B 13/30 Oct 4 Bel 3f fst :38^3 B 20/24 Sep 23 Bel 3f sly :38 B 4/4 Sep 18 Bel 5f my 1:01 H 7/11 Sep 14 Bel 4f my :48^2 Hg3/24

Flume
Own: Fox Hill Farm
SANTOS J A (165 28 18 28 .17)

Dk. b or br f. 2 (Mar)
Sire: Gulch (Mr. Prospector)
Dam: Linden Walk (Cox's Ridge)
Br: Foxfield (Ky)
Tr: Servis John C (10 1 2 0 .10)

L 117

Lifetime Record:	4 M 2 0	$9,010			
1995	4 M 2 0	$9,010	Turf	0 0 0 0	
1994	0 M 0 0		Wet	0 0 0 0	
Bel	1 0 0 0	$1,800	Dist	0 0 0 0	

8Oct95-4Bel fst 7f :23 :47 1:12 1:25^2 ⒻMd Sp Wt 53 8 1 4^5 4^{4}¼ 4^9 4^{10}¼ Luzzi M J L 117 13.30 63-17 Light Rain117^{nk} Ozena117^8 Strollinthepark1172¼ Four wide, no rally 8
12Sep95-6Med fst 6f :22^3 :46^1 :59 1:12^1 ⒻMd Sp Wt 32 1 4 5^{5}¼ 7^6 8^{9}¼ 5^9 Santagata N 117 *1.00 70-18 Aleutian Gold1175¼ Colorful Character1171¾ Rebeccavu117^1 No factor 8
2Aug95-2Mth fst 5½f :22^3 :46^2 :59 1:05^4 ⒻMd Sp Wt 56 7 2 5^{3}½ 5^{6}½ 5^{6}½ 2^{5}½ Marquez C H Jr 117 8.00 84-15 Salina Cookie1175¼ DH Break Through117 DH Flume117^2 5-wide, fin. well 8
19Jly95-6Mth fst 5½f :23 :47^2 1:00 1:06^2 ⒻMd Sp Wt 50 7 2 4^{1}¾ 2^{1}½ 2^3 2^4 Black A S 117 9.20 83-17 Dixie Slew117^4 Flume1173¼ Sinfully Delicious1121¾ Held place 7

WORKOUTS: Sep 28 Aqu 6f fst 1:17 B 1/2 Sep 6 Mth 4f fst :49^3 B 5/12 Aug 30 Mth 6f fst 1:17^2 B 1/2 Aug 16 Mth 4f fst :48^4 B 5/27 Jly 29 Mth 3f fst :36^3 B 7/52

Plum Thicket
Own: Humphrey G Watts Jr
SMITH M E (199 34 24 30 .17)

Dk. b or br f. 2 (Jan)
Sire: Wild Again (Icecapade)
Dam: Oh So Precious (Best Turn)
Br: Fawn Leap Farm (Ky)
Tr: Arnold George R II (34 4 10 5 .12)

117

Lifetime Record:	1 M 0 0	$900			
1995	1 M 0 0	$900	Turf	0 0 0 0	
1994	0 M 0 0		Wet	0 0 0 0	
Bel	1 0 0 0	$900	Dist	0 0 0 0	

10Sep95-2Bel fst 7f :23^1 :47 1:12 1:25^1 ⒻMd Sp Wt 36 2 6 6^{5}¼ 6^6 6^{11} 5^{16}¼ Velazquez J R 117 13.60 59-18 Winning Actress117^{nk} Newhall Road117^4 Ozena117^3 No threat 7

WORKOUTS: Oct 11 Bel 4f fst :50^2 B 37/45 Sep 19 Bel tr.t 4f fst :49^3 B 4/10 Sep 6 Bel 5f fst 1:00^4 H 14/43 Aug 23 Sar 5f fst 1:02^1 H 9/21 Aug 18 Sar 4f fst :50^2 Bg13/18 Aug 14 Sar tr.t 4f fst :51^2 B 20/38

Triple Search
Own: Aquilino & Bovino & Klopacz
CHAVEZ C R (76 5 5 7 .07)

B. f. 2 (Mar)
Sire: Regal Search (Mr. Prospector)
Dam: Triple Top (Topsider)
Br: Carl Bowling (Fla)
Tr: Aquilino Joseph (41 4 3 5 .10)

L 110^7

Lifetime Record:	2 M 0 0	$0			
1995	2 M 0 0		Turf	1 0 0 0	
1994	0 M 0 0		Wet	0 0 0 0	
Bel	1 0 0 0		Dist	0 0 0 0	

24Sep95-4Bel fst 7f :22^2 :45^2 1:10^2 1:23^3 ⒻMd Sp Wt 38 8 5 [illegible] 9^{11} 8^{16} 7^{22}¼ Davis R G L 117 68.25 61-15 StrtAtOnce117^3 MesbiMiden1171½ ScrltRinbow117^7 Four wide, no factor 10
7Sep95-9Bel fm 1 Ⓣ :23 :46 1:10^4 1:37 ⒻMd Sp Wt 35 11 8 [illegible] 6^{3}½ 8^{9}½ 9^{15}¾ Santos J A 117 25.50 62-21 Sinfully Delicious1171½ Illume117^{nk} Lizzy's Pleasure1174¼ Checked break 12

WORKOUTS: Oct 10 Aqu 5f fst 1:02 B 4/8 Sep 16 Aqu 4f fst :48^2 H 2/20 Sep 2 Aqu 5f fst 1:03^2 B 7/9 Aug 28 Sar tr.t 4f fst :53 B 20/24 Aug 23 Sar tr.t Ⓣ 5f fm 1:00^1 H (d)3/9 Aug 18 Sar tr.t 5f fst 1:05^2 B 8/9

Honorably
Own: Harbor View Farm
ALVARADO F T (120 15 18 14 .13)

Dk. b or br f. 2 (Feb)
Sire: Star de Naskra (Naskra)
Dam: Grateful Friend (Teddy's Courage)
Br: Harbor View Farm (Ky)
Tr: Kimmel John C (48 13 9 7 .27)

117

Lifetime Record:	3 M 1 0	$10,000			
1995	3 M 1 0	$10,000	Turf	0 0 0 0	
1994	0 M 0 0		Wet	1 0 1 0	$6,400
Bel	2 0 1 0	$8,200	Dist	1 0 1 0	$6,400

6Oct95-5Bel my 1 1/16 :23^4 :48^1 1:14 1:47 ⒻMd Sp Wt 63 6 3 4^2 2^{hd} 2½ 2^{1}½ Alvarado F T 117 11.40 62-35 WeekendInSeattle1171½ Honorably117^9 ReliableLdy117^{nk} Lost whip 1/8 pl 9
10Sep95-2Bel fst 7f :23^1 :47 1:12 1:25^1 ⒻMd Sp Wt 55 1 7 7^{7}½ 7^{6}¼ 4^{7}½ 4^{7}½ Alvarado F T 117 b 28.50 68-18 Winning Actress117^{nk} Newhall Road117^4 Ozena117^3 Broke slowly 7
25Aug95-2Sar fst 6f :22^4 :46^3 :58^3 1:11^4 ⒻMd Sp Wt 51 8 4 5^3 5^{6}½ 4^9 4^{13} Alvarado F T 118 b 11.80 69-22 OxfordScholr1181½ WinningActress118^{8}¾ NewhllRod118^3 No threat, wide 8

WORKOUTS: Sep 22 Bel tr.t 4f fst :50^1 B 15/20 Sep 4 Bel 5f fst 1:01 H 10/32 Aug 20 Sar 5f fst 1:01^1 H 6/28 Aug 14 Sar 4f fst :47^4 H 4/70 Aug 6 Sar 4f fst :50^1 Hg25/38 Aug 1 Sar 5f fst 1:03 B 17/24

Strollinthepark
Own: Pont Street Stable
BAILEY J D (197 44 27 22 .22)

Ch. f. 2 (Apr)
Sire: Roanoke (Pleasant Colony)
Dam: On the Stroll (Caracolero)
Br: Debbie Mallory & Helen O'Neal Hamilton (Ky)
Tr: Carroll Del W II (18 2 3 2 .11)

117

Lifetime Record:	1 M 0 1	$3,300			
1995	1 M 0 1	$3,300	Turf	0 0 0 0	
1994	0 M 0 0		Wet	0 0 0 0	
Bel	1 0 0 1	$3,300	Dist	0 0 0 0	

8Oct95-4Bel fst 7f :23 :47 1:12 1:25^2 ⒻMd Sp Wt 59 7 8 6^{6}¾ 3^{4}½ 3^6 3^{8}½ Bailey J D 117 7.70 66-17 Light Rain117^{nk} Ozena117^8 Strollinthepark1172¼ Pinched break 8

WORKOUTS: Oct 16 Bel 4f fst :49^2 B 21/50 Oct 3 Bel 5f fst 1:01^2 B 8/26 Oct 1 Bel 3f fst :37^2 Hg4/7 Sep 25 Bel 4f fst :48^3 Hg12/77 Sep 20 Bel 3f fst :36^3 Hg5/22 Sep 15 Bel 5f fst 1:02 H 21/33

Mackie Sarah
Own: Cornacchia & Dolan & Spielman

MIGLIORE R (89 9 6 16 .10)

Ch. f. 2 (May)		
Sire: Thirty Six Red (Slew o' Gold)		
Dam: Exceedingly Bold (Exceedingly)		
Br: Nick Zito (NY)		
Tr: Zito Nicholas P (65 11 10 10 .17)	L 117	

Lifetime Record :	1 M 0 0	$0
1995	1 M 0 0	Turf 0 0 0 0
1994	0 M 0 0	Wet 0 0 0 0
Bel	1 0 0 0	Dist 0 0 0 0

10Oct95- 2Bel fst 6f :22² :46² :58⁴ 1:11³ ⓅMd Sp Wt 24 4 10 10¹⁶ 10¹³ 10¹⁶ 9²⁶ Krone J A L 117 28.25 57- 19 Escena117⁴¼ Carly's Crown117⁹ Adoradancer117⁴ Broke slowly 10

WORKOUTS: Oct 16 Bel 4f fst :49³ B 24/50 Oct 11 Bel 5f fst 1:02⁴ B 26/29 Sep 25 Bel 5f fst 1:03 B 25/42 Sep 16 Bel 5f fst 1:03¹ B 23/29 Sep 9 Bel 5f fst 1:03 H 29/35 Sep 2 Bel 5f fst 1:02 H 17/32

Mesabi Maiden was a well-bred two-year-old filly making her second start for trainer Shug McGaughey. In her first, she broke from the nine post in a field of 10 and closed strongly from third by seven lengths to finish second by three lengths in a seven-furlong race which went in a lively 1:23³/₅. Her Beyer speed figure of 80 was 17 higher than anyone else in the race, and stretching out to 1¹/₁₆ miles made her look invincible. Keep in mind what Steve said about not avoiding Pick Sixes because there was a huge favorite. Instead, key that horse. Mesabi Maiden would go off at 3-10 and win by four lengths.

SIXTH RACE
Belmont

OCTOBER 19, 1995

1¹/₁₆ MILES. (1.39⁴) MAIDEN SPECIAL WEIGHT. Purse $32,000 (plus up to $12,560 NYSBFOA). Fillies, 2-year-olds. Weight, 117 lbs.

Value of Race: $32,000 Winner $19,200; second $6,400; third $3,520; fourth $1,920; fifth $960. Mutuel Pool $197,565.00 Exacta Pool $358,700.00 Minus Show Pool $1,329.92

Last Raced	Horse	M/Eql. A. Wt	PP St	¼	½	¾	Str	Fin	Jockey	Odds $1
24Sep95 4Bel²	Mesabi Maiden	2 117	3 6	1½	1½	1¹	1³	1⁴	Velazquez J R	0.30
8Oct95 4Bel³	Strollinthepark	2 117	7 5	3½	4hd	2³½	2⁶	2⁷	Bailey J D	6.60
24Sep95 4Bel⁵	Turn to the Queen	2 117	1 8	8	3½	5hd	3½	3²½	Stevens G L	39.75
6Oct95 5Bel²	Honorably	b 2 117	6 3	5hd	7½	4½	4⁴	4⁴½	Alvarado F T	4.80
6Oct95 5Bel⁴	Girton Gate	2 117	2 7	4½	2½	6¹½	5²	5³½	Samyn J L	27.75
10Sep95 2Bel⁵	Plum Thicket	2 117	4 4	2¹	6¹	7⁴	6½	6⁸	Smith M E	37.25
24Sep95 4Bel⁷	Triple Search	L 2 110	5 2	6½	5½	3½	7²⁰	7²³	Chavez C R⁷	73.25
10Oct95 2Bel⁹	Mackie Sarah	L 2 117	8 1	7½	8	8	8	8	Migliore R	55.75

OFF AT 3:29 Start Good. Won driving. Time, :23², :47, 1:12, 1:37¹, 1:43⁴ Track fast.

$2 Mutuel Prices:	3-MESABI MAIDEN	2.60	2.20	2.10
	8-STROLLINTHEPARK		3.30	2.10
	1-TURN TO THE QUEEN			2.20

$2 EXACTA 3-8 PAID $6.80

B. f, (Apr), by Cox's Ridge-Steel Maiden, by Damascus. Trainer McGaughey Claude III. Bred by Stuart S. Janney III & Ogden Phipps (Ky).

MESABI MAIDEN took the lead while well off the rail along the backstretch, opened a clear advantage on the turn then drew away while being ridden out. STROLLINTHEPARK settled just off the early pace, rallied five wide on the turn but was no match while clearly best of the others. TURN TO THE QUEEN moved up rapidly along the inside to reach contention nearing the far turn, dropped back on the turn and failed to threaten thereafter. HONORABLY raced within striking distance from outside on the turn and lacked a further response. GIRTON GATE showed speed for a half and gave way. PLUM THICKET forced the early pace, gave way before going a half. TRIPLE SEARCH steadily gained between horses to reach contention on the turn and flattened out. MACKIE SARAH was outrun. MACKIE SARAH wore mud caulks.

Owners— 1, Janney Stuart S III; 2, Pont Street Stable; 3, Jayaraman K K & B J; 4, Harbor View Farm; 5, Live Oak Plantation; 6, Humphrey G Watts Jr; 7, Aquilino & Bovino & Klopacz; 8, Cornacchia & Dolan & Spielman.

Trainers— 1, McGaughey Claude III; 2, Carroll Del W II; 3, Jolley Leroy; 4, Kimmel John C; 5, Kelly Patrick J; 6, Arnold George R II; 7, Aquilino Joseph; 8, Zito Nicholas P.

Scratched— Flume (30Oct95 4BEL⁴)

The second key would be in the fifth, a six-furlong allowance, non-winners of two, for New York-Bred fillies and mares at six furlongs. The scratch of Personal Nurse left a field of nine.

5 Belmont Park

6 Furlongs (1:07⁴) ALLOWANCE. Purse $32,000 (plus up to $12,560 NYSBFOA). Fillies and mares, 3-year-olds and upward foaled in New York State and approved by the New York State–Bred Registry which have not won a race other than maiden or claiming. Weights: 3-year-olds, 119 lbs. Older, 122 lbs. Non-winners of two races since September 7, allowed 3 lbs. A race since September 19, 5 lbs. A race since August 22, 7 lbs. (Races where entered for $40,000 or less not considered in allowances.)

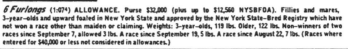

Flannel Sheets
Own: Flying Zee Stables
Dk. b or br f. 3 (Feb)
Sire: Triocala (Tri Jet)
Dam: Queen's Boudoir (Roman Reasoning)
Br: Flying Zee Stables (NY)
Tr: Martin Jose (39 5 4 6 .13)
114

	Lifetime Record :	5 1 1 2	$32,500
1995	3 1 1 1	$27,920 Turf	0 0 0 0
1994	2 M 0 0	$4,680 Wet	1 0 0 1 $3,520
Bel	3 1 1 1	$27,920 Dist	4 1 1 1 $29,080

Angel Kate
Own: Montanar: Marion G
B. f. 3 (Jun)
Sire: Mt. Livermore (Blushing Groom)
Dam: August Days (In Reality)
Br: Stone Ridge Farm (NY)
Tr: Terrill William V (27 4 4 3 .15)
L 112

	Lifetime Record :	9 1 4 1	$48,080
1995	9 1 4 1	$48,080 Turf	0 0 0 0
1994	0 M 0 0	Wet	2 0 0 0
Bel	5 1 3 0	$37,200 Dist	3 0 3 0 $18,800

Saratoga Capers
Own: Dubose Sandy
B. f. 3 (Mar)
Sire: Saratoga Six (Alydar)
Dam: Wind Capers (Mr. Prospector)
Br: Tom Bozek (NY)
Tr: Woodington Jamie (5 0 3 1 .00)
112

	Lifetime Record :	3 1 1 1	$23,120
1995	3 1 1 1	$23,120 Turf	0 0 0 0
1994	0 M 0 0	Wet	1 0 1 0 $5,400
Bel	2 0 1 1	$9,920 Dist	2 1 0 1 $16,720

Personal Nurse
Own: Caputo John
B. f. 4
Sire: Personal Flag (Private Account)
Dam: Double Jeux (Exclusive Native)
Br: Wilhelmina M. Combs (NY)
Tr: Schettino Dominick A (18 2 1 1 .11)
L 110⁵

	Lifetime Record :	18 1 0 1	$18,780
1995	11 1 0 0	$11,100 Turf	2 0 0 0
1994	7 M 0 1	$7,680 Wet	2 0 0 0 $1,920
Bel	3 0 0 0	$1,920 Dist	6 0 0 1 $9,420

Gallantress Ack
Own: DeMatteis Frederick
B. m. 5
Sire: Gallant Hour (Bold Hour)
Dam: Fabulous Ack (Ack Ack)
Br: Dematteis Fred & Prestia Charles (NY)
Tr: Priole Philip (7 1 0 1 .14)
115

	Lifetime Record :	38 1 4 2	$35,260
1995	8 0 0 0	$2,340 Turf	0 0 0 0
1994	11 0 1 2 1	$16,480 Wet	8 0 0 0 $960
Bel	10 0 0 0	$3,420 Dist	28 1 4 2 $32,800

Distinctly Patti
Own: Winbound Farms
VELAZQUEZ J R (207 32 23 26 .15)

B. f. 3 (Jan)
Sire: Distinctive Pro (Mr. Prospector)
Dam: Tournament Dancer (Lypheor)
Br: No L Stable (NY)
Tr: Sciacca Gary (70 7 5 12 .10)

L 112

Lifetime Record: 8 1 2 1 $39,000

1995	3	0	0	1	$5,380	Turf	0	0	0	0	
1994	5	1	2	0	$33,620	Wet	2	0	0	1	$3,520
Bel	4	0	2	1	$16,800	Dist	5	0	1	1	$16,040

6Oct95- 4Bel my 6f :23 :472 1:001 1:133 3+ Ⓕ[S]Alw 32000N1X 38 5 3 3½ 3¾ 35 3¾ Velazquez J R L 112 b *.65 65-23 InANutshell112¾ OurSecrtHrt1151½ DistinctlyPtti1123 Forced pace, wide 7
6Sep95- 6Bel fst 6f :223 :461 :582 1:111 3+ Ⓕ[S]Alw 32000N1X 59 7 12 104½ 94¾ 65 56¾ Velazquez J R 110 b 4.90e 78-14 LilMisGia1152½ AngelKate1132¾ SaratogaCpers1151½ Broke slowl, late gain 12
6Jan95- 8Aqu fst 6f [•] :222 :454 :584 1:13 Ⓕ[S]Alw 30000N1X 37 3 4 511 58½ 59 510½ Alvarado F T 116 b 2.40 67-18 Dancing Dawn1181½ Wolfe Island1162½ Lady By Design1162½ No factor 6
11Dec94- 8Aqu wf 1 1/16 [•] :231 :46 1:12 1:454 Ⓕ[S]East View54k — 1 3 46½ 612 625 — Alvarado F T 114 b 14.90 — 22 Rogues Walk1211½ Foxy Scarlet1142¾ Friendly Beauty1216 Outrun,eased 7
13Nov94- 7Aqu fst 6f :224 :464 :59 1:114 ⒻⓇN Y Stallion75k 59 6 5 85¾ 54½ 47 412½ Bravo J 114 b 8.60 71-22 Rogues Walk1161 Distinctive Ruby1145½ Foxy Scarlet1125¾ Four wide 8
26Oct94- 9Aqu fst 7f :231 :47 1:123 1:26 Ⓕ[S]Md Sp Wt 67 9 1 2hd 11 1½ 1½ Bailey J D 117 b *1.40 74-19 Distinctly Patti1171½ Foxy Scarlet112no Sammycat1121½ Driving 10
21Sep94- 3Bel fst 7f :23 :47 1:12 1:25 Ⓕ[S]Md Sp Wt 68 10 1 11 11 1hd 2nk Bailey J D 117 b *.50 78-17 Devilette117nk Distinctly Patti1179 Courtney Kelsey M.117hd Gamely 14
3Sep94- 3Bel fst 6f :222 :453 :58 1:104 ⒻMd Sp Wt 73 5 3 22 22 21½ 2½ Bailey J D 117 *1.90 86-14 Madame Adolphe117½ Distinctly Patti1171¾ Noble House1171½ Willingly 6

WORKOUTS: Oct 4 Bel 5f fst 1:013 Hg 9/34 Sep 19 Bel tr.t 3f fst :373 B 8/15 Sep 1 Bel 5f fst 1:024 Bg 24/35 Aug 24 Sar 4f fst :492 Hg 10/25 Aug 16 Sar 4f fst :491 Hg 8/28 Aug 10 Sar 4f fst :491 Hg 10/25

Homah J Simon
Own: Thor John
CHAVEZ C R (76 5 5 7 .07)

Dk. b or br f. 3 (Feb)
Sire: Distinctive Pro (Mr. Prospector)
Dam: Judy's Halo (Halo)
Br: John Thor (NY)
Tr: Sciacca Gary (70 7 5 12 .10)

L 1077

Lifetime Record: 14 1 1 2 $18,370

1995	13	1	1	1	$15,290	Turf	0	0	0	0	
1994	1	M	0	1	$3,080	Wet	2	0	0	0	
Bel	4	0	0	0	$1,800	Dist	11	1	1	2	$16,510

6Oct95- 4Bel my 6f :23 :472 1:001 1:133 3+ Ⓕ[S]Alw 32000N1X -0 4 2 21 22 712 725½ Alvarado F T L 116 b 12.10 48-23 InANutshell112¾ OurScrtHrt1151½ DistinctlyPtti1123 Altered course 5/16 7
12Sep95-12FL fst 6f :224 :47 1:003 1:153 3+ ⒻMd Sp Wt 30 8 2 1hd 13 14½ 12½ Winford S L L 118 b 5.50 66-24 Homah J Simon1182½ Prettiest Pink1181¾ Lucy Mcevil1183½ Kept to whip 10
31Aug95- 6FL fst 6f :222 :464 1:012 1:161 ⒻMd Sp Wt 9 2 2 1½ 14 15 26¾ Hiraldo J L 120 b 2.10 56-24 BillieBooBoo1206¾ HomahJSimon1206½ JustBrbr1204 Second best, tiring 6
22Aug95- 7FL fst 5½f :224 :481 1:024 1:094 3+ ⒻMd Sp Wt 3 6 2 1hd 2½ 34 511 Winford S L 116 fb 2.55 54-30 Iron Fence1221 Lucy Mcevil1164¾ Dana's Due122½ Gave way 6
11Aug95- 1Sar fst 6½f :22 :453 1:122 1:20 3+ Ⓕ[S]Md Sp Wt 23 12 1 44 43½ 68 816¾ Belmonte L A5 112 b 17.10 58-18 JeffreySupreme1216 MissyMims117no HoneyWatral1171 Stumbled break 12
28Jun95- 5Bel fst 6f :222 :464 1:00 1:131 3+ Ⓕ[S]Md Sp Wt 33 6 5 64½ 54 66½ 916½ Alvarado F T 114 b 16.20 59-22 Kacie's Favor1146 Angel Kate1143 Lil Mis Gia114½ Checked early, wide 13
2Jun95- 3Bel fst 6f :224 :47 1:00 1:132 3+ Ⓕ[S]Md Sp Wt 57 11 8 85¾ 44 32 45½ Ramos W S 114 b 27.50 68-25 Subversive Dancer1133½ Honey Watral113¾ Reelherin1151½ Flattened out 12
12May95- 2Bel my 6f :223 :471 1:002 1:131 3+ Ⓕ[S]Md Sp Wt 14 9 3 31 2½ 43 1115½ Ramos W S 114 b 10.00 59-15 GoGoGerver113½ DennieMe1087 LikeToShimmy122nk Forced pace, tired 14
19Apr95- 1Aqu fst 6f :221 :462 :593 1:124 3+ Ⓕ[S]Md Sp Wt 32 1 4 31 41½ 52¾ 89 Alvarado F T 114 b 7.60 69-13 Everythings O K114¾ Peacock Plume1144½ Saxifraga114no Speed, tired 14
5Apr95- 9Aqu fst 7f :232 :473 1:131 1:264 Ⓕ[S]Md Sp Wt 41 3 6 62¾ 42½ 44½ 410½ Alvarado F T 120 b 3.60 59-21 CommunicatorMadam1203½ DennieMae1132½ Escrrgot1204½ Saved ground 10

WORKOUTS: Aug 7 Bel tr.t 4f fst :491 H 7/17 ●Aug 1 Bel tr.t 3f fst :354 H 1/7 Jly 26 Bel 3f fst :361 H 3/14 Jly 20 Bel 3f fst :372 B 8/11

Watrals Ridge
Own: Watral Michael
ALVARADO F T (120 15 18 14 .13)

B. f. 4
Sire: Cox's Ridge (Best Turn)
Dam: Hester Bateman (Codex)
Br: Stone Ridge Farm (NY)
Tr: Brida Dennis J (35 4 2 3 .11)

115

Lifetime Record: 14 1 3 1 $45,880

1995	9	0	1	0	$14,080	Turf	1	0	0	0	
1994	5	1	2	1	$31,800	Wet	6	1	1	0	$24,600
Bel	8	0	2	1	$22,480	Dist	5	0	3	0	$22,360

29Sep95- 6Bel yl 1 1/16 Ⓣ :23 :464 1:12 1:45 3+ ⒻAlw 34000N2L 55 6 2 54¾ 103½ 812 813¾ Nelson D 115 b 47.00 59-29 Exposed114½ Mistress Hawk116½ Aesthete1126 Done early 10
18Sep95- 2Bel my 1 1/16 ⊗ :233 :471 1:122 1:441 3+ Ⓕ[S]Alw 34000N1X 57 5 1 2½ 2½ 45 57¾ Nelson D 116 b 6.40 70-23 Reel Talc1111 Work Of The Devil116nk Doroteo Arango1126 Dueled, tired 10
22Jun95- 9Bel sly 1 1/16 ⊗ :22 :45 1:103 1:451 3+ Ⓕ[S]Alw 34000N1X 51 2 3 42½ 3½ 43½ 57½ Migliore R 119 b 3.75 65-22 Lady Trilogy119hd Igobacktotheking1092½ Lovelines Gold1193½ Bid, tired 9
15Jun95- 7Bel wf 6f :222 :46 :584 1:121 3+ Ⓕ[S]Alw 32000N1X 67 3 1 810 910 66 54¾ Nelson D 119 b 15.20 75-20 SubversiveDncer1122 Infllible113nk PersonlCoup1112 Improved position 11
2Jun95- 9Bel fst 6½f :223 :464 1:13 1:194 3+ Ⓕ[S]Alw 32000N1X 54 5 10 107 1010 57 511½ Santos J A 119 b 8.50 64-25 StrliteSphire1122½ GrenStrwbrry1146½ OurGirlNss1192 Improved position 13
18May95- 6Bel gd 6f :214 :451 :573 1:104 3+ Ⓕ[S]Alw 32000N1X 72 4 6 87½ 74 45 26 Migliore R 119 b 5.70 81-16 Facing Reality1126 Watrals Ridge119hd Where Is It105hd Rallied wide 9
5May95- 7Bel fst 7f :223 :462 1:12 1:251 3+ Ⓕ[S]Alw 32000N1X 46 5 2 66 62¾ 44 49¾ Migliore R 119 b 1.85 65-17 CommunicatorMadam1125 ShellCrist1141¾ Jazzpcked1193 Flattened out 6
20Apr95- 9Aqu fst 6f :223 :47 1:00 1:131 3+ Ⓕ[S]Alw 30000N1X 53 5 3 53 31½ 51½ 44¾ Migliore R 119 b *1.80 71-16 Tara's Tempest1122¾ WhereIsIt1071 Jazzpacked1191 Wide, flattened out 7
31Mar95- 9Aqu fst 7f :224 :463 1:123 1:26 Ⓕ[S]Alw 32000N2X 36 7 5 64¾ 62½ 87½ 915 Migliore R 114 2.75 59-19 Needles Last114hd Bitta's Charm119no Distinct Manner1145½ No threat 9
6Nov94- 7Aqu wf 1 :23 :462 1:114 1:38 3+ Ⓕ[S]Alw 32000N1X 57 5 5 64 51½ 46½ 510¾ Nelson D 115 2.75 67-18 OurSpringwater110nk BlrneystoneLss1153¾ NowIHope1175¾ Dropped back 6

WORKOUTS: Sep 15 Bel 4f fst :484 H 13/38 Sep 7 Bel 3f fst :38 B 25/31

Tahila
Own: Taylor Joan M & Wilmot William B
SMITH M E (199 34 24 30 .17)

Dk. b or br f. 3 (May)
Sire: Slew the Knight (Seattle Slew)
Dam: Tristana (Bosun)
Br: Dr. William B. Wilmot (NY)
Tr: Wilmot William B (2 1 0 0 .50)

116

Lifetime Record: 5 1 1 1 $29,220

1995	4	1	1	1	$29,220	Turf	0	0	0	0	
1994	1	M	0	0		Wet	0	0	0	0	
Bel	2	1	0	0	$19,920	Dist	3	1	0	0	$19,920

6Oct95- 7Bel gd 6f :23 :47 :591 1:121 3+ Ⓕ[S]Alw 32000N1X 57 6 4 41½ 32 44½ 45½ Bailey J D 116 *.80 75-18 K. O. Lady1084½ Flannel Sheets116no Go With Flo113¾ Flattened out 6
20Sep95- 5Bel fst 6f :223 :463 :591 1:12 3+ Ⓕ[S]Md Sp Wt 66 5 1 23 2½ 1½ 1½ Sellers S J 117 4.00 81-19 Tahila117½ Lyric Opera1212½ Zesty1143 Repulsed challenge 11
24Aug95- 2Sar fst 7f :223 :462 1:133 1:273 3+ Ⓕ[S]Md Sp Wt 44 3 3 21½ 24 31 24 Sellers S J 117 2.35 64-18 Miz Off The Cuff1174 Tahila1172 Missy Mims117¾ Chased up for 2nd 8
11Aug95- 3Sar fst 6½f :221 :462 1:124 1:193 3+ Ⓕ[S]Md Sp Wt 47 10 3 1½ 2hd 31½ 38¾ Sellers S J 117 5.00 69-18 GabrielleDanielle117¾ TimeForAnother1217½ Thi117nk Dueled, weakened 12
31Jly94- 3Sar fst 6f :222 :464 :594 1:131 Ⓕ[S]Md Sp Wt 40 1 3 1½ 1hd 21 56¾ Sellers S J 117 *3.20f 68-16 PerfectArc1172½ CourtnyKlsyM.1172 DomintdWy1171½ Dueled, weakened 12

WORKOUTS: Oct 14 Sar tr.t 4f fst :502 B 1/1 Sep 13 Sar tr.t 5f fst 1:06 B 2/2 Sep 8 Sar tr.t 5f fst 1:063 B 1/1 Sep 2 Sar tr.t 4f fst :522 B 5/5 Aug 19 Sar tr.t 4f fst :521 B 8/15 Aug 8 Sar tr.t 3f fst :373 B 3/9

Leah Ray
Own: Jay Cee Jay Stable
STEVENS G L (82 17 10 14 .21)

Dk. b or br f. 3 (Apr)
Sire: Talc (Rock Talk)
Dam: Qui Square (Qui Native)
Br: Robert Greenhut (NY)
Tr: Destefano John M Jr (11 3 0 5 .27)

L 112

Lifetime Record: 6 1 1 0 $14,790

1995	6	1	1	0	$14,790	Turf	0	0	0	0	
1994	0	M	0	0		Wet	2	1	0	0	$8,400
Bel	1	1	0	0	$8,400	Dist	1	0	0	0	

18Sep95- 1Bel my 7f :23 :463 1:12 1:26 3+ ⒻMd 35000 54 3 2 1½ 1½ 16 12 Krone J A L 117 b 6.70 71-16 Leah Ray1172 Fairfield Miss1172¾ One Two Respect117nk Ridden out 7
23Mar95- 1Aqu fst 1 :233 :473 1:144 1:424 ⒻMd 25000 29 1 6 42 54 57½ 611 Martin G J7 113 b 5.70 44-34 Northern Five1206½ Heliopause115nk [DH]Stellina113 Saved ground 9
9Mar95- 9Aqu wf 170 [•] :24 :49 1:144 1:452 Ⓕ[S]Md Sp Wt 51 5 1 1½ 1hd 2½ 64¾ Martin G J7 113 b 6.20 67-24 Bo Bo's Sister1201½ Cool Babe120nk Razzita Margrita1202 Used in pace 9
24Feb95- 5Aqu fst 1 1/16 [•] :234 :493 1:16 1:491 Ⓕ[S]Md Sp Wt 53 6 1 11½ 1½ 1hd 31½ Martin G J7 114 b 8.10 58-29 Positive Tally116nk [D]Baby's In A Fog1211 Leah Ray114no Gamely 9
Placed second through disqualification.
5Jan95- 2Aqu fst 1 1/16 [•] :242 :494 1:16 1:51 ⒻMd 35000 29 2 2 1½ 1½ 31½ 54½ Martin G J7 114 b 48.25 46-27 CherokeeFable1171½ Gentlemn'sCopy1172½ NvITlk116hd Dueled, weakened 10
4Jan95- 5Aqu fst 6f [•] :23 :473 1:004 1:134 Ⓕ[S]Md Sp Wt 19 1 7 75 1210 1114 1028 Martin G J7 114 33.50 54-22 Patti's Purse1213½ Star Personality1219 Baroness B.1211¾ Outrun 12

WORKOUTS: Sep 30 Bel tr.t 4f fst :511 B 17/20 Sep 12 Bel 3f fst :371 B 7/15 Sep 7 Bel 5f fst 1:014 H 15/30 Aug 31 Bel 5f fst 1:013 H 12/34 Aug 23 Bel tr.t 4f fst :492 B 4/17 Aug 15 Bel tr.t 4f fst :513 B 19/28

The obvious favorite would be Angel Kate, who had been in the money six of nine starts, including three seconds in her only three tries at six furlongs. She had tired badly in her last start, despite the addition of Lasix, but that race was at one mile on a sloppy track. This would be her first sprint on Lasix.

Of the eight others in the race, Gallantress Ack was one for 38 and Homah J Simon and Watrals Ridge were each one for 14. Of the other five, Saratoga Capers was clearly the best off a win, a second and a third in her only three starts. But Angel Kate had beaten her by 2½ lengths in their only meeting. Angel Kate would be key No. 2. She would go off at even money and win by 1¼ lengths.

FIFTH RACE
Belmont
OCTOBER 19, 1995

6 FURLONGS. (1.074) ALLOWANCE. Purse $32,800. Fillies and mares, 3-year-olds and upward foaled in New York State and approved by the New York State–Registry which have not won a race other than maiden or claiming. Weights: 3-year-olds, 119 lbs. Older, 122 lbs. Non-winners of two races since September 7, allowed 3 lbs. A race since September 19, 5 lbs. A race since August 22, 7 lbs. (Races where entered for $40,800 or less not considered in allowances.)

Value of Race: $32,000 Winner $19,200; second $6,400; third $3,520; fourth $1,920; fifth $960. Mutuel Pool $235,119.00 Exacta Pool $298,640.00 Trifecta Pool $303,953.80

Last Raced	Horse	M/Eqt. A.Wt	PP	St	¼	½	Str	Fin	Jockey	Odds $1
5Oct95 5Bel8	Angel Kate	L 3 112	2	5	2½	2¹	1²	1¹½	Bailey J D	1.00
29Sep95 6Bel8	Watrals Ridge	b 4 115	7	8	5½	4¹	2¹½	2⁴	Alvarado F T	10.90
6Oct95 7Bel4	Tahila	3 116	8	7	4½	3hd	3¹½	3¹½	Smith M E	8.10
22Sep95 7Bel2	Saratoga Capers	3 112	3	1	3½	5½	5¹	4no	Davis R G	3.70
18Sep95 1Bel1	Leah Ray	Lb 3 115	9	9	8¹	7²	4¹½	5½	Stevens G L	20.70
6Oct95 4Bel3	Distinctly Patti	Lb 3 112	5	6	9	8½	7¹	6⁵	Velazquez J R	6.70
6Oct95 7Bel2	Flannel Sheets	b 3 114	1	2	6¹	6¹	8¹	7²	Perez R B	12.40
6Oct95 4Bel7	Homah J Simon	Lb 3 107	6	4	1hd	1½	6hd	8nk	Chavez C R7	82.00
22Sep95 7Bel9	Gallantress Ack	f 5 115	4	3	7½	9	9	9	Chavez J F	55.75

OFF AT 2:59 Start Good. Won driving. Time, :23, :46⁴, :59, 1:12 Track fast.

$2 Mutuel Prices:

2–ANGEL KATE	4.00	3.10	2.60
8–WATRALS RIDGE		6.60	5.00
9–TAHILA			3.80

$2 EXACTA 2–8 PAID $45.40 $2 TRIFECTA 2–8–9 PAID $237.50

B. f, (Jun), by Mt. Livermore–August Days, by In Reality. Trainer Terrill William V. Bred by Stone Ridge Farm (NY).

ANGEL KATE alternated for the lead along the inside for a half, shook off HOMAH J SIMON to get clear in upper stretch then turned back WATRALS RIDGE in the final eighth. WATRALS RIDGE settled just off the early pace, rallied between horses while four wide on the turn, then finished with good energy for the place. TAHILA raced in close contention while five wide to the top of the stretch and lacked a strong closing bid. SARATOGA CAPERS dueled early between horses, was shuffled back on the far turn, and failed to threaten thereafter. LEAH RAY outrun for a half, advanced six wide into the stretch and failed to threaten while improving position. DISTINCTLY PATTI checked along the backstretch, never reached contention. FLANNEL SHEETS saved ground to no avail. HOMAH J SIMON was used up battling for the early lead. GALLANTRESS ACK checked between horses nearing the far turn and was never close thereafter.

Owners— 1, Montanari Marion G; 2, Watral Michael; 3, Taylor Joan M & Wilmot William B; 4, Dubose Sandy; 5, Jay Cee Jay Stable; 6, Winbound Farms; 7, Flying Zee Stables; 8, Thor John; 9, DeMatteis Frederick

Trainers— 1, Terrill William V; 2, Brida Dennis J; 3, Wilmot William B; 4, Woodington Jamie; 5, Destefano John M Jr; 6, Sciacca Gary; 7, Martin Jose; 8, Sciacca Gary; 9, Priolo Philip

Overweight: Leah Ray (3).

Scratched— Personal Nurse (6Oct95 4BEL4)

Key No. 3 would be in the eighth, a 1¼-mile allowance race on turf. The scratches of Lemming and Crary left a field of nine:

8   Belmont Park

1¼ MILES. (Inner Turf). (1:57³) ALLOWANCE. Purse $36,000 (plus up to $14,130 NYSBFOA). 3-year-olds and upward which have not won two races other than maiden, claiming or starter. Weights: 3-year-olds, 117 lbs. Older, 122 lbs. Non-winners of $19,200 twice over a mile since September 9, allowed 3 lbs. $20,400 over a mile since September 22, 5 lbs. $9,000 over a mile since September 3, 7 lbs. (Races where entered for $60,000 or less not considered in allowances) (Condition eligibility preferred.)

Coupled - Watrals Sea Trip and Abi Yo Yo

Wave Your Flag
L 115

Own: Schettino Joseph A
B. g. 8
Sire: Lydian–Fr (Lyphard)
Dam: Wave in Glory (Hoist the Flag)
Br: A N W Enterprises & Swettenham (Ky)
Tr: Fisher Emmanuel (1 1 0 0 1.00)

STEVENS G L (12 17 10 14 .21)

Lifetime Record: 47 6 2 8 $134,090
1995 4 1 0 0 $21,600 Turf 31 5 1 6 $109,970
1994 6 1 0 2 $17,520 Wet 0 0 0 0
Bel ⊕ 20 2 1 2 $57,290 Dist ⊕ 7 0 0 1 $7,380

Super Twenty Five
L 115

Own: Live Oak Plantation
B. h. 4
Sire: Valid Appeal (In Reality)
Dam: Miss Angel T. (Talc)
Br: Live Oak Stud (Fla)
Tr: Kelly Patrick J (31 4 3 2 .13)

LEON F (54 8 5 8 .08)

Lifetime Record: 23 2 3 3 $59,130
1995 10 1 1 1 $19,810 Turf 14 2 3 2 $55,980
1994 8 1 2 2 $37,700 Wet 2 0 0 0 $340
Bel ⊕ 0 0 0 0 Dist ⊕ 0 0 0 0

Sunshine Spirit
L 110

Own: Nearing E H Jr & Sunshine Hill Farm
Ch. g. 3 (Mar)
Sire: Gold Alert (Mr. Prospector)
Dam: Snow all Knight (Snow Knight)
Br: Franks John (Fla)
Tr: Ribaudo Robert J (12 3 0 2 .25)

PEREZ R B (113 8 11 15 .07)

Lifetime Record: 12 4 1 0 $68,480
1995 11 4 1 0 $68,480 Turf 8 4 1 0 $68,000
1994 1 M 0 0 Wet 0 0 0 0
Bel ⊕ 4 2 0 0 $42,000 Dist ⊕ 0 0 0 0

O' Lucky Star
L 115

Own: Madura Angelo
Dk. b or br g. 4
Sire: Risen Star (Secretariat)
Dam: Can't Be Bothered (Stop the Music)
Br: Eaton & Thorne & Ronald Lamarque (Ky)
Tr: McGreevy James L (—)

SMITH M E (199 34 24 30 .17)

Lifetime Record: 15 2 1 6 $48,100
1995 3 1 0 1 $11,920 Turf 2 0 1 1 $8,580
1994 12 1 1 5 $36,180 Wet 4 1 0 1 $21,570
Bel ⊕ 1 0 1 0 $6,160 Dist ⊕ 0 0 0 0

Henry S.

Own: Bray Dana S Jr & McMillen Kevin
CHAVEZ J F (190 32 19 26 .17)

B. c. 4
Sire: Herat (Northern Dancer)
Dam: Secretary Road (Secretariat)
Br: Bray Dana S Jr (NY)
Tr: O'Brien Leo (58 6 9 6 .10)

L 115

Lifetime Record: 20 2 2 1 $51,480
1995 6 0 0 1 $6,120 | Turf 14 2 1 1 $48,540
1994 14 2 2 0 $45,360 | Wet 3 0 1 0 $2,660
Bel (T) 8 1 0 1 $21,780 | Dist (T) 3 1 0 0 $18,000

16Sep95-10Bel fm 1 1/16 (T) :25 2 :48 4 1:12 1 1:41 4 3+ Alw 36000N2X 85 5 9 9 11 10 7 7 6 6 6¼ Krone J A L 116 26.25 80-07 GrouchoGaucho116 2¾ GallopingThunder116¾ JellyRollJive115 2½ No threat 10
20Aug95-7Sar fm 1 3/8 (t) :48 1:12 1 1:36 1 1:53 2 3+ Alw 36000N2X 73 7 5 5 2½ 5 2½ 7 7 7 10½ Santos J A 114 b 11.70 87-12 Rory Creek114½ Easy Miner114nk Clearance Code113 2 Gave way 8
6Aug95-4Sar gd 1 (T) :24 1 :49 1:13 1 1:36 3 3+ Alw 36000N2X 68 7 8 8 4½ 8 3¼ 6 10 6 15 Velazquez J R 114 b 9.50 79-21 John's Call114 4 Rory Creek114 8 SuperTwentyFive114hd Lacked response 10
28Jly95-4Sar fm 1 1/16 (T) :23 1 :46 1:11 2 1:42 2 3+ Alw 36000N2X 83 7 10 9 8 9 5¾ 6 4½ 4 3½ Santos J A 114 b 6.10 83-07 Debonair Dan109½ Check Ride113nk Comstock Lode113 3 Steadied early 10
1Jly95-5Bel sly 1 1/16 (x) :22 4 :45 2 1:10 1:41 4 3+ Alw 36000N3L 39 4 7 6 9½ 7 15 6 24 7 41½ Martin G J5 115 b 10.00 48-18 Kerfoot Corner120 16 Crary113 3½ Spanish Charge111 14 No speed 7
17Jun95-7Bel fm 1 (t) :23 :45 4 1:10 1 1:34 1 3+ Alw 36000N2X 88 2 8 7 8 7 5½ 7 2½ 3 2 Martin G J5 115 b 18.40 90-12 Wavering Man120 1¾ Groucho Gaucho120nk Henry S.115 2 Closed late 9
11Nov94-7Aqu fst 1 (x) :23 2 :46 4 1:12 1 1:36 4 3+ Alw 34000N2X 23 1 7 7 15 8 15 8 24 8 37½ Alvarado F T 115 b 5.10e 46-21 Iron Gavel117 2 Five Star General117 6 Klondike Clem115 6 Outrun 8
30Oct94-7Aqu fm 1 1/8 (t) :48 2 1:12 2 1:37 1 1:50 3+ Alw 34000N2X 75 4 9 9 7½ 7 4 6 5 5 4¼ Chavez J F 114 b 16.40 84-12 Yokohama116 1¾ Green Gaitor117 2½ Indian Sun114¾ No threat 9
4Oct94-8Bel yl 1 1/16 (t) :23 4 :47 3 1:12 1:42 4 3+ Alw 34000N2X 76 5 9 9 6¼ 9 3¾ 8 5½ 6 9¼ Chavez J F 114 b 4.90 75-23 Grand Continental114 5 Geret's Jewel116 1½ Johnnys Glory117½ Wide turn 9
10Sep94-6Bel fm 1¼ (T) :47 2 1:11 3 1:36 2:00 1 3+ Alw 34000N2X 72 8 7 6 5¾ 6 4 6 7½ 6 9¾ Bailey J D 118 b 4.00 79-11 Same Old Wish117 2½ Doctor Disaster117 1½ Trevelyan115 2½ No threat 9

WORKOUTS: Oct 9 Aqu 5f fst 1:02 4 B 3/5 Oct 3 Aqu 5f fst 1:03 2 B 18/19 Sep 2 Bel 3f fst :36 1 H 8/27 Jly 24 Sar tr.t 4f fst :50 B 9/29

Validate

Own: Reineman Russell L Stable Inc
MAPLE E (145 11 18 19 .08)

B. c. 3 (Feb)
Sire: Alysheba (Alydar)
Dam: Danzig's Beauty (Danzig)
Br: Nuckols Charles Jr & Sons (Ky)
Tr: Stephens Woodford C (1 0 0 0 .00)

110

Lifetime Record: 7 2 3 0 $59,300
1995 6 2 3 0 $59,300 | Turf 2 2 0 0 $39,600
1994 1 M 0 0 | Wet 2 0 2 0 $12,400
Bel (T) 2 2 0 0 $39,600 | Dist (T) 0 0 0 0

16Jly95-10Bel fm 1 (t) :23 3 :46 4 1:11 1 1:35 2 3+ Alw 34000N2L 92 10 10 6 4 3nk 1hd 1 2 Maple E 114 3.70 86-13 Validate114 2 Basin Lane114nk Forest Thunder113¾ Wide, going away 10
3Jly95-10Bel yl 1 1/16 (T) :24 1 :47 3 1:11 4 1:43 1 3+ Md Sp Wt 90 8 4 4 5 3 2 1 1½ 1 6½ Maple E 114 3.95 80-26 Validate114 6½ Palm Freezer114 1 Mr Market114 3 Going away 10
15Jun95-6Bel wf 7f :23 2 :47 2 1:12 2 1:24 4 3+ Md Sp Wt 81 4 3 3 2 5 2 2½ 2 1¾ Maple E 113 *.90 75-20 Foreign Intrigue114 1¾ Validate113 7 Kadrmas113 5 Wide bid, hung 8
29May95-3Bel my 1 :23 1 :46 3 1:12 3 1:39 Md Sp Wt 80 6 5 5 3½ 2hd 1½ 2no Maple E 120 *1.15 68-33 Slip115no Validate120 13 Causeforall120 16 Five wide, game 6
13May95-2Bel fst 1 1/16 :22 3 :46 1:11 3 1:43 4 Md Sp Wt 88 4 5 4 4 2½ 2½ 2nk Maple E 121 3.35 80-26 Last Effort121nk Validate121 12 Clearance Code121 15 Four wide, game 8
7May95-5Bel fst 6f :22 2 :45 2 :57 3 1:10 1 3+ Md Sp Wt 66 7 6 10 6½ 10 6½ 7 5½ 5 5¼ Maple E 113 15.80 85-11 Runaway Brian122nk Scenturion113 3 Real Silk113 1½ Late gain 12
19Oct94-3Aqu fst 6f :22 3 :46 :58 3 1:11 4 Md Sp Wt 63 8 5 5 4½ 5 3¾ 5 5 5 4½ Maple E 118 7.10 79-20 Churka118no Blizzard118 3¾ Judge Me Not118½ Greenly 9

WORKOUTS: Oct 16 Bel 6f fst 1:16 B 2/7 Oct 8 Bel 6f fst 1:14 3 H 3/10 Oct 3 Bel 6f fst 1:18 B 5/5 Sep 29 Bel 5f fst 1:03 3 B 30/33 Sep 25 Bel 5f fst 1:02 2 B 22/42 Sep 22 Bel 4f fst :49 B 8/32

Watrals Sea Trip

Own: Watral Michael
ALVARADO F T (120 15 18 14 .13)

Dk. b or br g. 4
Sire: Transworld (Prince John)
Dam: Sea Trip (Sea Songster)
Br: Watral Michael (NY)
Tr: Brida Dennis J (35 4 2 3 .11)

115

Lifetime Record: 31 2 4 5 $86,410
1995 13 1 1 3 $43,510 | Turf 23 2 3 5 $80,470
1994 12 1 3 2 $42,900 | Wet 3 0 0 0
Bel (T) 14 2 3 3 $71,710 | Dist (T) 12 2 2 3 $63,160

30Sep95-5Bel gd 1 1/16 (T) :24 1 :48 1:12 3 1:44 2 3+ (S)Alw 36000N2X 78 8 9 5 7 5 3 6 4 5 5¾ Martinez J R Jr 116 14.20 68-22 Bellingham116 2¾ Mr. Baba116 1 Outlaw114no Evenly 10
25Sep95-6Bel yl 1¼ (T) :50 1:15 1 1:41 2:06 3+ Alw 36000N3L 69 1 6 6 6 7 3½ 7 2¾ 7 11½ Alvarado F T 117 13.10 47-31 Easy Miner117 2½ N B Forrest114nk Hawkeye Bay117 3 No threat 9
9Sep95-5Bel fm 1 3/16 (T) :47 1:11 1 1:35 4 2:00 1 3+ (S)Alw 36000N2X 80 4 8 7 6½ 5 2½ 3 5 3 5¾ Alvarado F T 119 3.65 81-11 No Secrets111 3 Bellingham117 2¾ Watrals Sea Trip119 1¾ Late gain 11
24Aug95-9Sar fm 1 1/8 (t) :45 1:09 1 1:34 1 1:46 3+ (S)West Point H86k 90 8 10 10 27 10 16 8 7½ 6 6¾ Pezua J M 111 32.25 90-04 Tiffany's Taylor114¾ My Mogul116 2¾ Bit Of Puddin113½ Broke slowly 10
14Aug95-5Sar yl 1 1/16 (t) :23 3 :47 1:12 4 1:44 3+ (S)Alw 36000N2X 79 8 7 6 7½ 7 3 4 1½ 3 3½ Alvarado F T 114 8.00 75-15 Identity113 2 Hello Sunshine109 1½ Watrals Sea Trip114¾ Took up 3/16 pl 10
29Jly95-5Sar fm 1 3/8 (T) :46 3 1:12 1 1:37 2 2:15 2 3+ Clm 50000 86 7 8 7 8½ 8 6¾ 6 3 7 3½ Alvarado F T 119 4.70e 86-08 DoctorDisaster116¾ HevyRin116 2 FwltyTowers116no Late gain, no threat 10
8Jly95-10Bel fm 1¼ (T) :48 3 1:13 3 1:38 1 2:01 4 3+ (S)Alw 34000N1X 87 1 8 9 4¾ 5 3 3 3 1nk Perez R B5 115 4.10 79-11 WatralsSeaTrip115nk Identity113 2½ SoundsLikeScott114 4 Up final strides 11
4Jly95-5Bel gd 1¼ (T) :49 2 1:14 1 1:39 2:03 3 3+ (S)Alw 36000N2X 75 2 9 8 7 7¾ 7 2¾ 5 3½ Nelson D 120 5.40 66-17 Demon Damon112 1½ Tamara R.120nk Outlaw112 2 Pinched break 10
3Jun95-7Bel fm 1 1/16 (T) :24 1 :48 2 1:12 3 1:42 4 3+ (S)Alw 34000N1X 73 8 4 3 1½ 4 1½ 4 3 4 2½ ‡ Nelson D 120 4.50 79-17 Mr. Baba120½ RevolutionaryEra110 1¾ RightForward122nk Four wide, tired 8
28May95-5Bel fm 1¼ (T) :48 1 1:12 1:36 4 2:02 2 3+ Alw 34000N1X 87 10 11 11 9¾ 7 4¾ 7 4½ 3½ Nelson D 120 11.10 75-14 GoneDncingAgin120hd SkteForJoy120½ WtrlsSTrip120nk Rallied five wide 12

WORKOUTS: Sep 21 Bel tr.t 4f fst :49 1 B 5/17

Abi Yo Yo

Own: Watral Michael
MOJICA R JR (6 0 0 1 .00)

Dk. b or br h. 5
Sire: Capote (Seattle Slew)
Dam: Jolivar (Herbager)
Br: Heinz Janice A & Lundy Robert A (Ky)
Tr: Brida Dennis J (35 4 2 3 .11)

115

Lifetime Record: 10 2 0 0 $34,720
1993 8 2 0 0 $34,720 | Turf 8 2 0 0 $34,720
1992 2 M 0 0 | Wet 0 0 0 0
Bel (T) 6 2 0 0 $34,320 | Dist (T) 1 0 0 0

17Oct93-4Bel sf 1 1/16 (T) :25 :49 1:13 4 1:46 2 3+ Alw 32000N2X 43 1 3 4 3½ 6 3 9 4½ 9 21½ Cruguet J 114 18.20 42-35 Ocean Wave114 1 Groovy Green114 2¾ It's A Runaway114¾ Done early 9
24Sep93-8Med yl 1 (t) :23 2 :47 1:12 2 1:40 Thompson40k 15 9 5 6 11 9 19 9 21 9 33¾ Mojica R Jr 117 8.60 39-28 Inagroove113¾ Winnetou122 1½ Bates Return115 1½ Outrun 9
13Sep93-8Bel gd 1 1/16 (T) :24 2 :47 3 1:12 1:43 3+ Alw 32000N2X 89 7 3 3 4 2 1 3 2 4 2 Mojica R Jr 113 24.50 79-14 (D)Victory Cross117nk Personal Draw112hd Talb117 1½ Bid, tired 8
29Aug93-7Sar fm 1 1/8 (T) :47 3 1:12 1 1:36 1 1:48 3+ Alw 30500N2X 77 5 2 2 2 2 1½ 4 4½ 8 8¾ Mojica R Jr 112 26.30 89-12 Dominant Prospect114 2 Personal Draw112¾ Al Karnak117no Used up 10
15Jly93-7Bel fm 1¼ (T) :49 1 1:14 1:38 1 2:01 4 3+ Alw 30500N2X 80 8 1 1 1 1 1½ 2 1 6 3½ Mojica R Jr 116 8.20 77-15 World Order117nk Cap White110no Hatta's Mill117no Speed, tired 8
4Jly93-4Bel yl 1 1/16 (t) :23 4 :47 2 1:12 2 1:44 1 3+ Alw 28500N1X 84 6 2 1hd 1 1 1 1½ 1 2¼ Mojica R Jr 111 10.30 75-23 Abi Yo Yo111 2¼ Baron Von Blixen111 1¾ Cadence Count113 1 Driving 9
13Jun93-4Bel fm 1 1/16 (T) :23 4 :47 3 1:11 1 1:41 1 3+ Alw 28500N1X 77 6 2 1½ 1½ 2½ 5 5¾ Mojica R Jr 111 2.00 84-09 Leningrad Symphony117nk Talb117 3 Cadence Count109 1½ Used up 8
28May93-7Bel fm 1 1/16 (t) :22 3 :46 1:10 1:41 2 3+ Md Sp Wt 80 7 2 2½ 2½ 1 2½ 1 2 Mojica R Jr 115 5.50 89-15 Abi Yo Yo115 2 Executive Crown115 2½ Schuerholz110 1 Driving 10
30Oct92-6Aqu fst 1 :23 3 :47 4 1:13 1 1:38 2 Md Sp Wt 24 3 1 4 1½ 6 7½ 6 21 9 33½ Mojica R Jr 118 47.90 37-31 Colonial Affair118 5¾ Castelli Street118 3½ Bull Inthe Heather118 3¾ Stopped 9
3Oct92-4Bel fst 7f :23 :47 1:12 2 1:25 3 Md Sp Wt 11 5 5 6 6 8 7½ 8 18 8 31¾ Romero R P 118 10.50 44-17 Ferociously118 5¾ Raglan Road118 3 Colonial Affair118 Outrun 8

WORKOUTS: Oct 8 Bel tr.t 4f fst :50 B 14/24 Sep 29 Bel 6f fst 1:17 2 B 18/20 Sep 22 Bel 5f fst 1:02 3 B 14/23

Islamabad

Own: Shoaib Hassan
SANTOS J A (165 28 18 28 .17)

Dk. b or br c. 3 (Feb)
Sire: Red Ransom (Roberto)
Dam: Turquoise Gal (Navajo)
Br: Dennis B. Swartz (Ky)
Tr: Clement Christophe (44 4 7 5 .09)

114

Lifetime Record: 5 2 0 1 $48,249
1995 1 1 0 0 $20,400 | Turf 3 2 0 1 $48,249
1994 4 1 0 1 $27,849 | Wet 0 0 0 0
Bel (T) 3 2 0 1 $48,249 | Dist (T) 0 0 0 0

30Sep95-10Bel gd 1 1/16 (t) :23 :46 1 1:11 3 1:44 1 3+ Alw 34000N1X 86 10 5 7 13 6 6½ 2hd 1 3 Sellers S J 112 9.30 77-22 Islamabad112 3 September Winds107nk Haagbah116 1 Driving 10
30Oct94-5Aqu fst 1 :23 :46 2 1:12 2 1:39 1 Alw 32000N1X 39 6 1 1 1 3 3½ 5 10 6 19½ Bailey J D 117 b 2.80 52-26 Akiba117 4 Fortunate Errol117 2 Crusader's Story117 2½ Used up 8
8Oct94-8Bel fst 1 1/16 :23 2 :46 1 1:11 1 1:44 Champagne-G1 75 2 10 10 11 10 4¾ 8 7½ 8 14½ Stevens G L 122 62.20 68-17 Timber Country122½ Sierra Diablo122 6½ On Target122nk No factor 11
25Sep94-6Bel sf 1 1/16 (T) :25 1 :49 1 1:14 1 1:46 3 Pilgrim-G3 59 5 5 5 17 5 11 5 17 3 18 Smith M E 115 3.40 45-37 DiplomaticJet117 12 HoustonConnection115 8 Islamabd115 3½ Broke slowly 5
8Sep94-9Bel fm 1 (t) :23 3 :46 4 1:11 3 1:35 3 Md Sp Wt 87 8 7 6 5½ 5 3 1½ 1no Bailey J D 118 5.50 84-13 Islamabad118no Claudius118 4¾ Noble 'n Heart118 3 Wide, driving 11

WORKOUTS: Oct 13 Bel (T) 5f fm 1:00 1 H (d) 1/7 Sep 20 Sar (t) 5f fm 1:03 3 B (d) 4/8 Sep 13 Sar (t) 4f sf :50 4 B (d) 5/6

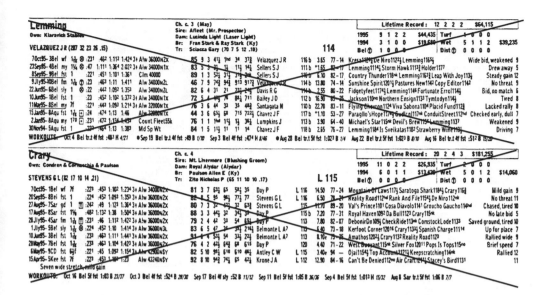

Validate had come from off the pace to win both of his shorter turf starts going away, by 6½ and two lengths, which was one indication he wouldn't mind stretching out. His breeding, by Alysheba out of a Danzig mare, was another, and the *Form* was kind enough to verify that by reporting his 2.16 dosage index in its analysis. His layoff of three months was mitigated by the fact that he had Hall of Fame trainer Woody Stephens in his corner and also by his sharp six-furlong work in 1:14⅗. Validate would go off the 8-5 favorite and only two other horses in the field of nine would go off at under 10-1. Wave Your Flag and Islamabad would both go off at 5-2. Wave Your Flag, though, had tried 1¼ miles on the grass seven times and lit the board only once, when he was third. Islamabad had won his shorter return easily from the difficult outside 10 post on the main turf course. Today, he again had the outside post, the nine, but it was on the inner turf course, where an outside post can be an even bigger disadvantage.

If you had decided to use three singles in the Pick Six, you couldn't be faulted for using Islamabad instead of Validate in the eighth. But Validate did win by 1½ lengths.

EIGHTH RACE
Belmont
OCTOBER 19, 1995

1¼ MILES. (Inner Turf)(1.57³) ALLOWANCE. Purse $36,000 (plus up to $14,130 NYSBFOA). 3-year-olds and upward which have not won two races other than maiden, claiming or starter. Weights: 3-year-olds, 117 lbs. Older, 122 lbs. Non-winners of $19,200 twice over a mile since September 9, allowed 3 lbs. $20,400 over a mile since September 22, 5 lbs. $9,000 over a mile since September 3, 7 lbs. (Races where entered for $50,000 or less not considered in allowances) (Condition eligibility preferred.)

Value of Race: $36,000 Winner $21,600; second $7,200; third $3,960; fourth $2,160; fifth $1,080. Mutuel Pool $244,188.00 Exacta Pool $240,963.00 Trifecta Pool $235,444.00

Last Raced	Horse	M/Eqt.	A.	Wt	PP	¼	½	¾	1	Str	Fin	Jockey	Odds $1
16Jly95 10Bel1	Validate		3	112	6	3hd	3½	2^1	2^1	1 1½	1 1½	Maple E	1.70
21Sep95 4Bel1	Wave Your Flag	Lbf	8	115	1	6^1	5hd	3^1	4hd	3^1	2¾	Stevens G L	2.65
30Sep95 10Bel1	Islamabad		3	114	9	5^1	6½	8^2	6^1	6 3½	3¼	Santos J A	2.85
4Oct95 9Med3	O' Lucky Star	Lb	4	115	4	4 1½	4½	6½	7½	5½	4^2	Smith M E	15.30
27Aug95 7Sar5	Super Twenty Five	L	4	115	2	2 2½	2 1½	4hd	5^1	2½	5^3	Leon F	38.00
17Oct93 4Bel9	Abi Yo Yo	b	5	115	8	1^2	1^2	1½	1½	4½	6½	Mojica R Jr	a-15.60
16Sep95 10Bel6	Henry S.	L	4	115	5	9	9	9	8hd	7^1	7 2¼	Chavez J F	18.20
30Sep95 5Bel5	Watrals Sea Trip		4	115	7	8^2	8 3½	7½	9	9	8^2	Alvarado F T	a-15.60
2Oct95 2Bel1	Sunshine Spirit	Lb	3	113	3	7^2	7^1	5½	3^1	8hd	9	Perez R B	21.80

a-Coupled: Abi Yo Yo and Watrals Sea Trip.

OFF AT 4:30 Start Good. Won driving. Time, :24³, :50⁴, 1:16³, 1:41³, 2:06¹ Course yielding.

$2 Mutuel Prices:			
7-VALIDATE	5.40	3.80	2.50
2-WAVE YOUR FLAG		3.40	2.70
8-ISLAMABAD			2.80

$2 EXACTA 7-2 PAID $17.00 $2 TRIFECTA 7-2-8 PAID $43.00

B. c, (Feb), by Alysheba–Danzig's Beauty, by Danzig. Trainer Stephens Woodford C. Bred by Nuckols Charles Jr & Sons (Ky).

VALIDATE settled just off the pace for five furlongs, made a run to challenge on the far turn, took charge in upper stretch then held sway under steady pressure. WAVE YOUR FLAG moved up steadily while saving ground along the backstretch, angled out leaving the turn, made a run to threaten in midstretch, but was no match for the winner. ISLAMABAD raced well back to the turn, rallied belatedly to gain a share. O' LUCKY STAR rated in the middle of the pack, while saving ground, dropped on the far turn, then failed to threaten with a mild late rally. SUPER TWENTY FIVE raced just behind the pacesetter while saving ground, was shuffled back midway on the turn, made a run along the rail to threaten in midstretch then flattened out. ABI YO YO set the pace along the inside for a mile and tired. HENRY S. checked early, never reached contention. WATRALS SEA TRIP was never a factor. SUNSHINE SPIRIT steadily gained from outsisde to threaten on the turn and gave way.

Owners— 1, Reineman Russell L Stable Inc; 2, Schettino Joseph A; 3, Shoaib Hassan; 4, Medure Angelo; 5, Live Oak Plantation; 6, Watral Michael; 7, Bray Dana S Jr & McMillen Kevin; 8, Watral Michael; 9, Nearing E H Jr & Sunshine Hill Farm

Trainers—1, Stephens Woodford C; 2, Fisher Emmanuel; 3, Clement Christophe; 4, McGreevy James L; 5, Kelly Patrick J; 6, Brida Dennis J; 7, O'Brien Leo; 8, Brida Dennis J; 9, Ribaudo Robert J

Overweight: Validate (2), Sunshine Spirit (3).

Scratched— Lemming (7Oct95 3BEL3), Crary (7Oct95 1BEL3)

$2 Pick-3 (3-6-7) Paid $26.20; Pick-3 Pool $125,151. $2 Pick-6 (6-6-2-3-6-7) 6 Correct 69 Tickets Paid $1,817.00 (including $37,750 Carryover); 5 Correct 1,077 Tickets Paid $27.00; Pick-6 Pool $155,824.

Angel Kate, Mesabi Maiden and Validate were three favorites who accounted for half of the Pick Six.

What about the other half?

The third, fourth and seventh races were won by the third choice, the second choice and the third choice, respectively.

3 Belmont Park

1 1/16 MILES. (1:394) CLAIMING. Purse $23,000. Fillies, 3-year-olds. Weight, 121 lbs. Non-winners of a race at a mile or over since September 23, allowed 2 lbs. A race since September 14, 4 lbs. A race at a mile or over since August 31, 6 lbs. Claiming price $30,000, if for $25,000, allowed 3 lbs. (Races where entered for $20,000 or less not considered.)

Birthday

Own: Harbor View Farm
SMITH M E (199 34 24 30 .17) $30,000
Ch. f. 3 (Jan)
Sire: Golden Act (Gummo)
Dam: Grateful Friend (Teddy's Courage)
Br: Harbor View Farm (Ky)
Tr: Jerkens H Allen (56 2 8 6 .04)
119

Lifetime Record: 9 2 0 1 $33,189
1995 9 2 0 1 $33,189 Turf 6 0 0 1 $9,969
1994 0 M 0 0 Wet 0 0 0 0
Bel 2 1 0 0 $15,420 Dist 0 0 0 0

15Sep95-5Bel fst 7f :224 :46 1:112 1.25 ⒻClm 35000 69 7 10 106½ 108 44 1¾ Smith M E 115 fb 6.30 76-14 Birthday115¾ Fine Wine113hd Emergency1172 Seven wide, going away 12
16Jly95-5Bel fm 1 1/16 Ⓣ :233 :471 1.112 1.421 ⒻAlw 34000N2L 65 5 6 63½ 62¾ 88¾ 812 Leon F 114 fb 11.10 75-13 Hawaiian Brave1176¾ Star Of Light1171 Lamplight117nk Four wide, tired 10
9Jly95-6Bel fm 1 1/16 Ⓣ :244 :49 1:13 1:432 ⒻClm 50000 69 4 2 21 2½ 43 74 Krone J A 116 fb 6.80 75-14 PagentPrincess112no JustFlirting116½ Aerosilver116½ Forced pace, tired 10
23Jun95-8Bel yl 1 1/16 Ⓣ :252 :483 1:121 1:43 ⒻSandsPoint H82k 61 1 3 46 47 417 420½ Krone J A 108 fb 9.90 60-19 Perfect Arc1175 Miss Union Avenue1233 Transient Trend11012 No threat 5
8Jun95-6Bel fm 1 Ⓣ :231 :463 1.111 1:36 ⒻClm 70000 65 6 4 56½ 62½ 55½ 37 Krone J A 112 f 2.50 76-17 Mega1121 Erins Reality1126 Birthday112no No late bid 7
3Jun95-2Bel fm 1 1/16 Ⓣ :24 :471 1:113 1:432 ⒻClm 35000 61 5 7 78 87½ 42½ 65 Krone J A 112 f 2.45 74-17 HalloweenMask1122 Domina115nk Gleholme112nk Stead, blocked stretch 8
3May95-5Bel gd 1¼ Ⓧ :494 1:151 1:40 2:04 3↑ ⒻAlw 34000N1X 51 2 3 32½ 45 57½ 518¼ Santagata N 113 f 6.80 56-16 Very True11211 Marigal1121½ Sam's Diary1193 Stumbled break 6
21Apr95-8Aqu fm 1 1/16 Ⓣ :241 :493 1:141 1:454 3↑ ⒻAlw 32000N2L 58 2 8 89½ 99½ 710 510 Leon F 110 f 7.20 70-18 MySpringLove1151½ PocketButy1174¾ BcusOfLov1202½ Improved position 10
2Apr95-1Aqu fst 6f :231 :474 1:002 1:132 3↑ ⒻMd 40000 53 1 5 23 2½ 1hd 11½ Santagata N 114 f 2.10 75-13 Birthday1141½ Aaron's Terms1123¾ Lucy Brown114hd Long drive 6

WORKOUTS: Oct 17 Bel 4f fst :48 H 7/34 Oct 10 Bel tr.t 5f fst 1:032 B 4/8 Sep 28 Bel 5f fst 1:002 H 4/29 Sep 9 Bel 7f fst 1:282 H 2/3 Aug 28 Bel 7f fst 1:292 B 1/1 Aug 15 Bel tr.t 5f fst 1:032 B 8/11

Blackburn

Own: Hauman Eugene E & Schwartz Barry K
MIGLIORE R (89 9 5 16 .10) $30,000
Dk. b or br f. 3 (May)
Sire: Sewickley (Star de Naskra)
Dam: Buckboard Bounce (Buckaroo)
Br: Robert S. Evans (Fla)
Tr: Hushion Michael E (38 6 6 6 .16)
L 117

Lifetime Record: 9 3 1 0 $42,920
1995 9 3 1 0 $42,920 Turf 0 0 0 0
1994 0 M 0 0 Wet 3 1 0 0 $10,320
Bel 7 2 0 0 $22,920 Dist 1 0 0 0 $1,020

5Oct95-8Bel sly 1 1/16 Ⓧ :223 :45 1:092 1:414 3↑ ⒻAlw 34000N1X 61 8 3 33 33½ 410 520½ Migliore R L 114 4.10 69-26 Nepta1122½ Winner's Edge11311 Crafty Lady1166 Wide, tired 8
15Sep95-5Bel fst 7f :224 :46 1:112 1:25 ⒻClm c-35000 58 3 11 84 64½ 74¾ 75½ Migliore R L 117 f 3.60 71-14 Birthday115¾ Fine Wine113hd Emergency1172 Flattened out 12
Claimed from October Moon Stable, Galluscio Dominic G Trainer
1Sep95-9Bel fst 1 :222 :452 1:103 1:361 ⒻClm c-25000 77 6 2 12 11½ 13 12½ Migliore R L 115 f *2.05 82-21 Blackburn1152½ A Wild Favor115nk Charmless1153½ Drift, remained clear 10
Claimed from Hauman Eugene E & Schwartz Barry K, Hushion Michael E Trainer
20Aug95-1Sar fst 6f :221 :463 :592 1:121 ⒻClm 35000 72 6 6 53½ 3nk 12 12 Migliore R 115 f 8.60 88-18 Blackburn1152 Really Wild1152½ Wilmick1155½ Four wide, drew clear 9
3Jly95-3Bel fst 7f :224 :464 1:122 1:252 ⒻClm c-25000 48 8 5 64½ 52½ 69 614 Santos J A 116 8.80 60-14 RideTheWind1152¾ AWildFvor115½ AmysingDine1148½ Four wide, no rally 8
Claimed from Evans Robert S, Schulhofer Flint S Trainer
14Jun95-1Bel sly 7f :222 :46 1:113 1:253 3↑ ⒻMd 35000 67 1 7 2hd 1hd 11½ 11¾ Santos J A 114 4.60 73-16 Blackburn1141¾ Capote's Cookie1131½ Jellyapple1129 Dueled, drew clear 8
31May95-3Bel fst 6f :224 :462 :59 1:123 3↑ ⒻMd 30000 37 3 6 73½ 65¾ 68 79½ Beckner D V 110 *1.80 68-16 ArctcPtnc1145 JrchoJnny109¾ HoustonElgnc1143½ Checked, bumped 1/2 12
18May95-4Bel my 6f :221 :454 :581 1:112 ⒻMd Sp Wt 42 1 3 32½ 44½ 57½ 514½ Beckner D V 120 4.70 69-18 Cappadocia1206 Just For Fun1152½ Garden Secrets1133 Tired 8
22Apr95-4Aqu fst 6f :221 :462 :59 1:12 ⒻMd Sp Wt 63 8 5 41¾ 3½ 22½ 24 Beckner D V 121 19.10 78-17 Ionlyhaveeyesforu1214 Blackburn1213½ Arctic Patience121nk Sharp try 8

WORKOUTS: Oct 1 Bel tr.t 4f fst :484 H 2/18 Aug 15 Sar 5f fst 1:013 H 23/47 Aug 11 Sar 4f fst :48 H 3/24 Jly 25 Sar 3f fst :38 B 16/27

Mae's Way

Own: Am W D Stable
CHAVEZ C R (76 5 5 7 .07) $30,000
Ch. f. 3 (Jan)
Sire: Strawberry Road*Aus (Whiskey Road)
Dam: Royal Lomond (Lomond)
Br: Paulson Allen E (Ky)
Tr: Schettino Dominick A (18 2 1 1 .11)
L 1087

Lifetime Record: 14 1 0 0 $24,690
1995 11 1 0 0 $24,690 Turf 7 0 0 0 $2,200
1994 3 M 0 0 Wet 2 1 0 0 $21,120
Bel 4 1 0 0 $22,140 Dist 3 0 0 0 $2,270

28Sep95-8Bel fst 1¼ Ⓧ :503 1:154 1:42 2:082 3↑ ⒻAlw 34204N1X 8 5 1 1hd 58 525 545½ Luzzi M J L 110 b 4.90 — 29 Select Account1104 Rabs Lil Brit Brit1171½ SpaceWarning11014 Gave way 5
9Aug95-10Sar fm 1⅛ Ⓣ :463 1:11 1:353 1:474 3↑ ⒻAlw 34000N1X 63 3 8 1110 1112 87¼ 912 Chavez J F 114 b 33.50 75-09 Just Wonderful1141½ Francia1143 Martha's Vineyard109½ Done early 11
23Jly95-9Sar fm 1 1/16 Ⓣ :234 :481 1:123 1:431 ⒻAlw 34000N2L 43 4 8 89½ 108¾ 1014 718 Bravo J 121 b 26.25 65-15 Lizzie Toon1182 Kay Bee Bee115nk Curtain Raiser1153 No threat 10
2Jly95-5Bel my 1¼ Ⓧ :47 1:121 1:401 2:071 3↑ ⒻMd Sp Wt 61 1 4 31½ 12 17 111 Chavez J F 113 fb 14.50 58-27 Mae's Way11311 Spectacular Affair122¾ ABlinkAndANod1176½ Ridden out 8
15Jun95-3Bel gd 1¼ Ⓣ :47 1:122 1:38 2:024 3↑ ⒻMd Sp Wt 53 1 7 713 74½ 48¾ 413¼ Decarlo C P 114 b 56.50 61-20 Gweibo11210 Hippy Hippy Heart1113 Winter Fling112nk Saved ground 10
31May95-5Bel fm 1¼ Ⓣ :48 1:132 1:383 2:031 3↑ ⒻMd Sp Wt 52 7 6 116½ 74¾ 610 915½ Decarlo C P 114 b 31.50 57-21 Kalfo1127½ A Rose For Shannon1125½ Social Sovereign112hd No speed 12
12May95-4Bel my 1 1/16 :224 :461 1:114 1:462 ⒻMd Sp Wt 33 2 6 64½ 56 49¾ 416¾ Decarlo C P 120 b 49.25 50-23 Head East1206 Bank Approval1159 Emergency1201¾ No threat 6
21Apr95-6Hia fm *1⅛ Ⓣ 1:532 ⒻMd Sp Wt 22 2 6 1018 923 816 618¼ Alligood M A L 121 6.00 47-27 Curling121nk Solo1215 Eappiality1211½ Belated bid 10
22Mar95-3Hia fm *1 1/16 Ⓣ 1:45 ⒻMd Sp Wt 44 7 6 77¼ 109 77½ 69¼ Alligood M A L 122 20.20 67-15 Alyinda122½ Rainy Day Woman1225 Supahnan1222 10
Checked bkstr, mild bid
25Jan95-2GP fst 1⅛ :243 :494 1:152 1:50 ⒻClm 10500 9 3 7 75½ 711 814 826½ Santos J A L 114 8.00 31-27 Eager Eater111nk Lady Char116nk Singahighnote1162½ No factor 8

WORKOUTS: Sep 16 Bel tr.t 4f fst :503 B 18/25 Sep 2 Bel tr.t 4f fst :532 B 28/29

A Wild Favor

Own: Dorsey Charles
VELAZQUEZ J R (207 32 23 26 .15) $30,000
Dk. b or br f. 3 (Apr)
Sire: Wild Again (Icecapade)
Dam: Curried Favor (Raja Baba)
Br: Sullivan Mary A (Ky)
Tr: Cordero Marjorie (2 0 0 0 .00)
115

Lifetime Record: 18 1 5 4 $47,120
1995 8 0 3 2 $20,400 Turf 2 0 0 0
1994 10 1 2 2 $26,720 Wet 4 0 1 0 $7,050
Bel 8 0 3 3 $19,170 Dist 4 0 2 1 $14,120

5Oct95-3Bel sly 1 1/16 :224 :454 1:103 1:451 ⒻClm 25000 68 2 2 2½ 1hd 2hd 21½ Velazquez J R 115 b 4.20 71-26 FineWine1151½ AWildFvor1153 Arunforyourmoney1158 Dueled, held 2nd 5
24Sep95-2Bel fst 1 1/16 :232 :47 1:114 1:434 ⒻClm 30000 69 8 4 43½ 42 31½ 32 Velazquez J R 115 b 2.10 78-20 Crafty Jenny115nk StreetCode1121¾ AWildFavor1152½ No match, four wide 8
1Sep95-9Bel fst 1 :222 :452 1:103 1:361 ⒻClm 25000 72 5 7 76½ 44½ 33½ 22½ Velasquez J 115 b 2.50 79-21 Blackburn1152½ A Wild Favor115nk Charmless1153½ Wide, up for 2nd 10
2Aug95-3Sar fst 7f :224 :462 1:124 1:261 ⒻClm 35000 67 6 5 92¾ 64 42½ 32¾ Velasquez J 115 b 4.90 72-19 Shrewd Penny1151½ Ride The Wind1211½ AWildFavor115¾ Five wide, hung 9
23Jly95-1Sar fst 6f :22 :454 :581 1:113 ⒻClm 35000 73 1 10 84½ 86½ 64¾ 41½ Velasquez J 115 b 7.10 82-11 Austrian Empress118nk Rich Seam114½ Wilmick115½ Belated rally 14
3Jly95-3Bel fst 7f :224 :464 1:122 1:252 ⒻClm 30000 72 2 6 33 41½ 32½ 22¾ Velasquez J 115 b 9.40 71-14 Ride The Wind1152¾ A Wild Favor115½ AmaysingDiane1148¾ Rallied inside 8
12May95-6Bel my 6f :221 :453 :573 1:101 ⒻClm 45000 40 5 6 58 69½ 611 621¼ Beckner D V 113 18.90 69-15 Daybydaybyday1138 Austrian Empress110nk Carson Kitty1197 No speed 6
21Jan95-2Aqu my 170 ⊡ :232 :464 1:114 1:424 ⒻClm 72500 55 6 6 611 511 516 520 Perez R B5 109 5.80 64-26 Varsity Gold11616 Tristam Baby1163½ Gone Grey108nk Bumped first turn 6
23Dec94-5Aqu fst 170 ⊡ :23 :471 1:14 1:462 ⒻAlw 32000N1X 50 5 5 513 59 311 215 Perez R B5 111 18.70 51-28 Foxy Scarlet11615 A Wild Favor1111½ Ring By Spring1161¾ Up for place 6
29Nov94-6Aqu wf 7f :231 :464 1:121 1:253 ⒻClm 75000 55 2 3 41¾ 53½ 46½ 48 Perez R B5 111 16.50 68-21 Ride The Wind116hd Linda's Crusade1143 Wonaria1075 Saved ground 5

WORKOUTS: Sep 19 Bel 3f fst :37 H 10/29 Aug 21 Sar tr.t 3f fst :371 B 2/9

Fine Wine

Own: Hough Stanley M & Team Canonie Stb
ALVARADO F T (120 15 18 14 .13) $25,000

Dk. b or br f. 3 (Mar)
Sire: Hooched (Danzig)
Dam: Raise'n Angel (Raise a Bid)
Br: Marilyn Lewis (Fla)
Tr: Hough Stanley M (37 6 7 4 .16)

L 118

Lifetime Record:	9 2 2 1	$29,870			
1995	6 1 2 1	$24,320	Turf	1 0 0 0	$260
1994	3 1 0 0	$5,550	Wet	2 2 0 0	$16,800
Bel	3 1 1 0	$18,000	Dist	1 1 0 0	$12,600

5Oct95-3Bel	sly	1 1/16		:224 :454 1:103 1:451	ⒻClm 25000	71	4	3	42	4¾	1hd	11½	Alvarado F T	L 115 fb	3.30	73-26	Fine Wine1151½ A Wild Favor1153 Arunforyourmoney1158	Split horses	5
15Sep95-5Bel	fst	7f		:224 :46 1:112 1:25	ⒻClm 30000	67	9	9	96	96½	34	2¾	Alvarado F T	L 113 fb	39.25	75-14	Birthday115¾ Fine Wine113nd Emergency1172	Rallied six wide	12
6Sep95-5Bel	fst	6½f		:231 :46 1:11 1:174	ⒻClm 25000	55	8	9	98¼	94	55¾	58	Belmonte L A5	L 110 fb	5.50	78-14	Emergency1194 FrontRowCntr1192 TimForAllir115½	Broke slowly, wide	10
11Aug95-2Sar	fst	6½f		:22 :454 1:111 1:181	ⒻClm 35000	67	2	8	44	32½	35	37½	Belmonte L A5	110 fb	6.10	77-18	Showsnap1216½ Emergency115¾ Fine Wine1101	Svd ground, willingly	9
1Feb95-8GP	fm	*1 1/16	Ⓣ	:232 :464 1:123 1:434+	ⒻAlw 26000N2L	46	10	2	25	21½	714	715¼	Boulanger G	118 b	3.20	74-03	Dove Song118hd Naughty Nana118no Transient Trend1214¼	Tired	10
7Jan95-4GP	fst	6f		:222 :453 :583 1:104	ⒻClm c-40000	72	1	6	41¾	22	23½	24½	Boulanger G	117 b	*1.30	82-13	How Bout Me1194½ Fine Wine1173¾ Lovely Gamble117¾	No match	7
Claimed from Levina B, Vivian David A Trainer																			
18Dec94-8Crc	fst	7f		:23 :471 1:132 1:27	ⒻAlw 15000N1X	65	7	1	42½	41½	63½	43	Boulanger G	117 b	5.30	74-23	Almmony1172 Formisty120¾ Coldhrtedprincess117nk	In close midstretch	9
24Nov94-7Crc	fst	6f		:221 :461 :591 1:132	ⒻClm 30000	64	7	3	74	53½	43½	4nk	Boulanger G	113 b	7.40	80-19	Coldhartedprincess114no Showsnap113hd College Girl115no	6 wide, gaining	8
24Oct94-3Pha	my	5½f		:223 :471 1:00 1:063	ⒻMd 25000	43	8	4	31½	21	1hd	1nk	Fiorentino C T	120 b	2.20	83-17	Fine Wine120nk Hanging Fire1203¼ Alien Strike1206¾	Bumped, driving	8

WORKOUTS: Sep 30 Bel 4f fst :511 B 46/53 Sep 1 Bel 5f fst 1:024 B 24/35 Aug 23 Sar tr.t 3f fst :384 B 7/13 Aug 7 Sar 5f fst 1:021 Hg 20/40 Aug 2 Sar tr.t 5f fst 1:06 B 6/8 Jly 27 Sar tr.t 3f fst :39 B 2/3

Crafty Jenny

Own: Austin Dale H & Heatherwood Farm
SANTOS J A (165 28 18 28 .17) $30,000

B. f. 3 (Apr)
Sire: Conquistador Cielo (Mr. Prospector)
Dam: Our Feast (Banquet Table)
Br: Dr. E. W. Thomas (Ky)
Tr: Schosberg Richard (30 8 7 3 .27)

L 121

Lifetime Record:	10 2 3 2	$56,380			
1995	10 2 3 2	$56,380	Turf	0 0 0 0	
1994	0 M 0 0		Wet	1 0 0 0	$960
Bel	4 2 0 0	$33,960	Dist	1 1 0 0	$13,800

24Sep95-2Bel	fst	1 1/16		:232 :47 1:114 1:434	ⒻClm 30000	72	5	2	22	2½	2hd	1nk	Santos J A	L 115	*2.10	80-20	Crafty Jenny115nk Street Code1121¾ A Wild Favor1152½	Fully extended	8
6Sep95-4Bel	fst	7f		:223 :453 1:11 1:241 3+	ⒻAlw 32000N1X	38	1	1	1hd	3nk	66	618	Smith M E	L 113 f	3.85	62-14	Hamba1162 Lafitte's Lady1162¾ Sarabi114¾	Dueled, tired	6
20Aug95-3Sar	fst	7f		:223 :461 1:114 1:251	ⒻAlw 32000N2L	71	2	3	1½	1½	2hd	21½	Smith M E	121	2.30	78-18	Good N Gorgeous1211½ Crafty Jenny121nk Canadian Halo1189	Held place	6
11Aug95-5Sar	fst	6f		:214 :451 :574 1:11 3+	ⒻAlw 32000N2L	39	4	5	86	911	811	821½	Santos J A	114	9.60	64-18	Hurricane Cat1093½ Deanna Bee1142½ Lafitte's Lady1151	No speed	9
21Jly95-1Sar	fst	7f		:22 :451 1:104 1:241 3+	ⒻAlw 32000N1X	81	8	1	44	42	31½	31½	Santos J A	114	9.20	83-10	Blind Trust107¾ Cana119¾ Crafty Jenny1147	Steady gain	9
3Jun95-4Bel	fst	1		:232 :471 1:124 1:393 3+	ⒻMd Sp Wt	70	1	2	1hd	1hd	11	13	Santos J A	114	4.50	65-26	CrftyJenny1143 SilentAllnte112nk SvnGoldStons11211	Dueled, drew clear	8
3May95-9Bel	wf	1	⊗	:224 :46 1:111 1:36 3+	ⒻMd Sp Wt	30	8	2	2½	32	413	527	Davis R G	112 b	2.50	56-16	Ravishing Raven11415 Bank Approval1105 Kalfo1127	Dueled, tired	8
17Apr95-3Aqu	fst	1		:231 :462 1:114 1:372	ⒻMd Sp Wt	67	4	1	1½	1½	21½	25¾	Santos J A	120 b	2.20	76-24	Lady Mondegreen1155¾ Crafty Jenny1205¼ Enchancement1205	Held well	7
6Apr95-5Aqu	fst	1		:232 :463 1:121 1:383	ⒻMd Sp Wt	62	5	3	1hd	1½	1½	34	Alvarado F T	120	6.20	72-26	Holley'sHeart1203¾ RvishingRven120hd CrftyJenny120no	Dueled, weakened	7
24Mar95-5Aqu	fst	6f		:224 :474 1:004 1:14	ⒻMd 45000	70	8	5	45	22½	21½	2¾	Alvarado F T	116	*1.80	71-29	Ray'sCraftyLady120¾ CrftyJenny1164¾ She'sADrgon1155	Bore out break	8

WORKOUTS: Oct 9 Bel tr.t 4f fst :503 B 16/25 Sep 24 Bel tr.t 5f fst 1:004 H 4/17 Sep 1 Bel tr.t 4f fst :502 B 18/22 Aug 7 Sar 4f fst :502 B 41/65 Aug 1 Sar 4f fst :493 B 10/30

Street Code

Own: Richards Robert J Jr
DAVIS R G (235 36 39 38 .15) $25,000

Ch. f. 3 (Jan)
Sire: Lost Code (Codex)
Dam: Shady Street (Shadeed)
Br: Wood Mr & Mrs M L (Ky)
Tr: Richards Robert J Jr (4 0 1 0 .00)

L 112

Lifetime Record:	16 1 5 0	$38,010			
1995	14 1 4 0	$34,790	Turf	1 0 0 0	
1994	2 M 1 0	$3,220	Wet	1 0 0 0	$1,260
Bel	4 0 1 0	$7,060	Dist	4 0 3 0	$19,010

5Oct95-3Bel	sly	1 1/16		:224 :454 1:103 1:451	ⒻClm 25000	50	1	1	1½	2hd	43½	412½	Davis R G	L 115 b	*1.75	60-26	Fine Wine1151½ A Wild Favor1153 Arunforyourmoney1158	Speed, tired	5
24Sep95-2Bel	fst	1 1/16		:232 :47 1:114 1:434	ⒻClm 25000	72	3	1	12	1½	1hd	2nk	Davis R G	L 112 b	11.60	80-20	Crafty Jenny115nk Street Code1121¾ A WildFavor1152½	Yielded grudgingly	8
6Sep95-5Bel	fst	6½f		:231 :46 1:11 1:174	ⒻClm 25000	59	2	6	53	63½	45½	46½	Davis R G	L 115 b	19.20	79-14	Emergency1194 Front Row Center1192 Time For Allaire115½	Evenly	10
20Aug95-1Sar	fst	6f		:221 :463 :592 1:121	ⒻClm 35000	47	3	3	2½	1hd	43	410	Davis R G	115 b	24.50	70-18	Blackburn1152 Really Wild1152½ Wilmick1155½	Dueled, weakened	9
11Aug95-2Sar	fst	6½f		:22 :454 1:111 1:181	ⒻClm 35000	63	4	5	22	54½	47½	59	Sellers S J	115 b	43.25	75-18	Showsnap1216½ Emergency115¾ Fine Wine1101	Chased, tired	9
23Jly95-1Sar	fst	6f		:22 :454 :581 1:113	ⒻClm 35000	47	14	1	3½	74½	1311	1311¾	Chavez J F	115	19.80f	71-11	Austrian Empress118nk Rich Seam114½ Wilmick115½	Gave way	14
24Jun95-4Bel	fst	6f		:221 :461 :584 1:113	ⒻClm 50000	39	4	3	85½	98½	912	817	Santos J A	114	17.40	66-15	Some Sweet116hd Facing Reality1183 Carson Kitty113nk	No speed	9
16Jun95-5Bel	fm	1 1/16	[T]	:241 :473 1:114 1:424	ⒻClm 50000	61	10	3	31	2½	43	79	Santos J A	116	6.40	73-12	Alyinda1165½ My Song114½ Aidan's Breath116½	Stalked, tired	10
25Mar95-6Hia	fst	1⅛		:481 1:123 1:38 1:512	ⒻCityOf Miami28k	53	3	3	41½	42	64¾	69½	Bravo J	L 112	4.70	75-05	Librada's Brigade1142½ Western Cowgirl114¾ Ayrial Delight112nk	Tired	7
25Feb95-10Tam	fst	1 1/16		:232 :473 1:124 1:462	ⒻSuncoast42k	72	4	5	3½	2hd	1hd	21½	Lopez C	L 109	2.80	88-07	Commando Dancer1091½ Street Code1092 Smooth Quest1124	2nd best	10

WORKOUTS: Sep 2 Aqu 5f fst 1:024 B 5/9

Bemmalou

Own: Bright View Farm
TREJO J (22 1 2 2 .05) $30,000

B. f. 3 (Apr)
Sire: Waquoit (Relaunch)
Dam: Louisa Jane (Vertex)
Br: Bright View Farm Inc (NJ)
Tr: Contessa Gary C (21 3 4 2 .14)

110[7]

Lifetime Record:	11 1 0 4	$28,220			
1995	11 1 0 4	$28,220	Turf	9 1 0 3	$24,700
1994	0 M 0 0		Wet	2 0 0 1	$3,520
Bel	2 0 0 1	$3,520	Dist	0 0 0 0	

4Oct95-2Bel	gd	1 1/16	[T]	:251 :491 1:133 1:442	ⒻClm 40000	63	2	5	41½	52	77	87¼	Beckner D V	118 b	27.25	67-20	Alyinda1152½ Mystic Mel115hd Passive Aggresive113nk	Tired	10
23Sep95-5Med	yl	1 1/16	Ⓣ	:233 :492 1:15 1:473 3+	ⒻAlw 22000N1X	39	5	4	53½	96¼	1017	1019¾	Beckner D V	112 b	5.60	44-37	Hello Mom1142 Lotsa Pasta1143¼ Every Bit A Lady116¾	Tired	10
6Sep95-10Med	fm	1 1/16	Ⓣ	:223 :464 1:12 1:443 3+	ⒻMd Sp Wt	65	5	4	31½	3½	1½	15¼	Beckner D V	116 b	*1.10	79-15	Bemmalou1165¼ Heirloom Majesty116nk Ministeress115¾	Mild drive	10
26Aug95-6Sar	fm	1 1/16	[T]	:23 :472 1:113 1:43 3+	ⒻMd Sp Wt	67	6	5	74	64½	64	32	Beckner D V	115 b	28.00	82-12	Sn'sWoodmn115no TwilightForst1152 Bmmlou1151	Stead, blocked 1/8 pl	10
7Aug95-3Sar	gd	1⅜	[T]	:484 1:143 1:40 2:183 3+	ⒻMd Sp Wt	35	6	3	32	55½	821	821¼	Luzzi M J	115 b	5.50	52-18	Winner's Edge1151¼ Sean's Woodman1152½ Shallah115no	Chased, tired	9
24Jly95-4Sar	fm	1 1/16	[T]	:23 :472 1:121 1:44 3+	ⒻMd Sp Wt	67	5	7	74	63½	36	38	Luzzi M J	117 b	29.00	71-12	Nabla1223 Tooth Fairy1175 Bemmalou117½	Steadied early, wide	10
17Jly95-6Bel	fm	1 1/16	Ⓣ	:231 :464 1:111 1:423 3+	ⒻMd Sp Wt	58	5	6	32	32	75¾	78	Santos J A	114	6.30	77-18	BankApproval1131¼ RisingReason1131 Whatawaytogo113¾	Flattened out	10
23Jun95-5Bel	wf	1	⊗	:224 :454 1:112 1:381 3+	ⒻMd Sp Wt	53	6	4	53	44	44	37	Chavez J F	112	4.50	65-23	Garden Secrets1125 Fairfield Miss1122 Bemmalou112hd	No threat	6
17Jun95-2Bel	fm	1 1/16	[T]	:242 :474 1:12 1:431 3+	ⒻMd Sp Wt	65	8	5	43½	32	44½	46½	Chavez J F	113	*2.95	73-12	Retained Earning113¾ Twilight Forest1134 Aesthete1131¾	Steadied early	10
24May95-3Bel	fm	1	Ⓣ	:22 :45 1:093 1:344 3+	ⒻMd Sp Wt	67	5	8	96½	53½	53	34¼	Chavez J F	112	27.00	85-07	SpaceWarning1123 BnkApprovl1071¼ Bemmlou112no	Steadied repeatedly	10

WORKOUTS: Sep 21 Bel 3f fst :37 B 4/20 Aug 20 Sar tr.t 4f fst :513 B 14/21

4 Belmont Park

1 1/16 MILES. (1:394) **MAIDEN SPECIAL WEIGHT. Purse $32,000 (plus up to $12,560 NYSBFOA). Fillies and mares, 3-year-olds and upward. Weights: 3-year-olds, 117 lbs. Older, 121 lbs. (Non-starters for a claiming price of $40,000 or less in their last three starts preferred.)**

Callas' Aria

Own: Jones John T L Jr
SANTOS J A (165 28 18 28 .17)

Dk. b or br f. 3 (Apr)
Sire: Nureyev (Northern Dancer)
Dam: Teacher's Joy (Daryl's Joy)
Br: Owens Norman D & Phil T (Ky)
Tr: Levine Bruce N (34 1 4 2 .03)

L 117

Lifetime Record:	4 M 2 0	$12,800			
1995	4 M 2 0	$12,800	Turf	3 0 2 0	$12,800
1994	0 M 0 0		Wet	0 0 0 0	
Bel	0 0 0 0		Dist	0 0 0 0	

4Oct95-5Bel	gd	1 1/16	[T]	:232 :472 1:121 1:442 3+	ⒻMd Sp Wt	77	10	1	1½	1hd	1½	2¾	Luzzi M J	117	13.40	73-20	Theyclimechrlie117¾ Clls'Ari1172 [DH]JustFlirting117	Pressured, gamely	10
14Sep95-1Bel	fm	1 1/16	[T]	:233 :471 1:12 1:443 3+	ⒻMd Sp Wt	67	3	1	1½	1hd	2½	24	Luzzi M J	116	3.50	69-23	Mistress Hawk1164 Callas' Aria1161 Whatawaytogo1163½	Held well	8
26Aug95-1Sar	fm	1 1/16	[T]	:224 :464 1:11 1:422 3+	ⒻMd Sp Wt	63	3	1	1½	2hd	31½	76	Perret C	115	*3.55	81-12	Soft Spot1211 Honey Watral115hd Shallah1151	Used in pace	10
22Jly95-3Sar	fst	6f		:221 :453 :574 1:102 3+	ⒻMd Sp Wt	48	2	9	85¾	88	910	915	Perret C	117	7.40	74-07	Deanna Bee1175 Playful Katie117hd Charge D'affaires1173	No rally	13

WORKOUTS: ●Sep 29 Aqu 5f fst 1:004 B 1/9 Sep 8 Aqu 5f fst 1:012 H 3/8 Aug 16 Sar tr.t Ⓣ 4f fm :492 B 6/14 Aug 8 Sar 5f fst 1:002 H 2/28 Aug 3 Sar 4f fst :484 H 6/40

Shallows
Own: Dinwiddie Farm
LOVATO F JR (27 2 9 4 .07)

B. f. 3 (Apr)
Sire: Cox's Ridge (Best Turn)
Dam: Brackish (Alleged)
Br: Dinwiddie Farms Ltd (Va)
Tr: Arnold George R II (34 4 10 5 .12)
L 117

Lifetime Record: 3 M 2 1 $16,320
1995 3 M 2 1 $16,320 Turf 0 0 0 0
1994 0 M 0 0 Wet 1 0 1 0 $6,400
Bel 3 0 2 1 $16,320 Dist 2 0 1 1 $9,920

27Sep95-5Bel my 1 1/16 ⊗ :23 :463 1:123 1:454 3+ ⒻMd Sp Wt 75 10 7 5 4½ 4 1½ 1hd 2 1½ Lovato F Jr 116 *1.55 68-24 Whatawaytogo116 1½ Shallows116 6½ Ionika109¾ Yielded grudgingly 10
11Sep95-4Bel fst 1 :23 :462 1:114 1:374 3+ ⒻMd Sp Wt 67 2 8 6 4½ 42 24 27 Lovato F Jr 116 *.35e 67-23 MryMcglinchy1167 Shllows116¾ PossblConsort116 2¾ Split horses, rallied 8
14Jly95-3Bel fst 1 1/16 :232 :464 1:122 1:454 3+ ⒻMd Sp Wt 60 5 6 54 5 3½ 33 3 1¾ Lovato F Jr 113 12.30 68-27 Sarabi114½ Winner's Edge113 1½ Shallows11312 Steady gain 6
WORKOUTS: Oct 16 Bel 4f fst :502 B 35/50 Oct 8 Bel 4f fst :52 B 45/49 Sep 22 Bel 4f fst :54 B 32/32 Sep 7 Bel 3f fst :37 B 7/31 Sep 1 Bel 3f fst :364 B 9/21 Aug 27 Sar 5f fst 1:024 B 10/17

In Conference
Own: Phipps Ogden Mills
VELAZQUEZ J R (287 32 23 26 .15)

B. f. 3 (Mar)
Sire: Dayjur (Danzig)
Dam: Personal Business (Private Account)
Br: Phipps Ogden Mills (Ky)
Tr: McGaughey Claude III (31 3 9 5 .10)
117

Lifetime Record: 3 M 0 2 $8,400
1995 3 M 0 2 $8,400 Turf 0 0 0 0
1994 0 M 0 0 Wet 1 0 0 1 $3,300
Bel 1 0 0 1 $3,300 Dist 0 0 0 0

17Sep95-3Bel sly 7f :223 :454 1:101 1:224 3+ ⒻMd Sp Wt 73 2 4 4 1½ 42 3 1½ 3 3½ Velazquez J R 117 7.30 83-11 CallAccount1171 VioletLdy117 2½ InConference117 3½ Check, lack room 1/4 5
19Aug95-4Sar fst 6f :222 :461 :582 1:111 3+ ⒻMd Sp Wt 51 5 6 6 2¾ 78 7 8½ 416 Day P 116 5.10 69-15 Penniless Heiress11611 La Gloria1164 Rich Seam116½ Six wide turn 11
10Aug95-5Sar fst 6½f :221 :452 1:101 1:164 3+ ⒻMd Sp Wt 54 5 11 911 813 412 3 16½ Day P 117 4.00 75-13 WishIMay11716 MasonDixie117nk InConference1173 Brk slowly, mild gain 11
WORKOUTS: Oct 17 Bel 4f fst :481 B 9/34 Oct 10 Bel 4f fst :494 B 17/38 Oct 1 Bel 3f fst :374 B 5/7 Sep 15 Bel 4f fst :492 B 21/38 Sep 9 Bel 4f fst :49 B 11/36 Sep 3 Bel 3f fst :372 B 10/22

Amaryllis
Own: Woodside Stud
DAVIS R G (235 36 39 30 .15)

B. f. 3 (May)
Sire: Cormorant (His Majesty)
Dam: Cupid's Play (Silent Screen)
Br: Eaglestone Farm, Inc (Ky)
Tr: Alpers Sue P (12 0 0 3 .00)
117

Lifetime Record: 1 M 0 0 $900
1995 1 M 0 0 $900 Turf 0 0 0 0
1994 0 M 0 0 Wet 0 0 0 0
Bel 1 0 0 0 $900 Dist 0 0 0 0

20Oct95-1Bel fst 6f :231 :461 1:002 1:133 3+ ⒻMd Sp Wt 58 2 11 8 8½ 10 8½ 8 4½ 5 3½ Krone J A 119 f 13.00 69-22 Playful Katie1191 Devil's Mine119½ Bali Magic1192 Bumped break 11
WORKOUTS: Oct 16 Bel 6f fst 1:17 B 5/7 Oct 11 Bel 4f fst :474 H 6/45 Sep 29 Bel 4f fst :483 H 10/61 Sep 22 Bel 6f fst 1:143 H 1/3 Sep 14 Bel 5f my 1:014 H 4/11 Sep 7 Bel 5f fst 1:02 Bg 17/30

Moll
Own: Port Sidney L
MIGLIORE R (89 9 6 16 .10)

Ch. f. 3 (May)
Sire: Criminal Type (Alydar)
Dam: Shamaritan (Sham)
Br: Shannon A. Wolfram & Jurgen Arnneman (Ky)
Tr: Clement Christophe (44 4 7 5 .09)
117

Lifetime Record: 2 M 0 0 $2,760
1995 2 M 0 0 $2,760 Turf 0 0 0 0
1994 0 M 0 0 Wet 0 0 0 0
Bel 1 0 0 0 $960 Dist 0 0 0 0

11Sep95-4Bel fst 1 :23 :462 1:114 1:374 3+ ⒻMd Sp Wt 60 4 4 5 2½ 5 2½ 5 7½ 5 10¾ Velazquez J R 116 12.10 63-23 Mary Mcglinchy1167 Shallows116¾ Possible Consort116 2¾ Chased, tired 8
16Aug95-4Sar fst 7f :223 :46 1:111 1:242 3+ ⒻMd Sp Wt 61 2 9 6 2½ 43 55 4 8½ Velazquez J R 117 50.00 75-14 Hamba1171 Mary Mcglinchy1176 Devil's Mine117 1½ Saved ground 10
WORKOUTS: Oct 13 Bel 4f fst :512 B 20/21 Sep 29 Bel 4f fst :492 B 23/61 Sep 21 Bel 4f fst :512 B 42/47 Sep 9 Bel 3f fst :384 B 16/17 Sep 2 Bel 3f fst :373 B 20/27 Aug 26 Bel tr.t 4f fst :502 B 15/22

Blonde Actress
Own: Jayaraman Devi & Kalarikkal K
STEVENS G L (82 17 10 14 .21)

Ch. f. 3 (Feb)
Sire: Lyphard's Ridge (Lyphard's Wish)
Dam: Stage Door Flirt (Stage Door Johnny)
Br: Jayaraman K K (Ark)
Tr: Jolley Leroy (25 3 2 2 .12)
117

Lifetime Record: 6 M 2 2 $17,051
1995 6 M 2 2 $17,051 Turf 1 0 0 0
1994 0 M 0 0 Wet 0 0 0 0
Bel 2 0 1 0 $8,200 Dist 1 0 1 0 $6,400

4Oct95-5Bel gd 1 1/16 Ⓣ :232 :472 1:121 1:442 3+ ⒻMd Sp Wt 18 4 9 8 9½ 89 921 9 27¾ Smith M E 117 3.80 46-20 Theycllmechrli117¾ Clls'Ari1172 DHJustFlirting117 Shuffled back early 10
24Sep95-3Bel fst 1 1/16 :232 :471 1:114 1:433 3+ ⒻMd Sp Wt 71 1 3 4 2½ 42 1½ 2 1½ Sellers S J 116 7.10 79-20 CrftyLdy116 1½ BlondActrss116 6½ PossiblConsort116nk Wide bid, weakened 7
9Sep95-4Bel fst 6f :224 :454 :58 1:103 3+ ⒻMd Sp Wt 56 4 5 4 2½ 5 4¾ 58 4 10½ Davis R G 117 6.60 77-19 La Gloria117 3¾ Devil's Mine117 5½ California Rush117 1½ No late bid 7
17Aug95-7Pim fst 6f :232 :472 :594 1:122 3+ ⒻMd Sp Wt 55 6 1 4 3½ 54 3 4½ 2 6½ Miller D A Jr 117 5.90 79-13 FlyingWaquoit117 6½ BlondeActress1176 GrandmaSdie110no Gained place 11
23Mar95-6OP fst 6f :22 :461 :591 1:124 ⒻⓈMd Sp Wt 57 11 10 10 12 8 13 58 3 2½ Gomez G K 120 *2.20 75-21 Snazzy Brick1202 Farewell Wish120nk Blonde Actress1202 Closed fast 12
20Jan95-2OP gd 6f :222 :471 1:002 1:141 ⒻMd Sp Wt 41 3 11 10 11 7 9½ 28 3 7½ Gomez G K 115 4.40 62-26 Fabulous Performer1206 Windy Lake120 1½ Blonde Actress1152 4-wide 11
WORKOUTS: Oct 12 Bel 4f fst :493 B 18/30 Oct 1 Bel 4f fst :51 B 25/28 Sep 20 Bel 4f fst :49 B 27/70 Sep 3 Bel 4f fst :48 H 13/46 ●Aug 1 Pim 4f fst :473 Hg 1/15

Deo Devil
Own: Paxson Mrs Henry D
BAILEY J D (197 44 27 22 .22)

Ch. f. 3 (Mar)
Sire: Devil's Bag (Halo)
Dam: Olden Charade (Hagley)
Br: Paxson Mrs Henry D (Ky)
Tr: Dickinson Michael W (14 2 4 0 .14)
L 117

Lifetime Record: 0 M 0 0 $0
1995 0 M 0 0 Turf 0 0 0 0
1994 0 M 0 0 Wet 0 0 0 0
Bel 0 0 0 0 Dist 0 0 0 0

WORKOUTS: Oct 12 Fai Ⓣ 5f fm 1:033 B (d) 3/4 Oct 3 Fai Ⓣ 5f fm 1:044 B (d) 10/11 Sep 18 Fai 5f (W) fst 1:042 B 8/9 Aug 21 Fai 5f (W) fst 1:043 B 6/8 Aug 14 Fai 4f (W) fst :521 B 5/5

Full Approval
Own: Humphrey G Watts Jr
SMITH M E (199 34 24 30 .17)

Ch. f. 3 (Mar)
Sire: Deputy Minister (Vice Regent)
Dam: Pentagram (Raise A Native)
Br: Windfields Farm (Ont-C)
Tr: Arnold George R II (34 4 10 5 .12)
L 117

Lifetime Record: 2 M 1 0 $7,800
1995 2 M 1 0 $7,800 Turf 0 0 0 0
1994 0 M 0 0 Wet 1 0 0 0 $1,800
Bel 1 0 0 0 $1,800 Dist 0 0 0 0

17Sep95-3Bel sly 7f :223 :454 1:101 1:224 3+ ⒻMd Sp Wt 66 4 2 3 1½ 3 1½ 4 3½ 47 Smith M E L 117 *1.55 80-11 Call Account1171 Violet Lady117 2½ In Conference117 3½ Checked 1/2 pl 5
28Aug95-4Sar fst 7f :23 :46 1:112 1:251 3+ ⒻMd Sp Wt 74 6 3 64 43 3 1½ 2 1½ Day P 117 15.50 79-18 Nepta117 1½ Full Approval117¾ Playful Katie1177 Finished well 7
WORKOUTS: Oct 11 Bel 4f fst :49 B 19/45 Sep 29 Bel 3f fst :363 B 5/30 Sep 14 Bel 4f my :484 B 7/24 Sep 6 Bel 4f fst :474 H 5/48 Aug 25 Sar 3f fst :364 Hg 4/8 Aug 14 Sar tr.t 4f fst :52 B 28/38

Friskies Tracy
Own: Ruvolo Michael
CHAVEZ J F (190 32 19 26 .17)

Ch. f. 3 (Mar)
Sire: Chromite (Mr. Prospector)
Dam: Friskies Empire (Vast Empire)
Br: JR Farm & Mike Ruvolo (Va)
Tr: Destasio Richard A (26 2 2 2 .08)
L 117

Lifetime Record: 3 M 0 0 $2,580
1995 3 M 0 0 $2,580 Turf 0 0 0 0
1994 0 M 0 0 Wet 0 0 0 0
Bel 2 0 0 0 $1,680 Dist 0 0 0 0

25Sep95-1Bel fst 6f :222 :453 :584 1:113 3+ ⒻMd 35000 51 3 9 56 55 45 48 Luzzi M J L 117 4.80 75-12 FinlyDcortd1175 FivToWon118 1½ StrOfAlxs114 1¾ Checked, bumped break 12
6Sep95-1Bel fst 6f :222 :472 :59 1:112 3+ ⒻMd 35000 49 5 4 31 3½ 32 4 9½ Luzzi M J 117 3.45 74-14 Christina B.117 8¾ Yul Babe118no Keep The Record117¾ Stalked, tired 9
29Jly95-4Sar fst 6f :223 :454 :58 1:101 3+ ⒻMd Sp Wt 16 6 6 5 2½ 4 4½ 516 5 29½ Luzzi M J 117 22.20 60-13 Mystriarch1176 Mason Dixie1175 Devil's Mine11714 Poor break 6
WORKOUTS: Oct 8 Bel tr.t 6f fst 1:182 B 3/3 Sep 15 Bel tr.t 4f fst :493 B 2/10 Sep 1 Bel tr.t 5f fst 1:022 B 4/15 Aug 15 Sar tr.t 4f fst :514 B 19/30 Aug 7 Sar 4f fst :492 Hg 25/65 Jly 19 Sar tr.t 4f fst :503 B 12/20

7 Belmont Park

6½ Furlongs (1:14³) CLAIMING. Purse $22,000. 3–year–olds. Weight, 122 lbs. Non–winners of three races since September 1, allowed 3 lbs. Two races since September 13, 5 lbs. A race since then, 7 lbs. Claiming price $30,000, if for $25,000, allowed 3 lbs. (Races where entered for $20,000 or less not considered.)

Is It Possible

Own: Hushion Michael E & Tramutola Tom

ALVARADO F T (120 15 18 14 .13) $25,000

Ch. g. 3 (Mar)
Sire: Premiership (Exclusive Native)
Dam: Frozen Honey (Better Bee)
Br: AbraCadabra Farms (Fla)
Tr: Hushion Michael E (38 6 6 6 .16)

L 112

	Lifetime Record: 22 4 4 4	$72,105
1995 14 3 2 3 $56,120	Turf 2 0 0 0	$320
1994 8 1 2 1 $15,985	Wet 4 0 0 2	$9,350
Bel 6 0 1 2 $10,660	Dist 2 1 0 0	$12,240

WORKOUTS: Aug 23 Sar 4f fst :50³ B 2/5

Manila Thriller

Own: Dogwood Stable

VELAZQUEZ J R (207 32 23 26 .15) $30,000

B. c. 3 (Feb)
Sire: Manila (Lyphard)
Dam: Promising Risk (Exclusive Native)
Br: Humphrey G W Jr & Louise I (Ky)
Tr: Alexander Frank A (28 4 5 5 .14)

L 115

	Lifetime Record: 11 1 2 3	$43,640
1995 3 0 0 1 $3,260	Turf 4 0 1 1	$13,280
1994 8 1 2 2 $40,380	Wet 2 1 0 0	$16,460
Bel 2 0 1 0 $5,500	Dist 0 0 0 0	

WORKOUTS: Sep 19 Bel 5f fst 1:03 B 36/52   Sep 6 Bel 3f fst :37³ B 12/18

Colossal Dream

Own: Carusillo Peter P

KING E L JR (2 0 0 0 .00) $30,000

Dk. b or br g. 3 (Feb)
Sire: Spare Card (Paris Dust)
Dam: Exault (Sham)
Br: San Martin & Llanes (Fla)
Tr: Allard Edward T (8 0 4 0 .00)

L 115

	Lifetime Record: 8 2 1 0	$17,320
1995 8 2 1 0 $17,320	Turf 2 0 0 0	$360
1994 0 M 0 0	Wet 2 1 0 0	$6,600
Bel 1 0 1 0 $4,000	Dist 0 0 0 0	

WORKOUTS: Oct 10 Med 4f fst :48 B 4/10   Sep 19 Med 4f fst :49 B 6/14

Easterwood

Own: Stewart Frank W

PEZUA J M (56 2 4 5 .04) $30,000

B. g. 3 (Apr)
Sire: Bailjumper (Damascus)
Dam: Paris Dawn (Mr. Redoy)
Br: Scott Kimbel & Pegasus Stud (Ky)
Tr: Meyer Jerome C (5 0 0 0 .00)

115

	Lifetime Record: 26 3 2 3	$61,874
1995 16 2 2 1 $45,640	Turf 4 0 0 0	$1,680
1994 10 1 0 2 $16,234	Wet 4 1 0 0	$17,193
Bel 7 1 0 1 $20,500	Dist 3 0 1 0	$17,800

WORKOUTS: Oct 12 Aqu 6f fst 1:15 B 2/3   ● Sep 19 Aqu 6f fst 1:14 H 1/6   Aug 9 Bel tr.t 6f fst 1:15⁴ B 3/3

Spanish Charge
Own: Paraneck Stable
RYDOWSKI S R (40 6 3 0 .15) $25,000

B. c. 3 (Mar)
Sire: War (Majestic Light)
Dam: Lady Romanee (Norcliffe)
Br: Crowell Howard G (Fla)
Tr: Aquilino Joseph (41 4 3 5 .10)

L 112

Lifetime Record:	11	2	2	1	$29,425						
1995	7	1	1	1	$18,660	Turf	3	0	1	0	$6,000
1994	4	1	1	0	$10,765	Wet	1	0	0	1	$3,960
Bel	2	0	0	1	$3,960	Dist	0	0	0	0	

8Sep95-9Bel	fst	1	:221 :451 1:101 1:361	Clm 37500	27	9	4	63¾	96¾	1122	1133¼	Rydowski S R	L 114 b	23.80	49-17	Country Thunder118nk Lemming1162¾ Leap With Joy113¾	Wide, tired	12
28Aug95-3Sar	fm	1 3/16 Ⓣ	:471 1:124 1:381 1:561	Clm 50000	61	2	1	14	13½	53¼	69¾	Perez R B	112 b	6.80	75-08	[D]Shotgun John112no Babylonian1122 Hard Charger1153	Used up	6
16Aug95-3Sar	fst	7f	:223 :46 1:11 1:24	Clm 50000	52	4	4	33½	65	77½	714¾	Davis R G	118 b	9.30	71-14	Kentucky Govenor1151 Dancing Gator1182½ Hail Orphan1151	Done early	7
27Jly95-7Sar	fm	1 1/16 Ⓣ	:224 :454 1:093 1:401	Alw 36000N2X	42	3	3	32½	78½	915	826	Rydowski S R	112 b	54.00	72-08	Dowty1121 No Secrets1144 Val's Prince1151½	Gave way	9
1Jly95-5Bel	sly	1 1/16 ⊗	:224 :452 1:10 1:414 3+	Alw 36000N3L	77	1	3	21½	22	28	320	Rydowski S R	111 b	12.00	70-18	Kerfoot Corner12016 Crary1133½ Spanish Charge11114	Chased, tired	7
15Jun95-5Bel	gd	1 Ⓣ	:222 :451 1:101 1:36	Clm 50000	81	4	4	21½	2hd	1hd	22	Rydowski S R	116 b	12.40	81-20	Timmons1162 Spanish Charge116½ Glittering Wolf1161½	Sharp try	11
3Jun95-8Pha	fst	6f	:214 :45 :572 1:102	Alw 15218N2L	78	5	7	32½	32	21	1nk	McCarthy M J	116 fb	9.50	89-13	SpanishCharge116nk ValidOmen1221½ Lyrlyrpantsonfire1162	Wide, just up	10
12Dec94-8Pha	fst	6f	:22 :45 :573 1:104	Alw 15000N1X	54	4	4	62¾	76½	76½	65½	Castillo F	122 f	7.60	81-19	Onto Luck1222½ Mr. Knowitall1161½ Paul D111nk	Outrun	7
8Nov94-1Pha	fst	170	:234 :483 1:143 1:46	Md Sp Wt	56	1	3	41	2hd	15	110½	Bisono J	121 f	*1.80	70-33	SpnishChrge12110 SirAlexnder121¾ GoldnLord1212½	Drifted out, drew out	7
22Oct94-5Lrl	fst	6f	:23 :464 :591 1:12	Md Sp Wt	49	1	10	118¾	98¼	78¾	63¼	Pino M G	120 f	8.90	71-17	Azurite Kid120¾ Carrigaline120½ American Wolf1204	Steadied 1/4	11

WORKOUTS: Oct 10 Aqu 4f fst :49 B 6/12 Aug 7 Sar tr.t 4f fst :494 B 3/40 Jly 21 Sar tr.t 5f fst 1:024 H 3/12

Pay Per Moon
Own: Pont Street Stable
LOVATO F JR (27 2 9 4 .07) $25,000

B. g. 3 (Apr)
Sire: Moon Prospector (Northern Prospect)
Dam: In Pay (Valid Appeal)
Br: Newmarket Ltd & Frank Yates Sr. (Fla)
Tr: Carroll Del W II (18 2 3 2 .11)

114

Lifetime Record:	9	1	0	1	$14,490						
1995	9	1	0	1	$14,490	Turf	3	0	0	0	$1,920
1994	0	M	0	0		Wet	1	0	0	0	
Bel	6	1	0	1	$12,570	Dist	1	0	0	1	$1,650

4Oct95-9Bel	fst	6f	:22 :46 :582 1:112	Clm 20000	57	8	6	810	87	56½	47	Davis R G	118 f	3.55	77-14	Explosive Ridge116no Is It Possible1165 Gold Toes1132	Late gain	8
21Sep95-1Bel	fst	6f	:221 :46 :583 1:113 3+	Md 35000	70	3	2	76½	53½	41½	1½	Lovato F Jr	118 f	8.70	83-20	PayPerMoon118½ Toner'sValue1151 CraftySum115nk	Bumped 1/2, up late	9
4Sep95-4Bel	fm	1 Ⓣ	:221 :451 1:094 1:344 3+	Md Sp Wt	60	4	7	811	97	98½	1010½	Lovato F Jr	117	31.25	79-14	Baroque1172 David Parson122nk Recorded1172	No threat	12
17Aug95-2Sar	fm	1 1/16 Ⓣ	:232 :464 1:11 1:422 3+	Md Sp Wt	53	7	9	911	710	78½	413½	Lovato F Jr	116	39.00	74-12	HrdChrger116nk [D]MrMrket1166 RoylGroomsmn1167	Improved position	10
15Jly95-3Bel	fm	1 1/16 Ⓣ	:231 :46 1:103 1:411 3+	Md Sp Wt	40	9	4	53	84½	810	820½	Lovato F Jr	114 b	31.75	71-08	The Author114hd The Greek One1137 Mr Market1141½	Tired	10
4Jly95-3Bel	fst	7f	:223 :453 1:114 1:253 3+	Md 50000	47	5	4	54	46½	57½	512	Lovato F Jr	115 b	30.50	61-17	Rank And File1123¾ Point Man1151¼ Kadrmas1151	No rally	8
22Jun95-4Bel	sly	7f	:221 :444 1:102 1:241 3+	Md 45000	24	5	2	33½	49	713	722½	Martinez J R Jr	112 b	6.40	57-16	Glenbeigh114no Hanging Road111½ Fat Lady's Encore1146	Gave way	7
25May95-1Bel	fst	6½f	:223 :462 1:132 1:202 3+	Md 40000	54	11	6	31½	32½	21	3½	Martinez J R Jr	114 b	8.40	73-20	Fleet Stalker121hd Believe It Seventy121nk Pay Per Moon114½	Bid, hung	11
13May95-2Bel	fst	1 1/16	:223 :46 1:113 1:434	Md Sp Wt	30	2	4	55	55	515	533¼	Velazquez J R	121	18.70	47-26	Last Effort121nk Validate12112 Clearance Code12115	No rally	8

WORKOUTS: Sep 30 Bel tr.t 4f fst :493 B 10/20 Sep 13 Bel tr.t 4f fst :491 B 4/15 Aug 31 Bel tr.t 4f fst :514 B 13/14 Aug 14 Sar 4f fst :483 Hg 17/70 Aug 8 Sar 5f fst 1:024 B 17/28 Aug 1 Sar 5f fst 1:06 B 24/24

Call Home
Own: Willis Sheldon
MIGLIORE R (89 9 6 16 .10) $30,000

B. c. 3 (Mar)
Sire: Phone Trick (Clever Trick)
Dam: Sweet Berry (Inverness Drive)
Br: Betty S. Brannen (Ky)
Tr: Domino Carl J (27 1 4 1 .04)

115

Lifetime Record:	4	1	0	0	$20,120						
1995	4	1	0	0	$20,120	Turf	0	0	0	0	
1994	0	M	0	0		Wet	0	0	0	0	
Bel	2	0	0	0	$960	Dist	1	0	0	0	$960

29Sep95-7Bel	fst	6f	:222 :451 :583 1:113 3+	Alw 32000N1X	66	5	4	31	41½	75¾	68¾	Davis R G	114	25.00	74-20	Mountain Of Laws113¾ Tenochtitlan120nk Dont Gamble1131¾	Used up	7
3Sep95-1Bel	fst	6½f	:222 :453 1:093 1:154 3+	Alw 32000N1X	72	3	2	63½	73½	53¾	59	Smith M E	116	19.20	87-07	Concoctor1162¼ Investor112½ Deputy Politan1164	No rally	8
20Aug95-4Sar	fst	6f	:223 :462 :584 1:114 3+	Md Sp Wt	78	4	2	2½	1hd	12	1½	Chavez J F	116	5.50	82-18	Call Home116½ As Time Flys By1161 Court Jester1162½	Fully extended	10
11Mar95-2GP	fst	6f	:222 :452 :574 1:094	Md Sp Wt	63	1	7	87¼	89¾	69½	413	Boulanger G	120	27.10	78-11	Defrere1201¾ Cayeli1207 Phidias Frieze1204¾	Belated bid, inside	12

WORKOUTS: Oct 16 Bel 5f fst 1:021 B 14/37 Sep 25 Bel tr.t 5f fst 1:03 B 5/9 Aug 14 Sar tr.t 5f fst 1:034 B 12/36 Aug 9 Sar 5f fst 1:01 H 9/48 Aug 2 Sar 5f fst 1:034 B 26/34 Jly 25 Bel 5f fst 1:03 B 4/6

Red Tom
Own: Gelb Ann & Heinlein Herman
SMITH M E (199 34 24 30 .17) $30,000

Ch. c. 3 (Mar)
Sire: Gemini Dreamer (Great Above)
Dam: Exclusive Secret (Exclusive Native)
Br: K. David Schwartz (Fla)
Tr: Tesher Howard M (39 4 6 2 .10)

L 115

Lifetime Record:	22	4	3	1	$60,950						
1995	14	3	1	1	$46,685	Turf	0	0	0	0	
1994	8	1	2	0	$14,265	Wet	5	1	1	0	$17,790
Bel	2	0	0	0	$690	Dist	1	0	0	0	$720

25Sep95-4Bel	fst	6f	:213 :434 :572 1:101	Clm 30000	81	6	10	910	87¼	42½	54	Smith M E	L 114 fb	15.70	86-12	Sheil'sIce1162 Winwithwlker116nk JudgeMNot1121¼	Brk slowly, mild rally	10
14Sep95-5Bel	fst	6f	:221 :46 :582 1:103	Clm 30000	56	6	3	3½	3nk	74½	1111½	Chavez J F	L 112 b	9.60	76-16	Wings Afire1161¼ Sutters Pond1161¾ Sheila's Ice1162¾	Dueled, tired	12
13Aug95-1Sar	my	6½f	:22 :452 1:11 1:173	Clm 35000	71	7	2	32	21	31	55¼	Bailey J D	121 fb	4.10	82-17	Hariki1151 Sheila's Ice1181½ Noble 'n Heart1152	Checked break	9
5Aug95-3Sar	wf	6f	:22 :452 :58 1:103	Clm 50000	54	1	4	41½	41½	74¾	715¼	Bailey J D	121 fb	5.70	73-13	Nightbreak1153½ Deputy Politan115no Dice Floe1122½	Gave way	7
26Jly95-3Sar	fst	7f	:221 :453 1:104 1:243	Clm 35000	67	13	1	11	2hd	22	85½	Bailey J D	121 fb	8.10	77-14	Dont Gamble114no Glenbeigh115hd Nightbreak1181	Dueled, tired	13
29May95-7Crc	fst	6f	:214 :453 :582 1:111 3+	Alw 16000N2X	65	2	6	54¼	63¾	55½	57½	Gonzalez M A	115 fb	4.40	84-07	Pro Brite119¾ Spot Tv119no Parella Fella1226½	Showed little	6
13May95-4Hia	fst	6f	:221 :451 :58 1:11 3+	Alw 19550N1X	78	4	3	47¼	43½	2hd	1nk	Gonzalez M A	111 fb	2.80	86-11	Red Tom111nk Request A Star1224½ Count Joseph116¾	Seven wide top str, driving	6
28Apr95-9Hia	fst	6f	:22 :442 :57 1:101	Alw 15000N1X	70	11	2	54	42	64¾	57¾	Coa E M	113 b	5.70	82-09	ConstantEscort1181¼ StayingFit1211½ TrvelingJeff1135	Lacked response	11
7Apr95-7Hia	fst	6f	:232 :454 :58 1:103	Alw 16500N1X	73	5	1	41½	4½	3½	32¾	Ramos W S	114 fb	*1.10	85-18	Willing To Cope113¾ Staying Fit1212 Red Tom1143	Weakened, inside	6
26Mar95-3Hia	fst	7f	:24 :47 1:111 1:242	Alw 16500N1X	73	5	1	3nk	3nk	1hd	2nk	Ramos W S	118 fb	*.50	87-10	Game Skipper113nk Red Tom1185 Hematite113¾	Gave way grudgingly	6

WORKOUTS: Oct 8 Bel tr.t 3f fst :364 B 4/27 Sep 1 Bel tr.t 4f fst :494 B 13/22

Crafty Jenny ($10) won the third, Blonde Actress ($8.30) the fourth and Call Home ($7.70) the seventh.

THIRD RACE

Belmont

OCTOBER 19, 1995

1½ MILES. (1.39⁴) CLAIMING. Purse $23,000. Fillies, 3-year-olds. Weight, 121 lbs. Non-winners of a race at a mile or over since September 23, allowed 2 lbs. A race since September 14, 4 lbs. A race at a mile or over since August 31, 6 lbs. Claiming price $30,000, if for $25,000, allowed 3 lbs. (Races where entered for $20,000 or less not considered.)

Value of Race: $23,000 Winner $13,800; second $4,600; third $2,530; fourth $1,380; fifth $690. Mutuel Pool $238,433.00 Exacta Pool $359,283.00

Last Raced	Horse	M/Eqt. A.Wt	PP	St	¼	½	¾	Str	Fin	Jockey	Cl'g Pr	Odds $1
24Sep95 2Bel¹	Crafty Jenny	L	3 121	5	2	5²	5²	5⁴	1¹	1¹	Santos J A	30000	4.00
5Oct95 3Bel¹	Fine Wine	Lbf	3 118	4	4	4½	4¹	1hd	2½	22½	Alvarado F T	25000	7.00
5Oct95 3Bel²	A Wild Favor		3 115	3	6	2¹	2¹	2½	3½	3hd	Velazquez J R	30000	5.30
15Sep95 5Bel¹	Birthday	bf	3 119	1	7	7	6¹½	6⁶	5³½	42½	Smith M E	30000	2.20
5Oct95 3Bel⁴	Street Code	Lb	3 112	6	1	3¹	3½	3¹	4³	57½	Davis R G	25000	7.40
5Oct95 9Bel⁵	Blackburn	Lf	3 117	2	5	1½	1²	4½	6⁵	64½	Migliore R	30000	2.95
4Oct95 2Bel⁶	Bemmalou	b	3 110	7	3	6¹	7	7	7	7	Trejo J⁷	30000	51.25

OFF AT 1:53 Start Good. Won driving. Time, :23, :46², 1:11³, 1:38, 1:44⁴ Track fast.

$2 Mutuel Prices:
6–CRAFTY JENNY	10.00	5.20	2.80
5–FINE WINE		6.50	3.80
4–A WILD FAVOR			2.90

$2 EXACTA 6–5 PAID $50.00

B. f, (Apr), by Conquistador Cielo–Our Feast, by Banquet Table. Trainer Schosberg Richard. Bred by Dr. E. W. Thomas (Ky).

CRAFTY JENNY reserved for a half, swung four wide to launch her bid on the turn, drew alongside the leaders to challenge in upper stretch then edged clear under pressure. FINE WINE raced in good position along the backstretch, surged to the front on the turn, battled between horses into upper stretch then held well for the place. A WILD FAVOR raced just behind the pacesetter, made a run between horses to challenge on the turn, remained a factor into upper stretch then lacked a strong closing bid. BIRTHDAY raced well back to the turn, failed to threaten with a mild late rally. STREET CODE stalked the pace from outside for six furlongs and lacked a further response. BLACKBURN sprinted clear in the early stages, gave way after going five furlongs. BEMMALOU never reached contention. BIRTHDAY and BLACKBURN wore mud caulks.

Owners— 1, Austin Dale H & Heatherwood Farm; 2, Hough Stanley M & Team Canonie Stb; 3, Dorsey Charles; 4, Harbor View Farm; 5, Richards Robert J Jr; 6, Hauman Eugene E & Schwartz Barry K; 7, Bright View Farm.

Trainers—1, Schosberg Richard; 2, Hough Stanley M; 3, Cordero Marjorie; 4, Jerkens H Allen; 5, Richards Robert J Jr; 6, Hushion Michael E; 7, Contessa Gary C.

Scratched— Mae's Way (28Sep95 9BEL⁵)

FOURTH RACE

Belmont

OCTOBER 19, 1995

1½ MILES. (1.39⁴) MAIDEN SPECIAL WEIGHT. Purse $32,000 (plus up to $12,368 NYSBFOA). Fillies and mares, 3-year-olds and upward. Weights: 3-year-olds, 117 lbs. Older, 121 lbs. (Non-starters for a claiming price of $40,000 or less in their last three starts preferred.)

Value of Race: $32,000 Winner $19,200; second $6,400; third $3,520; fourth $1,920; fifth $960. Mutuel Pool $252,052.00 Exacta Pool $364,457.00 Quinella Pool $77,950.00

Last Raced	Horse	M/Eqt. A.Wt	PP	St	¼	½	¾	Str	Fin	Jockey	Odds $1
4Oct95 5Bel⁹	Blonde Actress		3 117	6	4	5¹½	5²	4¹½	1hd	1⁴	Stevens G L	3.15
	Deo Devil	L	3 117	7	3	3¹½	3¹½	2hd	2⁴	2⁹½	Bailey J D	18.60
4Oct95 5Bel²	Callas' Aria	L	3 117	1	2	1½	2¹	1hd	3½	3½	Santos J A	10.10
11Sep95 4Bel⁵	Moll		3 117	5	8	9	9	8¹⁰	6¹½	4½	Migliore R	58.00
17Sep95 3Bel³	In Conference		3 117	3	9	2½	1hd	3¹½	4¹½	5nk	Velazquez J R	3.65
27Sep95 9Bel²	Shallows	L	3 117	2	6	4½	4¹	5²	5½	6³	Lovato F Jr	4.90
20Oct95 1Bel⁵	Amaryllis		3 117	4	7	6hd	7½	7½	7¹½	7¹½	Davis R G	12.10
17Sep95 3Bel⁴	Full Approval	L	3 117	8	5	7hd	6½	6hd	8³⁰	8	Smith M E	2.30
25Sep95 1Bel⁴	Friskies Tracy	L	3 117	9	1	8¹	8¹	9	9	—	Chavez J F	40.75

Friskies Tracy:Distanced

OFF AT 2:29 Start Good. Won ridden out. Time, :23², :46⁴, 1:12, 1:37³, 1:43³ Track fast.

$2 Mutuel Prices:
6–BLONDE ACTRESS	8.30	4.70	4.00
7–DEO DEVIL		14.80	8.90
1–CALLAS' ARIA			7.30

$2 EXACTA 6–7 PAID $132.00 $2 QUINELLA 6–7 PAID $89.50

Ch. f, (Feb), by Lyphard's Ridge–Stage Door Flirt, by Stage Door Johnny. Trainer Jolley Leroy. Bred by Jayaraman K K (Ark).

BLONDE ACTRESS reserved for a half, gradually gained while five wide leaving the turn, then wore down DEO DEVIL to win going away. DEO DEVIL stalked the pace from outside for a half, made a run to challenge midway on the turn, took the lead approaching the stretch, battled gamely into midstretch but couldn't stay with the winner through the final eighth. CALLAS' ARIA alternated for the lead between horses to the top of the stretch and weakened. MOLL outrun for six furlongs, failed to threaten while improving her position. IN CONFERENCE dueled along the inside for six furlongs and steadily tired thereafter. SHALLOWS raced just off the pace while saving ground to the turn, lacked the needed response when called upon. AMARYLLIS was never a factor. FULL APPROVAL never reached contention. FRISKIES TRACY was outrun. CALLAS' ARIA wore mud caulks.

Owners— 1, Jayaraman Devi & Kalarikkal K; 2, Paxson Mrs Henry D; 3, Jones John T L Jr; 4, Port Sidney L; 5, Phipps Ogden Mills; 6, Dinwiddie Farm; 7, Woodside Stud; 8, Firman Pamela & Humphrey G Watts Jr; 9, Ruvolo Michael.

Trainers—1, Jolley Leroy; 2, Dickinson Michael W; 3, Levine Bruce N; 4, Clement Christophe; 5, McGaughey Claude III; 6, Arnold George R II; 7, Alpers Sue P; 8, Arnold George R II; 9, Destasio Richard A

$2 Pick-3 (3-6-6) Paid $252.00; Pick-3 Pool $96,972.

SEVENTH RACE

Belmont

OCTOBER 18, 1995

6½ FURLONGS. (1.14³) CLAIMING. Purse $22,000. 3-year-olds. Weight, 122 lbs. Non-winners of three races since September 1, allowed 3 lbs. Two races since September 13, 5 lbs. A race since then, 7 lbs. Claiming price $30,000, if for $25,000, allowed 3 lbs. (Races where entered for $20,000 or less not considered.)

Value of Race: $22,000 Winner $13,200; second $4,400; third $2,420; fourth $1,320; fifth $660. Mutuel Pool $223,399.00 Exacta Pool $365,473.00

Last Raced	Horse	M/Eqt.A.Wt	PP	St	¼	½	Str	Fin	Jockey	Cl'g Pr	Odds $1
29Sep95 7Bel⁶	Call Home	3 115	6	1	1ʰᵈ	1ʰᵈ	1½	1½	Migliore R	30000	2.85
25Sep95 4Bel⁵	Red Tom	Lbf 3 115	7	2	2¹	2¹½	2³	2²½	Smith M E	30000	1.80
8Sep95 9Bel¹¹	Spanish Charge	Lb 3 112	4	4	5¹½	3¹½	3²	3⁵	Rydowski S R	25000	16.50
4Oct95 9Bel⁴	Pay Per Moon	f 3 115	5	3	7	5ʰᵈ	5¹½	4½	Lovato F Jr	25000	17.60
24Sep95 9Bel⁴	Easterwood	b 3 115	3	5	4½	4²	4½	5⁶	Pezua J M	30000	7.80
4Oct95 9Bel²	Is It Possible	Lbf 3 114	1	7	6ʰᵈ	7	6½	6¹	Alvarado F T	25000	2.35
8Oct95 9Bel⁸	Manila Thriller	L 3 115	2	6	3½	6½	7	7	Velazquez J R	30000	20.10

OFF AT 3:59 Start Good. Won driving. Time, :23, :45⁴, 1:10², 1:17 Track fast.

$2 Mutuel Prices:

6-CALL HOME		7.70	3.60	3.10
7-RED TOM			3.40	2.70
4-SPANISH CHARGE				5.80

$2 EXACTA 6-7 PAID $20.80

B. c, (Mar), by Phone Trick-Sweet Berry, by Inverness Drive. Trainer Domino Carl J. Bred by Betty S. Brannen (Ky).

CALL HOME dueled for the lead inside RED TOM the entire way and turned back that one under brisk urging. RED TOM battled heads apart into midstretch then yielded grudgigly. SPANISH CHARGE raced just behind the leaders while three wide for a half, then held for a share. PAY PER MOON unable to keep pace for a half while four wide, failed to threaten while improving his position. EASTERWOOD faded after going a half. IS IT POSSIBLE never reached contention. MANILA THRILLER up close while saving ground, gave way on the far turn.

Owners— 1, Willis Sheldon; 2, Gelb Ann & Heinlein Herman; 3, Paraneck Stable; 4, Pont Street Stable; 5, Stewart Frank W; 6, Hushion Michael E & Tramutola Tom; 7, Dogwood Stable

Trainers— 1, Domino Carl J; 2, Tesher Howard M; 3, Aquilino Joseph; 4, Carroll Del W II; 5, Meyer Jerome C; 6, Hushion Michael E; 7, Alexander Frank A

Overweight: Pay Per Moon (1), Is It Possible (2).

Scratched— Colossal Dream (24Sep95 9BEL2)

Let's consider how you might have constructed your ticket in those three races.

In the third, four horses went off at 5-1 or less, two at 7-1 and a longshot at 51-1.

In the fourth, four horses went off at 9-2 or less and the other five 10-1 or higher.

In the seventh, three horses went off at 5-2 or less, one at 7-1, and the other three at 16-1 or higher.

If your handicapping had come up with the three favorites in the third, fourth and seventh races, you'd have spent $54 on the Pick Six and connected.

But let's say your handicapping led you to use the four favorites in the third, fourth and seventh races. That cost $128 in Pick Six bets and, of course, you connected.

Here was the payoff in a Pick Six won by horses paying $10, $8.30, $4, $2.60, $7.70 and $5.40: $1,817.

Here's another carryover Pick Six which was eminently hit-table. I had four of the six winners picked on top in the *Gazette* and the two that I didn't won at odds of 7-2 and 8-5. And I'm still kicking myself for not playing Pick Sixes that day, December 2, 1995, at Aqueduct. You could have keyed three of the six races using singles. These three:

A field of six went to post in the third, a six-furlong maiden race.

3 Aqueduct

6 Furlongs (1:08) MAIDEN SPECIAL WEIGHT. Purse $29,000 (plus up to $11,382 NYSBFOA). 3-year-olds and upward. Weights: 3-year-olds, 120 lbs. Older, 122 lbs.

La Quinta
Own: Paulson Allen E
PEREZ R B (55 6 7 4 .11)
Ch. c. 3 (Jan)
Sire: Allen's Prospect (Mr. Prospector)
Dam: Daphne's Dancer (Northern Dancer)
Br: Paulson Allen E (Ky)
Tr: Mott William I (24 4 3 4 .17)
120

Lifetime Record: 2 M 0 1 $5,160

1995	2 M 0 1	$5,160	Turf	0 0 0 0	
1994	0 M 0 0		Wet	0 0 0 0	
Aqu	1 0 0 0	$1,860	Dist	1 0 0 1	$3,300

26Nov95-2Aqu fst 1 :23¹ :45⁴ 1:11 1:36² 3+ Md Sp Wt 72 6 4 42½ 41½ 45 48¾ Perez R B 118 3.45 78-15 Hasty Data1212½ Then Some1182½ Musical Connection118⁴ Steadied 1/2 pl 8
9Oct95-4Bel fst 6f :22⁴ :46² :58⁴ 1:11³ 3+ Md Sp Wt 65 4 6 5⁴ 32½ 35½ 3⁸ Perez R B 118 7.10 75-18 Paragram118⁵ Cossack Fighter118³ La Quinta118¾ Broke slowly, wide 6
WORKOUTS: Nov 23 Bel tr.t 3f fst :37³ B 11/16 Nov 17 Bel 3f fst :36³ B 4/13 Nov 11 Bel 4f fst :49² B 32/85 Oct 20 Bel 3f fst :37¹ B 9/17 Oct 1 CD 5f fst 1:01³ B 3/22 Sep 25 CD 5f fst 1:04² B 24/35

Real Silk
Own: Robsham Einar P
CHAVEZ J F (124 22 21 11 .18)
Ch. c. 3 (Feb)
Sire: Pentelicus (Fappiano)
Dam: Silk Stocks (Medieval Man)
Br: Robsham E Paul (Fla)
Tr: Terrill William V (25 2 3 2 .08)
L 120

Lifetime Record: 3 M 1 2 $12,600

1995	3 M 1 2	$12,600	Turf	0 0 0 0	
1994	0 M 0 0		Wet	1 0 0 1	$3,300
Aqu	0 0 0 0		Dist	3 0 1 2	$12,600

26Oct95-6Bel fst 6f :22⁴ :45⁴ :58 1:10⁴ 3+ Md Sp Wt 61 1 1 1¹ 2hd 2³ 2⁹ Davis R G L 119 *1.30 78-17 Confessor119⁹ Real Silk119¾ Promote1191½ Held place 6
27May95-2Bel wf 6f :22³ :45⁴ :57³ 1:10² Md Sp Wt 82 2 1 11½ 11½ 12½ 3nk Davis R G 120 *.90 89-09 Sutters Pond120hd Promote120hd Real Silk120⁶ Drifted, weakened 8
7May95-5Bel fst 6f :22² :45² :57³ 1:10¹ 3+ Md Sp Wt 71 9 5 4¹ 3¹ 3½ 33¼ Davis R G 113 *1.00 87-11 Runaway Brian122nk Scenturion113³ Real Silk1131½ Wide, no late bid 12
WORKOUTS: Nov 27 Bel tr.t 4f fst :48¹ H 6/40 Nov 18 Bel tr.t 5f fst 1:01³ B 4/22 Nov 11 Bel tr.t 5f fst 1:03 B 7/26 Nov 5 Bel tr.t 4f fst :48² H 15/58 Oct 20 Bel 4f fst :47¹ H 3/57 ●Oct 14 Bel 4f fst :47² H 1/60

The Old Guy
Own: Adie & Sedlacek & Tri Richard Sta
VELAZQUEZ J R (60 8 14 7 .13)
Ch. g. 3 (Apr)
Sire: North Prospect (Mr. Prospector)
Dam: Old Age (Broadway Forli)
Br: Roberts Bob (Ky)
Tr: Sedlacek Michael C (7 0 0 0 .00)
L 120

Lifetime Record: 5 M 0 0 $1,800

1995	5 M 0 0	$1,800	Turf	0 0 0 0	
1994	0 M 0 0		Wet	1 0 0 0	
Aqu	0 0 0 0		Dist	2 0 0 0	$900

2Sep95-3Bel fst 6½f :22² :45³ 1:10² 1:16⁴ 3+ Md Sp Wt 52 6 4 3³ 5⁴ 5¹¹ 510½ Velazquez J R L 117 fb 16.30 80-08 Zoom Cat117hd Musical Connection117³ Court Jester117² Brief speed 7
20Aug95-4Sar fst 6f :22³ :46² :58⁴ 1:11⁴ 3+ Md Sp Wt 64 3 7 3² 5² 4³ 55¼ Velazquez J R 116 fb 21.80 76-18 Call Home116½ As Time Flys By116¹ Court Jester1162½ Blocked turn 10
12Aug95-1Sar sly 7f :22¹ :45³ 1:12¹ 1:25⁴ 3+ Md Sp Wt 54 2 7 1hd 2hd 51¾ 88¼ Davis R G 117 fb 12.00 68-15 VictoryMill117² PlesntCourt117no CossckFightr117¾ Hustled, weakened 9
21Jly95-3Sar fst 6f :22 :45³ :58³ 1:11³ 3+ Md Sp Wt 55 10 6 4¹ 3½ 53¼ 7⁹ Davis R G 117 b 34.00 74-10 Nuclear Treaty117¹ Scenturion117¾ Prodigal Son117nk Forced pace 12
8Jly95-2Bel fst 7f :22² :46¹ 1:11² 1:24³ 3+ Md Sp Wt 37 3 7 2½ 3¹ 6¹⁰ 719¾ Davis R G 114 b 8.10 59-16 Dr.Guid122² CossckFighter114¾ CoupD'Argnt114¾ Checked break, tired 8
WORKOUTS: ●Nov 26 Aqu 5f fst 1:00³ H 1/12 Nov 18 Aqu 4f fst :52 B 16/19 Nov 11 Aqu 6f fst 1:17 B 1/3 Nov 5 Aqu 4f fst :51¹ B 8/8 Oct 27 Aqu 4f fst :49 B 5/12 Oct 18 Aqu 3f fst :39² B 5/5

Canonbury
Own: Valentine John
NELSON D (32 0 0 4 .00)
B. c. 4
Sire: He's Bad (Rambunctious)
Dam: Vintage Champagne (Iron Warrior)
Br: Valentine John (NY)
Tr: Ortiz Juan (5 0 0 0 .00)
122

Lifetime Record: 1 M 0 0 $0

1994	1 M 0 0		Turf	0 0 0 0
1993	0 M 0 0		Wet	0 0 0 0
Aqu	0 0 0 0		Dist	0 0 0 0

19Jly94-5Bel fst 7f :22⁴ :45⁴ 1:11² 1:24³ 3+ Md Sp Wt 48 9 4 42½ 64½ 88¼ 715¼ Mojica R Jr 116 22.00 65-19 Crafty Mist1161½ Level Land1165½ Fleet Stalker1163½ Brief speed 9
WORKOUTS: Nov 17 Aqu 6f fst 1:16² B 2/3 Nov 6 Aqu 6f fst 1:16² B 2/3 Oct 25 Aqu 4f fst :51¹ Bg7/11 Oct 13 Aqu 4f fst :49 B 3/4 Oct 1 Aqu 4f fst :48³ B 2/4 Sep 22 Aqu 3f fst :35⁴ H 1/3

Court Jester
Own: Hickory Tree Stable
ALVARADO F T (94 8 12 12 .09)
B. g. 3 (Apr)
Sire: Sovereign Dancer (Northern Dancer)
Dam: Cast the Die (Olden Times)
Br: Mills du Pont Alice (Va)
Tr: Reinacher Robert Jr (5 1 0 0 .20)
120

Lifetime Record: 3 M 0 3 $9,900

1995	3 M 0 3	$9,900	Turf	0 0 0 0	
1994	0 M 0 0		Wet	0 0 0 0	
Aqu	0 0 0 0		Dist	2 0 0 2	$6,600

15Sep95-4Bel fst 6f :22² :45³ :57² 1:09⁴ 3+ Md Sp Wt 72 5 6 6⁸ 6⁸ 3¹¹ 3¹¹ Smith M E 117 5.70 81-14 Dnjur117⁸ MusiclConnection117³ CourtJester117¹ Four wide mild rally 8
2Sep95-3Bel fst 6½f :22² :45³ 1:10² 1:16⁴ 3+ Md Sp Wt 70 4 7 66½ 43½ 3³ 3³ Smith M E 117 *1.30 88-08 ZoomCt117hd MusiclConnection117³ CourtJestr117² Broke slowly, wide 7
20Aug95-4Sar fst 6f :22³ :46² :58⁴ 1:11⁴ 3+ Md Sp Wt 74 8 10 9¹⁵ 9⁸ 6⁶ 31½ Smith M E 116 10.80 80-18 Call Home116½ As Time Flys By116¹ Court Jester1162½ Strong finish 10
WORKOUTS: Nov 30 Bel tr.t 4f fst :50² B 12/18 Nov 24 Bel tr.t 5f fst 1:02³ B 12/23 Nov 17 Bel tr.t 5f fst 1:04³ B 18/22 Nov 11 Bel 4f fst :49³ B 42/85 Nov 7 Bel tr.t 4f fst :51² B 31/39 Sep 11 Bel 5f fst 1:02¹ B 23/37

Chant Away
Own: Reineman Russell L
MAPLE E (51 5 8 8 .10)

Dk. b or br c. 3 (Jan)
Sire: Gulch (Mr. Prospector)
Dam: Sweetest Chant (Mr. Leader)
Br: Nuckols Charles Jr & Sons (Ky)
Tr: Stephens Woodford C (2 1 0 0 .50)

120

Lifetime Record:	0 M 0 0	$0		
1995	0 M 0 0		Turf	0 0 0 0
1994	0 M 0 0		Wet	0 0 0 0
Aqu	0 0 0 0		Dist	0 0 0 0

WORKOUTS: Nov 26 Bel tr.t 5f fst 1:01¹ H 3/24 Nov 18 Bel 4f fst :49¹ Hg 17/37 Nov 14 Bel 4f fst :51 B 19/27 Nov 10 Bel 4f fst :52 Bg 25/26 Nov 5 Bel 6f fst 1:15² B 3/5 Oct 25 Bel 5f fst 1:02² B 20/25 Oct 8 Bel 5f fst 1:04 B 35/38 Oct 3 Bel 4f fst :49³ B 13/31 Sep 29 Bel 4f fst :50³ B 42/61 Sep 25 Bel 4f fst :52² B 73/77 Sep 19 Bel 3f fst :38¹ B 23/29 Sep 16 Bel 3f fst :38 B 8/14

Blitzz U S A
Own: Kentucky Blue Stables & Sitt Eddie
CORDOVA D W (60 4 4 5 .07)

B. c. 3 (Apr)
Sire: Storm Cat (Storm Bird)
Dam: Thinghatab (Al Hattab)
Br: Muirfield Thoroughbred Breeders I (Ky)
Tr: Jolley Leroy (44 2 3 1 .14)

L 120

Lifetime Record:	4 M 1 0	$6,600			
1994	4 M 1 0	$6,600	Turf	0 0 0 0	
1993	0 M 0 0		Wet	1 0 1 0	$6,600
Aqu	1 0 1 0	$6,600	Dist	2 0 0 0	

25Oct94- 3Aqu wf 1 ⊗ :23² :47 1:12³ 1:38² Md Sp Wt 68 8 7 71½ 3½ 2½ 2¾ Bravo J 118 7.80 75-21 Hollywood Flash118¾ Blitzz U S A118¹½ Storm Hawk118¹½ Rallied wide 8
16Oct94- 3Bel fst 7f :23¹ :47² 1:12³ 1:25² Md Sp Wt 54 11 2 2½ 2hd 45½ 511¼ Carr D 118 19.00 65-18 Stauder113nk Devious Course118⁴¾ Slice Of Reality113⁴½ Dueled, tired 11
4Oct94- 5Bel fst 6f :22³ :45⁴ :58⁴ 1:12¹ Md Sp Wt 58 1 3 55½ 53½ 61½ 52¾ Luzzi M J 118 16.50 78-14 Pat N Jac118nk Judge Me Not118no Sosa118¹ Steadied 3/16 pl 9
29Aug94- 5Sar fst 6f :22¹ :45³ :58¹ 1:11² Md Sp Wt 38 10 6 7⁴ 6⁵ 6⁷ 716 Luzzi M J 118 b 8.70 68-13 Reality Road118⁸ Admiralty118⁵½ Cherokee Saga118nk No menace, wide 10

WORKOUTS: ●Nov 18 Bel tr.t 4f fst :48¹ H 1/41 ●Sep 22 Bel tr.t 4f fst :48 H 1/20 Sep 10 Bel 6f fst 1:16² H 4/6

The obvious standout was Real Silk. She'd been third, third and a distant second in her only three starts, the last off a layoff with Lasix. All her works since were strong, and she looked to be the lone speed. She was bet down to 3-5 and went wire to wire, winning by 3½ lengths.

THIRD RACE
Aqueduct
DECEMBER 2, 1995

6 FURLONGS. (1.08) MAIDEN SPECIAL WEIGHT. Purse $29,000 (plus up to $11,382 NYSBFOA). 3-year-olds and upward. Weights: 3-year-olds, 120 lbs. Older, 122 lbs.

Value of Race: $29,000 Winner $17,400; second $5,800; third $3,190; fourth $1,740; fifth $870. Mutuel Pool $261,851.00 Exacta Pool $306,542.00 Minus Show Pool $141.25

Last Raced	Horse	M/Eqt.	A.Wt	PP	St	¼	½	Str	Fin	Jockey	Odds $1
26Oct95 6Bel2	Real Silk	L	3 120	2	2	1¹	1²	1³	13½	Chavez J F	0.60
15Sep95 4Bel3	Court Jester		3 120	5	4	5⁸	514	2¼	25¼	Alvarado F T	5.20
19Jly94 5Bel7	Canonbury		4 122	4	3	4⁴	4¹	4¼	3³	Nelson D	43.00
2Sep95 3Bel5	The Old Guy	Lbf	3 120	3	5	3²	2¹	3½	44¾	Velazquez J R	14.30
26Nov95 2Aqu4	La Quinta		3 120	1	6	2hd	3¹	512	54¾	Perez R B	4.20
	Chant Away		3 120	6	1	6	6	6	6	Maple E	7.30

OFF AT 1:24 Start Good. Won ridden out. Time, :22³, :46², :58⁴, 1:11² Track good.

$2 Mutuel Prices:				
	2–REAL SILK	3.20	2.40	2.10
	5–COURT JESTER		3.30	2.10
	4–CANONBURY			3.30

$2 EXACTA 2–5 PAID $9.00

Ch. c, (Feb), by Pentelicus–Silk Stocks, by Medieval Man. Trainer Terrill William V. Bred by Robsham E Paul (Fla).

REAL SILK sprinted clear in the early stages, raced uncontested on the lead into the stretch then drew away while being ridden out. COURT JESTER reserved early, swung out while rallying on the turn, then finished well along the inside to best the others. CANONBURY raced within striking distance from outside for a half and lacked a strong closing bid. THE OLD GUY rushed up between horses, chased the winner to the top of the stretch and steadily tired thereafter. LA QUINTA showed speed while saving ground to the turn and gave way. CHANT AWAY never reached contention. BLITZZ U S A WAS ORDERED SCRATCHED AT THE GATE BY THE STEWARDS' ON THE ADVICE OF THE VETERINARIAN. ALL WAGERS INVOLVING BLITZZ U S A WERE REFUNDED AND ALL PICK-6 SELECTIONS OF BLITZZ U S A REVERT TO THE POST TIME FAVORITE, REAL SILK. A CONSOLATION PICK-3 WAS ALSO PAID.

Owners— 1, Robsham Einar P; 2, Hickory Tree Stable; 3, Valentino John; 4, Adie & Sedlacek & Tri Richard Sta; 5, Paulson Allen E; 6, Reineman Russell L

Trainers—1, Terrill William V; 2, Reinacher Robert Jr; 3, Ortiz Juan; 4, Sedlacek Michael C; 5, Mott William I; 6, Stephens Woodford C

Scratched— Blitzz U S A (25Oct94 3AQU2)

The scratches of Investor, Rampunch and Crusader's Story reduced the field to five in the seventh, a 6½-furlong allowance.

7   Aqueduct

6½ Furlongs (1:15) **ALLOWANCE. Purse $33,000** (plus up to $12,952 NYSBFOA). 3-year-olds and upward which have not won two races other than maiden, claiming or starter. Weights: 3-year-olds, 120 lbs. Older, 122 lbs. Non-winners of $18,000 twice since October 26, allowed 3 lbs. Such a race since then, 5 lbs. $9,900 since October 11, 8 lbs. (Races where entered for $60,000 or less not considered in allowances.)

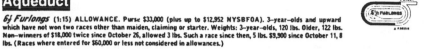

Investor

Own: Phipps Ogden Mills
Dk. b or br c. 3 (Mar)
Sire: Seeking the Gold (Mr. Prospector)
Dam: Arabian Miss (Damascus)
Br: Phipps Ogden Mills (Ky)
Tr: McGaughey Claude III (22 4 3 0 .18)

CASTILLO M JR (55 4 2 4 .07)   112

Lifetime Record: 9 2 3 3 $71,195

1995	7 1 2 3	$42,560	Turf	0 0 0 0
1994	2 1 1 0	$28,688	Wet	2 0 0 1	$3,520
Aqu	4 1 1 2	$35,676	Dist	1 0 1 0	$6,400

Turn West

Own: Stephens Lucille E
Dk. b or br c. 4
Sire: Gone West (Mr. Prospector)
Dam: Take a Turn (Danzig)
Br: Stephens Lucille E (Ky)
Tr: Stephens Woodford C (2 1 0 0 .50)

MAPLE E (51 5 8 8 .10)   L 119

Lifetime Record: 11 2 3 1 $53,820

1995	6 1 2 0	$29,640	Turf	1 0 0 0
1994	4 1 1 1	$22,680	Wet	1 1 0 0	$18,000
Aqu	4 2 0 1	$39,660	Dist	0 0 0 0

Proudest Romeo

Own: Jayaraman Kalarikkal K & Vilasini
Ch. h. 5
Sire: Proud Truth (Graustark)
Dam: Dearest Indy (Full Pocket)
Br: Jayaraman K K & Vilasini (Ky)
Tr: Jolley Leroy (14 2 3 1 .14)

CORDOVA D W (50 4 4 5 .07)   L 114

Lifetime Record: 16 2 4 2 $165,995

1995	1 0 1 0	$6,400	Turf	2 0 0 0	$1,140
1994	3 0 0 0	$1,140	Wet	0 0 0 0
Aqu	1 0 1 0	$6,400	Dist	0 0 0 0

Sunny Rican

Own: Grand Champ Stable
Ch. g. 3 (Feb)
Sire: Notebook (Well Decorated)
Dam: I'm For Dixie (I'm For More)
Br: Busamann Mr & Mrs Robert F (Fla)
Tr: Friedman Mitchell (27 3 3 6 .11)

MIGLIORE R (94 7 12 17 .07)   L 117

Lifetime Record: 22 4 3 2 $80,305

1995	16 3 3 2	$72,370	Turf	1 0 0 0	$155
1994	6 1 0 0	$7,935	Wet	3 1 0 1	$11,050
Aqu	3 1 0 0	$900	Dist	1 0 0 0	$900

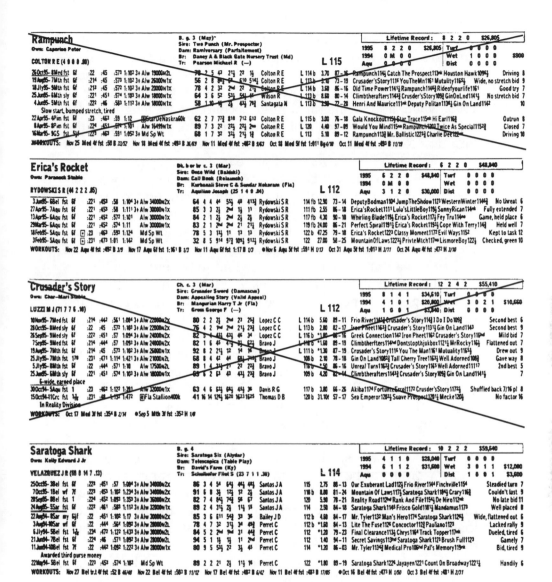

I absolutely loved Proudest Romeo, and expected him to be
an odds-on favorite. Instead, he went off at 5-2, as the other logical contender, Saratoga Shark, was bet down to 9-10.

Proudest Romeo had shown immense class in 1993, losing
the Jim Beam Stakes by just three-quarters of a length to Prairie

Bayou, who went on to win the Preakness Stakes. But Proudest Romeo's four-year-old season in '94 was a disaster, as he finished off the board in three starts. He'd obviously been hurt, since he didn't return to the races until his last PP, November 17, 1995, when, at 33-1, he ran a huge second by 4½ lengths to the very talented Finchville. In his first start in more than 17 months, Proudest Romeo made the lead, surrendered it, and held on for second by six lengths over third place Investor in a quick 1:10 for the six furlongs. His Beyer speed figure from that race was 100, higher than every Beyer of every other horse in the race, including the horses that got scratched. When a horse with back class throws in a race like that in his return, he's sending a message. We don't know what was wrong with him, but whatever it was, he had run a dynamite race. And he had to benefit from it.

Now, what about Saratoga Shark? He'd won two of 10 races lifetime, and had never even been in a stakes race. He hadn't raced since finishing a tiring fourth by 8½ lengths in a six-furlong allowance race, October 25, 1995. In that race, Finchville was third, beating Saratoga Shark by four lengths, though the *Form* noted that Saratoga Shark was steadied on the turn.

So we have Proudest Romeo losing to Finchville by 4½ lengths after Saratoga Shark lost to Finchville by four lengths.

Both Proudest Romeo and Saratoga Shark's defeats to Finchville were at six furlongs. Proudest Romeo had been stakes placed in route races, which suggested extending to 6½ furlongs today would not be a problem. Now look at Saratoga Shark's PPs. Five of his 10 races had been at six furlongs. He'd won two, tiring in the other three, including his last. In his five races longer than six furlongs, he'd tired in the stretch every single time, including one at 6½ furlongs.

So we know that Proudest Romeo has more back class than Saratoga Shark; Proudest Romeo needed his last race much more because of the long layoff, and that Proudest Romeo would be more adept at stretching out from six to 6½ furlongs. And Saratoga Shark goes off at odds-on, and Proudest Romeo at 5-2. Proudest Romeo won by 8½ lengths, returning $7.10. Saratoga Shark ran fourth.

SEVENTH RACE
Aqueduct
DECEMBER 2, 1995

6½ FURLONGS. (1.15) ALLOWANCE. Purse $33,000 (plus up to $12,952 NYSBFOA). 3-year-olds and upward which have not won two races other than maiden, claiming or starter. Weights: 3-year-olds, 120 lbs. Older, 122 lbs. Non-winners of $18,000 twice since October 26, allowed 3 lbs. Such a race since then, 5 lbs. $9,900 since October 11, 8 lbs. (Races where entered for $60,000 or less not considered in allowances.)

Value of Race: $33,000 Winner $19,800; second $6,600; third $3,630; fourth $1,980; fifth $990. Mutuel Pool $313,730.00 Exacta Pool $446,613.00

Last Raced	Horse	M/Eqt.	A.	Wt	PP	St	¼	½	Str	Fin	Jockey	Odds $1
17Nov95 8Aqu2	Proudest Romeo	L	5	114	2	2	2½	1½	17	18¼	Cordova D W	2.55
11Nov95 9Aqu1	Turn West	L	4	119	1	3	32½	3½	21	21	Maple E	5.10
17Nov95 8Aqu6	Sunny Rican	Lb	3	117	3	5	5	5	3½	31¼	Migliore R	8.20
25Oct95 3Bel4	Saratoga Shark	Lb	4	114	5	4	42½	41½	41½	45	Velazquez J R	0.90
3Jun95 6Bel4	Erica's Rocket	Lb	3	112	4	1	11	21	5	5	Rydowski S R	8.40

OFF AT 3:16 Start Good. Won ridden out. Time, :22¹, :45², 1:09³, 1:15⁴ Track wet fast.

$2 Mutuel Prices:				
	2-PROUDEST ROMEO	7.10	4.10	2.80
	1-TURN WEST		4.80	2.90
	3-SUNNY RICAN			3.30
	$2 EXACTA 2-1 PAID $31.00			

Ch. h, by Proud Truth–Dearest Indu, by Full Pocket. Trainer Jolley Leroy. Bred by Jayaraman K K & Vilasini (Ky).

PROUDEST ROMEO settled just off the early pace, took charge on the turn, then drew off while being ridden out. TURN WEST raced just off the pace while saving ground, angled out for room leaving the turn and finished willingly for the place. SUNNY RICAN outrun for a half, failed to threaten with a mild late rally. SARATOGA SHARK stalked three wide to the turn and lacked the needed response when called upon. ERICA'S ROCKET was used up setting the early pace.

Owners— 1, Jayaraman Kalarikkal K & Vilasini; 2, Stephens Lucille E; 3, Grand Champ Stable; 4, Kelly Edward J Jr; 5, Paraneck Stable

Trainers—1, Jolley Leroy; 2, Stephens Woodford C; 3, Friedman Mitchell; 4, Schulhofer Flint S; 5, Aquilino Joseph

Scratched— Investor (17Nov95 8AQU3), Rampunch (25Oct95 8MED1), Crusader's Story (10Nov95 7MED2)

The third key to the Pick Six was in the eighth race, a six furlong stakes, "The Garland of Roses Handicap," for fillies and mares. The scratches of Hurricane Cat and Madder Than Mad left a field of five.

8 **Aqueduct**

6 Furlongs **(1:08) 3rd Running of THE GARLAND OF ROSES HANDICAP. Purse $50,000 added. Fillies and mares, 3-year-olds and upward. By subscription of $50 each, which should accompany the nomination, $250 to pass the entry box, $250 to start, with $50,000 added. The added money and all fees to be divided 60% to the winner, 20% to second, 11% to third, 6% to fourth and 3% to fifth. Weights Sunday, November 26. Starters to be named at the closing time of entries. A trophy will be presented to the winning owner. Closed Saturday, November 18, with 20 nominations.**

Lottsa Talc
Own: McGuire Vincent & Werner Charles
NELSON D (32 8 0 4 .00)

Dk. b or br m. 5
Sire: Talc (Rock Talk)
Dam: Antilassa (Anticipating)
Br: K C V Stable (NY)
Tr: Kelly Timothy D (14 0 1 1 .00)

L 117

Lifetime Record:	46	15	6	9	$674,088						
1995	15	7	1	3	$372,930	Turf	3	0	0	0	$3,990
1994	12	4	1	2	$159,938	Wet	10	4	1	2	$157,901
Aqu	17	5	4	3	$184,276	Dist	20	9	4	3	$376,053

24Nov95-8Aqu	gd	1		:23	:45²	1:09³	1:35¹	3+ ⒻTopFlight H-G1	94	2	3	32½	34	38½	66	Nelson D	L 113	14.20	87-14	TwistAflet123 1½ ChposSprings118 1½ LottDncing114½	Checked early, tired	8
28Oct95-1Bel	my	7f		:22⁴	:46	1:10¹	1:22⁴	3+ ⒻFirstFlightH-G2	81	3	5	42	32½	37½	39	Nelson D	L 116	4.40	78-08	Twist Afleet121 2 Igotrhythm109 7 Lottsa Talc116 2½	Four wide, weakened	5
14Oct95-5Bel	fst	7f		:22	:45	1:10¹	1:23¹	3+ ⒻⓈIroquois H125k	93	10	8	83¾	1hd	13	11½	Nelson D	L 123 b	3.40	85-17	LottsaTlc123 1½ OurSpringwter112 3 MdderThnMd117 1¾	Five wide, gamely	14
17Sep95-8Bel	sly	6f		:22	:45	:56⁴	1:09¹	3+ ⒻⓈSchenectadyH55k	94	2	5	44	21	2½	1nk	Nelson D	L 122	3.40	95-11	LottsaTalc122nk MadderThnMd117 1 GreenStrwberry110 5½	Fully extended	8
13Aug95-6Mth	fst	6f		:22³	:45⁴	:58¹	1:10⁴	3+ ⒻAlw 40000N$Y	91	2	4	21	33	32½	1no	Nelson D	L 122	2.00	85-22	Lottsa Talc122no Up An Eighth117 1½ Fortune Wand117 2½	Got up	5
15Jly95-9Mth	fst	6f		:21⁴	:44³	:56⁴	1:09²	3+ ⒻW LongBranch40k	79	4	6	57½	56½	56½	36½	Nelson D	L 122	3.50	86-13	Zingadoon122 5 Up An Eighth117 1½ Lottsa Talc122 3½	Mild bid	6
22Jun95-8Bel	sly	1	⊗	:22¹	:44⁴	1:10¹	1:37²	ⒻAlw 46560C	-0	1	4	44½	413	424	439¾	Nelson D	115	*1.00	36-22	Unlawful Behavior112 1¾ Unreal Cupcake111 14 Tiffany's Taylor115 24	Bled	4
3Jun95-10Bel	fst	6f		:22³	:45⁴	:57⁴	1:11¹	3+ ⒻGenuinRiskH-G2	80	2	3	43½	45½	47	35	Nelson D	117	5.80	80-14	Classy Mirage122 3¾ Through The Docr111 1½ Lottsa Talc117 2	No threat	4
19Apr95-8Aqu	fst	1		:23¹	:45⁴	1:10	1:36¹	3+ ⒻⓈBroadway H54k	97	7	2	2hd	2hd	2½	1nk	Nelson D	122	*.85	88-20	LottsaTalc122nk Lilly'sMoment122 1¾ OurSpringwter112 6	Drifted, gamely	8
2Apr95-8Aqu	fst	6f		:22⁴	:46¹	:58¹	1:10³	3+ ⒻⓈHyde Park H54k	91	5	6	64	63	41½	2nk	Nelson D	122	1.65	89-13	Lilly's Moment121nk Lottsa Talc122½ Obligated Sue114 3	In traffic 1/4 pl	6

WORKOUTS: Nov 21 Bel tr.t 3f fst :35⁴ H *5/17* Nov 16 Bel 3f fst :38 B *9/16* Nov 9 Bel tr.t 4f fst :49⁴ B *6/16* Oct 23 Bel tr.t 3f fst :38¹ B *10/12* ●Oct 9 Bel 3f fst :35¹ H *1/24* Oct 4 Bel 3f fst :37¹ B *12/24*

~~**Hurricane Cat**~~
Own: Kupferberg Max & Saul J
CHAVEZ J F (124 22 21 11 .18)

B. f. 3 (Jan)
Sire: Storm Cat (Storm Bird)
Dam: Muriesk (Nashua)
Br: Overbrook Farm (Ky)
Tr: Margotta Anthony Jr (15 0 1 2 .00)

L 108

Lifetime Record: 8 2 4 1 $60,860
1995 8 2 4 1 $60,860 | Turf 1 0 0 0
1994 0 M 0 0 | Wet 2 0 1 1 $10,520
Aqu 1 0 0 1 $3,520 | Dist 5 2 2 1 $47,060

3Nov95-7Aqu sly 6f :22² :46 :58¹ 1:10⁴ 3↑ ⒻAlw 32000N2X 85 3 2 3¹ 3¹½ 3² 3¹½ Smith M E L 113 *.65 86-20 Wave Runner116½ Showsnap112¹ Hurricane Cat113¾ Best stride late 6
14Oct95-9Med sly 5f ⊗ :22 :45¹ :57¹ ⒻEgret35k 88 3 8 3¹ 2¹½ 2⁵ 2⁴½ Bravo J L 114 2.40 91-19 PhoneTheDoctor121⁴½ HurricaneCt114¹ Shnnie'sLight116¾ Second best 8
21Sep95-3Bel fst 6½f :22⁴ :46² 1:10³ 1:16⁴ 3↑ ⒻAlw 34000N2X 92 4 1 2hd 1hd 1½ 2no Smith M E L 114 1.80 91-20 QueenTutta112no HurricaneCt114¹¾ HipHipHurRhy112² Yielded grudingly 5
28Aug95-5Sar fm 1 [T] :23¹ :46¹ 1:10⁴ 1:35² 3↑ ⒻAlw 36000N2X 80 4 2 2²½ 3¹½ 5¹½ 7⁵ Day P 108 3.50 95-08 JustWonderful114² BldBeuty112½ MdmeAdolph112nk Forced pace, tired 10
11Aug95-5Sar fst 6f :21⁴ :45¹ :57⁴ 1:11 3↑ ⒻAlw 32000N2L 94 9 2 2¹ 2½ 2½ 1³½ Day P 109 3.95 86-18 Hurricane Cat109³½ Deanna Bee114²½ Lafitte's Lady115¹ Drew away 9
28Jly95-5Sar fst 6f :21⁴ :45² :57² 1:10³ ⒻAlw 32000N2L 74 3 6 3²½ 3³½ 4⁵½ 2⁷ Sellers S J 115 10.20 87-16 MybrideBarbara118⁷ HurricaneCat115½ MdmeAdolphe115¹ Up for place 11
20Feb95-6GP fst 6f :22² :46 :58⁴ 1:12 ⒻMd Sp Wt 78 3 4 1½ 1hd 1½ 1¾ Sellers S J L 120 2.30 80-23 Hurricane Cat120¾ My Winter Night120⁵½ EmmaLovesMarie120³ Driving 11
25Jan95-6GP fst 6f :22³ :46² 1:00 1:13⁴ ⒻMd Sp Wt 62 5 5 2hd 4½ 1¹½ 2²¾ Sellers S J L 120 *1.50 70-25 Hair Cut120²¾ Hurricane Cat120nk Jovial Joust120nk Gamely 10
WORKOUTS: Nov 26 Bel tr.t 4f fst :49 B 14/65

Manor Queen
Own: Behringer Edward C & Murray Thomas
MIGLIORE R (94 7 12 17 .07)

Dk. b or br f. 4
Sire: Wavering Monarch (Majestic Light)
Dam: Woodland Manor (Marine Patrol)
Br: Purdey William A (NJ)
Tr: O'Connell Richard (14 2 2 1 .14)

L 116

Lifetime Record: 32 11 4 2 $247,225
1995 15 6 1 2 $149,340 | Turf 0 0 0 0
1994 14 3 3 0 $72,685 | Wet 6 2 0 0 $36,170
Aqu 8 1 3 1 $48,860 | Dist 18 9 2 0 $185,545

22Nov95-8Aqu fst 6f :22⁴ :46¹ :58 1:10¹ 3↑ ⒻAlw 43860N$Y 101 2 1 2¹ 2½ 1hd 1²½ Chavez C R⁷ L 115 f 6.50 91-19 ManorQueen115²½ LucyEllen115² FntsticWomen115¹ Forced pace, clear 6
5Nov95-6Aqu fst 6½f :22² :45¹ 1:09⁴ 1:16² 3↑ ⒻAlw 38000N$Y 83 4 2 1½ 2¹½ 2² 3⁶½ Migliore R L 122 f 4.60 92-11 ShpelyScrpper114⁵½ Aly'sConquest119¹ MnorQun122² Speed, weakened 7
26Oct95-8Bel fst 6f :22² :45² :57³ 1:10¹ 3↑ ⒻAlw 42000C 92 4 5 1hd 1½ 1½ 1hd Migliore R L 119 f 3.80 90-17 ManorQueen119hd ShapelyScrapper117⁴ SusanVlley117³ Fully extended 5
8Oct95-7Bel fst 6f :22⁴ :46 :58¹ 1:10³ 3↑ ⒻAlw 40000N$Y 100 7 2 4¹¾ 4¹ 1hd 1nk Migliore R L 114 f 12.20 88-17 MnorQn114nk ShplyScrppr117³½ ThroghThDor117³ 5 wide, fully extended 7
16Jun95-8Bel fst 7f :23¹ :46² 1:11⁴ 1:25² ⒻAlw 44000N$Y 51 4 1 3¹½ 4²½ 7⁸ 7¹⁵¾ Smith M E 118 f 2.65 58-21 Unreal Cupcake113²½ Evi Bee112nk Future Answer112³ Rated, tired 7
3Jun95-8Mth fst 6f :22³ :46² :59¹ 1:11⁴ 3↑ Ⓕ[S]Handicap30k 80 1 4 2² 2² 2hd 1³½ Smith M E L 119 f *.90 80-21 Manor Queen119³½ Donna Doo116³½ Merri Tales120⁴ Drew clear 8
19May95-6Bel sly 6f :22¹ :45¹ :57 1:09⁴ ⒻClm 65000 90 6 1 2¹½ 1½ 1³½ 1⁸ Chavez J F 112 f 5.50 92-17 MnorQueen112⁸ SkipOne112nk OurShoppingSpree116³ Wide, ridden out 7
7May95-8Bel fst 1 :23¹ :46¹ 1:11¹ 1:37 ⒻAlw 40000N4X 66 8 4 5⁴ 4²½ 8⁷ 8¹⁶½ Velazquez J R 116 f 17.20 61-23 FuturePretense113³½ RegalSolution113½ ChattCode114¾ Four wide, tired 8
21Apr95-4Aqu fst 7f :23³ :46³ 1:11¹ 1:24¹ ⒻClm 55000 84 5 1 1¹ 1½ 1²½ 2½ Velazquez J R 116 f *2.30 82-15 Evi Bee112½ Manor Queen116³¾ Personal Girl116nk Couldn't last 6
1Apr95-7Aqu fst 6½f :23⁴ :46 1:10³ 1:16³ ⒻAlw 42000N$Y 77 3 2 3½ 3² 5³½ 6⁶¾ Velazquez J R 119 f 18.80 90-13 Incinerate117²½ Unreal Cupcake119¹¾ Via Dei Portici114¹½ Steadied 7/16 pl 7
WORKOUTS: Nov 18 Bel 5f fst 1:03⁴ B 26/31 Oct 1 Bel 5f fst 1:04 B 34/38 Sep 24 Bel tr.t 5f fst 1:00² H 2/16 Sep 19 Bel 5f fst 1:03³ B 48/52 Sep 13 Bel 4f fst :47⁴ H 4/54 Sep 9 Bel 5f fst :59⁴ H 4/35

Green Strawberry
Own: Perez Robert
ALVARADO F T (94 8 12 12 .09)

B. f. 3 (Feb)
Sire: Hamza (Northern Dancer)
Dam: Pescia (Strawberry Road (Aus))
Br: Perez Robert (NY)
Tr: Callejas Alfredo (12 0 0 1 .00)

109

Lifetime Record: 17 3 3 1 $96,177
1995 14 2 3 1 $77,697 | Turf 0 0 0 0
1994 3 1 0 0 $18,480 | Wet 3 1 0 1 $26,466
Aqu 2 0 1 0 $10,500 | Dist 8 1 1 1 $35,166

14Oct95-5Bel fst 7f :22 :45 1:10¹ 1:23¹ 3↑ Ⓕ[S]Iroquois H125k 47 11 5 2hd 4¹½ 13¹⁵ 13²¹ Chavez J F 110 b 31.75 64-17 LottsaTalc123¹½ OurSpringwater112³ MadderThanMad117¹¾ Dueled, tired 14
2Oct95-8Bel fst 1⅟₁₆ :22⁴ :46³ 1:12 1:45² 3↑ ⒻAlw 38570N3X 76 7 1 1⁴ 2hd 4⁴ 4⁸ Chavez J F 112 b 8.50 64-31 Full And Fancy116¹½ Dancing With Deb116¹½ BlindTrust114⁵ Used in pace 7
17Sep95-8Bel sly 6f :22 :45 :56⁴ 1:09¹ 3↑ Ⓕ[S]SchenectadyH55k 91 4 1 1³ 1¹ 1½ 3¹½ Chavez J F 110 b 12.30 94-11 LottsaTlc122nk MdderThnMd117¹ GreenStrwberry110⁵½ Speed, weakened 8
25Aug95-5Sar fst 6f :22³ :46 :58¹ 1:11¹ 3↑ ⒻAlw 38000N$Y 62 4 2 2½ 3² 8⁹½ 8¹⁰½ Velasquez J 117 b 13.30 74-22 ThroughTheDoor113nk ReglSolution121nk Confidentilly121hd Used in pace 8
31Jly95-8Sar fst 7f :22¹ :45³ 1:11 1:24¹ Ⓕ[S]SagamoreHill55k 70 7 1 1³ 1³½ 2¹½ 5⁶¾ Velasquez J 115 b *1.40e 78-16 Shebatim's Trick113³ Forested112no Friendly Beauty115²¾ Used in pace 8
24Jly95-6Sar wf 6½f :22 :45¹ 1:10² 1:17 3↑ Ⓕ[S]Alw 34000N2X 84 2 2 1½ 1² 1² 1³ Velasquez J 114 b 2.95 90-08 GreenStrwberry114³ MissHioCountry112⁶ SubvrsivDncr114hd Drew clear 9
29Jun95-8Bel fst 7f :22¹ :46¹ 1:12² 1:26 3↑ Ⓕ[S]Alw 32000N1X 81 6 1 2½ 1² 1⁴ 1² Velasquez J 113 b 4.20 71-22 GreenStrawberry113² Katie'sFlag112⁵½ BellaRansom112⁶ Fully extended 11
2Jun95-9Bel fst 6½f :22³ :46⁴ 1:13 1:19⁴ 3↑ Ⓕ[S]Alw 32000N1X 74 6 2 1½ 1¹ 1½ 2²½ Ramos W S 114 b 8.50 73-25 Starlite Saphire112²½ Green Strawberry114⁶½ Our GirlNessa119² Held well 13
18May95-6Bel gd 6f :21⁴ :45¹ :57³ 1:10⁴ 3↑ Ⓕ[S]Alw 32000N1X 71 8 3 2hd 2¹ 2⁴ 4⁶½ Madrid A Jr 114 b 5.60 81-16 Facing Reality112⁶ Watrals Ridge119hd WhereIsIt109hd Forced pace, tired 9
23Apr95-8Aqu fst 1 :22³ :45¹ 1:10⁴ 1:37⁴ Ⓕ[R]NY Stallion75k 59 6 3 4³ 4⁶ 4¹² 4¹⁵ Madrid A Jr 114 b 25.25 65-19 Dancin Renee118⁴ Varsity Gold116² Bien Sucre116⁹ Faded 7
WORKOUTS: ●Nov 22 Bel tr.t 3f fst :35 H 1/24 Nov 11 Bel tr.t 4f fst :48⁴ H 2/45 Sep 28 Bel [T] 4f sf :53 B (d)4/4 Sep 6 Bel 3f fst :35 H 2/18

Countess Steffi
Own: Filipowich T & Kates M & Lieberman
VELAZQUEZ J R (68 8 14 7 .13)

Dk. b or br m. 6
Sire: Geiger Counter (Mr. Prospector)
Dam: Steven's Treat (Raise a Bid)
Br: Whispering Hill Tb Brd Ltd Ptnrshp (Ont-C)
Tr: Charalambous John (—)

L 114

Lifetime Record: 33 12 8 3 $585,894
1995 8 3 4 0 $172,950 | Turf 1 0 0 0
1994 5 1 1 1 $31,079 | Wet 4 0 1 1 $20,549
Aqu 0 0 0 0 | Dist 15 4 5 2 $180,482

4Nov95-9WO fst 6f :21³ :44 :56⁴ 1:10² 3↑ ⒻOntFshionH-G3C 89 2 6 4¹½ 2¹ 1¹½ 1½ Dos Ramos R A L 115 8.00 92-15 CountessSteffi115½ HeavenlyPunch114¾ BarUMood120¹½ Driving off rail 8
9Oct95-4WO fst 7f :22 :45 1:10² 1:23⁴ 3↑ ⒻEtobicokeH-G3C 82 2 4 3¹½ 2¹½ 2⁴ 2⁴¾ Dos Ramos R A L 116 6.75 85-14 Early Blaze115⁴¾ Countess Steffi116¾ Heavenly Punch113³½ Chased speed 5
16Sep95-9WO fst 6f :22³ :45² :57³ 1:10² 3↑ ⒻRylNrthBCH-G3C 88 1 1 2hd 2hd 2hd 2²½ Dos Ramos R A L 117 5.85 89-13 Bar U Mood121²½ Countess Steffi117no Lynclar112½ Gamely 6
26Aug95-9WO fst 7f :22³ :45² 1:10² 1:23² 3↑ ⒻSeaway-G2C 84 3 1 2¹ 1hd 2³ 2⁵ Dos Ramos R A L 119 2.10 87-13 BarUMood115⁵ CountessSteffi119¹ FranssicaD'mour115¹½ Dueled, tired 6
13Aug95-6WO fst 6½f :22³ :45³ 1:09⁴ 1:16¹ 3↑ ⒻAlw 28712N$Y 97 3 1 1½ 1² 1³½ 1⁵ Dos Ramos R A L 117 *.90 96-12 CountessSteffi117⁵ FrnssicD'mour115⁶½ BlueSpruceLdy115½ Ridden out 4
18Jun95-7WO fst 6f :22 :44⁴ :57¹ 1:10¹ 3↑ ⒻHandicap42k 74 4 2 2hd 2½ 4³ 6⁵¾ Dos Ramos R A L 120 2.95 86-08 Brave Gal114½ Our Sweet Meg111² Showering120²½ Pressed inside 7
13May95-7WO fst 6½f :23¹ :46³ 1:11³ 1:18¹ ⒻGC Hendrie H86k 91 1 5 1hd 1¹ 1² 1no Dos Ramos R A L 113 8.45 86-18 Countess Steffi113no Mysteriously122hd EarlyBlaze121² Driving four path 9
26Apr95-8WO sly 5f :22² :46 :58² ⒻAlw 28200N$Y 89 1 3 1hd 1hd 1½ 2nk Dos Ramos R A L 117 4.20 90-21 Myrtle Irene122nk Countess Steffi117² Early Blaze122³ Weakened rail 5
5Nov94-4WO my 6f :22¹ :44⁴ :57² 1:10² 3↑ ⒻOntFshionH-G3C 87 4 1 1hd 2hd 1hd 3nk Dos Ramos R A L 112 5.90 93-08 EarlyBlze124no BrUMood109hd CountessSteffi112²½ Weakened late inside 6
10Oct94-4WO fst 7f :22² :45¹ 1:10 1:23¹ 3↑ ⒻEtobicokeH-G3C 84 6 3 3¹ 5¹¾ 3⁵ 4⁵¾ Landry R C L 112 5.15 89-09 Early Blaze120¹ Valiant Jewel115²½ Casual Rendezvous113²½ Lacked rally 8
WORKOUTS: Nov 22 WO tr.t 4f fst :48³ H 1/3 ●Oct 30 WO tr.t 4f fst :48¹ B 1/10 Oct 24 WO tr.t 4f gd :48² B 3/10 ●Oct 3 WO tr.t 5f fst 1:02 H 1/9 Sep 12 WO tr.t 4f fst :48² B 2/12

Madder Than Mad
Own: Siegel Jan & Mace & Samantha
MAPLE E (51 5 8 8 .10)

B. f. 4
Sire: Carr de Naskra (Star de Naskra)
Dam: Ackrimony (Ack Ack)
Br: Trowbridge Mr & Mrs Philip J (NY)
Tr: Jerkens H Allen (27 4 3 6 .15)

L 112

Lifetime Record:	12	4	5	1	$149,780						
1995	10	3	4	1	$129,330	Turf	1	0	1	0	$10,200
1993	2	1	1	0	$20,450	Wet	2	1	1	0	$34,130
Aqu	0	0	0	0		Dist	9	4	4	0	$125,830

14Oct95-5Bel	fst	7f	:22 :45 1:101 1:231 3↑	ⒻⓈIroquois H125k	83 4 4 52½ 51½ 23 34¾	Maple E	L 117	2.55	80-17	LottsaTalc1231½ OurSpringwter1123 MdderThnMd1171½	Even finish, wide 14
17Sep95-8Bel	sly	6f	:22 :45 :564 1:091 3↑	ⒻⓈSchenectadyH55k	93 1 3 33 32½ 3½ 2nk	Maple E	L 117	*1.10	93-11	LottsaTlc122nk MdderThnMd1171 GreenStrwberry1105½	Four wide, game 8
13Aug95-8Sar	gd	7f	:224 :46 1:10 1:222 3↑	ⒻBallerina H-G1	62 6 1 31 43½ 614 622½	Sellers S J	112	11.80	71-07	ClassyMirage1196 InsideInformation1264½ Lur'sPistolette1125	Gave way 6
15Jly95-3Hol	fst	6f	:221 :45 :57 1:084	ⒻAlw 54000N3X	101 1 3 2½ 2½ 2hd 1nk	Pedroza M A	LB 119	2.30	96-10	Madder ThanMad119nk IsleoBebe117no DancingOvation11511	Game on rail 5
22Jun95-8Hol	fm	5½f ⓣ	:211 :433 :554 1:014	ⒻAlw 51000N3X	90 2 5 44½ 55 44 24½	Pedroza M A	LB 122	5.90	95-02	Track Gal1204½ Madder Than Mad122hd Siyah Nara1161	Bobbled start 6
31May95-2Hol	fst	6f	:214 :444 :564 1:092 3↑	ⒻAlw 45000N2X	91 3 3 32 2hd 11 12½	Pedroza M A	LB 119	3.00	93-10	Madder Than Mad1192½ Afleet Floozie1161 Wild Jewel1165	Ridden out 6
16Apr95-6SA	wf	6f	:22 :453 :58 1:101	ⒻAlw 42000N1X	94 2 2 2½ 2hd 11 13½	Pedroza M A	LB 120	*.90	86-12	MadderThanMad1203½ Whatawomn1173½ Cee'sMrygne1202½	Clear, driving 5
19Mar95-3SA	fst	6f	:212 :441 :562 1:091	ⒻAlw 42000N1X	95 2 4 44 44½ 32½ 2hd	Pedroza M A	LB 121	2.70	91-06	MockOrange121hd MadderThnMd121½ Cthy'sDynsty1214½	4 wide into lane 6
15Feb95-7SA	fst	6f	:214 :444 :564 1:091	ⒻAlw 42000N1X	91 7 2 21½ 2½ 21 22	Pedroza M A	LB 120	7.60	89-12	WildJewel1212 MadderThanMad1202 Tht'llBeFine117no	Not good enough 7
16Jan95-5SA	gd	6f	:22 :452 :574 1:103	ⒻAlw 42000N1X	40 4 6 710 812 816 817½	Solis A	LB 120	*1.70	66-18	Queen Gen117½ That'll Be Fine1173 Carol117½	Wide, no threat 9

WORKOUTS: Nov 30 Bel tr.t 3f fst :39 B 7/7 Nov 25 Bel tr.t 6f fst 1:141 H 1/3 Nov 21 Bel tr.t 4f fst :491 B 11/47 Oct 9 Bel 5f fst 1:003 H 6/41 Oct 3 Bel tr.t 5f fst 1:023 B 3/4 Sep 29 Bel tr.t 5f fst 1:02 B 8/10

Beauty's Sake
Own: Jayaraman Kalarikkal K & Vilasini
CORDOVA D W (60 4 4 5 .07)

B. f. 4
Sire: Lyphard's Ridge (Lyphard's Wish)
Dam: Miss Rock Island (Explodent)
Br: Jayaraman K K & Vilasini (Ark)
Tr: Jolley Leroy (14 2 3 1 .14)

L 110

Lifetime Record:	12	3	3	2	$85,388						
1995	3	0	1	1	$12,020	Turf	0	0	0	0	
1994	6	2	1	1	$57,610	Wet	1	0	0	0	
Aqu	1	0	0	1	$3,740	Dist	8	3	2	2	$72,458

10Nov95-8Aqu	fst	6f	:222 :461 :583 1:112 3↑	ⒻAlw 34000N3X	67 1 4 11 11 32½ 34½	Smith M E	114	*1.25	75-17	KhalifaOfKushog1131½ Jonie'sHlo1128 Beuty'sSke1142¾	Speed, weakened 7
13Oct95-6Bel	fst	6f	:222 :452 :573 1:101 3↑	ⒻAlw 36000N3X	88 1 1 11½ 11 12½ 2nk	Stevens G L	115	5.70	90-18	FsibilityStudy113nk Buty'sSk1151½ KhlfOfKushog1132½	Yielded grudgingly 7
29Sep95-8Bel	fst	6½f	:22 :453 1:111 1:18 3↑	ⒻAlw 40320N3X	66 2 3 2hd 1hd 32 510½	Maple E	116	9.70	75-20	Lucy Ellen116hd Return Of Mom116hd Safe At Home11610	Dueled, tired 7
27Nov94-9TP	sly	6f	:22 :451 :574 1:104 3↑	ⒻHolidayInaug43k	50 5 6 75¾ 714 714 721	Gomez G K	L 112	9.50	68-17	Caznire1187 Bar U Mood1102 Dixie Band1121½	Outrun 8
17Nov94-8CD	gd	6f	:22 :453 :58 1:112 3↑	ⒻAlw 39500N$Y	92 2 4 1½ 1hd 11 31½	Gomez G K	112	4.10	87-15	Confidentially118nk Meryl'sMyth1211½ Beauty'sSake1121½	Pace, weakened 8
10Oct94-4WO	fst	7f	:222 :451 1:10 1:231 3↑	ⒻEtobicokeH-G3C	77 8 2 2½ 21 47 69	Hawley S	112	7.80	86-09	EarlyBlaze1201 VlintJewel1152½ CsulRendezvous1132½	Pressed early pace 8
15Sep94-9LaD	fst	6f	:22 :45 :574 1:102 3↑	ⒻAlw 15000N3L	82 5 3 22 2hd 12 15	Borel C H	113	*.70	94-14	Beauty's Sake1135 Cagna1212½ Platinum Whirl112hd	Ridden out 8
21Feb94-9OP	gd	6f	:22 :453 :58 1:101	ⒻM Washington55k	98 5 1 31½ 2hd 11½ 12	Gomez G K	112	1.90	90-16	Beauty'sSake1122 SmileOnMyFace1127 CapadesDancer112nk	Ridden out 7
21Jan94-8OP	fst	5½f	:213 :45 :564 1:024	ⒻDixie Belle59k	88 11 6 44 33 22 21½	Gomez G K	112	12.70	101-06	CurrentPassion1121½ Beauty'sSake1121 SmileOnMyFce1126½	4-wide 3/8's 12
27Nov93-6CD	fst	1 1/16	:233 :48 1:142 1:464	ⒻGolden Rod-G3	62 5 2 23½ 1hd 23½ 815½	Gomez G K	112	15.80	64-22	AtThHlf1225 Spiritofpochonts1153 MysticUnion1112½	Bid, led, gave way 9

WORKOUTS: Nov 27 Bel tr.t 4f fst :481 H 6/48 Nov 21 Bel tr.t 4f fst :493 H 19/47 ●Nov 6 Bel 4f fst :461 H 1/62 Oct 31 Bel 4f fst :48 B 3/56 ●Oct 8 Bel 4f fst :464 H 1/49 Sep 16 Bel 5f fst :592 H 2/29

Again, there was a horse I adored. Some horses, for some reason, never get the respect they deserve. Lottsa Talc was a prime example. In her last 10 PPs, she showed four wins, one at 4-5 and then three straight at 2-1, 3-1 and 3-1. She had won 15 times and been in the money 30 of 46 races lifetime. Following her three straight wins, she twice chased the ultra-talented Twist Afleet (10 for 12 lifetime), finishing third by nine lengths in the Grade II First Flight Handicap and sixth by six lengths in the Grade I Top Flight, in which the *Form* tells us she was checked early.

Lottsa Talc was now dropping from a Grade I stakes to an ungraded one and cutting back to her optimum distance of six furlongs, where she had a record of 9-4-3 in 20 starts.

She should have been about 2-5, but went off instead at 3-2, perhaps because her jockey, the underrated Diane Nelson, was then in a terrible slump at zero for 32. But Nelson had always ridden Lottsa Talc.

Of the other four in the race, Manor Queen was bet down to 9-5 as the second favorite. Manor Queen had won five of her last seven races, but they were a claimer, three allowance races, and a handicap for New Jersey-Breds. She'd never faced the competition Lottsa Talc had.

Nor had Countess Steffi, the 2-1 third choice shipping in from Woodbine off races in Grade II and III-Canadian stakes.

Beauty's Sake and Green Strawberry seemed overmatched.

Lottsa Talc won by a length and paid $5.10 over a game Manor Queen, who beat Countess Steffi by five lengths for second.

EIGHTH RACE
Aqueduct
DECEMBER 2, 1995

6 FURLONGS. (1.08) 3rd Running of THE GARLAND OF ROSES HANDICAP. Purse $50,000 added. Fillies and mares, 3-year-olds and upward. By subscription of $50 each, which should accompany the nomination, $250 to pass the entry box, $250 to start, with $50,000 added. The added money and all fees to be divided 60% to the winner, 20% to second, 11% to third, 6% to fourth and 3% to fifth. Weights Sunday, November 26. Starters to be named at the closing time of entries. A trophy will be presented to the winning owner. Closed Saturday, November 18, with 20 nominations.

Value of Race: $70,200 Winner $48,600; second $10,800; third $5,940; fourth $3,240; fifth $1,620. Mutuel Pool $298,826.00 Exacta Pool $349,482.00

Last Raced	Horse	M/Eql.A.Wt	PP	St	¼	½	Str	Fin	Jockey	Odds $1
24Nov95 8Aqu6	Lottsa Talc	L 5 117	1	5	5	4⁴	2½	1¹	Nelson D	1.55
22Nov95 8Aqu1	Manor Queen	Lf 4 116	2	2	41½	3¹	1¹	2⁵	Migliore R	1.80
4Nov95 9W01	Countess Steffi	L 6 114	4	1	2hd	2½	412	3½	Velazquez J R	2.30
10Nov95 8Aqu3	Beauty's Sake	L 4 113	5	3	1½	1½	3½	4¹¹	Cordova D W	9.50
14Oct95 5Bel13	Green Strawberry	b 3 113	3	4	3³	5	5	5	Alvarado F T	23.80

OFF AT 3:45 Start Good. Won driving. Time, :22¹, :45⁴, :58, 1:10 Track wet fast.

$2 Mutuel Prices:

1-LOTTSA TALC	5.10	2.70	2.10
3-MANOR QUEEN		2.70	2.20
5-COUNTESS STEFFI			2.30

$2 EXACTA 1-3 PAID $10.80

Dk. b. or br. m, by Talc–Antilassa, by Anticipating. Trainer Kelly Timothy D. Bred by K C V Stable (NY).

LOTTSA TALC checked after breaking slowly, moved up rapidly along the backstretch, angled in on the far turn, closed the gap on the turn, swung five wide at the top of the stretch then finished determinedly under steady right hand urging to wear down MANOR QUEEN in the final seventy yards. MANOR QUEEN shuffled back a bit along the backstretch, rallied four wide on the turn, accelerated to the front, opening a clear advantage in upper stretch, continued on the front into deep stretch and yielded grudgingly. COUNTESS STEFFI forced the early pace from outside, made a run to threaten at the quarter pole, weakened in the drive. BEAUTY'S SAKE sprinted clear in the early stages, set the pace for a half and steadily tired thereafter. GREEN STRAWBERRY showed only brief speed. LOTTSA TALC and GREEN STRAWBERRY wore mud caulks.

Owners— 1, McGuire Vincent & Werner Charles; 2, Behringer Edward C & Murray Thomas; 3, Filipowich T & Kates M & Lieberman; 4, Jayaraman Kalarikkal K & Vilasini; 5, Perez Robert

Trainers— 1, Kelly Timothy D; 2, O'Connell Richard; 3, Charalambous John; 4, Jolley Leroy; 5, Callejas Alfredo

Overweight: Beauty's Sake (3), Green Strawberry (4).

Scratched— Hurricane Cat (3Nov95 7AQU3), Madder Than Mad (14Oct95 5BEL3)

$2 Pick–3 (7–2–1) Paid $84.50; Pick–3 Pool $174,589. $2 Pick–6 (2–4–7–7–2–1) 6 Correct 61 Tickets Paid $4,737.00 (including $96,753 Carryover); 5 Correct 1,090 Tickets Paid $58.50; Pick–6 Pool $341,779

Those were the three singles: Real Silk in the third, Proudest Romeo in the seventh and Lottsa Talc in the eighth.

Let's handicap the other three Pick Six races.

The scratches of Lafitte's Lady, Book Of Fortune and Me And The Boys reduced the fourth race field to six filly and mare claimers ($45,000 to $50,000) going seven furlongs. In post position order:

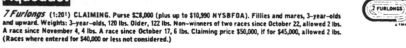

4 Aqueduct

7 Furlongs (1:20¹) **CLAIMING. Purse $28,000** (plus up to $10,990 NYSBFOA). Fillies and mares, 3-year-olds and upward. Weights: 3-year-olds, 120 lbs. Older, 122 lbs. Non-winners of two races since October 22, allowed 2 lbs. A race since November 4, 4 lbs. A race since October 17, 6 lbs. Claiming price $50,000, if for $45,000, allowed 2 lbs. (Races where entered for $40,000 or less not considered.)

Coupled – Sun Attack and Book Of Fortune

Lafitte's Lady — Ch. f. 4
Own: Foxwood
CHAVEZ C R (55 5 9 6 .08) $50,000 109⁷

Personal Girl — B. m. 5
Own: Marinos Jane E
PEZUA J M (50 8 5 11 .16) $50,000 L 116

Sun Attack — Ch. f. 4
Own: My Paradise Farms
MIGLIORE R (94 7 12 17 .07) $45,000 L 114

Z Rated — B. m. 5
Own: Camoti Thomas E
VELAZQUEZ J R (60 8 14 7 .13) $45,000 L 114

WORKOUTS: Sep 20 Aqu 4f fst :48¹ B 5/9   Sep 3 Aqu 5f fst 1:02 B 2/11
WORKOUTS: Nov 24 Bel tr.t 3f fst :37² B 12/17   Sep 15 Bel 4f fst :50 B 4/10
WORKOUTS: Sep 7 Bel tr.t 4f fst :58¹ B 15/24
WORKOUTS: Sep 7 Bel tr.t 4f fst :58¹ B 15/24   Jul 9 Mth fst 5f :59 B

Fawn's Angel
Own: Giorgi Vincent Jr & Saccone Joseph
LEON F (27 1 1 2 .04) $50,000

B. f. 4
Sire: Northern Prospect (Mr. Prospector)
Dam: Ellen's Ad (Our Michael)
Br: Saddle Home Farm (Ky)
Tr: Ortiz Pauline O (4 0 1 0 .00)

L 116

Lifetime Record:	20 3 5 3	$70,020			
1995	6 1 2 1	$32,640	Turf	0 0 0 0	
1994	12 2 2 2	$34,960	Wet	2 0 0 0	
Aqu	5 1 2 1	$18,980	Dist	1 1 0 0	$8,700

25Oct95-7Bel fst 1 1/16	:232 :461 1:111 1:442 3↑ ⒻAlw 34000N1x	74 5 6 510 53 11 12½	Cruguet J	L 116	10.00	77-24	Fawn's Angel1162½ Whatawaytogo1161½ Surprise Girl1124	Drew clear	6
1Oct95-1Bel fst 1 1/16	:234 :473 1:133 1:47 3↑ ⒻClm 18000	70 4 7 74½ 4¾ 1½ 2½	Cruguet J	L 116	3.30	63-36	Alkris116½ Fawn's Angel1164 Monster Order1141¾	Wide, couldn't last	7
20Sep95-3Bel fst 1	:231 :463 1:114 1:384 3↑ ⒻClm 18000	60 6 5 55½ 33½ 32½ 21	Cruguet J	L 114	5.40	68-21	Somthingscndlous1091 Fwn'sAngel1141½ MonsterOrder1143	Steady gain	7
12Mar95-4Aqu fst 1 1/16 ⊡	:241 :482 1:13 1:46 ⒻAlw 31040N1x	33 4 4 410 413 413 432½	Leon F	113	5.30	42-22	Smart Shopper11311 Jolie's Angel1085½ Fire Attack11416	Stumbled break	4
17Feb95-7Aqu fst 1⅛ ⊡	:49 1:143 1:41 1:544 ⒻAlw 32000N1x	37 5 6 77 78 614 622	Leon F	117	4.40	40-35	Swamp Cat117nk Bering Roses114nk Operator Assisted1101½	Never close	7
2Feb95-8Aqu fst 1 1/16 ⊡	:232 :48 1:143 1:493 ⒻAlw 32000N1x	67 3 7 68½ 22 23 35	Leon F	117	*2.50e	52-42	Doc's Josephine1174½ Swamp Cat112¾ Fawn's Angel1173	Bid, weakened	10
30Dec94-6Aqu fst 1⅛ ⊡	:484 1:144 1:421 1:553 3↑ ⒻAlw 32000N1x	75 3 5 73½ 43 33 43½	Cruguet J	115	5.70	54-39	Bounding Believer117¾ Fitnah1151½ Hidden Crest1151½	Some gain	9
18Dec94-6Aqu fst 1 1/16 ⊡	:242 :501 1:153 1:482 3↑ ⒻAlw 32000N1x	62 2 4 31½ 42½ 32½ 22	Cruguet J	115	7.00	61-29	Dixie Brat1152 Fawn's Angel115no Hidden Crest1152½	Up for place	7
7Dec94-7Aqu fst 1 1/16 ⊡	:231 :472 1:124 1:451 3↑ ⒻAlw 32000N1x	59 3 10 118½ 97½ 65½ 58¾	Cruguet J	115	8.30	69-21	GrabTheGlory112½ BlazingClearance1157 Doc'sJosephine112no	No threat	12
27Nov94-9Aqu fst 1	:24 :483 1:142 1:402 ⒻClm 30000	70 9 7 73¾ 2½ 22 24	Cruguet J	112	4.30	62-33	Cherry Glow1164 Fawn's Angel112nk Fighting Feather1162	Rallied wide	10

WORKOUTS: Nov 17 Bel tr.t 4f fst :513 B 31/32 Sep 8 Bel tr.t 5f fst 1:032 B 5/9

A Bimp in the Bye
Own: La Marca Stable
CHAVEZ J F (124 22 21 11 .18) $50,000

B. m. 5
Sire: Silent Screen (Prince John)
Dam: Staphie Brown Eyes (Explodent)
Br: Barge Marc (Ky)
Tr: Anderson William D (6 1 1 0 .17)

116

Lifetime Record:	32 9 5 2	$141,461			
1995	12 5 2 1	$102,086	Turf	1 0 0 0	
1994	7 0 1 1	$4,590	Wet	3 0 1 1	$7,755
Aqu	5 1 3 0	$34,460	Dist	3 0 0 0	

18Nov95-3Aqu fst 6½f	:23 :461 1:102 1:17 3↑ ⒻClm 40000	77 5 3 21½ 21 24 22½	Smith M E	116	2.30	93-10	Accipiter's Star1202½ A Bimp In The Bye116no S. S. Sparkle1141½	Held well	6
30Jly95-6Mth fst 6f	:214 :452 :58 1:104 3↑ ⒻAlw 38000N$Y	69 4 8 66 85½ 86 67	Colton R E	122	3.90	78-13	Donna Doo1162½ Wild Lady A.116½ My Sister Juliet1161¾		8
Broke bit slow, no bid									
17Jun95-8Mth fst 6f	:214 :451 :573 1:102 3↑ ⒻSafely Kept35k	81 2 5 32 32½ 44½ 33½	Wilson R	117	7.60	83-14	Zingadoon1192¾ Up An Eighth119¾ A Bimp In The Bye1177½	Willingly	6
6Jun95-9Mth fst 6f	:22 :451 :581 1:111 3↑ ⒻAlw 28000N$Y	78 2 5 41¾ 42½ 3½ 11	Wilson R	122	10.00	83-20	A Bimp In The Bye1221 Zingadoon1192½ Prosperous Lady1152½	Driving	6
13May95-7Bel fst 6f	:223 :453 :572 1:093 ⒻAlw 44000N$Y	72 5 5 32 42½ 45 412¾	Chavez J F	118	8.40	80-10	ClssyMirge1169 SusnVlley1162¾ MissProspctor1161	Checked break, wide	5
28Apr95-4GS fst 6f	:221 :452 :573 1:10 3↑ ⒻGS Bud BC H-G3	74 5 5 42½ 53¾ 67¾ 510	Chavez J F	109	14.10	84-16	Reet Petite1152½ Up An Eighth116½ Lilly's Moment118¾	No rally	7
22Mar95-8Aqu fst 6½f	:22 :46 1:113 1:181 ⒻAlw 34000N3x	83 9 2 2½ 1½ 1½ 11½	Chavez J F	117	6.60	89-20	A Bimp In The Bye1171½ Obligated Sue117nk Chow110¾	Dueled, gamely	9
4Mar95-6Aqu fst 6f ⊡	:224 :464 1:001 1:132 ⒻAlw 32000N2x	68 5 2 52 43½ 31 1nk	Chavez J F	122	3.00	76-24	ABimpInTheBye122nk Hppenchnc1123½ PromisdRlic1174	Wide, hard drive	5
19Feb95-6Aqu fst 6f ⊡	:224 :464 :593 1:124 ⒻAlw 30000N1x	83 3 2 2½ 31 31½ 1nk	Chavez J F	117	5.40	79-22	ABmpInThB117nk MssShplftr1173½ EphrcIntrld1176½	Altered course 1/2 pl	6
26Jan95-3Aqu fst 6f ⊡	:232 :48 1:01 1:141 ⒻClm 17500	77 1 4 2½ 11½ 12 14½	Chavez J F	117	4.70	72-26	A Bimp In The Bye1174½ Bunny's Touch1153 Miss Smart1136	Drew away	6

WORKOUTS: ●Nov 3 Med 5f sly 1:004 B 1/5 ●Oct 19 Med 6f fst 1:12 H 1/5 Oct 13 Med 5f fst 1:011 H 4/24 Oct 7 Med 5f fst 1:003 H 6/40 Sep 29 Med 4f fst :48 H 7/34 Sep 22 Med 3f fst :37 B 10/14

Just A Little Kiss
Own: Warswick Ronald J
CASTILLO H JR (55 4 2 4 .07) $50,000

Ch. f. 4
Sire: Mugatea (Hold Your Peace)
Dam: Pleasant Screams (Gallapiat)
Br: Yantis Laura J (Fla)
Tr: Schosberg Richard (20 3 1 4 .15)

L 116

Lifetime Record:	32 9 6 4	$197,883			
1995	11 2 0 2	$43,190	Turf	0 0 0 0	
1994	16 5 4 2	$128,633	Wet	4 1 1 0	$30,200
Aqu	2 0 0 0	$1,800	Dist	8 4 1 1	$89,828

22Nov95-6Aqu fst 6f	:223 :462 :582 1:11 3↑ ⒻClm 60000	79 6 4 74½ 74 74½ 64¾	Smith M E	L 113 b	5.10	82-19	UnrelCupck1141¾ RunwyFling1131½ ProudAccold115¾	Six wide, no threat	7
5Nov95-3Aqu fst 1	:232 :462 1:112 1:363 3↑ ⒻClm 60000	80 4 1 1hd 1hd 3nk 45½	Smith M E	L 116 b	*1.50	80-16	ADyToRemembr1162 SfAtHom114no Dncr'sGt1163½	Pressured, weakened	6
15Oct95-6Bel fst 1 1/16 ⊗	:232 :463 1:112 1:442 3↑ ⒻAlw 48000N$mY	73 5 5 31½ 32½ 35 37	Smith M E	L 113 b	15.00	70-23	Nappelon112hd Little Buckles1197 Just A Little Kiss1133½	No late bid	7
25Sep95-7Bel fst 6½f	:224 :454 1:101 1:164 3↑ ⒻAlw 38800N$Y	69 1 4 34½ 42 44½ 48½	Smith M E	L 114 b	5.30	83-12	ShplyScrppr1143½ JptrAssmbly1141½ Aly'sConqst1193½	Broke slowly, tired	4
11Sep95-5Bel fst 7f	:222 :451 1:10 1:231 3↑ ⒻClm 50000	83 1 9 97½ 54¾ 42 11¾	Smith M E	L 115 b	*1.70e	85-13	JustALittleKiss1151¾ JupitrAssmbly115nk UnrlCupck1163½	Best stride late	9
20Aug95-7Crc fst 6f	:22 :452 :581 1:114 3↑ ⒻAlw 19400NC	79 1 5 64¾ 65½ 68¾ 44½	Rivera J A II	L 115 b	4.90	83-18	Esplendita1172½ Sly Maid1221 Dance Chime1151½	Belated bid	6
29Jly95-8Crc fst 1 ⊗	:24 :473 1:122 1:394 3↑ ⒻVizcaya H40k	68 6 7 73½ 77 99¾ 912	Castillo H Jr	L 113 b	4.80	76-17	Prime Time Sunday1133 Easter Doll1151 Nezzie Baby112¾	No factor	9
9Jly95-8Crc sly 7f	:223 :461 1:114 1:251 3↑ ⒻClm 50000	87 2 4 48 42½ 22½ 12½	Rivera J A II	L 117 b	3.90	85-15	Just A Little Kiss1172½ Christinachristina1175 Mystic Union1171½	Driving	6
1Jun95-9Crc fst 1	:24 :471 1:12 1:392 3↑ ⒻHandicap21k	73 6 3 22½ 33½ 79 78½	Rivera J A II	L 114 b	2.20	82-19	Spectacular April115¾ Licorice Taffeta1113 Almond Isle113¾	Gave way	8
30Apr95-10Hia fst 7f	:232 :453 1:093 1:222 3↑ ⒻPoinciana H50k	39 2 5 2hd 3½ 912 926½	Castillo H Jr	L 114 b	5.30	71-11	Lady Honey Jo1151½ Sigrun1174 My Sister Juliet1142	Stopped	9

WORKOUTS: Nov 18 Bel tr.t 4f fst :49 B 9/41 Oct 30 Bel tr.t 4f fst :492 B 9/20 Oct 10 Bel tr.t 4f fst :493 B 8/22 Sep 7 Bel tr.t 4f fst :484 B 6/24

Book Of Fortune
Own: My Paradise Farms
MIGLIORE R (94 7 12 17 .07) $50,000

Dk. b or br f. 3 (Feb)
Sire: Notebook (Well Decorated)
Dam: Margaret Fortune (News Director)
Br: Swinderman J R & Kay (Fla)
Tr: Friedman Mitchell (27 3 3 6 .11)

L 114

Lifetime Record:	14 3 4 3	$85,594			
1995	14 3 4 3	$85,594	Turf	0 0 0 0	
1994	0 M 0 0		Wet	3 0 1 0	$15,604
Aqu	2 1 0 0	$15,720	Dist	3 2 0 0	$35,040

15Nov95-6Aqu gd 7f	:222 :451 1:11 1:242 ⒻClm c-40000	78 6 4 65 64½ 12 15½	Krone J A	L 116	2.15	82-18	BookOfFortune1165½ PssiveAggresive109nk HyHnn1201½	Wide, going away	6
Claimed from Dirienzo & Fellers & Guiyas Stables, Reid Robert E Jr Trainer									
3Nov95-7Aqu sly 6f	:222 :46 :581 1:104 3↑ ⒻAlw 32000N2X	83 6 3 44 35 44½ 42½	Krone J A	L 112	7.70	86-20	Wave Runner116½ Showsnap1121 Hurricane Cat113¾	Rallied wide	6
18Oct95-3Bel fst 6f	:23 :462 :574 1:104 ⒻClm 50000	72 4 7 4¾ 2½ 21½ 32½	Rydowski S R	L 116	*2.15	84-15	HyHnne1162½ Joe'sWorkingirl113nk BookOfFortun1162½	Dueled, weakened	7
25Sep95-3Bel fst 6½f	:224 :461 1:104 1:172 ⒻClm 60000	73 5 5 41½ 31 42½ 33	Luzzi M J	L 116	*1.45	85-12	Jon'sHlo1162¾ AstrnEmprss112nk BookOfFortn116hd	Checked brk, no rally	6
18Aug95-4Sar fst 6f	:22 :45 :573 1:103 3↑ ⒻAlw 34000N2X	87 1 2 21 31½ 33½ 35	Chavez J F	110	4.80	83-14	Holley'sHeart1154½ MybrideBarbara115½ BookOfFortune1103	No late bid	5
4Aug95-4Sar my 6f	:214 :451 :573 1:104 ⒻClm 75000	88 3 7 77¾ 65 35 25	Chavez J F	115	4.10	82-19	Holley's Heart1155 Book Of Fortune1151½ SomeSweet1185½	Rallied inside	7
13Jly95-8Bel fst 7f	:224 :46 1:11 1:24 3↑ ⒻAlw 34000N2X	79 4 2 53 31 21 43½	Migliore R	113	*1.60	77-17	Class Kris1121½ PrettyDiscreet1121¾ FullAndFancy111½	Bid, flattened out	6
24Jun95-9Bel wf 6f	:214 :45 :572 1:103 ⒻPrioress-G2	82 2 3 85¾ 73¾ 55½ 47¾	Migliore R	114	28.50	80-15	Scotzanna1211 Culver City1162¾ Miss Golden Circle1184	Mild gain	9
9Jun95-5Bel fst 6½f	:222 :454 1:11 1:173 3↑ ⒻAlw 34000N2X	91 10 6 74½ 52½ 2½ 23	Krone J A	112	3.15	84-19	RussnFlght1143 BookOfFortn1122½ FllAndFncy1124	Wide bid, no match	10
24May95-4Bel fst 7f	:222 :453 1:104 1:242 ⒻAlw 32000N1X	97 4 2 22½ 21½ 1½ 1½	Krone J A	112	3.65	79-19	BookOfFortune112½ Pleasntry1078½ ClerMndte11217	Stalked, drifted late	5

WORKOUTS: Sep 19 Bel 4f fst :49 B 14/46

Me And The Boys
Own: Smith Anne
LUZZI M J (71 7 7 6 .10) $50,000

Dk. b or br m. 5
Sire: Huckster (Mr. Prospector)
Dam: Silver's Xeda (Xeda)
Br: Larc's Wing Farm (Fla)
Tr: Lerman Michael (—)

L 116

Lifetime Record:	42 7 4 4	$129,675			
1995	12 1 1 3	$38,030	Turf	3 0 0 0	$1,125
1994	13 4 1 1	$58,820	Wet	3 0 0 1	$6,030
Aqu	2 1 1 0	$27,880	Dist	5 1 0 0	$12,375

Entered 10Dec95- 8 AQU

15Sep95-8Med fst 170	:233 :47 1:112 1:41 3↑ ⒻPrismatical40k	67 1 3 32 53 610 515	Wilson R	L 115 b	31.60	72-19	Footing1135½ Valiant Jewel113nk Why Be Normal1151½	Tired	6
2Sep95-8Mth fst 1 1/16	:234 :483 1:132 1:453 3↑ ⒻAlw 42000N$mY	75 6 5 3½ 1hd 34 36	Wilson R	L 115 b	5.60	71-18	Nasty Cure117hd Why BeNormal1175¾ MeAndTheBoys115no	Bid, weakened	7
19Aug95-5Mth fst 1	:234 :471 1:123 1:394 3↑ ⒻAlw 33000N4X	76 2 5 32 22 22 21	Wilson R	L 116 b	11.70	78-18	Z Rated1111 Me And The Boys1162½ Festive Star1166	Good try	7
30Jly95-9Mth fst 170	:23 :463 1:114 1:412 3↑ ⒻLadys Secret45k	79 2 5 54½ 53 45 69	Luzzi M J	L 113 b	23.80	86-09	Quaker Bonnet1132 Cavada1191½ Seeking The Circle119hd	Tired	8
16Jly95-8Mth fst 1 1/16	:231 :47 1:12 1:453 3↑ ⒻAlw 33000N$mY	74 6 4 43½ 32 53¾ 48¾	McCauley W H	L 117 b	12.40	68-18	Miss Gold Peace1157½ Why Be Normal1171½ Hooded Dancer115nk	Bid, tired	6
4Jly95-6Mth fst 1 1/16	:241 :482 1:124 1:451 3↑ ⒻAlw 30000N$Y	61 2 7 87½ 711 712 616	Black A S	L 117 b	6.10	63-21	Seeking The Circle115no Hooded Dancer1153½ Shouldnt Say Never117¾		7
Stumbled badly soon after start, appeared to clip heels									
13Jun95-9Mth fst 170	:231 :471 1:123 1:431 3↑ ⒻAlw 22000N3X	83 2 1 11½ 12 12 13½	McCauley W H	L 117 b	3.70	86-14	Me And The Boys1173½ Darned Alarming117¾ Nasty Cure1171½	Ridden out	6
3Jun95-6Mth fst 1	:234 :471 1:122 1:382 3↑ ⒻAlw 28000N1m	71 3 5 42½ 66 511 514¾	Turner T G	L 116 b	17.10	71-20	Stop Right Here11110 Why BeNormal1111½ Alphabulous1161¾	In tight early	7
9Mar95-10GP wf 1 1/16	:234 :471 1:122 1:441 ⒻAlw 36000N3X	76 3 4 46 42 35½ 39½	Bravo J	L 116 b	19.90	77-18	ExoticMoves1166¾ LicoriceTfft1163 MAndThBoys116½	Lacked response	7
20Feb95-8GP sly 1 1/16	:233 :48 1:132 1:461 ⒻAlw 30000N3X	59 3 3 31 43¾ 58¾ 612¾	Bravo J	L 116 b	11.80	64-20	High Mio Royal121no My Momma's Jolene1161½ Miss Aciss1164	Stopped	6

WORKOUTS: Nov 26 Bel tr.t 4f fst :501 B 48/65 Nov 21 Bel tr.t 4f fst :511 B 41/47 Nov 6 Pim 4f fst :493 B 7/11 Oct 10 Pim 4f fst :484 H 7/14

1 — Personal Girl — I have never seemed to be right on this erratic mare. You know the story: pick her and she runs poorly, ignore her and she wins. Although she was a closer, her best distance was six furlongs not seven, as reflected by her one-for-13 win record at seven. She needed a fast pace to set up her last run. Maybe.

2 — Sun Attack — Claimed for $35,000 when she was a dull fifth in her last start, and she was moving up while stretching out to a distance where she had just one third to show for five starts. In her lone dirt start at this claiming level, she'd been clobbered, but it was the first start off a layoff. Still didn't like her.

3 — Z Rated — I liked this mare, and I had a good reason. I'd picked her in the *Gazette* three starts back in her New York debut, when she gamely won a $40,000 claimer at 7-1, paying $17.20. She followed that race by running a pair of none-threatening fourths in allowance company at 6½ furlongs and a $60,000 claimer at six. Now she was dropping, but stretching out to seven furlongs. A quick glance at her PPs showed that eight of her last 10 races were at 6 furlongs, but note that she did show a wire-to-wire win in a non-winners of four allowance at one mile, and that her career record at seven furlongs was 4-2-0 in 12 starts. I picked her to win.

4 — Fawn's Angel — She had two seconds and a win in her last three starts, all routes, but the seconds were in $18,000 claimers, and the win in a non-winners of two. Since Z Rated had won a non-winners of four, she seemed overmatched. I passed.

5 — A Bimp In The Bye — This mare was a sharp and well-bet second in her return in a $40,000 claimer at 6½ furlongs. She was 5-2-1 in 12 '95 starts and was obviously going to have a shot here, except for one fact: in three starts at seven furlongs, she hadn't once finished in the money. I passed.

6 — Just A Little Kiss — This filly had lost her last four starts, but they were against tougher, and she was reasonably competitive in three of them with a third and two fourths. She showed three starts at seven furlongs in her PPs, two comfortable wins in $50,000 claimers, and a poor ninth in a stakes try. Her career record in eight starts at seven furlongs was four wins, a second and a third. I picked her second. (My third choice, Book Of Fortune, was scratched).

Z Rated and Just A Little Kiss would have been my first two choices for the Pick Six, and I likely would have added Personal Girl.

A Bimp In The Bye went off the favorite at 9-5 and finished a well-beaten fifth. Sent off at 7-2, Z Rated gamely held off 6-1 Personal Girl by a neck to return $9.20.

FOURTH RACE
Aqueduct
DECEMBER 2, 1995

7 FURLONGS. (1.20¹) CLAIMING. Purse $28,000 (plus up to $10,990 NYSBFOA). Fillies and mares, 3-year-olds and upward. Weights: 3-year-olds, 120 lbs. Older, 122 lbs. Non-winners of two races since October 22, allowed 2 lbs. A race since November 4, 4 lbs. A race since October 17, 6 lbs. Claiming price $50,000, if for $45,000, allowed 2 lbs. (Races where entered for $40,000 or less not considered.)

Value of Race: $29,400 Winner $16,800; second $7,000; third $3,080; fourth $1,680; fifth $840. Mutuel Pool $306,000.00 Exacta Pool $443,873.00 Quinella Pool $80,717.00

Last Raced	Horse	M/Eqt. A.Wt PP St	¼	½	Str Fin	Jockey	Cl'g Pr	Odds $1
22Nov95 6Aqu⁴	Z Rated	Lf 5 114 3 3	11½	11½	11½ 1ⁿᵏ	Velazquez J R	45000	3.60
5Nov95 6Aqu⁷	Personal Girl	Lb 5 116 1 4	2½	3ʰᵈ 2³	2⁵	Pezua J M	50000	6.10
22Nov95 6Aqu⁶	Just A Little Kiss	Lb 4 116 6 2	5⁵	4¹	3½ 3¾	Castillo H Jr	50000	3.90
25Oct95 7Bel¹	Fawn's Angel	L 4 116 4 6	6	6	5½ 4½	Leon F	45000	12.30
18Nov95 3Aqu²	A Bimp in the Bye	5 116 5 1	31½	5⁴	6 5½	Chavez J F	50000	1.80
18Nov95 3Aqu⁵	Sun Attack	Lb 4 114 2 5	4½	2½	41½ 6	Migliore R	45000	4.20

OFF AT 1:51 Start Good. Won driving. Time, :23¹, :47, 1:11³, 1:24¹ Track good.

$2 Mutuel Prices:

4–Z RATED	9.20	4.50	3.10
3–PERSONAL GIRL		6.60	3.90
7–JUST A LITTLE KISS			3.40

$2 EXACTA 4–3 PAID $48.60 $2 QUINELLA 3–4 PAID $27.60

B. m, by Sezyou–Vitriolic Lady, by Vitriolic. Trainer Rojas Osvaldo. Bred by Ersoff Stanley M (Fla).

Z RATED sprinted clear in the early stages, maintained a clear lead into midstretch, then turned back PERSONAL GIRL under brisk right hand urging. PERSONAL GIRL raced in close contention along the rail into upper stretch, angled out in upper stretch, then closed steadily but could not get up. JUST A LITTLE KISS raced within striking distnace while four wide to the top of the stretch and lacked a strong closing bid. FAWN'S ANGEL never reached contention. A BIMP IN THE BYE stalked early from outside, gave way on the turn. SUN ATTACK lodged a mild bid between horses to reach contention on the turn and flattened out thereafter.

Owners— 1, Camuti Thomas E & Sisko John F; 2, Marinos Jane E; 3, Worswick Ronald J; 4, Giorgi Vincent Jr & Saccone Joseph; 5, La Marca Stable; 6, My Paradise Farms

Trainers— 1, Rojas Osvaldo; 2, Moschera Gasper S; 3, Schosberg Richard; 4, Ortiz Paulino O; 5, Anderson William D; 6, Friedman Mitchell

Scratched— Lafitte's Lady (12Nov95 5AQU⁶), Book Of Fortune (15Nov95 6AQU¹), Me And The Boys (1Dec95 8AQU⁷)

$2 Pick-3 (1–2–4) Paid $32.40; Consolation Pick-3 (1–7–4) Paid $17.00; Pick-3 Pool $135,439.

This takes us to the fifth and sixth, two races I missed in the *Gazette*. Here they are:

The scratches of Vega's Secret and Leap With Joy left a field of nine three-year-old claimers ($40,000 to $50,000) in the seven-furlong fifth:

5 Aqueduct

7 Furlongs (1:201) **CLAIMING. Purse $28,000 (plus up to $10,990 NYSBFOA). 3-year-olds. Weight, 122 lbs. Non-winners of two races since November 1, allowed 2 lbs. Of a race since then, 4 lbs. Of a race since October 20, 6 lbs. Claiming price $50,000; for each $5,000 to $40,000, allowed 2 lbs. (Races where entered for $35,000 or less not considered.)**

Coupled - Vega's Secret and Leap With Joy

Traveling Jeff

Own: Ramsey Kenneth L & Sarah K
CASTILLO H JR (55 4 2 4 .07) $45,000
Ch. c. 3 (Feb)
Sire: Rajab (Jaipur)
Dam: Cute Cheryl (Trojan Bronze)
Br: Karutz Wallace S (Fla)
Tr: Plesa Edward Jr (3 1 0 1 .33)
L 114

Lifetime Record: 18 3 4 6 $57,465											
1995	14	3	2	5	$49,215	Turf	4	1	0	0	$14,605
1994	4	M	2	1	$8,250	Wet	1	0	0	1	$2,860
Aqu	1	0	0	1	$2,860	Dist	2	0	1	1	$4,960

2Nov95-5Aqu sly 6f :213 :45 :573 1:103	Clm 45000	87 11 6 43½ 32 11 31½	Castillo H Jr	L 112 f	18.00	88-14	Dontstopthjkbx109hd Wnwthwlkr1131¼ TrvlngJff1122	Yielded grudgingly 11
8Oct95-9Bel fst 6f :223 :46 :58 1:11	Clm 40000	86 3 3 31 1hd 21 33	Bailey J D	L 116	*1.95	83-17	SunnyRican1143 JudgeMeNot114hd TravelingJeff1165	Dueled, weakened 8
14Sep95-9Bel fm 1⅟16 ⓣ :233 :473 1:123 1:441	Clm 60000	73 7 3 1½ 1hd 21 55	Bailey J D	L 116	4.70	72-23	Palm Freezer118no The B Twelve Kid1143 King Konyo112no	Dueled, tired 10
27Aug95-10Crc gd 5f :214 :46 :59	3+ Alw 16000N3X	95 5 3 45 34 21½ 3½	Castillo H Jr	L 115	*1.40	93-12	PlyBothEnds115nk AspenFortun117nk TrvlingJff1152¼	Rallied, just missed 7
28Jly95-9Crc gd 5f ⊗ :22 :46 :59	3+ Alw 17700N2X	90 1 4 2hd 2hd 11½ 17¾	Castillo H Jr	L 114	3.50	94-16	Traveling Jeff1147¾ Sunshine Man119no Parella Fella119½	Driving 7
26Jly95-9Crc fst 7f :222 :454 1:112 1:242	3+ Alw 17700N2X	85 6 3 2hd 2hd 21 34¾	Castillo H Jr	L 114	9.40	85-15	No Lollygagging1173¾ Derivative122½ Traveling Jeff114nk	Weakened 7
15Jun95-5Crc gd *1⅟16 ⓣ 1:431	Clm 40000	70 5 2 21½ 21½ 23½ 49¾	Castillo H Jr	L 119	2.60	79-15	Tune M Up1225¼ Fiery Temper1172½ Sparkling Arctic1221½	Weakened 7
2Jun95-9Crc fm *7½f ⓣ 1:311	3+ Alw 17700N2X	83 7 6 1hd 1hd 1hd 52	Castillo H Jr	L 115	2.30	88-10	Shan's Ready122¾ Sir Carter122½ Flying Proof119hd	Faded 8
13May95-6Hia fm 1⅟16 ⓣ 1:433	Alw 19550N1X	81 1 1 1½ 11 11½ 13¾	Castillo H Jr	L 113	3.70	80-19	Traveling Jeff1133¾ Unreal Turn121¾ Roseman Bridge1142¾	Driving 10
28Apr95-9Hia fst 6f :22 :442 :57 1:101	Alw 15000N1X	83 4 5 32 1hd 1hd 32¾	Castillo H Jr	L 113	4.50	87-09	Constant Escort1181½ Staying Fit121½ Traveling Jeff1135	Weakened 11

WORKOUTS: ●Nov 27 Bel tr.t 5f fst 1:00 H 1/24 ●Oct 27 Bel tr.t 5f fst 1:001 H 1/20 Oct 18 Bel 5f fst 1:01 H 3/29 ●Oct 4 Bel 5f fst 1:001 H 1/34 Sep 28 Bel tr.t 5f fst 1:031 B 11/17 Sep 12 Bel 3f fst :364 B 3/15

Whirling Blade

Own: R Kay Stable
ALVARADO F T (94 8 12 12 .09) $50,000
Dk. b or br g. 3 (May)
Sire: Island Whirl (Pago Pago)
Dam: Bids and Blades (Blade)
Br: Gallagher Mrs James H (Fla)
Tr: Araya Rene A (5 0 1 2 .00)
116

Lifetime Record: 17 6 3 1 $87,750											
1995	11	5	2	0	$81,430	Turf	0	0	0	0	
1994	6	1	1	1	$6,320	Wet	3	1	1	0	$4,705
Aqu	5	3	0	0	$46,380	Dist	0	0	0	0	

16Nov95-6Aqu fst 6f :224 :462 :583 1:104	3+ Alw 46800N4X	81 4 3 44½ 43 52¾ 56	Flores F R7	105 b	10.20	82-15	Terrorist1192 Jericho Blaise114½ Rum'n Cope1192	No late bid 5
18Jun95-7Bel fst 6½f :223 :47 1:10 1:162	3+ Alw 34000N2X	58 4 2 47½ 45 47 618¾	Migliore R	114 b	5.00	74-20	Perfect Spiral110½ Scherbo1194¾ Ross Creek1115	Tired 6
20May95-3Bel gd 6½f :223 :453 1:102 1:17	3+ Alw 34000N2X	95 5 2 3½ 3nk 1hd 2½	Migliore R	114 b	4.10	89-10	Lake Ali116½ Whirling Blade1141½ Western Winter1142	Dueled, game 5
13May95-4Bel fst 6f :221 :453 :574 1:104	Clm c-55000	88 4 2 42½ 3½ 1½ 1¾	Migliore R	114 b	2.35	87-10	WhirlingBlde114¾ DiceFlo113nk SmrtLittlBoy1163¾	Four wide, drew clear 6
Claimed from My Paradise Farms, Friedman Mitchell Trainer								
28Apr95-3Aqu fst 1 :24 :471 1:12 1:372	Clm 60000	67 2 2 2½ 1hd 41½ 59½	Migliore R	117 b	3.30	72-18	Is It Possible1121½ Back Ring Al1124 Gold Toes1142	Dueled inside 6
13Apr95-6Aqu fst 6f :221 :452 :572 1:101	Alw 30000N1X	85 1 2 1½ 1hd 1½ 1½	Migliore R	119 b	*.70	91-10	Whirling Blade119½ Erica's Rocket117½ Fey Tru114no	Dueled, game 6
2Apr95-4Aqu fst 6f :232 :46 :58 1:104	Clm 45000	89 4 6 32½ 1hd 14 16½	Migliore R	120 b	*.90	88-13	WhirlingBlde1206½ Myfriendwtts1121 GoldToes115¾	Bobbled break, wide 6
19Mar95-2Aqu fst 6f :221 :454 :583 1:114	Clm c-35000	79 5 4 21 1½ 1hd 11½	Chavez J F	117 b	*1.70	83-19	WhirlingBld1171½ HnbnsJourny1199 GlttrngWolf117½	Gamely, drew clear 7
Claimed from Gallagher James H, Gullo Gary P Trainer								
16Feb95-4GP fst 6f :22 :443 :572 1:094	Clm 20000	77 3 4 21 21 22½ 26½	Fires E	117 b	9.00	85-15	Tar Buggy1176½ Whirling Blade1172¾ Pick A Dance1177¾	Best of others 9
16Jan95-4GP fst 6f :223 :454 :59 1:122	Clm 12500	75 3 6 2½ 1½ 13½ 14¾	Fires E	119 b	12.80	79-23	Whirling Blade1194¾ C. V. Tex117¾ Bet The Bookmaker113hd	Driving 8

WORKOUTS: Nov 25 Bel tr.t 4f fst :48 H 3/52 Nov 11 Bel tr.t 5f fst 1:043 B 15/26 Nov 4 Bel tr.t 3f my :364 B 2/8 Oct 27 Bel tr.t 3f fst :364 H 5/18

Spanish Charge

Own: Paraneck Stable
RYDOWSKI S R (44 2 2 2 .05) $40,000
B. g. 3 (Mar)
Sire: War (Majestic Light)
Dam: Lady Romanee (Nercliffe)
Br: Crowell Howard G (Fla)
Tr: Aquilino Joseph (25 1 4 0 .04)
L 112

Lifetime Record: 14 3 2 2 $39,540											
1995	10	2	1	2	$28,775	Turf	3	0	1	0	$6,000
1994	4	1	1	0	$10,765	Wet	1	0	0	1	$3,960
Aqu	1	0	0	0	$495	Dist	1	0	0	0	

10Nov95-5Med fst 1 :231 :461 1:111 1:38	Clm 20000	69 7 6 52¾ 2hd 1hd 1½	Rydowski S R	L 115 b	6.30	86-14	Spanish Charge115½ Peace Time115nk Call Me J. R.1141½	Driving 11
1Nov95-5Aqu fst 6f :222 :453 :574 1:11	Clm 20000	75 3 4 54½ 55 54 53½	Rydowski S R	L 116 b	4.00	83-16	Gold Toes1202 Easterwood116hd Fiddler107½	Evenly 8
19Oct95-7Bel fst 6½f :23 :454 1:102 1:17	Clm 25000	76 4 4 52 31½ 33½ 33	Rydowski S R	L 112 b	16.50	87-14	Call Home115½ Red Tom1152½ Spanish Charge1125	Willingly 7
8Sep95-9Bel fst 1 :221 :451 1:101 1:361	Clm 37500	27 9 4 63¾ 96¾ 1122 1133¼	Rydowski S R	L 114 b	23.80	49-17	Country Thunder118nk Lemming1162¾ Leap With Joy113½	Wide, tired 12
28Aug95-3Sar fm 1⅟16 ⓣ :471 1:124 1:381 1:561	Clm 50000	61 2 1 14 13½ 53½ 63½	Perez R B	112 b	6.80	75-08	ⒹShotgun John112no Babylonian1122 Hard Charger1153	Used up 6
16Aug95-3Sar fst 7f :223 :46 1:11 1:24	Clm 50000	52 4 4 33½ 65 77½ 714¾	Davis R G	118 b	9.30	71-14	Kentucky Govenor1151 Dancing Gator1182½ Hail Orphan1151	Done early 7
27Jly95-7Sar fm 1⅟16 ⓣ :224 :454 1:093 1:401	Alw 36000N2X	42 3 3 32½ 78½ 915 826	Rydowski S R	112 b	54.00	72-08	Dowty1121 No Secrets1144 Val's Prince1151¼	Gave way 9
1Jly95-5Bel sly 1⅟16 ⊗ :224 :452 1:10 1:414	3+ Alw 36000N3L	77 1 3 21½ 22 28 320	Rydowski S R	111 b	12.00	70-18	Kerfoot Corner12016 Crary1133½ Spanish Charge11114	Chased, tired 7
15Jun95-5Bel gd 1 ⓣ :222 :451 1:101 1:36	Clm 50000	81 4 4 21½ 2hd 1hd 22	Rydowski S R	116 b	12.40	81-20	Timmons1162 Spanish Charge116½ Glittering Wolf1161½	Sharp try 11
3Jun95-8Pha fst 6f :214 :45 :572 1:102	Alw 15218N2L	78 5 7 32½ 32 21 1nk	McCarthy M J	116 fb	9.50	89-13	SpanishCharge116nk ValidOmen1221½ Lyrlyrpantsonfire1162	Wide, just up 10

WORKOUTS: ●Nov 25 Aqu 4f fst :473 H 1/5 Oct 10 Aqu 4f fst :49 B 6/12

Cardsharp

Own: Doyle Richard B
MAPLE E (51 5 8 8 .10) $45,000
Dk. b or br g. 3 (Apr)
Sire: Stacked Pack (Majestic Light)
Dam: Tres Vrai (Believe It)
Br: Papert Frederic (NY)
Tr: Miceli Michael (7 1 0 0 .14)
L 116

Lifetime Record: 11 2 4 1 $48,686											
1995	11	2	4	1	$48,686	Turf	0	0	0	0	
1994	0	M	0	0		Wet	0	0	0	0	
Aqu	0	0	0	0		Dist	1	0	0	1	$2,541

11Nov95-6Lrl fst 1⅛ :473 1:121 1:374 1:504	3+ Alw 20500N2X	70 6 2 21 23 610 612½	Pino M G	L 119 b	9.40	72-25	Charlie Huff1175 Colonial Secretary1143 Lucky Trend114¾	Gave way 10
27Oct95-8Lrl fst 1⅟16 :242 :483 1:132 1:45	3+ Alw 19000N1X	72 5 2 21½ 21 21½ 11	Pino M G	L 118 b	*2.50	85-16	Cardsharp1181 Royal Silver114no Gala Show Biz114no	Driving 10
13Oct95-7Lrl fst 1⅟16 :241 :482 1:133 1:46	3+ Md Sp Wt	75 8 5 53 31 1hd 14	Pino M G	L 118 b	*1.70	80-19	Cardsharp1184 Easy Does It1193 Jarrettsville1222	Driving 8
19Aug95-11Pim fst 1⅟16 :231 :464 1:121 1:46	3+ Md Sp Wt	52 4 7 63 55 53 410	Pino M G	L 115	2.40	68-15	Electric Leix1154 Haveplanwilltravel115½ Broadstone1155½	Weakened 8
4Aug95-5Pim fst 1⅟16 :241 :48 1:121 1:45	3+ Md Sp Wt	73 7 2 2hd 2hd 1hd 2hd	Pino M G	L 115	2.90	83-12	Johnny Prospector115hd Cardsharp1155 Broadstone1101	Gamely 8
23Jly95-3Lrl fst 1⅟16 :24 :48 1:124 1:452	3+ Md Sp Wt	60 6 4 52¾ 53½ 45½ 43½	Pino M G	L 114	3.30	80-18	Armed Threat113hd Electric Leix114¾ Broadstone1082½	No threat 9
29Jun95-3Lrl fst 1⅟16 :232 :472 1:123 1:461	3+ Md Sp Wt	68 1 3 34 33 32 2¾	Pino M G	L 114	*1.40	78-19	Nawab113¾ Cardsharp114½ Armed Threat112nk	Rallied 9
15Jun95-7Lrl fst 7f :23 :462 1:112 1:242	3+ Md Sp Wt	60 11 2 21½ 22½ 25 37¾	Pino M G	L 114	3.10	79-20	Band Performance1145 Turn Say1142¾ Cardsharp114nk	Gave way 14
19May95-7Pim gd 1⅛ :464 1:113 1:383 1:52	3+ Md Sp Wt	65 1 3 32 32½ 45½ 49½	Pino M G	114	*1.80	69-14	Wave It115nk Danny's Crown1128½ Accusation114½	Gave way 9
7May95-5Pim fst 1⅟16 :241 :482 1:132 1:454	3+ Md Sp Wt	72 8 2 2½ 22 11½ 2¾	Pino M G	114	5.60	78-22	Best Party114¾ Cardsharp1142 War Hostage111nk	Tired 10

WORKOUTS: Nov 9 Lrl 4f fst :491 B 4/11 Nov 4 Lrl 4f fst :50 Bg 16/25 Sep 15 Lrl 4f fst :50 B 9/9 Sep 7 Lrl 5f fst 1:02 B 3/9

Vega's Secret

Own: My Paradise Farms
MIGLIORE R (94 7 12 17 .07) $50,000
Ch. c. 3 (Apr)
Sire: Clever Secret (Secretariat)
Dam: Extrusion (Lord Gaylord)
Br: Reynolds David P (Md)
Tr: Friedman Mitchell (27 3 3 6 .11)
L 116

Lifetime Record: 11 1 3 3 $39,960											
1995	9	0	3	3	$29,400	Turf	1	0	0	1	$3,080
1994	2	1	0	0	$10,560	Wet	1	0	0	0	$960
Aqu	5	0	1	2	$14,150	Dist	0	0	0	0	

18Nov95-9Aqu fst 1 :222 :444 1:094 1:354	Clm 40000	81 8 5 69¾ 46½ 34 34½	Migliore R	115	*3.30e	85-12	Country Thunder1172½ Babylonian1122 Vega's Secret115½	No late bid 11
1Nov95-6Aqu fst 1⅛ :472 1:123 1:373 1:501	3+ Alw 32000N1X	75 0 7 75½ 73½ 65 56	Alvarado F T	114	2.35e	83-12	Hawaii Star108½ Kadrmas112hd Point Man1121½	No threat 8
8Oct95-9Bel fst 6f :223 :46 :58 1:11	Clm 40000	72 5 6 74½ 79 510 59	Martinez J R Jr	110	4.00e	77-17	Sunny Rican1143 Judge Me Not114hd Traveling Jeff1165	No threat 8
21Apr95-9Aqu fm 1⅟16 ⓣ :231 :473 1:123 1:45	Clm 50000	59 6 6 57½ 45 46½ 310½	Migliore R	116	*1.60	73-18	Boyonette1053½ Chosen Reward1147 Vega's Secret116nk	No late bid 9
23Mar95-7Aqu fst 1 :231 :464 1:124 1:391	Alw 32000N1X	84 1 7 42½ 52½ 1½ 2no	Migliore R	113	1.75e	73-34	DancingGtor119no Veg'sSecret1134 TheGenerlsAngel122¾	Rail trip, game 8
16Mar95-4Aqu fst 1 :232 :47 1:12 1:38	Clm 51000	69 5 5 53½ 32 32 32¾	Migliore R	115 b	*1.90	76-24	Cn'tBelieveit1122 BckRingAl109¾ Veg'sSecret1155¼	Four wide, flattened 6
23Feb95-7Aqu fst 1⅟16 ⊡ :232 :48 1:13 1:45	Alw 32000N1X	89 3 6 55½ 43 39½ 213	Migliore R	117	2.80	67-25	HuskyHarry11713 Vega'sSecret117hd ScreenOscr1192½	Stead sharply 7/8 pl 7
3Feb95-6Aqu fst 6f ⊡ :223 :464 :594 1:133	Clm c-50000	56 7 10 118¾ 79 78 56¾	Migliore R	117	5.70	68-25	CrolinBlues1181¾ GetMyGlittr110no ThGnrlsAngl1203	Pinched break, wide 11
Claimed from Reynolds David P, Kelly Timothy D Trainer								
5Jan95-3Aqu fst 6f ⊡ :23 :464 :593 1:123	Clm 50000	68 1 4 54½ 53½ 31½ 21½	Migliore R	117	5.60	78-20	TheGeneralsAngel1171½ Veg'sSecret1171½ GetMyGlitter117nk	Second best 6
14Dec94-5Aqu fst 6f ⊡ :234 :48 1:003 1:132	Md 50000	62 6 5 62¾ 32 22½ 11½	Maple E	118	*3.35	76-21	Vega's Secret1181½ Fiddler1183 Ulterior1181	Driving 9

WORKOUTS: Oct 23 Bel tr.t 4f fst :484 B 8/20 Sep 29 Bel tr.t 5f fst 1:033 B 4/10 Sep 20 Bel 5f fst 1:043 B 55/57 Sep 8 Bel tr.t 4f fst :523 B 17/17

Sir Lovely

Own: Zuckerman Donald & Roberta M
PEZUA J M (50 8 5 11 .16) $50,000

Gr. g. 3 (Mar)
Sire: Carnivalay (Northern Dancer)
Dam: Lovely Child (Temperence Hill)
Br: Zuckerman Donald & Roberta T/E (Fla)
Tr: Moschera Gasper S (47 8 8 6 .17)

L 116

Lifetime Record:	10 3 2 1	$41,178			
1995	6 2 0 1	$32,043	Turf	0 0 0 0	
1994	4 1 2 0	$9,135	Wet	2 1 0 0	$9,000
Aqu	1 1 0 0	$12,600	Dist	1 0 0 0	

15Nov95-7Aqu gd 1	:222 :454 1:112 1:37	Clm 30000	86 10 4 42½ 1hd 11½ 12	Davis R G	L 114 b	4.70	84-28	Sir Lovely1142 Dancing Gator1185 Hail Orphan1161½	Four wide, clear 11
22Oct95-7Bel gd 1	:232 :47 1:113 1:363	Clm 50000	75 2 7 77 75½ 66½ 66	Davis R G	115 b	20.80	74-22	Paulo113¾ Blizzard1152 Flint And Steel1131½	No factor 7
7Oct95-1Bel wf 7f	:223 :453 1:102 1:234 3↑	Alw 34000N2X	68 8 5 94½ 97½ 611 611	Migliore R	113 b	56.25	71-24	Mountain Of Laws117½ Saratoga Shark1184½ Crary116¾	No threat 9
3Mar95-9GS fst 1	:233 :472 1:13 1:394	ChrHillMile-G3	72 3 5 67½ 66 58 55½	Lloyd J S	115 b	15.30	72-23	Sham Francisco115no Onto Luck1171 Country Squire115½	No factor 6
11Feb95-8Aqu fst 1 1/16 ⊡	:231 :474 1:144 1:492	Whirlaway BC81k	68 3 4 49½ 33 34½ 312½	Lloyd J S	115 b	22.70	45-38	Devil's Brew117½ Ave's Flag11912 Sir Lovely1153½	Saved ground 9
9Jan95-5Pha wf 170	:221 :462 1:113 1:421	Alw 16050N1X	76 7 3 32½ 12½ 2hd 1nk	Lloyd J S	116 b	*1.10	89-11	Sir Lovely116nk Arcentales1229 Defy The Devil116hd	Game win 7
23Dec94-8Pha fst 1	:231 :481 1:144 1:413	Alw 15000N1X	59 8 5 53½ 41 2hd 22½	Lloyd J S	116 b	2.20	67-25	Michael's Star1162½ Sir Lovely1163 Tray Try1163	Steadied, second best 8
14Nov94-6Pha fst 1	:232 :464 1:122 1:402	Alw 16500N1X	60 8 7 710 68 34 22½	Lloyd J S	115 b	17.90	73-31	ShamFrancisco1212½ SirLovely1151 RomanRaling1216½	Poor start, rallied 8
25Oct94-1Pha fst 6f	:233 :473 :594 1:123	Md 8000	57 7 2 1hd 11½ 13½ 18	Bisono J	120 b	3.00	78-22	Sir Lovely1208 Boogalu Billy1209½ Abe's Quadrant120nk	Ridden out 9
17Oct94-1Pha fst 6f	:23 :471 1:001 1:134	Md 10000	-0 4 6 2hd 1hd 45½ 513½	Bisono J	120 b	5.10	59-20	Poppies Shadow1182½ Lucky Chucky118½ Boogalu Billy1204½	8

Came in, bumped rival start, rushed, stopped

WORKOUTS: Nov 11 Bel 5f fst 1:02 H 19/56 Nov 1 Bel 4f fst :494 B 24/42 Sep 25 Aqu 5f fst 1:002 H 3/10 Sep 19 Aqu 5f fst 1:014 H 4/5 Sep 12 Aqu 5f fst 1:014 H 3/5 Sep 6 Bel 5f fst 1:034 B 41/43

Get My Glitter

Own: Filose Louis
CHAVEZ J F (124 22 21 11 .18) $40,000

B. g. 3 (Mar)
Sire: Glitterman (Dewan)
Dam: Exuberant Jane (Exuberant)
Br: Powell Arlene M (Fla)
Tr: Anderson William D (6 1 1 0 .17)

L 112

Lifetime Record:	33 4 9 2	$88,305			
1995	21 2 6 1	$59,250	Turf	6 0 2 0	$11,850
1994	12 2 3 1	$29,055	Wet	1 0 1 0	$5,200
Aqu	2 1 0 0	$15,240	Dist	0 0 0 0	

18Nov95-9Aqu fst 1	:222 :444 1:094 1:354	Clm 40000	80 10 1 12 11½ 2½ 45	Smith M E	L 115 b	4.40	85-12	Country Thunder1172½ Babylonian1122 Vega's Secret115½	Speed, tired 11
24Oct95-8Med fst 6f	:213 :44 :56 1:091 3↑	Alw 23000N3X	79 4 1 1hd 2hd 2hd 43½	Wilson R	L 115 b	5.30	89-14	Old Time Power1133 For All The Bills116½ Fleet Brass113no	Tired 6
12Oct95-9Med fst 6f	:22 :444 :564 1:091 3↑	Alw 23000N3X	69 1 6 2hd 22½ 37½ 414½	Bravo J	L 113 b	6.10	79-16	Heroic Pursuit11612 Unreal Turn114¾ For All The Bills1161	Tired 7
19Sep95-9Med fm 5f ⓣ	:221 :46 :583 3↑	Alw 26000N3X	86 1 3 22 2½ 1hd 2no	Bravo J	L 112 b	3.20	88-12	Wiloso111no Get My Glitter1122¾ Chris' TakeOff1161	Caught, final strides 9
4Sep95-5Med fm 5f ⓣ	:214 :46 :574	MercerRacabt40k	81 2 5 31 31½ 22 42	Bravo J	L 113 b	5.30	90-08	MneIngredient117½ CountDeMonnie1151½ RobinsGon114hd	Needed more 9
23Aug95-3Mth fst 6f	:223 :453 :574 1:102	Clm 35000	90 5 3 11 11½ 12 21¾	Bravo J	L 116 b	*1.00	85-21	Note Bandit1161¾ Get My Glitter1167½ Red Sovereign112nk	Second best 6
29Jly95-5Mth gd 1 ⓣ	:231 :47 1:113 1:372	Clm 40000	78 3 1 11 12 13 21½	Bravo J	L 115 b	3.10	81-15	Pot Of Brushes1151½ Get My Glitter1154 Note Bandit115¾	Good try 9
16Jly95-11Mth fst 6f	:213 :444 :573 1:111	Clm c-25000	80 2 6 15 15 14½ 21½	Black A S	L 116 fb	*1.30	82-15	Dontstopthejukebox1121½ Get My Glitter1164¾ Unfappable1143	2nd best 8

Claimed from Timber Creek Farm, Reese Cynthia G Trainer

2Jly95-8Mth fst 6f	:214 :452 :583 1:121 3↑	Alw 22000N3X	77 7 2 3½ 32 32½ 42¾	Black A S	L 114 b	7.20	75-18	Mr Miner116no Gallant Warfare1162½ Gulpha Gorge116½	Weakened 7
11Jun95-7Mth fm 5f ⓣ	:211 :433 :551 3↑	Alw 22000N3X	70 5 10 85½ 64½ 79 88½	Black A S	L 114	10.40	90-02	I'm Escapin1164½ Paragallo's Hope109nk Wiloso1162¾	10

Bit sluggish start, tired drive

WORKOUTS: ●Nov 16 Med 4f fst :48 H 1/8

Save The Whale

Own: Pont Street Stable
VELAZQUEZ J R (60 8 14 7 .13) $50,000

B. g. 3 (Apr)
Sire: Skip Trial (Balljumper)
Dam: Whale River (Northern Fling)
Br: Sunrise Stable South Inc (Fla)
Tr: Carroll Del W II (12 2 1 1 .17)

L 116

Lifetime Record:	19 4 2 3	$79,745			
1995	14 3 2 3	$72,545	Turf	5 0 0 0	$2,300
1994	5 1 0 0	$7,200	Wet	3 0 0 2	$7,700
Aqu	5 1 1 2	$20,860	Dist	1 0 0 0	$115

12Nov95-7Aqu wf 1⅛	:482 1:132 1:393 1:523 3↑	Alw 34000N2X	88 8 3 45 44 24 34	Smith M E	L 112	3.15	73-29	SliceOfRelity112hd JoRnExpress1154 SveTheWhle1121½	Even finish, wide 9
13Oct95-9Bel fst 1 1/16	:233 :464 1:112 1:431	Clm 40000	87 3 3 33 32 2hd 1¾	Smith M E	L 115	*1.05	83-17	Save The Whale115¾ Firm Decree1152 RobbyTwo113no	Split horses, clear 8
30Jly95-8Sar fst 1⅛	:47 1:112 1:373 1:51	Jim Dandy-G2	65 6 5 69 711 715 625	Smith M E	113	34.00	56-19	Composer1125 Malthus112¾ Pat N Jac1125	No threat 7
24Jly95-3Sar wf 1⅛	:49 1:123 1:37 1:492 3↑	Alw 36000N2X	90 1 1 1½ 11 2hd 33	Smith M E	113	3.05	86-13	HopkinsForest1063 Wayfarer113no SaveTheWhale1136½	Speed, weakened 5
8Jly95-4Bel fst 1⅛	:452 1:111 1:363 1:50 3↑	Alw 34000N1X	89 1 3 37½ 1½ 11 12	Smith M E	113	2.20	82-21	SveTheWhle1132 JoRnExprss1202½ CrssonSprings113nk	Well placed, clear 7
24Jun95-3Bel fst 1 1/16	:23 :461 1:11 1:44 3↑	Alw 34000N1X	84 6 3 43 1hd 2hd 21	Smith M E	113	5.40	78-24	Tymtodyn1131 Save The Whale113nk Slip111nk	Bumped 1/2, game 7
18Jun95-11Bel fm 1 ⓣ	:221 :451 1:102 1:34 3↑	Alw 34000N1X	71 1 5 53½ 72¾ 95½ 98½	Nelson D	112	19.60	85-10	Last Effort112hd Basin Lane114¾ Fleet Stalker120hd	Faded 12
20May95-9Bel gd 1 ⓣ	:222 :453 1:102 1:363 3↑	Alw 34000N1X	82 11 6 41¾ 53¾ 52½ 52	Nelson D	112	25.25	78-18	MrqueeStr110½ ⒹKeflonins112nk GoneDncingAgin120nk	Lacked response 11

Placed 4th through disqualification.

19Apr95-5Aqu fst 1⅛	:48 1:124 1:392 1:524 3↑	Alw 32000N1X	79 4 3 35 21½ 21½ 24	Velazquez J R	110	16.70	72-20	ScreenOscr1124 SveTheWhle1102 DeceptivStrok112nk	Bumped first turn 8
1Apr95-3Aqu fst 1⅛	:483 1:14 1:392 1:52	Alw 32000N1X	75 4 2 21 1½ 32 36½	Velazquez J R	112	23.00	74-17	HuntingHrd112nk ScrnOscr1126 SvThWhl112nk	Bumped break, weakened 6

WORKOUTS: Oct 25 Bel tr.t 3f fst :372 B 7/19 Sep 25 Bel tr.t 4f fst :502 B 15/26 Sep 13 Bel tr.t 5f fst 1:042 B 9/9 Sep 8 Bel 4f fst :494 B 24/36

Leap With Joy

Own: My Paradise Farms
BECKNER D V (29 8 2 2 .00) $45,000

B. g. 3 (Mar)
Sire: Premiership (Exclusive Native)
Dam: Bouncing Joy (Giboulee)
Br: Ocala Stud Farm (Fla)
Tr: Friedman Mitchell (27 3 3 6 .11)

L 114

Lifetime Record:	28 5 1 6	$75,335			
1995	16 3 1 2	$44,475	Turf	2 0 0 0	$250
1994	12 2 0 4	$30,860	Wet	6 1 1 0	$16,530
Aqu	2 0 0 0		Dist	3 0 0 1	$2,820

15Nov95-7Aqu gd 1	:222 :454 1:112 1:37	Clm 35000	50 11 3 31 4¾ 56 715	Migliore R	L 118 b	*2.30	69-28	Sir Lovely1142 Dancing Gator1185 Hail Orphan1161½	Chased, tired 11
1Nov95-6Aqu fst 1⅛	:472 1:123 1:373 1:501 3↑	Alw 32000N1X	68 4 4 31 3½ 78 710½	Velazquez J R	L 112 b	2.55e	79-12	Hawaii Star108½ Kadrmas112hd Point Man1121½	Chased, tired 8
22Oct95-3Bel my 1	:23 :46 1:103 1:361	Clm 45000	84 5 1 11 1½ 21½ 23	Santos J A	L 117 b	7.90	79-29	Slice Of Reality1153 Leap With Joy117nk Lemming1193	Speed, weakened 5
7Oct95-11Bel wf 1	:234 :47 1:113 1:363 3↑	Alw 34000N1X	66 5 2 31 52 97½ 914	Santos J A	L 113 b	20.90	66-14	Coup D' Argent1123½ Navillus1151½ Edgecombe Flyer112hd	Chased, tired 12
20Sep95-9Bel fst 1	:222 :452 1:102 1:371	Clm 45000	78 1 3 31½ 32 2½ 1¾	Smith M E	L 116 b	3.00	77-21	Leap With Joy116¾ Noble 'n Heart1162½ Dont TellDee118nk	Fully extended 9
8Sep95-9Bel fst 1	:221 :451 1:101 1:361	Clm c-35000	83 7 1 11½ 1hd 2hd 33	Smith M E	L 113 b	5.40	79-17	Country Thunder118nk Lemming1162¾ Leap With Joy113½	Weakened 12

Claimed from Lewis James Jr, Tortora Emanuel Trainer

26Aug95-8Crc gd 1 1/16	:232 :474 1:132 1:48	Clm 25000	82 1 2 21½ 1hd 16 15	Soodeen R5	L 112 b	2.50	79-14	Leap With Joy1125 Expeditious1172 Zabeel1172½	Driving 8
10Aug95-5Crc yl *1 1/16 ⓣ	1:45	Clm 32000	75 6 4 51½ 31 42½ 64½	Soodeen R5	L 114 b	58.70	74-28	The Old Khazor1151¾ Forest Thunder117½ Seattle's Spirit115¾	Faded 10
17Jly95-5Crc fm *1 1/16 ⓣ	1:421	Clm 32000	45 9 3 31 54 610 716½	Soodeen R5	L 114 b	10.40	77-11	General Gus1152¾ Seattle's Spirit115hd The Old Khazor1172¾	Faded 9
26Jun95-4Crc fst 1 1/16	:231 :463 1:114 1:454	Clm 40000	68 1 4 54½ 55½ 45½ 510	Soodeen R5	L 112 b	3.90e	80-15	Tune M Up122hd Fiery Temper1176½ Rough Runner1171½	Failed to menace 7

Jump The Shadow

Own: Dogwood Stable
PEREZ R B (55 6 7 4 .11) $50,000

Dk. b or br g. 3 (May)
Sire: Dayjur (Danzig)
Dam: Angel Island (Cougar II (Chi))
Br: Appleton Arthur I (Fla)
Tr: Alexander Frank A (18 0 0 5 .00)

L 116

Lifetime Record:	12 2 3 0	$75,118			
1995	10 1 2 0	$36,930	Turf	1 0 0 0	
1994	2 1 1 0	$38,188	Wet	0 0 0 0	
Aqu	1 0 0 0	$960	Dist	3 0 0 0	$2,170

17Nov95-8Aqu fst 6f	:223 :462 :582 1:10 3↑	Alw 32000N2X	75 7 7 95¾ 42 56½ 514¾	Perez R B	L 113	27.00	78-21	Finchville1124½ Proudest Romeo1146 Investor1131½	Steadied early 9
25Oct95-3Bel fst 6f	:223 :451 :57 1:084 3↑	Alw 34000N2X	69 2 6 43½ 33 58 615	Perez R B	L 113	19.80	82-13	OurExuberantLd112½ FrioRiver1144 Finchville1154	Saved ground, tired 7
24Aug95-8Sar fst 7f	:224 :454 1:101 1:223	Alw 34000N2X	47 5 2 31 3nk 49 529½	Bailey J D	115 b	4.10	63-18	Ghostly Moves1147 Porphyry1157 Dodge City1185½	Gave way 5
27Jly95-7Sar fm 1 1/16 ⓣ	:224 :454 1:093 1:401	Alw 36000N2X	40 1 4 42½ 56 814 927	Luzzi M J	112 b	5.80	71-08	Dowty1121 No Secrets1144 Val's Prince1151½	Checked 7/8 pl 9
3Jun95-6Bel fst 6f	:221 :453 :58 1:104 3↑	Alw 34000N2X	89 2 5 55 32 22 24	Luzzi M J	112 b	5.00	83-14	DeputyBodmn1104 JumpThShdow1123 WstrnWintr1146¾	Pinched break 6
21May95-7Bel fst 6f	:222 :461 :583 1:114 3↑	Alw 32000N1X	86 12 8 41¾ 3½ 1½ 11½	Bailey J D	112 b	*1.20	82-22	JumpTheShdow1121½ FriscoGold1211½ JoRnExpress114¾	Four wide, clear 12
7May95-4Bel fst 6f	:222 :452 :571 1:091	Alw 32000N1X	86 2 5 42 31 21½ 23¾	Bailey J D	114 b	*1.65	92-11	RealityRod1103½ JumpTheShdow1141¾ MountinOfLws1141½	Steadied turn 6
27Apr95-4Kee fst 6f	:22 :45 :564 1:091	Alw 32550N2L	87 7 4 31 32 44½ 44¾	Day P	L 118 b	7.70	87-12	Dodge City1211½ Once A Sailor1153 Zephaniah114nk	Flattened out 9
8Apr95-4Kee fst 7f	:221 :452 1:094 1:221	Alw 35000N2L	78 8 3 1½ 11 57½ 511	Gryder A T	L 121 b	7.90	79-15	Strategic Intent1152½ Dodge City1212 Hopkins Forest1211½	Pace, tired 10
11Mar95-6GP fst 7f	:221 :453 1:104 1:234	Alw 31000N1X	72 4 6 1hd 2hd 31½ 68	Day P	L 119	3.50	76-11	Fleet Brass1191¾ Bick1192 Mighty Magee1191½	Faded 11

WORKOUTS: Nov 26 Bel tr.t 4f fst :473 H 2/65 ●Nov 9 Bel 4f fst :472 H 1/13 Nov 2 Bel 4f sly :494 B 2/3 Oct 16 Bel 5f fst 1:02 H 16/20 Oct 9 Bel 5f fst 1:01 H 8/41 Oct 3 Bel 5f fst 1:02 B 13/25

Israelite

Own: Caliendo Philip
LUZZI M J (71 7 7 6 .10) $50,000

Dk. b or br g. 3 (Mar)
Sire: Broad Brush (Ack Ack)
Dam: Bushmaid (Bushido)
Br: Fisher Susan B (Ky)
Tr: Gorham Michael E (1 0 0 1 .00)

L 118

Lifetime Record:	9 4 0 1	$31,100			
1995	6 3 0 0	$23,400	Turf	0 0 0 0	
1994	3 1 0 1	$7,700	Wet	4 4 0 0	$30,000
Aqu	0 0 0 0		Dist	0 0 0 0	

20Nov95-8Suf fst 6f	:22 :452 :581 1:11 3↑	Alw 16660N$Y	75 8 5 42¾ 21½ 53¾ 79½	Vega H	LB 113 b	12.20	81-21	Detox1131½ Co Art1221½ Maudlin's Sunny1191	Speed, tired 8
28Oct95-11Suf sly 5f ⊗	:22 :453 :58 3↑	Alw 13720N3X	84 1 4 11 1½ 1hd 11	Vega H	LB 113 b	2.40	100-13	Israelite1131 Palecari1132½ Dr. Chopper1171	Hustled rail, driving 9
15Apr95-10Suf fst 6f	:22 :453 :581 1:104	Faneuil Hall25k	57 8 4 55½ 56½ 612 719	Campbell T M	B 119 b	8.40	72-24	Splendid Sprinter1195½ Satin Stride1206½ Dakota's Trick122¾	4 path, tired 8
8Mar95-3Suf sly 6f	:222 :462 :593 1:132	Alw 12740N2X	74 6 1 2½ 1hd 11 12½	Campbell T M	B 116 b	*1.10	78-24	Israelite1162½ Artistic Lad1163½ Silk Tie And Blaze1191½	Rallied outside 6
11Feb95-8Aqu fst 1 1/16 ⊡	:231 :474 1:144 1:492	Whirlaway BC81k	55 9 8 820 89 58 620¾	Migliore R	114 b	36.00	37-38	Devil's Brew117½ Ave's Flag11912 Sir Lovely1153½	Wide early 9
8Jan95-8Suf sly 6f	:231 :481 1:02 1:162	Alw 11760N2L	70 8 2 2hd 13 15 16	Vega H	B 119 b	2.10	66-40	Israelite1196 Change Colors1161¾ Adriatic King119¾	3 path, ridden out 8
16Dec94-8Suf fst 6f	:23 :481 1:014 1:16	Alw 11760N2L	34 2 5 22 2½ 4¾ 64¾	Vega H	122 fb	3.00	61-29	ArtisticLd122½ SilkTieAndBlze1174½ SecretServiceMn119nk	Off rail, tired 8
5Dec94-5Suf sly 6f	:23 :472 1:002 1:142	Md Sp Wt	55 7 1 3½ 11 14 11¾	Vega H	122 fb	*1.40	76-22	Israelite1221¾ Winlocsaceofmagic1223¾ Merrimack T. J.1225¾	3w, driving 8
25Nov94-4Suf fst 6f	:23 :474 1:012 1:151	Md Sp Wt	32 5 4 41 2hd 34 39½	Ma H C	122 b	2.70	62-25	Artistic Lad1226 Divine Courage1223½ Israelite122no	4w, stead ent stretch 8

WORKOUTS: ●Oct 24 Suf 3f fst :371 H 1/14 Sep 30 Rkm 6f fst 1:151 Hg2/7 Sep 22 Rkm 5f fst 1:021 B 5/14 Sep 8 Rkm 4f fst :50 B 4/8 Sep 2 Rkm 4f fst :521 B 20/20

1 — Traveling Jeff — In the money five of his last six starts, though only one was a win, and that was at five furlongs. Had one second and one third in two starts at seven furlongs. Versatile. Certainly a contender, but had weakened in the stretch in his last two starts at six furlongs, and wore fronts in his last. Contender. I initially picked him second, but then bumped him down to third in the paper.

2 — Whirling Blade — Showed three races longer than six furlongs and tired in all of them, two at 6½ and one at a mile. On the plus side, he'd won four of his last eight starts, one at $45,000 and another at $55,000. He'd been placed over his head in a non-winners of five in his return in his last start, and was fifth by six lengths. He was dropping today, but picking up 11 pounds. I liked his workout for this. I originally picked him third, reconsidered, and made him my top pick.

3 — Spanish Charge — Here was a horse I truly hated, a dislike which traced directly to the fact that I picked him at Saratoga in a similar race — seven furlongs in a $50,000 claimer — and he ran seventh by 14¾ lengths in a field of seven. He finally sank to his proper level, winning his last start at The Meadowlands in a $20,000 claimer. Now moving up to $40,000? No way.

4 — Cardsharp — Maryland shipper had been blown away in his last start, a non-winners of three, after winning his maiden and a non-winners of two with blinkers added. All his races were routes except for one try at seven furlongs, when he was a distant third. Didn't like him in this spot.

5 — Sir Lovely — I didn't know what to do with this horse. He'd graduated by winning an $8,000 maiden claimer at Philadelphia, then did well in three allowance tries. He ran a distant third in the Whirlaway Stakes behind a couple of real nice three-year-olds (Devil's Brew and Ave's Flag), then was fifth out of nine in the Cherry Hill Mile, a Grade III stakes. He returned from a six month vacation to run sixth twice, in a non-winners of three and in a $50,000 claimer, then, in his last race, won a $30,000 claimer at Aqueduct at one mile with the addition of Lasix. His only start at seven furlongs was in his return race when he lost 11 lengths in allowance company. I picked him first originally, then demoted him to second.

6 — Get My Glitter — A speedster who'd been fourth in his last three starts, the last in a $40,000 claimer at one mile at Aqueduct. He had four wins in 33 career starts with nine seconds and two thirds, and had never raced seven furlongs. In a one mile $40,000 claimer on turf, he'd led most of the way before tiring to second. He showed four races at six furlongs, tiring in each. I passed.

7 — Save The Whale — In the money five of his last six, with the only poor race in the Jim Dandy Stakes against Composer. He was a route horse cutting back to seven furlongs, a distance he'd tried only once without lighting the board. Following a layoff, he'd won a $40,000 claimer at $1\frac{1}{16}$ miles with Lasix added, then, in his last start, was third by four lengths in allowance company at $1\frac{1}{8}$ miles. I thought he had a big shot, but I passed.

8 — Jump The Shadow — He had been crushed in nonwinners of three allowance races in each of his last three starts. He hadn't lit the board in three starts at seven furlongs. He was dropping into a claimer for the first time, but I didn't like him a bit.

9 — Israelite — A shipper from Suffolk Downs who had won four of nine starts. He, too, was making his first start in a claimer. In his lone start longer than six furlongs, he was in the Whirlaway, finishing sixth by $20\frac{3}{4}$ lengths, $8\frac{1}{4}$ behind Sir Lovely. Uh-uh.

The betting for this race separated the field into two distinct groups: five contenders from 3-1 to 7-1 — who would run first through fifth — and four longshots (Spanish Charge, Israelite, Jump The Shadow and Cardsharp). Whirling Blade and Save The Whale both went off at 3-1, the former being a slight favorite. Get My Glitter went off at 7-2, Sir Lovely at 9-2 and Traveling Jeff at 7-1.

For the Pick Six, it made sense to use the five contenders.

Get My Glitter out-dueled Whirling Blade and went coast to coast, scoring by two lengths and returning $9.20. Traveling Jeff was a clear second, $2\frac{1}{2}$ lengths in front of Save The Whale. Sir Lovely and Whirling Blade checked in fourth and fifth, respectively.

FIFTH RACE
Aqueduct
DECEMBER 2, 1995

7 FURLONGS. (1.20¹) CLAIMING. Purse $28,000 (plus up to $10,950 NYSBFOA). 3-year-olds. Weight, 122 lbs. Non-winners of two races since November 1, allowed 2 lbs. Of a race since then, 4 lbs. Of a race since October 20, 6 lbs. Claiming price $50,000; for each $5,000 to $40,000, allowed 2 lbs. (Races where entered for $35,000 or less not considered.)

Value of Race: $28,000 Winner $16,800; second $5,600; third $3,080; fourth $1,680; fifth $840. Mutuel Pool $320,788.00 Exacta Pool $392,212.00 Trifecta Pool $346,216.00

Last Raced	Horse	M/Eqt.	A	Wt	PP	St	¼	½	Str	Fin	Jockey	Cl'g Pr	Odds $1
18Nov95 9Aqu⁴	Get My Glitter	Lb	3	112	6	4	1½	11½	1²	1²	Chavez J F	40000	3.60
2Nov95 5Aqu³	Traveling Jeff	Lf	3	114	1	9	4hd	3½	2²	22½	Castillo H Jr	45000	7.50
12Nov95 7Aqu³	Save The Whale	L	3	116	7	3	7²	6½	3½	3¹	Velazquez J R	50000	3.00
15Nov95 7Aqu¹	Sir Lovely	Lb	3	116	5	8	9	8⁵	5⁴	4⁴	Pezua J M	50000	4.70
16Nov95 6Aqu⁵	Whirling Blade	b	3	116	2	6	2½	2hd	4¹	5⁷	Alvarado F T	50000	*3.00
10Nov95 5Med¹	Spanish Charge	Lbf	3	112	3	7	6¹	7²	7½	6nk	Rydowski S R	40000	52.00
20Nov95 8Suf⁷	Israelite	Lb	3	118	9	1	5²½	5²½	6½	7⁵	Luzzi M J	50000	22.60
17Nov95 8Aqu⁵	Jump The Shadow	L	3	116	8	2	3hd	4½	8⁶	8½	Perez R B	50000	11.90
11Nov95 6Lrl⁶	Cardsharp	Lb	3	116	4	5	8½	9	9	9	Maple E	45000	27.50

*—Actual Betting Favorite.

OFF AT 2:20 Start Good. Won driving. Time, :22⁴, :45⁴, 1:10², 1:23¹ Track good.

$2 Mutuel Prices:

7-GET MY GLITTER	9.20	5.30	4.00
2-TRAVELING JEFF		7.70	3.90
8-SAVE THE WHALE			2.80

$2 EXACTA 7-2 PAID $62.50 $2 TRIFECTA 7-2-8 PAID $212.00

B. g, (Mar), by Glitterman—Exuberant Jane, by Exuberant. Trainer Anderson William D. Bred by Powell Arlene M (Fla).

GET MY GLITTER outsprinted rivals for the early advantage, extended his lead on the turn, then held sway under brisk urging. TRAVELING JEFF away a bit slowly, moved up steadily while saving ground, angled out while rallying on the turn, but couldn't gain on the winner through the stretch. SAVE THE WHALE outrun for a half, rallied along the inside to reach contention in upper stretch but was no match for the top two. SIR LOVELY outrun for a half, failed to threaten with a mild late rally. WHIRLING BLADE rushed up along the inside, forced the pace for a half and gave way. SPANISH CHARGE was never a factor. ISRAELITE up close early, while five wide, gave way on the turn. JUMP THE SHADOW chased the leaders while four wide for a half and tired. CARDSHARP never reached contention. TRAVELING JEFF and SAVE THE WHALE wore mud caulks.

Owners— 1, Filoso Louis; 2, Ramsey Kenneth L & Sarah K; 3, Pont Street Stable; 4, Zuckerman Donald & Roberta M; 5, R Kay Stable; 6, Paraneck Stable; 7, Caliendo Philip; 8, Dogwood Stable; 9, Doyle Richard B

Trainers— 1, Anderson William D; 2, Plesa Edward Jr; 3, Carroll Del W II; 4, Moschera Gasper S; 5, Araya Rene A; 6, Aquilino Joseph; 7, Gorham Michael E; 8, Alexander Frank A; 9, Miceli Michael

Scratched— Vega's Secret (18Nov95 9AQU³), Leap With Joy (15Nov95 7AQU⁷)

Now the sixth race, a field of eight two-year-old maidens (two were an entry) going six furlongs — Apotheosis, Barbican, Joe Jones, Air Supply, Allen's Rainbow and Dom McPeitz were all scratched:

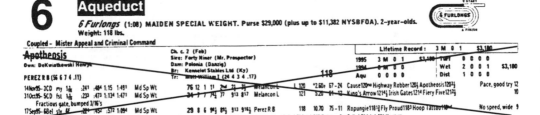

Canfield Casino
Own: Blue Goose Stbl & Hudson River Farm
LEON F (27 1 1 2 .04)

Dk. b or br c. 2 (Jan)
Sire: Fast Play (Seattle Slew)
Dam: Casino Babe (Golden Act)
Br: Green Curtis C (Ky)
Tr: Kelly Timothy D (14 0 1 1 .00)

118

Lifetime Record :	1 M 0 0	$0		
1995	1 M 0 0		Turf	0 0 0 0
1994	0 M 0 0		Wet	0 0 0 0
Aqu	0 0 0 0		Dist	1 0 0 0

30Sep95-2Bel fst 6f :222 :463 :592 1:124 Md Sp Wt 41 8 7 79¼ 99¼ 911 913¼ Perez R B 118 f 31.75 64-22 Citified1181 Turning Fifty11821 In The Rain1181 No speed 9
WORKOUTS: Nov 17 Bel 5f fst 1:022 B 14/35 Nov 9 Bel 4f fst :483 B 4/17 Oct 31 Bel 4f fst :483 H 7/56 Oct 26 Bel tr.t 6f fst 1:183 B 1/3 Oct 16 Bel 3f fst :381 B 16/26 Sep 26 Bel 3f sly :381 B 4/7

Mister Appeal
Own: Fertile Acres Farm
CHAVEZ J F (125 22 22 11 .18)

B. g. 2 (Mar)
Sire: Valid Appeal (In Reality)
Dam: Cuttin a Rug (Blade)
Br: Saint Francis Farm (Tex)
Tr: Sciacca Gary (36 4 2 4 .11)

118

Lifetime Record :	0 M 0 0	$0		
1995	0 M 0 0		Turf	0 0 0 0
1994	0 M 0 0		Wet	0 0 0 0
Aqu	0 0 0 0		Dist	0 0 0 0

WORKOUTS: Nov 26 Bel tr.t 3f fst :371 B 8/20 Nov 20 Bel tr.t 3f fst :354 H 2/13 ●Nov 14 Bel tr.t 3f fst :361 H 1/14 Nov 7 Bel tr.t 4f fst :491 B 8/39 Nov 1 Bel 4f fst :492 B 18/42 Oct 20 Bel tr.t 5f fst 1:023 B 5/10
Oct 13 Bel 5f fst 1:02 H 16/30 Oct 7 Bel 4f fst :49 H 5/29 Oct 1 Bel 4f fst :513 B 26/28 Sep 25 Bel 4f fst :492 B 42/77 Sep 19 Bel tr.t 3f fst :371 B 3/15

Sierra Grande
Own: Ellenberg & Kaster & O'Connor
ALVARADO F T (95 9 12 12 .09)

Ch. c. 2 (Feb)
Sire: Ogygian (Damascus)
Dam: Silver Valley (Mr. Prospector)
Br: Foxfield (Ky)
Tr: Lukas D Wayne (11 3 1 1 .27)

118

Lifetime Record :	2 M 2 0	$11,600			
1995	2 M 2 0	$11,600	Turf	0 0 0 0	
1994	0 M 0 0		Wet	1 0 1 0	$5,600
Aqu	1 0 1 0	$5,600	Dist	1 0 1 0	$5,600

19Nov95-2Aqu my 6f :222 :462 :583 1:11 Md Sp Wt 78 3 3 21 1½ 1½ 2½ Bailey J D 118 2.65 86-11 God's Village1181½ Sierra Grande1183½ Brouhaha1183 Yielded grudgingly 11
11Jun95-2Bel fst 5f :222 :463 :59 Md Sp Wt 75 1 1 11 1½ 21 25 Bailey J D 116 *.50 86-25 Grindstone1165 Sierra Grande1164 Fig Fest1161 Hustled, 2nd best 5
WORKOUTS: Nov 14 Bel 5f fst 1:012 B 5/16 Nov 6 Bel 5f fst 1:023 B 30/52 Oct 30 Bel 5f fst 1:014 B 16/36 Oct 23 Bel 5f fst 1:021 B 19/31 ●Oct 16 Bel 5f fst 1:00 H 1/30 Oct 10 Bel 4f fst :502 B 27/30

Turning Fifty
Own: Christiana Stables
MIGLIORE R (95 7 12 17 .07)

B. g. 2 (Jun)
Sire: Forty Niner (Mr. Prospector)
Dam: Broom Dance (Dance Spell)
Br: Christiana Stables (Ky)
Tr: Badgett William Jr (23 2 3 0 .09)

L 118

Lifetime Record :	2 M 2 0	$11,600			
1995	2 M 2 0	$11,600	Turf	0 0 0 0	
1994	0 M 0 0		Wet	1 0 1 0	$5,600
Aqu	1 0 1 0	$5,600	Dist	2 0 2 0	$11,600

19Nov95-4Aqu my 6f :223 :462 :582 1:104 Md Sp Wt 71 8 1 32 31½ 34½ 26 Migliore R L 118 3.50 83-11 SwingAndMiss1185 TurningFifty118½ UltimateSnction1189 Up for place 8
30Sep95-2Bel fst 6f :222 :463 :592 1:124 Md Sp Wt 72 7 5 42¾ 42 21½ 21 Chavez J F 118 5.50 76-22 Citified1181 Turning Fifty11821 In The Rain1181 Finished well 9
WORKOUTS: Nov 27 Bel tr.t 5f fst 1:05 B 20/24 Nov 18 Bel 3f fst :372 B 6/8 Nov 14 Bel 5f fst 1:012 B 5/16 Nov 1 Bel 5f fst 1:011 H 6/25 Oct 25 Bel 4f fst :52 B 46/49 Oct 19 Bel 4f fst :50 B 22/35

~~**Barbican**
Own: Lovinger Jeffrey S
SAMYN J L (50 3 4 6 .06)~~

~~B. c. 2 (Apr)
Sire: Irish Tower (Irish Castle)
Dam: Zimbaba (Bravest Roman)
Br: Carl William A (Ky)
Tr: Violette Richard A Jr (5 0 0 0 .00)~~

~~118~~

Lifetime Record :	2 M 0 0	$0		
1995	2 M 0 0		Turf	0 0 0 0
1994	0 M 0 0		Wet	2 0 0 0
Aqu	0 0 0 0		Dist	1 0 0 0

~~7Oct95-2Bel wf 7f :221 :453 1:122 1:262 Md Sp Wt 44 4 1 1½ 2hd 65½ 68¾ Luzzi M J 118 b 10.30 60-24 Saratoga Dandy118½ Fly Proud1183 Mesopotamia118¾ Used in pace 7
17Sep95-6Bel sly 6f :221 :452 :572 1:094 Md Sp Wt 46 3 4 54 66 610 610 Luzzi M J 118 21.30 82-11 Ropungie1181¼ Fly Proud1183 Hoop Tattoo118hd No rally 9
WORKOUTS: Nov 22 Bel 5f fst 1:022 H 5/6 Nov 14 Bel 3f fst :37 B 2/8 Nov 11 Bel 6f fst 1:193 B 7/8 Nov 7 Bel 4f fst :50 B 33/47 Oct 24 Bel 4f fst :484 B 23/65 Oct 18 Bel 4f fst :481 H 7/46~~

~~**Joe Jones**
Own: Dutrow Richard E & Roussel Louis
LUZZI M J (72 7 7 6 .10)~~

~~B. c. 2 (Apr)
Sire: Risen Star (Secretariat)
Dam: Your Hope (Mari's Book)
Br: Dutrow Richard E (Ky)
Tr: Dutrow Richard E (8 1 0 0 .17)~~

~~118~~

Lifetime Record :	1 M 1 0	$5,600			
1995	1 M 1 0	$5,600	Turf	0 0 0 0	
1994	0 M 0 0		Wet	1 0 1 0	$5,600
Aqu	1 0 1 0	$5,600	Dist	1 0 1 0	$5,600

~~4Nov95-2Aqu wf 6f :222 :461 :583 1:112 Md Sp Wt 77 5 1 1½ 1½ 1½ 2no Krone J A 119 3.40 85-14 Sea Horse119no Joe Jones1191½ Ultimate Sanction1196¾ Dueled, gamely 9
WORKOUTS: Nov 26 Aqu 5f fst 1:01 B 2/12 Oct 25 Aqu 5f fst 1:014 B 5/14 ●Oct 18 Aqu 5f fst 1:004 H 1/6 Oct 11 Aqu 5f fst 1:022 B 4/5 ●Oct 2 Aqu 5f fst 1:004 Hg 1/5 ●Sep 25 Aqu 4f fst :481 B 1/10~~

Devil's Cup
Own: Gold Spur Stable
MAPLE E (51 5 8 8 .10)

Dk. b or br c. 2 (May)
Sire: Devil's Bag (Halo)
Dam: Fun Forever (Never Bend)
Br: Floyd William H (Ky)
Tr: Kimmel John C (33 9 4 4 .27)

118

Lifetime Record :	0 M 0 0	$0		
1995	0 M 0 0		Turf	0 0 0 0
1994	0 M 0 0		Wet	0 0 0 0
Aqu	0 0 0 0		Dist	0 0 0 0

WORKOUTS: ●Nov 30 Bel tr.t 4f fst :484 Hg 1/18 Nov 25 Bel tr.t 5f fst 1:03 B 19/33 Nov 18 Bel 5f fst 1:012 Hg 2/31 Nov 13 Bel 5f fst 1:01 H 3/22 Nov 6 Bel 5f fst 1:001 H 3/52 Oct 30 Bel 5f fst 1:024 B 26/36
Oct 24 Bel 4f fst :491 B 44/65 Oct 16 Bel 4f fst :504 B 39/50 Oct 9 Bel 3f fst :382 B 20/24 Jly 1 Bel tr.t 3f fst :372 B 12/20 Jun 24 Bel tr.t 3f fst :362 H 4/21

~~**Air Supply**
Own: Dorsey Charles
CASTILLO H JR (56 4 2 4 .07)~~

~~Dk. b or br c. 2 (Apr)
Sire: Air Forbes Won (Bold Forbes)
Dam: Windita (Mari's Book)
Br: Anchel Mr & Mrs Michael (Ky)
Tr: Cordero Angel Jr (16 1 3 1 .06)~~

~~118~~

Lifetime Record :	0 M 0 0	$0		
1995	0 M 0 0		Turf	0 0 0 0
1994	0 M 0 0		Wet	0 0 0 0
Aqu	0 0 0 0		Dist	0 0 0 0

~~WORKOUTS: Nov 5 Bel tr.t 6f fst 1:15 B 2/6 Oct 26 Bel 5f fst 1:002 H 4/47 Oct 18 Bel 5f fst 1:01 H 3/29 Oct 11 Bel 5f fst 1:01 Hg 10/39 Sep 30 Bel 5f fst 1:013 Hg 21/52 Sep 22 Bel 4f fst :493 B 13/32
Sep 15 Bel tr.t 3f fst :38 B 8/40 Aug 31 Bel 5f fst 1:031 B 29/34~~

R.S.V.P. Requested
Own: Der-Sea Stable
BECKNER D V (30 0 2 3 .00)

Dk. b or br c. 2 (Mar)
Sire: Black Tie Affair (Ire) (Miswaki)
Dam: Flags Waving (Delta Flag)
Br: Mangurian Harry T Jr (Fla)
Tr: Moschera Gasper S (48 8 8 7 .17)

L 118

Lifetime Record :	4 M 0 0	$1,140			
1995	4 M 0 0	$1,140	Turf	4 0 0 0	$1,140
1994	0 M 0 0		Wet	0 0 0 0	
Aqu	0 0 0 0		Dist	0 0 0 0	

26Oct95-7Med gd 1 70 Ⓣ :223 :474 1:133 1:441 Md Sp Wt 42 3 11 119½ 1011 816 812¼ Santagata N L 118 b 15.30 57-31 Darn That Erica1184½ Belfour118½ Tanzia108½ Outrun 11
20Oct95-5Bel yl 1 1/16 Ⓣ :232 :463 1:114 1:444 Md Sp Wt 30 6 10 1016 1015 1017 924¼ Migliore R L 118 b 17.90 47-33 Optic Nerve1183 Value Investor118nk Hail To The Lion11817 No speed 10
13Sep95-6Bel fm 1 1/16 Ⓣ :23 :461 1:104 1:431 Md Sp Wt 58 8 5 53½ 54¾ 411 511¾ Migliore R L 118 b 49.00 68-20 Togher1187½ Going For The Gold118nk Bombardier1184 Evenly 8
25Aug95-6Sar fm 1 1/16 Ⓣ :23 :47 1:114 1:433 Md Sp Wt 35 4 11 1117 1115 1115 1115 Migliore R 118 b 11.80 66-07 Defcto118nk Bombrdier1184 Dontnswerthefour118nk Broke slowly, outrun 11
WORKOUTS: Nov 21 Bel tr.t 4f fst :513 B 43/47 Nov 11 Bel 5f fst 1:03 B 41/56 Oct 17 Bel 4f fst :491 B 19/34 Oct 11 Bel 4f fst :491 B 22/45 Sep 11 Bel 4f fst :501 B 36/44 Sep 6 Bel 3f fst :36 Hg 3/10

Criminal Command
Own: Cianciolo Margaret J
PEZUA J M (58 8 5 11 .16)
Ch. c. 2 (Mar)
Sire: Criminal Type (Alydar)
Dam: Jin's Command (Commadore C.)
Br: John Cianciolo (Ky)
Tr: Sciacca Gary (36 4 2 4 .11)
L 118
Lifetime Record: 5 M 0 0 $1,800
1995 5 M 0 0 $1,800 | Turf 1 0 0 0
1994 0 M 0 0 | Wet 1 0 0 0 $1,800
Aqu 1 0 0 0 $1,800 | Dist 1 0 0 0

4Nov95-5Aqu wf 1 :23 :463 1:13 1:392 Md Sp Wt 41 5 2 22 2hd 35 413 Velazquez J R L 118 fb 40.25 59-19 Mariner1183 Dothebucket1187 Beino Village1183 Bid, tired 9
27Oct95-1Bel fst 7f :223 :454 1:104 1:234 Md Sp Wt 38 8 2 41½ 84½ 1013 1021½ Alvarado F T L 118 fb 97.25 60-11 Robb1187¾ Traffic Circle1181¼ Footloose118½
Brief speed 12
11Oct95-2Bel yl 1 1/16 [T] :234 :483 1:142 1:452 Md Sp Wt 9 5 1 1½ 63 718 733 Smith M E L 118 33.25 36-29 Blushing Richard1186 Pugnatious118hd Dom Mcpeitz1187½ Used in pace 8
30Sep95-4Bel fst 6f :224 :463 :583 1:111 Md Sp Wt 44 6 3 54½ 77½ 814 820½ Chavez J F L 118 b 25.75 64-22 Cliveden Hall1189½ Favorable Ruling1182 Dom Mcpeitz1182 No threat 9
2Sep95-2Bel fst 1 :23 :454 1:103 1:37 Md Sp Wt 26 8 6 89½ 810 814 823¾ Chavez J F 118 b 30.50 55-16 Pirate Performer118¾ Fortitude1182 Hey You Weasel11810 No speed 8
24Aug95-6Sar fst 6½f :22 :454 1:113 1:182 Md Sp Wt 30 1 12 1224 1222 1119 1023 Chavez J F 119 b 17.80e 60-18 Gold Fever1198¾ Crafty Friend119hd Ide1191½ Took up break 12
WORKOUTS: Nov 17 Bel tr.t 3f fst :361 H 3/14

Our Theme
Own: Malmstrom Ivar W & Ivar W Jr
CORDOVA D W (60 4 4 5 .07)
B. c. 2 (Apr)
Sire: Our Native (Exclusive Native)
Dam: Durham's Theme (Lord Durham)
Br: Thomas Dooley & Mary Alice Dooley (Mich)
Tr: Destasio Richard A (17 1 1 1 .06)
L 118
Lifetime Record: 5 M 0 0 $1,920
1995 5 M 0 0 $1,920 | Turf 4 0 0 0 $1,920
1994 0 M 0 0 | Wet 0 0 0 0
Aqu 0 0 0 0 | Dist 0 0 0 0

11Oct95-6Bel yl 1 1/16 [T] :241 :483 1:132 1:454 Md Sp Wt -0 1 1 31½ 68 733 745¾ Davis R G L 118 17.70 — 29 Oh Bye Golly118¾ Cheerful Earful1183 Omission11816 Done early 8
8Sep95-6Bel fm 1 1/16 [T] :24 :483 1:131 1:44 Md Sp Wt 53 5 4 44½ 43 45½ 44½ Davis R G 118 14.30 68-14 StrOfThetricl1183 HilToTheLion1181¾ WvingGoodBye1183½ No rally wide 8
21Aug95-2Sar fm 1 1/16 [T] :233 :484 1:142 1:454 Md Sp Wt 52 9 5 56 62½ 63 64½ Davis R G 118 20.30 66-12 Officious118nk Togher1181 Green Manor118nk In traffic 5/16 pl 9
13Jly95-6Bel fm 6f (T) :22 :461 :583 1:11 Md Sp Wt 36 1 2 1½ 2hd 21 910 Davis R G 116 34.50 71-19 Harpsichord116¾ Old Chapel116hd Erskine1161 Dueled inside 12
24Jun95-2Bel fst 5f :22 :462 :594 Md Sp Wt 10 2 3 43 54 712 716 Davis R G 116 47.00 71-15 Cobb's Creek1161 Tax Break116¾ Game's On1161½ Brief speed 7
WORKOUTS: Nov 26 Bel tr.t 4f fst :52 B 61/65 Nov 18 Bel tr.t 5f fst 1:04 B 17/22 Nov 10 Bel tr.t 5f fst 1:051 B 2/4 Oct 30 Bel tr.t 4f fst :513 B 22/28 Sep 25 Bel tr.t 4f fst :52 B 24/25

~~**Allen's Rainbow**~~
Own: Vance Jeanne G
VELAZQUEZ J R (60 8 14 7 .13)
Dk. b or br c. 2 (Mar)
Sire: Allen's Prospect (Mr. Prospector)
Dam: Amerrico's Rainbow (Amerrico)
Br: Glegett Hal C B (Md)
Tr: Schulhofer Flint S (23 7 1 1 .30)
118
Lifetime Record: 2 M 0 1 $3,300
1995 2 M 0 1 $3,300 | Turf 0 0 0 0
1994 0 M 0 0 | Wet 1 0 0 0
Aqu 1 0 0 0 | Dist 2 0 0 1 $3,300

19Nov95-2Aqu my 6f :222 :462 :583 1:11 Md Sp Wt 53 10 4 32½ 3½ 44½ 611 Santos J A 118 1.70 76-11 God's Village1181½ Sierra Grande1183½ Brouhaha1183 Stalked, tired 11
25Oct95-6Bel fst 6f :224 :462 :582 1:103 Md Sp Wt 74 6 3 31 2hd 32 33½ Santos J A 118 7.60e 84-13 KnownAccomplc118½ SwngAndMss1183 Alln'sRnbw1183½ Bid, weakened 10
WORKOUTS: Nov 27 Bel tr.t 4f fst :50 B Nov 17 Bel 4f fst :494 B 18/42 Nov 10 Bel 4f fst :491 B 9/26 Nov 5 Bel 4f fst :50 B 37/55 Oct 23 Bel 3f fst :363 H 7/12 Oct 17 Sar tr.t 4f fst :50 Bg 2/10

~~**Dom McPeitz**~~
Own: Low Lawana L & Robert E
LUZZI M J (72 7 7 6 .10)
B. c. 2 (Jan)
Sire: Fortunate Prospect (Northern Prospect)
Dam: Moonlight Jet (Tri Jet)
Br: Farnsworth Farms & Saimer Joel (Fla)
Tr: Pelta Daniel C (6 0 1 1 .00)
L 118
Lifetime Record: 5 M 0 2 $6,820
1995 5 M 0 2 $6,820 | Turf 2 0 0 1 $3,520
1994 0 M 0 0 | Wet 0 0 0 0
Aqu 1 0 0 0 | Dist 1 0 0 1 $3,300

11Nov95-2Aqu fst 1 :234 :47 1:121 1:374 Md Sp Wt 49 3 4 52½ 53¼ 711 719½ Luzzi M J L 118 b 11.20 62-19 Prince Of Thieves1186¾ Circle Of Light1185½ Chenlo118½ Tired 9
11Oct95-2Bel yl 1 1/16 [T] :234 :483 1:142 1:452 Md Sp Wt 69 4 2 2½ 1½ 21 36 Luzzi M J L 118 b 7.70 63-29 Blushing Richard1186 Pugnatious118hd Dom Mcpeitz1187½ Bid, weakened 8
30Sep95-4Bel fst 6f :224 :463 :583 1:111 Md Sp Wt 67 3 2 21½ 22 27 311½ Luzzi M J 118 b 31.50 73-22 ClivedenHll1189½ FvorbleRuling1182 DomMcpitz1182 Chased, weakened 9
21Aug95-6Sar fm 1 1/16 [T] :232 :482 1:132 1:433 Md Sp Wt 43 7 8 75½ 85¾ 814 616¾ Velazquez J R 118 41.00 65-12 CrrncyArbtrg11810 CptnChrl1182 BlshngRchrd1181 Four wide, no threat 10
22Jly95-2Sar fst 5½f :224 :462 :584 1:051 Md Sp Wt 13 9 10 79½ 78 912 1020¾ Velazquez J R 120 7.40 74-07 Sunny Side1206 Northern Pursuit120nk Justinthemiddle1202 No threat 12
WORKOUTS: Nov 26 Bel tr.t 4f fst :484 H 10/65 Nov 21 Bel tr.t 4f fst :493 B 19/47 Nov 7 Bel tr.t 4f fst :513 B 32/39 Oct 31 Bel tr.t 4f fst :493 B 12/37 Sep 20 Bel 5f fst 1:001 H 5/57

1 — Canfield Casino — Ninth at 31-1 in debut while sporting front bandages. Next.

2 — Mister Appeal — A first-timer coupled with Criminal Command. From a high percentage two-year-old sire (Valid Appeal) with two strong three-furlong works, one of them a bullet. The other first-timer in here, Devil's Cup, looked better.

3 — Sierra Grande — Second by five lengths in his debut for Lukas at 1-2, then second by 1¼ lengths in his return. The one to beat. I picked him first.

4 — Turning Fifty — Strong second in his debut and also in his return race. Well bet each time. Tough not to like. I picked him second.

5 — Devil's Cup — A well-bred first-timer by Devil's Bag,

making his debut for an outstanding trainer with two-year-olds, John Kimmel. Worked a bullet. Contender. He became my third pick when Apotheosis scratched.

6 — R.S.V.P. Requested — All four of his races were on turf and were terrible. Next.

7 — Criminal Command — Fourth by 13 lengths in his last start at a mile was actually an improvement over his first five races. No thanks.

8 — Our Theme — Been idle off five bad races, the last four on grass. No way.

Sierra Grande, Turning Fifty, Devil's Cup were logical to use in the Pick Six. Sierra Grande was the even money favorite, Devil's Cup got bet down to 8-5, Turning Fifty went off at a generous 4-1 and the entry at 8-1. In an exciting three-horse battle, Devil's Cup edged Turning Fifty by a neck, with Sierra Grande another three-quarters of a length back, to return $5.40. There was a gap of 7¼ lengths back to Criminal Command in fourth.

SIXTH RACE   6 FURLONGS. (1.08) MAIDEN SPECIAL WEIGHT. Purse $29,000 (plus up to $11,382 NYSBFOA).

Aqueduct
2-year-olds. Weight: 118 lbs.

DECEMBER 2, 1995

Value of Race: $29,000 Winner $17,400; second $5,800; third $3,190; fourth $1,740; fifth $878. Mutuel Pool $325,522.00 Exacta Pool $516,399.00

Last Raced	Horse	M/Eqt. A.Wt	PP St	¼	½	Str Fin	Jockey	Odds $1
	Devil's Cup	2 118	5 4	4hd 2¹	2½	1nk	Maple E	1.70
19Nov95 4Aqu²	Turning Fifty	L 2 118	4 2	2½ 1½	1hd 2¾		Migliore R	4.10
19Nov95 2Aqu²	Sierra Grande	2 118	3 6	6⁹ 3½	3⁴ 3⁷¼		Alvarado F T	1.10
4Nov95 5Aqu⁴	Criminal Command	Lbf 2 118	7 1	3hd 5¹	4² 4²¼		Pezua J M	a-8.20
26Oct95 7Med⁸	R.S.V.P. Requested	Lbf 2 118	6 7	7¹² 7²⁴	6¹½ 5¹¼		Beckner D V	72.75
30Sep95 2Bel⁹	Canfield Casino	b 2 118	1 5	1hd 4hd	5¹ 6⁴		Leon F	71.25
11Oct95 6Bel⁷	Our Theme	Lb 2 118	8 3	5¹½ 6²	7³⁰ 7¹⁸		Cordova D W	73.50
	Mister Appeal	b 2 118	2 8	8 8	8 8		Chavez J F	a-8.20

a-Coupled: Criminal Command and Mister Appeal.

OFF AT 2:48 Start Good. Won driving. Time, :22³, :46², :58³, 1:11 Track good.

$2 Mutuel Prices:

7-DEVIL'S CUP	5.40	3.80	2.20
5-TURNING FIFTY		3.90	2.10
4-SIERRA GRANDE			2.10

$2 EXACTA 7-5 PAID $22.20

Dk. b. or br. c, (May), by Devil's Bag-Fun Forever, by Never Bend. Trainer Kimmel John C. Bred by Floyd William H (Ky).

DEVIL'S CUP settled just off the early pace, rallied four wide on the turn, made a run to challenge in midstretch, then wore down TURNING FIFTY under brisk urging. TURNING FIFTY dueled between horses for a half, maintained a slim lead into deep stretch and yielded grudgingly. SIERRA GRANDE reserved early, circled five wide on the turn, made a run to threaten in midstretch. CRIMINAL COMMAND forced the early pace between horses then tired on the turn. R.S.V.P. REQUESTED never reached contention after breaking slowly. CANFIELD CASINO dueled early along the rail then gave way on the turn. OUR THEME showed only brief speed. MISTER APPEAL checked in tight at the start and was never close thereafter. TURNING FIFTY wore mud caulks.

Owners— 1, Gold Spur Stable; 2, Christiana Stables; 3, Ellenberg & Kaster & O'Connor; 4, Cianciolo Margaret J; 5, Dor-Sea Stable; 6, Blue Goose Stbl & Hudson River Farm; 7, Malmstrom Ivar W & Ivar W Jr; 8, Fertile Acres Farm

Trainers—1, Kimmel John C; 2, Badgett William Jr; 3, Lukas D Wayne; 4, Sciacca Gary; 5, Moschera Gasper S; 6, Kelly Timothy D; 7, Destasio Richard A; 8, Sciacca Gary

Scratched— Apotheosis (14Nov95 3CD³), Barbican (7Oct95 2BEL⁶), Joe Jones (4Nov95 2AQU²), Air Supply, Allen's Rainbow (19Nov95 2AQU⁶), Dom McPeitz (11Nov95 2AQU⁷)

How should we have constructed our Pick Six ticket?

Real Silk in the third. Z Rated, Just A Little Kiss and Personal Girl in the fourth. Traveling Jeff, Whirling Blade, Sir Lovely, Get My Glitter and Save The Whale in the fifth. Sierra Grande, Turning Fifty and Devil's Cup in the sixth. Proudest Romeo in the seventh. Lottsa Talc in the eighth.

The cost was $90. (1 x 3 x 5 x 3 x 1 x 1 = 45 combinations.)

The Pick Six payoff with winners paying $3.20, $9.20, $9.20, $5.40, $7.10 and $5.10 was $4,737.

Now we all know that some of us — I don't want to use names — will not take Steve Crist's sound advice, and instead will play Pick Sixes when there isn't a carryover. Hey, we're only human, right?

Let's take a look at the Pick Six at Belmont, Friday, October 20, 1995. Only this time, we'll let you peruse the charts first, make your selections, construct your Pick Six tickets, and then we'll tell you whether or not you made a score.

But we will give you a clue. There was one vulnerable heavy favorite who crashed.

Here goes:

3 Belmont Park

6 Furlongs (1:074) MAIDEN SPECIAL WEIGHT. Purse $30,000 (plus up to $11,775 NYSBFOA). Fillies and mares, 3-year-olds and upward foaled in New York State and approved by the New York State-Bred Registry. Weights: 3-year-olds, 118 lbs. Older, 121 lbs.

Bob's Talc — Own: Juckiewicz Thomas E
B. f. 3 (May) Sire: Talc (Rock Talk) Dam: Diane's Kin (Kinsman Hope) Br: Gallagher Richard & Questroyal Farm (NY) Tr: Nieminski Richard (6 0 0 0 .00)
SANTAGATA N (55 2 5 7 .04)   L 118

| Lifetime Record: 13 M 1 1 $15,300 |
| 1995 9 M 0 1 $9,140 Turf 1 0 0 0 |
| 1994 4 M 1 0 $6,160 Wet 1 0 0 0 $900 |
| Bel 6 0 0 0 $4,500 Dist 10 0 1 1 $15,300 |

Diviso n'Belle — Own: Candow Robert A
Dk. b or br f. 3 (May) Sire: Cherokee Fellow (Funny Fellow) Dam: Stately Ms. (State Dinner) Br: Bolaro Farms (NY) Tr: Tesher Howard M (39 4 6 2 .10)
ALVARADO F T (123 15 18 15 .12)   L 118

| Lifetime Record: 3 M 0 1 $3,645 |
| 1995 3 M 0 1 $3,645 Turf 0 0 0 0 |
| 1994 0 M 0 0   Wet 1 0 0 1 $3,520 |
| Bel 2 0 0 1 $3,520 Dist 2 0 0 0 $125 |

Missy Mims
Own: Portier Patrick G
CHAVEZ C R (80 5 5 8 .06)
Dk. b or br f. 3 (May)
Sire: Love That Mac (Great Above)
Dam: Majestic Pleasure (What a Pleasure)
Br: Portier Patrick (NY)
Tr: Greco Emanuel J (5 1 0 0 .20)
L 1117
Lifetime Record: 9 M 2 2 $24,280
1995 9 M 2 2 $24,280 | Turf 0 0 0 0
1994 0 M 0 0 | Wet 1 0 0 0 $1,800
Bel 6 0 1 1 $13,300 | Dist 4 0 0 0 $3,480

20Sep95-5Bel fst 6f :223 :463 :591 1:12 3+ [F][S]Md Sp Wt 48 8 10 88½ 65 55 57 Smith M E 117 b 6.00 74-19 Tahila117½ Lyric Opera1212¾ Zesty1143 Brk slowly, five wide 11
24Aug95-2Sar fst 7f :223 :462 1:133 1:273 3+ [F][S]Md Sp Wt 40 5 6 11½ 14 2½ 36 Velasquez J 117 b 2.95 62-18 Miz Off The Cuff1174 Tahila1172 Missy Mims117¾ Rushed, weakened 8
11Aug95-1Sar fst 6½f :22 :453 1:122 1:20 3+ [F][S]Md Sp Wt 47 11 2 2½ 21 32½ 26 Velasquez J 117 b 6.90 69-18 JeffreySupreme1216 MissyMims117no HoneyWatrl1171 Dueled, held 2nd 12
16Jly95-1Bel fst 1116 :224 :454 1:12 1:452 3+ [F][S]Md Sp Wt 41 1 2 14 2hd 28 219 Velasquez J 113 b 10.40 53-22 ClypsoVuh11419 MissyMms1132 LghtBrghtHrt1151 Broke slowly, rushed 11
30Jun95-5Bel fst 6f :223 :463 :592 1:122 3+ [F][S]Md Sp Wt 42 4 7 54½ 57 56 514½ Migliore R 114 4.00 64-20 Crama1182½ Skaters Lustre1234 Honey Watral1144 Checked, green 10
14Jun95-3Bel sly 7f :224 :47 1:114 1:243 3+ [F][S]Md Sp Wt 32 3 11 2½ 11½ 28 422½ Migliore R 114 f 4.50 56-16 BellaRansom11317 LikeToShimmy1224 DominatedWay113¾ Dueled, tired 13
2Jun95-1Bel fst 6f :222 :464 1:00 1:134 3+ [F][S]Md Sp Wt 50 9 8 55½ 53½ 44 65¾ Beckner D V 113 f 16.70 66-25 Ireallyneededthis113¾ Pro Princess113½ IvanaMistress1131 Lacked rally 10
21May95-1Bel fst 7f :23 :464 1:121 1:252 3+ [F][S]Md Sp Wt 56 9 9 1hd 1½ 26 311 Beckner D V 113 f 4.30 63-22 Starlite Saphire1138 Toyaholic1083 Missy Mims1134½ Dueled, weakened 14
19Apr95-9Aqu fst 6f :222 :462 :583 1:111 3+ [F][S]Md Sp Wt 37 4 12 74¾ 45½ 39 415½ Samyn J L 114 24.25 70-13 Lucy Ellen1148 De Naskra's Dancer1147 Escarrgot114½ No late bid 14
WORKOUTS: Oct 9 Aqu 3f fst :383 B 6/6 Aug 2 Bel tr.t 4f fst :481 B 8/23

Distinctive Jeanne
Own: Timber Bay Farm
PEREZ R B (116 8 11 15 .07)
B. f. 3 (May)
Sire: Distinctive Pro (Mr. Prospector)
Dam: No Man (Majestic Prince)
Br: Timber Bay Farm (NY)
Tr: Entenmann William J (6 1 1 1 .17)
L 118
Lifetime Record: 3 M 0 1 $1,540
1995 3 M 0 1 $1,540 | Turf 1 0 0 0
1994 0 M 0 0 | Wet 0 0 0 0
Bel 1 0 0 0 | Dist 2 0 0 1 $1,540

7Oct95-9Pha fst 6f :221 :463 :592 1:123 3+ [F]Md Sp Wt 37 5 1 1½ 1½ 31 32½ Fiorentino C T 119 25.00 75-14 Ms. Melody1192½ Golden Key119hd Distinctive Jeanne119no Grudgingly 11
30Jun95-5Bel fst 6f :223 :463 :592 1:122 3+ [F][S]Md Sp Wt 26 9 10 74¾ 67 710 820¾ Martin G J5 109 6.80 58-20 Crama1182½ Skaters Lustre1234 Honey Watral1144 No rally 10
20May95-6Mgo fm *1½ [T] 2:233 3+ Alw 2500NC — 6 8 77 810 813 815 Chapman R 138 - — — Thunderstone1493 Summer Island1493 General Lark1496 Never a factor 10
WORKOUTS: Oct 4 Fai 3f fst :36 B 1/1 Sep 30 Fai 4f fst :501 B 1/3 Sep 24 Fai 3f fst :38 B 3/3 Sep 18 Fai 4f (W) fst :52 B 2/2

Rock The Media
Own: Peck Claudia
DECARLO C P (22 0 2 2 .00)
B. f. 3 (May)
Sire: Smart Style (Foolish Pleasure)
Dam: The Most Pleasure (What a Pleasure)
Br: Claudia S. Peck (NY)
Tr: Peck Claudia (—)
118
Lifetime Record: 0 M 0 0 $0
1995 0 M Q 0 | Turf 0 0 0 0
1994 0 M 0 0 | Wet 0 0 0 0
Bel 0 0 0 0 | Dist 0 0 0 0

WORKOUTS: Oct 10 Sar tr.t 3f fst :403 B 6/8 Sep 25 Sar tr.t 3f fst :39 B 3/5 Sep 12 Sar tr.t 3f fst :392 Bg4/4 Sep 9 Sar tr.t 5f fst 1:06 B 1/2 Sep 3 Sar tr.t 3f fst :384 B 1/3 Aug 28 Sar 4f fst :524 B 19/19
Aug 14 Sar 4f fst :522 Bg68/70 Aug 8 Sar 3f fst :372 B 13/16

Star Personality
Own: For J & D & Pond View Stable
NELSON D (52 5 5 7 .10)
B. f. 3 (May)
Sire: Star Gallant (My Gallant)
Dam: Peaxed (Personality)
Br: Pond View Farm (NY)
Tr: Nocella Vincent R (7 0 2 0 .00)
118
Lifetime Record: 4 M 3 0 $16,800
1995 3 M 2 0 $11,200 Turf 0 0 0 0
1994 1 M 1 0 $5,600 Wet 0 0 0 0
Bel 0 0 0 0 Dist 4 0 3 0 $16,800

19Mar95-9Aqu fst 6f :223 :463 :592 1:131 [F][S]Md Sp Wt 55 8 4 21½ 2½ 2½ 21½ Luzzi M J 120 *1.50 74-19 Facing Reality1201½ Star Personality1202½ Homah JSimon120½ Held place 11
4Mar95-1Aqu fst 6f [·] :234 :484 1:014 1:141 [F][S]Md Sp Wt — 1 6 — — — — Luzzi M J 121 *1.00 — 24 All Button1214 Saxifraga121nk Quaker Street121no Wheeled, lost rider 7
4Jan95-5Aqu fst 6f [·] :23 :473 1:004 1:134 [F][S]Md Sp Wt 59 12 1 3½ 1hd 1½ 23½ Carr D 121 *1.80 70-22 Patti's Purse1213½ Star Personality1219 Baroness B.1211¾ Second best 12
26Dec94-9Aqu fst 6f [·] :224 :47 1:00 1:133 [F][S]Md Sp Wt 55 7 4 43 41¾ 23 23 Carr D 117 10.10 72-21 GrenStrwbrry1173 StrPrsonlity117¾ RussinEnsign1172½ Circled, 2nd best 12
WORKOUTS: Oct 17 Aqu 3f fst :363 H 1/2 Oct 11 Aqu 5f fst 1:01 Hg2/5 Sep 29 Aqu 4f fst :48 H 2/17 Sep 9 Aqu 3f fst :382 B 8/8

Reelherin
Own: Valentine John
BELMONTE L A (30 1 1 3 .03)
B. m. 6
Sire: He's Bad (Rambunctious)
Dam: Alfa's Sunrise (Hoist the Silver)
Br: Valentine John (NY)
Tr: Ortiz Juan (8 1 0 0 .13)
L 1165
Lifetime Record: 18 M 5 3 $45,554
1995 7 M 2 1 $22,740 Turf 0 0 0 0
1994 7 M 3 2 $22,640 Wet 3 0 0 1 $5,040
Bel 5 0 0 1 $8,940 Dist 7 0 1 2 $11,320

18Sep95-3Bel my 1 :233 :473 1:13 1:39 3+ [F][S]Md Sp Wt 42 7 7 85½ 55½ 66½ 410½ Chavez C R7 L 114 b 7.70 57-23 FollowTheFlg1167 FigOfGold116½ DivisoN'belle1163 Four wide, no rally 12
9Jly95-3Bel fst 7f :23 :472 1:131 1:264 3+ [F][S]Md Sp Wt 32 7 4 63 62¾ 36 49½ Krone J A 122 b *1.15 57-18 TwentySixKrts1086½ DomintedWy1142½ FollowTheFlg114½ Flattened out 10
2Jun95-3Bel fst 6f :224 :47 1:00 1:132 3+ [F][S]Md Sp Wt 60 12 9 1014 99 46 34¼ Agosto R7 115 b 6.00 70-25 Subversive Dancer1133½ Honey Watral113¾ Reelherin1151½ Belated rally 12
14May95-2Bel fst 1116 :23 :461 1:131 1:473 3+ [F][S]Md Sp Wt 52 7 10 118¾ 52 32 47 Perez R B5 117 b 3.70 54-29 Forever Proud1126½ Hold You112no Stellina112½ Five wide, flattened 14
8Apr95-1Aqu fst 1 :234 :473 1:132 1:394 [F]Md Sp Wt 54 2 4 33 2hd 2½ 2¾ Martin G J7 114 b 4.10 69-22 PocketBeuty121¾ Reelherin1145¾ LerningTheRopes1211 Brief lead, game 8
18Mar95-9Aqu fst 1 :234 :482 1:153 1:43 [F]Md Sp Wt 47 4 4 52½ 42¼ 31 22 Martin G J7 114 b 3.60 52-31 Blind Truth1212 Reelherin1142 Be Reinvested121¾ Willingly 11
23Feb95-5Aqu fst 1⅛ [·] :494 1:15 1:42 1:554 [F]Md Sp Wt 49 6 3 2½ 2½ 32½ 44¾ Martin G J7 115 b *2.00 53-29 SesonsComernt1221¼ BlindTruth122no MissStrVrs1173 Forced pace, tired 10
30Dec94-9Aqu fst 1116 [·] :24 :492 1:162 1:511 3+ [F][S]Md Sp Wt 55 9 7 52¾ 1hd 11½ 21 Agosto R7 115 b 4.40 48-39 Ember's Girl1201 Reelherin1158 Taleum Flower1155½ Second best 12
3Dec94-1Aqu fst 6f :231 :474 1:004 1:133 3+ [F][S]Md Sp Wt 55 4 6 74½ 63½ 42 24 Agosto R7 115 b *1.20e 70-24 In Accordance1204 Reelherin1151½ Rumba Lession1201½ Finished well 9
22Apr94-9Aqu fst 1 :234 :481 1:142 1:401 3+ [F][S]Md Sp Wt 25 12 13 1312 129 1017 1018¾ Luttrell M G5 119 fb 8.80 48-27 Lois' Flag1157 Needles Last1156½ Lemon Chicken Lisa1151 Outrun 13
WORKOUTS: Oct 14 Aqu 4f fst :49 B 2/9 ●Oct 1 Aqu 4f fst :471 H 1/4 Sep 11 Aqu 6f fst 1:153 B 2/3 Sep 9 Aqu 3f fst :361 H 3/8

Knight Flight
Own: Moore Robert E & Robert J
AGOSTO R (6 0 0 1 .00)
Ch. f. 3 (Apr)
Sire: Slew the Knight (Seattle Slew)
Dam: Quickstar (To the Quick)
Br: Robert E. Moore (NY)
Tr: Shevy Michael J (3 0 0 0 .00)
1117
Lifetime Record: 0 M 0 0 $0
1995 0 M 0 0 | Turf 0 0 0 0
1994 0 M 0 0 | Wet 0 0 0 0
Bel 0 0 0 0 | Dist 0 0 0 0

WORKOUTS: Oct 17 Sar tr.t 4f fst :492 Bg1/7 Oct 10 Sar tr.t 4f fst :514 Bg6/8 Sep 28 Sar tr.t 3f fst :392 B 8/13 May 21 Bel 4f fst :54 B 113/113 May 17 Bel tr.t 4f fst :51 B 70/74 May 10 Bel 4f fst :494 Hg10/23
May 5 Bel tr.t 3f fst :39 B 8/10 Apr 29 Bel tr.t 3f fst :393 B 19/23

Marcy
Own: Tanrackin Farm
TREJO J (24 1 2 2 .04)
Ch. f. 3 (Mar)
Sire: Thin Slice (Damascus)
Dam: Cut the Wind (Shredder)
Br: Mrs. Thomas M. Waller (NY)
Tr: Freyer Donna J (4 0 0 0 .00)
1117
Lifetime Record: 0 M 0 0 $0
1995 0 M 0 0 | Turf 0 0 0 0
1994 0 M 0 0 | Wet 0 0 0 0
Bel 0 0 0 0 | Dist 0 0 0 0

WORKOUTS: Oct 10 Bel tr.t 3f fst :394 B 7/9 Oct 4 Bel 4f fst :482 Hg4/61 Sep 28 Bel tr.t 3f fst :374 B 10/14 Aug 18 Bel tr.t 4f fst :50 B 9/19 Aug 13 Bel tr.t 3f fst :37 B 8/12 Aug 8 Bel tr.t 3f fst :38 B 12/17
Jun 7 Bel 4f fst :50 Bg23/46 Jun 3 Bel 3f fst :38 Bg16/27

Great Beginnings
Own: Nolan Howard C Jr
MAPLE E (145 11 18 19 .08)

Ch. f. 3 (Mar)
Sire: Ends Well (Lyphard)
Dam: Alix de Bure (Lancastrian)
Br: Howard C. Nolan (NY)
Tr: Higgins W P (—)

L 118

Lifetime Record: 9 M 1 0 $7,570
1995 4 M 1 0 $6,240 | Turf 6 0 1 0 $7,330
1994 5 M 0 0 $1,330 | Wet 0 0 0 0
Bel 0 0 0 0 | Dist 1 0 0 0

14Jun95-6Bel gd 1 1/16 Ⓣ :233 :473 1:121 1:451 3+ Ⓕ[S]Md Sp Wt 54 7 6 52¾ 3½ 64¾ 77 Samyn J L 112 b 2.75 65-25 Lamplight114nk Watrals Finesse1142 DennieMae109hd Wide, flattened out 11
30Apr95-1Aqu fm 1⅛ Ⓣ :471 1:122 1:38 1:502 3+ Ⓕ[S]Md Sp Wt 70 2 4 34 32 24 26 Samyn J L 112 b *.80 82-09 Sweetzie1076 GretBginnings1124 WtrlsFinss1123 Bobb brk, check early 11
19Mar95-11Hia fm 1 1/16 Ⓣ 1:422 ⒻPatricia50k 66 2 6 68 68½ 59½ 613½ Maple E L 113 fb 93.30 73-12 MssUnonAvn1183 ShockngPlsr112nk AnothrLgnd1143 Failed to menace 8
16Jan95-5GP fst 1⅛ ⊗ :471 1:13 1:401 1:534 ⒻMd Sp Wt 10 3 11 1220 1125 1127 1040 Morales C E 120 142.10 28-23 Lil Merry Sunshine1201½ Head East1203 Just For Fun1204½ No threat 12
30Dec94-5Crc fm *1⅛ Ⓣ 1:542 ⒻMd Sp Wt 37 5 7 710 813 49½ 412¾ Morales C E 119 18.20 34-39 Remda119¾ Mistress Hawk1192 Rainy Day Woman11910 No threat 10
13Nov94-3CD fst 6f :212 :453 :583 1:124 ⒻMd Sp Wt 37 9 9 1112 1116 1117 1113 Morgan M R 121 36.80 69-15 [B]Miss Carson121hd Hip Hip Hur Rahy121hd Joop1213 Outrun 12
28Oct94-5Kee fst 6½f :222 :454 1:11 1:173 ⒻMd Sp Wt 24 7 11 1214 1017 814 721 Morgan M R L 118 25.20 67-16 Coffee Springs1182¾ Niner's Home1182 Francisco Road1188 12
Went to knees start, no factor
11Sep94-3Due fm *7f Ⓣ 1:234 ⒻBelle Starr50k 61 3 6 1010 98¾ 710 710 Thompson T J L 111 65.60 85-04 Blond Moment1133¾ Wild Linda111½ Pinpoint Control1201 No threat 11
4Sep94-4EIP fm 5½f Ⓣ :22 :46 :582 1:042 ⒻMd Sp Wt 47 9 12 1212 119½ 84½ 64¾ McKnight R E L 118 46.80 — — Beau Chapeau118no Silver Too118nk Dinababe1181 12
Bumped start, passed tired ones

WORKOUTS: Oct 2 Sar tr.t 4f fst :531 B 2/2 Sep 25 Sar tr.t 3f fst :384 B 2/5 Sep 9 Sar tr.t 4f fst :52 B 3/8 ●Sep 4 Sar 4f fst :511 B 1/5 Aug 24 Sar 4f fst :494 B 12/25 Aug 19 Sar 3f fst :37 B 11/22

Gray Dawn Pixie
Own: DeLuca & Lucas & Morrison
FEURTADO E E (2 0 0 0 .00)

Ro. f. 3 (Jun)
Sire: Highbinder (Rough'n Tumble)
Dam: Sharon Pixie (Vent du Nord)
Br: DeLuca Michael & Morrison Richard P (NY)
Tr: Streicher Kenneth (5 0 0 0 .00)

L 1135

Lifetime Record: 4 M 0 0 $0
1995 4 M 0 0 | Turf 1 0 0 0
1994 0 M 0 0 | Wet 1 0 0 0
Bel 3 0 0 0 | Dist 3 0 0 0

6Oct95-3Bel my 6f :231 :471 :593 1:121 3+ ⒻMd 30000 3 2 4 52½ 710 722 729¼ Santagata N L 115 fb 51.25 50-23 Rich Seam1186½ Fairfield Miss118¾ Bestofbothaccounts1182 No threat 8
8Sep95-3Bel fst 6f :224 :473 1:001 1:13 3+ Ⓕ[S]Md Sp Wt -0 1 1 21 2½ 1112 1122¾ Belmonte L A5 L 112 fb 45.50 53-17 FinnelSheets1171 ThrMilHrbor1173 StormyDwn1211¾ Forced pace, tired 12
30Jun95-5Bel fst 6f :223 :463 :592 1:122 3+ Ⓕ[S]Md Sp Wt -0 8 4 86¾ 910 920 941¾ Rydowski S R 114 b 76.75 37-20 Crama1182¼ Skaters Lustre1234 Honey Watral1144 Checked 1/2, green 10
8Jun95-5Bel fm 1 1/16 Ⓣ :233 :474 1:13 1:444 3+ Ⓕ[S]Md Sp Wt -0 9 9 97¾ 911 938 958 Persaud R10 102 61.25 — 17 Reel Talc1123¼ Hold You1127 Aspin Gal1222¼ Broke slowly 9

WORKOUTS: Oct 2 Aqu 5f fst 1:022 B 3/5 Sep 18 Aqu 3f sly :364 H 1/1 Sep 5 Aqu 3f fst :38 B 5/8 Aug 27 Aqu 5f fst 1:04 B 5/5 Aug 18 Bel tr.t 3f fst :371 B 5/13 Aug 15 Bel tr.t 5f fst 1:044 B 11/11

Zesty
Own: Edwards James F
PERSAUD R (12 1 1 2 .08)

Ch. f. 4
Sire: Exuberant (What a Pleasure)
Dam: Coz's Vigil (Coz's Ridge)
Br: Portier Patrick G (NY)
Tr: O'Brien Leo (60 6 9 7 .10)

L 11110

Lifetime Record: 7 M 0 1 $3,300
1995 6 M 0 1 $3,300 | Turf 0 0 0 0
1994 1 M 0 0 | Wet 3 0 0 0
Bel 4 0 0 1 $3,300 | Dist 4 0 0 1 $3,300

20Sep95-5Bel fst 6f :223 :463 :591 1:12 3+ Ⓕ[S]Md Sp Wt 58 4 7 76½ 54½ 33 33 Chavez C R7 L 114 34.50 78-19 Tahila117½ Lyric Opera1212½ Zesty1143 Rallied wide 11
11Aug95-3Sar fst 6½f :221 :462 1:124 1:193 3+ Ⓕ[S]Md Sp Wt 21 2 10 63½ 65 89½ 820 Cruguet J 121 27.25 57-18 Gabrielle Danielle117¾ Time For Another1217½ Tahila117nk No rally 12
1Jly95-1Bel sly 6f :224 :464 :584 1:112 3+ [S]Md Sp Wt 10 5 8 76 76¾ 612 625 Keim-Bruno P M10 108 35.50 59-14 New York Lights11412 Tri MyPatience1145½ Aspinwall1142½ Bobbled break 9
14Jun95-3Bel sly 7f :224 :47 1:114 1:243 3+ Ⓕ[S]Md Sp Wt -0 7 6 43 89½ 1327 1347 Martin G J5 117 20.20 31-16 Bella Ransom11317 Like To Shimmy1224 DominatedWay113¾ Brief speed 13
21May95-1Bel fst 7f :23 :464 1:121 1:252 3+ Ⓕ[S]Md Sp Wt 41 4 6 52½ 52½ 69½ 618 Velazquez J R 122 5.80 56-22 Starlite Saphire1138 Toyaholic1083 Missy Mims1134½ No rally 14
25Mar95-3Aqu fst 6f :224 :472 1:001 1:133 ⒻMd Sp Wt 33 2 11 77½ 78½ 811 613¾ Persaud R7 115 82.25 60-21 IFeelTheThunder1156 SrtogWethr1223½ Alytun1221¾ Checked break, wide 11
24Jly94-3Sar wf 6f :222 :462 :59 1:122 3+ Ⓕ[S]Md Sp Wt 24 9 8 93½ 113½ 118 1215¼ Richards G G 116 32.60 63-13 Lone Star Gale116nk Sara Paul1166 Z's Cover Girl1162½ Outrun 12

WORKOUTS: Oct 11 Aqu 4f fst :484 B 6/19 Sep 2 Bel 4f fst :49 B 21/47 Aug 8 Bel tr.t 7f fst 1:292 B 1/2 Aug 1 Bel tr.t 6f fst 1:13 H 1/1 Jly 24 Bel 5f fst 1:003 H 2/13

Time For Another
Own: Luckman Stanley M
SANTAGATA N (55 2 5 7 .04)

Ch. f. 4
Sire: Hay Halo (Halo)
Dam: Another Paddock (Darby Creek Road)
Br: Stanley Luckman (NY)
Tr: Streicher Kenneth (5 0 0 0 .00)

121

Lifetime Record: 8 M 2 0 $12,560
1995 5 M 2 0 $12,560 | Turf 1 0 0 0 $960
1994 3 M 0 0 | Wet 0 0 0 0
Bel 3 0 0 0 | Dist 4 0 1 0 $5,600

4Oct95-5Bel gd 1 1/16 [T] :232 :472 1:121 1:442 3+ ⒻMd Sp Wt 73 6 5 53½ 54 54½ 52¾ Santagata N 121 f 50.50 71-20 Theycallmecharlie117¾ Callas' Aria1172 [DH]Just Flirting117 Mild gain 10
20Sep95-5Bel fst 6f :223 :463 :591 1:12 3+ Ⓕ[S]Md Sp Wt 33 10 8 [illegible] 97½ 810 713 Luzzi M J 121 f *1.40 68-19 Tahila117½ Lyric Opera1212½ Zesty1143 Dull try 11
11Aug95-3Sar fst 6½f :221 :462 1:124 1:193 3+ Ⓕ[S]Md Sp Wt 64 11 2 31½ 3½ 1½ 2¾ Luzzi M J 121 f 7.40 76-18 Gabrielle Danielle117¾ Time For Another1217½ Tahila117nk Bid, game 12
27Jly95-5Sar fst 7f :224 :461 1:12 1:254 3+ Ⓕ[S]Md Sp Wt 44 11 4 85½ 76½ 74¾ 64¾ Luzzi M J 122 f 6.20 68-12 Lil Mis Gia117½ Lyric Opera122nk Skaters Lustre1223½ Evenly 14
12Mar95-5Aqu fst 6f [•] :231 :463 :591 1:122 ⒻMd Sp Wt 65 1 2 54½ 35½ 35 24 Luzzi M J 121 f 10.00 77-19 Compound Girl1144 Time For Another121hd MildAgain1218½ Gained place 7
9Sep94-9Bel fst 6f :23 :471 :593 1:12 3+ Ⓕ[S]Md Sp Wt 42 9 1 2½ 4½ 54 611 Lovato F Jr 118 b 7.80 70-18 Nanny Brow1182 Nicky's Amber1137½ High Tor118no Dueled, weakened 14
28Aug94-1Sar fst 7f :223 :454 1:11 1:24 3+ ⒻMd Sp Wt 54 2 7 54½ 51¾ 65½ 611½ Lovato F Jr 117 b 44.90 73-14 One Account1221 Faeula1173 Radiant Beams1224 Broke awkwardly 7
5May94-5Bel fst 6f :23 :464 :592 1:123 3+ Ⓕ[S]Md Sp Wt 36 8 8 63½ 63¾ 65 68¾ Lovato F Jr 115 54.10 70-18 Needles Last115no Miss Halo Country1152¾ Miss Diana A110¾ Four wide 9

WORKOUTS: ●Oct 18 Aqu 3f fst :363 B 1/5 Sep 13 Aqu 4f fst :523 B 4/4 Sep 6 Aqu 3f fst :38 B 2/5 Sep 1 Aqu 5f fst 1:021 B 3/8 Aug 22 Bel tr.t 4f fst :492 H 7/13 Aug 9 Bel tr.t 4f fst :513 B 18/22

Henry's Sunny Day
Own: Boeckmann Henry Jr
PERSAUD R (12 1 1 2 .08)

Ch. f. 3 (Apr)
Sire: Sir Wimborne (Sir Ivor)
Dam: Sunny Inspiration (Sunny North)
Br: Henry Boeckmann, Jr. (NY)
Tr: Koziarz Ted (4 0 0 0 .00)

10810

Lifetime Record: 1 M 0 0 $0
1995 1 M 0 0 | Turf 0 0 0 0
1994 0 M 0 0 | Wet 0 0 0 0
Bel 1 0 0 0 | Dist 1 0 0 0

8Sep95-3Bel fst 6f :224 :473 1:001 1:13 3+ Ⓕ[S]Md Sp Wt 7 12 10 1213 118¾ 1011 1018¼ Persaud R10 107 36.75 58-17 Flannel Sheets1171 Three Mile Harbor1173 Stormy Dawn1211¾ No speed 12

WORKOUTS: Oct 12 Aqu 4f fst :491 B 9/7 Sep 25 Aqu 4f fst :493 B 3/9 Sep 1 Aqu 5f fst 1:05 Bg 7/8 Aug 19 Bel tr.t 4f fst :52 B 25/28 Aug 12 Bel tr.t 3f fst :353 Hg 2/23 Aug 5 Bel tr.t 3f fst :38 B 10/19

Juniors Fortune
Own: Fuccille William B
PEREZ R B (116 8 11 15 .07)

B. f. 3 (Mar)
Sire: Imperial Falcon (Northern Dancer)
Dam: Greatly Shocked (Great Neck)
Br: Deiner-Ferguson (NY)
Tr: Hebert William (2 0 0 0 .00)

L 118

Lifetime Record: 2 M 0 0 $0
1995 1 M 0 0 | Turf 0 0 0 0
1994 1 M 0 0 | Wet 1 0 0 0
Bel 0 0 0 0 | Dist 0 0 0 0

5Aug95-10Sar wf 1 1/16 ⊗ :501 1:154 1:414 2:012 3+ Ⓕ[S]Md Sp Wt 15 4 4 63½ 78 1017 1032¾ Perez R B 115 47.75 30-25 Mon Drapeau1151¼ Follow The Flag1152½ Call To Prayer1153 Faded 11
24Nov94-3Aqu fst 7f :233 :472 1:132 1:27 Ⓕ[S]Md Sp Wt 18 6 7 812 819 820 727 Rodriguez O5 112 85.50 42-24 Foxy Scarlet1177 Sammycat1126½ Mon Drapeau1123 No menace 9

WORKOUTS: Oct 11 Sar Ⓣ 5f sf 1:043 B (d) 2/5 Sep 29 Sar tr.t 4f fst :514 B 5/7 Sep 18 Sar tr.t 4f gd :512 B 1/2 Sep 6 Sar Ⓣ 4f fm :492 H (d) 2/7 Aug 29 Sar 5f fst 1:044 B 7/7 Aug 22 Sar 4f fst :50 B 14/22

Accuracy
Own: Pomerantz Lawrence J
SMITH M E (204 36 24 31 .18)
B. f. 3 (Jan)
Sire: Duns Scotus (Buckpasser)
Dam: Affirming (Affirmed)
Br: Harbor View Farm (NY)
Tr: Barbara Robert (48 5 4 3 .10)
L 118
Lifetime Record: 4 M 0 0 $2,195
1995 4 M 0 0 $2,195 | Turf 0 0 0 0
1994 0 M 0 0 | Wet 1 0 0 0 $1,050
Bel 2 0 0 0 $1,470 | Dist 3 0 0 0 $2,070

6Oct95-3Bel my 6f :231 :471 :593 1:121 3+ ⒻMd 35000 54 5 7 74¾ 54 56 49¼ Smith M E L 118 b 5.20 71-23 RichSeam1186½ FirfieldMiss118¾ Bestofbothccounts1182 Pinched break 8
25Sep95-1Bel fst 6f :222 :453 :584 1:113 3+ ⒻMd 35000 47 8 3 2½ 31 55¼ 59¼ Smith M E L 117 b *3.05 73-12 Finely Decorated1175 Five To Won1181¼ Star Of Alexis1141¾ Dueled, tired 12
1Mar95-3GP fst 6½f :221 :454 1:122 1:194 ⒻMd c-32000 45 11 1 52½ 43¼ 57¼ 66 Samyn J L 120 b 6.60 70-18 CarsonKitty120½ Henbne'sGirl120hd ArcticPtience1203¼ Lacked response 11
Claimed from Voto Robert A, Pascucci Ambrose Trainer
9Feb95-6GP fst 6f :224 :464 :593 1:132 ⒻMd 32000 52 1 6 2½ 31½ 23¼ 44¼ Prosper G 120 b 7.10 68-22 Book Of Fortune1184¼ Mystery Of Love118no Little Doll118no Weakened 11
WORKOUTS: Sep 20 Bel 5f fst 1:022 Hg 33/57 Sep 7 Bel tr.t 4f fst :492 B 10/24 Aug 31 Bel 4f fst :502 B 40/54 Aug 17 Sar 4f fst :52 H 22/25 Aug 11 Sar 4f fst :513 H 23/24 Aug 5 Sar tr.t 3f fst :40 B 14/17

Come Like the Wind
Own: Amriati John J
SAMYN J L (89 9 10 14 .10)
B. f. 3 (Jun)
Sire: Compliance (Northern Dancer)
Dam: Windy Surf (In Reality)
Br: John J. Amriati (NY)
Tr: Ferraro James W (10 0 0 0 .00)
L 118
Lifetime Record: 2 M 0 0 $0
1995 2 M 0 0 | Turf 0 0 0 0
1994 0 M 0 0 | Wet 1 0 0 0
Bel 2 0 0 0 | Dist 1 0 0 0

5Oct95-1Bel sly 7f :222 :463 1:131 1:27 3+ ⒻⓈMd Sp Wt –0 6 1 2hd 53½ 814 833¼ Samyn J L L 118 fb 13.80 32-18 Only Forever1188 Easy Virtue1181½ Lucy Brown1214 Used up 10
15Sep95-4Bel fst 6f :222 :453 :572 1:094 3+ Md Sp Wt 43 6 7 710 714 717 622½ Samyn J L 114 f 104.25 70-14 Danjur1178 Musical Connection1173 Court Jester1171 No threat 8
WORKOUTS: Sep 2 Aqu 3f fst :38 Bg 4/4 Aug 15 Bel tr.t 3f fst :384 B 9/11 Aug 11 Bel tr.t 5f fst 1:061 B 7/7 Aug 5 Bel tr.t 4f fst :492 B 8/19 Jly 30 Bel 4f fst :504 B 41/46

Sunsational Girl
Own: Schwartz Herbert
NELSON D (52 5 5 7 .10)
Ch. f. 3 (Feb)
Sire: Sunny's Halo (Halo)
Dam: Jimmy's Girl (Proudest Roman)
Br: Arlene Schwartz (NY)
Tr: Schwartz Scott M (7 2 1 2 .29)
L 118
Lifetime Record: 4 M 0 0 $0
1995 4 M 0 0 | Turf 0 0 0 0
1994 0 M 0 0 | Wet 0 0 0 0
Bel 2 0 0 0 | Dist 2 0 0 0

20Sep95-5Bel fst 6f :223 :463 :591 1:12 3+ ⒻⓈMd Sp Wt 37 9 4 55½ 75 78¼ 611¼ Santagata N L 117 104.00 69-19 Tahila117½ Lyric Opera1212½ Zesty1143 No rally 11
11Aug95-1Sar fst 6½f :22 :453 1:122 1:20 3+ ⒻⓈMd Sp Wt 4 4 6 87½ 1013 1013 1025¼ Samyn J L 117 60.25 50-18 Jeffrey Supreme1216 Missy Mims117no Honey Watral1171 No factor 12
16Jly95-1Bel fst 1 1/16 :224 :454 1:12 1:452 3+ ⒻⓈMd Sp Wt — 11 1 24 1017 1038 — Martinez J R Jr 113 b 34.25 — 22 Calypso Vuh11419 Missy Mims1132 LightBrightHeart1151 Used up, eased 11
15Jan95-5Aqu fst 6f ⊡ :23 :471 1:001 1:134 ⒻⓈMd Sp Wt –0 6 6 64¾ 78 918 1022¾ Martin G J7 114 fb 13.20 51-19 June's Scout116½ Where Is It1212½ Escarrgot1211 Tired 11
WORKOUTS: Oct 3 Aqu 3f fst :36 B 3/13 Sep 9 Aqu 4f fst :492 B 4/7 Aug 28 Sar tr.t Ⓣ 5f fm 1:02 H 6/7 Aug 21 Sar tr.t Ⓣ 5f fm 1:012 B 8/15 Aug 8 Sar 4f fst :482 H 7/33 Aug 3 Sar 4f fst :492 B 19/40

Lucy Brown
Own: Goldstein Morton
LOVATO F JR (28 2 9 4 .07)
Ch. f. 4
Sire: Star Gallant (My Gallant)
Dam: Kinda Corny (Herb Water)
Br: Indigo Farm Inc (NY)
Tr: Goldstein Morton (6 0 0 1 .00)
121
Lifetime Record: 14 M 0 2 $10,520
1995 14 M 0 2 $10,520 | Turf 1 0 0 0
1994 0 M 0 0 | Wet 2 0 0 1 $3,750
Bel 6 0 0 1 $5,550 | Dist 8 0 0 1 $4,520

5Oct95-1Bel sly 7f :222 :463 1:131 1:27 3+ ⒻⓈMd Sp Wt 43 1 6 99¾ 64¼ 54¼ 39¼ Lovato F Jr 121 b 16.40 56-18 Only Forever1188 Easy Virtue1181½ Lucy Brown1214 Steady gain 10
8Sep95-3Bel fst 6f :224 :473 1:001 1:13 3+ ⒻⓈMd Sp Wt 38 2 11 86 73¼ 54¼ 45¾ Lovato F Jr 121 b 14.90 70-17 FinnelShets1171 TnrMilHrbor1173 StormyDwn1211¾ Brk slow, check 3/16 12
24Aug95-2Sar fst 7f :223 :462 1:133 1:273 3+ ⒻⓈMd Sp Wt 38 4 5 55 47 47 45¾ Lovato F Jr 121 b 5.90 61-18 Miz Off The Cuff1174 Tahila1172 MissyMims117¾ Saved ground, no rally 8
27Jly95-5Sar fst 7f :224 :461 1:12 1:254 3+ ⒻⓈMd Sp Wt 52 13 2 72¾ 54 44 55 Lovato F Jr 122 b 19.70f 72-12 Lil Mis Gia117½ Lyric Opera122nk Skaters Lustre1223¼ No late bid 14
7Jly95-5Bel fm 1 1/16 Ⓣ :241 :472 1:11 1:441 3+ ⒻⓈMd Sp Wt 11 6 2 55¼ 913 1028 1029¾ Graell A 122 b 68.00 45-22 Follow Joanne1222 Call To Prayer113nk Mapleline1131¾ Brief speed 10
28Jun95-5Bel fst 6f :222 :464 1:00 1:131 3+ ⒻⓈMd Sp Wt 34 5 6 1310 117¾ 1010 816 Graell A 123 62.25 58-22 Kacie's Favor1146 Angel Kate1143 Lil Mis Gia114¾ No threat 13
1Jun95-4Bel fst 1 :232 :471 1:134 1:42 3+ ⒻⓈMd Sp Wt 16 8 6 66 78¾ 713 721 Heredia J J 122 b 68.75 32-39 Peacock Plume112hd Calypso Vuh1127 Lyric Opera122¾ Lost whip 1/4 pl 9
21May95-1Bel fst 7f :23 :464 1:121 1:252 3+ ⒻⓈMd Sp Wt 31 1 14 137 119¼ 1014 1023 Ouellette S F10 112 b 20.50 51-22 Starlite Saphire1128 Toyaholic1083 Missy Mims1134¾ Broke slowly 14
10May95-3Bel wf 6f :223 :462 :582 1:124 3+ ⒻMd 40000 40 4 6 64 52 53¼ 55¼ Agosto R7 116 b 14.00 71-14 Charmless113nk Calais114¾ Houston Elegance114nk Evenly 11
28Apr95-9Aqu fst 6f :222 :463 :594 1:133 3+ ⒻⓈMd Sp Wt 37 7 5 65 64 65¾ 66¾ Agosto R7 115 b 35.00 67-18 De Naskra's Dancer1131¾ Go Go Gerver113no Bob's Talc1133¼ Evenly 12
WORKOUTS: Sep 30 Aqu 4f fst :53 B 5/5 Sep 5 Aqu 3f fst :37 B 3/8 Aug 12 Bel tr.t 3f fst :363 H 4/23

Sneezin Season
Own: Jackson Roy
CHAVEZ C R (80 5 5 8 .06)
B. f. 3 (Mar)
Sire: Cormorant (His Majesty)
Dam: Blossom Time (Flip Sal)
Br: M. Roy Jackson & Gretchen S. Jackson (NY)
Tr: Hertler John O (30 1 3 5 .03)
L 1117
Lifetime Record: 2 M 0 0 $0
1995 1 M 0 0 | Turf 0 0 0 0
1994 1 M 0 0 | Wet 2 0 0 0
Bel 1 0 0 0 | Dist 1 0 0 0

5Oct95-1Bel sly 7f :222 :463 1:131 1:27 3+ ⒻⓈMd Sp Wt –0 2 10 77¾ 98¼ 814 937 Nelson D L 118 b 11.70 29-18 OnlyForever1188 EsyVirtue1181½ LucyBrown1214 Checked, broke slowly 10
21Oct94-3Aqu wf 6f :231 :48 1:003 1:133 ⒻⓈMd Sp Wt 4 5 7 79 75 711 718¼ Luzzi M J 117 *2.25 56-18 Princess Sunny117nk Where Is It1173¼ Hold You1172¼ Dwelt 7
WORKOUTS: Oct 16 Bel tr.t 4f fst :49 B 2/20 Sep 29 Bel 5f fst 1:02 H 16/33 Sep 22 Bel 5f fst 1:013 H 8/23 Sep 11 Bel 4f fst :494 Bg 29/44 Sep 7 Bel tr.t 4f fst :501 B 15/24 Sep 2 Bel tr.t 3f fst :383 B 11/15

4 Belmont Park

6 Furlongs **(1:074) CLAIMING. Purse $24,000 (plus up to $9,420 NYSBFOA). 3-year-olds and upward. Weights: 3-year-olds, 119 lbs. Older, 122 lbs. Non-winners of two races since September 14, allowed 2 lbs. Of two races since September 2, 4 lbs. Of a race since then, 6 lbs. Claiming price $35,000, if for $30,000, allowed 3 lbs. (Races where entered for $25,000 or less not considered.)**

Coupled - Giant Leap, Miron's Gentleman and Carr Heaven; Farmonthefreeway and Limited War; Direct Satellite and Arz

Giant Leap
Own: Joques Farm
SANTOS J A (168 28 18 28 .17) $30,000
Dk. b or br g. 7
Sire: Conquistador Cielo (Mr. Prospector)
Dam: Leap of the Heart (Nijinsky II)
Br: Mellon Paul (Va)
Tr: Moschera Gasper S (61 14 7 11 .23)
L 113
Lifetime Record: 57 9 11 12 $187,685
1995 12 2 3 2 $46,100 | Turf 1 0 0 0
1994 16 2 4 2 $45,570 | Wet 13 2 4 4 $46,530
Bel 15 0 3 5 $33,600 | Dist 13 1 2 2 $25,150

23Sep95-2Bel my 1 1/16 :23 :464 1:111 1:42 3+ Clm 30000 43 3 4 57½ 78¼ 718 726¼ Davis R G L 116 fb 3.90 62-17 Klondike Clem1091½ Baypark1141½ A Call To Rise116¾ Done early 7
13Aug95-5Sar my 7f :223 :461 1:104 1:232 3+ Clm 35000 82 7 1 56 64 64¼ 37¾ Smith M E 113 fb 2.50 81-17 Carr Heaven1121¾ Concoctor1126 Giant Leap113¼ Improved position 8
3Aug95-5Sar fst 7f :213 :443 1:103 1:244 3+ Clm c-25000 86 8 7 65½ 53 2½ 11 Davis R G 112 fb *2.80 82-12 GiantLeap1121 ChngeOfFortune112½ NowhereMn1121 Four wide, game 12
Claimed from Jakubovitz Jerome R, Myer Pat Trainer
18Jly95-8Mth fst 1 1/16 :224 :461 1:11 1:45 3+ Clm 30000 73 1 3 34 24 34 34¼ Santagata N L 115 fb 3.70 75-21 Dynamic Brush1151¾ Halo Of Merit1152¾ Giant Leap1151¾ Saved ground 6
28Jun95-6Bel fst 7f :224 :461 1:112 1:242 Clm 30000 88 3 1 22¼ 21½ 2½ 22 Davis R G 112 fb *1.90 77-22 Baypark1122 Giant Leap1126¼ Wissie's Wish114nk Bid, clear 2nd 7
11Jun95-1Bel fst 7f :222 :453 1:112 1:244 Clm 25000 88 10 1 53¼ 44 22 22 Davis R G 116 fb 12.20 79-26 Heavenwood1162 Giant Leap1163 Inside Connection1163 Bid, no match 10
18May95-9Bel gd 7f :224 :46 1:11 1:241 Clm c-20000 65 6 2 31 43 85 89¼ Chavez J F 116 fb *2.05 71-16 Baypark116nk Le Risky1121½ Fire Devil116½ Used up 9
Claimed from Hagedorn Charles C & Rottkamp John, Odintz Jeff Trainer
10Apr95-7Aqu fst 6½f :222 :45 1:09 1:151 Alw 32000N2X 85 1 4 43½ 43 55 58¾ Chavez J F 114 fb 6.20 95-12 West Quest1192 Scherbo1191¾ Lake Ali1143 Stumbled break 5
26Mar95-4Aqu fst 7f :233 :464 1:114 1:241 Alw 32000N2X 89 4 2 31 42 2½ 2no Chavez J F 114 b 3.15 83-17 Here's Noah119no Giant Leap1141 Heavenwood1102 Four wide, gamely 5
16Mar95-8Aqu fst 1 :224 :454 1:111 1:373 Clm 30000 85 7 4 43 4¾ 1½ 1nk Chavez J F 116 fb 3.70 81-24 Giant Leap116nk A Call To Rise116½ Hot Slew1162 Wide, all out 8
WORKOUTS: Oct 10 Bel 4f fst :474 H 3/46 Oct 4 Bel 4f fst :512 B 58/61 Sep 16 Bel tr.t 4f fst :51 B 20/25

Miron's Gentleman

Own: Davis Barbara J
BAILEY J D (283 47 27 22 .23) $35,000
Ch. g. 4
Sire: Cutlass (Damascus)
Dam: Misstew (Crozier)
Br: Oaks Horse Farm Corp (Fla)
Tr: Moschera Gasper S (61 14 7 11 .23)
L 116

Lifetime Record: 27 6 8 2 $65,175										
1995	8	1	1	1	$20,130	Turf	0	0	0	0
1994	16	4	6	1	$39,595	Wet	3	2	0	0 $15,960
Bel	2	0	0	1	$3,190	Dist	11	3	5	1 $26,350

1Jun95- 7Bel fst 6½f :221 :452 1:111 1:18 Clm c-50000 75 6 7 42½ 54 74¾ 69¼ Velazquez J R 116 b 5.40 76-17 JerichoBlaise111no Gallapiat'sMoment1161¾ Expressed116hd No rally, wide 7
Claimed from Sommer Viola, Martin Frank Trainer
21May95- 6Bel fst 6f :221 :453 :581 1:111 Clm 45000 90 1 6 21½ 32½ 41½ 31½ Velazquez J R 112 b 27.00 83-22 Gllpit'sMoment114nk Expressed1161½ Miron'sGentlmn1121½ Saved ground 7
27Apr95- 6Aqu fst 7f :231 :454 1:11 1:24 Clm 35000 87 6 2 1hd 1½ 11½ 1no Velazquez J R 116 b 9.00 84-18 Miron's Gentleman116no Grey Chandon116hd Fabersham113¾ All out 6
6Apr95- 6Aqu fst 6½f :222 :452 1:10 1:162 Clm 37500 78 4 6 65 65½ 57 48½ Davis R G 114 b 7.70 89-08 Fabersham1111½ Gallapit'sMoment1123 MediclPro1164 Broke awkwardly 6
16Mar95- 4GP fst 7f :22 :443 1:093 1:231 Clm c-22500 78 7 7 43½ 38½ 56 56¾ Suckie M C L 115 b 6.80 80-14 Ocala Flame1192 John Willy117no Baron Mathew1173 9
Six wide top str, faded Claimed from Markel G, Hurtak Daniel C Trainer
4Mar95- 7GP fst 7f :223 :454 1:104 1:233 Clm 22500 88 4 10 52½ 75½ 34½ 24 Suckie M C L 115 b 28.30 81-14 Lake Ali1174 Miron's Gentleman115½ Hudson Bay1173¾ Rallied 12
5Feb95- 4GP fst 6f :214 :452 :582 1:112 Clm 25000 76 11 1 1015 119½ 108½ 77 Castillo H Jr L 117 b 20.90 76-16 Bet 'n Cash1172 Valid Blues117hd Sammy From Miami1151½ No threat 11
14Jan95- 6GP sly 7f :222 :453 1:104 1:241 Clm 30000 80 6 6 52¾ 85½ 96¾ 94 Castillo H Jr L 117 b 9.80 78-19 Hammermill117nk Thru The Roof117hd John Willy117¾ Gave way 11
31Dec94- 3Crc fst 6f :211 :443 :572 1:11 Clm 25000 70 7 2 67½ 310 311 212½ Santos J A L 119 b *1.30 80-15 Turf Star11712 Miron'sGentleman1193½ EliteExchange117nk Best of others 7
20Dec94- 9Crc fst 7f :224 :46 1:112 1:25 3↑ Alw 18200N2X 78 6 2 51½ 42½ 35½ 45½ Douglas R R L 121 b 13.30 81-21 Ultimate Don118no Pro Brite1195 Makeitsmooth118¾ Weakened 8

WORKOUTS: Oct 13 Bel 5f fst 1:014 H 14/30 Oct 2 Bel tr.t 4f fst :512 B 21/23 Sep 25 Bel tr.t 4f fst :514 B 23/26

Carr Heaven

Own: Joques Farm
ALVARADO F T (123 15 18 15 .12) $35,000
B. h. 5
Sire: Carr de Naskra (Star de Naskra)
Dam: Heaven Knows (Quadrangle)
Br: Payson Virginia Kraft (NY)
Tr: Moschera Gasper S (61 14 7 11 .23)
L 116

Lifetime Record: 28 8 6 5 $150,118										
1995	8	1	1	3	$30,436	Turf	0	0	0	0
1994	11	3	3	2	$37,592	Wet	6	3	1	1 $76,246
Bel	4	1	1	0	$20,650	Dist	20	4	4	5 $103,628

8Oct95- 5Bel fst 7f :22 :452 1:103 1:24 3↑ Clm 40000 82 8 5 610 54 33½ 25½ Luzzi M J L 116 b 2.85 76-17 Country Sky1145½ Carr Heaven116nk Imaging1162½ Rallied five wide 8
1Sep95- 8Bel fst 7f :23 :454 1:09 1:211 3↑ [S]GenDMacArthH55k 66 2 8 52½ 52 911 916 Martinez J R Jr 111 b 23.80 79-08 CormRy1204 RichmondRunner118nk FortEdwrd1141 Saved ground, tired 9
24Aug95- 3Sar fst 6f :222 :461 :582 1:11 3↑ Clm 50000 92 1 7 78½ 74¾ 43 31½ Chavez J F 113 b *1.05e 85-18 Expressed114hd Nicks Court1131½ Carr Heaven1132 Steadied, bumped brk 7
13Aug95- 5Sar my 7f :223 :461 1:104 1:232 3↑ Clm c-35000 99 6 5 43 41 12½ 11¾ Chavez J F 112 fb 6.10 89-17 Carr Heaven1121¾ Concoctor1126 Giant Leap113½ Four wide, game 8
Claimed from Bond H James & Payson Virgina Kraft, Bond Harold James Trainer
4Aug95- 5Sar my 6f :212 :444 :571 1:104 3↑ Clm 35000 86 4 7 66½ 77½ 55 63 Chavez J F 112 fb 2.95 84-13 Nicks Court112no Love Jazz112hd Unreal Mot1131 No threat 8
22Jly95- 8FL fst 6f :221 :45 :571 1:101 3↑ [S]WineCountryH30k 79 7 6 63½ 36 48 44½ Dominguez C V 115 fb 3.55 88-18 Chrioteer'sWnd1212½ Who'sGonnBRite1152 Lordofthmountin117hd Hung 7
11Jun95- 9FL fst 6f :214 :452 :581 1:12 3↑ [S]Handicap15k 87 3 5 66¾ 56½ 44½ 3¾ Dominguez C V 115 fb 1.95 83-24 Royal Ben116nk Who's Gonna BRite114½ CarrHeaven1151¾ Stumbled start 6
29Mar95- 9FL fst 6f :213 :444 :573 1:113 3↑ [S]GeorgeBarker30k 82 6 5 55 54¾ 45½ 33½ Dominguez C V 113 b 3.95 82-22 Royal Ben1132¾ Top End115¾ Carr Heaven113¾ Rallied 5 wide 8
5Dec94-12FL sly 6f :214 :442 :573 1:11 3↑ [S]Handicap15k 73 7 5 56 56 55½ 35 Dominguez C V 117 fb 3.85 86-18 Noble Sweetheart1141 Spent Shell1154 Carr Heaven1172½ 6 wide turn 7
6Nov94- 8FL fst 6f :211 :432 :57 1:103 3↑ Handicap10k 83 5 4 49 48 36½ 41½ Dominguez C V 118 fb 3.70 92-15 Royal Ben115½ Tea In My Eye112no Dacha113¾ Rallied rail 6

WORKOUTS: Sep 16 Bel 4f fst :481 H 2/52

Farmonthefreeway

Own: Hagedorn Charles G
DAVIS R G (243 37 42 30 .15) $35,000
B. g. 5
Sire: Talc (Rock Talk)
Dam: Screened (Alydar)
Br: Werblin David (NY)
Tr: Barbara Robert (48 5 4 3 .10)
L 116

Lifetime Record: 45 11 4 13 $449,075										
1995	16	5	1	3	$134,580	Turf	3	0	0	0 $4,560
1994	9	1	0	3	$41,526	Wet	6	1	1	4 $103,794
Bel	12	2	3	2	$97,165	Dist	21	6	1	7 $250,314

29Sep95- 5Bel fst 6f :224 :462 :581 1:103 3↑ Clm 45000 88 10 9 52½ 41 84½ 63½ Santagata N L 114 fb 4.80 84-20 Turn Now114hd Rum'n Cope114¾ Carsey's Pal116nk Four wide, tired 10
23Jly95- 4Sar fst 6½f :22 :443 1:092 1:16 3↑ Alw 38000N$Y 87 1 4 1½ 3½ 51¼ 47 Luzzi M J 122 b 5.80 88-11 Golden Tent122½ Bermuda Cedar1164 Barodet1132½ Dueled inside 6
12Jly95- 4Bel fst 7f :222 :444 1:092 1:223 Clm c-50000 97 1 5 2½ 31 11 11 Velasquez J 116 b *.55 88-14 Frmonthfrwy1161 Tnchttln1205 CncrdsPrspct120hd Saved ground, game 8
Claimed from R Kay Stable, Araya Rene A Trainer
29Jun95- 7Bel fst 7f :223 :45 1:103 1:24 Clm 70000 95 5 3 1½ 13 12 21¼ Velasquez J 113 fb 11.20 80-22 Golden Tent1161¼ Farmonthefreeway1132½ Late Guest112hd Held place 6
17Jun95- 6Bel fst 1 :231 :454 1:111 1:372 Alw 48000N$mY 85 5 3 32 31 42 57 Chavez J F 119 b 12.70 69-22 Richmond Runner1191½ Cantua Creek1161½ Aztec Empire1162 No rally 5
27May95- 9Bel fst 6f :22 :444 :57 1:093 3↑ Roseben H-G3 86 2 4 43 41½ 53½ 57½ Chavez J F 110 fb 20.40 85-09 Evil Bear1162 Rizzi117½ Vallata Lane1092½ Four wide, tired 5
17May95- 7Bel fst 6½f :23 :46 1:10 1:162 Alw 44000N$Y 76 2 5 32½ 2½ 56 511¼ Chavez J F 119 fb 3.60 82-13 Cantua Creek113¾ Virginia Rapids1221½ Boom Towner1198 Tired 6
22Apr95- 7Aqu fst 1 :233 :461 1:11 1:364 Alw 46000N$mY 98 1 3 1hd 1hd 12 1½ Chavez J F 119 fb *1.80 85-21 Farmonthefreewy119½ DibbsN'Dubbs1142 StormyJv117nk Fully extended 6
15Apr95- 8Aqu fst 1 :224 :452 1:10 1:352 Alw 46000N$Y 93 5 4 42 31 32½ 36 Chavez J F 116 fb 4.40 86-10 KyContndr112hd SlickHorn1166 Frmonthfrwy116nk Three wide, flattened 8
7Apr95- 3Aqu fst 1 :234 :471 1:121 1:363 Clm c-50000 98 4 2 22 1hd 12 14¾ Migliore R 116 fb *1.45 86-28 Frmonthefreewy1164¾ Vilmorin115nk CountrySky1123 Stalked, drew clear 5
Claimed from Pitino Rick & Zablowitz Karen S, Parisella John Trainer

WORKOUTS: Sep 28 Aqu 5f fst 1:021 B 6/13 Aug 31 Aqu 4f fst :483 B 4/17 Aug 13 Bel tr.t 4f fst :50 B 7/20

Direct Satellite

Own: Tam Ping W
VELAZQUEZ J R (214 32 23 28 .15) $35,000
Ch. c. 4
Sire: Mining (Mr. Prospector)
Dam: Balakhna (Tyrant)
Br: Hettinger John (NY)
Tr: Lake Robert P (28 3 6 7 .11)
L 116

Lifetime Record: 15 3 1 2 $74,210										
1995	6	0	1	1	$11,100	Turf	1	0	0	0 $1,750
1994	6	1	0	1	$31,360	Wet	3	0	0	1 $3,040
Bel	4	1	1	1	$23,340	Dist	9	1	1	2 $35,960

5Oct95- 9Bel sly 6f :22 :442 :562 1:084 3↑ Clm 25000 75 3 4 55 25 28 314½ Maple E L 116 4.00 82-18 Unreal Mot11613 Ocean Splash1161½ Direct Satellite116nk Weakened 8
29Sep95- 5Bel fst 6f :224 :462 :581 1:103 3↑ Clm 45000 77 8 10 74¾ 73 95¾ 98 Maple E L 114 5.00 80-20 Turn Now114hd Rum'n Cope114¾ Carsey's Pal116nk Checked break, wide 10
7Sep95- 4Bel fst 6f :22 :451 :571 1:092 3↑ Clm 50000 99 4 3 33½ 21½ 2hd 2½ Maple E L 113 10.20 93-13 One Big Hug117½ Direct Satellite1133 Tenochtitlan1138 Game effort 5
23Aug95- 4Sar fst 7f :224 :46 1:111 1:234 3↑ Clm c-35000 64 3 6 21½ 21 76¾ 814½ Luzzi M J 113 3.80 73-15 Concoctor113hd Ocean Splash113½ Taddarruj113hd Used up 9
Claimed from Tatta Anne, Nesky Kenneth A Trainer
5Aug95- 5Sar wf 6f :223 :46 :58 1:103 3↑ Clm 50000 85 6 6 41½ 3½ 31½ 53½ Santos J A 112 10.40 85-13 ColdExecution1121 TenochtitIn1121½ Expressed114½ Wide, flattened out 7
12Jan95- 6Aqu fst 6f [•] :222 :452 :581 1:104 Alw 34000N3X 89 2 6 33 33 42 55½ Pezua J M 119 5.20 84-20 Blum Gone117nk Justfortherecord1174 Mr Miner110no Lacked rally 8
30Dec94- 8Aqu fst 6f [•] :233 :474 :594 1:122 3↑ Alw 34000N3X 91 4 4 2hd 2hd 22½ 33¾ Pezua J M 117 10.10 77-24 Crafty1192½ Sonny's Bruno1151½ Direct Satellite1177 Finished evenly 7
14Dec94- 9Aqu fst 6f [•] :223 :461 :582 1:113 3↑ [S]Alw 32000N2X 86 8 1 2½ 2hd 11 1¾ Maple E 115 3.25 85-21 Direct Satellite115¾ Green Gaitor117nk Gulliviegold1151¾ Driving 9
23Nov94- 6Aqu fst 6f :221 :461 :582 1:104 3↑ Alw 32000N2x 85 5 3 3½ 3½ 44½ 48½ Beckner D V5 110 7.70 79-21 Thru'nThru115½ CatchinAir1157 BullIntheHether1171 Forced pace, tired 7
16Apr94- 8Aqu sly 6f :213 :441 :562 1:091 Best Turn-G3 59 6 6 31 76½ 710 616¾ Luzzi M J 115 f 8.50 79-09 Rizzi1175 Mr. Shawklit1172½ Memories Of Linda1151 Returned sore 7

WORKOUTS: Aug 16 Sar 3f fst :384 B 16/17 • Jly 24 Sar 5f gd :592 H 1/11

Codys Key

Own: Sheerin Raymond T
CHAVEZ J F (196 32 20 27 .16) $35,000
Ro. h. 6
Sire: Corridor Key (Danzig)
Dam: Go Thither (Cabin)
Br: Wilkinson Jon (NJ)
Tr: Contessa [illegible] C (21 3 4 2 .14)
L 118

Lifetime Record: 31 8 3 5 $236,348										
1995	6	1	1	2	$27,320	Turf	1	0	0	0 $400
1994	6	1	0	0	$34,580	Wet	2	0	0	0
Bel	11	4	1	1	$137,124	Dist	22	7	3	4 $214,098

30Oct95- 6Lrl fst 6f :222 :451 :564 1:09 3↑ Alw 32000NC 88 4 1 2 31 34 35 Nelson D L 117 8.10 90-13 Goldminer's Dream1191 Foxie G1194 Codys Key1174 Weakened 6
14Sep95- 7Bel fst 6f :221 :452 :571 1:094 3↑ Alw 42000N$Y 90 3 2 56 44½ 44 22½ Sellers S J L 114 6.40 89-16 In Case1192½ Codys Key114hd Cold Execution1194 Up for place 5
3Sep95- 9Bel fst 6½f :221 :452 1:092 1:154 3↑ Clm 30000 93 1 1 11½ 1½ 12 1¾ Sellers S J L 116 7.90 96-07 Codys Key116¾ Blum Gone1163½ Faviano120¾ Mild drive 12
21Aug95- 5Sar fst 6f :214 :452 :581 1:113 3↑ Clm 25000 84 8 4 43 42½ 2½ 3½ Chavez J F 113 4.40 82-15 Faviano113no I'm Reckless113½ Codys Key1133 Prominent throughout 12
26Jly95- 5Sar fst 6½f :214 :443 1:10 1:163 3↑ Clm 35000 78 11 2 63 42 53½ 86½ Bailey J D 112 4.20 86-14 Country Sky112no Tough Heart1121½ Unreal Mot113½ Tired 12
10Jun95- 4Bel fst 6½f :221 :451 1:10 1:162 Handicap48k 52 8 5 64 66 912 924¾ Chavez J F 110 24.00 68-14 Evil Bear1185½ [DH]Ulises112 [DH]Corma Ray1142 No threat 9
10Sep94- 9Med fst 6f :222 :453 :574 1:104 3↑ [S]Bold Josh H30k 84 7 4 41½ 31 32½ 54 Santos J A L 122 1.80 83-18 Munch N' Nosh117hd Toroweap115¾ Dr. Louis A.1132 No rally 7
29Aug94- 4Sar fst 6f :221 :452 :572 1:094 3↑ Handicap50k 101 5 1 2½ 2½ 1hd 12 Chavez J F 110 7.50 92-13 Codys Key1102 Chief Desire122hd Humbugaboo1162½ Driving 5
10Aug94- 6Sar fst 6f :214 :45 :571 1:10 Clm 75000 82 1 2 34½ 35 41½ 46 Chavez J F 117 3.10 85-09 Golden Tent113no Fabersham1132 Mining Burrah1174 Checked 3/16 pl 5
28May94- 8Bel fst 6f :22 :452 :572 1:093 3↑ Roseben H-G3 78 8 10 87½ 95½ 95¾ 911¼ McCauley W H 112 9.50 82-14 Boundary1132¾ Chief Desire117nk Birdonthewire1222 No factor 10

WORKOUTS: •Sep 30 Bel tr.t 3f fst :341 H 1/5 Sep 25 Bel tr.t 4f fst :483 B 3/26

Fabersham
Own: Scaglione Paul
TREJO J (24 1 2 2 .04) $35,000
Dk. b or br g. 7
Sire: Nepal (Raja Baba)
Dam: Snob Skate (Icecapade)
Br: Ken Mort Stables (NY)
Tr: Terracciano Neal (10 0 1 1 .00)
L 1097

Lifetime Record: 71 21 14 12 $634,241										
1995	16	1	3	5	$56,940	Turf	1	0	0	0
1994	14	5	2	3	$193,327	Wet	7	1	0	3 $48,812
Bel	20	4	3	3	$120,560	Dist	37	11	10	9 $398,931

25Sep95- 9Bel fst 6½f :221 :45 1:10 1:162 3+ Clm 35000 62 1 7 1110 1213 1211 1013 Graell A L 117 fb 19.90 80-12 Limited War110¾ Blum Gone1171 Country Sky117nk No speed 12
15Sep95- 6Bel fst 7f :23 :462 1:103 1:223 3+ Clm 35000 77 1 7 53 76¾ 57 510¾ Graell A L 114 fb 23.20 78-14 Late Guest1165 Fini Cassette1142¾ Blum Gone1161 Checked break 7
27Jly95- 3Sar fst 7f :221 :45 1:10 1:23 3+ Clm 50000 44 7 2 63½ 66½ 910 923¼ Graell A 112 fb 18.40 67-12 Rethink1121 Boom Towner114½ Brilliant Patriot1122 Wide, gave way 9
1Jun95- 7Bel fst 6½f :221 :452 1:111 1:18 Clm c-47500 75 3 6 67½ 65½ 64¼ 79¼ Santagata N 114 b 4.90 76-17 JerichoBlise111no Gllpit'sMoment1161¾ Exprssd116hd Four wide, no threat 7
Claimed from Hagedorn Charles C & Rottkamp John, Imperio Joseph Trainer
21May95- 6Bel fst 6f :221 :453 :581 1:111 Clm 50000 85 6 7 78 77 63¼ 53½ Alvarado F T 114 b 7.20 81-22 Gllpit'sMoment114nk Expressed1161½ Miron'sGentlemn1121½ Broke slowly 7
27Apr95- 6Aqu fst 7f :231 :454 1:11 1:24 Clm c-35000 87 1 6 52¾ 44 21½ 3nk Perez R B5 113 b *1.15 84-18 Miron's Gentleman116no Grey Chandon116hd Fabersham113¾ Willingly 6
Claimed from Davis Barbara J, Moschera Gasper S Trainer
14Apr95- 6Aqu fst 6f :22 :452 :572 1:092 Clm 50000 77 4 6 63½ 53 44 38 Perez R B5 111 b *2.40 87-10 One Big Hug1163 Carsey's Pal1165 Fabersham111nk Four wide, no rally 6
6Apr95- 6Aqu fst 6½f :222 :452 1:10 1:162 Clm 40000 98 2 5 53½ 53½ 1½ 11½ Perez R B5 111 b 3.40 98-08 Fabersham1111½ Gallapiat'sMoment1123 MediclPro1164 Four wide, clear 6
2Apr95- 9Aqu fst 6½f :222 :452 1:10 1:162 Clm 50000 85 2 7 84¾ 84¾ 56 56 Alvarado F T 114 b 4.50 92-13 OpeningPrayer1161½ JerichoBlaise116hd Farmonthefreewy1171 No threat 8
22Mar95- 6Aqu fst 7f :223 :451 1:102 1:232 Clm 47500 86 2 5 57 510 34¼ 26 Alvarado F T 115 b *.95 81-20 Farmonthefreeway1176 Fabersham115nk Jericho Blaise1197 Late gain 5
WORKOUTS: Oct 13 Aqu 4f fst :48 H 2/4 Sep 10 Aqu 6f fst 1:181 B 1/1 Sep 3 Aqu 5f fst 1:022 B 7/11 Aug 28 Aqu 3f fst :364 B 1/1 Aug 21 Sar tr.t 4f fst :533 B 21/22

Crystal Pistol
Own: McDonnell Francis C
SMITH M E (204 36 24 31 .18) $35,000
Gr. c. 4
Sire: Darn That Alarm (Jig Time)
Dam: Zuppa Inglesa (Iron Ruler)
Br: Big C Farms (Fla)
Tr: Lenzini John J Jr (12 1 1 2 .08)
L 116

Lifetime Record: 27 3 3 4 $91,510										
1995	15	2	2	2	$22,605	Turf	2	0	0	0 $135
1994	9	1	0	2	$66,305	Wet	4	0	0	0 $1,015
Bel	0	0	0	0		Dist	9	0	1	4 $10,940

13Sep95- 8Rkm fst 6f :213 :443 :57 1:093 3+ Alw 14700N$Y 74 4 9 75¾ 55 45 44¾ Caraballo J C LB 117 fb 9.20 91-08 Prolnzier1222¾ Mudlin'sSunny1164 QuickstBid1162 2w turn, flattened out 11
3Sep95- 8Rkm fst 6f :214 :442 :562 1:09 3+ Manchester H20k 80 2 1 34½ 47 46¼ 36¾ Thompson W A LB 116 fb 8.40 97-01 Prolanzier1156¼ Detox115hd Crystal Pistol1162 In tight start, rail 9
13Aug95- 5Sar my 7f :223 :461 1:104 1:232 3+ Clm 35000 80 4 6 33 31 45½ 59 Luzzi M J 118 fb 24.75 80-17 Carr Heaven1121¾ Concoctor1126 Giant Leap113½ Checked break, tired 8
2Aug95- 9Rkm fst 1⅛ :222 :454 1:111 1:44 3+ Alw 14700N$mY 58 4 1 2hd 3½ 710 713¾ Hampshire J F JrLB 116 fb 15.60 89-07 City OfDreams116½ Maudlin'sSunny116nk Slaymaker119no 2 wide, stopped 7
14Jly95- 8Rkm fst 1⅛ :231 :461 1:104 1:443 3+ Alw 14700N$mY 66 4 2 24 56 69¾ 712¾ Hampshire J F JrLB 116 fb 3.50 87-07 Slaymaker1161 Sabinal1161½ Maudlin's Sunny1192¾ Chased off rail, stppd 7
26Jun95- 9Rkm fst 140 :23 :47 1:121 1:423 3+ Alw 11760N3L 71 1 3 31½ 1½ 14 12½ Hampshire J F JrLB 119 fb *1.10 89-11 Crystal Pistol1192¾ Brian's Devotion1163 Spicy Hi1164¾ 3 path, driving 8
19Jun95- 5Rkm fm 1⅛ Ⓣ :232 :481 1:133 1:472 3+ Alw 11760N3L 54 5 8 94¾ 74 911 910¾ Hampshire J F JrLB 119 fb 3.30 67-21 AwyWthUStn1161½ HlksClbrty116nk NpomoDns1191 Bumped st, wide late 12
5Jun95- 7Suf fst 1 :233 :464 1:113 1:394 3+ Alw 11760N2L 75 1 2 21½ 12½ 15 14¾ Hampshire J F JrLB 116 fb 1.40 85-21 CrystlPstl1164¾ TllChrryTr116nk Shnnlkdmnds1192¾ 3 path 2nd turn, drvng 10
29Apr95-11Hia sly 1⅛ :464 1:104 1:35 1:481 3+ Seminole H50k 65 5 1 12½ 2½ 611 723¾ Gonzalez M A L 112 fb 57.30 77-09 Not Surprising1172¾ Pride Of Burkaan1171 Beyton1148 Tired 9
14Apr95-11Bir fst 170 :242 :473 1:13 1:454 3+ Alw 9500N2X 66 4 3 33 31½ 3½ 2nk Gonzalez M A LB 116 fb 1.80 80-20 Billy Three122nk Crystal Pistol1161 C B's Gem1163½ Aimed, just missed 6
WORKOUTS: Aug 31 Rkm 3f fst :353 B 2/9 ●Aug 24 Rkm 3f fst :363 H 1/7 Jly 28 Rkm 5f fst 1:034 B 6/16

Fighting Daddy
Own: Simon Steven
SANTAGATA N (55 2 5 7 .04) $35,000
Ch. g. 5
Sire: Fight Over (Grey Dawn II)
Dam: Daddyslittleangel (Rare Performer)
Br: Gallagher Mrs James H (Fla)
Tr: Imperio Joseph (21 2 3 1 .10)
L 116

Lifetime Record: 33 6 8 4 $159,028										
1995	4	0	1	2	$14,240	Turf	1	0	0	0
1994	18	3	5	2	$87,040	Wet	4	0	2	0 $11,660
Bel	6	1	0	0	$18,000	Dist	22	4	6	3 $116,898

26Feb95- 7Aqu fst 6f ⊡ :224 :462 :584 1:114 Alw 36000N4X 78 4 6 67 73½ 64½ 64¾ Perez R B5 112 b 4.10 79-19 Opening Prayer1171½ Tali Hai1171½ Yeckley117nk Checked 3/16 pl 7
11Feb95- 6Aqu fst 6f ⊡ :24 :473 1:001 1:133 Alw 36000N4X 90 1 4 21 31 32 3¾ Rydowski S R 117 b 5.50 74-33 Baypark119no Yeckley117¾ Fighting Daddy117nk Saved ground 7
3Feb95- 3Aqu fst 6f ⊡ :23 :47 :592 1:12 Clm 50000 92 1 5 33½ 2½ 2½ 31 Rydowski S R 115 b 3.50 82-25 Imaging113no Fabersham1171 Fighting Daddy1153 Bid, weakened 6
19Jan95- 8Aqu fst 6f ⊡ :233 :463 :581 1:102 Alw 36000N4X 88 1 5 42½ 21½ 24 24 Rydowski S R 117 b 7.80 87-18 Crafty1194 Fighting Daddy1171½ Tali Hai1174 Steadied 1/2 pl 5
30Dec94- 1Aqu fst 6f ⊡ :233 :48 1:01 1:134 3+ Clm c-25000 78 4 2 31 32 4½ 21½ Alvarado F T 122 b *1.30 73-24 Pension Fraud1171½ Fighting Daddy1222 Baypark1152¾ Second best 7
Claimed from Davis Barbara J, Moschera Gasper S Trainer
15Dec94- 7Aqu fst 6f ⊡ :23 :461 :581 1:104 3+ Alw 42000N$Y 65 6 6 66 66½ 610 614¼ Perez R B5 117 b 7.70 75-16 Medical Pro1112¾ Golden Tent119½ Chanels Titanic1131½ Outrun 7
7Dec94- 8Aqu fst 6f ⊡ :223 :454 :58 1:102 3+ Alw 34000N3X 90 1 6 52¾ 43 3½ 1no Perez R B5 112 b 2.15 91-12 Fighting Daddy112no Memories Of Linda115nk Blum Gone119½ Driving 7
2Dec94- 2Aqu fst 6f :213 :45 :574 1:11 3+ Clm 50000 98 2 2 36½ 34½ 31½ 1hd Perez R B5 112 b 4.10 87-21 Fighting Daddy112hd Unreal Mot113½ Imaging113hd Driving 6
22Nov94- 7Aqu wf 6f :222 :462 :583 1:11 3+ Alw 34000N3X 95 6 4 53½ 4¾ 1½ 2½ Santos J A 117 b 2.70e 86-24 More To Tell110½ Fighting Daddy1173½ Blum Gone1191 Wide, gamely 8
9Nov94- 5Aqu fst 7f :224 :46 1:111 1:233 3+ Alw 34000N3X 94 5 1 2½ 2½ 1½ 33½ Santos J A 117 b 1.95e 82-14 ⒹGoldnLrch1101 AdvncdPlcmnt1172½ FightingDddy1171¾ Bid, weakened 7
Placed second through disqualification.
WORKOUTS: Sep 24 Aqu 4f fst :491 H 4/10 Sep 16 Aqu 4f fst :501 B 7/21 Sep 9 Aqu 3f fst :364 B 4/8

Disaster Master
Own: Dark Horse Stables
MARQUEZ C H JR (—) $35,000
Ch. g. 4
Sire: Pappa Riccio (Nashua)
Dam: Eastern Witch (High Tribute)
Br: Wilkinson David N (NJ)
Tr: Tammaro John J III (—)
L 116

Lifetime Record: 32 5 6 5 $137,810										
1995	9	0	1	2	$13,120	Turf	2	1	0	0 $17,270
1994	16	4	4	2	$102,751	Wet	3	1	0	1 $23,250
Bel	0	0	0	0		Dist	20	3	5	5 $102,245

30Sep95- 7Med fst 170 :23 :462 1:111 1:41 3+ ⓈEscaped H30k 84 7 1 12½ 2hd 2hd 63¾ McCauley W H L 114 b 18.80 83-17 Halmandu116½ Slew You1162 Enlighten114¾ Tired 10
9Sep95- 9Med fst 6f :214 :444 :57 1:10 3+ ⓈBold Josh H35k 75 5 4 3nk 31 24 72½ Black A S L 114 b 9.90 90-12 Slew You1132½ Disaster Master1142 Is It Blinking1151¾ Second best 7
20Aug95- 5Mth fst 6f :214 :443 :572 1:094 3+ Alw 42000N$Y 76 12 1 5½ 52¾ 99½ 88 Black A S L 122 b 59.10 82-15 Jess C's Whirl1162¾ Chanels Titanic116½ Enlighten1171 Tired 12
5Aug95- 8Mth fst 6f :214 :444 :572 1:093 3+ Alw 40000N$Y 86 2 6 1hd 1hd 3½ 33½ Marquez C H Jr L 115 b 17.00 87-14 Old Tascosa1141 Poulain D'or1152½ ⒹⒽDisaster Master115 Weakened 7
22Jly95- 8Mth fm 5f Ⓣ :211 :441 :563 3+ Alw 35000N$Y 53 1 7 64 88¾ 811 813 Marquez C H Jr L 115 b 27.30 78-09 Distinctive Hat115nk Shananie's Boss122½ Mugabuck117no Thru early 8
24Mar95- 7GS fst 1 :231 :464 1:122 1:381 3+ ⓈVally ForgeH22k 66 8 2 2hd 3nk 56½ 714¼ Diaz L F L 117 b 8.80 72-25 Alladoreme1157 Papa Mijo1091½ Stokes State114no Tired 10
3Feb95- 3Aqu fst 6f ⊡ :23 :47 :592 1:12 Clm 50000 57 4 3 2½ 3½ 64½ 615 Diaz L F 115 b 3.85 68-25 Imaging113no Fabersham1171 Fighting Daddy1153 Forced pace, tired 6
21Jan95- 9GS my 6f :221 :451 :58 1:104 Alw 15000N$Y 78 6 1 2hd 5¾ 3nk 32½ Diaz L F L 122 b 2.70 88-16 Go Doc Go113nk Just A Lord1172 Disaster Master122hd Weakened 8
14Jan95- 9Lrl fst 6f :221 :453 :572 1:094 NorthernWolf54k 81 7 2 2½ 31½ 55¾ 69½ Diaz L F L 115 b 14.20 81-12 Who Wouldn't119hd Storm Tower1172½ Foxie G117¾ Gave way 7
10Dec94- 9Med sly 6f :222 :461 :582 1:104 3+ ⓈHandicap36k 90 9 1 11½ 12½ 12 11 Diaz L F L 114 b 6.10 87-17 Disaster Master1141 Merri Tales1184 Munch N' Nosh121no Driving 9
WORKOUTS: Oct 16 Med 4f fst :484 B 3/12 Sep 26 Med 6f sly 1:15 B 1/1 Sep 3 Mth 5f fst 1:013 B 2/14 Aug 15 Mth 4f fst :483 B 5/24 Jly 30 Mth 3f fst :361 B 2/9

Limited War
Own: Pomerantz Lawrence J
CHAVEZ C R (80 5 5 8 .06) $30,000
Dk. b or br g. 4
Sire: Vittorioso (Olden Times)
Dam: Act En Ciel (Coup de Chance)
Br: Landry Mr & Mrs Harry L (NY)
Tr: Barbara Robert (48 5 4 3 .10)
L 1087

Lifetime Record: 16 4 2 1 $94,850										
1995	8	2	1	0	$48,090	Turf	3	0	0	1 $8,160
1994	8	2	1	1	$46,760	Wet	2	1	0	0 $20,400
Bel	7	3	0	0	$51,210	Dist	2	1	0	0 $15,000

8Oct95- 5Bel fst 7f :22 :452 1:103 1:24 3+ Clm 35000 68 1 6 713 67 57½ 511½ Chavez C R7 L 111 10.80 69-17 Country Sky1145½ Carr Heaven116nk Imaging1162½ No threat 8
25Sep95- 9Bel fst 6½f :221 :45 1:10 1:162 3+ Clm 35000 93 4 12 1211 97½ 63½ 1½ Chavez C R7 L 110 34.00 93-12 Limited War110½ Blum Gone1171 Country Sky117nk Broke slowly, wide 12
18Sep95- 9Bel gd 1 :233 :463 1:111 1:362 3+ Clm c-18000 72 2 1 11 1½ 21½ 55½ Perez R B L 116 3.60 76-15 Le Risky1163 Northern T.1141 Eire Power116nk Dueled, weakened 12
Claimed from Happy Hill Farm, Kimmel John C Trainer
2Sep95- 9Bel fst 7f :224 :453 1:10 1:22 3+ Clm 18000 74 1 6 42½ 64½ 42½ 48 Perez R B 116 5.00 83-08 Maraud1144 Classi Envoy1162¾ Primordial1161½ No late bid 10
29Mar95- 8Aqu fst 1 :233 :462 1:104 1:354 Alw 36000N3X 74 5 3 42½ 41 54½ 510½ Perez R B5 108 7.70 79-19 Free Agent119nk Private Plan1133½ BermudaCedar1194 Checked 1/4, tired 5
20Feb95- 6Aqu fst 1⅟₁₆ ⊡ :242 :493 1:144 1:46 Alw 36000N3X 80 7 5 42½ 31 54 69¾ Perez R B5 112 9.10 65-29 Gallpit'sMoment117nk OcenSplsh112½ PrivtePln1173 Wide middle move 7
15Jan95- 4Aqu fst 170 ⊡ :233 :472 1:121 1:412 Alw 36000N3X 87 5 5 53½ 31½ 33½ 25½ Perez R B5 114 9.30 85-27 Five Star General1195½ Limited War114¾ Tanako1174½ Saved ground 5
7Jan95- 5Aqu my 1⅟₁₆ ⊡ :224 :473 1:142 1:482 ⓈAlw 34000N2X 82 5 4 47½ 33 1½ 12½ Perez R B5 112 *1.35 63-35 Limited War1122½ Vindicator11711 Klondike Clem1173½ Driving 7
18Dec94- 4Aqu fst 170 ⊡ :234 :48 1:141 1:44 3+ ⓈAlw 34000N2X 81 1 2 23 21½ 1hd 21½ Chavez J F 115 *1.10 77-29 Flying Groom1151½ Limited War1156 Lake11216 Second best 6
19Oct94- 8Aqu fm 1⅟₁₆ Ⓣ :242 :492 1:133 1:434 3+ Alw 34000N2X 80 6 2 31½ 31 41½ 43¾ Bailey J D 114 4.60 86-08 Gone For Real1142½ Flaming Falcon117no Sir Wollaston1141½ Lacked rally 6
WORKOUTS: ●Aug 28 Bel 4f fst :483 B 1/6 ●Aug 22 Bel tr.t 5f fst 1:01 H 1/10 Aug 15 Bel tr.t 5f fst 1:021 B 3/11 ●Aug 9 Bel tr.t 5f fst 1:011 B 1/9 Jly 30 Bel 5f fst 1:012 H 6/17 Jly 23 Bel 4f fst :502 B 12/17

Arz
Own: Haley Terrence W & Wickman Joseph F
VELAZQUEZ J R (214 32 23 28 .15) $35,000
Dk. b or br c. 4
Sire: Known Fact (In Reality)
Dam: Last Request*Ir (Dancer's Image)
Br: Shadwell Estate Co & Farm Inc (Ky)
Tr: Lake Robert P (28 3 5 7 .11)
L 116

Lifetime Record:	24	3	5	5	$66,379						
1995	12	2	2	2	$49,830	Turf	10	1	3	3	$18,469
1994	6	0	1	2	$5,403	Wet	3	1	0	0	$15,720
Bel	4	2	0	1	$38,050	Dist	5	0	2	1	$9,860

12Jly95-6Bel fst 1 1/16 ⊗ :23 :453 1:094 1:422 Clm 60000 75 5 2 2 1/2 1hd 3 4 1/2 3 12 1/2 Chavez J F 114 4.30 74-23 Dibbs N' Dubbs116 3 1/2 Sole Bird1163 Arz114no Dueled, tired 5
22Jun95-7Bel sly 1 1/16 :231 :463 1:11 1:421 Clm 27500 93 3 1 12 1 1/2 1 2 1/2 1 1/2 Velazquez J R 114 fb 4.30 88-22 Arz1141 1/2 Regal Mike1163 A Call To Rise112 1/2 Fully extended 6
9Jun95-10Bel fst 1 1/8 :471 1:113 1:374 1:511 Clm 35000 77 2 1 11 11 3 1/2 6 8 1/2 Velazquez J R 120 fb 4.00 66-24 D Klondike Clem116 2 1/2 Flying Groom116no Regal Mike1162 Used up 9
31May95-8Bel fm 1 Ⓣ :22 :452 1:104 1:354 3+ Alw 36000N3L 59 3 9 10 8 1/2 10 3 3/4 9 7 1/2 917 Perez R B5 117 b 25.50 67-21 Dutchess First1203 Kerfoot Corner1203 Moscow Magic1201 1/2 No threat 10
6May95-6Bel fst 1 1/16 :24 :47 1:112 1:433 3+ Alw 34000N2L 88 1 3 1hd 1 1/2 14 16 1/2 Velazquez J R 120 b 20.60 81-15 Arz1206 1/2 West Buoyant115hd Easy Miner1202 1/2 Brk slowly, going away 7
30Apr95-5Aqu fm 1 1/16 Ⓣ :224 :463 1:111 1:433 3+ Alw 32000N2L 73 8 8 711 6 5 1/2 4 2 1/2 4 6 1/2 Velazquez J R 120 b 27.50 85-09 Proceeded1203 1/2 Dial Trial1121 1/2 No Storm1201 1/2 Saved ground, weakened 10
22Apr95-9Aqu gd 1 1/16 Ⓣ :24 :48 1:124 1:442 Clm 50000 57 5 5 611 77 710 8 17 1/4 Santos J A 116 b 6.90 59-16 Bonus Award112nk Berseto1131 1/2 Royal Ninja110 1/2 No threat 9
7Apr95-2Aqu fst 6f :224 :472 :594 1:121 Clm 35000N2L 72 7 6 6 4 1/2 3 1/2 21 2 1/2 Velazquez J R 116 b 2.00e 79-19 Kris' Rainbow1141 1/2 Arz1163 Graduate School1161 1/2 Rallied four wide 8
31Mar95-2Aqu fst 6f :223 :464 :59 1:113 Clm c-25000N2L 70 3 4 55 66 44 35 Lovato F Jr 116 fb 8.80 79-19 Dependableness114no Metroplex1145 Arz1161 Checked 7/16 pl 7
Claimed from Schwartz Barry K, Hushion Michael E Trainer
24Feb95-1Aqu wf 6f ⊡ :23 :461 :581 1:104 Clm 35000N2L 64 3 6 7 5 1/2 89 57 49 Migliore R 116 fb 3.65 80-16 Plutonius1123 1/2 River Arly111 1/2 Robber Baron115no Steadied 5/16 pl 9
WORKOUTS: Oct 8 Bel tr.t 4f fst :494 B 12/24 Oct 2 Bel tr.t 3f fst :364 B 3/7

5 Belmont Park

1 1/16 MILES. (Inner Turf). (1:391) MAIDEN SPECIAL WEIGHT. Purse $32,000 (plus up to $12,560 NYSBFOA). 2-year-olds. Weight, 118 lbs. (Preference to horses that have not started for a claiming price.)

Coupled – Barlow and Trail City

Hail to the Lion
Own: Anchel Edward
DAVIS R G (243 37 42 30 .15)
Gr/ro c. 2 (Mar)
Sire: Sovereign Dancer (Northern Dancer)
Dam: Stark's Promise (Graustark)
Br: Daniel M. Galbreath (Ky)
Tr: Labeccetta Frank (10 1 1 1 .10)
118

Lifetime Record:	4	M	1	0	$9,100						
1995	4	M	1	0	$9,100	Turf	1	0	1	0	$6,400
1994	0	M	0	0		Wet	0	0	0	0	
Bel Ⓣ	1	0	1	0	$6,400	Dist Ⓣ	1	0	1	0	$6,400

8Sep95-6Bel fm 1 1/16 Ⓣ :24 :483 1:131 1:44 Md Sp Wt 64 3 3 33 3 2 1/2 3nk 23 Sellers S J 118 23.00 73-14 StrOfThetricl1183 HilToTheLion1181 1/2 WvingGoodBye1183 1/2 Bid, no match 8
2Sep95-2Bel fst 1 :23 :454 1:103 1:37 Md Sp Wt 31 4 7 78 7 6 1/2 711 7 20 1/2 Luzzi M J 118 12.50 58-16 Pirate Performer118 1/2 Fortitude1182 Hey You Weasel11810 No threat 8
27Jly95-2Sar fst 6f :22 :453 :574 1:104 Md Sp Wt 49 10 9 910 910 79 515 Luzzi M J 118 29.50 72-12 HonourAndGlory11810 BlshngJm1183 1/2 JttngRobrt118nk Improved position 12
14Jly95-2Bel fst 5f :23 :46 :583 Md Sp Wt 50 1 3 54 5 2 1/2 42 4 3 1/2 Agosto R7 109 20.30 90-07 Prospector'sPet116 1/2 TomN'Kath1161 1/2 ImGoodGmble1161 Bid, flattened 8
WORKOUTS: Oct 12 Aqu 4f fst :484 B 3/7 Oct 3 Aqu 5f fst 1:02 B 8/19 Sep 25 Aqu 5f fst 1:033 B 8/10 Aug 28 Aqu 5f fst 1:012 B 1/1 Aug 18 Sar 4f fst :482 H 2/18 Aug 5 Sar 4f fst :494 B 19/46

Waving Good Bye
Own: Giordano Ronald J
CHAVEZ J F (196 32 20 27 .16)
B. c. 2 (Apr)
Sire: Wavering Monarch (Majestic Light)
Dam: Woodmont Lass (Transworld)
Br: Thomas J. Carroll (Ky)
Tr: Terrill William V (27 4 4 3 .15)
L 118

Lifetime Record:	5	M	0	1	$3,520						
1995	5	M	0	1	$3,520	Turf	3	0	0	1	$3,520
1994	0	M	0	0		Wet	0	0	0	0	
Bel Ⓣ	2	0	0	1	$3,520	Dist Ⓣ	2	0	0	1	$3,520

20Sep95-6Bel fst 1 1/16 :224 :461 1:113 1:433 Md Sp Wt 16 9 2 2 1/2 710 729 7 39 3/4 Santos J A L 118 b 8.40 41-21 Blushing Jim11813 Lonsdale11810 Captain Charlie118 1/2 Forced pace 9
8Sep95-6Bel fm 1 1/16 Ⓣ :24 :483 1:131 1:44 Md Sp Wt 61 1 1 1 1/2 1 1/2 2hd 3 4 1/2 Chavez J F 118 18.90 71-14 StrOfThtricl1183 HlToThLon1181 1/2 WvngGoodBy1183 1/2 Pressed, weakened 8
21Aug95-6Sar fm 1 1/16 Ⓣ :232 :482 1:132 1:433 Md Sp Wt 36 4 2 21 22 714 8 19 1/2 Chavez J F 118 10.70 61-12 CurrncyArbitrg11810 CptnChrl1182 BlushngRchrd1181 Forced pace, tired 10
22Jly95-2Sar fst 5 1/2f :222 :462 :584 1:051 Md Sp Wt 12 2 9 911 10 9 1/2 1113 1121 Decarlo C P 120 31.00 74-07 SunnySide1206 NorthernPursuit120nk Justinthmiddl1202 Checked 1/2 pl 12
13Jly95-6Bel fm 6f Ⓣ :22 :461 :583 1:11 Md Sp Wt 36 12 11 6 2 1/2 4 1/2 9 6 1/2 1010 Chavez J F 116 9.70 71-19 Harpsichord116 1/2 Old Chapel116hd Erskine1161 Wide, tired 12
WORKOUTS: Oct 12 Bel 5f fst 1:02 B 10/19 Oct 4 Bel 4f fst :482 H 4/61 Sep 29 Bel tr.t 5f fst 1:024 B 5/17 Sep 16 Bel tr.t 4f fst :474 H 2/25 Sep 1 Bel 4f fst :484 B 20/40 Aug 15 Sar tr.t 5f fst 1:05 B 8/13

Aspen Ryder
Own: Due Process Stable
KRONE J A (137 16 21 9 .12)
B. c. 2 (Feb)
Sire: Deputy Minister (Vice Regent)
Dam: Two Rings (Round Table)
Br: Due Process Stable Inc (Ky)
Tr: Nobles Reynaldo H (15 0 1 0 .00)
L 118

Lifetime Record:	1	M	0	0	$0					
1995	1	M	0	0		Turf	1	0	0	0
1994	0	M	0	0		Wet	0	0	0	0
Bel Ⓣ	1	0	0	0		Dist Ⓣ	1	0	0	0

8Sep95-6Bel fm 1 1/16 Ⓣ :24 :483 1:131 1:44 Md Sp Wt 41 8 6 6 5 1/2 5 5 1/2 610 7 13 1/2 Bailey J D 118 10.50 62-14 StarOfTheatrical1183 HilToTheLion1181 1/2 WvingGoodBye1183 1/2 No factor 8
WORKOUTS: Oct 14 Mdl 5f fst 1:06 B 4/5 Oct 7 Mdl 4f fst :582 B 2/5 Oct 2 Mdl 4f fst :512 B 6/9 Sep 16 Mdl 5f fst 1:04 B 3/3 Sep 4 Mdl 5f fst 1:04 B 3/4 Aug 29 Mdl 5f fst 1:033 B 2/3

Lite Approval
Own: Live Oak Plantation
SAMYN J L (89 9 10 14 .10)
Gr/ro c. 2 (Apr)
Sire: With Approval (Caro)
Dam: Lunar Light (Majestic Light)
Br: Live Oak Stud (Fla)
Tr: Kelly Patrick J (31 4 3 2 .13)
118

Lifetime Record:	0	M	0	0	$0					
1995	0	M	0	0		Turf	0	0	0	0
1994	0	M	0	0		Wet	0	0	0	0
Bel Ⓣ	0	0	0	0		Dist Ⓣ	0	0	0	0

WORKOUTS: Oct 16 Bel tr.t 3f fst :381 B 4/7 Sep 29 Bel 3f fst :37 B 9/30 Sep 24 Bel tr.t 4f fst :504 B 35/44 ●Sep 19 Bel 4f fst :474 B 1/56 Sep 13 Bel tr.t 4f fst :501 B 7/15 Sep 7 Bel 4f fst :503 B 35/48
Sep 1 Bel 3f fst :371 Hg 13/21 Aug 27 Sar 3f fst :372 Bg 5/9 Aug 23 Sar 3f fst :372 Bg 9/23

Barlow
Own: Ramsey Kenneth L & Sarah K
BAILEY J D (283 47 27 22 .23)
B. c. 2 (May)
Sire: Dixieland Band (Northern Dancer)
Dam: Endicotta (Roberto)
Br: North Cliff Farms (Ky)
Tr: Mott William I (65 18 6 11 .28)
118

Lifetime Record:	2	M	0	0	$0					
1995	2	M	0	0		Turf	0	0	0	0
1994	0	M	0	0		Wet	1	0	0	0
Bel Ⓣ	0	0	0	0		Dist Ⓣ	0	0	0	0

5Oct95-2Bel sly 1 1/16 :224 :453 1:111 1:462 Md Sp Wt 29 2 5 45 511 626 6 28 1/2 Bailey J D 118 b 8.90 38-26 ChngePrtners1189 Lonsdl1181 1/2 CountryCuzzin1181 1/2 Bumped break, tired 9
19Aug95-6Sar fst 7f :23 :464 1:122 1:254 Md Sp Wt 41 2 9 4 1 1/2 5 2 1/2 5 6 1/2 6 12 1/2 Bailey J D 118 5.50 65-15 HeadMinister1182 Chenlo118 1/2 ChangePrtners118nk Broke slowly, rushed 9
WORKOUTS: Sep 29 Bel 4f fst :51 B 46/61 Sep 20 Bel 4f fst :473 H 8/70 Sep 13 Sar Ⓣ 7f sf 1:353 B (d) 3/4 Aug 30 Sar 3f fst :381 B 1/2 Aug 15 Sar 5f fst 1:023 B 31/47 ●Aug 6 Bel tr.t 5f fst 1:022 B 1/13

R.S.V.P. Requested
Own: Der-Sea Stable
MIGLIORE R (92 10 6 16 .11)
Dk. b or br c. 2 (Mar)
Sire: Black Tie Affair*Ire (Miswaki)
Dam: Flags Waving (Delta Flag)
Br: Mangurian Harry T Jr (Fla)
Tr: O'Connell Richard (36 5 4 7 .14)
L 118

Lifetime Record:	2	M	0	0	$960						
1995	2	M	0	0	$960	Turf	2	0	0	0	$960
1994	0	M	0	0		Wet	0	0	0	0	
Bel Ⓣ	1	0	0	0	$960	Dist Ⓣ	2	0	0	0	$960

13Sep95-6Bel fm 1 1/16 Ⓣ :23 :461 1:104 1:431 Md Sp Wt 58 8 5 5 3 1/2 5 4 1/2 411 5 11 1/2 Migliore R L 118 b 49.00 68-20 Togher1187 1/2 Going For The Gold118nk Bombardier1184 Evenly 8
25Aug95-6Sar fm 1 1/16 Ⓣ :23 :47 1:114 1:433 Md Sp Wt 35 4 11 1117 1115 1115 1115 Migliore R 118 b 11.80 66-07 Defcto118nk Bombrdier1184 Dontnswerthefour118nk Broke slowly, outrun 11
WORKOUTS: Oct 17 Bel 4f fst :491 B 19/34 Oct 11 Bel 4f fst :491 B 22/45 Sep 11 Bel 4f fst :501 B 36/44 Sep 6 Bel 3f fst :36 Hg 3/18 Aug 23 Sar tr.t Ⓣ 4f fm :49 B (d) 4/17 Aug 18 Sar tr.t Ⓣ 4f fm :491 H (d) 5/15

Marfada

Own: Nadanne Stables

BECKNER D V (60 2 5 5 .03)

B. c. 2 (Feb)
Sire: Marfa (Foolish Pleasure)
Dam: Pealing (London Bells)
Br: James B. Watriss & Pegasus Stud (Ky)
Tr: Contessa Gary C (21 3 4 2 .14)

L 118

Lifetime Record: 2 M 0 0 $180

1995 2 M 0 0 $180 Turf 2 0 0 0 $180
1994 0 M 0 0 Wet 0 0 0 0
Bel (T) 0 0 0 0 Dist (T) 1 0 0 0

12Oct95-7Med gd 1 (T) :233 :483 1:133 1:382 Md Sp Wt 45 3 7 83¼ 53 65½ 67¾ Beckner D V L 118 10.70 73-18 Why Change118¾ Coach Warner118¾ Gold Streak1181½ Even trip 10
28Aug95-2Sar fm 1 1/16 (T) :232 :481 1:13 1:432 Md Sp Wt 23 10 11 1212 1214 1115 1123 Nelson D 118 55.50 59-08 Jetting Robert118¾ Togher1183 Vibrations118nk No speed 12

WORKOUTS: Oct 9 Bel 4f fst :51 B 53/60 Sep 16 Bel 6f fst 1:18 B 6/6 Sep 11 Bel 6f fst 1:182 B 2/4 Sep 4 Bel 4f fst :501 B 36/47 ●Aug 27 Sar tr.t 3f fst :373 H 1/6 ●Aug 24 Sar tr.t 3f fst :372 B 1/6

Optic Nerve

Own: Oak Cliff & Sanders & Wade & Willis

SANTOS J A (168 28 18 28 .17)

Dk. b or br c. 2 (Apr)
Sire: Majestic Light (Majestic Prince)
Dam: Irreality Star (In Reality)
Br: Jaime S. Carrion (Ky)
Tr: Tesher Howard M (39 4 6 2 .10)

118

Lifetime Record: 1 M 0 0 $1,800

1995 1 M 0 0 $1,800 Turf 0 0 0 0
1994 0 M 0 0 Wet 0 0 0 0
Bel (T) 0 0 0 0 Dist (T) 0 0 0 0

30Sep95-2Bel fst 6f :222 :463 :592 1:124 Md Sp Wt 63 4 8 910 65 56 44½ Santos J A 118 3.85 72-22 Citified1181 Turning Fifty118¾ In The Rain1181 Check, awkward break 9

WORKOUTS: ●Oct 12 Bel [T] 5f gd 1:014 B (d) 1/10 Sep 25 Bel tr.t 4f fst :50 B 11/26 Sep 20 Bel 5f fst 1:003 H 11/57 Sep 8 Bel 6f fst 1:134 H 3/6 Sep 2 Bel tr.t 5f fst 1:02 B 2/6 Aug 27 Sar 5f fst 1:024 B 10/17

Tavito's Wish

Own: Friendship Stable

CHAVEZ C R (80 5 5 8 .06)

B. g. 2 (Mar)
Sire: Lyphard's Wish*Fr (Lyphard)
Dam: Catalina Way (Diplomat Way)
Br: Another Episode Farm (Fla)
Tr: Barbara Robert (48 5 4 3 .10)

L 111[7]

Lifetime Record: 4 M 0 0 $960

1995 4 M 0 0 $960 Turf 3 0 0 0 $960
1994 0 M 0 0 Wet 1 0 0 0
Bel (T) 2 0 0 0 $960 Dist (T) 2 0 0 0 $960

5Oct95-2Bel sly 1 1/16 :224 :453 1:111 1:462 Md Sp Wt 22 8 8 819 818 729 732¼ Chavez C R7 L 111 26.25 34-26 Change Partners1189 Lonsdale1181½ Country Cuzzin1181½ No threat 9
8Sep95-2Bel fm 1 1/16 [T] :233 :471 1:114 1:43 Md Sp Wt 46 8 7 87¾ 83½ 78½ 516¼ Sellers S J 118 17.60 65-14 Old Chapel1187 Cheerful Earful1181½ Hurry Home Halo1185 No threat 8
25Aug95-6Sar fm 1 1/16 (T) :23 :47 1:114 1:433 Md Sp Wt 46 3 7 63 74¾ 107¼ 1010 Beckner D V 118 10.70 71-07 Defacto118nk Bombardier1184 Dontanswerthefour118nk Tired, 11
13Jly95-6Bel fm 6f (T) :22 :461 :583 1:11 Md Sp Wt 36 8 7 1111 127¾ 119¾ 810 Santagata N 116 19.30 71-19 Harpsichord116¾ Old Chapel116hd Erskine1161 No threat 12

WORKOUTS: Sep 30 Bel 4f fst :494 B 30/53 Sep 20 Bel 5f fst 1:023 B 36/57 Aug 22 Sar (T) 6f fm 1:142 H (d) 2/2 Aug 15 Sar 4f fst :49 B 7/29

Trail City

Own: Mott William I & Verchota Robert

PEREZ R B (116 8 11 15 .07)

Dk. b or br c. 2 (Apr)
Sire: Red Ransom (Roberto)
Dam: Willow Runner (Alydar)
Br: Prestonwood Farm (Ky)
Tr: Mott William I (65 18 8 11 .28)

118

Lifetime Record: 2 M 0 0 $0

1995 2 M 0 0 Turf 1 0 0 0
1994 0 M 0 0 Wet 0 0 0 0
Bel (T) 0 0 0 0 Dist (T) 1 0 0 0

28Aug95-2Sar fm 1 1/16 (T) :232 :481 1:13 1:432 Md Sp Wt 45 6 2 34¼ 31½ 67¾ 813 Perez R B 118 19.20 68-08 Jetting Robert118¾ Togher1183 Vibrations118nk Stalked, tired 12
10Aug95-6Sar fst 6½f :222 :454 1:101 1:163 Md Sp Wt 43 5 9 31½ 32 611 722 Bailey J D 118 5.80 70-13 Diligence1184 Gold Fever118¾ Surround Sound1181 Used up 10

WORKOUTS: Sep 30 Sar tr.t 1f fst 1:443 B 2/2 Aug 26 Sar 4f fst :511 B 29/36 Aug 2 Sar 4f fst :511 Bg 32/38

Value Investor

Own: Klaravich Stables

STEVENS G L (86 17 13 14 .20)

B. c. 2 (May)
Sire: Cahill Road (Fappiano)
Dam: Northern Pine (Far North)
Br: Gainesway Thoroughbreds Ltd (Ky)
Tr: Sciacca Gary (73 7 5 12 .10)

L 118

Lifetime Record: 2 M 0 0 $0

1995 2 M 0 0 Turf 0 0 0 0
1994 0 M 0 0 Wet 0 0 0 0
Bel (T) 0 0 0 0 Dist (T) 0 0 0 0

9Sep95-6Bel fst 7f :23 :462 1:114 1:25 Md Sp Wt 7 3 5 2hd 43½ 1119 1027 Chavez J F 118 15.20 49-19 Peace Process1181 Tax Break1185 Dustin's Dream118¾ Brief speed 12
24Aug95-6Sar fst 6½f :22 :454 1:113 1:182 Md Sp Wt 41 7 8 82¾ 76 916 818 Velazquez J R 119 17.80e 65-18 Gold Fever119¾ Crafty Friend119hd Ide1191½ Steadied 1/2 pl 12

WORKOUTS: ●Oct 12 Bel 4f fst :473 H 1/30 Oct 5 Bel tr.t 4f gd :483 B 2/21 Sep 3 Bel 4f fst :471 H 4/46 Aug 20 Sar tr.t 4f fst :503 B 5/21 Aug 14 Sar 4f fst :49 Hg 24/70 Aug 8 Sar 5f fst 1:013 B 7/28

Country Cuzzin

Own: Morven Stud Farm

SAMYN J L (89 9 10 14 .10)

Dk. b or br c. 2 (Feb)
Sire: Cozzene (Caro)
Dam: Mint Spring (Key to the Mint)
Br: H.C. Groves Revocable Trust (Ky)
Tr: Schulhofer Flint S (58 8 8 14 .10)

118

Lifetime Record: 3 M 1 1 $11,320

1995 3 M 1 1 $11,320 Turf 0 0 0 0
1994 0 M 0 0 Wet 2 0 1 1 $9,520
Bel (T) 0 0 0 0 Dist (T) 0 0 0 0

5Oct95-2Bel sly 1 1/16 :224 :453 1:111 1:462 Md Sp Wt 59 9 3 31 21 27 310½ Samyn J L 118 4.60 56-26 ChangePrtners1189 Lonsdle1181½ CountryCuzzin1181½ Chased, weakened 9
23Sep95-6Bel my 7f :23 :46 1:101 1:221 Md Sp Wt 57 1 5 32 32½ 210 215½ Samyn J L 118 12.50 74-08 Crafty Friend11815 Country Cuzzin118¾ Mariner118¾ Held place 9
4Sep95-2Bel fst 5½f :223 :461 :58 1:041 Md Sp Wt 54 7 6 74½ 64¾ 78 411¾ Samyn J L 118 24.75 82-08 Sole City1186 Criminal Suit118nk Hashid118½ Carried wide 9

WORKOUTS: Oct 18 Bel 3f fst :361 B 4/25 Oct 13 Bel 3f fst :361 H 3/14 Oct 1 Bel 4f fst :49 B 10/28 Sep 17 Bel 4f sly :493 B 2/12 Sep 12 Bel 4f fst :492 B 23/43 Aug 30 Bel 4f fst :473 H 7/30

Wish You Goboy

Own: Mongru Madhan P

MAPLE E (145 11 18 19 .08)

Ch. g. 2 (Jan)
Sire: Lyphard's Wish*Fr (Lyphard)
Dam: Warm and Soft (Caracolero)
Br: Arnold Farms (Ky)
Tr: Barbara Robert (48 5 4 3 .10)

118

Lifetime Record: 3 M 0 0 $960

1995 3 M 0 0 $960 Turf 3 0 0 0 $960
1994 0 M 0 0 Wet 0 0 0 0
Bel (T) 2 0 0 0 $960 Dist (T) 2 0 0 0 $960

8Sep95-6Bel fm 1 1/16 [T] :24 :483 1:131 1:44 Md Sp Wt 46 7 5 64¼ 65½ 510 511¼ Smith M E 118 b 9.20 65-14 StarOfTheatrical1183 HiIToTheLion1181¾ WvingGoodBye118¾ No threat 8
21Aug95-2Sar fm 1 1/16 [T] :233 :484 1:142 1:454 Md Sp Wt 51 4 6 77 73 42 84¾ Maple E 118 14.20 65-12 Officious118nk Togher1181 Green Manor118nk Steadied 1/8 pl 9
16Jly95-6Bel fm 6f (T) :223 :462 :581 1:101 Md Sp Wt 41 11 4 810 97½ 89¾ 813¼ Maple E 116 38.50 72-15 Game's On116¾ Vibrations1161 Cornwall116nk No threat 12

WORKOUTS: Sep 30 Bel 4f fst :494 B 30/53 Sep 20 Bel 5f fst 1:023 B 36/57 Aug 15 Sar 4f fst :491 B 10/29 Aug 3 Sar 4f fst :50 H 26/40

Pro Doc

Own: Ruggeri George P

NELSON D (52 5 5 7 .10)

Gr/ro c. 2 (Mar)
Sire: Prospectors Gamble (Crafty Prospector)
Dam: Smile Softly (Prince Tenderfoot)
Br: Rosenthal Morton W (Fla)
Tr: Terrill William V (27 4 4 3 .15)

L 118

Lifetime Record: 4 M 0 0 $1,920

1995 4 M 0 0 $1,920 Turf 2 0 0 0 $1,920
1994 0 M 0 0 Wet 1 0 0 0
Bel (T) 1 0 0 0 Dist (T) 2 0 0 0 $1,920

13Sep95-6Bel fm 1 1/16 [T] :23 :461 1:104 1:431 Md Sp Wt 34 6 2 1½ 3nk 613 720¾ Nelson D 118 b 12.90 57-20 Togher1187¾ Going For The Gold118nk Bombardier1184 Dueled, gave way 8
25Aug95-6Sar fm 1 1/16 (T) :23 :47 1:114 1:433 Md Sp Wt 58 11 2 1hd 1½ 2hd 44½ Nelson D 118 b 51.50 76-07 Defacto118nk Bombardier1184 Dontnswerthefour118nk Dueled, weakened 11
12Aug95-2Sar sly 7f ⊗ :222 :463 1:12 1:251 Md Sp Wt -0 3 4 45 818 827 840 Smith M E 118 23.80 32-15 Spicy Fact118¾ Jetting Robert1184 Tuning Up118no Done early 8
29Jly95-6Sar fst 6f :22 :454 :584 1:114 Md Sp Wt — 8 9 912 919 929 — Luzzi M J 119 52.00 — 13 El Amante1191½ Hashid119¾ Head Minister118¾ Trailed, eased 9

WORKOUTS: Oct 11 Bel 4f fst :484 H 17/45 Oct 4 Bel 4f fst :512 H 50/61 Sep 29 Bel tr.t 4f fst :502 B 14/31 Sep 22 Bel tr.t 4f fst :492 B 10/20 Sep 9 Bel tr.t 4f fst :514 B 8/11 Sep 1 Bel 4f fst :502 B 35/40

Luckisasecret

Own: Beecher Aaron

DAVIS R G (243 37 42 30 .15)

Ch. g. 2 (May)
Sire: Huckster (Mr. Prospector)
Dam: Timeless Secret (Timeless Moment)
Br: Aaron Beecher (NY)
Tr: Gulle Gary P (31 4 3 3 .13)

L 118

Lifetime Record: 3 M 0 0 $0

1995 3 M 0 0 Turf 0 0 0 0
1994 0 M 0 0 Wet 0 0 0 0
Bel (T) 0 0 0 0 Dist (T) 0 0 0 0

29Sep95-1Bel fst 7f :224 :463 1:131 1:273 [S]Md Sp Wt 18 8 7 83½ 911 812 814 Sellers S J L 118 b 51.25 49-20 Hooray For Evan118no Tough One118¾ Ruletero118¾ No threat 9
13Sep95-4Bel fst 6f :224 :464 :591 1:12 [S]Md Sp Wt 19 12 10 86 87 910 918¼ Davis R G 118 b 39.25 62-20 Gotabe Inittowinit118¾ Iwillbking1181½ Rose's Lad118¾ No factor 12
31Jly95-2Sar fst 6f :224 :463 :591 1:12 [S]Md Sp Wt -0 11 10 109 1010 1015 1032 Rydowski S R 118 124.75 49-16 Carrbine Special118¾ Talc About June118hd Tri Line118nk No response 11

WORKOUTS: ●Oct 14 Aqu 3f fst :361 B 1/9 Sep 25 Aqu 3f fst :364 B 3/5 Aug 30 Aqu 4f fst :493 B 8/13 Aug 22 Bel tr.t 3f fst :37 B 2/9 Aug 14 Bel tr.t 5f fst 1:043 B 7/11 Jly 27 Sar tr.t 5f fst 1:064 B 6/6

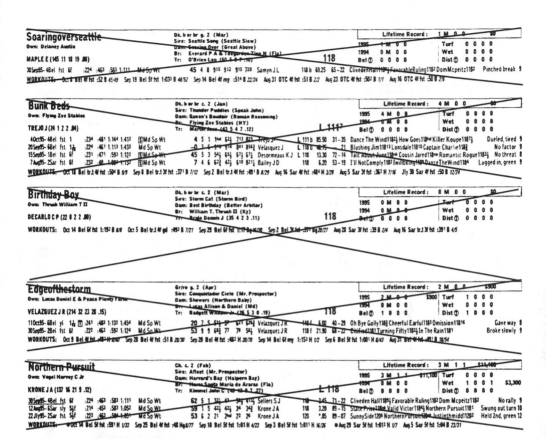

Soaringoverseattle
Own: Delaney Austin
MAPLE E (145 11 18 19 .08)

Dk. b or br g. 2 (Mar)
Sire: Seattle Song (Seattle Slew)
Dam: Soaring Over (Great Above)
Br: Everard P A & Taggardon Tina N (Fla)
Tr: O'Brien Leo (50 6 8 7 .10)
118

Lifetime Record: 1 M 0 0 $0
1995 1 M 0 0 | Turf 0 0 0 0
1994 0 M 0 0 | Wet 0 0 0 0
Bel① 0 0 0 0 | Dist① 0 0 0 0

30Sep95-4Bel fst 6f :224 :463 :583 1:111 Md Sp Wt 45 4 8 915 912 915 720 Samyn J L 118 b 69.25 65-22 ClivedenHall118¾ FavorableRuling1182 DomMcpeitz1182 Pinched break 9
WORKOUTS: Oct 8 Bel 4f fst :52 B 45/49 Sep 19 Bel 5f fst 1:033 B 48/52 Sep 14 Bel 4f my :514 B 22/24 Aug 31 OTC 4f fst :51 B 2/2 Aug 23 OTC 4f fst :502 B 1/1 Aug 16 OTC 4f fst :50 B 2/6

Bunk Beds
Own: Flying Zee Stables
TREJO J (24 1 2 2 .04)

Dk. b or br c. 2 (Jan)
Sire: Thunder Puddles (Speak John)
Dam: Queen's Boudoir (Roman Reasoning)
Br: Flying Zee Stables (NY)
Tr: Martin Jose (43 5 4 7 .12)
L 1117

Lifetime Record: 4 M 0 0 $0
1995 4 M 0 0 | Turf 0 0 0 0
1994 0 M 0 0 | Wet 0 0 0 0
Bel① 0 0 0 0 | Dist① 0 0 0 0

4Oct95-4Bel fst 1 :234 :481 1:144 1:412 [S]Md Sp Wt 4 5 1 1hd 62½ 713 825 Trejo J5 L 111 b 85.50 31-35 Dance The Wind118¾ How Goes118hd Killer Koupe1187½ Dueled, tired 9
20Sep95-6Bel fst 1⅛ :224 :461 1:113 1:433 Md Sp Wt -0 3 6 910 914 841 856½ Velasquez J L 118 b 40.75 — 21 Blushing Jim11813 Lonsdale11810 Captain Charlie118¾ No factor 9
15Sep95-1Bel fst 6f :231 :471 :593 1:122 [S]Md Sp Wt 45 5 3 54½ 65½ 67½ 67½ Desormeaux K J L 118 13.30 72-14 Talc About June118nk Cousin Jared118no Romantic Rogue1183½ No threat 8
7Aug95-2Sar fst 6f :232 :48 1:002 1:132 [S]Md Sp Wt 7 4 6 62¾ 42½ 610 821½ Bailey J D 118 6.20 53-19 I'll NotComply1182 IwillbeKing1183 DanceTheWind1184 Lugged in, green 9
WORKOUTS: Oct 18 Bel tr.t 4f fst :504 B 9/9 Sep 8 Bel tr.t 3f fst :371 B 7/12 Sep 2 Bel tr.t 4f fst :491 B 8/29 Aug 16 Sar 4f fst :484 H 3/28 Aug 5 Sar 3f fst :362 H 7/16 Jly 30 Sar 4f fst :50 B 12/24

Birthday Boy
Own: Thrush William T II
DECARLO C P (22 0 2 2 .00)

Dk. b or br c. 2 (Mar)
Sire: Storm Cat (Storm Bird)
Dam: Best Birthday (Better Arbitor)
Br: William T. Thrush II (Ky)
Tr: Brida Dennis J (35 4 2 3 .11)
118

Lifetime Record: 0 M 0 0 $0
1995 0 M 0 0 | Turf 0 0 0 0
1994 0 M 0 0 | Wet 0 0 0 0
Bel① 0 0 0 0 | Dist① 0 0 0 0

WORKOUTS: Oct 14 Bel 6f fst 1:192 B 4/4 Oct 5 Bel tr.t 4f gd :493 B 7/21 Sep 29 Bel 6f fst 1:17 Bg 16/20 Sep 2 Bel 3f fst :372 Bg 20/27 Aug 28 Sar 3f fst :39 B 2/4 Aug 16 Sar tr.t 3f fst :391 B 4/5

Edgeofthestorm
Own: Lucas Daniel E & Peace Plenty Farm
VELAZQUEZ J R (214 32 23 28 .15)

Gr/ro g. 2 (Apr)
Sire: Conquistador Cielo (Mr. Prospector)
Dam: Showers (Northern Baby)
Br: Lucas Allison & Daniel (Md)
Tr: Badgett William Jr (26 5 3 0 .19)
118

Lifetime Record: 2 M 0 0 $300
1995 2 M 0 0 $300 | Turf 1 0 0 0
1994 0 M 0 0 | Wet 0 0 0 0
Bel① 1 0 0 0 | Dist① 1 0 0 0

11Oct95-6Bel yl 1⅛ [T] :241 :483 1:132 1:454 Md Sp Wt 20 7 5 51½ 57 621 626½ Velazquez J R 118 f 6.00 40-29 Oh Bye Golly118¾ Cheerful Earful1183 Omission11816 Gave way 8
30Sep95-2Bel fst 6f :222 :463 :592 1:124 Md Sp Wt 53 9 9 68¾ 77 78 54½ Velazquez J R 118 f 21.90 68-22 Certified1181 Turning Fifty1182½ In The Rain1181 Broke slowly 9
WORKOUTS: Oct 9 Bel 4f fst :493 H 8/60 Sep 23 Bel 4f fst :51 B 28/30 Sep 20 Bel 4f fst :482 H 20/70 Sep 14 Bel 6f my 1:153 H 1/2 Sep 6 Bel 5f fst 1:001 H 8/43 Aug 31 Bel 4f fst :491 B 18/54

Northern Pursuit
Own: Vogel Harvey C Jr
KRONE J A (137 16 21 9 .12)

Ch. c. 2 (Feb)
Sire: Afleet (Mr. Prospector)
Dam: Harvard's Bay (Halpern Bay)
Br: Haras Santa Maria de Araras (Fla)
Tr: Kimmel John C (43 13 8 7 .27)
L 118

Lifetime Record: 3 M 1 1 $14,400
1995 3 M 1 1 $11,100 | Turf 0 0 0 0
1994 0 M 0 0 | Wet 1 0 0 1 $3,300
Bel① 0 0 0 0 | Dist① 0 0 0 0

30Sep95-4Bel fst 6f :224 :463 :583 1:111 Md Sp Wt 62 5 1 32½ 43 39½ 41½ Sellers S J 118 3.45 71-22 Cliveden Hall118¾ Favorable Ruling1182 Dom Mcpeitz1182 No rally 9
12Aug95-6Sar sly 5½f :214 :453 :583 1:052 Md Sp Wt 59 1 5 42½ 42½ 34 34½ Krone J A 118 3.20 89-15 State Prize118nk Valid Victor1184½ Northern Pursuit1181 Swung out turn 10
22Jly95-2Sar fst 5½f :222 :462 :584 1:051 Md Sp Wt 53 6 2 21 2hd 22 26 Krone J A 120 *.85 89-07 SunnySide1206 NorthernPursuit120nk Justinthmiddl1202 Held 2nd, green 12
WORKOUTS: ●Oct 14 Bel 5f fst :591 H 1/33 Sep 25 Bel 4f fst :48 Hg 4/77 Sep 10 Bel 5f fst 1:01 H 4/23 Sep 3 Bel 5f fst 1:011 H 16/26 ●Aug 29 Sar 5f fst 1:013 H 1/7 Aug 5 Sar 5f fst 1:04 B 23/31

6 Belmont Park

1¼ MILES. **(Inner Turf). (1:57³) CLAIMING. Purse $25,000 (plus up to $9,813 NYSBFOA). Fillies and mares, 3-year-olds and upward. Weights: 3-year-olds, 117 lbs. Older, 122 lbs. Non-winners of two races over a mile since September 9, allowed 2 lbs. Of such a race since September 27, 4 lbs. Of such a race since September 5, 6 lbs. Claiming price $35,000, if for $30,000, allowed 2 lbs. (Races where entered to be claimed for $25,000 or less not considered.)**

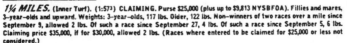

Flower Delivery
Own: Knight Landon
SMITH M E (204 36 24 31 .18) $35,000

B. f. 4
Sire: Stately Don (Nureyev)
Dam: Flew S. (Fluorescent Light)
Br: Knight Landon (Ky)
Tr: Badgett William Jr (26 5 3 0 .19)
116

Lifetime Record: 18 1 3 4 $45,145
1995 7 1 0 1 $15,090 | Turf 16 1 3 2 $39,725
1994 11 M 3 3 $30,055 | Wet 2 0 0 2 $5,420
Bel① 5 0 2 0 $15,240 | Dist① 6 0 2 1 $18,480

12Oct95-8Bel gd 1¼ [T] :483 1:131 1:384 2:032 3+ Ⓕ Alw 34000N2L 58 8 7 67 87½ 911 713 Velazquez J R 116 8.60 58-31 Francia1134 Star Of Light1114 Bella Dawn113nk Tired 12
18Aug95-3Sar fm 1⅜ [T] :472 1:111 1:354 1:481 3+ Ⓕ Clm 50000 81 5 7 77 77½ 56 32 Smith M E 114 *2.25 92-10 RoylPelliknow114nk ShesOurFstest1191½ FlowerDelivry1141½ Belated rally 8
22Jly95-4Sar fm 1⅜ [T] :483 1:133 1:38 2:152 3+ Ⓕ Clm 75000 86 6 5 53½ 45½ 43 52½ Velazquez J R 113 28.00 86-10 AssertiveDancer1181½ Knocknock113½ PrincessStrek113½ Checked break 8
17Jly95-7Bel fm 1¼ [T] :482 1:131 1:373 2:011 3+ Ⓕ Alw 34000N2L 66 4 12 119 105½ 109½ 910 Chavez J F 119 6.60 72-18 LookDaggers1122½ RoyalFndngo1191 RetinedErning1141½ Steadied early 12
7Jun95-7Bel gd 1¼ [T] :48 1:13 1:381 2:03 3+ Ⓕ Alw 34000N2L 77 9 9 97 44½ 44½ 41½ Alvarado F T 120 20.90 71-22 Cavalanche114nk Bella Dawn113nk Royal Fandango1201 Checked 3/8 pl 10
20Mar95-7Hia fm *1⅛ ① 1:49 Ⓕ Md Sp Wt 79 1 5 65 52½ 32 11 Fires E 122 *1.00 87-11 Flower Delivery1221 Major Momma1223½ Shes Our Fastest1224 Driving 11
9Feb95-10GP fm *1⅛ ① :482 1:131 1:37 1:492+ Ⓕ Md Sp Wt 50 5 9 94½ 86½ 712 712½ Sellers S J 120 4.50 86 — Sabbia Rosa1202 Dragon Miss120½ Mossy Path120nk 10
Raced wide most of trip, no threat
25Nov94-3Aqu sf 1⅛ ① :24 :493 1:153 1:483 3+ Ⓕ Md Sp Wt 64 4 6 64½ 63½ 45½ 45½ Chavez J F 120 b 2.40 60-31 Sheza Wild Again1203½ Crazy Fling1201½ She's Fine115¾ No threat 10
4Nov94-6Aqu yl 1⅛ ① :493 1:15 1:403 1:541 3+ Ⓕ Md Sp Wt 70 8 7 86½ 62½ 51½ 2nk Chavez J F 120 4.70 63-31 Polish Treaty115nk [DH]Flower Delivery120 [DH]Crazy Fling1204 10
Pinched break, lugged in stretch
11Oct94-3Bel fm 1¼ [T] :481 1:132 1:383 2:033 3+ Ⓕ Md Sp Wt 66 1 7 77 41½ 43 22 Chavez J F 119 4.30 70-17 Jodi'sLand1192 FlowerDelivery1191½ RiverbotPrincess119nk Rallied wide 8
WORKOUTS: Sep 30 Bel 4f fst :494 B 30/53 Sep 26 Bel 3f sly :39 B 5/7 Sep 16 Bel 4f fst :512 B 45/52 Sep 7 Bel 4f fst :51 B 38/48 Aug 16 Sar tr.t① 4f fm :493 B 7/14

Slew The Duchess
Own: Montanari Marion G
CHAVEZ J F (196 32 28 27 .16) $35,000
B. m. 5
Sire: Tsunami Slew (Seattle Slew)
Dam: Marquessa de Sade (Le Fabuleux (Fr))
Br: Montanari Marion G (Fla)
Tr: Terrill William V (27 4 4 3 .15)
L 120

Lifetime Record: 38 7 5 5 $147,320											
1995	10	2	1	0	$31,450	Turf	27	5	2	2	$86,300
1994	10	2	1	2	$41,040	Wet	4	1	1	1	$28,040
Bel Ⓣ	13	3	1	1	$51,960	Dist Ⓣ	5	1	1	0	$17,220

5Oct95- 6Bel sly 1¼ ⊗ :474 1:123 1:38 2:051 3↑ ⒻClm 40000 82 4 4 48½ 31½ 11½ 16 Chavez J F L 113 b 5.00 68-26 SlewTheDuchess1136 Majhuits1216½ RoylCozzene1132 Wide, going away 5
10Sep95- 3Bel fm 1¼ [T] :48 1:12 1:37 2:014 3↑ ⒻClm 35000 69 2 3 2½ 2hd 42½ 77½ Davis R G L 117 b 5.80 72-17 MissPocktCourt1171½ HighTlnt1192½ RoylPllknow121nk Dueled, rein broke 9
25Aug95- 1Sar fm 1⅛ [T] :47 1:113 1:353 1:473 3↑ ⒻClm 35000 72 8 9 98½ 96½ 57 67½ Lovato F Jr 114 16.90 89-07 Royal Pelliknow1191½ All Tango1145 High Talent114no No late bid 9
18Aug95- 3Sar fm 1⅛ [T] :472 1:111 1:354 1:481 3↑ ⒻClm 50000 72 4 8 810 88 77½ 76 Lovato F Jr 114 11.60 88-10 Royal Pelliknow114nk Shes Our Fastest1191¾ Flower Delivery1141½ No rally 8
6Jly95- 9Crc fm *1 1/16 Ⓣ 1:43 3↑ ⒻAlw 18300N3X 66 4 10 99¾ 910 98 89½ Castillo H Jr L 119 5.20 79-16 College Road1122½ Darnitallanyway1191½ Vaunted Vamp112¾ No threat 10
2Jun95- 8Crc fm *1 1/16 Ⓣ 1:45 3↑ ⒻClm 35000 75 5 6 610 62½ 42 22½ Castillo H Jr L 116 f 3.80 77-22 Madam Meadowlake1182½ Slew The Duchess116no Baby Millie116nk Rallied 7
22May95- 6Hia fst 1⅛ ⊗ :492 1:14 1:39 1:53 ⒻClm 35000 65 6 7 54 56 44 44 Castilic H Jr L 119 b 3.90 73-21 Madam Meadowlake116¾ Baby Millie1123 Cut The Pot114nk Belated bid 7
9May95- 8Hia fm *1 1/16 Ⓣ 1:433 ⒻClm 32500 78 1 10 1010 94¾ 84¾ 1nk Castillo H Jr L 114 *2.20 84-18 Slew The Duchess114nk Madam Meadowlake116no Reely Risky116nk 10
Wide top str, driving
15Apr95- 6Hia fm 1⅛ Ⓣ 1:481 ⒻAlw 17600N2X 58 1 6 613 610 510 514¾ Velez J A Jr L 114 5.50 77-12 LastBlood1121½ ChelseyFlower11410 GoodonyAmy1141½ Failed to menace 10
25Mar95- 7Hia fm 1 1/16 Ⓣ 1:42 ⒻAlw 16000N2X 79 4 7 87¾ 79 57½ 63¾ Bailey J D 114 4.80 84-06 Sherunsfornanny114no Gold Blossom117¾ Annie's Valentine114¾ Mild bid 10
WORKOUTS: Sep 21 Bel tr.t 4f fst :494 B 4/17 Sep 16 Bel tr.t 4f fst :50 B 14/25 Sep 4 Bel 5f fst 1:004 H 7/32 Aug 15 Sar tr.t 4f fst :54 B 25/30 Aug 2 Sar tr.t 4f fst :52 B 9/12 Jly 23 Sar tr.t 5f fst 1:054 B 7/8

High Talent
Own: Bertino & Mangine & Mariano E & P
BAILEY J D (283 47 27 22 .23) $35,000
Dk. b or br m. 6
Sire: Talc (Rock Talk)
Dam: Far and Above (Far Out East)
Br: Parsons Ron (NY)
Tr: Contessa Gary C (21 3 4 2 .14)
L 116

Lifetime Record: 45 7 8 6 $169,010											
1995	8	1	2	2	$31,420	Turf	29	5	6	5	$131,310
1994	19	2	4	3	$68,740	Wet	4	1	1	0	$21,480
Bel Ⓣ	17	3	4	4	$88,210	Dist Ⓣ	8	1	4	1	$41,250

Entered 19Oct95- 8 MED
10Sep95- 3Bel fm 1¼ [T] :48 1:12 1:37 2:014 3↑ ⒻClm 35000 82 4 1 1½ 1hd 11 21½ Bailey J D L 119 b *2.55 78-17 MissPocktCourt1171½ HighTlnt1192½ RoylPlliknow121nk Dueled, held well 9
25Aug95- 1Sar fm 1⅛ [T] :47 1:113 1:353 1:473 3↑ ⒻClm 35000 75 3 1 1½ 1½ 32 36½ Bailey J D 114 b *.90 90-07 Royal Pelliknow1191½ All Tango1145 High Talent114no Dueled, weakened 9
10Aug95-10Sar fm 1 1/16 Ⓣ :464 1:11 1:354 1:543 3↑ ⒻClm 50000 88 10 1 12 11½ 11½ 2nk Bailey J D 114 b 3.00e 92-06 Leo N' Me114nk High Talent114no Polar Princess1142 Yielded grudgingly 10
22Jly95- 4Sar fm 1⅜ [T] :483 1:133 1:38 2:152 3↑ ⒻClm 65000 83 8 2 2½ 2½ 32½ 74¾ Bailey J D 112 b 19.30 84-10 Assertive Dancer1181½ Knocknock113½ Princess Streak113½ Forced pace 8
13Jly95- 4Bel fm 1 1/16 [T] :231 :453 1:101 1:412 ⒻClm 40000 84 3 2 20 23 31½ 42¾ Santagata N 120 b 4.00 86-13 Madeline's Affair114¾ Leo N' Me1141½ A Demon A Day114½ Bid, tired 8
3Jly95- 4Mth fm 1⅛ Ⓣ :483 1:12 1:37 1:492 3↑ ⒻClm 40000 86 3 1 2½ 31 11½ 1¾ Santagata N L 115 b 5.30 84-15 High Talent115¾ Da Bounboun1151 Ruth's Revenge115hd Driving 8
1Jun95- 9Bel fm 1¼ [T] :481 1:124 1:38 2:034 ⒻClm 40000 74 5 2 42½ 21 21 31¾ Santos J A 116 b 3.15 67-20 Reinvesting Ada1161¾ Now I Hope109no High Talent116nk Saved ground 10
21May95- 4Bel fm 1 Ⓣ :223 :451 1:101 1:353 ⒻClm 45000 73 3 7 74½ 72½ 74½ 76½ Santos J A 114 b 10.10 79-15 Ski At Dawn109hd Turkolady1143½ Royal Pelliknow1121½ Even wide 11
8Dec94- 9Med fst 1 1/16 :232 :463 1:12 1:442 3↑ ⒻAlw 27000N3X 43 3 3 44 77 712 718¾ Santagata N L 116 b 11.90 70-16 Lasting Shore1132½ Cherokee Wonder1133½ Ruth's Revenge1142½ Tired 8
12Nov94- 7Med yl 1 70 Ⓣ :23 :48 1:124 1:432 3↑ Alw 26000N3X 75 7 4 53½ 52¾ 73¾ 65½ Colton R E L 115 b 3.30 68-22 Thorny Crown112¾ Balsam Bandit1161¾ Shipbird1181 No rally 9
WORKOUTS: Oct 9 Bel 5f fst 1:024 H 26/41 Oct 3 Bel 4f fst :492 B 10/30 Sep 29 Bel 4f fst :51 B 46/61 Sep 7 Bel 4f fst :493 B 21/40 Aug 20 Sar tr.t 4f fst :512 B 11/21 Aug 7 Sar tr.t 4f fst :52 B 27/40

Dinner Diamond
Own: Corrado Fred L
SANTOS J A (168 28 18 20 .17) $35,000
Dk. b or br m. 5
Sire: Diamond Shoal (Mill Reef)
Dam: After Dinner Mint (After Eight)
Br: Martin M T Racing Stable (NY)
Tr: DeBonis Robert (8 1 1 0 .13)
L 116

Lifetime Record: 45 5 3 5 $144,909											
1995	9	2	0	1	$52,659	Turf	30	5	2	5	$139,269
1994	11	1	0	3	$35,640	Wet	2	0	0	0	
Bel Ⓣ	19	3	1	3	$82,360	Dist Ⓣ	7	1	1	2	$32,130

13Oct95- 8Bel gd 1⅜ Ⓣ :492 1:14 1:383 2:161 3↑ ⒻHandicap50k 79 3 6 64¾ 65 47 412½ Luzzi M J L 111 26.25 74-25 Market Booster1227½ Caromana118no La Turka1215 No threat 6
15Sep95- 2Bel fm 1 1/16 [T] :244 :49 1:131 1:433 3↑ ⒻClm 50000 76 4 5 65½ 63½ 46½ 55½ Alvarado F T L 116 b 3.75 72-16 PrincessStreak1164 PolrPrincess116½ RockfordPech1141 Flattened out 8
16Aug95- 9Sar fm 1⅛ Ⓣ :462 1:104 1:35 1:472 3↑ Ⓕ[S]Yaddo H81k 81 1 6 68½ 55½ 46 49¾ Luzzi M J 112 b 12.60 80-11 Irish Linnet1248 Kris's Kiss1131¾ Casa Eire111no Late gain 6
22Jly95- 4Sar fm 1⅜ [T] :483 1:133 1:38 2:152 3↑ ⒻClm 75000 86 5 6 64½ 56 64½ 42½ Smith M E 113 b 4.20 86-10 AssertiveDancer1181½ Knocknock113½ PrincessStrek113½ Flattened out 8
3Jly95- 7Bel yl 1 Ⓣ :23 :463 1:111 1:362 3↑ ⒻAlw 38000N3X 88 4 8 67 63 43½ 33½ Luzzi M J 119 4.40 77-26 LadyReiko1211½ UnchartedWaters1192½ DinnerDimond1192½ Belated rally 8
17Jun95- 5Bel fm 1 Ⓣ :234 :47 1:11 1:341 ⒻClm 75000 85 6 9 95½ 94 63 53½ Luzzi M J 112 b 13.20 89-12 Symphony Lady1141½ CircusMusic113hd NewWave1172 Improved position 9
2Jun95- 5Bel fm 1 1/16 [T] :233 :471 1:11 1:42 ⒻClm 47500 88 4 7 75¾ 84¾ 42½ 12 Luzzi M J 116 b 3.20 86-13 DinnerDimond1162 SunshineLindjne112½ EeniMniMiny1122½ Going away 8
24May95- 7Bel fm 1 1/16 Ⓣ :231 :462 1:10 1:391 3↑ ⒻAlw 38000N3X 82 7 10 107½ 105¾ 66½ 59½ Luzzi M J 119 b 23.70 92-07 Perfect Arc1095 Joy Of Life1191½ Aucilla1192 No threat 10
23Apr95- 9Aqu fm 1⅛ Ⓣ :49 1:133 1:384 1:504 ⒻClm 45000 91 8 7 78½ 76½ 41½ 12½ Luzzi M J 114 b 9.70e 86-18 DnnrDmond1142½ EnMnMny1141¾ BonnShoppr116hd Altered course 3/16 pl 8
13Nov94- 3Aqu gd 1⅛ Ⓣ :47 1:12 1:382 1:511 3↑ ⒻAlw 36000N3X 80 4 9 920 912 57 45½ Perez R B5 112 b 13.70e 78-16 Knocknock1152½ Manila Lila117nk Waquoit's Tune1123 Mild gain 10
WORKOUTS: Sep 6 Bel 4f fst :492 H 25/48 Aug 11 Bel tr.t 4f fst :501 B 13/20 Aug 5 Bel tr.t 4f fst :50 B 9/19

Eenie Meenie Miney
Own: More-N-More Stable
MAPLE E (145 11 18 19 .08) $30,000
B. m. 6
Sire: Tunerup (The Pruner)
Dam: Yallah Miss (Yallah Native)
Br: Fairholme Farm Inc (Ky)
Tr: Sciacca Gary (73 7 5 12 .10)
L 114

Lifetime Record: 61 5 8 8 $225,717											
1995	8	0	1	1	$10,700	Turf	44	4	6	7	$184,939
1994	17	2	0	3	$55,870	Wet	7	0	1	1	$21,988
Bel Ⓣ	22	1	3	4	$64,298	Dist Ⓣ	5	0	2	0	$13,090

4Oct95- 8Bel gd 1 1/16 Ⓣ :231 :464 1:112 1:43 3↑ ⒻAlw 40000N4X 74 3 6 55 74½ 65½ 77½ Maple E L 116 26.75 75-20 Chelsey Flower1201¾ Jiving Around116¾ Ka Lae1161 Checked 1/2 pl 10
24Jly95- 1Sar fm 1 [T] :241 :481 1:13 1:373 3↑ ⒻClm 50000 72 7 6 53½ 53 75¾ 76¾ Sellers S J 113 *3.20e 82-12 Glorious Purple113¾ Light And Love113½ Leo N' Me1131¾ Lacked rally 9
7Jly95- 3Bel fm 1¼ [T] :501 1:144 1:39 2:03 ⒻClm 45000 74 4 4 32 41½ 64 74¾ Velazquez J R 114 7.80 68-22 Artful Pleasure1161½ Caroline Of Kent114no Mont Germont1121½ Tired 11
1Jly95- 7Bel sly 1 ⊗ :224 :46 1:11 1:37 ⒻAlw 40000N4X 57 1 3 33½ 45½ 59½ 518 Beckner D V 112 7.80 60-18 Dancer's Gate1084 Future Answer1122 Willspynow1129½ Tired 5
2Jun95- 5Bel fm 1 1/16 [T] :233 :471 1:11 1:42 ⒻClm 45000 82 1 3 32½ 42¾ 2½ 32½ Bailey J D 112 *2.95 83-13 DinnrDmond1162 SunshnLndjn112½ EnMnMny1122½ Inside bid, flattened 8
21May95- 4Bel fm 1 Ⓣ :223 :451 1:101 1:353 ⒻClm 50000 76 4 10 912 94½ 84¾ 65¼ Chavez J F 116 *1.80 80-15 Ski At Dawn108hd Turkolady1143½ RoyalPelliknow1121¼ Broke slowly, wide 11
23Apr95- 9Aqu fm 1⅛ Ⓣ :49 1:133 1:384 1:504 ⒻClm 45000 86 4 8 89½ 54¼ 3½ 22½ Chavez J F 114 2.90 84-18 DinnerDimond1142½ EenieMniMiny1141¾ BonniShoppr116hd Four wide bid 8
8Apr95- 6Hia fm 1 1/16 Ⓣ 1:423 ⒻClm 40000 69 2 11 96½ 106 86¼ 44¼ Vasquez J L 116 7.00 77-10 Forest Dunes1162¾ Litchfield Inn1162½ Uptown Show1163 12
Eight wide top str, belated bid
22Nov94- 8Aqu wf 1 ⊗ :233 :47 1:121 1:373 3↑ ⒻAlw 46000N$mY 61 1 4 31½ 45 414 415¼ Pezua J M 115 15.20 65-28 Lottsa Talc1151½ Blazing Kadie115nk Dixie Luck11313 Tired 4
13Nov94- 6Aqu gd 1 1/16 Ⓣ :232 :473 1:124 1:451 3↑ Ⓕ[R]Alw 46000N$YmT 74 7 7 714 710 712 411¾ Pezua J M 114 26.00 71-16 Caress1178½ Great Triumph115nk Blazing Kadie1173 No threat 7
WORKOUTS: Sep 29 Bel tr.t 4f fst :482 H 2/31 Sep 21 Bel 4f fst :49 B 18/47 Jly 20 Sar tr.t 3f fst :373 B 5/16

Royal Pelliknow

Own: O'Connell Richard

MIGLIORE R (92 10 6 16 .11) $35,000

B. m. 5
Sire: Raja's Revenge (Raja Baba)
Dam: I'm With Knowledge (King Pellinore)
Br: O'Connell Richard (NY)
Tr: O'Connell Richard (36 5 4 7 .14)

L 120

	Lifetime Record:	42 7 9 7	$210,117
1995	11 4 0 3	$93,177	Turf 16 6 5 7 $189,887
1994	14 1 6 3	$55,660	Wet 1 0 0 0
Bel ①	4 0 1 1	$87,047	Dist ① 4 0 1 1 $12,647

130ct95-5Bel gd 1⅛ ⓣ :25 :491 1:13² 1:44¹ 3↑ ⓕClm 40000 87 8 2 2½ 2hd 1hd 1hd Bailey J D L 114 *1.80e 75-25 RoylPelliknow114nk AllTango1½ Leo N' Me116½ Long drive, gamely 8
10Sep95-3Bel fm 1⅛ ⓣ :48 1:12 1:37 2:01⁴ 3↑ ⓕClm 35000 77 8 3 2½ 2¹ 33¼ Velazquez J R L 121 2.80 77-17 MissPocketCourt117½ HighTlent119²¼ RoylPelliknow121nk Bid, weakened 9
25Aug95-1Sar fm 1⅛ ⓣ :47 1:11³ 1:35³ 1:47³ 3↑ ⓕClm 35000 89 2 4 4²¼ 32 4¼ 1¼ Velazquez J R 113 5.00 97-07 RoylPelliknow119¼ AllTango1½ HighTalent114no Going away 9
18Aug95-1Sar fm 1⅛ ⓣ :47² 1:11¹ 1:35⁴ 1:48¹ 3↑ ⓕClm 35000 85 3 2 2¹¼ 1hd 1¹ 1nk Bailey J D 114 3.00 94-10 RoylPelliknow119nk ShesOurFstest119¹½ FlowerDlivry141¼ Drifted, all out 8
10Aug95-9Sar fm 1⅛ ⓣ :46⁴ 1:11 1:34¹ 1:54³ 3↑ ⓕClm 50000 80 5 2 2² 2¹½ 3¹½ 5¾ Nelson D 114 13.50 88-06 Leo N' Me114nk HighTalent114no Polar Princess114² Forced pace 10
24July95-1Sar fm 1 ⓣ :24¹ 1:13 1:37³ 3↑ ⓕClm 50000 72 4 2½ 2¹ 33 66¼ Bailey J D 116 5.90 86-12 Glorious Purple113⅞ Light And Love113¼ Leo N' Me113¹⅞ Forced pace 9
3July95-4Mth fm 1⅛ ⓣ :48³ 1:12 1:37 1:49² 3↑ ⓕClm 50000 69 2 2 1½ 2hd 42 5⅞ Nelson D 117 2.80 76-15 High Talent115¼ Da Bounbou115¹ Ruth's Revenge115hd Tired 8
18Jun95-5Bel fm 1⅛ ⓣ :22⁴ :45² 1:10¹ 1:41⁴ 3↑ ⑤Alw 36000N2X 82 7 5 5⁵ 4¹ 2¹ 1¹½ Bailey J D 120 *2.75e 89-10 RoylPelliknow120¹½ ADyToRmmbr120¹½ DrinDnk114nk 4 wide, fully extended 12
21May95-4Bel fm 1½ ⓣ :49 1:13¹ 1:36² 2:15³ ⓕClm 45000 79 5 6 6⁵½ 5¹½ 5½ 2¼ Bailey J D 112 6.40 81-15 Ski At Dawn108hd Turkolady114¼ RoyalPelliknow112¹½ Rallied wide 11
14May95-10Bel fm 1½ ⓣ :48 1:12¹ 1:36² 1:43³ 3↑ ⑤Alw 36000N2X 42 10 4 4²½ 5² 10¹¹ 10²⁰ Nelson D 120 5.70 60-12 Leo N' Me115¹½ Bien Sucre103¹ Very True112½ Four wide, tired 10

WORKOUTS: Oct 7 Bel tr.t 4f fst :52 B 21/22   Sep 30 Bel 4f fst :49² B 29/57   Sep 23 Bel tr.t 4f gd :49⁴ B 3/4   Aug 5 Sar 4f fst :50⁴ B 35/46

Dana's Wedding

Own: Leveen Leonard

DAVIS R G (243 37 42 30 .15) $35,000

Ch. m. 5
Sire: Compliance (Northern Dancer)
Dam: Dumb Donna (Honey Jay)
Br: Bemze Richard M (NY)
Tr: Kelly Michael J (9 2 0 0 .22)

L 116

	Lifetime Record:	32 5 3 4	$120,710
1995	10 2 0 0	$37,050	Turf 17 3 2 4 $76,350
1994	13 1 3 3	$42,560	Wet 4 0 1 0 $8,960
Bel ①	10 2 1 2	$45,480	Dist ① 3 1 1 0 $17,220

8Oct95-2Bel fst 1⅛ :23³ :471 1:12 1:44² 3↑ ⓕClm 35000 56 6 5 6⁹ 711 517 520¼ Davis R G L 116 8.70 57-25 Pastel Parade116⁶ Sun Attack116¼ Gliding Lark116½ No threat 7
10Sep95-3Bel fm 1⅛ ⓣ :48 1:12 1:37 2:01⁴ 3↑ ⓕClm 35000 70 7 2 4³ 7¹½ 84½ 67 Smith M E L 117 7.90 72-17 Miss Pocket Court117½ HighTalent119²¼ RoyalPelliknow121nk No late bid 9
25Aug95-1Sar fm 1⅛ ⓣ :47 1:11³ 1:35³ 1:47³ 3↑ ⓕClm 35000 75 1 5 6⁴½ 5¹½ 4⁴ 46¼ Davis R G 114 10.10 90-07 Royal Pelliknow119¼ All Tango1½ High Talent114no Saved ground 9
6Aug95-1Sar wf 1½ ⓣ :47⁴ 1:12³ 1:39³ 1:53² 3↑ ⓕClm 35000 69 4 6 64½ 51² 61¾ 610½ Davis R G 113 12.60 58-31 Bounding Believer113no Grab The Glory114²⅞ Proud Angela113⅞ No threat 7
22July95-1Sar fst 7f :22² :45² 1:10³ 1:24⁴ ⓕClm 35000 28 4 7 9⅝ 9⁹¼ 914 924 Decarlo C P 114 42.00 63-07 Susan Valley113no Runaway Fling116² Jupiter Assembly113⅞ Trailed 9
7May95-2Bel fm 1⅛ ⓣ :24⁴ :48³ 1:13 1:44² ⓕClm 35000 68 9 6 8⁹¾ 7⁷½ 6⁸ 5⁸ Krone J A 112 3.05 66-18 Joy Of Life116¼ Ski At Dawn108⁴² Saratoga April112²¼ No threat 10
23Mar95-8Aqu fst 1⅛ :48 1:14³ 1:43 1:49 ⑤ⓕAlw 34000N2x 51 2 4 5⁷ 55½ 3hd 11½ Santagata N 113 2.20 77-18 Dana's Wedding113¹½ Critical Crew113nk LoneStarGale113no Rallied inside 6
8Mar95-9Aqu fst 1⅛ ⓣ :24¹ :48hd 1:14 1:48 ⑤ⓕAlw 34000N2x 65 9 — 8⁵¼ 78¼ 58¼ 66¼ Santagata N 113 7.00 58-34 CarrStar108⁴ NewYorkFlq109no CriticlCrew113no Fog, improved position 9
18Feb95-7Aqu fst 1⅛ ⓣ :24² :49⁴ 1:14⁴ 1:48⁴ ⑤ⓕAlw 34000N2x 60 4 3 3⁴ 7⁷½ 76¼ 66 Santagata N 113 4.00 55-38 Hillis Lee119no Carr Star106² New York Flag108¹½ Four wide 11
25Jan95-9Aqu fst 1⅛ ⓣ :23³ :474 1:13³ 1:48⁴ ⓕClm 35000 80 2 5 55¼ 44½ 5⁴ 1hd Santagata N 117 20.10 61-40 Dana'sWedding117no S.S.Sparkle¹¼ UpstateFlyer117⅞ Wide, hard drive 8

WORKOUTS: Oct 3 Bel 4f fst :50⁴ B 21/30

Secretariatslegend

Own: Roberts Deborah P

NELSON D (52 5 5 7 .10) $30,000

B. m. 5
Sire: Nias (Secretariat)
Dam: Come On Eileen (Smoggy)
Br: Harding Virginia (Fla)
Tr: Roberts Deborah P (—)

L 114

	Lifetime Record:	34 5 6 5	$50,987
1995	9 2 1 1	$14,720	Turf 21 5 2 3 $39,700
1994	9 1 0 0	$9,170	Wet 3 0 2 0 $4,600
Bel ①	1 0 0 0		Dist ① 0 0 0 0

Entered 19Oct95–8 MED

110ct95-10Rkm fm 1 ① :23 :47² 1:13² 1:40 3↑ ⓕClm 16000 81 6 8 9¹¹ 86½ 5½ 12 Bermudez J E LB 119 f 5.60 85-15 Scrtritslgnd113² SuziDoWht113no PrimlyPropr116⅞ Rail turn, outside str 9
10ct95-6Rkm fm 1 ① :22³ :46⁴ 1:12³ 1:39¹ 3↑ ⓕClm 16000 81 9 10 10⁹¾ 77¼ 64 12 Bermudez J E LB 116 f 10.30 89-15 Secretritslgnd116² SuziDoWht112no GottBCIssi116no Stead nr str, driving 10
23Sep95-12Rkm fm 1⅛ ① :23 :471 1:12² 1:45³ 3↑ ⓕClm 16000 71 1 9 10¹² 9⁹½ 6¹¹ 37½ Bermudez J E LB 116 f 18.70 79-13 YouKnockout116½ PotntilDrmr119³ Scrtritslgnd116no Late gain between 12
18Sep95-8Rkm my 1⁴⁰ :24¹ :49 1:15¹ 1:45¹ 3↑ ⓕClm 12500 33 6 3 34 57 5⁸ 6¹4½ Guerra J A LB 116 f 13.80 62-24 See Leslie W.1194½ Fire Attack116½ Bidder's Pride116½ Wide, stopped 6
4Sep95-12Rkm fm 1⅛ ① :22⁴ :471 1:12¹ 1:45³ 3↑ ⓕClm 16000 72 5 2 2²½ 2¹½ 2² 4² Guerra J A LB 116 f 7.80 79-12 Glorymn'sDrm119no S2DWht112¹ PtntlDrmr119¹ Between, tired 9
26Aug95-12Rkm fm 1⅛ ① :22⁴ :471 1:12¹ 1:45³ 3↑ ⓕClm 16000 77 9 6 3¹½ 3¹½ 34 2²¼ Guerra J A LB 116 f 13.70 85-13 GottBCIssi112½ Scrtritslgnd116²¼ KokomoBrz114¹½ Blocked near stretch 10
20Aug95-10Rkm fm 1 ① :23¹ :47² 1:12² 1:38² 3↑ ⓕClm 16000 64 6 5 9¹½ 7⁹ 58¼ 4⁷½ Duys D C LB 116 f 21.20 86-12 PotentilDrmr116² QuivringLdy112¹¼ PowrHmmr116⁴ Bore out early, 2w 10
5Aug95-8Rkm fm 1 ① :23² :48² 1:13⁴ 1:39⁴ 3↑ ⓕAlw 12740N3x 57 1 6 56 5⁶ 8¹½ 8¹³⅞ Ramos A LB 116 f 18.80 72-21 Bidder'sPride116½ DancingMelnie113⁴ WrmingGlow119⁵ Stopped inside 10
8July95-12Rkm fm 1 ① :22 :45¹ 1:10⁴ 1:38² 3↑ ⓕAlw 12740N3x 54 4 1 21 5½ 8¾ 10¹⁵ Baez R LB 116 f 14.00 75-17 Other119⁷ Dancing Folly116no Power Hammer116hd Early pace 2 wide 10
15Oct94-11Rkm fm 1 ① :22² :46³ 1:12 1:39 3↑ ⓕAlw 12740N3x 66 9 9 7¹³ 6¹¹ 66¼ 5⅞¼ Jellison J A LB 116 f 16.40 83-10 Perfect Night116½ Catch A Flight116¹ Reality Ga1120² Wide early 10

WORKOUTS: ● Jly 24 Rkm 5f fst 1:01⁴ H 1/7

Curled Waters

Own: Carroll Del W II

STEVENS G L (86 17 13 14 .20) $35,000

Ch. m. 5
Sire: Ends Well (Lyphard)
Dam: Sunset Strait (Naskra)
Br: Rosenthal Mrs Morton (NY)
Tr: Carroll Del W II (18 2 3 2 .11)

L 116

	Lifetime Record:	50 2 3 2	$75,609
1995	12 1 2 0	$42,239	Turf 21 2 2 0 $56,639
1994	20 0 0 2	$10,200	Wet 3 0 0 0
Bel ①	15 2 2 0	$54,180	Dist ① 3 0 0 0

Entered 18Oct95–5 BEL

30Sep95-5Bel gd 1⅛ ⓣ :24¹ :491 1:12³ 1:44² 3↑ ⑤Alw 36000N2x 63 4 6 94½ 106¼ 1014 9¹²¼ Leon F L 113 16.10 61-22 Bellingham116²¼ Mr. Baba116¹ Outlaw118nk Tired 10
11Sep95-7Bel fm 1⅛ ⓣ :24³ :462 1:10⁴ 1:41⁴ 3↑ ⑤Alw 36000N2x 71 2 6 65¼ 4²¼ 3¹ 3⁴ Smith M E L 118 6.60 83-12 Darlin Danika113⅞ Curled Waters118½ New York Flag116⁴½ Up for place 8
27Aug95-4Sar gd 1⅛ ⓣ :24¹ 1:41 1:45 3↑ ⑤Alw 36000N2x 57 9 7 9⁴½ 106½ 9no 66¼ Davis R G 114 13.10 68-20 Bo Bo's Sister111nk Sweetzie113¹¼ Just Remind Her114½ No threat 10
16Aug95-5Sar fm 1⅛ ⓣ :462 1:10⁴ 1:35 1:47³ 3↑ ⑤Alw H81k 72 3 5 58¼ 6⁵ 5⁷ 5¹4¼ Leon F 107 33.50 74-11 Irish Linnet124⁸ Kris's Kiss113¹¼ Casa Eire111no No threat 6
10Aug95-10Sar fm 1⅛ ⓣ :46⁴ 1:11 1:34¹ 1:54³ 3↑ ⓕClm 50000 73 1 6 4⅝ 7⁴½ 74¼ 6² Day P 114 8.60 85-06 Leo N' Me114nk High Talent114no Polar Princess114² Saved ground, tired 10
16July95-4Bel fm 1⅛ ⓣ :454 1:10 1:34³ 1:40 3↑ ⑤Alw 36000N2x 69 3 5 5¹³ 5¹¹ 5¹⁶ 2⅝¼ Day P 121 4.30 75-15 Bien Sucre110¹6 Curled Waters121¹¼ Through The Tulips119³¼ Up for place 8
18Jun95-5Bel fm 1 ⓣ :22² :46¹ 1:10¹ 1:36¹ 3↑ ⑤Alw 34000N1x 78 9 6 6³ 64 1½ 1¹¾ Day P 119 4.00 82-14 Curled Waters119¹¾ Sweetzne114¹ Bid O'powdre111³ Rated, up late 10
18Jun95-5Bel fm 1⅛ ⓣ :45² 1:11 1:41² 1:49 3↑ ⑤Alw 36000N1x 76 5 7 6⁴ 52¼ 43 42¼ Valdivia J⁷ 113 36.00 86-10 RoyalPelliknow120¹½ ADayToRemember120¹¼ DarlinDanika114nk Willingly 10
25May95-5Bel fm 1⅛ ⓣ :24² :451 1:10¹ 1:35¹ 3↑ ⑤Alw 36000N1x 61 8 4 43 5¹¾ 7no 7⅝¾ Leon F 120 11.40 74-18 Bo Bo's Sister108¹ Funky Diva113¹¾ Russian Ensign114½ Bid, tired 10
14May95-10Bel fm 1⅛ ⓣ :24⁴ :481 1:12¹ 1:43³ 3↑ ⑤Alw 36000N2x 61 2 6 9⁴½ 93¾ 63¾ 7¹¹½ Leon F 120 53.50 69-12 Leo N' Me115¹¼ Bien Sucre103³ Very True112½ No response 11

WORKOUTS: Oct 10 Bel tr.t 4f fst :491 H 6/22   Sep 22 Bel tr.t 4f fst :48³ H 4/28   Sep 6 Bel 5f fst 1:02 B 26/43   Aug 7 Sar tr.t 4f fst :53¹ B 37/40   Aug 1 Sar tr.t 4f fst :512 B 6/15   Jly 26 Sar tr.t 4f fst :50 B 5/27

Miss Pocket Court

Own: Giambrone Anthony P & Silver Oak St
ALVARADO F T (123 15 18 15 .12) $30,000
B. m. 5
Sire: Court Trial (In Reality)
Dam: Pocket Power (Full Pocket)
Br: Mangurian Mr & Mrs H T Jr (Fla)
Tr: Moschera Gasper S (61 14 7 11 .23)
L 115

Lifetime Record: 76 15 15 16 $325,131											
1995	10	1	2	1	$33,017	Turf	17	3	1	6	$64,540
1994	17	4	5	4	$120,740	Wet	12	2	3	1	$53,837
Bel Ⓣ	7	2	1	3	$43,210	Dist Ⓣ	5	1	0	3	$24,150

5Oct95- 6Bel sly 1¼ ⊗ :474 1:123 1:38 2:051 3+ ⒻClm 40000 61 1 1 1½ 42¾ 47 414¾ Alvarado F T L 113 b *1.40 53-26 Slew The Duchess1136 Majahuitas1216½ Royal Cozzene1132 Used up 5
28Sep95- 5Bel fst 1 1/16 ⊗ :232 :471 1:121 1:442 3+ ⒻClm 30000 76 6 4 31½ 31½ 32½ 38½ Alvarado F T L 118 b *2.30 68-29 Grab The Glory1144½ Evi Bee1164 Miss Pocket Court1184 Bid, tired 8
10Sep95- 3Bel fm 1¼ [T] :48 1:12 1:37 2:014 3+ ⒻClm 35000 85 5 4 53½ 51½ 31½ 11¼ Alvarado F T L 117 b 10.10 79-17 MissPocktCourt1171¼ HighTlnt1192¾ RoylPlliknow121nk Well placed, clear 9
14Aug95- 1Sar wf 1⅛ :482 1:131 1:393 1:53 3+ ⒻClm c-25000 82 3 2 2½ 2hd 2hd 2no Bailey J D 112 fb 2.45 71-25 BoundingBelievr121no MissPocktCourt1121½ ProudAngl11813 Game effort 6
Claimed from Hauman Eugene E & Schwartz Barry K, Hushion Michael E Trainer
19May95- 9Bel sly 1 1/16 ⊗ :231 :462 1:113 1:433 ⒻClm 35000 41 8 3 32 31½ 79¾ 721¼ Luzzi M J 112 fb 3.60 59-21 GeorgiaAnna1135½ SunshineLindjne1124½ Lois'Flg1081 Forced pace, tired 9
23Apr95- 9Aqu fm 1 1/16 Ⓣ :49 1:133 1:384 1:504 ⒻClm 45000 46 3 3 43½ 44 810 820¼ Perez R B5 110 fb 5.30 65-18 DinnrDimond1142¼ EnMnMny1141¾ BonnShoppr116hd Steadied early, tired 8
6Apr95- 4Aqu fst 1⅛ :484 1:13 1:391 1:521 ⒻClm 50000 78 2 3 31½ 32 43¼ 46¼ Luzzi M J 112 fb 2.25 73-26 GrbTheGlory116nk MissGoldPece1145½ Gene'sGryGirl1073¼ Wide trip, tired 4
23Mar95- 3Aqu fst 1⅛ :491 1:141 1:394 1:523 ⒻClm 35000 84 5 2 2½ 2hd 2½ 21½ Migliore R 116 fb *1.20 75-34 MissGoldPece1161½ MissPocketCourt116nk Gn'sGryGirl1162¼ Up for place 5
28Jan95- 8Aqu fst 1 1/16 ⊡ :234 :483 1:14 1:464 3+ ⒻAffectnltlyH-G3 72 4 3 33½ 43½ 67½ 712¼ Migliore R 114 fb 7.10 59-34 Sea Ditty113nk Beloved Bea1142 Acting Proud1111¼ Gave way 9
7Jan95- 8Aqu my 170 ⊡ :243 :492 1:152 1:46 3+ ⒻWoodhaven H55k 78 7 2 2½ 2hd 2hd 41¾ Migliore R 116 fb 2.65 66-35 Starry Val112no Footing1131 Sterling Pound114¾ Tired 7
WORKOUTS: Aug 28 Sar tr.t 4f fst :522 B 17/24 Aug 11 Sar tr.t 4f fst :52 B 18/27 Jly 29 Sar tr.t 5f fst 1:064 B 10/10

Calling You (Fr)

Own: Englekirk Robert
VELASQUEZ J (52 2 8 5 .04) $35,000
Ch. m. 5
Sire: Don Roberto (Roberto)
Dam: Clear Speech (Dictus)
Br: Laurent Henry (Fr)
Tr: Lundy Sarah A (1 0 0 0 .00)
L 116

Lifetime Record: 38 5 6 2 $103,307											
1995	5	0	0	0	$10,575	Turf	37	5	6	2	$102,332
1994	13	0	3	0	$30,965	Wet	0	0	0	0	
Bel Ⓣ	1	0	0	0		Dist Ⓣ	9	2	3	2	$46,028

15Sep95- 2Bel fm 1 1/16 [T] :244 :49 1:131 1:433 3+ ⒻClm 45000 67 3 2 22 42½ 79¾ 79½ Velasquez J L 114 b 10.90 68-16 PrincessStreak1164 PolarPrincess116½ RockfordPech1141 Forced pace 8
6Aug95- 3Dmr fm 1⅛ Ⓣ :52 1:17 1:411 1:524 3+ ⒻAlw 50000N2X 82 1 2 21 1hd 43 46 Valdivia J5 LB 112 fb 42.60 66-16 Mille Nuits117hd Interim1171¾ Green Gates Magic1174 Rail,led,weakened 6
21Jly95- 6Hol fm 1⅛ Ⓣ :473 1:114 1:361 1:491 ⒻClm 47500 83 5 4 42 42 53½ 42¾ Valenzuela P A LB 118 b 13.50 76-19 East Liberty1161½ Ouzo Powered1161 Java Java117½ Bobbled start 9
12Jun95- 8Hol fm 1¼ Ⓣ :483 1:132 1:374 2:014 ⒻClm 57500 85 4 4 43½ 43 44 43½ McCarron C J LB 114 b 13.00 76-14 Lambent1131¾ Bibi Star116hd Iddy Biddy Dollar1191½ No late bid 7
24May95- 7Hol fm 1 Ⓣ :223 :46 1:104 1:36 ⒻClm 55000 74 4 8 813 810 711 710¾ Blanc B5 LB 108 b 60.30 72-17 Brendas Wildindian1161¾ Bonne Nuite1142¼ Bibi Star116¾ No threat 8
4Dec94- 7Hol fm 1⅛ Ⓣ :474 1:13 1:372 1:494 3+ ⒻClm 62500 85 3 4 46 3½ 4½ 22 Nakatani C S LB 116 10.00 73-25 Blue Tess1162 Calling You1161 Nat's Lea117hd 4 wide into lane 6
3Nov94- 3SA fst 1 1/16 :233 :48 1:122 1:434 3+ ⒻClm 45000 73 6 6 67 66 56½ 55¾ Stevens G L LB 114 11.80 70-18 RunningRen1142 IddyBiddyDollr1171¾ WingsOfDrms1161 Wide into lane 6
9Sep94- 8Dmr fm 1⅛ Ⓣ :504 1:152 1:392 1:51 3+ ⒻMatching66k 79 2 3 41½ 51¾ 65½ 67½ Vitek J J LB 117 42.70 74-13 Stellar Affair117hd Skiable1172 Fondly Remembered117no 4 wide 2nd turn 7
29Aug94- 2Dmr fm 1⅛ Ⓣ :501 1:151 1:394 1:52 3+ ⒻClm 45000 89 3 4 43½ 2½ 2hd 2hd Vitek J J5 LB 110 75.50 76-15 Bibi Star117hd Calling You110no Voluptuous117no Game effort 10
13Aug94- 7Dmr fm 1⅛ Ⓣ :482 1:121 1:37 1:49 34 Clm 45000 — 2 — — — — — Vitek J J5 LB 106 b 74.60 — 08 Seti L117hd Honor And Pride1171 Dream Of Fame117½ 10
Bumped into rail, lost rider leaving chute
WORKOUTS: Oct 18 Bel 3f fst :372 B 14/25 Oct 9 Bel 6f fst 1:15 B 2/8 Oct 1 Bel 5f fst 1:03 B 27/30 Sep 25 Bel 4f fst :51 B 66/77 Sep 11 Bel 4f fst :482 H 10/44 Sep 3 Dmr 4f fst :482 H 36/60

All Glory

Own: Sheringham John
DECARLO C P (22 0 2 2 .00) $35,000
Dk. b or br m. 6
Sire: One for All (Northern Dancer)
Dam: She's Dreamy (Cyane)
Br: Marsh Hazel B (Va)
Tr: Sheringham John (1 0 0 0 .00)
L 116

Lifetime Record: 33 2 1 4 $26,240											
1995	7	0	0	0	$3,060	Turf	24	2	1	4	$25,740
1994	12	1	1	4	$17,280	Wet	2	0	0	0	$500
Bel Ⓣ	16	0	0	0	$3,060	Dist Ⓣ	8	0	0	0	$3,060

10Sep95- 3Bel fm 1¼ [T] :48 1:12 1:37 2:014 3+ ⒻClm 35000 76 1 7 75½ 82½ 53 44 Decarlo C P 117 60.50 75-17 MissPocketCourt1171¼ HighTlent1192¾ RoylPelliknow121nk Rallied inside 9
13Jly95- 4Bel fm 1 1/16 [T] :231 :453 1:101 1:412 ⒻClm 40000 71 8 7 714 810 812 68¾ Persaud R10 106 53.75 80-13 Madeline's Affair114¾ Leo N' Me1141½ A Demon A Day114½ No threat 8
7Jly95- 3Bel fm 1¼ [T] :501 1:144 1:39 2:03 ⒻClm 50000 56 9 10 107¾ 118½ 1010 813¼ Decarlo C P 116 80.25 60-22 Artful Pleasure1161½ Caroline Of Kent114no Mont Germont1121½ No threat 11
11Jun95- 8Bel fm 1¼ [T] :48 1:12 1:361 2:002 3+ ⒻAlw 36000N2X 51 1 4 46½ 48 511 617¾ Decarlo C P 119 38.00 68-08 Assertive Dancer1194 Jodi's Land1161½ Sudana1196 Faded 7
1Jun95- 9Bel fm 1¼ [T] :481 1:124 1:38 2:034 ⒻClm 40000 73 6 10 109¾ 95¾ 65 42 Decarlo C P 116 83.00 67-20 Reinvesting Ada1161¾ Now I Hope109no High Talent116nk Belated rally 10
21May95- 4Bel fm 1 Ⓣ :223 :451 1:101 1:353 ⒻClm 45000 65 6 11 1116 1118 109¾ 910¼ Decarlo C P 114 86.25 75-15 Ski At Dawn108hd Turkolady1143½ Royal Pelliknow1121½ No speed 11
7May95- 7Bel fm 1 Ⓣ :222 :452 1:10 1:354 3+ ⒻAlw 36000N3L 24 9 12 1215 1217 1117 1031 Martin G J5 114 93.50 53-18 Lady She Is Too1093 Swamp Cat1192½ Wadaz119nk No speed 12
26Nov94- 5Aqu sf 1⅛ Ⓣ :482 1:141 1:402 1:53 3+ ⒻAlw 34000N2X 74 7 9 918 78 49½ 39¼ Martin G J10 108 85.25 66-29 Apolda1155½ Spectaculaire1174 All Glory1085 Improved position 10
31Oct94- 8Suf fm *1 Ⓣ 1:414 3+ ⒻAlw 12740N3L 64 5 6 54 78½ 63¾ 33 Rivera L Jr B 119 4.70 92-09 Dynamic Moment1121½ Other1191½ All Glory119¾ In tgt btwn 2nd turn 10
9Oct94-12Rkm fm 1 1/16 Ⓣ :232 :473 1:13 1:48 3+ ⒻAlw 11760N3L 68 12 11 1013 88 65 34¼ Rivera L Jr B 119 4.80 71-14 Femme Zi Zi1163 Other1191¼ All Glory1191¼ Inside, gaining 12
WORKOUTS: Oct 17 Bel tr.t 3f fst :37 B 2/12 Aug 15 Bel tr.t 3f fst :382 B 5/11

My Spring Love

Own: Santangelo Francis R
KRONE J A (137 16 21 9 .12) $35,000
Ro. f. 4
Sire: Jacques Who (Grey Dawn II)
Dam: My Dearest Love (T. V. Commercial)
Br: Pascuma J Jr & Santagelo Francis (NY)
Tr: Penna Angel Jr (12 4 1 1 .33)
L 116

Lifetime Record: 11 2 0 1 $44,300											
1995	4	1	0	0	$20,540	Turf	7	2	0	1	$42,380
1994	4	1	0	1	$23,760	Wet	1	0	0	0	
Bel Ⓣ	4	1	0	0	$19,080	Dist Ⓣ	0	0	0	0	

11Sep95- 7Bel fm 1 1/16 [T] :231 :462 1:104 1:414 3+ Ⓕ[S]Alw 36000N2X 50 6 8 75¾ 53 57 513¾ Krone J A L 116 *1.55 74-12 DrlinDnik1143½ CurledWters118¾ NewYorkFlg1164½ Pinched brk, flattend 8
14May95-10Bel fm 1 1/16 [T] :244 :481 1:121 1:431 3+ Ⓕ[S]Alw 36000N2X 61 8 8 63½ 41½ 77 811¼ Perez R B5 117 *3.00 68-12 Leo N' Me1151¾ Bien Sucre1103 Very True112½ Five wide, flattened 10
21Apr95- 8Aqu fm 1 1/16 Ⓣ :241 :493 1:141 1:454 3+ ⒻAlw 32000N2L 80 5 4 42 42 1½ 11¼ Perez R B5 115 4.70 80-18 MySpringLove1151¼ PocketBeuty1174½ BcusOfLov1202½ Well placed, clear 10
8Feb95- 5GP fm 1⅛ Ⓣ :483 1:131 1:37 1:491 + ⒻAlw 26000N1X 75 2 10 98 93½ 67½ 55 Castillo H Jr 118 8.10 81-09 Gold Blossom1181½ Dancer On Tour118¾ Slewveau1211½ Mild bid 12
26Nov94- 9Aqu fst 1 :232 :473 1:15 1:412 3+ Ⓕ[S]Alw 32000N1X 49 8 5 54 63 55 410 Santagata N 115 8.20 51-28 I'mabaroness110no Blarneystone Lass1151 Critical Crew1109 No late bid 10
30Oct94- 4Aqu fm 1⅛ Ⓣ :492 1:133 1:39 1:51 3+ ⒻAlw 32000N1X 75 6 10 74½ 63½ 54½ 34 Santagata N 116 33.50 81-12 Joy Of Ireland1171 Nobody PickedSix1143 MySpringLove116½ Willingly 11
4Oct94- 1Bel yl 1 1/16 [T] :234 :474 1:124 1:452 3+ Ⓕ[S]Md Sp Wt 71 8 5 54½ 43½ 1½ 14 Santagata N 119 4.70 69-23 My Spring Love1194 Vested Myth1191 Ember's Girl1196 Driving 8
16Sep94- 9Bel fm 1 1/16 Ⓣ :232 :463 1:111 1:423 3+ Ⓕ[S]Md Sp Wt 52 9 6 53 51¾ 64 76 Santagata N 118 26.70 79-13 Our Springwater1181½ Existentialism122nk Spectacular Affair113no Tired 10
21Oct93- 3Aqu sly 1 :224 :46 1:103 1:38 ⒻMd 35000 19 4 1 2½ 36 513 723¾ Santagata N 117 b 20.80 50-22 PlacidoPrincess1135½ Mggie'sLovebot11711 Midenbrooklyn1061 Used up 9
4Oct93- 3Bel fst 6f :23 :474 1:004 1:14 ⒻMd 35000 12 6 4 54½ 54½ 610 719½ Santagata N 117 23.90 50-28 Rosemarie'sJoy1172¾ AmericanCountess1171¾ Starrystrryflight1139 Tired 13
WORKOUTS: Oct 16 Bel 4f fst :494 B 27/50 Oct 10 Bel 5f fst 1:024 B 10/15 Oct 4 Bel 5f fst 1:02 B 13/34 Sep 29 Bel 6f fst 1:152 H 9/20 Sep 8 Bel 4f fst :51 B 34/36 Sep 3 Bel 6f fst 1:144 H 2/4

7 Belmont Park

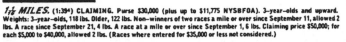

1¹⁄₈ MILES. (1:39⁴) CLAIMING. Purse $30,000 (plus up to $11,775 NYSBFOA). 3-year-olds and upward. Weights: 3-year-olds, 118 lbs. Older, 122 lbs. Non-winners of two races a mile or over since September 11, allowed 2 lbs. A race since September 21, 4 lbs. A race at a mile or over since September 1, 6 lbs. Claiming price $50,000; for each $5,000 to $40,000, allowed 2 lbs. (Races where entered for $35,000 or less not considered.)

A Call To Rise
Own: My Paradise Farms
SANTOS J A (168 28 18 20 .17) $45,000
B. g. 7
Sire: Poles Apart (Danzig)
Dam: A Bugle Command (Command Control)
Br: Manfuso John A (Md)
Tr: Friedman Mitchell (30 8 2 5 .27)   118

	Lifetime Record:	94 15 20 20	$514,381
1995	18 3 3 5	$76,290 Turf	3 0 0 1 $4,500
1994	21 3 6 4	$82,639 Wet	15 2 4 5 $78,421
Bel	21 4 5 5	$124,840 Dist	46 9 6 12 $258,034

Entered 19Oct95- 9 BEL
WORKOUTS: Aug 23 Sar 4f fst :45¹ H 4/23

Le Risky
Own: Frankel Richard M
STEVENS G L (86 17 13 14 .20) $45,000
Dk. b or br g. 6
Sire: Lejoli (Cornish Prince)
Dam: Frisky and Risky (Cormorant)
Br: Cuomo Michael (NY)
Tr: Galluscio Dominic G (16 4 0 0 .25)   L 113

	Lifetime Record:	75 12 7 15	$243,703
1995	17 4 4 1	$67,175 Turf	2 0 0 0
1994	23 2 2 8	$62,040 Wet	11 2 0 3 $40,386
Bel	23 3 2 6	$70,860 Dist	13 2 0 4 $43,116

WORKOUTS: Aug 22 Bel tr.4f fst :48⁴ B 4/13

Private Plan
Own: Jaques Farm
ALVARADO F T (123 15 18 15 .12) $45,000
Ch. g. 5
Sire: Private Account (Damascus)
Dam: Ericka Downs (Vaguely Noble)
Br: Firman Pamela N (Ky)
Tr: Moschera Gasper S (61 14 7 11 .23)   L 114

	Lifetime Record:	50 16 7 14	$297,365
1995	20 6 5 6	$162,160 Turf	3 1 0 0 $10,230
1994	18 8 0 4	$97,040 Wet	4 2 0 1 $40,255
Bel	15 6 3 5	$139,780 Dist	25 9 2 7 $152,655

Entered 19Oct95- 9 BEL
WORKOUTS: Oct 17 Bel 4f fst :49 B 36/34   Aug 28 Sar tr.4f fst :50 B 2/24   Jly 30 Sar tr.4f fst :51⁴ B 19/27

Copper Mount
Own: Kupferberg Max & Saul J
BAILEY J D (203 47 27 27 .23) $50,000
B. g. 4
Sire: Cormorant (His Majesty)
Dam: Damerella (King's Bishop)
Br: Nielsen Gerald A (NY)
Tr: Margotta Anthony Jr (24 4 4 3 .17)   L 116

	Lifetime Record:	16 4 2 1	$188,041
1995	5 0 1 0	$13,512 Turf	1 0 0 0
1994	10 4 1 1	$174,529 Wet	1 0 0 0
Bel	6 0 2 0	$37,234 Dist	5 1 1 0 $31,809

WORKOUTS: Sep 19 Bel 5f fst 1:03 B 26/52   Aug 27 Sar tr.4f fst :50⁴ N 2/10

Rocking Josh

Own: Dematteis Frederick

CHAVEZ J F (195 32 20 27 .16) $50,000

Ch. g. 6
Sire: Whitesburg (Crimson Satan)
Dam: Cold Carol (Run a Native)
Br: Farrow Edith D (Ky)
Tr: Priolo Philip (7 1 0 1 .14)

116

Lifetime Record:	68 11 14 14	$306,772			
1995	19 3 1 7	$96,750	Turf	2 0 0 0	$846
1994	18 1 6 4	$82,120	Wet	12 3 3 4	$69,732
Bel	14 1 3 3	$65,750	Dist	22 5 4 3	$115,934

8Oct95-3Bel	fst	1 1/16	:24	:471	1:12	1:442	3↑ Clm 50000	88	1	5	59	67¾	34	41¼	Chavez J F	117 f	3.15	75-25	A Call To Rise112½ Copper Mount116no Boots 'n Buck1171	Checked late	7
13Sep95-7Bel	fst	1	:231	:461	1:11	1:353	3↑ Clm 60000	86	2	6	68	63½	43½	34	Chavez J F	116 f	4.90	81-15	May I Inquire114hd Terrorist1164 Rocking Josh1162	Mild rally	6
7Sep95-4Bel	fst	6f	:22	:451	:571	1:092	3↑ Clm 60000	70	2	5	58	54½	47	411½	Santos J A	117 f	3.95	82-13	OneBigHug117½ DirectStellite1133 Tnochtitln1138	Brk slowly, no threat	5
3Aug95-8Sar	fst	7f	:222	:452	1:094	1:231	3↑ Alw 42000C	95	2	7	79	713	76½	65	Day P	114 f	11.20	85-12	Slick Horn119no Prenup1172½ Contract Court1141½	Brk slowly, no threat	7
24Jun95-6Bel	wf	1	:233	:461	1:104	1:364	Clm 75000	91	1	2	2hd	2hd	3nk	33½	Chavez J F	116 f	4.20	75-24	PrivatePlan109½ Gallapit'sMoment1123 RockingJosh1161	Dueled inside	7
14Jun95-7Bel	sly	6½f	:22	:452	1:10	1:162	Clm 75000	89	4	4	59½	59½	55½	44½	Krone J A	116 f	5.50	88-16	Dibbs N' Dubbs114½ Golden Tent1123 Lake Ali1071	No threat	5
4Jun95-8Bel	fst	1 1/16	:233	:464	1:104	1:422	Handicap50k	89	3	5	56½	63½	611	410	Krone J A	109 f	13.10	77-16	Slick Horn1185 Swindle1151 Electrojet1164	No rally	7
14May95-6Bel	fst	1 1/16	:224	:46	1:103	1:434	Clm c-50000	90	4	5	46	34	31	45½	Bailey J D	120 f	*.95	74-29	Private Plan1143 Five Star General1182 Stormy Java116½	No late bid	9
Claimed from Schwartz Barry K, Hushion Michael E Trainer																					
5May95-9Bel	fst	1 1/16	:224	:453	1:102	1:421	Clm c-40000	100	8	7	73½	1½	13½	14	Santos J A	116	3.10	88-21	RockingJosh1164 PrivatePln114nk AmbushAlley1164	Five wide, drew off	10
Claimed from Reese Walter C, Reese Cynthia G Trainer																					
21Apr95-8Pha	fst	6½f	:22	:444	1:094	1:162	Alw 21000N$Y	94	2	5	54½	65¾	44½	3½	Black A S	L 116	6.10	95-19	Conveyor116nk Lazy Luke116nk Rocking Josh1161½	Rallied	6

WORKOUTS: Aug 16 Bel tr.t 4f fst :502 B 12/20

Regal Mike

Own: Davidson Herbert S & Wendel Arthur

LEON F (55 0 5 8 .00) $40,000

B. h. 7
Sire: Regal Embrace (Vice Regent)
Dam: Ray Kay (Nehoc's Brother)
Br: Nolan Howard C (NY)
Tr: Wendel Arthur (13 1 0 1 .08)

L 112

Lifetime Record:	78 6 9 6	$156,655			
1995	19 1 2 2	$37,275	Turf	2 0 0 0	
1994	27 3 6 3	$71,740	Wet	10 0 3 3	$23,160
Bel	34 2 5 4	$61,455	Dist	28 1 2 0	$30,130

8Oct95-3Bel	fst	1 1/16	:24	:471	1:12	1:442	3↑ Clm 40000	84	6	6	69	54½	45	54¼	Leon F	L 113 b	16.50	73-25	A Call To Rise112½ Copper Mount116no Boots 'n Buck1171	No threat	7
15Sep95-6Bel	fst	7f	:23	:462	1:103	1:223	3↑ Clm 35000	80	7	4	710	66¾	46½	48¾	Leon F	L 114	9.10	79-14	Late Guest1165 Fini Cassette1142¾ Blum Gone1161	No threat	7
2Sep95-4Bel	fst	1 1/16	:234	:472	1:113	1:411	3↑ Clm 35000	71	2	4	33	62½	68	614½	Leon F	115 b	13.30	78-16	Sky Hero1172 Private Plan117nk Country Sky1175¾	Tired	7
16Jly95-8Bel	fst	1 1/16	:232	:462	1:104	1:43	3↑ Alw 38000N3X	84	5	8	77	86½	56	57	Leon F	120 b	13.10	77-22	Yourmissinthepoint120nk Wild Escapade1114 Fifth Set1202¾	No threat	8
1Jly95-6Bel	sly	1 1/8	:46	1:104	1:363	1:501	3↑ Alw 38000N3X	84	5	5	55	31½	32½	34	Leon F	120	11.80	77-18	Amathos1221 Fifth Set1203 Regal Mike1205½	Bid, weakened	5
22Jun95-7Bel	sly	1 1/16	:231	:463	1:11	1:421	Clm 30000	90	2	5	44½	43	22½	21¾	Leon F	116 b	7.80	86-22	Arz1141¾ Regal Mike1163 A Call To Rise112½	Steady gain	6
9Jun95-10Bel	fst	1 1/8	:471	1:113	1:374	1:511	Clm 35000	88	6	7	74½	55½	41	32½	Leon F	116 fb	7.90	73-24	[D]KlondikeClm1162½ FlyingGroom116no RglMik1162	Steadied, blocked 1/8	9
1Jun95-7Bel	fst	6½f	:221	:452	1:111	1:18	Clm 45000	92	1	5	710	76	42½	42	Leon F	112 b	16.50	83-17	Jericho Blaise111no Gallapiat's Moment1161¾ Express[illegible]116hd	Belated rally	7
14May95-6Bel	fst	1 1/16	:224	:46	1:103	1:434	Clm 45000	80	2	9	913	910	87	611¼	Leon F	114 b	16.10	69-29	Private Plan1143 Five Star General1182 Stormy Java116½	No factor	9
27Apr95-6Aqu	fst	7f	:231	:454	1:11	1:24	Clm 35000	85	2	5	65¾	67	52½	41	Leon F	116 b	6.10	83-18	Miron's Gentleman116no Grey Chandon116hd Fabersham113¾	Late gain	6

WORKOUTS: Aug 8 Bel tr.t 3f fst :372 B 7/17

Baypark

Own: Demola Dorothy & Nunzio P

NELSON D (52 5 5 7 .10) $50,000

Dk. b or br g. 6
Sire: Time To Explode (Explodent)
Dam: Here Come Some (Star Spangled)
Br: Anderson Farms (Ont-C)
Tr: Demola Richard (4 0 2 0 .00)

L 116

Lifetime Record:	68 10 7 12	$211,137			
1995	18 4 3 4	$91,050	Turf	3 0 0 0	$1,401
1994	21 3 1 4	$50,963	Wet	10 3 2 1	$52,109
Bel	13 2 2 3	$41,730	Dist	8 0 2 3	$17,033

9Oct95-3Bel	fst	1 1/16	:231	:463	1:113	1:442	3↑ Clm 35000	90	8	1	1½	1½	1hd	2¾	Nelson D	L 116	4.40	76-23	Le Risky116¾ Baypark116¾ Faviano114no	Dueled, gamely	9
23Sep95-2Bel	my	1 1/16	:23	:464	1:111	1:42	3↑ Clm 25000	88	2	1	14	11½	22	21½	Nelson D	L 114	22.20	88-17	Klondike Clem1091¼ Baypark1141¼ A Call To Rise1168¾	Held well	7
3Sep95-9Bel	fst	6½f	:221	:452	1:092	1:154	3↑ Clm 30000	50	3	5	43	116½	1214	1118	Martinez J R Jr	L 118	25.50	78-07	Codys Key116¾ Blum Gone1163½ Faviano120¾	Done early	12
12Jly95-4Bel	fst	7f	:222	:444	1:092	1:223	Clm 45000	55	6	8	64½	88	710	719	Chavez J F	114	5.60	69-14	Frmonthefrewy1161 Tnochtitln1205 ConcordsProspct120hd	Broke slowly	8
28Jun95-6Bel	fst	7f	:224	:461	1:112	1:242	Clm 30000	92	5	2	12½	11½	1½	12	Chavez J F	112	5.40	79-22	Baypark1122 Giant Leap1126½ Wissie's Wish114nk	Speed, game	7
11Jun95-1Bel	fst	7f	:222	:453	1:112	1:244	Clm 25000	61	2	8	98	1010	910	714½	Alvarado F T	118	10.10	62-25	Heavenwood1162 Giant Leap1163 Inside Connection1163	Never close	10
28May95-10Bel	fst	6½f	:222	:46	1:112	1:182	Clm c-18000	78	1	3	42½	42½	23½	32½	Luzzi M J	120	6.20	80-15	I'm No Quacker1122½ Appealing Tracy114hd Baypark1201¾	Willingly	12
Claimed from Sommer Viola, Martin Frank Trainer																					
18May95-9Bel	gd	7f	:224	:46	1:11	1:241	Clm 20000	83	1	1	1½	1½	12	1nk	Luzzi M J	116	4.00	80-16	Baypark116nk Le Risky1121½ Fire Devil116½	All out	9
6May95-5Bel	fst	6f	:222	:45	:57	1:092	Clm 25000	83	3	4	54	54	41½	44½	Luzzi M J	116	4.40	89-06	Bold Spector1161½ Groovy Attire1202¾ Publicized114½	Svd ground, evenly	8
12Apr95-3Aqu	fst	7f	:222	:451	1:101	1:23	Clm 25000	87	6	5	44½	42½	32	32	Luzzi M J	120	6.60	87-14	Regal Mike116hd Fabian1182 Baypark1201	Three wide, even late	9

WORKOUTS: Oct 3 Aqu 3f fst :38 B 9/13 Aug 26 Aqu 5f fst 1:014 B 1/2 Aug 9 Bel tr.t 3f fst :373 B 2/7 Aug 2 Bel tr.t 4f fst :472 H 3/23

8 Belmont Park

1 1/16 MILES. **(Inner Turf). (1:391) ALLOWANCE. Purse $36,000 (plus up to $14,130 NYSBFOA). Fillies and mares, 3-year-olds and upward which have not won two races other than maiden, claiming or starter. Weights: 3-year-olds, 118 lbs. Older, 122 lbs. Non-winners of $19,200 twice at a mile or over since September 13, allowed 2 lbs. $20,400 at a mile or over since September 28, 4 lbs. $9,000 at a mile or over since September 7, 6 lbs. (Races where entered for $60,000 or less not considered in allowances.) (Conditions eligibility preferred.)**

Exposed

Own: Low Lawana L & Robert E

SANTOS J A (168 28 18 28 .17)

Dk. b or br f. 3 (Apr)
Sire: Forty Niner (Mr. Prospector)
Dam: Look (Spectacular Bid)
Br: Claiborne Farm & The Gamely Corp (Ky)
Tr: Peitz Daniel C (12 1 1 2 .08)

L 116

Lifetime Record:	9 2 3 0	$51,600			
1995	6 2 2 0	$46,000	Turf	3 1 1 0	$27,200
1994	3 M 1 0	$5,600	Wet	0 0 0 0	
Bel (T)	2 1 1 0	$27,200	Dist (T)	3 1 1 0	$27,200

29Sep95-6Bel	yl	1 1/16 (T)	:23	:464	1:12	1:45	3↑ (F)Alw 34000N2L	85	1	6	44½	3½	12½	1½	Santos J A	L 114	11.70	73-29	Exposed114½ Mistress Hawk116½ Aesthete1126	Fully extended	10
15Sep95-9Bel	fm	1 1/16 (T)	:24	:474	1:114	1:43	3↑ (F)Alw 34000N1X	81	7	2	21½	21	31	22	Day P	L 111 f	16.70	81-16	Feel The Motion1112 Exposed111hd River Boogie1121	Up for place	10
25Aug95-9Sar	fm	1 1/16 (T)	:224	:454	1:102	1:413	3↑ (F)Alw 34000N2L	65	4	1	1½	11	1½	810¼	Nelson D	113 f	36.75	80-07	[D]Feel The Motion1143 Nabla1221 Mystic Mel1121	Used in pace	11
Placed 7th through disqualification.																					
13Aug95-10Sar	gd	1 1/8 (⊗)	:49	1:142	1:40	1:533	(F)Alw 34000N1X	74	5	1	13	13	2½	23½	Velazquez J R	112 f	8.20	64-32	Madame Adolphe1133½ Exposed11215 Fiery Kaye1125½	Bid, weakened	5
28Jly95-5Sar	fst	6f	:214	:452	:572	1:103	(F)Alw 32000N2L	46	6	8	43	76½	69½	718	Velazquez J R	115 f	56.25	70-15	Mybride Barbara1187 Hurricane Cat115½ Madame Adolphe1151	Tired	11
20Jan95-6OP	gd	6f	:221	:471	1:003	1:14	(F)Md Sp Wt	62	8	10	45¾	42	1hd	1nk	Gomez G K	L 120	*2.30	71-26	Exposed120nk Swing Set1202 Tejano's Pride1203	5-wide 3/8'ths	12
30Dec94-3Aqu	fst	6f [•]	:232	:474	1:004	1:142	(F)Md Sp Wt	47	6	3	22	23	36½	618½	Nelson D	117	*1.85e	60-24	Impish Saga1172 Ravishing Raven1124¾ Mystic Mel1171¾	Tired	9
7Dec94-5Aqu	fst	6f [•]	:223	:461	:583	1:111	(F)Md Sp Wt	69	7	4	31½	42	2½	21½	Davis R G	117	8.50	85-12	Some Sweet1171½ Exposed1171 Just For Fun117nk	Second best	11
16Nov94-3Aqu	fst	6f	:23	:472	:593	1:121	(F)Md Sp Wt	58	7	9	84½	71¾	52½	56½	Davis R G	117	14.60	74-14	Nubbins117no Love And Adore1171½ Country Cat1173	Pinched break	10

Kute Kris
Own: Sketchley John D
SMITH M E (204 36 24 31 .18)

Gr. m. 5
Sire: Kris S. (Roberto)
Dam: Golden Grey (Grey Dawn II (Fr))
Br: Red Oak Farm Inc (Fla)
Tr: Sketchley John D (—)

L 118

Lifetime Record: 32 3 5 7 $39,280

1995	12	1	0	4	$18,780	Turf	5	1	0	2	$12,890
1994	8	0	2	1	$8,440	Wet	6	1	1	1	$6,890
Bel(T)	0	0	0	0		Dist(T)	4	1	0	2	$12,750

10Oct95-7Pha gd 170 (T) :24 :482 1:134 1:463 3+ ⒻAlw 15000N1X 65 4 10 1012 96 42 12 Fiorentino C T L 115 fb 3.70 70-30 KuteKris1152 Herb'sProspect114nk MuttiMyLov1141½ Very wide, drew off 11
26Aug95-13Pha fm 1 1/16 (T) :224 :472 1:123 1:462 3+ ⒻAlw 19050N1X 62 1 11 1014 88¼ 65 33¼ Fiorentino C T L 115 fb 6.60 74-17 Stan's Boots1133 Sheza Sharp Danza114½ Kute Kris1151½ Rallied wide 12
29Jly95-12Pha fst 170 ⊗ :23 :474 1:132 1:444 3+ ⒻAlw 19793N1X 43 1 3 3½ 42 77¼ 79¾ Ferrer J C L 114 fb 2.90 67-22 Speedy Serenity1083 Patti's Gift114no Christina's Road1142¼ Inside, tired 8
17Jly95-6Pha fst 170 :223 :461 1:113 1:433 3+ ⒻAlw 19050N1X 53 1 5 56¼ 44¼ 34 34 Ferrer J C L 114 fb 4.80 78-12 Royal Divorce1142¼ Pick Up Sticks1141¾ Kute Kris1142 Off slow 7
25Jun95-8Pha fm 170 (T) :231 :47 1:123 1:434 3+ ⒻAlw 15000N1X 56 8 9 86½ 65¼ 54¼ 36¼ Unsihuay A L 113 fb 22.40 77-16 Ten Rifles1223¼ Rich Like Her1073 Kute Kris113¾ Wide 10
10Jun95-13Pha fm 1 1/16 (T) :231 :474 1:13 1:45 3+ ⒻAlw 19793N1X 33 5 11 1212 117¼ 613 519 Unsihuay A L 113 fb 12.40 66-15 Melee Melee11415 Golden Lucy114nk Miraglia1133 No factor 12
9May95-9Pha fst 1 :24 :471 1:112 1:381 3+ ⒻAlw 19050N1X 58 9 10 108¾ 77¼ 45¼ 45 Unsihuay A L 113 fb 24.90 82-07 First Halo1051¼ Alyssa's Hope115nk Dizzy Daughter1133¼ Off slow, wide 11
30Apr95-4Pha fst 7f :223 :453 1:111 1:244 3+ ⒻAlw 15000N1X 31 3 7 44 46 814 812¼ Unsihuay A L 116 fb 9.70 69-14 Alan's Turn1161½ Keep Dealing1163¼ Newshoesforbaby1061 Tired 9
18Apr95-9Pha fst 170 :232 :473 1:122 1:43 ⒻAlw 15000N1X 50 6 7 710 79¼ 59¼ 414 Unsihuay A L 113 fb 17.50 71-22 Miami Redskin1162¼ Loony Moon1149¼ Four Dancing Hoovs1142 Wide 8
21Mar95-7Pha sly 1 :24 :473 1:123 1:391 3+ ⒻAlw 15000N1X 48 2 4 55¼ 46 38 310¼ Unsihuay A L 114 fb 7.20 72-20 Strickly Elo1165¼ Cara R1124¾ Kute Kris1141½ No factor 7

WORKOUTS: Aug 23 Pha 3f fst :39 B 14/19

Feel The Motion
Own: Fink Morton & Teinowitz Philip
VELAZQUEZ J R (214 32 23 28 .15)

Ch. f. 3 (Mar)
Sire: Polish Navy (Danzig)
Dam: Adira (Affirmed)
Br: Carelaine Farm (Ky)
Tr: Schulhofer Flint S (58 6 6 14 .10)

114

Lifetime Record: 10 2 0 1 $48,552

1995	10	2	0	1	$48,552	Turf	9	2	0	1	$48,312
1994	0	M	0	0		Wet	0	0	0	0	
Bel(T)	6	1	0	1	$28,440	Dist(T)	6	1	0	1	$28,272

4Oct95-6Bel gd 1 1/16 (T) :233 :47 1:104 1:414 3+ ⒻAlw 36000N2X 82 5 4 44½ 33½ 36 36¼ Velazquez J R 116 5.30 82-20 Nabla1181½ Ring By Spring1135 Feel The Motion1163¼ No late bid 6
25Sep95-5Bel yl 1 1/16 (T) :24 :48 1:123 1:434 3+ ⒻAlw 48600N2X 53 1 5 31½ 52¼ 810 817¾ Krone J A 114 7.00 61-31 Rogues Walk114no Darlin Danika1142¼ ValorLady1142 Saved ground, tired 10
15Sep95-9Bel fm 1 1/16 (T) :24 :474 1:114 1:43 3+ ⒻAlw 34000N1X 85 10 5 53¼ 41½ 1½ 12 Velazquez J R 111 *1.80 83-16 Feel The Motion1112 Exposed111hd River Boogie1121 Wide, going away 10
25Aug95-9Sar fm 1 1/16 (T) :224 :454 1:102 1:413 3+ ⒻAlw 34000N2L 88 3 6 67½ 63¾ 31½ 13 Velazquez J R 114 15.80 91-07 [D]Feel The Motion1143 Nabla1221 MysticMel1121 Caused crowding 3/16 11
Disqualified and placed 10th
16Jly95-5Bel fm 1 1/16 (T) :233 :471 1:112 1:421 ⒻAlw 34000N2L 71 3 4 31½ 42 34½ 59¼ Santos J A 114 4.30 78-13 Hawaiian Brave1176¾ Star Of Light1171 Lamplight117nk Well placed 10
Placed 4th through disqualification.
15Jun95-8Bel gd 1 (T) :233 :464 1:112 1:354 3+ ⒻAlw 34000N1X 79 1 9 63¼ 5¾ 3nk 62 Santos J A 114 7.90 82-20 Sheza Wild Again119no Look Daggers1121 Ski AtDawn112¼ Steadied turn 12
28May95-6Bel fm 1 (T) :221 :452 1:101 1:351 ⒻAlw 34000N2L 78 4 2 21 1½ 1½ 44 Santos J A 114 12.00 83-14 Remda114½ Look Daggers1142¼ Bella Dawn1141 Bid, weakened 10
1Apr95-6Hia fm *1 1/16 (T) 1:404 ⒻBal Harbour31k 66 7 4 31 42 44 48¼ Sellers S J 113 19.20 89-02 Perfect Arc1142¼ Another Legend1142 Remda1134 Lacked response 12
10Mar95-11GP gd *1⅛ (T) :483 1:144 1:40 1:531+ ⒻMd Sp Wt 73 7 2 31½ 42¼ 13 1nk Santos J A 120 3.60 79-14 FeelTheMotion120nk ARoseForShannon1205 BoyntonCnyon1203¼ Driving 10
15Feb95-10GP fst 1 1/16 ⊗ :233 :483 1:14 1:46 ⒻMd Sp Wt 28 5 3 53 74¼ 919 1827¼ Santos J A 120 4.70 51-25 Two Elk1207 Whogunneddownbunny1202¼ Very True1204¾ No factor 10

WORKOUTS: Oct 17 Bel 4f fst :503 B 32/34 Oct 12 Bel 4f fst :493 B 18/30 Sep 12 Bel 4f fst :493 B 24/43 Sep 7 Bel 4f fst :50 B 29/48 Sep 2 Bel 4f fst :502 B 40/47 Aug 19 Bel tr.t 4f fst :511 B 17/28

Cant We Be Friends
Own: Whitney Wheelock
MAPLE E (145 11 18 19 .08)

B. f. 3 (May)
Sire: Sovereign Dancer (Northern Dancer)
Dam: Kerplop (Affirmed)
Br: Wheelock Whitney (Ky)
Tr: Lewis Lisa L (15 2 1 0 .13)

L 114

Lifetime Record: 5 2 1 1 $30,980

1995	5	2	1	1	$30,980	Turf	3	1	1	0	$24,860
1994	0	M	0	0		Wet	0	0	0	0	
Bel(T)	2	1	0	0	$22,560	Dist(T)	1	0	0	0	$2,160

25Sep95-5Bel yl 1 1/16 (T) :24 :48 1:123 1:434 3+ ⒻAlw 48600N2X 81 7 9 96¾ 94¾ 44 44¾ Maple E L 114 3.95 74-31 RoguesWalk114no DarlinDanika1142¼ ValorLady1142 Checked break, wide 10
8Sep95-5Bel fm 1 (T) :224 :454 1:094 1:343 3+ ⒻAlw 34000N1X 85 2 11 1111 96¾ 41½ 13¼ Maple E 112 21.10 90-14 CantWeBeFriends1123¼ SilentAllnte112hd RisingReson115no Strong finish 12
23Jly95-7Cby fm 7½f (T) :241 :481 1:13 1:312 3+ ⒻAlw 11500N3L 62 1 1 56¼ 64¼ 42¼ 2hd McNeil F A B 116 f 8.00 — — It'sOver116hd CntWeBeFrinds116½ [D]NicAccount1192 Led between calls 9
9Jly95-4Cby fst 6f :221 :453 :583 1:124 3+ ⒻAlw 10000N2L 57 3 6 58¼ 49¼ 48¼ 31 Stevens S A B 116 3.00 84-16 It's Over116hd Attention1171 Cant We Be Friends1164¼ 4 wide turn, rallied 6
24Jun95-4Cby fst 6f :223 :464 1:002 1:134 3+ ⒻMd Sp Wt 43 7 5 63¾ 64¾ 43½ 1½ Stevens S A B 114 *1.80 80-14 CntWBFrnds114½ IddyBttyBdw115¼ Ann'sHlo1141 Veer out strtch, 5 wd 9

WORKOUTS: ●Oct 14 Bel tr.t 5f fst 1:01 H 1/12 Oct 9 Bel tr.t 5f fst 1:052 B 12/12 Sep 20 Bel 4f fst :522 B 63/70 Sep 15 Bel 6f fst 1:143 H 3/12 Aug 15 Cby 3f fst :391 B 7/7 Aug 10 Cby 6f fst 1:142 H 1/2

Nepta
Own: Paulson Allen E
BAILEY J D (203 47 27 22 .23)

Ch. f. 3 (Feb)
Sire: Theatrical*Ire (Nureyev)
Dam: Art's Prospector (Mr. Prospector)
Br: Paulson Allen E (Ky)
Tr: Mott William I (65 18 6 11 .28)

116

Lifetime Record: 3 2 1 0 $45,800

1995	3	2	1	0	$45,800	Turf	0	0	0	0	
1994	0	M	0	0		Wet	1	1	0	0	$20,400
Bel(T)	0	0	0	0		Dist(T)	0	0	0	0	

5Oct95-8Bel sly 1 1/16 ⊗ :223 :45 1:092 1:414 3+ ⒻAlw 34000N1X 97 2 1 1½ 11½ 2hd 12¼ Bailey J D 112 b 2.40 90-26 Nepta1122¼ Winner's Edge11311 Crafty Lady1166 Drew clear, gamely 8
28Aug95-4Sar fst 7f :23 :46 1:112 1:251 3+ ⒻMd Sp Wt 77 7 1 53¼ 31 2hd 11½ Bailey J D 117 *.45 80-18 Nepta1171½ Full Approval117¾ Playful Katie1177 Fully extended, wide 7
1Jan95-6SA fst 6f :214 :443 :563 1:091 ⒻMd Sp Wt 95 5 4 41¾ 42¼ 33 21½ Take Y B 117 11.10 90-09 Smooth Charmer1171½ Nepta1171¾ Secret Harbor1176 Good effort 6

WORKOUTS: Oct 18 Bel 5f fst 1:033 B 26/29 Sep 29 Sar tr.t 1 fst 1:434 B 1/1 Aug 23 Sar 5f fst 1:024 Bg 15/21 Aug 17 Sar 4f fst :511 B 18/25 Aug 11 Sar 5f fst 1:014 H 13/35 Aug 5 Sar 4f fst :502 B 26/46

Skip One
Own: Cohn Seymour
CHAVEZ J F (196 32 20 27 .16)

B. f. 4
Sire: Skip Trial (Bailjumper)
Dam: Al Fayeza (Alydar)
Br: Burke Walter (Fla)
Tr: Terrill William V (27 4 4 3 .15)

L 116

Lifetime Record: 46 9 6 6 $202,050

1995	16	3	2	1	$78,350	Turf	11	3	2	0	$74,220
1994	18	4	4	1	$93,040	Wet	7	0	2	2	$17,850
Bel(T)	6	2	1	0	$42,800	Dist(T)	9	2	2	0	$50,940

11Oct95-7Bel fst 7f :223 :452 1:103 1:232 3+ ⒻAlw 34000N2X 79 6 2 31½ 21 3½ 43¾ Chavez J F L 115 b 4.70 80-16 HipHipHurRhy1121½ MrfSmerld114½ RvishingRvn1132 Forced pace, tired 7
18Sep95-7Bel gd 1 1/16 ⊗ :234 :47 1:11 1:421 3+ ⒻAlw 36000N2X 64 1 2 21½ 21½ 37 412¾ Chavez J F 120 b 3.40 75-15 Head East111¾ So Cheerful1118 Musicanti1164 Stumbled break 6
28Aug95-5Sar fm 1 [T] :231 :461 1:104 1:352 3+ ⒻAlw 36000N2X 82 6 4 34 53 2½ 54 Alvarado F T 122 b 11.00 96-08 JustWonderful1142 BldBeuty112½ MdmeAdolphe112nk Bid, flattened out 10
19Aug95-7Sar fm 1 [T] :242 :481 1:114 1:353 3+ ⒻClm 75000 88 2 1 1½ 1hd 2hd 12 Chavez J F 112 b 14.00 99-05 Skip One1122 Blazing Kadie116½ Sapor1161 Fought back gamely 8
11Aug95-9Sar fst 7f :223 :453 1:101 1:232 3+ ⒻClm 50000 89 3 3 21½ 22 34 11½ Bailey J D 112 b 23.10 89-18 Skip One1121½ Runaway Fling1152 You'renotlistening1123 Strong finish 9
22Jly95-1Sar fst 7f :222 :452 1:103 1:234 3+ ⒻClm 50000 72 3 4 43 43½ 42 54 Bailey J D 113 b 24.00 83-07 SusnVlley113hd RunwyFling1162 JupitrAssmbly1131½ Saved ground, tired 9
21Jun95-6Bel fst 7f :222 :453 1:111 1:25 ⒻClm 50000 70 2 4 33½ 41 54 56¼ Bailey J D 116 b 11.40 69-18 Personal Girl1162¼ Runaway Fling114½ Strategic Reward120½ No rally 7
31May95-4Bel fst 6½f :23 :462 1:113 1:181 ⒻClm 60000 38 4 7 42½ 66½ 711 719¼ Bailey J D 116 b 6.10 64-16 [DH]Unreal Cupcake111 [DH]Strategic Reward1143¼ Evi Bee1181 Gave way 7
19May95-6Bel sly 6f :221 :451 :57 1:094 ⒻClm 65000 69 2 6 33 33½ 35 28 Ramos W S 112 b 10.60 84-17 Manor Queen1128 Skip One112nk Our Shopping Spree1163 Rallied inside 7
27Apr95-8Aqu fm 1 1/16 (T) :23 :471 1:112 1:433 3+ ⒻAlw 34000N2X 59 6 2 35½ 74¾ 710 714 Davis R G 120 b 8.00 77-18 Shocking Pleasure1102 Swamp Cat1201½ Royal Pelliknow1131 Used up 7

WORKOUTS: Oct 4 Bel 4f fst :493 B 21/61 Sep 29 Bel 4f fst :514 B 56/61 Sep 13 Bel tr.t 4f fst :501 B 7/15 Sep 7 Bel tr.t 4f fst :501 B 15/24 Aug 26 Sar tr.t 4f fst :54 B 18/19 Aug 7 Sar tr.t 4f fst :52 B 27/40

Two Ninety Jones
Own: Matecumbe Stables
DAVIS R G (243 37 42 30 .15)

Dk. b or br f. 4
Sire: Sir Harry Lewis (Alleged)
Dam: Caromist (Care (Ire))
Br: Jones Mrs J G Sr (Ky)
Tr: O'Brien Leo (60 6 9 7 .10)

L 116

Lifetime Record:	15 2 1 3	$41,700			
1995	5 1 0 2	$16,840	Turf	10 2 0 3	$38,510
1994	8 1 1 1	$24,860	Wet	1 0 0 0	
Bel Ⓣ	4 1 0 0	$19,800	Dist Ⓣ	5 0 0 2	$6,310

29Sep95-4Med yl 5f Ⓣ :224 :464 :593 3+ⒻAlw 22000N2X 76 3 5 7¾ 8¼ 55 32 Ward J5 L 111 5.00e 81-17 In A Daydream1121¾ Outlaw Sweetie116hd Two Ninety Jones111nk Mild bid 11
6Sep95-7Med fm 1 1/16 Ⓣ :223 :47 1:11 1:421 3+ⒻAlw 24000N2X 74 6 9 96¾ 85 78¼ 35¼ Ward J5 L 111 b 15.10 85-15 BecuseI'mGold110¾ RemembrThNight1144¾ TwoNintyJons111hd Mild bid 10
2Aug95-6Sar fm 1 1/16 Ⓣ :232 :463 1:103 1:414 3+ⒻAlw 36000N2X 66 6 8 810 78¼ 87½ 818¼ Smith M E 113 b 16.30 79-08 ShezWildAgin1131¾ SrtogBid1081 HirloomWish113¾ Wide, flattened out 11
9Jly95-5Mth fm 1 Ⓣ :232 :471 1:112 1:364 3+ⒻAlw 20000N1X 75 8 7 73¾ 63¼ 33½ 1nk Santagata N 116 b 4.10 86-09 Two Ninety Jones116nk Make No Law111½ Please Dance112½ 9
Wide bid, got up
7Jun95-7Bel gd 1¼ Ⓣ :48 1:13 1:381 2:03 3+ⒻAlw 34000N2L — 7 2 1hd 109 1032 — Perez R B5 115 b 30.25 — 22 Cavalanche114nk Bella Dawn113nk Royal Fandango1201 Dueled, eased 10
29Nov94-6Crc fst 6f :221 :454 :584 1:123 ⒻClm 25000 52 6 3 4¾ 42¼ 44 59 Douglas R R 118 b 10.40 75-16 Be Myself116nk Orange Orchid1162¼ Copewithme1095 Tired badly 7
30Oct94-4Aqu fm 1⅛ Ⓣ :492 1:133 1:39 1:51 3+ⒻAlw 32000N1X 58 5 7 84¾ 95¼ 119¼ 1111¾ Alvarado F T 119 b 6.70 73-12 JoyOfIreInd1171 NobodyPickdSix1143 MySpringLov116¼ Steadied early 11
16Oct94-5Bel fm 1 Ⓣ :224 :46 1:101 1:344 3+ⒻMd Sp Wt 80 5 5 44 31½ 11 17¾ Alvarado F T 122 b 11.70 88-12 Two Ninety Jones1227¾ Sheza Wild Again119¼ Dragon Miss119¾ Drew off 12
8Oct94-1Bel fm 1 1/16 Ⓣ :241 :471 1:114 1:434 3+ⒻMd Sp Wt 56 9 5 59 44 56¼ 410 Velazquez J R 119 b 13.00 67-15 JerryBomb1191 VlleyOftheJolly1196 DnceOfSunshin1193 Saved ground 10
2Oct94-6Bel sf 1 1/16 Ⓣ :234 :481 1:14 1:462 3+ⒻMd Sp Wt 59 6 3 33½ 4¾ 65 58 Velazquez J R 119 b 11.80e 56-32 Apolda1143¾ Polish Treaty1193 Sheza Wild Again119nk Tired 8
WORKOUTS: Oct 9 Aqu 4f fst :492 B 3/7 Aug 31 Bel 4f fst :583 B 43/54 Aug 21 Bel tr.t 4f fst :48 H 3/22 Jly 24 Sar tr.t 4f fst :502 B 12/29

Hawaiian Brave
Own: Fares Farms
KRONE J A (137 16 21 9 .12)

B. f. 3 (Apr)
Sire: Lyphard (Northern Dancer)
Dam: Hawaiian Rain (Vaguely Noble)
Br: Fares Farm Inc (Ky)
Tr: Clement Christophe (44 4 7 5 .09)

112

Lifetime Record:	11 2 2 2	$69,548			
1995	7 2 0 1	$49,110	Turf	9 2 2 2	$67,038
1994	4 M 2 1	$20,438	Wet	2 0 0 0	$2,510
Bel Ⓣ	3 2 0 0	$41,100	Dist Ⓣ	4 1 1 0	$29,677

11Sep95-8Bel fm 1 1/16 Ⓣ :24 :471 1:102 1:412 ⒻAlw 50000NC 67 4 3 42 44 56¼ 510¾ Krone J A 112 5.00 80-12 Miss Union Avenue1222 Remda1172¼ My Oooo Aah1121¾ Done early 5
14Aug95-8Sar yl 1⅛ Ⓣ :463 1:104 1:36 1:483 ⒻAlw 50000NC 94 3 6 65½ 56¼ 32 33 Krone J A 112 2.75 81-15 Fashion Star1152¼ Class Kris120½ Hawaiian Brave1121½ Bumped 3/16 pl 7
2Aug95-9Sar fm 1 1/16 Ⓣ :231 :472 1:12 1:414 ⒻNijana-G3 84 2 7 73¾ 73 52 65½ Krone J A 112 4.20 85-08 Bail Out Becky115¾ Fashion Star1123 Grand Charmer120nk 9
Steadied turn, lacked room 1/16 pole. Run in divisions
16Jly95-5Bel fm 1 1/16 Ⓣ :233 :471 1:112 1:421 ⒻAlw 34000N2L 91 4 5 52¼ 1½ 14 16¾ Krone J A 117 *.95 87-13 Hawaiian Brave1176¾ Star Of Light1171 Lamplight117nk Ridden out 10
9Jun95-2Bel fm 1 Ⓣ :222 :452 1:11 1:341 3+ⒻMd Sp Wt 90 1 9 98 61½ 2½ 11½ Krone J A 112 3.45 92-08 HwiinBrve1121½ GrdenSecrts1127 MistrssHwk1124 Awaited room 5/16 pl 12
12May95-4Bel my 1 1/16 :224 :461 1:114 1:462 ⒻMd Sp Wt 26 6 4 52¼ 44¾ 59¼ 520¾ Bailey J D 120 f 2.85 46-23 Head East1206 Bank Approval1159 Emergency1201¾ Lacked response 6
23Apr95-2Kee wf 7f :224 :471 1:133 1:263 ⒻMd Sp Wt 58 6 11 117 73¾ 33 43½ Day P 119 f *2.40 64-21 Above Reproach1192 Mayhew1191½ GoodNGorgeous119no Came up empty 11
18Nov94♦ Evry(Fr) hy *1⅛ ⓉLH 2:091 Prix Saint-Roman-G3 53¾ Peslier O 128 6.50 Vaneyck123½ Bryntirion1231 Beau Temps123nk 7
Tr: Pascal Bary Stk 63700 *Raced in 5th,squeezed back over 1f out,unable to recover*
16Oct94♦ Longchamp(Fr) gd *1 1/16 ⓉRH 1:523 ⒻPrix de la Faisanderie-EBF 21½ Head F 128 *2.00 Sainte Aldey1281½ Hawaiian Brave1281½ Genovefa128¾ 9
Alw 32600 *Tracked in 3rd,5th 2f out,finished well but never catching winner*
18Sep94♦ Longchamp(Fr) sf *1 ⓉRH 1:452 ⒻPrix de la Lorie-EBF 21 Mosse G 128 2.50 Alleluia Tree1281 Hawaiian Brave1284 Chagrin d'Amour1282¼ 6
Alw 34100 *Tracked in 3rd,mild bid over 1f out,second best*
WORKOUTS: Oct 12 Bel Ⓣ 5f gd 1:024 B (d)5/10 Sep 8 Bel 3f fst :374 B 11/16 Sep 1 Bel 3f fst :373 B 16/21 Aug 24 Sar tr.t 4f fst :54 B 10/13 Aug 11 Sar tr.t 4f fst :533 B 22/27 Jly 31 Sar tr.t 3f fst :381 B 3/7

Shoop
Own: Davis Barbara J
NO RIDER (—)

Ro. f. 4
Sire: Double Sonic (Nodouble)
Dam: Noble Dream Maker (An Eldorado)
Br: Petrucione Joseph (Fla)
Tr: Moschera Gasper S (61 14 7 11 .23)

L 118

Lifetime Record:	11 2 1 1	$49,140			
1995	7 2 1 1	$46,020	Turf	1 0 0 0	
1994	4 M 0 0	$3,120	Wet	3 0 1 0	$5,820
Bel Ⓣ	1 0 0 0		Dist Ⓣ	1 0 0 0	

20Sep95-4Bel fst 1 1/16 :231 :46 1:114 1:451 3+ⒻAlw 34000N1X 69 6 3 31 31½ 2½ 1¾ Luzzi M J L 115 11.80 73-21 Shoop115¾ Winner'sEdge113nk Stephni'sRod115nk Four wide, determined 6
26Aug95-4Sar fst 7f :223 :461 1:113 1:243 3+ⒻClm c-25000 68 1 8 31 21½ 33 79 Decarlo C P 114 13.50 74-16 Safe At Home1131½ Midway Gal1211½ Gene's Gray Girl121hd Used up 8
Claimed from Capecci Bert & Louis & Kupferberg, Margotta Anthony Jr Trainer
5Aug95-1Sar wf 1⅛ :46 1:132 1:40 1:541 3+ⒻClm 25000 75 2 1 1½ 2hd 2hd 2hd Decarlo C P 114 29.50 65-25 Gene's Gray Girl120hd Shoop1144½ Muko1147 Speed, game 7
3Jly95-1Bel fst 1 :224 :46 1:113 1:391 3+ⒻClm 18000 57 6 4 36 47 46½ 39 Decarlo C P 117 18.00 58-23 Gene's Gray Girl114hd Yazma1109 Shoop117¾ No rally 7
9Jun95-4Bel fst 1 1/16 :223 :454 1:102 1:453 3+ⒻAlw 34000N1X 52 3 5 48½ 412 413 419¾ Decarlo C P 119 14.90 51-24 Spire1091¾ My Big Sis1092 The Big Strawberry11116 No threat 6
26Mar95-7Bel my 6f :223 :453 :572 1:10 3+ⒻAlw 32000N1X 63 4 5 79 77½ 79½ 712 Decarlo C P 119 30.25 79-10 Daybydaybyday1124 FantasticWomen1102½ AustrinEmpress105nk Trailed 7
16Mar95-1GP fst 6f :224 :461 :581 1:113 ⒻMd Sp Wt 75 5 2 41½ 2hd 11 14 Krone J A L 120 2.80 82-14 Shoop1204 Continued1202 Arc Of Colors1133 Ridden out 7
17Sep94-1Bel fm 1 1/16 Ⓣ :223 :451 1:094 1:414 3+ⒻMd Sp Wt -0 8 10 1016 1020 1027 1038½ Samyn J L 118 9.30 50-10 Philippine Queen118hd Valley Ofthe Jolly1182 Jodi's Land1181 Outrun 10
26Aug94-1Sar fst 7f :223 :454 1:11 1:24 3+ⒻMd Sp Wt 62 7 1 66½ 63¾ 54 48 Samyn J L 117 4.00 77-14 One Account1221 Facula1173 Radiant Beams1224 No threat 7
6Aug94-1Sar wf 1⅛ :493 1:143 1:40 1:522 3+ Md Sp Wt 66 1 4 42½ 62½ 41½ 48½ Samyn J L 112 17.20 66-17 Wayfarer1174¾ Private Cody117¾ Glitterati1172¾ Steadied early 6
WORKOUTS: Oct 14 Bel 4f fst :483 H 10/57 Oct 4 Bel 4f fst :49 H 13/61 Sep 16 Bel tr.t 4f fst :482 B 3/25 Sep 5 Bel tr.t 4f fst :49 B 3/11

Were your conclusions right? Did you hit the Pick Six? Here's what happened:

Second choice Accuracy ($7.20) won the third.

Favored Codys Key ($4.60) won the fourth.

Favored Optic Nerve ($4.50) won the fifth.

Favored High Talent ($5.40) won the sixth.

Favored Private Plan ($5) won the seventh.

Feel The Motion ($34.60), the fifth betting favorite in a field of eight, won the eighth.

THIRD RACE **Belmont** **OCTOBER 20, 1995**

6 FURLONGS. (1.07^{4}) MAIDEN SPECIAL WEIGHT. Purse $30,000 (plus up to $11,775 NYSBFOA). Fillies and mares, 3-year-olds and upward foaled in New York State and approved by the New York State-Bred Registry. Weights: 3-year-olds, 118 lbs. Older, 121 lbs.

Value of Race: $30,000 Winner $18,000; second $6,000; third $3,300; fourth $1,800; fifth $900. Mutuel Pool $251,623.00 Exacta Pool $405,481.00

Last Raced	Horse	M/Eqt.	A.	Wt	PP	St	¼	½	Str	Fin	Jockey	Odds $1
6Oct95 ^{3}Bel^{4}	Accuracy	Lb	3	118	12	8	$3\frac{1}{2}$	3^{2}	3^{5}	$1^{3\frac{1}{2}}$	Smith M E	2.60
20Sep95 ^{5}Bel^{5}	Missy Mims	Lb	3	111	3	4	1^{1}	1^{1}	$1\frac{1}{2}$	2^{nk}	Chavez C R^{7}	9.90
19Mar95 ^{9}Aqu^{2}	Star Personality		3	118	6	3	$2^{3\frac{1}{2}}$	2^{5}	2^{2}	$3\frac{3}{4}$	Nelson D	1.25
12Oct95 ^{2}Bel^{6}	Bob's Talc	Lb	3	118	1	2	6^{hd}	$6\frac{1}{2}$	$4\frac{1}{2}$	4^{1}	Santagata N	17.30
18Sep95 ^{3}Bel^{4}	Reelherin	L	6	121	7	7	8^{hd}	8^{2}	$6^{1\frac{1}{2}}$	$5^{1\frac{3}{4}}$	Leon F†	14.10
20Sep95 ^{5}Bel^{3}	Zesty	L	4	111	11	10	9^{1}	$7\frac{1}{2}$	7^{2}	$6^{1\frac{1}{2}}$	Persaud Randi^{10}	12.70
18Sep95 ^{3}Bel^{3}	Diviso n'Belle	Lb	3	118	2	1	5^{4}	$5^{1\frac{1}{2}}$	$5\frac{1}{2}$	7^{2}	Alvarado F T	24.75
	Marcy	f	3	111	8	6	10^{5}	9^{4}	$8\frac{1}{2}$	8^{6}	Trejo J^{7}	86.50
7Oct95 ^{9}Pha^{3}	Distinctive Jeanne	L	3	118	4	5	$4^{1\frac{1}{2}}$	4^{2}	9^{10}	9^{6}	Perez R B	11.40
14Jun95 ^{6}Bel^{7}	Great Beginnings	Lbf	3	118	9	11	$11\frac{1}{2}$	$11^{2\frac{1}{2}}$	10^{4}	10^{11}	Maple E	28.75
6Oct95 ^{3}Bel^{7}	Gray Dawn Pixie	Lbf	3	113	10	9	$7^{1\frac{1}{2}}$	10^{2}	11^{4}	11^{3}	Feurtado E E^{5}	203.25
	Rock The Media		3	118	5	12	12	12	12	12	Decarlo C P	165.25

OFF AT 1:59 Start Good. Won driving. Time, :21^{3}, :44^{2}, :58, 1:12 Track fast.

$2 Mutuel Prices:			
14-ACCURACY	7.20	5.00	3.00
3-MISSY MIMS		7.30	3.50
6-STAR PERSONALITY			2.60

$2 EXACTA 14-3 PAID $75.50

B. f, (Jan), by Duns Scotus-Affirming, by Affirmed. Trainer Barbara Robert. Bred by Harbor View Farm (NY).

ACCURACY raced just off the pace while four wide for a half, closed steadily in the middle of the track to win going away. MISSY MIMS sprinted clear in the early stages, set a brisk pace along the inside into the stretch, then weakened under pressure in the final eighth. STAR PERSONALITY forced the pace from outside into midstretch and weakened. BOB'S TALC unable to keep pace for a half, closed late between horses. REELHERIN failed to threaten while saving ground. ZESTY never reached contention while five wide. DIVISO N'BELLE faded after going a half. DISTINCTIVE JEANNE up close early, gave way on the turn. GREAT BEGINNINGS was never close.

Owners— 1, Pomerantz Lawrence J; 2, Portier Patrick G; 3, For J & D & Pond View Stable; 4, Juckiewicz Thomas E; 5, Valentino John; 6, Edwards James F; 7, Candow Robert A; 8, Tanrackin Farm; 9, Timber Bay Farm; 10, Nolan Howard C Jr; 11, DeLuca & Lucas & Morrison; 12, Peck Claudia

Trainers—1, Barbara Robert; 2, Greco Emanuel J; 3, Nocella Vincent R; 4, Nieminski Richard; 5, Ortiz Juan; 6, O'Brien Leo; 7, Tesher Howard M; 8, Freyer Donna J; 9, Entenmann William J; 10, Higgins W P; 11, Streicher Kenneth; 12, Peck Claudia

†Apprentice Allowance Waived: Reelherin (5).

Scratched— Knight Flight, Time For Another (4Oct95 ^{5}BEL^{5}), Henry's Sunny Day (8Sep95 ^{3}BEL^{10}), Juniors Fortune (5Aug95 ^{10}SAR^{10}), Come Like the Wind (5Oct95 ^{1}BEL^{8}), Sunsational Girl (20Sep95 ^{5}BEL^{6}), Lucy Brown (5Oct95 ^{1}BEL^{3}), Sneezin Season (5Oct95 ^{1}BEL^{9})

FOURTH RACE
Belmont
OCTOBER 20, 1995

6 FURLONGS. (1.07^4) CLAIMING. Purse $24,000 (plus up to $9,420 NYSBFOA). 3-year-olds and upward. Weights: 3-year-olds, 119 lbs. Older, 122 lbs. Non-winners of two races since September 14, allowed 2 lbs. Of two races since September 2, 4 lbs. Of a race since then, 6 lbs. Claiming price $35,000, if for $30,000, allowed 3 lbs. (Races where entered for $25,000 or less not considered.)

Value of Race: $24,000 Winner $14,400; second $4,800; third $2,640; fourth $1,440; fifth $720. Mutuel Pool $272,036.00 Exacta Pool $391,499.00 Quinella Pool $72,541.00

Last Raced	Horse	M/Eqt.	A.	Wt	PP	St	¼	½	Str	Fin	Jockey	Cl'g Pr	Odds $1
3Oct95 ^{6}Lrl^3	Codys Key	L	6	118	5	2	1^{hd}	1^{hd}	1^1	1^3	Chavez J F	35000	1.30
13Sep95 ^{8}Rkm^4	Crystal Pistol	L	4	116	7	7	$4^{\frac{1}{2}}$	$6^{\frac{1}{2}}$	$5^{\frac{1}{2}}$	2^{nk}	Smith M E	35000	24.50
26Feb95 ^{7}Aqu^6	Fighting Daddy	Lb	5	116	8	3	2^1	2^2	2^2	3^{nk}	Santagata N	35000	16.10
8Oct95 ^{5}Bel^5	Limited War	L	4	108	9	9	9	$8^{1\frac{1}{2}}$	6^1	4^{hd}	Chavez C R^7	30000	b-2.15
5Oct95 ^{9}Bel^3	Direct Satellite	L	4	116	4	5	5^{hd}	3^{hd}	3^{hd}	5^{nk}	Velazquez J R	35000	9.60
25Sep95 ^{9}Bel^{10}	Fabersham	Lb	7	109	6	8	$7^{2\frac{1}{2}}$	4^{hd}	$4^{\frac{1}{2}}$	$6^{\frac{1}{2}}$	Trejo J^7	35000	50.25
29Sep95 ^{5}Bel^6	Farmonthefreeway	Lb	5	116	3	4	$8^{1\frac{1}{2}}$	9	$8^{1\frac{1}{2}}$	7^3	Davis R G	35000	b-2.15
1Jun95 ^{7}Bel^6	Miron's Gentleman	Lb	4	116	1	1	$3^{1\frac{1}{2}}$	5^1	7^1	$8^{\frac{3}{4}}$	Bailey J D	35000	a-3.45
8Oct95 ^{5}Bel^2	Carr Heaven	Lb	5	116	2	6	6^1	$7^{1\frac{1}{2}}$	9	9	Alvarado F T	35000	a-3.45

a-Coupled: Miron's Gentleman and Carr Heaven.
b-Coupled: Limited War and Farmonthefreeway.

OFF AT 2:29 Start Good. Won driving. Time, :22^1, :44^4, :57^1, 1:10 Track fast.

$2 Mutuel Prices:				
	4-CODYS KEY	4.60	3.50	3.10
	6-CRYSTAL PISTOL		12.20	6.60
	7-FIGHTING DADDY			5.80

$2 EXACTA 4-6 PAID $70.00 $2 QUINELLA 4-6 PAID $52.50

Ro. h, by Corridor Key-Go Thither, by Cabin. Trainer Contessa Gary C. Bred by Wilkinson Jon (NJ).

CODYS KEY dueled along the inside into upper stretch, shook off FIGHTING DADDY to get clear in midstretch, then drew away under good handling. CRYSTAL PISTOL up close early, dropped back on the turn, swung out in upper stretch then finished well in the middle of the track to edge FIGHTING DADDY for the place. FIGHTING DADDY dueled outside the winner into the stretch and weakened. LIMITED WAR checked at the start, raced far back for a half, rallied belatedly along the inside. DIRECT SATELLITE raced within striking distance between horses for a half and lacked a strong closing kick. FABERSHAM outrun early, rallied five wide to threaten at the quarter pole, flattened out. FARMONTHEFREEWAY never reached contention. MIRON'S GENTLEMAN up close early while saving ground, gave way on the turn. CARR HEAVEN was never a factor.

Owners— 1, Sheerin Raymond T; 2, McDonnell Francis C; 3, Simon Steven; 4, Pomerantz Lawrence J; 5, Tam Ping W; 6, Scaglione Paul; 7, Hagedorn Charles G; 8, Davis Barbara J; 9, Joques Farm

Trainers—1, Contessa Gary C; 2, Lenzini John J Jr; 3, Imperio Joseph; 4, Barbara Robert; 5, Lake Robert P; 6, Terracciano Neal; 7, Barbara Robert; 8, Moschera Gasper S; 9, Moschera Gasper S

Codys Key was claimed by Davis Barbara J; trainer, Moschera Gasper S.,
Carr Heaven was claimed by Buhr Carl E; trainer, Barbara Robert.

Scratched— Giant Leap (23Sep95 ^{2}BEL^7), Disaster Master (30Sep95 ^{7}MED^6), Arz (12Jly95 ^{6}BEL^3)

FIFTH RACE
Belmont
OCTOBER 20, 1995

1$\frac{1}{16}$ MILES. (Inner Turf)(1.39^1) MAIDEN SPECIAL WEIGHT. Purse $32,000 (plus up to $12,560 NYSBFOA). 2-year-olds. Weight, 118 lbs. (Preference to horses that have not started for a claiming price.)

Value of Race: $32,000 Winner $19,200; second $6,400; third $3,520; fourth $1,920; fifth $960. Mutuel Pool $284,548.00 Exacta Pool $348,612.00 Trifecta Pool $340,296.00

Last Raced	Horse	M/Eqt.	A.	Wt	PP	St	¼	½	¾	Str	Fin	Jockey	Odds $1
30Sep95 ^{2}Bel^4	Optic Nerve		2	118	8	10	$5^{\frac{1}{2}}$	$5^{\frac{1}{2}}$	$4^{2\frac{1}{2}}$	3^9	1^3	Santos J A	1.25
9Sep95 ^{6}Bel^{10}	Value Investor	L	2	118	10	7	3^{hd}	$2^{\frac{1}{2}}$	$2^{1\frac{1}{2}}$	1^{hd}	2^{nk}	Velazquez J R	26.75
8Sep95 ^{6}Bel^2	Hail to the Lion		2	118	1	1	4^4	4^7	3^2	$2^{\frac{1}{2}}$	3^{17}	Davis R G	2.10
	Lite Approval		2	118	4	3	$9^{\frac{1}{2}}$	$9^{\frac{1}{2}}$	$7^{1\frac{1}{2}}$	6^3	$4^{1\frac{3}{4}}$	Samyn J L	16.90
12Oct95 ^{7}Med^6	Marfada	L	2	118	7	9	8^8	$7^{1\frac{1}{2}}$	$5^{\frac{1}{2}}$	4^{hd}	5^1	Beckner D V	82.00
5Oct95 ^{2}Bel^7	Tavito's Wish	L	2	111	9	6	7^1	$8^{3\frac{1}{2}}$	9^4	$7^{\frac{1}{2}}$	6no	Chavez C R^7	59.75
5Oct95 ^{2}Bel^6	Barlow	b	2	118	5	5	$1^{\frac{1}{2}}$	1^2	$1^{\frac{1}{2}}$	$5^{2\frac{1}{2}}$	$7^{\frac{3}{4}}$	Bailey J D	6.50
8Sep95 ^{6}Bel^7	Aspen Ryder	b	2	118	3	4	$6^{2\frac{1}{2}}$	$6^{\frac{1}{2}}$	$8^{1\frac{1}{2}}$	$8^{1\frac{1}{2}}$	$8^{\frac{3}{4}}$	Krone J A	21.60
13Sep95 ^{6}Bel^5	R.S.V.P. Requested	Lb	2	118	6	8	10	10	10	10	9^{12}	Migliore R	17.90
20Sep95 ^{6}Bel^7	Waving Good Bye	Lb	2	118	2	2	2^2	$3^{\frac{1}{2}}$	6^1	$9^{\frac{1}{2}}$	10	Chavez J F	13.20

OFF AT 2:59 Start Good. Won driving. Time, :23^2, :46^3, 1:11^4, 1:38^1, 1:44^4 Course yielding.

$2 Mutuel Prices:				
	8-OPTIC NERVE	4.50	3.80	2.40
	10-VALUE INVESTOR		15.00	5.70
	1-HAIL TO THE LION			2.60

$2 EXACTA 8-10 PAID $69.50 $2 TRIFECTA 8-10-1 PAID $285.50

Dk. b. or br. c, (Apr), by Majestic Light-Inreality Star, by In Reality. Trainer Tesher Howard M. Bred by Jaime S. Carrion (Ky).

OPTIC NERVE away a bit slowly, was unhurried for a half, closed the gap from outside on the turn, then sustaining his bid, wore down the leaders to win going away. VALUE INVESTOR stalked the pace from outside for five furlongs, made a run to challenge on the turn, surged to the front entering the stretch, battled heads apart into midstretch, then outfinished HAIL TO THE LION for the place. HAIL TO THE LION settled just off the pace while saving ground, angled out on the turn, made a run to threaten in upper stretch but couldn't sustain his bid. LITE APPROVAL far back for six furlongs, failed to threaten while improving his position. MARFADA unhurried early, gained a bit on the turn, then lacked a further response. TAVITO'S WISH was never a factor. BARLOW set the pace along the inside to the turn and tired from his early efforts. ASPEN RYDER faded after going five furlongs. R.S.V.P. REQUESTED never reached contention. WAVING GOOD BYE was used up trying to keep the early pace.

Owners— 1, Oak Cliff & Sanders & Wade & Willis; 2, Klaravich Stables; 3, Anchel Edward & Judith; 4, Live Oak Plantation; 5, Contessa Gary C & Nadanne Stables; 6, Friendship Stable; 7, Ramsey Kenneth L & Sarah K; 8, Due Process Stable; 9, Dor-Sea Stable; 10, Giordano Ronald J

Trainers—1, Tesher Howard M; 2, Sciacca Gary; 3, Laboccetta Frank; 4, Kelly Patrick J; 5, Contessa Gary C; 6, Barbara Robert; 7, Mott William I; 8, Nobles Reynaldo H; 9, O'Connell Richard; 10, Terrill William V

Scratched— Trail City (28Aug95 ^{2}SAR^8), Country Cuzzin (5Oct95 ^{2}BEL^3), Wish You Goboy (8Sep95 ^{6}BEL^5), Pro Doc (13Sep95 ^{6}BEL^7), Luckisasecret (29Sep95 ^{1}BEL^8), Soaringoverseattle (30Sep95 ^{4}BEL^7), Bunk Beds (4Oct95 ^{4}BEL^8), Birthday Boy, Edgeofthestorm (11Oct95 ^{6}BEL^6), Northern Pursuit (30Sep95 ^{4}BEL^4)

SIXTH RACE
Belmont
OCTOBER 28, 1995

1¼ MILES. (Inner Turf)(1.57³) CLAIMING. Purse $25,000 (plus up to $3,313 NYSBFOA). Fillies and mares, 3-year-olds and upward. Weights: 3-year-olds, 117 lbs. Older, 122 lbs. Non-winners of two races over a mile since September 9, allowed 2 lbs. Of such a race since September 27, 4 lbs. Of such a race since September 5, 6 lbs. Claiming price $35,000, if for $30,000, allowed 2 lbs. (Races where entered to be claimed for $25,000 or less not considered.)

Value of Race: $33,150 Winner $22,500; second $5,000; third $3,025; fourth $1,875; fifth $750. Mutuel Pool $320,249.00 Exacta Pool $482,837.00

Last Raced	Horse	M/Eqt.	A.	Wt	PP	¼	½	¾	1	Str	Fin	Jockey	Cl'g Pr	Odds $1
10Sep95 3Bel2	High Talent	Lb	6	116	3	1^{1}	1^{1}	$1^{1\frac{1}{2}}$	$1^{\frac{1}{2}}$	1^{3}	$1^{1\frac{1}{2}}$	Bailey J D	35000	1.70
4Oct95 8Bel7	Eenie Meenie Miney	L	6	114	5	7^{hd}	$7^{\frac{1}{2}}$	4^{2}	$3^{\frac{1}{2}}$	3^{3}	2^{3}	Maple E	30000	18.90
13Oct95 8Bel4	Dinner Diamond	L	5	116	4	$10^{\frac{1}{2}}$	10^{hd}	$7^{\frac{1}{2}}$	$5^{1\frac{1}{2}}$	$5^{2\frac{1}{2}}$	$3^{\frac{1}{2}}$	Santos J A	35000	3.40
11Sep95 7Bel5	My Spring Love	L	4	116	12	2^{1}	$2^{\frac{1}{2}}$	2^{1}	2^{1}	2^{hd}	$4^{\frac{1}{2}}$	Krone J A	35000	14.00
5Oct95 6Bel4	Miss Pocket Court	Lb	6	116	9	3^{2}	$3^{2\frac{1}{2}}$	$3^{\frac{1}{2}}$	4^{4}	4^{1}	5^{2}	Alvarado F T	30000	6.60
5Oct95 6Bel1	Slew The Duchess	Lb	5	120	2	12	12	12	9^{hd}	6^{2}	6^{1}	Chavez J F	35000	20.40
8Oct95 2Bel5	Dana's Wedding	L	5	116	6	5^{hd}	$5^{\frac{1}{2}}$	$6^{\frac{1}{2}}$	7^{hd}	7^{hd}	$7^{\frac{1}{2}}$	Davis R G	35000	28.75
12Oct95 8Bel7	Flower Delivery		4	116	1	11^{4}	11^{3}	11^{1}	12	10^{1}	8^{hd}	Smith M E	35000	6.20
10Sep95 3Bel4	All Glory	L	6	116	11	8^{1}	9^{1}	8^{hd}	11^{1}	8^{1}	9^{1}	Decarlo C P	35000	62.50
15Sep95 2Bel7	Calling You-FR	Lb	5	116	10	4^{2}	4^{2}	$5^{\frac{1}{2}}$	6^{hd}	$9^{\frac{1}{2}}$	10^{3}	Velasquez J	35000	30.75
30Sep95 5Bel9	Curled Waters	L	5	116	8	$6^{1\frac{1}{2}}$	$6^{\frac{1}{2}}$	$9^{\frac{1}{2}}$	10^{hd}	$11^{1\frac{1}{2}}$	11^{2}	Lovato F Jr	35000	29.00
11Oct95 10Rkm1	Secretariatslegend	Lf	5	114	7	$9^{1\frac{1}{2}}$	8^{1}	10^{1}	8^{hd}	12	12	Velazquez J R	30000	27.50

OFF AT 3:29 Start Good. Won driving. Time, :24², :49³, 1:15¹, 1:40², 2:06¹ Course yielding.

$2 Mutuel Prices:

3-HIGH TALENT	5.40	3.90	2.90
5-EENIE MEENIE MINEY		11.60	7.20
4-DINNER DIAMOND			3.20

$2 EXACTA 3-5 PAID $90.00

Dk. b. or br. m, by Talc-Far and Above, by Far Out East. Trainer Contessa Gary C. Bred by Parsons Ron (NY).

HIGH TALENT sprinted clear in the early stages, set the pace along the inside to the turn, shook off MY SPRING LOVE at the quarter pole then held sway under pressure. EENIE MEENIE MINEY under a snug hold early, was unhurried for five furlongs, moved up steadily while saving grond on the turn, then finished with good energy for the place. DINNER DIAMOND far back for seven furlongs while saving ground, closed late to gain a share. MY SPRING LOVE forced the pace outside the winner into upper stretch and weakened. MISS POCKET COURT chased the leaders while slightly off the rail for seven furlongs and lacked a strong closing bid. SLEW THE DUCHESS far back for six furlongs, angled five wide on the turn and failed to threaten while improving her position. DANA'S WEDDING faded after going six furlongs. FLOWER DELIVERY was never a factor. ALL GLORY never reached contention. CALLING YOU raced up close for five furlongs and tied. CURLED WATERS was finished after going six furlongs.

Owners— 1, Bertino & Mangine & Mariano E & P; 2, More-N-More Stable; 3, Corrado Fred L; 4, Santangelo Francis R; 5, Giambrone Anthony P & Silver Oak St; 6, Montanari Marion G; 7, Leveen Leonard; 8, Knight Landon; 9, Sheringham John; 10, Englekirk Robert; 11, Carroll Del W II; 12, Roberts Deborah P

Trainers—1, Contessa Gary C; 2, Sciacca Gary; 3, DeBonis Robert; 4, Penna Angel Jr; 5, Moschera Gasper S; 6, Terrill William V; 7, Kelly Michael J; 8, Badgett William Jr; 9, Sheringham John; 10, Lundy Sarah A; 11, Carroll Del W II; 12, Roberts Deborah P

Corrected weight: Miss Pocket Court (116).

Scratched— Royal Pelliknow (13Oct95 5BEL1)

SEVENTH RACE
Belmont
OCTOBER 28, 1995

1 1/16 MILES. (1.39⁴) CLAIMING. Purse $30,000 (plus up to $11,775 NYSBFOA). 3-year-olds and upward. Weights: 3-year-olds, 118 lbs. Older, 122 lbs. Non-winners of two races a mile or over since September 11, allowed 2 lbs. A race since September 21, 4 lbs. A race at a mile or over since September 1, 6 lbs. Claiming price $50,000 for each $5,000 to $40,000, allowed 2 lbs. (Races where entered for $35,000 or less not considered.)

Value of Race: $30,450 Winner $18,000; second $6,000; third $3,300; fourth $2,250; fifth $900. Mutuel Pool $319,313.00 Exacta Pool $448,987.00

Last Raced	Horse	M/Eqt.	A.	Wt	PP	St	¼	½	¾	Str	Fin	Jockey	Cl'g Pr	Odds $1
24Sep95 7Bel2	Private Plan	L	5	114	3	6	3^{hd}	$4^{1\frac{1}{2}}$	5^{2}	4^{3}	1^{hd}	Alvarado F T	45000	1.50
8Oct95 3Bel4	Rocking Josh	f	6	116	5	4	$5^{2\frac{1}{2}}$	$5^{3\frac{1}{2}}$	4^{hd}	3^{hd}	$2^{1\frac{1}{2}}$	Chavez J F	50000	4.70
9Oct95 3Bel2	Baypark	L	6	116	7	1	1^{4}	$1^{2\frac{1}{2}}$	$1^{\frac{1}{2}}$	$1^{\frac{1}{2}}$	$3^{\frac{1}{2}}$	Nelson D	50000	6.90
8Oct95 3Bel2	Copper Mount	L	4	116	4	3	2^{6}	2^{8}	2^{4}	$2^{1\frac{1}{2}}$	4^{1}	Bailey J D	50000	2.60
8Oct95 3Bel1	A Call To Rise		7	118	1	7	$6^{\frac{1}{2}}$	$6^{\frac{1}{2}}$	$6^{\frac{1}{2}}$	$5^{\frac{1}{2}}$	5no	Santos J A	45000	8.90
8Oct95 3Bel5	Regal Mike	Lb	7	112	6	2	7	7	7	$6^{\frac{1}{2}}$	6^{4}	Leon F	40000	35.50
9Oct95 3Bel1	Le Risky	L	6	112	2	5	4^{1}	$3^{\frac{1}{2}}$	3^{hd}	7	7	Smith M E	40000	11.90

OFF AT 3:58 Start Good. Won driving. Time, :23, :45², 1:09³, 1:35¹, 1:41⁴ Track fast.

$2 Mutuel Prices:

3-PRIVATE PLAN	5.00	3.00	2.50
5-ROCKING JOSH		4.50	3.30
7-BAYPARK			4.20

$2 EXACTA 3-5 PAID $24.20

Ch. g, by Private Account-Ericka Downs, by Vaguely Noble. Trainer Moschera Gasper S. Bred by Firman Pamela H (Ky).

PRIVATE PLAN reserved for five furlongs, launched a rally between horses on the turn, split rivals while gaining in midstretch, then outfinished ROCKING JOSH under brisk urging. ROCKING JOSH unhurried early, rallied four wide leaving the turn, battled heads apart outside the winner into deep stretch and yielded grudgingly. BAYPARK set the pace while racing well off the rail into the stretch then weakened in the final sixteenth. COPPER MOUNT raced just behind the early pacesetter while saving ground, made a run along the rail to threaten in upper stretch but couldn't sustain his bid. A CALL TO RISE far back for six furlongs, failed to threaten with a mild late rally between horses. REGAL MIKE never reached contention. LE RISKY raced just behind the leaders to the turn and gave way.

EIGHTH RACE

Belmont
OCTOBER 20, 1995

1¼ MILES. (Inner Turf)(1.39¹) ALLOWANCE. Purse $36,800 (plus up to $14,130 NYSBFOA). Fillies and mares, 3-year-olds and upward which have not won two races other than maiden, claiming or starter. Weights: 3-year-olds, 118 lbs. Older, 122 lbs. Non-winners of $19,200 twice at a mile or over since September 13, allowed 2 lbs. $20,400 at a mile or over since September 28, 4 lbs. $3,800 at a mile or over since September 7, 6 lbs. (Races where entered for $60,000 or less not considered in allowances.) (Conditions eligibility preferred.)

Value of Race: $36,800 Winner $21,600; second $7,200; third $3,960; fourth $2,160; fifth $1,080. Mutuel Pool $244,522.00 Exacta Pool $253,987.00 Trifecta Pool $268,238.00

Last Raced	Horse	M/Eqt. A.Wt	PP	St	¼	½	¾	Str	Fin	Jockey	Odds $1
4Oct95 6Bel³	Feel The Motion	3 114	3	2	3hd	3¹	3hd	2²	1¹	Velazquez J R	16.30
11Oct95 7Bel⁴	Skip One	Lb 4 116	6	5	1½	1¹	1½	1¹½	2¹½	Chavez J F	14.90
29Sep95 4Med³	Two Ninety Jones	Lb 4 116	7	7	7⁴	7⁵	7⁸	6½	3hd	Davis R G	41.50
25Sep95 5Bel⁴	Cant We Be Friends	L 3 114	4	4	4½	4hd	6¹½	5½	4¹½	Maple E	6.30
11Sep95 8Bel⁵	Hawaiian Brave	3 112	8	8	6³	6³	5¹	7¹²	5no	Krone J A	5.30
5Oct95 8Bel¹	Nepta	b 3 116	5	6	2²	2½	2¹	3½	6¹	Bailey J D	0.45
29Sep95 6Bel¹	Exposed	L 3 116	1	1	5²½	5²	4½	4½	7⁹	Santos J A	24.75
10Oct95 7Pha¹	Kute Kris	Lbf 5 118	2	3	8	8	8	8	8	Smith M E	49.00

OFF AT 4:30 Start Good. Won driving. Time, :24, :47³, 1:12¹, 1:38, 1:44⁴ Course yielding.

$2 Mutuel Prices:

3-FEEL THE MOTION	34.60	14.80	9.40
6-SKIP ONE		13.40	9.40
7-TWO NINETY JONES			10.80

$2 EXACTA 3-6 PAID $300.00 $2 TRIFECTA 3-6-7 PAID $3,094.00

Ch. f. (Mar), by Polish Navy-Adira, by Affirmed. Trainer Schulhofer Flint S. Bred by Carelaine Farm (Ky).

FEEL THE MOTION was rated just off the pace while saving ground to the turn, checked and angled out in upper stretch then closed strongly to wear down SKIP ONE in the final seventy yards. SKIP ONE set the pace under pressure for six furlongs, opened a clear advantage in upper stretch, but couldn't withstand the winner's late charge. TWO NINETY JONES outrun for six furlongs, advanced four wide into the stretch, rallied belatedly in the middle of the track. CANT WE BE FRIENDS raced in close contention between horses for a half, dropped back on the turn, then failed to threaten with a mild late rally. HAWAIIAN BRAVE reserved for a half, circled five wide on the turn, then closed some ground with a mild late rally. NEPTA angled out along the backstretch, forced the pace to the top of the stretch and gave way. EXPOSED under a snug hold while four wide for five furlongs, gave way on the turn. KUTE KRIS trailed throughout.

Owners— 1, Fink Morton & Teinowitz Philip; 2, Cohn Seymour; 3, Matecumbe Stables; 4, Whitney Wheelock; 5, Fares Farms; 6, Paulson Allen E.; 7, Low Lawana L & Robert E.; 8, Sketchley John D

Trainers— 1, Schulhofer Flint S; 2, Terrill William V; 3, O'Brien Leo; 4, Lewis Lisa L; 5, Clement Christophe; 6, Mott William I; 7, Peitz Daniel C; 8, Sketchley John D

Scratched— Snoop (20Sep95 4BEL¹)

$2 Pick-3 (3-3-3) Paid $279.50; Pick-3 Pool $144,101. $2 Pick-6
(14-4-8-3-3-3) 6 Correct 4 Tickets Paid $8,672.00; 5 Correct
153 Tickets Paid $75.50; Pick-6 Pool $61,673.

The Pick Six paid $8,672.

Could you have hit the Pick Six? Yes, by identifying Nepta as the vulnerable favorite in the eighth.

Nepta had two wins and a second in three dirt starts, and was making her turf debut for Billy Mott and Jerry Bailey. As a daughter of Theatrical, she obviously had grass breeding on her sire side. But her broodmare sire was Mr. Prospector, an outstanding sire, but one who is certainly better at producing dirt horses. And Nepta didn't show a single work on grass.

Three of Nepta's seven opponents had one win on turf. Feel The Motion, Two Ninety Jones and Hawaiian Brave each had two, and Skip One had three.

Nepta was asked to do something she hadn't done before: race on grass, against seven horses who had won on grass.

Nepta was bet down to 2-5, making every other horse in the race an overlay. She finished sixth by four lengths. Feel The Motion at 16-1 and Skip One at 14-1 combined for an exacta paying exactly $300. Two Ninety Jones was third at 41-1, completing a triple which paid $3,094.

But the biggest hit was in the Pick Six using four favorites, one second choice and one fifth choice in an eight-horse field.

Nobody expects you to always pick the right race to use all the horses in a Pick Six. You don't have to be right all the time. Be right once or twice by opening yourself up to the possibility of a big favorite losing.

Four-digit Pick Six payoffs and other huge exotic overlays pop up time after time at racetracks all over the country. Go for them!

About the Author

A multi-national award-winning writer, Bill Heller is a correspondent for *The Thoroughbred Times* and a columnist for the harness magazine *Hoof Beats*. He also writes regularly for *Street and Smith's Basketball Yearbook* and *Basketball Weekly*. He was elected second vice president of the United States Harness Writers Association in February 1996. Heller lives in Albany, New York, with his wife, Anna, and their seven-year-old handicapping wizard son, Benjamin (a.k.a. Bubba). *Exotic Overlays* is his seventh book.

Best Bets from Bonus Books

Overlay, Overlay: How to Bet Horses like a Pro
Leading trainers and jockeys share their handicapping secrets
Bill Heller
ISBN 0-93383-86-8
228 pages, paper, $9.95

Finding Hot Horses
How to pick horses that can win for you
Vincent Reo
ISBN 0-929387-96-1
135 pages, paper, $12.00

Workouts and Maidens
Inside betting info for those who want to win
Vincent Reo
ISBN 1-56625-000-5
165 pages, paper, $11.95

Break the One-Armed Bandits
How to come out ahead when you play the slots
Frank Scoblete
ISBN 1-56625-001-3
178 pages, paper, $9.95

Guerilla Gambling
How to beat the casinos at their own games
Frank Scoblete
ISBN 1-56625-027-7
339 pages, paper, $12.95

Harness Overlays: Beat the Favorite
How to win money at harness tracks
Bill Heller
ISBN 0-929387-97-X
139 pages, paper, $14.00

Woulda, Coulda, Shoulda
For anyone who has ever bet on a horse race or wanted to
Dave Feldman with Frank Sugano
ISBN 1-56625-069-2
316 pages, paper, $12.95

Victory at Video Poker
Combine strategy and chance for BIG WINS
Frank Scoblete
ISBN 1-56625-043-9
181 pages, paper, $12.95

Beat the Craps out of the Casinos
How to play craps and win
Frank Scoblete
ISBN 0-929387-34-1
152 pages, paper, $9.95

Bonus Books, Inc., 160 East Illinois Street, Chicago, Illinois 60611

TOLL-FREE: (800) 225-3775 FAX: (312) 467-9271
WEBSITE: http://www.bonus-books. com